An introduction to
POSITIVE ECONOMICS

fourth edition

an introduction to
POSITIVE
ECONOMICS

Richard G. Lipsey

Sir Edward Peacock Professor of
Economics, Queen's University,
Kingston, Ontario

Weidenfeld and Nicolson

London

© 1963 by Richard G. Lipsey

First printed October 1963

Second edition October 1966
Reprinted August 1967
Reprinted May 1968
Reprinted March 1969
Reprinted September 1970
Reprinted November 1970

Third edition August 1971
Reprinted March 1972

Paperback edition first published 1972
Reprinted September 1973
Reprinted May 1974

Fourth edition July 1975
Reprinted 1976
Part of this fourth edition appeared in the
United States in *Economics* by
Richard G. Lipsey and Peter O. Steiner,
© 1975, published by Harper and Row.

Weidenfeld and Nicolson
11 St John's Hill, London, SW11

ISBN 0 297 76898 0 cased
ISBN 0 297 76899 9 paperback

*Filmset by BAS Printers Limited, Wallop,
Hampshire and printed in Great Britain
by Redwood Burn Limited, Trowbridge & Esher*

To Diana

Contents

Part 3 The intermediate theory of demand

Part 4 The intermediate theory of supply

Part 5 The theory of distribution

Part 6 The economy as a whole

Fact and theory in economics

'... Einstein started from facts – the Morley Michelson measurements of light, the movements of the planet Mercury, the unexplained aberrancies of the moon from its predicted place. Einstein went back to facts or told others where they should go, to confirm or to reject his theory – by observation of stellar positions during a total eclipse.

'... It is not necessary, of course, for the verification of a new theory to be done personally by its propounder. Theoretical reasoning from facts is as essential a part of economic science as of other sciences, and in a wise division of labour there is room, in economics, as elsewhere, for the theoretician pure and simple, for one who leaves the technical business of verification to those who have acquired a special technique of observation. No one demanded of Einstein that he should visit the South Seas in person, and look through a telescope; but he told others what he expected them to see, if they looked, and he was prepared to stand or fall by the result. It is the duty of the propounder of every new theory, if he has not himself the equipment for observation, to indicate where verification of his theory is to be sought in facts – what may be expected to happen or to have happened if his theory is true, what will not happen if it is false.

'[Now consider by way of contrast the behaviour of the participants in a current controversy in economics.] ... None of them takes the point that the truth or falsehood of ... [a] ... theory cannot be established except by an appeal to the facts; none of them tests it by facts himself. The distinguishing mark of economic science as illustrated by this debate is that it is a science in which verification of generalizations by reference to facts is neglected as irrelevant. ... I do not see how ... [members of the public who survey the controversy] ... can avoid the conclusion that economics is not a science concerned with phenomena, but a survival of medieval logic, and that economists are persons who earn their livings by taking in one another's definitions for mangling.

'... I know that in speaking thus I make enemies. I challenge a tradition of a hundred years of political economy, in which facts have been treated not as controls of theory, but as illustrations. I shall be told that in the Social Sciences verification can never be clean enough to be decisive. I may be told that, in these sciences, observation has been tried and has failed, has led to shapeless accumulations of facts which themselves lead nowhere. I do not believe for a moment that this charge of barrenness of past enquiries can be sustained; to make it is to ignore many achievements of the past and to decry much solid work that is being done at this School and elsewhere. But if the charge of barrenness of realistic economics in the past were justified completely, that would not be a reason for giving up observation and verification. It would only be a reason for making our observations more exact and more numerous. If, in the Social Sciences, we cannot yet run or fly, we ought to be content to walk, or to creep on all fours as infants. ... For economic and political theorizing not based on facts and not controlled by facts assuredly does lead nowhere.

'There can be no science of society till the facts about society are available. Till 130 years ago we had no census, no knowledge even of the numbers and growth of the people; till fifteen years ago we had no comprehensive records about unemployment even in this country, and other countries are still where we were a generation or more ago; social statistics of every kind – about trade, wages, consumption – are everywhere in their infancy.

'... From Copernicus to Newton is 150 years. Today, 150 years from the *Wealth of Nations*, we have not found, and should not expect to find, the Newton of economics. If we have travelled as far as Tycho Brahe we may be content. Tycho was both a theorist and an observer. As a theorist, he believed to his last day in the year 1601 that the planets went round the sun and that the sun and the stars went round the earth as the fixed centre of the universe. As an observer, he made with infinite patience and integrity thousands of records of the stars and planets; upon these records Kepler, in due course, based his laws and brought the truth to light. If we will take Tycho Brahe for our example, we may find encouragement also. It matters little how wrong we are with our existing theories, if we are honest and careful with our observations.'

Extracts from Lord Beveridge's farewell address as Director of the London School of Economics, 24th June 1937. Published in *Politica*, September, 1937.

The use of this book

This is an introductory text book in economics, starting at an elementary stage and progressing, in some places, to an intermediate level. It is designed to be read as a first book in economics. I hope, on the other hand, that the book will not be without interest for someone who has already studied one of the many existing basic text-books written at a first year university standard.

The book had its beginnings when I was asked to give the basic economic theory lectures for the revised B.Sc.(Econ.) degree introduced at the London School of Economics in October 1961. I started to write my first few lectures and, almost before I knew it, a book was well under way. Had I appreciated at the outset what was involved in carrying such a project through to completion, I would never have begun it, but that is probably true of a great many enterprises in all fields.

There are three major themes of this text-book which should be mentioned here: first, an attempt to explain what economic theory is about and how one can go about criticizing it effectively and hence improving it; second, an attempt to elaborate, in so far as is possible within the confines of an introduction to economic theory, the relation between theory and real-world observations; and third, a consideration of the relation between economic theory and economic policy.

The first major theme of this book is how one can go about being intelligently and constructively critical of the existing body of economic theory. I have tried to address myself throughout to the intelligent student of honours-school quality. I have assumed that the student was interested in his subject and that he wished to know, at every stage, just what was going on and why. There is a tradition of trying to sneak quite complex bits of analysis past the student without telling him what is happening. This may be the best thing to do if the object is to get through an examination a large mass of people who have neither interest nor ability in economics, and who are hostile to the basic idea of a Social Science. I am not interested in reaching such a public. I have assumed that I am addressing an intelligent set of students, who may or may not be honours students and intending specialists, but who want to learn and who do not have closed minds. One of the troubles with the traditional approach of sneaking

analysis past the student is that, when the intelligent reader feels that there is some
thing wrong with what he has been taught, he does not know how to go about being
critical of it in an effective way. I have made a point of telling the student what is
going on, to say 'now we are doing comparative static equilibrium analysis' or whatever it might be, and I have devoted considerable space to an analysis of both sensible
and silly criticisms of the theories described. I do not accept the idea that the possibility of criticizing what he has learned should not be mentioned because if it is the
student will be led to make hasty and confused criticisms. A good student will always
attempt criticisms and evaluations of what he has been taught. It seems to me that his
criticisms are much more likely to be informed and relevant ones if he is given both
practice and instruction in how to set about effectively challenging what he has been
taught than if he meets a conspiracy of silence on this topic.

The second major theme is that of the relation between economic theory and
observation. One of the most unfortunate tendencies in the teaching of economics,
particularly in Britain, is that of making a clear split between economic theory and
applied economics. All too often economic theory is taught merely as logical analysis,
and is, at best, only vaguely related to the world, while applied economics becomes
description unenlightened by any theoretical framework. Economic theory is meant
to be about the real world. We seek, by the use of theory, to explain, understand and
predict phenomena in the real world, and our theory must therefore be related to,
and tested by, empirical observation of the world around us. The student of economic
theory needs to ask at every stage what are the relevant magnitudes and quantities
in the real world. This is the theme set by the quotation from Beveridge that opens
this book.[1]

The third major theme, which should be noted here, is that of the relation between
economic theory and economic policy. The distinction between positive and normative statements is well known to professional economists, but all too often we fail to
communicate its significance to our students. Even the best American text books
often manage to convey the idea that economic theory justifies the private-enterprise,
market economies, found in most Western countries. The experience of interviewing,
for admission to the London School of Economics and later to the University of Essex,
students who have done A-Level economics at school makes it painfully obvious that
from somewhere – I am never sure from where – students get such ideas as the ones
that the 'Law' of Comparative Advantage proves that nations *ought* to specialize in
the production of certain goods, that economics has proved that rent and price
controls are wicked and ought not to be used. The student who can think of good
reasons why, under some circumstances, price and rent controls and tariffs might be
desirable, reacts by dismissing economics as Medieval Scholasticism, or as a fraud
perpetrated by whichever political party he happens not to support; and so he should
do if economics did purport to prove such propositions. Economic theory cannot, of
course, ever show us what we ought to do, but only what will happen if we do do
certain things. The uses and the limitations of economic theory in dealing with
matters of public policy is a theme which recurs throughout the book.

1 I take it that in the last sentence quoted, Beveridge is saying that it does not matter how wrong present theories
may be as long as we make careful observations of the facts on which these theories stand or fall, and then discard
or amend theories when they are found to be inconsistent with the facts.

The study of economics can be both interesting and rewarding. To the student not intending to specialize in economics it can give some understanding of the functioning of the economy, and some appreciation of the issues involved in current controversies over economic policy. It may also give him some idea of the methods which have been applied with some modest success in one Social Science. To the would-be economics specialist the study of an introductory book, such as this one, can be the beginning of a real adventure. The scope of his chosen science opens up before him. At first he encounters theories which add to his understanding of the world, but very soon he begins to encounter problems: observations for which there are no satisfactory explanations, and theories which are generally agreed to be unsatisfactory, but which have not been adequately tested. Both of these constitute a challenge, in the first case for the development of new theories and in the second for the making of a careful set of observations to test an existing theory. One of the interesting things about economics in the 1970s is that the frontiers of knowledge in terms of unsolved problems can be reached very quickly, even though, as the reader of this book will soon learn, it may take a very long time to reach the frontiers of knowledge in terms of techniques available for the handling of problems.

Economics is a subject quite unlike some other subjects studied at school. Economic theory has a logical structure; it tends to build on itself from stage to stage. Thus the student who only imperfectly understands some concept or theory will run into increasing difficulty when, in subsequent developments, this concept or theory is taken for granted and built upon. Because of its logical structure, quite long chains of reasoning are encountered: if A then B, if B then C, if C then D, and if D then E. Each step in the argument may seem simple enough, but the cumulative effect of several steps, one on top of the other, may be bewildering on first encounter. Thus when, having followed the argument step by step, the reader encounters the statement 'now obviously if A then E', it may not seem obvious at all. This is a problem which almost everyone encounters with chains of reasoning. The only way to deal with it is to follow the argument through several times. Eventually, as one becomes familiar with the argument, it will become obvious that, *if* A *then* E.

Another problem is posed by the fact that economics has a large technical language or jargon. At first the student feels that all he is being asked to do is to put complicated names to common-sense ideas. To some extent this is true. At the beginning, economics consists largely of making explicit ideas which appeal strongly to common sense and which one has already held in a vague sort of way. This is an absolutely necessary step, because loose thinking about vaguely formed ideas is one of the quickest routes to error in economics. Furthermore, the jargon, the single word or phrase given to the common-sense idea, becomes necessary in the interests of brevity of expression as the subject is built up. The student should himself try the exercise of removing every technical term from the argument of one of the later chapters in this book and replacing these terms with the full verbal description of the ideas expressed. The argument would then become too cumbersome. If we are going to put several ideas together to see what follows from them, then the single clearly defined word or phrase to refer to these ideas becomes a necessary part of our equipment.

It follows from all of this that the student should use this book in quite a different way than he would use a book on many other subjects. A book on economics is to be worked at, and understood step by step, and not to be read like a novel. It is usually a good idea to read a chapter quickly in order to see the general run of the argument and then to re-read it carefully, making sure that the argument is understood step by step. The student should be prepared at this stage to spend a very long time on difficult sections. He should not be discouraged if, occasionally, he finds himself spending an hour on only two or three pages. A paper and pencil is a necessary piece of equipment in his reading. Difficult arguments should be followed by building up one's own diagram while the argument unfolds, rather than by relying on the printed diagram which is, perforce, complete from the beginning. Numerical examples should be invented to illustrate general propositions. At various stages the student is asked to put the book down and think out the answer to some problem for himself before he reads on: *the student should never read on without attempting to do what is asked.* He should also make his own glossary of technical terms, committing the definitions to memory. The first time a technical term is introduced, it is printed in capital letters so that it may easily be recognized as such.

After the book has been read in this detailed manner, it should be re-read fairly quickly from cover to cover; it is often difficult to understand why certain things are done until one knows the end product, and, on a second reading, much that seemed strange and incomprehensible, will be seen to have an obvious place in the analysis.

In short, one must seek to understand economics, not to memorize it (the technical vocabulary must, of course, be committed to memory). Memorization is the royal road to disaster in economics; theories, principles and concepts are always turning up in slightly unfamiliar guises. To one who has understood his economics this poses no problem; to one who has merely memorized it, this spells disaster. *The required approach is not more difficult than, but it is different from, that encountered in many other subjects.*

The first chapter of this book is a general essay on scientific method, particularly as it applies to the Social Sciences. None of the ideas is unduly difficult but each may seem rather abstract and 'up in the air' to someone unable to relate it to a detailed knowledge of some social science. The ideas are, however, of critical importance. The student, particularly the one who is just beginning his study of economics, should read the chapter carefully to get the general drift of the argument. He should refer back to it at times when the issues raised turn up in the contexts of particular bits of economics and, finally, when he has finished the whole book, he should re-read Chapter 1, making sure that he follows the argument fully. This last piece of advice is so important that, were it not for the costs of printing, I should be inclined to print Chapter 1 as both the first and the last chapter of the book. In the notes on fourth edition I allude briefly to an intended postscript discussing some of the doubts about economics as a science that have arisen in the early 1970s and taking note of some of the criticisms of Lord Beveridge's discussion of Einstein.

Chapter 2 deals with the economists' tools of analysis. It is not necessary to be a mathematician to learn economics, but it is necessary to have a mastery of the equivalent of O-Level mathematics. There is not room in an economics text-book to teach the elementary mathematics that is assumed in economics. Chapter 2 does, however, outline some of the most important bits of elementary mathematics commonly used. The student who is unsure of any of the points briefly outlined must go back to an elementary text-book and review these bits of necessary technique.

The student should seek to master completely one text-book, but, generally, he should not confine himself exclusively to this one book; he should read sections in other texts, particularly those sections dealing with ideas that he finds difficult. There are many first-class books to which he can make reference, and unfortunately there is an even larger number of not-very-good books and the student should seek expert advice before adopting a book for major study.

This is a book about economic theory. Although I have tried at all points to relate the theory to the world around us, I have not tried to fill in the institutional detail about any particular economy. For the UK the student should consult A. R. Prest and D. J. Coppock (editors), *The UK Economy: A Manual of Applied Economics* (Weidenfeld & Nicolson, 5th edition, 1974). This book gives a detailed and valuable survey of the UK economy that is descriptive rather than analytical.

Finally I should like to say a word of thanks to all those people who have made this book possible. In so far as the ideas and viewpoints expressed here are novel, they are the common property of all my colleagues who were members of the L.S.E. *Staff Seminar on Methodology, Measurement and Testing in Economics.* All that I did in the 1st edition was to give a slightly personal expression to this general viewpoint. Mr K. Klappholz read the manuscript of the 1st edition, removing countless blemishes, and contributed greatly to some of the novel ideas expressed herein. Mr R. Cassen read the proofs and contributed many last-minute improvements. Mr G. C. Archibald gave detailed scrutiny of the proofs of the second edition and his penetrating criticisms led to many improvements.

The executor of Lord Beveridge's estate has kindly granted permission to quote extracts from Beveridge's farewell address at the London School of Economics. Thanks are also due to Macmillan and McGraw-Hill for permission to quote from Lord Robbins' *Essay on the Nature and Significance of Economic Science* and Sir Roy Harrod's *The British Economy* respectively. Harper and Row has also been generous in giving their permission to quote at length from material first prepared for the American text book *Economics* written by Professor P. O. Steiner and myself.

I am also extremely grateful to the many users, students and teachers, who have taken the trouble to write to me pointing out errors, making comments and suggestions. Economics is a subject in which one never stops learning and it is always gratifying to realize that one can still learn from one's students. I hope that the readers of this book will continue to teach me with as many further comments and criticisms as they have in the past. Those who have done so are too numerous to mention, but I must at least single out Mr John Knapp of the University of Manchester who has, together with his students, contributed many constructive criticisms and suggestions for improvement. The largest single debt of all I owe to Professor P. O. Steiner who co-authored with me the American text book *Economics*. To Professor Steiner who was everywhere my severe critic and often my teacher I and the substance of the present book owe a very great debt. Mr M. V. Blandon and Mrs J. Wickens gave valuable research on the 1st edition, Mr P. Geary and Mr

J. Stilwell gave extensive research assistance to the 2nd edition, Mr Allan Popoff helped substantially with the 3rd edition and Mr Don Gilchrist assisted in the 4th edition. Mrs S. Craig, Mrs Evelyn Dean, Miss Tina Brown and Mrs Joanne Marlieb have shown unlimited patience in dealing with the manuscript. Proofs of the third edition were carefully scrutinized by Professor John Black who is responsible for removing countless blemishes and errors. Ms Claire Rubin has made many valuable suggestions for improvements based on a careful scrutiny of the third edition. The usual disclaimer of course holds here: for all shortcomings and mistakes remaining I am solely to blame.

R. G. LIPSEY
Sir Edward Peacock Professor of Economics
at Queen's University, Ontario

Notes on the fourth edition

The text of almost every Chapter has been rewritten in some detail to eliminate many passages teaching experience has shown to be rough or unclear in meaning. The micro half of the book remains unchanged in general approach and coverage except for some significant additions and updatings. A long overdue Appendix on the theory of discriminating monopoly has been added. More attention is paid to pollution and externalities in general, and also to Galbraith's views on the New Industrial State. The Chapter on Capital has been rewritten, and some scant attention paid to some Cambridge controversies – enough, at least, to make the student aware of their existence.

The major changes are concentrated in the macro half of the book. I have finally accepted the view of many teachers that I did not tell students enough about national income accounting concepts and have added a wholly new Chapter outlining these – albeit with a broad brush. The Chapter on equilibrium national. income is wholly rewritten. Although I believe the third edition told the story correctly, it proved excessively abstract. The present treatment starts with a numerical example of the approach to equilibrium in the simplest, easily understood, dynamic model. This allows the student to see the sense in which actual saving can be unequal to actual investment in a circular flow model while the two magnitudes remain identically equal in the national income accounting sense. Also the device of using four models that build one on the other allows equilibrium to be determined by the savings-investment approach which so many teachers find appealing while preserving the generalization of the withdrawals-injections approach which is introduced at a later stage. The Chapter on the consumption function has been enlarged to include a description and a discussion of the policy significance of the Permanent Income Hypothesis.

The monetary Chapters have been changed significantly to allow for some of the many developments in the theory and practice of monetary economies that have occurred since I first wrote this section.

The Part on International Trade remains essentially unchanged except for the addition to the Chapter on Exchange Rates of the model that makes the effect of devaluation a change in the relative price of traded and non-traded goods, rather than the relative price of imports and exports, and for an extension of the Chapter on postwar experience to cover the breakdown of the Bretton Woods System and the drift to a system of 'dirty floats'.

In the final section on policy I have added a wholly new Chapter covering some controversies between monetarists and neo-Keynesians. In the 'Conflicts' Chapter I have paid some attention to 'stagflation' and the current crisis in macro-economics. I have thought it important not to conceal this crisis from students, but since so many of the points of controversy are over relatively advanced points of macro and monetary theory, it would be a mistake to think that all the issues can be fully explained in an introductory text.

I have not had time to add an intended postscript dealing with the scientific method in economics and some criticisms of my use of Lord Beveridge's discussion of Einstein. That must wait for another edition. Suffice it to say that I was aware, when I first used the quotation, of the controversy over the extent to which Einstein was influenced by the Michelson-Morley experiment as against his own early thought experiment of the consequences of accelerating a body to the speed of light. I side with those commentators who do not place total reliance on what Einstein himself said about this later in his life. In any case the concern is, as Professor Popper has said, not with the *process* of scientific discovery but with the *logic* of scientific discovery. Anyone who has read all – and particularly the last chapters – of Koestler's *Sleep Walkers*, which I quote with approval, can hardly accuse me of having a mechanical view of the scientific process. Einstein, like Kepler, was a prime example of a scientist who was driven by intuition. His intuition, however, led him both to embrace the theory of relativity and to reject quantum theory (on the grounds that God does not play dice with the universe). It was empirical observation and experiment that led the scientific world to conclude that Einstein's intuition was sound in the first case and faulty in the second.

The call that economics should try to be scientific is only the call that we should try to test our theories against the world around us. If we will not do this, we should cease right now giving policy advice, since such advice must presuppose that our theories *are* related to the world of experience. If they are so related, then they *can* be tested against observations – and observations that are used as controls rather than merely as illustrations.

Queen's University
August 1974

Part one

Scope and method

1

Introduction

Why is the history of most capitalist countries one of several years of boom and plenty followed by several years of depression and unemployment with consequent poverty for a great many citizens? Why, during the 1930s in most capitalist countries, was there a ten-year period in which up to one person in four was unemployed while factories lay idle and raw materials went unused, when, in short, everything was available to produce goods which were urgently required and yet nothing happened? Are many Marxists correct in arguing that a return to such a situation of mass unemployment is something from which the capitalist countries are saved only by their high levels of arms expenditure? Or is it true that, largely because of the theories that grew out of the works of many British and Continental scholars but which were synthesized and further developed by an English academic economist writing nearly forty years ago from King's College, Cambridge, we have now learned how to prevent such situations of mass unemployment from ever occurring again?

Why do many countries have balance of payments crises? What is the point of international trade anyway, and would we not be better off if we made ourselves self-sufficient? Do devaluations (and revaluations) represent normal adjustments to the changing conditions of trade or are they the result of mismanagement of the economy by those in charge of it? What is wrong with the present international monetary system and why is it beset by periodic crises? What can be done to reform the system?

Why, in the past, have there been periods of rapidly rising prices alternating with periods of stable and sometimes falling prices? Why has the pace of world inflation so accelerated in the 1970s? Why do the prices of some commodities fluctuate widely while the prices of others are relatively stable? Why is it that, with many agricultural products, price fluctuations give rise to large variations in the incomes of the producers, while, with some other products, price fluctuations hardly cause any variation in producers' incomes?

What determines the level of wages and what influences do unions have on the share of income going to labour? What functions do unions fulfil in today's world?

3

Is it possible that they have already fully achieved their historical purpose of putting labour on an equal footing with management and that they have outlived their usefulness?

Must all modern economies make use of money? Could money easily be dispensed with in a truly Socialist state? How is it that new money can be created by ordinary commercial banks within broad limits, and by governments without limits? If money is valuable, why do economists insist that countries with large supplies of money are no richer than countries with small supplies of money?

What influence does government have on people's welfare? What are the effects of a government's taxation policies? What are the effects of public expenditures? How important to our welfare is the size of our national debt?

These are the types of questions with which economists concern themselves, and on which the theories of economics are supposed to shed some light. Such a list possibly gives the student a clearer idea of the scope of economics than can be obtained from an enumeration of the common textbook definitions.

The person who reads this book is setting out on a study of positive economics or, if we wish to use a slightly more accurate phrase, we might say that he is embarking on a study of POSITIVE ECONOMIC SCIENCE. The questions listed above give some idea of what is meant by *economics*. We must now consider in some detail what is meant by the two terms *positive* and *science*. Then we must ask whether or not it is really possible to conduct a scientific study of anything that is basically concerned with human behaviour. Economics is generally regarded as a social science, but can economics ever hope to be 'scientific' in its study of human behaviour? Economists make claims to be able to understand and to predict certain aspects of human behaviour. To someone who wishes to be able to evaluate these claims this introductory discussion is critical because the questions 'What can we hope to learn?' and 'How can we go about it?' are basic to the whole subject. They are also questions about which there is a vast amount of misunderstanding and even superstition.

POSITIVE AND NORMATIVE STATEMENTS

The ability to separate positive inquiries from normative ones has been one of the main reasons for the success of science in the last 300 years. If we are going to discuss science, the first thing we must do is to distinguish POSITIVE from NORMATIVE.

It is possible to classify statements as being positive or normative. Positive statements concern what *is*, *was* or *will be*. Positive statements, assertions or theories may be simple or they may be very complex but they are basically about what *is* the case. *Thus disagreements over positive statements are appropriately handled by an appeal to the facts.*

Normative statements concern what ought to be. They depend upon our judgements about what is good and what is bad; they are thus inextricably bound up with our philosophical, cultural and religious positions. We say that normative statements depend upon our VALUE JUDGEMENTS. Disagreements may arise over normative statements because different individuals have different ideas of what is good and bad and thus of what constitutes the good life. *Disagreements over normative statements cannot be settled merely by an appeal to facts.*

The distinction between positive and normative may be clarified by considering some assertions, questions and hypotheses that can be classified as positive or normative. The statement 'it is impossible to break up atoms' is a positive statement that can quite definitely be (and of course has been) refuted by empirical observations, while the statement 'scientists ought not to break up atoms' is a normative statement that involves ethical judgements. The questions 'What government policies will reduce unemployment?' and 'What policies will prevent inflation?' are positive ones, while the question 'Ought we to be more concerned about unemployment than about inflation?' is a normative one. The statement 'a government deficit will reduce unemployment and cause an increase in prices' is an hypothesis in positive economics, an hypothesis that could be tested by an appeal to empirical observation, while the statement 'in setting policy, unemployment ought to matter more than inflation' is a normative hypothesis which cannot be settled solely by an appeal to observation.[1]

The distinction between positive and normative follows from the fact that it is logically impossible to deduce normative statements from positive assumptions and *vice versa*. Thus if I think something ought to be done, and if I have some appropriate factual knowledge, I can deduce other things which, if I wish to be consistent, ought to be done; but I can deduce nothing about what is done (i.e., is true). On the other hand, if I know that two things are true, I can deduce other things that must be true, but I can deduce nothing about what is desirable (i.e., *ought* to be).

Consider a simple example. Suppose I believe (1) that it is a moral principle that one ought to be charitable to all human beings. Then if I am told (2) that the inhabitants of China are not Christians but are human beings then it follows (3) that one ought to be charitable towards Chinese. We have thus deduced from (1) and (2) a

1 Having grasped this distinction, the student must beware that he does not turn it into an inquiry-stopping, dogmatic rule. From the fact that positive economics does not include normative questions (because its tools are inappropriate to them) it does *not* follow that the student of positive economics must stop his inquiry as soon as someone says the word ought. Consider the statement: 'It is my value judgement that we *ought to have* rent control because controls are *good*.' Now it is quite in order for you as a practitioner of positive economics to ask 'Why?' It may then be argued that controls have certain consequences and it is these consequences which are judged to be good. But the statements about the consequences of rent control will be positive testable statements. Thus the pursuit of what appears to be a normative statement will often turn up positive hypotheses on which our *ought* conclusion depends. For example, although many people wax quite emotional for or against government control of industry, probably few of them believe that government control is good or bad in itself. Their advocacy or opposition will be based on certain beliefs about relations which can be stated as positive rather than normative hypotheses. For example: 'Government control reduces (increases) efficiency, changes (does not change) the distribution of income, leads (does not lead) to an increase of state control in other spheres.' A careful study of this emotive subject will reveal an agenda for positive economic inquiry that could keep a research team of economists occupied for a decade.

Philosopher friends have persuaded me that, when pushed to its limits, the distinction between positive and normative becomes blurred, or else breaks down completely. The reason for this is that when examined carefully most apparently normative statements reveal some positive underpinning (e.g., 'Unemployment is worse than inflation *because* the (measurable) effects of unemployment on human beings are judged by the majority of adult citizens to be more serious than the (measurable) effects of inflation'). I remain convinced, however, that, at this stage of the development of economics, the distinction is a necessary working rule the present abandonment of which would contribute more to confusion than to clarity. The justification for this view is that although we are not sure what to make of an apparently normative statement (because it may have a positive underpinning) we usually know a purely positive statement when we see one.

normative statement about how we ought to behave; no positive statement about how we do behave with respect to the Chinese can be deduced from (1) and (2). Now, suppose someone else comes along and says, 'You need not be charitable towards the Chinese because moral principles dictate that you should only be charitable towards Christians.' If we now get into an argument about whether or not we should be charitable towards the Chinese this argument will turn on our value judgements about how one ought to behave. These are questions on which reasonable people sometimes just have to agree to disagree. If both sides insist on holding to their views on charity, and even if both are perfectly reasonable men, there is no civilized way of forcing one to admit he is wrong.

Now, assume I say (1) that capital punishment is a strong disincentive to murder and (2) that the Chinese abolished capital punishment after the revolution so that (3) the number of murders must have risen in China since the revolution. The two factual statements, (1) and (2), and the deduction that follows from them are all positive statements. We can deduce nothing about the moral desirability of abolishing capital punishment from statements (1) and (2), even if we are certain they are factually correct. Now suppose someone else comes along and says, 'The number of murders has not risen in China since the revolution; in fact the number has fallen.' If he holds to this view he may be denying one or other of my first two positive statements. He might deny statement (1) by saying, for example, that capital punishment is actually an incentive to commit murder,[1] or he might deny statement (2) by saying that, although the Chinese pretended to abolish capital punishment as a propaganda move, in fact they retained it after the revolution. In both cases the disagreement is over factual statements. If we gathered enough facts and if both parties were reasonable, one side could be forced to admit it was wrong.

Thus positive economics deals with statements that could conceivably be shown to be wrong by actual observations of the world. This does not mean that it is possible to show them to be either wrong or consistent with the facts immediately, but only that it is possible to imagine factual evidence that could show them to be wrong. *Thus an appeal to the facts is an appropriate way in which to deal with them.* Normative questions cannot be settled by a mere appeal to empirical observation and it is thus necessary to deal with them by different techniques. It is therefore convenient to divide them off not because we think they are less important than positive questions, but merely because we handle them in different ways.

So far then, we have said that the separation of the positive from the normative is one of the foundation stones of science and that scientific inquiry, as we normally understand it, is usually confined to positive questions. We must now consider in more detail just what the scientific approach is and how scientific theories are developed and used.

---

1 Strange though it may seem at first sight, this view has been seriously advocated and a strong *prima facie* case may be made out in its favour. See Sidney Silverman, *Hanged but Innocent?* (Gollancz, 1953).

THE SCIENTIFIC APPROACH

Very roughly speaking, the scientific approach consists in relating questions to evidence. When presented with a controversial issue, the scientist will ask what is the evidence on both sides. He may then take a stand on the issue with more or less conviction depending on the weight of the evidence. If there is little or no evidence, the scientist will say that, at present, it is impossible to take a stand. He will then set about searching for relevant evidence. If he finds that the issue is framed in terms of questions about which it is impossible to gather evidence, he will try to recast the questions so that they can be answered by an appeal to evidence.[1] This approach to a problem is what sets scientific inquiries off from other kinds of inquiries.[2]

In some fields, the scientist is able to generate observations that will provide evidence for or against any hypothesis that he wishes to test. Experimental sciences, such as chemistry and some branches of psychology, have an advantage because it is possible for them to produce relevant evidence through controlled laboratory experiments. Other sciences, such as astronomy and economics, cannot do this. They must wait for time to throw up observations that may be used to test hypotheses.

The ease or difficulty with which one can collect or even manufacture evidence does not determine whether a subject is scientific or nonscientific, although many people have thought that it did; it is merely one of the factors determining the degree of ease with which the scientific inquiries of various fields can be pursued.[3] The way in which scientific inquiry proceeds does, however, differ radically between fields in which laboratory experiment is possible and those in which it is not. In this chapter we consider general problems more or less common to all sciences. In Chapter 3 we shall deal with problems peculiar to the nonexperimental sciences, which must accept observations in the forms in which they are thrown up by the world of actual experience.

The scientific attitude in everyday life

It is often said that we live in a scientific age. Over the last several hundred years the citizens of most Western countries have enjoyed the fruits of innumerable scientific discoveries. But the scientific advances that have so profoundly affected the average citizen have been made by an extremely small minority of the population. These advances have been accepted by most people without the slightest idea either of the technical nature of the discoveries involved, or of the attitude of mind that made

1 One of the really challenging problems to the scientist is to find out how to pose a question in the general spirit of the problem in which people are interested but in a form capable of being answered by reference to evidence. There is no formula for this; it is a real art and one of the most difficult of all problems.

2 Other approaches might be to appeal to authority, for example, to Aristotle or the Scriptures, to appeal by introspection to some inner experience (to start off 'all reasonable men will surely agree'), or to proceed by way of definitions to the 'true' nature of the problem or concepts under consideration.

3 It is often thought that scientific procedure consists of grinding out answers by following blind rules of calculation, and that only in the arts is exercise of real imagination required. This view is misguided. What the scientific method gives is an impersonal set of criteria for answering some questions. What questions to ask, exactly how to ask them and how to obtain the evidence are difficult problems for which there are no rules. They require, upon occasion, great feats of imagination and ingenuity.

them possible. If we take as a measure of the influence of science the degree of dissemination of the fruits of science, then we live in a profoundly scientific age, but if we take as our measure the degree to which the general public understands and practises the scientific approach, then we are definitely in a pre-scientific era. Indeed, the scientific method of answering questions by appealing to a carefully collected and coordinated body of facts is a method that is seldom adopted by the public.

Consider, for example, the current argument about capital punishment. It is possible to advocate capital punishment as an act of pure vengeance or because we believe that a good moral code requires *per se* that a person who kills *ought* himself to be killed. If we argue about capital punishment on these grounds, we are involved in normative questions depending upon value judgements. The great majority of arguments for capital punishment are not of this type, but rather are predictions about observable behaviour, and thus belong to the field of science. These are usually variants of the general argument that *capital punishment is a deterrent to murder*. In this general form it is probably very difficult to test the proposition and it will be necessary to state a number of more specific propositions which fall under this general hypothesis. Consider one such example:

> If there is capital punishment for murder involving robbery, then the robber will be less inclined to take a lethal weapon with him on his mission. If he does not take a lethal weapon with him, he will in fact commit fewer murders when surprised in the course of his robbery.

It is truly amazing how people can become committed to agreeing or disagreeing with such propositions without considering the available evidence. A survey of the press whenever the issue arises will show that most of the reasons given for agreeing or disagreeing with such statements are profoundly unscientific. How many of the participants know, for example, what proportion of murders in the course of robbery are made with lethal weapons brought by the criminal to the scene of the crime and what proportion are made with anything found at hand after the criminal has been discovered? Yet it would seem to be impossible to have an informed discussion on the issue without this elementary piece of factual knowledge.

Indeed a study of most of the arguments for and against capital punishment will usually reveal a maximum of empirical questions and a minimum of empirical evidence used to arrive at the answers given. If we really believed in a scientific inquiry into human behaviour we would try to state the arguments about capital punishment in terms of a specific set of propositions and would then set out systematically to gather evidence relating to each of these propositions. We may conclude that many hotly debated issues of public policy are positive and not normative issues, but that the scientific approach to such positive issues is very often ignored.

A SCIENCE OF HUMAN BEHAVIOUR

The preceding discussion raises the question of whether or not it is possible to have a scientific study in the field of human behaviour. When considering whether or not a scientific study of such subjects as the causes of unemployment and the consequences of capital punishment can be made, it is often argued that natural sciences deal with inanimate matter that is subject to natural 'laws', while the social sciences deal with man who has free will and cannot, therefore, be made the subject of (inexorable) laws.

Is human behaviour predictable?

Stated carefully the above view implies that inanimate matter will show stable responses to certain stimuli, while animate matter will not. For example, if you put a match to a dry piece of paper the paper will burn, while if you subject human beings to torture some will break down and others will not, and, more confusing, the same individual may react differently to torture at different times. Whether human behaviour does or does not show sufficiently stable responses to factors influencing it as to be predictable within an acceptable margin of error is a positive question that can only be settled by an appeal to evidence and not by *a priori* speculation.[1]

In fact it is a matter of simple observation that when we consider a group of individuals they do not behave in a totally capricious way but do display stable responses to various stimuli. The warmer the weather, for example, the higher the number of people visiting the beaches and the higher the sales of ice-cream. It may be hard to say when or why one individual will buy an ice-cream, but we can observe a stable response pattern from a large group of individuals: the higher the temperature the greater the sales of ice-cream.

Many other examples will come to mind where, because we can śay what the individual will probably do – without being certain of what he will do – we can say with quite remarkable accuracy what a large group of individuals will do. No social scientist could predict, for example, when an apparently healthy individual is going to die, but death rates for large groups are stable enough to make life insurance a profitable business. It could not be so if group behaviour were capricious. Also, no social scientist can predict what particular individuals will be killed in car accidents next holiday, but he can come very close to knowing how many in total will die, and the more objectively measurable data he is given concerning, for example, the state of the weather on the day, and the increase in car sales over the last year, the closer he will be able to predict the total of deaths. If group human behaviour were in fact random and capricious there would be no point in trying to predict anything on the basis of sample surveys. The fact that 60 per cent of the people sampled said they intended to vote for a certain candidate would give no information about the probable outcome of the election. Today's information might be totally reversed tomorrow. That there are discernible trends in election polls and by-elections is proof of the fact that in politics people do not act at random.[2]

1 *A priori* is a phrase commonly used by economists. It may be defined as that which is prior to actual experience, or as that which is innate or based on innate ideas.

2 Of course, it does not follow from anything that has been said so far that future events can be foretold by a casual study of the past. People sometimes think in terms of a simple dichotomy: either there are historical laws apparent to the casual observer or there is random behaviour. They observe a prophet extrapolating a trend (i.e., predicting that some change will take place in the future merely because it took place in the past) and, seeing him make an utterly mistaken prophecy, conclude that, because the prophet cannot prophesy, human behaviour is random and thus unamenable to scientific study. The stability we are discussing is a stable response to causal factors (e.g., next time it gets warm, ice-cream sales will rise) and not a mere stability of trend changes (e.g., ice-cream sales will go on rising in the future because they have risen in the past).

The 'law' of large numbers

We may now ask how it is that we can predict group behaviour while never being certain what a single individual will do. As a first step, we must distinguish between deterministic and statistical hypotheses. Deterministic hypotheses admit no exceptions. An example of such an hypothesis would be the statement: 'If you torture any man over this period of time with these methods he will *always* break down.' Statistical hypotheses admit of exceptions and purport to predict the probability of a certain occurrence. An example would be: 'If you torture a man over this period of time with these methods he will *very probably* break down – in fact if you torture a large number of men under the stated circumstances about 95 per cent of them will break down.' In such an hypothesis we do not purport to predict what an individual will certainly do but only what he will probably do. This does allow us however, to predict within a determinable margin of error what a large group of individuals will do.

Successful predictions about the behaviour of large groups are made possible by the statistical 'law' of large numbers. Very roughly this 'law' asserts that random movements of a large number of individual items tend to offset one another. The law is based on one of the most beautiful constants of behaviour in the whole of science, natural and social, and yet it can be derived from the fact that human beings make errors! This constant is the *normal curve of error* which the student will encounter in elementary statistics.

Let us consider what is implied by the law of large numbers. Ask one person to measure the length of a room and it will be almost impossible to predict in advance what sort of error of measurement he will make. Thousands of things will affect the accuracy of his measurements and, furthermore, he may make one error today and quite a different one tomorrow. But ask one thousand people to measure the length of the same room and we can predict with a high degree of accuracy how this *group* will make its errors! We can assert with confidence that more people will make small errors than will make large errors, that the larger the error the fewer will be the number of people making it, that the same number of people will overestimate as will underestimate the distance, and that the average error of all the individuals will be zero.[1] Here then is a truly remarkable constant pattern of human behaviour; a constant on which much of the theory of statistical inference is based.

If a common cause should act on all members of the group we can predict successfully their average behaviour, even though any one member of the group may act in a surprising fashion. If, for example, we give all our thousand individuals a tape measure which understates 'actual' distances, we can predict that, on the average, the group will now understate the length of the room. It is, of course, quite possible

---

1 For purposes of measuring the error we define the 'true' distance to be that measured by the most precise instruments of scientific measurement (whose range of error will be very small relative to the range of error of our one thousand laymen all wielding tape measures). Those familiar with statistical theory will realize that the predictions in the text assume that all the necessary conditions such as the existence of a large number of independent factors causing individuals to make errors, are fulfilled. The purpose of the discussion in the text is not to give the reader a full appreciation of the subtleties of statistical theory, but to persuade him that anyone is misguided who holds the common view that free will and the absence of deterministic certainty about human behaviour makes a scientific study of such behaviour impossible.

that one member who had in the past been consistently undermeasuring distance because he was depressed, will now overestimate the distance because the state of his health has changed; but something else may happen to some other individual that will turn him from an overmeasurer into an undermeasurer. Individuals may do peculiar things for reasons which, as far as we can see, are inexplicable, but the group's behaviour, when the inaccurate tape measure is substituted for the accurate one, will nonetheless be predictable, *precisely because the odd things that one individual does will tend to cancel out the odd things some other individual does.*

THE NATURE OF SCIENTIFIC THEORIES

So far we have seen that there is real evidence that human behaviour does show stable response patterns. Theories grow up in answer to the question 'Why?'. Some sequence of events, some regularity between two or more things is observed in the real world and someone asks why this should be so. A theory attempts to explain why. Whether or not a theory takes us any nearer to an understanding of 'ultimate reality' (whatever we may understand by this concept) is a very difficult philosophical question. Whatever may be the answer to this question, one of the main practical consequences of a theory is that it enables us to predict as yet unobserved events. For example, national income theory predicts that a government budget deficit[1] will reduce the amount of unemployment.[2] The simple theory of market behaviour predicts that, under certain specified conditions, the introduction of a sales tax will raise the price of the commodity concerned and that the price increase will be less than the amount of the tax. It also allows us to predict that, if there is a partial failure of the potato crop, the total income earned by potato farmers will increase!

The pervasiveness of theories

In common discussion a distinction is often drawn between theories which are thought to be academic and unreal, and hard facts which are thought to be the stuff of the real world. In practice all we ever actually observe in the world is a sequence of events. Any explanation whatsoever of how these events are linked together is a theoretical construct. Theories are what we use to impose order on our observations, to explain how the things we see are linked together. Without theories we would have only a shapeless mass of meaningless observations. If we are to make any sense at all of what we see, the choice is not one between theory and observation but between better or worse theories to explain our observations.

In a particular case we might see a change in company taxation followed by some change in the behaviour of companies. The practical man may think the link is obvious and indeed in some sense it may be, but nonetheless it requires a theoretical construction. Before we can link these two events together we need a theory of what the managers are trying to do, and of how they try to do it, plus the assumption that

1 A budget deficit arises when a government spends more than it raises by means of taxes.
2 This is not so simple a prediction as might appear at first sight. What it means and how it can be tested is considered in Chapter 36.

the managers know what behaviour will achieve their goals. Such theories of the behaviour of firms are considered in Part 4 of the present book.

Misunderstanding about the place of theories in scientific explanation gives rise to many misconceptions. One of the most common of these is the general prejudice against theories and the belief that they can be successfully dispensed with. This belief is often implied when someone makes the statement 'True in theory but not in practice'. The next time you hear someone say it (or, indeed, the next time you say it yourself) you should immediately reply, 'All right then, tell me what does happen in practice.' It is almost certain that you will not be told mere facts, but that you will be given an alternative theory – a different explanation of the facts. The speaker should have said, 'The theory in question provides a poor explanation of the facts' (i.e., it is contradicted by some factual observations) and that his alternative theory is a better one.

The construction of theories

A theory consists of a set of definitions, stating clearly what we mean by various terms, and a set of assumptions about the way in which the world behaves. Having defined terms and made assumptions about behaviour, the next step is to follow a process of logical deduction to discover what is implied by these assumptions. For example, if we assume that businessmen always try to make as much profit as is possible and if we make assumptions about how taxes affect their profits, we can derive implications about how they will behave when taxes change. These implications are the predictions of our theory; we predict for example that when taxes are next changed, businessmen will react in the way implied by our theory.[1]

The nature of scientific predictions

We have seen above that a successful theory enables us to predict as yet unobserved events. We must now consider with a little more care just what is the nature of a scientific prediction, and in particular if it is the same thing as a prophecy about the future course of events.

·1 Assumptions about behaviour often cause the student real concern. Consider a theory that starts out: 'Assume that there is no government.' 'Surely,' says the reader, 'this assumption is totally unrealistic and I cannot take seriously anything that comes out of the theory.' But this assumption may merely be the economist's way of saying that, whatever the government does, even whether or not it exists, *is irrelevant for the purposes of his particular theory*. Now, put this way, the statement becomes an empirical assertion, and the only way to test it is to see if the predictions which follow from the theory do or do not fit the facts that the theory is trying to explain. If they do, then the theorist was correct in his assumption that the government could be ignored; the criticism that the theory is un-realistic because we know that there really is a government is completely beside the point. Assumptions, however, are used in economics for other purposes, particularly to outline the set of conditions under which a theory is meant to hold. Consider a theory that assumes that the government has a balanced budget. This may mean that the theorist intends his theory to apply only when there is a balanced budget; it may *not* mean that the size of the government's budget surplus or deficit is irrelevant to the theory. The student may find it confusing that an assump-tion may mean many different things in economics. When he encounters an assumption in economic theory he should, therefore, do two things: ask what information the assumption is intended to convey, and remember that it is not always appropriate to criticize the simplifying assumptions of a theory on the grounds that they are un-realistic. *It is important to remember that all theory is an abstraction from reality*. If we did not abstract we would merely duplicate the world and would add nothing to our understanding of it. A good theory abstracts in a useful and significant way; a bad theory does not. If the student believes that the theorist has assumed away something that is important for the problem at hand, then he must believe, and try to show, that the implications of the theory are contradicted by the facts.

The critical thing to notice about a scientific prediction is that it is a conditional statement having the form '*if* you do this *then* such and such will follow'. *If* you mix hydrogen and oxygen under specified conditions, *then* water will be the result. *If* the government has a large budget deficit, *then* unemployment will be reduced. It is most important to notice that this prediction is very different from the statement: 'I prophesy that in two years' time there will be a large increase in employment because I believe the government will decide to have a large budget deficit.' The government's decision to have a budget deficit or surplus in two years' time will be the outcome of many complex factors, emotions, objective circumstances and chance occurrences, most of which cannot be predicted by the economist. If the economist's prophecy about the level of employment turns out to be wrong because in two years' time the government does not have a large deficit, then all we have learned is that the economist is not a good guesser about the behaviour of the government; we will not have found evidence that conflicts with any economic theory. However, *if* the government does have a large deficit (in two years' time or at any other time) and *then* unemployment does not fall, we have found evidence conflicting with a (conditional) scientific prediction in the field of economics.[1]

The testing of scientific predictions

If we wish to test any theory we confront its predictions with evidence. We seek to discover if certain events have the consequences predicted by the theory. Such a task is never lightly accomplished and some of the problems involved are the subject of Chapter 3. In the meantime we should notice that as with most other sciences it is never possible to prove or to refute any theory in economics with 100 per cent certainty.

Consider the simple economic theory that predicts 'if a sales tax is levied on the product of a competitive industry, *then* the price of the product will rise but by less than the amount of the tax'. It is not claimed that this prediction holds only for the years 1960–85, or only in odd-numbered years, nor is it claimed to hold in the USA and Germany but not in France and Paraguay. The prediction says that this result will hold *whenever a sales tax is levied in an industry that is competitive*. We may say that the theory is unbounded both in time and in space. But since we can make only a limited number of observations we can never prove conclusively that the theory is true. Even if we have made a thousand observations which agree with the prediction, it is always possible that in the future we will begin to make observations which conflict with the theory. Since this possibility can never be ruled out completely (no matter how unlikely we might think it to be), we can never regard any theory as conclusively proved.

It is also impossible to refute any theory conclusively. This matter is considered in

1 It is very important not to treat economic forecasting as synonymous with economic prediction. Forecasting is a type of conditional prediction which attempts to predict the future by discovering relations between economic variables of the sort that the value of Y at some future date depends on the value of X today, in which case future Y can be predicted by observing present X. Many conditional predictions are not of this form; those which relate the Y today to the value of X today provide significant and useful relations that allow us to predict 'if you do this to X you will do that to Y', without allowing us to forecast the future. The analogy often drawn between economics and weather forecasting suggests forecasting rather than the wider class of scientific predictions.

some detail in Chapter 3 and suffice it to say now that, since human beings make the tests, and since human beings are fallible, it is always possible that a piece of apparently conflicting evidence arose because we made a mistake in our observations. One conflicting observation does not worry us very much but as a mass of them accumulates we become more and more worried about our theory and will regard it as less and less likely to be true until eventually we shall abandon it even though we can never be 100 per cent certain we are not making an error in doing so.

WHEN IS A THEORY ABANDONED? As a generalization we can say that our theories tend to be abandoned when they are no longer useful, and that they cease to be useful when they cannot predict the consequences of actions in which we are interested better than the next best alternative.[1] When this happens the theory is abandoned and replaced by the superior alternative. In the process of upsetting existing theories we learn new, surprising facts.

Any developing science will continually be having some of its theories rejected; it will also be cataloguing observations that cannot be fitted into (explained by) any existing theory. These observations indicate the direction required for the development of new theories or for the extension of existing ones.[2] On the other hand, there will be many implications of existing theories that have not yet been tested, either because no one has yet figured out how to test them, or merely because no one has got around to testing them. These untested hypotheses provide agenda for new empirical studies.

The state of economics

Economics is no exception to this general rule. On the one hand there are many observations, for example the distribution of the national product among wages, profits and the rest, for which there are at present no fully satisfactory theoretical explanations. On the other hand, there are also many predictions (for example, that free international trade will make the earnings of labour less unequal between countries) which no one has yet satisfactorily tested. Thus the serious student of economics must not expect to find a set of answers to all possible questions as he progresses in his study. He must expect very often to encounter nothing more than a set of problems which provide agenda for further theoretical and empirical research. Even when he does find answers to problems, he should accept these answers as tentative and ask, even of the most time-honoured theory: 'What observations might I make that would be in conflict with this theory?' Economics is still a very young science and many problems in it are almost untouched. The student who ventures

1 In an advanced science the alternative will be another, competing theory. If there is no competing theory we can try the alternatives of comparing the theory with predictions based on a naive view such as 'this year will just be like last year', 'any change observed in the past will go on in the future', and so on.

2 The development of a new theory to account for existing observations is often the result of real creative genius of an almost inspired nature. This step in the development of science is the exact opposite of the popular conception of the scientist as an automatic rule-follower. One could argue for a long time whether there was more original creative genius embodied in a first-class symphony or a new theory of astronomy. Fascinating studies of the creative process may be found in A. Koestler, *The Sleep Walkers* (Hutchinson, 1959), especially the section on Kepler, and J.D. Watson, *The Double Helix* (Weidenfeld and Nicolson, 1968).

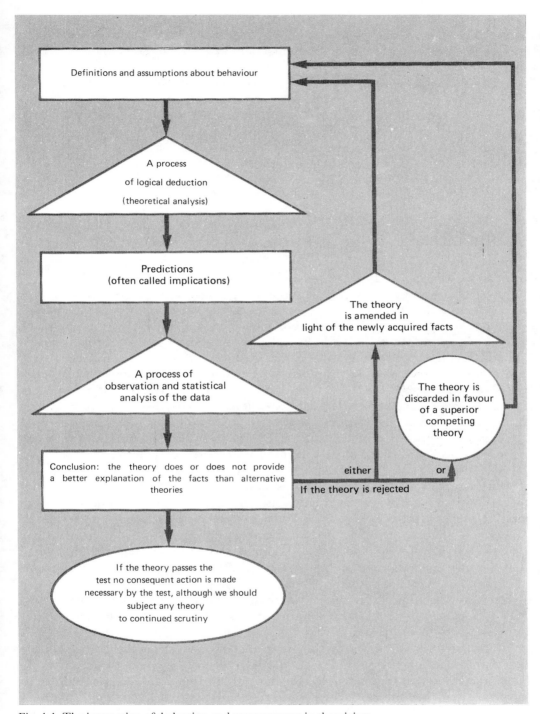

Fig. 1.1 The interaction of deduction and measurement in theorizing

further in this book may well find himself, only a few years from now, publishing a theory to account for some of the problems mentioned herein, or else he may find himself making a set of observations which will upset some time-honoured theory described within these pages.

One final word of warning: having counselled disrespect for the authority of accepted theory, it is necessary to warn against adopting an approach that is too cavalier. No respect attaches to the person who merely says: 'This theory is for the birds; it is *obviously* wrong.' This is too cheap. To criticize a theory effectively on empirical grounds one must demonstrate, by a carefully made set of observations, that some aspect of the theory is contradicted by the facts. This is a task that is seldom easily or lightly accomplished. Figure 1.1 provides a summary of the discussion of theories and it should be studied carefully.

SCIENTIFIC CRISES

Sciences often appear to evolve through a series of stages. At first, existing theories seem to be working well and the main scientific tasks are to extend the accepted theories in various directions. Then, gradually, observations begin to accumulate that conflict with existing theories. For a long time these conflicts are ignored or explained away on an *ad hoc* basis, but sooner or later the weight of conflicting evidence builds up to a crisis for the accepted theory. Finally a breakthrough occurs, and some genius develops a new theory that comprehends both what still seems right in the older theory *and* the observations that the older theory could not explain. Once the new theory is accepted, often after an interlude of uncertainty and heated controversy, a period of consolidation and extension occurs until new conflicts between theory and observation occur once again.

Economics appears to be currently in one of these times of crisis. After a long period of consolidation and development of the theories of 'macro-economics' (see Part 7), evidence that is not easily explained within the framework of existing theories is rapidly accumulating. As is usual in such times, there is substantial confusion and controversy. Some economists hold that only minor amendments to existing theories are needed to make them consistent with the new observations, others hold that major theoretical upheavals are necessary. In the heat of these controversies, economists tend to reveal what most scientists reveal in such situations: that they are first and foremost human beings with strong emotional commitments to various established positions and not dispassionate calculating machines.

Periods of scientific crisis can be profoundly disturbing for the scientists who become involved in them, to say nothing of those who depend on the scientists for answers to practical questions. Many economists are so committed to particular positions that they will never be convinced by new evidence and it seems that the best that can be hoped for is that one of the rules of the debate will remain 'try to see which theory best fits the evidence'. It is then possible that, as has happened in other sciences, a new generation of economists not committed to old and outdated positions will be able to judge the issues more dispassionately, and be able to assess correctly which of various competing theories best fits the facts.

The success of science does not require that individual scientists be totally objective. Individuals may passionately resist the apparent implications of evidence. The rule of the game that facts cannot be ignored and must somehow be fitted into the accepted theoretical structure, tends to produce scientific advance in spite of what might be thought of as unscientific, emotional attitudes on the part of many, or even most, scientists, particularly at times of scientific crisis.

But change the rules of the game by persuading people to ignore inconvenient facts or define them out of existence, and a major blow would be directed at scientific enquiry in economics.

2

The tools of theoretical analysis

If you look at the left-hand side of Figure 1.1 you will see two triangles indicating that something must be done in order to move in the direction indicated by the arrows. In order to accomplish these moves the economist needs two separate sets of tools. The first set is composed of all the apparatus of logical deduction used to discover the implications of theories. Logical deduction allows the economist to discover the implications of his assumptions, and thus to deduce from his theories predictions about observable events. The second set of tools is composed of the techniques of statistical analysis that the economist requires when he comes to test his theories against empirical observations. At that stage, he seeks to discover how well his theories stand up when confronted by the facts. This chapter is devoted to the tools of logical, or theoretical, analysis, while the tools of statistical analysis are considered in Chapter 3.

THE METHODS OF THEORETICAL ANALYSIS

We have already noted that an economic theory consists of definitions and hypotheses about the way in which the world behaves. The economic theorist has the task of discovering what is implied by these hypotheses. He seeks to make statements such as, '*If* costs vary in a certain way with output and *if* businessmen seek to make as much profit as they can, *then* a tax on the businessman's sales will have certain specified effects both on the level of output and on the price at which the product is sold.' The hypotheses of economic theory may be described in words, formulated symbolically or, if there are no more than three variables involved, illustrated graphically. Once formulated in a precise way, implications of the hypotheses may also be derived by verbal argument, mathematical analysis or geometry. Geometry is, of course, a branch of mathematics. Since we wish to distinguish geometrical from other mathematical techniques and to avoid the cumbersome expression 'mathematical techniques other than geometry', we shall hereafter distinguish between 'geometrical' and 'mathematical' methods.

To a great extent these methods are interchangeable; any piece of logical reasoning that can be done verbally or geometrically can also be done mathematically. Some things that are done in mathematics, however, cannot be done rigorously in verbal or in geometrical analysis. Where various methods can be used, the choice between them will be dictated by considerations of convenience, economy and the techniques at the command of the practitioner and the audience at which he is aiming.

EXPRESSING HYPOTHESES: THE CONCEPT OF A FUNCTIONAL RELATIONSHIP

The idea that one thing depends on another is one of the basic notions behind all of science. The gravitational attraction of two bodies depends on their total mass and on the distance separating them, attraction increasing with size and diminishing with distance; the number of murders in a country is thought to depend on, among other things, the severity of the penalties for murder; the amount of a commodity that people will buy is observed to depend on, among other things, the price of the commodity. When mathematicians wish to say that one thing depends on another, they say that one is a *function* of the other; thus we say that gravitational attraction is a function of the mass of the two bodies concerned and the distance between them; that the incidence of murder is a function of the severity of punishment for it; and that the quantity of a product demanded is a function of the price of the product.

There are two steps in giving compact symbolic expressions to the relations we have just described. First, we give each concept a symbol, and, second, we designate a symbol to express the idea of one factor's dependence on another. Thus, if we let g stand for gravitational attraction, M stand for the mass of two bodies, and d stand for the distance between two bodies, we may write

$$g = \mathrm{f}(M, d),$$

where f is read 'is a function of' and means 'depends upon'. The whole equation defines an hypothesis and is read 'Gravitational attraction is a function of the mass of the two bodies and the distance between them'. This is the same as the verbal statement with which we began.

The second hypothesis, that the number of murders depends on the severity of punishment for murder, may be expressed as

$$K = \mathrm{f}(S),$$

where K is a measure of the frequency of murders and S is a measure of the severity of punishment for being convicted of murder. The final hypothesis that the quantity demanded depends on the price of the product is written

$$q^d = \mathrm{f}(p),$$

where q^d is the quantity demanded of some commodity, and p is the price of the commodity.

The expression

$$Y = \mathrm{f}(X)$$

says that Y is a function of X. It means that Y depends upon or varies with X. The quantities X and Y in this functional relation are called *variables*. The notation often looks frightening to the student, especially to someone who did not get on well with his school mathematics. However, once one becomes familiar with it, this notation is extremely helpful, and since the functional concept is basic to all science, the notation is worth mastering.

The expression $Y = f(X)$ merely states that Y is related to X; it says nothing about the form that this relation takes. Does Y increase as X increases? Does Y decrease as X increases? Or is the relation more complicated? Take a very simple example where Y is the length of a board in feet, and X is the length of the same board in yards. Quite clearly, $Y = f(X)$. Further, in this case we know the exact form of the function, for length in feet (Y) is merely 3 times the length in yards (X), so we may write $Y = 3X$.

This example is not typical of all functional relationships because it is true by definition. It is not an hypothesis because it could not be challenged on the basis of empirical observations. It merely states in functional form the relation between the definitions of a foot and a yard. It is nonetheless useful to have a way of writing down relationships that are definitionally true.

Now consider a second example. Let C equal the total spending of a household on all consumption goods in one year, and Y equal the household's income. Now state the hypothesis

$$C = f(Y), \tag{1}$$

and, more specifically,

$$C = 0.8Y. \tag{2}$$

Equation (1) says that we hypothesize that a household's consumption depends upon its income. Equation (2) says, more specifically, that expenditure on consumption will be four-fifths as large as the household's income. The more specific equation, equation (2), expresses an hypothesis about the relation between two observable magnitudes. There is no reason why equation (2) *must* be true; indeed, it might not be consistent with the facts. But those are matters for testing. What we do have in the equation is a concise statement of a particular hypothesis.

Thus the existence of a relation between two variables, Y and X, is denoted by $Y = f(X)$, whereas any precise relation may be expressed by a particular equation such as $Y = 2X$, $Y = 4X^2$, or $Y = X + 2X^2 + 0.5X^3$.

If Y increases as X increases (e.g. $Y = 10 + 2X$), we say that Y is an INCREASING FUNCTION of X or that Y and X VARY DIRECTLY WITH each other. If Y decreases as X increases (e.g., $Y = 10 - 2X$), we say that Y is a DECREASING FUNCTION of X or that Y and X VARY INVERSELY WITH each other.

Economic theory is based on relations between various magnitudes (e.g., the quantity demanded of some commodity is related to the price of that commodity; the amount spent on consumption is related to national income). All such relations can be expressed mathematically. It is this fact that gives mathematical analysis importance in economics. Once our hypotheses are written down in terms of algebraic expressions we can use mathematical manipulation to discover what implications they have about behaviour.

THE ERROR TERM

The examples of functional relations considered above were all *deterministic* ones in the sense that they were expressed as if they held exactly: given the value of X we knew the value of Y exactly. The relations considered in economic theory are seldom of this deterministic sort.[1] When an economist says that the world *behaves* so that $Y = f(X)$, he does not expect that knowing X will tell him *exactly* what Y will be, but only that it will tell him what Y will be *with some margin of error*. This error in predicting Y from a knowledge of X arises for two quite distinct reasons. First, there may be other variables that also affect Y. When, for example, we say that the demand for butter is a function of the price of butter, $D_b = f(p_b)$, we know that other factors will also influence this demand. A change in the price of margarine will certainly affect the demand for butter, even though the price of butter does not change. Thus we do not expect to find a perfect relation between D_b and p_b that will allow us to predict D_b exactly, from a knowledge of p_b. Second, we can never measure our variables exactly, so that, even if X is the only cause of Y, our measurements will give various Ys corresponding to the same X. In the case of the demand for butter, our errors of measurement might not be large. In other cases, errors might be substantial as, for example, in the case of a relation between total spending on consumption goods, C, and total income, Y, earned in the nation: $C = f(Y)$. In this case our measurements of C and Y may be subject to quite wide margins of error, and we may observe various values of C associated with the same measured value of Y, not because C is varying independently of Y, but because our error of measurement is itself varying from period to period.

If all the factors other than X that affect the measured value of Y are summarized into an error term, ε, we write $Y = f(X, \varepsilon)$. This says that the observed value of Y is related to the observed value of X as well as to a lot of other things, both observational errors and other casual factors, all of which will be lumped together and called ε (the Greek letter epsilon). In economic theory, this error term is almost always suppressed, and we proceed as if our functional relations were deterministic. When we come to test our theories, however, some very serious problems arise precisely because we do not expect the functional relations of our theories to hold exactly.

It is extremely important, both when one comes to interpret a theory in terms of the real world and to test a theory formally against empirical observations, to remember that the deterministic formulation is a simplification, and that the error term is really present in all our assumed and observed functional relations.

---

1 Of course, an equation that expresses a definition will hold exactly. If, for example, we break up a person's income (Y) into spending (C) and saving (S), and define savings as all income not spent, then we write $Y = C + S$. This equation, which is called a definitional equation, is true exactly. We have defined our terms so that it must always hold; there is nothing anyone can do to invalidate the equation. On the other hand, if we believe that people always spend three quarters of their income and save the other quarter, we write $C = \frac{3}{4}Y$, $S = \frac{1}{4}Y$. These two equations are called behavioural equations because they tell us what we are assuming about people's behaviour. Such equations need not hold exactly; indeed they need not hold at all. We might, for example, observe someone spending only one tenth of his income and saving nine tenths, in which case neither of the latter equations would hold, although of course $Y = C + S$ is still true (by definition).

ALTERNATIVE METHODS OF REPRESENTING FUNCTIONAL RELATIONS

A functional relation states a relationship between two or more variables. Such relations can be expressed in words, in graphs or in mathematical equations. These are three alternative methods of expressing exactly the same thing.

As a simple example let us consider an assumed relation between the annual expenditure of a household on all the goods and services that it consumes (C) and its annual disposable income (Y). The assumed relation may be expressed in any one of three ways.

(1) VERBAL STATEMENT: When income is zero the household will spend £800 a year (either by borrowing the money or consuming past savings) and for every pound of income that the household obtains net of taxes (called disposable income) it will increase its expenditure by £0·80.

(2) GEOMETRICAL (GRAPHICAL) STATEMENT:

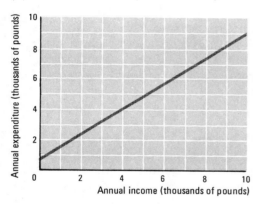

Fig. 2.1 A relation between a household's expenditure and its income

(3) MATHEMATICAL (ALGEBRAIC) STATEMENT: $C = 800 + 0·8Y$.

Since we shall make much use of the graphical representation of functional relations, it is convenient at this time to consider graphical techniques in a little more detail.

THE GRAPHICAL REPRESENTATION OF FUNCTIONAL RELATIONS[1]

In the previous section we considered a relation between annual expenditure and annual disposable income for a single hypothetical household:

$$C = 800 + 0·8Y. \tag{3}$$

It is convenient to refer to this as the household's consumption function. For any

1 Some students will find this section totally unnecessary in view of their previous background. It is included because the theoretical sections of this book rely heavily on graphical presentations, and there must be no doubt about what the graphs mean.

specified value of Y we can use the consumption function in (3) to determine the corresponding value of C. Let us start by taking five different levels of income, 0, £2,500, £5,000, £7,500 and £10,000, and calculating the level of consumption expenditure that would be associated with each. Table 2.1 shows these values and for further reference assigns a letter to each pair of values.

Table 2.1 Selected values of the function
$C = 800 + \cdot 8Y$

Y	C	Reference letter
£ 0	£ 800	A
2,500	2,800	B
5,000	4,800	C
7,500	6,800	D
10,000	8,800	E

We can, if we wish, show the data of Table 2.1 on a graph. To do this, we take each pair of values, i.e., a value of Y and the associated value of C and plot them as a point on a coordinate grid, which we do in Figure 2.2(i). In part (ii) of the figure we have plotted not only these five points but a line relating C to every value of Y in the range covered by the graph. You should take the equation $C = 800 + 0\cdot8Y$ and plot as many points as necessary to satisfy yourself that they all lie on the straight line that we have drawn in Figure 2.2(ii).

Once we have plotted this line, which *is* the function $C = 800 + 0\cdot8Y$ in the interval from $Y = 0$ to $Y = 10,000$, we have no further need for the coordinate grid, and the figure will be less cluttered if we suppress it, as in Figure 2.2(iii). For some purposes we do not really care about the specific numerical values of the function; we are content merely to represent it as an upward-sloping straight line. This is done in Figure 2.2(iv). We have replaced the specific numerical values of the variables C and Y with the letters C_1, C_2, Y_1 and Y_2 to indicate specific points. Figure 2.2(iv) tells us, for example, that if we increase the quantity of disposable income from OY_1 to OY_2, consumption expenditure will increase from OC_1 to OC_2.[1]

The beginning student may feel that we have lost ground at this stage, but it is in this form that most diagrams appear in economics texts. Let us see why. The great advantage of illustrating functional relations graphically is that we can easily compare different relations without specifying them in precise numerical form. Suppose that we wish to compare and contrast three households, R, S, and T, whose behaviour is described by the following general assumptions. (1) All three have the same amount of consumption expenditure when their disposable income is zero. The amount is greater than zero, which implies that they must be consuming past savings or going into debt. (2) In response to an increase in disposable income of £1,

1 In speaking of the quantity of Y as OY_1 or OY_2 we are following good geometric practice and recognizing that a *value* of Y is a *distance* on the Y axis. For brevity, we will usually use a shorter notation and speak of the quantity of Y as Y_1 or Y_2. This is somewhat less cumbrous, but it is important to remember that *any point on the axis represents the distance from the origin to that point* (e.g., Y_1 stands for the distance from 0 to Y_1).

household R increases its consumption expenditure by more than does household S and household S increases its consumption by more than does household T. (3) The response of each household's consumption expenditure to a change of £1 in its own disposable income is the same whatever its existing level of disposable income. These assumptions are cumbersome to state in words, but they are easily illustrated graphically. Figure 2.3 shows the postulated relations for the three households. The fact that the consumption lines all have the same intercept expresses the assumption that they all spend the same amount (Oa or simply a) when their disposable income is zero. The third assumption is shown by the fact that each household has a straight-line relation between C and Y; thus, for example, the change in C for a unit change in Y will be the same wherever we measure it on R's line. The second assumption is shown by the fact that R's line is steeper than S's line, which in turn is steeper than

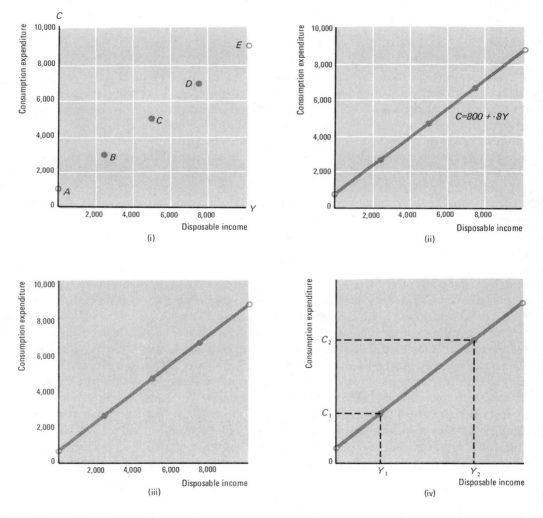

Fig. 2.2 Four different representations of the function $C = 800 + 0.8Y$

T's line. The steeper the line, the larger the change in C for a given change in Y. Thus general relations between two or more functions can be specified and analysed graphically without our having to commit ourselves to specific quantified relations such as the one illustrated in equation (3) on page 22.[1]

When we are dealing with hypotheses that are not specified quantitatively, we normally suppress most of the coordinate grid to prevent the figures from being cluttered up with irrelevant details. The grid is always understood to be there, of course, and, when required, we draw in the necessary grid lines. For instance, the coordinates of point p in Figure 2.3 are Ob and Oc, and the grid lines bp and cp are drawn in because they are needed. If you find this at all difficult, you should redraw all graphs on graph paper until you feel at home with graphical analysis.

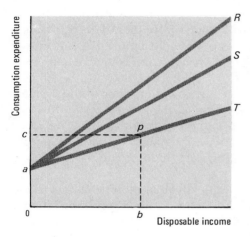

Fig. 2.3 Consumption functions for three hypothetical households

DERIVING IMPLICATIONS FROM FUNCTIONAL RELATIONSHIPS

So far, we have discussed how functional relations can be described verbally, geometrically and mathematically. When the economist has laid out the functional relations of his theory, he must then discover what is implied by these relations. He wishes to make statements such as 'If relations a and b hold, then relation c must necessarily hold as well'. In the process of making logical deductions from his theories, he may again employ verbal, geometrical or mathematical forms of reasoning. His main concerns will be to ensure that his reasoning processes are correct, so that the things he discovers are actually implied by his theory, and are efficient, so that he discovers everything that is implied by his theory.

---

1 The same general relations can also be specified algebraically. We have
$$C_r = a + b Y_r$$
$$C_s = c + d Y_s$$
$$C_t = e + f Y_t$$
where the subscripts r, s and t tell us whose income and consumption we are referring to. Assumption (1) means that $a = c = e$. Assumption (2) means that $b > d > f$. Assumption (3) means that the equations are all linear.

Many people – not just beginning students – are disturbed by the use of mathematics in economic reasoning. 'Surely,' they argue, 'human behaviour is too subtle and complex to be reduced to mathematical formulae.' At least four issues can be distinguished here.

First, we might wonder if we can ever understand enough about human behaviour to be able to build useful theories about it. This is an issue about our ability to understand, not about the language we should use to express what we do (or think we do) understand. Of course, if we don't know what we want to say, we cannot say it in any language whether verbal or mathematical. To begin to construct any economic theory, whatever language it is ultimately to be expressed in, we must assume that coherent assumptions about relevant human behaviour can be stated. (That we can make coherent assumptions about human behaviour is beyond question, since economic theory is full of them; whether or not they are relevant to the real world is an empirical question that will come up frequently in this book.) Verbal expression may sometimes be so vague as to hide our ignorance, but verbal expression can never overcome our ignorance of, or vagueness about, whatever is under consideration.

Second, we might wonder if it is *possible* to express assumptions about human behaviour in mathematical terms. If such assumptions can be stated at all, they can be stated mathematically since mathematics is just another language like English or Polish – albeit a more precise language than any of the languages of common speech. Any hypothesis about how two (or more) things are related can be expressed mathematically.

Third, we might wonder if the subtlety and complexity of human behaviour make mathematics a *less appropriate* language in which to express our assumptions than a verbal language such as English. Not only can any hypothesis about how two or more things are related be stated mathematically, but any qualification to that hypothesis that is clearly understood can also be so stated. It is always possible in words to state qualifications so vaguely that we do not know what to make of them. Indeed, verbal statements can often mask fuzziness in our concepts and assumptions. It is an advantage not a disability of mathematical formulation that it exposes what is being said and what is left unsaid. The language of mathematics turns out to be amazingly subtle and anything that we do understand clearly can be expressed in mathematical terminology.

Fourth, we might worry about the application of long chains of mechanical mathematical deductions in our theories. This worry is the source of some very serious confusions. Once the assumptions of a theory have been fully stated, all that remains for the theorist is to discover their implications. This is a stage solely requiring logical deduction proceeding from assumptions to implications. It is not a criticism to say that a technique is mechanical if by mechanical we mean that the technique does allow us to discover efficiently and accurately what is or is not implied by the assumptions of our theory. It is never an advantage to use a technique that leaves us in doubt whether or not a particular proposition is implied by our assumptions. If we accept the view that, somehow, verbal analysis (or 'judgement') can solve problems, even though we are unable to state clearly the considerations that lead to these solutions, then economics is no longer a science but has been turned instead into a medieval mystery, in which the main problem is to be able to distinguish between the true and the false prophet.

> **Mathematics is neither the maker nor the destroyer of good economic theory. Mathematics is a logical tool for deriving implications from assumptions. The advantages of mathematics are efficiency and power; but irrelevant or factually incorrect assumptions will yield irrelevant or factually incorrect implications, whatever the logical tools used to get from the former to the latter.**

Interesting examples of the process of logical deduction in economics cannot be given until we have a rigorously specified theory of some aspect of the economy. You will encounter many examples in later chapters. In the meantime we can illustrate the procedure with some very simple manipulation of the household's consumption function $C = 800 + 0.8Y$. First, it is clear that when its income is zero, the household is using up past savings or going into debt at the rate of £800 per year. Second, it is clear that an increase in income of £1 leads to an increase in consumption of 80p. Third, there will be a level of income at which the household is neither running into debt nor failing to spend all its income. This level is called the break-even level of income, and it is easily discovered by finding the level of Y such that C and Y are equal. Algebraically we need to solve the two simultaneous equations $C = 800 + 0.8Y$ and $C = Y$. The first tells us how the household's consumption expenditure varies with its income, and the second imposes the condition that consumption expenditure should equal disposable income. If you solve these two equations simultaneously, you will discover that the break-even level of income for this household is £4,000, and a little further experimentation will show that at any income less than £4,000, expenditure exceeds income, while at any income over £4,000, expenditure is less than income.

The graphical solution to this problem is shown in Figure 2.4.

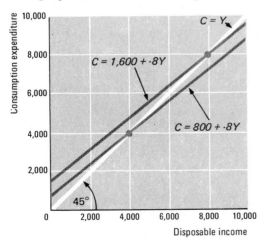

Fig. 2.4 The determination of the break-even level of income

As a final example of elementary theoretical reasoning, let us ask by how much the break-even level of income will increase if the household's behaviour changes so that, at each level of income, consumption expenditure is £800 higher than it was before. The changed behaviour is described by the new equation: $C = 1,600 + 0.8Y$. To find the new break-even level of income, we solve this simultaneously with $C = Y$ and find the solution to be £8,000. Thus, when consumption is increased by £800 at each level of income, the break-even level of income rises by £4,000. This result, which is illustrated in Figure 2.4, is perhaps a little less obvious than the previous ones. The first thing we must wonder is if it is an accident depending upon the numbers chosen or if there is some more general relation being illustrated by this particular example. A bit of experimentation with the algebra or geometry of this case should allow you to prove that, with the consumption function $C = a + 0.8Y$, any change in the constant a by an amount Δa will change the break-even level of income by $5(\Delta a)$. (Δ is the Greek capital letter *delta* and is the standard symbol for a *change* in something.) So the relation is constant for this function.

But now we must wonder about other consumption functions. To consider all linear ones we take the equation $C = a + bY$. Again a little experimentation will show you that if a is changed by an amount Δa, the break-even level of income will be changed by an amount $\Delta a/(1-b)$. This is a general result that holds for all straight-line consumption functions.

Notice how far we have come. We began with a very simple economic hypothesis relating two variables: consumption expenditure and disposable income. We took a numerical example and showed how it could be expressed algebraically and geometrically. We then showed how we could make certain simple logical deductions about what was implied by the hypothesis. At first, these deductions were obvious, but the last one – that if £800 more is spent at each level of income, break-even Y rises by £4,000 – was not quite so obvious as the others. We then wondered if this not-quite-so-obvious result was an accident depending on the particular numbers we chose. We first found that there was an unique answer for the function $C = a + 0.8Y$ (that the break-even level of Y rises by 5 times the rise in the constant a), and further experimentation showed that there was a single general result for all linear consumption functions (that break-even Y rises by $\dfrac{1}{1-b}$ times the rise in the constant a).[1]

All of this illustrates how the tools of logical analysis do allow us to discover what is implied by our assumptions. It also shows how theorizing tends to become cumulative: we obtain one result, possibly quite an obvious one, and this suggests another

---

1 This last result can be proved with simple algebra using the delta notation for changes explained in more detail on page 35. From equation (8) and $C = Y$, we at once derive that

$$Y = \frac{a}{1-b}.$$

Now let a increase by Δa, and Y must change:

$$Y + \Delta Y = \frac{a + \Delta a}{1-b} = \frac{a}{1-b} + \frac{\Delta a}{1-b}.$$

Subtracting the first equation from the second yields

$$\Delta Y = \frac{\Delta a}{1-b}.$$

possible result to us; we check this and find that it is true and this suggests something else. Then we wonder if what we have discovered applies to cases other than the one we are analysing, and before we know it we are led off on a long chase that ends only when we think we have found all of the interesting implications of the theory and have also found out how generally they apply outside the specific case we began by analysing. Of course, when we say the chase ends, we mean it ends for the particular investigator, for he is usually wrong when he thinks he has found all the implications of a theory. Some new and ingenious investigator is very likely to come up with new implications or generalizations and so the chase begins again.

THE QUANTITATIVE RELATION BETWEEN VARIABLES

The *magnitude* of the change that occurs in one variable in response to changes in another variable is extremely important in economics. We expect the quantity of any commodity that people wish to purchase (which we call quantity demanded and symbolize by q^d) to vary with its own price, $q^d = D(p)$, and we are interested in *how much* q^d changes for a given change in price. We expect the amount of a commodity produced and offered for sale, q^s, to vary with its own price, $q^s = S(p)$, and again it is important to know *by how much* q^s will change for a given change in price.[1] We expect the volume of unemployment (U) to vary with the difference between government revenue (R) and expenditure (E), $U = f(R - E)$, and we want to know *by how much* unemployment will change for a given change in the budget.

There is a precise mathematical method of handling problems arising from the question of how one variable changes as another variable on which it depends also changes. The branch of mathematics which deals with these problems is the *differential calculus*. A knowledge of the calculus is not necessary in order to read this book. In fact one can usually obtain a first degree in economics without such knowledge, but those who do have some idea of the calculus will find it a great help.[2]

The number of people obtaining a first degree in economics while remaining ignorant of mathematics is diminishing rapidly with the passage of time, and the serious student of economics is well-advised to learn at least some mathematics. For anyone going on to graduate work, who wishes to be able to read the literature of economic theory and of empirical testing, a knowledge of mathematics is for better or for worse, a necessity. It is still possible to do some kinds of specialized graduate research without a knowledge of mathematics, but without it a great deal of the literature on theoretical and applied research must remain forever a closed book.

1 Here we have two variables both related to price. To distinguish the two we use two letters, D and S to indicate the functional relationships. This is discussed further on pages 30–1.

2 An introduction to the ideas of the differential calculus plus a review of very elementary arithmetic, algebra and geometry can be found in W. W. Sawyer's excellent little book *Mathematicians Delight* (Penguin, 1943); a somewhat more advanced treatment may be found in J. Parry Lewis, *An Introduction to Mathematics for Students of Economics* (Macmillan, revised edn. 1969). A more rigorous treatment can be found in R. G. D. Allen's classic *Mathematical Analysis for Economists* (Macmillan, 1953). All these books are devoted mainly to mathematics with only passing references to economic applications. An introduction to mathematics with detailed applications to economics at each step can be found in G. C. Archibald and R. G. Lipsey, *An Introduction to a Mathematical Treatment of Economics* (Weidenfeld and Nicolson, 2nd edn., 1973).

Appendix

Some common techniques

Certain graphical and mathematical concepts are frequently encountered in economic analysis. In this appendix we deal briefly with the ones most frequently used in this book. Only the barest outlines are possible, and the student who wants a fuller treatment of the ideas expressed here should fill in his knowledge by reading the appropriate references listed in footnote 2, page 29.

Every student will need to master the elementary techniques described in this appendix before he completes his study of introductory economics. Those who find they can manage it at this stage should study the appendix carefully now. Those who had difficulty with simple mathematics at school should read carefully as far as the section entitled *Straight Lines, Slopes and Tangents*, up to which point there is no algebraic manipulation. They should then skim through the rest of the material making a list of the concepts discussed. When these concepts are encountered later in the text they should be reviewed carefully again in the Appendix.

(1) TERMINOLOGY OF FUNCTIONAL RELATIONS

It is standard terminology in modern mathematics to state that Y is a *function* of X if and only if to every value of X there corresponds at most one value of Y. This makes the concept of a function narrower than the concept of a relation, the latter allowing more than one value of Y to be associated with a given value of X. In this usage Y is a function of X in the parabola shown in Figure 2.7, page 36 since to every value of X there corresponds no more than one value of Y, but X is not a function of Y since to many Y values (e.g., $Y = 100$) there correspond two X values.

An alternative terminology uses the term function to apply to any relation and then distinguishes single-valued and multi-valued functions. In this book we use the term function to refer to a relation between X and Y whether it is single-valued or multi-valued.

In Chapter 2 we used the expression $Y = f(X)$ to denote a functional relation between X and Y. Sometimes we wish to deal with more than one functional relation and to denote that, although we do not know their exact form, the two relations may be different. It could be, for example, that in one case $Y = 3X$, whereas in the other $Y = 0.5X$. This may be indicated in any one of several ways, for example:

$$Y = f(X)$$

and

$$Y = g(X),$$

where the f and g indicate that we are dealing

with two different relations between X and Y.

The choice of letters used to indicate a functional dependence is, of course, arbitrary, but sometimes letters can be selected to indicate the particular dependence in question. Assume, for example, that both X and Z are functions of Y, e.g., $X = 10 + 3Y$ and $Z = 5 - 2Y^2$. It is often more convenient to write

$$X = X(Y)$$

and

$$Z = Z(Y).$$

On the other hand we might wish to deal simultaneously with two different relations between X and Y, for example, $X = 3Y$ and $X = 2 - 6Y$. In this case we could write

$$X = X_1(Y)$$

and

$$X = X_2(Y),$$

where the numerical subscripts distinguish the two different relations. This choice of letters to indicate the particular functional relation in question will be illustrated many times throughout this book.

(2) NECESSARY CONDITIONS AND SUFFICIENT CONDITIONS

It is common in popular discussion to confuse necessary and sufficient conditions. Many futile arguments have been caused by one person arguing that a condition was sufficient for a result and another arguing that it was not necessary, each thinking he was contradicting the other when, in fact, both were correct. Consider, for example, a club that normally admits only males who are graduates of Oxford, but that is also willing to admit all male MPs, whatever their background. Being a male MP is thus sufficient to admit you to the club, but it is not necessary to be one. Being a male is a necessary condition for admission (since no females are admitted on any terms), but it is not a sufficient condition. Being a graduate of Oxford is by itself neither necessary (since

non-Oxford graduates who are MPs can be admitted) nor sufficient (since female graduates of Oxford are not admitted). We may summarize the conditions for admission as follows:

To be male is necessary but not sufficient.
To be a male MP is sufficient but not necessary.
To be both a male and an Oxford graduate is sufficient but not necessary.
To be an Oxford graduate is neither necessary nor sufficient.
To be an MP is neither necessary nor sufficient.
To be *either* a male graduate of Oxford *or* a male MP is necessary and sufficient.

In general, a necessary condition is something that must be present but by itself may not guarantee the result. A sufficient condition is something that, if present, does guarantee the result but that need not be there for the result to occur. A condition (or set of conditions) that is necessary *and* sufficient must be there and, if there, is enough to guarantee the result.

In this club, the necessary and sufficient condition for entry is a compound either-or condition: to be either a male graduate of Oxford or a male MP. If, however, another club were set up that was open to all former members of the House of Commons and to no one else, then to have been an MP would be a necessary and sufficient condition for entry into the club.

(3) DEPENDENT AND INDEPENDENT VARIABLES

Suppose we say that Y is always 3 times as large as X. Two other ways of saying the same thing are to say that X is one third as large as Y and that Y minus $3X$ must be zero. We can write

$$Y = 3X,$$
$$X = \tfrac{1}{3}Y,$$

and

$$Y - 3X = 0.$$

These are three ways of expressing the same relation between Y and X. To express the same three forms in general terms; we can write

$$Y = g(X), \qquad (1)$$
$$X = h(Y), \qquad (2)$$

and

$$f(X, Y) = 0. \qquad (3)$$

Equations (1) and (2) are called the explicit forms of the function. In (1) Y is written as an explicit function of X. Equation (3) is called the implicit form of the function. All the terms are gathered onto the left-hand side and the whole expression is thus equal to zero. In which of the three forms we choose to write the function is clearly only a matter of convenience[1].

The term on the left-hand side of (1) and (2) is called the DEPENDENT VARIABLE and the terms on the right-hand side are called the INDEPENDENT VARIABLES. As far as mathematics is concerned the distinction between dependent and independent variables is quite arbitrary: $Y = f(X)$ necessarily implies $X = g(Y)$. The convention may be used, however, to express information we have about the causal relation between the variables. Assume for purposes of illustration, that crop yield (C) depends *solely* on the amount of rainfall (R). This allows us to write

$$C = C(R). \qquad (4)$$

But if knowing the amount of rainfall is sufficient to allow us to deduce the amount of crop, then knowing the amount of crop is sufficient to let us deduce the amount of rainfall. Thus we also have

$$R = R(C). \qquad (5)$$

As far as mathematics is concerned, it does not matter which of these two ways we choose. But, of course, the causal relation is clearly defined in this case. The amount of

1 It is not always possible to write a relation in each of these forms. Consider, for example, $x + 2y - 10 = 0$ and $x^2 + xy + y^2 = 0$.

rainfall influences the crop yield; the crop yield does not influence the amount of rainfall.

As a matter of convention, whenever we think we know the direction of the causal link between variables we write the causes as independent variables and the effects as dependent ones. Thus, as a matter of convention, we would use equation (4) instead of equation (5). Again, if we wanted to say crop yield (C) depended on fertilizer (F), sunshine (S) and rainfall (R) we would write

$$C = C(F, S, R). \qquad (6)$$

In equation (6), C is the dependent variable and F, S and R are the independent variables.

(4) EXOGENOUS AND ENDOGENOUS VARIABLES

In economic theories it is convenient to distinguish between EXOGENOUS and ENDOGENOUS VARIABLES. Endogenous variables are ones that are explained *within* a theory; exogenous variables are ones that influence the variables but are themselves determined by factors outside the theory. Assume, for example, that we have a theory of what determines the price of apples from day to day in London. The price of apples in this case is an endogenous variable – something determined within the framework of the theory. The state of the weather, on the other hand, is an exogenous variable. It will influence apple prices but will be uninfluenced by these prices. The state of the weather will not be explained by our theory; it is something that happens from without, so to speak, but it nonetheless influences our endogenous variables, apple prices, because it affects the demand for apples. Exogenous variables are sometimes referred to as AUTONOMOUS VARIABLES.

(5) STOCKS AND FLOWS

Some of the most serious confusions in economics have arisen from a failure to distinguish between STOCKS and FLOWS. Imagine a bathtub half full of water with the tap turned on and the plug removed; you have in mind a model similar to many simple economic theories. The level of water in the bath is a stock – an amount that is just there. We could express it as so many gallons of water. The amount of water entering through the tap and the amount leaving through the drain are both flows. We could express them as so many gallons *per minute* or *per hour*. A flow necessarily has a time dimension – there is so much flow *per period of time*. A stock does not have a time dimension – it is just so many tons or gallons or heads.

The amount of wheat produced is a flow; there is so much flow per year or per month. The amount of wheat sold is also a flow – so much per month or year. The amount of wheat stored (produced but unsold) in the granaries of the world is a stock; it is just so many millions of tons of wheat. The distinction between stocks and flows will arise many times throughout this book.

(6) IDENTITIES AND EQUATIONS

The distinction between *definitional identities* and *equations* is important and subtle. A definitional identity is true for all values of the variables; no values can be found that would contradict it. An example of such an identity is

1 Yard ≡ 3 Feet.

It should be noted that identities are often written with a three-bar sign and that the expression $y \equiv x$ is read 'y is identical with x'.

Equations are relations that are true only for some values of the variables but that can be contradicted by other values. Thus the expression $y = 10 + 2x$ is an equation. It is written with a two-bar or equals sign and is read y is equal to ten plus two x. This expression is true, for example, for $x = 2$ and $y = 14$, but not for $x = 2$ and $y = 2$. Equations can be used to state testable hypotheses, since they make statements that are true for some states of the universe but false for other states;

definitions do not state testable hypotheses, since they make statements that are true by virtue of our use of words.

Definitional identities, therefore, tell us nothing about the world. They cannot be the 'basis' of any theory (although they can be used very helpfully to convey definitions of terms) and they can usually be reduced to the form $y \equiv y$ which, although true, is hardly very enlightening. Consider, for example, the statement

$$y = c + s, \qquad (7)$$

where y is a man's income, where c is his expenditure on goods and services, and where s is the amount he saves. As it stands we do not yet know if this is an identity or an equation. If y is defined as the amount of money the man earns, c as the amount he actually spends on goods and services, and s as the amount he puts in the bank, then the equation expresses an hypothesis about what people do with their incomes. This is because there are other things the man might do with his income, such as giving it to his nephew. Now, however, let us keep the above definitions of y and c, but define s in terms of y and c: s is defined to be all income not spent on consumption. Thus by definition we have

$$s \equiv y - c. \qquad (8)$$

Equation (7) is a definitional identity,

$$y \equiv c + s. \qquad (9)$$

We fool ourselves if we think we have learned anything from (9), for, if we substitute (8) into it, we get

$$y \equiv c + y - c,$$

which, of course, reduces to

$$y \equiv y,$$

which is true for *any* values of y, c and s.

Confusion between equations and definitional identities is a source of error in economics. One of the most perplexing habits of economists is to warn the student about the nature of identities and then to introduce national-income theory with several pages of definitional identities claimed to be the foundation of the theory.[1]

(7) SOME CONVENTIONS IN FUNCTIONAL NOTATION

Assume we are talking about some sequence of numbers, say, 1, 2, 3, 4, 5,.... If we wished to talk about one particular term in this series without indicating which one, we could talk about the ith term, which might be the 5th or the 50th. If we now want to indicate terms adjacent to the ith term, whatever it might be, we talk about the $(i-1)$th and the $(i+1)$th terms.

By the same token we can talk about a series of time periods, say, the years 1900, 1901 and 1902. If we wish to refer to three adjacent years in any series without indicating which three years, we can talk about the years $(t-1)$, t and $(t+1)$.

Now consider some functional relation, say, one between the quantity produced by a factory and the number of workers employed. In general, we can write $Q = Q(W)$, where Q is the amount of production and W is the number of workers. If we wished to refer to the value of output where ten workers were employed, we could write $Q_{10} = Q(W_{10})$, whereas, if we wished to refer to output when some particular, but unspecified, number was employed, we wrote $Q_i = Q(W_i)$. Finally, if we wished to refer to output when the number of workers is increased by one above the previous level, we can write $Q_{i+1} = Q(W_{i+1})$. This use of subscripts to refer to the value of the variables where they take on particular numbers is a most useful notation and one that we shall use at various points in this book.

We may also use time subscripts to indicate a lagged relation between variables. A lagged relation between X and Y is one in which the

value of Y at any point of time depends on the value of X at some previous point of time. Let us say that the amount produced of a product is a function of its price; so we write $Q = Q(p)$, where Q is the amount produced and p is the price of the product. Production takes time, and what is produced today may not be much influenced by today's prices. If we divide time into months and assume a three-months' lag in output, then we have $Q_t = Q(p_{t-3})$, which says that the amount produced today depends on what the price was three time periods ago, which in this case is three months ago.

Another convention is used to save space when there are many independent variables in a function. Let us say that Y depends on six variables X_1 to X_6. We could write this as

$$Y = Y(X_1, X_2, X_3, X_4, X_5, X_6),$$

but this is rather cumbersome, so, instead, we write

$$Y = Y(X_1, \ldots, X_6),$$

where the dots indicate that the intervening terms are understood to be present.

Now assume that Y is a function of some number of variables but we do not wish to say exactly how many. We can say that Y is a function of n variables X_1 to X_n. Now the omission of intermediate variables is necessary, for, until we know what number n stands for, we cannot say how many variables there are. In this case we write

$$Y = Y(X_1, \ldots, X_n).$$

(8) GRAPHING FUNCTIONS

A coordinate graph divides space into four quadrants, as shown in Figure 2.5. The upper right-hand quadrant, which is the one in which both X and Y are positive, is usually called the positive quadrant. Very often in economics we are concerned only with the positive values of our variables, and in such cases we confine our graph to the positive quadrant. Whenever we want one or both of our variables to be allowed to take on negative values we must include some or all of the

1 A criticism of this practice, and reference to places where it is used, is given in K. Klappholz and E. J. Mishan, 'Identities in Economic Models', *Economica*, May 1962, and R. G. Lipsey in *Essays in Honour of Lord Robbins*, ed. by M. Peston and B. Corry (Weidenfeld & Nicolson, 1971).

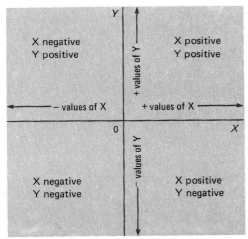

Fig. 2.5 A coordinate graph divides space into quadrants

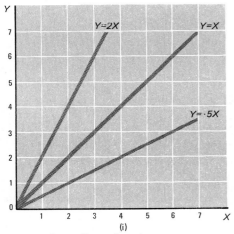

(i)

Fig. 2.6 Some linear functions

see that they are all straight lines through the origin. This is also obvious from the fact that if we let $X = 0$ in each of the above relations Y also becomes 0. In the first equation, Y goes up half a unit every time X goes up by one unit; in the second equation, Y goes up one unit every time X goes up one unit; and in the third equation, Y goes up two units every time X goes up one unit.

We now introduce the symbol Δ to indicate a change in a variable. Thus ΔX means the value of the change in X and ΔY means the value of the change in Y. In the first equation if $X = 10$ then Y is 5 and if X goes up to 16, Y goes up to 8. Thus, in this exercise, $\Delta X = 6$ and $\Delta Y = 3$.

Next consider the ratio $\Delta Y / \Delta X$. In the

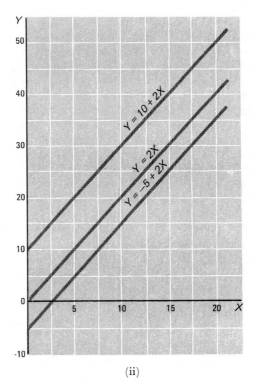

(ii)

other quadrants. For example, one of the functions in Figure 2.6(ii) is extended into the quadrant in which X is positive and Y is negative, while the remaining two functions are not extended beyond the positive quadrant.

(9) STRAIGHT LINES, SLOPES AND TANGENTS

Consider the following functional relations:
$$Y = \cdot 5X,$$
$$Y = X,$$
$$Y = 2X.$$
These are graphed in Figure 2.6(i). You will

above example it is equal to $\cdot 5$. In general, it will be noted that, for any change we make in X in the first equation, $\Delta Y / \Delta X$ is always $\cdot 5$. In the second it is unity and in the third the ratio is always 2. In general, if we write

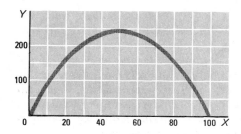

Fig. 2.7 A parabola with a maximum value of Y

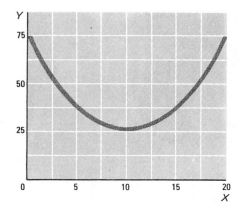

Fig. 2.8 A parabola with a minimum value of Y

$Y = bX$, then, as is proved below, the ratio $\Delta Y/\Delta X$ is always equal to b.

We now define the slope of a straight line to be the ratio of the distance moved up the Y axis to the distance moved along the X axis. We start at the point (X_1, Y_1) and then move to the point (X_2, Y_2). The change in X is $X_2 - X_1$ or ΔX as indicated. The change in Y is $Y_2 - Y_1$ or ΔY. Thus the ratio $\Delta Y/\Delta X$ is the slope of the straight line. This slope tells us the ratio of a change in Y to a change in X.

In trigonometry the tangent of an angle is defined as $\Delta Y/\Delta X$; thus the slope of the line is equal to the tangent of the angle between the line and any line parallel to the X axis. In general, the larger the ratio $\Delta Y/\Delta X$ the steeper the graph of the relation. In Figure 2.6(i) three lines corresponding to $\Delta Y/\Delta X = \frac{1}{2}$, 1 and 2 are shown. Clearly, the steeper the line the larger the change in Y for any given change in X.

Now consider the following equations:

$$Y = 2X$$
$$Y = 10 + 2X$$
$$Y = -5 + 2X.$$

These are graphed in Figure 2.6(ii). It will be observed that all three lines are parallel, i.e., they have the same slope. In all three $\Delta Y/\Delta X$ is equal to 2. Clearly, the addition of a (positive or negative) constant does not affect the slope of the line. This slope is influenced only by the number attached to X. In general, we may write the equation of a straight line as

$$Y = a + bX.$$

Now, by inserting two values of X, say X_1 and X_2, and finding the corresponding Ys, we get

$$Y_1 = a + bX_1$$

and

$$Y_2 = a + bX_2,$$

and, by subtraction,

$$Y_2 - Y_1 = b(X_2 - X_1)$$

or

$$\Delta Y = b\Delta X$$

$$\frac{\Delta Y}{\Delta X} = b.$$

The constant a disappears when we subtract and so does not influence the slope of the line. What the constant does is to shift the line upward or downward parallel to itself.

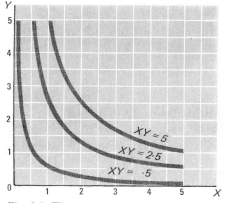

Fig. 2.9 Three rectangular hyperbolae

(10) NONLINEAR FUNCTIONS

All of the examples used so far in this appendix and most of the examples in the text of Chapter 2 concern linear relations between two variables. A linear relation is described graphically by a straight line, and algebraically by the equation $Y = a + bX$. It is characteristic of a linear relation that the effect on Y of a given change in X is the same whatever the values of X and Y from which we start. The graphical expression of this is that the slope of a straight line is constant.

Many of the relations encountered in economics are nonlinear. In these cases the relation will be expressed graphically by a curved line and algebraically by some expression more complex than the one for a straight line. Two common examples are as follows:

$$Y = a + bX + cX^2$$

and

$$Y = \frac{a}{X^b}.$$

The first example is a parabola that can take up various positions and shapes depending on the signs and magnitudes of a, b and c. Two examples of parabolas are given in Figures 2.7 and 2.8. The second example becomes a rectangular hyperbola if we let $b = 1$, and then the position is determined by the value of a. Three examples where $a = 0.5$, 2.5 and 5 are shown in Figure 2.9.

There are, of course, many other examples of nonlinear relations between variables. In general, whatever the relation between X and Y, as long as it can be expressed on a graph it can also be expressed by means of an algebraic equation.

(11) MAXIMUM AND MINIMUM VALUES

Consider the function

$$Y = 10X - 0.1X^2,$$

which is plotted in Figure 2.7. It will be observed that Y at first increases as X increases, but after a while Y begins to fall

as X goes on rising. We say that Y rises to a *maximum*, which is reached in this case when $X = 50$. Until $X = 50$, Y is rising as X rises, but after $X = 50$, Y is falling as X rises. Thus Y reaches a maximum value of 250 when X is 50.

A great deal of economic theory is based on the idea of finding a maximum (or a minimum) value. Since Y is a function of X, we speak of *maximizing the value of the function*, and by this we mean that we wish to find the value of X (50 in this case) for which the value of Y is at a maximum (250 in this case).

Now consider the function

$$Y = 75 - 10X + 0.5X^2,$$

which is graphed in Figure 2.8. In this case, the value of Y falls at first while X increases, reaches a *minimum*, and then rises as X goes on increasing. In this case, Y reaches a minimum value of 25 when X is 10. Here we speak of *minimizing the value of the function*, by which we mean finding the value of X for which the value of Y is at a minimum.

(12) FUNCTIONS OF MORE THAN ONE VARIABLE

In most of the examples used so far Y has been a function of only one variable, X. In many cases the dependent variable is a function of more than one independent variable. The demand for a good might depend, for example, on the price of that good, on the prices of a number of competing products, on the prices of products used in conjunction with the product with which we are concerned, and on consumers' incomes.

When we wish to denote the dependence of Y on several variables, say, V, W and X, we write $Y = Y(V, W, X)$, which is read Y is a function of V, W and X.

In mathematics and in economics we are often concerned about what happens to Y as X varies on the assumption that the other factors that influence X are held constant at some stated level. There are many ways to denote this and we shall use the following notation:

$$Y = Y(X) \quad \bigg|\, \begin{array}{l} V = V^0 \\ W = W^0. \end{array}$$

The symbols to the right of the bar tell us what is being held constant and at what level. The above example is read Y is a function solely of X with V held constant at the level V^0 and W held constant at the level W^0. In a particular example, we might state the actual levels of V and W. If, for example, W were held constant at 10 and V at 5 we would write

$$Y = Y(X) \quad \bigg|\, \begin{array}{l} V = 5 \\ W = 10. \end{array}$$

(13) PARTIAL DERIVATIVES

Students who do not know mathematics are often disturbed by the frequent use in eco-nomics of arguments that depend on the qualification 'other things being equal' (for which we often use the Latin phrase *ceteris paribus*). Such arguments are not peculiar to economics. They are used successfully in all branches of science and there is an elaborate set of mathematical techniques available to handle them.

When mathematicians wish to know the approximate ratio $\Delta Y/\Delta X$ (i.e., how Y is changing as X changes) when other factors that influence Y are held constant, they calculate what is called the *partial derivative of Y with respect to X*. This is written symbolically as $\partial Y/\partial X$. We cannot enter here into a discussion of how this expression is calculated. We only wish to note that finding $\partial Y/\partial X$ is a well-recognized and very common mathematical operation, and the answer tells us approximately how Y is affected by small variations in X when *all other relevant factors are held constant*.

3

The tools of statistical analysis

If you look once again at the left-hand side of Figure 1.1 you will see that the second of the two processes contained in triangles is the process of statistical analysis used to test the predictions of theories. The role of statistical analysis is twofold. First, we wish to use observations from the real world to test our theories. Second, we wish to use such observations to give us measures of the quantitative relations between economic variables. Testing and measurement are the purposes for which statistical tools are needed. In this chapter we consider them both.

TESTING

In order to determine whether or not they do give us predictions that are correct within some acceptable margin of error, we must test our theories against the evidence of what actually happens in the economy. Testing theories against observations is not a task that is lightly accomplished (or briefly described). As a first step in seeing how we go about testing theories, we must distinguish between laboratory and non-laboratory methods.

Laboratory sciences

In some sciences, it is possible to obtain all observations needed for testing a theory from controlled experiments made under laboratory conditions. In such experiments, we hold constant all the factors that are thought to affect the outcome of the process being studied. Then we vary these factors one by one while we observe the influence that each variation appears to have on the outcome of the experiment.

Suppose, for example, we have a theory that predicts that the rate at which a substance burns is a function of the chemical properties of that substance and the rate at which oxygen is made available during the process of combustion. To test this theory, we can (1) take a number of identical pieces of some substance and burn them, varying the amount of oxygen made available in each case. This allows us to see how combustion varies with the quantity of oxygen used. We can then (2) take a number of substances with different chemical compositions and burn them, making available identical amounts of oxygen in each case. This allows us to see how combustion varies with chemical composition.

In such an experiment, we never have to use data that are generated when both chemical composition and the quantity of oxygen are varying simultaneously. Laboratory conditions are used to hold other things constant and to produce data for situations in which factors are varied one at a time.

Non-laboratory sciences

In some sciences we cannot isolate factors one at a time in laboratory experiments. In these sciences observations are still used to establish relationships and to test theories, but such observations appear in a relatively complex form, because several things are usually varying at the same time.

Consider, for example, the hypothesis that one's health as an adult depends upon one's diet as a child. Clearly, all sorts of other factors affect the health of adults: heredity, conditions of childhood other than nutrition, and various aspects of adult environment. There is no possible way to examine this hypothesis in the manner of a controlled experiment, for we are unlikely to be able to find a group of adults whose diet as children varied but for whom all other influences affecting health were the same. Should we conclude that the hypothesis cannot be tested because other factors cannot be held constant? If we did we would be denying the possibility of many advances in medicine, biology and other sciences concerned with humans that have actually been made during the last hundred years. Testing is harder when one cannot use laboratory methods, but, fortunately, it is still possible.

In a situation in which many things are varying at once, we must be careful in our use of data. If we study only two people and find that the one with the better nutritional standards during his youth has the poorer adult health record, this would not disprove the hypothesis that a good diet is a factor leading to better health. It might well be that some other factor had exerted an overwhelming influence on these two individuals. The less healthy man may have lived most of his adult life in a disease-ridden area of the tropics, whereas the more healthy may have lived in a relatively congenial northern climate. Clearly, a single exception does not disprove the hypothesis of a relation between two things as long as we admit that other factors can also influence the outcome.[1]

How can we test an hypothesis where many things vary at once? If we cannot select data chosen in such a way that other things are held equal, we have to fall back

---

1 Note how often in ordinary conversation a person advances a possible relation (e.g., between education and some facet of a man's character) and how someone else will 'refute' this theory by citing a single counterexample (e.g., 'my friend went to that school and did not turn out like that'). It is a commonplace in everyday conversation to dismiss an hypothesis with some such remark as 'Oh, that's just a generalization'. All interesting hypotheses are generalizations and it will always be possible to notice some real or apparent exceptions. What we need to know is whether or not the mass of evidence supports the hypothesis as a statement of a general tendency for two or more things to be related to each other. This issue can never be settled one way or the other by the casual quoting of a few bits of evidence that just happen to be readily available.

on more formal statistical techniques that have been designed to unscramble the separate effects of several influencing factors all of which are changing simultaneously.

> **The techniques of statistical analysis show how, given enough observations, it is generally possible to identify the relationship, if one exists, between two variables, even though other things which affect the outcome are also varying.**

THE STATISTICAL TESTING OF ECONOMIC THEORIES: an example

Economics is a non-laboratory science. It is rarely if ever possible to conduct controlled experiments with the economy. Millions of *uncontrolled experiments* are, however, going on every day: housewives are deciding what to purchase in the face of changing prices and incomes; firms are deciding what to produce and how to produce it; and government bodies are intervening in the economy with taxes, subsidies and controls. All of these acts can be observed and recorded. Thus a mass of data is produced continually by the economy. Most things in which economists are interested, such as the volume of unemployment, the level of prices and the distribution of income, are influenced by a large number of factors, many of which vary simultaneously. If we are to test our theories about relations in the economy, we will have to use those statistical techniques that were designed for situations in which other things are not held constant.

Consider the simple hypothesis that there is a strong relation between the incomes of American households and the quantities of beef they purchase.[1] To begin with, we need to make observations of household income and purchase of beef. We realize that we cannot enumerate all the individual households in the American population, so we must take a smaller number of observations (called a *sample*) and hope that it is typical of all US households.

The sample

We start by observing three households. Our data are recorded in Table 3.1. These data may lead us to wonder if our hypothesis is wrong, but, before we jump to that conclusion, we should also note that 'by chance' we may have happened to select three households that are not typical of all the households in the country. The expenditure on food is undoubtedly influenced by factors other than income and possibly these other factors just happen to be the dominant forces in these three cases selected.

To check on this possibility, we select a large number of households in order to reduce the chances of consistently picking untypical ones. Suppose we do this by selecting 100 households from among our friends and acquaintances. A statistician points out, however, that our new group is a very *biased sample*, for it contains households from only a limited geographical area, probably with only a limited occupational range, and possibly with very similar incomes. It is unlikely that this sample

---

1 The data for this example are adapted from Daniel B. Suits, *Statistics: An Introduction to Quantitative Economic Research* (Rand McNally, 1963) p. 169.

Table 3.1 Beef consumption and total
income for three US households

Household	Household income $	Consumption of beef, pounds per week
1	4,500	5·10
2	5,500	5·05
3	6,500	4·93

of households will be representative of all households in the United States, which is
the group in which we are interested.

The statistician suggests that we take a *random sample* of households. A random
sample is chosen according to a rigidly defined set of conditions that guarantees,
among other things, that every household in which we are interested has an equal
chance of being selected. Choosing our sample in a random fashion has two important consequences. First, it makes it unlikely that our sample will be very unrepresentative of all households, and, second, it allows us to calculate just how likely it is
that our sample is unrepresentative in any given aspect by any stated amount. The
reason for this second result is that our sample was chosen by chance, and chance
events are predictable. This is extremely important because the predictability of
chance events allows us, for example, to determine the probability that all households
in the United States will differ by any quantitative amount from the households in
our sample.

That chance events are predictable may sound surprising. But if you pick a card
from a deck of ordinary playing cards, how likely is it that you will pick a heart? an
ace? an ace of hearts? You play a game in which you pick a card and win if it is a
heart and lose if it is anything else; a friend offers you £5 if you win against £1 if you
lose. Who will make money if the game is played a large number of times? The same
game is played again, but you get £3 if you win and pay £1 if you lose. Now who will
make money over a large number of draws? If you know the answers to these
questions, you know that chance events are in some sense predictable.

Once we have chosen our random sample we collect the information we require
from it, including, in this case, the income of each household and its purchases of
beef. In this example we are dealing with a random sample of 4,827 households.

The analysis of the data

We first plot the data on a *scatter diagram*. In Figure 3.1, we measure household
income along the horizontal axis and purchases of beef along the vertical one. Each
dot represents one household, and its position on the graph tells us the income and
beef purchases of that household. [1]

1 There are 4,827 observations in our sample. A scatter diagram with this number of points would be unintelli-
gible when reduced to the size of a printed page. We have drawn the scatter diagram by taking a 5 per cent random
sample of the 4,827 households. Each of the dots is to be thought of, therefore, as standing for 20 of the households
in our sample.

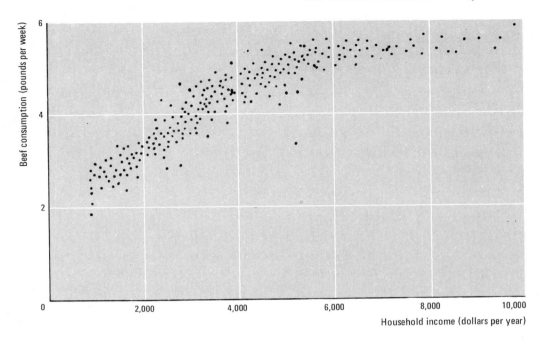

Fig. 3.1 A scatter diagram showing income and expenditure on food of 242 American households

The scatter diagram in Figure 3.1 suggests that there is a strong tendency for purchases of beef to be higher, the higher is household income. The relationship is not perfect, however, for there is considerable variation in beef purchases that cannot be associated with variations in households' incomes. These 'unexplained variations' in beef purchases occur for two main reasons: first, there are factors other than income that influence beef purchases, and some of these other factors will undoubtedly have varied between the households in our sample; second, there will inevitably be some errors in our measurements (e.g., a household might have incorrectly recorded its beef purchases).

In order to make the data somewhat more manageable, we have grouped them into classes. In Table 3.2, we grouped together in the first row all the households with incomes between zero and $999 a year and calculated their average weekly beef consumption. In the second row we did the same for households with incomes between $1,000 and $1,999 per year, and so on. This reduces a mass of 4,827 observations to a mere 10 observations. At the loss of some considerable amount of detail, the table makes clearer the general tendency for beef purchases to rise with income.

We can estimate the specific relation between beef purchases and household income from the data at hand if certain conditions are fulfilled.[1] Given that these conditions are approximately fulfilled, we can do three things. First, we can fit to the data a line that represents the best estimate of the actual relation between household

---

1 These must be left in detail to courses in statistics and econometrics. One such condition is that other factors causing beef purchases to vary among households are not themselves systematically related to income. In that case they will tend to average out in a large sample.

Table 3.2 Beef purchases and income for a sample
of US households

Household income $	Average weekly beef consumption, pounds	Number of families
0–999	2·13	532
1,000–1,999	2·82	647
2,000–2,999	3·70	692
3,000–3,999	4·25	867
4,000–4,999	4·86	865
5,000–5,999	5·16	513
6,000–6,999	5·20	371
7,000–7,999	5·30	159
8,000–8,999	5·52	121
9,000–9,999	5·90	60

income and beef purchases.[1] This line will describe the tendency for higher household incomes to be associated with higher beef consumption. (The equation of a line so fitted is $B = 2·35 + 0·47Y$, where B is purchases of beef in pounds and Y is income in thousands of dollars per year. The line shows that for every increase of $1,000 in household income, beef consumption tends to increase by about half a pound per week.)

Second, we can obtain a measure of the percentage of the variations in household expenditure on food that can be accounted for by variations in household income. This is the commonly encountered r^2, which is called the coefficient of determination and which, in this case, tells us the proportion of the variance[2] in beef purchases that can be 'explained' by associating it with variations in household incomes.

Third, we can apply a 'significance test'. This allows us to discover the chances that the relation we have discovered has arisen only because our sample is not representative of all households in the United States. In the present case, there is less than one chance in one million that we could have made the observations that we did if, in fact, there were no relation between income and beef purchases for all US households. Thus we can have a great deal of confidence in the hypothesis that these two variables, beef purchases and household income, are in fact positively related in the United States.

It is clear from the scatter diagram that we cannot account for *all* of the variation in households' purchases of beef by observed variations in household income. If we could, all the dots would lie on a line. We may wish to look for some other factor that might also exert a systematic influence on beef expenditure. What could make one household with an income of $6,000 buy 20 per cent more beef than another household with the same income? One possible factor is that households in different

1 Before we fit the line, we must decide if the relation is best described by a straight line or a curve. Fortunately there are tests that allow us to tell if we made an error in thinking that the relation was linear when it really was curvilinear. In the example considered here, the correct relation is slightly curvilinear, but a straight line is a reasonable approximation to the correct relation over the range of most of the data.

2 *Variance* is a precise statistical measure of the amount of variability (dispersion) in a set of data.

parts of the country may have been faced with very different prices of beef. Of course, there will be many other factors, such as size of family and religion, but we shall select price for the purpose of illustrating how to handle more than one factor simultaneously. Assume that the US Department of Agriculture survey also collected data on the prices of various cuts of beef in each city or town from which a household in the sample bought its meat. These data were then used to calculate the average price of beef facing each household.

We now have three observations for each one of our 4,827 households – their annual income, their weekly purchases of beef, and the average price of the beef that they purchase. How should we handle these data? Unfortunately, our scatter-diagram technique has now let us down, since we cannot easily show the relation among three things on a two-dimensional graph. We can, however, group the data in a fashion similar to the way they were grouped in Table 3.2. This time we have two variables that are thought to influence beef consumption, and we have to *cross-classify* the data as shown in Table 3.3. To prevent the table from becoming too large, we have grouped households into income groups of $2,000 rather than $1,000, as in Table 3.2, but this is only a matter of convenience, and the classification can be made as detailed as is required for any particular purpose.

Table 3.3 Average household purchases of beef in pounds per week, classified by household income and the average purchase price of beef

| Household income $ | Average price of beef per pound | | | |
	$0·80–0·99	$1·00–1·19	$1·20–1·39	$1·40–1·59
0–1,999	2·65	2·59	2·51	2·43
2,000–3,999	4·14	4·05	3·94	3·88
4,000–5,999	5·11	5·00	4·97	4·84
6,000–7,999	5·35	5·29	5·19	5·07
8,000–9,999	5·79	5·77	5·60	5·53

Each row of this table exhibits the effect of *price* on the purchases of beef for a given level of income. Reading across the second row, for example, we see that households with incomes between $2,000 and $3,999 bought an average of 4·14 pounds of beef when the 'price' was between 80 and 99¢ per pound, 4·05 pounds when the price was between $1 and $1·19, and so on. Each column of the table shows the effect of *income* on purchases of beef for given prices of beef. For instance, the last column shows how beef purchases varied with income for those households that were subject to a very high average price of beef. It should be clear that this device of cross-classification manages to catch observationally much of the idea of *holding other things constant* that is sometimes thought to be possible only in laboratory sciences. [1] Reading across any row, we are holding income constant within a specified range, which can be made smaller by making the classification finer, and varying price; reading down any column, we are holding price constant within a specified range and varying income.

1 See the discussions on page 37, 'Functions of More than One Variable', and on page 38, 'Partial Derivatives'.

If we wish to estimate a numerical relation between household income, average price and beef purchases, we may use the technique of *multiple regression analysis*. This technique allows us to estimate the effects of variations in the price of beef and in household income on beef purchases. It also permits us to measure the proportion of the total variation in beef purchases that can be explained by associating it with variations both in income and in price. Finally, it permits us to estimate how likely it is that the relations we have found in our sample are the result of chance rather than an underlying relationship for all US households. Chance enters because we might by bad luck have chosen an unrepresentative sample of households.

TESTING HYPOTHESES

Statistical techniques can help us to measure the nature and strength of economic relationships, and can tell us how probable it is that a certain result has occurred merely by chance. What they cannot do is to *prove* with certainty that an hypothesis is either true or false. We have already discussed this matter in Chapter 1, but we now summarize the earlier discussion and then take it a step further.

Can we prove an hypothesis is true?

Most hypotheses in economics are what may be called universal hypotheses. They say that, whenever certain specified conditions are fulfilled, cause X will always produce effect Y. We have already pointed out that universal hypotheses cannot be proved to be correct because we can make only a finite number of actual observations and we can never rule out the possibility that we shall in the future make a large number of observations that conflict with the theory.

Can we prove an hypothesis is false?

By the same token, we cannot get a categorical disproof of an hypothesis. Consider the hypothesis 'Most crows are black'. We observe 50 crows; 49 are grey and only one is black. Have we disproved the hypothesis? The answer is no, for it is *possible* that this was just bad luck, and that if we could observe all the crows in the world it would indeed prove to be the case that most are black. Although we have not disproved the hypothesis, we have learned something from our study of 50 crows and, if we have to make a decision about the blackness of all crows, we may be better off for having this information. In particular, we are likely to suspect that our hypothesis is not correct. The question of decision-taking is considered below but in the meantime we must ask if it is ever possible categorically to refute an hypothesis. To do this we need two conditions. First, the hypothesis must admit of no exceptions: it must say, for example, all crows are black, or in the language of Chapter 1, it must be a deterministic hypothesis. Second, we must be certain that any apparently refuting observations are not mistaken. The observation of 49 black crows and one grey refutes the hypothesis *all* crows are black provided we are sure that we genuinely saw a grey crow. But are we sure that the odd bird really was a crow? Are we sure that what looked like a grey crow was not a dusty black crow.[1] Errors in observation may always be present. For this reason, an hypothesis cannot be refuted on the basis of a single conflicting observation, and indeed it can never be categorically refuted no matter how many conflicting observations we make. If we observe 49 grey crows and only one black one, our faith in the hypothesis that all crows are black may well be shaken and as a practical measure we may choose to abandon the hypothesis (see below). We can never be certain, however, that all 49 cases were not due to errors of observation[2] and had we persisted we might have ended up with 999,950 black crows and 50 grey ones. (This would make the hypothesis look pretty good, since a measurement error on 0·005 per cent of our cases might not seem at all improbable.[3])

Rules for decision-taking

We have seen that in general we can neither prove nor refute an hypothesis conclusively, no matter how many observations we make. Nonetheless, we have to make decisions and act as if some hypotheses were refuted (i.e., we have to reject them) and we have to act as if some hypotheses were proved (i.e., we have to accept them). Such decisions are always subject to error but by using statistical analysis we can control the possibility of making errors even if we cannot eliminate it. This is an extremely valuable thing to be able to do. The method of control is to choose the risk we are willing to take of rejecting an hypothesis if it is in fact correct. Conventionally, we use a cut-off point of 5 per cent or 1 per cent. If we use the 5 per cent cut-off point, we say that we will regard an hypothesis as rejected if there exists less than one chance in twenty that we could have made the set of observations we actually made if the hypothesis were correct. Using the 1 per cent decision rule we give the hypothesis a greater measure of reasonable doubt: we reject hypotheses only if there is less than one chance in one hundred that the observations we made could have occurred if the hypothesis were true.

Consider an example. When studying expenditure on beef our hypothesis might have been that the expenditure on beef of US households *falls* as their income rises.

1 Even if we satisfy ourselves fully that we saw a grey crow, future generations may not accept our evidence unless they go on observing the occasional grey crow. After all we no longer accept the mass of well-documented evidence accumulated several centuries ago on the existence and power of witches, even though it fully satisfied most contemporary observers. Clearly the existence of observational errors on a vast scale has been shown to be possible even though it may not be frequent.

2 It has been said that there is hardly an accepted theory of physics that is not 'refuted' daily by some schoolboy operating in a school laboratory somewhere in the country. Such isolated 'refutations' do not worry physicists, although they would be worried if some day almost every schoolboy in the country should begin to make observations that appeared to refute some accepted theory.

3 Advanced students may notice that the above differs from the view expressed by Professor Popper in *The Logic of Scientific Discovery* (Hutchinson, 1959). The difference arises from the fact that I take all empirical hypotheses to be statistical ones because of the universal existence of errors of observation. We do of course make arbitrary decisions to reject statistical hypotheses but so also do we make arbitrary decisions to accept them. These rules of thumb for practical decision-taking have nothing to do with the methodological questions of whether any hypothesis can be conclusively refuted and whether any hypothesis can be conclusively proved. My answer to both questions is no. Those who are not convinced by my arguments may proceed with the text as long as they are prepared to accept that most hypotheses in economics are statistical hypotheses.

We would then ask what the chances were of making the observations shown in Figure 3.1 if the hypothesis were correct. There is always some chance that our sample was untypical of all US households or that the relationship appears as it is because of measurement errors. If we calculate that there is *less* than one chance in 100 of making the observations in Figure 3.1 if the hypothesized relation that beef purchases fall as income rises actually holds for all US households, then we would abandon the hypothesis and for practical purposes regard it as refuted.

When action must be taken, some such rule of thumb is necessary. But it is important to understand, first, that we can never be certain that we are right in rejecting a statistical hypothesis and, second, that there is nothing magical about our arbitrary cut-off points. The cut-off point is a device used because some decision has to be made. Notice also that decisions can always be reversed should new evidence come to light.

QUANTITATIVE MEASUREMENT OF ECONOMIC RELATIONS

So far we have considered whether certain observations support certain general hypotheses. The actual data do, for example, support the hypothesis that households' expenditure on beef increases as their incomes increase. This, however, is not enough. It is important to quantify such qualitative statements. In this case, we should like to be able to say that American household expenditure on beef increases by some definite amount, for every $1·00 that household income increases. [1]

Economic theories are seldom of much use until we are able to give quantitative magnitudes to our relations. For estimating such magnitudes, our common sense and intuitions do not get us very far. Common sense might well have suggested that expenditure on beef would rise rather than fall as income rose, but only careful observation is going to help us to decide by how much it typically rises.

One of the major uses of statistical analysis is to help us to quantify our relations. In practice, we can use actual observations both to test the hypothesis that two things are related and to estimate the numerical values of the function describing those relations that do exist.

Very often the result of a statistical test of a theory is to suggest a new hypothesis that 'fits the facts' better than the previous one. Indeed, in some cases just looking at scatter diagrams (or making a regression analysis) uncovers apparent relations that no one anticipated, and leads the economist to formulate a new hypothesis. You should look back to Figure 1.1 on page 15 once again, this time to see where such hypotheses enter the picture. [2]

---

1 The actual quantitative relation is somewhat more complex and this simple one is used solely for purposes of illustration.

2 Hypotheses that originate from data are sometimes called *inductive* hypotheses in contrast to *deductive* ones. But in any science, the sequence of theory and testing is continuous. The question of which came first, theory or observation, is analogous to the debate over the chicken and the egg.

SOME WORDS OF WARNING

In the first three chapters of this book I have been concerned to argue that economics can be a scientific enquiry. Some words of caution are now in order.

First, it is important to point out that there are many major differences among the various sciences, of which the ability to make controlled experiments is only one. Because these differences exist, methods that work well in one science may not be suitable in another. In particular, what works in physics, the Queen of all sciences, may not work well in a social science such as economics. What unites all sciences, however, is the view that they are meant to explain and predict observed phenomena, and that their successes and failures are to be judged by their abilities to do so.

Second, because this is not a text-book in economic statistics, the problems involved in collecting reliable observations, or 'facts', against which to judge our theories, are not stressed.[1] Such problems can be formidable, and there is always the danger that we may reject a theory on the basis of mistaken observations. Unreliable observations are all too frequently encountered. It is important to note, however, that if, on the one hand, we think all our observations are totally unreliable, then we have nothing to explain and, hence, no need for any economic theory. If, on the other hand, we believe that we do have observations reliable enough to require explanation, then we must also believe that we have observations reliable enough to provide tests for the predictive powers of our theories.

Third, I have been concerned in Chapter 3 to dispel the common view that economists cannot be scientific in their use of data because they cannot make controlled experiments. The reader should not be left with the view that the statistical tasks described in this chapter are easily accomplished. In fact they are often very difficult and the pitfalls ready to trap the unwary user of inappropriate statistical procedures are too numerous to mention. Indeed a whole new subject, econometrics, has grown up to amend existing techniques and to develop new ones able to handle the special data problems that occur in economics and other social sciences. To launch into a career in economic or social research without a full knowledge of the field of statistical analysis is to take a severe risk that one's work will be useless or even downright misleading.

---

1 Although I have not stressed this problem, the question of the reliability of observations is either explicit or implicit in the discussion on pages 6, 10, 14, 21 and 46–7.

4

The problems of economic theory

We are now ready to begin our study of economics. So far we have considered the general nature of social science and the two major sets of tools of theoretical and statistical analysis. This concluding chapter of the Introduction provides a general view of the subject matter of economics. It is intended to give the student an idea of the relation between the main divisions of economics which we shall study in subsequent chapters. Theory is meant to relate to problems. If the student cannot think of a set of problems to which the theory he is studying might help to provide answers, then either he or the theory has failed. The student is advised to refer back to this chapter during the course of his study of the remainder of the book, such references being particularly advisable when he feels that he has lost sight of the problems to which a particular part of economic theory is directed.

THE SOURCE OF ECONOMIC PROBLEMS
Wants and resources

Most of the problems of economics arise out of the use of resources to satisfy human wants. The resources of a society consist not only of the free gifts of nature, such as land, forests and minerals, but also of human resources, both mental and physical, and of all sorts of man-made aids to further production, such as tools, machinery and buildings. It is sometimes useful to divide the resources of any country into three main groups: (1) all those free gifts of nature such as land, forests, minerals, etc., commonly called NATURAL RESOURCES and known to the economist as LAND; (2) all human resources, mental and physical, of both an inherited and acquired sort, called by the economist LABOUR; and (3) all those man-made aids to further production, such as tools, machinery, plant and equipment, including everything man-made which is not consumed for its own sake but is used in the process of making other goods, called by the economist CAPITAL. Economists call these resources FACTORS OF PRODUCTION because they are used in the process of production. Often a fourth factor, ENTREPRENEURSHIP (from the French word *entrepreneur* meaning

50

the one who undertakes tasks) is added to the three (land, labour and capital) already mentioned. The entrepreneur is the only one who takes risks by introducing both new ways of making old products and wholly new products. Thus he is the one who organizes the other factors of production and directs them along new lines.

The things that are produced by the factors of production are called COMMODI-TIES. Commodities may be divided into GOODS and SERVICES: goods are tangible, like cars or shoes, and services are intangible, like haircuts or education. This distinction, however, should not be exaggerated: any good is valued because of the services it yields to its owner. In the case of an automobile, for example, the services consist of such things as transportation, mobility and, possibly, status. [1]

In most societies goods and services are not regarded as desirable in themselves; no great virtue is attached to piling them up endlessly in warehouses, never to be consumed. [2] Usually the end or goal that is desired is that the individual should have at least some of his wants satisfied. Goods and services are thus regarded as *means* by which the *goal* of satisfaction may be reached. The act of making goods and services is called by the economist PRODUCTION, and the act of using these goods and services to satisfy wants is called CONSUMPTION.

Scarcity

The human wants that can be satisfied by consuming goods and services may be regarded, for all practical purposes in today's world, as insatiable. [3] In relation to the known desires of individuals, for better food, clothing, housing, schooling, vacations, entertainments, etc., the existing supply of resources is woefully inadequate; it is sufficient to produce only a small fraction of the goods and services that people desire. This gives rise to one of the basic problems encountered in most aspects of economics, the problem of SCARCITY.

CHOICE: Choices are necessary because resources are scarce. Because there are not enough resources to produce everything we would like to consume, there must exist some mechanism by which it is decided what will be done and what left undone;

1 The division of resources into land, labour and capital, and the division of consumption commodities into goods and services are matters of definition. Definitions are to be judged not as matters of fact but on the grounds of usefulness and convenience. The question: 'Is this threefold division of resources the right one?' is one that has no meaning for the scientist. The question: 'Is this division likely to be a useful one?' is a question that can fruitfully be discussed. Arguments about definitions are one of the most common sources of futile debates in all fields. Such arguments are so common that they have been given a name, *essentialist arguments*. An essentialist argument takes place whenever we have no disagreement about the facts of the case but we argue as to what name to use to indicate the agreed facts. We might, for example, be in complete agreement on what goes on in Soviet Russia and Communist China but we might get into an argument as to which should be referred to as true Socialism. Such an essentialist argument is a waste of our time and we would be better to call what goes on in Russia X and China Y and see if we can get on with defining some arguments of substance (e.g., does X provide more freedom for the expression of dissent than Y?).

2 This is intended as a statement of fact, a statement about what is; it is not intended to imply any value judgement about what ought to be.

3 Whether or not it would ever be possible to produce enough goods and services to satisfy all human wants is a question we need not consider here. It would take a vast increase in production (a percentage increase in the thousands) to raise all members of society to the standard at present enjoyed by the richer members. It is doubtful that, even if this could be done, all members of society would find their wants fully satisfied so that there would be no one who would desire more commodities.

what goods will be produced and what left unproduced; what quantity of each good will be produced; and whose wants will be satisfied and whose left unsatisfied.

The decision to have more of one thing necessarily implies the decision to have less of something else. All societies face these problems and somehow decisions on them must be reached. In most societies many different people and organizations either make or influence these choices. Individual consumers, business organizations, labour unions and government officials all exert some influence. One of the differences among various economies such as those of the United States, the United Kingdom, India and the Soviet Union is in the amount of influence that different groups have upon these choices.

OPPORTUNITY COST: Because resources are scarce, we are forced to choose. If you choose to have more of one thing, then, where there is an effective choice, it will be necessary for you to have less of the other. Think of the members of an individual household with a certain amount of resources answering the question: 'How shall we use our resources?' If we have more of this then we must have less of that. If by cost we mean what must be given up in order to obtain something then the cost of having more bread is having less of something else. Say that in this case the household decides to give up some cinema attendances. If the price of a loaf of bread is one third of the price of a cinema seat then the cost of three loaves of bread is one cinema attendance foregone or, put the other way around, the cost of one cinema attendance is three loaves of bread foregone.

Now consider the same problem at the level of the whole society. If the government elects to build more roads, and thereby finds that it must cut down on its school construction programme, then the cost of the new roads can be expressed as so many schools per mile of road. If the government decides that more resources must be devoted to arms production then less will be available to produce civilian goods and a choice will have to be made between 'guns and butter' with the cost of one expressible in terms of the amount of the other foregone. The economist's term for expressing costs in terms of foregone alternatives is OPPORTUNITY COST.

Our discussion may now be summarized briefly. Most of the problems of economics arise out of the use of resources, land, labour and capital, to satisfy human wants. Resources are used to produce goods and services which are then consumed by households to satisfy their wants. The problem of choice arises because resources are scarce in relation to the virtually unlimited wants which they could be used to satisfy.

> **The concept of opportunity cost emphasizes the problem of choice by measuring the cost of obtaining a quantity of one commodity in terms of the quantity of other commodities that could have been obtained instead.**

BASIC ECONOMIC PROBLEMS

Most of the specific questions posed at the beginning of Chapter 1 (and many other questions as well) may be regarded as aspects of six more general questions that must be faced in all economies, whether they be capitalist, socialist or communist. Economists have been interested to find out how decisions on these questions are arrived at in various societies, and how governments and other organizations can intervene to change the answers currently being given.

BASIESE EKONOMIESE PROBLEME

(1) ARE THE COUNTRY'S RESOURCES BEING FULLY UTILIZED, OR ARE SOME OF THEM LYING IDLE?: We have already noted that the existing resources of any country are not sufficient to satisfy even the most pressing needs of all the individual consumers. It may seem strange, therefore, that we must ask this question at all. Surely, the reader will say, if resources are so scarce that there are not enough of them to produce all of those goods which are urgently required, there can be no question of leaving idle any of the resources that are available. Certainly no individual would consciously decide to waste resources which are so scarce. Equally certainly, in a socialist society the government would not consciously plan to leave quantities of all kinds of these useful resources lying idle. Yet it is one of the most disturbing characteristics of free-market economies that such waste sometimes occurs. When this happens the resources are said to be involuntarily unemployed (or, more simply, unemployed). Unemployed workers would like to have jobs, the factories in which they could work are available, the managers and owners would like to be able to operate their factories, raw materials are available in abundance, and the goods that could be produced by these resources are urgently required by individuals in the community. Yet, for some reason, nothing happens: the workers stay unemployed, the factories lie idle and the raw materials remain unused. The cost of such periods of unemployment is felt both in terms of the goods and services that could have been produced by the idle resources, and in terms of the terrible effects on human beings who are unable to find work for prolonged periods of time.[1]

It is one of the most important problems of economics to discover why free-market societies produce such periods of involuntary unemployment *which are unwanted by virtually everyone in the society*. Once it is discovered why this is so, the next problem is to investigate how such unemployment can be prevented from occurring in the future.

These problems have long been the concern of economists, and have been studied under the heading of TRADE CYCLE THEORY. Their study was given renewed importance by the Great Depression of the 1930s. For more than ten years almost all Western countries experienced heavy unemployment. In the USA and the United Kingdom, for example, this unemployment was never less than one worker in ten, and it rose to a maximum of approximately one worker in four. This meant that, during the worst part of the depression, one quarter of these countries' resources were lying involuntarily idle, while many millions of people remained without employment for a period of more than ten years. A great advance was made in the study of these phenomena with the publication in 1936 of the *General Theory of Employment, Interest and Money*, by J. M. Keynes. This book, and the whole branch of economic theory that grew out of it, has greatly widened the scope of economic theory and

---

1 The student with no personal experience of unemployment or depression should attempt to gain some idea of this experience by reading one or two of the many books on the Great Depression of the 1930s. Two such books are George Orwell's *The Road to Wigan Pier* (Harcourt, Brace & World, 1958), and John Steinbeck's *The Grapes of Wrath* (Viking, 1958). Both are also available in paperback.

greatly added to our knowledge of the problems of unemployed resources. This branch of economics is called MACRO-ECONOMICS.

More recently, quite high levels of unemployment have been suffered in the United States. Between 1958 and 1964 the unemployment rate fluctuated between 5 and 7 per cent of the labour force. After a long political debate, the remedies which Keynesian economics predicted would cure the unemployment were adopted, and within a very short time unemployment fell as predicted. Here is a striking example of the power of economic theory in allowing us to control our environment instead of remaining passive victims of it.

(2) WHAT GOODS ARE BEING PRODUCED AND IN WHAT QUANTITIES?: This question arises directly out of the scarcity of resources which creates a situation in which, when there is full employment of resources, the decision to use more resources to produce more of one thing necessitates producing less of something else. The question concerns the allocation of scarce resources among alternative uses (a shorter phrase, resource allocation, will often be used). The questions 'What determines the allocation of resources in various societies?' and 'What are the consequences of conscious attempts to change resource allocation?' have occupied economists since the earliest days of the subject. Any economy in which resources are scarce in relation to human wants, whether it be capitalist, socialist or communist, must have some mechanism to produce decisions about resource allocation. In free-market economies, the majority of decisions concerning the allocation of resources is made through the price system and hence the study of the workings of the price system is an extremely important branch of our subject. This study is dealt with in the THEORY OF PRICE.

(3) BY WHAT METHODS ARE THESE GOODS PRODUCED?: This question arises whenever there is more than one technically possible way in which goods can be made. Generally there are many such ways. Agricultural commodities, for example, can be produced by farming a small quantity of land very intensively, using large quantities of fertilizer, labour and machinery, or by farming a large quantity of land extensively, using only small quantities of fertilizer, labour and machinery. Both methods can be used to produce the same quantity of some good; one method is frugal with land but uses larger quantities of other resources, whereas the other method uses large quantities of land but is frugal in its use of other resources. The same is true of manufactured goods: it is usually possible to produce the same output by several different techniques, ranging from ones using a large quantity of labour and only a few simple machines to ones using a large quantity of highly automated machines and only a very small number of workers. Questions about why one method of production is used rather than another, and the consequences of these choices about production methods, are dealt with in the THEORY OF PRODUCTION.

(4) HOW ARE THE SUPPLIES OF GOODS ALLOCATED AMONG THE MEMBERS OF THE SOCIETY?: The distribution of the national product among various individuals and groups in the society is clearly of great general interest. Economists have long asked what governs the division of the national product among various groups, such

as labourers, capitalists and landowners.[1] We also wish to know to what extent active government intervention can, within the framework of a free-market society, succeed in altering the distribution of income, and what the consequences are of such interventions.

Such questions have been of great concern to economists since the beginning of the subject, and interest in them is as active today as it was almost two centuries ago when Adam Smith and David Ricardo made their path-breaking attempts to solve them. These questions are the subject of the THEORY OF DISTRIBUTION.

(5) HOW EFFICIENTLY ARE THE RESOURCES BEING USED?: This question sub-divides into two questions: is the production efficient? and, is it allocated efficiently? These questions quite naturally arise out of questions 2, 3 and 4. Having asked what quantities of goods are produced, how they are produced and to whom they are allocated, it is natural to go on to ask whether the production and allocation decisions are efficient. Production is said to be inefficient if it would be possible merely to reallocate resources and to produce more of at least one good without simultaneously producing less of any other good. The goods that are produced are said to be in-efficiently allocated if it would be possible to redistribute them among the individuals in the society, and make at least one person better off without simultaneously making anyone worse off.

There is reason to believe that such inefficiencies exist in all economies. If they could be removed it would be possible to increase the production of everything simul-taneously and to make everyone in the society better off. The importance of such inefficiencies, however, depends on their *quantitative* significance. It would not be worth while spending time and effort to remove them unless the costs of so doing were more than made up by the gains resulting from their removal. In fact, not enough is known about the quantitative significance of such inefficiencies.

Questions about the efficiency of production and its allocation belong to the branch of economic theory called WELFARE ECONOMICS. A detailed study of this very difficult branch of economics is beyond the scope of this book.

Questions 2 to 5 are related to the allocation of resources and the distribution of goods and are intimately connected, in a market economy, to the way in which the price system works. They are sometimes grouped under the general heading of MICRO-ECONOMICS.

(6) IS THE ECONOMY'S CAPACITY TO PRODUCE GOODS AND SERVICES GROWING FROM YEAR TO YEAR OR IS IT REMAINING STATIC?: This question is one of great concern. If the capacity to produce does grow steadily, as it has in most Western countries over the last few centuries, then a steady increase in living standards is made possible. The horror and poverty described in the England of 140 years ago by Charles Dickens is no longer with us as a mass phenomenon; and this is largely due to the fact that the capacity to produce goods and services has grown about 2 per cent

1 In the eighteenth century when the theory of distribution was first developed, the three great social classes were workers, capitalists and landowners, and the problem of distribution was to explain how the national product was split up among these classes. In modern times we are concerned with explaining distribution among all the various groups in which we may be interested.

per year faster than population since Dickens' time. Why the capacity to produce grows rapidly in some economies, slowly in others, and not at all in yet others is a critical problem which has exercised the minds of some of the best economists since the time of Adam Smith. Although a certain amount is now known in this field, a great deal remains to be discovered. Problems of this type are dealt with in the THEORY OF ECONOMIC GROWTH.

There are, of course, other questions that arise, but these six are the major ones common to all types of market economies. Most of the rest of this book is devoted to a detailed study of these questions. We shall study among other things how decisions on these questions are made in free-market societies, and the (often unexpected) consequences of settling these questions through the price system.

The questions distinguished diagrammatically

It has been a common source of error in the past to confuse these questions. An answer appropriate to one has often been accepted uncritically as an answer to another, merely because the two questions could be stated in words which sounded similar.

The distinction between the four questions that are most commonly confused can

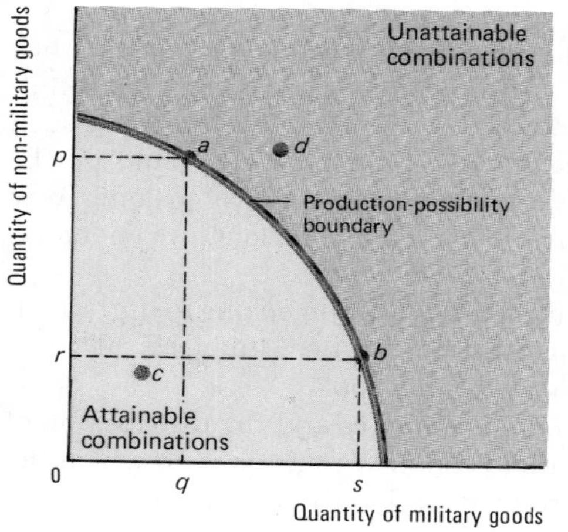

Fig. 4.1 The choice between armaments and consumers' goods

be emphasized by introducing a simple diagram. Consider the choice that faces all economies today, between producing armaments and producing goods for civilian use. This is a problem in the allocation of resources: how many resources to devote to producing 'guns for defence' and how many to devote to producing goods for all other purposes. We illustrate this choice in Figure 4.1. On one axis we measure the quantity of military goods produced and on the other axis the quantity of all other goods. Next we plot all those combinations of military and civilian goods that can be produced if all resources are fully employed. We join up these points and call the resulting line a PRODUCTION-POSSIBILITY BOUNDARY. Points inside the boundary such as *c* show the combinations of military and civilian goods that can be obtained given the society's present supplies of resources. Points outside the boundary such as *d* show combinations that cannot be obtained because there are not enough resources to produce them. Points on the boundary such as *a* and *b* are just obtainable; they are the combinations that can just be produced using all the available supplies of resources.

The downward slope of the boundary indicates that there is an opportunity cost of producing more of one type of commodity, cost being measured in terms of the quantity foregone of the other type of commodity. Thus if we move from point *a* to point *b* we are reallocating resources out of civilian production and into military production. The amount of military goods produced rises from *q* to *s*, while the quantity of civilian production falls from *p* to *r*. Thus the opportunity cost of getting *s* − *q* more arms produced is *p* − *r* civilian goods sacrificed. When we talk about moving between points *a* and *b* we are talking of the allocation of resources discussed in question 2.

It is, of course, always possible for the economy to be at some point inside the production-possibility boundary. If the economy could be at point *b* then it could also be at point *c* producing less of both military and civilian goods than at *b*, or indeed at any point inside the boundary. The reader can easily check that, when the economy is located at a point inside the boundary, production of both types of commodity is less than it would be if some points on the boundary were attained.

An economy can be producing at some point inside its production-possibility boundary either because some of its resources are lying idle (question 1), or because its resources are being used inefficiently in production (question 5). Figure 4.2 shows the production-possibility boundary on the assumption that one third of the economy's resources are lying idle. The higher the proportion of resources unemployed the closer will the white line be to the origin.

Let us now ask: 'How can an economy produce more military goods?' Clearly we must know whether the present position is on the boundary or inside it. If the economy is on the boundary, then, assuming for the moment that the boundary cannot

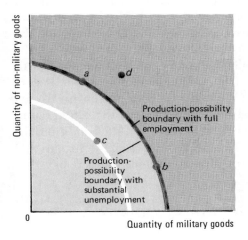

Fig. 4.2 The choice between armaments and consumers' goods when there is full employment and when there is substantial unemployment

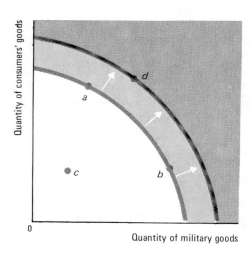

Fig. 4.3 Economic growth shifts the boundary outward and makes it possible to have more of all commodities

be shifted, the answer is: more arms can be obtained only at the cost of producing less civilian goods (e.g., by moving from point *a* to point *b*). If, however, the economy is at some point, such as *c*, inside the boundary, then more of both goods can be produced simultaneously. If the economy is inside the boundary because there is heavy unemployment, then the measures which succeed in reducing unemployment will allow the economy to have more of both goods. If, on the other hand, the economy is inside the boundary because, although existing resources are fully employed, they are being used inefficiently, then measures which increase the efficiency of resource utilization will allow the economy to produce more of both goods.

Finally we come to the question of economic growth (question 6). If the economy's capacity to produce goods is increasing through time, then the production-possibility boundary is being pushed outwards over time as illustrated in Figure 4.3.[1] In this case, if the economy remains on the possibility boundary, it will be possible to increase the production of all goods over time, moving for example from point *a* to point *d*.

Thus we see that in order to increase the production of all goods in an economy, it is necessary to do one of two things. If production is at a point inside the production-possibility boundary, then it may be moved to a point closer to, or actually on, the boundary, from *c* to *b* in Figure 4.2, for example. If the economy is already on the boundary, then it is necessary to take steps which will move the boundary outwards so that production can expand, for example from *b* to *d* in Figure 4.3. It is very important to distinguish between two sorts of movements: (i) a movement from a point within, to a point on, the boundary, and (ii) a movement of the actual boundary. The conditions for doing the former are very different from the conditions for doing the latter. The fact that in both cases we speak of an increase in national income (total production in the economy) can cause confusion. But a policy that

1 Anything that increases labour productivity will push the production-possibility boundary outwards from the origin. This could be done, for example, by the invention of new machines which increased the hourly output of each worker.

would succeed in increasing national income if the object were to move from a point within the boundary to a point on the boundary might be a failure if what was really necessary was to increase national income by moving the actual boundary. The student will avoid confusion if he uses the phrase ECONOMIC GROWTH to refer to an outward shift of the production-possibility boundary, and the phrase A CHANGE IN THE LEVEL OF ACTIVITY to refer to a movement of actual production away from (activity declining) or towards (activity rising) the boundary due to a change in the amount of resources employed.

ECONOMICS: A WORKING DEFINITION

The six-way classification just discussed does not cover all of the things that interest economists. Additional topics such as the problems of international trade or comparative economic systems might be included in one or more of these categories, or they might be treated separately. Similarly, the theory of economic policy might be regarded as affecting all of the problem areas mentioned, or it might be treated separately.

Our purpose in listing these problem areas is to outline the scope of economics more fully than can be done with short definitions. Economics today is regarded much more broadly than it was even half a century ago. Earlier definitions stressed the alternative and competing uses of resources. Such definitions focused on choices between alternative points on a stationary production-possibility boundary. Important additional problems concern failure to achieve the boundary (problems of inefficiency or underemployment of resources) and the outward movement of the boundary over time (problems of growth and development).

Broadly defined economics is now thought of as concerning:

> 1. **the ways in which a society uses its resources and distributes its output among individuals and groups in the society;**
> 2. **the ways in which production and distribution change over time; and**
> 3. **the efficiencies and inefficiencies of economic systems.**

Part two

The elementary theory of price

5

A general view of the price system

The economic problem as we know it today is a mere eight or nine thousand years old; little more than an instant compared to the millions of years humanoid creatures have been on earth. It arose when the first agricultural revolution – dated at between 6000 and 8000 BC – conclusively reinforced already-existing tendencies for man to change from a nomadic food gatherer into a settled food producer, tending crops that he himself had planted and animals that he, or his forebears, had domesticated.

SURPLUS AND SPECIALIZATION: Along with permanent settlement, the agricultural revolution brought surplus production: the farmer could produce substantially more than he required to satisfy his own needs for survival. The agricultural surplus permitted the growth of new classes of people – such as soldiers, priests, government officials and skilled artisans. These people produced other goods and services while consuming the surplus food produced by farmers. Economists call this allocation of different jobs to different people SPECIALIZATION OF LABOUR. Specialization has proven extraordinarily efficient compared to a system in which each person is self-sufficient, producing for himself everything that he consumes. The efficiency of specialization has at least two distinct sources. First, individual talents and abilities differ and specialization allows each person to do the thing he can do relatively best, while leaving everything else to be done by others. Not only do people do their own thing; they do their own best thing. Second, a person who concentrates on one job has a better chance of becoming efficient at it than does a jack-of-all-trades.

Specialization must be accompanied by trade. People who produce only one thing must trade most of it in return for all of the other things they require.

Voluntary agreements between those who wished to exchange goods with each other were undoubtedly the most common way in which this exchange of produce took place in early societies. Naturally, trading became centred in particular gathering places. These places were called markets, and even today we use the term market economy to refer to economies in which people specialize in productive activities and meet most of their material wants through exchanges voluntarily agreed upon by the contracting parties.

MONEY: The earliest free-market economies depended on barter, which means that goods were traded directly for other goods. But barter can be very costly in terms of time spent searching out satisfactory exchanges. Money evolved to facilitate exchanges. The institution of money eliminates the cumbrousness of barter by placing money between the two sides of each barter transaction. If a farmer has wheat and wants a hammer, he does not have to search for an individual who has a hammer and wants wheat; he merely has to find any individual who wants wheat; the farmer takes money in exchange. He then finds another individual who wishes to trade a hammer and gives up the money for the hammer.

FACTOR SERVICES: Market transactions in early economies involved mostly goods and services for consumption. An individual specialized in making some commodity and traded it for all the other products that he required. Most labour services were provided directly by the maker, by apprentices who were learning to become crafts-men themselves, and by slaves who did most of the domestic work. Over the last several hundred years many technical developments have encouraged specialization in the methods of production and have made it efficient to organize agriculture and industry on a very large scale.

THE DIVISION OF LABOUR: The technical developments over the last few hundred years have been based on what is called the DIVISION OF LABOUR. This term refers to the specialization of tasks within the production process of a particular commodity. The labour involved is divided into a series of repetitive tasks and each individual does one task that may represent a minute fraction of the tasks necessary to produce one commodity. Indeed it is possible today for an individual to spend his whole life doing a production line job without ever knowing what commodity he is helping to produce!

The division of labour made it necessary to organize production in large and expensive factories. With this development the individual worker lost his status as a craftsman or as a peasant and became a member of the urban proletariat. He became wholly dependent for his income on his ability to sell his labour to the factory owner and without any plot of land to fall back on for subsistence in times of need.

The day of the small craftsman who made and sold a commodity for himself is over. Today's workers do not earn their incomes by selling goods they themselves have produced, rather they sell their labour services to firms and receive money wages in return.

SCARCITY: All economies that have existed, at least since the original agricultural revolution, have been faced with the problem of scarcity because there are not enough resources to produce all of the goods and services that could be consumed.

It is therefore necessary to allocate the available resources among their various possible uses, and in so doing to choose what to produce and what not to produce.

> **In a market economy, the allocation of resources is the outcome of millions of independent decisions made by consumers and producers, all acting through the medium of markets.**

HOW MARKET ECONOMIES WORK

Early economists observed the market economy with wonder. They saw that most commodities were made by a large number of independent producers and yet in approximately the quantities that people wanted to purchase them. Natural disasters aside, there were neither vast surpluses nor severe shortages of products. They also saw that in spite of the ever-changing requirements in terms of geographical, industrial and occupational patterns, most labourers were able to sell their labour services to employers most of the time.

How does the market produce this order in the absence of conscious coordination by some central coordinating body? It is one thing to have the same thing produced year in and year out when people's wants and incomes do not change; it is quite another thing to have production adjusting continually to changing wants, incomes and techniques of production. Yet this *relatively* smooth adjustment is accomplished by the market – albeit with occasional, and sometimes serious, interruptions. The great discovery of the eighteenth-century economists was that the price system is a *social control mechanism*.

Adam Smith, whose classic *The Wealth of Nations* published in 1776 was the high point of this development, spoke of the price system as 'the invisible hand'. It allows decision-making to be decentralized to millions of individual producers and consumers, but nonetheless to be coordinated. Two examples may help to illustrate how this coordination occurs.

A change in demand

First consider how the market reacts to a change in the tastes of individual consumers. Let us say, for example, that consumers develop a greatly increased desire for Brussels sprouts and a diminished desire for carrots; it might be a matter of fashion, sparked off by some quite minor cause, or it might be the result of a successful advertising campaign on the part of an association of the Brussels sprout producers: 'Carrots may be good for you, but Brussels sprouts *taste* good.' Whatever the reason, we can take it that there has been a major shift in tastes in favour of sprouts and away from carrots.

What will be the effects of this change? Consumers will buy more Brussels sprouts and fewer carrots. With production unchanged, a shortage of Brussels sprouts and a glut of carrots will develop. In order to unload their surplus stocks of carrots, merchants will reduce carrot prices, on the argument that it is better to sell them at a reduced price than not to sell them at all. On the other hand, merchants will find that they are unable to satisfy all their customers' demands for Brussels sprouts;

sprouts will become a scarce commodity and the merchants will raise the price. As the price rises, fewer people will be able and willing to purchase sprouts. Thus the demand will be limited to the available supply by the means of making the commodity more expensive.

Farmers will now observe a rise in the price of Brussels sprouts and a fall in the price of carrots. Brussels sprout production will be more profitable than in the past, for the costs of producing them will be unchanged, while their market price will have risen. Similarly, carrot production will be less profitable than in the past because costs will be unchanged but prices will have fallen. Thus the change in consumers' tastes, working through the price system, causes a reallocation of resources out of carrot production and into Brussels sprout production.

As the production of carrots declines, the glut on the market will diminish, and carrot prices will begin to rise. On the other hand, the expansion in Brussels sprout production will reduce the shortage and the price will fall. These price movements will continue until it no longer pays farmers to reduce carrot production and to increase the production of sprouts.

Let us review this last point. When the price of carrots was very low and the price of sprouts very high, carrot production was unprofitable and sprout production was very profitable. Therefore more sprouts and fewer carrots were produced. These production changes caused sprout prices to fall, and carrot prices to rise. Once the prices of these goods became such that it no longer paid farmers to transfer out of carrots into sprouts, production settled down and price movements ceased.

We can now see how the transfer of resources takes place. Carrot producers will be reducing their production, and they will therefore be laying off workers, and generally demanding fewer factors of production. On the other hand, Brussels sprout producers will be expanding production by hiring workers and generally increasing their demand for factors of production. Labour can probably switch from carrot to sprout production without much difficulty. If, however, there are certain resources, in this case say certain areas of land, which are much better suited for sprout-growing than for carrot-growing, and other resources, say other areas of land, which are much better suited for carrot-growing than sprout-growing, then their prices will be affected. Since farmers are trying to increase sprout production, they will be increasing their demand for those factors which are especially suited for this activity. This will create a shortage and cause the prices of these factors to rise. On the other hand, carrot production will be falling, and hence the demand for resources especially suited for carrot-growing will be reduced. There will thus be a surplus of these resources and their prices will be forced down.

Thus factors particularly suited to sprout production will be earning more than previously, and they will obtain a higher share of total national income than before. Factors particularly suited for carrot production, on the other hand, will be earning less than before and so will obtain a smaller share of the total national income than before.

These changes may now be summarized.

(1) A change in consumers' tastes causes a change in purchases which causes a shortage or a surplus to appear. This in turn causes market prices to rise in the case

of a shortage and to fall in the case of a surplus.

(2) The variations in market price affect the profitability of producing goods, profitability varying directly with price. Producers will shift their production out of less profitable lines and into more profitable ones.

(3) The attempt to change the pattern of production will cause variations in the demand for factors of production. Factors especially suited for the production of commodities for which the demand is increasing will themselves be heavily demanded so that their own prices will rise.

(4) Thus the change of consumers' tastes sets off a series of market changes which causes a reallocation of resources in the required direction and in the process causes changes in the shares of total national income going to various factors of production.

We shall study changes of this kind more fully later; for now the important thing to notice is how a change initiated in consumers' tastes causes a reallocation of resources in the direction required to cater to the new set of tastes.

A change in supply

Now consider another change – this time on the side of producers. We assume that, at existing prices, farmers become more willing to produce sprouts than in the past and less willing to produce carrots. There are many things that could cause such a change. It might be brought about by a change in *the costs of producing* the two goods: a rise in carrot costs and a fall in sprout costs. Whatever the reason, we take it that, at existing prices of the two goods, farmers are more willing to produce sprouts and less willing to produce carrots than previously.

Now what will happen? For a short time, nothing at all; the existing supplies of sprouts and carrots are the results of decisions taken by farmers some time in the past. But farmers will now plant fewer carrots and more sprouts, and soon the quantities coming on to the market will change. The amounts available for sale will rise in the case of sprouts and fall in the case of carrots. A shortage of carrots and a glut of sprouts will result. The price of carrots will rise and the price of sprouts will fall. As carrots become more expensive and sprouts become cheaper, fewer carrots and more sprouts will be bought by consumers. On the other hand, the rise in carrot prices and the fall in sprout prices will act as an incentive for farmers to move back into carrot production and out of sprout production. We started from a position in which there was a shortage of carrots which caused carrot prices to rise. The rise in carrot prices removed the shortage in two ways: first by reducing the demand for the increasingly expensive carrots, and second by increasing the output of carrots which became increasingly profitable to produce. We also started from a position in which there was a surplus of Brussels sprouts, which caused their price to fall. The fall in price removed the surplus in two ways: first by encouraging the consumers to buy more of this commodity which became less and less expensive, and second by discouraging the production of this commodity, which became less and less profitable.

WHO CONTROLS THE FREE MARKET?

These examples illustrate many important features of the price system. The first thing to notice is that the market responds to the collective decisions of either consumers or producers even though it is completely unaffected by the individual decision made by any one of them. There are millions of purchasers of carrots and Brussels sprouts and the effect on market prices and resource allocation of the change in the tastes of a single purchaser will be negligible. But if all consumers change their tastes the effect on prices and resource allocation will be significant. The situation is similar for producers, at least for producers of the type of product described in this chapter. There are millions of farmers and the effect on market prices and resource allocation of the change in the behaviour of a single one of them is negligible. But if all farmers alter their behaviour the effect on prices will be significant, and there will be changes in the allocation of resources of the sort we have already discussed.

The second point to notice is that systematic adaptations to changes in the demand and supply can, and do, take place without being consciously coordinated by anyone. When shortages develop, prices rise and profit-seeking farmers are led to produce more of the good in short supply. When surpluses occur, prices fall and supply is voluntarily contracted. The price system produces a series of automatic signals so that a large number of different decision-making units (firms and households) do, in fact, produce coordinated reactions to some change.

We have seen that although no single individual may be able to exert any significant control over a free market the decisions of two groups, producers and consumers, do determine what is produced and sold. Thus the decisions of both producers and consumers influence the allocation of resources. A change in either consumers' demand or producers' supply will affect the allocation of resources and thus also the final pattern of production and consumption in the economy. The *mechanism* by which these changes occur is through changes in prices and profits.

> **It is often remarked that in a free-market society the consumer is king. Such a maxim reveals only half the truth. Prices are determined by both demand and supply. A free-market society gives sovereignty to two groups, producers and consumers, and the decisions of both groups affect the allocation of resources.**

Under certain very special conditions, known to the economist as conditions of PERFECT COMPETITION, the producer loses his sovereignty and becomes a mere automaton responding to the will of the consumer. These very special conditions are described in Chapter 20. Aside from this special case, however, the producer has at his command, and actually does exercise, considerable power in the allocation of resources in the economy.

This general picture of the working of the price system has left untouched many problems. Before we can handle these problems, we must formulate the ideas given in this chapter into a more precise theory of price. This will be done in the following chapters.

THE EMPIRICAL EVIDENCE

There is a great deal of empirical evidence showing that, for many agricultural commodities and industrial raw materials, the price system works very much as

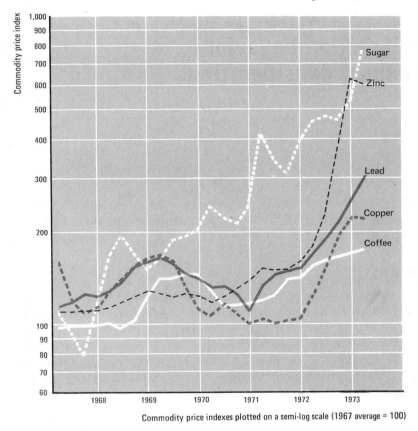

Commodity price indexes plotted on a semi-log scale (1967 average = 100)

Fig. 5.1 A time series for five commodities showing that prices in the primary sector change frequently. *Source:* Based on *National Institute Economic Review.*

described in this chapter. In any retail or wholesale produce market, prices can be observed to react to the state of demand and supply, rising when there is a shortage and falling when there is a surplus. Even the most casual observation of agriculture will show farmers varying their production of different crops as market prices vary. A much more difficult question is whether or not it is valid to generalize this view of the price system into a theory of the prices of all commodities: agricultural goods, manufactured goods, and services. This question must be postponed until after the theory of price has been developed more fully.

Figure 5.1 shows that the prices of some commodities do change frequently. Of course, this does not prove that they change in response to the factors described in this chapter. The figure does show, however, that the price changes that we have described as signals do occur frequently, at least for a number of commodities.

6

The theory of market behaviour: some preliminary considerations

In this chapter we introduce some of the concepts and assumptions which form the basis of a theory of market behaviour. This is the first step in developing the formal theory that occupies us for the next five chapters.

THE DECISION-TAKERS

Economics is about the behaviour of individuals. We assume that anything we observe in the world and anything we assume in our theories can be traced back to decisions taken by individuals. There are millions of individuals in most economies and to reduce things to manageable proportions they are consolidated into three important groups: HOUSEHOLDS, FIRMS and CENTRAL AUTHORITIES. These are the *dramatis personae* of economic theory and the stage on which much of their play is acted is called the MARKET.

THE HOUSEHOLD: By a household we mean all the people who live under one roof and who make, or are subject to others making for them, joint financial decisions. In the *theory of demand* we ignore the problem of how individuals within a household reach decisions and, taking the household as a basic atom of behaviour, we assume that it behaves consistently with respect to all of the choices that it must make. As with most assumptions of this type, the test of its value is to be judged by whether or not the predictions that follow from it are consistent with the facts. This we shall consider in a later chapter. In the meantime we notice that many interesting problems concerning conflict within the family and parental control over the fate of minors are neglected because we take the household as a basic decision-taking unit. These intra-family problems are discussed by other disciplines such as sociology, anthropology and psychology and we should not expect to find all problems handled within the field of economics. However, it is very important to remember that when economists speak of *the* consumer or *the* individual they are in fact referring to the group of individuals composing the household. Thus, for example, the commonly-heard phrase *consumer sovereignty* really means *household sovereignty*. These two concepts are, however, quite distinct: it is one thing to say that individuals should be free to decide their own fate and quite another thing to say that the head of the household should be free to decide the fate of all the members of the household some of whom will usually be minors.

The above is just a warning not to confuse households with individuals in certain general discussions. In the theory of market behaviour we assume that households are consistent decision-taking units behaving as if they contained only one individual. The problem of how such consistent decisions are arrived at (e.g., by paternal dictatorship or by complete democracy) is not considered in our theory.

Households are assumed to act so as to maximize their well-being, satisfaction, or utility, as it is variously called. This can sometimes be a slippery concept, and it is considered in detail in Part 3. It is sufficient for our present purposes to say that we assume that households know what they want, and, so far as they are able, do what they want.

THE FIRM: The firm is defined as the unit that uses factors of production to produce commodities that it then sells either to other firms, to households, or to the central authorities. The firm is thus the unit that makes the decisions regarding the employment of factors of production and the output of commodities. It cannot decide what its sales shall be, but, through advertising and other media, it can try to influence the purchasing decisions of households which themselves determine the firm's sales. The firm is considered in much more detail in Chapter 17. In the meantime we note the assumption analogous to the one made for households: that the firm makes consistent decisions in relation to the choices open to it, and that the internal problems of who reaches particular decisions and of how they are reached can be ignored. In short the firm is taken as our atom of behaviour on the supply side just as the household is taken as our atom of behaviour on the demand side.

The firm is assumed to be motivated by a desire to make profits in as large amounts as it can. We say that the firm seeks to maximize its profits. This is analogous to the assumption that the household seeks to maximize its satisfaction. It is, however, a little more explicit, since it says that the firm's satisfaction depends only on its current level of profits. This assumption has, as we shall see in Chapter 25, come under serious attack, and there are several competing theories that we shall consider in detail later. In the meantime, we can go quite a long way using the very simple assumption that firms seek to maximize their profits.

CENTRAL AUTHORITIES: This comprehensive term includes all public agencies, government bodies and other organizations belonging to or under the direct control of the government. It includes such bodies as the central bank, the civil service, commissions and regulatory bodies, the cabinet, the police force and all other bodies by which control can be exercised over the behaviour of firms and households. It is not important for the student to draw up a comprehensive list of all central authorities but only to have in mind the general idea of a group of organizations that exist at the centre of legal and political power and exert some control over individual decision-takers and over markets. It is *not* a basic assumption of economics that the central authorities always act in a consistent fashion as if they were a single individual. Indeed conflict between different central bodies is the subject of much intermediate analysis of the theory of the control of the economy.

THE INDIVIDUAL MARKET

Originally the word MARKET designated a place where certain things were bought and sold. Petticoat Lane (for many consumer goods) and Covent Garden (for whole-sale fruit and produce) are two world-famous examples of markets in the everyday sense. Indeed much of economic theory was originally based on an attempt to explain price behaviour in such markets. Why, for example, can you sometimes obtain at the end of the day tremendous bargains, and at other times only get what you want at prices which appear exorbitant in relation to prices ruling a few hours before? The student who takes the trouble to visit any nearby street market will see many other interesting forms of behaviour most of which can be explained by the theory of price that he is in the process of studying.

Once theories of market behaviour had been developed they were easily extended to cover commodities such as wheat, which can be purchased anywhere in the world and the price of which tends to uniformity the world over. Clearly when we talk about 'the wheat market' we have extended our concept of a market well beyond the idea of a single place to which the housewife goes to buy something. The theory was even extended to cover markets where things which have not yet been produced are bought and sold, called futures markets.

Constructing a satisfactory definition[1] of a market is not an easy task. For present purposes we define a MARKET as *an area over which buyers and sellers negotiate the exchange of a well-defined commodity*. We have already noted that the actual geographical area covered by a single market will vary greatly with the commodity. In the case of wheat, the market is the whole Western world; in the case of strawberries, it may only be a small area including and surrounding one city, in the case of haircuts, it may be one small neighbourhood in a city.

Throughout Part 2 we shall confine ourselves to markets in which the number of buyers and sellers is large enough so that no one of them has any appreciable influence on price. This is a very rough definition of what economists call COMPETI-TIVE MARKETS. Thus, the theory developed in Part 2 is the theory of competitive markets. In Part 4 we shall consider the behaviour of markets that do not meet this competitive requirement.

---

1 By talking of a satisfactory definition we do not mean to imply that there are true and false definitions (see note 1, page 51) but only that the problem is to include what we want to include and to get a theoretical construct that can be related to the world of experience, so we will be able to identify the places where we expect the predictions of our theory to hold.

DIFFERENT KINDS OF ECONOMIES

A FREE-MARKET ECONOMY is a collection of individual free markets. Such an economy is one in which the allocation of resources is determined by production, sales and purchase decisions taken by firms and households. The way in which these decisions influence the allocation of resources has been discussed in Chapter 5.

At the opposite extreme from a completely free-market economy is a CENTRALLY-CONTROLLED ECONOMY in which all the decisions about the allocation of resources are taken by the central authorities, and in which firms and households produce and consume only as they are ordered.

Neither the completely free-market economy nor the completely controlled economy has ever existed, at least in recent history. In practice all economies are MIXED ECONOMIES in the sense that some decisions are taken by firms and households, and some by central authorities. In some economies, however, the influence of the central authorities is substantially less than it is in others. Not only may the average amount of central control vary among economies, it may also vary among markets within one economy. Thus, in Britain the day-to-day behaviour of the stock market is free from central control, while the market for rented housing is subject to quite substantial amounts of regulation and control by the central authorities.

The economic theory that we are developing is about the behaviour of free markets, but it can also deal with many types of central control commonly found in Western economies. We shall use the phrase free-market economy to indicate economies for which the decisions of individual households and firms exert a substantial amount of influence over the allocation of resources. The dividing line is an arbitrary one and we must always remember that every possible mixture of centralized and decentralized control exists, and that the economies of Poland and Russia differ from those of France and the UK only in the degree to which the central authorities exert an influence.[1]

1 Free-market economies are sometimes called capitalist economies and we shall occasionally use capitalist as a synonym for free market. The latter term is, however, the more descriptive, since free market and centrally controlled economies are not differentiated by the extent of their use of capital (indeed there is more capital per head in Soviet Russia than in many Western countries), but by the extent to which individual markets are controlled or not by the central authorities.

7

The elementary theory of demand

We have seen that the market price of a commodity is influenced by the demand of households to purchase the commodity, and by the supply of the commodity that firms offer for sale. The first step, therefore, in developing a formal theory of market prices is to consider the determinants of households' demand and firms' supply. Demand is considered in this chapter and supply in the next.

Some definitions

The amount of a commodity that households wish to purchase is called the QUANTITY DEMANDED of that commodity. We must at the very outset notice two important things about the quantity demanded. First, it is a *desired* quantity. It is how much households wish to purchase, not necessarily how much they actually succeed in purchasing. If sufficient quantities are not available, the amount households wish to purchase may exceed the amount they do purchase. To distinguish between these two concepts, we use the term quantity demanded to refer to desired purchases, and we use phrases such as QUANTITY ACTUALLY PURCHASED or QUANTITY ACTUALLY BOUGHT AND SOLD to refer to actual purchases. The second thing to note is that quantity demanded is a flow. (See page 32.) We are concerned not with a single isolated purchase, but with a continuous flow of purchases, and we must therefore express demand as so much per period of time – one million oranges *per day*, say, or seven million oranges *per week*, or 365 million *per year*.

This approach would appear to raise difficulties when we deal with the purchases of durable consumer goods that are bought only occasionally. It makes obvious sense to talk about consuming oranges at the rate of thirty per month but what can we say of someone who buys a new television set every five years or a new car every two? This apparent difficulty disappears if we measure the demand for the *services* of the consumer durable. Thus, the television purchaser is using the services of television sets at the rate of $\frac{1}{60}$ of a set per month. If a fall in the price of television sets makes him discard his old set every four years instead of every five we say that his consumption of the services of television sets has gone up from $\frac{1}{60}$ to the rate of $\frac{1}{48}$ of a set per month.

WHAT DETERMINES THE QUANTITY OF A COMMODITY THAT WILL BE DEMANDED BY AN INDIVIDUAL HOUSEHOLD?

We now introduce four hypotheses about what determines the quantity of a commodity demanded by an individual household.

(1) Quantity demanded is influenced by the price of that commodity.
(2) Quantity demanded is influenced by the size of the household's income.
(3) Quantity demanded is influenced by the prices of other commodities.
(4) Quantity demanded is influenced by the household's tastes.

This list of factors influencing the household's demand may conveniently be summarized, using the notation developed in Chapter 2. What we have said is that the amount of a commodity a household is prepared to purchase is a function of (i.e., depends upon) the price of the good in question, the prices of all other goods, the household's income and its tastes. This statement may be expressed in symbols by writing down what is called a DEMAND FUNCTION:

$$q_n^d = D(p_n, p_1, \ldots, p_{n-1}, Y, T),$$

where q_n^d is the quantity that the household demands of some commodity, labelled 'commodity n', where p_n is the price of this commodity, where $p_1, \ldots, p_{n-1}$ is a shorthand notation for the prices of all other commodities, where Y is the household's income and T the tastes of the members of the household.[1]

This is quite a complicated functional relationship, and we shall not succeed in developing a simple theory of demand or price if we consider what happens to the quantity demanded when these things – prices, income and tastes – all change at once. To get around this problem we use a device that is very frequently employed in economic theory. We assume that all except one of the terms in the right-hand side of the above expression are held constant; we then allow this one factor, say p_n, to vary, and consider how the quantity demanded (q_n^d) varies with it, *on the assumption that all other things remain unchanged*, or, as the economist is fond of putting it, *ceteris paribus*. We then allow some other term, say income (Y), to vary, and consider how, *ceteris paribus*, quantity demanded varies as income varies. We can now consider the relation between quantity demanded and each of the variables on the right-hand side of the demand function, taking them one at a time.[2]

1 Quantity demanded depends on the price of the commodity

In the case of almost all commodities, the quantity demanded increases as the price of the commodity falls; income, tastes and all other prices remaining constant. As its price falls, a commodity becomes cheaper relative to its substitutes, and it is therefore easier for the commodity to compete against these substitutes for the household's

---

1 This functional notation is merely a shorthand notation; it is not of itself mathematics. If you still find this · troublesome you should read pages 19–20 and 30–1 of Chapter 2 and its Appendix now.

2 This technique is further discussed on pages 37–8.

attention. Thus, the household does not always buy the same bundle of goods; it substitutes one commodity for another in its budget as prices change. If, for example, carrots become very cheap, the household will be induced, up to a point, to buy more carrots and less of other vegetables whose prices are now high relative to the price of carrots.

THE DEMAND SCHEDULE: To illustrate the relation between the quantity of a commodity demanded and its price, we shall take imaginary data for the prices and quantities of carrots. Table 7.1 shows the quantity of carrots that a household would demand at various prices. At any price, such as £40 per ton, there is a definite quantity demanded, 10·25 lbs per month in this case. The table gives the quantities demanded for six selected prices. Each of the price–quantity combinations in the table is given a letter for easy reference.

Table 7.1 A household's demand schedule
for carrots

	Price per ton £	Quantity demanded in lbs per month
n	20	14·0
p	40	10·25
q	60	7·5
r	80	5·25
s	100	3·5
t	120	2·5

THE DEMAND CURVE: We can now plot the data from Table 7.1 on a graph with price on the vertical axis and quantity on the horizontal one. In Figure 7.1 we have shown such a graph and have plotted the six points corresponding to each price–quantity combination shown in Table 7.1. Point n on the graph shows the same information as does the first row of the table: at £20 a ton, 14 lbs of carrots will be demanded by the household each month. Point t shows the same information as does the last row of the table: when the price is £120 a ton, the quantity demanded will be only 2·5 **lbs per month.**

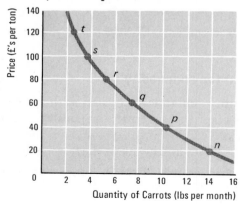

Fig. 7.1 A household's demand curve for carrots

We now draw a smooth curve through these points. This curve is called the DEMAND CURVE for carrots. The curve shows the quantity of carrots that the household would like to buy at every possible price of carrots; its downward slope indicates that the quantity demanded increases as the price falls.

A single point on the demand curve indicates a single price–quantity combination. *The whole demand curve shows the complete functional relation between quantity demanded and price.* Economists often speak of the conditions of demand in a particular market as given or as known. When they do so they are not referring just to the particular quantity that is being demanded at the moment (i.e., not just to a particular point on the demand curve). They are referring rather to the whole demand curve, to the complete functional relation whereby desired purchases are related to all possible alternative prices of the commodity.

> **The demand curve for a commodity shows the relation between the price of that commodity and the quantity the household wishes to purchase. It is drawn on the assumption that income, tastes and all other prices remain constant, and its downward slope indicates that the lower the price of the commodity the greater will be the quantity that the household will desire to purchase.**

2 Quantity demanded depends on the price of other commodities

There are three possible relations between the demand for one good and the prices of other goods: a fall in the price of one good may lower the household's demand for another good, it may raise it or it may leave it unchanged. If a fall in the price of one good, Y, causes a fall in the demand for another good, X, the two goods, X and Y, are said to be SUBSTITUTES. When the price of one good falls, the household buys more of it and less of goods that are substitutes for it; thus the demand for a good varies directly with the price of its substitutes. This relation is illustrated by our imaginary carrot example in Figure 7.2(i). The curve slopes upwards, indicating that as the price of a substitute rises, the household's demand for carrots rises, while, when the price of a substitute falls, the demand for carrots falls. Examples of goods which are substitutes are butter and margarine, carrots and cabbage, cinema seats and theatre seats, public transport and private cars.

If a fall in the price of one good raises the demand for another good, the two goods are said to be COMPLEMENTS. In this case, when the price of one good falls, more of that good is consumed and also more of those goods that are complementary to it. This relation will obtain between goods that tend to be consumed together, goods such as motorcars and petrol, cups and saucers, bread and butter, rail trips to Austria and skis. This is illustrated in Figure 7.2(ii) for our carrot example. The curve slopes downwards, indicating that when the price of a complement falls there is a rise in the quantity of carrots demanded.[1]

---

1 Readers familiar with more advanced works will realize that the definition given in the present text does not conform exactly to ones used in intermediate theory books, where, following J.R. Hicks, the definition used involves sliding a budget plane around a single indifference surface. Such a definition may be of use in theoretical work but it is non-operational. Also, since in practice most income effects are very small, the theoretical definition will be indistinguishable from the one we have adopted for most practical problems of measurement.

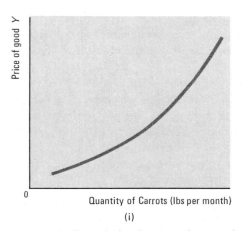
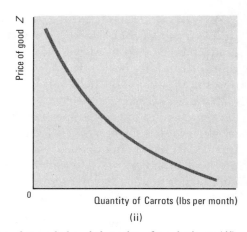

Fig. 7.2 (i) The relation between the quantity of carrots demanded and the price of a substitute (Y)
(ii) The relation between the quantity of carrots demanded and the price of a complement (Z)

3 Quantity demanded depends on the household's income

Normally we would expect a rise in income to be associated with a rise in the quantity of a good demanded. There are two possible exceptions. In some cases a change in income might leave the quantity demanded completely unaffected. This will be the case with goods for which the desire is completely satisfied after a certain level of income is obtained. Beyond this level, variations in income have no effect on the quantity demanded. This is possibly the case with many of the more inexpensive foodstuffs. It is unlikely, for example, that the demand for salt would be affected by either an increase in a household's income from £2,000 to £2,100 per annum, or by a decrease in its income from £2,000 to £1,900 (although salt purchases might be influenced by income changes if income were as low as, say, £200 per annum). In the cases of other commodities it is possible for a rise in income beyond a certain level to lead to a fall in the quantity that the household demands. Such a relation is likely

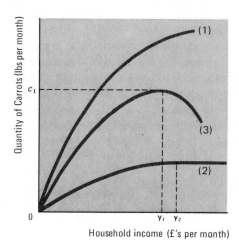

Fig. 7.3 The relation between the quantity of carrots demanded and household income

to occur when one commodity is a cheap but inferior substitute for some other com-modity. Commodities the demands for which rise as income rises are usually called NORMAL GOODS. Commodities the demands for which falls as income rises are called INFERIOR GOODS.

All three possible relations are illustrated in Figure 7.3 for our example of carrots. The three curves indicate alternative relations between income and the demand for carrots under the assumption that all factors other than income remain constant. Curve 1 illustrates the case in which a rise in income brings about a rise in purchases at all levels of income. Curve 2 illustrates a case in which purchases rise with income up to a certain point (income y_2) and then remain unchanged as income varies above that amount. Curve 3 illustrates the case in which purchases first rise with income up to a certain level (at income y_1 where purchases are c_1), but then fall as income goes beyond that level: the good becomes inferior at incomes higher than y_1. We have discussed these curves as the three possible alternative relations between the quantity of carrots demanded and income. In fact, each separate commodity will have its own characteristic curve: many commodities will have curves similar to 1, some may have curves similar to 2, and some will have curves that look like 3.

4 Quantity demanded depends upon the household's tastes

If it becomes fashionable amongst middle-class households to have a second car, the flow of expenditure on cars will increase. This does not mean that everybody will buy a second car, but some people will, and quantity demanded will rise. When there is a change in tastes in favour of a commodity, more of the commodity will be demanded even though the price of that commodity, the prices of all other commodities and household income do not change. Some changes in tastes are passing fads, like 'flower power' and Nehru jackets; other changes in tastes are permanent, or at least long lasting, such as the switch to filter cigarettes and ball point pens.

The economist often regards tastes as given and changes in these tastes as exo-genous and therefore outside his province. Tastes do to some extent arise out of the basic wants and needs of human beings, and as such they are more nearly in the realm of the biologist and the psychologist than of the economist. Changes in taste may, however, be the result of economic activities. One of the major purposes of advertis-ing is not only to inform the household about what products will best suit its present wants but also to try to set fashions and to change tastes. There is little doubt that, at least within limits, the attempt is successful. When tastes do change, for whatever reason, there are increases in the quantities demanded for some commodities and decreases in the quantities demanded for others.

MARKET DEMAND CURVES

So far we have discussed how the quantity demanded by an individual household depends on such things as prices and income. In the theory of price we are concerned with the total demand for some commodity on the part of all households. For each individual household there is a relation between the price of a commodity and the quantity of the commodity that it will demand. To obtain a market demand schedule from the demand schedules for individual households we merely sum the quantities demanded by each household at a particular price to obtain the total quantity demanded at that price; we repeat the process for each price to obtain a schedule of a total or market demand at all possible prices. A graph of this schedule is called the MARKET DEMAND CURVE.

The relation between the demand curves of households and the market demand curve is illustrated in Figure 7.4, where, for simplicity, we deal with a market containing only two households. We assume that we know the complete demand curve for each household and we show these in Figures 7.4(i) and (ii). From these individual demand curves we have derived the market demand curve, which merely shows how much will be demanded at each price by both households. Geometrically, the market demand curve in (iii) is derived by a horizontal summation of the two individual curves in (i) and (ii). At a price of £40, for example, household (i) demands 10·25 lbs of carrots and household (ii) demands 10 lbs; the total demand is 20·25 lbs, which quantity is plotted in Figure 7.4(iii) against the price of £40. At a price of £100 household (i) demands 3·5 lbs while household (ii) demands 6·25 lbs, and total demand is 9·75 lbs. Thus the market demand curve is to be thought of as the horizontal sum of all the demand curves of the households in the market. [1]

We have illustrated the market demand curve by summing the demands for only two households. In practice the market demand curve will represent the demands not just of two households but of all the households that are located in some area that makes up a market for a commodity. Since we will use the carrot example in subsequent chapters, we shall assume here that we have data for the total market demand for carrots in a particular area. These data are shown in Table 7.2 and are plotted in Figure 7.5. For reference the six points for which data are given in Table 7.2 are each referred to by a letter.

In practice we seldom obtain market demand curves such as the one shown in Figure 7.5 by summing the demand curves of individual households as illustrated in Figure 7.4. Our knowledge of market curves is usually derived by observing total quantities. The derivation of market demand curves by summing individual curves is a theoretical operation. We do it because we wish to understand the relation between curves for individual households and market curves.

When we go from the individual household's demand curve to the market demand curve we must add two new determinants of demand to the four already given: the size of the population and the distribution of income.

1 When summing curves, students sometimes become confused between vertical and horizontal summation. Such a confusion can only result from the application of memory rather than common sense to one's economics. *Consider what would be meant by vertical summation*: Measure off equal quantities, say 7·5 lbs. in Figure 7.4(i) and (ii). Now add the price to which this quantity corresponds on each household's demand curve. This gives £60 + £82 = £142. If we now plot the point corresponding to £142 and 7·5 lbs. in Figure (iii) we have related a given quantity of the commodity to the sum of the prices which households (i) and (ii) are separately prepared to pay for this commodity. Clearly, this information is of no interest to us in the present context. *Every graphical operation can be translated into words*. The advantage of graphs is that they make proofs easier; the disadvantage is that they make it possible to make silly errors. To avoid these, the student should always translate into words any graphical operation he has performed and ask himself: 'Does this make sense and is this what I meant to do?' For example, a market demand curve is meant to tell us total purchases at each price, and hence it is obtained from individual curves by adding up the *quantities* demanded by each consumer at given prices, not by adding the *prices* which each consumer would pay for some given quantity.

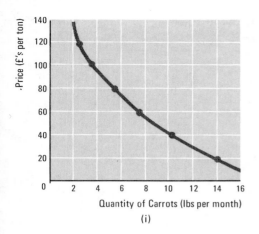

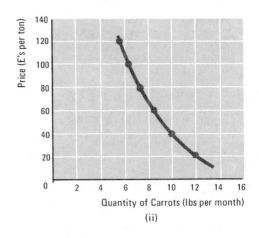

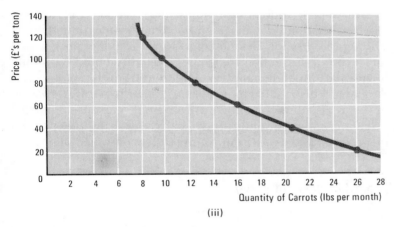

Fig. 7.4 Aggregation of individual demand curves to obtain a market demand curve (i) First household's demand curve (ii) Second household's demand curve (iii) Total demand curve for the two households

5 Quantity demanded depends upon the size of the population

As population grows, more people need to be fed, clothed, housed and entertained, and thus for most commodities quantity demanded increases as population does.[1] Economists treat population change as another exogenous determinant of demand.

6 Quantity demanded depends upon the distribution of income among households

We have already seen that household demand depends upon household income.

1 The relation is not quite as simple as this since we not only need more people, they must be able to buy things before demand increases. But a change in total population without any change in the percentage of total resources unemployed will increase the demand for most commodities.

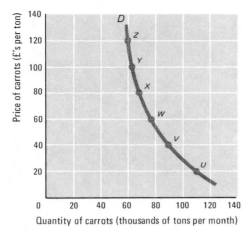

Fig. 7.5 A market demand curve for carrots

Table 7.2 A market demand schedule for carrots

	Price per ton £	Quantity demanded in thousands of tons per month
u	20	110·0
v	40	90·0
w	60	77·5
x	80	67·5
y	100	62·5
z	120	60·0

Thus market demand will depend upon total household income. Let us now imagine a society, an oil-rich sheikdom, say, in which the total income, though high, has been obtained by adding the very low incomes of a large number of poor households and the very high incomes of the few enormously wealthy ones. We would expect this society to have a pattern of demand very different from that of a society in which the same total income is distributed more evenly. Closer to home, we would expect for example that any redistribution of income from single persons to married couples would change demand in favour of furniture, baby goods and other things bought by couples with children, and away from commodities consumed mainly by bachelors.

The importance of the market demand curve

The market demand curve relates the quantity of a product demanded to the product's price and of all the relations in the demand function shown on page 75 it is the one most emphasized by economists. The emphasis does not reflect any belief that changes in prices are the largest single determinant of the changes in quantity demanded. Indeed changes in income, due to the variations in the level of employment and to economic growth (see points 1 and 6 on pages 53–5), probably account for a larger proportion of total variations in quantity demanded than do changes in price. Demand curves relating quantity demanded to price are emphasized at this stage because we are developing a theory of how resources are allocated between their various possible uses by the price mechanism, and for this purpose it is the relation between price and quantity demanded that is most important.

Shifts in the market demand curve

We must now consider the effect on the demand curve of a change in each of the other factors that were held constant when we drew the curve. These effects are, of course, implicit in what has been said about the relation between demand and each of these other factors.

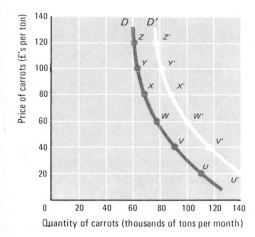

Fig. 7.6 The effect of a rise in household income on the demand for carrots

(1) THE EFFECT ON THE DEMAND CURVE OF A CHANGE IN INCOME: It has already been argued that, in the case of most commodities, a rise in income, *ceteris paribus*, will cause an increase in demand. Therefore, if household income rises, we shall find that, whatever the price we consider, there will be an increase in the quantity that is demanded at that price.

Table 7.3 shows, for our hypothetical example of carrots, the possible effect of an increase in the income of each household that purchases carrots. These new data are plotted in Figure 7.6 as the demand curve D'. The original demand curve is also shown and is labelled D. We say that the demand curve for carrots has shifted (in this case it has shifted to the right). The shift from D to D' indicates an increase in the desire to purchase carrots at each possible price. At the price of £40 a ton, for example, 116,000 tons are demanded, whereas only 90,000 were demanded at the lower income.[1] A rise in income thus shifts the demand curve to the right, whereas a

Table 7.3 Two alternative demand schedules for carrots

	Price of carrots (£ per ton)	Quantity of carrots demanded at the original level of household income (thousands of tons per month)	Quantity of carrots demanded when household income rises to a new level. (thousands of tons per month)	
u	20	110·0	140·0	u'
v	40	90·0	116·0	v'
w	60	77·5	100·8	w'
x	80	67·5	87·5	x'
y	100	62·5	81·3	y'
z	120	60·0	78·0	z'

1 Thus a rightward shift in the demand curve indicates an increase in demand in the sense that more is demanded at a given price and that a higher price would be paid for the original quantity. It is, of course, true that the amount demanded at Point Y' on D' is less than the amount demanded at Point U on D. This comparison merely shows that, in spite of the increased desire to purchase the good, a sufficiently large rise in price can reduce the quantity actually demanded to an amount lower than it was originally.

fall will have the opposite effect of shifting the curve to the left. In the case of an inferior good, a rise in income will cause a reduction in the quantity demanded at each market price, and the whole demand curve moves to the left.

(2) THE EFFECT ON THE DEMAND CURVE OF A CHANGE IN THE PRICES OF OTHER GOODS: Here the effect depends on whether the good, whose price changes, is a complement or a substitute. Consider, for example, the effect on the demand curve for electric cookers of a rise in the price of electricity. Electricity and electric cookers are complementary commodities and the rise in the price of electricity makes cooking with electricity more expensive than previously. Some households will switch to gas when they come to replace their existing cookers and some newly formed households will buy a gas rather than an electric cooker when they are setting up their household. Thus the rise in the price of electricity leads to a fall in the demand for electric cookers. Now consider the effect of a rise in the price of gas cookers. Gas and electric cookers are substitutes for each other and when gas cookers rise in price some households will buy electric rather than gas cookers, and the demand for electric cookers will thus rise.

For a general statement we may refer to commodity X rather than to electric cookers. A rise in the price of a commodity complementary to X will shift the demand curve for X to the left, indicating that less X will be demanded at each price. A rise in the price of a commodity that is a substitute for X will shift the demand curve for X to the right, indicating that more X will be demanded at each price.

(3) THE EFFECT ON THE DEMAND CURVE OF A CHANGE IN TASTES: This relation, of course, is quite simple. A change in tastes in favour of a commodity will mean that, at each price, more will be demanded than previously, so that the whole demand curve will shift to the right. On the other hand, a change in tastes away from a commodity will mean that, at each price, less will be demanded than previously, so that the whole demand curve will shift to the left.

Figure 7.7 summarizes the preceding discussions in which we have considered the effects on the demand curve of changes in the other things which are assumed constant when one curve is drawn. It is, of course, possible to do the same things for the curves illustrated in Figures 7.2 and 7.3, and the reader should check that he understands the analysis by showing the shifts in these curves caused by variations in the other factors that were assumed to be constant when the particular curve was constructed. (For example, what will happen to the curves in Figure 7.3 if there is a fall in the price of the product in question?)

Movements along curves versus shifts of curves

It is most important to distinguish between a *movement along* a demand curve and a *shift* of the whole curve. A movement along a demand curve indicates that a different quantity is being demanded *because* the price has changed. A shift of a demand curve indicates that a different quantity will be demanded at each possible price because something else, either incomes, tastes or the price of some other good, has changed.

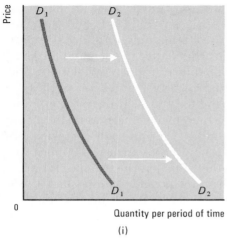
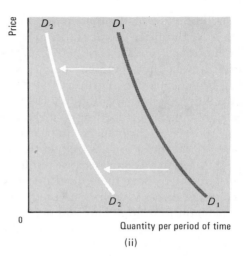

Fig. 7.7 Shifts in demand curves

(i) A rise in demand – the demand curve shifts to the right indicating a larger quantity is demanded at each price. This can be caused by (1) a rise in income, (2) a rise in the price of a substitute, (3) a fall in the price of a complement, (4) a change in tastes in favour of this commodity

(ii) A fall in demand – the demand curve shifts to the left indicating a smaller quantity is demanded at each price. This can be caused by (1) a fall in income, (2) a fall in the price of a substitute, (3) a rise in the price of a complement, (4) a change in tastes against this commodity

There is no generally agreed terminology to distinguish between these two quite different occurrences, a movement along one curve and a shift of the whole curve. This absence of agreement on the use of words can be confusing. When the economist speaks of an increase or a decrease of demand, he is usually referring to a shift of the whole curve, because he is more concerned with the whole functional relation between demand and price than with the particular quantity that happens to be demanded at any one moment. We shall follow this usage, and when we speak of *an increase or a decrease in demand* we shall be referring to a *shift* in the whole curve – to a change in the quantity that will be demanded at each possible price. When we refer to a movement along a curve we shall refer to a change in the *quantity demanded*, specifically, to an increase in the quantity demanded, indicating a movement down the curve because of a fall in price, or a decrease in the quantity demanded, indicating a movement up the curve because of a rise in price.

THE DEMAND FOR PETROL: AN EXAMPLE

The preceding discussion of the factors influencing demand may be reviewed by considering, as an example, the demand for petrol. The quantity of this commodity demanded will vary inversely with its price: as the price falls, more petrol will be consumed. This will occur because existing car owners will use more petrol, because new purchasers of cars will worry less about obtaining cars with low petrol consumption, and because some non-car owners will now feel they are able to afford to run a car. For these reasons the quantity of petrol demanded is expected to rise as its price falls. The quantity demanded may also be expected to vary inversely with the price of cars. As the price of cars falls, more households will purchase cars and there will be increased purchases of petrol (the price of petrol remaining unchanged). Petrol and cars are thus complementary goods. On the other hand, the demand for petrol can be expected to vary directly with the price of public transport – a fall in the price of public transport leading to a fall in the demand for petrol, and a rise in the price of public transport leading to a rise in the demand for petrol. If the price of public transport rises, car owners can be expected to use their own vehicles more frequently and public transport less frequently and it is possible that some non-car owners will be induced to buy cars because public transport is now more expensive. Public transport and petrol are thus substitutes for one another. Finally, the demand for petrol will vary directly with household incomes, a rise in incomes leading to a rise in petrol consumption. This will occur because car owners will use their existing cars more frequently, because some households will switch to more expensive cars which generally use more petrol per mile than do the less expensive ones, and because some non-car owners will now purchase cars as their incomes rise.

8

The elementary theory of supply

The term supply of a commodity refers to the amount of that commodity that producers are able and willing to offer for sale. Like demand, supply measures *desired* quantities, and it measures them as a *flow*, as so much per day, week, month or year.

We shall make a very superficial study of supply in this chapter, establishing only what is necessary for a simple theory of price. In Part 4 we shall devote considerable attention to the theory of production, which is the branch of economics concerned with the determination of supply.

WHAT DETERMINES THE QUANTITY SUPPLIED?

We now introduce five hypotheses about the most important factors influencing the quantity of a commodity that will be supplied.

(1) QUANTITY SUPPLIED DEPENDS UPON THE PRICE OF THE COMMODITY: *Ceteris paribus*, the higher the price of any commodity, the more profitable will it be to make it. We expect, therefore, that the higher the price, the greater will be the quantity supplied.

(2) QUANTITY SUPPLIED DEPENDS UPON THE PRICES OF OTHER COMMODITIES: Generally, an increase in the price of other commodities will make production of the commodity whose price does not rise relatively less attractive than it was previously. We thus expect that, *ceteris paribus*, the supply of one commodity will fall as the prices of other commodities rise.

(3) QUANTITY SUPPLIED DEPENDS UPON THE PRICES OF FACTORS OF PRODUCTION: A rise in the price of one factor of production will cause a large increase in the costs of making those goods that use a great deal of that factor, and only a small increase in the costs of producing those commodities that use a small amount of the factor.

For example, a rise in the price of land will have a large effect on the costs of producing wheat and only a very small effect on the costs of producing motor vehicles. Thus
a change in the price of one factor of production will cause changes in the relative
profitability of different lines of production and this will cause producers to shift
from one line to another, and so cause changes in the quantities of the various
commodities that are supplied.

(4) QUANTITY SUPPLIED DEPENDS UPON THE GOALS OF FIRMS: If producers of
some commodity want to sell as much as possible, even if it costs them some profits
to do so, more will be sold of that commodity than if they wanted to make maximum
profits. If producers are reluctant to take risks, we would expect smaller production
of any good the production of which was risky.

In elementary economic theory we assume the goal of the firm is to make as much
profit as possible. The full implications of this hypothesis, the implications of alternative hypotheses and the consequences of the rejection of the 'profit-maximizing
hypothesis' are considered in great detail in Part 4.

(5) QUANTITY SUPPLIED DEPENDS UPON THE STATE OF TECHNOLOGY: The
enormous increase in production per worker that has been going on in industrial
societies for about 200 years is very largely due to improved methods of production.
These in turn have been heavily influenced by the advance of science. Discoveries
in chemistry have led to lower costs of production of well-established products, like
paints, and to a large variety of new products made of plastics and synthetic fibres.
The new electronics industry rests upon transistors and other tiny devices that are
revolutionizing production in television, high-fidelity equipment, computers and
guidance-control systems. Atomic energy may one day be used to build canals and
to extract fresh water from the sea. At any time what is produced and how it is
produced depend upon what is known. Over time, knowledge changes and so do the
supplies of individual commodities.

THE SUPPLY FUNCTION

We may now summarize the preceding discussion: the quantity supplied of a
commodity is a function of the price of that commodity, the prices of all other
commodities, the prices of the factors of production, technology and the goals of
producers. This statement may be expressed in symbols by writing down what is
called a SUPPLY FUNCTION,

$$q_n^s = S(p_n, p_1, \ldots, p_{n-1}, F_1, \ldots, F_m, G, T)$$

where q_n^s is the supply of commodity n, p_n is the price of that commodity, $p_1, \ldots, p_{n-1}$
is shorthand for the prices of all other commodities, $F_1, \ldots, F_m$ is shorthand for the
prices of all factors of production, G the goals of producers and T is the state of
technology.

Quantity supplied and price

For a simple theory of price we wish only to know how the quantity supplied of a commodity varies with its own price, all other things being held constant.[1] We are only concerned, therefore, with the *ceteris paribus* relation, $q_n^s = S(p_n)$. There is much to be said on the relation between quantity supplied and price. For the moment we shall content ourselves with the intuitively plausible hypothesis that, *ceteris paribus*, the quantity of a commodity produced and offered for sale will increase as the price of the commodity rises and decreases as the price falls (i.e., quantity supplied and price will vary directly with each other). This hypothesis has a strong common-sense appeal, since the higher is the price of the commodity, the greater are the profits that can be earned, and, thus, the greater is the incentive to produce the commodity and offer it for sale.

The hypothesis is known to be correct in a large number of cases and we shall proceed for the next few chapters assuming it to be generally correct. The exceptions to the hypothesis and their implications will be studied when we come to the theory of production.

THE SUPPLY SCHEDULE: To illustrate this hypothesis, we extend the numerical example of the carrot market to include the quantity of carrots supplied. The supply schedule given in Table 8.1 is analogous to the demand schedule in Table 7.1, but it records the quantities producers wish to sell at a number of alternative prices rather than the quantities consumers wish to buy. At a price of £80 a ton, for example, 100,000 tons of carrots would come onto the market each month; at a price of £40 a ton, only 46,000 would be forthcoming.

Table 8.1 A supply schedule for carrots

	Price of carrots (£'s per ton)	Quantity supplied (thousands of tons per month)
u	20	5·0
v	40	46·0
w	60	77·5
x	80	100·0
y	100	115·0
z	120	122·5

THE SUPPLY CURVE: We can now plot the data from Table 8.1 on a graph similar to the one we used to show the demand curve. In Figure 8.1 price is plotted on the vertical axis and quantity on the horizontal one, and the six points corresponding to each price-quantity combination shown in the table are plotted. The point labelled *u*, for example, gives the same information that is on the first row of the table: when the price of carrots is £20 a ton, 5,000 tons will be produced and offered for sale each month.

1 We do this because we are concerned at this stage to develop a theory of price. We do not mean to imply that price is quantitatively the most important determinant of supply. Over any long period technology is probably the most important determinant although as we shall see in Chapter 18 the question of the extent to which technological changes themselves occur in response to price changes is a difficult one to answer.

Now we draw a smooth curve through the six points. This is the supply curve for carrots. It shows the quantity of carrots that will be produced and offered for sale at each price of carrots.

> **The supply curve for a commodity shows the relation between the price of that commodity and the quantity producers wish to sell. It is drawn on the assumption that all other factors that influence quantity supplied remain constant, and its upward slope indicates that the higher the price the greater the quantity producers will wish to sell.**

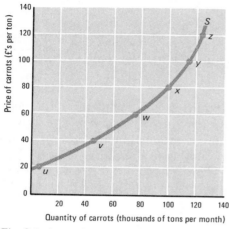

Fig. 8.1 A supply curve for carrots

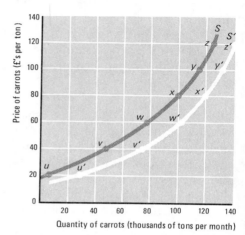

Fig. 8.2 A shift in the supply curve for carrots

Shifts in the supply curve

A shift in the supply curve means that, at each price, a different quantity will be supplied than previously. An increase in the quantity supplied at each price is illustrated in Table 8.2 and graphed in Figure 8.2 as the curve S'. This change appears as a rightward shift in the supply curve for carrots. On the other hand, a decrease in the quantity supplied at each price would appear as a leftward shift. A bodily shift in the supply curve, such as the one shown in Figure 8.2, must be the result of a change in one of the factors other than the price of the commodity that influence the quantity supplied. The major possible causes of such shifts are summarized under Figure 8.3.

Table 8.2 Two alternative supply schedules for carrots

	Price of carrots (£s per ton)	Original quantity supplied (tons per month)	New quantity supplied (tons per month)	
u	20	5	28	u'
v	40	46	76	v'
w	60	77·5	102	w'
x	80	100	120	x'
y	100	115	132	y'
z	120	122·5	140	z'

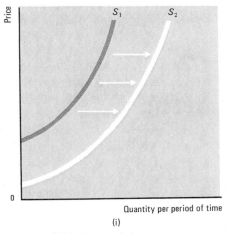

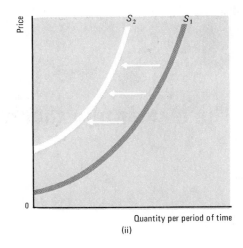

Fig. 8.3 Shifts in supply curves

(i) A rise in supply – the supply curve shifts to the right indicating that producers wish to make and sell more at each price. This can be caused by (1) improvements in technology, (2) decreases in the prices of other commodities, (3) decreases in the prices of factors of production used in making this commodity, (4) some kinds of changes in the goals of producers

(ii) A fall in the supply – the supply curve shifts to the left indicating that producers wish to make and sell less at each price. This can be caused by (1) loss in technical knowledge (unlikely), (2) increases in the prices of other commodities, (3) increases in the prices of factors of production used in making this commodity, (4) some kinds of changes in the goals of producers

As with demand, it is essential not to become confused between a movement along the supply curve (caused by a change in price) and a bodily shift in the curve (caused by a change in factor other than the commodity's own price). To avoid confusion, we adopt the same terminology as with demand: SUPPLY refers to the whole relation between price and quantity supplied, and QUANTITY SUPPLIED refers to a particular quantity actually supplied at given values of all the variables that influence supply. Thus, when we speak of *an increase or a decrease in supply*, we are referring to shifts in the supply curve, such as the ones illustrated in Figures 8.2 and 8.3. When we speak of a movement from one particular point on the supply curve to another point such as a movement from *w* to *y* in Figure 8.1, we shall speak of *a change in the quantity supplied*; in this particular case quantity changes from 77,500 to 115,000 tons per year in response to a rise in price from £60 to £100 per ton.

Now that we have studied the basic concepts of demand and supply, we can go on, in the next chapter, to study the theory of the determination of market prices by the interaction of demand and supply.

9

The elementary theory of market price

In this chapter we shall combine our theories of demand and supply into a theory of the determination of market prices. We begin by considering the example of carrots.

The determination of the equilibrium price

Table 9.1 brings together the market demand and supply schedules for carrots from Tables 7.2 and 8.1. In Figure 9.1 the data for both demand and supply are plotted on a single graph.

Table 9.1 Demand, supply and excess demand schedules for carrots (thousands of tons per month)

	Price per ton (£s)	Quantity demanded	Quantity supplied	Excess demand (quantity demanded minus quantity supplied)
u	20	110·0	5·0	+ 105·0
v	40	90·0	46·0	+ 44·0
w	60	77·5	77·5	0·0
x	80	67·5	100·0	− 32·5
y	100	62·5	115·0	− 52·5
z	120	60·0	122·5	− 62·5

THE RELATION BETWEEN QUANTITY SUPPLIED AND QUANTITY DEMANDED AT VARIOUS PRICES: Consider first the point at which the two curves in Figure 9.1 intersect. This point corresponds to a market price of £60; the quantity demanded is 77·5 thousand tons and the quantity supplied is the same. Thus at the price of £60 the amount consumers wish to buy is exactly the same as the amount producers wish to sell. Provided that the demand curve slopes downwards and the supply curve slopes upwards throughout their entire ranges, there will be only one price, £60 in this case, at which the quantity demanded is equal to the quantity supplied.

Now consider any price higher than £60, say a price of £100. At this price consumers wish to buy 62·5 thousand tons while producers wish to sell 115 thousand tons; thus supply exceeds demand by 52·5 thousand tons. It is easily seen, and the reader should check a few examples, that for any price above £60, quantity supplied exceeds quantity demanded. It is also clear that the higher is the price, the greater is the excess of the one over the other. Such situations are referred to as ones of EXCESS SUPPLY.

Finally, consider prices below £60, say a price of £40. At this price consumers' desired purchases of 90 thousand tons far exceed the producers' desired sales of 46 thousand tons. There is an excess of 44 thousand tons. It is easily seen, and the reader should again check one or two examples, that at all prices below £60, the quantity demanded exceeds the quantity supplied. Furthermore, the lower the price, the larger the excess of the one over the other. Such situations are referred to as ones of EXCESS DEMAND.

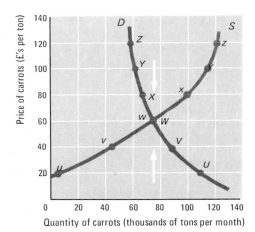

Fig. 9.1 The determination of the equilibrium price of carrots

CHANGES IN PRICE WHEN DEMAND DOES NOT EQUAL SUPPLY: We now introduce two hypotheses about how price changes when the quantities demanded and supplied are not equal to each other. First we assume that, when there is excess supply, the market price will fall. Producers, unable to sell some of their goods, may begin to ask lower prices for them; purchasers, observing the glut of unsold commodities, may begin to offer lower prices. For either or both of these reasons prices will fall. This hypothesis is illustrated in Figure 9.1 by the arrow indicating a downward pressure on price at all prices above £60.

The second hypothesis is that when there is excess demand, price will rise. Individual households, unable to buy as much as they would like to at present prices, offer higher prices in an effort to get more of the available goods for themselves, and suppliers, who could sell more than their total production, may begin to ask higher prices for the quantities that they have produced. For either or both of these reasons prices will rise when quantity demanded exceeds quantity supplied. This hypothesis is illustrated in Figure 9.1 by the arrow indicating an upward pressure on price for all prices below £60.

THE EQUILIBRIUM PRICE: For any price above £60, according to our theory, the price tends to fall, and for any price below £60, the price tends to rise. At a price of £60, there is neither an excess of quantity demanded creating a shortage, nor an excess of quantity supplied creating a glut; quantity supplied is equal to quantity demanded and there is no tendency for the price to change. The price of £60, where the two curves intersect, is the price that equates quantity demanded and quantity supplied; it is the only price at which there is neither a shortage nor a surplus; and it is the price towards which the actual market price will tend. This price is called the EQUILIBRIUM PRICE. The term *equilibrium* means a state of balance; such a state of balance occurs when demanders desire to buy the same amount as suppliers desire to sell.

When quantity demanded equals quantity supplied we say that the market is in a state of EQUILIBRIUM. When quantity demanded does not equal quantity supplied we say that the market is in a state of DISEQUILIBRIUM.

We may now summarize our simple theory of price as follows:

> **Hypotheses**
> **(1) Demand curves slope downward continuously.**
> **(2) Supply curves slope upward continuously.**
> **(3) An excess of the quantity demanded over the quantity supplied causes price to rise; an excess of quantity supplied over quantity demanded causes price to fall.**
>
> **Implications**
> **(1) There is no more than one price at which quantity demanded equals quantity supplied. In the language of economic theory, equilibrium is unique.**
> **(2) If either the demand or supply curve shifts, the equilibrium price and quantity will change. (The actual changes are considered below.)**[1]

The excess-demand function

We have drawn demand and supply curves and shown that the equilibrium is at the point at which the two curves intersect. It is very often useful to work with an EXCESS-DEMAND CURVE which shows the relation between the price of the commodity and excess demand, defined as quantity demanded *minus* quantity supplied.

The excess demand curve for our carrot example is shown in Figure 9.2. It is obtained by plotting the data in the last column of Table 9.1 against the appropriate prices of the carrots. The equilibrium price occurs where the excess demand curve cuts the price axis. At prices below the equilibrium there is positive excess demand

---

1 For a long time it was thought that the following inference could be drawn from these hypotheses: the market will be *stable* in the sense that, if the price moves away from its equilibrium level, it will move back toward and will eventually return to, the equilibrium level. This inference cannot be drawn from this theory. The problem of stability is mentioned briefly in Chapter 12.

since quantity demanded exceeds quantity supplied. At prices above the equilibrium, excess demand is negative. It is common to refer to negative excess demand as excess supply.

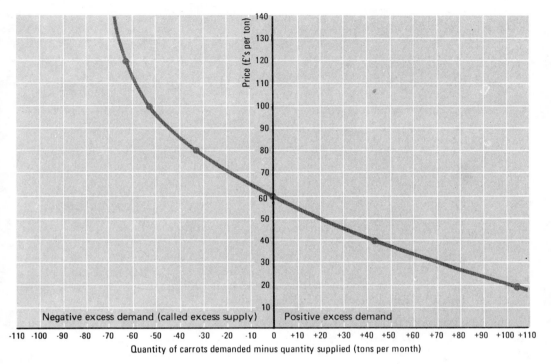

Fig. 9.2 An excess demand curve for carrots

SHIFTS IN DEMAND AND SUPPLY

We may now consider the effect of shifts in the demand and supply curves on the equilibrium price and quantity. In Figure 9.3 the original demand curve is D_1 and the supply curve is S_1. Now assume that the demand curve shifts to D_2. This increase in demand might, for example, be the result of a rise in incomes. The original equilibrium price is p_1 and the quantity q_1. When the demand curve shifts, excess demand develops because, at price p_1, the quantity demanded is now q_3, whereas the quantity supplied remains at q_1. As a result of the excess demand, $q_3 - q_1$, price will rise towards the new equilibrium price of p_2. At this price the quantity demanded equals the quantity supplied. The new equilibrium quantity bought and sold is q_2; the rise in price from p_1 to p_2 reduces the quantity demanded from q_3 to q_2, whereas it increases the quantity supplied from q_1 to q_2. This gives rise to the first implication of our theory.

> **(1) A rise in the demand for a commodity (i.e., a rightward shift of the demand curve) causes an increase in both the equilibrium price and the equilibrium quantity bought and sold.**

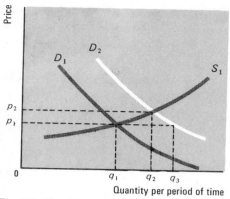

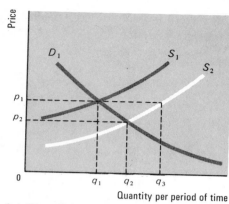

Fig. 9.3 The effects of shifts in the demand curve   Fig. 9.4 The effects of shifts in the supply curve

When the demand decreases (i.e., when the demand curve shifts to the left), there will be a decrease both in the equilibrium price and in the equilibrium quantity. This can also be seen in Figure 9.3 if we visualize a shift in the demand curve from D_2 to D_1. Equilibrium price decreases from p_2 to p_1 and equilibrium quantity from q_2 to q_1. This gives us our second implication.

> **(2) A fall in the demand for a commodity (i.e., a leftward shift of the demand curve) causes a decrease in both the equilibrium price and the equilibrium quantity bought and sold.**

The effect of a rise in supply is shown in Figure 9.4. The shift in the supply curve to the right, from S_1 to S_2, indicates an increase in supply; at each price more is now offered for sale than was previously offered. This time, however, the shift of the curve causes a glut to develop at the old equilibrium price. When the curve shifts, the quantity offered for sale increases from q_1 to q_3 but the quantity demanded remains unchanged at q_1. The excess supply causes prices to fall. As prices come down, the quantity supplied diminishes and the quantity demanded increases. The new equilibrium price is at p_2, where the quantity supplied and the quantity demanded are equal to q_2. This gives us our third implication.

> **(3) A rise in the supply of a commodity (i.e., a rightward shift of the supply curve) causes a decrease in the equilibrium price and an increase in the equilibrium quantity bought and sold.**

The effect of a decrease in supply can be seen in Figure 9.4 by assuming a shift in the supply curve from S_2 to S_1. Equilibrium price increases from p_2 to p_1 and the equilibrium quantity bought and sold decreases from q_2 to q_1.

> **(4) A fall in the supply of a commodity (i.e., a leftward shift in the supply curve) causes an increase in the equilibrium price and a decrease in the equilibrium quantity bought and sold.**

We now have a theory that is beautiful in its simplicity and yet, as we shall see, unusual in its wide range of applications. The theory of the determination of price by demand and supply is one of the finest examples of a theory that is both very simple and very powerful.

The 'laws' of supply and demand

It is very common to refer to the four propositions that we have just developed as the 'laws' of supply and demand. The notion of natural law as something which is proven to be true, is an eighteenth- and early nineteenth-century concept. It has long been discarded from the natural sciences, although traces of it still linger on elsewhere. Even the great 'laws' of Newton were upset after 200 years, and scientific theories are now accepted not as laws but as tentative hypotheses which will sooner or later be discovered to be in conflict with the facts and replaced by other more embracing hypotheses.

As with all theories, the implications of the theory of market price may be looked at in two ways. First they are logical deductions from a series of assumptions about behaviour. We may say that the implications are true in the sense that they represent logically valid deductions from a series of assumptions. Second, they are predictions about observable behaviour in the world. To make them such we assume that the behavioural assumptions of the theory conform to actual behaviour in our world, and it then follows that any logical implication of these assumptions must also conform to actual behaviour. We could say that such predictions are 'true' in the empirical sense if they have been tested against evidence and found to be consistent with our observations of actual behaviour.

The use of the word 'law' implies that the four implications are true in the empirical sense. We must always remember that these 'laws' are nothing more than predictions that follow from price theory and that, as such, they are open to testing. There is considerable evidence that, in many markets, the predictions are consistent with the facts; in other markets – especially those for manufactured goods – it is not so

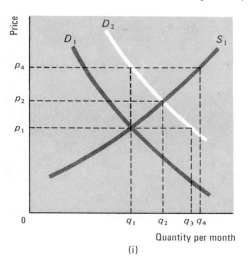
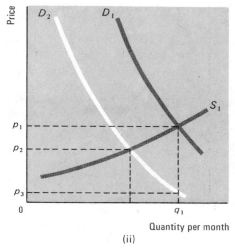

Fig. 9.5 The effects of shifts in the demand curves for carrots and brussels sprouts (i) A rise in the demand for sprouts (ii) A fall in the demand for carrots

clear that they do come near to being consistent with our observations. In general, however, we should not speak of 'laws'; we should speak rather of predictions that appear to be at least somewhere near the mark in a considerable number of cases.

AN EXAMPLE

In Chapter 5 we discussed in a preliminary and intuitive way the effects of various changes in the demands for and supplies of Brussels sprouts and carrots. We can now formalize part of this discussion in terms of our newly-developed theory. We do this to gain practice by using our new tools of demand and supply curves in the context of an already familiar problem.

(1) THE EFFECTS OF A RISE IN THE DEMAND FOR SPROUTS AND A FALL IN THE DEMAND FOR CARROTS: The market for sprouts is illustrated in Figure 9.5(i). The original demand and supply curves are D_1 and S_1 so that the original equilibrium price is p_1 and quantity q_1. Now the demand curve shifts to D_2. At the original price of p_1 there is now an excess of demand over supply of $q_3 - q_1$. If, for the time being, the supply of sprouts is fixed at q_1, then prices will rise to p_4, which price equates the original supply with the increasing demand. Equilibrium is obtained at first solely by choking off demand through price increases. The supply curve of sprouts is, however, S_1. At the price p_4 producers would like to grow and sell the quantity q_4. Production will begin to increase and, as the increased flow comes on to the market, the price will fall, for no more than q_1 can be sold at the price p_4. The new equilibrium price is p_2 where the quantity demanded and supplied is q_2.

The effects on carrots, which are shown in Figure 9.5(ii) are the reverse of the effects on sprouts. The leftward shift in demand causes price to fall to p_3 as long as the quantity supplied remains at its original level of q_1. The fall in price, however,

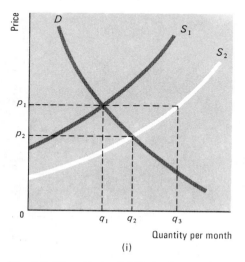

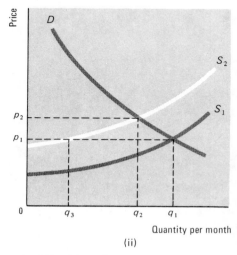

Fig. 9.6 The effects of shifts in the supply curves for carrots and brussels sprouts
(i) An increase in the supply of brussels sprouts (ii) A decrease in the supply of carrots

causes a contraction in output and then a rise in price to its new equilibrium level of p_2. The fall in demand thus causes both the new equilibrium price and quantity to be lower than their original levels.

(2) THE EFFECTS OF AN INCREASE IN THE SUPPLY OF SPROUTS AND A DECREASE IN THE SUPPLY OF CARROTS: These effects are illustrated in Figure 9.6. The increase in the supply of sprouts from S_1 to S_2 causes a surplus to appear. In Figure 9.6(i), the surplus is equal to $q_3 - q_1$ at the original equilibrium price of p_1. The surplus causes the price to fall and, as it falls, the quantity supplied decreases and the quantity demanded increases. The new equilibrium price of p_2 is lower than the original price, while the new equilibrium quantity of q_2 is higher than the original quantity.

The decrease in the supply of carrots is illustrated by the leftward shift in the supply curve in Figure 9.6(ii) from S_1 to S_2. At the original price of p_1 there is now a shortage of $q_1 - q_3$, because the quantity supplied has fallen from q_1 to q_3 while the quantity demanded has remained unchanged. As a result of the shortage the price rises. This rise in price reduces the quantity demanded and increases the quantity supplied. The new equilibrium price is at p_2, which is higher than the original price by $p_2 - p_1$. The new equilibrium quantity is q_2 which is lower than the original equilibrium quantity by $q_1 - q_2$.

10

Elasticity of demand and supply

In this chapter we shall consider the degree to which the quantity demanded and the quantity supplied respond to changes in price. This question is a most important one, because it arises many times in practical applications of the theory of demand and supply.

THE IMPORTANCE OF THE RESPONSIVENESS OF DEMAND TO PRICE

Consider the effects of the decrease in the supply of carrots analysed in the previous chapter. In Figure 10.1(i), the fall in the supply from S_1 to S_2 is seen to result in a large fall in the quantity of carrots sold from q_1 to q_2, and a small rise in the price of carrots from p_1 to p_2. Figure 10.1(ii) shows the same shift in the supply curve as that shown in Figure 10.1(i), but the demand curve is different. In this case the price of

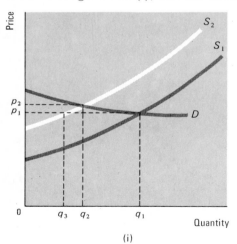 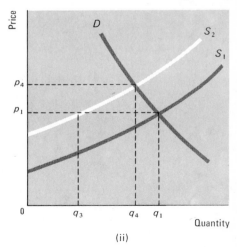

Fig. 10.1 The effects on price and quantity of a shift in supply when combined with demand curves of various slopes

carrots rises considerably from p_1 to p_4, while the quantity traded falls only by the small amount of $q_1 - q_4$. Clearly, a given shift in supply has very different effects depending on the slope of the demand curve.

Let us consider how the different results illustrated in Figures 10.1(i) and (ii) come about. At the initial equilibrium position, price is p_1 and quantity is q_1. A leftward shift in the supply curve occurs and, at the existing price of p_1, there is now an excess demand of $q_1 - q_3$. This shortage causes the price to rise. In the case illustrated in Figure 10.1(i), even a small rise in price is sufficient to choke off most of the excess demand. The quantity demanded responds greatly to price changes; equilibrium is restored by only a small change in price and a large reduction in quantity demanded. In the case illustrated in Figure 10.1(ii), a rise in price has much less effect on the quantity demanded. Price therefore continues to rise until sufficient supply is called forth to match the only slightly reduced quantity demanded. Price rises considerably but quantity bought and sold falls by only a small amount.

Since the supply-curve shifts are the same, the difference between the two cases clearly lies in the different ways in which demand responds to changes in price. In the first case, the quantity demanded varies greatly with price, and a small rise in price restores equilibrium by choking off the excess demand. In the second case, the quantity demanded is very insensitive to price changes and equilibrium is restored only when the price rise has been sufficient to call forth the extra supply necessary to satisfy the almost unchanged quantity demanded. Evidently, the geometrical shape of a demand curve is of some importance.

ELASTICITY: A MEASURE OF THE RESPONSIVENESS OF DEMAND

When considering the responsiveness of the quantity demanded to changes in price, we may wish to make statements such as the following: 'The demand for carrots was more responsive to price changes ten years ago than it is today', or 'The demand for meat responds more to price changes than does the demand for green vegetables.'

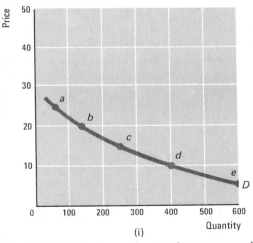 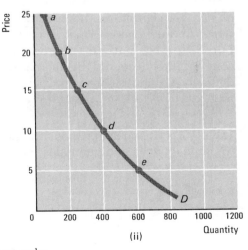

Fig. 10.2 A single demand curve drawn on two different scales

In Figures 10.1(i) and (ii) we were able to make direct comparison of the responsiveness of quantity demanded along the two curves because they were drawn on the same scale. Certainly, you should not try to compare two curves without making sure the scale is the same. Also, you must not leap to conclusions about responsiveness of quantity demanded on the basis of the apparent steepness of a single curve without noting the scale and the quantitative effect of price changes. To illustrate the hazards look at the demand curve in Figure 10.2(i). This curve appears rather flat, but, by a mere change in scale, we can make the demand curve *showing the identical information* appear to be rather steep. This is done in Figure 10.2(ii).

Assume that we are concentrating on actual quantities and that, for example, we have the information shown in Table 10.1. Does this give us enough information to

Table 10.1 Changes in prices and quantities for
three commodities

Commodity	Reduction in price	Increase in quantity demanded
Beefsteak	£0·05 per pound	7,500 tons
Men's cotton shirts	£0·05 per shirt	4,500 shirts
Radios	£0·05 per radio	20 radios

make meaningful comparisons of the responsiveness of quantities demanded to price changes among the three commodities? Can we conclude, for example that the demand for radios is not as responsive to price changes as is the demand for beefsteak because a £0·05 cut in price gives quite a large increase in demand for beefsteak, while an equal price cut has very little effect on the demand for radios? There are two problems here. First, a reduction in price of 5p will be a large price cut for a low-priced commodity and an insignificant price cut for a high-priced commodity. The price reductions listed in Table 10.1 probably represent something in the order of a 15 per cent fall in the price of beefsteak, a 3 per cent fall in the price of cotton shirts, and less than a 1 per cent fall in the price of radios. It is more revealing for purposes of comparison to know the percentage change in the price of the various commodities. Secondly, by an analogous argument, knowing the quantity by which demand changes is not very revealing, unless we also know the level of demand. An increase of 10,000 tons is quite a significant reaction of demand if the quantity

Table 10.2 Changes in prices and quantities related
to original prices and quantities for three commodities

Commodity	Original price	Change in price	Original quantity	Change in quantity
Beefsteak (lb)	£0·40	− £0·05	108,750	7,500
Men's shirts	£1·66	− £0·05	144,750	4,500
Radios	£50·00	− £0·05	10,000	20

formerly bought was, say, 15,000 tons, while it is but a drop in a very large bucket if the quantity formerly demanded was, say, 10,000,000 tons.

Table 10.2 records the original levels of, as well as the changes in, price and quantity. What we really need to know is: how large is the price decrease, expressed as a percentage of the original price, and how large is the increase in quantity, expressed as a percentage of the quantity originally being sold? This information is recorded in Table 10.3.

Table 10.3 Percentage changes in prices and quantities for three commodities

Commodity	% Change in price	% Change in quantity
Beefsteak	− 12·50	6·90
Men's shirts	− 3·01	3·11
Radios	− 0·10	0·20

It is now seen that quite a large percentage change in the price of beefsteak brought about a much smaller percentage change in quantity purchased. On the other hand, although the increase in the number of radios purchased was only twenty, this is seen to be quite a large percentage change in the quantity *in comparison to the percentage change in price that brought it about.*

A formal definition of elasticity

In the above example we were led to compare for each commodity the percentage change in quantity demanded with the percentage change in price that brought it about. The simplest way to do this is to divide the one percentage by the other. When we do this, and express the result as a positive number, we obtain what is called the ELASTICITY OF DEMAND and usually symbolized by the Greek letter eta, η. Writing out the definition in full we have

$$\eta = (-1) \frac{\text{Percentage change in quantity demanded}}{\text{Percentage change in price}}.$$

There are two problems that arise when this formula is applied to calculate numerical measures of elasticity. First, when we deal with a percentage change, we must define the change as a percentage of something. Should it be the original amount? This is a simple procedure but has the disadvantage of making the percentage change, and hence the elasticity between two points on a demand curve, depend on the direction of the movement. Thus if we define the percentage change in price as the change from the original price, a movement from £1·00 to £1·20 is a 20 per cent change (price increased by $\frac{1}{5}$), while a movement from £1·20 to £1·00 is only a $16\frac{2}{3}$ per cent change (price decreased by $\frac{1}{6}$). If, however, we take the percentage change to be the change in price divided by the average price (£1·10), both the change from £1·00 to £1·20 and the change from £1·20 to £1·00 give a percentage change of 18·18 per cent. Since we want the elasticity between two points on a curve to be a single value, independent of the direction of movement between the two points, we shall take all percentage changes to be the change in price or quantity divided by the average of the original and the new prices or quantities.

The second problem arises from the fact that every change has a sign attached to it; it is either an increase ($+$) or a decrease ($-$). Since demand curves slope downwards, the change in quantity will always have the opposite sign to the change in price. The minus sign in the definition of elasticity is simply to make elasticity of demand a positive number. This is a matter of convenience only; it has no more profound justification than that. The convenience lies in being able to equate 'more responsive' with 'more elastic'. If the negative sign is retained then the more responsive is quantity demanded to a change in price the smaller is the elasticity.

Consider an example in which commodities X and Y have elasticities of $+10$ and $+0.5$ (calculated according to the above formula). The demand for commodity X is more responsive to price changes than is the demand for commodity Y, and X has the larger measured elasticity ($+10 > +0.5$). But if we did not multiply by (-1) the two elasticities would be -10 and -0.5 so that the commodity with the more responsive demand, X, would have a smaller elasticity than $Y(-10 < -0.5)$.

Having dealt with these two problems we can now proceed to calculate the elasticities for the three examples given in Table 10.2. These calculations are shown in detail in Table 10.4.

We now have a precise measure of elasticity. According to this measure, the demand for radios is more responsive to a price change than is the demand for beefsteak and men's shirts. The percentage change in the quantity of radios demanded was twice as large as the percentage change in price that brought it about ($\eta = 2$); the percentage change in the quantity of men's shirts demanded was the same as the price change that brought it about ($\eta = 1$); but the percentage change in the quantity of beefsteak demanded was only half as large as the price change that brought it about ($\eta = 0.5$).[1]

Interpreting numerical values of elasticity of demand

The numerical value of elasticity can vary from zero to infinity. Elasticity is zero if there is no change at all in quantity demanded when price changes, i.e., when quantity demanded does not respond to a price change. The larger the elasticity, the larger the percentage change in quantity for a given percentage change in price. As long as the elasticity of demand has a value of less than one, however, the percentage change in quantity is less than the percentage change in price. When elasticity is equal to one, then the two percentage changes are equal to each other. When the percentage change in quantity exceeds the percentage change in price, then the value for the elasticity of demand will be greater than one.

When the percentage change in quantity is less than the percentage change in price (elasticity less than one), the demand is said to be INELASTIC. When the percentage change in quantity is greater than the percentage change in price (elasticity

---

1 The measure of elasticity defined in the text is called *arc elasticity*. In theoretical work the elasticity is defined not between two points on a curve but at each point. This measure is called *point elasticity* and it makes use of derivatives. The relation between arc and point elasticity is further considered in the appendix to this chapter.

Table 10.4 Calculation of elasticities of demand for beefsteak, men's shirts and radios from the data given in Table 10.2

	Old amount	New amount	Change in amount	Average amount	Percentage change	Elasticity
Beefsteak						
price(£'s)	0·40	0·35	−0·05	0·375	$\frac{-0·05}{0·375}100=-13·33$	$\eta=-\frac{+6·67}{-13·33}=+0·5$
quantity (lbs)	108,750	116,250	7,500	112,500	$\frac{7,500}{112,500}100=+6·67$	
Men's shirts						
price (£'s)	1·66	1·61	−0·05	1·635	$\frac{-0·05}{1·635}100=-3·06$	$\eta=-\frac{+3·06}{-3·06}=+1·0$
quantity	144,750	149,250	4,500	147,000	$\frac{4,500}{147,000}100=+3·06$	
Radios						
price (£'s)	50·00	49·95	−0·05	49·975	$\frac{-0·05}{49·975}100=-0·10$	$\eta=-\frac{+0·20}{-0·10}=+2·0$
quantity	9,980	10,000	20	9,990	$\frac{20}{9,990}100=+0·20$	

greater than one), the demand is said to be ELASTIC. The previous discussion is summarized in Table 10.5. This terminology is most important, and the student should spend time in becoming familiar with it.

Table 10.5 Price elasticity: measures, meaning and nomenclature

Numerical measure of elasticity	Verbal description	Terminology
Zero	Quantity demanded does not change as price changes	Perfectly (or completely) inelastic
Greater than zero, but less than one	Quantity demanded changes by a smaller percentage than does price	Inelastic
One	Quantity demanded changes by exactly the same percentage as does price	Unit elasticity
Greater than one, but less than infinity	Quantity demanded changes by a larger percentage than does price	Elastic
Infinity	Purchasers are prepared to buy all they can obtain at some price and none at all at an even slightly higher price	Perfectly (or infinitely) elastic

We may now consider briefly the graphical representation of demand curves of various elasticities. These are summarized in Figure 10.3. Zero elasticity occurs when

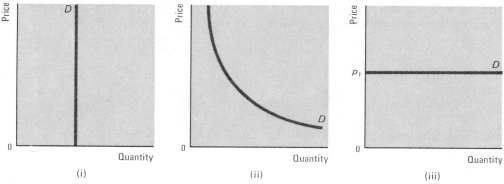

Fig. 10.3 (i) A demand curve of zero elasticity (ii) A demand curve of unit elasticity (iii) A demand curve of infinite elasticity

the quantity demanded does not change as the price changes: purchasers wish to buy the same amount at all prices. The graph of a demand curve of zero elasticity will thus be a vertical straight line indicating that the same quantity is demanded whatever the price. Unit elasticity occurs when a given percentage change in price brings about an equal percentage change in quantity at all points on the curve. The graph of a curve of unit elasticity over its whole range is shown in Figure 10.3(ii).[1] A demand curve of infinite elasticity means that there exists some small price reduction which raises the demand from zero to infinity. This case occurs when, at some price, consumers will buy all that they can obtain of the commodity (an infinite amount if they could get it), while at an even slightly higher price they would buy none at all. In Figure 10.3(iii), demand is zero for all prices above p_1, but *at price p_1* demand is infinite. This very unlikely looking case turns out to be a very important one when, in the theory of production, we come to study the demand for the output of a single firm.

Elasticity of demand and changes in total expenditure and total revenue

Money spent by purchasers of a commodity is received by the sellers of the commodity. The total amount spent by purchasers is thus the gross revenue of the sellers. Often in economics we are interested in how total expenditure by purchasers of a commodity or total gross receipts of sellers of the commodity, reacts when the price of a product is changed.

If the price of a product falls there will be an increase in quantity sold; what happens to total revenue depends on the amount by which sales rise in response to a given price cut. The simplest example is sufficient to convince us that total revenue may rise or fall in response. One hundred units of a commodity are being sold at a

1 Beginners often wonder why a curve of convex shape is implied by constant elasticity. The reason is that if the ratio $\dfrac{\text{percentage change in quantity}}{\text{percentage change in price}}$ is to be kept constant, equal absolute price cuts must be met with larger and larger absolute increases in quantity. Thus, geometrically, the curve must get flatter and flatter as price becomes lower and lower. This increasing flatness of the demand curve indicates, of course, an increasing responsiveness of the *absolute* quantity demanded to successive *absolute* price changes.

price of £1·00; the price is then cut to 90p. If the quantity sold rises to 101, the total revenue of the sellers falls (from £100 to £90·90), but if quantity sold rises to 120, total revenue rises (from £100 to £108).

You should now take the earlier example of radios, shirts and beefsteak, and calculate what happened to total revenue when price fell in each case. When you have done this you will see that in the case of beefsteak, where the demand was inelastic, a cut in price lowered the revenue of sellers; in the case of the radios, where the demand was elastic, a cut in price raised the revenue earned by sellers. The border-line case is provided by men's shirts; here the demand elasticity is unity, and the cut in price leaves total revenue unchanged. These relations are no accident. Total consumer expenditures (or total receipts of sellers, which is the same thing), are related to elasticity in the following way. If the demand is inelastic, a change in price causes a less than proportionate change in the quantity demanded, so that total revenue falls when price falls and rises when price rises. If the demand is elastic, a change in price causes a more than proportionate change in quantity, so that total revenue rises when price falls and falls when price rises. When the elasticity of demand is unity, a change in price is met by an exactly proportionate (and therefore an exactly offsetting) change in quantity, and hence total revenue remains constant when price changes. These results are summarized below.

> **If elasticity of demand exceeds unity, a fall in price increases total consumer expenditure, and a rise in price reduces it. If elasticity is less than unity, a fall in price reduces total expenditure and a rise in price increases it. If elasticity of demand is unity, a rise or a fall in price leaves total expenditure unaffected.**

What determines elasticity of demand?

One of the most important determinants of elasticity is undoubtedly the degree of availability of close substitutes. Some commodities, like margarine, cabbage, pork and Fords, have quite close substitutes – butter, other green vegetables, beef and other similar makes of cars. A change in the price of these commodities, *the prices of the substitutes remaining constant*, can be expected to cause quite substantial substitution – a fall in price leading consumers to buy more of the commodity in question and a rise in price leading consumers to buy more of the substitute. Other commodities, such as salt, housing and all vegetables taken together, have few, if any, satisfactory substitutes, and a rise in their price can be expected to cause a smaller fall in quantity demanded than would be the case if close substitutes were available.

The following hypothesis about elasticity of demand is commonly advanced: there are certain commodities, called luxuries, which can easily be dispensed with and which have highly elastic demands because, when their prices rise, consumers stop purchasing them. There are other commodities, called necessities, which are essential to life, and which have almost completely inelastic demands because, when their prices rise, the consumer has no choice but to continue to buy them. Most goods fall into one or other of these classes, entertainment being an example of the former and food an example of the latter.

There is nothing logically wrong with this hypothesis; it is quite easy to imagine a world that behaved like this. The only problem is that the hypothesis does not describe *our* world; the hypothesis is refuted by the facts. In all the demand studies that have been made, there is no observable tendency for commodities to fall into two groups, one with very low elasticities and one with very high elasticities. There seem to be goods with all possible sorts of elasticity, a few are very low, a few high and the remainder are spread out between these extremes.

To a great extent elasticity depends on how widely or narrowly a commodity is being defined. It is true, of course, that food and shelter are necessities in the sense that life cannot go on without some minimum quantity of them, and it is possibly true that foods as a whole would have an inelastic demand. It does not follow from this, however, that any one food, for example white bread or cornflakes, is a necessity in the same sense. Thus, there is no reason to believe that the quantity of any one food demanded cannot and will not fall greatly as a result of a rise in its price.

INCOME AND CROSS ELASTICITY OF DEMAND

The purpose of measuring demand elasticity is to discover the degree to which the quantity demanded responds to a change in any one of the factors that influence it. So far, we have considered the response of the quantity of a commodity demanded to changes in the commodity's own price. It is also important to know how demand responds to changes in incomes and the prices of other goods.

INCOME ELASTICITY: The responsiveness of demand for a commodity to changes in income is termed *income elasticity of demand*, and is defined as

$$\eta_Y = \frac{\text{percentage change in quantity demanded}}{\text{percentage change in income}}.$$

For most goods, increases in income lead to increases in demand, and income elasticity will be positive. In the case of inferior goods, where a rise in income leads consumers to demand less of the commodity, income elasticity will be negative.

If you look back now to Figure 7.3 on page 78, you will see plotted several curves relating demand to income. Whenever a curve is rising, income elasticity is positive. When demand is unaffected by the level of income, as in the right-hand portion of the curve labelled (2), income elasticity is zero. When the curve declines, as in (3), income elasticity is negative.

The reaction of demand to changes in income is extremely important. In most Western economies economic growth is important, with the level of total income doubling every 20 or 30 years. This rise in income is shared more or less equally by all the households in the country. As they find their income increasing they increase their demand for all but inferior commodities. The demand for some commodities such as food and basic clothing will not increase nearly so much as the demand for other commodities. In the UK and most of Western Europe it is the demand for durable goods, such as cars, refrigerators, washing machines that is increasing most rapidly as household incomes rise, while in the United States it is the demand for services that is rising most rapidly.

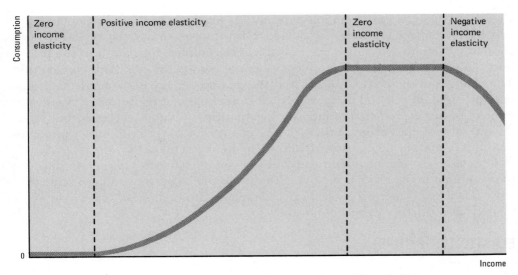

Fig. 10.4 A relation between expenditure on a single commodity and household income

Income elasticity measures this response of demand to changes in income. The variability of the response is one of the major causes of resource reallocation in any Western economy, and one of the major reasons why we always have with us contracting and depressed industries as well as expanding and buoyant ones. Industries with low income elasticities will find the demands for their products expanding only slowly while industries with high income elasticities find the demands for their products expanding rapidly. This relation is an extremely important one and we shall return to it many times in this book. In the meantime, the main relations are summarized in Table 10.6 and illustrated in Figure 10.4.

Table 10.6 Income elasticity, measures and meaning

Numerical measure of income elasticity for a particular commodity	Verbal description
Negative	Demand for the commodity falls as income rises
Zero	Demand for the commodity does not change as income changes
Greater than zero but less than one	Demand for the commodity rises by a smaller proportion than does income
Unity	Demand for the commodity rises by the same proportion as does income
Greater than unity	Demand for the commodity rises by a larger proportion than does income

CROSS-ELASTICITY: The responsiveness of demand to changes in the price of another commodity is called CROSS-ELASTICITY OF DEMAND. It is defined as

$$\eta_X = \frac{\text{percentage change in quantity demanded of commodity } X}{\text{percentage change in price of commodity } Y}.$$

Cross-elasticity can vary from minus infinity to plus infinity. Complementary goods will have negative cross-elasticities and substitute goods will have positive cross elasticities. Bread and butter, for example, are complements, a fall in the price of butter is predicted to lead to an increase in the consumption of both commodities. The changes in the price of butter and the quantity of bread demanded will have opposite signs. Butter and margarine, on the other hand, are substitutes. A fall in the price of butter is predicted to increase the quantity of butter consumed but reduce the quantity of margarine consumed. The changes in the price of butter and in the quantity of margarine demanded will, therefore, have the same sign.

The closer the relation of substitutability or complementarity, the larger the quantity reaction for any given price change and thus the larger the absolute value of the cross-elasticity. If the two goods bear little relation to each other, we would expect their cross-elasticities to be close to zero.

ELASTICITY OF SUPPLY

The ELASTICITY OF SUPPLY is defined as the percentage change in quantity supplied divided by the percentage change in price, and it is a measure of the degree to which the quantity supplied responds to price changes. Figure 10.5 illustrates three cases of supply elasticity. The case of zero elasticity is one in which the quantity supplied does not change as price changes. This would be the case, for example, if suppliers persisted in producing a given quantity, q_1 in Figure 10.5(i), and dumping it on the market for whatever it would bring. Infinite elasticity is illustrated in Figure 10.5(ii). The supply elasticity is infinite at the price p_1, because nothing at all is supplied at lower prices, but a small increase in price to p_1 causes supply to rise from zero to an indefinitely large amount, indicating that producers would supply any amount demanded at that price. The case of unit elasticity of supply is illustrated in Figure 10.5(iii). Any straight-line supply curve drawn through the origin has, in fact, an elasticity of unity. For a proof of this, see the appendix to this chapter, page 114.

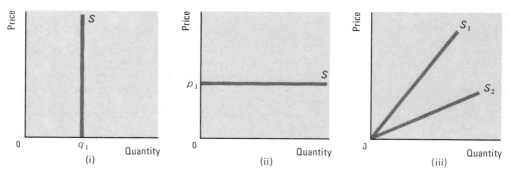

Fig. 10.5 Supply curves of zero, infinite and unit elasticity

What determines supply elasticity?

Supply elasticities are very important for many problems in economics. The brevity of our treatment here reflects two main facts: first, that much of the treatment of demand elasticity carries over to the case of supply and does not need repeating, and, second, that we will have more to say about the determinants of supply elasticity in Part 4. In the meantime, we may note that supply elasticity depends to a great extent on how costs behave as output is varied. If costs per unit of product rise rapidly as output rises, then the stimulus to expand production in response to a price rise will quickly be choked off by increases in costs. In this case, supply will tend to be rather inelastic. If, on the other hand, costs per unit of product rise only slowly (or not at all) as production increases, a rise in price that raises profits will call forth a large increase in quantity supplied before the rise in costs puts a halt to the expansion in output. In this case, supply will tend to be rather elastic.

Appendix

A formal analysis of elasticity

Arc elasticity of demand is defined as the ratio of the percentage change in the quantity demanded to the percentage change in price. In Chapter 10, as in most elementary treatments, we defined elasticity of demand as the negative of this amount so that it would be a positive number. It is convenient in formal analysis to maintain this simplification.

In Chapter 10 we also took price and quantity to be the average of the prices and quantities before and after the change being considered; for the more formal treatment in this appendix it is more satisfactory to take price and quantity to be the ones ruling before the change being considered. The difference between taking p and q as original or as average amounts diminishes as the magnitude of the change being considered is diminished.

Arc elasticity may be regarded as an approximation to the elasticity measure commonly used in theoretical treatments. This latter measure is called POINT ELASTICITY.

We shall consider arc and then point elasticity, but first we must define some symbols:

$\eta \equiv$ elasticity of demand
$\varepsilon \equiv$ elasticity of supply
$q \equiv$ the original quantity
$\Delta q \equiv$ change in quantity
$p \equiv$ the original price
$\Delta p \equiv$ the change in price.

We can now express the definition of arc elasticity in symbols:

$$\eta \equiv -\frac{\Delta q/q}{\Delta p/p}.$$

By inverting the denominator and multiplying, we get

$$\eta \equiv -\frac{\Delta q}{q} \cdot \frac{p}{\Delta p}.$$

Since it does not matter in which order we do our multiplication (i.e., $q.\Delta p \equiv \Delta p.q$), we may reverse the order of the two terms in the denominator and write

$$\eta \equiv \frac{\Delta q}{\Delta p} \cdot \frac{p}{q}. \tag{1}$$

We have now split elasticity into two parts: $\Delta q/\Delta p$, the ratio of the change in quantity to the change in price, which is related to the slope of the demand curve, and p/q, which is related to the place on the curve at which we made our measurement.

Figure 10.6 shows a straight-line demand curve by way of illustration. If we wish to measure the elasticity at point 1, we take our p and q at that point and consider a price change, taking us, say, to point 2, and measure our Δp and Δq as indicated. The slope of the straight line joining points 1 and 2 is $\Delta p/\Delta q$ (if you have forgotten this, refer to

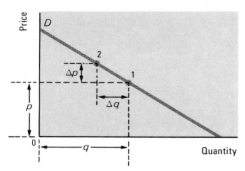

Fig. 10.6 A straight-line demand curve

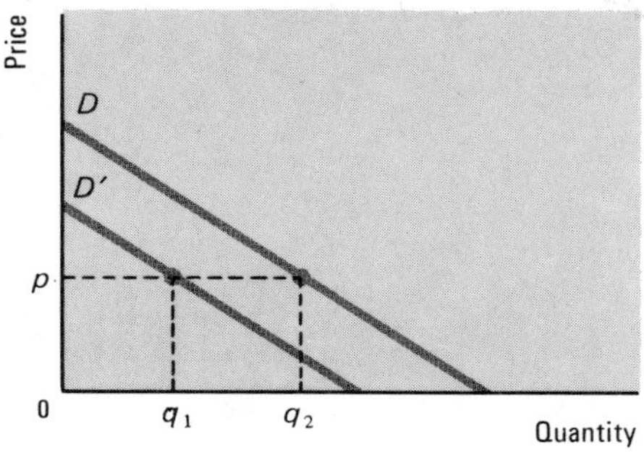

Fig. 10.7 Two parallel straight-line demand curves have unequal price elasticities at p

the appendix to Chapter 2, p. 35), and the term in equation (1) is $\Delta q/\Delta p$, which is the reciprocal of $\Delta p/\Delta q$. We conclude, therefore, that the first term in our elasticity formula is the reciprocal of the slope of the straight line joining the two price–quantity positions under consideration.

We may now develop a number of theorems relating to the elasticity of demand and supply.

(1) *The elasticity of a downward-sloping straight-line demand curve varies from infinity* (∞) *at the price axis to zero at the quantity axis.* We first notice that a straight line has a constant slope so that the ratio $\Delta p/\Delta q$ is the same anywhere on the line. Therefore, its reciprocal, $\Delta q/\Delta p$, must also be constant. We can now infer the changes in η by inspecting the ratio p/q. At the price axis $q = 0$ and p/q is undefined, but as we let q *approach* zero without ever quite reaching it, the ratio p/q increases without limit. Thus $\eta \to \infty$ as $q \to 0$. As we move down the line, p falls and q rises steadily; thus p/q is falling steadily so that η is also falling. At the q axis the price is zero, so the ratio p/q is zero. Thus $\eta = 0$.

(2) *Comparing two straight-line demand curves of the same slope, the one farther from the origin is less elastic at each price than the one closer to the origin.* Figure 10.7 shows two parallel straight-line demand functions. Pick any price, say p, and compare the elasticities of the two curves at that price. Since the curves are parallel, the ratio $\Delta q/\Delta p$ is the same on both curves. Since

we are comparing elasticities at the same price on both curves, p is the same, and the only factor left to vary is q. On the curve farther from the origin, quantity is larger (i.e., $q_2 > q_1$), and hence p/q is smaller; thus η is smaller.

It follows from Theorem 2 that a parallel shift of a straight-line demand curve lowers elasticity (at each price) if the line shifts outward, and raises elasticity if the line shifts inward.

(3) *The elasticities of two intersecting straight-line demand curves can be compared at the point of intersection merely by comparing slopes, the steeper curve being the less elastic.* In Figure 10.8 we

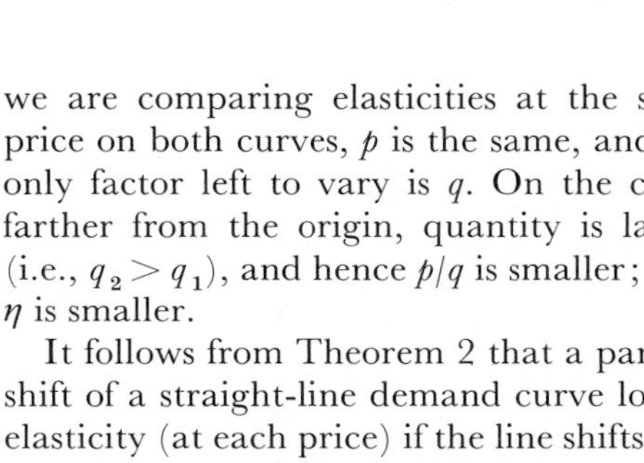

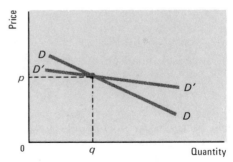

Fig. 10.8 Two intersecting straight-line demand curves have different elasticities where they cross

have two intersecting curves. At the point of intersection p and q are common to both curves, and hence the ratio p/q is the same. Therefore η varies only with $\Delta q/\Delta p$. On the steeper curve $-\Delta p/\Delta q$ is larger than on the

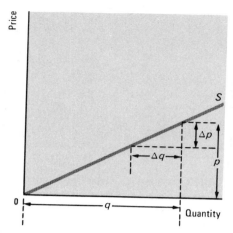

Fig. 10.9 A straight-line supply curve through the origin has an elasticity of one

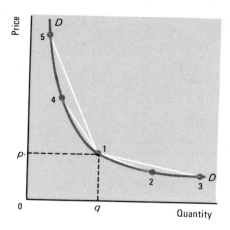

Fig. 10.10 Arc elasticity measured from a particular point (1) on a demand curve that is not a straight line

flatter curve; thus the ratio $-\Delta q/\Delta p$ is smaller on the steeper curve than on the flatter curve, so that elasticity is lower.

(4) *Any straight-line supply curve through the origin has an elasticity of one.* Such a supply curve is shown in Figure 10.9. Consider the two triangles with the sides p, q, and the S curve, and Δp, Δq, and the S curve. Clearly these are similar triangles. Therefore the ratios of their sides are equal, i.e.,

$$\frac{p}{q} = \frac{\Delta p}{\Delta q}. \qquad (2)$$

Elasticity of supply is defined as

$$\varepsilon = \frac{\Delta q}{\Delta p} \cdot \frac{p}{q}, \qquad (3)$$

which, by substitution from (2), gives

$$\varepsilon = \frac{q}{p} \cdot \frac{p}{q} \equiv 1. \qquad (4)$$

(5) *With a straight-line demand curve, the elasticity measured from any point p, q, according to equation (1) above, is independent of the direction and magnitude of the change in price and quantity.* This follows immediately from the fact that the slope of a straight line is a constant. If we start from some point p, q, and then change price, the ratio $\Delta q/\Delta p$ will be the same whatever the direction or the size of the change in p.

(6) *The elasticity measured from any point p, q,*

according to equation (1) above, is in general dependent on the direction and magnitude of the change in price and quantity. Except for a straight-line demand curve (for which the slope does not change) the ratio $\Delta q/\Delta p$ will not be the same at different points on a demand curve. Figure 10.10 shows a demand curve that is not a straight line. We desire to measure the elasticity from point 1. The figure makes it apparent that the ratio $\Delta q/\Delta p$, and hence the elasticity, will vary according to the size and the direction of the price change. This result is very inconvenient. The reason for it is that we are averaging the reaction of Δq to Δp over a section of the demand curve, and,

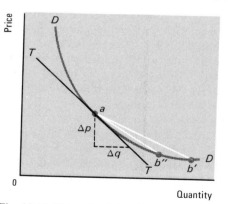

Fig. 10.11 Point elasticity of demand measured from a particular point (a) on the demand curve

depending on the range that we take, the *average reaction* will be different.

If we wish to measure the elasticity at a point, we need to know the reaction of quantity to a change in price at that point, not over a whole range. We call the reaction of quantity to price change at a point dq/dp, and we define this to be the reciprocal of the slope of the straight line (i.e., $\Delta q/\Delta p$) tangent to the demand curve at the point in question. In Figure 10.11 the point elasticity of demand at a is the ratio p/q (as it has been in all previous measures) now multiplied by the ratio of $\Delta q/\Delta p$ measured along the straight-line tangent to the curve at a. This definition may now be written

$$\eta = -\frac{dq}{dp} \cdot \frac{p}{q}. \qquad (5)$$

The ratio dq/dp as we have defined it is in fact the differential-calculus concept of the derivative of quantity with respect to price.

This elasticity is the one normally used in economic theory. Equation (1) may be regarded as an approximation to this expression. It is obvious by inspecting Figure 10.11 that the elasticity measured from (1) will come closer and closer to that measured from (5) the smaller the price change used to calculate the value of (1). From (1), change the price so that we move from a to some point b'; the ratio $\Delta q/\Delta p$ is the reciprocal of the slope of the straight line joining a and b'. The smaller the price change that we make, the closer the point comes to point a and the closer the slope of the line joining the points comes to the slope of the line tangential to the curve at a. If the slopes of these two lines get closer together, so also do the reciprocals of the slopes and, thus, so do the elasticities measured by equations (1) and (5). Thus, if we consider (1) as an approximation to (5), the error will diminish as the size of Δp diminishes.

11

Some predictions of the theory of price

In this chapter we shall study the theory of price that we have developed over the last five chapters to see if it can be made to yield useful predictions about actual behaviour in the world. When developing our formal theory we concentrated first on the determination of equilibrium prices, and, second, on the effects of various shifts in demand and supply curves. The propositions that we have derived in Chapters 9 and 10 and others that we shall derive in this chapter can be viewed in two different ways. First, they may be considered merely as logical implications of our theory of price. For example, the proposition that an increase in demand raises the equilibrium price and quantity traded is a logical deduction from our theory and, unless generations of economists have all made the same gross error of logic, we must accept it as being incontrovertible. From the second point of view, however, these propositions may be regarded as predictions about what will happen in the world under certain stated circumstances. From this point of view the correctness of our theory is an empirical matter.

In order to make contact between our theory and the real world, we advance three hypotheses: (1) that the assumptions of our theory (e.g., about the shapes of demand and supply curves) adequately describe relations that exist in the real world; (2) that unless some curve shifts, the actual price in the real world stays at or near the equilibrium price; and (3) that if there is a change in the equilibrium price, the actual price will move fairly quickly towards the new equilibrium. *If* these hypotheses are correct *then* the propositions of our theory will provide useful predictions about how real prices and quantities will actually behave under certain conditions; if not, the predictions of our theory will frequently be contradicted by the evidence.[1]

1 The student should now re-read two earlier passages.
(a) The paragraph on 'True in Theory and not in Practice' on page 12. It is, of course, quite possible that a proposition follows logically from the postulates of a theory but that the proposition is refuted by experience. We then conclude that the whole theory is a bad one and that at least one of its assumptions about behaviour must incorrectly describe what actually happens.
(b) The section on the 'laws' of supply and demand on pages 97 and 98. Of course, *given the theory*, certain conclusions about equilibrium prices necessarily follow. But this does nothing to establish whether or not these conclusions allow us to predict correctly what will happen in the world. The ability of a theory to predict is a matter that can be judged only on empirical grounds – i.e., by actually looking to see if what does happen is what the theory predicts will happen.

The cases studied in this chapter are examples chosen both to illustrate the use of price theory and to give the reader practice in using it. It is a mistake to try to commit particular examples to memory; what the practice of working through these examples should develop is your own facility with the tools of price theory, so that you can use it yourself to analyse any new problems that you may encounter.

PRICE CONTROL AND RATIONING
Maximum price legislation

It is very common in wartime, and not unknown in peacetime, for governments to pass laws fixing the maximum prices at which a number of commodities may be sold. In this section we shall confine ourselves to the setting of maximum prices (sometimes called ceiling prices) while in the next section we shall go on to consider the effects of setting minimum prices.

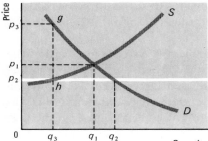

Fig. 11.1 Maximum price controls

What would you expect to be the consequences of a system in which some prices are fixed by law and not by demand and supply in a free market?

Figure 11.1 shows the demand and supply curves for some commodity. The equilibrium price is p_1 and the equilibrium quantity is q_1. We now wish to predict what would happen if the central authorities were able to enforce a maximum price at which this commodity was to be sold. If the maximum price were set above the equilibrium price, the intervention would have no effect. The equilibrium price would still be attainable and the market equilibrium would be in no way inconsistent with the maximum price law. On the other hand, suppose the maximum price is set at a level below the equilibrium one, say at p_2. The equilibrium price will no longer be legally obtainable. Prices must be reduced from p_1 to p_2, and as a result the quantity demanded will expand by $q_2 - q_1$, from q_1 to q_2; the quantity supplied, on the other hand, will fall by $q_1 - q_3$, from q_1 to q_3. Thus a shortage of the commodity will develop, the quantity demanded exceeding the quantity supplied. (In Figure 11.1 the excess demand is equal to $q_2 - q_3$).

We now have our first predictions about the effect of price control in a competitive market.

The setting of maximum prices either will have no effect (maximum price set at or above the equilibrium) or will cause a shortage of the commodity and reduce both the price and the quantity actually bought and sold below their equilibrium values.

ALLOCATION OF AVAILABLE SUPPLY: In the case of effective price ceilings, production is not sufficient to satisfy everyone who wishes to buy the commodity. Price is not allowed to change so as to allocate the available supply amongst the would-be purchasers from which it follows that some other method of allocation will have to be adopted. Our theory does not predict what this other method will be, but it is not difficult to enumerate those alternatives which experience has shown likely to arise. If shops sell their available supplies to the first customers that arrive, then people are likely to rush to those stores which are rumoured to have supplies of any commodity of which there is a severe shortage; long queues will develop and allocation will be on the basis of being lucky or knowledgeable enough to gain from the principle of 'first come first served'.[1] Another system may develop if shopkeepers themselves decide who will get the scarce commodities and who will not. Goods may be kept under the counter and sold only to certain customers. The shopkeeper might sell only to regular customers who bought a wide range of goods, or he might sell only to people of a colour or religion of which he approved. All kinds of rules could be adopted by the storekeeper and these may be given the general name 'allocation by sellers' preferences'.[2]

If the central authorities dislike the somewhat arbitrary system of allocation that grows up, they can ration the goods, giving out ration coupons sufficient to purchase the quantity q_3 in Figure 11.1. The authorities can then determine, as a conscious act of policy, how the available supply is to be allocated: the coupons might be distributed equally amongst the population, or they might be distributed on the basis of age, sex, marital status, number of dependants or any other criterion that the authorities wish to adopt. Thus we are led to predict the following

> **Where there is a feeling against allocation on the basis of first come first served and of sellers' preferences, effective price ceilings will give rise to strong pressure for a centrally-administered system of rationing.**

BLACK MARKET: Next we observe that, under certain circumstances, price control with or without rationing is likely to give rise to a BLACK MARKET, a market in which goods are sold illegally at prices which violate the legal restrictions (either above a legal maximum price or below a legal minimum). For many products there are only a few large producers but very many retailers and, although it is easy to police the producers, it is difficult even to locate all those who are, or could be, retailing the product, much less to police them. Although the central authorities may be able to control the price that producers get, they may not be able to control the price at which retailers sell to the public. What would you predict about this case? First, the amount produced would remain unchanged at q_3 in Figure 11.1 because the producer would continue to receive the controlled price for his product. At the

1 In wartime Europe the rumour that some shop was selling supplies of some very scarce commodity was sufficient to cause a local stampede. Housewives often spent days tracking down such rumours and then hours standing in line before being able to gain entrance to a shop. Usually the supplies would be exhausted while many housewives remained unserved.

2 In wartime Britain, to move from one town to another meant losing one's status as a 'regular' in many shops. Unless one was a long-term regular at some shop it was very difficult indeed to obtain cigarettes or beer, both of which were subject to price control while being unrationed.

retail level, however, a black market would arise, because purchasers would be willing to pay very much more than the controlled price for the limited amounts of the commodity available. If the whole quantity were sold on the black market, it would fetch a price of p_3 per unit. The total amount paid by consumers would be p_3 times q_3 which in the diagram is the rectangle bounded by Op_3gq_3. The total amount of the illegal receipts of black marketeers would be the rectangle bounded by $p_2\ hg\ p_3$. The theory predicts that the potential for a profitable black market will always exist whenever effective price ceilings are imposed. The actual growth of such a market depends on there being a few people willing to risk heavy penalties by running a black-market supply organization and a reasonably large number of persons prepared to purchase goods illegally on such a market. It is an interesting comment on the strengths of various human motives that there has never been a case documented in which effective price ceilings were not accompanied by the growth of a black market.

It is unlikely that all goods will be sold on the black market both because there are some honest people in every society and because the central authorities always have some power to enforce their price laws. Thus we would normally expect not the extreme result given above but rather that some of the limited supplies would be sold at the controlled price and only some would be sold at the black market price.

An economist's evaluation of a black-market situation can be made only when it is known what objectives the central authorities were hoping to achieve with their price-control policy. If they are mainly concerned with an equitable distribution of a scarce product, it is very likely that effective price control on manufacturers plus a largely uncontrolled black market at the retail level produces the worst possible results. If, however, they are mainly interested in restricting the total supply available for consumption in order to release resources for other more urgent needs, such as war production, the policy works effectively if somewhat unfairly. Where the purpose is to keep prices down, the policy is a failure to the extent that black marketeers succeed in raising prices, and a success to the extent to which transactions do take place at controlled prices.

There is much evidence confirming these predictions which we have shown to follow from our simple theory of price. Practically all belligerent countries in both the First and the Second World Wars set ceilings on many prices well below free-market, equilibrium levels. The legislation of maximum prices was always followed by shortages, then by either the introduction of rationing or the growth of some method such as allocation by sellers' preferences, and finally by the rise of some sort of black market. The ceilings were more effective in limiting consumption than in controlling prices, although they did restrain price increases to some considerable extent. Peacetime price controls have been less frequent and have probably been less successful in obtaining their major objectives. Many countries, for example, have tried to control rentals of houses and apartments for private use usually with the same results: a shortage, private allocation systems and a black market.[1]

---

1 For example, a grossly inflated sum may be paid for a few shoddy bits of furniture. In this case, the landlord is receiving the difference between the controlled rent and the free market one as a lump sum payment at the beginning of the tenancy.

Minimum price legislation

Governments sometimes pass laws stating that certain goods and services cannot be sold below some stated minimum price. In many Western countries today there are minimum wage laws which specify 'floors' for the wages to be paid to different kinds of labour. Resale price maintenance, which exists in many countries, gives the manufacturer power to prevent the retailer from selling below prices set by the manufacturer. Before reading on, see if you can work out for yourself what our theory predicts about the effects of minimum price laws.

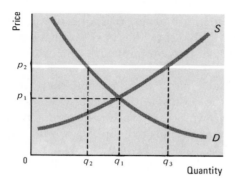

Fig. 11.2 Minimum price controls

The case of a commodity subject to minimum price legislation is illustrated in Figure 11.2. The free-market equilibrium price is p_1, and the equilibrium quantity traded is q_1. If the minimum price is set below the equilibrium price then it has no effect on the market. The attainment of the free-market equilibrium and the fulfilment of the minimum price law are perfectly compatible. On the other hand, if the minimum price is set above the equilibrium, say at p_2, the free-market equilibrium will be legally unobtainable. The actual price will be p_2, and at that price there will be an excess of supply over demand. Suppliers would like to sell q_3, but purchasers are only willing to buy q_2 at the price p_2. The actual amount bought and sold will thus be q_2 and there will be excess supply of $q_3 - q_2$. This leads us to our first prediction about minimum prices.

> **The setting of minimum prices will either have no effect (minimum price set below the equilibrium) or cause a surplus of the commodity to develop, with the actual price above its equilibrium level but the actual quantity bought and sold below its equilibrium level.**

In this case there is, at the legally enforced price, no scarcity of the controlled commodity. Therefore we do not predict that alternative allocative systems will grow up. There will, however, be a shortage of purchasers and potential suppliers may compete in various ways for the available customers. Methods of price cutting will be searched for, some of which find loopholes in the law and some of which merely flout it. For example, clubs and other organizations have grown rapidly in order to take advantage of cheap group rates which the airlines are not legally allowed to offer the single passenger. There will be no opportunity for a set of black-market operators to take over the distribution of the product since there is nothing to be gained by buying at the controlled price and selling at the free-market price. There will of course be an incentive for an individual producer to sell his product at less than the controlled price as long as his alternative is not to sell it at all. Thus in this case we predict the absence of an organized black market but the existence of some clandestine selling by individual producers at prices below the legal minimum.

As an example of minimum price policies consider the case of minimum wage laws which are found in most Western countries. Applying our theory to the labour market is a bit of a jump in the dark, but we can note in passing that the theory developed in Part 5 does allow us to use a downward-sloping demand curve for each type of labour. If we hypothesize that our theory of competitive markets will apply to a labour market, we have the following predictions about minimum wage laws when applied in only a few markets of the economy.

(1) Where the law is effective it will raise the wages of some of those who remain in employment.

(2) It will lower the actual amount of employment (by $q_1 - q_2$ in Figure 11.2).

(3) It will create a surplus of labour which would like to but cannot obtain jobs in the occupation affected ($q_3 - q_2$ in Figure 11.2).

(4) It will create an incentive for some workers to try to evade the law by offering to work at wages below the legal one.

(5) It will not lead to the rise of an independent group of black marketeers who buy at the controlled price and sell at a black-market one.

There is ample evidence confirming most of these predictions. The illegal offering of their services for part-time and evening work is a well established reaction of many workers to union regulation of minimum allowable wages. The empirical validity of prediction (2) is a matter of dispute when minimum wage laws are applied across the whole economy. We cannot go into this controversy here but we shall raise it again in Chapter 28.

It is remarkable how many predictions our simple theory yields about the effects of price control and how often these predictions have been confirmed by evidence. It is also interesting, and not a little depressing, to see how often governments are prepared to pass price-control laws without showing any apparent appreciation of their likely effects.

A digression on methods of allocating scarce commodities

In the previous section we raised the question of alternative methods of allocating scarce commodities amongst potential consumers. Since it is almost always true that people would like to have more of a commodity than is in fact available, it is necessary to have some way of rationing out the available supply. In a free-market society this is done by the price mechanism. When there is excess demand, price rises and this encourages production and discourages consumption. Price continues to rise until, at its equilibrium level, the rate of consumption is equal to the rate of production. Thus market price does the rationing. If price is held constant at a level below equilibrium, the available quantity must be allocated in some other way: by store-keepers on the basis of sellers' preferences, by queues on a first come first served basis or by government rationing, with coupons distributed according to any one of a number of principles.

Because goods are scarce, there must be some system of allocating them amongst potential consumers. It is sometimes argued that the price system provides the best (in an ethical sense) way of doing this. Certainly there is nothing in positive economics that can prove that the price system as it functions in the real world provides what is ethically the best method of allocating goods. Positive economics attempts to show the consequences of allocating scarce goods by various methods. Any decision about what method ought to be adopted will be a better-informed one if taken in the light of knowledge of the actual effects of various methods.

It is sometimes said that the price which equates demand and supply, p_1 in Figure 11.1, is the *natural* price, while other prices are *artificial* ones. This is very emotive language which is likely to give the impression that the natural price is in some sense the best price. All that can be said on the basis of economics is that the price p_1 is the one that equates quantity demanded to quantity supplied *through the mechanism of price*. If other prices are enforced, alternative methods of equating demand to supply will have to be employed.

TAX INCIDENCE

What is the effect of taxes placed on the sale and purchase of commodities, such as the excise tax on jewellery, petrol or whisky? Do such taxes leave prices unchanged or do they cause prices to rise? Does the producer pay the tax or is he able to pass it on to the consumer through higher prices? Many such age-old controversies are to be found in the field of tax theory.

As a first step in discovering what our theory predicts about these issues, consider the effect of a tax on the supply of a commodity. Look at Table 11.1, which repeats in

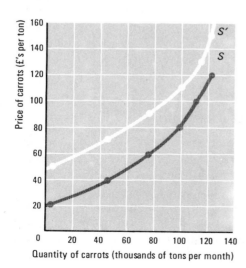

Fig. 11.3 The effects of a tax of £30 per ton on the supply curve for carrots

columns (1) and (2) the supply schedule for carrots from Table 8.1, page 89.

The supply schedule indicated by columns (1) and (2) is graphed in Figure 11.3 and is labelled S. The schedule shows the relation between the price that farmers get for their carrots and the total amount that all farmers are willing to produce and sell. If no tax is levied, then sellers receive the whole market price for which the commodity is sold. If a tax is levied, however, then sellers will receive on each unit sold the market price of the commodity *minus* the amount of the tax. *If producers are to receive the same amount per unit as they were receiving prior to the tax, the market price will have to rise by the full amount of the tax.*

To illustrate this, we assume that a tax of £30 a ton is placed on the sale of carrots. Every time a producer sells a ton of carrots, he must pay £30 to the government and can keep for himself only what is left after that. The table shows that producers were prepared to supply 5,000 tons of carrots a month when they received £20 a ton for themselves. Thus 5,000 tons a month will be supplied at a market price of £20 a ton when there is no tax, but at a market price of £50 a ton when there is a tax. Taking another example from the table, we see that producers are prepared to grow and to sell 115,000 untaxed tons a month at a market price of £100 a ton, but they will grow and offer for sale this amount only at a market price of £130 a ton when a tax is levied.

We may summarize this change in more general terms as follows. Assuming that the willingness of sellers to supply the commodity is unchanged, then, after a tax has been levied, every quantity supplied will be associated with a market price higher by the full amount of the tax than the one previously required.

Table 11.1 Derivation of a supply schedule when a tax is levied on the sale of the commodity

Pre-tax supply schedule		If a tax of £30 per ton is placed on the sale of carrots, they must be *sold* for the price listed in column 3 if the seller is to *receive* the amount listed in column 1 (Col. 1 +£30)
If the seller receives the price listed below he will offer for sale the quantity listed below		
Column 1 £'s per ton	Column 2 Thousands of tons supplied per month	Column 3 £'s per ton
20	5·0	50
40	46·0	70
60	77·5	90
80	100·0	110
100	115·0	130
120	122·5	150

The no-tax relation between the quantity of carrots supplied and their market price is shown in columns (1) and (2) in Table 11.1 and by the supply curve labelled S in Figure 11.3. The after-tax relation is shown in columns (2) and (3) of the table and by the supply curve S' in Figure 11.3.

The effect of a tax on a commodity is to shift every point on the supply curve vertically upward by the amount of the tax.

So far, we have only shown what would have to happen to market price if the quantity supplied were to remain the same. But what actually happens to price depends on demand as well as on supply. Before we can say anything about the price, we must add a demand curve. (In Figure 11.4 we plot the demand curve for carrots as well as the pre- and post-tax supply curves.) The original equilibrium price is £60 and the quantity traded is 77,500 tons a month. If, following the imposition of the tax, the price were to rise by the full amount of the tax from £60 to £90, the quantity demanded would fall, and there would be an excess of quantity supplied over quantity demanded. This would cause the price to fall until it reached the equilibrium point where the new supply curve cuts the demand curve. In the example illustrated in Figure 11.4, the new equilibrium price is £82 a ton. This is the price that will be

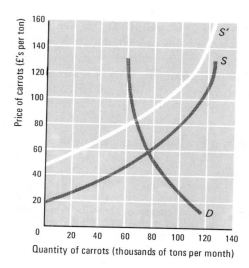

Fig. 11.4 The effect of a tax of £30 per ton on the equilibrium price and quantity of carrots

paid by consumers. When the tax of £30 a ton is deducted, the producers will receive a price of £52. Thus, in this example, the tax has the effect of raising the price paid by consumers by £22 and lowering the price received by producers by £8. The *incidence* of the tax falls just under three quarters on the consumers and just over one quarter on producers. The term *incidence* is used to describe who actually bears the burden of the tax in terms of higher prices paid or lower prices received.

If we drop the specific numerical example of the carrot market, the following more general prediction is easily established.

As long as the demand curve slopes downward and the supply curve upward, the imposition of a tax will raise the price paid by consumers and lower the price received by producers in both cases by less than the amount of the tax.

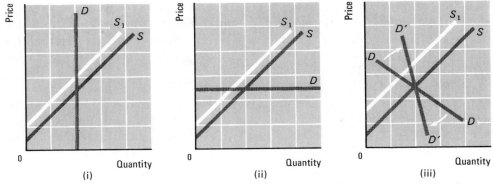

Fig. 11.5 The effect of a tax on price and quantity, given demand curves of various elasticities

The influence of elasticity of demand and supply

Figure 11.5, like Figure 11.4, shows two supply curves representing before- and after-tax situations. It combines them with different demand curves. Figure 11.5(i) shows a perfectly inelastic demand curve, Figure 11.5(ii) a perfectly elastic one and Figure 11.5(iii) two intermediate cases. In the case of the perfectly inelastic curve, the equilibrium price increases by the full amount of the tax; in the case of the perfectly elastic curve, the equilibrium price is unchanged in spite of the shift in the supply curve. This suggests the following general prediction.

> **The more inelastic the demand for a commodity, the greater the rise in the price paid by the consumer and the less the fall in the price received by the producer as a result of the imposition of any given tax.**

The derivation of this prediction is illustrated in Figure 11.5(iii). Look at demand curve D, which intersects the original supply curve, S, to determine the equilibrium price. Note the post-tax equilibrium price given by the intersection of the original demand curve with the new supply curve S_1. Now consider *pivoting* the demand curve through the original equilibrium point, as shown in the figure. Clearly, the steeper, and thus also the more inelastic, the demand curve at the equilibrium point, the greater the rise in price paid by consumers and the smaller the fall in the price received by producers.[1]

These tax predictions are quite general ones applying to all more or less competitive markets. As an illustration of their wide range of applicability, we may consider some of the major effects of real estate taxes.

Real-estate taxes

Property taxes, which are a percentage of the assessed market value of land and buildings, are commonly levied by local governments throughout the world. Property owners often protest that the crushing burden of these taxes makes real estate in-

1 We have earlier warned against confusing the slope of a demand curve with its elasticity. When two or more demand curves intersect, however, their relative elasticities at the point of intersection can be inferred from their slopes: the steeper the curve the more inelastic it is. (See page 113 of the appendix to Chapter 10 for a proof.)

vestment unprofitable, while many tenants believe that the taxes are borne fully by them in terms of higher rents. Both groups cannot be right in alleging that they each bear the whole burden of the tax! The theory of competitive markets suggests that the truth lies somewhere between these two extremes and that part of the tax is borne by landlords and part passed on to tenants.

To see what is involved, start with a situation in which there is no real estate tax and then assume that one is imposed. If each one of the thousands of landlords in the city decides to raise rents by the full amount of the tax, what does the theory predict will happen? There will be a decline in the quantity of rental accommodation demanded. Higher rents will induce some city dwellers to move outside the city limits where rents for equivalent accommodation are lower, and will induce some of those who stay to economize on space now that it has become more expensive. The same two effects will also be observed with storekeepers and other commercial users of the city's real estate. The decline in the quantity demanded without any change in the quantity supplied will cause a surplus of rental accommodation. Landlords will find it difficult to replace tenants who move out, and the typical unit will remain empty between tenancies longer than previously. Prospective tenants will find many alternative sites from which to choose and will become very particular in what they expect from landlords eager to rent their accommodation.

This situation will lead some prospective tenants to offer to pay rents below the going ones and will lead some landlords to accept the offer rather than earn nothing from vacant premises. Once some landlords cut their rentals, many others will have to follow suit or else leave their properties unrented for long periods of time. As the rents received by landlords fall, there will be a gradual contraction in the quantity of rental accommodation supplied. Home-owners will be less willing to rent out parts of their homes, and when blocks of flats are replaced, as they are continuously, it may not pay to build them quite as high as previously, now that the after-tax rents received by landlords are lower. This reduction in the quantity supplied prevents the price from coming down to its original pre-tax level.

Eventually, rentals will reach a new equilibrium at which the quantity demanded equals the quantity supplied. This equilibrium will be higher than the original pre-tax rent but lower than the rent that passes the whole tax on to tenants. Thus the burden of the tax is shared by landlords and tenants, the proportion in which it is shared depending on elasticities.

Notice that this result can emerge even though neither the landlords nor the tenants realize what is happening. Both sides may think, for example, that the landlord is fully passing the tax on, even though this is not the case. In fact, in Britain and parts of Europe it is common for the tenant, rather than the landlord, to be sent the tax bill and to pay the tax directly to the city; even in this case, however, the landlord bears part of the burden of the tax. As long as the existence of the tax reduces the quantity demanded below what it otherwise would be, the tax will depress the amount received by landlords, and for this reason they will bear part of its burden. The reason why this can occur without landlords and tenants being aware of it is that neither of them is likely to have much idea of what equilibrium rentals would be in the absence of the tax. It doesn't do much good to look at what happens immediately after tax rates are changed, since, as we have already seen, landlords may begin by raising rents by the full amount of the tax. This creates a disequilibrium, however, and in the final position, prices will have risen by less than the tax. Furthermore, rentals are changing for many reasons, including general inflationary pressures, local changes in costs, and shifts in demand resulting from changes in living habits. In such a situation in which many things are changing at once only careful statistical analysis can sort out the influence of one particular variable, in this case changes in tax rates.

THE PROBLEMS OF AGRICULTURE

To the casual observer, the agricultural sector of almost any advanced Western economy presents a series of seeming paradoxes. Food is one of the truly basic necessities of life. Yet over the last century agricultural sectors have been declining in relative importance, and those persons who have remained on the land have continued to receive incomes often well below national averages.

Governments have felt it necessary to intervene and, as a result, a bewildering array of controls, supports and subsidies has been built into agricultural markets. Subsidies and price floors have led to the accumulation of vast surpluses which have sometimes rotted in their storage bins and sometimes been sold abroad at prices well below their costs of production.

All of this has gone on against a backdrop of endemic malnutrition and occasional outbursts of famine in the 'Third World'. Today the spectre of undernourishment and starvation is growing as the world's population increases and it looks like the problem of surplus agricultural production may give way – indeed in the US, if not in Europe, it already has given way – to the problem of deficient agricultural production.

Why has agriculture so often been a problem industry in the past, and is it really possible that it may cease to be one in the near future?

Short-term fluctuations in prices and incomes

The production of many agricultural goods is subject to quite large variations due to factors completely beyond human control: lack of rainfall, invasion of pests, floods and other natural causes are capable of reducing output to a level well below that planned by farmers, while exceptionally favourable conditions can cause production to be well above the planned level. We may now ask what our theory predicts about the effect of these unplanned fluctuations on the price of agricultural commodities and on the revenues earned by farmers for the sale of their crops.

A supply curve is meant to show desired output and sales at each market price. If there are unplanned variations in output then actual production and sales will diverge from their planned level. The supply curve drawn in Figure 11.6 shows the total quantity farmers desire to produce and offer for sale at various prices. If the price were p_1, then planned production would be q_1, but actual production would vary around this planned amount, owing to causes beyond the farmers' control. Two demand curves are drawn in Figure 11.6; one is relatively elastic and the other is relatively inelastic over the quantity range from q_2 to q_3. In a world in which plans

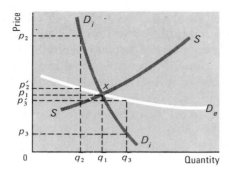

Fig. 11.6 Variations in price caused by
unplanned variations in supply operating on
elastic and inelastic demand curves

were always fulfilled, price would settle at the equilibrium level of p_1 with output q_1. But unplanned fluctuations in output will cause the actual price to fluctuate. If, for example, the crop is poor so that the actual production is q_2, then a shortage will develop; prices will rise to p_2 in the case of demand curve D_i, and p'_2 in the case of curve D_e. In each case the quantity demanded will be reduced to a point at which it is equal to the available supply. If, on the other hand, conditions are particularly favourable, actual production will exceed planned production, a surplus will occur and price will fall. For example, when production is q_3, price falls to p_3 in the case of curve D_i and to p'_3 in the case of curve D_e. In each case the fall in price increases the quantity demanded sufficiently to absorb the extra unplanned supply but the fall in price is larger when the demand curve is D_i than when it is D_e.

We have now derived the following prediction.

> **Unplanned fluctuations in output will cause price variations in the opposite direction to the output changes (the bigger the output the lower the price) and, for given output fluctuations, the price fluctuations will be larger the lower is the elasticity of demand for the product.**

Now consider the effects on the revenues received by farmers from the sale of their crops.[1] Here the relations are a bit more complex, but they all follow immediately from the results established on page 106. If the good in question has an elasticity of demand greater than unity, then unplanned increases in supply raise farmers' revenues while unplanned decreases lower them. If, on the other hand, the good has an inelastic demand, consumers' total expenditure on the product, and thus farmers' revenues, will rise when price rises and fall when price falls. Thus, good harvests will bring reductions in total farm revenues while bad harvests will bring increases in farm revenues![2] If the demand elasticity happened to be unity, then farmers' revenues would not vary as output and prices varied because every change in output would be met by an exactly compensating change in price so that total expenditure would remain constant.

---

1 While we can make predictions in this section about the revenues, such receipts are closely related to the incomes of farmers. We can without risk of serious error extend these predictions to incomes.

2 It does not follow that every individual farmer's income must rise (after all, some farmers may have nothing to harvest); it follows only that the aggregate revenue earned by all farmers must rise.

We now have the following predictions:

(1) Unplanned fluctuations in output can cause every conceivable type of fluctuation in farmers' revenue.

(2) Farm revenue and farm output will vary in the same direction whenever demand for the product is elastic.

(3) Farm revenue and farm output will vary in opposite directions whenever demand for the product is inelastic.

(4) The fluctuations in revenue will be larger the further the elasticity of demand for the product diverges from unity in either direction.

Evidence on these predictions is fairly abundant. Unplanned fluctuations in output do occur frequently in agriculture. Where the prices of the products are left to be determined by the free market, large price fluctuations do occur. In the case of many agricultural goods, the demand is quite inelastic. In these cases we find very large price fluctuations together with the peculiar situation that when nature is unexpectedly kind and produces a bumper crop, farmers see their incomes dwindling, while when nature is moderately unkind so that supplies fall unexpectedly, farmers' incomes rise. The self-interests of the farmer and of the consumer appear to be exactly opposed in such cases.

Cyclical fluctuations in prices and incomes

Agricultural markets are subject not only to short-run instabilities due to uncontrolled output changes, but also, like most raw materials, to cyclical instability due to shifts in demand. In periods of prosperity, full employment prevails, incomes are high, and demands for all goods are high. In periods of depressed business activity, there is substantial unemployment, total incomes earned fall, and the demand for most goods falls as a result. As the pulse of business prosperity ebbs and flows, we thus find demand curves for all goods rising and falling. What effect will this have on commodity prices? Industrial products typically have rather elastic supply curves, so that demand shifts cause fairly large changes in outputs but only small changes in prices. Agricultural commodities often tend to have rather inelastic supplies. Thus, when demand falls due to a recession in general business activity, prices tend to fall drastically in agriculture but to remain fairly stable in the manufacturing sector.

This phenomenon is illustrated in Table 11.2 with data for the United States,

Table 11.2 Farm and industrial prices and
production, 1929 = 100

Year	Agriculture		Industry	
	Production	Prices	Production	Prices
1929	100	100	100	100
1932	99	44	53	70
1937	108	83	103	85

Source: A. L. Meyers, *Agriculture and the National Economy,*
Temporary National Economic Committee, Monograph No. 23
US Government Printing Office (Washington, 1940)

where agriculture still accounts for a significant proportion of total output and employment. The data allow a comparison of the experience of agriculture and manufacturing during the largest cyclical decline in demand that Western economies have suffered in modern times. The price and quantity data in the table confirm the hypothesis that agricultural commodities tend to have very inelastic supplies, while manufacturing commodities tend to have much more elastic ones. To the public, the relatively large fall in agricultural prices is likely to signify that the farmer has fared relatively poorly compared to the typical manufacturer. But, of course, it is revenues, not prices, that matter in deciding how badly various sectors have fared relative to each other. A very different picture emerges if we look at gross receipts rather than at prices alone. Table 11.3 shows the gross-receipts position of the two sectors. Agriculture fared better in revenue than industry relative to 1929. Since we

Table 11.3 Value of farm and industrial production

Year	Agriculture°	Industry
1929	100	100
1932	43·6	37·1
1937	89·6	87·6

° The figures are index numbers calculated from Table 11.2 by multiplying together one sector's price-and-quantity indexes for a given year and dividing by 100.

do not have cost figures, we cannot reach a final conclusion about incomes. But from the point of view of fluctuations in total receipts caused by cyclical fluctuations in demand, it is just as much a curse to have a very elastic supply as it is to have a very inelastic one!

Agricultural stabilization programmes

In free-market economies, agricultural incomes often tend to fluctuate around a low *average* level. Agricultural stabilization programmes have two goals: to reduce the fluctuations and to raise the average level of farm incomes. Most countries have some sort of scheme to reduce agricultural fluctuations. The two policies, producing stable incomes and producing reasonably high incomes, can, as we shall see, often conflict. We shall illustrate the workings of stabilization schemes for unplanned fluctuations in supply. A similar analysis could be carried out for cyclical fluctuations in demand.

Figure 11.7 shows the demand and supply curves for some agricultural product. According to its definition the supply curve shows the amount firms would be willing to produce and offer for sale at each price. Thus it shows the total *planned production* of all farmers. If there were no uncertainties in the agricultural world, actual production would be equal to planned production and price and quantity would settle at p_1 and q_1 respectively. We know, however, that many uncertain events affect agricultural production. Thus when planned production is q_1 actual production will fluctuate, say between q_2 and q_3. If the price fluctuates so as to equate demand to

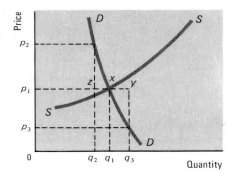

Fig. 11.7 Policies designed to stabilize price
in the face of unplanned fluctuations in supply

actual production, the market price will fluctuate between p_2 and p_3.

In this section we shall make the simplifying assumption that planned production remains at q_1 and that actual output varies around q_1 only because of unplanned fluctuations. In Chapter 12 we shall reconsider this example under the less rigid assumption that planned production itself changes in response to changes in market price.

One method of preventing these fluctuations in prices and incomes is for the individual farmers to form a producers' association which tries to even out the supply actually coming on to the market, in spite of variations in production.[1] There is no point in an individual farmer holding some of his production off the market in an effort to force up the price. Since one farmer's production is a completely insignificant part of total production, the farmer who sold less would only reduce his income without having any noticeable effect on price. But if all farmers get together and agree to vary the supply coming on to the market, then, collectively, they can have a major effect on price.

Under the conditions illustrated by Figure 11.7, a producers' association might be quite successful in keeping the price at p_1 and incomes at the level indicated by the area of the rectangle Op_1xq_1. What would the association's policy have to be? Any excess of production over q_1 would have to be stored away unsold. If, for example, production for one year were q_3, then $q_3 - q_1$ would have to be added to the association's stocks while q_1 was sold at the price p_1. Any deficiency of production below q_1, on the other hand, would have to be made good by sales out of the association's stocks. If production were q_2, for example, then $q_1 - q_2$ would be sold out of stocks, making total sales again equal to q_1 at a price of p_1. In this way the producers' association could keep sales, price and incomes stabilized in spite of fluctuations in production. Provided that the level of sales to be maintained (q_1 in Figure 11.7) were equal to average production, then the policy could be carried on indefinitely. If, on the other hand, an attempt were made to keep the price too high, so that sales were less than the average amount produced, then, over a number of years, additions to stocks would exceed sales from stocks, and the level of stocks held would tend to

1 We are concerned here only with action to stabilize prices. After we have studied the theory of perfect competition in Chapter 20 we shall return to the topic of producers' organizations and study their attempts to raise the average level of their members' incomes. At that time we shall develop a theory of the inherent instability of producers' cooperatives.

increase. The successful policy is one that keeps sales constant at q_1 (by adding to or subtracting from stocks) and, since income accrues to the producers when the goods are actually sold, incomes will be stabilized at p_1 times q_1 which graphically is the area of the rectangle Op_1xq_1.

What will happen if a producers' association is not formed but the government attempts to stabilize the incomes of farmers by itself entering the market, buying and adding to its own stocks when there is a surplus, and selling goods from its stocks, when there is a shortage? If the government wishes to stabilize farmers' incomes, what policy should it adopt? Should it aim, like the producers' association, at keeping prices constant at all times? Before reading further, the reader should attempt to work out for himself the consequences of a government policy designed to keep price fixed at the level p_1 in Figure 11.7 by buying goods when production is in excess of q_1 and by selling goods when production falls short of q_1. The government is assumed not to consume any of the commodity but only to hold stocks, adding to them when it buys and subtracting from them when it sells.

If the average level of production around which the year-to-year figure fluctuates is q_1, then there is no reason why the government should not successfully stabilize the price at p_1 indefinitely. This policy would not, however, have the result of stabilizing farmers' incomes. Farmers will now be faced with an infinitely elastic demand at the price p_1: whatever the total quantity produced, they will be able to sell it at the price p_1; if the public will not buy all the production, then the government will purchase what is left over. If total production is q_3, then q_1 will be bought by the public and $q_3 - q_1$ by the government to add to its own stocks. Total farm income in this case will be the amount indicated by the area of the rectangle Op_1yq_3 (the quantity q_3 multiplied by the price p_1). If total production in another year is only q_2, then this quantity will be sold by farmers and the government also will sell $q_1 - q_2$ out of its stocks so that price will remain at p_1. Total farm income will then be the amount indicated by the rectangle Op_1zq_2 (quantity q_2 multiplied by the price p_1). It is obvious that if prices are held constant and farmers sell their whole production each year, then farmers' incomes will fluctuate in proportion to fluctuations in production. This government policy therefore will not eliminate income fluctuations but it will reverse their direction. Now bumper crops will be associated with high incomes while small crops will be associated with low incomes.

What, then, must the government's policy be if it wishes to stabilize farmers' revenues through its own purchases and sales in the open market? Too much price stability causes revenues to vary directly with production, as in the case just considered, while too little price stability causes them to vary inversely with production, as in the free-market case originally considered. It appears that the government should aim at some intermediate degree of price stability. In fact, if it allows prices to vary exactly in proportion to variations in production, then revenues will be stabilized. A 10 per cent rise in production should be met by a 10 per cent fall in price, and a 10 per cent fall in production by a 10 per cent rise in price.

The government policy necessary to achieve the requisite price fluctuations is shown in Figure 11.8. The analysis becomes a bit difficult at this stage and the student should draw his own graph, building it up step by step as the argument

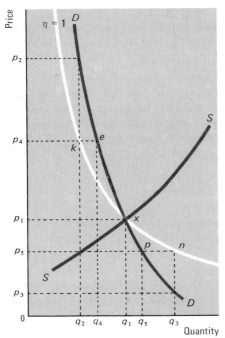

Fig. 11.8 Government policies designed to stabilize income in the face of unplanned fluctuations in supply

proceeds, using Figure 11.8 only as a guide. DD and SS should first be copied from Figure 11.8. As before, planned production is q_1, and the price which equates demand with planned production is p_1. Actual production, however, fluctuates between q_2 and q_3, and these fluctuations, given the very inelastic demand curve DD, could cause price to fluctuate between p_2 and p_3. Now construct through the point x (the equilibrium point when actual production is equal to planned production) a curve of unit elasticity throughout its whole range. This constructed curve is the white rectangular hyperbola in Figure 11.8, labelled $\eta = 1$. If q_1 is produced and sold at price p_1, total income is that indicated by the rectangle Op_1xq_1. The white curve now tells the market price that must rule if production and sales are allowed to vary but income is to be held constant.

Consider first what happens if production is q_3. Market price must be held at p_5 if income is to be unchanged. But, at market price p_5, the public only wishes to purchase q_5 and it is therefore necessary for the government to buy up the remaining production, $q_3 - q_5$ and add it to its stocks. Farmers' total sales are q_3 at price p_5, and since the white curve is a rectangular hyperbola, it follows that income p_5 *times* q_3 is equal to income p_1 *times* q_1.

Now consider what must happen if production is equal to q_2. If farm income is to be unchanged, then the price must be allowed to rise to p_4 (by construction the area of rectangle Op_4kq_2 is equal to the area of rectangle Op_1xq_1. But at the price p_4, the public will wish to buy q_4 so that the government must sell $q_4 - q_2$ out of its stocks.

If this policy is successful, it will have the following results. First, there will be smaller fluctuations in the price of this product than there would be if price were determined on a completely free market. Secondly, total revenues of the producers will be stabilized in the face of fluctuations in production. Finally, the government scheme should be self-financing. In fact, if we ignore costs of storage, the scheme will show a profit, for the government will be buying at low prices (below p_1) – the lower the price the more it buys – and it will be selling at high prices (above p_1) – the higher the price the more it sells. Whether or not the scheme actually shows a profit will depend on the costs of storing the crops from the periods of glut when they are purchased until the periods of shortage when they are sold. In any case, this scheme has the financial advantage over the previous one in which the government completely stabilized prices. In that case there would necessarily be a loss; since all purchases and sales would be made at the same price, p_1, there would be no trading profit to set against the costs of storage.

Problems with stabilization policies

The above analysis is meant merely to illustrate some of the many types of schemes that could be operated and to show how, once the details of the schemes are specified, the theory of price can be used to predict the consequences of each. If such schemes have all of the advantages outlined above, why is it that there is so much trouble with most stabilization programmes that are actually operated? One of the major problems with these schemes arises from the absence of perfect knowledge, combined with political pressure applied by farmers. Demand and supply curves are never known exactly, so the central authorities do not know what will be the average production forthcoming over a number of years at various prices. The central authorities do not, therefore, know exactly what level of income they can try to achieve while also keeping sales from stocks approximately equal to purchases for stocks, over a large number of years. Since farmers have votes there is strong pressure on any government to err in the direction of fixing the income to be stabilized at too high a level. If the level of income, and hence price, is fixed too high, then the central authorities will find it necessary to buy unsold crops most of the years and will find only a few years when production is low enough for sales to be made out of stocks. In this case, stocks will build up more or less continuously, and the time will come when no more can be stored. When this happens, the stored crops will either have to be destroyed, given away or dumped on the market for what they will bring, thus forcing the market price down to a very low level. If the crops are thrown on the market and allowed to depress the price, then the original purpose for which the crops were purchased, price stabilization, is defeated. If the crops are destroyed or allowed to decay, the efforts of a large quantity of the country's scarce factors of production (the land, labour and capital that went into producing the stored goods) have been completely wasted. Furthermore, the authorities' plan will now show a deficit, for goods will have been purchased which cannot be sold at all. This deficit will have to be made up by taxation, which means that people in cities will be paying farmers for producing goods which are never consumed.

When schemes get into this sort of difficulty, the next step is often to try to limit the production of each farmer. Quotas may be assigned to individual farmers and penalties imposed for exceeding them. Or else, as has been done very many times in the past, bonuses may be paid for leaving land idle, for ploughing crops under without harvesting them, or for other means of cutting back on production. Such measures attempt to get around the problem that too many resources are allocated to the agricultural sector by the device of preventing these resources from producing all that they are capable of producing. The interesting question of the morality of such measures takes us outside the scope of positive economics, but that does not, of course, mean that the reader should not pursue the question.

RESOURCES IN AGRICULTURE: THE LONG-TERM PROBLEM: Even if the temptation to set too high a price is avoided, there is still a formidable problem waiting to wreck many agricultural-stabilization programmes. This problem results from the fact that the productive capacity of almost all economies is growing over time. In the United Kingdom, the increase in *per capita* production has averaged almost 2 per cent a year over the last 100 years. Owing to better health, better working conditions, and more and better capital equipment, workers in most sectors of the economy can produce more per head than they previously did. If the allocation of resources were to remain unchanged, there would be an increase in the production and hence in the supply of each commodity in proportion to the increase in productivity in that industry.

The real incomes of the population will also increase, on the average at a rate equal to the production increase. How will the people wish to consume their extra income? The relevant measure in this case is the income elasticity of demand, which measures the effect of increases in income on the demands for various goods. If, to take the simplest case, all goods have unit income elasticities of demand, then the proportion in which the various goods are demanded will not change with income, and an x per cent rise in income will lead to an x per cent rise in the demand for every good. It is known, however, that income elasticities vary considerably among goods, and that most goods tend to have different income elasticities at various levels of income. For example, at the level of income achieved in advanced industrialized countries, many foodstuffs have very low income elasticities, and many manufactured goods have high income elasticities.

Assume that productivity expands more or less uniformly in all industries: the demands for goods with low income elasticities will be expanding slower than the supplies; excess supplies will develop, prices and profits will be depressed, and it will be necessary for resources to move out of these industries. Exactly the reverse will

Table 11.4 Surpluses and shortages resulting from uniform increases in productivity and differing income elasticities of demand

	Agriculture	Manufacturing
Production originally was	50·0	50·0
Production after productivity change, if there were no reallocation of resources, would be	100·0	100·0
Income elasticity of demand is	0·50	1·5
Therefore quantity demanded after rise in income is	75·0	125·0
Therefore surplus or shortage is	25·0 (surplus)	25·0 (shortage)

happen for goods with high income elasticities: demand will expand faster than supply, prices and profits will tend to rise, and resources will move into the industries producing these goods. Table 11.4 illustrates the point just made. It gives a simple numerical example of an economy divided into an agricultural and a manufacturing sector. Originally, resources are divided equally between the two sectors. Productivity then doubles in both sectors. The incomes of all consumers double and the income elasticity of demand for manufactured goods is higher than the income elasticity of demand for agricultural goods. The rise in productivity causes a surplus equal to one quarter of the agricultural production, and a shortage equal to one quarter of the manufactured goods production. Furthermore, if the productivity increases are going on continuously, there will be a *continual tendency* toward excess supply of agricultural goods and excess demand for manufactured goods. Thus it will be necessary to have a continuous movement of resources out of the agricultural and into the manufacturing industries.

In a free-market economy, this reallocation will take place under the incentives of low prices, wages and incomes in the declining sector, and high prices, wages and incomes in the expanding sector. Look at Table 11.4 again. Because there is excess supply in the agricultural sector, prices will fall and incomes of producers will fall. Because too much is being produced there will be a decline in the demand for farm labour and the other factors of production used in agriculture, and the earnings of these factors will decline. At the same time, exactly the opposite tendencies will be observed in manufacturing. Here demand is expanding faster than supply; prices will rise; incomes and profits of producers will be rising. There will be a large demand for the factors of production used in manufacturing industries, so that the price of these factors, and consequently the incomes that they earn, will be bid upward. In short, manufacturing will be a buoyant expanding industry and agriculture will be a depressed and contracting industry.

> **In a free-market society, the mechanism for a continued re-allocation of resources out of low-income-elasticity industries into high-income-elasticity ones is a continued depressing tendency on prices and incomes in contracting industries, and a continued buoyant tendency on prices and incomes in expanding industries.**

Now what is the effect that all this will have on the kind of government stabilization policy considered earlier? Generally, there are two motives behind agricultural stabilization policies: first, to secure a *stable level* of income, and, second, to provide a *high level* of income. Frequently, in a wealthy society where real incomes are expanding year by year, people feel that the agricultural sector *ought* to share in this prosperity. Stabilization programmes often aim at providing the farmer with an income on a parity with incomes earned in the urban sector of the economy.

Positive economics has nothing to say about the ethics of such a policy; it merely tries to discover its consequences. The main problem is that a programme that succeeds in giving the rural sector a high level of income may frustrate the reallocation mechanism and, unless some other means of reducing the size of the rural sector is found, the discrepancy between demand and supply will continue to grow until it reaches unmanageable dimensions. If productivity continues to increase in the rural sector while income elasticities of demand for its products are low, the excess of supply over demand will get larger and larger as time passes. If the government insists on trying to maintain agricultural prices and incomes, it will find that, as time goes by, it is necessary to purchase ever-larger surpluses. If incomes are guaranteed, there will be no monetary incentives for resources to transfer out of the agricultural sector. Unless some other means is found to persuade resources to transfer, then a larger and larger proportion of the resources in agriculture will become redundant. If, on the other hand, the government does not intervene at all, leaving the price mechanism to accomplish the resource reallocation, it will be faced with the problem of a more or less permanently depressed sector of the community. The government may not be willing to accept all of the social and political consequences of leaving this sector to fend for itself.

The reader should not jump to the conclusion that economics proves that governments ought not to interfere with the price mechanism because the risks are too large. Such a conclusion cannot be *proved*; it is a *judgement*, which depends on a valuation of the gains and losses of such intervention. Positive economics, by providing some insight into the workings of the price mechanism, can be used to predict some of the consequences of intervention and thus to point out problems that must be solved in some way or another if it is to be successful. If the problem of reallocating resources out of the rural sector is not solved, then intervention to secure high and stable levels of farm incomes will be unsuccessful over any long period of time.

A BETTER FUTURE FOR AGRICULTURE?

The demands for agricultural products produced by advanced Western countries have recently been soaring. A few of the reasons are: (i) the rise in world population (although it is not enough that people should want more to eat – they must also be able to pay for it at a price that will cover costs of production); (ii) the sale of large quantities of agricultural commodities from Western stockpiles to the USSR, where rising population and disappointing output have created serious food shortages; and (iii) the very high income elasticity of demand for meat, which is a method of producing food value out of feed grains that is technically inefficient compared with the food value that can be obtained by direct consumption of grains in such forms as bread.

World grain reserves have fallen to their lowest levels in two decades and in 1974 were equal to only one month's consumption. At the same time the rise in petroleum prices has created a worldwide shortage of nitrogen fertilizers and has also greatly increased the cost, in poor countries sometimes to prohibitive levels, of pumping water for irrigation.

The United States, a leading supplier of food exports for the rest of the world, has reduced its payments to farmers for keeping land out of production (the payments were designed to reduce surpluses caused by supporting agricultural prices above their equilibrium levels) and has brought nearly all of its idle crop land back into production. For the United States three decades of agricultural surpluses which grew to seemingly unmanageable proportions have given way to several years of excess demand. It is possible that rising world demand will push agricultural prices to a level such that European agriculture will no longer need the complex structure of supports it now has, and where it faces excess demand rather than mounting surpluses that can never be sold at prices that would cover costs of production.

Whatever the future has in store for agriculture, many of the problems facing the industry and many of the complications caused by government intervention will continue to be rendered understandable and predictable by relatively simple price theory.

12

The elementary dynamic theory of price

STATICS AND DYNAMICS

All the theories developed in previous chapters have one characteristic in common. The theory of taxes provides an example of the method employed, and it may be recalled by referring back to Figure 11.4 on page 124. A tax on a commodity shifts its supply curve vertically upwards by the amount of the tax. The new equilibrium price is above the old one, but not by the full amount of the tax. This theory thus produces the prediction that the effect of a tax is to raise the price paid by consumers by less than the full amount of the tax, and to lower the price received by producers, again by less than the full amount of the tax.

It will be noticed that the predictions are derived by comparing the new equilibrium position with the original equilibrium position. A moment's reflection will show that this is the method of analysis used throughout all of the previous chapters. We wish to form a hypothesis about the effect of some change in the data, for example the introduction of a tax or a change in the conditions of demand. We start from a position of equilibrium and then introduce the change to be studied. The new equilibrium position is determined and compared with the original one, the differences between the two being due to the change that was introduced. This analysis, which is based on a comparison of two positions of equilibrium, is called COMPARATIVE STATIC EQUILIBRIUM ANALYSIS. This is a rather cumbersome expression and it is usually abbreviated to COMPARATIVE STATICS.

Theories based on the technique of comparative static analysis are adequate for dealing with many problems. Comparative statics, however, cannot be used to handle two important classes of problem: first, it cannot be used to predict the path which the market follows when moving from one equilibrium to another, and second, it cannot predict whether or not a given equilibrium position will ever be attained. In many cases we are not so much interested in the position of equilibrium as we are in how the market behaves when it is out of equilibrium. For these purposes we require DYNAMIC ANALYSIS, which may be defined as *the study of the behaviour of systems, single markets or whole economies, in disequilibrium situations.*

139

Agricultural price fluctuations

In the previous chapter, we applied comparative static analysis to a very simple case of agricultural price fluctuations. In that example planned production was constant and price fluctuations were caused by unplanned exogenous changes in supply. After each change there was time for the price to settle at its new equilibrium level, equating demand with the current supply well before supply was subject to another unplanned change. The price fluctuations in the market could thus be viewed as movements between a series of successive equilibrium positions, each one equating the current supply with demand.

Some agricultural markets exhibit regular oscillations in price which cannot be accounted for by unplanned shifts in supply. In such markets there is definite evidence that the fluctuations in price result from *planned* fluctuations in farmers' output, these fluctuations following a definite cyclical pattern. Such phenomena have been discovered in many markets. The classic example is the corn-hog cycle in the United States which was first documented in the 1930s by Professor M. Ezekiel. Here we have a different phenomenon from that studied in Chapter 11. In the present case farmers' output plans are fulfilled and yet these very plans give rise, not to a movement towards equilibrium, but to a set of continuing oscillations. This phenomenon requires explanation.

Supply lags

All supply decisions take time to implement. Supply coming on to the market at any one time is thus the result of decisions taken in the past, while decisions taken about production in the present will have their effect on the actual supply coming forward to the market only at some time in the future. We say that supply reacts with a *time lag*.

Every commodity has its own characteristic, and often quite complex, supply lag. In cases in which the lag is short, it may not matter if it is ignored, but in many cases the lag is of critical importance. Consider one or two examples. If the owner of a rubber plantation wishes to produce more rubber in response, say, to a rise in the market price of rubber, he will be able to increase actual production fairly rapidly if there exist stocks of mature trees not now being tapped for raw rubber. But once such stocks of unused capacity are utilized (and often they will not exist at all) then it will take at least five years before newly planted rubber trees can reach maturity and begin to yield latex. To take another example, an increase in the demand for raw milk can be met to some extent almost immediately by diverting milk from other uses, to a greater extent within 27 months by not slaughtering calves at birth and waiting for them to reach maturity, and, to an ever-increasing extent, by allowing the larger population of adult cows to give birth to a larger number of calves.

In the case of agricultural commodities, the time interval between successive crops is one factor which helps to determine the time lag with which supply adjusts to price. The simplest possible time lag is one in which this year's price has no effect whatsoever on this year's supply. Farmers look to the existing market price when deciding what crops to plant this year, and thus *next year's* supply depends on *this year's* price, while this year's supply depends on last year's price. In the terminology of the Appendix to Chapter 3 (page 34) we may write

$$S_t = f(p_{t-1})$$

which reads: supply at time period t depends on the price ruling in the previous time period, $t-1$, where time periods are measured in years.

It is also typical of many agricultural commodities that the (lagged) adjustment of supply to a price change comes in a sudden jump. If there are heavy plantings this year nothing happens to supply at all for a year and then, when the harvest is in, there is a sudden rise in supply. This is to be contrasted with many manufacturing industries in which the supply reaction is spread out over time, production building up slowly to its new planned level. In the former case we speak of a *one-period time lag* while in the latter case we say that there is a *distributed time lag* in the reaction of supply to a change in price.

MARKET FLUCTUATIONS

In Chapter 5 we discussed in an intuitive fashion the effect of an increase in the demand for Brussels sprouts. In Chapter 9 we were able to formalize some of this discussion in terms of the theory of equilibrium price. You should now re-read the discussion on pp. 98–99 before reading on. We were not able at that time to formalize the discussion of the movement between the initial and the final equilibrium because we did not have a dynamic theory. Let us study this problem in more detail, with reference to Figure 12.1.

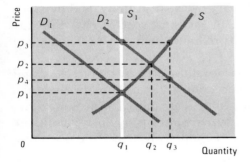

Fig. 12.1 The quantity of sprouts supplied reacts to changes in prices with a time lag

Let us now consider how the movements from the initial to the new equilibrium position might take place. In Figure 12.1, the curve labelled S is an ordinary supply curve for sprouts. The rise in the demand for Brussels sprouts raises the equilibrium price from p_1 to p_2 and the equilibrium quantity bought and sold from q_1 to q_2. When the original increase in demand occurs, it is not possible to produce any more sprouts until another crop can be raised. In the intervening period, the whole effect of the rise in demand will have to be taken out in a price increase. Until the rate of output begins to increase, supply will continue to come onto the market at the rate of q_1 per period; we show this complete inelasticity of supply by drawing a vertical supply line S_1 at the output of q_1. Since the demand for sprouts has shifted from D_1 to D_2 and the market price will rise to p_3, this is the price that equates the new demand to the unchanged supply. If price reacts quickly it may rise to p_3 within a week or two after the rise in demand and stay there until more sprouts can be raised.

But if p_3 is to be the market price of sprouts, farmers would like to produce at the rate of q_3. They are very likely to plan to increase output to that rate and, indeed, there is as yet no signal to tell them that a lower rate, q_2, is the 'correct' rate of output at which to produce.

When the newly planted sprouts reach maturity, the rate of production will suddenly expand to q_3, and price will fall drastically. Indeed, the price that will clear the market is now p_4. But once the price stabilizes at p_4 farmers will wish to produce and sell a quantity much less than q_3. They will cut back on next year's plantings not only to a level below q_3 but to a level below the equilibrium level of q_2 and, when the new crop is harvested, the quantity supplied will fall drastically. At this point we may well begin to wonder whether the market will ever reach equilibrium.

THE COBWEB

We shall now introduce an elementary dynamic theory that accounts for some of the aspects of behaviour discussed above. In this theory, we assume that producers' output plans are fulfilled, but with a time lag, and we show how *planned* changes in supply can give rise to oscillations in market behaviour. In order to introduce the ideas of dynamic theory, we shall consider only the simplest possible time lag, but even this will be quite sufficient sometimes to upset the smooth working of the market adjustment mechanism. This simple time lag is the one already discussed, in which this year's price has no effect whatsoever on this year's supply, and in which the full adjustment to this year's price is made all at once next year. We have already seen that such lags are typical of agricultural products, such as wheat, oats and barley, that give one crop annually.

Markets subject to simple one-year time lags are illustrated in Figures 12.2 and 12.3. Look first at Figure 12.2. The demand curve shows the relation between the price ruling in any year and the quantity that will be demanded in the same year; the supply curve shows the relation between the price ruling in any one year and the quantity that will be supplied to the market in the following year. The price that

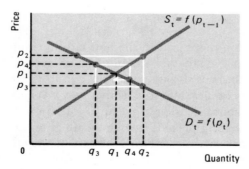

Fig. 12.2 A stable cobweb

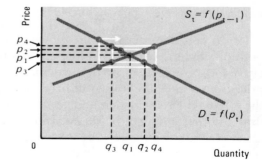

Fig. 12.3 An unstable cobweb

equates demand and supply is p_1. At this price q_1 units will be produced and sold.

What will happen if this equilibrium is disturbed by, for example, a temporary fluctuation in either of the curves? If in one year, year t, the price is p_2, farmers will plan to produce q_2 in the following year. In that year, year $t+1$, q_2 will come on the market, and, in order that q_2 may be sold, the price must fall to p_3. The price of p_3 will induce farmers to produce the quantity q_3. When this quantity comes on the market in the following year, year $t+2$, the price will rise to p_4. This price will call forth a supply of q_4 the next year, year $t+3$, and this will depress the price below p_4. It is clear from this that, in the market described by Figure 12.2, the price and quantity will oscillate around their equilibrium values in a series of diminishing fluctuations, so that, if nothing further disturbs the market, price and quantity will eventually approach their equilibrium levels, p_1 and q_1.

Now consider the case illustrated in Figure 12.3. Exactly the same argument as the previous paragraph applies here, and the text of that paragraph should be re-read to describe the process in this market. In this case, however, the oscillations get larger and larger so that the equilibrium is never restored.

The market in Figure 12.2 has an adjustment mechanism which is *stable*, while that of Figure 12.3 has one which is *unstable*. A stable equilibrium is one which will be restored if it is disturbed, thus the actual price and quantity will tend towards their equilibrium levels (Figure 12.2); an unstable equilibrium is one which will not be restored if it is disturbed, thus the actual price and quantity will tend away from their equilibrium levels (Figure 12.3). What is the difference between these two markets that makes one stable and the other unstable? The student should try to answer this question for himself before reading further.

The difference between the two markets is in the relation between the slopes of the demand and the supply curves. In Figure 12.2 the demand curve is flatter than the supply curve. The absolute quantity demanded changes more as price changes than does the absolute quantity supplied. An excess demand or supply can be eliminated with only a small price change, and the price change in turn causes only a very small change in supply in the following year. Hence the supply change has only a small effect on next year's price. In Figure 12.3 the supply curve is flatter than the demand curve: the quantity supplied responds more to price changes than does the quantity demanded. When there is excess supply, a large price fall is necessary to call forth the required demand. This price fall causes a large reduction in next year's supply (because supply is very responsive to price). Next year there is a large shortage and a very big price increase is necessary to reduce demand to the level of the available supply. This price rise causes a very large increase in quantity supplied in the following year and so we go on in a series of alternating periods of ever-increasing surplus and shortage.[1]

In the case of the unstable equilibrium the oscillations get bigger and bigger. There is nothing in our theory so far to prevent these oscillations from becoming infinitely large. In practice, however, we should not expect this to happen; we should

---

1 This argument is, of course, only an intuitive one. Mathematical analysis, however, easily shows that the market is in fact stable if the supply curve is steeper than the demand curve and unstable if the supply curve is flatter than the demand curve.

expect that the oscillations would tend to reach limits. A full theory of such a market would require an analysis of these limits.

> **What we have established is that in the unstable case the operation of the competitive price system itself does not tend to remove any disequilibrium; it tends rather to accentuate it.**

We shall call a system in which this happens an *unstable system*.

This cobweb model is a very simple one in which supply plans are always fulfilled (actually quantity supplied always equals planned quantity supplied), planned supply in one year depends solely on the price ruling in the previous year, and the market price is always such as to equate the quantity currently being demanded with that currently being supplied. It is evident that more interesting and complex models arise if: (i) we allow actual supply to deviate from planned supply due to such uncontrollable factors as weather conditions; (ii) we allow for a time lag in the adjustment of *price* to the state of excess demand; and (iii) we allow for some form of learning process on the part of farmers so that planned supply does not depend solely on the price of the previous period. Situations of this sort become quite complex and they cannot be handled without the help of mathematical analysis. [1] The study of the simplest cobweb model does, however, serve to introduce dynamic theory, and to illustrate its value by providing a reasonably satisfactory explanation of an interesting real-world phenomenon. It also shows in a fairly dramatic way that even very simple competitive markets may show unstable oscillatory behaviour. [2]

---

1 The interested student should consult Chapter 1 of R.D.G. Allen, *Mathematical Economics* (Macmillan, 1966).

2 It was thought for a very long time that the static theory of Chapter 9, summarized on page 94, permitted the inference that the market would always be stable. (See note 1, page 94.) The present analysis shows why this inference cannot be drawn. That excess demand should cause price to rise and excess supply should cause price to fall is not sufficient to ensure stability. Such models as the one illustrated in Figure 12.3 contain all the assumptions listed in Chapter 9, yet they are unstable. In these models excess demand pushes the price up towards equilibrium *but it pushes it too far*; excess supply pushes price down towards equilibrium *but it also pushes it too far*. Thus an endless series of oscillations around the equilibrium is possible.

13

A postscript and a preview

THE INTERRELATIONSHIPS OF MARKETS: A POSTSCRIPT

In Part 2 we have developed a theory of the behaviour of individual, competitive markets.

The economy does not, however, consist of a series of self-contained markets functioning in isolation. It is to be viewed, rather, as an interlocking system in which anything happening in one market has profound effects on many other markets and could, potentially, influence every other market in the economy. Thus our study of the behaviour of one market in isolation is only a first step towards understanding the behaviour of a whole economy. We also need a theory of how the individual markets are linked together and of how they act and react on each other. We shall consider this, albeit very briefly, in Part 6, but in the meantime it is desirable to obtain an intuitive picture of the linking together of the economy market.

Consider, for example, the effects of a rise in the demand for motor cars. This will be met fairly soon by a rise in car production. If the rise in demand is considerable, and judged to be permanent, there will also be a planned increase in capacity in the car industry. Employment will rise and an attempt may be made to attract labour from elsewhere by offering higher wages. Thus, one of the first impacts on other industries will be a loss of labour and possibly a need to raise wages in order to compete with the car industry for labour. This may cause profits to fall in these other industries. The increased employment in the car industry may occasion some geographical movement of labour. In this case there would be a rise in the demand for housing in the car centres and a corresponding fall in demand elsewhere. New housing construction in the car-producing areas would lead to a rise in the demand for construction workers and materials. Quarries and brickworks may have to take on additional labour and expand output. Further, there will be a rise in the demand for raw materials used in car construction and the effects of this may be felt in such diverse spots as the glass-making areas of the Midlands, the steel-manufacturing sections of Wales and the rubber plantations of Malaya. If new investment in plant and equipment takes place in the car industry, there will be a rise in the demand for many capital goods; shortages and bottlenecks may develop, and other industries which use these goods may experience increases in their costs and trouble with delivery dates. There will also be a change in consumers' expenditure because some people's earnings will be increased and other people's reduced. Thus the effects of this one change will spread out through the economy rather like the ripples which spread out over the smooth surface of a pond after a pebble has been dropped into it.

The price system is a control mechanism

The example considered above illustrates two very important points. First the various markets of the economy are interrelated: a single initial change in demand has numerous repercussive effects throughout the economy. Second, adaptations to the initial shift take place without being consciously coordinated by any single central authority. When shortages develop, prices rise and profit-seeking entrepreneurs are led to produce more of the good in short supply. When surpluses occur, prices fall and supply is voluntarily contracted. It was the great discovery of the eighteenth-century economists that a competitive price system produced a coordination of effort in which by seeking their private gains and responding to such public signals as prices, costs and profit rates, individuals produce coordinated reactions to changes in demand and supply.

> **The price system was not consciously created. With a price system it is not necessary to foresee and to coordinate all necessary changes; such changes occur automatically as a result of the separate decisions taken by a large number of individuals, each seeking his own private profit, but all responding to changes in demands and prices.**

Efficient and inefficient control mechanisms

Having grasped this idea, the student must beware of jumping to the conclusion that the price system has been shown to be the *best* system of regulating the economy; one must beware of equating the word 'automatic', which we have used, with the phrase 'perfectly functioning', which we have not used. It is easy enough to control the heat in your house by means of an automatic thermostatic control, but it is equally easy to have such a badly designed or imperfectly functioning system that the heat control you actually achieve is worse than you would have had by 'stoking up' and 'damping down' by hand. To observe that the price system functions automatically, i.e., without conscious centralized coordination, does not tell us how *well* it functions. We have seen, for example, in the case of the 'cobweb' (see Chapter 12), how the automatic working of the price system can produce violent fluctuations in price and output.

The reader who believes that behaviour in a free-market economy is unplanned and uncoordinated must dispel this notion. The existence of a coordinating mechanism is beyond dispute. The question of how well it works in comparison with practical alternative coordinating systems has been a matter of dispute for 200 years and is still a great unsettled social question.

DEMAND AND SUPPLY: A PREVIEW

In developing a theory of the behaviour of competitive markets, which are markets in which no single buyer or seller is important enough to exert any significant influence on prices, we first introduced a theory of households' demands (Chapter 7) and then (Chapter 8) a theory of firms' supply. We must now consider in much more detail the theory of demand and the theory of supply. Demand is considered in Part 3 and supply in Part 4. The theory of demand occupies us for only three chapters because we never need to depart from our competitive assumption that each household is a price-taker, being totally unable to influence by any action of its own the market prices of the commodities it purchases. The theory of supply occupies us for a much longer time. This is because many interesting issues of economic policy are encountered in the theory of supply, and also because very serious complications are encountered when it is realized that a large proportion of production is in the hands of firms in noncompetitive situations, in the sense that each firm is able to exert a significant influence on price and total quantity bought and sold by altering its own price-output decisions. Indeed, although we do not need to alter any of the hypotheses about demand introduced in Chapter 7, it becomes necessary, as a result of the existence of these noncompetitive situations, to abandon the hypothesis of Chapter 8 that there always exists a simple relation between market price and firms' supply. But first we must turn our attention to the theory of demand.

Part three

The intermediate theory of demand

14

Some basic theorems and predictions

Is the effect on a household's consumption different if its money income falls than if the price it pays for goods rise? Does an increase in the level of all prices hurt everybody? Does it hurt anybody? Can we predict the effect of changes in prices on a household's behaviour? To answer these and other similar questions, we must go behind the demand curve to look in more detail at the behaviour of millions of independent decision units whose aggregate behaviour is summarized in market demand curves.

In this chapter we consider the different effects on a household's consumption of changes in relative prices, absolute prices and incomes. In the following chapter we show some alternative methods of deriving from assumptions about household behaviour the basic prediction that the demand curve for a product slopes downwards. We have already discussed in Chapter 6 the general assumptions made about the household, which is the basic decision unit on the side of demand. You should now review pages 70–1 of that chapter to refresh your memory on these basic assumptions.

CHOICES FACING THE HOUSEHOLD

We shall consider a single household allocating the whole of its money income between only two goods X and Y. We assume that the household spends all of its income on the purchase of X and Y for current consumption; it neither spends more than its income nor saves any of it.[1] We start by considering numerical examples, but later go on to state the argument in general terms.

In Figure 14.1, the quantity of X is measured on the horizontal axis and the quantity of Y on the vertical one. Any point on the graph represents a combination of the two goods. Point m, for example, represents 40 units of X and 60 units of Y.

---

1 These assumptions are not as restrictive as they might at first seem. Two goods are used so that the analysis can be handled geometrically; the argument can be generalized to n goods with the use of mathematics. Savings are ignored because it is the allocation of expenditure between goods for current consumption in which we are interested. The possibility of borrowing or using up past savings can be allowed for, but it should soon be apparent to the reader that none of the results in which we are interested here would be affected by this.

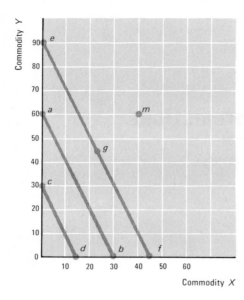

Fig. 14.1 Shifts in the budget line caused by changes in household income

We now construct the household's BUDGET LINE, which shows all those combinations of the goods that are just obtainable, given the household's income and the prices of the two commodities. [1] Assume, for example, that the household's income is £120 per month, that the price of Y is £2 per unit, and the price of X is £4. What combinations of X and Y are open to the household? First, it could spend all its money on Y, obtaining each month $60Y$ and no X (this combination is indicated by point a on Figure 14.1). It could also buy $30X$ and no Y (point b on the figure). Other combinations open to it are $58Y$ and $1X$, $56Y$ and $2X$, $54Y$ and $3X$; in fact, since X costs twice as much per unit as Y, the household must forego the purchase of $2Y$ in order to be able to purchase one more X. In the language of Chapter 4, the *opportunity cost* of X is $2Y$. All the possible combinations of X and Y open to the household are shown by the straight line ab in Figure 14.1. Points between ab and the origin do not use all the household's income, points beyond ab would require more than the household's income, while points on ab are just attainable in the sense that they just require all the household's income.

The effects of changes in income

We may now ask what happens to the budget line when income changes? If, for example, the household's income is halved from £120 to £60 per month, prices being unchanged, then the amount of goods the household can buy will also be halved. If it spends all its income on Y, it will now get $30Y$ and no X (point c); if it

1 This budget line is analogous to the production possibility boundary shown in Figure 4.1 on page 56. The budget line shows the combinations of goods available to one household given prices and its income, while the production-possibility curve shows the combinations of goods available to the whole society given its techniques of production and supplies of resources.

spends all its income on X, it will get $15X$ and no Y (point d). All possible combinations open to the household appear on budget line cd. Note that this line is parallel to budget line ab, but closer to the origin. Since prices are unchanged, the household must give up $2Y$ for every additional X it wishes to purchase. The fact that ab and cd both have the same slope indicates that the opportunity cost of X in terms of Y is the same in both situations.

If the household's income rises to £180, it will be able to buy more of both commodities than it could previously. If it buys only Y it can now have $90Y$ (point e); if it buys only X it can have $45X$ (point f); if it divides its income equally between the two goods it can have $45Y$ and $22\frac{1}{2}X$ (point g): All the combinations of X and Y now available to the household appear on budget line ef.

We conclude that variations in the household's income, with prices constant, shift the budget line parallel to itself, inward towards the origin when income falls, and outward away from the origin when income rises. The reader should now draw his own figure similar to Figure 14.1 and sketch budget lines for incomes of £100 and £40 per month.

The effects of changes in prices

We may now consider what happens when prices change. Since Figure 14.1 is rather cluttered, we transfer the line ef (illustrating income £180, price of $X = £4$, and price

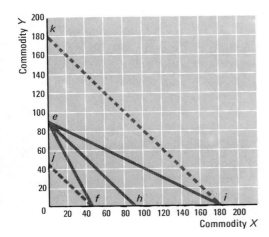

Fig. 14.2 Shifts in the budget line caused by changes in prices

of $Y = £2$) to Figure 14.2. Now assume that the price of Y remains unchanged while the price of X changes. Say, for example, that it falls from £4 to £2. The household can now buy either $90X$, if it devotes its whole income to that commodity, or $90Y$, if it purchases only Y. The combinations available to the household are given by the budget line eh. A few points on this line should be checked to see that the combinations of X and Y indicated exactly exhaust the household's income of £180 when X and Y are both priced at £2.

Now assume that the price of X falls to £1, the price of Y remaining constant at £2. The new budget line indicating all the combinations available to the household is *ei*. A comparison of the budget lines *ef*, *eh* and *ei* shows that changing one money price changes the *slope* of the budget line; the lower is the price of X the flatter is the budget line.

Next let us try changing both prices in the same proportion. If we start from budget line *eh* (income £180, X and Y priced at £2) and double both prices, then we will halve the amount of both goods that the consumer can purchase. The budget line now becomes *jf*, because the income of £180 will now buy $45Y$ and no X, $45X$ and no Y, or any combination of X and Y on the straight line joining these two points.

Now let us go back to line *eh* (£180 income and a £2 price for X and Y) and halve both prices. The consumer can now have twice as much of both commodities as previously and the budget line moves outward to *ki*.

We notice that changing both prices in the same proportion shifts the budget line parallel to itself in the same way as a change in income shifted it. Before reading further the student should go back to Figure 14.1, take budget line *ab* (income = £120, $Y = £2$ and $X = £4$), and determine what *price changes* would shift the budget line to *cd* and to *ef*.

This last result suggests that we can have off-setting changes in money prices and money income. Consider the budget line *eh* in Figure 14.2. This budget line was originally obtained from an income of £180 with prices of £2 for both X and Y. What will happen if the household's income doubles to £360? The budget line will shift to *ki*, since the household can buy twice as many units of both commodities as it could previously. But what if prices double from £2 to £4? This cuts the household's consumption possibilities in half, and the budget line is back to budget line *eh*. A rise in money income and a proportionate rise in both money prices leave the position of the budget line unchanged.

Relative prices and opportunity costs

The reason why changing both prices in the same proportion shifts the budget line parallel to itself is that the slope of the budget line indicates the opportunity cost of one commodity in terms of the other and an equal proportionate change in both prices leaves this opportunity cost unchanged. For example, if Y costs £2 and X costs £4 then $2Y$ must be foregone in order to be able to purchase $1X$; if Y costs £4 and X costs £8 it is still necessary to forego $2Y$ to be able to purchase one more X. In fact, as long as the price of X is twice the price of Y, it will be necessary to forego two Y in order to be able to purchase one more X. More generally, the amount of Y that must be given up to obtain another unit of X depends only on *the relation between the price of Y and the price of X*. If we take the money price of X and divide it by the money price of Y we have the opportunity cost of X in terms of Y (the quantity of Y that must be foregone in order to be able to purchase one more X). This may be written:

$$\frac{p_x}{p_y} = \text{opportunity cost of } X \text{ in terms of } Y,$$

where p_x and p_y are the money prices of X and Y. It is apparent that changing both prices in the same proportion leaves the ratio p_x/p_y unchanged. In economics, this ratio is called a RELATIVE PRICE, which is the term used when any price is expressed as a ratio of another price. Relative prices must be distinguished from money prices, which are called ABSOLUTE PRICES.

Conclusions and predictions

We have now reached a number of conclusions. You should re-read the relevant parts of this chapter if you cannot prove each of these for yourself.

> **(1) A change in money income, with money prices (and thus necessarily relative prices) constant, shifts the budget line parallel to itself, inward towards the origin when income falls, and outwards away from the origin when income rises.**
> **(2) An equal percentage change in all absolute prices leaves relative prices unchanged, and, if money income remains unchanged, it will shift the budget line parallel to itself, inward towards the origin when prices rise, and outward away from the origin when prices fall.**
> **(3) Multiplying all money prices by the same constant, λ, while holding money income constant, has exactly the same effect on the budget line as multiplying money income by $1/\lambda$, while holding money prices constant. For example, doubling all money prices has the same effect on the budget line as halving money income.**
> **(4) A change in relative prices causes the budget line to change its slope.**
> **(5) An equal percentage change in all absolute prices combined with a percentage change in income of the same magnitude, and in the same direction as the price change, leaves the budget line exactly where it was before the changes occurred.**

The five conclusions listed above are matters of logic. The effects of various changes on the budget line are incontrovertible. In order to translate these conclusions into predictions about household behaviour, we advance the hypothesis that a household's market behaviour depends solely on the tastes of the members of the household and on the location of the household's budget line. This behavioural hypothesis along with the five propositions above will allow us to make testable predictions about the behaviour of households. The following are two important examples.[1]

> **The change in a household's market behaviour will be the same if either its income changes by λ or all money prices change by $1/\lambda$.**

> **The household's market behaviour will be unaffected if its money incomes and all money prices change simultaneously by λ.**

1 Strictly speaking, these predictions apply only to households that do not have any significant quantities of bonds, cash or other assets whose value is fixed in money units and whose real value thus changes when money prices change. (For example, the real value of a cash hoard would be halved by a doubling of the price level.) The predictions apply to those households for which income is the main determinant of current expenditure, probably the majority.

REAL AND MONEY INCOME

We now make the important distinction between REAL INCOME and MONEY INCOME. Money income measures a household's income in terms of some monetary unit, so many dollars or so many pounds sterling; real income measures a household's income in terms of the command over commodities that the money income confers. A rise in money income of x per cent combined with an x per cent rise in all money prices leaves a household's ability to buy commodities, and hence its real income, unchanged. When we speak of the real value of a certain amount of money, we are referring to the goods and services that can be bought with the money; we are referring, that is, to the PURCHASING POWER of the money.

Allocation of resources: the importance of relative prices

Price theory predicts that the allocation of resources depends on the structure of relative prices. If the money value of all prices, incomes, debts and credits were doubled, there would, according to our theory, be little noticeable effect. The economy would function as before. The same set of relative prices and real incomes would exist, and there would be no incentive for any reallocation of resources; the only difference would be that the money level of all prices and incomes would be doubled.

This prediction is an implication of the theories of the behaviour of households and firms. We have already seen that doubling all money prices and money incomes leaves the household's budget line unchanged and so, according to the theory of household behaviour, the change gives households no incentive to vary the quantity of each commodity that they purchase. As far as producers are concerned, if all prices, both of final goods and of factors of production, double, then the relative profitability of different lines of production will be unaffected, as indeed will the real level of profits in all lines of production.[1] Thus producers will have no incentive to alter production rates so as to produce more of some things and less of others.

If, on the other hand, relative prices change, then our theory predicts that resources will be reallocated. Households will buy more of the cheaper goods and less of the expensive ones, and producers will expand production of those goods whose prices have risen relatively and contract production of those goods whose prices have fallen relatively (since the latter will be relatively less profitable lines of production).

The theory of prices and of resource allocations is a theory of relative, not of absolute, prices.

Inflation and deflation: the importance of absolute prices

The average level of money prices is called the PRICE LEVEL. If all money prices double, we say that the price level has doubled. An increase in the price level is called an INFLATION, a decrease is called a DEFLATION. If a rise in all money prices and incomes has little or no effect on the allocation of resources, it may seem surprising

---

1 Since all prices and costs will have doubled, money profits will have doubled, but the purchasing power of these profits will be just what it was before the change occurred.

that so much concern is expressed over inflation. Clearly, a person who spends all of his income, and whose money income goes up at the same rate as money prices go up, loses nothing from inflation. His real income is unaffected. There are, however, two problems that make inflation more serious than it might seem from the above discussion. First, in our society, many contractual obligations are fixed in money terms. Second, when money incomes rise during an inflation they do not all rise at the same speed; there are important leads and lags in the adjustment process and these affect the relative positions of different groups in the society while the price level is adjusting from one level to the other.

If I borrow from the bank enough money to buy a new car, I do not promise to pay back in two years' time enough money to buy a new car; I promise, rather to pay back the same sum of money as I borrowed. If prices have doubled in the meantime, I will pay back to the bank only half as much as is needed to buy a car at that time, while if prices have halved I will pay back enough money to buy two cars. If I pay money to buy ordinary life insurance, the company enters into a legal obligation to pay me or my heirs so much money when I retire or die. The purchasing power of this money will depend on the prices that exist when the money is paid. Old-age pensions, all borrowing and lending contracts, mortgages and hire-purchase agreements, are but a few examples of contractual obligations fixed in money terms, the real value of which fluctuates with the price level.

One dramatic example is found in wartime borrowing by governments. A household which bought a British War Bond for £75 in 1940 may have been pleased to know that the bond could be redeemed for £100 in 1950. But this £100 in 1950 bought it only £41 worth of goods at 1940 prices. In other words, by not buying £75 worth of goods in 1940 the household secured the right to buy £41 worth of goods 10 years later. This is a rate of interest in real terms of *minus* 2 per cent per year over the period of ten years! To take another example, a British Naval Lieutenant Commander who joined the Service in 1915 at the age of 18, and served his country through two world wars, retiring on a pension of £800 per year in 1945 would have found that by 1965 the real value of his pension had shrunk drastically. Indeed, at the prices ruling in 1965 his pension would buy considerably less than half the goods and services it would have bought in 1915. Since it is very unlikely that the possibility of such a dramatic change in the price level ever occurred to him, it is not stretching a point to say that in return for a lifetime of service, through two wars, he received less than one half of what he had every reason to expect and ended his life with a standard of living not far above a bare subsistence level.

Thus we see that inflation lowers the real value of all debts, savings, and money incomes by reducing the quantity of goods and services that can be purchased. The person who borrows money gains from unexpected inflation because the sacrifice in terms of goods and services in repaying the debt is reduced, whereas the person who has loaned money loses because the real value of the money returned is less than the real value of the money originally given up.[1] By the same token, anyone who saves

---

1 The qualification 'unexpected' is important. In the case of a fully anticipated inflation both sides in any bargain can adjust their money prices and interest rates to compensate for the inflation and thus bring about any real result that is agreed on independent of the rate of inflation.

money, buys ordinary life insurance, or in any other way disposes of his savings so that he gets a fixed money return, loses by inflation. An inflation of 10 per cent per year will reduce the purchasing power of a sum of money to one-half its original amount in about 7 years.

The second consequence of inflation that was mentioned above arises from the fact that all adjustments do not take place instantaneously. If there were to be a once and for all doubling of the price level, most money incomes would probably double eventually, so that the real value of all incomes would be restored to their original level. In the process, however, some groups will manage to increase their incomes quickly, whereas other groups will increase theirs only slowly. But the price level does not suddenly double and then remain constant, and in a state of continuous inflation, those groups whose money incomes rise quickly gain at the expense of those whose money incomes rise only slowly.

The theory of the determination of the absolute price level is discussed in Part 8.

Appendix

Some basic theorems on the budget line

In this appendix we shall use simple algebra to prove the five propositions given on p. 155 of the text. For a given money income, M, and given money prices p_x and p_y the household has a budget equation in which the quantities of X and Y purchased appear as independent variables.

THE EQUATION OF THE BUDGET LINE

$$p_x X + p_y Y = M$$
$$p_y Y = M - p_x X$$
$$Y = \frac{M}{p_y} - \frac{p_x}{p_y} X. \quad (1)$$

Equation (1) is a linear equation of the form

$$Y = a + bX, \quad (2)$$

where $a = M/p_y$ and $b = -p_x/p_y$. The intercept a is the number of units of Y that can be purchased by spending all of M on Y i.e., money income divided by the price of Y. The slope depends on the relation between p_x and p_y. Proofs of five propositions on page 155 of the text are now easily provided.

PROPOSITION (1): A change in money income with money prices (and thus necessarily relative prices) constant, shifts the budget line parallel to itself, inward towards the origin when income falls, and outwards away from the origin when income rises.

PROOF: If we change the value of M in (1) we change the value of a in (2) in the same direction: $\Delta a = \Delta M/p_y$ but b is unaffected since M does not appear in that term; thus changing M shifts the budget line inwards ($\Delta M < 0$) or outwards ($\Delta M > 0$) but leaves the slope unaffected.

PROPOSITION (2): An equal percentage change in all absolute prices leaves relative prices unchanged, and, if money income remains unchanged, it will shift the budget line parallel to itself, inward towards the origin when prices rise, and outward away from the origin when prices fall.

PROOF: Multiplying both prices in equation (1) by the same constant λ gives

$$Y = \frac{M}{\lambda p_y} - \frac{\lambda p_x}{\lambda p_y} X.$$

Since the λs cancel out of the slope term, b is unaffected; the a term is however changed. If $\lambda > 1$ then a is diminished while if $\lambda < 1$ then a is increased.

PROPOSITION (3): Multiplying all money prices by the same constant, λ, while holding money income constant, has exactly the same effect on the budget line as multiplying money income by $1/\lambda$, while holding money prices constant.

159

PROOF: Multiply both money prices in (1) by λ:

$$Y = \frac{M}{\lambda p_y} - \frac{\lambda p_x}{\lambda p_y} X.$$

Cancelling the λs from the slope term gives:

$$Y = \frac{M}{\lambda p_y} - \frac{p_x}{p_y} X.$$

Finally bringing the λ from the denominator to the numerator of the constant term gives:

$$Y = \frac{(1/\lambda)M}{p_y} - \frac{p_x}{p_y} X.$$

PROPOSITION (4): A change in relative prices causes the budget line to change its slope.

PROOF: One way to change relative prices is to multiply one money price, say p_x, by $\lambda(\lambda \neq 1)$ leaving the other money price unchanged.

Firstly selecting p_x gives:

$$Y = \frac{M}{p_y} - \frac{\lambda p_x}{p_y} X.$$

Obviously the slope of the budget line is changed. Secondly if p_x is held constant and

p_y multiplied by $\lambda(\lambda \neq 1)$, then the slope changes once again and the constant term changes as well. (As a bit of practice in algebraic manipulation one might show that in this case the intercept in the X axis does not change – this intercept is the constant if the equation of the budget line is written $X = c + dY$ rather than as in (2) $Y = a + bX$.)

PROPOSITION (5): An equal percentage change in all absolute prices combined with a percentage change in income of the same magnitude, and in the same direction as the price change, leaves the budget line exactly where it was before the changes occurred.

PROOF: Multiply M and both prices in equation (1) by λ:

$$Y = \frac{\lambda M}{\lambda p_y} - \frac{\lambda p_x}{\lambda p_y} X.$$

Cancel out the λs from the intercept and the slope terms to obtain:

$$Y = \frac{M}{p_y} - \frac{p_x}{p_y} X.$$

which is equation (1) once again.

15

Theories of household demand

In this chapter we shall consider two of the three most important theories of household behaviour with respect to demand. The purpose of the discussion is to derive from assumptions about household behaviour the prediction that the household's demand curve for a product is downward sloping. For many purposes in positive economics we can take the downward sloping demand curve as a basic assumption for which there is much confirming evidence. For completeness, however, we wish to trace this relation back to individual behaviour on the part of the decision-taking units described in Chapter 6. In the process we can develop some other important insights.

This chapter outlines two theories of demand. The theory described first is the oldest theory of household behaviour, that of marginal utility. It is included because of the widespread significance of the distinction it makes between marginal and total utility. The second theory described is that of revealed preference, which provides a simple and operationally useful way of distinguishing between the effects of a change in real income and the effects of a change in relative prices. In the appendix to this chapter the third major theory of demand, the indifference-preference theory, is outlined.

MARGINAL UTILITY THEORY

(1) If you had to choose between giving up one of the following, which would you choose: water or attendance at the cinema?
(2) If you had to choose between one of the following which would you choose: to increase your consumption of water by 35 gallons (the amount required, e.g., for one average size bath) a month or to attend one more cinema performance each month?

In (1) you are comparing the value you place on your total consumption of water with the value you place on the total of your attendances at the cinema. In economics we say you are comparing the TOTAL UTILITY of all water consumption with the TOTAL UTILITY of all cinema attendances. There is little doubt that everyone would answer (1) in the same way, revealing that the total utility derived from consuming water exceeds the total utility derived from attending the cinema.

In (2) you are comparing the value you place on a small addition to your water consumption with the value you place on a small addition to your cinema attendances. In economics we say you are comparing the MARGINAL UTILITY of water with the MARGINAL UTILITY of cinema performances. We encounter marginal concepts many times in economics, the marginal unit being the one right on the border. If, for example, we talk about a marginal change in your consumption of water we are talking about consuming a little bit more or a little bit less, and the unit of water affected is called the marginal unit. In the case of choice (2) we cannot be as sure how different individuals will choose as we were with choice (1). Some might select the extra cinema performance, while others might say that they already had seen all the cinema performances they could stand (marginal utility of another cinema attendance, *zero*) and they would select the extra water. Furthermore, their choice would depend on whether they made it in a time when water was plentiful so that they had more or less all the water they wanted (marginal utility of a little more water, *zero*) or when water was scarce so that they might put quite a high value on obtaining a bit more water (marginal utility of a little more water, *high*).

In our purchasing decisions we are very seldom faced with choices of type (1), but we are very often faced with choices of type (2). If our income rises a bit we have to decide whether to have a bit more of one thing or the other. If we find that we are overspending, or if our income falls, we have to decide what to cut down on, to have a little less of this or a little less of that. Choices in the world are thus rarely conditioned by total utilities; it is marginal utilities that are relevant in deciding between a bit more of this or a bit more of that.

The hypothesis of diminishing marginal utility

We now introduce the basic hypothesis of utility theory.

> **The value that any household attaches to successive units of a particular commodity will diminish steadily as its total consumption of that commodity increases, the consumption of all other commodities being held constant.**

This is called the hypothesis of diminishing marginal utility. Another way of stating the hypothesis is to say that the total utility that is derived from consuming the commodity increases as more of it is consumed, but at a diminishing rate so that, for example, the 100th unit consumed per month will add less to the household's total utility than did, say, the 10th unit.

If we assume we have some index with which to measure utility we can illustrate these hypotheses in the following figures. Figure 15.1(i) shows that the total utility derived from consuming the commodity rises as more of it is consumed, but Figure 15.1(ii) shows that the amount of utility derived from consuming each additional unit of the commodity gets less and less the more of the commodity that is already being consumed. For instance when x_1 is consumed per month *total utility* is t_1 but *marginal utility* is only m_1, showing that when x_1 is already consumed the utility of consuming a bit more is quite low.[1]

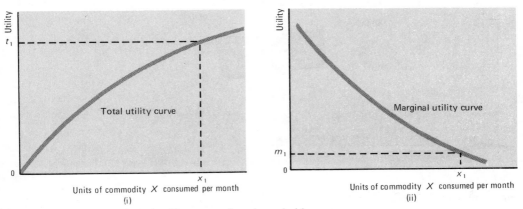

Fig. 15.1 Marginal and total utility curves for a household

WATER, AN EXAMPLE: As an example of the difference between total and marginal utility consider the example of water. Some minimum quantity of water is absolutely necessary to sustain life and a person would give up all his income and wealth to obtain that quantity: the marginal utility of that quantity is infinite. Much more than this bare minimum can be drunk and the marginal utility of successive glasses of water will decline steadily. But water has many other uses. A fairly high marginal utility will be attached to some minimum quantity for bathing but much more than this minimum will be used for frequent baths and for having a water level in the bath higher than is absolutely necessary. The last gallon used for bathing is likely to have quite a low marginal utility. Again, some small quantity of water is necessary for cleaning one's teeth but the many people who leave the tap running while scrubbing their teeth can hardly pretend that the water so consumed between wetting and rinsing the brush has a high utility. Similarly for cleaning one's car. A couple of pails of water per week for this purpose probably have high utility. But the gallons poured down the drain if the hose is left on between successive rinses provide no more than a minor convenience. When we consider all the extravagant uses of water for the modern consumer we can hardly doubt that the marginal utility of the last, say, 30 per cent of all the units consumed is very low even though the total utility of all the units consumed is infinitely high. The marginal utility curve is probably of the shape shown in Figure 15.2. (This is more than idle speculation for it leads to the prediction that there will be a large increase in the amount of water consumed if water is provided free rather than at a modest price. This prediction, as we shall see later, is in conformity with many empirical observations.)

CAN MARGINAL UTILITY EVER REACH ZERO?: With many commodities there is

---

1 Mathematicians will recognize marginal utility as the first derivative of total utility with respect to the quantity consumed. If $U = f(X)$ describes total utility as a function of the quantity of X consumed then marginal utility is $dU/dX = f'(X)$.

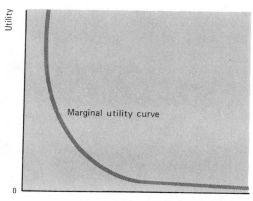

Fig. 15.2 Hypothetical marginal utility curve for water consumed by a typical household

some maximum consumption after which additional units would confer no additional utility, and if the individual were forced to consume more this would actually reduce his total utility. Tobacco and food are obvious examples. There is some maximum number of cigarettes that most people would smoke per day even if they did not have to worry about the cost. Long before consumption reached the point of continuous chain-smoking, additional cigarettes would cease to add to utility and would begin to reduce total utility, i.e., they would confer a negative marginal utility or as it is sometimes called a DISUTILITY. The same is undoubtedly true of many other commodities such as food, alcoholic beverages and most recreations.

The equilibrium of a household

We now recall the basic assumption about the motivation of households first introduced in Chapter 6: *The members of a household will seek to maximize their total utility.* This is just another way of saying that the members of households try to make themselves as well off as they possibly can in the circumstances in which they find themselves.[1] From this we can immediately derive one prediction that turns out to be important at a later stage.

> **Consumption of any free good will be pushed to the point at which its marginal utility is zero.**

A free good is one for which no price needs to be paid. As long as a further unit confers a positive marginal utility, total utility can be increased by consuming more of the commodity. In Figure 15.3 if cigarettes were a free good the consumer would consume c_1 of these per day, making total utility from smoking as large as possible (u_1). Beyond this point, further cigarettes have a negative marginal utility.

We can now restate the proposition about scarcity on page 51.

---

1 This is sometimes taken to mean that individuals are assumed to be narrowly selfish and devoid of any altruistic motives. This is not so. If the individual derives utility from giving his money away to others, this can be incorporated into the analysis and we can compare, for example, the marginal utility of 50p that he gives away with the marginal utility of 50p that he spends on himself.

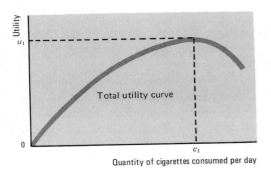

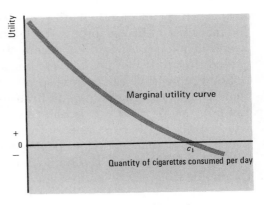

Fig. 15.3 Hypothetical total and marginal utility curves for cigarettes consumed by
a typical household

**There are not enough resources to produce the amounts of all com-
modities that people would wish to consume if commodities were free.
Therefore marginal utilities will remain positive for at least some
goods, i.e., households would get additional utility from consuming
more of them.**

We may now ask how a household will adjust its expenditure so as to maximize its
total utility when it has to pay for the goods it consumes.[1] Should it go to the point at
which the marginal utility of all commodities is the same? At this point it would
value equally the last unit of each commodity consumed. This would make sense only
if each commodity had the same price per unit.

**The household maximizing its utility will allocate its expenditure
among commodities so that the utility of the last penny spent on each
is equal.**

To understand this point quickly, imagine that the household is in a position in
which the utility of the last penny spent on carrots yields three times the utility of the
last penny spent on Brussels sprouts. In this case, total utility can be increased by
switching a penny of expenditure from sprouts to carrots and gaining the difference
between the utilities of a penny spent on each.

The utility-maximizing household will continue to switch its expenditure from
sprouts to carrots as long as a penny spent on carrots yields more utility than a penny
spent on sprouts. But this switching reduces the quantity of sprouts consumed and
so raises the marginal utility of sprouts; at the same time it increases the quantity of
carrots consumed and so lowers the marginal utility of carrots. Eventually, the
marginal utilities will have changed enough so that the utility of a penny spent on
carrots is just equal to the utility of a penny spent on sprouts. At this point there is
nothing to be gained by a further switch of expenditure from sprouts to carrots. If
the consumer did persist in a further reallocation of his expenditure, he would

1 The justification for personifying a household in this context is given in Chapter 6, pages 70–1.

further reduce the marginal utility of carrots (by consuming more of them) and raise the marginal utility of sprouts (by consuming less of them). Further reallocations would then lower total utility, because the utility of a penny spent on sprouts would exceed the utility of a penny spent on carrots.

Let us now leave carrots and sprouts and deal with commodities in general. We represent the marginal utility of the last unit of X as MU_x, and the price of X as p_x. Let MU_y and p_y refer to a second commodity. The marginal utility per penny of X will be MU_x/p_x. For example, if the last unit adds 30 units to utility and costs 10 pence, its marginal utility per penny is $30/10 = 3$.

The condition required for a household to maximize its utility is, for any pair of commodities,

$$\frac{MU_x}{p_x} = \frac{MU_y}{p_y}. \tag{1}$$

This is just another way of writing the condition that the household will so allocate its expenditure that the utilities gained from the last penny spent in each direction are equal. What it shows us, however, is that the utility-maximizing household, faced with a set of prices, will so adjust its expenditures that the utilities of the last units of all types of goods consumed will be proportional to their prices. Only simple cross-multiplication is now needed to obtain another important relationship:

$$\frac{MU \text{ of a unit of } X}{MU \text{ of a unit of } Y} = \frac{\text{price of a unit of } X}{\text{price of a unit of } Y}. \tag{2}$$

Here we have an equation relating what the household can control (the marginal utilities) to what is given to it by the market (the market prices).

The derivation of the household's demand curve

To derive the household's demand curve for a commodity we need only ask what happens when there is a change in the price of that commodity. To do this for, say, carrots, we take equation (2) and let X stand for carrots and Y for all other commodities. We also assume that carrots take up such a small proportion of the consumer's total expenditure that the marginal utilities of all other goods are unaffected when the household spends a little more or a little less on carrots. If, for example, total expenditure on carrots rises from £1 a month to £2 in response to a 10 per cent fall in price, this represents a large increase in carrot consumption, and the marginal utility of carrots must fall, but the extra pound spent on carrots will be made up by less spent on each of a hundred different commodities, and the reduction in the consumption of each of them is so small that it will have a negligible effect on their marginal utilities.

What will happen if, with all other prices constant, the price of carrots rises? The household that started from a position of equilibrium will now find itself in a situation in which

$$\frac{MU \text{ of carrots}}{MU \text{ of } Y} < \frac{\text{price of carrots}}{\text{price of } Y}. \tag{3}$$

(The symbol $<$ is read 'is less than'.)

To restore equilibrium it will buy fewer carrots, thus raising their marginal utility until once again (2) is satisfied (where X is carrots). The common sense of this is that the marginal utility of carrots *per penny* falls when their price rises. Thus if the household began with the utility of the last penny spent on carrots equal to the utility of the last penny spent on all other goods, the rise in carrot prices makes this no longer true. The household must buy fewer carrots until the marginal utility has risen to the extent that the utility of a penny spent on carrots is the same as it was before. Thus if carrot prices have doubled, the quantity purchased must be reduced until the marginal utility of carrots has doubled.

This analysis leads to the basic prediction of marginal utility theory.

> **A rise in the price of one commodity (with income and the prices of all other commodities held constant) will lead to a decrease in the quantity of the commodity demanded by each household. If this prediction is valid for each household, it is also true for all households taken together. Thus the market demand curve for every commodity will be downward sloping.**

ELASTICITY OF DEMAND: We often want to know not only the direction in which quantity demanded will change when price changes, but also by how much. When the price of eggs rises, will the consumer cut his purchases a lot or a little? If the price of eggs doubles, for example, we predict that the consumer will reduce his purchase of eggs until their marginal utility has doubled, but we do not yet know if this will be accomplished by a large or a small reduction in purchases. Figure 15.4 shows two possibilities. If eggs have a marginal utility curve such as X' that is flat over the relevant range, consumption is cut from q_1 to q_3 before the marginal utility is doubled from u_1 to u_2. Up to that point there is a clear gain in transferring expenditure from eggs to other goods. If eggs have a steep marginal utility curve over the relevant range, such as X'', only a slight reduction in purchases, from q_1 to q_2 suffices to double their marginal utility. In both cases the household reaches an equilibrium that satisfies relation (2), but in one case purchases fall by a large amount whereas in the other case, they fall only a little.

Curve X' is shown in two forms in Figure 15.4. The solid version has a higher total

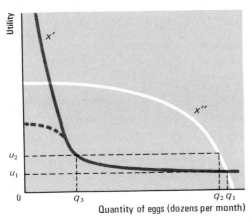

Fig. 15.4 Two alternative marginal utility schedules for eggs

utility than X'' because the utility of the first units consumed is very high. The dashed version has a much lower total utility than X''. Notice that the reactions to the rise in price are independent of the shape of the curve outside the relevant range. Curve X' could be as shown by the solid line or it could be as shown by the broken line, and the result would be the same.

This leads to the following important conclusion.

> **The response of quantity demanded to a change in price (i.e., the elasticity of demand) depends on the marginal utility over the relevant range and has no necessary relation to the total utility of the good.**

Confusion between total and marginal utilities: some examples

THE PARADOX OF VALUE: Early economists struggling with the problem of what determined the relative prices of commodities encountered what they considered to be a paradox: very necessary commodities such as water were observed to have prices that were low relative to the prices of many luxury commodities such as diamonds. These early economists argued somewhat as follows: 'Water is necessary to our very existence, whereas diamonds are a frivolous luxury that could disappear from the face of the earth tomorrow without causing any real upset. Does it not seem odd, therefore, that water is so cheap relative to diamonds?' It was seventy-five years before this apparent paradox was satisfactorily resolved, and so we should not be too surprised to find that the confusion that so long ensnared economists still persists in popular discussions today. Since its policy implications are important it is worthwhile investigating how the confusion arises.

The 'paradox of value' arose because an intuitively appealing hypothesis is obviously refuted by any number of day-to-day observations. The early economists believed that expensive goods should be ones with high total utilities and cheap goods ones with low total utilities. They were thus arguing that market values should be related to total utilities. These economists referred to market values as *exchange values* and to total utilities as *use values*. They posed their problem by saying that use values should be, but were observed not to be, related to exchange values.

The hypothesis compares the total market value of two commodities with their total utilities.[1] A precise statement of it would be:

$$\frac{p \times q \text{ of diamonds}}{p \times q \text{ of water}} = \frac{\text{total utility of diamonds}}{\text{total utility of water}}. \tag{4}$$

This relation does not hold in the real world since the total utility of diamonds is always less than the total utility of water while at many times and places the total market value of diamonds traded exceeds the total market value of water.

We have seen already that we do not expect market behaviour to have any relation to total utility. When, in Figure 15.4, the price of eggs doubled, for example, the

---

1 We cannot relate the total utilities of two commodities simply to their relative market *prices*, since we can make the latter be anything we want by choosing our units appropriately. For example, a bushel of diamonds is expensive relative to a gallon of water, but a small industrial diamond is cheap relative to a million gallons of purified water.

reaction of quantity demanded was the same with the broken marginal utility curve X' as with the solid X' curve. Yet these two curves imply very different total utilities of eggs. The paradox of value is thus explained by saying that relation (3) is not a valid deduction from the assumption that households are utility maximizers. Utility maximization depends on equating market prices with marginal utilities (equation 2), not total market values with total utilities (equation 4).

To see this intuitively, remember that water is cheap because there is so much of it that people consume it to the point at which its *marginal* utility is very low, and they are not prepared to pay a high price to obtain a little more of it. Diamonds are very expensive because they are scarce (the owners of diamond mines keep diamonds scarce by limiting output), and people have to stop consuming them at a point where marginal utility is still high. Thus people are prepared to pay a high price for an additional diamond.[1]

NECESSITIES, LUXURIES AND TOTAL UTILITY: The general public tends to rank goods on a scale as luxuries or necessities. Students usually do the same and often expect to find market behaviour bearing some relation to this classification. The argument might proceed somewhat as follows: 'There are certain commodities, called luxuries, that have low total utilities. Since they can easily be dispensed with they have highly elastic demands because, when their prices rise, consumers can stop purchasing them. There are other commodities, called necessities, that are essential to life and have high total utilities. These commodities have almost completely inelastic demands because, when their prices rise, the consumer has no choice but to continue to buy them. Many goods fall into one or other of these classes, entertainment being an example of a luxury and food an example of a necessity.'

The trouble with this hypothesis is that it tries to predict elasticity, which is the reaction of the quantity demanded to a small change in price, from a knowledge of total utilities. But as we saw above, elasticity is related to marginal, not total, utility. The hypothesis is not a valid inference from the theory of household utility maximization. Persons who predict relative demand elasticities on the basis solely of relative total utilities can thus be expected to be wrong as often as they are right, since we do not expect elasticities and total utilities to be related one way or the other.

PRICING POLICIES RELATED TO TOTAL UTILITIES: There is very little doubt that the emotional reaction of people to goods is in response to their total utilities rather than to their marginal ones. We often hear an argument such as the following: 'Water is a necessity of life, and it would be wrong to make people pay for it.' Such views often produce curious results. If, for example, water is provided free instead of at a modest cost, the additional consumption that will occur will be on account of the many uses that yield a relatively low utility (such as letting the water run while cleaning one's teeth and one's car). The relevant question when deciding between a

---

1 If you consider a cut in the price of a good with an elasticity of demand of less than unity you will realize that use value and market value can vary in *opposite* directions. In such cases the increased quantity consumed results in a higher total utility but the less than proportionate increase in quantity results in a lower total market value (price *times* quantity).

zero and a modest price for water is not 'Is water so necessary that we would not want to deprive anyone of *all* of it?' but rather 'Are the marginal uses of water which our policy will encourage so necessary that we want to encourage them in spite of the fact that it is costly to provide the water for these uses?' Clearly, these two questions can be given different answers.

Evidence about the consumption of water at various prices suggests that the marginal utility curve for water is shaped somewhat like the curve in Figure 15.2, so that much more water is consumed at a zero price than at a modest positive price. This additional water has an opportunity cost since its provision requires resources. If the utility of the commodities foregone is higher than the utility of the extra water consumed, then people are worse off as a result of receiving water free. A charge for water would release resources from water production to produce goods that yield a higher utility. [1]

The observation that some minimum quantity of water is so important that no one should be deprived of it is quite irrelevant to the policy decision about whether to provide water free or at a modest price. One may, indeed, wish to provide some minimum of water free to the very poor, but this would not be the primary effect of making water generally free. Extreme caution should be used in basing policies on a consideration of total utilities. Usually, if not always, it is marginal utilities that are relevant, rather than total utilities.

THE MEASUREMENT OF TOTAL UTILITIES BY ATTITUDE SURVEYS: Consider the type of attitude surveys that are so popular these days in sociology and political science. These surveys take the form of asking such questions as:

'Do you prefer blondes or brunettes?'

'Do you like the Conservatives more than the Socialists?'

'In deciding to live in area A rather than B what factors influenced your choice? List the following in order of importance: neighbours, schools, closeness to swimming area, price, quality of house, amount of free land, play areas for children, general amenities.'

'In choosing a university what factors were important to you? List in order of importance; environment, academic excellence, residential facilities, parents' opinion, school opinion, sports facilities, clubs.'

The reader of the Sunday papers and popular books will be able to add many other examples to their list (all of which are drawn from real cases rather than the author's imagination). *All of the above surveys, and most of the others the reader will be able to add, attempt to measure total rather than marginal utilities.* [2] There is, of course, nothing wrong with this *per se*. Anyone is free to measure anything that interests him and in some cases knowledge of total utilities may be of practical value. But in many cases actual behaviour will, as we have already seen, be determined by marginal utilities, and if one attempts to predict such behaviour from a (correct) knowledge of total utilities one will be hopelessly in error.

1 Against this, of course, would have to be set the cost of metering water consumption and collecting the accounts.

2 I am indebted to Professor G.C. Archibald for making this penetrating point when we were discussing the practical value of a particular attitude survey.

Where the behaviour being predicted involves an either-or decision, such as a vote for the Socialist or the Conservative candidate, the total utility that is attached to each party or candidate will indeed be what matters, because the voters are choosing one or the other. Where the decision is a marginal one between a little more or a little less, however, total utility is not what will determine behaviour.

We shall consider two examples in which the correct measurement of total utilities leads to incorrect predictions about actual behaviour.

Assume that University X is disturbed that its staff is spread around over many far flung villages so that there is no tendency for an 'academic community' to develop nearby the University site. Some sociologists are employed to study the causes of this, and the researchers conduct the third study suggested above (of course it will be more detailed than we have suggested). Assume that they find that most people have located away from the University in order to be near the sea, being influenced by the proximity of swimming for themselves and their children. The University wants to attract new staff members to locate close to the site; will it suffice to build swimming facilities on the University housing estate?

The surveyors have measured the relative total utilities of the quantities of the various attributes actually consumed. The quantity consumed is of course a function of the price. If swimming is free, as it is at the seaside, the total utility from it may be large. But if a charge is to be levied for it (and somehow the University must recoup the cost of providing swimming pools on its estate) the total utility people will then get from it depends on the shape of their marginal utility curve. If typical curves are like curve A in Figure 15.5, then at even a modest price people would consume no swimming and would *not* be attracted to an area which provided such facilities at a price in excess of the marginal valuation they placed on the first unit consumed. If the curve is like B, then at a modest price total consumption would not be much less than when the price was zero and total utility would remain quite high.

Much more can be said but the above should be enough to show that the knowledge provided by these surveys is little guide to the policy makers in deciding how to

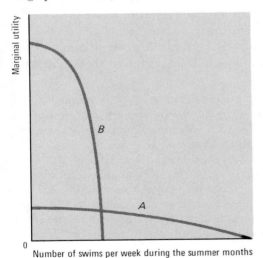

Fig. 15.5 Two alternative marginal utility curves for swimming for a typical household

attract staff back to the proximity of the University. On the other hand, two relevant questions are 'How much less would the price of housing have to be near the site to lead you to locate here rather than near the sea (i.e., what is the money value you place on the *margin of advantage* of the seaside location over a nearby one)? and '*At existing prices*, by how much would we have to change the attractions of the nearby location to make you move from the seaside?' Both of these are marginal questions. All too often social investigators think that by measuring total utilities (at existing prices) they can infer something about what is needed to change behaviour (at unspecified prices).

Now consider the second example. A recent newspaper poll in an American town showed that two thirds of the voters rated its (good) school system as one of its important assets. Yet in a subsequent election the voters turned down a school bond issue. Is this irrational behaviour (as the newspaper editorials charged)? Does it show a biased sample in the poll? It demonstrates neither. The poll measured the people's assessment of the total utility derived from the school system, while the bond-issue vote depended on the people's assessments of the marginal utility of a little more money spent on the school system. There is, of course, nothing contradictory in any-one feeling that the total utility of the city's fine school system is very large, but that the city has other needs that have a higher marginal utility than further money spent on school construction.

The 'law' of diminishing marginal utility of income [1]

So far we have been discussing the hypothesis of diminishing marginal utility from the consumption of successive units of a single commodity. It is often stated that it is a 'law' of economics that the utility or satisfaction gained from the expenditure of an extra pound's worth of income diminishes steadily as income rises. Thus, it may be stated that an extra pound of income will increase a man's satisfaction more when he is poor than it will when he is rich.

If the 'law' is a testable proposition, then it must tell us that some things can happen in the world while other things cannot happen. In order to see if this is the case, let us imagine how we might go about refuting it. Assume, for example, that we go to an individual and ask him if his satisfactions from spending additional units of income have diminished as his income rose. The individual might then tell us the following story:

I suffer from stomach trouble which results in intense agony after every meal; in fact I positively dislike eating. Also I seldom notice my surroundings so I don't much care where I live. However, my doctor tells me I must eat well to keep my stomach functioning at all, and it is necessary to live in a tolerably comfortable place in order to keep healthy. Thus, when I had a very low income I spent most of it on food and shelter, and derived very little satisfaction from so doing. After my income rose beyond a certain level, I was able to afford a few small luxuries and these brought me real pleasure; when my income rose still further, I was able to buy large items of luxury; a fast car, holidays abroad and a telescope to pursue my hobby of amateur astronomy. Clearly, the satisfaction that I receive from the expenditure of additional increments of income has been increasing steadily as my income has risen.

1 This section can be omitted without interrupting the flow of the argument.

Now, how might a defender of the 'law' of diminishing utility of income react to this attack? There is one very common defence which needs careful attention here. Let us imagine a supporter of the 'law' replying as follows:

This person is only fooling himself. If he really got more satisfaction from his luxuries than from food and shelter, he would have bought the luxuries when he was poor. His behaviour shows that he values his health more than the other satisfactions that he mentions. The fact that he chose food and shelter in preference to these luxuries *proves* that he gets more utility from the food and shelter.

Now this appears to be a very strong defence, but let us see what effect it has on our 'law'. The 'law' states that successive increments of income bring progressively diminishing utility *because* they are used to purchase goods which bring successively smaller amounts of utility. How do we know which goods bring the consumer most utility? We do this by observing which goods he purchases when his income is low. But if we state that the consumer will choose first the goods which bring him most utility and define the goods which bring him most utility to be those which he chooses first, we have done nothing more than to discover our own definitions; we have uttered a tautology which is compatible with *any* state of the universe.

Clearly such a defence of the 'law' reduces it to a useless tautology; it does not matter what consumers do; no matter how masochistic, selfless or selfish, rational or irrational they are, all behaviour is compatible with this tautology. Clearly, if the 'law' is to tell us something about the world, we need to have an independent indicator of utility or satisfaction. If we have this, we can then say 'good A gives this consumer more satisfaction than does good B (at equivalent prices) and we therefore predict that he will buy good A when his income is low, and good B only when his income rises'. In the absence of such a measure of utility, we have no theory at all. Until a measure has been put forward, and until the predictions of the theory have been tested against observed consumers' behaviour, it is extremely misleading even to talk about the 'law' of diminishing marginal utility of income, in fact it is not even clear that we are making a positive (i.e., potentially testable) statement when we say that the marginal utility of money is declining.[1]

REVEALED PREFERENCE THEORY

We now discuss the theory of household behaviour called revealed preference. We shall use this theory to distinguish between what is called an income effect and a substitution effect of a price change, which is a distinction we have not yet made, and then to give an alternative derivation of the downward sloping household demand curve based not on the assumption of diminishing marginal utility but rather on the assumption that the household behaves consistently.

---

1 It is not my purpose in this section to reject the hypothesis of diminishing marginal utility of income. All that I wish to do in the text is to make the general point that unless we are very careful, we can argue in a circle, thereby making our statement true by definition, which robs it of all empirical content (i.e., it then says nothing about the world) and makes it uninteresting for positive economics.

A change in relative prices: the income and substitution effects

We now wish to investigate in more detail the consequences of a change in relative prices. We consider a household whose initial budget line is *ab* in Figure 15.6 and assume that initially it chooses the combination indicated by the point α (*v* of *Y* and *s* of *X*). Now assume that the price of *X* falls, the money price of *Y* and the household's income remaining constant. The new set of possibilities open to the household is indicated by the budget line *ac*. Assume that the household now chooses the combination β (*t* of *Y* and *u* of *X*) from all of those available to it. More of both *X* and *Y* are consumed.

Now it is possible, and it turns out to be useful, to analyse this movement from α to β into two constituent parts, one called the SUBSTITUTION EFFECT and the other called the INCOME EFFECT. It will be noted that this fall in the price of *X* does have something of the same effect as a change in income because it makes it possible for the household, if it so wishes, to have more of all commodities. In Figure 15.6 the price fall makes the total shaded area newly available; combinations indicated by points within this area were not available at the original set of prices. Points within area (1) indicate newly available combinations containing more *Y* but less *X* than was being consumed at α. Points within area (2) indicate newly available combinations containing more *X* but less *Y* than was consumed at α. Points within area (3), however, indicate newly available combinations containing more *X* and more *Y* than was consumed at α.

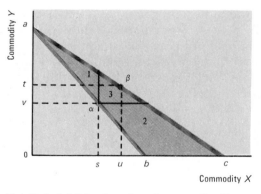

Fig. 15.6 A fall in the price of commodity *X*   Fig. 15.7 The income and the substitution effect

We are considering a fall in the price of *X* and the movement of the household from α to β. What we now wish to do is to break up this movement into two parts, one due to the pure change in relative prices and the second due to the income effect (the household being able to have more of all goods). To do this we can imagine ourselves reducing the household's income until there is no income effect of the change in price – i.e., until it is no longer able to consume more of all goods than it was consuming originally. To do this we reduce its income until, *at the new set of prices*, it is just able to buy its original bundle of goods. Graphically, reducing income with relative prices constant means that the line *ac* slides inwards towards the origin, parallel to itself until it passes through the point α. This is shown in Figure 15.7 by the broken line $a'c'$.

The total effect of this price change may now be broken up into the income and the substitution effects.

(1) X becomes cheaper relative to Y but simultaneously income is reduced, so that the household can just buy the bundle of goods that it was buying originally. The household may move from α to some other point on $a'c'$, say the point ε. The change in the quantity of X purchased (from q to m) is defined as the substitution effect; it is the effect solely of a change in relative prices. Generally we expect the household to buy more of the relatively cheaper good, X.

(2) Relative prices are now held constant at their new level and the household's income is returned. Graphically the budget line is moved outwards, parallel to itself, until it is returned to the position ac. The movement from the intermediate position ε to the final position β is defined as the income effect; mn more of X is bought because, with relative prices constant, the household's income rises. In practice, of course, the household moves directly from α to β. Our theory, however, says that demand is a function both of relative prices and of real income. A change in the money price of one good changes both relative prices and real income and what we have done here is to separate out the effects of the two changes.

The direction of the substitution effect

We are now able to derive the basic prediction of revealed preference theory:

> **The substitution effect can never cause a reduction in purchases of the commodity whose price has fallen.**

To derive this prediction we introduce the behavioural hypothesis that the household always acts consistently. This makes it necessary to define carefully the idea to which we are attaching the word 'consistent'. Once we know the household's income and the market prices facing it, we know the combinations of goods which it is possible for the household to choose; these will be all the points on, or inside, its budget line. In Figure 15.8 the combinations available to the household are those within, or on the border of, the shaded triangle Oab. (For simplicity we shall speak of the points *in* the triangle Oab.) The household must choose one combination out of all those open to it. We denote the actual combination chosen by z and the *whole set of combinations rejected* by S. (S thus stands for *all* points in the triangle Oab other than the point z.) We now define consistent behaviour as follows: *if the household chooses the combination z in preference to all the combinations in S it will never subsequently choose any combination from S in a situation in which z is also available.*

Let us now consider a fall in the price of X accompanied by a sufficient reduction in the household's income so that it can just purchase its original combination of goods indicated by the point z. In Figure 15.8, the budget line moves from ab to $a'c'$. Now the household can choose any point on the budget line $a'c'$. Consider first the segment za' of this new budget line. Points to the left of z were available in the first situation; they are therefore part of the set S which was originally rejected in favour of z. Since z is still available in the new situation it follows from our consistency assumption that z cannot be rejected in favour of any point on the segment $a'z$. On the other hand points on the segment zc' lie outside the original set S; they were not available in the original position and there is thus no inconsistency in choosing any point to the right of z in preference to z. Thus the household either stays at z or moves to the right along the segment zc' which means that, either it consumes the same amount of X (the good whose price has fallen), or it consumes more of it. We conclude therefore that, given our assumptions, the substitution effect can never lead the household to buy less of the commodity whose price has fallen. Since price and quantity cannot move in the same direction, we say that the substitution effect is non-positive.

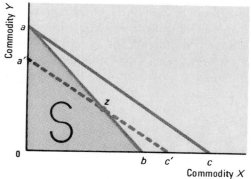

Fig. 15.8 Proof that the substitution effect is non-positive

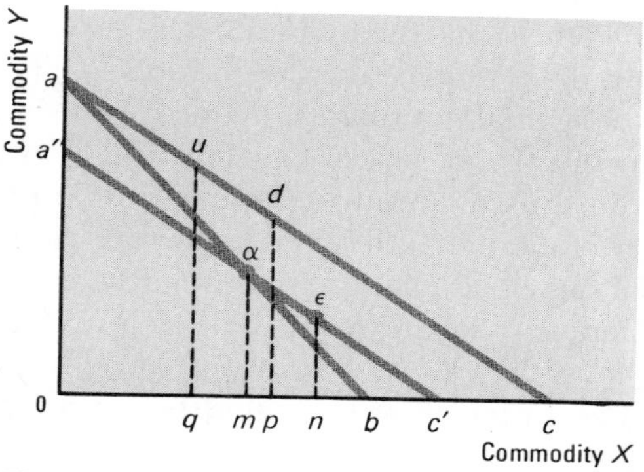

Fig. 15.9 Negative income effects

THE SLOPE OF A HOUSEHOLD'S DEMAND CURVE: We have seen that, when the price of X falls, there is an income effect as well as a substitution effect. If X has an income elasticity of demand greater than zero (i.e., it is not an inferior good) the income effect will lead to an increase in the purchases of X (the point β will lie to the right of the point ϵ in Figure 15.7). Since the substitution effect cannot be positive, an income elasticity of demand larger than zero is sufficient to ensure that more X will be purchased when its price falls (i.e., the point β lies to the right of the point α in Figure 15.7).

> **This means that the demand curve, which shows the quantity of X demanded at alternative prices of X, will slope downward to the right.**

On the other hand, a negative income elasticity is not sufficient to ensure that the household will buy less of the good when its price falls; this will only happen if the negative income effect is *large enough* to outweigh the substitution effect. In Figure 15.9 we have illustrated two cases of a negative income effect. The initial budget line is ab and the household's initial position is at α, purchases of X being m. The price of X now falls so that the budget line shifts to ac. To measure the substitution effect we reduce income until the household is just able to buy its original combination of X and Y indicated by the point α; this gives the budget line $a'c'$. Assume that it now buys the bundle indicated by ε, purchasing mn more X on account of the substitution effect. Assume further that X is an inferior good so that the income effect will be negative, and examine two possible cases. In the first case the income effect causes the household to move from ε to d on the new budget line ac. It buys np less X on account of the income effect, but this is not sufficient to overcome the substitution effect, *and the household is observed to increase its purchases of X by mp as a result of the fall in its price.* In the second case, the income effect is stronger and the household moves from ε to u as a result of the rise in its income, thus reducing purchases of X by an amount nq. *The household will be observed to reduce its purchases of X from m to q as a result of the fall in price.* [1]

We conclude, therefore, that, on the assumption that the household acts consistently as defined above, its demand curve for any product will be downward sloping unless the income effect is negative (the good is inferior) and of sufficient magnitude [2] to overcome the substitution effect.

The terminology of the reaction of demand to income changes is not standardized and can be confusing. In Table 15.1 we present a table of equivalents which should help the reader to understand overlapping terminology.

Table 15.1 Terminology used to describe the reaction of the quantity demanded to a change in income

Numerical measure of income elasticity	Verbal description of income elasticity	Income effect	Type of good
$\eta_y < 0$	negative	negative	inferior
$0 < \eta_y < 1$	positive but inelastic	positive	normal
$1 < \eta_y < \infty$	positive and elastic	positive	normal

CONSUMER RATIONALITY

It is often said that economic theory is based on the assumption of rational behaviour. There are three points that need to be made in this context. First, rational behaviour is often used in a value sense to say that certain forms of behaviour (called rational ones) are better than others (called 'irrational' ones). Second, if rational is meant in a positive rather than a normative sense, then it is very difficult to establish by casual observation that certain behaviour is not rational. Third, if by rational we mean 'consistent' behaviour then such an assumption is necessary not only for economics but for any subject which attempts to build theories about human behaviour. Let us consider these points one at a time.

Positive economics cannot assert that certain forms of consumer satisfaction are rational while other forms are irrational. We cannot demonstrate, for example, that

1 This case in which a fall in price lowers the consumption of a commodity is called the Giffen case, after the Victorian economist Sir Robert Giffen who is reputed to have observed an actual example of it. The significance of this Giffen case is considered at some length in the next chapter.

2 The income effect of a given price change depends partly on the importance of the commodity in the household's budget. If, for example, the household's income is £1,000 per annum and it is spending £10 (i.e., 1 per cent of its income) on some commodity, then a 50 per cent fall in the price of the commodity is equivalent to allowing it to purchase the original bundle and raising its income by £5 per annum, i.e., by $\frac{1}{2}$ of 1 per cent.

it is sensible or rational for the consumer to derive satisfaction from consuming a good in isolation and silly or irrational for him to derive satisfaction from showing the good off to his neighbours and boasting about how much he paid for it. Positive economics can be used to analyse any form of known consumer behaviour no matter how immoral, misguided or chauvinistic it may seem to be to the person conducting the analysis.

If by rational behaviour we mean something like choosing appropriate means to arrive at given ends, then this is something that economists, and others can study. It is important to notice, however, that it is by no means easy to discover by casual observation that a certain behaviour pattern is irrational. It is sometimes said, for example, that it is irrational for the consumer to judge the quality of an article by its price. Certainly the consumer who does this can occasionally be very greatly misled. The typical consumer can, however, have only very imperfect knowledge of the wide range of articles from which he has to choose. If he trusts his own amateur technical knowledge, he may sometimes go very badly astray. It *may* well be that price is in fact the best single indicator of quality available to the consumer. Such an index is un-doubtedly less than perfect, but a consumer who used it consistently *might* do better on average than a consumer who used his own judgement based on incomplete and often mistaken technical knowledge. If this were the case, we would have to conclude that the consumer who judged quality by price was rational in the sense defined, even though we might sometimes observe him making mistakes. The moral to this story is that it is very difficult, by looking at the very best means of making a few choices, to decide what is a rational means of choosing when one is faced with the need to make a great many choices based on an imperfect knowledge of a complex world.

Finally, if by rational we mean consistent (i.e., the individual does not have contradictory preferences), then any *theory* of behaviour necessarily assumes this, for, if we make inconsistent assumptions about the consumer's preferences, we will have no theory at all but a set of contradictory propositions. Thus, to say that we assume consistency (i.e., rationality) is only to say that we have a theory. The extent to which people do behave consistently in the real world is, as we have already seen in Chapter 1, a matter that can only be established by careful, detailed observation.[1]

1 The beginner need not worry very much about this paragraph. The idea contained in it does, however, help to dismiss a lot of misguided criticism of economics. The advanced student should notice however that the use of the word consistent here is different from that in the revealed preference theory on page 175. The general rationality principle in this section is that the person should act consistently *in respect to the variables that do influence his action*. This very general statement is given empirical content when we specify the variables that do influence his action. In revealed preference theory, as in other theories of demand, the number of variables is severely restricted and all the consumer is assumed to care about is the quantities of the various commodities that he consumes. The consumer is then assumed to take consistent decisions with respect solely to the quantities of the commodities available to him. To take an example, the consistency assumption on page 175 would be refuted if the consumer cared not only about what he gets but also about who sold it to him, and in situation (1) he took z and rejected the other points in S because he liked the man selling the bundle z and in situation (2) he took some other point from S even though z were available because he did not like the new salesman for the bundle z. This does not violate the general rationality principle discussed in the text above, but it does violate the revealed preference consistency assumption because the latter amounts to assuming that nothing influences the consumer other than the quantities he is able to consume.

Appendix

Indifference theory

In utility theory, we start by asking what happens to the consumer's satisfactions if he consumes more or less of one commodity. In indifference theory, we start by asking a different, but quite closely related question: 'If the household is consuming two commodities, how much more of one commodity must we give it to compensate for reducing its consumption of the other commodity by some small amount?' To parallel the questions with which we opened our discussion of utility theory, we now ask: 'How many extra movies would you need to see per month to compensate you for reducing your consumption of water by 35 gallons per month?' We can interpret the term *compensate* to mean 'leave your total utility unchanged by the change in goods and services consumed' or, in other words, 'leave you indifferent as to a choice between the two alternative sets of goods and services'.

An indifference curve

Let us say that the household starts with some quantity of each of two goods, say 10 units of food and 18 of clothing. We refer to such a set of quantities as a combination (or bundle) of goods.

We now offer the household some alternative bundle of goods, say 15 units of food and 13 of clothing. This alternative has 5 fewer units of clothing and 5 more of food than the first one. Whether the household prefers this bundle to the first one depends on the relative valuation that it places on 5 more units of food and 5 fewer units of clothing. If it values the extra food more than the foregone clothing, it will prefer the new bundle to the original one. If it values the food less than the clothing, it will prefer the original bundle to the new one. There is a third alternative. The household may value the extra food the same as it values the foregone clothing. If this were the case, the household would gain equal satisfaction from the two alternative bundles of food and clothing. In other words, the household is *indifferent* between the two bundles.

Now let us try further alternatives. Suppose, after much trial and error, we have identified a number of bundles, all of which give equal satisfaction and among which the household will thus be indifferent. The bundles identified are shown in Table 15.2.

These bundles are graphed in Figure 15.10. There will, of course, be other combinations of the two commodities that will give the same level of satisfaction to the household. All of these combinations are shown in the figure by the smooth curve that passes through the points plotted from the table. This curve is called an *indifference curve*.

Any points above and to the right of the

Table 15.2 Combinations of food and clothing that give equal satisfaction to a hypothetical household

Combination	Clothing	Food
a	30	5
b	18	10
c	13	15
d	10	20
e	8	25
f	7	30

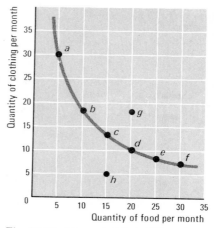

Fig. 15.10 A household's indifference curve showing combinations of food and clothing that yield equal satisfaction and among which the household is indifferent

curve show combinations of food and clothing that the household would prefer to combinations indicated by points on the curve. Consider, for example, the combination of 20 units of food and 18 clothing, which is represented by point g in the figure. Although it might not be obvious that this bundle must be preferred to bundle a (which has more clothing but less food), it is obvious that it will be preferred to bundle c, because there is both less clothing and less food represented at c than at g. Inspection of the graph shows that *any* point above the curve will be obviously superior to *some* points on the curve in the sense that it will contain both more food and more clothing than those points on the curve. But since all points on the curve are equal in the household's eyes, the point above the curve must thus be superior to *all* points on the curve. By a similar argument, points below and to the left of the curve represent bundles of goods that are inferior to bundles represented by points on the curve.

THE HYPOTHESIS OF A DIMINISHING RATE OF SUBSTITUTION: Now look closely at the shape of the indifference curve in Figure 15.10. The downward slope of this curve indicates that, if the household has its clothing purchases reduced, it must have its food purchases increased if its overall level of satisfaction is to remain constant. Not only is the indifference curve downward sloping, it is also convex viewed from the origin (i.e., the slope becomes flatter and flatter as one moves down and to the right).

This convex shape represents the basic hypothesis of indifference theory. *The hypothesis of a diminishing rate of substitution* says that the less of one good and the more of another that a household has, the less willing it will be to give up some of the first good to get further units of the second good.

The example of clothing and food illustrates this hypothesis. We start by imagining the household moving from the combinations a through f that were shown in Table 15.2 (and graphed in Figure 15.10). When the household moves from a to b, it gives up 12 units of clothing and gains 5 units of food; it remains at the same level of overall satisfaction. The household at point a was prepared to sacrifice 12 clothing for 5 food (i.e., 12/5 = 2·4 units of clothing per unit of food obtained). When the household moves from b to c, it sacrifices 5 clothing for 5 food (this involves a rate of substitution of one unit of clothing for each unit of food). These calculations, together with similar ones for movements through the points $d, e,$ and f, are shown in Table 15.3.

The last column shows the rate at which the household is prepared to sacrifice clothing per unit of food obtained. At first, the household will sacrifice 2·4 units of clothing to get one more unit of food, but as its con-

Table 15.3 Rate of substitution of clothing for food

Movement	Change in clothing	Change in food	Rate of substitution = $\dfrac{\text{Change in clothing}}{\text{Change in food}}$
From a to b	−12	5	−2·4
From b to c	− 5	5	−1·0
From c to d	− 3	5	− ·6
From d to e	− 2	5	− ·4
From e to f	− 1	5	− ·2

sumption of clothing diminishes and that of food increases, the household becomes less and less willing to sacrifice further clothing for more food, and finally, when it moves from e to f, it is willing to sacrifice only one fifth of a unit of clothing for an extra unit of food.

We have looked at movements between widely separated points on the indifference curve. If we think of making a very small movement from any of the points on the curve, the rate at which the household will give up clothing to get food is called the MARGINAL RATE OF SUBSTITUTION and is shown by the slope of the tangent to the curve at that point.[1] The tangent at a tells us the rate at which the household will sacrifice clothing per unit of food obtained when it is currently consuming 30 clothing and 5 food (the co-ordinates of point a). As we move down the curve from a to f, the slope of the curve diminishes. This shows that the more food and the less clothing the household has, the less willing it will be to sacrifice further clothing to get more food.

The indifference map

So far we have constructed but a single indifference curve. There must, however, be a similar curve through every point in Figure

1 The ratios shown in Table 15.3 are the slopes of the chords joining the two points on the indifference curves. As point b is moved closer to point a, for example, the slope of the relevant chord approaches the slope of the tangent to the curve at a. (See a similar discussion concerning elasticities in the appendix to Chapter 10, pages 114–15.)

15.10. If we start at point g, which corresponds to 18 units of clothing and 20 units of food, there will be other combinations that will yield satisfaction to the household and, if we connect the points indicating all of *these* combinations, we will obtain an indifference curve through g. Similarly, we could find all the combinations of food and clothing that gave that household a level of satisfaction equal to what is obtained from the bundle represented by point h in Figure 15.10. If we plotted the points corresponding to these bundles and connected them, we would obtain an indifference curve through point h. We can repeat this exercise as many times as we wish and generate as many indifference curves as we wish. The farther away any indifference curve is from the origin, the higher is the level of satisfaction given by any of the combinations of goods indicated by points on the curve.

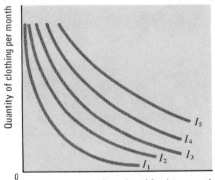

Fig. 15.11 An indifference map for a household: the higher the number on the curve, the higher the level of satisfaction indicated by all of the points on that curve

A set of indifference curves is called an IN-DIFFERENCE MAP, an example of which is shown in Figure 15.11. It specifies the household's tastes by showing its rate of substitution between the two commodities for every level of current consumption of these commodities. When economists say that a household's tastes are *given*, they do not mean merely that the household's current consumption pattern is given; rather they mean that the household's entire indifference map is given.

THE EQUILIBRIUM OF THE HOUSEHOLD

An indifference map describes the preferences of households. The budget line (see pages 151–2) describes the possibilities open to the household, given its money income and the money prices of commodities. We can represent the budget line on an indifference map. If we assume, for example, that the household has an income of £75 a month, that food costs £3 a unit, and that clothing costs £2·5 a unit, the household's budget line takes the position of the straight line shown in Figure 15.12. Any point on the

line can be attained. Which one will the satisfaction-maximizing household actually choose?

Suppose that it starts at point *a* in Figure 15.12, where it is on indifference curve I_1. If it moves to point *b*, it is still just on its budget line, but it has moved to a preferred position – i.e., to a combination of goods on a higher indifference curve than the first combination. The household can continue this process, moving down the budget line through point *c* and attaining higher curves until it reaches point *d*. If it moves further, however, to points *e*, *f*, and *g*, it will begin to move to lower indifference curves.

If we start the household at a point to the right of *d*, say at *g*, the same argument will apply: the household can attain higher curves by moving up its budget line to the left. As it moves, it attains higher curves until it reaches *d*, but if it persists beyond *d*, it moves to lower curves. This leads to the following conclusion:

Satisfaction is maximized at the point at which an indifference curve is tangent to a budget line. At such a position the slope of the indifference curve (the marginal rate of substitution of the goods in the household's preferences) is the same as the slope of the budget line (the marginal rate of substitution in the market).

The common sense of this result is that, if the household values goods at a different rate than the market does, there is room for profitable exchange. The household can give up the good it values below the market and take in return the good it values more highly than the market does. When the household is prepared to swap goods at the same rate as they can be traded on the market, there is no further opportunity for it to raise its utility by substituting one commodity for the other.

Notice that this result is very similar to the one we had with marginal-utility theory. The household is presented with market information (prices) that it cannot itself change. It adjusts to these prices by choosing a bundle

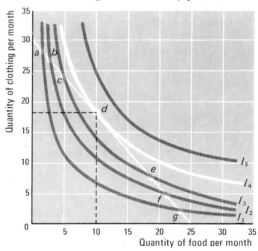

Fig. 15.12 The equilibrium of a household. The household has an income of £75 a month, faces prices of £2·5 a unit for clothing and £3 for food, and is in equilibrium at *d*, where it consumes 10 units of food and 18 of clothing and has reached its highest attainable indifference curve

of goods such that, at the margin, its own subjective evaluation of the goods conforms with the evaluations given by market prices.

We have so far described graphically the nature of satisfaction-maximizing equilibrium for a household that knows its tastes and the market conditions facing it. Let us now use this apparatus to study the effect on the household of changes in its income and in the market prices of the commodities that it purchases.

THE REACTION OF THE HOUSEHOLD TO A CHANGE IN INCOME: A change in income leads to parallel shifts of the budget line – inward towards the origin when income falls, and outward away from the origin when income rises (see page 153). For each level of income there will, of course, be an equilibrium position at which an indifference curve is tangent to the relevant budget line. Each such equilibrium position means that the household is doing as well as it possibly can for that level of income. If we move the budget line through all possible levels of income, and if we join up all the points of equilibrium, we will trace out what is called an income-consumption line, an example of which is shown in Figure 15.13. This line shows how consumption bundles change as income changes, with relative prices held constant.[1]

THE REACTION TO A CHANGE IN PRICE: We saw in the previous chapter that a change in the relative prices of the two goods changed the slope of the budget line. Assume now that the money price of food falls, the money price of clothing being held constant. This is shown by the pivoting of the budget line in Figure 15.14 from *ab* to *ac* to *ad*. The household moves from position *e* to position *e'* to *e"*. If we now vary the price of food continuously,

1 We can use this income-consumption line to derive the curve relating consumption of one commodity to income that we first introduced on page 78. To do this, we merely take the quantity of either good consumed at the equilibrium position on a given budget line and plot it against the level of money income that determined the position of the particular budget line. By repeating this for each level of income, we produce the required curve.

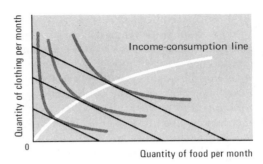

Fig. 15.13 The income-consumption line showing the reaction of the household to changes in its money income with money prices constant

we will find an equilibrium position for each price, and by connecting these, we trace out what is called a price-consumption line. This line shows how consumption of the two goods varies as the price of one changes, the price of the other and the household's money income being held constant. Such a line is shown in Figure 15.14.

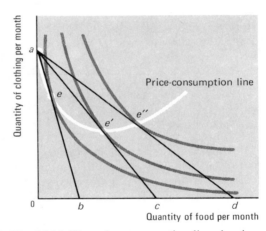

Fig. 15.14 The price-consumption line showing the reaction of the household to changes in the price of food with the price of clothing and money income held constant

The individual household's demand for a commodity

To derive the household's demand curve for any commodity we need to depart from our world of two commodities. We are interested in what happens to the household's demand for some commodity, say carrots, as the price of that commodity changes, *all other prices being held constant* (see page 75). We plot a new indifference map in Figure 15.15 in which we represent the quantity of carrots on the horizontal axis and the value of all other goods consumed on the vertical axis. The indifference curves tell us the rate at which the household is prepared to swap carrots for money (which allows it to buy all other goods) at each level of consumption of carrots and of other goods.

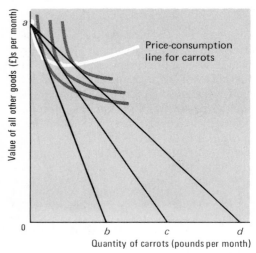

Fig. 15.15 The derivation of a household's demand for carrots

We now take the household's income and plot it on the money axis, so that in Figure 15.15 the household has £a of income per period (months in this case) and is thus able to consume £a worth of all other goods, if it keeps its carrot consumption at zero. Given the money price of carrots and the household's income, we obtain a budget line showing all those combinations of carrots and other goods that the household can consume. We now change the money price of carrots (thus changing the slope of the budget line through a). By joining the points of equilibrium, we trace out a price-consumption line between carrots and all other commodities in just the same way as we traced out such a line for food and clothing in Figure 15.14.

Note that Figure 15.15 is very similar to Figure 15.14. The axes are labelled differently and the price-consumption line in Figure 15.15 is crowded into the upper part of the diagram, indicating that, whatever the price of carrots, the household does not spend a large part of its income on them.

Every point on the price-consumption line corresponds to one price and one quantity of carrots demanded. When we plot these pairs of values on a new figure with price on one axis and quantity on the other, we have the household's demand curve for carrots. In Figure 15.15 the quantity of carrots consumed increases as the price of carrots falls, so the demand curve has a downward slope.

CAN THE HOUSEHOLD'S DEMAND CURVE EVER SLOPE UPWARD? THE INCOME AND THE SUBSTITUTION EFFECT: The demand curve that we derived above had a downward slope. A fall in the price of carrots increased the quantity demanded. Is this a necessary result or merely a consequence of the way in which we happened to draw the graph? To answer this question we must distinguish between the income and the substitution effects. As we saw on page 174, a fall in the price of carrots has something of the effect of a rise in income since it makes it possible for the household to have more of all goods.

We can imagine removing this *income effect* of a price change by insisting that the household remain on its original indifference curve in spite of any change in price. A change in relative prices changes the slope of the budget line, but, if the household is to remain on its original indifference curve, money income must be changed just enough so that the budget line slides around the same curve, always remaining tangent to it.

Assume, for example, that the price of carrots is cut in half, so that the slope of the budget line becomes only half as steep, the actual line pivoting from ab to ac in Figure 15.16. The household was initially in equilibrium at point e_1 on Figure 15.16. If we adjust the position of the budget line after the

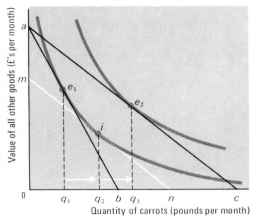

Fig. 15.16 The income and the substitution effect of a fall in the price of carrots

price fall so as to keep the household on its initial indifference curve, the new position of equilibrium is at i. (The line mn is parallel to ac, and thus its slope conforms to the new set of relative prices.) The increase in the consumption of carrots from q_1 to q_2 can be termed the *substitution effect* – the effect on carrot consumption of a fall in the price of carrots, household *utility* held constant. Because the indifference curve slopes downward to the right, it follows that a fall in the price of carrots necessarily raises the quantity bought, if the level of utility is held constant. The substitution effect is thus a negative one: a change in price leads quantity demanded to change in the opposite direction.

We have said that halving the price of carrots would cause the household to move from e_1 to i on the *same* indifference curve. But this, of course, is not what happens when the price of carrots falls in the real world. No economic dictator reduces everyone's money income to ensure that they get no increase in utility from the change. We have seen that the budget line actually pivots through a, indicating that the household could obtain more of all goods if it wished. In Figure 15.16 the new budget line is ac and the new equilibrium position is e_2. Thus, when the price falls, carrot consumption rises from q_1 to q_3. This movement can, however, be broken up conceptually into a substitution effect from

q_1 to q_2, which is the result of a change in relative prices, and the increase from q_2 to q_3 between points i and e_2, which is called the *income effect*. This income effect is equivalent to the increase in consumption from q_2 to q_3 that would have occurred owing to an outward shift in the budget line, relative prices held constant at their new level.[1]

This distinction permits a concise statement of the conditions under which the demand curve is expected to slope downward. The change in demand for one commodity in response to a change in its price can be thought of as a composite of the income and the substitution effects. The theory predicts that the substitution effect is negative. Thus a fall in the relative price of a commodity, with the level of utility held constant, leads to a rise in the demand for the commodity. Unless we expect an increase in income to lead to a reduction in consumption of the good, because it is an inferior good, the theory gives the unambiguous prediction that more of the commodity will be demanded when its price falls.

A sufficient condition of our theory to predict that the household's demand curve slopes downward is that the good

1 Notice the difference between these two effects as defined by revealed preference theory and by indifference theory. In revealed preference theory the price of X is lowered and income is reduced *until the original combination of goods can just be purchased*; any increase in the purchase of X is now ascribed to the substitution effect. In indifference theory the price of X is lowered and the household's income is reduced *until the original level of satisfaction can just be attained*; any increase in the purchase of X is then ascribed to the substitution effect. In indifference theory it is shown that the substitution effect must be negative (i.e., price and quantity must vary in opposite directions). In revealed preference theory it is shown that the substitution effect is non-positive (i.e., price and quantity cannot vary in the same direction). The difference between the statement that something is negative and that it is non-positive (i.e., zero or negative) is, for *practical* purposes, trivial. The great advantage of using the definitions in revealed preference is that they are operational. We saw in footnote 2 to page 177 that the income effect of a price change can readily be calculated in revealed preference terms, whereas it is quite immeasurable in indifference curve terms.

in question should not be an inferior one. A decrease in its price will lead to an increase in quantity demanded due both to substitution and to the increase in income.

In the case of an inferior good, however, we cannot obtain a definite prediction about what will happen. The income effect of a fall in price leads to a tendency for a decrease in the consumption of the good. But the substitution effect still works for an increase in the quantity demanded. Thus the final result depends on the relative strengths of the two effects. Two cases of a negative income effect are shown in Figure 15.17. The original equilibrium is at e_1 with q_1 pounds of carrots consumed per month. The price of carrots falls, and the pure substitution effect would move the household to i (with $q_1\ q_2$ *more* carrots consumed each month). The income effect is negative, but if it moves the household only to e'_2, the net effect is for household consumption to rise from q_1 to q_3. In the second case, the negative income effect is stronger than in the first case, and the final equilibrium is at e''_2 with the consumption of carrots falling by $q_1 - q_4$ per month as a result of the fall in the price of carrots.

We conclude from this analysis that the case of an upward-sloping demand curve for a product is a theoretical possibility. It re-

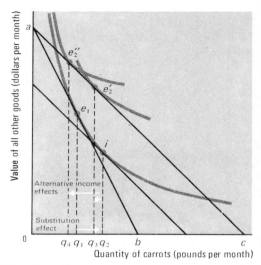

Fig. 15.17 Two alternative negative income effects for carrots. With e'_2 the demand curve for carrots still slopes downward, but with e''_2 the demand curve slopes upward

quires a change in price to have a large enough negative income effect to offset the substitution effect. We do not expect a combination of circumstances that makes this possible to occur often, and therefore we must expect an upward-sloping market demand curve to be a rare exception to the general prediction that demand curves will slope downward. We shall examine this exception further in Chapter 16.

16

The theory of demand: measurements and tests

In this chapter we shall first consider the problems that arise when we attempt to test the theory of demand. Then we consider attempts to measure quantitatively the relation between quantity demanded and prices and incomes. Finally, we go on to discuss the critical importance to economic theory of such quantitative measures.

CAN DEMAND THEORY BE TESTED?

The main problem encountered in deciding whether or not demand theory can be tested is to discover if the theory makes any predictions that are precise enough to be tested. To study this question we shall consider the relation between demand and each of the variables that are supposed to influence it; but before doing this we must dispose of one common but misguided means of testing the theory.

Testing by observing the behaviour of isolated households

It is common to criticize demand theory by arguing from personal experience that people do not always behave in the rational manner assumed by the theory. Cases in which consumers do not behave consistently can usually be multiplied from casual observation of one's self and one's acquaintances. What can we make of such observations? The answer depends on what we want demand theory to accomplish. Three uses of demand theory may be distinguished. First, we may be interested in the aggregate behaviour of all households – as graphically illustrated, for example, by the market demand curve for a product. Second, we may want to make probabilistic statements about an individual household's actions under certain circumstances. Third, we may want to make statements about what all households always do. The first-mentioned use – the aggregate use – of the theory of demand is the most common one in economics. All of the predictions developed in Chapter 11, you will recall, depend on having some knowledge of the shape of the relevant market demand curves, yet they do not require that we be able to predict the behaviour of each individual household. The second use, though much less common than the first, is sometimes important; we do sometimes want to be able to say what a single house-hold will probably do. The third use is by far the least important of the three, since it is rare that we wish to make categorical statements about what all households will always do.

Fortunately, the criticisms cited above apply only to the third use of demand theory. The observation that households sometimes behave in an inconsistent fashion would, if carefully documented, refute the prediction that *all* households *always* behave as assumed by the theory.

Neither the existence of a relatively stable downward-sloping market demand curve, nor our ability to predict what a single household will probably do requires that all households invariably behave in the manner assumed by the theory. Such fully consistent behaviour on the part of everyone at all times is sufficient but not necessary for a stable market demand curve. Consider two other possibilities. First, some households may always behave in a manner not assumed by the theory. Households whose members are mental defectives or have serious emotional disturb-ances are obvious possibilities. The inconsistent or erratic behaviour of such house-holds will not cause market demand curves for normal goods to depart from their downward slope, provided these households account for a minority of purchasers of any product. Their erratic behaviour will be swamped by the normal behaviour of the majority of households. Second, an occasional irrationality or inconsistency on the part of every household will not upset the downward slope of the market demand curve for a normal good. As long as these isolated inconsistencies are unrelated across households, occurring now in one and now in another, their effect will be swamped by the normal behaviour of the majority of households.

> **The downward slope of the demand curve requires only that at any moment of time most households are behaving as is assumed by the theory. This is quite compatible with behaviour contrary to the assump-tions of the theory on the part of some households all of the time and on the part of all households some of the time.[1]**

Thus we cannot test the theory about the behaviour of market demand by observ-ing the behaviour of only a few individual households, and we must consider what can be learned by observing such things as market demand for a product, the price of the product, other prices, and the total income of all consumers, which are the variables, that appear in our theory of market demand. This is best done by considering in turn the relationship between demand and each of the influencing variables.[2]

The relationship between demand and tastes

A change in tastes causes demand to change. The proposition that demand and tastes are related is not really testable unless we have some way of measuring a change in

1 We have relied here on intuitive argument but this result can be shown rigorously by the use of mathematics. It is desirable at this stage to review pages 9–11 on the prediction of individual and group behaviour.

2 These hypothesized relations are described in detail in Chapter 7.

tastes. We do not have an independent measure of taste changes and what we usually do is to infer them from the data for demand. We make such statements as: 'In spite of the rise in price, quantity purchased increased, so there must have been a change in tastes in favour of this commodity.' More generally, we are likely to account for all of the changes in demand that we can, in terms of prices and incomes and then assert that the residual must be due to changes in tastes (and to errors of measurement). This does not concern us unduly because we are not greatly concerned to establish precise relations between tastes and demand and we are prepared to take it as obvious from even the most casual observation that tastes do influence demand.

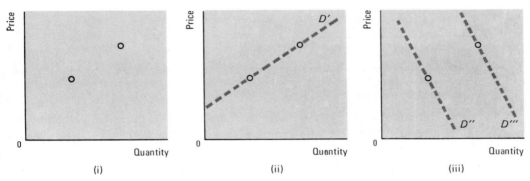

Fig. 16.1 Alternative interpretations of two price-quantity observations: either the demand curve slopes upwards or it has shifted

The fact that we cannot identify those changes in demand that are due to changes in tastes, because we cannot measure taste changes, does, however, cause us much trouble when we come to consider the relation between demand and other factors. Whenever we see something happening that does not agree with our theory it is always possible that a change in tastes accounted for what we saw. Say, for example, *incomes and other prices were known to be constant*, while the price of some commodity rose and, at the same time, more was observed to be bought. This gives us observations such as the ones illustrated in Figure 16.1(i). It may be that the demand curve for the product has a shape similar to that shown by the broken line D' in Figure 16.1(ii), but it may also be that the rise in price coincided with a change in tastes so that the demand curve shifted from D'' to D''' in Figure 16.1(iii). If we only have two observations we will not be able to distinguish between these two possibilities since we have no independent way of telling whether or not tastes changed. If, however, we have many observations we can get some idea of where the balance of probabilities lies between these two situations. If we have 26 observations (say the price changed each week over a period of six months) which, allowing for the influence of other prices and incomes,[1] look like those illustrated in Figure 16.2 we will have to stretch the point a great deal to avoid the conclusion that the evidence conflicts with the hypothesis of a downward-sloping demand curve.

---

1 This can be done through multiple regression analysis or other more sophisticated statistical techniques in the manner alluded to in Chapter 3.

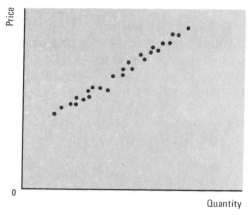

Fig. 16.2 Twenty-six price quantity observations for which one explanation, that the demand curve slopes upward, is very much more likely than the alternative explanation, that the demand curve has shifted between each of the 26 observations

Of course, we can always explain away these observations by saying that tastes must have changed in favour of this commodity each time that its price rose and against the commodity each time that its price fell. This 'alibi' can certainly be used with effect to explain away a single conflicting observation, but we shall be uncomfortable in using the same alibi 26 times in six months, and we shall begin to suspect a fault in the hypothesis that demand and price vary inversely with each other. What we now have is a problem in statistical testing of the sort described in Chapter 3. We are not prepared to throw away a theory after only one conflicting observation, but we are prepared to abandon it once we accumulate a mass of conflicting observations that were very unlikely to have occurred if the theory was correct.[1] Thus, statistically, the theory is testable. Fortunately, there is, as we shall see, a great deal of evidence that most demand curves do slope downward. The predictions of the theory have – with a few possible exceptions – been found to be in agreement with the facts.

The influence of the prices of other commodities

In Chapter 7, we made a distinction between goods that are complements to one another and those that are substitutes. Consider the demand for commodity X. This demand will *vary inversely* with the price of a complement (i.e., when the price falls demand for X will rise), and will *vary directly* with the price of a substitute (i.e., when the price falls, demand for X will fall). There may also be a group of commodities, variations in the price of which leave demand for X unchanged. These commodities

---

1 If changes in tastes are not related to changes in price, we can easily calculate the odds on the observations in Figure 16.2 being consistent with a downward-sloping but continually shifting demand curve. If tastes changed each week, there is a 50–50 chance that they changed in favour of or against the commodity. Then there is a 50–50 chance that tastes changed in the direction to offset the first week's price change. In the second week there is also one chance in two. The chances that they changed the 'right' way in both weeks are $\frac{1}{2} \cdot \frac{1}{2} = \frac{1}{4}$ and the chances that they changed the right way for 26 successive weeks are $(\frac{1}{2})^{25} = 1/33,554,432$.

lie on the boundary that divides the goods that are substitutes for X from those that are complements to X.

These three reactions – demand for X rises, falls or remains unchanged when the price of some other good varies – cover all conceivable possibilities: there is nothing else that could possibly happen. So far we merely have a set of labels to attach to all possibilities. We do not have a testable theory unless we have a way of *deciding in advance* which goods are substitutable for, and which are complementary to, X.

We can do this sometimes from technical knowledge alone. This is particularly important if we consider the demands for inputs in production. Steel plates, electric welders and welder operators are complementary. Thus, we can predict that a fall in the price of any one will lead to an increase in the demand for all three. Cranes and crane operators, steam shovels and lorries, trains and rails, roads and fences, any piece of equipment and its human operator are all examples of pairs of goods that are complements to each other. The reader will be able to expand this list more or less indefinitely. A similar list could be drawn up for inputs that are substitutes and it would include such things as wood, bricks and concrete in construction, manure and artificial fertilizers, a building full of statistical clerks with desk calculators and a small electronic digital computer.

There are also many consumers' goods for which we can predict complementarity or substitutability in advance. Complementarity would exist, for example, between electric razors and preshave lotion, ordinary razors, razor blades and shaving cream, golf clubs and golf balls, grass seed and lawn mowers, electric stoves and electricity, and marriage and services of obstetricians, marriage guidance counsellors and divorce court judges.[1] The list of substitute goods would include such obvious examples as various green vegetables, beef and pork, private automobiles and public transport, open fireplaces and central heating, gas and electric cookers, holidays in Spain and on the Italian Riviera, skiing in Switzerland, Austria and Norway, and it could be extended to cover many pages. If the technical data tell us which goods are substitutes and which are complements, then we can predict in advance the effect of a change in the price of one good on the demand for the other. As the above examples show, we are able to do this in a very large number of cases.

The relation between demand and household income

Just as with demand and other prices, our theory says it is possible for a change in income to have any conceivable effect on demand: a rise in income may cause the demand for a product to rise, to fall or to remain unchanged. Since we cannot rule out any possibility, the theory is of no use to us unless we have a way of knowing in advance what the reaction will be to a change of income in the case of a particular commodity – otherwise we can predict nothing and can only classify changes after they have occurred.

1 A somewhat high-minded reader once objected to this passage and her objection illustrates the difference between positive and normative economics. Whatever we may think of the ethics of divorce, if we know that a fairly stable fraction of marriages end in divorce, we can predict with some confidence that an increase in marriages now will lead to an increase in the demand for the services of divorce lawyers and judges in the future.

In this situation there are two facts that help to give content to the theory. *First, we observe that income elasticities are fairly stable over time.* If, over the last 20 years, the income elasticity of demand for some agricultural product has been observed to fall from 0·70 to 0·40 we are pretty safe in predicting that a rise in income next year will be met by a less than proportionate rise in the demand for that product. If, on the other hand, the income elasticity of demand for cars and electricity are both observed to have been above 2·0 for several years and also to be rising, it is fairly safe to predict that rises in income in the next few years will be met by more than proportionate rises in the demand for cars and electricity. The fact that these elasticities are observed not to change rapidly or capriciously allows us to predict into the near future from a knowledge of the level and direction of change of existing income elasticities.

The second observation that helps give empirical content to the theory, is that all households throughout the Western world tend to behave in a broadly similar fashion. (Indeed it is not even clear that the qualification Western is necessary.) At low levels of income food tends to have a fairly high income elasticity of demand but as the level of income rises, the income elasticity of demand for food tends to fall well below unity, so that very little of any additional amount of income is spent on food. The phenomenon has been observed in every growing country that has approached the levels of income currently enjoyed by the countries of Western Europe. Thus we can confidently predict (1) that as long as productivity growth continues in agriculture the long-run drift from the land will continue in Western countries (unless they have a large export market for their agricultural goods), and (2) that when other countries of the world achieve sustained positive rates of growth they will soon encounter the problem of a declining agricultural sector. Households in the United States currently enjoy an average level of income higher than that enjoyed by households anywhere else in the world. By observing broad changes in the pattern of demand in the United States we can get some idea what will happen to demand in other countries 20 or 30 years from now when they achieve the level of per capita income currently being enjoyed in the United States. A significant phenomenon in the United States in the past two decades is the decline in the income elasticity of demand for durable consumer's goods and the rise in the income elasticity of demand for services. This has necessitated a continued transfer of resources that is not being accomplished with perfect smoothness. If there is stability in household behaviour in these broad patterns across countries, then the countries of Western Europe can look forward to similar pressures on the pattern of resource allocation within a generation or two.

The incomes of Western countries are doubling every 30 years or so. Over such periods of time, changes in income exert a major influence on changes in demand. Indeed, some knowledge of what income elasticities are and are likely to be is one of the most potent tools at the economist's command for predicting the future needs of the economy.

Demand for the commodity and the commodity's own price

The marginal utility theory of demand predicted that all demand curves must always slope downward (see p. 166). This prediction has long been known as the law of demand: the price of a product and the amount demanded vary inversely with each other.

Great interest was therefore attached to an apparent refutation of this law supposedly made by the Victorian economist Sir Robert Giffen. Giffen was reputed to have observed that an increase in the price of wheat led to an increase in the consumption of bread by nineteenth-century English peasants.

If this observation is correct (i.e., if Giffen really made it, about which there now appears to be some doubt, and if there is only a low probability of errors in his measurement of a magnitude sufficient to account for the result[1]) it does refute the hypothesis that all demand curves always slope downwards. Does it refute the modern theory of demand? The answer is 'No' because this is just the type of rare exception to the normal case that is envisaged by the modern theory. Wheat accounted for a very large fraction of the total expenditure of the households affected by the price change. If wheat is an inferior good so that the income effect is negative it is possible that the large negative income effect overcame the normal substitution effect.

Thus the modern theory of demand only makes an unequivocal prediction when we have extraneous information about income elasticities of demand. Since incomes change continuously due to economic growth we are fortunate in having such information about most commodities. When, as in the case of most commodities, we know that the income effect is positive (income elasticity of demand exceeds zero) we can predict in advance that the quantity demanded will vary inversely with its price. Where we know the income effect to be negative (i.e., we know that we are dealing with an inferior good) we cannot be sure of this result. The only thing we can say is that the smaller the proportion of total expenditure accounted for by this commodity, the less important is the income effect and the more likely are we to get the normal result of price and quantity varying inversely with each other. Finally, if we have no knowledge about the income effect we can still hazard a probabilistic statement. The great weight of existing evidence suggests that, if with no prior knowledge you had to guess whether the demand curve for some commodity X was downward or upward sloping, the former choice would be the odds-on favourite.

A very different set of possible exceptions has been suggested in some of the theories of demand developed in the last 20 years. Several possibilities have been suggested, and they all depend on the assumption that the consumer is influenced by factors other than the position of his budget line.[2] Consider an example.

Assume that a household's satisfaction depends not only on the quantity of the commodity that it consumes but on the price it has to pay for the commodity. The household may, for example, buy diamonds not because its members particularly like diamonds *per se*, but because they wish to show off their wealth in an ostentatious but socially acceptable way. In the words of Thorstein Veblen, 'they indulge in *conspicuous consumption*, and when their neighbours copy them they are indulging in

1 In this connection is it interesting to read footnote 1 page 46 concerning the impossibility of absolutely conclusive refutations even in the face of evidence that convinces contemporary observers.

2 See footnote 1, page 178.

pecuniary emulation.[1] The household values diamonds precisely because they are expensive; thus, a fall in their price might lead it to stop buying them and to switch to a more satisfactory object of ostentatious display. If enough households acted similarly, this could lead to an upward rather than a downward-sloping demand curve for diamonds.

But an upward-sloping market demand curve for diamonds and other similar products has never been observed. Why? A moment's thought about the industrial uses of diamonds, and the masses of lower-income consumers who could buy diamonds only if they were sufficiently inexpensive, suggests that upward-sloping demand curves for some individual households are much more likely than is an upward-sloping market demand curve for the same commodity. Recall the discussion on page 188 about the ability of the theory of the downward-sloping demand curve to accommodate odd behaviour on the part of a small group of households (this time the 'odd' group is the rich, rather than the mentally defective or the emotionally disturbed).

Not only do we believe that most demand curves slope downward, we have a reasonable idea of the value of demand elasticity in many cases. Reasonably precise knowledge about demand curves is a necessity if we are to make real-world applications of the demand and supply theory developed in this book. If we knew nothing at all empirically about these curves, the theory would be devoid of any real-world application. If we do have this knowledge, then we can predict in advance the effects of changes in many factors such as taxes, costs, the amount of competition in a particular market, and so forth. The more accurate is our knowledge of the shape of these curves, the smaller will be the margin of error in such predictions.

MEASUREMENT OF DEMAND

The above discussion leads us directly to a consideration of the problems of the measurement of demand. Three of the most famous names in this field are Henry Schultz of the University of Chicago, Richard Stone of Cambridge University and Herman Wold of the University of Uppsala, Sweden.[2] Many difficult problems must be overcome before we can obtain even an approximate measure of the response of demand to price changes from empirical data. Most of these problems are of a very technical nature and cannot be appreciated without a knowledge of statistical theory. We must, however, mention two of the most important of these.

EVERYTHING IS VARYING AT ONCE: When we observe changes in market demand over time many of the factors assumed to influence demand will be varying simultaneously. What, for example, are we to make of the observation that the quantity of butter demanded rose by 10 per cent over a period in which household income rose by 5 per cent, the price of butter fell by 3 per cent and the price of margarine rose by

---

1 These phrases are drawn from a book which is worth browsing because of its many insights which are still relevant to today's world. Thorstein Veblen, *The Theory of the Leisure Class* (1899) now available in paperback.

2 H. Schultz, *The Theory and Measurement of Demand* (University of Chicago Press, 1938; reprinted, 1957); R. Stone, *The Measurement of Consumers' Expenditure and Behaviour in the United Kingdom*, 1920–38 (Cambridge University Press, 1954); H. Wold and L. Jureen, *Demand Analysis: A Study in Econometrics* (John Wiley, 1953).

4 per cent? How much of the change is due to income elasticity of demand, how much to price elasticity and how much to the cross elasticity between butter and margarine.[1] The answer is that we cannot tell if all we have is this one observation. If, however, we have a large number of observations showing, say quantity demanded, income, price of butter and price of margarine every month for two or three years we can hope to discover the separate influence of each of the variables. This general problem is discussed in Chapter 3 but the development and elaboration of the solution belongs to a course on statistics. The most frequently used technique for estimating the separate effect of each of these variables on demand is called multiple regression analysis, but in certain cases more complex techniques become necessary.

THE IDENTIFICATION PROBLEM: Another characteristic problem arises when we try to estimate the relation between demand for a commodity and the price of that commodity from data for quantity purchased and price. In this case we are interested in the reaction of the quantity demanded to only one of the variables that influence it, and the problem would seem relatively simple. As we shall see, this is not the case. The solution to this problem is beyond the scope of this book but the present discussion should serve as a warning against the very common practice of trying to infer something about the shape of the demand curve from price and quantity data alone.

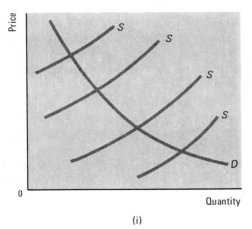
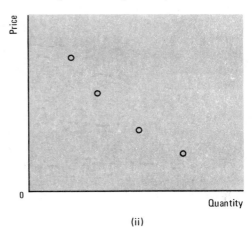

Fig. 16.3 (i)   A shifting supply curve and a fixed demand curve
        (ii)   Observations generated by (i)

The nature of the problem can be illustrated simply. We start by assuming that all situations that we observe in the real world are equilibrium ones, in the sense that they are produced by the intersection of demand and supply curves. If, as in Figure 16.3(i), the demand curve stays put while the supply curve moves up and down, possibly because of crop variations in some agricultural commodity, then the price-quantity observations illustrated in Figure 16.3(ii) will be generated. If we draw a line through these observed points, we will have a good approximation to the demand curve in Figure 16.3(i).

1 If you are not completely clear on the meaning of these three important elasticities you should review pages 103 and 108–10.

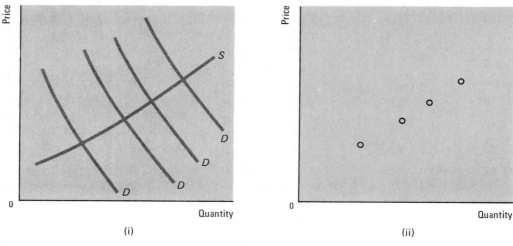

Fig. 16.4 (i) A shifting demand curve and a fixed supply curve
        (ii) Observations generated by (i)

Now assume, as in Figure 16.4(i), that the supply curve stays put while the demand curve moves about, owing perhaps to changes in the number of consumers or in their incomes. Now the price-quantity relations that will be observed are those given in Figure 16.4(ii). If we draw a curve through these points, we will obtain a fair approximation to the supply curve in Figure 16.4(i).

So far so good. But now what happens if both curves shift, as in Figure 16.5(i)? In this case we will obtain a series of points that will be very unlike either the demand or the supply curves that generated them. A few such points are shown in Figure 16.5(ii).

This difficult problem is not insurmountable. The key to *identifying* both the demand and supply curves in Figure 16.5(i), given the observations in Figure 16.5(ii),

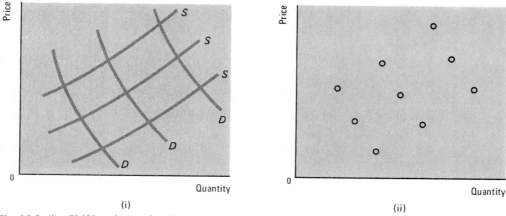

Fig. 16.5 (i) Shifting demand and supply curves
        (ii) Observations generated by (i)

is to relate them to other variables as well as price – supply to one variable and demand to *some other variable*. For example, we might relate supply of the commodity not only to the price of the commodity but also to its cost of production, and we might relate demand not only to the price of the commodity but also to consumers' incomes. Provided that both of these other factors, cost of production and income, vary sufficiently, it will now be possible to determine the relation between supply and price as well as the relation between demand and price.

In serious work, concern is usually given to identifying the various relations. In some applied work, however, the problem is often ignored. Whenever you see an argument such as the following: 'Last year the price of whisky rose by 10 per cent and whisky exports hardly fell at all, so we know that the foreign elasticity of demand must be very low', you should ask if the author has really identified the demand curve. If the rise in price was due to a rise in foreign demand for whisky we may actually have discovered that the short-run *supply curve* of whisky is very inelastic (since whisky takes several years to manufacture). The general result to keep in mind is that unless we have some additional information telling us which curve shifted and which curve has stayed put, we can tell nothing about the shape of either the demand or the supply curve from price and quantity data alone.

WHY IS THE MEASUREMENT OF DEMAND IMPORTANT?

Much work has been done on the measurement of demand and demand elasticity. This work is of great value because it provides our theory of price with empirical content. If we knew *nothing* about demand elasticities, then all of the exercises we have gone through in previous chapters would have very little application to the real world.

A somewhat different view of the importance of empirical measures of demand is held by some economists. We shall quote from a classic statement of this view by Lord Robbins:[1]

Our *a priori* deductions do not provide any justification for saying that caviar is an economic good and carrion a disutility. Still less do they inform us concerning the intensity of the demand for caviar or the demand to be rid of carrion. . . . But is it not desirable to transcend such limitations? Ought we not to be in a position to give numerical values to the scales of valuation, to establish quantitative laws of demand and supply? . . . No doubt such knowledge would be useful. But a moment's reflection should make it plain that we are here entering into a field of investigation *where there is no reason to suppose that uniformities are to be discovered*.

A simple illustration should make this clear. Suppose we are confronted with an order fixing the price of herrings at a point below the price hitherto ruling in the market. Suppose

---

1 L. Robbins, *An Essay on the Nature and Significance of Economic Science* (Macmillan, 1932), pages 98–101. Every economics specialist should read this provocative work. It contains the classic statements of many views still held by economists. It also states a view on the nature of economic theory and its relation to empirical observations that is directly contradictory to the one presented in this book. Many other economists at the time shared this view and we have quoted from Robbins because it is such a clear statement of the view then commonly held and not unknown even today. For a similar statement see, for example, L. von Mises, *Human Action* (Hodge, 1949), Chapter 2. For a view much closer to the one presented here, however, see Lionel Robbins 'The Present Position of Economics', *Rivista Di Economica*, September 1959.

we are in a position to say, 'According to the researches of Blank (1907–8) the elasticity of demand for common herring (*Clupea harengus*) is 1·3, the present price-fixing order therefore may be expected to leave an excess of demand over supply of two million barrels.'

But can we hope to obtain such an enviable position? Let us assume that in 1907–8 Blank had succeeded in ascertaining that, with a given price change in that year, the elasticity of demand was 1·3. What reason is there to suppose that he was unearthing a constant law? It is possible reasonably to suppose that coefficients derived from the observation of a particular herring market at a particular time and place have any *permanent* significance – save as Economic History?

The above argument runs somewhat as follows: 'I can think of no reasons why the relationship in question (e.g., the relation between demand and price) should be a stable one; I can in fact think of several reasons why it should not be stable; I conclude, therefore, that in the real world the relationship will not be stable, and attempts to *observe* whether or not it is stable can be ruled out on *a priori* grounds as a waste of time.' This argument is rather a curious one, and it appears, although it may not have been the author's intention, that it could have been used to stop at an early stage the investigations that produced *observations* of practically every stable relation we now know.[1]

The first criticism of the passage quoted is, thus, that *a priori* arguments, although they may strongly suggest the hypothesis that certain relationships will not be stable ones, can never establish this. Only empirical observations can demonstrate such propositions about the real world. Even if the *a priori* arguments turn out to be correct most of the time, there always exists the possibility that in a few cases they will be wrong. Only empirical observation is capable of discovering the cases in which the *a priori* argument is wrong.

The second major criticism of the passage is that it is of critical importance to *economic theory* to know just how variable any given relationship is. If, for example, tastes are so variable that demand curves shift about violently from day to day, then all of the comparative static-equilibrium analysis of the previous chapters would be useless, for only by accident would any market be near its equilibrium and this would only occur momentarily. If, on the other hand, tastes and other factors change extremely slowly, then we might do very well to regard the relation between demand and price as constant for purposes of all predictions of, say, up to 20 or 50 years. Even if we could show, on *a priori* grounds, that every relation between two or more variables used in economic theory was necessarily not a stable one, it would be critical for purposes of theory to know the quantitative amount of the lack of stability. Only empirical observations can show this, and such observations are thus important for economic theory as well as for economic history.

Let us consider an example of this point. The relation between the demand for herrings and their price might have been so variable that the elasticity of demand was 1·37 in 1903, 0·01 in 1905, 8·73 in 1906, 1·00 in 1907 and 41·2 in 1908. If demand for all goods varied in such a capricious way, price theory would be of very little use,

---

1 For example consider all the factors that influence a falling body [append a list of 20 or so factors which do, or could be imagined to, influence such a body]; clearly, since most of these are variable, we will find no constant, stable relations in the realm of falling bodies.

for we would be unable to predict the effects of the sort of shift in costs, taxes, etc., that we have been considering. If, on the other hand, all the measures of the elasticity of demand for herrings over a period of 20 years lay between 1·2 and 1·45, then we could predict the effects of various changes in the herring market with a close degree of accuracy and with a high degree of confidence. We would be astounded, and indeed we would suspect a fraud, if a large number of measures of the elasticity of herring demand, made in several places and over a large number of years, all produced the value of, say, 1·347. What we want to know, however, is *how much* spatial and temporal variation there is in the demand for herrings. Only empirical observations can settle this question.

Finally, even if we find substantial variations in our relations, we want to know if these variations appear capricious or if they display a systematic pattern that might lead us to expect that herring demand is related to other factors. We might, for example, find a strong but sometimes interrupted tendency for the elasticity of demand for herrings to fall over time. We might then find that this systematic variation in price elasticity could be accounted for by income variations (as the population gets richer its demand for herrings is less and less affected by price variations and so the demand becomes more and more inelastic). We might now find that a high proportion of the changes in herring demand could be accounted for by assuming a *stable relation* between demand on the one hand and price *and* income on the other. In general, what looks like a very unstable relation between two variables may turn out to be only part of a more stable relation between three or more variables.

All of this leads us to the following conclusion: the theory of demand and price can have few applications to the real world without some empirical observations of quantitative magnitudes. Empirical measurements are critical to economic theory. Without some knowledge of the stability or instability of a particular relation (e.g., the relation between price and quantity), we cannot use economic theory to make useful predictions about the real world.

Modern measures of demand[1]

The solution of many of the statistical problems associated with demand measurement has led to the development of many refined techniques. It has also led to a large accumulation of data on demand elasticities.

Food products

PRICE ELASTICITIES FOR FOOD PRODUCTS: Table 16.1 shows a few estimated elasticities for foodstuffs.

The data are merely examples of the very large number of elasticities for agricultural commodities that have been measured. Both British and American data tend to confirm the general picture of low price elasticities for most foodstuffs.

---

1 The data for this section are drawn from R. Ferber, 'Research on Household Behaviour', *American Economic Review*, March 1962; E. Mansfield (ed.) *Managerial Economics and Operational Research* (Norton, 1966) and R. Stone (see Source to Table 16.1).

Table 16.1 Price and income elasticities for selected foodstuffs in the UK

Commodity	Income elasticity	Price elasticity	Percentage of variation accounted for by changes in income, own price, and prices of related goods
Flour	—	0·79	53
Home-produced mutton and lamb	0·70	1·47	70
Bacon and ham	0·55	0·88	71
Poultry	1·17	0·27	33
Cream	1·71	0·69	69
Oranges	0·92	0·97	52
Sugar	0·09	0·44	74
Meals away from home	2·39	Not estimated	Not estimated

Source: Richard Stone, *The Measurement of Consumers' Expenditure and Behaviour in the United Kingdom, 1920–38* (Cambridge University Press, 1954), Vol. 1.

Professor Stone's data do reveal a few interesting exceptions to this general rule. One shown in Table 16.1 is home-produced mutton and lamb. Why should the demand for this product be elastic? The answer is that British households can choose between two close substitutes: locally produced lamb and mutton and imported lamb and mutton, which typically has a somewhat lower quality and price than the home-produced product. This is just the sort of situation in which we would expect either one of a pair of close substitutes to have an elastic demand, even though the demand for the two together (all mutton and lamb) is inelastic.

INCOME ELASTICITIES FOR FOOD PRODUCTS: Stone also measured income elasticities of demand in the United Kingdom and found these typically to be well below unity for most foodstuffs, thus confirming the general picture of the long range agriculture problem described in Chapter 11. Two interesting exceptions were cream (1·71) and restaurant meals (2·39). At the time when these estimates were made, cream was still regarded as an expensive luxury by most British households. This is just the sort of situation in which we would expect a rise in income to bring the commodity within the range of acceptable purchases for more and more households, so that demand would be very responsive to a rise in income. The data confirm this expectation. The case of restaurant meals is even more interesting. Meals eaten away from home are almost always more expensive, calorie for calorie, than meals prepared at home. We would thus expect that, at lower ranges of income, restaurant meals would be regarded as an expensive luxury, the demand for which would, however, expand substantially as households became richer. This is, in fact, what happens. Does this mean that the market demands for the foodstuffs that appear on restaurant menus will also have high income elasticities? Generally, the answer is 'No', because, when a household buys meals out rather than preparing them at home, the main change is not in what is eaten but in who prepares it. The additional expenditure on 'food' mainly goes to pay the wages of cooks and waiters and to yield a return on the owner's capital. Thus, when a household expands its expenditure on restaurant food by 2·4 per cent in response to a 1 per cent rise in its income, most of this represents an increased demand for a service to replace the housewife's unpaid work, rather than an increased demand for food. Most of the extra expenditure on 'food' thus goes to persons in the service industry, and little, if any, finds its way into the pockets of farmers. What we have here is a striking example of the general tendency for households to spend a higher proportion of their income on services as their income rises.

NONFOOD PRODUCTS: Although the importance of the agricultural problem led early investigators to concentrate on the demand for foodstuffs, modern studies have expanded to include virtually the whole range of commodities on which the household spends its income. Particular interest has attached to the demand for consumers' durables, such as cars, radios, refrigerators, television sets and houses. Demands for these types of goods are particularly interesting because they constitute a large fraction of total demand and because such demands can be quite variable from one year to the next. Since the commodity is durable, it can always be made to 'make do' for another year; thus purchases can be postponed with greater ease than can purchases of nondurables such as food and services. If enough households decide simultaneously to postpone purchases of durables for even six months, this decision can have a major effect on the economy.

These modern studies have shown that demand is often influenced by a wide variety of socioeconomic factors – family size, age, geographical location, type of employment, wealth and income expectations – not included in the traditional theory of demand. Although significant, the total contribution of all of these factors to changes in demand tends to be small. Typically, less than 30 per cent of the variations in demand are accounted for by these 'novel' factors and a much higher proportion by the traditional variables of prices and current incomes.

INCOME ELASTICITIES FOR NONFOOD PRODUCTS: A great deal of information on income elasticities has been accumulated for many countries. It tends to confirm the view expressed earlier in this chapter that, as incomes rise, household expenditures follow broadly similar paths in most Western countries. Summarizing the many studies, Robert Ferber wrote that they 'tend to bear out earlier findings on income elasticity yielding low elasticities for food and housing, elasticities close to unity for clothing and education, and higher elasticities for various types of recreation, personal care, home operation and other services'.

PRICE ELASTICITIES FOR NONFOOD PRODUCTS: The main lesson economists have learned in measuring price elasticities of manufactured goods is that they tend to be fairly elastic. Millinery, for example, has been estimated to have an elasticity of 3·0, which implies a large response of quantity demanded to price changes.

An interesting study was made of the elasticity of demand of a number of staple items sold by the R. H. Macy Co. in New York. This study was a controlled experiment in which prices of many products were varied over quite wide ranges. The controlled nature of the experiment meant that prices could be changed in the most favourable circumstances – e.g., not at the same time as a change in the prices of a competing product. The measured elasticities were all high, probably because very close substitutes were available in identical or very similar products sold by other department stores.

Most businessmen have an intuitive idea of the elasticities they face, although they seldom use the economist's language in referring to them. There does also seem to be evidence that they do sometimes underestimate their elasticities and thus over-price their commodities. When the Columbia Record Company of America took a great gamble in 1938 and cut the price of its classical records in half, it turned them overnight from a high-priced luxury into a commodity available to the ordinary person. The response was enormous, and, to the surprise of many of the other record producers, sales expanded so much that total consumers' expenditure on classical records increased greatly. Opposite cases in which companies have raised prices and been surprised at the resulting drop in sales have also been documented (see e.g., page 304).

Clearly, modern research has revealed a great deal about the determinants of demand. Any economist who wishes to make an applied study of a particular market is very likely to have some established evidence on which to draw. Even more important, many methodological problems have been resolved and techniques sharpened. As time goes by, further evidence accumulates at a rapid rate, and we find ourselves far beyond merely wondering if demand curves slope downward. Not only do we now know the approximate shape of many demand curves, we also have information about how demand curves shift. As each year goes by our knowledge of demand relations increases significantly.

Part four

The intermediate theory of supply

17

Background to the theory of supply

In Part 2 very little was said about production. We merely assumed that there existed a supply curve relating the quantity of a commodity producers would wish to make and offer for sale to the price of that commodity. We now wish to inquire in more detail into the theory of supply; and in particular we wish to explain the supply curve in terms of the decisions of individual producers. We wish to develop a theory which will tell us how production will respond to changes in consumer demand. We also need a theory to help us deal with a whole host of questions such as: What is the effect of various forms of competition or monopoly on the efficiency and level of production in an industry? What are some of the causes and consequences of advertising? Why do firms combine? Is there a tendency for monopoly to replace competition as the dominant form of production? What are the causes and consequences of take-over bids? Is the policy of taxing the domestic consumption of a good in order to encourage its export a sensible policy? This is but a sample of the many questions which belong in the field of supply or production theory, as it is variously called. In an introductory textbook we can do little more than outline the basic theory and show a few applications. This chapter presents some background material. A formal theory is constructed in subsequent chapters.

THE NATURE OF THE FIRM

In Chapter 6 we assumed that all firms, whatever their nature, take consistent decisions directed solely to maximizing their profits. This amounts to assuming that the decisions taken by firms are unaffected by their institutional set-up. This assumption that the structure of the firm can be ignored has come under frequent and sustained attack. Once we have developed the standard theory, we shall devote some attention to such criticisms. In order to understand what we are abstracting from, and in order to consider the criticisms of our abstractions, it is necessary at this stage that the reader should understand something of the nature of the modern business organization.

Forms of business organization

There are three major forms of private business organization: the single proprietorship, the partnership and the joint-stock company, which in America is called the corporation. In the single proprietorship, there is one owner who is personally responsible for everything done by the business. In the partnership, there are two or more joint owners each of whom is personally responsible for everything done by the firm. In the joint-stock company, the firm is regarded in law as having an identity of its own and the owners are not each personally responsible for everything that the firm does.

In most Western countries it is necessary to add two other forms of organizing production, nationalized industries and goods and services provided without direct charge by the state. Nationalized industries are owned by the state and are usually under the direction of a more or less independent board appointed by the state. Although their ownership differs, the organization and legal status of these firms is very similar to that of the joint-stock company and they are perforce very large firms. Their activity is similar also in the sense that they gain their revenue by selling to the public the product that they produce. In the United Kingdom about 20 per cent of total production is accounted for by these firms, the most important of which in 1974 were railways, coal, airlines, electricity, gas, postal and telephonic communication.

The final form of production is quite dissimilar from all those considered above because revenue is obtained from general taxation and the product is provided free to the public. Important examples found in all countries are defence, roads and education. In the U K we must also add the National Health Service which provides medical and hospital services free (or at very small charges) to the general public. In countries without nationalized medical services, hospitals and doctors behave just as do other firms: they purchase factors of production on the open market and gain revenue by selling their services to those people who wish to, and can afford to, purchase them. In the next few chapters we shall confine our attention to the privately owned sector of the economy, but we shall return to the publicly owned sector in Chapter 32.

PROPRIETORSHIPS AND PARTNERSHIPS, ADVANTAGES AND DISADVANTAGES: The major advantage of the single proprietorship is that the owner can readily maintain full control over the firm. He is the Boss. The disadvantages are, first, that the size of the firm is limited by the capital the owner can personally raise, and, second, that he is personally responsible in law for all debts of the firm.

The partnership overcomes to some extent the first disadvantage of the proprietorship but not the second. Ten partners may be able to finance a much bigger enterprise than could one owner, but they are still subject to what is called UNLIMITED LIABILITY. Each partner is fully liable for all of the debts of the firm. As a direct consequence of unlimited liability, it is difficult to raise money from many persons through a partnership. An investor may be willing to risk £1,000, but not be willing to jeopardize his entire fortune; if, however, he joins a partnership in order to do the former, he cannot avoid doing the latter.

A further disadvantage of an ordinary partnership is that any time a partner dies, or resigns, the partnership agreement must be redrawn. This makes it difficult to have as a partner someone who is not genuinely interested and involved in the business, but who is willing merely to invest in it, for such a partner may wish, at any time, to liquidate his interest by selling it to someone else. While this is not impossible under partnership law, it is not easy.

The *limited partnership* is designed to avoid some of these difficulties. General partners continue to have unlimited authority and unlimited liability. But it is possible to have a second type of partner whose liability is limited to the amount that he has invested in the firm. He may not participate in the management of the firm, nor engage in agreements on behalf of the partnership. In effect the limited partnership permits some division of the functions of decision-making, provision of capital and risk-taking.

In most respects this division of responsibility is more effectively managed through the joint-stock company. But there are certain professions in which the partnership form is traditional and in which its survival is made feasible by use of limited partnerships. These traditional partnership areas include law, medicine and brokerage.

THE JOINT-STOCK COMPANY, ADVANTAGES AND DISADVANTAGES: The joint-stock company is regarded in law as an entity separate from the individuals who own it. It can enter into contracts, it can sue and be sued, it can own property, it can contract debts, and its obligations are not those of its owners. This means that the company can enter into contracts in its own right, and that its liability to adhere to such contracts can be enforced only by suing the company, not by suing the owners. The right to be sued may not seem to be an advantage, but it is this right that makes it possible for others to enter into enforceable contracts with the company.

Some joint-stock companies are very small, or have their stock owned by a very small group that also manages the firm; the form of the joint-stock company that we are chiefly interested in is one that issues shares that are purchased by the general public. The company obtains the money paid for the shares, and the shareholders become the owners of the company. They are entitled to share in the profits of the company, which, when they are paid out, are called DIVIDENDS. They are also entitled to split up the assets of the company, should it be liquidated, after all debts are paid off.

This method of finance usually means that the owners of the firm cannot all be the managers. The line of control is as follows. The shareholders (and there may be tens of thousands of them) elect a board of directors. The board of directors is supposed to act as a cabinet. It sets broad lines of policy and appoints senior managers. The managers are supposed to carry out the wishes of the directors, translating the broad lines of policy laid down by them into a series of detailed decisions.

The most important aspect of a joint-stock company from the point of view of its owners is that they have limited liability. Should the company go bankrupt, the personal liability of any shareholder is limited to whatever he has actually invested in the firm. Usually this is the money he spent to purchase its shares. The great advantage of the joint-stock company is that it can raise capital from a very large number of individuals, each of whom gets a share in the firm's profits, but who, beyond risking the loss of the amount he actually invests, has no liabilities. Thus each investor may sit back and collect his dividends without knowing anything about the firm that he, along with many others, owns. Because of this, large quantities of capital can be raised. Because shares are readily transferable among individuals (a form of exchange that stock markets are organized to facilitate), a joint-stock company can have a continuity of life that is unaffected by frequent changes in the identity of its owners.

The disadvantages of the joint-stock company from the point of view of the investor are, first, that he may have little say in the management of the firm. (For example, if the directors decide that the company should not pay dividends, an individual investor cannot compel them to pay him his share of the earnings.) Second, the company is subject to income taxation, as are the investor's dividends. This 'double taxation' of corporate income is much discussed in the public finance literature. Some view it as clearly unfair and discriminatory. Others view it as the price to be paid for the advantage of incorporation. Judging from the importance of the company in our society, the price, whether just or unjust, has not been prohibitive. This form of organization is even now spreading to the service industries and agriculture as these grow to the point where they need large quantities of capital to function effectively.

The financing of the modern firm

The above discussion has emphasized the raising of money from the owners of the firm. It should not be thought, however, that all the money needed by the firm to carry on its business is subscribed by the owners. The most important sources of funds for modern firms are (1) selling *shares, stocks* or *equities* (as they are variously called) either by private or public sale; (2) borrowing by the sale of *bonds*; (3) borrowing from banks and other financial institutions; and (4) reinvesting the firm's profits.

STOCK AND STOCKHOLDERS: The owners of the firm are its stockholders, persons who have put up money to purchase shares in the firm. They make their money available to the firm and risk losing it in return for a share in the firm's profits. Stocks in a firm often proliferate into a bewildering number of types. Basically, however, there is *common stock* and *preferred stock*. Common stock usually carries voting rights and has a residual claim on profits. After all other claims have been met, including those of holders of preferred shares, the remaining profits, if any, belong to the common-stock holders. Firms are not obliged by law to pay out any fixed portion of their profits as dividends, and indeed the practice among companies as to the *payout ratio* varies greatly.

Preferred stocks may be voting or nonvoting, cumulative or noncumulative. Basically, the difference between preferred stock and common stock is that preferred stocks carry with them a right to a preference over common stocks to any profits that may be available after other obligations have been met. If profits are earned, the company is obliged to pay a dividend to preferred-stock holders, but there is a stated maximum to the rate of dividends that will be paid per pound originally invested.

BONDS AND BONDHOLDERS: The bondholders are creditors, not owners of the firm. They have loaned money to the firm in return for a *bond*, which is a promise to pay a stated sum of money each year by way of *interest* on the loan, and also to repay the loan at some stated time in the future (say, five, seven or ten years hence). This promise to pay is a legal obligation on the firm's part whether or not profits have been made. If these payments cannot be met, then the bondholders can force the firm into liquidation. Should this happen, the bondholders have a claim to the firm's assets prior to that of any of the stockholders. Only if the bondholders and all other creditors have been repaid in full can the stockholders recover anything for themselves.

The disadvantage to the company of raising capital through the sale of bonds is that interest payments must be met whether or not there are any profits. Many a firm that would have survived a temporary crisis had all its capital been share capital has been forced into liquidation because it could not meet its contractual obligation to pay interest to its bondholders.

OTHER BORROWING: Many short-term needs and some long-term ones are met by borrowing from banks and other financial institutions. This is true of giant companies and small businesses. Indeed making commercial and industrial loans is one of the major activities of the banking system. Little needs to be said about such loans at this stage, except to note that 'term' (i.e., short-term) borrowing tends to be expensive to firms and that they usually prefer to raise money in other ways for long-term purposes. Banks often limit the amounts they are willing to lend companies to specified fractions of their total financial needs. Some companies are forced to seek funds from other financial institutions, at yet higher rates of interest. Many small businesses which are not well established cannot sell stocks to the public and must rely mainly on bank loans to finance their activities.

REINVESTED PROFITS: For the established firm, as distinct from the new one, an additional very important means of obtaining funds is through the reinvesting, or ploughing back, of the firm's own profits. One of the easiest ways for the controllers of the firm to raise money is to retain some of the firm's own profits rather than pay them out as dividends to shareholders. This has become an extremely important source of funds in modern times. If the shareholder does not wish his profits to be reinvested there is very little that he can do about it. In many cases, firms pay out a standard dividend to their common-stock holders year after year, holding back any profits in excess of this amount, and paying dividends out of reserves when current profits fall short of the amount necessary to make such dividend payments. Common stocks on which a standard payment is made year in and year out in spite of fluctuating profits are a very far cry from the original idea of a common stock, which yielded little or nothing in bad times and very high returns in good times.

THE FIRM IN ECONOMIC THEORY

In Chapter 6 we defined the firm as the unit that takes decisions with respect to the production and sale of commodities. This single concept of the firm covers a variety of business organizations from the single proprietorship to the joint-stock company, and a variety of business sizes from the single inventor operating in his garage and financed by whatever he can extract from a reluctant bank manager to vast undertakings with many thousands of shareholders and creditors. We know that in large firms decisions are actually taken by many different individuals. We can, nonetheless, regard the firm as a single consistent decision-making unit because of the assumption that all decisions are taken in order to achieve the common goal of maximizing the firm's profits. This assumption is critical to the whole traditional theory of the firm and we may state it formally as follows:

> **We assume that the same principles underlie each decision made within a firm and that the decision is uninfluenced by who makes it. Thus we can abstract from the peculiarities of the persons making the decisions and the kinds of organization in which they work.**

Whether a decision is made by a small independent proprietor, a plant manager, or a Board of Directors, that person or group is, as far as the theory goes, the firm for the purposes of that decision. This is a truly heroic assumption. It amounts to saying that for purposes of predicting their behaviour, at least in those aspects that interest us, we can treat the farm, the corner grocery, the large department store, the small engineering firm, the giant chemical combine, the vast oil firm and that largest of all business organizations the General Motors Corporation of America, all under the umbrella of a single theory of the behaviour of the firm. Even if this turns out to be only partially correct it will represent an enormously valuable simplification which will show the power of theory in revealing some unity of behaviour where to the casual observer there is only a bewildering diversity.[1]

Criticisms of the theory of the firm because it neglects to identify either decision-takers or the institutional structure within which decisions are taken, are discussed in Chapter 25. Some competing hypotheses about actual business behaviour are also discussed at that time. The final test of whether or not such factors can be legitimately ignored is an empirical one: if the theory that we develop by ignoring these factors is successful in predicting the outcome of the kind of events in which we are interested, then we can conclude that we were correct in assuming that these factors could be safely ignored.

The motivation of the firm

We assume that the firm makes decisions in such a way that its profits will be as large as possible. In technical language, we assume that the firm *maximizes its profits*. The assumption of profit maximization enables us to predict the behaviour of the firm in regard to the various choices open to it. We do this by studying the effect that making each of the choices would have on the firm's profits. We then predict that the firm will select from the alternatives open to it the one that produces the largest profits.

At this point the reader is entitled to ask if we are justified in going ahead to build

---

1 The student must not be surprised if at first encounter the theory seems rather abstract and out of touch with reality. Because it does generalize over such a wide variety of behaviour it must ignore those features with which we are most familiar and which in our eyes distinguish the farmer and the grocer from Royal Dutch Shell. Any theory that generalizes over a wide variety of apparently diverse behaviour necessarily has this characteristic, because it ignores those factors that are most obvious to us and which create in our minds the appearance of diversity.

an elaborate theory based on such a crude assumption about the motives of the businessmen. It is well known that some businessmen are inspired some of the time by motives other than an overwhelming desire to make as much money as they possibly can. Cases in which businessmen have gone after political influence, and others in which decisions have been influenced by philanthropic motives, are not difficult to document. Should we not, therefore, say that the assumption that businessmen seek to maximize profits is refuted by empirical evidence?

The real world is complex. A theory picks on certain factors, and deals with them on the assumption that they are the important ones, and that the ones ignored are relatively less important. If it is true that the key factors have been included, then the theory will be successful in predicting what will happen under specified circumstances. It follows that it is not an important criticism to point out that a theory ignores some factors known to be present in the world; this tells us nothing more than that the theory is a theory and not just a photographic reproduction of reality in its full complexity. If the theory has ignored some important factors, then its predictions will be contradicted by the evidence, at least in those situations in which the factor ignored is quantitatively important.

How does all of this relate to profit-maximizing theory? First, this theory does not say that profit is the only factor that ever influences the businessman. It is believed only that profits are an important consideration, important enough so that a theory that assumes profit maximization to be the sole motive of the businessman will produce predictions that are substantially correct. It follows from this that to point out that businessmen are sometimes motivated by considerations other than profits does not constitute a relevant criticism of the theory. It may well be that profit-maximizing theory is substantially wrong but, if so, the way to demonstrate this is to show that the predictions that follow from the theory are refuted by the facts. This, of course, requires that we have mastered the theory first. We shall therefore press on to discover the implications of the assumption that businessmen seek only to maximize profits; when we have completed this task we shall ask how the theory might be tested against empirical evidence. Finally, in Chapter 25 we shall consider several alternative theories that have been put forward.

Nationalized industries

We have already noted (see page 206) that a significant amount of total production is in the hands of industries that are owned by the state. Do we need a separate theory of the behaviour of nationalized industries? Usually these industries are run by boards that are appointed by the state but given considerable autonomy within the framework of broad directives on what goals to pursue. If the nationalized industries seek to maximize their profits then their behaviour will be indistinguishable from that of private firms. If, however, they are given other goals, such as always to try just to cover all their costs so as to make neither profits nor losses, then their behaviour will differ from that of the private sector. Once we know the objectives of these industries we will be able to predict their response to changes in market signals. In the next few chapters we shall confine ourselves to the behaviour of privately-owned firms, but in Chapter 32 we shall return to the question of nationally-owned ones.

A PREVIEW OF THE THEORY OF SUPPLY

Firms are assumed to seek to maximize their profits. Profits (π) are the difference between revenues derived from the sale of commodities (R) and the cost of producing these commodities (C):

$$\pi = R - C.$$

Thus, a theory of the behaviour of profits may be broken down into a theory of the behaviour of revenues and of costs.

In developing the theory of supply, we first explain the special meaning that economists give to the concept of costs and then develop a theory of how costs vary with output. This theory is common to all firms. We then consider how revenues vary with output and find that it is necessary to deal separately with firms in competitive and in monopolistic situations. Once this has been done, costs and revenues are combined to determine the profit-maximizing situation for firms in various competitive and monopolistic situations. When the firm has maximized its profits it is said to be in a position of equilibrium.

Once the theory of the equilibrium of the firm (and groups of firms that compose industries) has been developed, it can be used to predict the outcome of changes in such things as demand, costs, taxes and subsidies. These predictions can then be tested against observations. It is the steps of deriving predictions and testing them in which we are really interested, and towards which all previous steps are directed. We must be prepared, however, for some quite hard work before these last steps can be taken. The necessary theory is built up over the next few chapters.

18

The theory of costs

Profits are the difference between revenues and costs and we must now ask how to calculate the cost associated with a given level of output, produced with given techniques. Any rate of output will have a set of inputs associated with it. In order to arrive at the cost of producing this output we need to be able to put a value on each of the separate inputs used. The assignment of monetary values to physical quantities of inputs may be very easy in some cases and very hard in others. Furthermore, different people or different groups may assign different values to the same input.

Economists might study production behaviour of firms for a variety of reasons:
(1) to predict how the firm's behaviour will respond to specified changes in the conditions it faces;
(2) to help the firm make the best decisions it can in achieving its goals;
(3) to evaluate how well from society's point of view firms use scarce resources.
The same measure of cost need not be correct for all of these purposes. For example, if the firm happens to be misinformed about the value of some resource, it will behave according to that misinformation. In predicting the firm's behaviour, the economist should use the information the firm actually uses, even if he knows it to be incorrect. But in helping the firm to achieve its goals, the economist should substitute the correct information.

Economists know exactly how to define costs in order to solve problems (2) and (3) above. If we assume that businessmen use the same concept, the economist's definition will also be appropriate for problem (1). We shall make this assumption for the moment; the consequences of being in error are discussed in Chapter 25 below.

THE MEASUREMENT OF THE FIRM'S COST

Any firm that wishes to maximize its profits must assign costs to each of its inputs according to the following principle.

> **The cost of any input is what the firm must give up in order to obtain the use of that input.**

213

To assign a cost to a given amount of production the firm must decide what inputs it has used and assign to each a monetary value equal to what it has given up in order to have the use of that input. Although easy enough to state in general, the application of the principle to specific cases can pose difficult problems.

The cost of purchased and hired factors

Assigning cost is perhaps most straightforward for those factors that the firm buys on the market, and *uses up* entirely during the period of production. Many raw material and intermediate products fall into this category. If the firm pays £5 per ton for coal delivered to its factory, it has sacrificed its claims to whatever £5 can buy, and thus the purchase price is a reasonable measure of the opportunity cost of using that ton of coal. For hired factors of production the situation is identical: the cost to the firm of having a week's labour is what the firm must pay out to obtain that much labour.[1]

The cost of owned factors

In the case of factors of production that the firm neither purchases nor hires for current use, the cost must also be assessed, but, since no payment is made to anyone outside of the firm, these costs, which are called IMPUTED COSTS, are not so obvious. If the firm is to discover what behaviour will maximize its profits, it must be able to impute a cost to its owned factors equal to what the firm gives up in order to use these factors. Since the firm has the alternative of renting out its owned factors for someone else's use it must charge itself for the use of its owned factors, the amount that it could have obtained by renting the factor to someone else. Although at first sight it seems strange that the firm charge itself for using its own factors this is necessary in order for it to obtain a true picture of what it gives up in order to use the factor.[2] In practice the imputation of costs is fraught with difficulties which may be illustrated by two examples of particular cost imputations and then by some general pitfalls.

THE COST OF MONEY: A firm that borrows money in the open market pays the current rate of interest for it, and the rate of interest, therefore, indicates what the firm must give up in order to obtain the use of the money. But what if a firm uses its own money? Consider, for example, a firm that uses £10,000 worth of its own money. If the interest rate is 10 per cent this money could have been loaned out to someone else yielding £1,000 per year to the firm and this £1,000 should be deducted from the firm's revenue as a cost to the firm of using its own funds. If, to continue the example, the firm makes only £800 over all other costs, then we should say not that the firm

---

1 It is worth noticing that typically labour cost is more than the wages actually paid to the labourer because employers usually contribute to such things as pension funds and various kinds of unemployment and disability insurance. Frequently, there are 'fringe benefits' as well. The cost of all these must be added to the direct wage paid to the employee in order to determine the cost to the firm of obtaining a given amount of labour.

2 The amount that the firm could obtain by renting out (or selling outright) its owned factors on the open market represents a *minimum* estimate of the costs to the firm of using its own factors. If the factor has more than one use within the firm then the firm must be careful to value the factor at a price that reflects the alternative uses to which it could be put in the firm. If the factor is used for use *A* then it is not available for uses *B*, *C* or *D*. The cost to the firm of using the factor in use *A* is thus the value that the firm could have obtained by using it in the most profitable alternative available whether inside or outside of the firm.

made a profit of £800 by producing, but rather that it lost £200, for if it had closed down completely and merely loaned out its £10,000 to someone else, it could have earned £1,000.

> **The market rate of interest gives the minimum for the imputed cost of money to the firm, since the firm always has the opportunity of lending out its money at that rate.**

SPECIAL ADVANTAGES: Suppose a firm owns a valuable patent or a highly desirable location, or has a brand name such as Coca Cola, Ford, or Players. Use of any of these involves a cost to the firm, because if the firm does not itself choose to use it, it could lease or sell it to others.

   If, for example, a family grocery store is being run on a particularly valuable piece of land, acquired by the store's founder for £1,000 over a hundred years ago, but now worth £5,000 a month if rented out, then the grocery store must charge itself £5,000 a month for use of its especially advantageous piece of land. If the store cannot show a profit when charging itself £5,000 a month for use of its land then the store is not a profitable venture (after all the store could be moved to another location and the present land rented out for £5,000). Similar considerations apply to a firm that acquired a patent for next to nothing: the current cost to the firm of using the patent is the price that could be obtained by leasing its use or selling it outright on the open market.

Two common errors in imputing costs of owned factors

(1) THE COST OF AN OWNED FACTOR IS SOMETIMES THOUGHT TO BE EQUAL TO WHAT THE FIRM MUST CURRENTLY PAY OUT TO SECURE USE OF THE FACTOR: Usually the current payment for an owned factor is zero, while the cost incurred by using the factor is correctly measured by what the factor could earn if it were leased (or sold) on the open market. This proposition has already been illustrated in the two examples considered above but it is mentioned here to remind you of one of the two most prevalent errors in imputing costs of owned factors.

(2) THE CURRENT COST OF USING AN OWNED FACTOR IS SOMETIMES THOUGHT TO BE RELATED TO THE PRICE THAT WAS PAID WHEN THE FACTOR WAS ORIGINALLY PURCHASED: Probably the most common mistake in calculating opportunity cost is to take historical costs into consideration. This is the error that seems to die hardest and which still pervades some business practices. The point is so important that we shall consider two examples. In the first, the current cost is higher than one might think from considering historical cost and in the second, it is lower.

Example 1. A man buys a £2,000 motor car that he intends to use for six years after which it will be scrapped. He may think that this will cost him £333·33 per year but if after one year the value of his motor car on the used-car market is only £1,400 it has cost him £600 to use the car during the first year. Should he charge himself £600 as a cost of using the car in its first year? After all, he expects the car to last for six years. The answer is 'yes' because one of his alternatives was to buy a one-year old car initially. Indeed, being the owner of a one-year old car is the very position he is in after the first year of running his new car. Whether he likes it or not, he has paid £600 for the use of the car during the first year of its life. If the market had valued the car at £1,900 after one year the cost to him of using the car for the first year would have been only £100. The cost of using the new car in its first year of life is the £600 that the business man could have had for other uses if a one-year old car had been used instead.

Example 2. A firm has just purchased a set of machines for £100,000. They have an expected life time of 10 years and the firm's accountant calculates the 'depreciation cost' of these machines at £10,000 per year. The machines can be used to make only one product and since they are installed in one part of the firm's whole factory, they can be leased to no one else and they have a negligible secondhand or scrap value. Assume that, if the machines are used to produce the firm's product, the cost of all other factors utilized will amount to £25,000 per year. Immediately after purchasing the machines the firm finds that the price of the commodity that the machines make has unexpectedly fallen so that the output can now only be sold for £29,000. What should the firm do?

If in calculating its costs the firm adds in the historically determined 'depreciation costs' of £10,000 a year, the total cost of operation comes to £35,000; with revenue at £29,000 this makes a loss of £6,000 per year. It appears that the goods should not be made! But this is not correct. Since the machines have no alternative use whatsoever, the imputed cost to the firm of using them is zero. The total cost of producing the output is thus only £25,000 per year and the whole current operation shows a return over cost of £4,000 per year rather than a loss of £6,000.

Of course, the firm would not have bought the machines had it known that the price of the product was going to fall, but having bought them, the cost of using them is zero, and it is profitable to use them as long as they yield any net revenue whatsoever over all other costs.

The principle illustrated by both of these examples may be stated in terms of an important maxim:

> **Bygones are bygones and should have no influence in deciding what is currently the most profitable thing to do.**[1]

The opportunity cost principle of valuing inputs

The preceding discussion may be summarized by saying that the profit-maximizing firm values its inputs of factors of production according to the principle of opportunity cost: the cost of anything is measured by the value of the foregone alternatives.[2]

---

1 This is a very important principle that extends well beyond economics and is often ignored in these other areas as well. In many poker games, for example, the cards are dealt a round at a time and betting proceeds after each player's hand has been augmented by one card. Players who bet heavily on early rounds because their hands looked promising often stay in through later rounds on indifferent hands because they 'already have such a stake in the pot'. The professional player knows that, after each round of cards, his bet should be made on the probabilities that the hand he currently holds will turn into a winner when all the cards have been dealt. If the probabilities look poor after the fourth card has been dealt (five usually constitutes a complete hand), he should abandon the hand and refuse to bet further whether he has put 5p or £5 into the pot already. The amateur who bases his current decisions on what he has put into the pot in earlier rounds of betting will be a long-term loser if he plays in rational company. In poker, war and economics bygones *are* bygones, and to take account of them in current decisions is to court disaster!

2 See page 52 for a more general discussion of opportunity cost.

The cost of using inputs in particular ways is measured by the value that could have been produced if the inputs were used in alternative ways.

In the case of factor services currently purchased, the firm is sacrificing what it could have obtained by spending the money in other ways. The money spent on these factors thus correctly states the value of the foregone alternatives. In the case of owned factors, the current market value of the services of these factors places a minimum on the opportunity cost to the firm of using these factors for itself.

The cost of capital

Once capital is installed in a firm, it may, as the preceding example showed, have little or no opportunity cost. But capital wears out over time and has to be replaced. Capital will not be maintained in an industry unless it is expected to yield a return at least equal to what it can earn in comparable uses in other industries. Thus, over an extended period of time, the firm's activities must yield a return to its capital equal to what it could earn in other comparable industries. If not, the owners will move their capital elsewhere.

It is helpful to think of the return to capital being divided into a pure return, a risk premium and pure profit. The PURE RETURN is what the capital could earn in a riskless investment. The RISK PREMIUM is what must be paid to compensate the owners for the risks of losing their capital, which is a risk that accompanies *any* business venture in a world of less than perfect certainty. Both of these elements are costs when viewed over a long enough period of time for capital equipment to be replaced. If the firm does not produce a return on its capital sufficient to cover the return on a riskless investment and a sufficient compensation for any riskiness, the owners of the capital are not covering their opportunity costs. The owners will be able to do better by transferring their capital elsewhere, which they can do by not replacing old machinery as it wears out and by investing in other industries the funds that could have been used for replacement.

If capital earns any further return, this is in the nature of PURE PROFIT which is often just called profit for short. Pure profit is a return to capital in excess of its opportunity cost and if such profits exist, capital is covering more than its opportunity costs.

Profit

Profit as the term is used in economics refers to pure profit, i.e. any excess of revenues over all opportunity cost. To discover if such profits exist, take the revenues of the firm and deduct the cost of all factors of production other than capital. Then deduct the pure return on capital and any risk premium necessary to compensate the owners of capital for the risks associated with its use in this firm and industry. Anything that remains after deducting all costs listed above is a pure profit. It belongs to the owners of the firm and therefore may be regarded as an additional return on their capital investment; it is a return in excess of all the opportunity costs including those of capital.

THE PRODUCTION FUNCTION

We have now seen how to put a money value on the inputs used by the firm in the process of production. The next stage in our inquiry is to develop the theory of how the firm's outputs are related to its inputs. This is the theory of the production function.

The relation between the factor services used as inputs in the productive process and the quantity of output obtained can be expressed in functional notation as follows:

$$q = q(f_1, \ldots, f_m),$$

where q is the quantity produced per period of time and where $f_1, \ldots, f_m$ are the quantities used of the services of m different factors of production. This relation between input and outputs is usually referred to as the PRODUCTION FUNCTION. The production function depends solely on technical conditions; it describes the purely technological relation between what is fed in by way of inputs of factor services and what is turned out by way of product.

It must not be forgotten that production is a flow: it is not just so many units but so many units per period of time. If we speak of raising the level of monthly production from say, 100 to 101 units, we do not mean producing 100 units this month and one unit next month, but going from a rate of production of 100 units each month to a rate of 101 units each month.

Three decision periods

In deciding what factor services to use as inputs the firm must make many decisions. In order to reduce these to theoretically manageable dimensions we distinguish three time periods and group all actual decisions into one of these three periods. We think of the firm as making decisions about (1) how best to employ its existing plant and equipment (the *short run*); (2) what new plant and equipment and production processes to select, given the framework of known technical possibilities (the *long run*); and (3) what to do about encouraging the invention of new techniques (the *very long run*). These time periods ('runs') are theoretical constructions. They abstract from the more complicated nature of real decisions and focus only on the key factor that restricts the range of choice in each set of decisions. We now consider these three periods in more detail.

THE SHORT RUN: The short run is defined as the period of time over which the inputs of some factors cannot be varied. The most usual meaning is that the firm cannot get the use of more of the FIXED FACTORS than it has on hand, and that it is committed to pay any costs that are associated with this quantity of the fixed factors. This is the meaning we shall use. The factors that can be varied in the short run are called VARIABLE FACTORS.

The factor that is fixed in the short run is usually an element of capital (such as plant and equipment), but it might be land, or the services of management, or even the supply of skilled salaried labour. What matters is that at least one significant factor should be fixed.

The short run does not correspond to a fixed number of months or years. In some industries it may extend over many years; in others it may be only a matter of months or even weeks. In the electric-power industry, for example, where it takes three or more years to acquire and install a steam-turbine generator, an unforeseen increase in demand will involve a long period during which the extra demand must be met as well as possible with the existing capital equipment. At the other end of the scale, a machine shop can acquire new equipment (or sell existing equipment) in a matter of a few weeks, and thus the short run is correspondingly short. If there is an increase in demand, it will have to be met with the existing stock of capital for only a short time, after which the stock of equipment can be adjusted to the level made desirable by the higher demand. The length of the short run is influenced by technological factors such as the speed of manufacture and installation of equipment. But these things are not totally fixed and may be influenced by the price the firm is willing to pay.

THE LONG RUN: The long run is defined as the period long enough for the inputs of all factors of production to be varied, but not so long that the basic technology of production changes. Again, it does not correspond to a specific period of time, but varies among industries.

The special importance of the long run in production theory is that it corresponds to the situation facing the firm when it is *planning* to go into business or to expand substantially the scale of its operations, or to branch out into new products or new areas, or to modernize, replace, or reorganize its method of production.

The *planning decisions* of the firm characteristically are made with fixed technical possibilities but with freedom to choose whatever factor proportions seem most desirable. Once these planning decisions are carried out – once a plant is built, equipment purchased and installed, and so on – the firm has fixed factors and makes operating decisions in what we have called the short run.

THE VERY LONG RUN: Unlike the short and the long run, the very long run is concerned with situations in which the technological possibilities open to the firm are subject to change, leading to new and improved products and new methods of production. The firm may bring about some of these changes itself, particularly through its programmes of research and development. In the first part of this chapter we ignore the possibility that the firm may incur costs in an effort to change its own technology, and consider only its choice of techniques of production under the assumption of a constant technology.

THE SHORT RUN

In the theory of the short run we are concerned with what happens to output as more or less of the variable factors are applied to given quantities of the fixed factors. For simplicity in developing our theory we shall use an example in which a manufactured commodity is produced by two factors of production, capital and labour, and in which capital is fixed and labour is variable in the short run. Assume that a firm starts with a fixed amount of capital (say 10 units) and contemplates applying various amounts of labour to it. Table 18.1 shows the output that can be produced when various quantities of the variable factor are employed. As a preliminary step to understanding the table, we shall define the terms it uses.

Table 18.1 Variation of output (one fixed, one variable factor), with capital fixed at 10 units

(1) Quantity of labour L	(2) Total product TP	(3) Average product AP	(4) Marginal product[a] MP
1	43	43	43
2	160	80	117
3	351	117	191
4	600	150	249
5	875	175	275
6	1,152	192	277
7	1,372	196	220
8	1,536	192	164
9	1,656	184	120
10	1,750	175	94
11	1,815	165	65
12	1,860	155	45

[a] Marginal product here represents $TP_n - TP_{n-1}$, where n is the number of units of labour. For *graphical* purposes, *MP* should be viewed as occurring in the interval between the nth and $(n-1)$th unit. For example, the *MP* of 117 covers the interval from $L=1$ to $L=2$ and would be represented graphically as halfway between them.

Total, average and marginal product

Table 18.1 shows three different ways of looking at how output varies with the quantity of the variable factor.

(1) TOTAL PRODUCT (TP) means just what it says: the total amount produced during some period of time by all the factors of production employed over that time period. If the inputs of all but one factor are held constant, total product will vary with the quantity used of the variable factor. Columns (1) and (2) of Table 18.1 represent a total product schedule, and Figure 18.1(i) shows this schedule graphically. (We shall discuss its shape very soon.)

(2) AVERAGE PRODUCT (AP) is merely the total product per unit of the variable factor:

$$AP = TP/L.$$

It is shown as a schedule in column (3) of Table 18.1. The level of output where *AP* reaches a maximum is called the POINT OF DIMINISHING AVERAGE RETURNS.

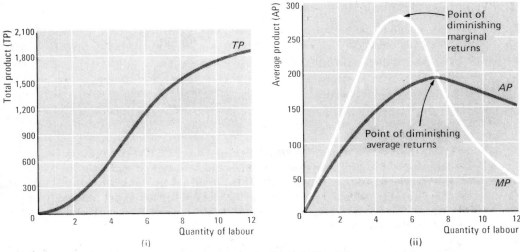

Fig. 18.1 (i)   Total product curve plotted from Table 18.1 ($k = 10$)
    (ii) Average and marginal product curves plotted from data in Table 18.1

(3) MARGINAL PRODUCT (MP) is the change in total product resulting from the use of one more (or one less) unit of the variable factor.[1]

$$MP = \Delta TP/\Delta L.$$

Computed values of the marginal product appear in the last column of Table 18.1. For example, the MP corresponding to 4 units of labour is given as 249 bushels. This reflects the fact that the increase in labour from 3 to 4 units ($\Delta L = 1$) increases output from 351 to 600 ($\Delta TP = 249$). MP in the example reaches a maximum between $L = 5$ and $L = 6$ and thereafter declines. The level of output where marginal product reaches a maximum is called the *point of diminishing marginal returns*.

Figure 18.1(ii) shows the average and marginal product curves plotted from the data in Table 18.1. Notice (1) that MP reaches its maximum at a lower level of L than does AP, and (2) that $MP = AP$ when AP is a maximum.[2]

Although three different curves are presented in Figure 18(i) and (ii), there is, of course, only one relationship between output and labour input. Fully specifying the average product schedule, for example, would let us derive the total product and marginal product schedules as well. We may use whichever of total, average or marginal concepts as proves most convenient.

---

1 The marginal product thus measures the rate at which total product is changing as one factor is varied. Students familiar with elementary calculus will recognize the marginal product as the partial derivative of the total product with respect to the variable factor. In symbols:

$$MP = \frac{\partial TP}{\partial L}.$$

In the text we refer only to finite changes, but the phrase 'a change of one unit', should be read 'a very small change'.

2 This is a matter of mathematics. We shall prove and make intuitively plausible a proposition directly analogous to this one, a proposition about average and marginal cost concepts, a few pages hence (see pages 224–5).

The hypotheses of diminishing returns

The variations in output that result from applying more or less of a variable factor to a given quantity of a fixed factor that are illustrated in Table and Figure 18.1, are the subject of a famous economic hypothesis. Most frequently, it has been called the LAW OF DIMINISHING RETURNS, but it has also been given other names, including the law of variable proportions and the HYPOTHESIS OF EVENTUALLY DIMINISHING RETURNS. It may be stated in terms of marginal and/or average products; we shall state it as two hypotheses rather than one.

> **Hypothesis of Eventually Diminishing Marginal Returns: If increasing amounts of a variable factor are applied to a fixed quantity of another factor, the amount added to the total product by each additional unit of the variable factor will eventually decrease, after which each additional unit of the variable factor will add less to the total product than did the previous unit.**

> **Hypothesis of Eventually Diminishing Average Returns: If increasing amounts of a variable factor are applied to a fixed quantity of another factor, the output per unit of the variable factor will eventually decrease.**

We state both hypotheses, since it is logically possible to have diminishing marginal

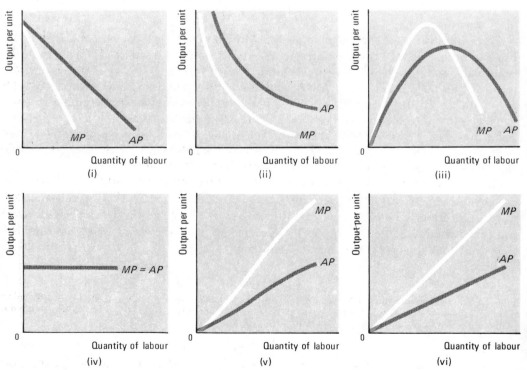

Fig. 18.2 The hypotheses of eventually diminishing productivity admit the possibility of (i) (ii) and (iii) but not, indefinitely, (iv) (v) and (vi)

returns without diminishing average returns. In the present chapter we shall be concerned with diminishing average returns, but in other places in your study of economics you will encounter the hypothesis of diminishing marginal returns. In any case both hypotheses are assumed to be true throughout.

Empirical evidence in favour of the hypothesis of diminishing returns is strong in many fields. Indeed, were the hypothesis incorrect, there would need to be no fear that the present population explosion will bring with it a food crisis. If the marginal product of additional workers applied to a fixed quantity of land were constant, then world food production could be expanded in proportion to the increase in population merely by keeping the same proportion of the population on farms. As it is, diminishing returns means an inexorable decline in the marginal product of each additional labourer as an expanding population is applied, with static techniques, to a fixed world supply of agricultural land. Thus, unless there is a continual and rapidly accelerating improvement in the techniques of production, the population explosion must bring with it declining living standards over much of the world, and eventual widespread famine.

The hypotheses of diminishing marginal and average returns are illustrated in Figure 18.2. If the hypotheses of diminishing productivity are correct, it is conceivable that marginal and average returns might diminish from the outset, so that the first unit of labour contributes most to total production and each successive unit contributes less than the previous unit. This is so, for example, in the cases illustrated in Figure 18.2(i) and (ii). The case in Figure 18.2(ii) is of particular interest, because it reflects the short-run shape of one widely used production function that is called the Cobb-Douglas production function. Situations such as that pictured in Figure 18.2(iii) are possible and have been extensively studied. In such cases, both marginal and average returns increase for a while and only later diminish. This would happen if it were impossible to use the fixed factor efficiently with only a small quantity of the variable factor (if, say, one man were trying to farm 1,000 acres). In this case increasing the quantity of the variable factor makes possible a better organization and a more efficient division of labour, so that the addition of another unit of the variable factor would make all units more productive than they were previously. According to the hypotheses of diminishing returns, the scope for such economies must eventually disappear, and sooner or later the marginal and average product of additional workers must decline. Another way of describing this situation is to recognize that, as we increase the amount of labour on 1,000 acres from 1 to 10 to 100 to 1,000 men, we are *varying* the proportions of the two factors. This is why the hypotheses are sometimes called the *laws of variable proportions*.

Short-run variations in costs

We now wish to pass from our theory of returns to a theory of costs. To do this we confine ourselves to a consideration of firms that are not in a position to influence the prices of the factors of production which they employ. These firms must take the market prices of the factors as given and can purchase all that they require at the going price; or, to put the same thing in more technical language, we confine ourselves to the study of firms that face perfectly elastic supply curves of all factors of production.

Given this assumption, we can now go from physical returns to short-run costs, for once we have specified both the returns to the variable factor and the price of the factor, we know by implication the cost of producing any given output. Let us start by defining three cost concepts analogous to the three production concepts already introduced.

(1) TOTAL COST means just what it says: the total cost of producing any given level of output. Total cost is conveniently divided into two parts, total fixed costs and total variable costs. FIXED COSTS are those costs that do not vary with output; they will be the same if output is one unit or one million units. The cost of any fixed factor is a fixed cost. Fixed costs are also often referred to as *overhead costs* or *unavoidable costs*. VARIABLE COSTS are all those costs that vary directly with output, rising as more is produced and falling as less is produced. In our previous example, since labour was the variable factor of production, the wage bill would be a variable cost. Variable costs are often referred to as *direct costs*.[1]

(2) AVERAGE COST is the total cost of producing any given output divided by the number of units produced so as to give the cost per unit. Average total cost may be divided into average fixed costs and average variable costs in just the same way as total costs were divided.[2]

Although average *variable* costs may rise or fall as production is increased, it is clear that average fixed costs decline continuously as output increases. A doubling of output always leads to a halving of fixed costs per unit of output. This is a process popularly known as 'spreading one's overheads'.

(3) MARGINAL (OR INCREMENTAL) COST is the increase in total cost resulting from raising the rate of production by one unit.[3] Since fixed costs do not vary with output,

---

1 In symbols we may write

$$TC = TFC + TVC$$
$$TFC = \bar{K}$$
$$TVC = w_i X_i,$$

where TC is total cost, TFC is total fixed cost, TVC is total variable cost, $\bar{K}$ is some constant amount, X_i is the quantity of the variable factor used, and w_i is the price per unit of this factor. Since fixed costs are constant and since variable costs necessarily rise as output rises, total costs must rise with output or, to put the point more formally, TC is a function of total product and varies directly with it: $TC = f(q)$.

2 In symbols:

$$ATC = \frac{TC}{q} = \frac{TVC + TFC}{q} = AVC + AFC.$$

3 In symbols:

$$MC = \frac{\Delta TC}{\Delta q}.$$

For a one-unit change, $MC_n = TC_n - TC_{n-1}$, i.e., the marginal cost of the nth unit of output is the total cost of producing n units minus the total cost of producing $n-1$ (i.e., one less) units of output. If we are producing a number of identical units of output, we cannot, of course, ascribe a separate (and different) cost to each unit. When we speak, therefore, of the marginal cost of the nth unit we mean nothing more than the change in total costs when the rate of production is increased from $n-1$ units to n units per period of time.

marginal fixed costs are always zero. Therefore marginal costs are necessarily marginal variable costs, and a change in fixed costs will leave marginal costs unaffected. For example, the cost of producing a few more potatoes by farming a given amount of land more intensively is the same, whatever the rent paid for the fixed amount of land.[1]

These three measures of cost are merely different ways of looking at a single phenomenon, and they are mathematically interrelated. Sometimes it is convenient to use one, and sometimes another.

Short-run cost curves

Let us take the production relationships in Table 18.1 and assume the price of labour is £20 per unit and the price of capital is £10 per unit. In Table 18.2, we present the cost schedules computed for these values. (If you do not see where any of the numbers come from, review Table 18.1 and the definitions of cost just given.) These data are graphed in Figure 18.3. Figure (i) shows the total curves; Figure (ii) plots the average and marginal cost curves.

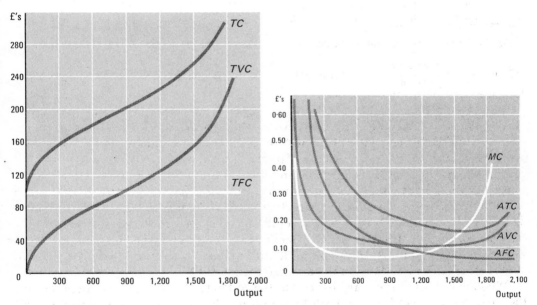

Fig. 18.3 (i) Three short-run total cost curves
(ii) Marginal and average cost curves

1 Only the simplest bit of algebra is necessary to prove this important proposition:

$$MC_n = TC_n - TC_{n-1}$$
$$= (TVC_n + TFC_n) - (TVC_{n-1} + TFC_{n-1}),$$

but

$$TFC_n = TFC_{n-1} = \bar{K};$$

therefore,

$$MC_n = (TVC_n + \bar{K}) - (TVC_{n-1} + \bar{K})$$
$$= TVC_n - TVC_{n-1}$$

Hence marginal costs are independent of the size of fixed costs.

Table 18.2 Cost schedules for data in Table 18.1 (price of labour, £20 per unit; price of capital, £10 per unit)

		Total cost			Average cost			Marginal cost[a]
(1)	(2)	(3)	(4)	(5)	(6)	(7)	(8)	
Labour	Output	Fixed	Variable	Total	Fixed	Variable	Total	
L	q	TFC	TVC	TC	AFC	AVC	ATC	MC
1	43	£100	£ 20	£120	£2·326	£·465	£2·791	£·465
2	160	100	40	140	·625	·250	·875	·171
3	351	100	60	160	·285	·171	·456	·105
4	600	100	80	180	·167	·133	·300	·080
5	875	100	100	200	·114	·114	·229	·073
6	1,152	100	120	220	·087	·104	·191	·072
7	1,372	100	140	240	·073	·102	·175	·091
8	1,536	100	160	260	·065	·104	·169	·122
9	1,656	100	180	280	·060	·109	·169	·167
10	1,750	100	200	300	·057	·114	·171	·213
11	1,815	100	220	320	·055	·121	·176	·308
12	1,860	100	240	340	·054	·129	·183	·444

[a] 'Marginal' cost is really 'incremental' cost, $MC = \dfrac{\Delta TC}{\Delta q}$, for intervals indicated in the table. Thus the MC of ·171 in line 2 is $\dfrac{£140 - £120}{160 - 43} = ·171$. For graphical purposes this should be plotted at the level of output halfway between 43 and 160.

THE RELATION BETWEEN AVERAGE AND MARGINAL CURVES: One point requires some emphasis. Notice that in the figure marginal cost cuts both average variable and average total costs at their minimum points. The relation between marginal and average curves is a mathematical one and not a matter of economics. Although it is a purely formal relation, it is very important to understand how these curves are related. The average cost curve slopes downward as long as the marginal cost curve is below it; it makes no difference whether the marginal cost curve is itself sloping upward or downward. When AC is declining, MC is below it. The common-sense interpretation is that, if the cost of an additional unit of output lowers the average cost, it must itself be less than the average cost.

If you will think of the marginal cost as the cost of the last unit, and remember that the average cost is influenced both by it and by all past units, you will find it self-evident that the marginal cost must cut the average cost curve at the lowest point on the AC curve – a valuable proposition one to remember.[1] A precisely analogous

1 The propositions of this paragraph are easily proved using calculus.
Let C = average cost per unit
   q = quantity of output,
   Total cost = C·q

$$MC = \frac{d(C \cdot q)}{dq} = q\frac{dC}{dq} + C.$$

$\dfrac{dC}{dq}$ is the slope of the average cost curve. Since quantity of output (q) is positive,

relationship holds between any average curve and the marginal curve corresponding to it. Previously, we met marginal and average products when we saw that marginal product cut average product when AP was a maximum. We shall meet other marginal curves later.

We have drawn the average cost curves as U-shaped. Focus for the moment on the shape of the average variable cost curve. It reaches a minimum at an output of 1,372 units, the same output at which AP reached a maximum in Table 18.1. This is no accident, for with fixed factor prices, when average product per worker is a maximum, average variable cost must be a minimum.[1]

The common sense of this proposition is that each additional worker adds the same amount to cost but a different amount to output. When average productivity is rising, the cost per unit of output will be falling, and vice versa.

The hypothesis of eventually diminishing average productivity thus implies the hypothesis of eventually increasing average variable costs.

For rising average total costs, all that is additionally required is that average variable costs should eventually rise faster than average fixed costs fall.

The hypothesis of diminishing average returns implies only that average costs will *eventually* rise. 'Eventually' may not mean that they rise whenever output is increased. An important empirical question that has long concerned students of cost behaviour is whether the average cost curve rises in the range of output that is relevant to the

---

$$\frac{dC}{dq} < 0 \text{ means } MC < C \qquad (1)$$

$$\frac{dC}{dq} > 0 \text{ means } MC > C \qquad (2)$$

$$\frac{dC}{dq} = 0 \text{ means } MC = C. \qquad (3)$$

Condition (3) is, of course, a necessary condition of minimum C, and proves that marginal cost is equal to average cost at its minimum point. The reader should now be able to prove in an analogous fashion that, when average product is a maximum, $MP = AP$.

1 This point is easily seen if a little algebra is used:

$$AVC = \frac{TVC}{q}$$

but

$$TVC = L \cdot w$$

and

$$q = AP \cdot L,$$

where L is the quantity of the variable factor used and where w is its cost per unit.

Therefore

$$AVC = \frac{L \cdot w}{AP \cdot L}$$

$$= \frac{w}{AP}.$$

In other words, average variable cost equals the price of the variable factor divided by the average product of the variable factor. Since w is constant, it follows that AVC and AP vary inversely with each other, and when AP is at its maximum value AVC must be at its minimum value.

firm's plans. The empirical evidence does show rising costs, but often the shape of the curve is very flat – more like a saucer than a cup – in the relevant range of outputs.

THE DEFINITION OF CAPACITY: The level of output that corresponds to the minimum level of short-run total cost is often called *optimal capacity*, *plant capacity*, or just *capacity*. Capacity in this sense is not an upper limit on what can be produced, as you can see by looking again at Table 18.2. In the example, capacity output is between 1,500 and 1,600 units, but higher outputs can be achieved. A firm producing with *excess capacity* is producing at an output smaller than the point of minimum average total cost. A firm producing *above capacity* is producing above this output and is thus incurring higher costs per unit. These concepts give the term CAPACITY a meaning different from its meaning in everyday speech, but the concepts will prove useful and need cause you no confusion.

THE LONG RUN

In what way does the long run differ from the short run? In the short run, with only one factor variable, there is only one way to produce a given output: by adjusting the input of the variable factor until the desired level of output is achieved. Thus, in the short run, the firm must make a decision about its output, but once it has decided on a rate of output, there is only one technically possible way of achieving it. In the long run all factors are variable. If a firm decides on some rate of output, it has an additional decision to make: by which of the many technically possible methods will the output be produced; should the firm adopt a technique that uses a great deal of capital and only a small amount of labour or should it adopt one that is less capital intensive but uses more labour?

Since there are almost always many ways of achieving the same total output, we need some method of choosing between them. The hypothesis of profit maximization provides a simple rule for this choice: any firm that is trying to maximize its profits will select the method of producing a given output that produces it at the lowest possible cost. This is an implication of the hypothesis of profit maximization, and we term it the implication of COST MINIMIZATION. It can be stated formally as follows:

> **For any specific output the firm chooses the least costly way of achieving that output from the alternatives open to it.**

If there is a known stable required output rate, and if the costs of factors are known, this is all there is to it.

Graphical representation of the cost-minimizing choice[1]

We assume that in the long run the firm can choose to use the factors in a wide range of different proportions. Table 18.3 shows a numerical example in which 6 units of output can be produced by a range of different methods. The first method uses much labour and very little capital, we say it is a very labour-intensive method of production. As we move down the table, capital is being substituted for labour in such a way

1 This section can be omitted without loss of continuity.

as to keep output constant; we say the method of production is becoming more capital intensive. Finally, at the bottom of the table, we reach the most capital-intensive method where almost all of the labour has been replaced by (probably highly automated) capital.[1]

Some of the combinations shown in Table 18.3 are plotted in Figure 18.4. A smooth curve is drawn between the points to indicate the assumption that, in the long run, the firm can choose *any* combination of labour and capital should it be profitable to do so. This curve is derived from the production function by finding all combinations of the inputs that will yield a given output. The curve is called an 'equal product curve' or an ISOQUANT and it shows the whole set of technically-efficient possibilities for producing 6 units of output. It is analogous to a contour line on a map joining all points of equal altitude.

Table 18.3 Alternative ways to produce six units of output*

L	K
144	$\frac{1}{4}$
72	$\frac{1}{2}$
36	1
18	2
12	3
9	4
6	6
4	9
3	12
2	18
1	36
$\frac{1}{2}$	72
$\frac{1}{4}$	144

* These are points for an isoquant for 6 units of output for the production function $q = \sqrt{L \cdot K}$.

We started arbitrarily with the isoquant for 6 units of output. But there is another isoquant for 7 units, for 7,000 units, or for any other rate of output. If we plot a number of these isoquants, say at output intervals of 1,000 units, on a single graph we have what is called an isoquant map. Each isoquant refers to a specific output and connects alternative combinations of factors that are shown by the production function to be capable of achieving that output.

To find the least-cost way of producing any given output we need to represent factor costs. Suppose, to continue our example, that capital costs £4 per unit and labour costs £1 per unit. In Chapter 14 we used a budget line to show the alternative combinations of goods a household could buy; now we use an *isocost line* to show alternative combinations of factors a firm can buy for a given outlay. For example, the line labelled $TC = 18$ in Figure 18.4 is an isocost line that represents all combinations of the two factors that the firm could buy for £18. Point *a* represents 3 units of *K* and

1 If you are worried about using fractions of a unit of labour, remember that our units are undefined and could just as easily be 100 man-months as 1 man-month.

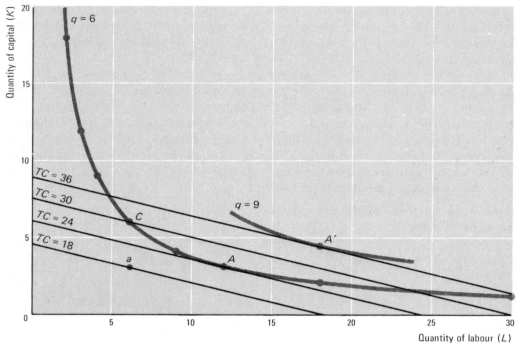

Fig. 18.4 Choice of the least-cost factor proportion

6 units of L. The slope of this line reflects relative factor prices just as did the slope of the budget line in Chapter 14 (see page 154). We also show in Figure 18.4 the isocost lines for £24, £30 and £36.

Now consider the point labelled A in the Figure. It is on the 6-unit isoquant and on the £24 isocost line. Thus it is possible to achieve the output $q = 6$ for a total cost of £24. There are other ways to achieve this output, as we saw. One such way to produce 6 units is shown at point C, where $K = 6$, $L = 6$ and $TC = £30$.

A least-cost way of producing any output must be represented by a point such as A. It must be a point on an isoquant that just touches an isocost line. If it cuts the isocost line (as happens at point C), it is possible to move along the isoquant and reach a lower level of cost. Only at point A (where $K = 3$ and $L = 12$) is a movement in *either* direction a movement to a higher cost level. The lowest attainable cost of producing 6 units is £24, and the lowest average cost of producing six units is £24/6 = £4 per unit of output.

> **The least-cost method of producing any given output can be described graphically as the tangency point between the relevant isoquant and an isocost line.**

The intuitive sense of this tangency solution is that the isoquant represents the technical ability to substitute labour for capital in production, and the isocost line represents the ability to substitute labour for capital in the market place. At a point such as C it pays to substitute labour for capital, because the technical gain is larger than the market-exchange rate of labour for capital.[1]

THE LONG-RUN OUTPUT EXPANSION: Suppose a firm is in the position indicated by point A in Figure 18.4, but wishes to produce more output. Clearly it will have to spend more money. Suppose it is prepared to spend £36 instead of £24. The isocost line shifts outward to Total Cost = £36 in the figure. What is the highest output the firm can achieve for this cost? Clearly it wants the highest isoquant that it can reach on the isocost line, and this will be the isoquant that is just tangent to the isocost line. It is shown as point A' in Figure 18.4, where output is 9 units. If we connect all such tangency points, we have an *output-expansion path* that shows the least-cost way of producing each level of output.

Figure 18.5 shows three different output-expansion paths for three different iso-quant maps. In each diagram the points A, A' and A'' represent the least-cost way of producing the level of output of the isoquant they are on. In Figure 18.5(i) the output-expansion path is a straight line from the origin (a *ray*). The distinguishing characteristic of a ray is that the proportion of L to K is everywhere the same. This indicates that the least-cost factor proportions are unchanged as output changes. This happens to be true of the Cobb-Douglas function and of a number of other so-called homogeneous functions. But it need not be the case. In Figure 18.5(ii) the output-expansion path shows that the best factor proportions change as output increases, with capital being increased relative to labour. In other words, in Figure 18.5(ii) capital is substituted for labour. In Figure 18.5(iii) a reverse situation is pictured in which labour is substituted for capital as output increases. We shall return to the question of changing factor proportions shortly.

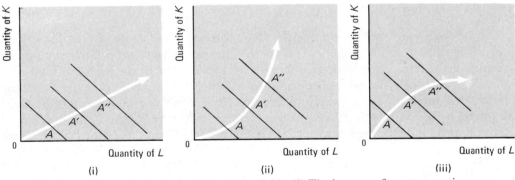

Fig. 18.5 Output-expansion paths, both factors variable. (i) The least-cost factor proportions are unchanged as output changes (ii) Capital is substituted for labour as output increases (iii) Labour is substituted for capital as output increases

Long-run cost curves

In the long run it is possible to attain the least-cost factor combination of producing any output. For given factor prices a least-possible cost can be associated with each

1 Remember that at point A in Figure 18.4 we have both (1) the lowest level of cost for six units of output, and (2) the highest level of output for £24 of cost.

level of output and the result is a long-run cost curve. A long-run average cost curve is shown in Figure 18.6. The rate of output is measured on the horizontal axis, and the cost per unit of output (i.e., total cost divided by the number of units) is measured on the vertical axis.

This curve is related to the production function. You should be absolutely clear as to its meaning. There are several technically feasible ways of producing any output, say q_2; for the given factor prices there is one least-cost technique. The level of cost per unit using that technique is c_2. Levels of cost below c_2 are not technically possible at that output; levels above c_2 (such as c_2'), while possible, are not economically efficient. The curve is the boundary between what is feasible and what is not feasible, given the production function and the costs of the factors of production.

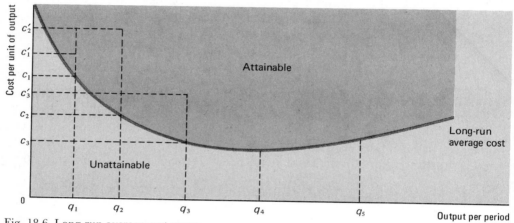

Fig. 18.6 Long-run average cost curve

To be sure you understand Figure 18.6, compare the levels of cost shown for outputs q_2 and q_3. This cost curve shows the cheapest way to produce each of those outputs if the firm is perfectly free to vary all factors and thus attain the least-cost factor combination for each output. Output q_3 is larger than q_2 and the least-cost method of producing it is likely to require more capital and more labour than required by q_2. This may mean a larger plant of different design. Thus if a firm is actually producing output q_2 at cost c_2 and wishes to increase its output to q_3, it will only achieve the lowest cost level (c_3) if it is prepared to change its plant and equipment. It would take time to do this, and in the meantime q_3 can only be produced by applying more labour to a plant designed to produce q_2 so that factor proportions would not be those designed to produce q_3 at c_3.

THE SHAPE OF THE LONG-RUN COST CURVE: What can be said about the shape of the long-run cost curves? Figure 18.7 shows sections of the long-run average cost curves of three imaginary firms. Let us begin with some definitions.

Increasing returns: Firm *A* in Figure 18.7 is what is called a DECREASING-COST FIRM. An expansion in production will, once sufficient time has elapsed for all desired

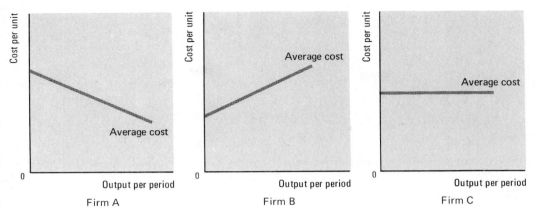

Fig. 18.7 Long-run average cost curves of three firms. Firm A: decreasing costs, increasing returns. Firm B: increasing costs, decreasing returns. Firm C: constant costs, constant returns

adjustments to be made in the techniques of production, result in a reduction in costs per unit of output. Since the prices of factors are assumed constant, the fall in costs per unit must be because output increases faster than inputs as the scale of the firm's production expands. Such a firm is often said to be encountering INCREASING RETURNS TO SCALE.

Advantages of large-scale production may arise simply as a result of the scale of output (with no change in factor proportions), owing to such things as the specialization of tasks that division of labour makes possible. They may also arise because of factor substitution. Even the most casual observation of the differences in production technique used in large- and small-sized plants supports the existence of the differences in factor proportions. This is because large, specialized machinery and equipment, which uses a different ratio of labour to capital than does smaller, less specialized equipment, is useful only when the volume of output that the firm can sell justifies its use.

Decreasing returns: Firm *B* in Figure 18.7 is called a RISING-COST FIRM. An expansion in production will, even after sufficient time has elapsed for all adjustments to be made, be accompanied by a rise in average costs per unit of output. If costs per unit of input are constant, this rise in costs must be the result of an expansion in output less than in proportion to the expansion in inputs. Such a firm is said to be encountering DECREASING RETURNS TO SCALE.

Decreasing returns are easy to understand where there are fixed factors (such as high-quality management) that get overutilized as output rises, or where the cost of factors rises as the firm tries to acquire more of them. But if the theory of long-run costs is taken literally to mean that all factors are fully variable and that all factor prices are fixed, it is difficult to see why cost per unit need rise. After all, one way of producing twice today's output is to *replicate* – to build an identical plant elsewhere and operate it identically. Rising output costs usually imply either some hidden fixed factors or rising factor costs.

Constant returns: Firm *C* is a CONSTANT-COST FIRM. Its average costs per unit of output do not change as the scale of output changes. This means that output must be increasing exactly as fast as inputs are increased; the firm is said to be encountering CONSTANT RETURNS TO SCALE.

Once a firm reaches an output sufficiently large that there are no longer advantages of yet larger production open to it, it may expect to be able to double or treble its output by replicating – i.e., by increasing its number of identical plants.

The modern theory of long-run costs leads to the prediction that, *except for changes in factor prices*, firms that are free to vary all factors of production should experience increasing or constant returns. They may be able to take advantage of larger output to introduce specialized techniques that lead to increasing returns and decreasing costs. When these opportunities are exhausted, they should have to do no worse than replicate their existing methods of production.

The relation between the long- and the short-run cost curves

The various short-run cost curves and the long-run curve are all derived from the same production function, plus given prices for all factor inputs. In the long run all factors can be varied, in the short run some must remain fixed. The long run cost-curve shows the lowest cost of producing any output when all factors are variable. In Figure 18.8, we have reproduced a fragment of the long-run cost curve of Figure 18.6. The level of output, q_2, and its associated cost level, c_2, are the same as in Figure 18.6. We know that the cost level, c_2, is the lowest attainable cost of producing the

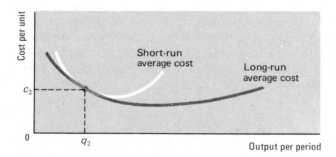

Fig. 18.8 A short-run and a long-run average cost curve

output q_2. But the best technique for achieving this output uses *some* quantity of each factor. Now suppose the firm builds a plant appropriate to this output. What happens if the firm then varies output using this (fixed) plant? The short-run cost curve shows the answer to this question. As output is varied from q_2, by applying more or less of the variable factors, costs will vary also. As output is changed from q_2, a different size plant would be required to achieve the lowest attainable cost. Thus we expect that short-run costs will rise above the long-run costs as shown in the figure. All this means is that the firm's average costs will be higher if it is forced to produce one output with a plant designed for another output than they are if it can produce the output with a plant optimally designed for that level of output. Note that the short-run cost curve is tangent to (touches) the long-run curve at the level of output for which the fixed factor is appropriate and lies above it for all other levels of output.

If we now repeat the whole process, assuming that the firm is fully adjusted to some different level of output and that it then has to vary output in the short run, we shall generate a new short-run cost curve. If we repeat this process for every level of output, we will find that every point on the long-run cost curve has associated with it a short-run cost curve that touches it at that point. Each such curve shows how costs vary as output is varied, holding some factors fixed at the level most appropriate to that output. This is illustrated in Figure 18.9.[1] The long-run curve is sometimes called an 'envelope' that encloses the short-run curves.

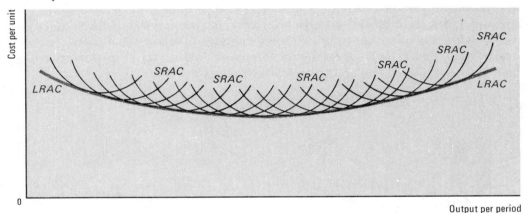

Fig. 18.9 The relation between the long-run average cost curve and the short-run average cost curves

Variations in factor prices: the principle of substitution

What will happen to the least-cost method of production if there is a change in factor costs? We should expect that if one factor becomes cheaper relative to the other, the least-cost method of producing any given output will change in the direction of using more of the now relatively cheaper and less of the now relatively more expensive factor. This is exactly what happens and, on the assumption that firms try to minimize their costs, we have the following prediction:

> **Methods of production will tend to change if the relative prices of factors change. More of the relatively cheaper factor will be used and less of the relatively more expensive one.**

The principle illustrated graphically

Consider the example first given in Figure 18.4 and repeated in Figure 18.10. Let

1 Each short-run curve touches the long-run curve at one point and lies above it everywhere else. We say the short-run curves are tangent to the long-run one. This has an important, though subtle, consequence. Two curves that are tangent at a point have the same slope at that point. If *LRAC* is decreasing where it is tangent to *SRAC*, then *SRAC* must also be decreasing. Thus the point where *SRAC* = *LRAC* need not be the minimum point of *SRAC*. Unless *LRAC* is horizontal at the point of tangency, it will not be tangent at the minimum point of *SRAC*. The economic sense of this rests upon the subtle distinction between the most efficient way to utilize a given plant, and the most efficient way to produce the amount of output required. It is the *second* that interests us as economists. If bigger plants can achieve lower costs per unit, we will gain by building a bigger plant and underutilizing it whenever the gains from using the bigger plant are big enough to offset the costs of being inefficient in our use of the plant. If there are *some* gains from building bigger plants there is always some underutilization that is justified.

the price of labour rise from £1 to £4, the price of capital being constant at £4 per unit. The optimal factor combination for producing 6 units originally was 12 units of labour and 3 units of capital (shown at point *A* of Figure 18.10). It cost £24. To produce that same output in the same way would now cost £60 at the new factor prices. But the new £60 isocost line is not tangent to the isoquant. A substitution of labour for capital by shifting to point *C* makes it possible to produce 6 units for £48 (6 units of labour at £4, 6 units of capital at £4). Thus we see (1) that the increase in the price of one factor increased the cost of production (from £24 to £48 in the example), but (2) substitution of the relatively cheaper factor, labour, kept the cost below what it would have been (£60) if no change in factor proportions had been made. *An increase in the price of one factor shifts all relevant cost curves upwards and causes a substitution of relatively cheap factors for relatively expensive factors.*

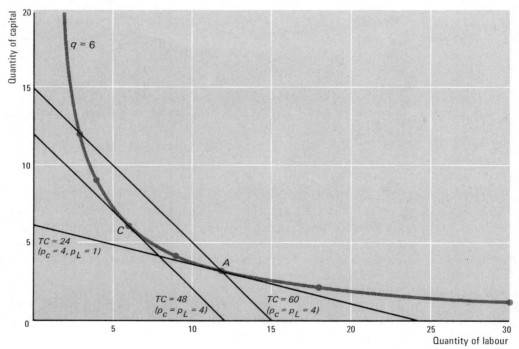

Fig. 18.10 The effect of a change in factor price on least-cost factor proportions

A digression on the significance of the principle of substitution to the economy as a whole

The relative prices of factors of production in an economy will tend to reflect their relative scarcities. In a country with a great deal of land and a small population, for example, the price of land will be low while, because labour is in short supply, the wage rate may be high. In such circumstances firms producing agricultural goods will tend to make lavish use of (cheap) land and to economize on (expensive) labour; a production process will be adopted that is labour extensive and land intensive. On the other hand, a small country with a large population will be one in which the demand for land will be high relative to its supply. Thus, land will be very expensive and firms producing agricultural goods will tend to economize on land by using a great deal of labour per unit of land. In this case a productive process will tend to grow up that is labour intensive and land extensive.

Thus we see that relative factor prices will reflect the relative scarcities (in relation to demand) of different factors of production: abundant factors will have prices that are low relative to the prices of factors that are scarce. Firms seeking their own private profit will be led to use much of the factors with which the whole country is plentifully endowed, and to economize on the factors that are in scarce supply in the whole country.

This discussion provides an example of what we mean when we say that the price system is an automatic control system. No single firm needs to be aware of national factor surpluses and scarcities. Prices determined on the competitive market tend to reflect these, and individual firms that never look beyond their own private profit are nonetheless led to economize on factors that are scarce to the nation as a whole.

The above suggests that we should not be surprised to discover that methods of producing the same commodity differ in different countries. In the United States, where labour is highly skilled and very expensive, a steel company may use very elaborate machinery to economize on labour. In China, where labour is abundant and capital very scarce, a much less mechanized method of production may be appropriate. The Western engineer who feels that Chinese are way behind Westerners because they are using methods discarded in the West as inefficient long ago may be missing the truth about economic efficiency in use of resources. The suggestion, often made, that to aid underdeveloped countries we need merely to export Western 'know-how' may be incomplete.

It appears that the price system does lead profit-maximizing firms to take account of the nation's relative factor scarcities when deciding which of the possible methods of production to adopt. One must avoid jumping to the conclusion that whatever productive processes are produced by the market are always the best possible ones and that they should never be interfered with. There is, however, a strong common-sense appeal in the idea that any society interested in getting the most out of its resources should take account of their relative scarcity in deciding what productive processes to adopt.

THE VERY LONG RUN

Changes in supply over the very long run are strongly influenced by changes in the techniques of production, by changes in the goods being produced, and by changes in the quality of factor inputs. Most economic theory focuses attention on short- and long-run decisions taken within the context of given factor supplies, given products, and known techniques of production. These decisions are important but, if we are interested in the performance of the economic system over long time periods, questions concerning the causes and consequences of very long-run changes cannot be ignored. In this section we confine ourselves to the question of how the economic system will respond in the very long run to changes in demands, prices and costs such as we have considered in the short and long run and in doing this we shall concentrate on changes in *productivity*. Many of the wider aspects of very long-run changes must be postponed until Chapter 48, which deals with the whole problem of long-term economic growth.

Productivity

There is no doubt whatever that over the last years, the material standard of living of the typical family has increased enormously in all of the world's industrialized countries. Much of this increase has been due to the invention of new, improved ways of making products. This causes an increase in output per unit of input employed, and it is referred to as an increase in PRODUCTIVITY.

The magnitude of increases in productivity deserves some attention. The apparently modest rate of increase of output per man-hour of labour of 2·0 per cent per year leads to a doubling of output per man-hour every 35 years. Productivity in the United Kingdom has increased at approximately this rate over the last 100 years.

Between 1945 and 1970 productivity growth in the UK was closer to 3 per cent per year (which doubles output every $23\frac{1}{2}$ years) while in other countries it has been much higher. In Japan, for example, it has been increasing at about 10 per cent per year, a rate which doubles output per man-hour approximately every seven years.

PRODUCTIVITY CHANGES AND THE THEORY OF SUPPLY: There is no doubt that productivity changes affect the supplies of commodities. What is in doubt is the extent to which productivity changes themselves are an endogenous response to economic signals and incentives and the extent to which they are an endogenous consequence of the spontaneous creative activity of scientists, inventors and many other researchers. The answer to the question will greatly influence our judgement of the ability of the economy to adjust to various disturbances that impinge on it.

SOURCES OF INCREASES IN PRODUCTIVITY: Long-run increases in efficiency are due to, and can be divided into, scale effects, increases in the quality of the inputs, changes in the known techniques of production and improvements in products. Mere population growth, other things equal, will permit higher productivity if most products are subject to increasing returns to scale. Substitution of more and more capital for labour as the level of production expands is likely to lead to greater productivity. Better raw materials, better trained or educated labour, or better machines will increase productivity even if no changes in factor quantities or proportions take place. Better organization of production alone can account for increases in productivity. New ideas can raise efficiency by being applied to new products: imagination can design a better mousetrap, with no change in the quantity, quality or proportions of factors.

Inventions and innovations

An INVENTION is defined as the discovery of something new, such as a new production technique or a new product. An INNOVATION is defined as the introduction of an invention into use.

It is generally accepted that innovation responds to economic incentives. New products and methods will not be introduced unless it appears profitable to do so, and a change in economic incentives can change the apparent profitabilities of various possible innovations.

But innovation can only occur when there has already been an invention. If there is a dramatic rise in labour costs, firms may now decide to take up some labour-saving process that hitherto had been ignored since its invention, but they cannot do so if the invention has not yet been made. If we are concerned with the response of the economy to such economic signals as changes in the relative prices both of consumer goods and of inputs, then we need to know the extent to which invention responds to such incentives. A number of hypotheses about the sources of invention have been put forward.

(1) INVENTION IS A RANDOM PROCESS: Some men are by nature both curious and clever. Thousands of attempts will be made to invent better ways of doing things. Many men will fail, and they remain nameless, but a few succeed. These are the Hardwicks, Stephensons, Whitleys, Edisons and Fords. The successful inventions become a pool of potential innovations, and, when the climate is right, they are introduced into production.

(2) INVENTION IS A RESPONSE TO THE INSTITUTIONAL FRAMEWORK: Things like the patent laws, the tax structure, or the organization of business enterprise stimulate or retard the process of invention. Invention, in this view, is not exogenous to society, but it does not respond primarily to economic variables, and it certainly is exogenous to the individual *firm*.

(3) INVENTION AND INNOVATION ARE THE PRODUCT OF THE INHERENT LOGIC AND MOMENTUM OF SCIENCE: Science has a logic and momentum of its own. There was a time for the discovery of the steam engine, the aeroplane, hybrid corn, the electron tube and the rocket. Particular men are the instruments, not the causes, of scientific discovery. Had Edison never been born we would still have had, at about the same time, both the light bulb and the gramophone. According to this view, the present is the electronic age, and automation is its industrial application.

(4) NECESSITY IS THE MOTHER OF INVENTION: Ignorance is only skin deep. With enough expenditure of funds, men can do anything – split the atom, conquer cancer, fly to Mars or cultivate the desert. The pace and rate of invention depend upon how many resources are devoted to solving problems, and resources are devoted according to needs. A firm for which a certain factor is becoming scarce will discover ways to economize on using it, or will develop a more plentiful substitute for it. (For example, the scarcity of high-grade iron ore led to the development of ways of using low-grade ores.) In this view, automation is a response to expensive labour. The impetus for invention may thus come from within the firm. But it may also come from without: governments may set priorities and do the research that leads to major discoveries and innovations. Atomic energy, for example, is the result of the United Kingdom's

and later of the United States' desire to develop superweapons during the Second World War.

(5) PROFITS ARE THE SPUR: The profit motive not only leads men and firms to seize the best known methods, but to develop new ways to meet both old and new needs and wants.

Which of these hypotheses is correct? Possibly all of them are. They are not self-contradictory and the evidence for one cannot be regarded as disproving the others. The fact that some firms spend millions of pounds on research and development to overcome specific problems or invent new products does not change the fact that many discoveries are made in university laboratories by men who have little knowledge of, or interest in, current prices and scarcities. The fact that many patentable discoveries are given to the world does not prove that others are not motivated by the prospect of huge personal gain. And so on.

We have asked whether the direction of invention responds to economic incentives. We are also critically interested in the pure volume of invention. Even if its direction does not exactly respond to current market signals it is still a potent source of increases in living standards. Inventions that reduce the quantities of all inputs required to gain a given output are absolutely efficient and will raise living standards even if they save just as much on plentiful as on scarce factors of production.

Invention and economic incentives

Does it matter how invention is determined? Consider a single example to illustrate why it does.

Hypothesis 1: This hypothesis accepts the third view of invention listed above. This is the age of electronics and automation, and scientists just go on inventing methods that replace unskilled labour with capital, thereby creating unemployment among the unskilled. The normal corrective of the price system is for the relative price of unskilled labour to fall, thus inducing a substitution in favour of unskilled labour until the unemployment is eliminated. But, so goes the hypothesis, scientists just go on inventing labour-saving techniques, uninfluenced by the incentives of relative factor prices. Now assume that each new technique invented is *absolutely* more efficient than its predecessors in the sense that it uses less of *all* factors than does its predecessors – but at the same time it uses less unskilled labour *relative* to other inputs. Firms will now be motivated to adopt the absolutely more efficient new techniques, but in so doing they will adopt a factor combination that increases the unemployment amongst the unskilled.

Hypothesis 2: This hypothesis accepts the fifth view of invention given above. When unemployment amongst the unskilled drives down their relative wage, firms will be led to select from amongst existing techniques those that are more intensive in the use of unskilled labour. If there is still unemployment amongst the unskilled, their factor services will remain cheap and there will be a profit incentive to develop *new* techniques that substitute cheap unskilled labour for the more expensive factors of production.

Thus, in the case of hypothesis 1, the long-term effects of invention and innovation are to increase the problem of 'structural unemployment' of the unskilled, while in the case of hypothesis 2, the effect of the same inventive activity is to reduce this unemployment. Clearly it matters whether in the long run invention proceeds more or less autonomously or under the influence of such economic incentives as relative factor prices.

SUMMARY OF THE BASIC THEORY OF COSTS

This concludes our study of the theory of costs. A number of the subjects covered, although important, are digressions from the point of view of developing a theory of the behaviour of the firm. We shall now summarize the basic points that the student needs to know before proceeding to the next few chapters on the theory of supply. Anyone who is not clear about the following points should review his understanding of them by re-reading the relevant parts of the preceding two chapters.

(1) We hypothesize that firms strive to maximize their profits, and, since profits are the difference between the costs and revenues of the firm, it is necessary to consider what we mean by costs and how these vary as output varies.

(2) The cost to the firm of any input that it uses is given by what the firm must give up to have the use of the input.

(3) In the case of any factor service that the firm hires from outside, the cost to the firm is adequately measured by the price paid, since that sum of money cannot be used for other purposes.

(4) In the case of factors owned by the firm, the cost is measured by what the factor could be leased out (or sold) for on the open market. This cost may bear little relation to the cost originally paid to purchase these factors.

(5) Points (2)–(4) summarize an opportunity cost principle of input valuation: the cost of using an input is the cost of the alternatives that are foregone by so doing.

(6) So far we have seen how to value inputs. To see how costs vary as production varies we need to see how inputs vary as production varies. This relation is described by the production function. When we have costed the inputs we can derive a cost function showing how costs vary as production varies.

(7) In the short run some factors are fixed and some are variable. The variations in output that accompany variations in the variable input are described by the hypothesis of eventually diminishing returns. Given the price of the variable factor, we can move directly from returns curves to cost curves. The short-run marginal and average cost curves are assumed to be U-shaped with the MC curve cutting the AC curve at the lowest point on the latter curve.

(8) In the long run all factors are variable and the long-run average cost curve shows the lowest attainable average cost for each level of output on the assumption that the proportion in which inputs are used is so adjusted as to make costs as low as possible.

(9) The principle of substitution says that the long-run effect of a change in factor prices is to cause a substitution of the relatively less expensive factors for the relatively more expensive ones. Thus a change in price induces an economizing of factors whose prices rise and a more lavish use of factors whose prices fall.

(10) Each short-run cost curve touches the long-run cost curve at one point and elsewhere lies above the long-run curve. If the *LRAC* is falling, the tangency point is to the left of the minimum point on the *SRAC*; if the *LRAC* is rising, the tangency point is to the right of the minimum point on the *SRAC*. Only at the minimum point of the *LRAC* is the tangency at the minimum point on the *SRAC*.

(11) In the very long run technological knowledge changes, and the question of how costs change as output changes depends on the question of how changes in technological knowledge respond to changes in economic incentives.

19

The equilibrium of a profit-maximizing firm

In Chapter 17 we hypothesized that firms seek to maximize their profits, such profits being the difference between total revenues derived from selling their product and the total cost of making it. In Chapter 18 we developed a theory of the variation of cost with output. This theory is meant to apply to all firms. In the present chapter we consider the firm's revenues and profits, and develop the rules for profit-maximizing behaviour as they apply to all firms. When we come to apply these rules, however, we find that we cannot develop a single theory of the relation between revenue and output that is applicable to all firms. In subsequent chapters we develop separate theories of revenue for firms in different market situations. In the meantime we confine ourselves to what can be said for all firms.

VARIOUS REVENUE CONCEPTS

The revenues of the firm are the receipts that it obtains from selling its products. We can look at these revenues as totals, averages or marginal quantities in exactly the same way as we looked at costs as totals, averages and marginal quantities in the previous chapter.

(1) TOTAL REVENUE refers to the total amount of money that the firm receives from the sale of its products, i.e., to gross revenue. This will vary with a firm's sales so we may write:

$$TR = R(q),$$

where TR is total revenue and, as in the last chapter, q is total production over some period of time. [1] Total revenue is obviously equal to the quantity sold multiplied by the selling price of the commodity, i.e.,

$$TR = q \cdot p,$$

where p is price per unit. The unqualified term *revenue* is often used to refer to

1 We are not considering problems of the holding of stocks of commodities so, in this simple theory, we can equate production with sales.

total revenue and whenever we speak of revenue or use the symbol R we shall mean total revenue.

(2) AVERAGE REVENUE is total revenue divided by the number of units sold so as to give the average revenue per unit sold. Quite obviously, the average revenue is the price of the commodity, so we may write:

$$AR = p.$$

It follows from this that the curve which relates average revenue to output is identical with the demand curve that relates price to output.

(3) MARGINAL REVENUE is the change in total revenue resulting from an increase in the rate of sales per period of time (say per annum) by one unit. The marginal revenue resulting from the sale of the nth unit of a commodity is thus the total revenue resulting from the sale of n units per annum minus the total revenue that would have been earned if only $n-1$ (i.e., one less) units had been sold per annum. The reader should not think that $n-1$ units are sold at some time and an extra unit at some later time. Marginal revenue refers to alternative sales policies *at the same period of time.* Thus, to find the marginal revenue of the 100th unit we compare the total revenue resulting when 100 units are sold over some period of time with the total revenue that would have resulted if 99 units had been sold over the same period of time. In general we may write[1]:

$$MR_n = TR_n - TR_{n-1}.$$

BEHAVIOURAL RULES FOR PROFIT MAXIMIZING

We have assumed that the firm tries to maximize its profits. We now translate this behaviour into several formal rules. We do not assume that the firm necessarily uses these rules in coming to its decision, but, as long as the firm succeeds somehow in maximizing its profits, these rules will allow us to predict its behaviour.

A rule to decide whether or not to produce at all

A firm always has the option of producing nothing. If it produces nothing, it will have an operating loss equal to its fixed costs. Unless production adds as much to revenue as it *adds* to costs, it will increase the loss suffered by the firm.

> **Rule 1. A firm should produce output only if total revenue is equal to or greater than total variable cost.**

Another way of stating this rule is that the firm should produce output only if average revenue (price) is equal to or greater than average variable cost.

---

1 This definition invokes finite changes. Students familiar with the calculus will recognize marginal revenue as the *derivative* of total revenue with respect to quantity sold:

$$MR = \frac{dTR}{dq} = f'(q).$$

A rule to ensure that profits are either at a maximum or at a minimum[1]

If the firm is going to produce at all according to Rule 1, it is necessary to decide how much it should produce. If, on the one hand, the firm finds that at its present level of production the cost of making another unit (marginal cost) is less than the revenue that that unit would bring in (marginal revenue) it is clear that the firm could increase its profits by producing more. Thus, whenever a firm finds that at the current level of output marginal revenue exceeds marginal cost it can increase its profit by producing more. If, on the other hand, the firm finds that at the present level of production the cost of making the last unit exceeds the revenue gained by selling it, total profit could clearly be increased by not producing the last unit of output. Thus, whenever the firm finds that marginal cost exceeds marginal revenue it can increase its total profit by reducing its output.

Now we have the result that the firm should change its output whenever marginal cost does not equal marginal revenue, raising output if $MR > MC$ and lowering output if $MC > MR$. Rule 2 follows from this.

> **Rule 2. If a firm is to be in a position where it does not pay it to alter its output – i.e., in a profit-maximizing position – it is necessary that marginal revenue should equal marginal cost.**

At the profit-maximizing output the last unit produced should add just as much to revenue as it adds to cost.

A rule to ensure that profits are maximized rather than minimized

It is possible to fulfil Rule 2 and have profits at a minimum rather than a maximum. Figure 19.1 illustrates. The firm has a short-run marginal cost curve similar to the ones derived in Chapter 18 and it is assumed to be able to sell all its output at the going market price so that the market price is the firm's marginal revenue. (If all units can be sold at the prevailing market price then each unit adds that price to the firm's total revenue.)

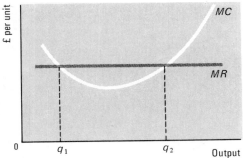

Fig. 19.1 Marginal cost = marginal revenue is a necessary but not a sufficient condition for a profit maximum

---

1 Advanced students will realize that the possibility of a stationary point of inflexion in the profits function is ignored in this treatment.

There are two outputs in the Figure, q_1 and q_2 where marginal cost equals marginal revenue. Output q_1, however, is a minimum profit position because a change of output in either direction would increase profit: for outputs below q_1 marginal cost exceeds marginal revenue and profits can be increased by *reducing* output while for outputs above q_1 marginal revenue exceeds marginal cost and profits can be increased by *increasing* output.

Output q_2, however, is a maximum profit position since at outputs just below q_2 marginal revenue exceeds marginal costs and profits can be increased by increasing output towards q_2, while at outputs just above q_2 marginal cost exceeds marginal revenue and profit can be increased by *reducing* output towards q_2.

Rule 3 is needed to distinguish minimum profit positions such as q_1 from maximum positions such as q_2.

Rule 3. For an output for which $MC = MR$ to be a profit-maximizing output rather than a profit-minimizing output it is sufficient that $MC < MR$ at slightly smaller outputs and that $MC > MR$ at slightly larger outputs.

The geometric statement of this condition is that at the profit-maximizing output the marginal cost curve should intersect the marginal revenue curve from below (thus ensuring that $MC < MR$ to the left of, and $MC > MR$ to the right of, the profit-maximizing output).

A mathematical derivation of the rules of profit maximization

Students familiar with elementary calculus may like to see these conditions derived formally, others may skip this section.

Condition 1: Profits π are defined as follows:

$$\pi = R - (FC + VC), \tag{1}$$

where R is total revenue, FC is total fixed cost and VC is total variable cost. Now let subscripts n and p stand for a state where there is no production and one where there is production respectively. It pays the firm to produce if there is some level of production for which

$$\pi_p \geqslant \pi_n. \tag{2}$$

When the firm does not produce, R and VC are zero so the profit condition (2) becomes

$$R - FC - VC \geqslant - FC$$

or

$$R \geqslant VC \tag{3}$$

or, dividing both sides by output, Q, we get: price $\geqslant AVC$.

Condition 2:

$$\pi = R - C \tag{4}$$

but both revenues and costs vary with output, i.e., $R = R(Q)$ and $C = C(Q)$. Thus we may write

$$\pi = R(Q) - C(Q).$$

A necessary condition for the maximization of profits is

$$\frac{d\pi}{dQ} = R'(Q) - C'(Q) = 0$$

or

$$R'(Q) = C'(Q).$$

But these derivatives define marginal revenue and marginal cost so we have

$$MR = MC.$$

Condition 3: To ensure that we have a maximum and not a minimum for profits we require

$$\frac{d^2\pi}{dQ^2} = \frac{dMR}{dQ} - \frac{dMC}{dQ} < 0$$

or

$$\frac{dMR}{dQ} < \frac{dMC}{dQ}$$

which means that the algebraic value of the slope of the marginal cost curve must exceed, at the point of intersection, the algebraic value of the slope of the marginal revenue curve. This translates into the geometric statement that the marginal cost curve should cut the marginal revenue curve from below.

THE MEANING AND SIGNIFICANCE OF PROFITS

We have talked of the firm maximizing its profits, which are the difference between its revenue and its cost, but the special meaning that we have given to the concept of cost implies the special meaning for the concept of profits that we first discussed on page 217. Positive profit means an excess of revenues derived from the sale of output over the full opportunity costs of all the factors used to produce the output; while negative profits, more commonly called losses, implies that revenues fall short of opportunity costs.

This use of the words *profit* and *loss* gives specialized definitions to words that are in everyday use. They are, therefore, a potential source of confusion.

Other definitions of profits

The businessman defines profits as the excess of revenues over the costs with which his accountant provides him. The major differences are that, since the accountant does not include as costs, charges for risk-taking and use of the owners' own capital, these items are recorded by the businessman as part of his profits. When the business-man says he *needs* profits of such and such an amount in order to stay in business, he is making sense within his definition, for his 'profits' must be large enough to pay for those factors of production that he uses but does not account for as costs.

The economist would express the same notion by saying that the businessman needs to cover *all* of his costs, including those not included by accounting conventions. If the firm is covering all its costs (in the sense that we have defined costs), then it follows that it could not do better by using its resources in any other line of activity than the one currently being followed. Indeed, it would probably do worse in most other lines of activity; it certainly would do no better. Thus a situation in which revenues equal costs (profits of zero) is a satisfactory one – because all factors, hidden as well as visible, are being rewarded at least as well as in their *best* alternative uses.

The income-tax authorities have yet another definition of profits, which is implicit in the thousands of rules as to what may be (and what may not be) included as a deduction from revenue in arriving at taxable income. In some cases, the taxing authorities allow more for cost than the accountant recommends; in other cases they allow less. [1]

It is important to be clear about different meanings of the term *profits* not only to avoid fruitless semantic arguments but also because a theory that predicts that certain behaviour is a function of profits defined in one way, will not necessarily predict behaviour accurately, given some other definition. For example, if the economist predicts that new firms will enter an industry whenever there are profits, his prediction will frequently be wrong if he is working from the businessman's definition of profits. The economists' definition of profits is for many purposes the most useful, but if you wish to apply it to business behaviour or to tax policy, you must be prepared to make the appropriate adjustments. Also if you wish to apply accounting or tax data to particular economic theories, you must be prepared to rectify the data.

Profits and resource allocation

When resources are valued by the opportunity cost principle, we have seen that the amounts assigned show how much these resources might earn if used in their best alternative uses. If there is some industry in which revenues typically exceed opportunity costs, the firms in that industry will be earning profits. This will mean that profit-maximizing firms will want to move resources into this industry, because the earnings potentially available there are greater than in alternative uses of the resources. If, in some other industry, firms are incurring losses, some or all of this industry's resources are more highly valued in other uses, and profit-maximizing firms will want to reallocate some of the resources at their command.

---

1 In some economics texts of an earlier generation the pure return to capital and the risk premium are not called costs. When this is done these returns are included in profits and profits are divided between normal profits and super-normal profits. Normal profits are what must be earned to induce a firm to remain in an industry and they are thus the same thing as the returns to capital and risk-taking. Super-normal profits are anything in excess of normal profits and are thus the same thing as our profits. The difference is purely semantic. To say that an industry is in equilibrium when its firms are just earning normal profits, where such profits include returns to capital and risk-taking, is the same thing as saying that an industry is in equilibrium when its firms are earning neither profits nor losses when costs include returns to capital and risk-taking.

Profits in some activity are the signal that resources can profitably be moved into that activity. Losses are the signal that they can profitably be moved elsewhere. Profits and losses thus play a crucial signalling role in the workings of a free-market system. Only if there are zero profits (revenues equal to opportunity costs) is there no incentive for resources to move into or out of an industry.

20

The theory of perfect competition

In the previous chapter we derived the rules for maximizing profits. These general rules apply to all firms. The actual relation of revenue to output, however, is not the same for all firms. It depends on how much competition the firm has. We shall distinguish four basic market situations, often called MARKET FORMS. For each situation we shall develop a theory of how revenue varies with output, and of how firms consequently behave to maximize profits. The market form of PERFECT COMPETITION is discussed in this chapter; the three other forms, monopoly, monopolistic competition and oligopoly, are dealt with subsequently.

THE DEMAND FOR A FIRM'S PRODUCT

We may begin by illustrating how the market situation may influence the demand, or revenue curve that the firm faces. Consider first an automobile manufacturer. He will be aware that his own policies can influence the market for his product. He will know that, if he makes a substantial increase in his price, his sales will fall off, while if he lowers his price substantially, he will be able to sell more of his product. If he contemplates making a large increase in his production that is not in response to some known or anticipated rise in demand, then he is likely to have to reduce his price in order to sell the extra output. Thus he cannot control both price and quantity in any way that he wishes; the quantity that he is able to sell will depend on the price that he charges. Let us now make the point more formally: the manufacturer of automobiles is faced with a downward-sloping demand curve for his product. He is able to determine *either* the price of his product *or* the quantity that he sells; he may fix his price, in which case the maximum quantity that he can sell is determined, or he may fix the quantity that he will sell, in which case the maximum price that he may charge is determined.

Now, by way of contrast, consider an individual producer of wheat. He will be one of a very large number of farmers, all growing wheat; his own contribution to the total production will be but a very, very small drop in an extremely large bucket. The elasticity of demand facing the wheat farmer is, of course, the elasticity of the market demand curve for wheat. Taking a typical estimate of 0·25 for the elasticity of world demand for wheat, this means that, if the farmer succeeded in increasing the world supply of wheat by $\frac{1}{4}$ per cent, he would bring down the world price by 1 per cent. The farmer is, however, not interested in the relation between changes in *world* output and the price of wheat, but rather in the relation between changes in *his own* output and the price of wheat, and, of course, large percentage changes in his own output will represent only very small percentage changes in world output. The elasticity of the market demand for a product is defined as

$$\eta_M = (-1) \frac{\text{percentage change in total quantity}}{\text{percentage change in market price}}.$$

What we now need is a new concept to measure the reaction of world price to changes in one farmer's output. We call this the *firm's elasticity of demand*, and define it as

$$\eta_F = (-1) \frac{\text{percentage change in one producer's output}}{\text{consequent percentage change in market price}}.$$

Although the denominators of these two elasticities are the same, the numerators are not. Any change in one farmer's wheat production will represent a larger percentage change in his own production than it will in world production. Thus, in the case of the wheat farmer, η_F will be substantially larger than η_M.

To see this, let us roughly calculate the firm's elasticity of demand for a very large wheat farmer. Total world production of wheat was approximately 13,000 million bushels in 1973; the output of a very large Canadian wheat farm would have been in the order of 125,000 bushels. Now suppose that this wheat farm increased its production by 62,500 bushels, a 50 per cent increase in its own production but an increase of only 1/1000 of 1 per cent in world production. Table 20.1 shows that this increase would lead to a decrease in the world price of 1/500 of 1 per cent, and give the farm an elasticity of demand of 25,000! This is a very high elasticity of demand. The farmer would have to increase his output 1,000 times to bring about a 1 per cent increase in world output of wheat. Since the farmer is quite unable to vary his output this much, it is not surprising that he regards the price of wheat as being unaffected by any changes in output that he could conceivably make. Clearly we will not be far off the truth if we say that, for all practical purposes, one wheat farmer is unable to affect the world price. If he doubles, triples or quadruples his production at one extreme or stops producing altogether at the other, this will have but a negligible effect on the world price. We therefore assume, as only a very slight simplification of reality, that the farmer is *totally* unable to influence the world price of wheat and is able to sell all that he could conceivably produce at the going world prices. This gives us the first of the two major assumptions of the theory of perfect competition:

Assumption 1: The individual firm in perfect competition is assumed to be faced with a perfectly elastic demand for its product, meaning that at some price it can sell all it produces, and at higher prices none.

The difference between the wheat farmer and the automobile producer is one of degree of *power* over the market. The wheat farmer, because he is an insignificant part of the whole market, has no power to influence the world price of wheat. The automobile manufacturer, on the other hand, does have the power to influence the price of automobiles, because his own production represents a quite significant part of the total supply of automobiles.

Students sometimes confuse the individual firm's demand curve under perfect competition with the market demand curve for the product. The market demand curve is downward sloping, indicating that if there is an increase in supply, prices will fall. The demand curve facing a single producer is assumed to be perfectly elastic, because variations in his production, *over the range which we need to consider for all practical purposes*, will have such a *small* effect on price that the effect can safely be assumed to be *zero*. Of course, if the single producer increased his production by a vast amount, say ten-thousand-fold, then this would cause a significant increase in supply and he would be *unable* to sell all he produced at the going price. The perfectly elastic demand curve does not mean that the producer could actually sell an infinite amount at the going price, but rather that the variations in production *which it will normally be practicable for him to make* will leave price virtually unaffected.

Table 20.1 Calculation of a firm's elasticity of demand*

Given: $\eta_M = 0.25$

World output = 13,000 million bushels

Firm's output increases from 125,000 to 187,500 bushels

Step 1. Find the percentage change in world price:

$$\eta_M = -\frac{\text{percentage change in world output}}{\text{percentage change in world price}}$$

Percentage change in world price $= -\dfrac{\text{percentage change in world output}}{\eta_M}$

$$= -\frac{5/10{,}000 \text{ of 1 per cent}}{0.25}$$

$$= -1/500 \text{ of 1 per cent.}$$

Step 2. Compute the firm's elasticity of demand:

$$\eta_F = -\frac{\text{percentage change in firm's output}}{\text{percentage change in world price}}$$

$$= -\frac{50 \text{ per cent}}{-1/500 \text{ of 1 per cent}} = \frac{.5}{.00002} = +25{,}000.$$

* In this calculation, we depart from the procedure for arc elasticity recommended on page 103 and use the original quantities in computing percentage changes. This is done only for arithmetic convenience in the example.

Total, average and marginal revenue of the firm in perfect competition

In perfect competition the individual firm faces a perfectly elastic demand curve for its product. Since the market price is unaffected by variations in the firm's output, it follows that the marginal revenue resulting from an increase in the volume of sales by one unit is constant and is equal to the price of the product. If, for example, a farmer faces a perfectly elastic demand for wheat at a market price of £2 a bushel, it follows that each additional unit sold will bring in that amount, i.e., the marginal revenue is £2, and the average revenue (equals total revenue/number of units sold) is also £2. The demand curve facing the firm is thus identical with both the average and the marginal revenue curves. All three of these curves coincide in the same straight line showing that $p = AR = MR$ all remain constant as output varies. Total revenue does, of course, vary with output; since price is constant, it follows that total revenue rises steadily as output rises. (The student should satisfy himself that, if he draws a graph relating a perfectly competitive firm's total revenue to its output, he will obtain an upward-sloping straight line which passes through the origin.)

PROFIT-MAXIMIZING OUTPUT OF THE COMPETITIVE FIRM

We saw in the previous chapter that profit maximization implies that marginal cost equals marginal revenue. Since, for the perfectly competitive firm, marginal revenue equals the market price, it follows that (if the firm maximizes profits) marginal cost will equal price.

This is illustrated in Figure 20.1. At output q_1 the cost of making an extra unit is

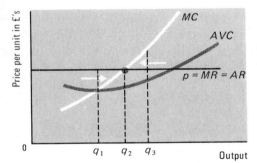

Fig. 20.1 The equilibrium of a competitive firm

less than the revenue gained from selling that unit. It therefore pays the firm to increase its rate of production and, by so doing, to increase its profits by the difference between MC and MR. This relation holds for any point to the left of q_2, and the incentive to raise production is indicated by the arrow. At output q_3, on the other hand, the cost of making an extra unit exceeds the revenue gained from the sale of that unit. It therefore pays the firm to reduce its rate of production and, by so doing, to increase its profits by the amount of the difference between MC and MR. This relation holds for any point to the right of q_2, and the incentive to lower production is indicated by the arrow. At output q_2 the firm cannot increase profits either by raising or by lowering output. Output q_2 is thus the rate of output for which profits are maximized. When the firm is maximizing profits, it has no incentive to change its output policy. Unless prices or costs change, the firm will stay put, since it is doing as well as it can do; we say that the *firm* is in *equilibrium*. Economists are not usually interested in equilibrium positions as such. Such positions are required in order to do comparative static analysis which allows us to predict the consequence of various changes in which we are interested. Through comparative static analysis we hope to generate testable hypotheses about actual behaviour. First, however, we must discover the equilibrium for the whole industry before we can use our theory to produce hypotheses about how competitive industries will react to the changes in which we are interested.

THE DERIVATION OF THE SUPPLY CURVE
The firm's supply curve

Figure 20.2(i) shows a numerical example of a firm's marginal cost curve, together with four *alternative* demand curves: D_1 if the market price is £2; D_2 if the market price is £3; D_3 if the market price is £4; and D_4 if the market price is £5.

The firm's marginal cost curve gives the marginal cost corresponding to each level of output. We desire a supply curve that gives the quantity the firm will supply at every price. At prices below AVC the firm will supply zero units (rule 1). At prices above AVC the firm will equate price and marginal cost (rule 2) producing q_1 at p_1, q_2 at p_2, q_3 at p_3 and so on. From this it follows that:

> **In perfect competition the firm's marginal cost curve above AVC has the identical shape of the firm's supply curve.**

This proposition is so obvious that it sometimes causes difficulty to the student who is looking for something very difficult and very profound. Any reader who is not absolutely certain that he understands it should construct for himself the firm's supply curve. Given perfect competition, profit maximization, and the actual cost curve of Figure 20.2(i), the reader can discover the output of the firm corresponding to any

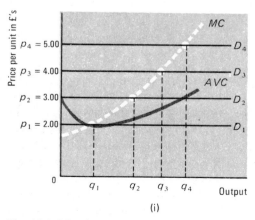
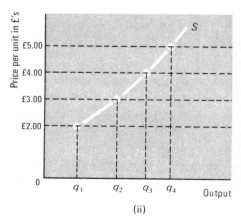

(i)   (ii)

Fig. 20.2 Marginal cost and supply curves for a price-taking firm

given market price. He can then plot the firm's curve on a graph of his own by relating market price to quantity produced by the firm. Once he has done this he will see that the supply curve he has constructed is identical in shape to the marginal cost curve in Figure 20.2(i) and the supply curve in Figure 20.2(ii).

The short-run supply curve for a competitive industry

Now that we have derived the supply curve for each firm in a competitive industry, we have to derive the supply curve for the whole industry. To do this, we find the sum of the amounts supplied by each firm for each given price.

Consider the simple numerical example illustrated in Figure 20.3. Firm A's supply curve is shown in the first diagram and firm B's in the second. The problem is to

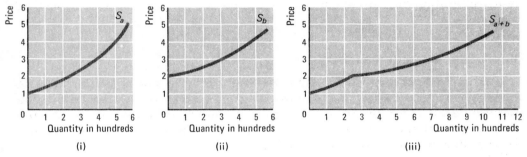

Fig. 20.3 The derivation of the supply curve for a competitive industry

construct an aggregate supply curve showing how the total supply of these two firms will vary with price (on the assumption that they are in a perfectly competitive industry). Below the price of £1, nothing is produced. Between £1 and £2, only firm A produces, so the aggregate supply curve is identical with firm A's curve. At a price of £3, firm A produces 400 units and firm B produces 300 units; the total production at £3 is 700 units. For any given price the aggregate quantity is the sum of the two quantities produced by the two firms at that price.

If there are hundreds of firms the process is the same: each firm's MC curve shows what the firm will produce at any given price, p; the industry supply curve relates the price p to the sum of the quantities produced by all the firms. Thus we have the following result.

> **The supply curve for a competitive industry is the horizontal sum of the marginal cost curves of all the individual firms in the industry.**

In Part 2 we used short-run industry supply curves as part of our theory of price. We have now derived these curves for a competitive industry, and we have seen how they are related to the behaviour of individual, profit-maximizing firms.

An industry is said to be in short-run equilibrium when price is such that supply equals demand. This was discussed in detail in Chapter 9. Figure 20.4 illustrates such an equilibrium. We know that at price p_E the quantity supplied by each firm setting $p_E = MC$ will add up to the quantity from E. This is true by definition: we constructed the industry supply curve in such a way as to make it true. The industry is said to

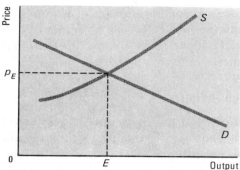

Fig. 20.4 The equilibrium of a competitive industry

be in equilibrium when supply equals demand and thus when, for each firm, marginal cost equals price.

Profits and losses in the short run

We have shown that the firm is in short-run equilibrium at a rate of output for which its marginal cost equals its marginal revenue. Although we know from this that the firm is maximizing its profits, we do not know how large these profits are. It is one thing to know that a firm is doing as well as it can in the circumstances; it is quite another thing to know how well it is doing.

Indeed it is quite possible that a firm in short-run equilibrium will be making profits, incurring losses, or just covering costs. Providing that losses are not more than fixed costs, all three situations represent possible short-run equilibrium positions for *all* of the firms in some perfectly competitive industry. But only the position of zero profits represents a possible long-run equilibrium. We saw in the last chapter that profits and losses provided a signal that resources should enter or leave an industry. Thus, if existing firms are showing profits, there will be an incentive for new firms to enter the industry – since resources employed in this industry are earning more than they can earn in their next best alternative use. If existing firms are making losses, there is an incentive for profit-maximizing firms to leave the industry, since the resources they are employing could earn more in other uses. When revenues equal costs, resources in this industry will be earning just as much as they could earn in their best alternative use, and only then will there be no incentive for the industry either to expand or to contract.

Now to make the transition to the long run, we introduce the second of the two important assumptions of the theory of perfect competition.

> **Assumption 2: Any new firm is free to set up production if it so wishes and any existing firm is free to cease production and leave the industry if it so wishes. We say that the industry has freedom of entry and exit.**

This assumption ensures that there are no legal or other institutional barriers to prevent profit-maximizing firms reacting to the incentives provided by the existence of short-run profits and losses.

CAN PROFITS DIFFER AMONG FIRMS?: In perfect competition all firms face the same price, therefore, their profits can differ only if their costs differ. There are two main reasons why, at first sight, one might expect costs to differ among perfectly competitive firms. First, some firms may have access to superior technology not available to others and, second, some may have access to superior factors not available to others (e.g. an especially talented manager).

The first reason is ruled out by the assumptions of the model of perfect competition. It is assumed that there are no monopolies of knowledge: anything that one firm knows another firm can know, and any technology that is available to one firm is available to all other firms. This is not as unlikely as it might sound at first sight. These conditions are roughly fulfilled, for example, in agriculture when every farmer can buy the same tractors, use the same fertilizer and read the same technical books as every other farmer.

> **In perfect competition all firms have access to the same technology so that costs cannot differ among firms on this account.**

The second reason, access to superior factors, will cause factor earnings *but not profits* to differ among firms. For example, a superior manager will run his firm better than an average one. The manager, however, should be able to collect the whole of his extra productivity in terms of a higher-than-average salary because other firms will be willing to pay him more than the average manager to obtain his services. But what if the manager had been unfortunate enough to sign a long-term contract with his employer at only the average managerial salary before he realized he had superior abilities? Surely when the firm costs the manager at the average salary that it pays him, the firm will earn extra profits equal to the manager's extra productivity? The answer is 'no' because the firm must cost its use of the manager at his opportunity cost, and the firm always has the option of taking on an average manager and then hiring out the services of the superior manager at a wage that reflects his ability.

The moral to this story is that the fruits of superior factors of production adhere to the factors, they are extra income resulting from the use of the factor; they are not a source of extra profits to firms. (If a firm owns a superior factor, as in the case of the manager under contract or an owner-manager, the firm can earn the extra return on the manager's skill but it does so by virtue of owning the factor, not as an addition to the profits earned on its capital.)[1]

> **Different qualities of factors may be a source of differences in gross revenues and in factor earnings among perfectly competitive firms but they are not a source of different costs and profits.**

In perfect competition all firms must have identical cost curves. As a check assume that the manager of one firm suddenly became super-efficient and managed to reduce his firm's costs so that his firm was making $10,000 a year more than all other firms. That manager is himself immediately worth the extra $10,000. Any firm that could bid him away for anything less than $10,000 would add to their profits by so

1 This important principle is discussed in much more detail in Chapter 27.

doing. Thus the costs of the firm for whom the manager works go right back where they were initially once the manager's services are properly costed.[1]

Profits as defined by the accountant or the tax collector may differ greatly among perfectly competitive firms, but costs defined as opportunity costs will be identical.

In perfect competition all firms have identical cost curves.

LONG-RUN EQUILIBRIUM OF THE COMPETITIVE FIRM AND INDUSTRY

First assume that existing firms in the industry are making losses when they are in their profit-maximizing, short-run equilibrium position. When average revenue is below average total cost, the typical firm in this industry is not using its resources to maximum advantage. When it gets the chance, it will shift them to other uses. It gets this chance as its fixed factors, such as machines, gradually are used up. If the firm does not replace them; it will gradually liquidate its investment and withdraw (or exit) from the industry. As firms withdraw, the short-run supply curve of the industry, which is the sum of the marginal cost curves of all the firms remaining in the industry, will shift to the left and prices will rise. Firms will continue to withdraw and price will continue to rise until the firms remaining in the industry are able to cover all their costs – until, that is, they are no longer making losses.

Now assume that in short-run equilibrium the firms in the industry are making profits. These profits will attract new investment into the industry in the form either of new firms entering the industry and/or of existing firms expanding their plants. For simplicity we shall illustrate for the case of new firms entering the industry.

Suppose, in response to high profits for 100 existing firms, ten new firms enter an industry. Market demand does not change, and the market supply curve that formerly added up to the outputs of 100 firms now must add up the outputs of 110 firms. At any price, more will be supplied because there are more suppliers. But this shift in supply will mean that the equilibrium price must fall. As the price falls, so will profits fall. The new entry will continue, however, until the extra supply has driven price down sufficiently to eliminate all profits; only then will there be no further incentive for entry.

Finally, assume that in short-run equilibrium there are neither profits nor losses. Now there is no incentive for exit since resources can do no better elsewhere; and neither is there any incentive for entry since resources do no better here than elsewhere. Thus, if we define long-run equilibrium to be a situation in which the industry is neither expanding nor contracting but is fully adjusted to the present state of demand and costs, a long-run equilibrium will have the following characteristics.

---

1 The point is subtle and it is a source of considerable confusion. It is therefore worth re-emphasizing that the firm may get the extra $10,000 if it has control over the manager through a long-term contract but it gets it because it owns the manager's services, it does not receive an extra return on its capital. To understand this *vary the example* to assume that the firm could hire out the manager's services to other firms for a premium of $11,000 over the average manager's salary but the manager could only save this firm $10,000. Now if the firm uses the manager itself and correctly costs his services at the market premium over the average manager's salary of $11,000 it shows a loss of $1,000. This is because the firm had the alternative of hiring in an average manager and losing the $10,000 the superior manager could have saved it, while renting out the services of the superior manager and gaining $11,000 thereby. For the firm now to use the superior manager itself does, therefore, show a loss of $1,000 over the best alternative plan.

(1) Firms will be equating short-run marginal cost to price; i.e., they must be in short-run, profit-maximizing equilibrium.

(2) Price must equal average total cost; i.e., firms must be making neither profits nor losses so there is a tendency neither for expansion nor contraction.

Economies of scale[1]

The previous section gives enough of the long-run theory of a perfectly competitive industry to enable us to do many comparative static exercises. There is, however, a third characteristic of competitive industries in long-run equilibrium that is important in some contexts:

(3) If a perfectly competitive industry is in long-run equilibrium, each individual firm must be producing at the minimum point of its long-run average total cost curve – i.e., it must not have further unexploited economies of scale within its grasp. (These would be shown by a downward slope of the long-run cost curve at the firm's present level of output.)

To understand the reasoning behind this proposition start by assuming that a firm is just covering its average total costs of production with its present quantity of the fixed factor, but that it has unexploited economies of scale. This means that it will be able to reduce its average total costs of production by increasing the quantity of its factor that is fixed in the short run (say, by building a larger plant). Since it can sell all it produces at the going market price, it can increase its profits by this policy (average total costs fall while average revenue remains constant). Thus a firm will increase its size by increasing the quantity of its fixed factor whenever it is subject to falling long-run costs at its present level of output.

Next assume that a firm is just covering its costs, but that it is in the range of diseconomies of scale so that its long-run average cost curve is rising at its current level of output. Now the firm could increase its profits by reducing the size of its fixed factor, thus reducing average total costs below its (constant) average total revenue.

The argument can be shown graphically. Figure 20.5 shows a perfectly competitive firm's long-run average cost curve (the white curve labelled *LRATC*) and short-run average and marginal cost curves for three different quantities of the fixed

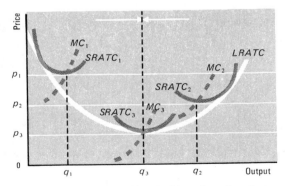

Fig. 20.5 Three short-run equilibria but only one long-run equilibrium

1 This section can be skipped without loss of continuity.

factor. Assume first that the firm's current amount of capital gives it short-run marginal and average total cost curves of $SRATC_1$ and MC_1. If the market price of the product is p_1, the firm would be in short-run equilibrium at output q_1 where it is just covering its total costs – given the present quantity of its fixed factor. But since at q_1 the firm's long-run average cost curve lies below p_1, output q_1 could be produced at a lower cost if the firm changed the quantity of its fixed factor. In this case the firm needs to increase the fixed factor: the present size of the firm is too small.

Second, assume that the firm has a much larger quantity of the fixed factor so that its short-run curves are $SRATC_2$ and MC_2. If the price were p_2, the firm would be in short-run equilibrium at output q_2 where it would be just covering all its costs. But again the long-run cost curve at q_2 is below p_2. The firm could achieve lower costs by changing the size of its fixed factor. In this case the present size of the firm is too large.

Only when the firm's fixed factor is such that its short-run curves are $SRATC_3$ and MC_3 is it possible for it to be in long-run as well as in short-run equilibrium. This will occur when the price is p_3: the firm is in short-run equilibrium at output q_3 and it is also on its long-run cost curve. Any variation in quantity of the fixed factor would raise long-run average costs, and given the price p_3, would produce losses.

We have seen that since in a perfectly competitive industry the same technology is available to all firms, all firms have the same cost curves. For a given set of factor prices, $LRATC$ in Figure 20.5 will thus be the cost curve of *each* firm in the perfectly competitive industry. This means that each firm can be in long-run equilibrium when its fixed factors are such that its short-run curves are $SRATC_3$ and MC_3 when market price is p_3 and each firm's output is q_3. The total output of the industry will depend on the number of identical individual firms that are in the industry. (There will have to be just enough firms so the sum of their individual outputs equals the quantity demanded at a price of p_3. If quantity supplied is less than quantity demanded at p_3 the price will rise, profits will be earned and new firms will be attracted into the industry. If quantity supplied exceeds quantity demanded at p_3 then price will fall, losses will occur and some existing firms will leave the industry.)

21

The theory of monopoly

The market form of MONOPOLY is at the opposite extreme from that of perfect competition. It exists whenever an industry is in the hands of a single producer. In the case of perfect competition there are so many individual producers that no one of them has any power whatsoever over the market; any one producer can greatly increase or diminish his production without affecting the market price significantly. A monopolist, on the other hand, has power to influence the market price; by reducing his output he can force up the price, and by increasing his output he can force it down. In the first half of this chapter we confine ourselves to the case of monopolists who must charge a single price for the goods that they sell; in the second half we consider cases in which the monopolist can sell his goods at different prices either to different classes of customers or to different geographical markets.

A MONOPOLIST WHO SELLS HIS COMMODITY AT A SINGLE MARKET PRICE
Average and marginal revenue for a monopolist

The reader should now review the section on total, average and marginal revenue on pages 243–4. Since the monopolist is the only producer of the product, the demand curve that the firm faces *is* the market demand curve. Also, since a 10 per cent variation in the monopolists' output *is* a 10 per cent variation in the industry's output, it follows that the firm's elasticity of demand (see pages 250–2) is the same as the market elasticity of demand.

In perfect competition the price is unaffected by variations in the firm's output, and it follows that the addition to revenue resulting from increasing the level of sales by one more unit is the market price of that unit (see page 253). Thus the marginal and average revenue curves coincide in the same horizontal straight line. In the case of monopoly, however, the average revenue curve, which is the same as the market demand curve, is *downward* sloping. Furthermore, the marginal revenue curve does not coincide with the demand curve: since the sale of *an extra unit* forces down the price at which all units already being sold can now be sold, the sale of an extra unit results in a net addition to revenue of an amount less than its own selling price.

We must now inquire in more detail into the relation between the average and marginal revenues of a monopolist. We may start by considering the simple example illustrated in Table 21.1.

Table 21.1 Alternative price and sales combinations for a monopolist together with the corresponding marginal revenues

	Price	Rate of sales per year	Total revenue	Marginal revenue
Situation 1.	£2	100	£200	
				£0·99
Situation 2.	£1·99	101	£200·99	
				−£0·05
Situation 3.	£1·97	102	£200·94	

We assume that the monopolist is selling each year 100 units of some commodity at a price of £2. This yields a total revenue of £200. He then steps up his rate of sales to 101 units per year, but, as a consequence of the downward-sloping demand curve, he drives the price down to, say, £1·99. This makes his new total revenue £200·99. Thus, the increase in revenue resulting from the sale of an additional unit per year is only £0·99 even though the extra unit sells for £1·99. A moment's thought will show that there is no mystery about the fact that the marginal revenue (£0·99) is less than the price (£1·99) at which the extra unit is sold. One hundred units per year could have been sold for £2, but, in order to sell the extra unit, the price *on all units* is driven down by 1p. Thus, there is a loss of 1p per unit on each of the 100 units. This makes a total loss of £1·00 which must be deducted from the extra revenue of £1·99 from the sale of the 101st unit. Thus, the net increase in revenue associated with the sale of the 101st unit is only £0·99.

The sceptical reader may construct similar numerical examples in order to illustrate for himself the proposition that, whenever the demand curve slopes downward, the marginal revenue associated with an increase in the rate of sales by one unit per period will be less than the price (or average revenue) at which that unit is sold.[1]

---

1 It is easy to prove algebraically that, if the demand curve slopes downwards, marginal revenue is always less than price. Let subscripts n and $n+1$ indicate the revenue associated with the sale of n and $(n+1)$ units, so that, e.g., TR_n is the total revenue associated with the sale of n units per period.

$$\begin{aligned} MR_{n+1} &= TR_{n+1} - TR_n \\ &= (n+1)P_{n+1} - nP_n \\ &= nP_{n+1} + P_{n+1} - nP_n \\ &= n(P_{n+1} - P_n) + P_{n+1}. \end{aligned}$$

Since the demand curve slopes downwards P_{n+1} (the price ruling when $n+1$ units are sold) will be less than P_n (the price ruling when n units are sold). Thus the MR of the $n+1$th unit is less than P_{n+1}.

Using calculus, the proof is as follows:

$$\begin{aligned} P &= P(q) \\ TR &= q.P = q.P(q) \\ MR &= \frac{dTR}{dq} = q.P'(q) + P(q) \end{aligned}$$

But $P(q)$ is the price and $P'(q)$ is negative, since the demand curve slopes downward. Thus $MR < P$, and the difference is the marginal fall in price, $P'(q)$, multiplied by the quantity already being sold, q.

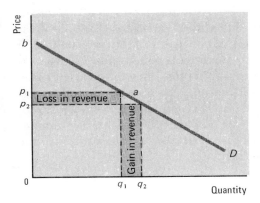

Fig. 21.1 The change in a monopolist's revenue resulting from a small increase in the amount sold

Exactly the same argument may be illustrated graphically. In Figure 21.1 sales are assumed to increase from the rate of q_1 units per year to q_2 units. The extra revenue gained from the sale of the extra unit is equal to the area of the rectangle marked 'Gain in revenue'. This, however, does not represent pure gain, for q_1 units could have been sold at price p_1, but they must now be sold at price p_2, because the extra unit is to be sold as well. This makes a loss of p_1-p_2 per unit on all q_1 units, which is indicated by the area of the rectangle 'Loss in revenue'. Marginal revenue of selling the additional amount q_1-q_2 is equal to the difference between these two areas.

Figure 21.2 shows a numerical example of a demand curve for a monopolist and his corresponding marginal and total revenue curves. The D curve shows the price corresponding to any given rate of sales, and the MR curve shows the change in total revenue that is brought about by increasing the rate of sales by one unit per period.

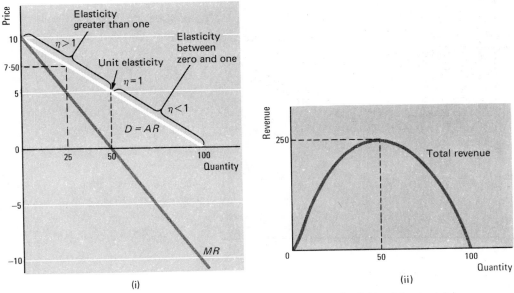

Fig. 21.2 The relation of total, average and marginal revenue to elasticity of demand (η)

Thus, for example, for $q = 25$ units the price is £7·50, but the MR is £5, which means that the 25th unit adds £5 to total revenue. When $q = 50$, price is £5, but MR is zero. To sell the last unit costs as much in lost revenue (because of the price reduction necessary to persuade the extra buyer to buy) as the price it commands. For quantities greater than 50 units MR is negative, meaning that total receipts are decreased by additional sales. (That an increase in sales could reduce revenue should not be surprising; if a given percentage fall in price is met by a smaller percentage rise in sales, total revenue earned will decline. As we saw on pages 106–7, this corresponds to elasticity of demand less than 1.) Such a case is illustrated by the example of the move from situation 2 to situation 3 in Table 21.1.

The equilibrium of a monopolist

To describe the profit-maximizing position of a monopolist we need only bring together information about the monopolist's revenues and his costs and apply the rules developed in Chapter 19.

This is done graphically in Figure 21.3. The technological facts of life are the same for the monopolist as for a competitive firm, so that the short-run cost curves have the same shape in both cases. (The monopolist's curves are assumed to be AVC, ATC and MC – the curve ATC' relates to a later argument.) The difference lies in the demand conditions. The perfectly competitive firm (of Figure 20.1) is faced with a

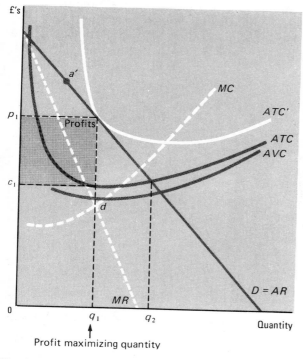

Fig. 21.3 The equilibrium of a monopolist

perfectly elastic demand for its product while the monopolist of Figure 21.3 is faced with a downward-sloping demand curve.

The equilibrium output is q_1 and this output meets the several conditions for profit-maximizing behaviour described in Chapter 19. Marginal cost equals marginal revenue; marginal cost cuts marginal revenue from below; and price is greater than average variable cost. The aggregate amount of profits is represented by the shaded rectangle which represents the output, q_1, multiplied by the gap between average revenue, p_1, and average total cost, c_1.

There are two common misconceptions about monopoly profits that need to be cleared at this point. First, nothing guarantees that a monopolist will make profits in the short-run. If you shift the ATC curve upward, but leave all other curves unchanged, you will see that profits shrink as the curve moves up. When it gets as high as ATC', so that it is tangent to the demand curve, the monopolist earns zero profits. All that the condition $MC = MR$ tells us is that the monopolist does better at that output than at other levels of output. It is possible for the firm to continue producing in the short run, even if its ATC curve were to lie everywhere above D, as long as its AVC curve lies somewhere below D. In these circumstances the firm can set a price in excess of AVC and lose less by producing than by letting its fixed factors stand idle.

The second common misconception about monopoly profits is that a monopolist who is not maximizing his profits must be making losses. This is, of course, not correct. At output q_1, where $MC = MR$, total profits are as large as possible. If output is increased beyond q_1, $MC > MR$, any additional units sold are *reducing* total profits, but *total* profits are still positive. In fact total profits remain positive until output reaches q_2 units. At that level average total cost equals average revenue, so that total cost equals total revenue. Should output be increased beyond q_2, total profits would finally become negative.

Firm and industry, short run and long run

A monopolist, as we have defined him, is the only producer in an industry. There is, thus, no need to have a separate theory of the firm and the industry. The monopolist *is* the industry.

In a monopolized industry, as in a perfectly competitive one, profits provide an incentive for new firms to enter the industry. If the monopoly is to persist in the long run, other firms must be discouraged from entering. We saw that there are BARRIERS TO ENTRY. These barriers may take several forms: patent laws may create and perpetuate monopolies by conferring on the patent holder the sole right to produce a particular commodity. The government may grant a firm a charter or a franchise that prohibits competition by law. Monopolies may also arise because of economies of scale. The established firm may retain a monopoly through a cost advantage because it can produce at a lower cost than could any new, and necessarily small, competitor. A monopoly may also be perpetuated by force, or by threat: potential competitors can be intimidated by threats ranging from sabotage to a price war in which the established monopoly has sufficient financial resources to ensure victory.

Because there is no entry into a monopolistic industry, the profits of a monopolist may persist over time. In perfect competition, the long run differs from the short run because the process of entry forces profits down to zero in the long run. There is no such tendency under monopoly, and the long run differs from the short run only in terms of the cost curve on which the monopolist is operating. Consider a monopolist fully adjusted to a given demand curve: the appropriate sized plant has been constructed and *long-run marginal cost* has been equated to marginal revenue. Now assume that there is a permanent rise in demand. The best the monopolist can do in the short run is to work his existing plant more intensively, expanding output until the short-run marginal cost curve associated with his fixed plant intersects the marginal revenue curve. In the long run, however, a larger plant could be built, and any other relevant adjustments made to 'fixed' factors until the monopolist is again in a position at which long-run marginal cost equals marginal revenue.

Absence of a supply curve under monopoly

The next stage in our study is to consider the relation between the price of the product and the quantity supplied under monopoly. In the case of perfect competition we were able to discover a unique relation between price and quantity supplied, and this gave rise to a supply curve for each firm and, by aggregation, to a supply curve for the industry.

In monopoly, a unique relation between market price and quantity supplied does not exist. Like all profit-maximizing firms, the monopolist equates marginal cost to marginal revenue, but, unlike firms in perfect competition, marginal revenue does not equal price; hence the monopolist does *not* equate marginal cost to price. Under these conditions it is possible for different demand conditions to give rise to the same output but to differing prices. In order to know the amount produced at any given price, we need to know the demand curve as well as the marginal cost curve.

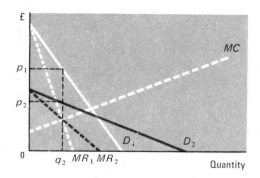

Fig. 21.4 Two different prices associated with the same output

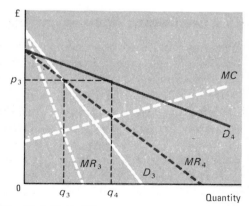

Fig. 21.5 Two different outputs associated with the same price

The proposition that when a firm faces a downward-sloping demand curve, there is no unique relation between price and output is illustrated in Figures 21.4 and 21.5.

In Figure 21.4 two different demand curves both result in the same output, q_2, but in two different prices. When demand is D_1 marginal revenue equals marginal cost at output q_2 and price is p_1. When demand is D_2 marginal cost again equals marginal revenue at output q_2 but price is at p_2. Thus, it is possible to have the same output sold at various prices.

In Figure 21.5 we illustrate the same general point by showing a case in which the same price is associated with two different quantities; when demand is D_3 marginal revenue equals marginal cost at output q_3 and the resulting price is p_3. When demand is D_4 marginal revenue equals marginal cost at output q_4 but price is again p_3.

PRICE DISCRIMINATION

So far in this chapter we have assumed that the monopolist charges the same price for every unit of his product no matter to whom, or where, he sells it. But other situations are possible. Milk is often sold at one price if it is for drinking, but at a lower price if it is to be used to make ice cream or cheese. Doctors, lawyers and business consultants sometimes charge rates for their services that vary according to the incomes of their clients. Cinemas charge lower admission prices for children. American railways charge different rates per ton mile for different kinds of products. Firms often sell their products abroad cheaper than at home. Electrical companies in many countries sell electricity more cheaply for industrial use than for home use. All of these are examples of PRICE DISCRIMINATION. In general we may say that price discrimination occurs when a producer sells a commodity to different buyers at two or more different prices *for reasons not associated with differences in costs.*

Why price discrimination pays

A formal analysis of price discrimination is given in the Appendix. In the text we give only an intuitive discussion of the common sense of price discrimination.

Price discrimination occurs because different units of a commodity can be sold at different prices, and it will be profitable for the seller to take advantage of this if he can. Some of the issues involved in discriminatory pricing can be seen looking at the demand curve in Figure 21.1 on page 263 and thinking of it as describing a market containing a large number of individual buyers, each of whom wishes to buy one unit, and each of whom has indicated the maximum price he is prepared to pay for it. Suppose a single price, p_1 is charged. The quantity q_1 will be sold because the buyers of each of the p_1 units are willing to pay at least q_1 per unit. Although one buyer was willing to pay only p_1 all of the other buyers were willing to pay more. They have benefited because the price was limited to p_1. If the seller could negotiate with each buyer individually, he might be able to charge some buyers more than p_1. In fact, by charging each person the maximum that he is prepared to pay, the seller could greatly increase his profits.[1] If he must charge a single price and if he wishes to

---

1 The area under the demand curve above the line at p_1 in Figure 21.1 (= the area p_1ba) is sometimes called *consumers' surplus.* It represents the amount consumers would have been willing to pay, unit by unit, for the quantity q_1, *above the amount they actually paid* when the price was set at p_1.

raise his rate of sales from q_1 to q_2 he would have to lower the market price from p_1 to p_2. Marginal revenue is less than the new price charged because of the effect that the reduction in price has on the revenues from the first q_1 units, a reduction that was not necessary to sell *them* (since *they* were already being sold at the higher price). If the seller had been able to sell the extra amount q_2-q_1 at p_2 without reducing the price on the first q_1 units (if, in other words, he had been able to discriminate), he would have profited thereby.

When is price discrimination possible?

The conditions under which a seller can succeed in charging discriminatory prices are, first, that he can control the supply of the product in the sense of controlling what is offered to a particular buyer, and, second, that he can prevent the resale of the commodity by one buyer to another. However much the local butcher would like to charge the banker's wife twice as much for a lamb chop as he charges the street sweeper he cannot succeed in doing so. The banker's wife can always go into the supermarket for her meat where her husband's occupation is not known. Even if the butcher and the supermarket agreed to charge her twice as much, she could hire the street sweeper to do her shopping for her. The surgeon, on the other hand, may succeed in discriminating (if all reputable surgeons will do the same) because it will not do the banker much good to hire the street sweeper to have his operations for him.

The first of the two conditions – control over supply – is the feature that makes price discrimination an aspect of the theory of monopoly. Monopoly power in some form is necessary (but not sufficient) for price discrimination.

The second of the two conditions – ability to prevent resale – tends to be associated with the character of the product, or the ability to classify buyers into readily identifiable groups. Services are less easily resold than goods; and those goods requiring installation by the manufacturer (like heavy equipment) are less easily resold than are movable commodities (like household appliances).[1] Transportation costs, tariff barriers or import quotas serve to separate classes of buyers geographically and may make discrimination possible.

To summarize, price discrimination will be both profitable and possible where the supplier(s) can control the amount and distribution of supply, where the buyers can be separated into classes among which resale is either impossible or very costly,[2] and where there are significant differences in the willingness to pay among the distinct classes of buyers.[3]

1 An interesting example of nonresalability occurs in the case of plate glass. Small pieces sell much more cheaply per square foot than bigger pieces, but the person who needs a 6' × 10' plate window cannot use four pieces, each of which is 3' × 5'.

2 The discussion of this paragraph relates directly to discrimination among *classes of buyers*. Discrimination among *units of output* follows similar rules. Thus the tenth unit purchased by a given buyer in a given month can be sold at a different (higher or lower) price than the fifth unit *only* if the seller can keep track of who buys what. This can be done by the seller of electricity through his meter readings, or by the magazine publisher, who can distinguish between renewals and new subscriptions. The owner of a car-wash establishment and the manufacturer of aspirin find it more difficult, although by such devices as coupons or 'one-penny' sales, they too can determine which unit is being purchased.

3 'Willingness to pay' is reflected in the demand curves. The fact that demand curves slope downward shows that some units could always be sold at a higher price if sellers are permitted to deviate from a single price.

The positive effects of price discrimination

The positive consequences of price discrimination are summarized in the following two propositions, which we state and try to make intuitively plausible, but do not prove:

> **(1) For any given level of output the best system of discriminatory prices will provide higher total revenue to the firm (and thus also higher average revenue) than the best single price.**

If this is not obvious you should review the first pages of this chapter.

> **(2) Output under monopolistic discrimination will generally be larger than under single-price monopoly.**

It may be a help at this stage to review the discussion on pages 261–4. Marginal revenue will tend to be higher, given the possibility of price discrimination, because the lower price the producer must charge in order to sell an additional unit will not apply to all previous units sold. The common sense of this is as follows: the monopolist who must charge a single price produces less than the perfectly competitive industry, because he is aware that by producing and selling more he drives down the price against himself. Price discrimination allows him to avoid this disincentive. To the extent that he can sell his output in separate blocks, he can sell another block without spoiling the market for the block already being sold. In the case of *perfect* price discrimination, where every unit of output is sold at a different price, his output would be the same as the output of a perfectly competitive industry. This is easily seen as follows. If each unit can be sold at a separate price, the seller does nothing to spoil the market for previous units by selling an additional unit. The marginal revenue of selling an additional unit is the price of that unit. Thus, the demand curve becomes the marginal revenue curve, and the monopolist reaches equilibrium at a point at which the price (in this case, marginal revenue) equals marginal cost. This is also the point of competitive equilibrium.

The normative aspects of price discrimination

Price discrimination often has a bad reputation. The very word discrimination has connotations of undesirability to many. In the UK, railways have been prevented by law from charging discriminatory prices since the time of their original construction. In the US, the Robinson-Patman Act makes many kinds of price discrimination illegal. Much of the impetus for railroad regulation in the US came from the outraged cries of farmers that they were being discriminated against and forced into bankruptcy by the railways, who were not legally prohibited from charging discriminatory prices as were their British counterparts.

Whether or not an individual judges price discrimination to be good or bad is likely to depend upon the details of the case, as well as upon his own personal value judgements. Certainly there is nothing in economic theory to suggest that price discrimination is always in some sense worse than non-discrimination under conditions of monopoly or oligopoly. The following examples should serve to illustrate the varying aspects of price discrimination.

EXAMPLE 1: A very large oil refiner agrees to ship his product to a market on a given railway, but only if the railway gives his company a secret rebate on the transportation cost and does not give a similar concession to rival refiners. The railway agrees, and is thus charging discriminatory prices. This rebate gives the oil company a cost advantage that it uses to drive its rivals out of business or to force them into a merger on dictated terms. (John D. Rockefeller is alleged to have used similar tactics in forming the original Standard Oil Trust in the US in the late nineteenth century.)

EXAMPLE 2: In an earlier period British Rail was not allowed to discriminate between passengers in different regions. To prevent discrimination, a fixed fare per passenger mile was laid down and had to be charged on all lines whatever the density of their passenger traffic and whatever the elasticity of demand for the services of the particular line. In the interests of economy, branch lines which could not cover costs were often closed down. This meant that some lines closed even though the users preferred rail transport to any of the available alternatives and the strength of their preference was such that they would voluntarily have paid a price sufficient for the line to have covered its costs. The lines were nonetheless closed because it was thought inequitable to charge the passengers on their line more than the passengers on other lines. More recently British Rail has been allowed to charge prices that take some account of market conditions and this seems to have increased profits.

EXAMPLE 3: When the Aluminium Company of America (ALCOA) had a virtual monopoly on the production of aluminium ingots, it sold both the raw ingots and fabricated products (such as aluminium cable) made from the ingots. At one time, ALCOA sold cable at a price 20 per cent below the price it charged for ingots. It did so because users of aluminium cable could substitute copper cable, but many users of ingots had no substitute for aluminium. In return for its bargain price for cable, ALCOA made the purchasers of cable agree to use it only for transmission purposes. (Without such an agreement, any demander of aluminium might have bought cable and melted it down.)

EXAMPLE 4: Doctors in private practice very often charge discriminatory prices for their services. When they are accused of behaving unfairly they point out that, if they had to charge a uniform fee for all patients, it would have to be high enough – if the doctors were to obtain a reasonable income – to price their services out of the reach of the lower-income groups. The discriminatory price system, they argue, is what allows them to make their services available to all income groups while still securing an income sufficiently high to ensure a continued supply of doctors.

EXAMPLE 5: A product that a number of people want has the cost and demand structure pictured in Figure 21.6. There is no single price at which a producing firm can cover total costs. However, if the firm is allowed to charge discriminatory prices, it will be willing to produce output, and it will make a profit.[1] (Public utility companies are often thought to operate under these conditions.)

1 Given perfect discrimination, total revenue would be the shaded area $OdcA$, whereas total costs are $OabA$. As long as the triangle ade is larger than ebc, there are profits.

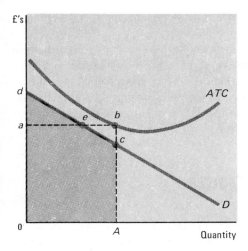

Fig. 21.6 No single price will cover total costs but a set of discriminatory prices will do so

EXAMPLE 6: The government decides to offer primary school education to all children. The cost per child is estimated at £300 per child per year. Instead of charging tuition to each child's parents, the government chooses to make the school free and to raise the money by a school tax that is proportional to the value of the houses of the people who live in the community, whether or not they have children.

Each of these examples, as well as those at the beginning of this chapter, involves price discrimination. Few readers would regard them all as equally good or bad. There are two points to be stressed. First, the consequences of price discrimination can differ in many ways from case to case; and, second, no matter what any individual's values are, he is almost bound to evaluate the individual cases differently.

Price discrimination: systematic and unsystematic

We have discussed systematic and persistent price discrimination. Systematic price discrimination most often consists of classifying buyers according to their age, location, industry, income and so forth, or according to the use they intend to make of the product, and in charging different prices for the different classes of buyers even though costs do not vary according to these classifications. Such discrimination may also take other forms, such as charging an individual more for the first unit he buys than for subsequent units, or *vice versa*, or by setting an all-or-nothing price on a specified quantity of the product that is different for different quantities of the product.

Another sort of price discrimination is frequently found. A seller who occasionally gives a favourite customer a few pennies off, or shades his price to secure a new account, is engaged in price discrimination. If these practices are used infrequently, they are called *unsystematic discrimination*. Such discrimination is not really part of the price structure and we have ignored it in this chapter. This does not mean that it is unimportant – indeed, unsystematic price discrimination plays a very real role in the dynamic process by which prices do change in response to changed conditions of supply and demand.

The causes and consequences of systematic and unsystematic price discrimination are very different. Control legislation will, however, generally be unable to distinguish between them and will hit at both. If legislation is motivated solely by a desire to attack systematic discrimination, it may have unforeseen and possibly undesired effects on unsystematic discrimination. For example, if unsystematic price discrimination is important for the working of competition, prohibiting it by legislation may aid the maintenance of monopoly power.

THE NATURE AND EXTENT OF MONOPOLY POWER
A perfect monopoly

The concept of monopoly has certain difficulties. No firm has complete monopoly power. Some firms which have fairly close competitors will face quite elastic demand curves; other firms with fewer close competitors will face less elastic demand curves. In order to clarify the concept of monopoly, some economists have tried to define a perfect monopoly that would be at the opposite end of the spectrum from perfect competition. Two ideas have been put forward; both are unsatisfactory. Some people have said that a perfect monopolist would be a firm selling a good for which the demand was perfectly *inelastic* (this seemed the opposite of a perfect competitor who faces a perfectly *elastic* demand). The reader should be able to see the contradiction in the idea of a profit-maximizing monopolist facing a perfectly inelastic demand curve.

Such a case would never come about. No profit-maximizing monopolist would ever sell at a price at which the demand for his product was perfectly inelastic. Clearly he would go on raising price while not losing sales and thus go on increasing profits. In fact he would continue to raise his price, not only until the demand ceased to be perfectly inelastic, but until the demand ceased to be inelastic at all (for marginal revenue is negative as long as elasticity of demand is less than one, see page 264).

The second idea put forward was that a perfect monopolist would be a firm that had a monopoly of all goods and hence a firm that took in the consumer's entire income (ignoring saving). The monopolist would thus be faced with a demand curve of unit elasticity: any increase in price would be met by a proportional fall in quantity bought, so that total expenditure (= total consumers' income) would remain constant.

The problems here are more subtle than in the case of the completely inelastic demand. Let us first consider what a profit-maximizing monopolist would do if faced with a demand curve of unit elasticity. The marginal revenue corresponding to such a demand curve is, of course, zero. A 1 per cent increase in sales is always accompanied by a 1 per cent fall in price, while a 1 per cent reduction in sales causes a 1 per cent rise in price, so that total revenue remains unchanged. Clearly the monopolist will cut down output, thus reducing costs but leaving revenue unaffected, and hence increasing profits. If the demand curve were truly of unit elasticity throughout its whole range the monopolist's output would approach zero, while his price would approach infinity, until finally he sold virtually nothing at all and sold it at an infinitely high price, absorbing the whole of income as his profits! Now all of income becomes the monopolist's profits and, since nothing is produced, no money will be paid out to factors of production. Thus next period the only purchaser left for the monopolist to exploit would be the monopolist himself!

What is the reason for these absurdities? The whole theory of the firm is based on *ceteris paribus* assumptions. Other things, prices, incomes, etc., are assumed to be constant, i.e., not affected by any change in the industry under consideration. The assumption that the total income of purchasers is constant depends upon the industry being small. If the industry is very large, then a change in the level of production will affect factor earnings, and thus incomes, significantly and so cause a *shift in the demand curve*. Clearly, we could not use the theory of the last few chapters if the demand curve for a firm's product shifted every time the firm's output changed.

The attempt to consider a perfect monopolist as one who takes all income founders on the rock that it is no longer a situation in which the *ceteris paribus* assumptions hold. The attempt to apply our tools of analysis to such a situation can only produce absurd results. The theory of the firm that we have outlined here is concerned with productive units which are *small* in relation to the total economy. We conclude that the two ideas of a perfect monopoly considered here are self-contradictory.

Monopoly power as a variable

We have seen that the attempt to define a perfect monopolist runs into impossible complications. Indeed it is really impossible to imagine a firm without any significant competition. A firm may have a complete monopoly of a particular product, but for every product there are some substitutes that can provide the same services. Some products have fairly close substitutes, and even a single seller producing such a product will have close rivals for his customers' expenditure. Not only will his demand be relatively elastic, but new entrants into closely allied fields may shift his demand curve. Even if there is no very close substitute for his product at the moment, high profits may induce rivals to develop substitutes to cut into his market.

If other firms in other industries influence the monopolist's behaviour, they must do so by shifting his demand curve. The less the influence of other firms on the monopolist, the less will their actions cause shifts in his demand curve and the more insulated will he be from them (i.e., the more monopolistic will he be). Thus, it may be useful to think of monopoly as a variable rather than as an absolute. In general, the extent of monopoly power will be greater, the smaller the shifts in demand caused by the reactions of sellers of other products, and the smaller the shifts in demand caused by the entry of new sellers. How large these shifts will be depends upon a great variety of other variables, which will be considered in Chapter 22.

MEASURING MONOPOLY POWER: Our theory predicts that behaviour in monopolistic markets will differ from behaviour in perfectly competitive markets. We have also seen that it is more reasonable to regard monopoly power as a variable rather than as an absolute. Thus if we are to apply the theory of monopoly we must be able to measure the extent of monopoly power in various markets. Also, it is often felt by government agencies (acting on behalf of the people) that uncontrolled mono-poly power is undesirable. These governmental agencies must know where monopoly power exists if they are to control or eliminate it. For both of these reasons, and for others as well, it becomes important to measure the extent of monopoly power in various markets.

Ideally, one would like to compare the prices, outputs and profits of firms in any industry with what prices, outputs and profits would be if all firms were under unified (monopoly) control and were fully insulated from entry. But this hypothetical comparison does not lend itself to measurement.

Concentration ratios: In practice, two alternative measures are widely used. The first of these is the *concentration ratio*. A concentration ratio shows the fraction of total market sales controlled by the largest group of sellers. Common types of concentra-tion ratios cite the share of total industry sales of the largest four or eight firms. The inclusion in concentration ratios of the market shares of several firms rests upon the possibility that large firms will adopt a common price-output policy that is no different from the one they would adopt if they were in fact under unified manage-ment. But of course they may not, thus high concentration ratios may be necessary for the exercise of monopoly power, but they are not sufficient. It is nevertheless interesting to know where potential monopoly power does exist.

Profits as a measure of monopoly power: Many economists, following the lead of Professor Joe S. Bain, use profit rates as a measure of monopoly power. By 'high' profits the economist means returns sufficiently in excess of all opportunity costs that potential new entrants desire to enter the industry. If profits are *and remain* high, so goes the logic of this measure, it is indirect evidence that neither rivalry among sellers nor entry of new firms prevents existing firms from pricing as if they were monopolists.

Using profits in this way requires care, because, as we have seen (page 247), the profits reported in firms' income statements are not pure profits over opportunity cost. In particular, allowance must be made for differences in risk and in required payments for the use of the owners' capital.

While neither concentration ratios nor profit rates are ideal measures of the degree of market power that a firm, or group of firms, actually exercises, both are of some value and both are widely used. In fact, concentration ratios and high profit rates are themselves correlated. Because of this, alternative classifications of industries according to their degree of monopoly power, measured in these two ways, do not differ very much from one another.

Appendix

A formal analysis of price discrimination

Consider a monopolist who sells a single product in two distinct markets A and B. Customers in one market cannot buy in the other, either directly or by having a customer in the other market resell the product to them; the two markets are completely insulated from each other. The demands and marginal revenue curves are shown in Figure 21.7.

Since the monopolist can price discriminate he is under no necessity to set $p_A = p_B$. How then will he behave in each market? The simplest way to discover what he should do is to imagine him deciding how best to allocate *any* given output, Q^*, between the two markets. Since output is fixed (arbitrarily at Q^*), there is nothing the monopolist can do about costs. The best thing he can do therefore is to maximize the revenue that he gets by selling Q^* in the two markets. *To do this he will allocate his sales between the markets until the marginal revenues of the last unit sold in each are the same.* Consider what would happen if he did not. If the marginal revenue of the last unit sold in market A exceeded the marginal revenue of the last unit sold in market B the monopolist would keep his overall output constant at Q^* but reallocate a unit of sales from market B to market A gaining a net addition in revenue equal to the difference between the marginal revenues in the two markets. Thus it will always

pay a monopolist to reallocate a given total quantity between his markets as long as marginal revenues are not equal in the two markets.

If we assume that marginal cost is constant, we can determine the profit-maximizing course of action from Figure 21.7. The MC curve in both figures shows the constant marginal cost. The monopolist's total profits are maximized by equating MR in each market to his constant MC thus selling q_A at p_A in market A and q_B at p_B in market B. Marginal revenue is the same in each market $(c_A = c_B)$ so that the monopolist has his total output correctly allocated between the two markets and marginal cost equals marginal revenue showing that the monopolist would lose profits if he produced more or less total output.

Now assume that marginal cost varies with output, being given by MC' in Figure 21.8(iii). Now we cannot just put the MC curve onto the diagram for each market since the marginal cost of producing another unit for sale in market A will depend on how much is being produced for sale in market B and vice versa. To determine what overall production should be, we need to know overall marginal revenue. To find this we merely sum the separate quantities in each market that correspond to each particular marginal revenue. If, for example, the 10th

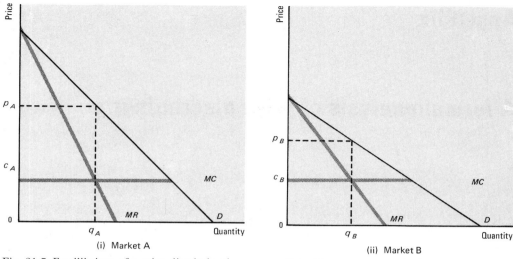

Fig. 21.7 Equilibrium of a price-discriminating monopolist with constant marginal costs

unit sold in market A and the 15th unit sold in Market B each have a marginal revenue of £1 in their separate markets then the marginal revenue of £1 corresponds to over-all sales of 25 units (divided 10 units in A and 15 in B).

The overall marginal revenue curve to the monopolist is the horizontal sum of the marginal revenue curves in each market.

The new marginal revenue curve shows the marginal revenue associated with an increment to production on the assumption that

sales are divided between the two markets so as to keep the two marginal revenues equal.

This total MR curve is shown in Figure 21.8(iii) and is labelled MR'. The firm's total profit maximizing output is at Q_1 where MR' and MC' intersect (at a value of c_1). By construction, marginal revenue is c_1 in each market although price is different. To find the equilibrium prices and quantities in each market find the quantities, q_A and q_B where $MR = c_1$ in each market. Then find the prices, p_A and p_B that correspond to these quantities. All of this is illustrated in parts (i) and (ii) of the Figure.

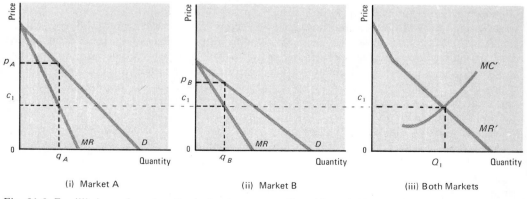

Fig. 21.8 Equilibrium of a price-discriminating monopolist with variable marginal costs

AN APPLICATION

In some industries firms sell competitively on international markets while enjoying a home market that is protected from foreign competition by tariffs or import quotas. The degree of competition abroad, and protection at home, varies from case to case, but to illustrate the issues involved consider the following extreme case.

A firm is the only producer of product X in country A. There are thousands of producers of X in other countries so that X is sold abroad under conditions of perfect competition. The government of country A grants the firm a monopoly in the home market by prohibiting imports of X. The firm now can be a discriminating monopolist. It is faced with a downward-sloping demand curve at home and a perfectly elastic demand curve abroad at the prevailing world price of X.

What will it do? Can we be sure that it will always sell at a higher price in the protected home market than in the world market? The answer is 'yes'. To maximize profits the firm will divide its sales between the foreign and the home market so as to equate marginal revenues in each market. On the world market its average and marginal revenues are equal to the world price. Thus the firm will equate marginal revenue in the home market with the world price and since price exceeds marginal revenue at home (because the demand curve slopes downward), price at home must exceed price abroad.

The argument is illustrated in Figure 21.9. The home market is shown in (i) the world market in (ii) and the sum of the two marginal revenue curves in (iii). Providing the marginal cost curve cuts the marginal revenue curve to the right of the kink (i.e., MC does not exceed the world price when only the home market is served), both markets will be served at prices of p_H at home and p_F abroad. The total quantity sold will be Q of which q_H is allocated to the home market and the rest $(q_F = Q - q_H)$ is sold abroad.[1]

1 It is an interesting exercise to consider the effect on the firm's exports of a tax on the sale of X in the home market.

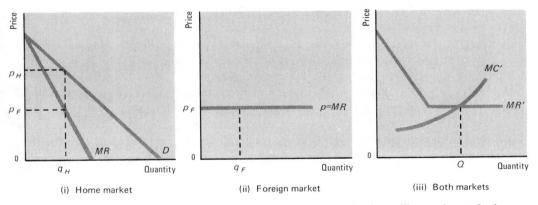

(i) Home market   (ii) Foreign market   (iii) Both markets

Fig. 21.9 Equilibrium of a firm with a monopoly in the home market but selling under perfectly competitive conditions abroad

22

Theories of imperfect competition

Up to now we have dealt with the two extremes of monopoly and perfect competition. In this chapter we shall give some consideration to the whole range of market forms that lie between these two extremes. A detailed consideration is beyond the scope of this book, and we shall do nothing more than provide a general introduction to the two main divisions within this range, monopolistic competition and oligopoly.

IMPERFECT COMPETITION AMONG THE MANY

Consider an industry in which there is a large number of producers with free entry into, and exit from, the industry, but in which *each producer sells a product which is somewhat different from that sold by his competitors*. We say that the product is differentiated. There might, for example, be a large number of competing firms selling soap. The products of the firms would be rather similar but by no means identical. Each soap would differ in physical composition from competing products; it would also have a different packaging, and, as the advertisers say, it would have a different 'brand image' from its competitors. Industries of this kind are referred to as being MONO-POLISTICALLY COMPETITIVE. The term MONOPOLISTIC COMPETITION describes a situation similar to perfect competition, with the single important difference that each producer sells a product that is somewhat differentiated from the products sold by his competitors.

This means that each firm does not face a perfectly elastic demand curve. We may now construct the demand curve of such a firm *on the assumption that competing firms hold their prices constant*. On the one hand if the firm raises its price, it will lose business to its competitors, but it will not lose all of its customers just because its prices go slightly above those of its competitors. The fact that the product is differentiated from competing products means that some people will prefer it to other products even though it is somewhat more expensive. As prices are raised higher and higher above those of similar products, the firm can expect that fewer and fewer customers will persist in buying its product. On the other hand, if the firm lowers its price below that charged by competitors, it can expect to attract customers, but not everyone will be attracted by a small price differential. Thus the firm will be faced with a downward-sloping demand curve. Generally the less differentiated is the product, the more elastic will the firm's demand curve be. (If there is no differentiation, the demand curve will be perfectly elastic because the smallest increase in price above those of competitors will lose *all* the firm's customers while the smallest decrease in price below those of competitors will attract *all* the competitors' customers.)

Thus we must picture, as in Figure 22.1, a firm faced with a downward-sloping, but rather flat demand curve, for its product. The firm will, of course, have the usual U-shaped short-run cost curve. The short-run equilibrium of the firm is exactly the same as that of a monopolist. The firm is not a passive price taker; it may juggle price and quantity until profits are maximized. This is at output q_1 and price p_1 in the figure.[1]

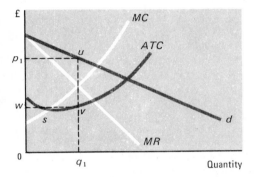

Fig. 22.1 The short-run equilibrium of a firm in monopolistic competition

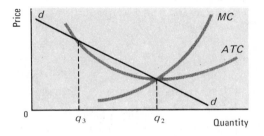

Fig. 22.2 The firm can make profits for any output between q_3 and q_2

We may now ask about the long-run equilibrium of the industry. The firm that we have shown in Figure 22.1 is earning profits ($= p_1 uvw$) and, if this firm is typical of the others in the industry, there will be an incentive for new firms to enter the industry. As more firms enter, the total demand for the product must be shared out amongst this larger number of firms, so that each can expect to have a smaller share of the market. Thus at any given price, each firm can expect to sell less than it could before the influx of new firms: the demand curve for the firm's product shifts to the left. This must continue until no profits are being earned; for as long as profits exist, there is an attraction for new firms to enter, so that the industry will continue to expand.

Before the student reads further he should make a genuine effort to see if he can discover for himself the final equilibrium position. Start from Figure 22.1 and observe

1 The complete theory of monopolistic competition also deals with a type of price cutting that leads to a short-run equilibrium of the *industry*. We jump straight from the short-run equilibrium of the firm to the long-run equilibrium of the industry because we only wish to develop those predictions of the theory that follow from the long-run equilibrium positions. Readers already familiar with the theory may assume that the point *u* in Figure 22.1 is at the intersection of the *dd* and the *DD* curves, so that there is no further tendency for short-run price competition.

that, as new firms enter the industry, the demand curve, *dd*, facing our one firm will shift to the left. Also observe that this will continue until there are no further profits. What will be the position of final equilibrium?

Assume, to begin with, that the demand curve shifts to the position indicated in Figure 22.2 in which the average revenue curve intersects the average total cost curve at the point of lowest average cost. Will this do? Surely, if the firm produces output at q_2 then it will just be covering its costs. But if it restricts output below q_2 it will increase average revenue more than average costs and, hence, it will move into a range of output at which profits can be earned. In Figure 22.2 costs are just covered at outputs q_2 and q_3, while profits are earned at any output between these levels.

The final position must be that indicated in Figure 22.3. The average revenue curve touches the average cost curve at only one point, the point *x* corresponding to quantity q_4 and price p_4; the average revenue curve is *tangential* to the average cost curve at point *x*. When output is at q_4 costs are just being covered since average revenue equals average total costs. At any other level of output losses occur, since average revenue is less than average total costs.

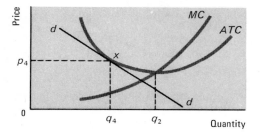

Fig. 22.3 The long-run equilibrium of a firm in monopolistic competition

Thus we see that a zero-profit equilibrium is possible under conditions of monopolistic competition, in spite of the fact that the individual firm is faced with a downward-sloping demand curve. Each firm is forced into a position in which it has EXCESS or UNUSED CAPACITY. (Recall the definition of capacity given on page 228.) The firm in Figure 22.3 could expand its output from q_4 to q_2 and reduce average costs, but it does not make use of this productive capacity because doing so would reduce average revenue by even more than it would reduce average costs. If the demand curve *cuts* the average total cost curve, as in Figure 22.2, it is always possible to make profits by producing in the range over which the demand curve lies above the cost curve. An equilibrium in which profits cannot be earned but total costs can be covered requires that the demand curve should be tangential to the average total cost curve and this in turn implies that in equilibrium the firm will have some unused capacity (equal to q_2–q_4 in Figure 22.3).

Predictions of the theory

In this section we shall consider those major predictions of the theory of monopolistic competition that differ from those of the theory of perfect competition. Other predictions of the theory which are similar to those of perfect competition are considered in the following chapter.

> **(1) The equilibrium output of the firm is less than the one at which average total cost is a minimum. (This is known as the excess capacity theorem.)**

This is one of the more important insights in the whole theory of the firm. It tells us that a long-run, zero-profit equilibrium can occur even though each firm is like a monopolist in the sense of having a downward-sloping demand curve. It will occur because so many firms will enter the industry that each individual firm will be unable to utilize all of the capacity at its command. The theory predicts that industries in monopolistic competition will exhibit a continual tendency towards excess capacity.

The next two predictions can be established directly by inspection of Figure 22.3 plus the recollection that in a long-run, perfectly-competitive equilibrium, price is equal to minimum average cost.

> **(2) Prices at equilibrium will be higher and output will be lower, *ceteris paribus*, than under perfect competition.**
> **(3) Equilibrium price will be greater than marginal cost.**

The fourth prediction is related to product differentiation.

> **(4) Firms in monopolistically competitive industries will offer consumers a wider variety of brands, styles and possibly qualities than will firms in perfect competition.**

Monopolistic competition is predicted to produce more products, but less cheaply, than perfect competition. Whether the added cost of differentiated output (and production at less than capacity) is 'worth it' to buyers is a question involving empirical estimates of costs and value judgements about various benefits.

A fifth prediction of the theory is as follows.

> **(5) It may pay the monopolistically competitive firm to engage in non-price competition of a kind that it would not pay it to use in perfect competition.**

To see that this is a prediction, recall that a firm in perfect competition can sell as much as it wishes at the going price and that it regards itself as a price-taker. Therefore, it does not pay it to spend money to increase the amount the firm can sell. But in monopolistic competition, expenditures on product differentiation, product quality or advertising can change the position of the firm's demand curve and thereby increase short-run profits. We are thus led to the prediction that firms in industries characterized by the conditions of monopolistic competition will engage in non-price competition, whereas those in perfect competition will not.

The great debate

A great debate exists between the devotees and critics of the theory of monopolistic competition. The devotees call the theory 'a revolution of major importance'; the

critics say: 'In the general case [the theory does not help us to] make a single statement about the economic events in the world we sought to analyse.'[1]

The student may find it hard to understand why such a debate exists. The two
theories make different predictions and, presumably, one or the other must predict
more accurately. Part of the trouble, however, is that it is difficult to get the two sides
to agree on what is a fair test.

Consider the market for soaps and detergents. Among the well-known brands on
sale in the United States are Ivory, Dash, Joy, Comet, Cascade, Camay, Lava, Duz,
Tide, Cheer, Dreft, Oxydol, Spic 'n' Span and Zest. Surely this is an impressive
array of differentiated products? On first glance, this might appear to be a perfect
example of monopolistic competition. But every one of the products named above is
manufactured by a single company, Procter and Gamble, which alone accounts for
more than half of the American sales of soaps, cleansers and detergents.[2] Will Procter
and Gamble really believe that if it lowers its prices its largest rival, Lever Brothers,
will not lower theirs? Does the soap industry exhibit revenues that do not exceed
costs and does it have free entry? The answer is *no* to each question. Clearly we do not
have a case of monopolistic competition.

Many examples of intense competition between a multitude of only slightly differentiated manufactured products turn out to be similar to the soap case: many
brands are produced but by only a few large firms. Such cases cannot be handled by
the theory of monopolistic competition, but we shall say more about them under
theories of oligopoly.

Many branches of retailing, however, are much closer to the concept of a mono-
polistically competitive industry. Every shop selling a particular line of goods,
whether groceries, men's clothing or drugs is differentiated from every other shop
selling the same line of goods, both by the location of the shop and the personality of
the manager and his staff. Each is a monopolist to some extent, yet there is freedom
of entry and a consequent long-run tendency for profits to be pushed to zero. Profits
are forced to zero because in long-run equilibrium there are more outlets than are
necessary to handle the custom, so that each shop and its staff operate for most of the
time at substantially less than full capacity. Whatever the detractors of the theory
may say, it seems that the model of a downward-sloping demand curve resulting
from product differentiation, with the additional condition of freedom of entry, is a
very useful one for the economist to have in his tool kit, because he will sometimes
encounter industries that do come close to fulfilling these two conditions.

IMPERFECT COMPETITION AMONG THE FEW: THEORIES OF OLIGOPOLY

We now need to consider the behaviour of firms that have only a few close competitors. An industry containing only a few firms is called an OLIGOPOLY and it has, as

1 The first quotation is from Robert L. Bishop, 'Monopolistic Competition After Thirty Years: The Impact on
General Theory', *American Economic Review*, May 1964, p. 33. The second is from George Stigler, *Five Lectures on
Economic Problems* (Longmans, 1948), p. 18.

2 The three-firm concentration ratio exceeds 80 per cent. This illustration comes from J. W. Markham's article
in the *American Economic Review*, May 1964, p. 54. His point is that the multi-product firm is not the multi-product
industry of monopolistic competition, and that we require a different theory to explain its behaviour.

a special case, an industry with only two producers which is called a DUOPOLY. A high proportion of manufacturing industries in all Western countries are oligopolistic. In the British car industry, for example, 90 per cent of the production is in the hands of five large firms. Similar patterns are to be found in many other industries such as the motor-tyre, the chemical, the synthetic fibre, the electric wire and cable and the match industries.

When we move from competition amongst the many to competition amongst the few, the whole price-output problem of the firm takes on a new dimension: that of the possible reaction of the firm's few competitors. The firm's policy now depends on how it *thinks* its competitors will react to its moves, and the outcome of the firm's policy depends on how they *do* in fact react. There is now no simple set of rules for the equilibrium either of the firm or of the small group of firms that constitutes the industry. Neither is there a set of simple predictions about how the firms will react, either individually or collectively, to various changes in taxes, costs and demand. Everything depends on the policy each firm pursues, on the policy its competitors pursue, on how each reacts to the other's moves, and on how each *thinks* the other will react.

It is often said that, under these circumstances, price and output are *indeterminate*. Such a statement is misleading (the price and output do, of course, get determined somehow), and what is meant by the statement is that, under oligopoly, price and output are not determined by the same factors as in large-group cases. In small-group cases an additional set of factors – competitors' real and imagined reactions to each other's behaviour – contributes to the determination of price and output. Because the problem is complex, it is not surprising that there is no single well-developed theory of the functioning of oligopolistic markets. Indeed, the oligopoly problem has been attacked in two quite different ways.

Developing theoretical models by assuming how firms react

One attempt has been to develop a series of models by assuming that individual firms will react in particular ways, and then seeing what follows from these assumptions. A. A. Cournot, in 1838, developed the first known theory of duopoly. He had each seller choose his profit-maximizing output on the assumption that the other seller would hold his own output constant. He then showed that, if each seller in turn adjusted to the last move made by his competitor, on the assumption that the competitor would make no further moves, a stable equilibrium would be reached in which the market was divided between the two in a deterministic way. The assumption that each firm expects no reaction from its competitors although the competitor always does react seems rather naive, and in the 135 years since Cournot, economists have advanced many models of oligopolistic behaviour, and have sought to make these models more seemingly relevant than Cournot's rather special, though path-breaking, one. The German economist Stackelberg developed a theory in the 1930s that included Cournot's model as a special case and in which it was possible to handle the question of whether it would pay the firm to be a price leader or a price follower. A follower is one who lets the leader set any price and then passively adjusts to it, while a leader sets his own price confident that the follower will accept it.

Also in the 1930s the American economist Harold Hotelling approached the oligo-poly problem from a novel direction and developed a series of models in which there was a tendency for competition among a few oligopolists to produce a result that was, in a clearly definable way, less socially desirable than the result produced by a single monopolist.

Some of the most recent developments in the theory of oligopolistic behaviour have been in the Theory of Games. This theory, which is a study of rational strategies in small-group situations, has done a great deal to increase our knowledge of how to behave rationally – i.e., choose actions that maximize the chance of obtaining our stated objectives, in such diverse fields as cold war military strategy and card games, and some economists feel that the theory shows promise of providing an analytical structure suitable for the handling of oligopoly problems.[1] *But an analytical technique is only as useful as the real-world information that it is used to analyse.* Even the most powerful new techniques will be empty without empirical knowledge of how firms actually behave in typical small-group situations.

So far the attack on oligopolistic behaviour through the development of general models has produced disappointingly few results. There are few clear predictions that are capable of being tested against evidence. Many economists feel that what is required is much more empirical knowledge of how firms actually do react in small-group situations. They believe that, until such knowledge can be used to narrow drastically the range of cases shown to be possible by general theoretical models, there can be little hope of developing genuinely useful theories of oligopolistic behaviour. These economists have been champions of what may be called the piece-meal empirical attack on the oligopoly problem, and we may now attempt a very brief summary of some of the aspects of their work.

Generalizing from hypotheses about observed behaviour

The second major attack on the problem of understanding oligopolistic behaviour has been an attempt to build up a theory piecemeal by developing testable hypotheses to explain actual aspects of observed behaviour. The hope is that these piecemeal explanations will eventually produce the necessary elements for a general theory that will be successful in explaining and predicting oligopolistic behaviour. Although we cannot enter into a detailed discussion of these elements in this book, we can (1) describe a general hypothesis that serves as a framework for integrating many sub-sidiary hypotheses, (2) give examples of some of the subsidiary hypotheses in order to illustrate their general nature, and (3) discuss two or three hypotheses at greater length.

THE HYPOTHESIS OF QUALIFIED JOINT PROFIT MAXIMIZATION: The hypothesis of qualified joint profit maximization is the key general hypothesis. If all the firms in an industry maximize their joint profits then their combined profits are the same as those that would be earned by a single profit-maximizing monopolist running the

---

1 For an entertaining general introduction to the theory in its many established applications see J. D. Williams, *The Compleat Strategyst* (McGraw-Hill, 1954).

industry. Thus an industry in which all firms practise unqualified joint profit maximization, behaves in exactly the same way as it would if it were controlled by a single monopolist. Firms cannot, however, always attain the unqualified joint profit-maximizing position. Usually the best they can do is to achieve a position of qualified joint profit maximization. We may now state the hypothesis of *qualified* joint profit maximization as follows.

> **Firms that recognize that they are in rivalry with one another will be motivated by two opposing forces; one moves them towards policies that maximize the combined profits of the existing group of sellers, the other moves them away from the joint profit-maximizing position. Both forces are associated with observable characteristics of firms, markets and products, and thus we can make predictions about market behaviour on the basis of these characteristics.**

To make the hypothesis testable, we need to identify the forces that lead the firm towards joint profit maximizing and the forces that lead it away.

HYPOTHESES ABOUT OLIGOPOLY BEHAVIOUR: Below are eight hypotheses about behaviour in oligopolistic markets. These hypotheses concern several dependent variables (level of price and profits, flexibility of price and extent of nonprice competition). The first five concern relationships of a firm with the group of identified existing sellers that are its present rivals; the last three concern the effect on a firm's behaviour of potential entrants into the industry.

Hypothesis 1. The industry will tend to be closer to the joint profit-maximizing price and profits, the greater the degree of mutual recognition of interdependence. Mutual recognition of interdependence will tend to be greater (a) the smaller the number of sellers, (b) the more nearly equal the sellers are in market shares and in methods of production, and (c) the more nearly identical the products of the sellers.

The argument here is that when sellers are few, nearly equal in size, and producing closely similar products, they are sure to be in direct rivalry. They will soon discover this fact and their reaction will be to minimize the profit-reducing effects of direct competition.

Hypothesis 2. The easier it is for firms in an industry to reach a tacit agreement, (i.e., the adoption of a common policy without explicit discussion or agreement), the closer the firms will come to the joint profit-maximizing price. The ability to reach and abide by tacit agreements will tend to be greater (a) the greater the degree of mutual recognition of interdependence, (b) in an industry with a dominant firm rather than in an industry without one (the large firm is the obvious leader for the others to follow), (c) in a market in which the price that maximizes joint profits is stable or rising rather than falling, since it is easier to get orderly agreements on maintaining or raising prices than on reducing them, (d) the less the degree of uncertainty attached to the firms' estimates of future demands, costs and other relevant factors (given much uncertainty, different firms may evaluate things differently), and (e) among firms with similar expectations of the future than among firms with widely differing expectations (different evaluations will lead to different views of appropriate policy).

The reasoning behind these hypotheses is that it is easier to reach agreements (1) if there is a natural leader for all to follow, (2) in raising prices than in cutting them, and (3) under circumstances in which all the sellers perceive the future more or less similarly and with some confidence. Put differently, agreement can be viewed as a search for order, and order is more easily achieved when the postulated conditions are met.

Hypothesis 3. Prices will tend to be more inflexible in the face of changes in demand or cost, the more uncertain the firm is about what its rivals' responses will be. This uncertainty in turn will be greater (a) with a substantial number of rivals than with only a few, and (b) in periods of slack demand and industry-wide excess capacity, when rivals will be tempted to 'steal' one another's customers.

Hypothesis 4. Prices will tend to be more inflexible, the more effective is tacit agreement. This hypothesis is based on the established evidence that it is costly to change prices often. Frequent price changes may occur when firms are actively competing with each other, but monopolists will change prices only infrequently. This hypothesis is in conflict with hypothesis 3 and it makes price inflexibility the actual goal of collective behaviour. It is an aspect of the ADMINISTERED PRICE HYPOTHESIS which states that firms with discretion over their prices will seek not to change their prices in response to every variation in demand and costs.

Hypothesis 5. Nonprice competition will tend to be more vigorous, the greater the limitation on price competition. Thus nonprice competition will tend to be greater under the conditions of hypotheses 1(a), (b) and (c), and 2(b), (c), (d) and (e). The argument here is that firms may well agree tacitly to avoid price cutting in order to avoid expensive and potentially explosive 'price wars', in which each of two or more sellers attempts to undersell the other, but that the basic rivalry of the sellers for customers will find other outlets as firms seek to maintain or improve their market positions.

Hypothesis 6. The industry will tend to be closer to the joint profit-maximizing price, the greater the barriers to entry of new firms. This is because the threat of entry may force existing firms to adopt policies (such as lowering prices) aimed at keeping entrants out. We shall examine such policies in some detail below.

Hypothesis 7. Prices will tend to be less flexible upward and more flexible downward the less the barriers to entry of new firms. The reason is that an imminent threat of entry may lead existing firms to forego opportunities to raise prices, and at other times force them into price reductions to forestall entry. This hypothesis has been advanced mainly to explain the behaviour of companies who supply a major portion of their output to identified large buyers, and who fear their customers may enter the industry and provide their own supply. There are many examples of such entry by customers into their suppliers' industries. The Ford Motor Company at one time entered the glass business because it felt it was being over-charged for safety glass. American steel companies now mine most of the iron ore and much of the coal they use in production. They are said to be 'vertically integrated'.

Hypothesis 8. Nonprice competition will tend to be greater, the weaker the other barriers to entry. The argument here is that advertising or product differentiation may give an established firm an advantage over potential entrants that is a crucial deterrent to entry. This motive for advertising is greater, the greater the threat of entry.

While we cannot discuss all of these hypotheses, we shall look carefully at entry.

Barriers to entry

As with so much in the field of industrial organization and oligopoly, this topic was first and most fully developed by Professor Joe S. Bain. He studied many ways in which existing firms may have advantages over potential entrants. We shall consider two of these advantages.

ABSOLUTE COST ADVANTAGES: An absolute cost advantage means that existing sellers have average cost curves that are significantly lower over their entire range than those of potential new entrants. Among possible sources of such an advantage are 'going-concern value', control of crucial patents or resources, and knowledge that comes only from 'learning by doing' in the industry. Each of these may be regarded as a source of only temporary disadvantages of new firms, which, given time, might develop their own know-how, patents, etc. In Figure 22.4, at any price below p_L, the level of minimum cost for an entrant, entry would prove unattractive to new firms, although existing firms will earn profits. Thus if the existing firms should price their output at p_L or below, new entrants would face losses. The price p_L is known as a LIMIT PRICE.

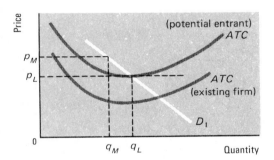

Fig. 22.4 A cost advantage of existing firms over a potential new entrant

Suppose the marginal revenue and marginal cost curves are such that the joint profit-maximizing price is p_M. Existing firms may be better off in the long run if they price at p_L and supply the quantity q_L, rather than setting price at p_M and supplying quantity q_M. The reason is that p_M may induce entry, thus shifting the demand curves of existing firms to the left and in this way reducing their earnings. One would have to examine the level of demand for the individual firm's product before and after entry, as well as the length of time before entry occurred, before one could say whether the existing firms would be better off to charge the limit price or the price that maximized profits, ignoring entry. In general the greater the barrier to entry, the closer is the limit price to the joint profit-maximizing price.

SCALE ADVANTAGES OF EXISTING SELLERS: Suppose existing firms have no absolute cost advantage, but that they are large in size and that the technology of the industry is such that there are economies of large-scale production.

Such economies imply that new firms, which inevitably begin with only a small share of the market, will have high costs. They will thus find it hard to compete with large established firms that will have low costs because they are large enough to exploit existing economies of scale. This important point is illustrated in Figure 22.5. The ATC curves show the long-run average costs of a single firm subject to decreasing costs.

The established firm has a demand curve D_e, and it is able to earn profits above all its opportunity costs. For the situation pictured in Figure 22.5(i), if a new firm enters the industry with a demand curve D_{n1} there is no output at which it can cover its costs. If it takes time for the firm to establish itself in the market and to have the demand for its product build up to a higher level, the firm must accept losses. These losses will continue until its demand has shifted to D_{n2}, at which time it can cover all its costs by producing at the output corresponding to the point of tangency between D_{n2} and ATC. Figure 22.5(ii) differs from Figure 22.5(i) in that quite a small level of output is sufficient to exploit all the significant economies of scale. The curve D_{n1} for the new entrant is shown in exactly the same position as in Figure 22.5 (i), but this time the firm can make profits even though it has a very small share of the market. Clearly, entry is much easier in an industry whose costs are like those in (ii) than in an industry where costs are like those in (i). The industry pictured in (ii) is said to exhibit lower *minimum efficient scale* (MES).

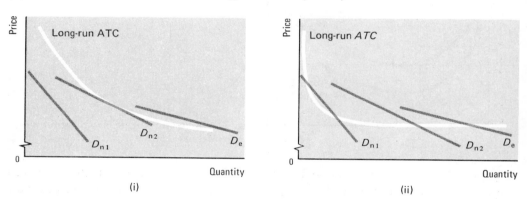

Fig. 22.5 Two alternative long-run cost curves compared with given demand curves

BARRIERS TO ENTRY IN THE ABSENCE OF SCALE ADVANTAGES IN COST CURVES: Is there any way in which firms with small minimum efficient scales may be able to forestall entry? We may examine two possibilities. First, if consumers switch brands frequently, then increasing the number of brands sold by existing firms will reduce the expected sales of a new entrant (thus keeping D_{n1} as far over to the left as possible). Say, for example, that an industry contains three large firms, each selling one brand of cigarettes, and suppose that each year 30 per cent of all smokers abandon their existing brand allegiance and choose new brands in a random fashion. If a new firm enters the industry, it can expect to pick up 25 per cent of these smokers (it has one brand out of a total of four available brands). This gives it $7\frac{1}{2}$ per cent (25 per cent of 30 per cent) of the total market as a result merely of picking up its share of the random switchers. If, however, the existing three firms had five brands each, then there would be fifteen brands already available, and a new small firm selling one new brand could expect to pick up only one-sixteenth of the brand switchers, giving it less than 2 per cent of the total market on this account.

A second defensive policy that may be adopted by an industry that faces potential entrants owing to a low *MES*, is to attempt to shift the cost curves (of itself *and* of potential entrants) upward and to the right by advertising. If there is much brand-image advertising, then a new firm will have to spend a great deal on advertising its product in order to bring it to the public's attention. If the firm's sales are small, advertising costs *per unit sold* will be very large. Only when sales are large, so that the advertising costs can be spread over a large number of units, will costs per unit be brought down to a reasonable level. Thus, heavy advertising expenditures in an industry without economies of scale in production, have the effect of changing total cost curves from the general shape illustrated in Figure 22.5(ii) to that illustrated in Figure 22.5(i).

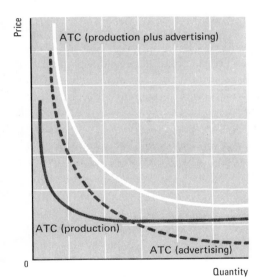

Fig. 22.6 Average total cost curves allowing for both production and advertising costs

This proposition is illustrated in Figure 22.6. The curve labelled *ATC* (production) is copied from Figure 22.5(ii) and it shows a case in which economies of scale are all exhausted at a quite modest level of output, with constant long-run average costs beyond that level. Such an industry is easy to enter. We now add a fixed level of advertising costs necessary to establish a new brand against the heavy advertising of existing brands. When we divide this fixed cost by the number of units produced, we obtain the curve *ATC* (advertising), which shows how advertising cost per unit sold declines as output is raised, thus spreading the fixed cost over more and more units. If we add these two curves together, we obtain the curve *ATC* (production plus advertising), which shows how *all* costs vary as output varies. The curves are drawn to scale, and it is clear from inspection that there are substantial scale economies up to a much higher level of output than when advertising was not a component of costs. A small new entrant will now be at a substantial cost disadvantage when competing against a large established firm.

These hypotheses about nonprice competition creating barriers to entry help clarify two apparently paradoxical aspects of everyday industrial life: the fact that one firm may sell many different brands of the same product, and the fact that each firm spends much money on advertising, competing not only against the products produced by rival firms but also against other products that are produced by the same firm. The soap and cigarette industries provide classic examples of this behaviour. In both of these industries there is only a small number of firms, but there is a very large number of only slightly differentiated products. The explanation is that technological barriers to entry are weak in these industries – a small plant can produce at an ATC just about as low as that of a large plant. Product differentiation and brand-image advertising create substantial barriers where technological ones are weak, and they thus allow existing firms to move in the direction of joint profit maximization, without fear of a flood of new entrants attracted by the high profits.

The final word

Of course, there is a great deal more to the theory of oligopoly than can be summarized here, but enough should have been said to show that the counsel of despair 'you will never explain something so complex as small-group behaviour' should be rejected. The assertion that something is impossible is a powerful challenge to the creative mind. Enough has already been established in this field to show not only that we can already explain and predict some parts of oligopoly behaviour, but also that 20 years from now we shall probably be able to explain and predict much more. There can be no doubt, however, that even in our introductory treatment of this subject we have come very close to one of the frontiers of modern economics.

23

Some predictions of the theories of competition and monopoly

In this chapter we shall use comparative static analysis to derive some implications of the theories of competition and monopoly. The propositions that we shall derive can be viewed in two different ways. First, they are implications of the theories already developed. From this point of view we are engaged in a purely logical process of finding out what propositions are implied by the assumptions we have made in previous chapters. This is a simple matter of right or wrong: either a certain proposition is or is not implied by our theory. This is a matter on which we can come to a perfectly definite conclusion, and the student must accept that the probability of errors in logic still remaining in this well worked-over field is extremely small.

If we wish, however, to see how well our theory fits the real world, if we wish, that is, to test our theories, then the propositions developed in this chapter must be taken as empirical hypotheses. Whether or not these hypotheses are consistent with the facts is a matter for testing and, in the absence of strong empirical evidence, it is not necessary to accept the propositions as statements about what actually happens in the world.

Thus whether or not a given proposition is implied by, or follows from, some theory, is a purely logical question that can be settled definitely without reference to facts; but the question whether or not a given proposition (which follows from a theory) fits the facts or is inconsistent with them is an empirical question that can only be settled by an appeal to real-world observations. In this chapter we are concerned solely with questions of the former type; in subsequent chapters we shall consider those of the latter type.

We shall begin by re-examining those problems of perfectly competitive industries that we first illustrated in Chapter 11. In that chapter we considered producers' cooperatives that were designed to iron out year-to-year fluctuations in incomes. Most producers' cooperatives have a second objective, to raise as well as to stabilize producers' incomes.

THE DRIVE TO MONOPOLIZE PERFECTLY COMPETITIVE INDUSTRIES

Cocoa producers in West Africa, wheat producers in the United States and Canada, coffee growers in Brazil, the Arab oil producers, taxi drivers in many cities and labour unions throughout the world have all sought to obtain, through collective action, some of the benefits of departing from perfectly competitive situations.

The motivation behind this drive for monopoly power is not hard to understand. The equilibrium position of a perfectly competitive industry is *invariably* one in which a restriction of output and a consequent increase in price would raise the profits of *all* producers. This is particularly obvious when, as is so often the case with agricultural goods, the demand for the product is inelastic at the equilibrium price. In this case marginal revenue for a variation in the industry's output is negative and marginal cost positive. Thus a reduction in output will not only raise the total revenues of all producers but will also reduce total costs, and if costs fall and revenues rise, total profits must rise. It is equally true, although not so obvious, that total profits can be increased if demand is elastic at the competitive equilibrium price. At any competitive equilibrium, each firm is producing where marginal cost equals price (see page 253). But as long as the demand curve slopes downward, marginal revenue for the industry is less than price and thus also less than marginal cost. Thus, in competitive equilibrium the last unit sold necessarily contributes less to revenue than to costs. From this we derive the basic prediction that it would always pay the producers in a perfectly competitive industry to enter into an output-restricting agreement. We shall call an association formed for such a purpose a producer's cooperative, or a coop. for short.

Once an output-restricting agreement has been concluded there is a force tending to break down the producers' cooperative behaviour. Clearly, any one farmer can raise his output without affecting the market price. Since this farmer's actions would not affect the price, his income would rise because he could sell his pre-coop. output at the post-coop. prices. Thus, unless the coop. is very carefully policed and has the power to enforce its quota restrictions on everyone's output, there will be a tendency for members to begin to violate quotas once prices have been raised. Furthermore, the coop. must have power over all producers, not merely over its members; otherwise a producer could avoid the quota restrictions on his output merely by leaving the coop.

These two tendencies are illustrated graphically in Figure 23.1. Figure 23.1(i) represents the market conditions of supply and demand; Figure 23.1(ii) represents the conditions of demand and cost for an individual farmer. Before the coop. is formed, suppose that the market is in competitive equilibrium at price p_1 and output Q_1 (where the demand curve intersects the supply curve), and the individual farmer is producing output q_1 and just covering costs. The coop. is formed in order to allow producers to exert a monopolistic influence on the market. By persuading each farmer to reduce his output, it reduces market output to Q_2 (where the marginal revenue curve intersects the supply curve, which is also the industry's marginal cost curve) and achieves the price p_2. The farmer in Figure 23.1(ii) has a quota of q_2, but even though he has reduced his output, he has improved his position. He is now earning profits in the amount shown by the darker section of the area shaded. This leads to

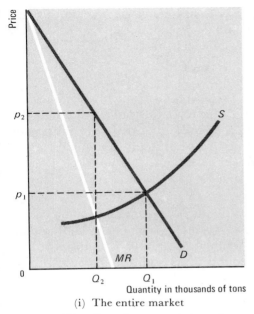

(i) The entire market

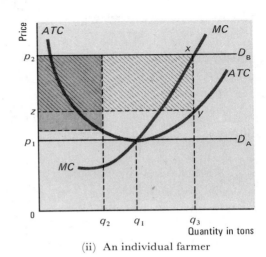

(ii) An individual farmer

Fig. 23.1 The effect of crop restriction schemes

our first prediction, that every farmer will be better off if a coop. is formed and succeeds in raising price to p_2 than if no coop. is formed and price remains at p_1.

But, once price is raised to p_2, the individual farmer would like to increase his output because price is greater than his marginal cost. At q_2, price (and thus the single producer's marginal revenue) exceeds marginal cost, and it follows that, left to himself, the producer would like to increase his output. He would like to move to output q_3 where marginal cost equals his marginal revenue and where he would earn the profits shown by the shaded area p_2xyz in Figure 23.1 (ii). This leads to our second prediction, that each coop. member can increase his profits by violating his output quota, provided the other members do not violate theirs.

These two predictions highlight the dilemma of the producers' coop. Each farmer is better off if the coop. is formed and is effective. But each is even better off than that if everyone else cooperates and he does not. Yet if everyone cheats (or stays out of the coop), all will be worse off.

This leads to the following summary prediction.

> **Producers' coops. formed to raise prices by restricting output in competitive industries will be able to raise producers' incomes, provided they are able to enforce quotas on the outputs of all producers. Such coops. will, however, exhibit unstable tendencies, for it will always be in the interest of any single member to raise his output. If many producers do so, the coop. will collapse and all producers will lose.**

The history of schemes to raise farm incomes by limiting crops bears ample testimony to the empirical applicability of this prediction. Very often crop restriction breaks down, and prices fall as individuals exceed their quotas. The great bitterness and occasional violence that is sometimes exhibited by members of crop-restriction schemes against non-members and members who cheat is readily understandable.

CHANGES IN DEMAND AND COSTS

We must now spend some time studying the response of both competitive and monopolistic industries to changes in their demand and cost functions. Although the analyses may seem highly formal and abstract at the outset, they are important because they set the stage for a study of the effects of taxes, subsidies, innovations and a host of other things, all of which affect either the revenues or the costs of firms.

Changes in demand

A RISE IN DEMAND IN COMPETITION : Figure 23.2 shows the cost and demand conditions for a single firm (i) and for a whole industry (ii) under perfect competition. When the demand curve is D_1, both the individual firm and the industry are in equilibrium at price p_1. (If you have any doubts about this, you should review Chapter 20 now.) There is no incentive for any firm to change its output, nor is there incentive for entry or exit of firms.

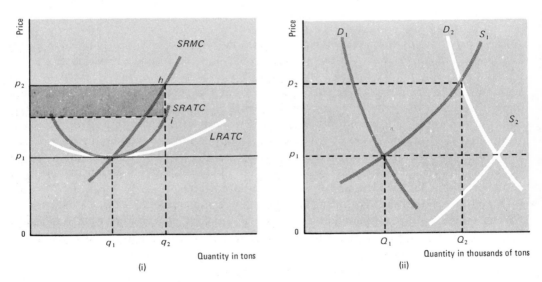

Fig. 23.2 The effects of an increase in demand under perfect competition:
(i) equilibrium of a single firm (ii) equilibrium of the industry

Now assume that the market demand curve in Figure 23.2(ii) shifts from D_1 to D_2. This demand shift causes a shortage to develop. The shortage causes a rise in price, which in turn causes firms to increase their output. In the short run, the market price rises to p_2, the individual firm that we are considering will produce q_2 units, and the total production of all firms will be Q_2. The individual firm will be making profits on each unit equal to the difference between the price per unit and its short-run average total cost $(q_2h - q_2i = hi)$. Thus the firm's total profit is equal to the area of the shaded rectangle in (i).

These then are the predictions about the short-run effects of a rise in demand:

(1) Price will rise.
(2) There will be an increase in the quantity supplied by each firm and hence by the industry.
(3) Each firm will now be earning profits.

The long-run effects follow from prediction 3. Since firms are now making profits, this industry becomes an attractive one in which to invest. New firms will enter the industry, and there will be an increase in supply that will tend to bring the price below the previously established short-run equilibrium level p_2. Supply will increase and price will fall until the profits are eliminated so there is no longer any incentive for new firms to enter the industry.

We have already noted that since in perfect competition all firms have access to the same technology, all firms have the same costs. It follows that each new firm that enters the industry will have costs identical to those of the firm shown in Figure 23.2. Thus new firms as well as old will be able to earn profits as long as price exceeds p_1. The process of entry will stop when price is driven back to p_1, each original firm is producing its original quantity q_1 but the whole industry's output has expanded because there are more firms in the industry. When the expansion has come to a halt the new short-run supply curve in Figure 23.2(ii) is S_2 which is the sum of the marginal cost curves of the now larger number of firms in the industry.

In the long run this leads to an expansion of output at a constant price. The argument is simple: if p_1 is the price equal to the minimum point on the long-run average total cost curve of all existing and potential firms, then p_1 is the only price consistent with long-run equilibrium (all firms just covering total costs).

Are other results possible? The main reason for answering 'yes' is that the industry's expansion may bid up the prices of factors of production heavily used in that industry.[1] If this happens then each firm's *LRATC* curve will shift upwards (see page 236) and the expansion of the industry will come to a halt before price is driven down to p_1. Such an industry will have an increase in price associated with a long-run expansion of output.

It is also conceivable, although rather unlikely, that the expansion of the industry could cause factor prices to fall.[2] This would cause the *LRATC* curves to shift downwards and expansion would continue until prices were driven below p_1 (to the minimum points on the new *LRATC* curves).

Thus the long-run consequences of a rise in demand are as follows:

1 It is also possible that costs could rise if there were real diseconomies of scale external to the firm so that with *factor prices constant* the expansion of the industry caused existing firms' *LRATC* curves to shift upwards. This possible, but rather unlikely, case can be left for more advanced treatments that need to cover all logical possibilities.

2 It is a well known result in more advanced theory that if all industries have constant returns to scale (the location of minimum point on a firm's *LRATC* curve is independent of the size of the industry) and if different industries use factors of production in different proportions the production-possibility surface will be concave to the origin which means that all industries will find their costs and long-run equilibrium prices rising as they expand.

(1) The scale of industry will expand.
(2) Profits will eventually return to zero.
(3) Price may be above, below or equal to its original level but (i) constant factor prices and (ii) costs for new entrants being the same as costs of the original firms before entry ensures that price will return to its original level.

A FALL IN DEMAND IN COMPETITION: Consider a fall in demand. Figure 23.3 shows the firm and the industry in long-run equilibrium with price at p_1 before the fall. When demand falls to D_2, a glut of the commodity is created; supply exceeds demand at the original price p_1; price then falls to p_3. At price p_1, the individual firm was just covering all opportunity costs. At the new price, p_3, the firm will produce q_3, the output for which marginal cost equals marginal revenue.

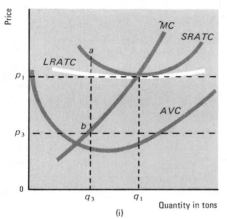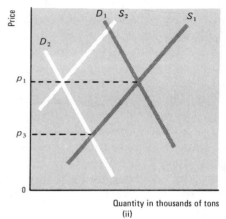

Fig. 23.3 The short-run effects of a fall in demand: competition. (i) Short-run equilibrium of a firm in perfect competition (ii) Short-run equilibrium of a perfectly competitive industry

The firm will now be suffering losses. Average total cost is q_3a, and average revenue is q_3b $(=p_3)$; losses per unit are ab. Would it not be worth the firm's while to close down its operations altogether, instead of running at a loss? The answer to this is 'No'. We have already seen on page 244 that it pays the firm to continue producing in the short run as long as price is greater than average variable costs.

We conclude, therefore, that if price falls below average total cost but exceeds average variable cost, the firm will make losses, but will stay in production at least in the short run. Only if price falls below average variable cost will the firm cease production.

Thus the short-run effects of a fall in demand in a competitive industry are as follows:

(1) Price will fall.
(2) There will be a decrease in the quantity supplied by each firm and hence by the industry.
(3) Each firm will now be making losses.
(4) Firms will go out of production immediately only if they are unable to cover their variable costs of production.

The long-run effects follow from point (3). Since firms in the industry are not covering all costs, the industry is not an attractive place in which to invest. No new capital will enter the industry; as old plant and equipment wears out, it will not be replaced (because the expected profits on the funds used for this equipment will be negative). Thus the scale of the industry will contract. The short-run supply curve, showing how production varies with price, capital equipment being held constant, shifts to the left. But, as the supply diminishes, the price of the product begins to rise. This price rise will continue until the firms remaining in the industry can just cover their total costs.

The analysis for a rise in demand applies in this case with only minor changes. If factor prices remain constant, then price must return to p_1 before the remaining firms can reach the minimum points on their $LRATC$ curves. If, however, the contraction of the industry causes a fall in the prices of factors of production used especially heavily by the industry, the cost curves of the remaining firms will shift down and price need not rise as far as p_1 before costs can be covered thus stopping further contraction. In the unlikely event that the contraction causes the industry's heavily used factors to rise in price, cost curves rise and price must rise above p_1 before the remaining firms can cover their costs.

We have established the following long-run implications of a fall in demand.

(1) **The scale of the industry will contract.**
(2) **Losses will eventually return to zero.**
(3) **Price may be above, below or equal to its original level but (i) constant factor prices and (ii) costs for new entrants being the same as costs of the original firms before entry ensures that price will return to its original level.**

A CHANGE IN DEMAND IN MONOPOLY: On page 266 in the section on the absence of a supply curve under monopoly we saw that we cannot predict that a rise in demand will always cause an increase in both price and output, even in the short run. It is possible, providing the elasticity of the demand curve changes sufficiently, for a rise in demand to cause a fall either in price or in output.

At this level of generality, we are left with the conclusion that a rise in demand for a monopolist can cause both his price and his output to rise, but that it is possible for either his price or his output to fall. This may seem a disappointingly vague conclusion, but it is all the theory implies. In order to get a more specific prediction we would need to know more about the demand curve than that it merely sloped downwards. If, for example, we knew the slopes of the demand curves before and after the shift, we would be able to make a definite prediction.

There are some interesting cases in which we can make definite predictions: (1) every point on the demand curve shifts upwards or downwards by the same amount and (2) the demand curve pivots through its point of intersection on the price axis. In both these cases price and quantity rise when demand rises, and fall when demand falls. These cases are important because they can be adapted to study the effects of a per unit and an *ad valorem* tax on the monopolist's output, and they are illustrated in Figures 23.4(i) and (ii).

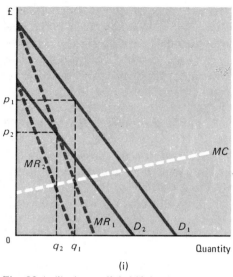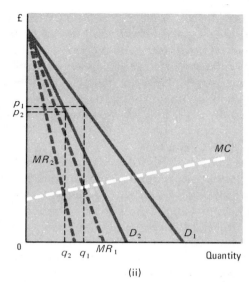

Fig. 23.4 (i) A parallel shift in the monopolist's demand curve changes the price and quantity in the same direction as the change in demand (ii) A pivoting of the monopolist's demand curve through the price intercept changes the price and quantity in the same direction as the changes in demand

Changes in costs

COMPETITION: Consider a case in which marginal costs are reduced by a given amount at all levels of output for all firms. This is shown by a downward shift in the marginal cost curves. In a competitive industry the short-run supply curve will shift downwards by the amount of the downward shift in the firm's marginal cost curves, and this will lead to a greater output at a lower price. But the price will fall by less than the vertical downward shift in the marginal cost curve, while profits will now be earned because of the lower costs of production. Thus, in the short run, the price comes down by less than the reduction in marginal cost, and the benefit of the cost reduction is shared between the consumers, in terms of lower prices, and the producers, in terms of profits.

In the long run, however, profits cannot exist in an industry having freedom of entry, and new firms will enter the industry; the influx of new firms will increase output and drive price downward until all profits are eliminated. In the long run, therefore, all of the benefits of lower costs in competitive industries are passed on to consumers in terms of higher output and lower prices.

The case of a rise in costs is just the reverse, and, in the short run, the effects will be shared between the consumer, in terms of higher prices, and the producer, in terms of losses. In the long run, however, firms will leave the industry until those remaining can cover all their costs. Therefore, the effects of higher costs are borne fully by the consumer in terms of lower output and higher prices in the long run.

MONOPOLY: In a monopoly a fall in marginal costs will cause a reduction in price and an increase in output. (You should draw a graph to illustrate this for yourself.) Thus, the direction of the change in price and output in response to a change in costs is the same in monopoly as in perfect competition. But the magnitude of the change will be less in monopoly than in competition. Since a monopolist necessarily has barriers to entry (or he wouldn't be a monopolist), the higher profit that he earns as a result of a fall in his costs does *not* attract new entrants whose competition then drives profits down to their original level. Thus, in monopoly we expect the benefit of lower costs, and the burden of higher costs, to be shared between the consumers in terms of price and output variations and the producer in terms of profit variations both in the short run and in the long run.

We now have a powerful tool at our command: once we can relate anything in which we are interested to a change in either costs or revenues, we have a series of predictions already worked out. We shall see examples of how this can be done in the next section of this chapter and in the following chapter.

The effect of taxes on price and output

There are many kinds of taxes which affect the costs of a firm. We shall here consider only three of them: a tax that is a fixed amount per unit produced; a tax that is a fixed amount; and a tax that is a fixed percentage of profits. The first is called a per unit tax, the second a lump-sum tax and the third a profits tax.

PER UNIT TAX: A per unit tax increases the cost of producing each unit by the amount of the tax. The marginal cost curve of every firm shifts vertically upward by the amount of the tax. In perfect competition, this means that the industry supply curve shifts upward by the amount of the tax. Now all we need is to refer to the results of the previous section in order to derive the required predictions. (1) In the short run, a per unit tax will raise the price but by less than the amount of the tax so that the burden will be shared by consumers and producers. (This prediction has already been derived in Chapter 11.) (2) In the long run the industry will contract, profits will return to normal and the whole burden will fall on consumers. (3) If cost curves of firms remaining in the industry are unaffected by the contraction in the size of the industry, then price will rise in the long run by the full amount of the tax.

Although the monopolist has no supply curve the tax does shift his marginal cost curve. The analysis given earlier in the chapter allows us to state the following prediction immediately. In the short run and in the long run, the burden of the tax will be shared between consumers in terms of lower output and higher prices and the monopolist in terms of lower profits.

Prediction (2) is one example of a most important general prediction that recurs constantly: in an industry with freedom of entry or exit, profits must be forced to zero in the long run. Thus, any temporary advantage or disadvantage given to the industry by government policy, by private conniving or by anything else, must be dissipated in the long run since free entry and exit will ensure that surviving firms earn zero profits. Intervention can influence the size of the industry, the total volume of its sales, and the price at which its goods are sold; but intervention cannot influence the long-run profitability of the firms that remain in the industry. Many a government policy has started out to raise the profitability of a particular industry and only ended up increasing the number of firms operating at an unchanged level of profits.

LUMP-SUM TAX: Consider now the effect of a lump-sum tax. Such taxes increase the fixed costs of the firm but do not increase marginal costs. [1] The short-run effect on price and output of a change in fixed costs is zero, both in perfect competition and in monopoly. Since both marginal costs and marginal revenues remain unchanged, the profit-maximizing level of output cannot be affected. Hence we deduce the implication that a lump-sum tax leaves price and output unchanged in the short run. [2]

In the long run, the tax has no effect on a monopolist's price and output. Assuming that the monopolist was previously making profits, then the tax merely reduces the level of these profits. But, since the monopolist was making as much money as he possibly could before the tax, there is nothing that he can do to shift any of the tax burden onto his customers. (Of course, if the lump-sum tax is so large that, even at the profit-maximizing level of output, profits are reduced to less than zero, the monopolist will cease production in the long run.)

In the case of perfect competition, we would expect the tax to affect price and output in the long run. If the industry was in equilibrium with zero profits before the tax was instituted, then the tax would cause losses. Although nothing would happen in the short run to price and output, equipment would not be replaced as it wore out. Thus, in the long run, the industry would contract, and price would rise until the whole tax had been passed on to consumers and the firms remaining in the industry were again covering total costs.

PROFITS TAX: A famous prediction is that a tax on profits (as the term is defined in economics) will have no effect on price and output. Let us first see how the prediction is derived and then consider its application to real-world situations.

In perfect competition there are no profits in long-run equilibrium. Since profits taxes would not be paid by a perfectly competitive firm when it was in long-run equilibrium, it follows that the existence of the tax would not affect the firm's long-run behaviour. A monopolist usually earns profits in the long run and therefore would pay the profits tax. The tax will reduce his profits but it will not cause him to alter his quantity produced nor (hence) his price. This is illustrated in Figure 23.5 in which profits are shown as varying with the quantity the monopolist sells. (Since

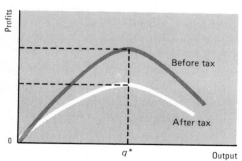

Fig. 23.5 A tax on pure profits will affect neither price nor output

1 See page 225 where we showed that marginal costs were necessarily marginal *variable* costs.
2 Unless the tax is so high that it causes the producers simply to abandon the business at once. Because of this, a lump-sum tax is different from some fixed costs because it can be avoided by quitting the industry.

he faces a downward-sloping demand curve every quantity implies a particular price.) Before the income tax the monopolist maximizes profits by selling the quantity q^*. Now assume that a 20 per cent profits tax is imposed. Since every level of output is associated with 20 per cent less profit than before, the level of output, q^*, that produced the highest profits before the tax still does so after the tax has been imposed. Since q^* remains the profit-maximizing output, the monopolist's price does not change.

Thus a tax on profits, as they are defined in economics, affects neither price nor output. Hence it has no effect on the allocation of resources.

Does this prediction apply to 'profits taxes' as they are levied in the real world? The answer is an emphatic 'no' because profits as they are defined in tax law are very different from profits as defined in economics. In particular the tax-law definition includes earnings of the factor of production, capital, and the reward for risk-taking. To economists these are a part of costs but for tax purposes they are a part of profits.

We may notice one or two of the many consequences of such 'profits' taxes. First, perfectly competitive firms will pay 'profits' taxes even in long-run equilibrium since they use capital and must earn enough money to pay a return on it. Second, the tax will affect costs differently in different industries. Assume one industry is very labour intensive so that 90 per cent of its costs of production go to wages and only 10 per cent to capital and other factors, while another industry is very capital intensive so that fully 50 per cent of its costs (in the economist's sense) are a return to capital. The 'profits' tax will take a very small bite of the total earnings of the first industry and a large bit out of those of the second industry. If the industries were equally profitable (in the economist's sense) before the 'profits' tax, they would not be afterwards and there will be a tendency for producers to be attracted into the first industry and out of the second one. This will cause prices to change until both industries become equally profitable, after which no further movement will occur. The tax does not leave the allocation of resources unaffected.

Many further ways in which real-world taxes on profits influence the allocation of resources could be mentioned but enough has been said to suggest that those who fail to make the distinction between taxes levied on what the economist means by profits and taxes levied on what the tax inspector means by profits will make predictions about the real world that do not in fact follow from their own theory. The theory predicts that a tax on 'pure profits' will have no effect on the price and output policy of firms, but that a tax on 'profits' as they are defined by the taxing authorities will have a definite effect on these decisions. Clearly, great care must be taken when the same term is given one meaning by economists and another meaning by the general public or by government officials.

A COMPETITIVE INDUSTRY THAT BECOMES MONOPOLISTIC

As well as yielding certain testable predictions based on the minimal amount of knowledge normally assumed, the theory of the firm and industry provides a framework into which more detailed knowledge can be fitted. Further testable predictions can then be extracted from the theory. If, for example, we know the elasticity of demand, and how the demand curve is shifting through time, and if we have detailed information about costs, the theory will yield a large number of predictions. In this section we shall consider one example of the use of the theory in a specific context. This example, although hypothetical, is not unlike many actual situations, particularly those in the retail trades.

Assume that in a particular city the barbers all belong to a single trade association. There is freedom of entry into the industry in the sense that anyone who has obtained a stated set of qualifications can set up as a barber. All barbers, however, must join the association and must abide by its rules. The association sets the price of haircuts and strictly enforces this single price. Thus there is no price competition between barbers.

Periodically the association raises the fixed price of haircuts in an attempt to raise the incomes of its members. The association is strong enough to prevent any illicit price-cutting and to resist all attempts to secede. The question is: will the barbers succeed in raising their incomes by raising the price of haircuts? If you were a consulting economist called in to advise the barbers' association, what would you predict to be the consequences of this price rise? You should not read on until you have tried to develop these predictions for yourself.

Clearly we need to distinguish between the short- and the long-run effects of this increase in the price of haircuts. In the short run the number of barbers is fixed. Thus in the short run the answer is simple enough: it all depends on the elasticity of the demand for haircuts. If the demand elasticity is less than one, total expenditure on haircuts will rise and so, therefore, will the income of barbers; if demand elasticity exceeds one, the barbers' incomes will fall. The problem in the short run amounts to that of getting some empirical knowledge about the elasticity of demand for haircuts. If you were actually advising the barbers' organization you might be lucky enough to be able to refer to a full-scale econometric study of demand. In the case of haircuts this is unlikely and you would probably have to try to gain some idea of demand elasticity by studying the effects of changes in haircut prices either at other times or in other places. We cannot go into this matter except to mention that you should not fall into the trap of reasoning as follows: 'Haircuts are a necessity for no one goes without one. Therefore the demand for haircuts will be almost perfectly inelastic.' The reader should easily spot the fallacy in this argument. There are many reasons why the demand for haircuts is not perfectly inelastic. For example, the time between haircuts is by no means a constant. An increase in the average period between haircuts from three to four weeks would cause a $33\frac{1}{3}$ per cent decline in demand; if this change in habits were occasioned by a 20 per cent rise in price, then the demand elasticity over this price range would be 1·66! Furthermore, habits can change drastically, as the recent fashion for long hair shows. Sometimes such changes may be caused by noneconomic factors, but they can also occur in response to a price change.

Let us say, however, that, on the basis of the best available evidence, you estimate the elasticity of demand *over the relevant price range* to be substantially less than one, say 0·3. You then predict that the barbers will be successful in raising incomes in the short run; a 20 per cent rise in price will be met by a 6 per cent fall in custom, so that total revenue of the typical barber would rise by about 13 per cent. In predicting the consequences you would also need to estimate the length of the short run for this industry (a couple of years?).

Now what about the long run? If barbers were just covering all costs before the price change, they will now be earning profits. Barbering will become an attractive trade relative to others requiring equal skill and training, and there will be an inflow of barbers into the industry. As the number of barbers rises, the same amount of business must be shared out among more and more barbers, so that a typical barber will find a steady decrease in the amount of trade that he does. His profits will thus decrease. Profits may also be squeezed from another direction. Faced with increasing excess capacity – a typical barber could handle much more business than does in fact come his way – barbers may compete against each other for the limited number of customers. Since they are unable to compete through price cuts, they can only compete in service. They may redecorate their shops, and buy expensive magazines. In these ways competition will raise costs. Thus, the profits of the individual barber will be attacked from two directions; falling revenues and rising costs. This movement will continue until barbers are once again just covering all costs. Once this comes about there will be no further attraction to new entrants. The industry will settle down in a new position of long-run equilibrium in which individual barbers are just covering all of their opportunity costs. There will be more barbers than in the original situation, but each barber will be working a lower fraction of the day and will be idle for a larger fraction (i.e., there will be excess capacity); the total number of haircuts given by each barber will be diminished, and possibly the level of costs and service will have increased. Thus your report would say 'you may succeed in the short run (if demand is sufficiently inelastic) but the policy is bound to be self-defeating in the long run'.

The general moral of the story is the now-familiar one that if you cannot control entry, you cannot succeed in keeping earnings above opportunity costs in the long run. If price competition is ruled out, then profits will be driven down by the creation of excess capacity. Producers' associations that are successful in keeping earnings up are those that are successful in restricting entry.

IS OLIGOPOLY THEORY NECESSARY?

So far in this chapter we have managed to analyse a number of cases using only the theories of perfect competition and monopoly – plus some of the concepts of mono-polistic competition, in the barber example. Some economists argue that these two polar theories are all that are necessary to predict the outcome of any situation in which we might be interested. These economists recognize the existence of small-group industries, but they believe that such industries will behave either like perfectly competitive ones or like monopolies; thus no other theories will be needed to understand and predict their behaviour. Probably the majority of economists do not accept this view and believe that much behaviour, particularly in the industrial sector, cannot be understood without an explicit theory of oligopoly. These economists would point to such cases as the two following.

CIGARETTES: The American cigarette industry is one of the most highly concentrated of manufacturing industries. It has three dominant firms: the American Tobacco Company, R.J.Reynolds and Liggett & Myers. If we were to analyse it using the theory of monopoly, we would predict that the cigarette companies would avoid competing with one another either in buying tobacco or in setting the price of cigarettes. We also predict that substantial profits would persist for many years. These things *have* happened. In an antitrust suit against these three companies, it was shown that they conspired to purchase tobacco in auctions without bidding against one another, and that all kept their prices of cigarettes high relative to the costs of production. A dramatic (and monopolistic) episode occurred in June 1931, when, in the depths of the Depression and in the face of the lowest tobacco-leaf prices in a quarter of a century, the three big cigarette companies (which then controlled 90 per cent of the market among them) all raised their prices.

But here the monopoly analogy begins to break down. The policy proved spectacularly unsuccessful. Smokers shifted in large numbers to cheaper brands made by other companies, and ultimately prices fell well below the May 1931 level as the big three tried to regain their market shares. (They have not since achieved as large a share as they held in May 1931.)

The profits of these cigarette companies were, and remain, well above the average for all manufacturing industries. In this respect, the theory of monopoly predicts well. It is also successful in predicting the lack of competition in the leaf market, and the absence of serious price competition in the last 45 years.

But there are other characteristics of the industry that are readily observable and that are not predicted by the theory of monopoly. The most notable is the enormous expenditure on advertising by each of the companies. Advertising expenditure raises costs and lowers profits. It has two aspects. First, it represents intense nonprice competition among the existing sellers, who recognize that it does not pay to compete by price cutting, and, second, it represents an attempt to raise barriers against potential competitors.

The high cost of establishing a new brand name represents a really substantial barrier to entry. The theory of oligopoly predicts that advertising will occur for these reasons. (See page 288.) Some kinds of advertising are also consistent with monopoly theory. If a monopolist, through advertising, can change consumers' preferences towards his product in such a way as to shift the demand curve to the right, or make it more inelastic, he may increase revenues by more than the cost of the advertising. But such advertising is product-oriented advertising, not brand-name advertising. It certainly would not pay a monopolist to advertise two of his brands in competition with each other. Neither the kind nor the amount of cigarette advertising is of the sort predicted by the theory of monopoly.

STEAM TURBINE GENERATORS: Three electrical manufacturers, General Electric, Westinghouse and Allis-Chalmers, produce more than 95 per cent of all the steam turbine generators in the United States. In 1960, these three firms were charged with having held a series of meetings beginning at least as early as June 1957, for the purpose of agreeing on prices and sharing the market among themselves. Subsequently each of the firms pleaded guilty. Do we need a theory of oligopoly to explain this behaviour, or is the theory of monopoly sufficient? Certainly, the behaviour as charged in the indictments is fully consistent with the theory of monopoly. For the period from July 1957 to May 1958, the conspiracy apparently succeeded in producing something very close to joint-profit-maximizing behaviour, including extensive price discrimination.

Midway in 1958, however, the cooperative behaviour broke down; prices fell very drastically, and the three sellers became involved in vigorous price competition among themselves. Among the reasons for this change was the threat by the Tennessee Valley Authority to ask for foreign bids on a turbine generator it required, a slackening of demand, and rumours of antitrust prosecution. All attempts to stop the price cutting were in vain. Behaviour had ceased to be monopolistic.

In analysing the market behaviour in this industry, the monopoly model would have led to accurate predictions for one period and to very poor predictions for another period. Simple models that predict with accuracy under some circumstances but not under others are useful if we know, or can define, the situations in which they will work and those in which they will not work. *But defining these situations is precisely the purpose of more complex or elaborate theories.* For example, if the theory of oligopoly were to tell us that the monopoly model will work well for steam turbine generators in periods of strong demand, but will not work when firms develop excess capacity, it would be useful in itself and would also increase the usefulness of monopoly theory.

THE PREDICTIONS OF THE THEORY OF THE FIRM AND INDUSTRY

In this chapter we have developed a number of quite general predictions of the theory of the firm and industry, and we have also illustrated the use of the theory in yielding predictions after certain specific information has been added to its general assumptions. It is fashionable these days amongst professional economists to emphasize the inadequacies and the failures of the traditional theory of the firm. Such shortcomings, real though they are, should not be allowed to obscure the fact that this theory is an outstanding intellectual achievement. The theory of perfect competition shows in a quite general way how a large number of separate profit-maximizing firms can, with no conscious coordination produce an equilibrium which depends only on the 'technical data' of demand and costs. Individual attitudes and eccentricities of producers and a host of other factors are successfully ignored, and it is shown how an equilibrium follows solely from the conditions of costs and demand. The analysis extends *mutatis mutandis* to the cases of monopolistic competition and monopoly. It does not extend, however, to oligopoly. In the case of competition amongst the few, it is no longer true that the solution depends only on the 'objective' factors of costs and market demand. The attitudes of each competitor to the stratagems of his few opponents becomes important, and, for the same costs and market demand, the equilibrium of the industry will vary considerably as the psychology of the competitors varies. It is here that the traditional theory has had the least success, and it may be true that an entirely different framework will have to be worked out in order to deal successfully with the problems of oligopoly.

The consumer goods with which the ordinary citizen is most familiar – cars, radios, TV sets, washing machines, cookers etc. – are mostly produced by oligopolistic industries. For this reason the casual observer must beware of reaching the false conclusion that the perfectly competitive model is not applicable to any significant number of markets. This is emphatically not so. Markets where buyers and sellers adjust quantities to a given price that they cannot change by their own individual efforts abound in the economy. Foreign exchange markets, markets for raw materials, markets for many agricultural commodities, most futures markets, the markets for gold and other precious metals and stock markets are but a few whose behaviour is comprehensible with, but makes no sense without, the basic model of perfect competition (possibly augmented by one or two specific additional assumptions to catch the key institutional details of each case).

Manufactured consumer goods are, as already mentioned, dominated by oligopolistic industries. Retail trades and many service industries come close to the conditions of monopolistic competition in that there is free entry, a large number of competing firms and product differentiation (the person who provides service matters and each person is different).

Clearly, the whole armoury of market forms is relevant to our economy. Happily, as illustrated in this chapter, theories do make many important predictions about how our economy behaves but, unhappily, there are all too many questions to which current theory does not provide clear answers that have already stood up to serious testing.

24

Monopoly versus competition: predictions about performance

Monopoly has been regarded with suspicion for a very long time. It is often held that modern economic theory has proved that monopoly is a system whereby the powerful producer exploits the consumer, while competition always works to the consumer's advantage. Indeed, the founder of English classical economics, Adam Smith, in his *Wealth of Nations*, developed a ringing attack on monopolies and monopolists and, since that time, most economists have been advocates of free competition and critics of monopoly. In this chapter we shall first consider this classical case against monopoly, and then go on to see what else can be said about monopoly and competition on the basis of positive economics.

THE CASE AGAINST MONOPOLY

The classical case against monopoly is based on the static theory of resource allocation *within the context of a given technology*. The case is to a very great extent based on a single prediction: if a perfectly competitive industry should be monopolized, and the cost curves of all productive units are unaffected by this change, the price will rise and the quantity produced will fall. Thus, given identical cost and demand conditions, monopoly leads to a lower output and a higher price than does perfect competition. We made use of this proposition in the first section of Chapter 23 and we need only briefly rehearse its derivation here.

Equilibrium under perfect competition occurs where supply equals demand. Since the supply curve is the sum of the marginal cost curves, it follows that in equilibrium, marginal cost equals price. This is illustrated in Figure 24.1 in which the competitive supply curve is labelled MC to remind us that it is the sum of the marginal cost curves of the individual firms; the competitive output is q_c and the competitive price p_c. Now assume that this industry is monopolized as a result of a single firm buying out all the individual producers. Further assume that each plant's cost curve is unaffected by this change. In other words we assume that there are neither economies nor diseconomies resulting from the coordinated planning of production by a single decision

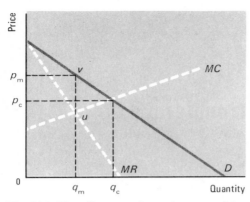

Fig. 24.1 The effect on price and output of the monopolization of a perfectly competitive industry

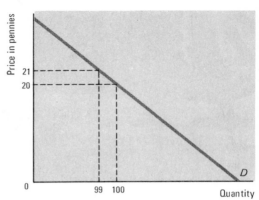

Fig. 24.2 An individual demand curve: the household is prepared to pay more than the market price for all but the last unit bought

unit. This means that the marginal costs will be the same to the monopolist as to the competitive industry: the competitive industry's supply curve will be the marginal cost curve to the monopolist. But the monopolist who seeks to maximize profits will equate marginal cost not to price, but to marginal revenue. Now the output of the industry falls from q_c to q_m while the price rises from p_c to p_m.

> **A monopolist facing the same costs and market demand as a competitive industry, will have a lower output and a higher price than would the competitive industry.**

THE CASE FOR PERFECT COMPETITION[1]

Are we justified in saying that a lower-price, higher output situation is *in any sense* better, or more nearly optimal, than the reverse? The second prong of the classical case against monopoly consisted in showing that perfect competition led, *in equilibrium*, to a use of resources that was, in a clearly defined sense, the 'best' one.

We cannot go into this inquiry in any detail here, and we shall have to satisfy ourselves with a rather intuitive statement of why the allocation of resources resulting from perfect competition was regarded as superior to the one resulting from monopoly. The argument is based mainly on two predictions about production under conditions of perfect competition: (1) at equilibrium, the level of cost is the lowest level attainable, given the technology of the society, and (2) marginal cost equals price.

1 This discussion is taking us in the direction of welfare economics, a subject usually thought to be a normative one founded on value judgements. Personally, I accept the case argued by G.C. Archibald, 'Welfare Economics, Ethics and Essentialism', *Economica*, Vol. 26, 1959, that welfare economics is either mathematics (the conditions for an optimum) or positive economics (predictions about what changes will expand the consumer's range of choice). My reason for omitting a detailed discussion of welfare economics at this stage, is not that it isn't (or can't be made to be) positive economics but that it is a rather subtle subject to be given detailed consideration in an introductory text.

Competition produces output at least average total cost

The first prediction follows from the proposition that perfectly competitive firms must, in long-run equilibrium, be producing at the minimum point on their long-run average total cost curves. The significance of producing outputs at their lowest possible cost is obvious: the fewer are the resources used to produce any one commodity, the greater is the total output that can be obtained from our limited supply of resources.

Competition produces output where marginal cost equals price

The price of the commodity indicates the money value that consumers place on the last unit of the commodity that they purchase. Consider the individual demand curve in Figure 24.2. As the price rises, the consumer buys fewer units. If the market price settles at 20p, he will buy 100 units; thus he gets all but the last unit at a price *less* than he would be prepared to pay for them. (He is prepared, for example, to pay 21p each to get 99 units.) Thus, assuming his demand curve to be downward sloping, the price measures what he is prepared to pay for the last unit he purchases; he would be prepared to pay more than the current price in order to obtain all but the last unit (which is why he would continue to buy them at higher prices); to obtain additional units, he is prepared only to pay an amount less than the market price (which is why he does not at present buy these additional units).

Under perfect competition, marginal cost equals price in equilibrium. It follows that consumers are prepared to pay for the last unit they actually purchase an amount exactly equal to the cost of producing that last unit. In monopoly, price exceeds marginal cost. From this it follows that consumers pay, for the last unit they actually purchase, an amount greater than the cost of producing it. Furthermore, consumers would be prepared to buy further units for an amount greater than the cost of producing these units; consumers are, however, not allowed to purchase these extra units because the monopolist is restricting output in order to maximize his profits. In Figure 24.1, for example, the marginal cost at the monopolist's equilibrium is $q_m u$ and price is $q_m v$ so that consumers are prepared to pay uv more for another unit than the actual cost of producing that unit. They would also be willing to buy at a price in excess of the marginal costs of production a total of $q_m q_c$ units more than they are permitted to buy.

There is a strong intuitive appeal to the idea that consumers will in some sense be 'better off' when marginal cost equals price, than when it is less than price. It can in fact be shown, and it is a well-known proposition in welfare economics, that, given a large number of very strict conditions, the equating of marginal costs to price in all lines of production, will yield an optimal situation *in the sense that it will be impossible to make some consumers better off without simultaneously making others worse off*; when marginal costs do not equal prices in some industries, this will result in a non-optimal situation *in the sense that it will be possible to make some consumers better off without making others any worse off by changing some prices and outputs in the economy.*

The demonstration of the above proposition can be found in any textbook of welfare economics. There is no doubt that the proposition has had a strong effect on the attitudes of economists and students of economics towards the value of the price system. If the unhindered price system operating through perfect competition produces an optimal situation, then interference by the central authorities can only move us away from this optimum, and it may be condemned for this reason. Because the proposition has exerted so much influence and has led so many to the conclusion stated above, it is probably worth while pointing out just how far away it is from applicability to the world of our experience.

Requirements for an optimum to be achieved

The proposition that perfect competition leads to an optimum allocation of resources requires among other things, the following:

(1) There should be no divergence between private and social costs anywhere in the economy (see Chapter 32). From society's point of view it pays to produce a good up to the point at which the revenue gained from the last unit just equals the opportunity cost of making it, only if the firms' private costs reflect the opportunity costs to society of using the resources elsewhere, and if the firms' private revenues reflect the gains to society of having an extra unit of this good produced. We shall see in Chapter 32 that social and private costs often diverge. This critical condition is therefore by no means always fulfilled.

(2) There should be perfect competition in all sectors of the economy, ensuring that the correct result obtains throughout. This we know to be at variance with the facts (see pages 305–6).

(3) There should be no external economies or diseconomies of scale. An external economy or diseconomy is beyond the influence of a single firm and thus does not enter into the firm's calculations even though it may be important for society.

(4) The process of innovation and growth should be strictly autonomous. (See Chapter 18, pages 238–9 for a discussion of possible hypotheses about innovation.) If market forms other than perfect competition are more conducive to growth, future income will be higher if they are allowed to exist.

(5) The conditions necessary to produce this optimum should exist simultaneously everywhere in the economy. If this is not so, we have no idea what the effect will be of fulfilling them somewhere in the economy. Specifically, if in a world of mixed market structures, we break up one monopoly and make it into a competitive industry, we have no general presumption even in a theoretical model that this will move us closer to an optimum position.[1]

It must be clear, even to the casual observer, that this set of conditions is wildly at variance with actual facts. Of course, we do not have a world of perfect competition, and the above theory does little to help us decide whether a bit more or less oligopoly would improve or worsen things in any clearly defined way. Nonetheless we can still pass judgements on certain implications of competition and monopoly, that as ordinary citizens we do or do not like. What we cannot do is to assume that economic

---

1 This important proposition upsets much of the basis of piecemeal welfare economics. We know how to identify the best of all possible worlds (from the limited point of view of the optimum we are discussing), but we have little clear idea how to order two states of the very imperfect world in which we live. If this were not so economists could not disagree as much as they do about specific policy measures.

theory predicts that *any* increase in the degree of competition in the economy will necessarily increase the efficiency of resource allocation.

The political appeal of perfect competition

Why is the proposition that perfect competition leads to an optimum allocation of resources, still so potently attractive? Perhaps it can be explained by the great appeal of the perfectly competitive model to the liberal who is frightened by the exercise of power either by private organizations or by the state. To someone who believes in the individual and hates all power groups, the perfectly competitive model was almost too good to be true.

In the perfectly competitive world, no single firm and no single consumer has any power over the market whatsoever. Individual consumers and producers are both members of a group of many similar consumers or producers, and no single one can affect the market. Individually they are passive quantity adjustors. If we add to this the assumption that firms are profit maximizers, all firms become passive responders to market signals, always doing what is most desirable from the society's point of view. The great impersonal force of the market produces an appropriate response to every important change. If, for example, tastes change, prices will change and the allocation of resources will move in the appropriate direction, but throughout the whole process no one will have any power over anyone else. Millions of firms are reacting to the same price changes. If one refuses to react there will be countless other profit-maximizing firms all eager to make the appropriate changes. If one firm refuses to take coloured employees or makes any other decision based on prejudice, there will be millions of other firms that will recognize that profit-maximization is not consistent with discrimination on the basis of race, colour or creed or anything other than how hard a man is prepared to work.

It was a noble model: no one had power over anyone, and yet the system behaved in a systematic and purposeful way. Many will feel that it is a pity that it corresponds in so few aspects to reality as we know it. Also we should not be surprised to find that it still has a very strong appeal and that some people still cling tenaciously to belief that it describes the world in which we live; it would remove so many problems if only it did.

Is monopoly really evil?

Looking only at the theories of perfect competition and monopoly, some have been tempted to conclude that economic analysis has proved that monopoly is evil, that it exploits the consumer and that it should be condemned and stamped out whenever possible. Nothing in positive economics allows us to speak of monopoly as an evil. Positive economics seeks to establish valid predictions about the real world; it tells us the consequences of our actions. If our economics is done well, we shall be able to say with some confidence that, if an industry is monopolized, certain changes will occur in price and output. Whether or not we like these consequences is a subjective matter. We can be in complete agreement about the consequences and yet disagree irreconcilably about whether they are desirable or undesirable, good or evil. Whether we prefer the consequences of competition to those of monopoly *and whether our margin of preference is sufficient to justify incurring any substantial costs involved in moving from one to the other*, are matters that involve value judgements and that take us beyond the scope of positive economics.

Policy implications of accepting the classical position

The belief that competition produced ideal results and monopoly nonideal ones led at once to the notion of prohibiting *by law* the practice of monopoly. *Antimonopoly laws*, perhaps the first manifestation of the classical down-with-monopolies policy, give the courts the power to dissolve an existing monopoly into a larger number of independent companies.

A second policy – *public-utility regulation* – grew out of the belief that, in some sectors (for example, in transportation and public utilities), competition was impossible. We saw in Chapter 20 that unexploited economies of scale were incompatible with perfect competition (see pages 259–60). Perfect competition can only exist in industries in which the output at which the *ATC* curve reaches its minimum is small in relation to the total market demand. In this case the total necessary output can be produced by many competing firms, all producing at minimum average total costs. If, on the other hand, the output at which the *ATC* curve reaches a minimum is large in relation to the market demand, then perfect competition is impossible and firms will expand under the incentive of falling long-run costs until the market is dominated by a few large producers, or possibly by only one. Such industries were regarded as natural monopolies since competition among many firms would be unstable and would quickly give way to oligopoly or monopoly. The advantage of having one or a few large firms producing at a lower cost than could be achieved by many small firms is evident but, in order to prevent monopolistic exploitation, the policy advice was that the central authorities should regulate prices in such a way that the industry would only earn the normal rate of return on its capital. Thus costs would be lowered by the monopolization, but the price would be held to its competitive level by the State's intervention. In practice there are many difficulties in deciding on what is a 'reasonable' or 'normal' rate of return for a natural monopoly to earn on its capital. Nonetheless many countries exercise a great deal of this sort of regulation of naturally monopolistic industries, particularly in the case of public utilities such as gas, electricity, transportation and communications.

SOME UNSETTLED QUESTIONS OF MONOPOLY VERSUS COMPETITION

The classical condemnation of noncompetitive forms of behaviour was based on the belief that the alternative to monopoly was perfect competition. Today we realize that very often the effective choice is not between monopoly and perfect competition, but between more or less oligopoly, so that we are not sure what effects a specific intervention will have on price and output. Thus, even if we accept the perfectly competitive result as being more desirable than a completely monopolistic one, this does not in itself tell us much about the real decisions that face us. In the remainder of this chapter we shall talk about competitive and monopolistic situations in general terms, with a view to considering the effects of encouraging a little more or less competition than we now have.

The importance of the given-cost assumption

The classical predictions about monopoly depend critically on the assumption that costs are unaffected when an industry is monopolized. If any savings are effected by combining numerous competing groups into a single integrated operation, then the costs of producing any given level of output will be lower than they were previously. If this cost reduction does occur, then it is possible for output to be raised and price to be lowered as a result of the monopolization of a perfectly competitive industry. Such a situation is illustrated in Figure 24.3. The competitive equilibrium price is

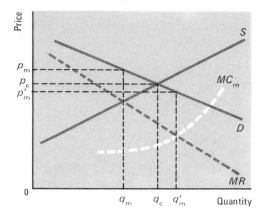

Fig. 24.3 The effects on price and output of a monopoly that is more efficient than a large number of competing firms

p_c and quantity is q_c. If the industry was monopolized and costs were unaffected, production would fall to q_m, and price would rise to p_m. If, however, the integration of the industry into a single unit causes some increase in the efficiency of organization and thereby reduces costs, then the marginal cost curve will shift downward. If it shifts to MC_m, then production will rise to q'_m and price will fall to p'_m. This shows that the monopolization of an industry, combined with a sufficiently large consequent increase in efficiency, can result in a fall in price and a rise in quantity produced, as compared to the competitive industry.[1]

Of course, it is also possible that the monopolization of an industry may reduce the efficiency of production, and so shift the marginal cost curve upward. In this case, monopolization will, *a fortiori*, raise price and lower output as compared to the competitive industry. The reader should draw his own diagram showing the effects on price and output of a monopolization that caused costs to rise above those ruling under competition.

On the one hand, it is sometimes argued that monopolization will lower costs because wasteful duplication will be eliminated, and because economies of scale will result from, for example, establishing one coordinated management body for the industry. On the other hand, it is also sometimes argued that competition forces the individual firm to be efficient because the firm will not survive unless it keeps its costs

---

1 The reader should be able to show for himself that, if the elasticity of demand were less than one at the competitive price, the monopolist would reduce output and raise price, no matter how large the reduction in his costs.

as low as its competitors', whereas inefficiency is more common under monopoly because, although inefficiency reduces profits, it need not drive the monopolistic firm out of business. What is certain is that we cannot predict the effects on price and output of monopolizing a competitive industry unless we know the effect of this change on the industry's costs. This is as far as our theory can take us; it can predict what empirical magnitudes are important, but, until we have some evidence of the effects of monopolization on an industry's cost structure, we cannot predict the effect that it will have on price and output.

The effect of market structure on innovation: the very long run

We have seen that, if monopoly results in lower costs than does perfect competition, output may be higher and price lower than under competition. We may now ask if economic theory predicts anything about the relative incentives to develop, and to introduce, cost-reducing innovations under various market forms.

We may note first that both the monopolist and the perfect competitor have a profit incentive to introduce cost-reducing innovations. A monopolist can always increase his profits if he can reduce his costs. We saw in Chapter 23 (pages 298–9) that a cost reduction will cause the monopolist to produce more, to sell at a lower price, and thus to increase his profits. Furthermore, since he is able to prevent the entry of new firms into his industry, these additional profits will persist into the long run. Thus, from the standpoint of maximizing his profits, the monopolist has both a short- and a long-run incentive to reduce his costs.

The firm in perfect competition or in monopolistic competition has the same incentive in the short run, but not in the long run. In the short run, a reduction in costs will allow the firm that was just covering costs to earn profits. In the long run, other firms will be attracted into the industry by these profits. Existing firms will copy the cost-saving innovation and new firms will enter the industry using the new techniques. This will go on until the profits of the innovator have been eliminated. The effectiveness of profits as an incentive to reduce costs for a firm in competition will thus depend on the magnitude of the extra profits and the length of time over which they persist. If, for example, it only takes a few months for existing firms and new entrants to copy and install the new invention, then the original firm's profits will be above normal for only a very short time, and the extra profits may not be sufficient to compensate for the risks and the costs of developing the innovation. In all such cases, the direct incentive to innovate would be absent from a competitive industry. On the other hand, if it takes several years for other firms to copy and install the cost-saving innovation, then the profits earned over these years by the innovating firm may be more than sufficient to compensate for all costs and risks, and yield a handsome profit as well. In this case, the incentive to innovate is present in a competitive industry.

So far we have considered the profit incentive to introduce new innovations. Another consideration is the availability of the resources needed to finance research to invent new methods and new products. It is often held that the large profits available to monopolistic firms provide a ready fund out of which to finance research and development. The typical, perfectly-competitive firm, so goes this argument, is only earning enough money to yield a normal return on its capital, and it will have few funds to spare for research and development. Supporters of this view can point to much illustrative evidence. They can point out, for example, that few of the innovations that have vastly raised agricultural productivity over the last century were developed by the typical competitive farming unit; they were developed rather by a few oligopolistic or monopolistic manufacturers of farm equipment and by researchers in government-financed, research institutions.

One argument on the other side is that competitive firms *must* innovate or they will lose out to their competitors, while, although monopolists have an incentive to innovate, they do not need to do so because they are insulated from potential competitors by their barriers to entry. There is lack of agreement on how important this argument is. Opponents of it would argue, first, that it is wrong to regard a monopolist or oligopolist as shielded from all competition. It is always possible that some new firm will be able to break into the market by developing some new, similar, but superior product that evades existing patents and other barriers to entry. Furthermore, the larger the monopoly profits of the existing firm(s), the larger is the incentive for new firms to break into the market. Thus, it is argued that all monopolies are in potential competition with possible new entrants, and the monopolist who sits back and does not innovate will not long remain a monopolist. The second argument that opponents would advance is that the necessity to innovate is by no means universal under perfect competition. If an innovation is hard to copy, then there *is* a strong incentive for a competitive firm to innovate and a big penalty for firms who do not innovate because a long time will be needed before the non-innovator can copy and catch up with the innovator. On the other hand, if the innovation is easy to copy, there is a smaller incentive for the competitive firm to innovate and a smaller penalty for the firm that fails to innovate, since it is easy for the non-innovator to copy and catch up with the innovator. The above discussion may be summarized as follows:

> **All firms have an incentive to innovate since they can increase their profits with a successful innovation. The greater the barriers to entry and the harder it is for other firms already in the industry to copy the innovation, the longer will the profits of innovating persist and, thus, the larger is the incentive to innovate. In competitive industries without barriers to entry there will be little incentive to make innovations that are very easily copied since both the profits of innovating and the losses from not innovating before other firms innovate will be very short-lived.**

Economists of the classical view were not unaware of these considerations and they usually supported *patent laws*. Patent laws represent an attempt to lengthen the short-run period during which the innovating firm can earn profits as a reward for its innovation. Once the patent expires, other firms can copy the innovation and, when they do so, production will expand until revenues fall to just cover all costs. There is little doubt that, were there no patent laws, many innovations could be copied with greater speed than at present, and that the original innovators would not earn as much extra revenue to compensate them for the costs and risks of development. On the other hand, patents can be imitated, so their real advantage to the small firms should not be exaggerated. Indeed, it has been argued that patents are of greater advantage to the monopolist who has the resources to develop, patent and 'keep on the shelf' processes that might enable a potential competitor to challenge his position.

The classical case against monopoly concerns the allocation of resources within the context of a fixed technology. The above discussion has concerned the very long run where the production function is changing due to the discovery of lower-cost methods of producing old products and the introduction of new and improved products. The issue that we are faced with is the extent to which market organization affects the rate of innovation. Before reading on it would be helpful to refresh your memory of the discussion of invention and innovation by rereading pages 238–41.

The greatest opponent of the classical position on monopoly was the distinguished Austrian (and later American) economist, Joseph A. Schumpeter.[1] Schumpeter's argument was, first, that innovations that lower costs of production, thus increasing output per head and creating economic growth, have a much larger effect on living standards than any 'misallocation' of resources causing there to be at any one time too much production of one kind of commodity and too little of another. The second part of Schumpeter's argument is based on his theory that innovation is functionally related to market forms in such a way that there is likely to be much more innovation under monopoly and oligopoly than under monopolistic and perfect competition. Let us look at each of these points in turn.

According to the classical case against monopoly, it results in a misallocation of resources with too few resources devoted to producing goods in the monopolistic sector and too many in the competitive sector. Schumpeter believed that the losses due to this misallocation were small relative to the gains and losses due to variations in the rate of economic growth. Modern measures made since Schumpeter wrote have tended to support him in this contention. It appears very unlikely that the losses due to monopolistic and oligopolistic misallocations can amount to more than 2 or 3 per cent of a country's national income.[2] But the national income of most countries is growing at that rate each year, and a growth rate of 3 per cent per year doubles material living standards in less than 25 years.

The second part of Schumpeter's argument was that monopolistic and oligopolistic market forms were more conducive to growth than is perfect competition. His argument was that only the incentive of profits led men to take the great risks of innovation and that monopoly power was much more important than competition in providing the climate under which innovation occurred. The large short-run profits of the monopolist provided the incentive for others to try to usurp some of these for themselves. If a frontal attack on the monopolist's barriers to entry was not possible, then the barriers would be circumvented by such dodges as the development of similar products against which the monopolist would not have patent protection. The pro-

---

1 His most famous book is *The Theory of Economic Development* (English edn.; Harvard University Press, 1934). The beginning student is referred to the lucid but less technical *Capitalism, Socialism and Democracy* (3rd edn.; Harper, 1950). Both works are available in paperback.

2 In one of the most famous of these studies Professor Harberger of the University of Chicago puts the figure at about $\frac{1}{10}$ of 1 per cent of the US national income!

cess of one monopoly replacing another through the invention of new products or new production techniques Schumpeter called the *process of creative destruction*.

Since, in Schumpeter's theory, monopoly is more conducive to growth-creating innovations than is perfect competition, it follows that the 'worse' the allocation of resources at any moment of time, i.e. the greater the amount of monopolization, the more rapid is the rate of innovation which leads to economic growth and thus the more rapid the long-run rise in living standards. This very important hypothesis cannot be handled with normal long-run theory because long-run theory *assumes* constant technology.

Schumpeter put part of his argument in the following words.

What we have got to accept is that it [monopoly] has come to be the most powerful engine of progress and in particular of the long-run expansion of total output not only in spite of, but to a considerable extent through, this strategy [of creating monopolies] which looks so restrictive when viewed in the individual case and from the individual point of time. In this respect, perfect competition is not only impossible but inferior, and has no title to being set up as a model of ideal efficiency. It is hence a mistake to base the theory of government regulation of industry on the principle that big business should be made to work as the respective industry would work in perfect competition.[1]

Schumpeter's theory leads to the policy conclusion that the attempt to break up monopolies and oligopolies and to try to make the economy behave as if it were perfectly competitive is undesirable since it will reduce rather than raise living standards. A breaking up of all monopolies and oligopolies might result in a maximum once-for-all rise in living standards of up to 5 per cent due to the removal of the misallocation of resources, but the cost of this would be very high since, according to his theory, this would reduce the rate of innovation and thus have a serious retarding effect on the growth rate.

Consider an illustrative example. Let there be two countries each with a national income of 100 and growing at 3 per cent per annum. Country *A* breaks up its monopolies and thereby achieves an immediate rise of national income to 105 but a fall in its growth rate to 2 per cent. Country *B* lives with its monopolies and continues to have a 3 per cent growth rate. Country *B* will catch up to country *A* in five years' time, and in 50 years time country *B* will have an income of just over 1·5 times that of country *A*. Clearly, given these figures, the cost of breaking up *A*'s monopolies was very large indeed.

The effect of alternative market forms on the process of innovation and economic growth is an extremely important question. Unfortunately it is one on which existing theory and empirical studies shed all too little light. Here is a largely unexplored area, knowledge of which cannot help but affect seriously our evaluation of the entire issue of monopoly *versus* competition.

BALL-POINT PENS: AN EXAMPLE OF SCHUMPETERIAN CREATIVE DESTRUCTION: Much of the previous discussion can be illustrated by the rather spectacular case of the behaviour of the economy in response to the introduction of a revolutionary new technique for writing, the ball-point pen. In 1945, Milton Reynolds acquired a

1 *Capitalism, Socialism and Democracy* (Harper, 1950), page 106.

patent on a new type of pen that used a ball bearing in place of a conventional point; he formed the Reynolds International Pen Company, capitalized at $26,000 and began production on 6 October 1945.

The Reynolds pen was first introduced with a good deal of fanfare by the New York department store, Gimbels, who guaranteed that the pen would write for two years without refilling. The price was set at $12.50 (the maximum price allowed by the wartime Office of Price Administration, which was the body with which the American central authorities sought to control prices during and after the Second World War). Gimbels sold 10,000 pens on 29 October 1945, the first day they were on sale. In the early stages of production, the cost of production was estimated to be around 80¢ per pen.

The Reynolds International Pen Company quickly expanded production. By early 1946, it employed more than 800 people in its factory and was producing 30,000 pens per day. By March 1946 it had $3 million in the bank. Demand was intense. Macy's, Gimbels' traditional department-store rival, introduced an imported ball-point pen from South America. Its price was $19.98 (production costs unknown).

The heavy sales quickly elicited a response from other pen manufacturers. Eversharp introduced its first model in April, at $15.00. In July 1946, the business magazine, *Fortune*, reported that Schaeffer was planning to put out a pen at $15.00, and Eversharp announced its plans to produce a 'retractable' model priced at $25.00. Reynolds introduced a new model, but kept the price at $12.50. Costs were estimated at 60¢ per pen.

The first signs of trouble emerged. The Ball-point Pen Company of Hollywood (disregarding a patent infringement suit) put a $9.95 model on the market, and a manufacturer named David Kahn announced plans to introduce a pen selling for less than $3.00. *Fortune* reported fear of an impending price war in view of the growing number of manufacturers and the low cost of production. In October, Reynolds introduced a new model, priced at $3.85, that cost about 30¢ to produce.

By Christmas, 1946, approximately 100 manufacturers were in production, some of them selling pens for as little as $2.98. By February 1947, Gimbels was selling a ball-point pen made by the Continental Pen Company for 98¢. Reynolds introduced a new model priced to sell at $1.69, but Gimbels sold it for 88¢ in a price war with Macy's. Reynolds felt betrayed by Gimbels. Reynolds introduced a new model listed at 98¢. By this time ball-point pens had become economy items rather than luxury items, but still were highly profitable.

In mid-1948, ball-point pens were selling for as little as 39¢, and costing about 10¢ to produce. In 1951, prices of 25¢ were common. Today there is a wide variety of models and prices, ranging from 10¢ to $5.95, and the market appears stable, orderly and only moderately profitable. Ball-point pens were no passing fad, as every reader of this book knows. Their introduction has fundamentally changed the writing-implement industry in America and in the world.

The ball-point pen example has interested observers in many fields. Lawyers have been concerned about the ease with which patent rights were circumvented. Psychologists have noted the enormous appeal of a new product even at prices that seemed very high. Advertising men have regarded it as a classic case of clever promotion.

From the point of view of economic theory, it illustrates several things:

(1) That a monopoly (in this case a patent monopoly) can in the short run charge prices not remotely related to costs and earn enormous profits.

(2) That entry of new firms (even in the face of obstacles) will often occur in response to high profits.

(3) That where it does occur, entry will in time drive prices down to a level more nearly equal to the costs of production and distribution.

(4) That the lag between an original monopoly and its subsequent erosion by entry may nevertheless be long enough that the profits to the innovator, as well as to some of the imitators, may be very large indeed. (It is estimated that Reynolds earned profits as high as $500,000 *in a single month* – or about 20 times its original investment.)

The effect of market structure on consumer's range of choice

It is sometimes argued that one of the virtues of competition among several producers is that it presents the consumer with a wide range of differentiated commodities, while complete monopoly with only one producer tends towards uniformity of product. We shall not ask here to what extent a variety of products is desirable, but will ask if we would in fact expect competition to produce more diversity of product than monopoly.

AN EXAMPLE FROM RADIO AND TELEVISION: A very interesting case in which competition tends to produce a nearly uniform product while monopoly tends to produce widely differentiated ones, has been studied in detail.[1] This is the case of radio and television. The explanation runs somewhat as follows: consider a case in which there are two potential radio audiences; one group, comprising 80 per cent of the total audience, wishes to hear pop music; the other group, comprising 20 per cent wishes to listen to a concert of chamber music; and in which each individual radio station seeks to maximize its own listening audience.

If there is only one station, it will produce pop music. If a second competing station is now opened up, its most profitable policy will be to produce a similar pop-music programme on the grounds that half of the large audience is still better than all of the small one. A third station would also prefer a third of the large audience to all of the small one. In fact five stations would be needed before it would be profitable for any one station to produce a programme of chamber music. Thus competition between two or three stations would tend to produce two or three almost identical pop-music programmes, each competing for its share of the large audience.

A monopoly controlling two stations would not, however, pursue this policy. The policy to maximize its total listening audience would be to produce pop music on one channel and chamber music on the other. The monopoly might spend more money on preparing the programme for the larger audience, but it would not spend money to produce a similar programme on its second channel – the optimal policy for its second channel would be to go after the other 20 per cent of potential listeners so

1 P.O. Steiner, 'Monopoly and competition in TV: some policy issues', *The Manchester School* (1961); 'Program Patterns and Preferences and the Workability of Competition in Radio Broadcasting', *Quarterly Journal of Economics,*' May 1952.

that, between the two channels, the monopoly would have the largest possible audience.

In both the cases of monopoly and competition each individual firm tries to maximize its own listening audience, but when there are two competing stations they both go after the same large audience, ignoring the minority group, while, when there are two stations owned by one monopoly, they go after both audiences, one for each station. Under these circumstances, competition produces a uniformity of product which ignores the desires of the minority, while monopoly produces a varied product catering for the desires of both the majority and the minority group.

At the time that the case was studied, British radio was a three-station monopoly, and British television was based on competition between two stations, each taking as its criterion of success its own listening audience. It was found that the three stations of the monopolized radio produced very little similarity between the products offered at any one time, while the two competing stations of British television produced almost identical products a great deal of the time. Thus at a randomly selected time of the day the radio listener was likely to have two or three varied possibilities open to him, while the television viewer was often forced to choose between two quite similar programmes.

THE PRINCIPLE OF MINIMUM DIFFERENTIATION: In some ways this radio example is a special case[1] and we may now consider the problem in somewhat more general and abstract terms.

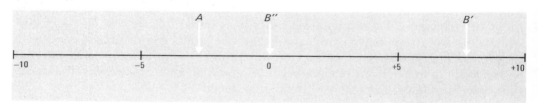

Fig. 24.4 The differentiation of a product with one independent characteristic

Consider a product with only one independent characteristic which we can measure on a scale from -10 to $+10$. This is illustrated in Figure 24.4. The product might, for example, be soap powder in which harshness was associated with cleansing power and mildness with lack of it. A $+10$ rating might indicate a soap which had great cleansing power but removed the skin from the unfortunate user's hands, and -10 a soap which was positively beneficial to the hands but which would not remove the merest speck of grease.[2] Let us assume that firm A has settled its product on the scale at -2. If firm B now wishes to produce a competing product, what will be its optimal policy? It might go to an extreme, producing a soap which had strong cleansing power but was also rather harsh on the hands, going out as far as, say, $+8$

1 The case is certainly sufficient to refute the proposition that some degree of competition always produces more product differentiation than does monopoly. One must be very careful not to dismiss refutations as merely special cases.

2 This product has two characteristics, cleansing power and effect on skin, but they are not independent of each other; we have assumed that they vary directly with each other.

on the scale (indicated by B' in Figure 24.4). Consumers whose tastes lead them to prefer something *between* the two products would, presumably, choose the product which came closest to satisfying their tastes. Firm A would get all customers who preferred a product ranging from -10 to $+3$, while B would get all those who preferred a product in the range $+3$ to $+10$. Now let us assume that, having decided to make a product with more cleansing power and more harshness than the competitor's product, firm B goes only a little way in this direction, just enough to make the difference noticeable but not enough to cause a major difference between the two products. Let us say it goes to zero on our scale (see B'' Figure 24.4). Now firm B should get all customers who would like a product rating between -1 and $+10$. Clearly firm B does better to place its product at B'' rather than at B', and equally clearly the best policy is to locate the product to the right of A on the scale just enough for the difference to be noticeable. That the optimal policy is often to make your product different enough from your competitor's product for the difference to be noticeable but no more so, is sometimes referred to as the PRINCIPLE OF MINIMUM DIFFERENTIATION.[1]

AN EXAMPLE OF OLIGOPOLISTIC COMPLEXITY: If we now add a third competing firm, any simple competitive strategy will lead to an unstable process. If, for example, A is at -1 and B at zero then the optimal strategy for the new firm C is to produce a product rated at $+1$. But now, assuming that the customers are distributed evenly along the scale according to their tastes, firm B will have only 5 per cent of the market (i.e., those customers preferring a product between $-\frac{1}{2}$ and $+\frac{1}{2}$) and it will pay it to move outside either A or C. Say B goes to $+2$. Now C has only a small part of the market and it will pay it to go to -2, putting A in the position of being bracketed by the other two so that it goes to $+3$ (or to -3). The student can be left to prove for himself that if each firm moves in sequence and makes the move which will give it the biggest share of the market without worrying about what its competitors might then do, an unstable situation will develop so that the process of move and counter-move will not lead to an equilibrium position. In this example the addition of a third firm removes the tendency towards minimum differentiation and replaces it by a tendency towards perpetual oscillation.

If we drop the assumption that each firm does not look beyond its next move, a host of interesting possibilities are opened up. The reader should consider the consequences of at least a few of the possible strategies. What happens if each firm looks ahead to its competitors' next move? What happens if two firms look beyond their next move and one firm does not? What happens if only one firm looks ahead? What happens if two firms collude? It is interesting to note that in this last case the two colluding firms can take the lion's share of the market by locating at $+5$ and -5, thus leaving the third firm unable to retaliate, but that the third firm can, by locating anywhere between -4 and $+4$ determine how this share is split up between the two colluding partners.

---

1 The principle of minimum differentiation has applicability well beyond the scope of economics. It goes a long way, for example, in explaining why in a two-party system both parties tend to gravitate towards a middle-of-the-road position that minimizes the real choice given to voters.

All of this is a simple illustration of the general point made in Chapter 22 that the outcome of an oligopolistic situation is influenced by the strategies adopted by the competing firms.[1]

MONOPOLY VERSUS COMPETITION: A CONCLUSION

We have been concerned in this chapter with what could be said about monopoly and competition on the basis of positive economic theory. On many crucial points we have no accepted theory at all,[2] and, on other points, existing theory has been inadequately tested. It is obviously necessary to keep an open mind on the subject and to admit that, on the basis of existing theory, it is impossible to make out an overwhelming case either for or against monopoly as compared with competition. Everyone will have his own guess, hunch or prejudice on the subject, often based on bits of personal experience. But, from the point of view of economic science, we are interested in carefully documented, objective evidence and on these grounds a great deal remains to be discovered, even at a most elementary level, about the comparison of the effects of monopoly with those of competition.

---

1 At this point in previous editions I have had a section asserting what seemed obvious to me that, if a second independent characteristic was added so that products were differentiated in two-dimensional space, the principle of minimum differentiation would reassert itself for any number of firms. This assertion, which is now better regarded as a conjecture, turns out to be wrong. The applicability of the principle including an explanation of why the above-mentioned conjecture is wrong is presented in B. C. Eaton and R. G. Lipsey 'The Principle of Minimum Differentiation Reconsidered', *Review of Economic Studies*, February 1975. (Much, although by no means all, of the article is not accessible to beginning students.)

2 See the list of questions on page 205. A casual reading of the newspapers will raise many questions in the field of the theory of the firm, which cannot be handled by any existing theory.

25

Some criticisms and tests of the theory of supply

In previous chapters we have derived a number of testable implications from our theory. The theory itself is tested every time one of these implications is confronted with facts, in such a way that a conflict between theory and observation is possible. In many cases, if a particular implication were in conflict with the facts, this would necessitate only a minor change in the basic theory. We might, for example, discover that firms did not always close down when they were unable to cover their variable costs of production. This is in conflict with the theory of short-run profit maximization as we have presented it; but only minor changes might be required to make the theory consistent with these new facts. In other cases, however, empirical observations have been alleged that strike at the very core of the theory. If these conflicting observations were substantiated it would be necessary either to make very drastic amendments to, or to abandon completely, the theory as we know it.

In this chapter we shall first discuss some general approaches to testing the theory and then consider a number of criticisms that have been raised against it. The final criticism relates to the work of Professor J. K. Galbraith who has attacked the very basic assumption that the market demand curves represent given data for firms so that firms must react to *given* demand conditions.

APPROACHES TO TESTING THE THEORY

Each of the following three approaches has often been used in criticizing and testing the theory of the firm:

(1) *Formulate an alternative (and competing) theory that makes different predictions.* Given an alternative theory, one can discover the areas in which the two theories make conflicting predictions, and choose the one that comes closer to predicting what actually is observed to happen. We might hypothesize, for example, that firms choose to maximize their sales rather than their profits, and we would then have two competing theories. We could then derive conflicting predictions from the two theories and could confront these with the evidence. This is a satisfactory way of choosing between two theories.

(2) *Observe decision-takers to see if they behave as the theory predicts they will behave.* We might observe, for example, how a certain executive takes a decision: what records he consults, what questions he asks, and so on. Or we might create a laboratory situation and give 'subjects' a chance to take decisions, then record and analyse their decisions.

Although this approach may give rise to new theories, it does not by itself provide a test of an existing theory, since it does not tell us whether the procedure actually employed by the decision-taker really makes any difference in his decision.

If, for example, an executive systematically discusses proposed price changes with his sales manager and his lawyer, but rarely with his cost accountant, it may suggest the hypothesis that demand and anti-monopoly considerations loom larger in his mind than cost conditions, but it does not demonstrate that these things play a more important role than cost in pricing decisions. Other explanations are possible. For example, the executive might be an expert on cost conditions, or he might need less time to acquaint himself with cost data than with demand data, or his cost accountant may provide him with lucid memos, whereas his sales manager can only communicate orally.

(3) *Ask decision-takers how they take decisions.* Another approach to testing the theory of profit maximization is merely to ask businessmen: 'Do you seek to maximize profits?' This approach has from time to time been tried and it will not surprise you to learn that, when asked if their sole motive was to make as much money as possible, businessmen replied that it was not, and that they sought to charge a fair price, to make only a reasonable profit, and generally to conduct their affairs in a manner conducive to the social good. Asking people what they do and why they do it may well provide some interesting hunches and suggest hypotheses about behaviour for further testing. If you have always taken it for granted that people do a certain thing and inquiry shows that everyone denies it, then this may make you suspicious and lead you to check your ideas further. But it can never show that your original idea was wrong. Consider what the denials might mean: (1) the people were lying; they did try to do the thing assumed but would not admit to it; (2) the people told what they thought was the truth, but they were not aware of their own motives and actions; (3) the people were correct in saying that they did not try to do it. Now how are we to judge which of these possibilities is correct? One needs only a nodding acquaintance with elementary psychology to realize that we are not likely to discover very much about human motivation by asking a person what motivates him. Generally, he will have either no idea at all, or else only a pleasantly acceptable rationalization.

Direct questioning at best (assuming the subject tries to be scrupulously honest) tells us what the person questioned thinks he is doing. Such information may be extremely interesting and useful, but it can never refute an hypothesis about what the person actually is doing. To challenge such an hypothesis, we must observe what he does, not ask him what he thinks he does.

CRITICISM 1: FIRMS DO NOT HAVE ADEQUATE INFORMATION

One group of critics says that profit-maximizing theory will prove inadequate because businessmen, however hard they may try, cannot reach decisions the way the theory predicts. This criticism has a number of aspects, some of them very crude and some quite sophisticated.

One of the crudest forms of this criticism is based on the observation that businessmen do not calculate in the manner assumed by the theory. Sometimes businessmen are interviewed and it is discovered (apparently to the surprise of the interviewer) that they have never even heard of the concepts of marginal cost and marginal revenue. It is then argued: (1) the theory assumes businessmen equate marginal cost to marginal revenue; (2) empirical observations show that businessmen have never heard of marginal cost and marginal revenue; (3) therefore the theory is refuted, because businessmen cannot be employing concepts of which they are unaware.

This observation, assuming it to be correct, does refute the theory that businessmen take decisions by calculating marginal values and consciously equating them. But it does not refute the theory that businessmen maximize profits. The mathematical concepts of marginal cost and marginal revenue (these are just the *first derivatives* of the total cost and total revenue functions by another name) are used by the economic theorist to discover what will happen as long as, by one means or another – by guess, hunch, clairvoyance, luck or good judgement – the businessman does approximately succeed in maximizing his profits. The constructs of the theory of the firm are purely logical tools employed by the economist to discover the consequences of certain behaviour patterns. They are not meant to be a description of *how* the businessman reaches his decisions. If the businessman is maximizing his profits, then the tools of economic theory allow us to predict how the businessman will react to certain changes – e.g., the introduction of a tax – and this prediction is independent of the thought process by which he actually reaches his decision.

A similar argument stems from the observation that businessmen do not calculate down to single units with such a nice degree of accuracy as is assumed. In the verbal presentation of the theory of the firm it is usually stated that the businessman will increase production until the cost of producing the very last unit is just equal to the revenue gained from its sale. This is merely a verbal statement of the mathematical conditions for the maximization of the net revenue function. The observation that businessmen do not calculate down to single units, is not of itself relevant as a test of the theory. The marginal analysis allows us to predict how the businessman will respond to certain changes in the data; if he is maximizing his profits he will be observed to respond in this way even though he calculates in a much cruder fashion than does the mathematician.

More sophisticated critics point out that the information available to the decision-taker is simply not adequate to permit him to reach the decisions that the economist predicts he will reach. This argument generally takes one of three forms: that the businessman is the victim of his accountants, and bases decisions on accounting concepts, which differ from economic ones; that the natural lag between accumulating and processing data is such that important decisions must be made on fragmentary and partially out-of-date information; and that, because acquiring full economic information is costly, firms cannot afford to acquire as much information as economists assume them to have. [1]

THE HYPOTHESIS OF FULL-COST PRICING: Out of these lines of criticism has come the hypothesis of *full-cost pricing*, which was originally suggested by businessmen's answers to questions on how they set prices.

This hypothesis explicitly denies that businessmen will charge the price that will maximize their profits. According to the full-cost hypothesis, businessmen use available data to compute full costs per unit (variable costs plus overhead) and add to this a conventional mark-up; price is set at this figure and sales are determined by what the market will absorb at that price. [2] Thus firms are conceived of as having a perfectly elastic supply curve set at the level of 'full costs'. The student should be able to verify for himself that the full-cost theory leads to different predictions than does profit-maximizing theory. The full-cost hypothesis portrays the businessman as a rather conservative creature, a prisoner of his habits and his accounting records, instead of the alert profit-seeker of traditional theory.

Although full-cost theory has occasioned considerable heated argument, no generally accepted authoritative test of it exists. In so far as the theory is made to rest on the inadequacy of accounting records, it has been effectively refuted by showing that modern accounting procedures do not limit firms to the use of average costs. [3] But the belief that the theory is appropriate for some firms cannot be refuted either by showing that firms are not forced to be full-costers by modern accounting methods, or by showing that some firms do not choose to follow full-cost methods.

It is still possible within a single academic institution to find some competent economists who accept the full-cost theory and others who assert that no one in his right mind could take such a theory seriously. The fact that some people take it seriously while others say that it is so silly that it is not worth testing is cogent argument for subjecting every theory, no matter how little confidence one has in it, to empirical tests. As long as testing is left to judgement based on individuals' casual and private observation, there will be disagreement. If, however, the choice between the two is as clear as most people think, then a carefully documented set of tests would settle the matter once and for all.

Many economists believe, and this may well be the final assessment of the controversy, that the full-cost theorists discovered the rule of thumb by which day-to-day decisions are taken within the firm, but that the critical decision as to the 'customary' mark-up is one taken periodically by management at a high level, with profit maximization as an important objective.

1 The growing importance of business consultants and of economic research departments within firms suggests that firms may not always have been successful in maximizing profits, and that they are making serious efforts to improve performance in this direction. The evidence from such consultants suggests that the businessman aided by his accountant has often been led to take many decisions which are not profit-maximizing ones.

2 The theory may also be regarded as an attack on the *desire* of businessmen to maximize profits. A paper by R.L. Hall and C.J. Hitch, 'Price Theory and Business Behaviour', *Oxford Economic Papers*, May 1939, generated a long debate that is well summarized in R.A. Gordon, 'Short-Period Price Determination in Theory and Practice', *American Economic Review*, June 1948.

3 See, for example, James S. Earley, 'Recent Developments in Cost Accounting and the "Marginal Analysis"', *Journal of Political Economy*, June 1955.

CRITICISM 2: DECISIONS MADE BY THE FIRM ARE STRONGLY INFLUENCED BY THE INSTITUTIONS WITHIN THE FIRM

A major attack on profit-maximizing theory comes from a group of economists whose concern is with ORGANIZATION THEORY. They argue that in big organizations decisions are made after much discussion by groups and committees and that the structure of the *process* affects the *substance* of the decisions; so that different decisions will result from different kinds of organization, even if all else is unchanged. Thus the firm cannot be regarded as an entity taking consistent decisions in respect of definite and unchanging goals. The firm will take different decisions faced with identical situations but using different decision-taking institutions.

Although it has proved easier for organization theorists to express their central point of view than to formulate specific testable hypotheses, they have formulated a number of the latter. One is that a large and diffuse organization finds it necessary to develop standard operating procedures to help it in making decisions. These decision rules arise as a compromise among competing points of view and, once adopted, are changed only reluctantly. One prediction following from this hypothesis is that the procedures used may be nonoptimal and will persist for long periods of time, despite changes in conditions affecting the firm. For either reason, profits will not be maximized. Another prediction is that this procedure will lead large firms to adopt conservative policies and avoid large risks. Smaller firms will take bigger risks.

Hypotheses like these are very hard to test. Proponents of organization theory feel that the evidence supports them: critics feel that they are undemonstrated. It is hard to avoid the view that at the present time the evidence is inconclusive.

CRITICISM 3: FIRMS DO NOT SEEK TO MAXIMIZE SHORT-RUN PROFITS

A major class of these criticisms strikes directly at the assumption of profit maximization. 'Businessmen', it is argued, 'do not seek to maximize profits at all; of course they must make some profits or they will go out of business but, after that, they pursue some totally different goal; the actions necessary to achieve this goal are substantially different from those necessary to achieve profit maximization.' 'Thus', it is argued, 'all the deductions based on the assumption of profit maximization will be at variance with the facts, except in those cases in which the actions necessary to achieve the goal actually being pursued happen, by chance, to coincide with the actions necessary for profit maximization.' This is stronger than saying that firms are prevented from achieving maximum profits by the lack of information available to businessmen or by the organization's structure. This hypothesis states that the firm does not even try to maximize profits.

The first set of criticisms under this general heading centre around the question of who actually controls the firm. The owners of the firm are the firm's ordinary shareholders, and they are the ones who, presumably, have most to gain from a policy of profit maximization. Perhaps the great bulk of ordinary shareholders are not able to exercise any significant control over the firm's behaviour. Many investigators have forcefully advocated the view that groups other than the majority of ordinary shareholders exert the determining influence on the firm's behaviour. For this to matter to positive economics, the controlling group must wish to pursue goals other than profit maximization so that their behaviour will be different from that desired by the majority of ordinary shareholders.

We shall now consider three hypotheses about the control, as opposed to the ownership, of the modern firm.

THE HYPOTHESIS OF MINORITY CONTROL: *Because of the widespread distribution of shares, the owners of a minority of the stock are usually able to control a majority of the voting shares and thus to exercise effective control over the decisions of the company.*

Let us see how these results might occur. Each share of common stock has one vote in a company. Any individual or group controlling 51 per cent of the stock clearly controls the majority of the votes. Shareholders vote at the annual meeting and they may vote in person or they may assign a 'proxy' to someone who will be attending. But suppose one group owns 30 per cent of the stock, with the remaining 70 per cent distributed so widely that few of the dispersed group even bother to vote; in this event 30 per cent may be the overwhelming majority of the shares *actually voted*. How large a percentage is actually required to control the majority depends on the pattern of ownership and on whether there has been a major effort to collect proxies. A colourful, but rare, phenomenon in business history is the 'proxy fight' in which competing factions of stockholders (or management) attempt to collect the voting rights of the dispersed and generally disinterested stockholders. In general, a very small fraction of shares, sometimes as small as 5 per cent, actively voted may exercise dominant influence at meetings of stockholders.

Another aspect of minority control is made possible through the *holding company*. Suppose, in a certain company, call it A, ownership of 20 per cent of the stock would give dominant control. Now a new company, which we shall call B, is formed. B purchases 20 per cent of the stock in A. Company B can now control A. But no more than 51 per cent of the stock of B is required to control the stock in A. Indeed, if 20 per cent ownership of B is sufficient to control B's affairs, an amount of money equal only to 4 per cent of the value of A's stock (20 per cent of 20 per cent) is required for a group to gain control of B and thus of A. Now suppose a new company, C, is formed to purchase 20 per cent of company B! This pyramiding of control via holding companies has no limits in logic, but it is limited in both law and in practicality. (It should also be mentioned that holding companies serve many purposes other than the rather suspect one described here.)

Dispersed ownership and minority control are well established in the corporate sector of most advanced free-market economies. Does it matter?

As far as the behaviour of the firm is concerned, the hypothesis of minority control is important only if the shareholders are able to exert a significant influence on its behaviour, *and* if the controlling minority have interests and motives different from the holders of the majority of the firm's shares. If all shareholders are mainly interested in having the firm maximize its profits, then it does not matter, as far as market behaviour is concerned, which set of shareholders actually influences the firm's policy. There is no accepted evidence to show that controlling groups of shareholders habitually seek objectives different from those sought by the holders of the majority of the firm's shares.

THE HYPOTHESIS OF INTERCORPORATE CONTROL GROUPS: *Whole sectors of the economy are effectively controlled by small groups of people through the mechanism of interlocking directorships.*

If each member of a small group holds directorships in several companies, the group can control the boards of directors of many different companies without being so obvious as to have the identical set of persons on each and every board. By controlling the boards of directors, this group can exert effective and relatively unostentatious control over the companies themselves.

The factual basis of this hypothesis is that many individuals are directors of many companies. These 'interlocking directorships' have been widely studied.

There is no law against a particular individual being a director of many companies. Some individuals are wanted by many companies for the prestige that their name conveys. Certain bank officers appear on many different boards of directors. They represent their bank's interest in companies to which they have loaned money. The hypothesis of intercorporate control groups is only important to positive economics if boards of directors are able to control the policies of companies in ways that would not be approved of by managers or by shareholders. Indeed, there does not seem to be any evidence that the common directors exert any significant influence altering the firm's behaviour from what it would be if no such interlocking existed.

THE HYPOTHESIS OF THE SEPARATION OF OWNERSHIP FROM CONTROL: *Because of diversified ownership and the difficulty of assembling shareholders or gathering proxies, the managers rather than the shareholders exercise effective control over the decisions of the company.*

The argument offered in support of this hypothesis is as follows. Shareholders elect directors who appoint managers. Directors are supposed to represent shareholders' interests and to determine broad policies that the managers merely carry out. In order to conduct the complicated business of running a large firm, however, a full-time professional management group *must* be given broad powers of decision. Although managerial decisions can be reviewed from time to time, they cannot be supervised in detail. In fact, the links are typically weak enough so that top management often does truly control the destiny of the company over long periods of time. As long as directors have confidence in the managerial group, they accept and ratify their proposals, and shareholders characteristically elect and re-elect directors who are proposed to them. If the managerial group behaves badly, it may later be removed and replaced, but this is a drastic action and a disruptive one, and it is infrequently employed. Within very wide limits then, effective control of the company's activities does reside with the managers, who need not even be shareholders in the company. Although the managers are legally the employees of the shareholders, they are able to remain largely unaffected by them. Indeed, the management group characteristically asks for, and typically gets, the proxies of a very large number of shareholders and thus perpetuates itself in office.

This hypothesis was put forcibly about thirty years ago by Professors A. A. Berle and G. C. Means in a pioneering study of the large company. The study showed that in nearly 60 per cent of the largest companies no dominant ownership group could be identified with as much as 10 per cent of the shareholdings. Professor Robert

Larner has recently shown that this percentage is much higher today – above 80 per cent – than it was in the 1930s. But again, what is the significance of the fact?

For the hypothesis of the separation of ownership and control to be important, it is necessary not only that the managers should be able to exert effective control over business decisions, but also that they should wish to act differently from the way the shareholders and directors wish to act. If the managers are motivated by a desire to maximize the firm's profits – either because it is in their own interests to do so or because they voluntarily choose to reflect the shareholders' interests – then it does not matter that they have effective control over decisions. If the managers wish to pursue goals different from those of the owners, the behaviour of the firm will be different according to whether the managers or the owners exercise effective control.

This is a genuinely competing hypothesis to that of profit maximization, but before we go on to consider it in detail we should notice that it is also in conflict with the two hypotheses outlined previously. Clearly one cannot hold simultaneously that managers take the effective decisions, ignoring the interests of shareholders and directors, and that directors take the effective decisions, ignoring the interests of managers and shareholders, and that a minority of shareholders take effective decisions ignoring the interests of the other groups.

SALES MAXIMIZATION: One theory based on the assumption that it is managers rather than shareholders who really control the firm uses the hypothesis that the firm seeks to maximize its gross sales revenue rather than its profits. Faced with a choice between profits and sales, it is assumed that the firm would choose to increase its sales rather than its profits.

This theory rests on the separation of management and ownership. In the giant company, the managers need to make some minimum level of profits to keep the shareholders satisfied; after that they are free to seek growth unhampered by profit considerations. This is a sensible policy on the part of management, so the argument runs, because the manager's salary, power and prestige all depend more on the size of the firm than its rate of profit; generally, the manager of a large, normally profitable company will earn a salary considerably higher than that earned by the manager of a small but highly profitable company. Thus we may assume that firms seek to maximize their sales revenue, subject to some minimum profit constraint.

This theory is a genuine alternative to the profit-maximizing theory because it yields different predictions. The fact that it predicts larger output and lower prices than profit-maximizing theory does not help to provide a test, however, because in a particular situation we do not know what the profit-maximizing price and output would have been. But the theories do have different implications about the elasticity of demand at the firm's market price. Sales-maximizing theory implies that (if profits are above the minimum required level) a firm with substantial monopoly power will tend to charge a price where the elasticity of demand is unity, whereas profit-maximizing theory implies that elasticity will be greater than unity. Observations of industries where elasticity of demand tends to be consistently above unity, but in which the firms continue to earn profits above the required minimum, would cast doubt upon the sales-maximizing hypothesis.

Satisficing

Organization theorists have already been mentioned under criticism (2) above. As well as advancing the criticisms already mentioned, they have advanced their own alternative theory of the firm's motivation, called *satisficing*. Professor Herbert Simon says, 'We must expect the firm's goals to be not maximizing profits but attaining a certain level or rate of profit, holding a certain share of the market or a certain level of sales.' According to this theory, firms will strive very hard to achieve certain *minimum* (or 'target') levels of profits, but, having achieved them, they will not strive aggressively to improve their position further. This means that the firm could come to rest in a large number of situations rather than in only one unique situation (the profit-maximizing or the sales-maximizing one). In the language of economic theory, we say that equilibrium is not unique.

The satisficing theory is potentially an important alternative to the profit-maximizing theory. Perhaps Simon exaggerates when he says, 'The satisficing model vitiates all the conclusions about resource allocation that are derivable from the maximizing model when perfect competition is assumed', but very probably it does lead to differences in expected behaviour.

To test the satisficing theory, one must specify the 'targets' of the firm. This has not been done carefully enough to permit us to specify the precise areas of conflict between satisficing and profit-maximizing theory. Until we know precisely what predictions of the two theories are in conflict with each other, we do not know to what extent the theories differ, and thus we cannot test them. One case that is cited by proponents of satisficing is that, immediately after the Second World War, prices of new cars were lower than prices of used cars. As viewed by the proponents of satisficing, manufacturers of automobiles were satisfied with (even possibly embarrassed by) their high profits and were content not to take advantage of the excess demand to increase profits.

Long-run profit maximization

Many of the alternative theories of the firm's behaviour were put forward to account for observations which were in definite conflict with the theory that the firm always strives to maximize its *short-run* profits.[1] One alternative sometimes used in an effort to make the theory of profit maximization consistent with this conflicting evidence is that firms seek to maximize long-run rather than short-run profits. Short-run profit maximizing predicts, for example, that a rise in price will accompany any temporary shortage of a commodity. If it is observed that the price rise does not occur in such circumstances, it might be argued that although the firm *is* a profit maximizer, to exploit the temporary shortage by raising prices would engender such ill will and consequent loss of custom later, that it is not worth while to cash in on this transitory situation. The firm is still a maximizer but it is maximizing long-run profits. This is

---

1 Here are some examples of conflicting observations: for some time after the Second World War the prices of new cars in Britain were lower than the prices of second-hand cars; prices commonly increase by the full amount of the tax (this is somewhat suspect as a 'fact'); prices of manufactured goods do not change so as to reflect every fluctuation in demand and supply as do the prices of agricultural goods.

how long-run maximizing theorists would explain the observation about the relative price of new and used cars referred to above.

No doubt the extension of the theory of short-run profit maximization in a perfectly competitive market, into markets in which each producer sets his own price, requires extensive modification in the theory. If we are not careful, however, whenever we find a firm not maximizing profits we shall merely assert that, clearly, it was maximizing over some other time period than the one we were considering. Unless we work out our theory carefully and include in it a means of identifying the long-run period over which profits are supposed to be maximized, we will have a universal untestable alibi for all evidence that conflicts with profit-maximizing theory. If this is what happens, then our theory becomes consistent with absolutely any behaviour on the part of businessmen and as a result becomes totally uninteresting.

CRITICISM 4: A CRITICISM BASED ON THE OBSERVED SHAPE OF THE SHORT-RUN COST CURVE

In Chapter 18, we argued that the marginal-cost curve would be U-shaped, falling at first as a more efficient combination of the fixed and variable factors became possible, and then rising as diminishing returns set in. Empirical evidence has several times suggested that many marginal cost curves were flat up to the capacity level of output, so that each extra unit would cost as much to produce as did the previous unit, until the plant was operated at capacity, after which costs would begin to rise.

The economic theorist should ask three questions when faced with such evidence about the shape of the marginal cost curves: (1) Is the evidence reliable? (2) What part of my theory does it refute? and (3) Does this upset any important predictions that I have previously relied on? We shall not consider question (1) here, but see what follows if we assume the answer to be 'Yes'. A careful look at the theory of costs shows that the declining part of the marginal cost curve occurs if the fixed factor is *indivisible*. The argument (see pages 222–3) runs in terms of having too low a ratio of the variable factor to the fixed factor. As production is increased more of the variable factor is used and a better combination with the fixed factor achieved. This argument clearly implies that all of the fixed factor must be used all of the time. If the fixed factor is *divisible* so that part of it may go unemployed, then there is no need, as production is decreased, to depart from the optimum ratio of the actually employed quantities of the fixed to the variable factor. Thus, costs will be constant up to the point at which all the fixed factor is used. Beyond this point, production can only be increased by combining more of the variable factor with the constant (total) amount of the fixed factor. Under these circumstances costs would be rising. Consider as a simple example a 'factory' that consists of 10 sewing machines in a shed, each with a capacity of 20 units per day when each is operated for 8 hours by one girl. If 200 units per day are required, then all 10 machines are operated on a normal shift. If demand falls to 180 units then one girl is laid off. But there is no need to combine the 9 girls with 10 machines. Clearly one machine can be 'laid off' as well, and in production the ratio of labour/machines is not varied. Clearly, production can go from 1 to 200 without any change in factor proportions. In this case we would expect the factory to have constant marginal costs up to 200 units, and only then to encounter rising costs, as production was expanded, by means of overtime and other methods of combining more labour with the 10 machines.

Thus, the first answer that the theorist gives is that constant marginal costs do not refute any part of the theory of costs, provided the fixed factor is divisible. Constant marginal costs with an indivisible fixed factor would, however, refute the theory of costs *which predicts that marginal and average costs must vary when factor proportions vary*.

To deal with the final question, the economist places the new cost curve (flat up to capacity and then rising) in his theoretical models in place of the former U-shaped one. Here the reader can be left the exercise of showing that few if any of the predictions of the theory of the firm and industry (such as those developed in Chapter 23) are affected if a flat section of the marginal and average short-run cost curves is substituted for the declining sections.

We conclude, therefore, that the observations, if true, are not radically upsetting to the traditional theory of the firm.

CRITICISM 5: FIRMS HAVE A DEGREE OF POLITICAL AND ECONOMIC POWER OVER THE MARKET THAT IS NOT RECOGNIZED IN CONVENTIONAL ECONOMIC THEORY

Conventional theory and the alternatives to it discussed so far are alike in one important respect. In each, the firm is regarded as responding to market demands in one way or another. Thus, although the firms' managers may have a range of discretion, they are constrained to some extent by the market and by consumers' preferences.

A very different hypothesis is possible, and is given its most prominent expression by the economist John Kenneth Galbraith and the American consumer's advocate Ralph Nader who first came to public attention when he published his blistering attack on the safety of American automobiles *Unsafe at Any Speed*. In this view, it is *not* consumer's wants that create market signals, which, in turn, provide profit opportunities, which motivate business behaviour. Instead, large corporations have power to create and manipulate demand. Their need to invest and plan into a distant future is threatened by the vagaries of market demand and the threat of political interference with their objectives. The first threat is met by manipulating wants by advertising, by choice of products to produce and by pricing policies. The political threat is minimized by coopting or corrupting the government agencies that should control them. These tasks, and the requirements of production, create a class of managers – a technostructure – which exerts the dominant influence in the corporation. Because they have great power, corporations earn large profits, which are reinvested to further the achievement of the values of the ruling technostructure – values that emphasize industrial production, rapid growth and highly materialistic aspirations at the expense of better things of life such as cultural and aesthetic values and the quality of the environment.

Further, according to this theory, these corporation managers are indirectly subverting public institutions (from universities to regulatory agencies) to these values.

Government, instead of regulating business and protecting the public interest, has become the servant of the technostructure. It supplies the corporate sector with such essential inputs into its productive process as educated, trained, healthy and socially secure workers. Government also serves the giant corporations through policies concerning tariffs, import quotas, tax rules, subsidies and research and development. These policies protect and insulate the industrial establishment from competitive pressures and reinforce its dominance and its profitability.

Even more importantly, the industrial managerial group joins with the military in a *military-industrial complex* that utilizes, trains and elevates the technicians to positions of power and prestige not only in industry, but also in the Army, in the defence establishment and in the highest positions of government. In so doing, the corporations and their managers threaten to dominate if not subvert our foreign policies as well as our domestic ones. This is the nightmare of the 'new industrial state'.

These views did not, of course, originate with the publication of Galbraith's *The New Industrial State* in 1967, or with the formation in the United States of 'Nader's Raiders'. James Burnham wrote much earlier of *The Managerial Revolution* and Robert Brady sounded an alarm against *Business as a System of Power.* Indeed, Thorstein Veblen predicted the technocratic takeover of society in *The Engineers and the Price System* in 1921, and Karl Marx predicted the subversion of the government bureaucrat by the businessman over a century ago. It is not the originality of these views that matters, but the insight that hypotheses based upon them may shed on current problems. Many of today's social critics find such hypotheses persuasive. If they are substantially correct, they do indeed render much of conventional economic theory irrelevant.

There are several hypotheses here:

> **The largest corporations, (a) tend to dominate the economy, (b) largely control market demand rather than being controlled by it, (c) coopt governmental processes instead of being constrained by them, and (d) utilize their substantial discretionary power in ways that are against the interests of society.**

The evidence for the hypothesis

Although the hypotheses are relevant to any Western Industrial economy the major discussion has related to the US economy and it is best to discuss them in relation to that economy.

Superficially, at least, many of the facts of the American economy lend support to this hypothesis. Corporations do account for approximately two thirds of all business done in the United States today, and large corporations dominate the corporate sector. Of nearly 200,000 manufacturing corporations, roughly 1 per cent of them have $10 million or more in assets. These large corporations (2,600 in 1970) hold 86 per cent of manufacturing assets. The 200 to 250 largest corporations – $\frac{1}{10}$ of 1 per cent of all manufacturing corporations – control approximately 50 per cent of the total assets of manufacturing.

The giant corporations are well known: General Motors, Standard Oil, US Steel,

Sears Roebuck, General Electric, Du Pont, and so on. Many of them are highly profitable, and most are so widely owned that managers, rather than stockholders, exercise effective control. If power comes with size, a 'few' men – several thousand strategically placed executives of a few hundred leading corporations – have great power over economic affairs. As to political influence, individual corporations and trade associations have lobbyists and exercise whatever persuasion they can. Executives of many of these corporations serve on public commissions and frequently take important governmental positions. Executives often make large contributions to political campaigns.

Much of the pollution of the environment is associated with industries which consist of well-known large firms. If automobiles, electric power, steel, oil, industrial chemicals, detergents and paper are the primary sources of all pollution, surely Ford, Consolidated Edison, Bethlehem Steel, Texaco, Monsanto, Proctor and Gamble and International Paper are significantly to blame. Each of these is among the 100 largest nonfinancial corporations.

Doubts about the hypothesis

SENSITIVITY TO MARKET PRESSURES: Even the largest and most powerful industries are not immune to market pressures. Ford's Edsel – a new car introduced in the 1960s after an unusually elaborate promotion campaign but nonetheless a total market flop – is a classic example of consumer rejection of a product. The penetration of small foreign cars into the American market forced the automobile industry into the production of smaller cars. The decline of railroading as a mode of passenger travel is manifest in many ways, as the financial history of once great railroading corporations shows. The failure of Penn Central Railroad is one example. Another is reflected in the fact that the Pullman Company was the nation's tenth largest firm in 1909; today, it is not in the top 300. The rise of air and motor travel and the decline of railroading were accompanied by the rise in the use of oil and the decline in the use of coal. More recently, the upsurge in demand for electric power and the shortage of oil has revitalized the coal industry. And so on.

The influence of changing demands may be seen in many ways. Turnover in the list of leading companies is continuous and revealing. Only two companies (US Steel and Standard Oil of New Jersey) were in the top ten both in 1909 and half a century later. Consider these giants of 1909, none of them among the largest 250 today: International Mercantile Marine (today United States Lines), United States Leather, American Sugar Refining, American Cotton Oil, American Hide and Leather, American Ice, Baldwin Locomotive, Cudahy, International Salt, United Shoe Machinery and Wells Fargo. Largely, they have slipped or disappeared because of the relative decline in the demand for their products. Today's giants include automobiles, oil and airline companies and electric power producers for the obvious reason that demand for these products is very strong.

Are these demand shifts explained by corporate manipulation of consumers' tastes or by more basic changes? Clearly, advertising seeks to and does influence consumers' demand. If Ford stopped advertising, it would surely lose sales to GM and Chrysler, but it is less clear that the automotive society itself was conjured up by

Madison Avenue, or that when travellers are persuaded to 'Fly the Friendly Skies of United' their real alternative was to use a stagecoach, a bicycle, or even a Greyhound bus – more likely, they are foregoing American, Eastern or Northwest Airlines. Careful promotion can influence the success of one rock group over another, but could it sell the waltz to today's teenager? Advertising – taste-making – unquestionably plays a role in shaping demand, but so, too, do more basic human attitudes, psychological needs and technological opportunities. The important empirical question is, 'How much?'

Was the birth control pill and the enormous social change that it produced something forced on an unwilling or indifferent public by clever advertising?

Changes in demand and in taste are sometimes sudden and dramatic, but, in the main, they are gradual and continuous and less noticeable month by month than decade by decade. On the average, about two new firms enter the top 100 every year, and as a consequence two others leave. This means a significant change in a decade. Moreover, the products produced by existing firms change, and thus just listing companies understates the changes that occur. R.J. Reynolds, once exclusively a tobacco manufacturer, now earns less than half its revenue from tobacco or tobacco products; International Telephone and Telegraph is only incidentally in the telephone equipment business – and so on.

Managerial discretion is limited by these shifts in demand. A further restraint on existing managements is the threat of a stockholder revolt or a takeover bid. As we shall see in some detail in Chapter 29, the maximum amount one can afford to pay for any asset depends on how much it is expected to earn. If I can make an asset produce more than you, I can rationally outbid you for it.

A management that fails to come close to achieving the profit potential of the assets it controls becomes a natural target for acquisition by a firm that specializes in taking over inefficiently run firms. The management of the acquiring firm makes a TENDER OFFER (or TAKEOVER BID as it is sometimes called) to the stockholders of the target firm, offering them what amounts to a premium for their shares, a premium it can pay because it expects to increase the firm's profits. Managers who wish to avoid takeover bids cannot let the profits of their firm slip far from the profit-maximizing level – because their unrealized profits provide the incentives for takeovers. Some, though by no means all of the so-called conglomerate firms, have specialized in this kind of takeover. In the last decade, the example par excellence of this has been International Telephone and Telegraph which has acquired (among other companies) Avis Car Rental, Continental Baking, Sheraton Hotels, Canteen Food Service and Hartford Life Insurance. In each case, it has substantially increased the operating profits of the acquired company after the takeover. The presence of the threat of takeovers must be regarded as limiting the discretion of corporate management.

WHO CONTROLS THE GOVERNMENT: Is government subservient to big business? Clearly, big business does benefit from many government policies and does lobby for them. Lobbying is a large-scale and a legal activity, and is engaged in by many groups. Big business has its influence, but so too do farmers, labour unions and small business groups. Whether corporations exercise undue or improper influence is an important question that requires serious examination. It is easy to assert that 'everyone knows that the oil lobby dominates the American Congress', but such assertions do not resolve empirical questions. Lobbying and influence may well help explain why for years America imposed quotas on foreign oil imports, but lobbying by the oil companies did not prevent a delay of the Alaska pipeline for many years, the decreases in valuable depletion allowances, or restrictions imposed on off-shore oil drilling. Relaxation of all of these restrictions came because of the oil shortages of the 1970s, not political pressure. (Of course to the extent that oil companies caused the oil shortage, they may be said to have indirectly put pressure on the government.) Government contracts bolster the aerospace industry, but Boeing and Lockheed are in deep financial trouble, partly as a result of government decisions. Tobacco companies have seen government agencies first publicize the hazards of their principal product and, more recently, restrict their advertising.

Thus, while business clearly often succeeds in its attempts to protect its commercial interests by political activity, it does so within limits. Where the truth lies between the extremes of 'no influence' and 'no limits' is a matter now being subjected to substantial research. It is a matter that will be clarified by research, not by mere assertion.

NEGLECT OF THE PUBLIC INTEREST: One aspect of the Galbraithian critique has found a receptive public: This concerns the apparent disregard by large corporations of the adverse effect of productive activities on the environment. The problems of pollution arise from activities of small corporations as well as large, and from the activities of government units and cities and citizens as well. Do such polluting activities represent in a significant degree irresponsible behaviour by corporations, which can be countered by such things as Campaign GM, a 'campaign to make General Motors responsible'? Are they, instead, to be regarded as examples of the type of market failure discussed in Chapter 32? If the latter, they require not an exhortation to responsible behaviour, but some form of governmental policy action.

What has come to be known as the 'consumerist' view, or CONSUMERISM, is that corporations ought to be forced to serve the consumers' or general public interest, not merely the interests of their stockholders. Thus, for example, GM's directors must be made to recognize that automobiles both pollute and cause accidents and that GM's abundant resources should be invested in developing and installing both safety and antipollution devices. This, consumerists argue, is a good and proper use of GM's profits, even if GM's stockholders do not see it that way, and even if automobile purchasers do not want to pay the cost of the extra safety and antipollution devices.

The basic arguments *for* this position are that only the company can know the potentially adverse effect of its actions and that by virtue of holding a corporate charter, the corporation assumes the responsibility to protect the general welfare while pursuing private profits. The argument *against* this view is that managers of companies have neither the knowledge nor the ability to represent the general public interest. They are largely selected, judged and promoted according to their ability to run a profit-oriented enterprise, and the assumption that they are especially competent to decide broader *public* questions is unjustified. According to this argument, moral (as distinct from economic) decisions such as whether to make or use Napalm, to make or use internal combustion engines, to manufacture or smoke cigarettes, or to manufacture or utilize DDT cannot properly be delegated to individual corporations or their executives. Some of them are individual decisions. Others require either the expertise or the authority of a public regulatory agency, and whoever makes decisions on behalf of the public must be politically responsible to the public.

In this view, most required changes in corporate behaviour should be accomplished not by exhorting business leaders to behave responsibly, nor by placing consumer representatives on the corporation's board of directors, but by regulations or incentives that force or induce the desired corporate behaviour. Let corporations pursue their profits, but subject to public laws. The central authorities can require all cars to have seat belts, or require auto manufacturers to install antipollution valves or to meet specified standards of emission levels. Another alternative is to open the way for law suits against corporations that either enjoin certain behaviour or force corporations to pay for the damages their products cause.

Which strategy to follow, or which combination, represents an important policy choice, and surely depends upon notions of relative effectiveness. An overlooked irony is that the 'make-them-behave-responsibly' view of the corporation is an uneasy bedfellow of the view that 'corporations have too much discretion already', unless there seems no effective way to limit or channel corporate power.

The controversy about policy alternatives is both current and important, and much of the credit for the dialogue is due to Galbraith and Nader. It is essential to recognize that the policy issues at stake – whether and how to change the behaviour of corporations – can arise whether corporations are primarily responding to market signals, or whether they are impervious to them. If society does not approve the results of corporate behaviour, it will want to control the behaviour, whatever the cause. Knowing the cause, of course, helps in designing a remedy. But the controversy about *results* does not reveal whether the conventional theory of the firm (which is about behaviour) is or is not irrelevant. This can be determined only by a closer testing of the competing theories. Few economists today are prepared to reject conventional theory and accept instead the vision of the new industrial state. But this view may change as more evidence is evaluated.

THE GENERAL DEMAND AND SUPPLY THEORY OF A MARKET ECONOMY

In Chapter 5 we noted that there was evidence that markets for agricultural goods and other primary products did function as assumed in the theory of demand and supply. We also stated that the generalization of this demand-and-supply theory to a theory of the whole economy was a rather speculative leap in the dark. We have now studied the theory of production sufficiently to realize that we cannot in fact apply our simple demand-and-supply theory to the whole economy. This theory is a theory of *competitive* markets, i.e. markets in which there is a large number of buyers and sellers. Most manufactured goods, however, are produced under conditions of oligopoly in which there are a very few firms. These firms may or may not compete actively with each other, and in cases in which they do compete they are quite likely to change their prices only occasionally and to compete from day to day by adjusting such things as service, delivering dates, quality and special features of the product.

How important is it that the manufacturing sector is primarily oligopolistic? Does this fact undermine our ability to use economic theory as a successful predictive device? At least two things seem fairly clear.

First, we do have difficulty predicting the detailed effects on the manufacturing industries of such things as changes in tax rates, changes in the number of firms in an industry, and small changes in demands, costs and government regulations. In administered price situations there is considerable non-price competition. Since we do not have a single well-tested theory of non-price competition, it is often, although by no means always, unclear what will be the effects of changes such as those just listed.

Second, if we wish to predict general long-term trends our theory is more helpful. There is substantial empirical evidence to support each of the following statements. The prices of most primary products are set on competitive markets and these prices do fluctuate in response to shifts in demands and supplies. Large changes in the relative prices of inputs do cause firms to change the proportions in which they use factors, since *whatever* the firm's objectives they can usually be better served by minimising costs rather than by wasting money unnecessarily. Continual changes in the prices of inputs sooner or later lead firms to change the prices of their outputs. (Even a non-profit maximizing monopoly cannot afford to let its profits become significantly negative.) This means that over the long term relative prices of manu- factured commodities do change to reflect major changes in the relative costs of producing these commodities. When relative commodity prices change, consumers react, and many long-term changes in consumption patterns that are casually ascribed to changes in tastes, fashions and habits, are responses to changes in relative prices. Observers who predict the broad reactions to such major changes as the recent increases in the price of oil from the Middle East make disastrous errors when they ignore this general long-term adaptability of the economy which makes it behave in broad outline as would a perfectly competitive economy. (An example of one such blunder is considered in the concluding section of Chapter 48.)

This general assessment seems fairly clear and would probably command majority, although by no means universal, acceptance among economists. But just how bad is our ability to predict in detail (especially in the oligopolistic part of the economy) and just *how* good is our ability to predict long-term trend reactions to major events? (Do not forget that we are not trying to foretell the future as would a fortune-teller, but to make conditional predictions about the reactions of the economy to given events. See pages 12–13.) Because it is hard to assemble the mass of available evidence so as to focus it on this issue, economists are left to their personal assessment of the balance between success and failure and debate goes on among those who assess it differently. About all that it seems safe to say is that when judged by its ability to predict the outcome of events in which we are interested, the theory of the allocation of resources reveals both substantial successes and major failures.

Part five

The theory of distribution

26

The demand for and supply of factors of production

PROBLEMS OF DISTRIBUTION

Are the poor getting poorer and the rich richer as Karl Marx thought they would? Are the rich getting relatively poorer and the poor relatively richer as Alfred Marshall hoped they would? Is the inequality of income a social constant determined by forces possibly beyond man's understanding and probably beyond his influence as Vilfredo Pareto thought?

Each year the economy produces a certain total output. This output gets divided – more or less unequally – among the individuals and groups in the society. The theory of income distribution is concerned with what determines the fraction of total income that goes to any particular individual or group.

The founders of classical economics, Adam Smith and David Ricardo, were concerned with the distribution of income among what were then the three great social classes: workers, capitalists and landowners. To deal with this question they defined three basic factors of production: labour, capital and land. The return to each of these factors was the income of each of the three classes in society. Smith and Ricardo were interested in two questions: (1) What determines the income of each group relative to the total income, and (2) how will the economic growth of society affect this distribution of income? Their theories predicted that landlords would become relatively better off and that capitalists would become relatively worse off as society progressed. Karl Marx accepted this classical pair of questions but provided very different answers. He concluded that capitalists would become relatively better off and workers relatively worse off as society developed. These and other nineteenth-century debates focused on the distribution of income among the major factors of production.

THE FACTUAL BACKGROUND OF DISTRIBUTION

Income takes many forms: wages and salaries, rental income from property, interest and profits, to name the major ones. Table 26.1 shows the distribution of income in

343

the United Kingdom by major types for 1972. This table shows the amounts of income paid to the various factors of production rather than the amounts paid to various individuals or households. A single individual may receive incomes from several different factors of production, he might get income for his own labour services, from renting property that he owns, and from his holdings of shares in various joint-stock companies. When we classify income according to the factor of production that is its source, we are dealing with the FUNCTIONAL DISTRIBUTION of income.

Table 26.1 Functional distribution of income
in the UK, 1972 (before tax)

	£ million	Percentage of total
Income from employment	37,138	68·2
Income from self-employment	4,764	8·8
Gross trading profits of companies	6,584	12·1
Gross trading surplus of public corporations	1,612	3·0
Gross trading surplus of other public enterprises	178	0·3
Rent	4,182	7·7
Total domestic income before providing for depreciation and stock appreciation	54,458	100·1

Source: National Income and Expenditure, HMSO 1973

Table 26.2 Distribution of personal
incomes (before tax)

Income in £s	Percentage of earning persons	
	1969/70 Quinquennial Survey	1970/71 Annual Survey
0–499	9·1	4·13
500–599	6·23	5·43
600–699	6·24	5·94
700–799	6·13	5·67
800–999	12·40	10·87
1,000–1,499	28·53	26·77
1,500–1,999	19·40	20·10
2,000–2,999	8·58	15·64
3,000–4,999	2·52	3·91
5,000–9,999	0·94	1·26
10,000–19,999	0·19	0·24
20,000 upwards	0·04	0·04

Source: Annual Abstracts of Statistics, HMSO 1973.

Most of the theory of distribution that we discuss in this part is concerned with the functional distribution of income. But economists are also interested in the distribution of income among individuals and families. When we classify income according to the size of income received by each earner irrespective of the sources of that income, we are dealing with the SIZE DISTRIBUTION of income. Many economic policies are designed to modify the size distribution of income.

The basic facts about the size distribution of income are given in Tables 26.2 and 26.3. Table 26.2 shows the distribution of incomes in the UK by income level.

Table 26.3 Inequality in income distribution (before tax)

1969/70 Quinquennial Survey		1970/71 Annual Survey	
Percentage of earning persons	Percentage of income	Percentage of earning persons	Percentage of income
9·1	2·82	4·13	1·23
15·33	5·35	9·56	3·17
21·57	8·35	15·50	5·67
27·70	11·76	21·17	8·42
40·10	19·80	32·04	14·74
68·63	46·04	58·81	36·19
88·03	70·77	78·91	58·77
96·61	85·65	94·55	82·54
99·13	92·58	98·46	91·86
100·00	100·00	100·00	100·00

Source: Annual Abstract of Statistics, HMSO 1973.

Table 26.3 focuses on the inequality in the size distribution of income: the 20 per cent of the population at the bottom of the income scale receive only 7 per cent of the nation's income; the 20 per cent at the top receive 35 per cent of it.

It is tempting to give superficial explanations of differences in income. People often say: 'A man is paid what he's worth.' But the economist must ask: 'Worth what to whom?', 'What gives him his value?' Sometimes people say: 'Men earn according to their ability.' But note that incomes are distributed in a very much more unequal fashion than any measured index of ability such as IQ or physical strength. In what sense is Tom Jones 20 times as able as the promising new pop singer? He gets paid 20 times as much. In what sense is a lorry driver more able than a schoolteacher? In what sense is a football player more able than a wrestler?

If answers couched in terms of worth and ability are easily refuted, so are answers like 'It's all a matter of luck', or 'It's just the system'. We are concerned now to discover whether or not the theories of economics provide explanations of the functional distribution of income that are more satisfactory than the ones mentioned above.

FACTOR PRICES AND FACTOR INCOMES

The traditional theory states that distribution is simply a special case of price theory.

The income of any factor of production (and hence the amount of the national product that it is able to command) depends on the price that is paid for the factor and the amount that is used. If we wish to build up a theory of distribution we thus need a theory of factor prices. Such a theory involves little that is not already familiar.

The free-market price of any commodity is determined by demand and supply. In Figure 26.1 the original demand and supply curves for some factor of production

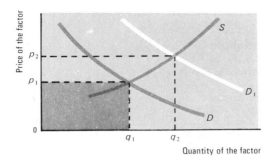

Fig. 26.1 The determination of the price, quantity and income of a factor of production

are D and S. The equilibrium price is p_1 and quantity q_1. The total income earned by the factor is the shaded area. If we now assume that the prices of all other factors of production, the prices of all goods, and the level of national income are given and constant, then fluctuations in the equilibrium price and quantity will cause fluctuations in the money earnings of the factor, in the relative earnings (compared to other factors) and in the share of national income going to the factor. Assume, for example, that the demand curve for the factor in question rises from D to D_1. Now the money price of the factor rises from p_1 to p_2, and the relative price rises from p_1/F to p_2/F where F is the (given) price of some other factor or an average price of *all* other factors. The total earnings rise from p_1q_1 to p_2q_2 and, if the total income in the whole economy remains constant at Y, then the share of income going to this factor rises from p_1q_1/Y to p_2q_2/Y. Thus the problem of distribution in a free market reduces to the question of the determinants of the demand and supply of factors of production plus the problem of determining the effect of the departures from a free market caused by monopolistic organizations, government action, unions, etc.

THE DEMAND FOR FACTORS

Producers require land, labour, raw materials, machines and other factors of production because these are needed to produce the goods and services that firms sell. So the demand for any factor of production depends on the existence of a demand for the goods that it helps to make. We say that the demand is a DERIVED DEMAND.

Obvious examples of derived demand are not hard to find. The demand for computer programmers is growing as industry turns increasingly to electronic computers. The demand for university teachers increases whenever the number of students going to university increases. The demand for coal miners and coal-digging equipment declines as the demand for coal declines. Indeed, anything that increases demand for a commodity – population changes, changes in tastes, etc. – will increase the demand for the factors required to make it. Typically one factor will be used in making many goods, not just one. Steel is used in dozens of industries, as are the services of carpenters. The total demand for a factor will be the sum of the derived demands for it in each productive activity.

In this section we are mainly concerned to derive the prediction that the demand curve for a factor is downward sloping. We do this because derived demand provides a link between pricing of factors and the pricing of products. This allows us to connect our theory of the behaviour of the firm to our theory of distribution.

The quantity of a factor demanded in equilibrium

We first derive a famous relation that will hold in equilibrium for every factor employed by a wide class of firms. To do this we first recall that in Part 4 we established a set of conditions necessary for the maximization of profits in the short run. Some factor was fixed (usually capital) and some other factor was allowed to vary, and we saw that the profit-maximizing firm would increase its output to the level at which the last unit produced added just as much to cost as it did to revenue or, in technical language, until marginal cost equalled marginal revenue. *Another way of stating exactly the same thing is to say that the firm will increase production up to the point at which the last unit of the variable factor employed adds just as much to revenue as it does to cost.* Just as it is true that all profit-maximizing firms, whether they are selling under conditions of perfect competition, monopolistic competition or monopoly, produce to the point at which marginal cost equals marginal revenue, so it is true that all profit-maximizing firms will hire units of the variable factor up to the point at which the marginal cost of the factor (i.e., the addition to the total cost resulting from the employment of one more unit) equals the marginal revenue produced by the factor. Since we have already used the term marginal revenue to refer to the change in revenue resulting from the sale of an additional unit of production, we shall use another term, MARGINAL REVENUE PRODUCT, to refer to the addition to revenue resulting from the sale of the product contributed by an additional unit of the variable factor. It is true, therefore, of all profit-maximizing firms that are in equilibrium:

Marginal cost of the variable factor = marginal revenue product of that factor. (1)

This must be true for every factor that the firm can vary, and thus in the long run it must hold for all factors. If there were a single factor for which (1) did not hold, the firm could increase its profits by varying the employment of that factor. Thus (1) is a relation that must hold in equilibrium for *all* profit-maximizing firms with respect to all variable factors of production.

Now let us consider all those firms that are unable to influence the prices of the factors that they purchase (i.e., they buy their factors in a perfectly competitive market). In this case the marginal cost of the factor is merely its price. The cost, for example, of obtaining an extra man on the payroll is the extra wage that must be paid for that man. For firms that take factor prices as given we may now state the condition of (1) above in the following form:

Price of the factor = marginal revenue product of the factor. (2)

The firm's demand curve for a factor[1]

Conditions (1) and (2) describe relations that hold in equilibrium. We now wish to derive the demand curve for a factor of production. We shall do this assuming that the firm is unable to influence the price of the factor (we drop this assumption in Chapter 28). For the moment we shall assume that there is only a single variable factor of production. This allows us to use condition (2) to derive the firm's demand for a factor as soon as we have its marginal revenue product curve. As an example we assume in Figure 26.2 that we have the marginal revenue product curve for some factor. This shows us how much would be added to revenue by employing one more unit of the factor for each level of total employment of the factor. Condition (2) states that the profit-maximizing firm will employ additional units of the factor up to the point at which the marginal revenue product equals the price of the factor.

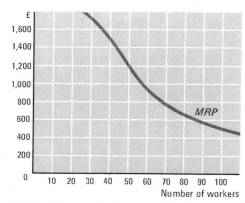

Fig. 26.2 A marginal revenue product curve for a factor

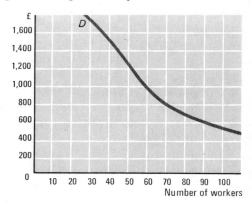

Fig. 26.3 A firm's demand curve for a factor of production when only one factor can be varied is the marginal revenue product curve of that factor

If, for example, the price were £1,200 per year, then it would be most profitable to employ 50 workers. (There is no point in employing a fifty-first since he would add only £1,180 to revenue but £1,200 to costs, and hence he would *reduce* total profits by £20.) The curve in Figure 26.3 shows the quantity of labour employed at each price of labour. Such a curve can be derived from Figure 26.2 by picking various prices of the variable factor, and reading off the amount used from the marginal revenue product curve in just the way described above for the price of £1,200.

Note that this curve is identical with the marginal revenue product curve in Figure 26.2. The curve in Figure 26.3 relates the price of the variable factor to the quantity employed, and hence it is the demand curve for the variable factor. *The marginal revenue product curve of a factor is the firm's demand curve for that factor.*

THE DERIVATION OF THE MARGINAL REVENUE PRODUCT CURVE: We have related the firm's demand for a single variable factor to the marginal revenue product curve, and we must now inquire into the derivation of this latter curve. The marginal

1 This is a difficult section and it may be omitted without loss of continuity by skipping directly to the summary on page 353.

revenue product of the factor is defined as the addition to total revenue resulting from the employment of an additional unit of the variable factor. This may be broken up into two components, a physical component and a value one, and we must now consider how each of these varies as the quantity of the factor varies.

The physical component: We have assumed that we have only one variable factor of production. As we vary the quantity of this factor, output will vary. The hypothesis of diminishing returns that we developed in Chapter 18 predicts that as we go on adding more and more units of the variable factor to the given quantity of the fixed factor the extra output produced by successive increments of the variable factor will decline. The hypothesis is illustrated in Figure 26.4.

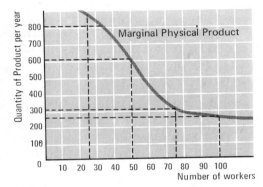

Fig. 26.4 The marginal physical product curve

The value component: Now, to convert this curve into a marginal revenue product curve we need to know the value of the extra physical product. The marginal physical product depends solely on the technical conditions of production, but the value to the firm of this extra product depends on the price of the product. There are two cases to consider. If the firm sells its products in a perfect market, the price of the product is given and accurately measures the value to the firm of an additional unit of output. Thus, in the case of perfect competition, the marginal revenue product is given by

Marginal physical product *multiplied by* price of the product. (3)

If, on the other hand, the firm faces a downward-sloping demand for its product, the value to the firm of an extra unit of output will be less than its price because, to sell the extra unit, the price will have to be reduced on all units sold (see page 261). In this case the gain in revenue due to an extra unit of output is its marginal revenue which is less than its price. Thus, where any firm faces a downward-sloping demand curve for its product, the marginal revenue product is given by:

Marginal physical product *multiplied by*
marginal revenue associated with the sale of the extra units. (4)

Expression (4) is less than (3), and (3) is often called *the value of the marginal product* to distinguish it from (4) for which the name *marginal revenue product* is sometimes reserved.

All of this no doubt sounds very forbidding at first reading. It is an example of a chain of reasoning referred to in the Introduction (see page xv) where each step is simple enough but the cumulative effects of several steps can seem complex. And there are more steps to come! Perhaps it would be best before going on to summarize the argument so far:

> **Any profit-maximizing firm will hire a variable factor up to the point at which the last unit hired adds as much to its revenue as it does to its costs. The addition to costs is the price of the factor (if the firm buys factors in a competitive market). The addition to revenue is the marginal physical product multiplied by price of product if the firm sells in a perfectly competitive market, and marginal physical product multiplied by marginal revenue if the firm faces a downward-sloping demand curve. In either case, the curve showing the addition to revenue resulting from the employment of an additional unit of the factor is the firm's demand curve for the factor on the assumption that only one factor can be varied.**

The industry's demand for the factor

When we derived the market demand for a commodity we merely summed the demands of individual households. We cannot rely on such a simple procedure in the case of a factor of production. The individual firm's demand curve shows how the quantity of the factor demanded varies with the factor's price *on the assumption that the price of the firm's output remains constant.* This assumption is only valid if all other firms keep their output fixed. If the price of the variable factor changes, however, we should expect all firms to vary their production. If, for example, the price of the factor falls, then all firms will hire more of the variable factor and the resulting rise in output will cause a fall in the market price of the commodity. This fall in price will cause the marginal revenue product of the factor – the amount added to total revenue by the employment of one more unit of the factor – to be less than it would have been if the price of the product had remained unchanged. We must now derive a demand curve on the assumption that, when factor prices change, all firms in the industry vary their output in order to maximize their profits. We assume that we know the marginal physical product curves for all firms in the industry, and also the demand curve for the product produced by the industry and we proceed in the following manner.

(1) Assume some particular price of the factor and find the equilibrium price for the product. This is done in the manner of Chapter 20; once the factor price is known, the marginal physical product curves can be translated into marginal cost curves; these cost curves are then summed, giving us an industry supply curve which, together with the demand curve, determines the equilibrium price of the product.

(2) Next take the marginal physical product curve of the firm in which we are interested, and multiply each quantity by the market price determined in (1) above. This gives a marginal revenue product curve on the assumption that market price remains constant as output is varied. This is the curve derived in Figure 26.2, and reproduced in Figure 26.5. Locate the point *A* in Figure 26.5 corresponding to the

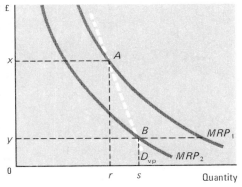

Fig. 26.5 Derivation of the firm's demand curve for a factor on the assumption that all firms change their output so that the price of a product changes when the price of the factor changes

existing price of the factor and the quantity actually being employed. *This MRP curve is the firm's demand curve for the variable factor, on the assumption that the price of the commodity is fixed; its slope depends solely on the technical conditions of production, i.e., on the slope of the marginal physical product curve.*

(3) Now consider a lower price of the factor, say y, instead of x. Our firm, in an effort to maximize profits, will hire more labour. But so will all other firms and, as a result, the price of the product will fall. This causes the curve showing marginal physical product (MPP) multiplied by existing market price to *shift inwards towards the origin*. Thus the firm moves towards equilibrium in two ways: (i) by hiring more labour and (ii) by having its curve showing MPP times market price shift inwards. A possible equilibrium is illustrated by point B. The lower price of the product gives rise to a new curve showing MPP times market price and the new quantity of labour hired is s instead of r. We repeat the procedure for each possible price of labour and generate a set of points like A and B. We then join up these points and obtain a demand curve for labour allowing for the price changes in the final product. This curve is steeper than any of the fixed-price demand curves. How much steeper this curve is depends upon how much the price of the product falls as all firms expand output, i.e., on the elasticity of the market demand for the product. In order to derive the industry's demand curve for the factor we merely aggregate the demand curves developed for individual firms under (3) above.

An alternative derivation of the industry's demand curve

Alternatively we could derive the industry demand curve for a factor in the following way. Take the MPP curve for each firm. Assume some specific price of the variable factor. Derive a marginal cost curve for each firm in the manner of Chapter 18. Sum these to obtain an industry supply curve. Now repeat the process for each possible price of the variable factor. This gives rise to a whole family of industry supply curves each corresponding to a particular price of the variable factor. Such a family of curves is illustrated in Figure 26.6 (S_{10} corresponding to a factor price of £10 a week, S_8 to a factor price of £8, etc.). Assume a particular factor price, say £6. By using the market demand curve and the supply curve S_6, the equilibrium price and quantity can be

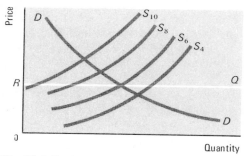

Fig. 26.6 Derivation of the demand curve for a factor
on the part of a perfectly competitive industry

derived. Now draw a horizontal line, RQ, through the point of intersection of S_6 and DD. Points of intersection of RQ and the various supply curves tell how production would vary as factor prices varied, *if the market price did not change*. Points of intersection of the actual demand curve, DD, and the various supply curves show how production would vary if market prices are allowed to vary. Since we now know the amount of production corresponding to each particular price of the variable factor, we know the amount of the variable factor that must be employed. Plotting this amount against its price gives the industry demand curve for the factor. Clearly, the variations in production are less when prices are allowed to change than when they are fixed. We conclude that, for given changes in factor prices, the variations in production, and hence the elasticity of demand for the variable factor, are less when goods prices vary than when they are assumed to be constant. The student should now draw for himself a diagram similar to Figure 26.6, but with a much steeper demand curve than the one in the printed figure. He will then be able to show for himself that *the elasticity of demand for a factor is lower, the lower is the elasticity of demand for the product.*

One other important relation can be derived from this analysis. Consider two factors of production: expenditure on factor A accounts for 2 per cent of the total costs of production, while expenditure on factor B accounts for 50 per cent of total costs. Consider 1 per cent changes in the price of each factor. Clearly, the supply curves in Figure 26.6 will shift less in response to the change in factor A's price than in response to the change in B's. The smaller the shift in the marginal cost curve, the smaller the change in equilibrium output. The smaller the change in output, the smaller the change in the quantity of the variable factor required as an input. This leads to the conclusion that *the smaller the proportion of total cost accounted for by a given factor of production the more inelastic will be its demand.*[1]

---

1 This is necessarily true when we have only one variable factor of production, but care must be taken when there are many variable factors. The elasticity of demand depends in such cases both on the proportion of costs accounted for by the factor, and the ease with which other factors can be substituted for it. Thus, we would not expect there to be an inelastic demand on British building sites for Irish labourers from the city of Cork because, although they account for a low proportion of total costs, other labourers are perfect substitutes for them. On the other hand we would expect there to be an inelastic demand for door handles because, not only are they a small proportion of the total costs of building a house, but it is very hard to build a satisfactory house without them.

Demand for a factor when more than one factor is variable

If there is more than one variable factor the marginal revenue product curve is no longer the firm's demand curve for the factor. This curve shows what happens to revenues as the factor is varied but *all other factors held constant*. If there is more than one variable factor, a change in the price of one factor will lead to a substitution between the factors and more of the now cheaper factor will be bought *even if the firm's output is unchanged*. Thus, the firm's demand curve for a factor will be more elastic than the marginal revenue product curve of the factor, the amount of additional elasticity depending on the ease with which one factor can be substituted for another. How easy it is to substitute one for another depends on the technical conditions of production. It is important to emphasize that it is very easy to underestimate the degree to which factors can be substituted one for another in the production. It is fairly obvious that a bushel of wheat can be produced by combining land either with a lot of labour and a little capital, or with a little labour and a lot of capital. When he comes to manufactured goods, however, the student often tends to think in terms of using inputs in pretty well fixed proportions. A bit of casual observation of an industry over time will show just how factor proportions can be varied to produce a given product. There is, for example, the case in which glass and steel turn out to be very good substitutes for each other. One would never guess this by considering their physical qualities in general, but in the case of car manufacture one can be substituted for the other over a wide range merely by varying the dimensions of the windows.

Summary of the theory of the demand for a factor

The elasticity of the demand for a factor depends on both the technical conditions of production and the market demand for the commodity that the factor produces. The main influences may be summarized as follows:

(1) An industry's demand for a factor is more elastic the more elastic is the demand for the commodity produced by the industry.

(2) An industry's demand for a factor will be more elastic the larger is the proportion of total costs accounted for by payments to that factor.

(3) An industry's demand for a factor will be more elastic the easier it is to substitute other factors for the one in question.

We have some further relations that necessarily hold in equilibrium provided the firm buys its factors in a perfect market.

(1) If the firm sells its product in a perfect market the price paid to a factor will be equal to the value of that factor's marginal product, i.e., marginal physical product *multiplied by* the price of the product.

(2) If the firm faces a downward-sloping demand curve for its product the price of a factor will be equated in equilibrium with the marginal revenue product of the factor, i.e., marginal physical product *multiplied by* the marginal revenue resulting from the sale of the extra product. This amount is necessarily less than the value of the marginal physical product *multiplied by* the price of the product.

Finally, we note that although the above relations hold in all equilibrium situations, it does not follow that the sum of the firm's marginal revenue product curves is the industry's demand curve for the factor.

THE SUPPLY OF FACTORS OF PRODUCTION

In dealing with the supplies of factors of production we make a distinction between the total supply of a factor to the whole economy and the supply to some small part of the economy, say to one industry or to one firm. We shall deal first with the total supply of factors to the economy.

The total supply of factors

At first glance it may seem plausible to assume that the total supply of most factors is fixed. After all, there is only so much land in the world, or in England, or in London. There is an upper limit to the number of workers; there is only so much coal, oil, copper and iron ore in the earth. These considerations do indeed put absolute maxima upon the supplies of factors. But in virtually every case we are not near these upper limits, and the problem of changes in the total effective supply of land, labour, natural resources or capital deserves discussion.

LABOUR: By the total supply of labour we mean the total number of hours of work that the population is willing to supply. This quantity, which is often called the supply of effort, is a function of three things: the size of the population, the proportion of the population willing to work, and the number of hours worked by each individual; and we may ask what are the determinants of each?

(1) Population: Populations vary in size, and these variations may be influenced to some extent by economic factors. There is some evidence that the birth rate is higher in good times than in bad. Much of the variation in population is, however, not explained successfully by economics.

(2) The labour force: The proportion of the population entering the labour market, the LABOUR FORCE, as it is called, varies considerably in response to variations in the demand for labour. Generally, a rise in the demand for labour, and an accompanying rise in earnings, will lead to an increase in the proportion of the population willing to work. Married women and elderly people are inclined to enter the labour

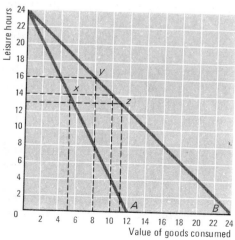

Fig. 26.7 The choice between income and leisure

force when the demand for labour is high. The dramatic increase in the proportions of married women and persons over 65 who were employed during the Second World War is a case in point.

(3) Hours worked: Variations in the number of hours people are willing to work have resulted in a substantial reduction in the supply of labour over a long period of time. Generally, a rise in real wages, such as has occurred in most Western countries over the last two centuries, leads people to consume more goods *and also to consume more leisure.* This means that people will be willing to work fewer hours per week, a fact that, unless offset by a rise either in total population or in the proportion of the population in the labour force, will lead to a decline in the supply of labour. Workers are in the position of trading their leisure for goods; by giving up leisure (i.e., by working), they obtain money and, hence, goods. A rise in the wage rate means that there is a change in the relative price of goods and leisure. Goods become cheaper relative to leisure, since each hour worked results in more goods than before, and each hour of leisure consumed is at the cost of more goods forgone.

This is illustrated in Figure 26.7. Leisure is measured on the vertical axis and the money value of goods consumed on the horizontal axis. Each individual starts with 24 hours of his own time. If the wage rate is 50p per hour, he can have 24 hours of leisure and no goods, or £12 worth of goods and no leisure (much less any sleep), or any combination of goods and leisure indicated by points on *budget line A.* Assume, first, that he chooses the position indicated by point *x*, so that he consumes 14 hours of leisure and trades the other 10 (at 50p per hour) for £5 worth of goods. Now assume that the wage rate doubles to, say, £1 per hour. He can now have any combination of goods and leisure indicated by points on budget line *B*. If he continues to work for 10 hours per day, he now gets £10 worth of goods, but there is nothing to stop him from moving to a point above and to the right of *x*, in which case he can have more goods *and* more leisure. If, for example, he moves to the position indicated by *y*, he will have an extra two hours of leisure and an extra £3 worth of goods. On the other hand, the extra income that can be obtained *per unit of leisure sacrificed* might make him more willing to give up leisure to get goods. He might, for example, move to point *z* and work one more hour, getting £11 worth of goods.[1]

Thus our standard theory makes no prediction about the effect of an increase in wage rates on the supply of effort. We must now wonder what actually happens in the world: do increases in wages cause people to work fewer hours or more hours? Attempts to increase the supply of effort offered by coal miners in post-war Britain have consistently been thwarted, for the miners have wished to take out part of their increased real income by consuming more leisure. They can do this without departing from the agreed upon work-week merely by increasing their absenteeism. Most

1 The movement from his original position on *A* to his new position on *B* is the result of an income effect and a substitution effect. When the wage rate rises, the substitution effect works to increase the supply of labour, because giving up leisure to get goods is now a more profitable occupation than before. The income effect works to decrease the supply of labour (i.e., increase the consumption of leisure), because the person can consume more of everything, including leisure. Whether the rise in wages causes a rise or a fall in the number of hours people will wish to work depends on the relative strengths of these two effects. If the reader prefers to use indifference curves in his analysis (see the Appendix to Chapter 15) he can draw a curve tangent to *A* at *x* and two *alternative* curves tangent to *B* at *y* and *z*. But this will add nothing further of substance to the argument already given.

of the long-run evidence confirms that as real earnings per hour rise, people wish to reduce the number of hours they work. This is of course concerned with the supply of effort to the whole economy; there is plenty of evidence that a rise in earnings in one industry will increase the supply of effort to that industry by attracting workers from other industries.

TAXES AND THE SUPPLY OF EFFORT: Do income taxes reduce the supply of effort? People complain and always have complained about high taxes. Many people believe that today's high income taxes tend to reduce the supply of effort by reducing the incentive for people to work. They protest that it is not worth their while to work because of the crushing tax burdens they have to shoulder. Such objective evidence as exists on this subject suggests, however, that high taxes do not always reduce the supply of effort. A good deal of research has shown that while some persons may reduce their work effort in response to rising taxes, others feel poorer and thus work harder to be able to maintain their after-tax incomes. The most recent research suggests at most a small net disincentive at least up to a level of tax rates of 50 per cent. The problem is more complex where there is international movement of labour and there does seem to be some evidence that very high rates of tax contribute towards 'brain drains' to countries with lower tax rates.

A similar question is whether welfare payments and other forms of aid to the poor make them less willing to accept employment. This question is receiving a good deal of current attention. No large disincentives have been found, primarily because many of those receiving payments are unable to work and most of those who can work find it worthwhile to do so for their sense of participation in society as well as for the extra income; in other words, there appear to be nonpecuniary (as well as pecuniary) benefits to working.

LAND: If by land we mean the total area of dry land, then the supply of land in a country is, in this definition, pretty well fixed. A rise in the earnings of land cannot result in much of an increase in the supply of land, unless we can drain land that is at present covered with water. The traditional assumption in economics is that the supply of land is absolutely inelastic. However, if by land we understand all the fertile land available for cultivation, then the supply of land is subject to large fluctuations. Considerable care and effort is required to sustain the productive power of land and, if the return to land is low, the fertility of the land may be destroyed within a short period of time. On the other hand, a high return to land may make worth while irrigation, drainage and fertilization schemes that can greatly increase the supply of arable land.[1]

There is no value in debating which is 'real' land: the total land area or the total supply of arable land. The magnitude we are interested in depends on the problem at hand. For most problems in agricultural economics, however, it is the total supply of cultivable land that is relevant. If we are interested, for example, in the effect of

---

1 It is common practice, following David Ricardo, a British economist of the early nineteenth century, to define land as the *original and inexhaustible powers of the soil*. Ricardo wrote before the phenomenon of dust bowls, which turn large tracts of land into barren deserts, was widely known, and before men were aware that the deserts of North Africa had once been fertile areas. Clearly, as we know today, the fertility of land is not inexhaustible.

land taxes on the prices of agricultural goods, then it is of no help to be told that the total land area of a country is fixed; what we need to know is the effect of such taxes on the supply of cultivable land. The total supply of cultivable land is by no means perfectly inelastic; it can be expanded greatly by irrigation and other forms of reclamation and it can be contracted drastically and rapidly – as many farmers have found to their sorrow – by neglecting the principles of soil conservation.

Natural resources: Land is usually defined to include the natural resources found in or on the land. The quantity of a given natural resource existing in the world is of course limited, and it can be totally exhausted. But the problem of actual exhaustion does not arise as often as one might think. There is often a large undiscovered or unexploited quantity of a given resource. A shortage of the resource will raise its price and encourage exploration and the development of previously unprofitable sources. The world's proven and exploitable supply of a resource thus usually varies considerably with the price of the resource. Of course there is an upper limit, and resources can be totally exhausted, and, even worse, they can be polluted or otherwise despoiled so that they are rendered useless long before they have been consumed.

CAPITAL: Capital is a man-made factor of production. The supply of capital in a country consists of the stock of existing machines, plant, equipment, etc. This capital is used up in the course of production, and the supply is thus diminished by the amount that wears out each year. On the other hand, the stock of capital increases each year as a result of the production of new capital goods, the expenditure on which is called INVESTMENT EXPENDITURE. New machines and new buildings replace ones that wear out (although they will rarely be identical with the capital they are 'replacing'). The total amount of capital goods produced is called GROSS INVESTMENT. Capital goods that are not replacing worn-out ones, and that therefore represent net additions to the capital stock, are called NET INVESTMENT.

The supply of capital has been observed to increase considerably over time in all modern countries. The volume of net investment determines the rate of increase of the capital stock. There is considerable evidence that net additions to the stock of capital vary considerably over the trade cycle, being low in periods of slump and high in periods of boom. Taking the long view, however, and ignoring cyclical fluctuations, there has been a fairly steady tendency for the stock of capital to increase over a very long period of time. The theory of investment, which we shall develop in subsequent sections of this book is thus a theory of changes in the stock of capital.

The supply of factors to particular uses

The question of what determines the allocation of factors of production among various possible uses is a very general one. Even if all factors had only one use, it would still be necessary to allocate them among competing firms in the same industry. As it is, factors have many uses; a given piece of land can be used to grow a variety of crops, and it can also be subdivided for a housing development. A machinist from Coventry can work in a variety of automobile plants, or in a dozen other industries, or even in the physics laboratories at Cambridge. Factors must be allocated among different industries and they must also be allocated among different firms in the same industry.

If the owners of these factors are mainly concerned with making as much money as they can, they will move their factor to that use in which it earns the most money; this movement out of one use into another will continue until the earnings of a factor in each of its various possible uses are the same. Since owners of factors take other things besides money into account – things like risk, convenience and a good climate – factors will be moved among uses until there is no net advantage in further movement, allowing for both the monetary and nonmonetary advantages of different uses. We may now restate this discussion as the *hypothesis of equal net advantage*.

> **Owners of factors will choose that use of their factors that produces the greatest net advantage to themselves. Net advantage includes both monetary and nonmonetary elements.**

This hypothesis plays the same role in the theory of distribution as the hypothesis that firms seek to maximize profits plays in the theory of production. It leads to the prediction that factors of production will be allocated among various uses in such a way that they receive the same net return in each use. This hypothesis is, however, unsatisfactory as it stands.

Difficulties arise unless we can measure nonmonetary advantages. Suppose we observe that a mechanic is working in London for £200 a year less than he could make in Newcastle. Is this evidence against the hypothesis, or does it merely mean that the nonmonetary benefits of living in London (or of not living in Newcastle) are worth £200 to him? A moment's thought will make it clear that any conceivable observation could be rationalized to fit the hypothesis as long as we do not have an independent measure of nonmonetary advantages. To make the hypothesis useful we must do one of two things: either we must define in a measurable way the nonmonetary benefits that we believe are important to choices; or we must make an assumption about the relative stability of monetary and nonmonetary advantages. The first alternative is generally regarded as impossible, unless we assume that the hypothesis is correct in which case whatever monetary difference occurs between the earning of a factor in two uses is assumed to measure the extent of the difference in nonmonetary advantages. The second alternative, to make an assumption about the relative stability of monetary and nonmonetary advantages is more promising. If, for example, we assume that the difference in nonmonetary advantages between two uses of a factor remains constant over time, we can predict that variations in monetary advantages will cause variations in net advantage and that some resources will flow in response to the change.

It is not necessary, of course, to make the strong assumption that nonpecuniary advantages are constant. Instead, we can assume that they change, but more slowly than pecuniary ones. In this case, we can still extract predictions about behaviour.[1] This weaker assumption leads us to the following fundamental prediction:

---

1 It would be sufficient to assume that pecuniary and nonpecuniary advantages vary independently of each other. See Chapter 3. But this is an assumption that is likely to prove incorrect.

Any change in the relative price paid to a factor in two uses will lead owners of factors to increase the quantity they wish to supply to the use in which the relative price has increased, and decrease the quantity they wish to supply to the use in which it has decreased.

This prediction implies a rising supply curve for a factor in any particular use. Such a supply curve (like all supply curves) can shift in response to changes in other variables. One of these is the size of the nonmonetary benefits.

FACTOR MOBILITY: We now inquire into the speed with which factors move between uses in response to changes in their relative prices in the different uses. The key concept here is that of FACTOR MOBILITY. Factor mobility, or immobility, is an important aspect of how well resources respond to the signals that indicate where factors are wanted. If a factor is highly mobile in the sense that the owners of this factor will quickly shift from use A to use B in response to a small change in the relative factor price, then supply will be highly elastic. If, on the other hand, factor owners are 'locked in' to some use and cannot respond quickly, the supply will tend to be inelastic, even though owners may genuinely wish to take advantage of the higher prices offered elsewhere. Factor mobility is dependent on the speed with which factors will respond. The barriers to mobility vary substantially from factor to factor.

Mobility of land: Land, which is physically the least mobile of all factors, is paradoxically one of the most mobile in an economic sense. Consider agricultural land. Within a year at most, one crop can be harvested and a totally different crop planted. A farm on the outskirts of a growing city can be sold for subdivision and development on very short notice. Once land is built upon, as urban land usually is, its mobility is much reduced. One can convert a site on which a hotel has been built into an office-building site but it takes a very large differential in the value of land use to make it worth while because the hotel must be torn down.

Although land is highly mobile between alternative uses it is completely immobile as far as location is concerned. There is only so much land within the borders of any given city and no increase in the price paid can induce further land to locate within the city. This locational immobility has, as we shall see, some important consequences.

Mobility of capital: Most capital equipment, once constructed, is immobile. A great deal of machinery is specific; once built, it must either be used for the purpose for which it was designed, or else not used at all. This is, of course, not true of all pieces of capital equipment – a shed, for example, may be used for a large number of purposes – but much capital equipment is extremely immobile among uses during its physical lifetime. It is the immobility of capital equipment that makes exit of firms from declining industries a slow and difficult process. During the life of a piece of capital, the firm may make allowances for depreciation that allows the firm to replace the capital good when it wears out. If conditions of demand and cost have not changed, the firm may spend money to replace the worn-out piece of equipment with an identical one. The firm may, however, do many other things with its funds: it may buy a newly designed machine to produce the same goods; it may buy machines to produce totally different goods; or it may lend the money to some other firm for the latter's uses. In this way, the long-run allocation of a country's stock of capital among various uses changes.

In popular discussion, sums of money are often referred to as capital. Money represents a claim on resources. A firm or a household that has accumulated money savings can spend these on anything that it desires. It can buy beer or machines and, by so doing, will direct the nation's resources to the production of beer or machinery. Also, the firm or household can lend its money to other firms or households and thereby allow the borrowers to determine what the nation's resources will be used to produce.

Mobility of labour: Labour is unique as a factor of production in that the supply of the service implies the physical presence of the owner of the source of the service. Absentee landlords may obtain an income from renting out their land located in remote parts of the world while continuing to live in the place of their choice. Investors can shift their capital from one firm to another so that their income is earned from activities throughout the world while they themselves never leave New York or Tokyo or wherever they may desire to live. But if a worker employed by a firm in Coventry decides to offer his labour services to a firm in South London he must physically travel to South London to do so. If a capitalist decides to invest in steel mills he need never visit one, while if a labourer decides to work in a steel mill he must be physically present. This is, of course, all quite obvious but it has the important consequence that nonmonetary factors are much more important in the allocation of labour than in the allocation of other factors of production. If the rate of return is even slightly higher in steel mills than it is elsewhere, other things being equal, capital will move into steel. But the wage paid in steel mills can be substantially above that in other industries without inducing an analogous flow of labour into the steel industry provided that people find working in steel mills unpleasant.

Although labour is in a substantial degree influenced by nonwage considerations, we should still expect that labour would respond to changes in the wage structure. But we must be careful. If doctors' earnings go up and farmers' earnings go down, would farmers move into medicine? No, for it is not easy for a farmer to become a doctor (or for that matter for a doctor to become a farmer). The very obvious barriers between various occupations have led some economists to speak of labour as consisting of a series of *noncompeting groups* and to explain differential pay between occupations as the consequence. Since, as we all know, the sons of farmers can and do become doctors, the notion of impassable walls between various occupations is not a very satisfactory explanation of the immobility of labour. In addition, not all occupational shifts are as difficult as that between medicine and farming.

An important variable with labour mobility is *time*. In the short run, it is difficult for people to shift occupations. It is not hard for a secretary to shift from one company to another, and it is not hard to persuade her to take a job in London instead of in Colchester, but it will be difficult for her to become an editor or a fashion model in a short period of time. There are two considerations here: ability and training. Lack of either will stratify some people and make certain kinds of mobility difficult.

Over long periods, labour mobility between occupations is very great indeed. In assessing the mobility of labour, it is important to remember that the labour force is not static. At one end, young people enter the labour force from school, and at the other end older persons exit from retirement or death. The turnover due to these causes, is about 3 to 4 per cent per year. Thus, even if no one ever changed jobs, it would be possible to reallocate 3 or 4 per cent of the labour force annually merely by directing new entrants to jobs other than the ones left vacant by persons leaving the labour force. Over a period of 20 years, a totally different occupational distribution could appear without a single individual ever changing his job.

Various studies have been made to determine the amount of mobility shown by labour in moving from job to job and place to place. In times of heavy depression, mobility from place to place is very low. In periods with more or less full employment, there appears to be some evidence that differentials in wages between areas and occupations do reflect relative scarcities and that labour does tend to some extent to move from low-wage sectors of the economy to high-wage ones; there seems to be even stronger evidence, however, that labour is more attracted by the chance of obtaining a job than by the wage rate actually paid for that job. By way of contrast, studies of labour mobility over the generations, or *social stratification* as the sociologists call it, indicate impressive mobility. The data show very substantial mobility both up and down the scales of education, skilled training and social status over the course of two or three generations.

> **Labour is much more mobile in the long run than in the short run. Over a given time period, it is more mobile between jobs in the same location and occupation than between different locations (where movement of the family is a deterrent) or between different occupations (where lack of skills is a deterrent).**

Man-made barriers to labour mobility: Many organizations, private and public, adopt policies that affect their personnel and influence their mobility as workers. When labour unions negotiate seniority rights for their members, they protect the old employee from being laid off in a cutback of production, but they also make him very reluctant to change jobs. If an employer provides his employees with a non-transferable pension plan, the employees may not want to forfeit this benefit by changing jobs. When the governments of individual states in the US provide compensation to unemployed residents, these residents may be reluctant to leave the state, even to find work.

There are other barriers as well. Licensing is required in dozens of trades and professions. Barbers, electricians, doctors and, in some places, even pedlars must have licences. There is, of course, a generally acceptable reason for requiring licences in cases in which the public must be protected against the incompetent or the quack or the nuisance. But licensing can also have the effect of limiting supply. The fact that, in countries without national health services, medicine is often one of the highest paid occupations and that doctors have long been in short supply, are a result of the difficulties in getting into medical schools, the long internship and residency requirements, the rules concerning certification, and so forth. It is at least possible that in these countries doctors' earnings are high because the barriers to entry into the profession prevent even long-run increases in the proportion of the population being admitted to medical practice. Whether such barriers as exist are required by the standards of the profession or are designed to keep the supply limited (and the earnings high) is a matter open to debate. Trade unions may impose barriers to mobility. The 'closed shop', for example, which requires all employees of a plant or a trade to be a member of a particular union, gives unions the power to limit the supply of labour that they represent. Racial prejudice, discrimination against women and other similar attitudes, also limit the mobility of labour.

27

The pricing of factors in competitive markets

We have now developed theories of both the demand for, and the supply of factors of production. This is all we need to develop a theory of the pricing of factors in a free market: given that factor prices are free to vary, they will move to a level at which quantity demanded equals quantity supplied. Furthermore, shifts in either the demand for, or the supply of factors will have the effects on prices, quantities and factor incomes predicted by normal price theory.

The theory of factor prices is an absolutely general one. If one is concerned with labour, one should interpret factor prices to mean wages; if one is thinking about land, factor prices should be interpreted to mean rent, and so on. In this chapter we assume that factors are bought and sold on a competitive market by a large number of buyers and sellers. In Chapter 28, we shall introduce monopolistic elements into factor markets.

MONEY, REAL AND RELATIVE PRICES: Changes both in relative factor prices and in the share of national income going to a factor are likely to be brought about through changes in the *money prices* of a factor; but the mere knowledge that the money price of a given factor has risen tells us very little about what has happened either to the income of the factor relative to another factor, or to its income relative to the whole national income. Only if money national income and all other money prices are constant can variations in the money price of one factor give us direct information about the factor's relative price and its share in the national income. In partial equilibrium analysis, it is simplest to assume that total income and all other prices remain constant. In this case a variation in the money price of a factor causes a simultaneous variation both in its relative price (compared to any other single factor) and in the share of the national income going to the factor.

RELATIVE FACTOR PRICES UNDER COMPETITIVE CONDITIONS

If there were only one factor of production, all the units of which were identical, and if the nonmonetary advantages accruing to this factor were the same in all its uses, then the prices of all the units of this factor would tend towards the same level. Units of the factor would tend to move from low-price to high-price occupations. The supply of the factor would diminish in occupations in which prices were low, and the resulting shortage would tend to force the price up; the supply of the factor would increase in occupations in which prices were high, and the resulting surplus would force the price down. The movement would continue until there was no further incentive to transfer, i.e., until the price of the factor was the same in all its uses. This equality would be established whatever the states of demand in the various industries, This proposition is illustrated by example in Figure 27.1 which shows that, given the states of demand, most of the factor would flow into the second industry until prices were equalized.

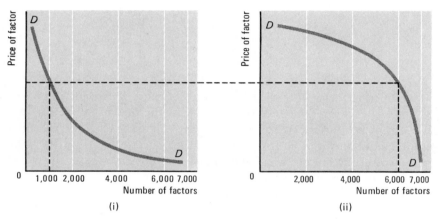

Fig. 27.1 The distribution of 7,000 workers between two industries with different demand curves

Causes of differences in factor prices are of two sorts, dynamic or disequilibrium ones, and static or equilibrium ones. The dynamic differences are associated with changing circumstances, such as the rise of one industry and the decline of another. Such differentials set up movements in factors that will themselves act to remove the variations. The differences in prices may persist for a long time, but there is a tendency for them to be reduced, and in equilibrium they will be eliminated. Equilibrium differences in prices, on the other hand would persist in a state of equilibrium without there being any tendency for them to be removed by the competitive forces of the market.

Dynamic differentials and factor mobility

First consider dynamic differentials. If there were a rise in the demand for product A and a fall in demand for product B, there would be an increase in the (derived) demand for factors in industry A and a decrease in the (derived) demand for factors in industry B. Factor prices would go up in A and down in B. This is an example of a dynamic change in relative prices, for the changes themselves will cause factors to move from industry B to industry A, and this movement will cause the price differentials to lessen and eventually to disappear. How long this process takes depends on how easily factors move from one industry to the other, i.e., on factor mobility. Some factors, particularly labour, may be relatively immobile in the short run and thus dynamic differentials can last for a long time even if there are no barriers to movement. The factors that affect labour mobility and thus determine the duration of dynamic differentials have been discussed in more detail in Chapter 26.

Equilibrium differentials

Equilibrium differentials in factor prices are related to differences in the factors themselves (e.g., land of different fertilities, and labour of different abilities) or to different nonmonetary advantages of different factor employments. *Ceteris paribus* a job with high nonmonetary rewards will have a lower equilibrium wage rate than a job with low nonmonetary rewards. Thus it is often possible, for example, to pay people in academic and research jobs less than they would be able to earn in the world of commerce and industry, because there are substantial nonmonetary advantages associated with university employment. If labour were paid the same in both jobs, then it would move out of industry and into academic employment. Excess demand for labour in industry and excess supply in universities would then cause industrial wages to rise relative to academic ones until the movement of labour ceased.

Equilibrium differentials may also be caused by differences between factors. Thus the high pay of skilled workers relative to unskilled workers reflects the fact that there is a shortage of skilled workers relative to the demand for them. No movement from unskilled to skilled jobs eliminates this differential, because it is difficult for most adult unskilled workers to become skilled ones. It is important to realize that the high pay of the skilled man relative to the unskilled one merely reflects demand and supply conditions for these two types of labour. There is nothing in the nature of competitive markets that ensures that the skilled worker always get high pay just because he is skilled. If, for example, the demand for skilled workers fell off so much that, even though the supply was small, there was a glut of such workers, their wages would come down. On the other hand, if there was a change in education so that unskilled workers could now acquire skills more easily, the wages of skilled workers would fall relative to those of unskilled workers. History is replete with examples of particular groups of skilled workers who have lost their privileged position when there was a change in the demand for their services. Many middle-class people feel that it is both unjust and incomprehensible that, since the Second World War, lorry drivers and coal miners have made much more money than many relatively highly educated office workers. Whatever the justice of the matter, it is certainly not incomprehensible. A rise in the supply of office workers relative to the demand for their services and a decline in the supply of lorry drivers and coal miners relative to the demand for their services will, according to the normal workings of the market, raise the earnings of lorry drivers and coal miners relative to those of office workers. If there are substantial nonmonetary benefits to being an office worker rather than a coal miner or a lorry driver then the earnings differentials will not set up a flow of labour out of the latter occupations into the former and the differential will persist (i.e., it will be an equilibrium one).

TRANSFER EARNINGS AND ECONOMIC RENT

Some differentials in factor prices will, as we have seen, persist even in equilibrium. In order to study further the differences in factor earnings between alternative uses, we need to distinguish between the amount that a factor must earn in its present use in order to prevent it from transferring to another use which is called the factor's TRANSFER EARNINGS, and any excess that the factor actually earns over this amount, which is called the factor's ECONOMIC RENT. The meaning of rent in this context differs greatly from its everyday usage, and we must first try to understand how this rather specialized meaning arose.

THE HISTORY OF THE CONCEPT OF ECONOMIC RENT: In the early part of the nineteenth century, when British economics was in its infancy, there was a controversy about the high price of corn (the generic term for all grains). One group held that corn had a high price because the landlords were charging very high rents to the farmers who were growing corn on their land. It was held that, in order to meet these high rents, the price that farmers charged for their corn had to be raised to a very high level. Thus, it was argued, the price of corn was high because the rents of agricultural land were high. The second group, which included David Ricardo, one of the great figures of British classical economics, held that the situation was exactly the reverse. The price of corn was high because there was a shortage of corn caused by the Napoleonic Wars. Because corn had a high price there was keen competition amongst farmers to obtain land and this competition bid up the rents of corn land. If the price of corn were to fall so that corn growing became less profitable, then the demand for land would fall, and the price paid for the use of land, i.e., rent, would fall as well. Thus, this group held that the rent of corn land was high because the price of corn was high and not *vice versa*. The modern student of economics will recognize in the Ricardian argument the idea of *derived demand*. Landlords, Ricardo was saying, cannot just charge any price they want for land; the prices they get will depend on demand and supply. The supply of land is pretty well fixed and the demand depends on the price of corn. The higher the price of corn, the more profitable it will be to grow corn, the higher will be the demand for corn land, and the higher will be the price paid for its use.

The argument was elaborated by considering land to have only one use, the growing of corn. The supply of land was given and virtually unchangeable, i.e., land was in perfectly inelastic supply and landowners would prefer to rent out their land for some return rather than leave it idle. Nothing had to be paid to prevent land from transferring to uses other than growing corn, because it had none. Therefore, so went the argument, all of the payment to land, i.e., rent, is a surplus over and above what is necessary to keep it in its present use. *Given the fixed supply of land*, the price will depend on the demand for land which is itself a function of the price of corn.

Rent, which was the term for the payment for the use of land, thus became the term for a surplus payment to a factor over and above what was necessary to keep it in its present use. Subsequently two facts were realized. First, factors of production other than land often earn a surplus over and above what is necessary to keep them in their present use. Movie stars, for example, are in very short and pretty well fixed supply, and their possible earnings in other occupations are probably quite moderate; but, because there is a huge demand for their services, they may receive payments greatly in excess of what is needed to keep them from transferring to other occupations. Secondly, it was realized that land itself often has many alternative uses and, from the point of view of *any one use*, part of the payment made to land would *necessarily* have to be paid to keep the land in its present use. Thus it appeared that all factors of production were pretty much the same: part of the payment made to them would be a payment necessary to keep them from transferring to other uses, and part a surplus over and above what was necessary to keep this factor in its present use. This surplus came to be called ECONOMIC RENT.

TWO MEANINGS OF THE TERM RENT: The term economic rent is a most unfortunate one. The adjective 'economic' is often dropped and the economist often speaks of rent when he means economic rent, thus causing a confusion between the concept of a surplus over and above transfer earnings, and the payment made to landlords for the hiring of land and buildings. When a tenant refers to his rent he is referring to what he pays his landlord, much of which is a transfer earning necessary to prevent the land and buildings in question from being transferred to some other use. It is important to guard against confusing the two concepts.

THE MODERN DISTINCTION BETWEEN TRANSFER EARNINGS AND ECONOMIC RENT: In most cases the actual earnings of a factor of production will be a composite of transfer earnings and economic rent; it is possible, however, to imagine limiting cases in which all earnings are either one or the other. Consider some individual firm or some industry faced with a perfectly elastic supply curve of a factor of production; it will be able to obtain all that it wants at the going price but, if it does not pay this price, it will be unable to obtain any of the factor. In such a case, which is illus-

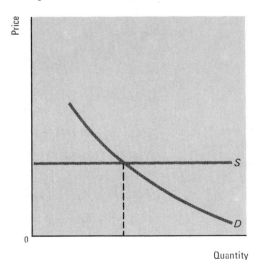

Fig. 27.2 All of the income earned by the factor is transfer earnings

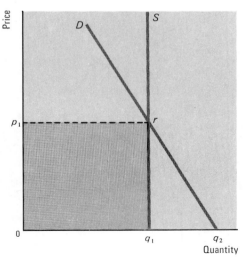

Fig. 27.3 All of the income earned by the factor is an economic rent

trated in Figure 27.2, the whole price paid to the factor represents transfer earnings; the amount that is actually paid must be paid to prevent the factor from transferring to another use.

Now consider the case of a factor that is fixed in supply and has only one use. Assume that this factor is put on the market by its owners and sold for whatever it will fetch, on the grounds that some income is better than none. The whole supply is owned by thousands of different owners so there is no point in any one of them withholding his own (small) supply from the market in an effort to raise the price. Such a factor will be in perfectly inelastic supply: the amount offered for sale will be the same whatever the price. This case is illustrated in Figure 27.3. The whole of the price that is paid to the factor is an *economic rent* because, if a lower price were paid, the factor would not transfer to an alternative use. It might be thought that, in such a case as this, the factor would not command any price, but this is not so. The price, as in all other free-market cases, is determined by demand and supply. The fixed quantity available is the amount q_1 in Figure 27.3, while, if the price were zero, the amount demanded would be q_2. Thus at a price of zero there would be excess demand for the factor, and competition amongst buyers would force the price upwards until it reached p_1 and the excess demand disappeared. The equilibrium is at r, the price paid to the factor is p_1, the quantity employed is q_1 and, hence, total factor income is indicated by the area of the shaded rectangle.

Finally consider a factor with an upward-sloping supply curve such as the one shown in Figure 27.4. Given the demand curve, D, the equilibrium would be at z, the price would be p_5 and the employment q_5; total factor earnings would be p_5 *times* q_5. If q_5 units of the factor are to be attracted into the industry, and if a single price must be paid, then it is necessary to pay the price p_5. However, all but the last unit would be prepared to remain in the industry for a price less than p_5. In fact, q_1 of these units would be prepared to remain if the price were as low as p_1. If the price

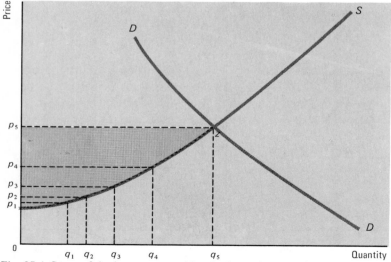

Fig. 27.4 Some of the income earned by the factor is a transfer earning and the remainder is economic rent

rose from p_1 to p_2, an additional $q_2 - q_1$ units would be attracted into the industry; if the price rose to p_3, an additional $q_3 - q_2$ units would enter the industry. Clearly, for any unit that we care to pick, the point on the supply curve corresponding to it shows the minimum price that must be paid in order to keep that unit in the industry (i.e., its transfer earnings). Equally clearly, if the supply curve slopes upward, all previous units have lower transfer earnings. Thus the total transfer earnings of the q_5 units is the unshaded area *below* the supply curve. Since the total payment made is the rectangle Op_5zq_5, it follows that the economic rent earned by the factor is the shaded area *above* the supply curve and below the line p_5z.

The following example illustrates why a rising supply curve involves rents: if universities increase the salaries paid to professors of economics in order to attract additional economists into university teaching (and away from industry and government), those economists who are persuaded to shift into university teaching will be receiving only transfer earnings. But those economists who were already content to be university professors will find their salaries have increased as well, and this increase will be a rent to them.

Figures 27.2, 27.3 and 27.4 suggest the following important conclusion:

> **The more elastic the supply curve, the less the amount of the payment to factors that is a rent and the more that is a transfer earning.**

Kinds of transfers

How much of a given payment to a factor is an economic rent and how much is a transfer earning depends on what sort of transfer we are considering.

If we consider the transfer of a factor from one firm to another within a single industry for which the supply of the factor should be highly elastic, then pretty well all of the factor's earnings will be transfer earnings. If the firm in question did not pay the factor the going price, then the factor would transfer to another firm in the same industry. If we are considering the transfer of a factor from one industry to another, then part of the payment may be a transfer earning and part an economic rent, since mobility will be less, and thus the supply curve less elastic. We cannot point to a given factor, a labourer, say, and assert that of his income of £1,000, £800 is a transfer earning and £200 a rent, for it all depends on what transfer we are considering.

ECONOMIC RENT AND TRANSFER EARNINGS IN THE PAYMENT TO LABOUR: Labour is able to move from job to job and something must be paid to keep a given unit of labour in its present use; what has to be paid for this reason is a transfer earning to labour. How much has to be paid to keep labour in its present use depends upon what the use is. Let us say, for example, that carpenters receive £6 for working a normal 8-hour day. Then a single small construction firm will have to pay £6 per day or it will not obtain the services of any carpenters. To that one firm the whole £6 is a transfer payment; if the whole £6 were not paid, carpenters would not remain with that firm. But consider what would happen if the construction industry encountered difficulties so that all construction firms were forced to reduce the wages offered to carpenters. In this case carpenters could not move to other construction firms to get more money. If they do not like the wages offered, they will have to move to another industry. If the best they can do elsewhere is £4·50 per day, then they will not begin to leave the construction industry until wages in that industry fall below £4·50. In this case the transfer earnings of carpenters in construction are £4·50 and, when they were receiving £6 (presumably because there was a heavy demand for their services), the additional £1·50 was an economic rent from the point of view of the construction industry. Now consider what would happen if there was a decline in the demand for carpenters in all industries. The only thing left to do, if one did not like the wages, would be to move to another occupation: in other words one must cease to be a carpenter. If no one was induced to do this until the wage fell to £4, then £4 would be the transfer earnings for carpenters in general. The wage of £4 must be paid to persuade people to be carpenters at all.

Some very highly specialized types of labour are in inelastic supply. This is particularly true of persons such as singers and actors who have a special talent which cannot be duplicated, whatever the training. The earnings that such persons receive are mostly in the nature of economic rent: they enjoy their occupations and would pursue them for very much less than the high remuneration that some of them actually receive. Their high rewards occur because they are in *very scarce supply relative to the demand for their services*. If the demand for their services were to rise their earnings would rise permanently, while if the demand fell their earnings would fall permanently.

R ENT AND TRANSFER EARNINGS IN THE RETURN TO CAPITAL: If a piece of capital equipment has several uses, then the analysis of the last section can be repeated for the case of the machine. Many machines, however, once they are constructed, are utterly specific, having only one use. In this case, any income that is made from the operation of the machine is in the nature of a rent. Assume, for example, that when a machine was installed it was expected to earn £500 per annum in excess of all its operating costs. If the demand for the product now falls off so that the machine can earn only £200, it will still be worthwhile operating it rather than throwing it away. In fact, assuming the machine to have only one use, it will pay to keep it in operation rather than scrap it, as long as it yields any return at all over its operating costs.[1] Thus, if the machine does yield a return of, say, £500 per annum in any one year, we can say that all of the return is an economic rent because the machine would still have been allocated to its present use – it has no other – as long as it yielded even £1 above its operating costs. Thus, *once the machine has been installed*, any net income that it earns is a rent (i.e., a payment not necessary to keep it in its present use). However, the machine will in time wear out and it will not be replaced unless it is expected to earn a return over its lifetime sufficient to make it a good investment for its owner. Thus, over the long run, some of the revenue earned by the machine is a transfer earning; if the payment is not made, a machine will not continue to be allocated to that use in the long run. In any one year, however, the income earned can sink to zero without affecting the allocation of existing machines to different uses in the economy.

1 This is just another way of stating the proposition given in Chapter 23, page 296, that it pays a firm to continue in operation in the short run as long as it can cover its variable costs of production.

In this case, whether a payment made to a factor is an economic rent or a transfer earning depends on the time span under consideration. In the short run all of the income of a machine is in the nature of a rent, while in the long run some of it is in the nature of a transfer payment. Factor payments which are economic rents in the short run and transfer payments in the long run are called QUASI-RENTS.

ECONOMIC RENT AND TRANSFER EARNINGS IN THE PAYMENT TO LAND: The formal analysis is identical to that given in the case of labour. How much of the payment made to a given piece of land is a transfer payment depends upon the nature of the transfer. Consider, first, the case of an individual wheat farmer. He must pay the going price of land in order to prevent the land from being *transferred to the use of other wheat farmers*. From his point of view, therefore, the whole of the payment that he makes is a transfer payment. Now consider a particular industry that uses land. In order to secure land for, say, wheat production, it will be necessary to offer at least as much as the land could earn when put to other uses. From the point of view of the wheat industry, that part of the payment made for land which is equal to what it could earn in its next most remunerative use is a transfer payment. If that much is not paid, then the land will in fact be transferred to the alternative use. If, however, land particularly suitable for wheat growing is scarce relative to the demand for it, then the actual payment for the use of this land may be above the transfer payment; any additional payment is an economic rent. Assume, for example, that the maximum payment that can be offered by farmers wishing to use land for the crop next most remunerative to wheat is £10 per acre. Now wheat farmers must offer £10 per acre to secure the land. But it may be that the price of wheat is such that the profits of wheat growing are very high when only £10 per acre is paid for the land. A large number of farmers will wish to hire land at this price in order to grow wheat: the demand for wheat land will exceed its supply. Competition will bid up the rent offered until the demand is equal to the supply. The rental finally established might be, say, £13 per acre. In this case, from the point of view of the wheat industry as a whole, £10 is transfer earnings and the remaining £3 is economic rent. If the price of wheat falls and, as a result, the demand for wheat land falls, then the rent paid for wheat land will also fall. This will continue until the rent offered falls to £10 and then land will begin to be transferred out of wheat into other uses. This transfer will continue and the supply of wheat will diminish until the price of wheat rises sufficiently, so that the remaining wheat farmers can offer to pay the £10 transfer cost to keep the land out of other uses.

Land is very mobile between agricultural uses because its location is usually of little importance. In the case of urban uses, however, location of the land is critical and, from this point of view, land is of course completely immobile. If there is a shortage of land in central London, such land as is available will command a high price but, no matter what the price paid, this will not cause land in rural areas to move into central London. The very high payments made to urban land are in the nature of economic rents. The land is scarce relative to demand for it, and it commands a price very much above what it could earn in agricultural uses. The payment that it receives is thus well in excess of what is necessary to prevent it from transferring from urban back to agricultural uses. From the point of view, however, of one parti-cular type of urban use, high rents are a transfer payment that must be paid to keep the land from transferring to other urban uses. Cinemas, for example, account for but a small portion of the total demand for land in central London; if there were no cinemas at all, rentals of land would be about what they are now. Thus the cinema industry faces a perfectly elastic supply of land in central London, and the whole of the price that it pays for its land is a transfer payment which must be paid to keep the land from transferring to other urban uses. [1]

Some implications of the distinction between transfer earnings and economic rent

INCREASING THE SUPPLY OF A FACTOR: An important policy implication of the distinction between rents and transfer earnings concerns the effect of wage increases on the quantity of labour supplied. For example, if the central authorities want more physicists, should they subsidize physicists' salaries? As we have seen, such a policy may well have an effect on supply. It may influence schoolboys uncertain about whether to become engineers or physicists to become physicists. But it will also mean that a great deal of money will have to be spent on extra payments to people who are already physicists. And these payments will be economic rents, since existing physicists have demonstrated that they are prepared to be physicists at their old salaries. Although some may have been considering transferring to another occupa-tion, such movements are not common. [2] An alternative policy, which may produce more physicists per £, is to subsidize scholarships and fellowships for students who will train to become physicists. This policy tends to operate at the margin on persons just deciding whether or not to enter the occupation. It avoids the payment of addi-tional rents to persons already in the occupation. Graphically, it is shown by a rightward shift in the supply curve because there will now be more persons in the occupation without any change in earnings. If the supply curve is quite inelastic, an increase in the quantity supplied may be achieved more easily and at less cost by shifting the supply curve to the right than by moving along it.

URBAN LAND VALUES AND LAND TAXES: The high payments made to urban land are largely economic rents. The land is scarce relative to the demand for it, and it commands a price very much above what it could earn in agricultural uses. The pay-ment it receives is thus well in excess of what is necessary to prevent it from transfer-ring from urban back to agricultural uses. A society with rising population and rising per capita real income tends also to have steadily rising urban land prices. This fact has created a special interest in taxes on land values.

---

1 Thus the old examination question, 'Discuss the view that the price of cinema seats is high in central London because the price of land is high', should be answered in the affirmative, not in the negative as examiners often seemed to expect. The view that the prices of *all* goods and services in central London are high because rents are high can, however, be denied.

2 International mobility, it is clear, is another matter. One of the reasons for the considerable migration of trained physicists of all ages from Britain to the United States is the very much higher monetary rewards to be earned in the United States compared with the United Kingdom. Clearly, many British physicists are being paid less than their transfer earnings, and the result is a steady one-way 'brain drain' from Britain to America.

TAXES ON LAND: Who pays taxes on the value of land? If the same tax rate is applied to all uses of land, the relative profitability of different uses will be unaffected, and thus a landlord will not be tempted to change the allocation of land among uses. Land will not be forced out of use, because land that is very unprofitable will command little rent and so pay little tax. Thus there will be no change in the supply of goods that are produced with the aid of land, and, since there is no change in supply, there can be no change in prices. *The tax cannot be passed on to consumers.* Farmers will be willing to pay just as much (and no more) as they would have offered previously for the use of land. Agricultural prices and rents will be unchanged, and the whole of the tax will be borne by the landlord. The net rents earned by landlords will fall by the full amount of the tax, and land values will fall correspondingly (because land is now a less attractive investment relative to, say, bonds than it was previously).

THE SINGLE-TAX MOVEMENT: Taxation of land values has had enormous appeal in the past. The peak of its appeal occurred 80 years ago, when the 'single-tax movement' led by Henry George commanded great popularity. George's book *Progress and Poverty* is, as books on economic issues go, an all-time best seller. His idea was to tax away the 'unearned increment' that accrued to landowners and to finance *all* government undertakings thereby. George pointed out that the fixed supply of land, combined with a rapidly rising demand for it, allowed the owners of land to gain from the natural progress of society without contributing anything. He, along with many others, was incensed at this 'unearned increment' reaped by landowners. Observing the huge fortunes accruing to landlords, he calculated that most of government expenditure could be financed by a single tax that did nothing more than remove the landlords' unearned increment.

A further appeal of taxes on land values arises from the fact that economic rent can be taxed away without affecting the allocation of resources. Thus, for someone who does not wish to interfere with the allocation resulting from the free play of the market, the taxation of economic rent is attractive.

Two problems arise, however, in any attempt to tax this economic rent. First, the theoretical statement refers to *economic rent, not* to the payment actually made by tenants to landlords. What is called rent in the world is partly an economic rent and partly a return on capital invested by the landowner. The policy implications of taxing rents depend on being able to identify *economic rent* in practice. At best, this is a very difficult thing to do; at worst, it may be impossible.

The second problem is a normative one. If, in the interests of justice, we want to treat all recipients of economic rent similarly, we will encounter insurmountable difficulties because economic rent accrues to factors other than land. It accrues to the owners of any factor that is fixed in supply and that faces a rising demand. If there is, for example, a fixed supply of first-class opera singers in the country, they will gain in exactly the same way as the society becomes richer and the demand for operas increases, without there being any corresponding increase in the supply of singers. No one has yet devised a scheme that will tax the economic rent but not the transfer earnings of such divergent factors as land, patents, football players and high court judges.

The appeal of the single tax has now receded, both because of the difficulties mentioned above and because, with the great increase in the size of the government, even an effective tax on economic rent could hardly be expected to finance the majority, let alone the entirety, of government expenditures. The movement has left one curious anachronism behind in the tax policies of those American cities that levy their real-estate taxes at a higher rate on the assessed value of the land than on the assessed value of the buildings erected on the land.

The failure of the *single*-tax idea does not change the fact that a large increment of value does accrue to the owners of land, particularly in or near urban areas, as a result of the natural growth of the economy without the landlord having to contribute any additional productive services in order to obtain the increment. Indeed someone could buy a piece of land, leave it idle for ten years and then sell it and collect the increment in the land's value. Thus, the failure of the single-tax movement as a general theory of how to finance the government does not necessarily discredit the idea of attempting to design taxes that will recapture some of this increment in value and allow it to be employed for general social uses rather than leave it for the landlord's private use.

28

Wages and collective bargaining

A great deal of the analysis of factor pricing in the last chapter applies to the factor, labour, and to its price the wage rate. So far, however, we have concentrated on factor pricing in perfectly competitive markets. Although most non-human factors of production are sold in perfectly competitive markets, labour is more commonly sold in imperfect or monopolistic markets. Many types of workers sell their services in markets containing at most only a few potential employers. Many employers hire a particular type of labour service from a single seller – the trade union. Furthermore, even if there were many firms and many non-unionized workers the degree of market information available to a typical worker would be substantially less than that available to a single seller of, say, iron ingots. Because labour markets are characteristically imperfectly competitive, and sometimes monopolistic, we must extend our theory somewhat before we can apply it to the full range of problems concerning the determination of wages. In this chapter we shall mainly consider labour markets that are small in relation to the whole economy; at the end of the chapter we consider more general questions about the share of national income going to labour as a whole.

THE DETERMINATION OF WAGES WITHOUT UNIONS

We first consider the determination of wages in the absence of unions. There are two important cases to study: first, where there are many purchasers of labour, and second, where there are only a few purchasers (or possibly only one). In both cases labour is assumed to be supplied competitively, in the sense that there are many individual workers each one of whom must take the existing wage rate as being beyond his control, and who needs to decide only how much of his labour services to provide at the going wage rate.

Labour purchased competitively

In the first case we also assume that there is a large number of purchasers of labour services none of whom can influence the wage rate. The labour market is now perfectly competitive, and thus it is similar to the markets analysed in the previous chapter. As we saw in Chapter 27, the wage rate and the volume of employment in such a market will be determined at the intersection of the demand and the supply curve. Although the demand curve is *not* the marginal revenue product curve, it *is* true that in equilibrium the wage rate will be *equal to* the value of the marginal product of labour. This is illustrated in Figure 28.1 where the equilibrium wage and the marginal value product are w_c and quantity of employment is q_c.

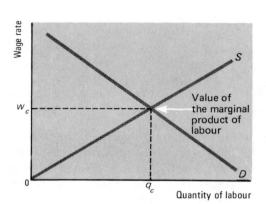

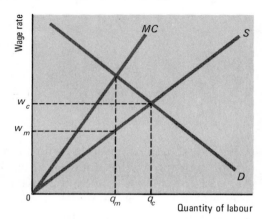

Fig. 28.1 The determination of wages in a competitive market

Fig. 28.2 The determination of wages when labour is sold competitively but bought monopsonistically

Labour purchased monopsonistically

In the second case there are so few purchasers of labour that each one realizes he is able to influence the wage rate by varying the amount that he purchases: the purchasers of labour are *not* price-takers in the labour market. For simplicity we deal with a case in which the few purchasers form an employers' association and act as a single decision-taking unit in the labour market. The sole purchaser in the market is called a MONOPSONIST.

The sole purchaser of labour can offer any wage rate that he chooses and the labourers must either work for him or move to other markets (i.e., change occupation or location). For any given quantity that is purchased, the labour supply curve shows the price per unit that must be paid; to the monopsonist, this is the average cost curve of the factor. But the marginal cost of employing extra units exceeds average cost. If, for example, 100 units are employed at 50p per hour, then total cost is £50 and average cost per unit is 50p. If 101 units are employed and the factor price is driven up to 52p, then total cost becomes £52·52; the average cost per labourer is 52p, but the total cost has increased by £2·52 as a result of hiring one more labourer. The marginal cost of obtaining an extra labourer will exceed the wage paid, because the increased wage rate necessary to attract him must also be paid to all the labourers already employed. Thus, in Figure 28.2 we can draw a marginal cost curve for labour that will lie above the average cost curve. The profit-maximizing monopsonist will equate marginal cost of labour with its marginal revenue product; in other words, he will go on hiring labour until the last unit increases total costs by as much as it increases total revenue.

Thus, in equilibrium, marginal cost and not the wage rate will be equated with the marginal revenue product of labour. Since marginal cost exceeds the wage rate, it follows that the wage rate will be less than the marginal revenue product. Also, since the supply curve of labour is upward sloping, the volume of employment must be less than it would be if the market were perfectly competitive.

This analysis is illustrated in Figure 28.2 in which w_c and q_c would be the competitive wage and volume of employment, while w_m and q_m are the corresponding values under monopsony. Since the monopsonist only wishes to employ a quantity of labour equal to q_m, he need only pay a wage of w_m to call forth that quantity.

This analysis leads to the following general conclusion:

> **Monopsonistic conditions in the factor market will result in a lower level of employment and a lower wage rate than would rule when the factor was purchased under competitive conditions.**

The reason for this is that the monopsonistic purchaser is aware that, by trying to purchase more of the factor, he is driving up the price against himself. He will, therefore, stop short of the point that is reached when the factor is purchased by many different firms, none of which can exert an influence on its price.

THE DETERMINATION OF WAGES WITH UNIONS

Now let us consider the effect of introducing a labour union into each of the two markets described above. For the moment we assume that the union is able to fix, as a result of unilateral action or negotiation, any price of labour that it wishes, but that the volume of employment is determined by the amount employers would like to hire at the union-determined wage.

Labour purchased competitively

The union might fix the same wage as would arise from a competitive market (w_c in Figure 28.1). This has no effect on the average wage ruling in the market but, if

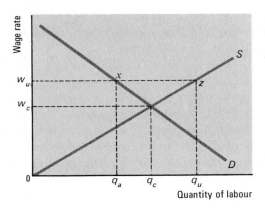

Fig. 28.3 The effect on wages and employment of the entry of a union into a competitive labour market

ignorance of wages offered by other firms or slowness of adjustment causes a dispersion of wages around the mean, the union announcement of an agreed wage of w_c
will reduce or eliminate this dispersion of wage rates. In effect, by increasing
workers' knowledge of the going rate, the union creates a result closer to the one that
would arise in a market that was truly perfectly competitive.

It is more likely, however, that the union will attempt to raise wages above their
competitive level. In Figure 28.3 we assume that the union raises the wage from w_c
to w_u. This creates a perfectly elastic supply of labour up to the quantity q_u (since
this is the quantity of labour supplied at the union wage). The supply curve now
becomes $w_u zS$ and the equilibrium is at x where the demand curve cuts the new
supply curve. The union has succeeded in raising the wage rate above its competitive
level but only at the cost of reducing employment from q_c to q_a.

Notice also that there are workers who would like to work at the going wage and
cannot get employment (excess supply equals $q_a q_u$ or xz). Indeed, these unemployed
workers would be prepared to work for a wage *less than* w_u. (For example, at w_c the
quantity supplied would still equal q_c and thus would be in excess of the actual
quantity of employment of q_a). Thus there will be workers prepared to accept less
than the going wage, and it is clearly to the employer's advantage to hire them at
some lower rate. Thus, unions can be successful in perfectly competitive industries
only when they are able strictly to enforce the union wage on workers and employers,
and to resist wage-cutting pressure from workers who cannot get work at the union
rate. The history of attempts to unionize American migrant fruit pickers and other
workers in competitive labour markets shows that these predictions are frequently
borne out in practice.

> **A union entering a perfectly competitive labour market can raise the
> wage above the free-market level but only at the cost of lowering the
> amount of employment. The new wage will create an excess supply of
> labour at the going rate and consequent pressure for wage-cutting that
> the union must be powerful enough to resist, if it is to be successful in
> holding wages up.**

Labour purchased monopsonistically

We now consider the effects of introducing a union into the labour market illustrated
in Figure 28.2. This will give us the surprising prediction that the union can raise
wages by a substantial margin and at the same time raise the volume of employment!
The analysis is just a little tricky and we shall take it in two steps.

As a first step we consider the effect on the supply curve (i.e., the average cost
curve) and the marginal cost curve of labour when the union enforces some wage on
the market. This creates a perfectly elastic supply curve up to the point at which the
union wage cuts the supply curve. In Figure 28.4 we have copied the S and MC curves
for labour from Figure 28.2. Assuming that the union wage is w_1, the supply curve for
labour now becomes $w_1 xS$. Up to an employment of q_1 the marginal cost curve is also
$w_1 x$ (since the wage rate is constant, the marginal cost of the extra worker is only the
wage that must be paid to him). We now assume, however, that if the employer wants
more than q_1 of labour he can obtain it by paying everyone a wage in excess of the

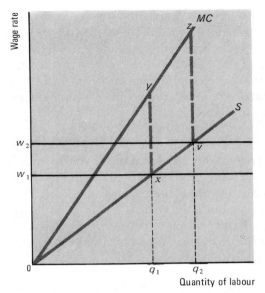

Fig. 28.4 The effect of a union determined wage on the average and marginal cost curves of labour

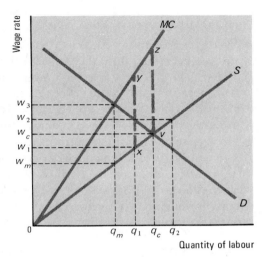

Fig. 28.5 The effect on wages and employment of the entry of a union into a monopsonistic labour market

union wage – to which the union will have no objection. The supply curve now is w_1xS: it has a kink at x. The marginal cost of labour jumps from x to y (i.e., it has a discontinuity at q_1) and thereafter becomes yMC. This is easily seen by the fact that once the employer is operating on the segment xS of the supply curve the existence of the union minimum wage w_1 is irrelevant to him (because he is already paying more than that), and so his situation is exactly the same as if a union had not existed, i.e., S is the supply curve of labour that he faces and MC is its marginal cost curve. If, to take one more example, the union negotiates a new minimum wage of w_2, the supply curve becomes w_2vS and the marginal cost curve becomes w_2vzMC with a discontinuous jump at an employment level of q_2.

We are now in a position to analyse the effects of the entry of a union into a market in which labour is purchased by a single buyer. In Figure 28.5 the curves S, MC and D are reproduced from Figure 28.2. The wage and employment level without a union are w_m and q_m. Now assume that the union negotiates a wage of w_1. This creates a supply curve of w_1xS and a marginal cost curve of w_1xyMC. The monopsonistic purchaser of labour will now be in equilibrium at employment q_1 since for levels of employment up to q_1 the marginal cost of labour is less than the marginal revenue product, while for levels above q_1 the reverse is true. The union has raised both wages and employment! The reason for this result is that before the entry of the union, the employer kept employment down because he was aware of the fact that as he increased employment he forced up the wage that he must pay to those already employed; but the introduction of the union wage faces him with a perfectly elastic supply curve so that there is no point in holding employment low for fear of driving up the wage that must be paid to everyone.

The maximum level of employment q_c is reached at a negotiated wage of w_c, which duplicates the perfectly competitive result. Here the supply curve is $w_c vS$ and the MC curve $w_c vzMC$. Above this wage a conflict emerges between wages and employment, with further wage increases being obtained at the cost of lowered employment. The wage w_2, for example, is associated with the same employment as is the wage w_1. Note, however, that until the wage is raised as high as w_3 the volume of employment is higher than it was before the union was introduced.

Also note that up to the wage w_c there is no excess supply of labour. At w_1, for example, q_1 of labour is supplied and q_1 is employed. Only when the wage passes the competitive level of w_c does an excess supply of labour appear. Thus there is a range w_m to w_c over which the union can raise both wages and employment, and also not create a surplus of labour anxious to work at less than the union rate. There is a further range, w_c to w_3, over which both wages and employment can be raised over what they were in the absence of the union, but over which an excess supply of labour occurs, forcing the union to resist a downward pressure on wages exerted by the unsatisfied group. For example at a wage of w_2 the excess supply is $q_2 - q_1$.

> **A trade union entering a monopsonistic market will have a range over which it can raise wages and employment without creating a surplus of labourers who would like to work at the going rate. There will be a further range over which it can raise both wages and employment above the level existing in the absence of the union but at the cost of creating an excess supply of labour.**

So far we have dealt with the simple case of a union that fixes a wage and allows employment to be determined by demand. Other methods of raising wages are available, and unions also have other goals in addition to that of raising wages. Before we consider these further we shall embark on a slight digression to fill in a few necessary institutional and historical details about the labour market. In the process of doing this we will be able to use the theory already developed to understand the reasons for some of the events that have occurred in the past and some of the institutions that have finally emerged.

LABOUR MARKET INSTITUTIONS

(1) POTENTIAL MONOPSONISTS: FIRMS AND EMPLOYERS' ASSOCIATIONS: The large firm has some degree of monopsony power by virtue of its size and the number of employees that it hires. It recognizes that its actions affect the wage rate, especially the rates received by those kinds of labour that are in some way limited to the industry in which the firm operates. Employers' associations are groups of employers who band together for the purpose of adopting a common policy in labour negotiations. This allows a group of firms to achieve the same result as could be obtained by a single monopsonistic buyer of labour.

(2) POTENTIAL MONOPOLISTS: UNIONS: A union is many things: a social club, an educational instrument, a political club, a bargaining agent for an individual worker, and, to some, a way of life. For the purposes of our discussion of labour markets, a

union (or trade union, or labour union) is an association of individual workers that speaks for them in negotiations with their employers.

Unions today have two different principles of organization: the trade (or craft) unions, in which workers with a common set of skills are joined in a common association, no matter where or for whom they work, and industrial unions, in which all workers in a given plant or a given industry are collected into a single union, whatever their skills.

Industrial unions became common in the United States with the rise in the 1930s of the Congress of Industrial Organizations (CIO). Among the prominent industrial unions in the US are the United Auto Workers and the Steel Workers Unions. The existence of these industrial unions means that the great automobile and steel companies have only one union with which to deal. A single agreement over wages, working conditions or union practices is sufficient to change the situation throughout the entire firm.

A single union covering an entire industry is less common in the UK and in many other countries than in the US. When the employer has to deal with many unions, and twenty or more unions are not uncommon within a single firm in the UK, agreement between labour and management can be very hard to reach and sometimes *jurisdictional disputes* break out over which union is to be responsible for which jobs. An experienced observer of the British industrial scene has said: 'On occasion, new capital instruments have been inadequately used, and production has been held up by disputes among rival unions about the types of workers to be employed on new operations or new materials. The shipbuilding, printing and building industries have provided examples of this obstruction.'[1]

Of course, such jurisdictional disputes may merely reflect power struggles between the managements of various unions. They do, however, have at least one substantial economic cause and this lies in forces that we have already studied. In situations in which unions are holding wages in a particular occupation above their competitive level, we have seen that there will be an excess supply of labour at the going wage rate. Since more people would like to work in the occupation than can do so, both the union leaders and the rank and file will be acutely aware of the trade off between wages and unemployment, and of the possibility that some workers who are currently employed may find themselves without work. (This does not mean, of course, that they must become permanently unemployed but only that they must move to less remunerative occupations). In terms of Figure 28.3, if the union shown loses a jurisdictional dispute, the demand curve for its members shifts to the left and the excess supply rises, while, if the union wins the dispute, the demand curve shifts to the right and the excess supply diminishes.

Such problems could not arise if the wage were set so that quantity demanded equalled that supplied, but, whenever the wage is such that excess supply develops, then the outcome of jurisdictional disputes genuinely affects the employment opportunities and the amount of downward pressure on the wage rate exerted by unsatisfied suppliers of labour in a particular occupation. Clearly, however undesirable the

1 G.C. Allen, *The Structure of British Industry* (Longmans, 2nd edition, 1966), page 170. Such disputes possibly receive a degree of publicity out of proportion to their actual harmful effect on the economy.

consequences of such disputes might be, the caricature of them as Alice-in-Wonder-land people acting like children and squabbling about trivia is wide of the mark. Economic analysis predicts that there are general situations in which matters of very real importance to the welfare of the participants are involved in jurisdictional disputes.

(3) KINDS OF BARGAINING ARRANGEMENTS: OPEN, CLOSED AND UNION SHOPS: In an open shop, a union represents its members, but does not have exclusive bargaining jurisdiction for all the workers of one kind. Membership in the union is not a condition of getting or keeping a job. Unions usually oppose such an arrangement and economic theory explains why they do so. Consider an open-shop bargaining situation. If, on the one hand, the employer accedes to union demands, the nonmembers achieve the benefits of the union without paying dues or sharing the risks or responsibilities. If, on the other hand, the employer chooses to fight the union, he can run his plant with the nonunion members, thus weakening the power of the union members in the fight.

Now consider what will happen if the union does succeed in obtaining a wage above the competitive level. We have already seen that, when wages exceed the competitive level, there arises an excess supply of labour *willing to work at less than the union wage* (see page 378). If there is an open shop there is nothing to prevent these workers from accepting a wage below the union wage and thus undermining the union's power to maintain high wages. If it is necessary for all workers to join the union, then the union can prevent its members from accepting less than the union wage, and so have the power to maintain high wages in spite of the existence of excess supply. Positive economics cannot, of course, tell us whether to approve or disapprove of such practices but it can help us to understand them. The desire to avoid the open shop leads to two other arrangements, the *closed shop* and the *union shop*.

In a closed shop, only union members may be employed and the union controls its membership however it sees fit. Employers sometimes regard this as an unwarranted limitation on their right to choose their employees. This often leads to the compromise solution of the union shop. In a union shop, the employer may hire anyone he chooses, but every employee must join the union within a specified period. This leaves the employer free to hire those individuals whom he wishes to hire, but gives the union the power to enforce its union wage since union members can be prevented from accepting employment below that wage.

(4) WEAPONS OF CONFLICT: STRIKES, PICKET LINES, STRIKE BREAKERS, LOCK OUTS, BLACK LISTS: The strike is the union's ultimate weapon. It consists in the concerted refusal to work of the members of the union. It is the strike or the threat of a strike that backs up the union's demands in the bargaining process. Picket lines are made up of striking workers who parade before the entrance to their plant or firm. Other union members will not often 'cross' a picket line. This means that if bricklayers strike against a construction firm, carpenters may not work on the project although they may have no grievance against the firm, nor will any lorry driver deliver supplies to a picketed site. Pickets represent an enormous increase in the

bargaining power of a small union. (Much of the very strong feeling expressed by employers against jurisdictional disputes arises from the fact that an employer may be unable to settle with *either* union without facing a picket line from the other, and that a picket line from either may be sufficient to bring his entire plant to a stop.) The lock-out is the employer's equivalent of the strike. By closing his plant, he locks out the workers until such time as the dispute is settled. Strike breakers are workers who are used by management to operate the plant while union members are on strike. A black list is an employer's list of workers who have been discharged for union activities, and who are not supposed to be given jobs by other employers. All of these employers' weapons are much less commonly used today than in the past, and the modern employer relies mainly on his organization's skill at the bargaining table and its resources to withstand a strike as his main weapons in resisting union demands.

(5) COLLECTIVE BARGAINING: This term is used to describe the whole process by which unions and employers (or their representatives) arrive at and enforce agreement. It usually describes a situation of bilateral monopoly in which there is one seller, the union, and one buyer, either a single firm or an employers' association.

The basic difference between collective bargaining and the theoretical analysis with which we began this chapter, is that in collective bargaining both sides must agree to the wage, while in our analysis we assumed that the union set a wage and the employer decided how much labour to buy at that wage. In collective bargaining there is always a substantial range over which an agreement can be reached and in particular cases the actual range will depend on the goals of the two bargaining parties. Thus, economic theory does not predict a precise outcome to the collective bargaining process. By analysing the effects on unions and management it can, however, isolate some of the economic factors that will strongly influence the final bargain but, as in oligopolistic competition between firms (see Chapter 22), the outcome will be significantly influenced by such political factors as skill in bargaining, ability to bluff and such psychological factors as one side's assessment of the reaction of the other side to its own moves. (For example, the employers will ask 'How much can we resist without provoking the unions into calling a costly strike?' and the unions will ask 'Will the employers force us to strike only for a token period so they can tell their shareholders they *tried* to resist, or do they think this is a really serious matter so that they intend to hold out to the bitter end against any strike that we might call?'). It is just because bilateral monopoly admits of more than one acceptable economic solution that these non economic factors become so important.

The evolution of the modern union

Unionism today is both stable and fairly widely accepted. It was not always so. No more than 80 years ago unions were fighting for their lives, and union organizers and members were risking theirs.

Trade unionism had its origin in the pitifully low standard of living of the average nineteenth-century worker and his family. Much of the explanation of the low standard of living throughout the world lay in the small size of the total national output relative to the population. Even in the wealthiest of countries, an equal division of national income among all families in 1800 would have left them all in poverty by our present standards.

Poverty had existed for centuries. It was accentuated, however, by the twin processes of urbanization and industrialization. The man who was moderately content working his land, usually became restive and discontented when he moved into a grimy, smoky, nineteenth-century city, took employment in a sweatshop or a factory, and settled with his family in a crowded, insanitary slum. Of course many of them moved because they had no choice, having been driven off their land by the enclosure movements. Thus, we cannot assume that they made a free choice in the belief that the urban life was preferable to their former rural one. Their rural life had been destroyed and the urban life was preferable to their new rural situation of probable starvation, but not necessarily superior to their original rural condition.

Stories of the workers' very real suffering during the industrial revolution could fill many volumes, but an example will at least illustrate some of the real horrors that lay behind the drive for change and reform.

In the cotton-spinning work, these creatures [the workers] are kept, fourteen hours in each day, locked up, summer and winter, in a heat of from *eighty to eighty-four degrees*. The rules which they are subject to are such as no negroes [i.e., slaves] were ever subjected to. ... The door of the place wherein they work, is *locked, except half an hour*, at tea-time, the work-people are not allowed to send for water to drink, in the hot factory; even *the rain water is locked up*, by the master's order. ... If any spinner be found with his *window open*, he is to pay a fine of a shilling! ... for a large part of the time, there is the abominable and pernicious stink of the *gas* to assist in the murderous effects of the heat. ... the notorious fact is, that well constituted men are rendered old and past labour at forty years of age, and that children are rendered decrepit and deformed, and thousands upon thousands of them slaughtered by consumption [tuberculosis], before they arrive at the age of sixteen. ...[1]

Out of these conditions came the full range of radical political movements from revolutionary socialism, which today we call Marxism or Communism, to Fabian socialism, which tried to effect change gradually through existing political systems. Out of them also came the union which was to some extent a club providing some protection for those workers who were unemployed, disabled or retired, and to some extent a bargaining agent. Unions were for a long time resisted by the full power of both the employers and the central authorities.

The union organizers perceived that ten or a hundred men acting together had more influence than one acting alone. The union was the organization that would provide a basis for confronting the monopsony power of employers with the collective (i.e., monopoly) power of the workers. But it was easier to see the solution than to achieve it. Organizations of workers would hurt employers and they did not accept them passively. Agitators who tried to organize other workers were often dismissed and black-listed, and in some cases they were physically assaulted or even killed.

1 William Cobbett, *Political Register*, vol. LII, 20 November 1824, as quoted by E. Royston Pike, *Human Documents of the Industrial Revolution in Britain* (Allen & Unwin, 1966), pages 60–61. This fascinating book chronicles some of the most common horrors of the nineteenth-century industrial revolution. Every student of society should spend at least one evening browsing its pages. When he is finished he should have little trouble understanding the militant reforming attitudes of early Marxists and trade unionists. Whatever he may think of the solution offered by the Marxists he will hardly be able to doubt that they were trying to deal with, rather than to ignore as so many others did, a very real human problem.

Requirements of a successful union

In order to realize the ambition of creating some effective power over the labour market it was necessary to gain control of the supply of labour and to have the financial resources necessary to outlast the employer in a struggle for strength. There was no 'right to organize', and the union had to force a usually hostile employer to negotiate with it. Since early unions did not usually have large resources, it was necessary to attack on the front where the employer was weakest.

All of these considerations explain why it was unions of the highly skilled and specialist types of labour, that first met with any success, and the previous discussion can be summarized into two main reasons for this. First, it was easier to control the supply of skilled rather than unskilled workers. Organize the unskilled or the semi-skilled and the employer could find replacements for them. But the skilled workers – the coopers, the bootmakers, the shipwrights – were another matter. There were few of them, and they controlled the access to their trade by controlling the conditions of apprenticeship. The original unions were in effect closed shops: one had to belong to the union to hold a job, and the union set the rules of admission. The second main reason was that a union of a small number of highly skilled specialists could attack the employer where he was most likely to give in, and thus would need fewer resources to withstand employer resistance than would be needed by unions of the unskilled. In Chapter 26 (page 353) we discussed the determinants of the elasticity of demand for a factor. A particular skilled occupation is very difficult to dispense with in an industrial process, so that other factors cannot easily be substituted for it. Also labour in a particular skilled occupation is likely to account for a relatively low proportion of total costs, so that the effects on the employers' overall costs of giving in to a demand for a wage increase of, say 20 per cent, would be much less than the effects of giving in to an equivalent demand from the very numerous unskilled workers. Thus a low ability to substitute other factors plus a small contribution to total costs combined to give the unions of skilled workers an advantage in fighting the employer, not enjoyed by other groups (see note 1, page 352). Thus there are good theoretical reasons that help us to understand why the union movement showed its first real power in the sectors of small groups of relatively skilled workers.

Even in such cases unions had their ups and downs. When employment was full and business booming, the cost of being fired for joining a union was not so great, for there were other jobs. During periods of depression and unemployment, however, the risks were greater. The individual worker knew that other unemployed members of his trade would be there to take his job if he caused trouble. Slowly during the course of the nineteenth century unions grew in size and power but not at a steady pace. A clear cyclical swing in membership is observable with gains in periods of prosperity, and setbacks in periods of business depression. By the interwar period the union had established itself as an integral part of the industrial scene.

THE METHODS AND THE OBJECTIVES OF THE MODERN UNION
Wages

Unions are to a great extent interested in the wages obtained by their members. At the beginning of this chapter we considered the case of a union that could set the wage rate but had to take the supply of labour as given, and let the employer decide how many workers to employ at the union wage rate. Unions can also attempt to influence both of these variables that we first took to be outside their control. In this section we shall consider the supply of labour to a particular occupation or industry. An alternative to setting the wage and letting that determine the quantity of labour provided, is to try to determine the quantity of labour supplied and then let the wage be that which equates demand and supply. This is illustrated in Figure 28.6, which for

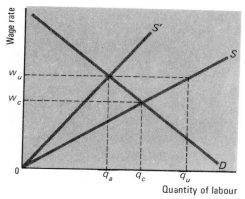

Fig. 28.6 An increase in wages caused by an entry restriction into a particular labour market

simplicity describes a labour market that would be perfectly competitive in the absence of the union. The union can raise its wage above the perfectly competitive level, w_c, by two alternative policies. First, as already analysed, it can negotiate a wage of w_u and let the volume of employment fall from q_c to q_a and allow there to develop an excess supply of labour of $q_u - q_a$. The second policy is to restrict entry into the occupation by any one of a number of possible methods, such as lengthening apprenticeship periods, rationing places for trainees, etc. Such tactics will make it more expensive, or otherwise more difficult to enter the occupation. Thus, at any given wage rate, the quantity supplied will be reduced; the supply curve shifts to the left, and if it is shifted to S', the wage w_u emerges from the competitive market without the union having to intervene in the process of wage setting. Furthermore, there is no excess supply at w_u since the supply curve has been shifted. Thus, there is no wage-reducing pressure from unemployed persons who are trained for the occupation but unable to find jobs.

Which of the two tactics will appeal to a particular union will depend on many factors, such as the ease with which supply can be restricted, the ease with which union wages can be negotiated and enforced, and the public's reaction to these two tactics in particular situations. As an example of the force of the last consideration we can examine the case of doctors in countries such as the United States where medical services are not nationalized. It is inconceivable that the public or the central authorities would accept a situation in which doctors raised the price of their services above the competitive level by collective agreement and then allowed an unemployed surplus of doctors to develop. So many people clearly need more medical services than they get, that the existence of any substantial amount of unemployed medical talent would be very unlikely to be tolerated. Thus, doctors are forced back on the second alternative, which produces the same result, but by more socially acceptable methods. They raise training periods and training costs and restrict entry into medical schools. By these and other tactics they shift the supply curve of qualified doctors to the left. If they shift it to S' in Figure 28.6, they give themselves the same wage as if they had left the supply curve at S and regulated the wage at w_u, but they avoid what would be a very embarrassing surplus of unemployed doctors. In both cases the actual supply of doctors to the public is less (by $q_c q_a$) than it would have been under competitive conditions.[1]

Wages versus employment

We have already seen that in many situations the union faces a trade-off between wages and employment: an increase in wages can only be obtained at the cost of lowered employment. In some cases it is possible to avoid this conflict by bargaining with the employer about *both* wages and employment. The rise of the guaranteed-annual-wage type of agreement in the US in recent years represents an attempt to

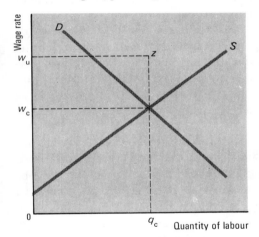

Fig. 28.7 The effect of bargaining for both the wage rate and the volume of employment

do just this. This situation is illustrated by point z in Figure 28.7. The demand curve shows for each wage rate the amount of labour the employer would like to hire. But he may prefer to hire some other amount rather than to go without labour altogether. When wages are w_c and employment is q_c the union might offer the employers the alternative of employing q_c labour, at a wage of w_u or of facing a strike. If the employer accepts the former alternative, then he will move to point z, which is off his demand curve. In this case, the union raises the per capita wages and total real earnings of its members without causing any reduction in employment. The union's success in pursuing such a policy will probably depend on the size of the profits in the industry (i.e., on the extent to which the industry departs from the perfectly competitive equilibrium), and also on the state of the market, which will determine the

1 Of course, some of the high standards for entry into the medical profession are needed to protect the public from incompetent doctors, but most investigators have concluded that restrictions on entry are much greater than they need to be and serve partly the function analysed in the text.

relation between the losses resulting from hiring more than the desired quantity of labour at the agreed wage rate, and the expected losses resulting from a strike.

Wages versus job security

Unions vary greatly in the extent to which they adopt a defensive or an offensive attitude to the labour market. The people who were in their twenties during the Great Depression of the 1930s until recently dominated the leadership of unions, management and government. Not surprisingly, the labouring members of this age group have been strongly conditioned to a defensive attitude to jobs. They lived through a period when unemployment never fell below 20 per cent of the labour force as a national average, and when it was over 50 per cent in many of the hardest-hit areas. They saw people grow up, marry and raise children on the dole. They saw young people who were eager to work but were totally unable to find any form of employment, slowly have their spirit broken as they had to confess their failure to wives and children. They suffered the humiliation of being read lessons on hard work, thrift and patience by a London-based middle-class bureaucracy that had not itself had direct experience of unemployment. When occasionally they rose up in a general strike or a hunger march the troops were called out against them.

In such a situation of mass unemployment the installation of a new machine in a factory that removed someone's job condemned the job holder to a possibly indefinite future of existence on the dole. It is little wonder that new machines and rationalization that might reduce costs by removing jobs were opposed bitterly, and that job-saving restrictive practices were adhered to with tenacity. In a period of heavy unemployment technological change is likely to mean unemployment for those whose jobs are lost by the change.

The defensive attitude which was so understandable in the 1930s survived (not surprisingly) into the post-war period in which circumstances were very different. The post-war period was a time of full employment and a time in which new jobs were available to replace old ones that were destroyed by technological change. In such a world the attitude of defending existing jobs at all costs made much less sense than in the 1930s. Furthermore sustained economic growth necessarily means change both in the techniques of production and in the pattern of demand, and the defence of all existing jobs is doomed to failure in such a changing world. Slowly over the last 30 years the attitude of some unions has changed from one of resisting technological change to one of collaborating with it, and of trying to reduce some of its costs to individuals who are adversely affected. The acceptance of such change can then be used as an offensive base from which to launch a concentrated attack for higher wages and better working conditions. We must never forget, however, that as long as people are alive who suffered through the 1930s, the heritage of the mismanagement of that period (see page 505) will leave a set of defensive attitudes which it is well to try to understand.

Unions and the structure of relative wages

So far we have considered the influence on the wages of its members of one particular union operating in a small section of the total labour market. Our theory predicts that a powerful union can in such circumstances raise the wages earned by its members, possibly at the expense of lowering the volume of employment. This prediction does seem to be supported by some substantial empirical evidence that unions do influence the structure of relative wages by raising wages in some industries and occupations, where they are particularly strong without there being a corresponding rise in wages elsewhere. For example, the American economist Albert Rees, one of the leading students of the influence of unionism on wages, concluded, 'I would say that perhaps a third of the trade unions have raised the wages of their members by 15 to 20 per cent above what they might be in a nonunion situation, another third by 5 per cent to 10 per cent, and the remaining third, not at all'.[1]

UNIONS AND THE FUNCTIONAL DISTRIBUTION OF INCOME

The functional distribution of income concerns the division of national income into such broad aggregates as wages, rent and profits (including the return to capital). A question in which trade unionists and many other observers have been interested for a very long time is: Are unions able to influence the share of total national income going to labour in general? In this case we are not interested in the power of one small union to raise the wages of its members, possibly at the expense of workers in less powerful situations; we are interested, rather, in the ability of unions to raise the earnings of labour in general at the expense of the earnings of land and capital. Much of the efforts of the early classical economists were directed towards developing a theory that would explain the functional distribution of income, and a great deal of the concern of early trade unionists was over increasing the share of total national income going to labour – helping one group of labourers at the expense of other groups would not have had nearly the general appeal as helping all the workers at the expense of the capitalists and the landowners. It may seem surprising that in spite of all this early, and continued interest, we cannot say very much about this question even now.

We have seen that we do have a well-developed, micro-market theory that allows us to predict the effect on relative wages of a particular intervention of a union, an employers' organization, or the central authorities in any one market. We do not, however, have an accepted theory of the overall distribution of national income, that allows us to predict the consequences of a particular intervention, such as the growth of trade unions, on the functional distribution of income.

To illustrate this problem let us consider the effect of trade union intervention to raise wages above their competitive level in all industries. The predictions for one industry are illustrated in Figure 28.3: the wage rate rises but employment falls. But if this occurs simultaneously in *all* industries we cannot apply the same analysis. The analysis of Figure 28.3 was based on demand curves which are in turn based on assumptions of other things being equal. If unions raise the wage rate of even a significant part of the labour force, they will cause incomes to change significantly; this will cause demand curves for consumers' goods to *shift*; this will cause outputs to vary; and this, in turn, will cause shifts in the derived demand curves for labour.

1 Albert Rees, *Wage Inflation* (National Industrial Conference Board, 1957).

Unless we have a theory of how each of these changes is related to the other, we cannot attempt to answer this question. In fact, there is no generally accepted, well-worked-out theory which would allow us to deal with it. Here then is a real challenge to the advanced student interested in questions of labour and income: to develop and test a theory which would shed light on this important question.

A study of Figure 28.8 may, however, make us a bit sceptical of the proposition that unions have had an enormous effect in shifting the distribution of income towards labour. If labour as a whole is to gain relative to other groups, its share of the total of national income must grow. The fact is, however, that the share of income going to labour has not shown any marked long-term tendency to increase as is shown in Figure 28.8.

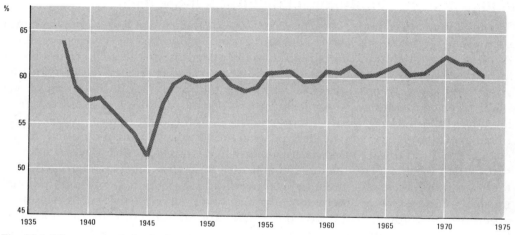

Fig. 28.8 Wages and salaries in the UK as a percentage of GNP, 1938–73

The economy is, as we have already observed, a complicated mechanism allowing for many reactions and interactions. The effect of any change on the whole system must necessarily be fairly complex, and in the absence of a well-tested theory we cannot be confident about the final outcome. Union power that seems so obvious and forceful to the lay observer is a case in point. There is little doubt that unions do have some significant influence on economic variables, but just where, and how much is something about which we cannot yet be dogmatic, however 'clear' it may seem to the outside observer.

29

Interest and the return on capital

One of the major components of the functional distribution of income is the return on capital. In this chapter we shall study this return and see how it is related to the rate of interest. Interest is the payment made for the use of money. An annual interest rate of 6 per cent means that one must pay 6p for the use of one £ of money for one year. One does not buy money; one hires its services and then returns it, and the interest rate is the price paid for those services.

THE PRODUCTIVITY OR EFFICIENCY OF CAPITAL

As a first step in our study we must notice the sense in which we can say that capital is productive. Most modern production techniques make extensive use of capital goods: instead of making all consumers' goods directly with the aid only of such simple tools as nature provides, productive effort goes into the manufacture of tools, machines and other goods that are not desired in themselves but only as an aid to making other goods. The use of capital goods renders production processes *roundabout*. Instead of making what we want directly, we engage in an indirect process: that of first making the goods that we need to use in making what we finally want.

In many cases, production is very roundabout indeed. For example, a worker may be employed in a factory making machines that are used in mining coal; the coal may be burned by a power plant to make electricity; the electricity may provide power for a factory that makes machine tools; the tools may be used to make a tractor; the tractor may be used by a potato farmer to help in the production of potatoes; and the potatoes may be eaten by a consumer. This kind of indirect production is worthwhile *if* the farmer using his tractor can produce more potatoes than could be produced if all the factors of production involved in the chain were applied directly to the production of potatoes (using only such tools as were provided by nature). In fact, the capital-using, roundabout method of production is very often more efficient than the direct method, and the difference between the flows of output that result from the two methods is a measure of the productivity of capital.

Of course, the extra output is not achieved without cost. Generally speaking, a decision to increase the amount of capital available entails a current sacrifice and a future gain. The current sacrifice occurs because resources are diverted from producing consumption goods to producing capital goods, and the future gain occurs because production is higher with the new capital than without it (even after allowing for maintenance of consumption goods and replacement of worn-out capital).

The rate of return on capital

Take the receipts from the sale of the goods produced by a firm and subtract the appropriate costs for purchased goods and materials, for labour, for depreciation and for the manager's own contributed talents. Subtract from this an allowance for the taxes the firm will have to pay, and what is left may be called the gross return to capital. To the businessman, this provides an amount with which to pay interest on borrowed capital, to pay dividends to the owners of the company, and to provide undistributed profit to reinvest in the firm.

We saw in Chapter 18 (page 217) that the economist finds it convenient to divide the gross return to capital into (1) the pure return on capital, which is the amount that capital could earn in riskless investment; (2) a risk premium, which compensates the owners for the actual risks of the enterprise; and (3) the economic profits.

Risk-taking and economic profits were discussed in detail in Chapter 18. Owners must be compensated for the risks they take in order to induce them to commit their capital to risky ventures; risk-taking is thus to be regarded as an input into the production process and payment for it a necessary (though imputed) cost. This is the second item in the above list.

Economic profits from the sale of a good are defined as the excess of revenues over the opportunity cost of *all* the resources required to produce the good. They provide a signal in a market system that additional resources could be efficiently employed in the production of the good. This is the third item in the above list.

The first item listed above – the pure return to capital – is an element of cost and requires more extensive discussion. What determines its size? Why is it high in some time periods and low in others? What causes it to change?

In discussing such questions, it is usual to deal not with the total return on capital, but with a rate of return *per unit* of capital employed. This concept requires placing a money value on a unit of capital (the 'price of capital goods') and a current money value on the stream of earnings that the productivity of capital leads to. If we let X stand for the current annual value of the productivity of a unit of capital, and P for the price of the capital good, the ratio X/P may be defined as the rate of return on capital. As a preliminary to understanding the determinants of the rate of return on capital, we must define two key concepts: the marginal efficiency of capital and present value.

The marginal efficiency of capital

It is convenient to think of society as having a stock of capital, often referred to as that society's CAPITAL STOCK, that can be given a single value.[1] If this stock of capital is increased in a fully employed economy, the productivity of capital is predicted to change. The rate of return on the last unit of capital employed is called the marginal efficiency of capital (MEC). A schedule that relates the return on each additional unit of capital stock to the size of the capital stock is called the marginal-efficiency-of-capital schedule.

The MEC schedule is constructed on the assumptions that the population is fixed and that technology is unchanging. This allows us to focus on the effect of changes in the quantity of capital, other things remaining constant. As more and more capital is accumulated with given technical knowledge and a constant population, the ratio of capital to labour increases. This is called CAPITAL DEEPENING. To see why this must occur, consider the difference between a single firm and the whole economy.

When a single firm wants to expand its output it can buy another piece of land, build a factory identical to the one it has now, and hire new labour to operate it. In this way, the firm is able to replicate what it already has. Each worker in the new factory can have the same amount of capital as each worker in the old factory, and output per worker and per unit of capital can remain unchanged. Increasing the quantity of capital without changing the proportions of factors used is called CAPITAL WIDENING. For the economy as a whole, this is possible only as long as there are unemployed quantities of all factors of production. The additional workers, for example, must be drawn from somewhere; and in a fully employed economy, what one small firm can do the whole economy cannot do. If the size of the capital stock is to increase while the total labour force remains constant, the amount of capital per worker must increase. This means that more capital-intensive methods of production will have to be adopted, that is, capital deepening must occur.

As long as capital deepening is productive the marginal efficiency of capital will be positive. But capital is assumed to be subject to diminishing returns, just as are all other factors of production. As more and more capital is employed, the output per unit of capital will fall because each unit of capital is combined with fewer and fewer units of labour. As more and more capital-intensive methods are used, marginal product declines, and thus any MEC schedule when plotted graphically is downward-sloping. An example is illustrated in Figure 29.1.

THE PRESENT VALUE OF FUTURE INCOME

How is the productivity of capital related to the price of capital? Because the productivity of capital takes the form of producing a *future* flow of output, it is necessary in answering this question to decide what value to place on income that is to be received at some time in the future.

The value of a single future payment

Let us assume, for purposes of illustration, that the rate of interest on a perfectly safe

---

1 The idea of a stock of capital being measured by a single number is a simplification. Society's stock of capital goods is made up of a diverse bundle of factories, machines, bridges, roads and other man-made aids to further production. For expository purposes, it is useful to make the heroic assumption that all of these can be reduced to some common unit and summed to obtain a measure of the society's *physical* stock of capital.

loan is 5 per cent and then ask three separate questions. (1) *How much money would you have to invest today if you wished to have £100 in one year's time?* Letting X stand for this amount we have: $X(1 \cdot 05) = £100$. Or $X = £100/1 \cdot 05 = £95 \cdot 24$. What this tells us is that if you lend out £95·24 today at 5 per cent interest you will receive £100 a year from now (£95·24 as repayment of the principal of the loan and £4·76 as interest). (2) *What is the maximum amount you would be prepared to pay now to acquire the right to £100 in cash in one year's time?* Surely this is £95·24. If you paid more you would be losing money since you can loan out £95·24 at 5 per cent and receive £100 in a year's time. If you could buy the right to £100 cash for anything less than £95·24 it would be profitable to do so since you could borrow £95·24 now in return for your promise to repay £100 one year from now.[1] (3) *What is the most you could borrow today in return for your promise to repay £100 a year from now?* If lenders were perfectly certain you would meet your promise, they would lend you £95·24. No one would lend you any more since the lender has the option of lending his or her money elsewhere at 5 per cent. If you offered to take less (say £90) then everyone would rush to lend you money since lending to you would yield more than the going rate of return on safe loans of 5 per cent.

These three questions can be reduced to one question: 'How much money now is equivalent to £100 payable for certain a year from now when the interest rate on perfectly safe loans is 5 per cent?' This sum is called the present value of £100 a year from now at a 5 per cent interest rate. In general PRESENT VALUE (PV) refers to the value now of payments to be received in the future. The present value clearly depends on the rate of interest that is used in the calculation. When a future sum is turned into its equivalent present value we say that sum is DISCOUNTED. Discounting always takes place at some particular rate of interest.

Of course the numerical example given above depended on the 5 per cent interest rate that was chosen to illustrate the calculations. If the interest rate is 7 per cent, the present value of the £100 receivable next year is £100/1·07 = £93·45. In general, the present value of X pounds one year hence at an interest rate of i per cent per year is

$$PV = \frac{X}{(1 + i)}.$$

Now consider what would happen if the payment date is further away than one year. If we lend £X at 5 per cent for one year we will be paid £$(1 \cdot 05)X$. But if we immediately relend that whole amount, we would get back at the end of the second year an amount equal to 1·05 *times* the amount lent out, i.e. £$(1 \cdot 05)(1 \cdot 05)X$. Thus £100 payable two years hence has a present value (at 5 per cent) of

$$\frac{£100 \cdot 00}{(1 \cdot 05)(1 \cdot 05)} = £90 \cdot 70.$$

---

1 Suppose, for example, you were offered the right to £100 a year from now for £90 now. If the market rate of interest is 5 per cent, you could borrow £95·24 now, buy the right to £100 next year for £90 and pocket £5·24 as your profit. Next year you claim the £100 which is just enough to repay the loan of £95·24 plus interest (at 5 per cent) of £4·76.

The amount of £90·70 lent out now with the interest that is paid at the end of the first year lent out for the second year would yield £100 in two years.[1] In general, we may write, for the present value of £X after t years at i per cent,

$$PV = \frac{X}{(1+i)^t}.$$

The present value of a given sum payable in the future will be smaller the further away the payment date and the higher the rate of interest.

THE VALUE OF AN INFINITE STREAM OF PAYMENTS: So much for a single sum payable in the future; now consider the present value of a stream of income that continues indefinitely. While at first glance that might seem very high since as time passes the total received grows without reaching any limit, considerations of the previous section suggests that one will not value highly the far distant payments. To find the present value of £100 a year, payable forever, we need only ask how much money would have to be invested now at an interest rate of i per cent per year to obtain £100 each year. This is simply $i \times X = £100$, where i is the interest rate and X the sum required. This tells us that the present value of the stream of £100 a year forever is

$$PV = \frac{£100}{i}.$$

If the interest rate were 10 per cent, the present value would be £1,000, which merely says that £1,000 invested at 10 per cent would yield £100 per year, forever. Notice that here, as above, PV is *inversely* related to the rate of interest: the higher the interest rate, the less is the (present) value of distant payments.

THE VALUE OF A FINITE STREAM OF INCOME: It is also possible to obtain the present value of some finite stream of income and then convert it into an *equivalent* infinite stream. This is of considerable theoretical value, since we can always deal with the equivalent infinite stream, even if the problem we are considering concerns a finite stream. Consider, for example, a machine that yields the following stream of income, £100 now, £275 in one year's time, £242 in 2 years, £133·10 in 3 years, £87·84 in four years and nothing thereafter. The present value of this flow of income, when the market rate of interest is 10 per cent, is

$$PV = £100 + \frac{£275}{1·1} + \frac{£242}{(1·1)^2} + \frac{£133·10}{(1·1)^3} + \frac{£87·84}{(1·1)^4}$$

$$= £100 + £250 + £200 + £100 + £60$$

$$= £710.$$

But £710 invested at 10 per cent interest will yield a flow of £71 per annum in perpetuity. Thus the irregular finite flow listed above is equivalent to, i.e., it has the same present value as, the smooth flow of £71 forever. Thus, in any practical problem concerning an irregular flow we can substitute the equivalent regular flow, which can be handled with much greater ease.

---

1 Readers familiar with this type of calculation will realize that the argument in the text is based on an annual compounding of interest.

The value of an asset

Now consider how to determine the market value of an asset that produces a stream of valuable services. The asset might be a piece of land, a machine, a slave or a block of flats. We saw in Chapter 27 that the market conditions of demand and supply will determine the price of the asset's output. This allows us to convert the stream of output into a stream of money. We saw in the previous section of this chapter how to calculate the present value of a future stream of income, and it only remains to make the obvious point that the equilibrium market price of an asset will be equal to the present value of the stream of income, conferred by ownership of the asset. Thus the present value of a machine that produces the equivalent of £100 a year net income indefinitely is £2,000 if the appropriate rate of interest is 5 per cent, because £2,000 invested at 5 per cent per year would yield £100 a year, and it would pay anyone with money to invest to buy the machine for any price up to and including £2,000. (Of course the machine will not produce income indefinitely, but we are making use of the result in the previous section that for any finite, and possibly irregular, stream of income actually produced by the machine there will be an equivalent constant, infinite stream.) If the price were less than £2,000 everyone would be eager to buy the machine and its price would rise. On the other hand, if the price were more than £2,000, say £2,500, it would not pay anyone to buy the machine. If it was bought with borrowed money, the purchaser would have to pay £125 a year to borrow the money necessary to purchase an asset that would yield only £100. If it were bought with the purchaser's own money, the purchaser could have lent the £2,500 out at the going rate of interest and earned £125 a year rather than buying the machine and getting only £100. Thus no one would be willing to buy the machine and its price would fall. The only price at which people would be prepared to both buy and sell the machine is £2,000.

In general, if the market price of any asset is greater than the present value of the income stream it produces no one will want to buy the asset, while if the market price is below its present value everyone will want to buy it. Thus,

> **in a competitive market the equilibrium price of any asset will be the present value of the income stream produced by the asset.**

When we obtain the present value of any asset that yields a stream of future income, we speak of *discounting the future income stream* to get the CAPITALIZED VALUE of the asset. This capitalized value of the asset is nothing other than the present value of the stream of income that is yielded by the asset.[1]

A SIMPLE THEORY OF THE RELATION BETWEEN INTEREST AND THE RETURN ON CAPITAL

Given the concepts just developed, we can now outline a simple theory that relates

---

1 A major problem in arriving at the present value of a future stream of money income is to decide on the appropriate interest rate to use in discounting the future stream. If the firm can borrow as much money as it wants at i per cent per year, it should discount at i per cent per year. If the firm is subjected to credit rationing, its internal rate of return on an extra £ invested may be substantially above the market rate of interest. In this case the firm should discount at its own opportunity cost of capital. The general principle is that the rate of discount should reflect the genuine opportunity cost of capital to the firm.

the *MEC* to the rate of interest. It is helpful to begin with the behaviour of an individual firm.

The demand for capital by a firm

Suppose that for £8,000 a firm can purchase a machine that yields £1,000 a year net of all costs into the indefinite future. Also suppose that the firm can borrow (and lend) money at an interest rate of 10 per cent. The present value of the stream of income produced by the machine (the capitalized value of the machine) is £1,000/$0.10 = $£10,000; the present value of £8,000 now is (of course) £8,000. Clearly, the firm can make money by purchasing the machine. Another way to see this is to suppose that the only uses a firm has for its money are to buy the machine or to lend out its £8,000 at 10 per cent interest. Buying the machine is the superior alternative since this yields £1,000 per annum while lending out the £8,000 purchase price yields only £800 per annum.

In general, if X is the annual stream of net income produced by the machine, if P is its purchase price, and if i is the interest rate that correctly states the opportunity cost of capital to the firm, then the capital good should be purchased if

$$\frac{X}{i} > P.$$

The term X/i is the present value of the stream of income produced by the capital good or, in other words, the capitalized value of the asset.

> **It pays to purchase a capital good whenever the present value of its future stream of net income exceeds the purchase price of the capital good.**

This same relationship can be looked at in another way, by rearranging the terms in the algebraic inequality above:

$$\frac{X}{P} > i.$$

The expression X/P shows the annual net income produced by the capital good as a fraction of the price of the good, which we defined earlier as the rate of return on the capital. In this form the condition is restated to say:

> **It pays to purchase a capital good whenever its rate of return exceeds the interest rate that could be earned on the money invested in it.**

If the firm purchases all assets for which the rate of return is greater than the opportunity cost of capital, its equilibrium position will be where its rate of return, X/P, on the marginal asset purchased is just equal to the opportunity cost of its capital, i.

The equilibrium condition for the firm, $X/P = i$, indicates that the last (and least profitable) unit of capital purchased just covers the opportunity cost of the capital invested in it.[1]

1 This is, of course, a specialized form of the *MRP = price of the factor* condition developed on page 347. The marginal rate of return on capital is, in effect, the marginal revenue product of capital, and the interest rate is the price of capital.

The aggregate demand for the capital stock

The equilibrium condition just derived applies to every profit-maximizing firm and hence it applies to the economy as a whole. The society's *MEC* schedule relates the entire capital stock to the marginal return on another unit of capital. If the rate of interest, i, is below the *MEC everyone* will wish to borrow money and buy capital equipment. If the rate of interest is above the *MEC no one* will wish to do so. Thus equilibrium is only possible where $i = MEC$.

To see why this is the equilibrium condition, suppose that the society is in a position where the *MEC* is significantly greater than i. In such a situation it will pay investors to borrow funds at i per cent per year to acquire capital stock that will earn an amount in excess of i per cent per year. This, in turn, will tend to push the economy towards equilibrium either by increasing the capital stock, thus moving down the *MEC* schedule and decreasing the *MEC*, or by increasing interest rates, or by some of each.

These possibilities are illustrated in Figure 29.1. The marginal efficiency of capital is indicated by the *MEC* curve, and with the existing stock of capital at k_1, the marginal efficiency is m_1. If the current rate of interest is m_2, it will pay everyone to borrow money and invest it in capital equipment. This must be a state of dis-equilibrium. Equilibrium can be established by: (i) raising the capital stock to k_2 while holding the rate of interest constant at m_2, (ii) raising the rate of interest to m_1 while holding the capital stock constant at k_1 or (iii) any combination of increases in the interest rate and the capital stock which equates the marginal efficiency of capital and the rate of interest.

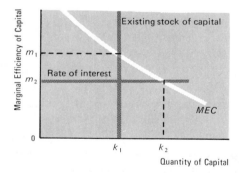

Fig. 29.1 In equilibrium the rate of interest is equal to the marginal efficiency of capital

To the extent that interest rates tend to be fixed within narrow limits, this simple theory tends to be a theory of the determination of the stock of capital. To the extent that the stock of capital tends to change only slowly, the simple theory tends to be a theory of the determination of interest rates. Generally, both interest rates and the stock of capital vary, and the relative ease and speed of the adjustment of capital stock and interest rates (and the elasticity of the *MEC* schedule) determine whether most of the adjustment falls on the interest rate or on the stock of capital.

One implication of this simple theory that has played an important role in economic debate is that in a world of static knowledge, the return on capital and the rate of interest is predicted to fall steadily as more capital is accumulated and society moves down its *MEC* schedule. This prediction, however, has not been borne out in the history of capitalist economies. Despite both capital accumulation and apparent capital deepening, there has been no such tendency for the rates of interest observed in capitalist economies to fall. One obvious explanation is that knowledge has not remained static; technological innovation has played a major role in determining the return on capital. Since it shifts the *MEC* schedule outwards it is possible for increasing amounts of capital not to result in a declining marginal efficiency.

THE SIMPLE THEORY AS A THEORY OF THE MARKET RATE OF INTEREST

The theory developed above predicts the mutual determination of the equilibrium *MEC*, the capital stock and the pure rate of interest. In equilibrium the *MEC* must equal the pure rate of interest. Any disequilibrium can be removed either by changing the capital stock (and hence the *MEC*) or by changing the rate of interest (or both). The capital stock is very large in relation to current investment and thus it changes slowly. For this reason the major adjustment to remove a disequilibrium will have to be in the rate of interest rather than in the *MEC*. Thus, the theory is sometimes described as a theory of the determination of the rate of interest. Within this theory, in order to explain variations in interest rates over time, one should look at those factors affecting the *MEC* schedule and those factors affecting the size of the capital stock.[1]

This pure rate of interest is not, however, the same thing as the market rate of interest, the rate actually paid to borrow money. To move from the pure to the market rate of interest a number of important assumptions that were either explicit or implicit in the previous discussion need to be relaxed.

Uncertainty

So far we have discussed the present value of a *certain* future stream of income. In reality uncertainty will be attached to (i) the physical stream of goods the capital will produce; (ii) the *value* of the stream of goods (i.e. the net income) the capital will produce; and (iii) the ability of a person who borrows money to invest in capital (or for any other purpose) to repay the loan.

THE PHYSICAL OUTPUT OF CAPITAL: Generally one can be fairly clear on the flow of goods one expects to gain from a piece of capital equipment. In these days of shortages of many raw materials and the possible outright exhaustion of others, however, some uncertainty must inevitably be attached to the flow of goods that the capital good will produce.

THE VALUE OF THE NET INCOME PRODUCED BY CAPITAL: Even if everyone were perfectly certain about the physical productivity of capital, great uncertainty would inevitably attach to the expected stream of net income associated with the capital good. Even in a world of full employment the prices of outputs and inputs fluctuate

1 A theory that determines the pure rate of interest also determines the price of a unit of capital since its price, *P*, equals its annual productivity divided by the rate of interest.

greatly. A favourable combination of changes, output prices up and input prices down, can greatly increase the net income produced by the capital good. An unfavourable combination can reduce net income or even eliminate it completely. In times of major depressions demand for consumers' goods declines drastically as unemployment rises. Even if capital is physically productive it can produce no stream of net income if the goods that it produces cannot be sold.

All of these uncertainties vary among firms and among industries. For an example of extreme variation between two firms in the same industry consider British Petroleum (BP) and a firm set up to drill a single wild cat oil well. For an example of variation between two industries consider an industry that produces a stable commodity such as milk and an industry that is subject to many varied uncertainties such as aircraft.

People investing their own money (e.g., by buying equities) in firms that are in high-risk industries will only do so if they expect a high yield from the capital their money will be used to purchase. People lending their money (e.g., by purchasing bonds) to firms in high-risk industries will only do so if they are offered a high rate of interest in return. For these reasons the return on capital and the rate of interest paid on borrowed money will differ among firms and industries.

The rate of interest will also differ systematically with the TERM (i.e. the duration) of the loan for reasons that are ultimately related to uncertainty. Borrowers are usually willing to pay more for long-term loans than for short-term loans because they are certain of having use of the money for a longer period. Lenders usually require a higher rate of interest the longer is the time before the borrower must repay because the risk element (will the borrower be able to repay? What will happen to the price level?) is larger the longer is the period of the loan. Thus, other things being equal, the shorter the term of a loan, the lower the interest rates.

Inflationary expectations

So far we have implicitly assumed a constant price level. In a world in which the purchasing power of money is constantly changing, it is necessary to distinguish between the real rate and the money rate of interest. The MONEY RATE OF INTEREST is measured simply in money paid. If you pay me £8 interest for a £100 loan for one year, the money rate is 8 per cent. The REAL RATE OF INTEREST concerns the ratio of the *purchasing power* of the money returned to the *purchasing power* of the money borrowed, and it may be different from the money rate.

Consider further my £100 loan to you at 8 per cent. The real rate that I earn depends on what happens to the overall level of prices in the economy. If the price level remains constant over the year, then the real rate that I earn is also 8 per cent. This is because I can buy 8 per cent more real goods and services with the £108 that you repay me than with the £100 I lent you. If, however, the price level were to rise by 8 per cent, the real rate would be nil because the £108 you repay me will buy the same quantity of real goods as did the £100 I gave up. If I were unlucky enough to have lent money at 8 per cent in a year in which prices rose by 10 per cent, the real rate would be minus 2 per cent.

The real rate of interest is the difference between the money rate of interest and the rate of change of the general price level.

In discussing the relation between the real and the money rates of interest it is important to distinguish between an inflation that is fully anticipated by everyone (as might be the case when say a steady 5 per cent inflation has been going on for a long time) and an inflation that is unanticipated (as might be the case when the rate of inflation suddenly accelerates). Consider first the case of a fully anticipated inflation. The relation between real and money rates of interest often leads to much misunderstanding during times of anticipated inflation. Say, for example, that the equilibrium value of the real rate of interest is a modest 3 per cent and that the rate of inflation is now, and is expected to continue, at 5 per cent. The money rate should then be 8 per cent. Now assume that the rate of inflation accelerates to 15 per cent per year and is expected to remain at that figure. The money rate should now rise to 18 per cent. The 18 per cent money rate combined with a 15 per cent inflation rate represents the same real burden on borrowers as did the 8 per cent money rate combined with a 5 per cent rate of inflation. Yet when such changes occur it is common for the public to become very concerned at the 'crushing' burden of the rising interest rates on those with mortgages and other debts. But consider what would happen if in response to this worry the government legislated maximum interest rates of say 12 per cent in the face of the 15 per cent inflation. Now the real rate of interest would be negative: in real terms *lenders* would be paying for the privilege of being able to lend their money to the *borrowers*! This seems counter-intuitive to many people but consider the example of a person who borrows £100 and repays £112 one year hence in the face of a 15 per cent inflation. The purchasing power of the £112 returned is less than the purchasing power of the £100 borrowed so that the real rate of interest has in fact proved negative in spite of the seemingly high money rate paid on the loan.

If there is uncertainty about the rate of inflation there is an added complication because people are uncertain about what the real rate of interest will be. If the rate of inflation accelerates unexpectedly borrowers gain; if it decelerates unexpectedly lenders gain. The effect on the current money rate of interest depends on how both borrowers and lenders react to uncertainty about the real rate of interest.

Other demands to borrow money

So far we have only considered the purchase of new capital as a reason to borrow money. While capital equipment is a major source of the demand for funds it is not the only source. Households borrow money to buy goods. The central authorities at all levels are major borrowers. Shifts in the demand to borrow money on the part of households or central authorities can cause the market rate of interest to change with no immediate change in the marginal efficiency of capital.

The influence of the central bank

Central banks often have active policies about what interest rates should be. The bank will intervene in the market for bonds in an attempt to influence the yield of these bonds. The central bank is a large enough potential buyer and seller of bonds to be able to do just this, and the exact way in which it is accomplished is analysed in Chapter 42.

Bank administration of interest rates

The rate of interest does not fluctuate in response to every minor fluctuation in the demand to borrow money. Banks, for example, consider many factors when they fix the rate of interest that they charge on loans. They are reluctant to change these rates every time changes occur in the demand to borrow money. If there is an excess demand for loanable funds (because the *MEC* is greater than i), rather than raise the rate of interest banks often ration the available supply of funds among their customers according to such criteria as the borrower's credit rating, how long the banker has known him, and the amount of business he does. Credit rationing is commonly found in lending institutions in most Western countries. When the market rate of interest is below the pure return on capital, money will appear 'tight' – hard to borrow – to the typical businessman.

Differences in the costs of administering credit

So far we have not considered what it costs the lender to earn his money. There is, in fact, great variation in the costs of different kinds of credit transactions. It is almost as cheap (in actual numbers of pounds) for a bank to lend £1 million to an industrial firm that agrees to pay the money back with interest after one year as it is for the same bank to lend you £1,200 to buy a new car on a loan that you agree to pay back over two years in 24 equal instalments. The difference in the cost *per pound* of each loan is considerable. The bank may very well make less profit per pound on a £1,200 loan at 18 per cent per year than on a £1 million loan at 8 per cent per year. In general, the bigger the loan and the fewer the payments, the less the cost per pound of servicing the loan. Why, then, do banks and loan companies usually insist that you repay the loan in frequent instalments? They worry that, if you do not pay regularly, you will not have the money when the loan comes due.

RECAPITULATION

(1) The efficiency of capital is measured by the stream of income (net of all other factor costs) produced by capital expressed as a rate per unit of capital.
(2) The marginal efficiency of capital is the efficiency of the marginal unit of capital.
(3) As more capital is added to a fixed amount of labour and land the marginal efficiency of capital is assumed to decline over a period of time because of the operation of the law of diminishing returns.
(4) The amount that firms will be willing to pay for a piece of capital equipment is the present value of the stream of net income produced by the capital.
(5) If the *MEC* exceeds the pure rate of interest everyone will wish to borrow money and buy capital equipment. If the *MEC* is less than the pure rate of interest no one will wish to borrow money to buy capital equipment. Thus in equilibrium the pure rate of interest will be equal to the marginal efficiency of capital.

(6) The income earned by an owner of capital, whether he uses it himself and gains the marginal efficiency of capital or lends it to someone and earns the pure rate of interest, is thus determined by the marginal efficiency of capital.

(7) The total return to capital includes, in addition to the pure return on capital, a risk premium and pure profits. If there are no barriers to entry, pure profits are a disequilibrium phenomenon which exist only until new capital enters the industry, expanding output and reducing prices so that the pure profits disappear (if there are barriers to entry the pure profits may persist in the long run).

(8) Actual interest rates differ from the pure rate of interest for a number of identifiable reasons such as risk and term of the loan.

A POSTSCRIPT ON BOND PRICES AND INTEREST RATES

We saw on page 396 that the equilibrium price of an asset is the present value of the stream of income that it confers. This has one important corollary that we shall use frequently and which we discuss here in relation to two types of bonds.

CONSOLS: A CONSOL, or *perpetuity*, is a bond that pays a fixed sum of money each year forever. It has no redemption date. The price of a consol promising to pay for example, £100 per year, is £2,000 when the interest rate is 5 per cent and £1,000 when the rate is 10 per cent. *The price of a consol varies inversely with the rate of interest.*

Now consider a world in which consols are the only interest-earning asset, and assume that many people have excess money balances that they wish to invest. If everyone tries to buy consols their price will be bid up. If the price of consols paying £100 a year rises from say, £5,000 to £10,000, this means that the interest rate that lenders are prepared to accept has fallen from 10 per cent to 5 per cent. (If existing consols sell at £10,000 any new borrower can also sell a newly issued consol for £10,000.) *Any action of investors that causes the price of consols to change also causes the rate of interest to change in the opposite direction: a rise in the price of consols is the same thing as a fall in the rate of interest.*

REDEEMABLE BONDS: Most bonds are not consols; instead, most bonds pay a fixed sum of money in interest each year but they also have a redemption date on which the principle of the loan will be repaid. A bond with a redemption value of £1,000 payable ten years hence and yielding £100 a year in the interim, would be worth the present value of a ten-year stream of £100 per year *plus* the present value of £1,000 payable in ten years. It is obvious that the same principles apply to redeemable bonds as to consols: (i) **the price of bonds and the rate of interest vary inversely with each other and (ii) any action of investors that bids up the price of bonds means that the rate of interest lenders are prepared to accept has fallen.**[1]

1 A redeemable bond differs from a consol in that the present value of the former becomes increasingly dominated by the fixed redemption value as the redemption date approaches. Taking an extreme case, if a bond is to be redeemed for £1,000 in a week's time its value will hardly change if the rate of interest goes from 5 to 10 per cent. *The change in the value of a bond associated with a given change in the rate of interest is less the nearer to the present is its redemption date.*

30

Criticisms and tests of the theory of distribution

In previous chapters we have developed the traditional theory of distribution in a number of different contexts. It is no doubt valuable to repeat what is basically the same analysis in a number of different guises. Repetition helps in developing the 'feel' for the workings of a price system that is so important to the economist. It has the disadvantage, however, of making the theory appear to have much more content than it actually has. In fact, the whole of distribution theory is based on only two or three basic hypotheses about the behaviour of factor owners and firms. In this chapter we lay out the basic structure of the theory and then go on to consider various criticisms and tests.

THE THEORY RESTATED

The traditional theory of distribution asserts that factor prices can be explained by demand and supply.

The theory of factor supply predicts that factors will move between occupations in search of the highest net advantage. Factors will move among uses, industries and places, taking both pecuniary and non-pecuniary rewards into account. Factors will move in such a way as to equalize the net advantages to the owners of factors. Because there are impediments to the mobility of factors, there may be lags in the response of factors to changes in relative prices. Thus, the elasticity of supply will depend on what factor is being discussed and what time horizon is being considered.

The demand for a factor is a derived demand, depending for its existence on the demand for the product produced by the factor. The elasticity of an industry's demand curve for a factor will vary directly with (i) the elasticity of demand for the product produced by the industry; (ii) with the proportion of total production costs accounted for by the factor; and (iii) the extent to which it is technically possible to substitute other factors for the one in question.

In equilibrium *all* profit-maximizing firms will employ *all* variable factors up to the point at which the marginal unit of each type of factor adds as much to revenue as to costs. All profit-maximizing firms that are price-takers in the factor market will employ factors up to the point at which the price paid for the last unit of the factor equals the increase in revenue caused by its employment. For firms selling goods in competitive markets, the increase in revenue is the marginal physical product *times* the price; for firms facing a downward-sloping demand curve for their products, the increase in revenue is marginal physical product *times* marginal revenue.

It is important to emphasize that the equilibrium relations summarized in the previous paragraphs necessarily apply to all firms that are successfully maximizing their profits. A firm that is not equating the marginal revenue product of each of its factors with that factor's price is not maximizing its profits. On the other hand, if the firm is maximizing its profits, then it is necessarily equating each factor's price to the corresponding marginal revenue product. The theory thus stands or falls with the theory of profit maximization. It is merely an implication of profit maximization, and the only reason for spelling it out in detail is that this may help us to develop interesting and useful hypotheses about the effects of various changes in the economy on the markets for factors of production.

When one thinks of all the heated arguments over the traditional theory of distribution, and of all the passionate denunciations and defences that it has occasioned, it is surprising to observe how few predictions it makes, and how uncontroversial most of them are. The theory predicts that demand for a factor depends on, and varies with, the demand for the products made by the factor. This was undoubtedly a great discovery when it was first put forward; now, however, it is almost a platitude. The theory also asserts that the technical conditions of production will influence the demand for a factor. The theory predicts that (assuming the supply curve of the factor has not shifted) changes in the factor price must reflect changes in the demand for the commodities made by the factor. On the supply side, the theory predicts that movement of resources between firms and between industries will occur in response to changes in factor prices. It is very hard to quarrel with any of these predictions; in fact, they seem so obvious as to be trite. They are, nevertheless, important and often arise in practical issues of policy.

CRITICISMS OF THE THEORY

We have seen that marginal productivity theory relates to the demand for factors of production; it constitutes half of the traditional theory of distribution. The other half is the theory of supply, which asserts, as we have seen, that factors will move between occupations in search of the highest net advantage. It is the marginal productivity half of the theory that has been subject to most criticism and about which there exist so many misconceptions. In order to illustrate these, and to show what is wrong with them we shall discuss four common misconceptions – all of which have been drawn from real sources and not the author's own imagination.

(1) *The theory assumes perfect competition in all markets.* This is just not correct. The relationship between the marginal physical product and the marginal value product will be altered if the degree of competition alters, but the marginal value product will be equated with the price of the factor in perfect competition, imperfect competition and monopoly, provided only that the firm is a price-taker in the factor market.

(2) *The theory assumes that the amount and value of the marginal product of a factor is known to the entrepreneur.* The theory assumes no such thing! Critics argue that the firm will not pay any factor the value of its marginal product, because the firm will generally have no idea what that marginal product is and would be unable to calculate this magnitude even if it tried. This criticism is irrelevant. It has already been pointed out that payment according to marginal revenue product occurs *automatically* whenever the firm is maximizing its profits. It does not matter *how* the firm succeeds in doing this – by guess, luck, skill or by calculating marginal quantities. As long as profits are maximized, factors will be getting the value of their marginal products. The theory does not purport to describe how businessmen calculate; it merely predicts how they will react to various situations on the assumption that they are maximizing profits.

(3) *The theory is inhuman because it treats human labour in the same way as it treats a ton of coal or a wagonload of fertilizer.* One must be careful to distinguish one's emotional reaction to a procedure that treats human and nonhuman factors alike from one's evaluation of it in terms of positive economics. Anyone who accepts this criticism must explain carefully why separate theories of the pricing of human and nonhuman factors are needed. He must also show that his 'human' theory makes predictions that differ from those made by the marginal productivity theory. The marginal productivity theory is only a theory of the *demand* for a factor. It predicts only what employers would like to buy. It predicts that employers' desired purchases of labour (and all other factors) depend on the price of the factor in question, the technical conditions of production, and the demand for the product made by labour. *Supply* conditions may differ between human and nonhuman factors, but these differences are accommodated within the theory. No evidence has yet been gathered to indicate that it is necessary to have separate theories of the *demand* for human and nonhuman factors of production.

(4) *When all factors are paid according to their marginal products the resulting distribution of income will be a just distribution.* Some supporters of the theory of marginal productivity have held that not only was the theory correct, but that it described a functional distribution of income that was a *just* one because factors were rewarded according to the value of their contributions to the national product. Many critics of the low levels of wages that prevailed in the nineteenth century reacted with passion against a theory that was claimed to justify these rates of pay.

It is beyond the scope of a book on positive economics to enter into normative questions of what constitutes a just distribution of income. It is, however, worth getting the facts straight. According to the marginal productivity theory, each labourer (or each unit of any other factor) does *not* receive the value of what he personally contributes to production. Each labourer, instead, receives the value of what the last labourer employed would add to production *if all other factors were held constant*. If one million similar labourers are employed, then each of the one million receives as a wage an amount equal to the extra product that would have been contributed by the millionth labourer if he had been hired while capital, etc., had remained unchanged. Whatever the justice of the matter, it is not correct to say that each factor receives the value of *its own* contribution to production. Indeed, where many factors cooperate in production, it is generally impossible to divide up the *total production* into the amounts contributed by each factor.

DO MARKET CONDITIONS DETERMINE FACTOR EARNINGS?
Factors other than labour

Most nonhuman factors are sold on competitive markets. The theory predicts that changes in the earnings of these factors will be associated with changes in market conditions. The overwhelming preponderance of evidence supports this. Consider some examples:

(1) RAW MATERIALS: A dramatic example was provided during the Korean War when a rapid increase in the demand for many strategic materials sent their prices soaring, to the extent that the incomes earned by their owners soared as well. The prices of copper, tin, rubber, and hundreds of other materials fluctuate daily in response to changes in the demand and supply of these products. Current shortages of certain key raw materials are almost always signalled by price increases. There is little question that the competitive market theory of factor pricing provides a good explanation of raw-material prices and hence of the incomes earned by their producers.

(2) LAND VALUES: Land in the heart of growing cities is clearly fixed in supply, and values rise steadily in response to increasing demand for it. The value of the land itself often makes it worthwhile to destroy durable buildings to convert land to more productive uses. The New York skyscraper and the new London skyline are monuments to the high value of urban land. In many smaller cities, the change in tastes from shopping in town to shopping in outlying shopping centres has lessened the demand for land downtown and influenced relative land prices. The increase in the price of land on the periphery of every growing city is a visible example of the workings of the market.

Agricultural land appears at first glance to provide counterevidence. The classical economists predicted 150 years ago that, as population and the demand for agricultural products grew, the price of the fixed supply of land would rise enormously. The price of agricultural land, however, has *not* skyrocketed. Although the demand for agricultural produce did expand in the predicted fashion because of the rise in population, the productivity of agricultural land has increased in quite unexpected ways due to the invention of the vast range of machines and techniques that characterize modern agriculture. The prediction was falsified, not because the price of agricultural land is not determined by market forces, but rather because some of the market forces were incorrectly foreseen.

(3) TAXICABS: The system of regulating taxicabs in London is very different from the one in use in New York. The theory successfully predicts the consequences of these different regulatory rules in each city.

The supply of New York taxicabs is rigidly controlled by a licensing system, and the number of cabs is kept well below what it would be in a free-market situation. The medallion, which confers the right to operate a cab, acquires a scarcity value (presently over $30,000). As the demand for services of taxicabs rises due to increases in population and average incomes, the price of medallions rises correspondingly, so that new entrants earn only normal returns on their investment. If fares are increased and the demand proves inelastic, so that gross income from operating a cab rises, the price of the medallion also rises correspondingly. The fare increase thus amounts to a free gift to the current holders of medallions; it does nothing to raise the net incomes of cab operators newly entering the industry.

In London, fares are rigidly regulated but entry is free to anyone who can pass a set of tests. Periodically fares are raised in an effort to raise incomes. If demand is inelastic incomes rise in the short run, but this attracts new entrants who continue to come in until each existing cab is carrying just enough fares to cover its full opportunity cost, at which price profits have been reduced to zero. This case is in fact analytically identical to that of the barber discussed on pages 301–3.

Labour

When we apply our theory to labour we encounter two important sets of complications: first, labour markets are a mixture of competitive and noncompetitive elements, the proportions of the mixture differing from market to market; and, second, labour being the human factor of production, nonmonetary considerations loom large in its incentive patterns. These complications make labour economics one of the most difficult fields of all economics. Monopolistic elements and nonmonetary rewards, both of which are difficult to measure, require careful specification if the theory that labour earnings respond to market prices is to be made testable. Nevertheless, we do have a mass of evidence to go on. We do have cases in which a strong union – one able to bargain effectively and to restrict entry of labour into the field – has caused wages to rise well above the competitive level. The West Coast longshoremen in the US could never have hoped to obtain their present privileged position were it not for the extremely effective operations of Harry Bridges, president of the union. When Bridges was mobbed in San Francisco in Spring, 1964, by unemployed labourers wanting jobs as longshoremen, we were given impressive evidence that, if entry could not be restricted, the high earnings of longshoremen could not be long maintained. Many other similar cases have been documented. Unions can and do succeed in raising wages and incomes when they operate in small sections of the whole economy; the high earnings do attract others to enter the occupation or industry; and the privileged position can be maintained only if entry can be effectively restricted.

Earnings do respond, at least to some extent, to monopoly power. Do they respond to normal fluctuations of demand and supply? Here the evidence is mixed. The competitive theory predicts that a decline in the demand for some product will cause a decline in the derived demand for the factors that make the product, a decline in their income, and the exit of factors to other uses. Cases come easily to mind. With the advent of the motor car, many skilled carriage-makers found the demand for their services declining rapidly. Earnings fell, and many craftsmen who were forced to leave the industry found that they had been earning substantial rents for their scarce, but highly specific, skills. These men were forced to suffer large income cuts when they moved to other industries. Many silent-screen stars whose voices were unsuitable for the talkies suffered disastrous cuts in income and fell into oblivion when the demand for silent films disappeared. A similar but less dramatic fate hit many radio personalities who were unable to make the transition to television and had to compete in the greatly reduced market for radio talent. Much earlier, the same fate met those music-hall stars whose talents did not project onto the flat, flickering screen of the early silent movies. How soon will television entertainers, who have enormous incomes due to the high demand for their services, go the same way when a yet newer mass entertainment medium sweeps away the present one? When in a competitive, changing society you hear the bell toll for some once wealthy and powerful group, you should always remember that someday it could easily be tolling for you!

These variations in factor earnings are caused by changes in market conditions, not by changes in our notions of the intrinsic merit of various activities. To illustrate, ask yourself why, if you have the talent, can you make a lot of money writing copy for a London advertising agency, whereas, if you have the talent, you are unlikely to make a lot of money writing books of poetry? Not because any economic dictator or group of philosophers has decided that advertising is more valuable than poetry, but because in the British economy there is a large demand for advertising and only a tiny demand for poetry. A full citing of all such evidence would cover many pages, and it would all point to the conclusion that earnings of factors do very often respond to changes in market forces.

On the other hand, not only can monopoly elements raise incomes above their competitive levels, but they can also prevent incomes from falling and reflecting decreases in demand. Of course, if the demand disappears more or less overnight (as it did in the case of silent-movie stars and carriage makers), there is nothing any union can do to maintain incomes. But the story may be different if, as is more usually the case, demand shrinks steadily over a few decades. In this case powerful unions *who are able virtually to prohibit new entry of labour into the industry* can often hold wages up in the face of declining demand. The industry's labour force thus declines, through death and retirement, in spite of the relatively high wage being paid to the employees who remain. Cases in which this has occurred are found in railways and coal mining in the US.[1]

Thus the competitive theory does help to explain the relative earnings of different groups of labour; clearly, however, a strong dose of monopoly theory must be added if we hope to explain much of what we see.

DO FACTORS MOVE IN RESPONSE TO CHANGES IN EARNINGS?

In the previous section we saw that earnings do tend to change in response to the conditions of demand and supply. Changes in earnings are signals whose purpose is

---

1 I cannot suppress the conjecture that the 'restrictive behaviour' of unions in these cases has led to a more orderly, humane and civilized phasing out than would have occurred had the adjustment been left to a free market, in which case those who remained in the industry and who were needed by it, would all have suffered depressed conditions in order that the disincentive could operate on those who did leave and on those who might otherwise have entered. This is similar to the point made on page 372 about the payment of additional rents to those already in an industry or occupation in order to encourage new *entry*.

to attract resources into those lines of production in which more are needed and out of lines in which less are needed.

Land

In the case of land, there is strong evidence that the theory is able to predict the actual course of events quite accurately. Land is transferred from one crop to another in response to changes in the relative profitabilities of the crops. Recently in the US, for example, the price of meat was held down as part of an unsuccessful attempt to control inflation by a system of direct price controls. A shortage of meat quickly developed as farmers switched their land to more profitable lines of production. When the controls were removed prices rose in response to the shortage, and in response to the rise in prices output expanded as land was brought back into meat production. Countless similar examples of the effects of controlling some but not all prices (and hence of changing relative prices) have been documented.

Land on the edge of town is transferred from rural to urban uses as soon as it can earn substantially more as a building site than as a corn field. Although physically immobile, land is constantly transferred among its possible uses as the relative profitabilities of these uses change. Little more needs to be said here; the most casual observation will show the allocative system working with respect to land much as described by the theory.

Capital

There is no doubt that in the long run capital moves in response to market signals. The patterns of location of, and of products produced by, the nation's factories have changed greatly over the last two centuries. Over a period of say fifty years the change is dramatic; from one year to the next it is small. Most plant and machinery is relatively specific. Once installed it will be used to produce the product for whose output it was primarily designed as long as the variable costs of production can be covered. But if full, long-run opportunity costs are not covered, the capital will not be replaced as it wears out and investment will take place in other industries instead. Long-run movements in the allocation of capital clearly occur in response to market signals.

The mechanism will work so long as there is freedom of entry and exit. Exit is hard to prevent (other than by government legislation and subsidy) but monopolies and oligopolies do try to erect barriers to entry. Profits in a monopolized industry where entry is blocked do not induce flows of new investment, and they therefore serve no apparent long-run allocative function. The opposition to monopoly and to monopoly profits rests in part upon those profits existing without inducing the resource flows that would eliminate them.

Although monopoly profits appear to play no role in long-run allocation, we are not certain that they have no function in the *very long run*. In Chapter 24 we saw that one eminent economist, Joseph Schumpeter, felt that they were the mainspring of capitalist economic growth in the very long run. He believed that monopolistic (and oligopolistic) profits cause the technological changes that have made living standards in market economies double every twenty or thirty years. Schumpeter saw monopoly profits as an inducement to people to innovate and run large risks in the knowledge that the few who succeed will earn large profits. Furthermore, he saw innovation and the rise of new products and industries, and the accompanying destruction of apparently well-entrenched monopolies, as a very-long-run process that makes the economy much more competitive and amenable to change than it appears to be when viewed at any moment in time. This is an issue on which economists do not have enough knowledge to give a final answer, but it should serve as yet another warning about the dangers of ignoring the very long run in which the main cause of changes in per capita output is changes in technology.

Labour

Labour is the factor for which the evidence on the movement of factors in response to changes in earnings is most mixed. Countless studies of labour mobility have been made, but they do not point to a simple answer to the question of how much labour moves in response to monetary incentives. On the one hand, it is clear that the great migration of Americans to the West Coast during the Second World War was induced by expanding employment opportunities and soaring wages in the shipyards and aircraft factories of California. On the other hand, why were the depressed areas of Wales not depopulated ten years ago when the coal mines began to shut down?

At the risk of grossly simplifying a complex situation, it may be said that the existing evidence is consistent with the following hypotheses.

(1) There exists a fairly mobile component in any group. This mobile component tends to consist of the youngest, the most adaptable and often the most intelligent members of the group.

(2) This mobile group can be attracted from one area, occupation, or industry to another by relatively small changes in economic incentives.

(3) Providing the pattern of demand for resources does not shift too fast, most of the necessary reallocation can be accomplished by movements of this mobile group. Of course, the same individual need not move over and over again. The group is constantly replaced by new entrants into the labour force.

As we go beyond these very mobile persons, we get into ranges of lower and lower mobility until, at the very bottom, we find persons who are virtually completely immobile. The most immobile are the very old, those with capital sunk in non-marketable assets, the timid, the weak and those who receive high nonmonetary rewards in their present occupation or location. It is difficult for them to move; in extreme cases, only the threat of starvation will move them. Even this may not be enough since some people believe, rightly or wrongly, that they will starve even if they move. Thus, it may be relatively easy to create a substantial inflow of workers into an expanding occupation, industry or area and an outflow of workers from a depressed occupation, industry or area by a shift in earnings. Outflows from depressed areas such as Appalachia and parts of New England in the US, the Maritime Provinces of Canada, Sicily and Southern Italy, the Highlands of Scotland, declining areas of north-east England, and rural parts of central France have been observed over long periods of time.

Although it is relatively easy to get *some* outmigration, it is difficult to get large transfers in a short period of time. When demand falls rapidly, pockets of poverty tend to develop. In each of the geographical areas mentioned above, labour has been leaving, but poverty has increased. The reason is that the rate of exit has been slower than the rate of decline of the economic opportunities in the area. Indeed, the exit itself causes further decline, for, when a family migrates, both the supply of labour and the demand for labour decline. This is because all the locally provided goods and services that the family consumed before they migrated now suffer a reduction in demand.

The effects of direct government intervention: Recently the governments of several countries have been controlling wages in an attempt to control inflation. Since it is easier to control the earnings of labour in some sectors of the economy than in others these controls inevitably influence the structure of relative earnings. Furthermore, in Britain the controls seem to have been used in a conscious attempt to redistribute income from the middle class to the working class. There seems to be some evidence that this has been successful and that the real incomes of many middle-class households has actually fallen relative to the real incomes of working-class households. The theory predicts that a change in the allocation of labour will occur as a result: there will be a shortage of persons to fill jobs whose relative prices have been held down and no shortage of persons to fill jobs whose relative prices have risen. The theory also predicts that the reallocation of labour will be larger the longer is the policy maintained. Presumably those applying the policy hope that this shift in the allocation of labour will be small or that it will not adversely affect the country's economic performance. Only time, and careful study, will tell if either of these hopes are to be fulfilled.

Alternatives to income differentials as an allocative device for labour: One of the main functions of inequalities in earnings is to signal labour to reallocate. It is sometimes asserted that if this signal is removed, government compulsion would be the only allocative device available. This assertion is not correct.

One alternative signal, still largely within the free-market mechanism, is to keep the earnings of the employed from varying, but to let unemployment rates vary. The mechanism we have been studying for reallocating labour from industry A to industry B in the face of a shift in demand is a rise in earnings in B and a fall in A. But what if wage rates in A and B are fixed by powerful unions or by government decree? Unemployment will develop in A, and severe shortages will develop in B. Even though there is no difference in the earnings of labour in A and B, the chance of obtaining a job is much higher in B than in A. This may well induce new entrants into the labour force to train for B rather than A, and it may induce some unsuccessful applicants for jobs in A to transfer to B. This allocative system could work, although it would be at the cost of a higher average rate of unemployment than when relative earnings are used as the allocative signal.

Thus, it is possible to imagine allocative signals other than differentials in earnings and government compulsion. The question is now an empirical one: to what extent does labour respond to these differentials and to what extent does it respond to other signals? On the one hand, some recent studies have suggested that the regional movement of labour responds more to relative regional unemployment rates than to relative earnings. On the other hand, the unemployment in Appalachia, north-east England and southern Italy seems to be as ineffective as wage differentials in inducing sufficient movement, and there is some evidence that farm unemployment in many countries does not drive people off the farms as rapidly as the decline in the demand for farm labour requires.

MARGINAL PRODUCTIVITY THEORY AND THE MACRO-DISTRIBUTION OF INCOME

The theory of distribution outlined in this part concentrates on the pricing of factors in each of the many markets of the economy. We have seen over and over again that the theory does successfully predict the consequences on particular prices and quantities of changes that impinge on particular markets. (E.g., what will be the effects of holding down the salaries of headmasters of state schools at a time when all other wages and salaries are increasing?)

The concept of macro-distribution

We have referred several times to the functional distribution of income among such broad classes of factors as land, labour and capital. Can we say anything about what determines the distribution of income at this level of aggregation? What, for example, determines the share of total income going to labour as a class? What influences do unions and government policy have on this share? Questions of distribution at this level of aggregation are often referred to as questions about *macro-distribution* (as opposed to *micro-distribution* which refers to such questions as what determines the share of total income going to headmasters of state schools). Figure 28.8 on page 390, for example, shows some data for the macro-distribution of income: it shows the share of national income going to the total of all wage and salary earners (i.e., to labour as a factor of production).

Marginal analysis and macro-distribution

Questions of the macro-distribution of income between the great social classes of the society, labourers, rentiers and capitalists, were of great concern to classical economists such as Ricardo, Malthus and Marx. With the development of marginal analysis in the last half of the nineteenth century emphasis shifted to the determination of factor prices and quantities in millions of individual markets. The theory that grew out of this development (often called the marginal productivity theory after the demand half of the theory) offers few general predictions about the macro-distribution of income. It holds that to discover the effect of some change, say a tax or a new trade union, on the macro-distribution between wages, profits and rent, we would need to be able to discover what would happen in each individual market of the economy and then aggregate to find the macro-result. To do this we would need to know the degree of monopoly and monopsony in each market, we would need to be able to predict the effect on oligopolists' prices and outputs of changes in their costs, and we would need to have a theory of the outcome of collective bargaining in situations of bilateral monopoly (see page 383). We would also need to know how much factor substitution would occur in response to any resulting change in relative factor prices. Finally, we would need a general equilibrium theory linking all of these markets together (see Chapter 31). Clearly we are a long way from being able to do all this: with our present state of knowledge, the marginal productivity theory provides few if any predictions about the effects on macro-distribution of such changes as shifts in total factor supplies, taxes on one factor, and the rise of trades unions.

This conclusion is not necessarily a criticism of the theory. It may well be that relative shares are determined by all the detailed interactions of all the markets in the economy, and that general predictions about the effects of various events on macro-distribution can be obtained only after we have enough knowledge to solve the general equilibrium problem outlined in the previous paragraph.

Many economists would argue that we should not expect to get further than this. They would hold that the great macro-questions on the scale of *labour versus capital* are largely unanswerable, and pedestrian though it may seem, the ability of the traditional theory to deal with micro-questions is a remarkable triumph. One reason advanced for the view that the great macro-distribution questions are unanswerable is that it only makes sense to talk about laws governing macro-distribution if labour, capital and land are each relatively homogeneous and each subject to a common set of influences not operating on the other two factors whereas, in fact, (so goes the view) there is likely to be as much difference between say two different types of labour as between one kind of labour and, say, one kind of machine. On the one hand, the micro-distribution of income can be thought of as subject to understandable influences because it deals with innumerable relatively homogeneous factors. On the other hand, macro-distribution is nothing more than the aggregate of the micro-distributions, and there is no more reason to expect that there should be simple laws governing the macro-distribution of income between land, labour and capital than to expect that there should be simple laws governing the macro-distribution between people with light hair and people with dark hair.[1]

Alternative theories of distribution

Many economists have been dissatisfied with the answer that there is no answer to the great social questions of macro-distribution (at least in free market economies). This dissatisfaction has lead to attempts to formulate theories which deal explicitly with macro-distribution problems.

MACRO-MARGINAL PRODUCTIVITY THEORIES: An attempt that is in the tradition of marginal productivity theory is based on the postulated existence of a *macro-production function* for the whole economy. Assume that total national output can be

1 In case it is not obvious to the reader trying to guard against the author's biases, I am in general (if not complete) agreement with this view. (Although like most other economists who believe that their subject can explain some of what we see in society, I should be overjoyed if someone did succeed in getting a workable theory of macro-distribution that stood up to some serious empirical tests.)

treated as a simple composite commodity that varies in amount according to the inputs of homogeneous labour, homogeneous land and homogeneous capital. This allows us to write for the economy as a whole

$$P = P(Ld, L, K),$$

where P stands for output and Ld, L, K for inputs of land, labour and capital respectively. If the total supplies of each factor are fixed at any one time and if the economy is usually at or near the full employment of all factors, then the quantities of Ld, L and K inputs are determined and so, through the production function, is P.

Each factor of production will have a marginal product – the change in output that would occur if the quantity of the factor were varied slightly, the quantity of the other factors being held constant – and this will determine the price of the factor. The total payment going to the factor measured in real terms will be the quantity of the factor multiplied by its marginal product. The macro-distribution of income is thus determined by the nature of the production function (which determines marginal products) and the supplies of the three factors that are available in the economy.

Although aggregate production functions of this sort are commonly used in theoretical models, there is little evidence that they are good descriptions of the behaviour of total output over long periods of time or that they isolate important forces that determine the macro-distribution of income. [1]

THE DEGREE OF MONOPOLY AND KEYNESIAN THEORIES: A more radical departure from traditional theory was expounded by Michael Kalecki, who sought to explain labour's share in terms of the overall degree of monopoly in the economy. Mention should also be made of the many 'macro-theories' that follow from Keynes's general theory. Theories of this sort make use of the Keynesian aggregates that we shall not study until Part 7, so we will say no more about them here. We can observe, however, that, in spite of the obvious appeal of being able to relate distribution to only a few measurable variables, such theories have not yet received much significant empirical support.

---

1 The Cobb-Douglas production function was an early attempt to explain labour's share. In the two factor version real national output (Y) is determined by inputs of labour (L) and capital (C), according to the production function

$$Y = AL^aC^{1-a}.$$

Notice that this is a single (macro) production function for the whole economy.
The real wage of labour (w) is its real marginal product:

$$w = \frac{\partial Y}{\partial L} = aAL^{a-1}C^{1-a}.$$

The total wage bill is

$$wL = \frac{\partial Y}{\partial L} \cdot L = aAL^{a-a},$$

and the share of wages in the national product is

$$\frac{wL}{Y} = \frac{aAL^aC^{1-a}}{AL^aC^{1-a}} = a.$$

Thus the Cobb-Douglas national production function leads to the prediction that labour's share of the total national product will be a constant, a, and independent of the size of the labour force.

PROFESSOR ROBINSON'S VIEWS: Finally, and perhaps most important in the list of dissenters from orthodox distribution theory, we should mention Professor Joan Robinson of Cambridge University. Professor Robinson has for many years propounded the view that distribution theory went off on the wrong track with the late nineteenth-century development of marginal productivity theory. In her view we need to go back to the classical theories of Ricardo and Marx and develop them into satisfactory theories of macro-distribution. It is impossible to do justice to Professor Robinson's view, to say nothing of criticizing it in depth, within the confines of this book. Rather than present a capsule summary that would inevitably be a caricature it is probably fairer to refer the interested reader to Professor Robinson's own writings in which she attacks the traditional theory of distribution and propounds her own 'classical' alternative.[1]

The Quantity of Capital: One criticism made by the Cambridge School does, however, require explicit mention. In the simple development of the theory of capital and interest in Chapter 29 we talked of changes in 'the' quantity of capital and we invoked the 'law' of diminishing returns to predict that the marginal efficiency of capital would decline as the stock of capital grew.

But society's stock of capital is in fact a very heterogeneous collection of tools, factories, equipment, etc. How can we speak of 'the' stock of capital? How can we reduce this heterogeneous collection of capital goods to a single number so that we can say that the capital stock is increasing or decreasing?

The obvious way is to use a price. If we take the price of capital we can value all these diverse physical things and obtain the total value of the economy's capital stock. But if we then use this quantity of capital in combination with the *MEC* schedule to determine the price of capital (i.e., the pure return on capital which in equilibrium is equal to the pure rate of interest) we may be involved in circular reasoning: If we wish to use 'the' quantity of capital in conjunction with 'the' production function *to determine the price of capital* (and hence the share of total income going to the owners of capital) we cannot use the price of capital to determine the quantity of capital.

For over a decade a debate has raged over the possibility of calculating a single measure of the quantity of capital that could, without circularity, be placed into a macro-production function to determine the price of capital. The outcome of the debate appears to be that this cannot be done.[2]

1 See, in particular, Joan Robinson and John Eatwell, *An Introduction to Modern Economics* (McGraw-Hill, 1973). Cambridge critics are often unwilling to give any points at all to the 'marginal productivity theory'. It seems to me, however, that when new theories replace old ones they should save what is valid in the old theories as well as discard what is invalid. Traditional theory is very successful in explaining micro-distribution problems. If it were to be supplanted by new theories, it would be a serious blunder to throw away the baby of successful micro-applications along with the admittedly dirty bath water of unsuccessful macro-applications. Furthermore, it is not clear to me how Cambridge-style classical distribution theories can even be brought to bear on the sort of micro-distribution problems outlined earlier in this Chapter.

2 It is worth noting at this point what is not so often pointed out: the same problems exist with land and labour. The society's stock of land is a heterogeneous collection of good, bad and indifferent land, some suited for some crops and some for other crops. The society's stock of labour is a heterogeneous collection of human beings no two of whom are the same: if identical quantities of other factors are combined first with individual *A* and then with individual *B*, very different quantities of output may result. To talk about 'the' quantity of labour and 'the' quantity

For the economist who wishes to combine marginal productivity theory with macro-production functions to deal with the macro-distribution of income, this is a serious matter. To the economist who accepts only the traditional micro-theory of distribution this is not so upsetting. Such an economist believes that there are thousands of distinct factors – which it may be convenient sometimes to group into such broad classes as land, labour and capital – but which get separately priced and which are each more or less substitutable one for another. Thus there is no particular reason to believe that labour as a whole will be subject to one set of influences, land as a whole to another distinct set and capital as a whole to yet a third distinct set. To such an economist the inability to measure *the* quantity of capital (and *the* quantities of labour and land) is not a particularly serious matter.

For the traditional theorist these are at least two distinct issues: (a) does a demand and supply model of factor pricing shed any light on micro-distribution problems and (b) does the *marginal productivity theory* adequately explain the demand for factors of production, particularly the demand for capital? Some traditional theorists would answer 'yes' to both questions, others would say that the answer to (b) may be 'no' but that the answer to (a) is surely 'yes'.

---

of land is just as heroic an oversimplification as to talk about 'the' quantity of capital. Furthermore to obtain 'the' quantities of labour and land by aggregating their values (i.e., multiplying each kind of labour by its price and then aggregating, and similarly for land), and then using these aggregate quantities to determine the prices of land and labour is to engage in circular reasoning just as it is with capital.

Part six

The economy as a whole

31

The interaction among markets: general and partial analysis

THE INTERRELATIONSHIP OF MARKETS

The economy of any country consists of thousands upon thousands of individual markets. There are markets for agricultural goods, for manufactured goods and for all types of consumers' services; there are markets for semi-manufactured goods, such as steel and pig iron, which are outputs of some industries and inputs of others; there are markets for raw materials such as iron ore, trees, bauxite and copper; there are markets for land, and for thousands of different types of labour; there are markets for the lending of new capital and for the transfer of existing loans. So far we have studied these markets more or less in isolation (although in the case of the markets for factors of production we have been concerned to stress the relation between the demands for consumers' goods and the demands for factors of production through the idea of the *derived demand for a factor*).

The economy should not, however, be viewed as a series of markets functioning in isolation. It should be viewed instead as an interlocking system in which anything happening in one market will greatly affect many other markets. The markets of the economy are linked together and what goes on in each is coordinated (more or less well) by the price system. Changes in surpluses and scarcities are reflected in price changes; these price changes signal to decision takers what is happening in other markets and they alter their behaviour in response to these changes in signals.

AN EXAMPLE OF INTERRELATED MARKETS: The demand for cars has been rising fairly rapidly in most Western countries. A particular rise in demand will be met fairly soon with a rise in output using existing plant and equipment but working it harder by means of overtime and other expedients. If the rise in demand is considerable, and judged to be permanent, there will also be a planned increase in capacity in the car industry. Employment will rise and an attempt may be made to attract labour from elsewhere by offering higher earnings. Thus, one of the first impacts on other industries will be a loss of labour and possibly a need to raise wages in order to compete with the car industry for labour. This may cause profits to fall in these other industries. The increased employment in the car industry may occasion some geographical movement of labour. In this case there would be a rise in the demand for housing in the car centres and a corresponding fall in demand elsewhere. New housing construction in the car-producing areas would lead to a rise in the demand for construction workers and materials. Quarries and brickworks will have to take on additional labour and expand output. There will also be a rise in the demand for banking services, cinemas, haircuts and the thousands of other things that households moving to the car-producing areas will want to consume. Furthermore, there will be a rise in the demand for raw materials used in car construction, and the effects of this may be felt in such diverse places as the glass-making areas of the Midlands, the steel-manufacturing sections of Wales and the rubber plantations of Malaya. If new investment in plant and equipment takes place in the car industries, there will be a rise in the demand for many capital goods; shortages and bottlenecks may develop and other industries which use these materials may experience increases in their costs and troubles with delivery dates. There will also be a change in consumers' expenditure because some people's earnings will be increased and other people's reduced. Thus the effects of this one change will spread out through the entire economy.

The price system allows the adaptations to the initial shift to take place without being consciously coordinated by some single central authority. When shortages develop, prices rise and profit-seeking entrepreneurs are led to produce more of the good that is in short supply. When surpluses occur, prices fall and supply is voluntarily contracted. The price system produces a series of automatic signals so that a large number of different decision-taking units (firms) do, in fact, coordinate their efforts. How well they coordinate them depends on how well prices reflect current and future scarcities and surpluses, and on how fast and effectively firms respond to the changing price signals.

Feedback

One of the characteristics of the interrelated set of markets that forms the economy is that a change in one market will affect many other markets and the changes in these other markets may in turn affect (we say feed back onto) the original market.

In the example given above, we showed that the decision to expand capacity in the car industry would have many repercussions throughout the economy. The changes in these other markets might well feed back onto the car industry. To predict the precise effects of this feedback is very difficult. There is no doubt that the regional pattern of car sales will be affected. Sales will rise in the car-producing areas as workers migrate to these, and sales will fall in areas which the migrating workers leave. It is also possible that an overall national increase in car sales could occur if the increase in employment in the car industry brings more workers into the income range at which they will buy a new car, rather than a second-hand one.

These feedbacks, where they are significant, make it difficult to use the sort of economic theory that we have relied on completely up to this point. This theory is best described as PARTIAL EQUILIBRIUM THEORY. We have already distinguished in Chapter 12 between equilibrium (static) theory and disequilibrium (dynamic) theory, and we must now distinguish between partial and general equilibrium theory.

Partial equilibrium theory

The distinguishing features of partial and general equilibrium are illustrated in Figure 31.1. We start by considering some *sector* of the economy – possibly the market

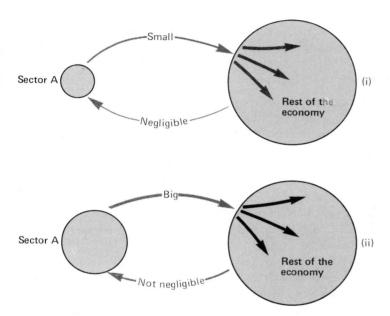

Fig. 31.1 (i) Partial equilibrium analysis is possible (ii) General equilibrium analysis is necessary

for cabbages, for carpenters or for cars, and we call this sector *A*. If there is some change in sector *A*, this will cause changes in the rest of the economy and these changes will in turn reflect back on sector *A*, causing further changes in that sector. Let us assume, for example, that the initial change in sector *A* is a fall in the supply of cabbages. This will cause an increase in their price and a fall in the quantity bought. The rise in the price of cabbages will cause other demands to change; in general, we would expect to find an increase in the demand for goods that are close substitutes for cabbages and a decrease in the demand for goods that are complementary with cabbages. As a result, the prices of all these other goods will change. These are the induced changes in the rest of the economy. The original demand curve for cabbages, that we used to derive our prediction, was based on the assumption that all other prices were given. Now, however, prices of substitutes for cabbages have risen and this will cause a *shift* in our original demand curve for cabbages. This is the reflection back of the induced changes in the rest of the economy on to the original sector. *It is a basic assumption of partial equilibrium analysis that such effects are small enough to be ignored.*

All partial equilibrium analyses are based on the assumption of *ceteris paribus*. Strictly interpreted, the assumption is that all other things in the economy are unaffected by any changes in the sector under consideration (sector A). This assumption is always violated to some extent, for anything that happens in one sector must cause changes in some other sectors. What matters is that the changes induced throughout the rest of the economy are sufficiently small and diffuse so that the effect they in turn have on sector A can safely be ignored. There is no simple rule telling us when partial analysis can safely be employed. The final test is in whether or not the predictions of partial theory are refuted by the facts. As a first approximation it is probably safe to say that the smaller is the sector under consideration, the more likely is it that its behaviour can successfully be predicted by partial analysis.

General equilibrium analysis

General equilibrium analysis attempts to deal explicitly with interrelationships between sectors. The micro-economic theories of Parts 1 to 5 are all partial theories (interrelations are dealt with, but only in an impressionistic, intuitive way). The macro-economic theories of Parts 7 and 8 are of the general equilibrium type.

The father of general equilibrium analysis was Leon Walras. It was his great insight to conceive of the economy as a system of simultaneous equations describing the demands and supplies of each commodity. The prices of all commodities occurred in each equation so that a change in any one of the demand or supply equations would cause changes in all prices and quantities. Thus, the general interrelation of all markets was illustrated.

Today a great deal of modern theory makes use of general equilibrium models. Pure theorists concern themselves with such problems as the conditions under which a unique general equilibrium can exist, while others, concerned with a wide range of problems from international trade to monetary theory, find it necessary to handle their problems in general equilibrium models. To get far with general equilibrium theory requires mathematical tools, so we must confine ourselves in this book to the present intuitive statement of the problem.

EMPIRICAL KNOWLEDGE ABOUT GENERAL EQUILIBRIUM

In recent decades a number of ambitious attempts have been made to breathe the life of empirical applicability into general equilibrium models. A typical problem would be to determine what would happen to the economy if we wished to produce an extra million tons of steel for export. An increase in the production of steel would require an increase in the output of many other industries such as iron ore, coal and glass. These industries will themselves require steel and each other's products as their own inputs. Thus the steel industry must expand its output not only because more steel is required for export but because more coal is required to make steel and the output of coal requires steel as an input. Furthermore, more steel requires more iron ore and this requires more coal to feed the engines to transport the ore and this in turn requires yet more steel. The problem is to discover, when all actions and reactions have been allowed for, what will be the necessary changes in the outputs of all the industries, including steel, in order that a *net* increase in steel production (for export) of 1 million tons may be produced.

Input-output models

The most important attempt to deal with these general-equilibrium problems of the interrelations between markets is that of Nobel Prize winning Professor Wassily Leontief. His pioneering work on the structure of the American economy has resulted in empirical measurements of the interrelations in the economy. These measurements allow us to predict the effects throughout the economy of changes in any one sector. The theoretical structure of *input-output models* (as they are called) is based on many simplifications. The basic unit is a broadly defined *sector* (or industry) that is assumed to use both labour and the products of other industries. It is assumed that sectors use their inputs in fixed proportions. Actual interrelations are measured empirically and then used to predict the outcome of various changes.

The basic concepts of input-output can be seen in a highly simplified example. Table 31.1 represents an economy with three sectors. Every sector appears in the table twice. It appears in a column as a purchaser and user of goods and services, and it appears in a row as a producer and seller. By moving along any row, we can see the value of production of a particular sector. Agriculture, for example, produced £250 (million is always understood) for use within the agricultural sector, £300 for use by the manufacturing sector (raw materials, etc.), £50 for use as an input by the service sector, and £400 for final demand. (In our simple example all final demand is accounted for by household purchases, but in more realistic cases there would be

Table 31.1 An input-output table for a hypothetical economy

	Purchasers				
	Agriculture	Manufacturing	Services	Final demand (e.g. household consumption)	Gross production, including commodities used up
Agriculture	£ 250	£ 300	£ 50	£ 400	£1,000
Manufacturing	250	150	150	600	1,150
Services	80	120	50	500	750
Primary inputs (e.g. labour)	420	580	500	1,500	
Total value of inputs	1,000	1,150	750		2,900

exports, inventory accumulation, and other sources of demand for the output of the system.) The last item in the row shows that the total production of agricultural goods was £1,000. Looking back, we see that £600 of this was used up as inputs by the three sectors, while £400 was available for consumption.

Reading down any column we see a particular sector as a user of goods and services, provided by itself and by other sectors of the economy. The first column, for example, shows agriculture as a consumer. It uses £250 of its own output (e.g., feed, seed, natural fertilizer), £250 of manufactured goods (e.g., ploughs, petrol), £80 from the service industries (e.g., repairs and transport), and £420 worth of labour as a production input. (For simplicity labour is assumed to be the only unproduced, or primary, input in the system.) The total value of all inputs (shown at the end of the column) is equal to the total value of goods produced (shown at the end of the first row). This reflects the accounting convention that the total value of output must be accounted for as a cost of production. This implies that profits are included as a factor of production. In our table they are included in payments to labour, which are to be interpreted as payments to workers, managers and owners for services provided. You should now be able to interpret any row or column in the table, remembering that the value in each cell indicates the amount of *output* of the industry in whose row it appears, that was used as an *input* by the industry in whose column it occurs.

Now look at the totals. The total value of all the goods produced in the economy is shown in the lower right-hand cell to be £2,900. This can be arrived at by adding the total values of the goods produced by the three sectors (agriculture, £1,000; manufacturing, £1,150; and services, £750), or since all value produced is accounted for as a cost, by adding the total value of all inputs used by each sector. These columns are shown in the outer row and column of the table.

But much of this £2,900 worth of production is itself used up as an input in further productive process, and hence it is not available to satisfy final demand. For example, pigs, not people, are the largest single consumer of corn. If we subtract production that is subsequently used up for further production, we are left with the values in the row and column for final demand and primary inputs. The final-demand column shows the amount of production that is *not* subsequently used up as a further input, and hence the amount that is available to satisfy demand in the system. There is

Table 31.2 Direct-requirements matrix calculated
from Table 31.1

	Purchasers		
	Agriculture	Manufacturing	Services
Agriculture	0·25	0·26	0·07
Manufacturing	0·25	0·13	0·20
Services	0·08	0·10	0·07
Primary inputs (e.g., labour)	0·42	0·51	0·66
Total value of inputs	1·00	1·00	1·00

£400 of agricultural goods, £600 of manufacturing goods, and £500 of services. These are the outputs that are available to satisfy consumers' wants. They total £1,500, a sum that can, by virtue of accounting conventions, also be arrived at by adding up the total value of primary inputs in each of the three sectors. (We shall later call this total *Gross National Product*.) The total value of incomes earned by primary inputs, is, by definition also, £1,500.

THE INTERPRETATION OF INPUT-OUTPUT TABLES: If we are interested in the economy's capacity to produce goods for final demand and to generate income, it is the primary input row and the final demand column with which we are concerned. Why, then, should we be interested in the upper left-hand block of entries that shows the requirements, as inputs, of each industry for the products of every other industry? These entries can be estimated by observing actual output and consumption for the various sectors of the economy, but of what use are they?

To begin answering this question, consider what would happen if we wished to raise the output of agriculture for final demand by £100 from £400 to £500. How much more agricultural output, manufactured output, services and labour would be required? Since the production of agricultural goods requires agricultural goods, we expect that output in this sector will have to rise by more than £100. But by how much must it rise? The first column of the table tells us that £100 more final output of agricultural goods would require £25 more agricultural goods as inputs for further agricultural production, £25 more manufactured goods to help produce the £100 worth of agricultural output for final demand, £8 more from the service industries, and £42 more of labour. But this is only the beginning. The extra manufacturing and service output will require extra inputs from all three sectors, plus labour.

To begin to solve for the final outcome we first convert Table 31.1 into a set of ratios called input coefficients, so that we know the value of each input required to get £1 worth of output. The resulting table[1], which is called a direct-requirements matrix, is shown in Table 31.2. We use this matrix to calculate the total changes in output required to produce the extra £100 of agricultural goods for final demand.

Table 31.3 Final-requirements matrix after increasing the output of agricultural goods for final demand by £100 over Table 31.1

		Purchasers			
	Agriculture	Manufacturing	Services	Final demand (e.g. house-hold con-sumption)	Gross produc-tion, including commodities used up
Agriculture	£ 288	£ 313	£ 51	£ 500	£1,152
Manufacturing	288	156	154	600	1,198
Services	92	125	51	500	768
Primary inputs (e.g., labour)	484	604	512	1,600	
Total value of inputs	1,152	1,198	768		3,118

At this stage, we need some technique beyond what we can assume here. There do exist, however, standard procedures for discovering from the direct-requirements matrix the overall increases in the outputs of the various sectors, and the additional demand for labour required to get a £1 increase in agricultural goods (or any other goods) available for final demand.

1 The first column is obtained as follows: $\frac{250}{1,000} = 0.25$; $\frac{250}{1,000} = 0.25$; $\frac{80}{1,000} = 0.08$; $\frac{420}{1,000} = 0.42$.

This tells us that £1 worth of agricultural output requires 25p of agricultural inputs, 25p of manufactured inputs, 8p of service inputs and 42p of labour.

These results can then be used to discover what must happen when, as in our case, an extra £100 of agricultural output is required for final demand. The new solution is shown in Table 31.3. The differences between Tables 31.1 and 31.3 represent the net changes. Overall, the increase in final demand for agricultural output of £100 requires an increase in gross production of agriculture of £152, of gross production of manufacturing of £48, and of services of £18. Clearly, in this system a change in one sector causes changes throughout the whole economy.

APPLICATIONS AND SHORTCOMINGS: Input-output tables are derived from actual observed data for production and consumption in the various sectors of the economy. They are a convenient way of laying out social data concerning inputs, outputs and transactions in the economy. They give us a picture of the interrelations that exist at a moment of time. They allow us to discover what is required in order to produce an extra unit of output of any product, allowing for all the induced reactions, as well as for the inputs directly used by a sector whose net expansion is desired. In the preceding example, for instance, it was not enough to know what £1 of agricultural output required as direct inputs, because the production of these inputs themselves entailed further increases in the output of all sectors.

The answers we get can sometimes be surprising. Consider a simple example. Industry X uses 10p of imported goods and 90p of domestically produced commodities per £ of its direct inputs, while industry Y uses 20p of imports and 80p of domestic commodities. Are we to conclude that Y is more import-using than X? Not necessarily, for the domestic goods used by X directly or indirectly may have a higher import content than the domestic goods used by Y. For example, X may purchase domestically produced steel made with imported iron ore. If its domestic purchases have a high import component, industry X may, after all direct and indirect effects have been allowed for, use more imports than Y per £ of output.

One way to discover which good entails more imports in a system of complex interrelations is to solve the input-output matrix to find the total import cost incurred by raising, by one unit, the output of X and then of Y. Such answers cannot easily be guessed, even if one has all the relevant data. Trying to guess the solution if one has data breaking the economy down into, say, 200 interdependent sectors is trying to guess the numerical solution to a system of 200 simultaneous equations.

Now assume we want to know what would happen to the structure of the economy if there were a change in the pattern of final demand, possibly due to a decline in military expenditure or a rise in exports of machinery to underdeveloped countries. Our question might be, 'If there is a fall in the output of other goods by £1 million, by how much could machinery output be increased if the labour released is to be devoted to increasing machinery output?' The input-output table can provide an answer. The techniques for solving this problem are fairly sophisticated, but we can see what is involved by imagining the following steps. We first solve the system for the reduction in final demand for goods. This tells us, among other things, how much labour would be freed because of the induced declines in output everywhere in the system. We next discover, allowing for all the direct and indirect effects, the labour input required to get £1 of output of machinery for final demand. This allows us to determine how much more machinery output can be sustained from a given amount of unused labour.

An input-output table is extremely valuable to planners who are investigating the effects of relatively small, but nonetheless important, changes in the economy. It is also helpful in predicting where bottlenecks will occur (and thus which sectors will need to expand fastest) if a general expansion or large change in the pattern of output is to be thrust on the economy.

The basic limitations of the input-output table lie in the assumptions of fixed input requirements per unit of output and of constant returns to scale. When we calculate the basic-requirements matrix, we build into it the assumption that the direct input requirements of £1 of output of any product do not change as the pattern of final demand changes. The economic theory that we have studied so far predicts that this is not the case. It predicts that a large change in the pattern of final demand will lead to changes in the pattern of derived demands for factors and changes in relative factor prices. In response to such changes, industries are predicted to change the ratios in which the various inputs are used. Such input substitution in response to a change in the pattern of final demand is ruled out by standard input-output analysis. How important this limitation is quantitatively depends on many considerations, but it is clear that the assumption of fixed coefficients is more nearly acceptable for analysing the effects of marginal changes in the patterns of demand over short periods of time, than for analysing large changes over long periods of time.

That input-output tables assume constant returns to scale is clear enough. The direct-requirements matrix implies that multiplying all inputs by the same constant also multiplies the output by that constant. Of course, we do not expect this to be always true, but the applicability of these tables requires only that the departures from the assumption be relatively insignificant. Once again, the departures are more likely to be negligible for small changes than for large ones.

After so cursory a study we cannot give a full evaluation of input-output analysis. Suffice it to say that the technique has proved very valuable to central planners both in highly centrally-controlled economies such as Poland and Czechoslovakia and in mixed economies such as the UK and the US. The limitations referred to above are nonetheless serious, and many modifications designed to avoid the static and linear nature of the technique have been developed.

Simulation techniques

Another relatively new approach to measuring the behaviour of complex general equilibrium systems is to use *simulation models*[1]. In essence, the approach builds an artificial and simplified representation or model of an economy in much the same way as aeronautical engineers build wind tunnels to simulate the atmosphere. Experiments can then be performed on the model. In economics, simulation models have used water in pipes and electric currents in wires to simulate the flows of goods and services, as well as the stock of goods. With the development of large-scale computers, very elaborate models can be represented electronically. Hypotheses about

1 The interested student will find an excellent and nontechnical survey of this field in the paper by Guy H. Orcutt, 'Simulation of Economic Systems', *American Economic Review*, December 1960.

how individual units behave can be placed into the memory of a computer, and the economist can observe how large numbers of simulated households and firms interact in the simulated markets. (The behaviour of markets is also governed by rules programmed into the computer.) The results of such interactions over time become outputs of the machine. Experiments can be performed on the system: for example, the economist can increase 'taxes' and trace out the effects of the increase month by month over many 'years'. Since months of actual time can be simulated in a few seconds on a computer, the economist will be able to run many experiments (for example, he can try out *different* tax policies) and compare the results of each. This approach is in its infancy, and it is too early to evaluate its success, but it certainly is one of the most exciting of the recent developments on the frontiers of economic theory.

A FINAL WORD

There is no doubt that the millions of households and firms in an economy are interrelated and that their decisions, individually small, impinge upon one another through the market mechanism. It is clear that the economy does adjust, sometimes imperfectly, often slowly, to the changing demands upon it. An enormous part of the adjustment process is handled by the price system, which no one planned and which is (by and large) unregulated. To say we do not understand the price system nearly well enough does not mean that we do not have a good idea of the way it works, the speed with which it works, the places where it appears to be least satisfactory, and the places where it appears to do very well. Dissatisfactions with the workings of the price system have led policy-makers, even in the most market-oriented of economies, to adopt policies that interfere with the free working of markets. Some of the great efficiencies of the price system have led policy-makers in economies where everyone is ideologically committed to planning, to introduce pricing schemes to guide a significant part of the decision-making process.

32

Micro-economic policy

Most people live in mixed economies: on the one hand, the market mechanism is given substantial freedom to influence the allocation of resources and the distribution of income; on the other hand, the central authorities intervene in many different ways and exert substantial influence on the workings of the market. We observed at the end of the last chapter that dissatisfaction with the workings of the unhampered market has led to substantial central intervention even from governments committed to accepting the general idea of the free market, while, at the same time, a growing awareness of the advantages of the price system as a coordinating mechanism for decentralized decision-taking has led to a reintroduction of many aspects of the price system by central authorities in countries committed to the basic idea of central planning.

In this chapter, we are concerned with the activities of the central authorities that impinge upon the unrestricted workings of the free-market system. We are particularly concerned at this time with policies that affect the allocation of resources and the distribution of income, rather than with those that have as their primary concern the overall level, stability and growth of national output. We shall start by considering some of the main reasons for public intervention in free markets.

THE CASE FOR THE FREE MARKET

The major case for the free market is that it provides a reasonably efficient and impersonal method of determining the ever-changing pattern of the allocation of resources. The great value of the market is in providing automatic signals *as a situation develops*, so that all of the changes consequent on, say, building a new car plant do not have to be anticipated and allowed for by a body of central planners. Millions of adaptations to millions of changes in tens of thousands of markets are required every year, and it would be a Herculean task to anticipate these and plan for them centrally. Should we produce yellow hats or green hats or both, and if both, in what proportion? Such matters, so goes the argument, do not need to be decided centrally, and are best left to be decided by the market. The great advantage of the free market is that it allows for some decentralized (but nonetheless coordinated) decision-taking. The experience of planned economies such as those in the Soviet bloc is that it is very difficult and very expensive (in terms of scarce manpower) to try to plan centrally *everything* about the economy. This is particularly so as per capita output rises, and an increasing variety of consumers' goods is produced. The observable trend in these centrally planned countries is to keep important decisions, such as the decision about the division of resources between the production of capital goods and consumers' goods, in the hands of the central authorities but to try to decentralize such decisions as how many resources should be devoted to the production of yellow hats in relation to the number devoted to the production of green hats. If such decisions are to be decentralized, then (a) some form of market signals must exist, and (b) there must be some incentive for firms and the owners of factors of production to react appropriately to these signals.

Allocation by the market also tends to be more impersonal than allocation by many other methods. We have observed earlier that the control of prices at non-equilibrium values without rationing tends to create allocation by sellers' preferences (see pages 118–19). If the market is determining prices, the tobacconist will sell cigarettes to anyone who enters his shop. If the price of cigarettes is well below the equilibrium value, the tobacconist will be unable to satisfy everyone who comes into his shop, and he will be forced to decide who he is going to satisfy. He might work on the first-come-first-served principle, or he might serve people whose colour, manner, dress or sex he liked and refuse to serve others.

Furthermore, the incentive for bribery and corruption is clearly present in situations of excess demand. If, for example, state housing is available at prices well below the market price, there will be a queue to get into the flats that do become available. The official who controls the allocations from the waiting list will be in a position of power and could take bribes for pushing someone up in the list. If the state charged the market price for its housing, this opportunity for corruption would be removed because, temporary and unforeseen fluctuations aside, everyone who was prepared to pay the price could obtain accommodation.

In addition to these general considerations there is the more technical argument coming from welfare economics that the competitive price system leads to an optimal allocation of resources. This theory of optimal resource allocation has not been fully developed in this book, but it was mentioned briefly during the discussion of monopoly versus competition. At that time we mentioned that the conditions needed to obtain this optimality, e.g., perfect competition throughout the economy – were a long way from being fulfilled. Thus the case for the price system in the oligopolistic world in which we live must rest mainly on more general considerations of which the most important is that it provides a method for decentralizing decision-taking while assuring that such decisions are at least moderately well coordinated.

THE CASE FOR INTERVENTION

A great deal of intervention into the free workings of the price system does in fact occur in all Western economies. There are many reasons for such interventions, and we must now consider the most important of them.

(1) Divergences between private and social costs

When the firm is calculating the profitability of alternative production plans, it will have to estimate the revenue gained from selling the output and the costs of producing it. In assessing the costs of producing a given output, the firm must estimate the opportunity cost of the required factor services. The opportunity cost to the firm will normally be related to the market prices of the factor services. If the market prices of the resources used adequately reflect their alternative uses from the whole society's point of view, then the firm's decisions will be based on a consideration of the value of the alternative uses of these resources in the whole society. There are many reasons why this may not be so, and this leads us to distinguish two concepts of cost.

PRIVATE COST: Private cost measures the opportunity cost to the firm of the resources that it uses. This opportunity cost is based on the alternatives that are available to the firm. If a firm uses a resource for which it has absolutely no alternative use, then the private cost is zero. Private cost is usually based on the market value of the factors currently purchased by the firm and the price that could be obtained by selling to outsiders the services of factors owned by the firm.

SOCIAL COST: Social cost measures the opportunity cost to the whole society of the resources that the firm uses. This opportunity cost is based on the alternatives that are available to the whole society. If a firm uses a resource for which the society had alternative uses then the social cost of these resources is not zero, it is rather the value of the resource in its best alternative use.

The divergence between private and social cost is one of the most important reasons for intervening in the free market. The social value of resources in alternative uses is measured by social costs; the value to the firm is measured by private costs. If the two do not coincide the firm will base its decisions about the allocation of resources on considerations that do not reflect the interests of the society as a whole and not even perfect competition would lead to an optimum allocation of resources.

Perhaps the best way to proceed is to give a number of examples of divergences between private and social costs, and to show the consequences of taking decisions on the basis of private costs.

(1) A factory discharges its waste into a river. The resulting pollution destroys fish living downstream, and forces several communities to install costly water purification plants and to build swimming pools since the river is no longer safe for swimming. The private cost to the factory of using the river as a waste disposal unit is zero since there is no alternative use for the river to the factory and no price has to be paid for the privilege. The social cost consists of the fish that are destroyed and the resources used in the purification plants and the swimming pools (plus the costs incurred by a host of other consequences of water pollution). The social cost of using the river to dispose of waste may well be greatly in excess of the social cost of having the factory's waste disposed of in a chemical treatment plant. Yet there will be no

incentive for the private firm to adopt what is socially the least costly method, since the private costs of the two alternative methods do not reflect the social costs.

(2) An industrial complex discharges smoke into the atmosphere; private cost: zero; social cost, when done on a large scale: prodigious. Over the last hundred and fifty years very large amounts of industrial waste have been disposed of into the atmosphere at a very high social cost. The cost shows up in a great many ways: extra laundry and cleaning bills, the periodic sandblasting of grime-encrusted buildings, smog blankets which often slow and sometimes even halt all of the city's business, chronic diseases caused by air pollution, and a general shortening of life expectancy. The list can be extended almost indefinitely.

(3) An offshore oil well disposes of its waste oil by dumping it into the sea. The private cost is virtually zero. The social cost is very high, and is measured in terms of ruined beaches, fish and birds destroyed, tourist industries damaged, and general destruction of the environment.

(4) An oil company proposes to send tankers from Alaska down the West Coast of Canada to American ports. Assume that the risks are such that approximately one voyage every 10 years will end in disaster. The private cost of taking this risk is the small insurance premium necessary to insure against it. The oil firm will be led to use this route if all costs including the insurance premium are less than the value of the oil shipped. The social cost is measured both in terms of the destruction that will be caused to the coastline environment when a tanker sinks and in terms of all of the (government financed) resources that will be used to cope, in so far as one can cope, with the resulting pollution. Clearly, it would be less costly to society to exploit some alternative source of energy even if it has substantially higher private costs, as long as it did not result in the additional social costs.

(5) A private timber firm cuts a forest which had an alternative use of providing a nature sanctuary and a national recreation area. The citizens valued the park highly, but there was no way for the firm to bring this alternative use into its calculations since public parks are not bought or sold on any market.

(6) Another timber firm cuts a forest and thereby destroys a natural watershed bringing drought and destruction on neighbouring farms. Social cost exceeds the private cost by all the foregone agricultural output, plus resources subsequently used to provide a stable water supply to the farms.

(7) The choice between alternative transport systems is usually made after comparisons of private costs. For instance, in deciding whether to ship his goods by rail or road, a manufacturer will consider, amongst other things, the relative prices charged by each. These relative charges will in turn be related to the relative private costs of the railroad and the road haulage firm of moving the goods. It is sometimes argued that the social costs of transporting freight by road greatly exceed the private costs. People who hold this view point to the facts that trucks use the roads free, that the cost of roads would be greatly reduced if they did not have to be built strong enough to sustain the pounding of heavy lorries and that road congestion, which is aggravated by lorry traffic, imposes heavy costs on other users, particularly where a road goes through a town. A classic case of the failure of the unhindered price system would occur *if* the cost situation for freight transport were as follows:

ROAD HAULAGE

private cost < revenue

social cost > revenue

RAIL HAULAGE

private cost > revenue

social cost < revenue

If this were the case the free market would divert traffic onto the roads, while from society's point of view the margin of advantage lies with rail traffic.

(8) Another example concerns zoning laws. If A owns a building lot in a residential area (on which he intends to build a house in five years) and decides to get some money out of it in the meantime by leasing it to a farmer to pasture his goats, or to a fairground operator, the neighbours may well object. In a society that values individual freedom, we have a predisposition not to interfere with bargains freely negotiated between adults. But if, as in the above example, these bargains confer substantial costs on third persons not party to the bargain, there is a case for intervention.

THE REMEDY FOR SOCIAL AND PRIVATE COST DIVERGENCES: In cases in which social and private costs can be clearly identified and measured it is possible to adjust for any divergence between the two by taxes and subsidies. Where social costs exceed private costs, a tax on the production of the good may bring private costs more in line with social costs, and where the opposite relation occurs a subsidy can be used. Road and petrol taxes provide an example, although many feel that they still leave private costs well below social ones. Free parking in the centre of urban areas creates a situation of zero private costs in the face of substantial social costs. Parking meters are thus more than just another way of raising money; they are used to bring private and social costs into line and make the person who imposes the cost on society bear it himself. The recent discussion of means of charging cars for the use of urban roads represents another attempt to bring the private cost to the road user into line with the social cost of accommodating private cars in congested urban areas. Taxes on cigarettes may to some extent reflect the fact that the social costs of cigarette consumption – in terms of expensive medical and hospital services required for smokers in later life – exceed the private cost of the cigarette to the consumer. On the other hand, subsidies on housing and medical services reflect the belief held by some that the social cost of removing slums and producing a high standard of health is less than the private cost.

Problems arise where divergences cannot be identified, or where they cannot be quantitatively measured even when they are located. In such cases the situation cannot be remedied by simple tax or subsidy policies because the extent of the divergence between private and social cost is not known.

Much environmental pollution falls into this category. Up to a very few years ago most experts had very little idea of the far-reaching consequences of the pollution caused by many industrial activities. Only now are we beginning to get an appreciation of the devastating consequences of some of our polluting activities, and thus of the vast divergence between the private and the social costs. Even today we are ignorant of many long-run effects and thus cannot say by how much we should raise private costs by taxation to make them conform to social costs. In such cases, where we have a substantial margin of ignorance, but a risk that major, possibly irreversible, damage may be caused by a given activity, it may be considered prudent to ban the activity altogether until more knowledge of its consequences is gained. Thus, a second policy reaction is to prohibit certain activities by law. This will generally recommend itself in cases in which we are uncertain of the social costs, and there exists some distinct possibility that they may be extremely high.

(2) Market imperfections

FACTOR IMMOBILITY: If factors are relatively immobile, the supply will tend to be inelastic in the short run, and even large increases in the price offered may induce only small movements. As we saw in Chapters 28 and 30, if theoretical physicists are in short supply their pay will rise, and an increase in the payments made to existing physicists may ultimately lead to an increase in the total supply of physicists (for example, by persuading students who had planned to become economists or engineers to go into physics instead). But such increases in pay may have only a small effect on supply for several years, in view of the training required. Meanwhile, existing physicists will earn high salaries, and will command a larger share of national income than they otherwise would have done. It may well be that public policy can bring about an increase in the supply of physicists more quickly and at lower cost than can the unhampered market. The central authorities might, for example, provide very generous scholarships and studentships to encourage students to take degrees in physics. These provide incentives for new entrants to the labour force to become physicists without providing extra earnings to all these who are already in the profession.

Factors may be immobile for reasons other than time lags required for education. For example, unemployed workers may be uninformed about job opportunities or inadequately trained to take jobs that are available. Agencies such as Employment Exchanges can increase the speed with which such workers can find jobs by collecting data on what kind of jobs are available in what places, and informing unemployed workers about them. Special programmes of retraining are also provided by some governmental units. Factors may often be reluctant to move from one location to another because of the heavy moving expenses, or the difficulties in finding housing, or racial prejudice in hiring. Public policies may lessen these imperfections by giving subsidies for expenses incurred in moving from one job to another, by building public housing (or subsidizing private housing) in areas that have labour shortages, and by legally prohibiting various forms of discrimination with respect to the hiring of minority groups.

Markets may also be poor allocators of labour among possible uses if labour is ignorant of the signals being provided by the market. Signals do not work if they are not seen. Before you dismiss this imperfection as trivial, ask yourself if you have any clear idea of the expected lifetime income of a person following the subject of study you have chosen, and that of persons following the subjects your friends have chosen. Also, do you know enough to be able to compare lifetime earnings of the few people who are unusually successful with the earnings of those who are only averagely successful in each of the relevant occupations?

FIRM BEHAVIOUR: Profit maximization in a world of perfect competition makes firms into passive adjusters who follow market signals without exerting any personal pressure on the outcome. When we depart from perfect competition and/or profit-maximizing behaviour, firms achieve the power to interfere with the behaviour of the market. Profit-maximizing monopoly presents one pure case. Monopoly power prevents resources from moving in response to market signals. A rise in demand for a monopolist's product will cause a rise in the monopolist's profits; in a perfectly competitive industry this would lead to an increase in resources allocated to the production of this good until profits fell to zero, but if the monopolist can restrict entry into his industry, no such resource reallocation will occur – except insofar as the monopolist finds it profitable to increase his own output.

If the firm is not concerned with profit maximization, the market mechanism may not work in anything like the manner described by our theory. A rise in demand will not even necessarily be met by a rise in output of the existing monopolist if he is not a profit maximizer.

Oligopoly can also cause market reactions that are not in accordance with the perfectly competitive result. Since firms are conditioned by the real and imagined reactions of their very few rivals, almost any conceivable result can follow even from such an unambiguous change in market signals as a rise in the price of some commodity, or the fall in the price of some factor of production. Thus in oligopolistic situations we are unsure about how satisfactorily firms will respond to changes in market signals.

CONSUMER BEHAVIOUR: Economists usually do not try to pass judgement on the tastes of consumers. A market system is said to work if it responds to consumers' tastes whatever the nature of the tastes. But the market will not work effectively if consumers are misinformed about the products they buy. Providing market information, or enforcing a requirement that others provide it, is a major activity of many government agencies whose function is to make markets work better. These activities range from requiring food manufacturers to identify the contents and the net weight of their product, through the government inspection and grading of meat and grain, to the provision of information on changes involved in consuming particular products such as cigarettes.

(3) Collective consumption goods

Certain goods or services, if they provide benefits to anyone, necessarily provide them to a large group of people. Such goods are called COLLECTIVE CONSUMPTION GOODS. National defence is a prime example of a collective consumption good. If we have an adequate defence establishment, it protects us all. It protects you, even if you do not care to 'buy' any of it. The quantity of national defence to be provided must be decided collectively, and there is no market where you can buy more or less of it than your neighbour. A compromise quantity must be generally agreed on and then the government must acquire the funds to pay for it by taxation.

There are many other examples. The beautification of a city provides a service to all residents and visitors. A barrage that protects a city from a flood is also a collective consumption good. So also is a hurricane-warning system. Another important example is police protection. If a police force reduces the number of crimes, everyone gains. In a market system even if you did not pay to have the police watch your house you would gain from the fact that your neighbour did.

In general, market systems cannot compel payment for a collective good, since there is no way to prevent a person from receiving the services of the good if he refuses to pay for it. Only governments, through their power to tax, can compel payments by all. Indeed, it is the existence of collective consumption goods that necessitates putting some of our production into government hands, and that prevents the government from selling everything it produces on the free market just as any other firm does (and as the government does with postal services but does not and cannot do with military and police services).

(4) The costs of collecting revenue

In some cases a good that is not a collective consumption good will still not be suitable for private production because the cost of collecting revenue from individual consumers is prohibitively high. If so the free market will not provide the good even if consumers would rather have this good than any other that could be produced with the same quantity of factor services. In such cases the government can provide the good and pay for it out of general tax revenue without having to use resources to collect a payment from each consumer of the good.

Consider an example. Suppose motorists in a metropolitan area are willing to pay to have a high-speed urban motorway system leading into and out of town. Suppose that there are enough people willing to pay 6p a mile to cover the costs of building such a road system, but that different groups of them want to use different sections of the system. A private company would find it profitable to build and operate the road if it could collect 6p a mile from everybody willing to pay that much. But if it must build a toll house at every entrance and exit to the road in order to collect this money, the costs of the system would be increased and the venture might seem an unprofitable one. Intra-urban motorways with many access points and many short-journey travellers are often unsuitable for private ventures, because the cost of collecting tolls is too high. It is no accident that in countries where privately built toll roads are common, virtually all toll roads are *inter-urban* roads which require relatively few access points and where the average journey is a long one.

(5) The desire to protect some individuals from decisions taken on their behalf by others

In economics the household is taken to be the basic decision-taking unit. We must not forget that most households contain several persons and that the choice problem within the household is a political one. Whose desires are to be favoured and by how much in making the purchasing decisions for the household? One example should suffice to show how important this point is. In an unhindered free market the adult members of the household will make decisions about how much education to buy, and thereby exert a profound effect on the lives of their children. A selfish parent may buy no education, while an egalitarian one may buy the same quantity for all his children. The central authorities may interfere in this choice both to protect the child and to ensure that some of the scarce educational resources are unequally distributed according to intelligence rather than wealth. We force all households to purchase education for their children and we provide strong inducements, through scholarships, etc., for the gifted to consume much more education than either they or their parents might voluntarily select if they had to pay the whole cost themselves. The latter is done probably because of a divergence between social and private costs, but the former is done in the belief that the head of the household should not have perfect freedom to take decisions that affect the welfare of other members of the household, particularly when they are minors.

(6) The belief that some obligations transcend the market criteria

In a market system, if you can pay for something you can have it. If you have to clean your house and if you can persuade someone else to do the job for you in return for £2, presumably both parties to the transaction are better off: you would prefer to part with £2 rather than clean the house yourself and your cleaning woman prefers £2 to not cleaning your house. Normally we do not interfere with people's ability to negotiate such mutually advantageous contracts.

Most people do not feel this way, however, about activities which are regarded as social obligations. A prime example is military service. At times and places in which military service is compulsory, contracts similar to the one between the housewife and her cleaning woman could also be struck. Some persons faced with the obligation to do military service could no doubt pay enough to persuade others to do their turn of service for them. By exactly the same argument as we used above, we can presume that both parties will be better off if they are allowed to negotiate such a trade. But such contracts are usually prohibited. Why? We do this because we feel that there are values other than those that can be expressed in a market. In times when it is necessary, military service by all healthy males is usually held to be an obligation independent of their tastes, wealth, influence or social position. It is felt that everyone *ought* to do this service, and trades between willing traders are prohibited.

(7) Compassion

A free-market system rewards certain groups and penalizes others. The workings of the market may be stern, even cruel; consequently, it may seem humane to intervene. Should unproductive farmers be starved off the farm? Should men be forced to bear the full burden of their misfortune, if, through no fault of their own, they lose their jobs? Indeed, even if they lose their jobs through their own fault, should they and their families have to bear the whole burden, which may include starvation? Should the ill and aged be thrown on the mercy of their families? What if they have no families? Should small businessmen have to compete with the chain store and the discount house? A great many government policies are concerned with modifying the distribution of income that results from such things as where one starts, how able one is, how lucky one is and how one fares in the free-market world.

In the discussion above, we noted some of the reasons why people acting through their government may wish to achieve a different quantity, quality and distribution of goods than the free market provides. This is the case against *complete laissez-faire*. But members of a society may have other goals as well. One of these may be a belief in the individual's freedom to act on his own and to make his own choices. Multiple goals often involve conflicts, and conflicts require choices. The decision on when and where and to what extent to interfere with the free-market system must require value judgements about the relative values to be placed on alternative policy goals whenever they come into conflict.

The optimal correction of market failure

The spirit of our times has led many to treat all problems of market failure, such as pollution, as a national scandal and perhaps even as an imminent crisis of survival. The problems in fact, run the whole range from threats to our survival down to minor nuisances. Virtually all activity leaves some waste product behind it. To say that all pollution must be removed whatever the cost is certainly to try for the impossible and probably to get a vast commitment of society's scarce resources to projects some of which will yield a low utility. If, by emitting smoke, a factory is appreciably lowering the life expectancy of those in surrounding communities, it is clearly worthwhile investing a great deal in purifying the effluent. But suppose that the smoke from another factory is not a health hazard, but does smell badly. Further assume that the 10,000 local residents affected by this pollution would be willing to pay on average no more than £10 a year to be rid of the smell. The social cost of the present smoke emission is thus £100,000 a year. Say that the firm was forced to adopt an alternative disposal method at a cost of £500,000 a year. This means that £500,000 worth of society's scarce resources will be used to create a result that society values at only £100,000. Because these resources could have produced other goods valued at £500,000, there is an overall loss of £400,000.

This example points to an important problem: control of pollution and other externalities is costly; it makes sense where the benefits have a higher value than the cost. Pollution control, as with other services, may have great benefits at first and then run into diminishing returns. Instances of the need for external control where social costs are great (e.g., control of nuclear wastes) are obvious and dramatic; in other cases social costs are more nearly equal to private costs.

Which activities to prohibit, which to modify, which to clean up after and which to tolerate, are important choices. The economist can help those who have to make these choices by carefully designating costs and benefits. It is important to note that the choices made may vary among communities and over time. As a society gets wealthier the value placed on improvements in the quality of life relative to material gains may rise. Poor communities may welcome new industries for the employment and tax revenues they bring, while richer communities may seek to remove these same industries in order to avoid the unpleasant social costs they bring with them.

ECONOMIC ANALYSIS AND ECONOMIC POLICY

So far we have considered some of the very important general considerations involved in the question of central-authority intervention into a basically free market economy.

We may now pass on to a general consideration of the role of the economist in policy issues. Like all interesting questions this one is the subject of disagreement and debate. All that is done here is to outline a view that does, I think, approximately reflect the majority view of economists. The student should be warned against accepting this as the only view.[1]

Economists sometimes speak as if economic theory justified certain policy objectives and showed others to be wrong. It is not uncommon to hear such phrases as: 'Rent control is economically *unsound*'; 'The policy of running transport services free is *economic nonsense*'; 'The only *valid* economic policy is to charge a price which covers costs'. Of course such phrases might be a loose way of making the reasonable point that the policy is 'unsound' for any one of several reasons which are outlined below. It is, however, quite likely that such phrases will be employed in an effort to dismiss a policy without thinking through its consequences; and if they are not a cover for such sloppy thinking they are quite likely to be used in an attempt to persuade someone that economics proves what policy goals we ought to seek, and which ones we should eschew. Every time a student encounters such catch phrases as 'economic nonsense', his every critical faculty should be aroused. 'What does this really mean?', he should ask, 'and why, exactly, is it dismissed as "nonsense"?' We have stated in Chapter 1 that it is impossible to deduce a statement about what ought to be from statements about what is. Positive economics concerns what is and cannot therefore produce statements about what ought to be.

Rent control: an example

What then can we expect from economics when we come to consider problems of economic policy? Consider, for example, the position of an economist asked to examine the case for and against rent control (i.e., the fixing by the central authorities of the rentals of private dwellings). First, he should ask what policy goals rent control is meant to achieve. He might find, for example, that rent control is intended to redistribute income from rich to poor, and to ensure a minimum standard of housing for everyone. Next, he must ask if rent control does in fact help to realize these policy goals. If the answer is 'No', then the case against rent control is clear: it does not achieve the objects for which it is intended. If the answer is 'Yes', then further study is necessary. Consider, as an example, the goal of income redistribution. Rent control, if effective, means that the tenant pays less rent than he otherwise would, and the landlord receives less income than he otherwise would; thus rent control redistributes income from landlord to tenant. But do landlords tend to be richer than their tenants? If a survey shows that most tenants are in fact richer than their landlords, the economist can conclude that there is a case against rent control, not because it is unjust or unethical, but because it does not achieve the policy goal for which it was being used. If, however, the survey indicates that most tenants have lower incomes than their landlords, then the economist will conclude that rent control *is* a means of obtaining the desired goal of income redistribution.

1 The injunction 'be critical and keep an open mind' applies of course, everywhere. For a view very different from the one expressed here, see, G. Myrdal, *Value in Social Theory: A Selection of Essays on Methodology*, edited by Paul Streeten (Routledge, 1958).

The economist must next ask if rent control has effects that conflict with other policy objectives. It may be, for example, that, although rent control provides low-cost housing, it simultaneously causes the appearance of more slum areas. When a measure helps to achieve one goal but hinders the attainment of another, it is necessary to decide which of these goals is preferred. The economist must then consider the alternative policies to see if there are any measures that will achieve the goal at a lower sacrifice in terms of setbacks to other policy objectives. It may be, for example, that the progressive income tax redistributes income from rich to poor with more certainty and precision and with fewer undesired side effects than rent control.

The economist must now determine if it is feasible to adopt the alternative means. In other words, when faced with evaluating a policy measure for achieving some goal, he must ask whether other measures *that are feasible at the time and place* would better achieve the desired goal.

If, having done all this, the economist concludes that rent control *does* achieve the desired policy, that the undesirable effects in other directions are judged (by the policy-makers) to be less important than the desirable effects in achieving the stated policy goal, and that there are no other practicable measures that would better achieve the goals, he will conclude that there is a strong case in its favour.

There are many pitfalls in applying this procedure. Most importantly, the economist himself will usually have strong views on the particular measure he is attempting to assess. If he does not like the measure, he is likely to be relentless in searching out possible unwanted effects, and somewhat less than thorough in discovering effects that help to achieve the desired goals. It is difficult to guard against an unconscious bias of this sort; the best method of doing so is to ensure that many economists of different political persuasions all examine the issue.

Suggesting new policies

It is the role of the economist not only to analyse the consequences of a proposed policy (or to compare two or more policies), but also to suggest new policies. Given a statement of the objectives, economic analysis can be used to invent or publicize proposed policies that have not previously been under consideration. The economist might, for example, point out that some radical new measure such as running all public transport in urban areas free of charges might be a hitherto-unthought-of means of achieving a number of generally accepted goals. [1] Free public transport in all major urban areas might vastly relieve congestion, by dissuading people from bringing private cars into these areas; it might also relieve urban overcrowding by persuading people to live further out of town; and there might be a large social saving in time and effort brought about on both these counts; finally there would be a direct saving in resources because conductors, ticket salesmen, ticket collectors, inspectors and many traffic policemen could be dispensed with. [2] This labour would be freed for use elsewhere to produce needed goods and services. The case for and

1 This is by no means a novel policy suggestion and it is chosen for illustrative purposes only. A carefully conducted *quantitative* study would be necessary before one could come to any conclusion on the net advantage of this scheme.

2 The discussion on the costs of raising revenue (see page 438) is relevant at this point.

against this particular policy would need much more careful consideration than can be given here, but the point is made that the economist has a function in suggesting quite new ways of achieving old goals. In this case the goal of relieving transport congestion might be achieved together with additional savings resulting from the freeing of labour for other uses.

One of the greatest advantages of the economist in dealing with policy matters such as those mentioned here is that he is trained to look for *consistency* in people's ideas about the world. Where someone else may look at ideas and policies one at a time, the economist has a predisposition to look at them all at once, to see if they make a pattern, and to ask if they are consistent one with the other. Indeed, the training of economic theorists often leads them to value consistency above all else. This is, of course, a great strength for it is seldom useful to hold inconsistent ideas: to act, for example, at one time as if all relevant demand curves were inelastic and then immediately afterwards to introduce a policy which would make sense only if they were all elastic. The demand for consistency – that we do not contradict ourselves – is a necessary one for satisfactory explanation in economics as in other fields. However, it is not enough. A perfectly consistent theory may be utterly wrong, and this can be found out only by testing it against observations. A significant advance in the use of economics in policy matters would be achieved if people accepted the statements of economists only after they had asked 'What is the evidence?' and 'Has this theory been subjected to a test *where it had a real chance of meeting with conflicting evidence?*'.

Possible conflicts of policy

It may be quite impossible to fulfill all of our policy goals simultaneously. It may well be that a measure will bring us closer to some of our objectives, but take us further away from others. In such cases we say that there is a TRADE OFF between policy objectives: they conflict with one another in the sense that we can get closer to one goal only at the cost of moving further away from another. It is then not sufficient for governments to decide which objectives are worth pursuing, they must also decide on some *rate of substitution* between them; they must decide how much of one it is worth sacrificing in order to get more of the other. Many of today's controversies over matters of economic policy are concerned with this issue of the relative importance of different objectives, each objective being accepted as desirable, *ceteris paribus*. Practically everyone, for example, accepts a high level of employment and control of inflation as desirable goals of policy. There is real disagreement, however, over the relative importance of these two goals, over the rate at which one should be substituted for the other.

MAJOR POLICY TOOLS

The central authorities have three main tools to affect the nature of what goods are produced and how they are distributed: rule-making, taxation and public expenditures. We shall consider each of these separately.

Rule-making as a tool of policy

Rules pervade our society. Shop hours and working conditions are regulated.

Children cannot be served alcoholic drink. Parents are required to send their children to school in most countries and to have them inoculated against certain communicable diseases in some. Laws prohibit people from selling or using certain drugs. Prostitution is prohibited in many societies even when it is between a willing buyer and a willing seller. In many countries you are forced to purchase insurance for the damage you might do with your private motor car even if you don't want to carry insurance. In many countries a person who offers goods for sale cannot refuse to sell them just because he does not like the customer's colour or dress. There are rules against fraudulent advertising and the sale of substandard, adulterated or poisonous foods. In some countries, such as the United States, anyone who wants to can purchase a wide variety of weapons ranging from pistols to machine guns. In other countries, such as the United Kingdom, it is extremely difficult for a private citizen to obtain a gun.

Many business practices are controlled by rules and prohibitions. In many countries agreements between oligopolistic firms to fix prices or to divide up markets are illegal. The mere existence of monopoly is also often outlawed and monopoly firms are forcibly broken up into several independent ones, who will, it is presumed, compete with each other. When the cost advantages of monopoly resulting from scale economies are considerable, the monopolistic firm is often regulated as to the prices it can charge and the return it can earn on its capital investment. The reality of such control is beyond question; its advisability and its effectiveness are subject to substantial debate.[1]

Tax structure as a tool of policy

Taxes raised in Britain amounted to nearly 30 per cent of the value of all incomes earned in the country in the year 1974. As we saw in Chapters 11 and 23, taxes have some effect on prices; for this reason, we expect the pattern of taxes to have an effect on the allocation of resources among uses. There is much evidence about the effect of particular taxes on the allocation of resources to particular markets. We do not, however, have sufficient knowledge to assess the total effect of the whole tax system on the economy, and we are thus unable to answer such questions as: 'How different would the allocation of resources and the distribution of income be if all taxes were removed?'

TAXES AND THE SIZE DISTRIBUTION OF INCOME: In order to discuss the effect of taxes on distribution we need to define three types of taxes.

A tax is called PROPORTIONAL if it takes amounts of money from people in direct proportion to their income. A tax is called REGRESSIVE if it takes a larger percentage of income from people the lower their incomes. A tax is called PROGRESSIVE if it takes a larger percentage of income from people the larger their incomes. The words proportional, progressive and regressive are treated as positive terms. Nothing in the definition implies that one is better than another.

When dealing with rates of tax, we need to distinguish between what is called the

---

1 For an outline of British anti-monopoly policy see the relevant chapter in Prest, the *UK Economy: A Manual of Applied Economics* (5th edn., Weidenfeld & Nicolson, 1974).

AVERAGE RATE OF TAX and the MARGINAL RATE OF TAX. Referring to the income tax, the average rate of tax paid by some individual is his total tax divided by his total income. His marginal rate of tax is the rate he would pay on another unit of income. To take an example, an individual in Britain with an income of £1,000 per year would pay about £122 in tax, making an average rate of 12 per cent. If his income rose to £1,001 he would pay 30p in tax on the extra one pound of income making a marginal rate of 30 per cent.

Consider first the progressivity of some individual taxes. On the one hand, the income tax is steeply progressive as illustrated in Table 32.1. On the other hand, the heavy taxes on cigarettes and beer are regressive since the proportion of income spent on cigarettes and beer, and hence the proportion paid in tobacco and beer tax, tends to decline as income rises. A government uses many individual taxes to make up its tax system. This is because different taxes have different strengths and weaknesses, and catch different income levels or types of incomes with varying degrees of efficiency. Popular discussion often concentrates on the progressivity or regressivity of a particular tax: certain taxes, such as the tobacco tax, are often condemned because they are regressive; also, the image of the United Kingdom as a steeply progressive-tax country is often based solely on the progressivity of the income tax, without any correction for the influence of other taxes which are either less progressive or even regressive. Clearly, if we wish to judge the effect of the tax system on the size distribution of income we need to look at the progressivity of the whole tax system. We wish to ask of a typical household what happens to the proportion of its income that is absorbed by all taxes as income rises.

Studies made in several countries suggest that the overall tax system is usually very much less progressive than is the personal income tax considered on its own. Indeed in spite of steeply progressive rates of income tax, the American tax system appears to be regressive up to the middle ranges of income.

The tax system distinguishes among households not only according to the size of household income, but also according to a host of other characteristics, such as size of family, age, occupation and source of income. The tax system undoubtedly does redistribute income among households when they are classified by some of these other characteristics. Consider two examples.

Deductions for wives and children: By giving deductions for wives and children, the tax system tends to redistribute income away from households with only one person, and towards households with many children. The grounds for this redistribution are probably normative, involving considerations of equity. The incentive effect, however, is to reduce the private cost of raising children. As the world population explosion causes more and more concern, some people are being led to question the desirability of creating such an incentive. They argue that the social cost of a rapidly rising population greatly exceeds the private cost to the household of raising its own family, and they argue for taxes on children rather than subsidies. By raising the private cost nearer to the social cost, they seek to provide an incentive to have smaller rather than larger families. Here is a policy issue that will probably be strongly debated over the next decade or so.

Table 32.1 UK income tax, 1973–4

UK Income Tax, 1973–4 (Single person, no dependants)			
Earned income £	Amount of tax £	Average tax rate %	Marginal tax rate %
500	—	—	—
750	46	6	30
1,000	121	12	30
1,500	271	18	30
2,000	421	21	30
3,000	721	24	30
4,000	1,021	25	30
6,000	1,662	27	40
10,000	3,743	37	60
20,000	10,453	52	75
50,000	32,953	65	75

Earned Income Allowance: The second example is that in the United Kingdom, incomes arising from the sale of the services of labour (called earned income) is taxed more lightly than incomes of more than £2,000 per year arising from the sale of the services of capital (called unearned income). This tends to redistribute income from people whose income arises from investing their capital, towards people whose income arises from the sale of labour services.

THE STRUCTURE OF TAXES AND THE GOODS THE ECONOMY PRODUCES: Resources move, in a market economy, in response to changes in the *relative* prices of different goods and factors, and in response to the relative profitability of different industries. A *neutral* tax is defined as one that does not change any of the signals to which resources respond. It is clear that the tax system of any Western country is not neutral in this sense. It would be surprising if it were. The central authorities may wish to allocate resources in a way different from the way the market allocates them, and taxes can be used to that end.

One way in which tax structure affects resource allocation is through the deductions allowed on the personal income tax. An allowable deduction is an expenditure that may be deducted from income before computing the amount of taxes payable. Consider a wealthy man in the 75 per cent marginal tax bracket (see Table 32.1). Every £100 he spends on an item that is tax deductible costs him £25 in after-tax income. Every £100 he spends on items that are not tax deductible costs him £100 in after-tax income. In many countries contributions to charitable and educational institutions are tax deductible, as are interest payments on a mortgage, while contributions to political parties are not, nor is rent paid on a home. The effect of these laws is to *restructure* incentives by making the relative cost of giving to educational institutions less than the cost of giving to political parties, and the 'price' of owning a home relatively less than the price of renting one. Empirical studies leave no doubt that actual behaviour responds to these incentives in just the way that theory predicts it will.

Some taxes are designed to influence the behaviour of firms. The 'investment credit' found in various forms in both the UK and the US provides special tax relief for firms that are engaging in new investment. In the United States and Canada, income received from the production of minerals is given favourable tax treatment, through the so-called depletion provisions, which allow a mineral producer to deduct from his income amounts that often exceed the costs actually involved. Because of this, explorers and producers of minerals earn greater profits after taxes; and empirical studies leave no doubt that the depletion provisions have greatly increased investment in discovering and developing mineral supplies.

Excise and sales taxes raise the relative prices of taxed commodities. Commodities such as cigarettes, alcoholic beverages and petrol are taxed particularly heavily. As we saw in the discussion of tax incidence in Chapter 11, excise and sales taxes will have some effect on prices and quantities consumed. It is not clear whether taxes of these kinds are *intended* to curtail consumption or merely to raise revenue. The more inelastic the demand for a product (*ceteris paribus*), the less the curtailment of consumption and the greater the revenue yield for any given tax.

The quantitative extent to which tax policies actually change the pattern of goods and services produced by affecting relative prices is not really known. It is clear that many prices are higher than they would be without taxation and that some are lower. On the basis of our theory, we are led to predict that this leads to less production and consumption of the former commodities and more of the latter, but the question of *how different* is the bill of goods, is an empirical one that requires, but has not received, extended study. Nor is it clear whether such effects as have occurred are intended consequences of a policy designed to achieve them, or are incidental side effects of policies designed to achieve other ends.

Public expenditure as a tool of economic policy

Much government expenditure is devoted to TRANSFER PAYMENTS. These are payments made *not* in return for any goods or services. They transfer money from one person or group to another without adding to total production. Public welfare, old age, unemployment and disability payments are all examples of transfer payments.

Much government expenditure is allocated to the provision of goods and services, many of which are provided free to the households that consume them. Some of these goods are collective consumption goods such as defence and police, and some are goods for which the cost of collecting payment would be too high, such as urban roads. For these commodities there is no problem of choice between the public and private sector: either they are provided by the state or not at all. Other goods and services such as education, hospital and medical care, rural roads and motorways are provided by private firms in some countries, but are nonetheless provided free by the state in other countries. Yet other commodities such as postal and telephone services, and the products of nationalized industries are provided by the state but are sold to consumers on a commercial basis just as if a private firm were producing them.

A full consideration of the pros and cons of state versus private production of these goods and services belongs to a more advanced course. We can only mention a few of the most important points here.

COLLECTIVE GOODS: There is no problem here since private firms cannot adequately provide them.

FREE GOODS: The considerations involved here are many and complex. The case for subsidizing goods such as medical care and education rests partly on a divergence between social and private costs, partly on compassion, and partly on more subtle welfare arguments. There is nonetheless a very strong argument against the provision of *free* goods (as opposed to subsidized goods) and we must now consider it. This case is based on the theory of household demand and before reading on the student should re-read pages 162–8 of Chapter 15.

If a good is provided free and all demand is met, then households will go on consuming it until the last unit consumed has a zero marginal utility. As long as extra units consumed have a positive marginal utility (no matter how small) and a zero marginal private cost, households can raise their total utility by raising their consumption of the commodity. Thus, resources will have to be used up in producing units of the commodity which have zero marginal utility to each and every household. Since resources are scarce, they must be taken from the production of other goods that have positive marginal utilities for all households (i.e., households would like to have more of them). To use scarce resources to produce goods with zero or even very low marginal utilities when the same resources could produce goods with higher marginal utilities ensures that all households will have lower total utilities than they could have. If a price were charged for the commodity, its consumption would decline and resources would be freed to move to uses where their product had a higher marginal utility.[1]

The quantitative extent of this problem depends on the shape of the marginal

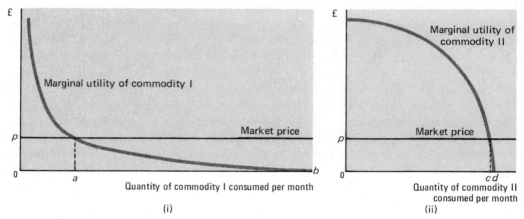

Fig. 32.1 (i) Providing the commodity free greatly increases the amount of resources allocated to producing it
(ii) Providing the commodity free increases only slightly the number of resources allocated to producing it

1 This case against free goods can be maintained *without* having to accept that the proposition that perfect competition provides an optimal allocation of resources has any relevance to practical policy problems.

utility schedule. Commodity I in Figure 32.1(i) has a very flat schedule, the difference between the consumption (a) when the market price is charged and consumption (b) when the commodity is free is very great. Commodity II has a steep schedule and the consumption at zero price (d) is not much higher than at the market price (c). The case against providing commodity I free is that this will absorb some of the nation's scarce resources in providing units of the commodity which have a very low marginal utility. The case against providing commodity II free is the same, but quantitatively it is much less serious.

Why then does the state provide so many goods free? We have already discussed the case of water (see pages 169–70).[1] This is an example of a very weak case. Water undoubtedly has a flat marginal utility schedule of the sort illustrated in Figure 32.1(i), thus the no-price policy means that a great deal of the economy's scarce resources must be committed to producing units of water which have a very low marginal utility. Furthermore, water does not provide a case where there are obvious social gains from encouraging consumption beyond what the individual would voluntarily choose. Indeed, if a commercially profitable market price were charged there is little reason to believe there would be serious divergencies between social and private costs. Here is a case in which it is hard to see a rationale behind existing policy.[2]

The case of hospitals and schools is somewhat different. First, there is some doubt that many people would waste free hospital care in the way they are observed to waste free water. Studies that have been made suggest a low incidence of unnecessary hospitalization in a free-hospital system. In the case of education up to the statutory age, consumption is compulsory in any case.[3] Secondly, there is compassion. Necessary medical and hospital care can sometimes be very expensive, the annual cost can easily be in excess of a household's annual income. This is different from water where it is not a great burden for a household to pay a commercial rate for all the water that is necessary to a moderately civilized life. Thus, to charge a price that covered costs of production would deny medical and educational services to many.[4] In both these commodities, social and private costs and benefits are thought to diverge substantially. Thus, if I choose not to, or am unable to, afford to buy a cure for an infectious disease, the effects are not felt by me alone. If all children are better educated, not only they and their parents gain; everyone gains from any rise in output that results from an increase in their labour productivity. Thus, there are good reasons accepted

1 In many countries a flat charge is levied on domestic water users. The flat charge is irrelevant from our point of view. It is absence of any charge on additional units consumed that is important.

2 There is one other consideration that could be important. It might be that the costs of recording domestic water consumption and collecting the water fees would exceed the gains from the reduction of water consumption that provided a low marginal utility. If so water would come under case 4 on page 438.

3 Indeed, there is some evidence that the consumption of 'free' education paid for by all taxpayers whether or not they are parents of school-age children leads to a lower consumption of education than would result from education paid for solely by the households that were consuming it, and obviously benefiting from it.

4 Of course it is possible to insure against medical expenses in countries without nationalized medicine. But as everyone who is acquainted with aged people on average incomes in the United States knows many insurance policies tend to let the client down in just those disasters in which they are most needed. When this happens, the life savings of even the most frugal labouring household can be eaten up by medical and hospital bills in an alarmingly short period of time.

by everyone for reducing the private cost of these services below the market rate by means of a subsidy. The only argument is whether the cost should be merely lowered or actually reduced to zero. Many people feel that the costs of making agonizing choices between a bit more medical care for one member of the household or a bit more education for another are degrading, and far greater than the costs of making the service free (the cost being measured in terms of the extra resources devoted to the provision of these services). Others disagree. The provision of free welfare services is still hotly debated, and the full set of arguments cannot be set out here. Enough should have been said to show that the case for and against providing a commodity free varies greatly with the nature of the commodity being considered.

GOODS SOLD ON THE OPEN MARKET: Finally we come to public expenditure used to produce goods that are then sold on the open market. Typically these industries produce goods and sell them to the public, just as any other firm does. They do not, however, have to seek to maximize profits, and they often seek just to cover costs. Various reasons for nationalizing industries have been put forward and we can only give very brief mention to these.

(1) *To confiscate the profits for the general public's welfare instead of for the capitalists'.* In so far as nationalized industries are profitable, and in so far as they are not much less efficient under nationalization than in private hands, this is an achievable objective. Quantitatively, however, it is insignificant beside such redistributive devices as the progressive income tax. In so far as unprofitable and declining industries are nationalized (e.g., coal, railways, airlines in Britain) this motive cannot be a dominant one since there are few, if any profits available for general distribution.

(2) *To get more coordination where private costs do not reflect social costs.* Nationalization of all forms of transport, for example, might be used to produce a single transport policy wherein decisions made by railways took into account the costs imposed on the road haulage industry and vice versa. Whatever the facts of such interrelationship there can be little doubt that the nationalized industries in Britain have up to the present time made little attempt to look beyond their own parochial boundaries when taking decisions.

(3) *To obtain a radically different pattern of production than would obtain under private enterprise.* If this were a goal, the nationalized industries would require a clear directive as to how their output and prices were to be determined. In fact they have usually been given the major task of trying to avoid losses, which requires that they make average revenue equal to average costs. In industries presently making losses, the attempt to cut losses is profit-maximizing behaviour. Thus behaviour in these industries is indistinguishable from what the private firm's behaviour would be. In the case of a profitable industry, on the other hand, the directive 'cover costs' ($AR = ATC$) will lead to a higher output and a lower price than the directive 'maximize profits' ($MR = MC$) and the student should not read on until he has drawn a graph to demonstrate this. But if more of something is produced there will be less of something else, and the extra production of nationalized industries pricing at average costs represents a gain only if this production is valued higher than the production foregone elsewhere.

(4) *To control effectively a natural monopoly.* Industries such as the postal, telegraph, telephone, gas and electricity inevitably are natural monopolies. The alternatives here are public regulation of a privately-owned industry or public ownership. One of the main arguments for nationalization is to secure effective control over such natural monopolies. All countries seem to accept this argument in the case of the post office and many countries also accept it for the great public utility industries such as gas and electricity.

(5) *To get greater efficiency and a more dynamic growth policy than under private industry.* The relative efficiency of private versus public production is still the subject of heated debate. Although universal agreement is not forthcoming, I would hazard the personal guess that the experience of nationalized industries in the United Kingdom suggests that they have neither been vastly better nor vastly worse in running their day-to-day affairs than were their private predecessors.

COAL MINING – AN EXAMPLE: The view that public control was needed to save an industry from the dead hand of third-rate, unenterprising, private owners was very commonly held about the British coal industry in the inter-war period, and was undoubtedly a factor leading to its nationalization in 1946. This view was clearly held by the Commission which reported in 1926 on the state of the coal industry when they said:

It would be possible to say without exaggeration of the miners' leaders that they were the stupidest men in England, if we had not had frequent occasion to meet the owners.[1]

On the other hand, Sir Roy Harrod has argued that the rundown state of the coal industry in South Wales and Yorkshire and the advanced state of the pits in Nottinghamshire and Derbyshire represented the correct response of the owners to the signals of the market. He writes:

The mines of Derbyshire and Nottinghamshire were rich, and it was worth sinking capital in them. If similar amounts of capital were not sunk in other parts of the country, this may not have been because the managements were inefficient, but simply because it was known that they were not worth these expenditures. Economic efficiency does not consist in always introducing the most up-to-date equipment that an engineer can think of but rather in the correct adaptation of the amount of new capital sunk to the earning capacity of the old asset. In not introducing new equipment, the managements may have been wise, not only from the point of view of their own interest, but from that of national interest, which requires the most profitable application of available capital ... it is right that as much should be extracted from the inferior mines as can be done by old-fashioned methods (i.e., with equipment already installed), and that they should gradually go out of action.[2]

Declining industries always present a sorry sight to the observer. Revenues have fallen below long-run total costs, and, as a result, new equipment is not brought in to replace old equipment as it wears out. The average age of equipment in use thus rises steadily. The superficial observer seeing the industry's very real plight is likely to

---

1 Quoted in David Thomson, *England in the Twentieth Century* (Pelican Books, 1965), p. 110. But see also L. S. Amery's reply that the Commission had ignored the very strong claim of the government to be so considered. Some of the policies that gave the government that claim are discussed on pages 504–6.

2 Roy Harrod, *The British Economy* (McGraw-Hill, 1963), p. 54.

blame it on the antiquated equipment in use, whereas the antiquated equipment is the effect, not the cause, of the industry's decline. To modernize at high capital costs merely makes the plight worse, since output and costs will rise in the face of declining demand and prices. The correct response to a steadily declining demand is indeed not to replace old equipment, but to continue to operate what exists as long as it can cover its variable costs of production.

It would take a major, and carefully planned, econometric study to determine who was right about the British coal industry, but, whatever the merits of this particular case, the general point is an extremely important one: a declining industry will always display an old age structure of capital and thus 'antiquated' methods; this is the consequence and not necessarily the cause of decline. To install new plant and equipment in a genuinely declining industry is to use the nation's scarce resources where they will not lead to large increases in the value of output. Capital resources are scarce: if investment occurs in mines, there is less for engineering, schools, roads, computer research and a host of other things. To re-equip a declining industry which cannot cover its capital costs, is to use scarce resources where by the criterion of the market their product is much less valuable than what it would be in other industries.

This of course is a very brief discussion of the reasons for having a sector of nationalized industries. But enough has been said to show that there are many possible motives for nationalization and judging from the behaviour of the industries, some of the most publicized motives cannot have been the real ones since the action necessary to give effect to them has not occurred.

MICRO-POLICY: A CONCLUSION
The overall progressivity of government policies

Looking at *tax* progressivity alone may be misleading. For example, a regressive tax (say a sales tax) may be used to provide funds for increasing welfare payment to the needy and thus end up redistributing income to the poor.

Studies made in many countries suggest that when government expenditure is considered along with taxes the overall effect is fairly progressive. Tax systems tend to be proportional or even mildly regressive up to the middle or upper middle levels of income, but government expenditures do favour the poor. When the two effects – taxes and expenditure – are combined, government activity does appear to redistribute real income from rich to poor.

An assessment of government intervention

Governments intervene in the operation of the market system in countless ways and with many purposes. In an introductory treatment we can do little more than illustrate these. Hopefully, enough has been said to demonstrate one or two main points:

(1) There are general reasons following from economic analysis as to why government intervention can improve the efficiency of what is basically a free-market system.

(2) For these reasons, and no doubt for others as well, all governments intervene to some extent in the operations of the market.

(3) Although there are many valid reasons for such intervention, there may also be misguided intervention based on mistaken economic analysis of cause and effect, or a mis-assessment of the consequences of a particular intervention. Thus, the student must always strive to keep an open mind on issues of public policy, and decide them on their merits rather than in relation to such dogmas as 'all interventions are necessarily harmful' or 'all interventions necessarily bring net benefits'.

33

From micro- to macro-economics

So far in this book we have made a detailed study of the workings of individual markets. We have dealt with problems of the relation between prices of various commodities and those of various factors of production, and problems of the allocation of scarce resources between alternative uses. These, and related problems, fall into the field of MICRO-ECONOMIC THEORY. In micro-economics, we start with households whose members have needs and desires for goods and services. They have, in varying amounts, resources – income, assets, time and energy – with which to attempt to satisfy these wants. But, their resources are insufficient to permit them to satisfy all their needs and desires. They are forced, therefore, to make choices, and this they do through markets where they are offered many ways to spend their money, their energy and their time. The signals to which the households respond are market prices; given a set of prices, each household will make a given set of choices. In so doing, they also, in the aggregate, affect those prices. The prices signal to firms what goods they may profitably provide. Given technology and the cost of factors, firms must choose among the products they might produce, among the ways of producing them, and among the various quantities (and qualities) they can supply. In so doing, they affect prices. Firms demand factors of production, in quantities depending on their output decisions, which, in turn, depend upon consumers' demands. These derived demands for factors will in turn affect the prices of labour, managerial skill, raw materials, buildings, machinery, use of capital, land and all other factors. The owners of factors (or the possessors of the skills that can provide the factor services) respond to factor prices and make their choices about where to offer their services. These choices determine factor supplies. Payments by firms to factor owners provide the owners of the factors with incomes. The recipients of these incomes are people who have needs and desires for goods and services and we have now come full circle.

The process described above is often referred to as the *circular flow* of income: money passes from households to firms in return for goods and services produced by firms, and money passes from firms to households in return for factor services provided by households. We now wish to raise a number of new questions concerning

454

this flow. We want to know, for example, why it varies in volume so that sometimes the production and sale to households of goods and services, as well as employment of factor services by firms, is large in total volume whereas at other times output, sales and employment are small in volume. We want to know why the average price at which these transactions occur varies, and why it has been rising in most countries over the last twenty years. Questions of this sort relate to the overall or aggregate behaviour of the circular flow and the branch of economics that deals with these is called MACRO-ECONOMICS.

There is no clear-cut dividing line between macro- and micro-economics and perhaps the best way of showing the scope of macro-economics is to list the most important sets of problems with which we shall be concerned in the remainder of this book, and to contrast these where possible with the related problems dealt with in micro-theory.

(1) *Problems relating to fluctuations in the level of resource use, particularly fluctuations in the level of employment of labour.* In micro-economics we take the total volume of employment as given and consider how it is allocated between various sectors of the economy.

(2) *Problems relating to fluctuations in the average level of prices; problems, that is, of inflation and deflation.* In micro-economics we take the absolute price level as given and account for the structure of relative prices.

(3) *Problems relating to fluctuations in the average level of money wages.* In micro-economics we take the average level of wages as given and account for the relation among wages in different areas, occupations and industries.

(4) *Problems relating to the allocation of resources between the production of consumers' goods, on the one hand, and the production of capital goods, on the other.* This is an allocation problem similar to the one encountered in micro-economic theory. The level of aggregation is, however, different; here we are dealing with the allocation of resources between two sectors which together account for the whole economy, while in micro-theory we split the economy up into many small sectors.

(5) *Problems relating to the rate of growth of productive capacity.* We have touched on these problems every time we have dealt with the very long run. We have yet, however, to make any systematic study of the causes and limits of economic growth.

(6) *Problems concerning the relation between international trade and the levels of employment, prices, and growth in the economy.* We have so far neglected the important matter of international trade although, as we shall see, international trade has both its micro- and its macro-economic aspects. Sets 5 and 6 could be handled almost equally well within the framework of micro-theory. Set 6 is dealt with here because international trade is an important determinant of aggregate employment, output and income.

The division between macro- and micro-economics is not a matter of right and wrong but rather a matter of convenience. It does prove convenient to make this distinction partly because the problems differ, and partly because the method of analysis differs between these two branches. The basic problem in micro-economics is the determination of the allocation of resources, and the basic theory is that of the determination of relative prices through demand and supply. The basic problem in macro-economics is the determination of the flow of income, and the basic theoretical structure is the model of the circular flow of income. It is to a study of this model that we must now turn our attention.

Part seven

The circular flow of income

34

National income

GOODS AND MONEY FLOWS

In our economy, both commodities and factors of production are constantly being exchanged for money. If one household buys a currently-produced commodity from a second, it hands over money in return. The selling household has now earned this money; it is the household's income. It may in turn spend the money, passing it on to a third household in exchange for some other currently-produced commodity. The third household has now earned the money, and it may in turn spend it. And so it goes on, the money passing from household to household in exchange for commodities: each time money changes hands in return for currently-produced goods and services, it is income for the recipient. The money flows from hand to hand in much the same way as water flows through a pipe or electricity through a circuit.

Flows between individual households

Imagine a simple economy that consists of four households, A, B, C and D, each of which makes a different commodity. Assume that there is only one pound note in the economy. Household A buys goods valued at £1 from B, giving the pound note in return. This pound is income for household B, and it spends it by buying a pound's worth of goods produced by household C. Household C has now earned a pound that it uses to buy goods produced by D, and D in turn buys a pound's worth of goods produced by A. The flows of goods and money in this economy are illustrated in Figure 34.1. Goods flows are shown with broken lines and money flows with solid lines. A single pound note has passed round the circle and has been used for four separate transactions. Each household has earned £1 as its income, and each has spent £1. If these are all the transactions over, say, a week, then the total income earned by all households in our economy over the week is £4. Note that the total income exceeds the quantity of money (£1) because the same pound note was used for more than one transaction. This illustrates an important fact: total income is not necessarily equal to the total quantity of money, because a single unit of money can

Total income ≠ Total how. geld.

create income each time it changes hands. Thus, if the typical unit of money changes hands more than once during the period under consideration, income earned will be greater than the amount of money in existence. When we refer to the number of times that money changes hands over some time period, we speak of the velocity of circulation of money. (This concept is discussed in more detail in Chapter 43.)

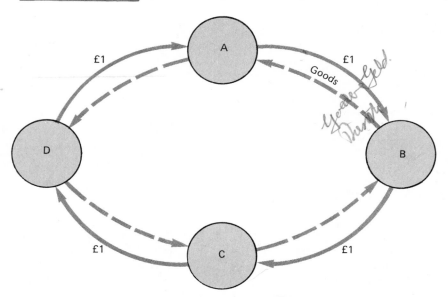

Fig. 34.1 Flows of goods and money between four households

Flows between households and firms

In a real economic system, production is organized by firms; each separate household does not earn its income by making its own goods for sale. Instead, firms make the commodities that households consume. Firms purchase the services of factors of production from the households that own them, paying wages, rent, interest and profits in return, and then use these factors to make commodities that are sold to households. Households earn income by selling factor services to firms; they spend this income by buying goods and services from firms.[1]

In this Chapter we deal with the fundamental concepts that are used in the theory of the circular flow of income. In the following Chapters we build a model of the circular flow and use it to derive predictions concerning the behaviour of the economy. The most important concept with which we must deal is that of national income itself.

NATIONAL INCOME is the basic concept in macro-economics. It refers to the total market value of all goods and services produced in the economy during some specific period of time and to the total of all incomes earned over the same period of time. NATIONAL INCOME ACCOUNTING is the measuring of the total flow of output (goods

1 This is usually but not always the case. People in domestic service, for example, earn their income by selling their services directly to other households.

and services) and of the total flow of inputs (factors of production) that pass through all of the markets in the economy during a specific period. To see exactly what national income includes, how it is measured and what it can tell us, we must study it in some detail. Let us start with the national income of a very simple economy and then introduce, one by one, the complications needed to make it applicable to real-world economies. [1]

THE SPENDTHRIFT ECONOMY

In the simple Spendthrift economy, there are only two groups of decision makers – households and firms; each group earns all of its income by selling goods and services to the other group, and each group spends all of its income by buying goods and services from the other group. Households earn their income by selling the services of factors of production (land, labour, and capital) to firms, and they spend all of their income by purchasing goods and services produced by firms. Firms sell all of their output to households and receive money in return. All of the money received by firms is in turn paid out to households. Part goes to the households that sell factor services to firms, and the rest is profit paid out as DIVIDENDS to the owners of the firms. [2] In short, neither households nor firms save anything in the Spendthrift economy; everything that one group receives goes to buy goods and services from the other group. Expenditure is the rule of the day!

The Spendthrift economy is illustrated in Figure 34.2. Payments are shown flowing from households to firms in return for goods and services purchased and from firms to households in return for factor services purchased.

Now suppose we wish to calculate the total value of the economy's annual output. We can do this by making calculations based on either side of the circular-flow diagram shown in Figure 34.2. The output-expenditure approach uses calculations based on the flows on the right-hand side of the figure, while the input-factor income approach uses calculations based on the flows on the left-hand side of the figure.

The output-expenditure approach to national income

When we use the output-expenditure approach to measure the total value of output, we calculate the total expenditure needed to purchase the nation's output. In the simple Spendthrift economy all output is sold to households, and we can get the total we require by measuring the actual expenditure of households on currently produced goods and services. In more complex economies many groups other than households purchase a part of the economy's output, while another part is not sold at all (rather it is held by the firms that produce it for sale in the future). In such economies it is

1 This method of argument is common in economics and is based on the idea that it is easier to study things one at a time rather than all at once. Indeed, early economists made this explicit when they spoke of abstractions from reality followed by a build-up to realism through a series of 'successive approximations'. This is a useful method of discussion provided one remembers that the second step is as essential as the first.

2 The owners of firms provide much of the money that firms need to carry on business. The owners risk the loss of their money if the firm fails in return for the profits they earn if the firm succeeds. The owners provide factor services to firms in return for the profit income that they receive, just as do the households that sell labour services to firms in return for wage income.

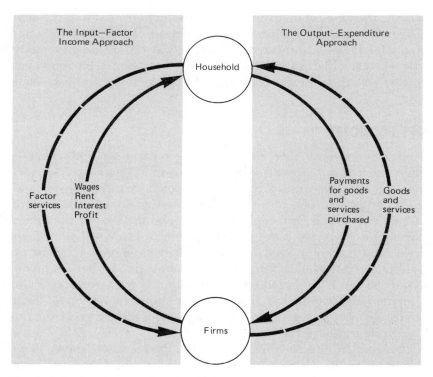

Fig. 34.2 Real and money flows between firms and households

often simpler to calculate the total value of all firms' output directly rather than to calculate the expenditure on that output by those who purchase it.

Calculating the economy's *total* output from the outputs of *individual* firms raises a new and difficult problem. If we merely added up the market values of the outputs of each firm in the simple Spendthrift economy, we would obtain a total greatly in excess of the value of output actually available to be consumed by the households in the Spendthrift economy. Suppose, for example, that we took the value of all farmers' outputs of wheat and added to it the value of all flour mills' outputs of flour, plus the value of the outputs of bakeries, plus the value of the sales of bread by all retail shops. The resulting total would be much larger than the value of the final product – bread – produced by the economy. We would have counted the value of the wheat four times, of the flour three times, of the bread produced by the bakery twice, and of the services of the retail shop once.

To avoid this problem of *double counting*, national income accountants use the important concept of the value added. Each firm's VALUE ADDED is the value of its output *minus* the value of the inputs that it purchases from other firms. Thus a flour mill's value added is the value of its output of flour *minus* the value of the grain it buys from the farmer and the values of any other inputs such as electricity and fuel oil that it buys from other firms. The relation between value added and total value of sales is illustrated in the example given in Exhibit 1.

Exhibit 1
VALUE ADDED THROUGH STAGES
OF PRODUCTION: AN EXAMPLE
Because the output of one firm often becomes the input of other firms, the total
value of goods sold by all firms greatly exceeds the value of the output of final goods.
This general principal is illustrated by a simple example in which firm R starts from
scratch and produces goods (raw materials)
valued at £100; the firm's value added is
£100. Firm I purchases raw materials valued
at £100 and produces semi-manufactured
goods that it sells for £130. Its value added
is £30 because the value of the goods is increased by £30 as a result of the firm's activities. Firm F purchases the semi-manufactured goods for £130 and works them
into a finished state, selling them for £180.
Firm F's value added is £50. The value of
final goods, £180, is found either by counting the sales of firm F or by taking the sum
of the values added by each firm. This
value is less than the £410 that we obtain
by adding up the market value of the
commodities sold by each firm. The following table summarizes the example.

Transactions between firms at three different stages of production

	Firm R	Firm I	Firm F	All firms
A. Purchases from other firms	£ 0	£100	£130	£230 = Total inter- firm sales
B. Purchase of factors of pro duction (wages, rent, interest, profits)	100	30	50	180 = Value added
Total A+B = value of product	£100	£130	£180 = Value of final goods and services	£410 = Total value of all sales

In macro-economics a firm's output is defined as its value added; the sum of all
values added must be the value of all goods and services produced by the economy.
   The idea of value added suggests an important distinction between intermediate
and final products. INTERMEDIATE PRODUCTS are all goods and services used as
inputs into a further stage of production. FINAL PRODUCTS are the outputs of the
economy after eliminating all double counting. In the previous example, grain, flour,
electricity, and fuel oil were all intermediate products used at various stages in the
process that led to the production of the final product, bread. In the Spendthrift
economy, all final products are produced by firms and sold to households for
consumption.[1]

1 Thus, the earlier statement that in the Spendthrift economy all output is sold to households refers to final
products. Intermediate products can, of course, be sold from one firm to another.

The input-factor-income approach to national income

The second way in which national income can be calculated is by measuring the value of factor inputs or, what is the same thing, the factor incomes generated by the process of production. This approach is based on the flows on the left-hand side of Figure 34.2, and it is usually referred to simply as the factor-income approach.

It is usual in macro-economics to distinguish four main components of factor incomes: RENT, which is the payment for the services of land; WAGES AND SALARIES (often referred to simply as wages), which are the payment for the services of labour; and interest and profits, both of which are payments for the services of capital. In order to obtain its capital goods a firm requires money. This is made available by those who lend money to the firm and by those who put up their own money and risk its loss in order to become the firm's owners. INTEREST is earned by those who lend money to the firm, and PROFITS are earned by those who own the firm.[1]

The relation between the two approaches to national income

We have seen that the value of the output produced over a specific period can be obtained by looking at *either* the output-expenditure *or* the input-factor-income side of the economy. Can the two approaches yield different answers? The answer is 'No' because of the definition of profits. The profits on a firm's output are defined by the national income accountant as the value of that output minus all claims for rent, wages, and interest that arise out of its production. This definition ensures that the sum of rent, wages, interest and profit is equal to the value of output.[2] The relation between the two approaches is illustrated in Exhibit 2.

> **Because the value of output produced is equal to the value of income earned (by virtue of the definition of profits), we can talk about either national income or national product. National income emphasizes the input, or factor-income, aspect of production, while national product emphasizes the output of final goods aspect of production.**

Since both terms refer to the same total they are used interchangeably.

An example of the calculation of national income in the Spendthrift economy is

---

1 The concepts of rent, wages, interest, and profits used in macro-economics do not correspond exactly to the micro-economic concepts that go under the same names. The details of the differences need not detain us in an introductory treatment, but the reader should be warned that differences exist. (For example, profits in macro-economics correspond closely to the everyday use of the term as the return to the owners of firms, while in micro-economics profits have a more technical definition. See page 217.)

2 The definitional identity of factor earnings and the value of output is easily shown for those who prefer algebraic demonstrations. Let P, R, W and I stand for profits, rent, wages and interest respectively and let O stand for the value of output. Using the three bar identity sign to indicate that all this is a matter of how we define terms (not a matter of how the world does and does not behave) we write the *definition* of profits as:

$$P \equiv O - (R + W + I),$$

rearranging terms:

$$P + R + W + I \equiv O,$$

i.e., factor earnings ≡ value of output.

Exhibit 2

VALUE ADDED, VALUE OF OUTPUT, AND FACTOR INCOMES: AN EXAMPLE

Last year in the Spendthrift economy a tenant farmer produced £25,000 worth of wheat. His wage bill was £10,000 (including a payment for his own labour services); his rent was £3,500; and he paid interest of £1,250 on a bank loan. He also spent £7,000 on seeds, electricity, fertilizer, and a host of other inputs that were themselves produced by other firms. This left him a profit of £4,500 in return for supplying and risking his own capital in his farming enterprise. His transactions are summarized below.

Take	Total value of sales	£25,000	
Subtract	Cost of materials purchased	7,000	
To obtain	Value added		£18,000
Take	Rent	3,500	
Plus	Wages	10,000	
Plus	Interest	1,250	
Subtract them from value added		−£14,750	
To obtain	Profits	3,250	
Add back profits to rent, wages, and interest			
To obtain	Factor earnings		£18,000

The wheat farmer's contribution to total national income is £18,000. This figure can be obtained by calculating the farmer's value added or by calculating the factor income generated by his productive activities.

given in Table 34.1. In the Spendthrift economy goods and services produced and sold for consumption account for the total value of all production. Factor incomes earned by the households who supply the services of land, labour and loan capital account for most of the total value of goods produced, while the remainder is profits. Both sides of the table add up to the same total by virtue of the definition of profits.

Table 34.1 National income in the Spendthrift economy (millions of pounds)

Factor income		Value of output	
Rent	£ 100	Consumption goods	
Wages	650	and services (C)	£1,000
Interest	160		
Profits	90		
	£1,000		£1,000

THE FRUGAL ECONOMY

The Spendthrift economy is an economy of the here and now; all income is spent on goods and services for current consumption and all current output is consumed. In the Frugal economy households and firms look to the future, and as a result both saving and investment occur.

Saving

SAVING is income not spent on goods and services for current consumption. Both households and firms can save. Households save when they elect not to spend part of their current income on goods and services for consumption. Firms save when they elect not to pay out to their owners some of the profits that they have earned. All profits belong legally to the owners, but only some are actually paid out while the rest are withheld by the firm to finance part of its gross investment.

DISTRIBUTED PROFITS are profits actually paid out to the owners of firms, and UNDISTRIBUTED PROFITS are profits held back by firms for their own uses. Undistributed profits constitute saving made on behalf of the owners of firms since they are incomes of the owners not spent on current consumption.

Investment

The terms investment and investment goods are used in the same way in macro- as in micro-economics. INVESTMENT is defined as the production of goods not for immediate consumption. All such goods are called INVESTMENT GOODS. They are produced by firms and they may be bought either by firms or by households. Most investment is done by firms, and in this chapter we shall concentrate solely on such investment. Firms can invest either in capital goods, such as plant and equipment, or in inventories. We shall consider inventories first.

INVESTMENT IN INVENTORIES: Virtually all firms hold inventories of their inputs and of their outputs. Inventories of inputs allow production to continue at the desired pace in spite of short-term fluctuations in the deliveries of inputs bought from other firms. Inventories of outputs allow firms to meet orders in spite of temporary, unexpected fluctuations in the rate of output or sales.

Inventories are an inevitable part of the productive process, and they require an investment of the firm's money since the firm has paid for them but has not yet sold them. An accumulation of inventories counts as current investment because it represents goods produced but not used for current consumption, while a drawing down – often called a decumulation – counts as *dis*investment because it is a reduction in the stock of goods produced in the past.

INTENDED AND UNINTENDED INVENTORY INVESTMENT: Inventory investment may be either intentional or unintentional. If the firm produces and holds goods that it planned to use to build up its inventories, then its investment is intentional, or planned. If the firm produces goods that it planned to sell but does not because expected orders do not materialize, then its inventory investment is unintentional, or unplanned. Similarly, inventory disinvestment may be intentional or unintentional. If the firm plans to produce less than it sells its inventory disinvestment is intentional, while if sales are unexpectedly greater than output then the resulting inventory disinvestment is unintentional.

INVESTMENT IN CAPITAL GOODS: All production uses capital goods: man-made aids to production such as hand tools, machines, and factory buildings. The total amount of capital goods in the country is called the capital stock. The production of new capital goods is called investment. The act of creating new capital goods is an act of investment. Newly-produced capital goods may either replace capital that has been used up in the process of production (or otherwise consumed) or else it can make net additions to the stock of capital.

TOTAL INVESTMENT: The total investment that occurs in the economy is called GROSS INVESTMENT. The amount necessary for replacement is called the CAPITAL CONSUMPTION ALLOWANCE and is often loosely referred to as DEPRECIATION; the remainder is called NET INVESTMENT. It is net investment that increases the economy's total stock of capital, while the replacement investment keeps the existing stock intact by replacing what has been worn out or otherwise used up.

Income and output in the Frugal economy

The current production of final commodities in the Frugal economy can be divided into two sorts of output. First, there are consumption goods and services actually sold to households. Second, there are investment goods that consist of capital goods plus inventories of semi-finished and finished commodities still in the hands of firms. The symbols C and I stand for currently produced consumption goods and currently produced investment goods respectively.

In an economy that uses capital goods, as does the Frugal economy, it is helpful to distinguish between two concepts of national income (or national product). GROSS NATIONAL INCOME (or GROSS NATIONAL PRODUCT, GNP) is the sum of all values added in the economy; it is the sum of the values of all final goods produced for consumption and investment, and thus it is also the sum of all factor incomes earned in the process of producing the nation's output. NET NATIONAL INCOME (or NET NATIONAL PRODUCT, NNP) is GNP minus the capital consumption allowance. NNP is thus a measure of the net output of the economy after deducting from gross output an amount necessary to maintain the existing stock of capital intact.

An example of the calculation of national income in the Frugal economy is given in Table 34.2. The value of output means the value of final commodities produced. In the Frugal economy this is the value of consumption goods and services and investment goods, which include capital goods and inventory accumulation. GNP and NNP differ by the amount of the capital consumption allowance.

Table 34.2 National income in the Frugal economy
(millions of pounds)

Factor income		Value of output	
Rent	£ 120	Consumption goods and services (C)	£1,000
Wages	780	Investment goods (I)	
Interest	190	Capital goods	175
		Inventory	
Profits	110	accumulation	25
Gross National Product (GNP)	£1,200	Gross National Product (GNP)	£1,200
Capital consumption allowance	105	Capital consumption allowance	105
Net National Product (NNP)	£1,095	Net National Product (NNP)	£1,095

Output and expenditure in the Frugal economy

In the Spendthrift economy all currently produced goods and services are sold to households, so obviously the value of final output is equal to the value of expenditure on that output. In the Frugal economy some final output is sold to households, some – such as plant and equipment – is sold to other firms, and some – newly produced inventories of a firm's own output – is not sold at all. The national income accountant includes production of goods for inventories as part of total expenditure since the firm certainly spends money on the factor services necessary to produce goods for its own inventories. The accountant calculates the economy's total expenditure as the actual expenditure on final goods and services sold, plus the market value of final commodities currently produced and added to inventories. This definition makes total expenditure the same thing as the value of all final commodities produced and thus ensures that the measured value of expenditure is identical with the measured value of output in any economy.

THE GOVERNED ECONOMY

We now give our economy a government. The Governed economy contains central authorities – often simply called 'the government' – who levy taxes on firms and households and who engage in numerous activities such as defending the country, making and enforcing the laws, building roads, running schools, and predicting the weather. When the government produces goods and services that households desire such as roads and air traffic control, it is obviously engaged in useful activity and is obviously adding to the sum total of valuable output; but with other government activities the case may not seem quite so clear, and everyone knows people who feel that many of the activities of government are wasteful or even downright harmful. The national income statistician does not enter into such speculation but instead counts as part of the GNP every government expenditure on goods and services whether it is to build Concorde, to provide police protection, or to pay a civil servant to file and refile papers from a now-defunct ministry. The statistician does that not only because no two people could ever agree on precisely which government expenditures were productive and which wasteful, but also, and more fundamentally because GNP is meant to measure total output and total use of factors of production, regardless of individual opinions about the value of the things produced. Thus the GNP includes all of these government expenditures, along with the outputs of gin, Bibles and contraceptives.

Total national income of the Governed economy includes all factor incomes generated by the activities of firms and governments. Just as wheat production uses factors and generates factor incomes, so do the activities of any branch of government such as the Department of the Environment.

TRANSFER PAYMENTS: There is one exception to the rule that all government expenditure is included in the GNP. If the government taxes a wage-earner and uses the money to make payments to a mother of five children whose husband has deserted her, income is transferred from the taxpayer to the recipient. The government does not receive any productive services from the deserted mother in return for the payments. The expenditure itself adds neither to employment of factors nor to total output. Indeed, this is true whether the government raises this money by taxes, by borrowing, or by printing brand new money (which, as we shall see in a later Chapter, is something that it can do). The term GOVERNMENT TRANSFER PAYMENTS refers to any payments made to households by the government that are not made in return for the services of factors of production. Such payments do not lead directly to any increase in output and for this reason they are not included in the nation's GNP. Thus, whenever government expenditure is included in a measurement of the GNP, it is understood to be net of any 'transfer payments'.

DISPOSABLE INCOME: One magnitude that national income statisticians are concerned to measure is the amount of income that households actually have available to spend or to save. This is called DISPOSABLE INCOME. To calculate disposable income the statistician must make several adjustments to GNP. First he deducts all those elements of the value of output that are not paid out to households: business savings represent receipts by firms from the sale of output that are withheld by firms for their own uses, and corporation taxes are receipts that are paid over to the government. Second, personal income taxes must be deducted from the income paid to households in order to obtain the amount households actually have available to spend or save. Finally, it is necessary to add government transfer payments made to households; although these are not themselves a part of GNP, they are made available to households to spend and save and are thus a part of disposable income. To sum up, disposable income is GNP *minus* any part of it that is not actually paid over to households, *minus* the personal income taxes paid by households, *plus* transfer payments received by households.

Government expenditure is usually given the symbol G, and the GNP in the Governed economy can then be expressed as $GNP = C + I + G$. A simplified set of national accounts for this economy is shown in Table 34.3. For the Governed

Table 34.3 National income in the Governed
economy (millions of pounds)

Factor income		Value of output	
Rent	£ 140	Consumption goods	
Wages	920	and services (C)	£1,000
Interest	225	Investment (I)	
Profits	125	Capital goods	175
	———	Inventory	
		accumulation	25
		Government	
		Total government	
		expenditure 250	
		Less transfer	
		payments 40	
		Government contri-	
		bution to GNP (G)	210
GNP	£1,410	GNP	£1,410
Depreciation	105	Depreciation	105
	———		———
NNP	£1,305	NNP	£1,305

economy the value of output is made up of consumption, investment and government
goods and services. Transfer payments, unlike all other government expenditures,
are not made in return for factor services used for the output of goods or services. All
government expenditures other than transfer payments are counted as part of
current GNP.

THE OPEN ECONOMY

None of the three economies considered so far engaged in trade with foreign countries. Such economies are often referred to as CLOSED ECONOMIES. In contrast, OPEN
ECONOMIES engage in significant amounts of foreign trade, so that some of the goods
produced at home are sold abroad while some of the goods sold at home are produced
abroad.

The GNP of any economy, open or closed, is the total value of final goods and
services produced in that economy. Some care is required, however, when the
expenditure approach is used to measure the GNP of an Open economy. It is
necessary to allow for the facts that part of the expenditure on the domestic economy's GNP comes from foreign firms, households, and governments and that part
of the expenditure of domestic firms, households, and governments goes to the GNP
of foreign countries.

ACCOUNTING DEFINITIONS: To allow for these facts the GNP of an Open economy
may be thought of as being calculated in three steps. First, the total expenditure by
domestic firms, governments, and households on all final goods wherever they are
produced is calculated. (This is $C + I + G$). Second, the value of all imported commodities, M, is deducted. This gives the total purchases of domestic spending units
on all domestically produced goods and services. Third, the value of all exports, X,

which indicates domestic production sold abroad, is added in to total expenditure. The resulting figure is the nation's GNP.

In symbols the GNP for the Open economy is GNP $= C + I + G + (X - M)$. (1)

The value $X - M$ is called NET EXPORTS. This value is usually small in relation to the total value of either X or M. Thus, the correction to GNP when we move from a closed economy, where GNP $= C + I + G$, to an Open economy, where GNP $= C + I + G + (X - M)$, will not usually be large. However, a change in either X or M, not matched by a change in the other, will cause the GNP to change in the same way as would a change in C, I, or G.

AN ALTERNATIVE DEFINITION: There is an alternative method of allowing for imports and exports in national income. This method is closer to the concepts required in a theoretical model of the behaviour of national income, but it is very difficult to apply when making actual measurements. To use this method we calculate national income as the amount of expenditure on consumption, investment, and exported goods and services that falls on commodities actually produced domestically. The rest we call the *import content* of consumption, investment, government expenditure and exports. Thus we can define four new concepts

$$C^* = C - C_M$$
$$I^* = I - I_M$$
$$G^* = G - G_M$$
$$X^* = X - X_M$$

Where C_M, I_M, G_M and X_M are the import contents of C, I, G and X respectively. You should not be surprised to hear that exports can have an import content. An exported car, for example, may have imported steel and rubber in it.

With these new definitions, GNP is defined by the following relation:

$$GNP = C^* + I^* + G^* + X^*.$$ (2)

The four terms give us the values of *domestic outputs* of consumption, investment, government commodities and exports.

It is easy to show that the two approaches come to the same thing by substituting the definitions of each of the starred terms into the second expression for GNP, numbered (2) above. The substitution yields

$$GNP = C - C_M + I - I_M + G - G_M + X - X_M.$$

Gathering up all the import terms gives

$$GNP = C + I + G + X - (C_M + I_M + G_M + X_M),$$

and using M to stand for the sum of all imports yields

$$GNP = C + I + G + (X - M)$$

which is the first expression for GNP, numbered (1) in the previous subsection.

Thus the two ways of allowing for imports and exports come to the same thing. That of equation (1) is usually used in applied work since it is much easier to measure C, I, G and X than C^*, I^*, G^* and X^*. If we wish, however, to get the demands for domestic production under each of these categories, it is the starred rather than the unstarred terms that we require.

A SUMMARY OF APPROACHES TO MEASURING THE GNP

Because the GNP can be looked at in various ways, students do not always find it immediately apparent that there is one, and only one, value of the GNP for any one year. Basically, GNP measures the total value of the economy's output of final goods, O. We may look at this output either in terms of expenditure required to purchase it, E, or in terms of the expenditure required to produce it, FI.

First, consider the expenditure required to purchase the economy's total output. When currently-produced final commodities are sold, the market value of the output is equal to the amount actually spent to purchase the output. When currently-produced final commodities are added to the inventories of their producers, and not sold, the market value of the output is equal to the amount that would have to be spent if this output were purchased. The national income accountant defines expenditure not as what is actually spent, but as what would have to be spent to purchase all of the nation's output of final goods and services. By including the value of goods and services produced but not sold (as well as those that are produced and sold) in the definition of 'actual expenditure', the statistician ensures that[1]

$$O \equiv E.$$

When we measure GNP by measuring the value of output or the value of expenditure on that output, we are using the output-expenditure approach to measuring the GNP.

Second, consider the expenditure on factor services required to produce the GNP. This expenditure is the income of households who sell their factor services to producers. Factor incomes are divided into rent, wages and salaries, interest, and profits. The national income accountant defines rent, wages and salaries, and interest as the value of land, labour and borrowed capital used in the course of production, whether or not payments were actually made to the owners of these factors of production during the year; and he defines profits as the total value of output minus rent, wages and salaries, and interest. This definition ensures that

$$O \equiv FI$$

where FI stands for total factor incomes.

When we measure GNP by measuring the value of factor incomes generated in the process of producing total output, we are using the input-factor-income approach to measuring the GNP (usually referred to as the factor-income approach for short).

The definitions are such that output can be measured by expenditure or by factor incomes. It follows that the national income statistician uses terms in such a way that total expenditure and total factor incomes are identical with each other.

The definition used by the national accountant are such that $FI \equiv O \equiv E$, all three of which are alternative ways of looking at the nation's GNP.

---

1 The three-bar identity sign emphasizes that these two values are equal by definition.

Appendix

Interpreting national income measures

We have seen that national income represents the total flow of production of final goods and the total flow of factor services used to produce these goods over some period of time, usually taken as a year. The information provided by this measure can be extremely useful for many purposes, but unless it is carefully interpreted it can also be seriously misleading. Furthermore, each of the definitions we have considered – GNP, NNP, DI, and others that we shall consider shortly – gives us slightly different information, so that each may be the best statistic for studying a certain range of problems.

MAJOR CHARACTERISTICS OF GNP

We shall now consider some of the major characteristics of the GNP that give it both its strengths for some purposes and its weaknesses for others. Where the GNP has serious weaknesses in a particular application, we will ask if there is a better alternative.

Money values versus real values

The GNP measures the total *money* value of final goods produced during a year. Thus, it has a price and a quantity component, and a particular change in the GNP can be caused by many different combinations of price and quantity changes. A 10 per cent rise in GNP might, for example, have been caused by a 10 per cent rise in prices, all quantities

remaining unchanged; a 10 per cent rise in output, all prices remaining unchanged; or smaller increases in both prices and quantities. For some purposes the money value of national income is just the measure required. This is, however, not always the case. Sometimes we wish to know what is happening to the actual quantity of output and then we need to separate changes in the GNP that were caused by changes in market prices from changes that were caused by variations in the quantities of output. Over any long period of time, changes in the GNP reflect both real quantity changes and money price changes and if, for example, we wish to assess the change in real output of an economy whose GNP had increased by 10 per cent, it will make a great deal of difference if over the period money prices have increased by 10 per cent, increased by 5 per cent, or remained constant.

To answer this question, the GNP series has to be 'deflated', which means adjusting it for the change in the level of prices. This is done by an index number developed for that purpose and called the GNP DEFLATOR. When the GNP is measured in terms of the prices prevailing at the time of measurement, it is measured in current values. When it is deflated to give a real series, it is measured in real or constant values.

473

Total output versus per capita output

The rise in real GNP over this century has had two main causes: first, an increase in the amounts of land, labour and capital used in production; second, an increase in output per unit of input. In other words, more inputs have been used, and each input has become more productive. For many purposes, we do want the measure of total output provided by the real GNP discussed in the previous section: for example, if we wish to assess a country's potential military strength or to know the total size of its market. For other purposes, however, we will need per capita measures, which are obtained by dividing GNP by the number of persons in some group. GNP divided by the total population gives us a measure of how much output there is on average for each person in the economy; this is called PER CAPITA GNP. GNP divided by the number of persons employed tells us the average output per employed worker. GNP divided by the total number of hours worked measures output per hour of labour input.

Total output versus parts of output

So far, we have distinguished between real and money measures of GNP and between total and per capita measures. In each case, however, it was the total GNP that we manipulated. We now come to a series of characteristics of GNP that suggest the use of only parts of the GNP when studying particular problems.

GROSS VERSUS NET OUTPUT: Whether we express it in current or constant dollars, as a total or as a per capita figure, the GNP is basically a measure of total output. Net national product, NNP, is a measure of the economy's net output after allowing for what must be produced to maintain intact the stock of capital inherited from the past. NNP is GNP minus capital consumption.

Each measure is appropriate for certain purposes. If, for example, we wish to measure the total demand for factor services implied by the level of output in the country, it is the

GNP that we require. If, however, we wish to measure the output available for such purposes as consumption and new investment, after ensuring that the capital stock is maintained intact, it is the NNP that we require.

TOTAL INCOME VERSUS DISPOSABLE INCOME: The GNP measures the total factor incomes generated by the productive activities of the economy. It does not measure the income actually received by households. We have already noted that because of business saving, various taxes on business, and personal income taxes, much of the income generated through production never reaches households. For many purposes, therefore, a narrower measure of income than GNP is useful. If, for example, we wish to relate the saving and spending decisions of households to their income, it is disposable income (DI) that we require rather than total national income. (You should recall that not only does DI exclude much of what is in GNP, but it includes government transfer payments, which are not included in GNP.)

AVERAGES VERSUS MEASURES OF DISPERSIONS: Per capita figures for GNP, NNP, and DI tell us about the average levels of various income measures. Such information is of great interest, and it is useful to be told, for example, that per capita real GNP is rising at 5 per cent in country A and only 1 per cent in country B.

Average measures, however, conceal great variations among individuals. If we wish to know how wide is the spread of individual incomes around the national average, we require a *measure of dispersion*. Macro-economics largely ignores measures of dispersion and concentrates on total and average measures of income. The concentration on such measures is acceptable – on the principle of dealing with one problem at a time – as long as it is not forgotten that much important information is suppressed when measures of dispersion are ignored. We should not forget, for example, that many individuals in advanced countries are hungry today, and some are no better off than were their fathers and grandfathers, in spite of the high and rising *average* level of real GNP, NNP, and DI.

Omissions from GNP

Finally, we come to a series of omissions from the GNP, and thus also from the NNP, DI, and other measures based mainly on parts of the GNP. The importance of these omissions can be assessed only when we know the purpose for which the income data is to be used.

ILLEGAL ACTIVITIES: The GNP does not measure illegal activities even though many of these are ordinary business activities in that they produce goods and services that are sold on the market and generate factor incomes. The American liquor industry during the 1920s when the production and sale of all alcoholic drinks was prohibited was an important example because it accounted for a significant part of the nation's total economic activity. Today, the same is true in many countries of some forms of gambling, prostitution and the production and distribution of soft and hard drugs from grass to opium. If we wish to have a measure of the total demand for factors of production in the economy or of the total marketable output – whether or not we as individuals approve of particular products – we should include these activities. Probably the main reason for leaving them out is that because of their illicit nature, it would be hard to find out enough about them to include them even if we wanted to.

NON-MARKETED ECONOMIC ACTIVITIES: When a bank teller hires a carpenter to build a bookshelf in his house, the value of the bookshelf enters into the GNP; if the teller builds the bookshelf himself, the value of the bookshelf is omitted from the GNP. In general, any labour service that does not pass through a market is not counted in the GNP. Such omissions include, for example, the services of housewives, any do-it-yourself

activity, and voluntary work such as canvassing for a political party, participating in the operation of a day-care centre, or leading a Boy Scout troop.

Does the omission of non-marketed economic activities matter? Once again, it all depends. If we wish to measure the flow of goods and services through the market sector of the economy, or to account for changes in the opportunities for employment for those households who sell their labour services in the market, this omission is desirable. If, however, we wish to measure the overall flow of goods and services available to satisfy people's wants, whatever the source of the goods and services, then the omissions are undesirable and potentially serious. In most advanced industrial economies the non-market sector is relatively small, and it can be ignored even if GNP is used for purposes for which it would be appropriate to include non-marketed goods and services. The omissions become serious, however, when one is using GNP or DI figures to compare living standards in very different economies. Generally, the non-market sector of the economy is larger in rural than in urban settings and in underdeveloped than in developed economies.

FACTORS AFFECTING HUMAN WELFARE BUT NOT INCLUDED IN THE VALUE OF OUTPUT: Many things that contribute to human welfare are not included in the GNP – leisure, for example. In fact, although a shorter working week may make people happier, it will tend to reduce measured GNP.

GNP does not allow for the capacity of different goods to provide different satisfactions. A million pounds spent on a bomber or a nuclear missile makes the same addition to GNP as a million pounds spent on a school or concert hall, expenditures that may produce very different levels of satisfaction for consumers.

GNP does not measure the quality of life. To the extent that material output is purchased at the expense of overcrowded cities and roads, polluted environments, defaced countrysides, maimed accident victims, longer delays in public services and a more complex life that entails a frantic struggle to be happy, GNP measures only part of the total of human well-being. Ironically, payments to remedy pollution or to treat the ills of the cities and its citizens are included in the GNP. Thus, the unfortunate by-products of material advances themselves generate national income.

A MEASURE OF ECONOMIC WELFARE

GNP does not measure human welfare, nor was it designed to do so. The philosophy of the national income statistician might be expressed in the observation 'Man may not live by bread alone, but it is nonetheless important to know how much bread he does have to live by'. But GNP is often used as if it were a measure of human welfare. For example, fast growth rates of real GNP are usually regarded as desirable irrespective of the political and environmental factors that may make a country with a slow growth rate a happier place in which to live than a country with a fast growth rate.

Can a statistic that comes closer to measuring human welfare than does GNP be designed? If this could be done, GNP could be kept as the measure of market activity whenever one was needed, and the new measure could be used to indicate human welfare, at least by those bold or foolhardy enough to do so.

A pioneering attempt to develop such a measure has been made by Professors William Nordhaus and James Tobin.[1] They call their measure MEW, for MEASURE OF ECONOMIC WELFARE.

The basic philosophy behind MEW is that the end product of economic activity is household welfare, which in turn depends on consumption rather than on production. GNP is a measure of output, while MEW is

1 William Nordhaus and James Tobin, 'Is Economic Growth Obsolete?' in *Economic Growth*, NBER, Fifth Anniversary Colloquium V (New York, 1972). Professor Paul Samuelson calls it NEW, for net economic welfare.

an attempt to measure all consumption that contributes to human welfare. To derive their estimate of MEW, Nordhaus and Tobin start with consumption as defined by the national income accountant, deduct items that they argue do not contribute to welfare, and add items that they argue do contribute to welfare but are not included in consumption as measured in the national income accounts.

They make three kinds of deductions: (1) expenditures that they argue do not yield utility directly (examples are public expenditures such as police protection, sanitation services, road maintenance and national defense, and private expenditures such as commuting to work[1]); (2) all household expenditures to purchase durable consumer goods such as cars, TV sets and washing machines (they argue here that the utility that these goods confer is derived over the lifetime of the goods and not just when they are purchased); (3) estimated allowances for what is called 'negative externalities', which are the losses in welfare connected with urbanization, pollution, and congestion.[2]

Nordhaus and Tobin also make three kinds of additions: (1) estimates of the value of the services of consumers' durables – such as cars, TV sets and washing machines – actually consumed during the period (although the money spent to buy a new car this year does not all count as current consumption, the value of the services of the car used this year does count as consumption); (2) estimates of the value of work, such as do-it-yourself activities, that does not pass through the market; (3) estimates of the value of leisure. This last addition is extremely

1 Clearly, there are enormous complications in judging the effect of such expenditures on welfare, and to say that the effect is always zero is to make a heroic assumption.

2 Although most people think congestion, pollution, and so on are undesirable, most people, given a voluntary choice, elect to live in an urban rather than a rural setting. Presumably, therefore, the possibility of being able to live in an urban setting, which is not provided by countries that are primarily agricultural, should receive a *positive* welfare weight.

important quantitatively, and two of the many difficult problems associated with it are: first, a higher value should undoubtedly be placed on leisure consumed voluntarily, because people prefer leisure to more income, than on leisure consumed involuntarily, because work is not available; second, it is not at all obvious what value to put on leisure voluntarily consumed.

If we wish to arrive at a single total for consumption of the things that give people utility, we cannot just add up an hour of leisure and a ticket to the opera. To arrive at our single figure for total consumption, we need to value everything consumed in terms of money. The opera ticket is simple enough: We value it at its market price. But what of leisure? Two of the many possible approaches to valuing leisure are the *opportunity-cost* and the *intrinsic-value* approaches. The opportunity-cost approach measures the value of leisure at what is given up in order to obtain it. A person who elects to consume an extra hour of leisure each week is giving up the opportunity of working for that hour. This causes him to sacrifice the income that he could have earned from an hour's work. Since the real wage rate – the goods and services that can be bought with the income earned from an hour's work – has been rising steadily over the years, the value of leisure measured by the opportunity-cost approach has also been rising steadily over the years. The intrinsic-value approach seeks to measure the value of leisure according to the enjoyment that it actually provides. Although it may be difficult to measure such intrinsic values, the approach does open up the possibility that an hour's leisure might have an unchanging value over time, because an hour *with a book of verse, and a jug of wine beneath a bough* yielded as much utility in 1929 as it does in 1975. Indeed, this approach is at least consistent with the heretical thought that 50 years ago when we knew how to use our leisure, an hour's leisure might have yielded more utility than it does in the hectic present when we have lost the gentle art of doing nothing.

Nordhaus and Tobin try three different methods of valuing leisure, and the importance of this one calculation is illustrated by the fact that in 1965 the index of MEW (with 1929 = 100) has three widely different values – 119, 143 and 126 – depending on which measure of valuing leisure is chosen.[1] The first indicates a virtual standstill, the last a major increase in MEW.

WHICH MEASURE IS BEST?

To ask which is *the* best national income measure is something like asking which is *the* best carpenter's tool. The answer is 'It all depends on the job to be done'.

There are many related national income measures. There is no true, or best, measure for all purposes. The advantages and disadvantages of each can be assessed only in relation to the particular problem for which it might be used.

If we wish to compare living standards across countries and over time, then some measure such as MEW, or a further refinement of it, will very likely be superior to the GNP. It would surely be desirable if the widespread use of MEW stopped politicians from judging their country's economic performance simply by comparing the level and rate of growth of their measured GNP with those of other countries.

No matter how refined future measures of economic welfare become, they are unlikely ever to replace the GNP completely. Economists and politicians interested in the ebb and flow of economic activity that passes through the market and in the rise and fall in employment opportunities for factors of production whose services are sold on the market will continue to use GNP as a measure that comes closest to telling them what they need to know.

1 Your fathers would be very interested to learn that MEW was higher in 1935 than in 1929 on two of the three ways of valuing leisure in spite of the fact that in 1935 the Western world was in the middle of the worst depression in recorded history, during which millions of labourers suffered the indignity of prolonged periods of involuntary unemployment.

35

The determination of national income

The tale told by the real GNP series for any Western market economy throughout the present century is one of steady long-term increase interrupted by short periods of constant or falling GNP. The two major themes in the GNP story are thus long-term trend increases and short-term fluctuations.

The short-term fluctuations bring serious problems with them. A downturn in the GNP brings unemployment in its wake: fewer goods produced mean fewer factors employed. A sharp rise in GNP which brings output to the point of full employment of the nation's productive capacity may be accompanied by a severe inflation.

Inflation and unemployment are regarded by most people as undesirable. Why do they occur? Can the central authorities adopt policies that will make them occur less often or with less severity? To address ourselves to these sorts of questions we need to develop a theory of the circular flow of income. In the present chapter we develop the basic model, and examine the forces in the model that determine the size of equilibrium GNP. In the next Chapter we use this theory to explain why GNP changes. In subsequent Chapters we investigate what governments can do to influence the short-term fluctuations in, and the long-term growth of, the GNP.

PRELIMINARY DEFINITIONS AND ASSUMPTIONS
National income

In measuring national income, distinctions are made among such concepts as GNP and NNP. In their theories, economists usually use the generic concept of national income (indicated by the symbol Y) rather than such specific concepts as the GNP, or the NNP. Usually, however, Y may be thought of as interchangeable with GNP.[1]

1 Economists have sometimes debated whether the basic concept should be GNP or NNP. If we wish to explain employment and inflation GNP would appear to be the relevant concept since both jobs and pressure on the nation's productive capacity depend on the economy's total output, whether the output is being used to produce capital to replace what has worn out or for any other purpose.

Equilibrium income

Equilibrium is a state of rest, usually brought about by a balance between opposing forces. National income is said to be in equilibrium when there is no tendency for it either to increase or to decrease. The actual national income achieved at that point is referred to as the EQUILIBRIUM NATIONAL INCOME. In this chapter we study the forces that determine the size of the equilibrium national income which is often described as the problem of the *determination of national income*.

Autonomous and induced expenditure

Any expenditure that is taken as a constant unaffected by any economic variables within our theory is called AUTONOMOUS EXPENDITURE. Any expenditure that is determined by, and thus varies with, economic variables within our theory is called INDUCED EXPENDITURE. For example, in the simple theory of the determination of national income, investment expenditure is taken as a constant while consumption expenditure is assumed to vary directly with national income. In the terminology just introduced, investment is autonomous and consumption is induced expenditure. (Note that, using the terminology introduced on page 32, autonomous and induced are the same things respectively as *exogenous* and *endogenous*.)

Unemployment

One of the main variables that concerns us in macro-economics is the amount of unemployment (U). We define the labour force as the number of persons willing to work (n), which number is made up of those actually working (l) and those willing to work but unable to find jobs, i.e., unemployed, (u). Thus $n = l + u$. We define the percentage of the labour force unemployed as

$$U = \frac{u}{l+u} \times 100$$

and the percentage of the labour force employed as

$$L = \frac{l}{l+u} \times 100 = 100 - U.$$

(Notice that lower case letters refer to absolute numbers and capitals to percentages.)

Actual income and full-employment income

We have already noted that national income data show a long-term upward trend and short-term fluctuations. To separate these, a concept called FULL-EMPLOY-MENT NATIONAL INCOME or POTENTIAL NATIONAL INCOME is used. This is the national income that could be produced when the country's factors of production are fully employed.[1] This concept is given the symbol Y_F. Actual national income,

---

1 Because there must always be some unemployment due to people changing jobs, entering and leaving the labour force etc., there will always be some unemployment. This unavoidable minimum amount of unemployment is called frictional unemployment and 'full employment' is defined to occur when there is no more than this minimum amount of frictional unemployment. In America full employment is said to occur when 4 per cent of the labour force is unemployed. In Britain it was defined in 1944 as occurring at 3 per cent unemployment, but postwar experience suggested a figure closer to 2 per cent.

symbolized by Y, can be below or equal to Y_F and, by working resources overtime and otherwise harder than normal, it can occasionally rise above Y_F. The concept of Y_F is extremely important and the terms potential and full-employment national income will occur throughout the analysis.

Basic assumptions

We start with some simplifying assumptions (noting once again that it is easier to study things one at a time rather than all at once). These assumptions are designed to isolate the main forces that determine national income. (The consequences of dropping them are considered later in this book.)

(1) POTENTIAL NATIONAL INCOME IS CONSTANT: Potential national income changes very slowly from one year to the next. Although the cumulative effects of small annual changes in potential income can be dramatic over several decades, the effects are relatively minor over a period of a year or two. Assuming full-employment income to be constant allows us to isolate the forces that strongly influence national income over short periods of time. When full-employment income is constant, actual income changes only because of changes in the amount of employment of factors of production. The theory of national income in the short term is thus a theory of the degree to which the economy's full-employment productive capacity is actually utilized. [1]

(2) THERE ARE UNEMPLOYED SUPPLIES OF ALL FACTORS OF PRODUCTION: This assumption implies that output can be increased by employing land, labour and capital that is currently unemployed. In subsequent chapters we shall study the behaviour of national income when unemployment has reached such a low level that it is difficult, if not impossible, to increase output by putting to work factors of production that are currently unemployed.

(3) THE LEVEL OF PRICES IS CONSTANT: The reason for making this assumption now is that it allows us to isolate the causes of changes in *real national income*. [2] When prices are fixed, any change in national income must reflect a change in real quantities produced, whereas if prices increase, a change in national income will reflect a mixture of price and quantity changes. Later, when we come to study the causes of inflation, we will wish to drop this assumption. Once again, it is a case of studying things one at a time rather than all at once.

Armed with the three assumptions just stated, we can focus on the problem of what determines the equilibrium level of real national income. The procedure is to take a model of an economy and discover what determines the equilibrium level of national income in that model economy. How the behaviour of national income in the model

---

1 The constancy of Y_F follows from two more basic assumptions. The total supply of inputs, and the output produced per unit of input used (productivity) are both assumed constant. Given these assumptions full employment of all inputs, including labour, implies a particular quantity of employment, and this quantity of employment in turn implies a particular quantity of real output. Later, when we study the long-term behaviour of national income, we will be concerned with the changes in productivity and in factor supplies that cause Y_F itself to change.

2 The distinction between real and money national income is discussed on page 473.

relates to the behaviour of national income in the real world and the insight that the one gives us into the other is discussed in subsequent chapters. It is convenient to start by studying the simplest of the hypothetical economies that were introduced in the last Chapter.

NATIONAL INCOME IN THE SPENDTHRIFT ECONOMY

Recall the three essential features of this simplified economy. First, there are only two groups of decision-takers, firms and households. Second, households spend all of their incomes buying consumption goods and services produced by firms. Third, firms pay all of their earnings out to households in the form of rent, wages, interest and distributed profits; there are no deductions for taxes (since there is no government), for depreciation (since if capital exists it lasts forever) or for business saving (since there is no investment in new capital).

The CIRCULAR FLOW OF INCOME is *the flow of payments and receipts between domestic firms and domestic households*. It is shown for the Spendthrift economy in Figure 35.1.

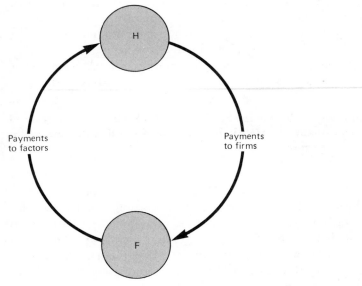

Fig. 35.1 The circular flow of income in the Spendthrift economy

For this economy the circular flow is a genuinely closed circuit: whatever is received by households is passed on to firms and whatever is received by firms is passed on to households. No existing expenditure is ever withdrawn from the flow and no new expenditure is ever injected into it from outside.

If we start national income at any level in this economy, that level will persist indefinitely. If, for example, firms produce £1,000 worth of goods per week they will pay out £1,000 in factor incomes, and households will spend £1,000 on buying the output of firms. Households will just be able to spend all their income at current market prices and firms will be just able to sell all of their output at these same prices.

Thus there is no reason for anyone to alter his or her behaviour. The same would be true if we started production at £10,000 per week, at £1 million per week or any other figure (as long as resources were available to produce the output, i.e. actual output, Y, is less than or equal to full employment output, Y_F).

Any level of national income once set going, will persist forever, since there is no reason for it to change. Since Y can be in equilibrium at any level there is nothing – except accident – to explain why it is at one level rather than another.

Unreal though this economy is, using it as a model allows us to isolate the forces that do determine the level of national income in more complicated economies such as the Frugal economy to which we now turn.

NATIONAL INCOME IN THE FRUGAL ECONOMY

The simplest version of the Frugal economy differs from the Spendthrift economy in two essentials. First, households spend only part of their incomes on consumption, and they save the rest. Second, firms devote only part of their efforts to producing consumption goods for sale to households, and the remainder goes to producing investment goods. The firms that purchase the new capital goods are said to be *investing*. To simplify matters at the outset, we assume that all saving is done by households and all investing is done by firms. To indicate these magnitudes we use the symbols C for consumption, S for saving and I for investment.

Note that in the Frugal economy, saving and investment decisions are made by different groups: saving decisions are made by households, and investment decisions are made by firms.[1] Thus

> **there is no reason why a change in the desire of households to save or of firms to invest should automatically be matched by a similar change in the desire of the other group.**

Investment decisions

Firms make plans about how much to invest in new capital equipment. For this chapter it is convenient to study how the level of national income adjusts to a fixed level of investment. Thus we assume that firms plan to make a constant amount of investment in plant and equipment each year and that they plan to hold their inventories constant. In Chapters 38 and 39 we shall drop these assumptions and study the important effects on national income caused by changes in the level of investment.

Consumption-saving decisions

Each household makes plans about how much to spend on consumption and how much to save. These are not, however, independent decisions. Since saving is income not spent on consumption, it follows that households have to decide on a single division of their income between saving and consumption.

1 When we later allow for business saving and household investment it will remain true that many, even if not all, saving decisions are made by different groups from those making the investment decisions.

How do households in the aggregate actually divide their income between C and S? This is an empirical question. The evidence suggests that over the long term there is a remarkably stable division of income between C and S.[1] This suggests that we assume C to be constant fraction of Y. We shall make this assumption now although we shall need to amend it later.

Withdrawals and injections

Saving and investment are examples of two more general categories of expenditure called withdrawals and injections. A WITHDRAWAL *is any income that is not passed on in the circular flow*. Thus if households earn income and do not spend it on domestically-produced goods and services this is a withdrawal from the circular flow. Similarly, if firms receive money from the sale of goods and do not distribute it as payments to factors, this is a withdrawal from the circular flow. An INJECTION *is an addition to the income of domestic firms that does not arise from the expenditure of domestic households or an addition to the income of domestic households that does not arise from the spending of domestic firms*. If, for example, firms gain income by producing investment goods which they sell to other firms this is an injection, because the income of firms rises without households having increased their expenditure.

Withdrawals, by reducing expenditure, exert a contractionary force on national income. If, for example, households decide to increase their saving and correspondingly reduce the amount they used to spend buying consumption goods from firms, this reduces the income of firms, and reduces the payments they will make to factors of production. Injections, by raising expenditure, exert an expansionary force on national income. If, for example, firms sell machines to other firms, then incomes and their payments to households for factor services will rise without there having been an increase in household expenditure.

In the Frugal economy saving is the only withdrawal. It is income that households receive but do not spend buying goods and services from firms. Also investment is the only injection. It is income of firms that does not arise from the spending of households. The circular flow in this economy is shown in Figure 35.2. The black circuit is the basic circular flow from domestic firms to domestic households[2] and back again; the white arrows show the flow of saving as a withdrawal and the flow of investment as an injection.

The behaviour of the circular flow

We now consider how income is determined in this model. If we are ever to observe income out of equilibrium there must be lags in the flow around the circuit pictured in Figure 35.2, because if all adjustments were instantaneous, the economy could never be out of equilibrium. The way in which the flow behaves out of equilibrium will depend critically on these lags. Since we are mainly interested in equilibrium

1 If we take averages of the actual observed data for C, S and disposable income for a ten-year period we find the fraction of income devoted to C and S over that decade. If we obtain such an average for each decade we find that the proportions of income devoted to C and S have remained remarkably constant over the whole of this century in spite of large increases in national income. These observations are discussed in more detail in Chapter 37.

2 Domestic is used to mean *not foreign*.

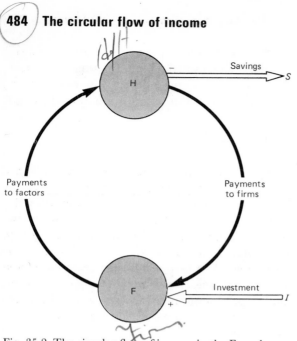

Fig. 35.2 The circular flow of income in the Frugal economy

income, we will make the simplest assumptions that are sufficient to reveal the forces determining equilibrium income.

(1) Time is divided into weeks.

(2) Production adjusts to demand with no time lag. Thus, whatever is demanded this week is produced and sold this week without any need for inventories of goods produced in the past to change.

(3) Income is paid to households one week in arrears. Thus if production rises this week, more factors are employed but household disposable income does not rise until pay day which is at the last instant of the week. The income received on pay day is not therefore available for spending until the following week.

(4) Households save a constant proportion of their disposable income each week and spend the remainder purchasing currently-produced goods and services.

(5) Investment expenditure is an exogenous constant.

A NUMERICAL ILLUSTRATION: Table 35.1 illustrates the behaviour of the Frugal economy with the added specific assumptions that households save 20 per cent of their disposable incomes and consume the remaining 80 per cent, while investment expenditure is constant at 20 per week.[1] The example is not difficult but it is critical to everything that follows so it will repay very careful study. The first two rows of the Table display an equilibrium situation in weeks 1 and 2. The value of national income is constant at 100 per week. Because national income is the same last week as this week, disposable income is also constant at 100. Saving is 20 and consumption is 80. Total demand is for 80 of consumption goods and 20 of investment goods. Thus

---

1 All quantities are measured in monetary units, and since prices are constant, values change only when real quantities change. The unit is left undefined since it could just as well be an index number as a sterling or a dollar value.

demand is just sufficient to purchase the output of 100 that is produced. National income is in equilibrium because, unless it is disturbed, the situation will repeat itself week after week with output of 100, disposable income of 100, induced consumption expenditure of 80, and autonomous investment expenditure of 20. Notice that the amount households save is exactly equal to the amount firms invest (so that all investment could be financed by selling bonds and equities to households).

Table 35.1 The behaviour of the circular flow of income in the Frugal economy: an example of a rise in investment

Col. 1	Col. 2	Col. 3	Col. 4	Col. 5	Col. 6
Week	Disposable income, Y^d (=the value of last week's national income)	Saving, S (=0·2 Y^d)	Consumption, C (=0·8 Y^d)	Investment, I (=an exogenous constant)	National income, Y (=value of this week's production, i.e., $C+I$)
1	100	20	80	20	100
2	100	20	80	20	100
3	100	20	80	40	120
4	120	24	96	40	136
5	136	27·2	108·8	40	148·8
.	.	.	.	.	.
.	.	.	.	.	.
.	.	.	.	.	.
n	200	40	160	40	200

A RISE IN INVESTMENT: Now let us disturb the equilibrium with a sudden investment boom. At the beginning of week 3 firms become more optimistic about the future and decide to double their investment expenditure. (They cannot borrow this new amount from households and will have to borrow from financial institutions or else use their own accumulated reserves.)

Now let us look carefully at what happens in weeks 3 and 4. In week 3 household disposable income is the 100 earned from production in week 2. Therefore, household saving remains at 20 and consumption expenditure at 80. Firms, however, now demand 40 of investment goods and output expands immediately to meet this demand. Thus national income rises to 120 in week 3. Investment made by firms (col. 5) exceeds saving made by households (col. 3), and this discrepancy exerts a net expansionary force on the circular flow of income.

In week 4 household disposable income rises to 120 as households are paid for the extra work done in week 3. Their saving rises to 24, and their consumption expenditure rises to 96. The output of consumption goods rises immediately to meet this extra demand. The value of total output rises to 136 ($96C + 40I$). In the following week this 136 is paid out to households and as a result their expenditure rises once again.

A moment spent checking, by substituting in any intermediate values, will show that at any income less than 200, (a) income will rise period by period and (b)

savings as recorded in col. 3 are less than investment as recorded in col. 5.[1] Once income rises to 200, however, all expansionary forces are spent. At that income, households will spend 160 and save 40. The withdrawal of saving will just match the injection of investment and income will repeat itself period by period until something happens to disturb it. This is shown by week n in the Table.

A FALL IN INVESTMENT: Now let us briefly consider a disturbance that lowers national income. Table 35.2 repeats the original situation for weeks 1 and 2 but then assumes that in week 3 there is a sudden rush of pessimism, rather than of optimism, and a halving of investment rather than a doubling. In week 3 investment falls from 20 to 10 and total output falls from 100 to 90. In the following week disposable income falls to 90, and as a result, saving falls to 18 and consumption to 72. Because output adjusts immediately to this fall in consumption expenditure, national income falls to 82 in week 4 ($72C + 10I$). Notice that in weeks 3 and 4 investment as defined by col. 4 is less than saving as defined by col. 2. This excess of saving over investment exerts a net contractionary force on the circular flow and causes national income to fall.

Table 35.2 The behaviour of the circular flow of income in the Frugal economy: an example of a fall in investment

Col. 1	Col. 2	Col. 3	Col. 4	Col. 5	Col. 6
Week	Disposable income, Y^d (=the value of last week's national income)	Saving, S (=0·2 Y^d)	Consumption, C (=0·8 Y^d)	Investment, I (=an exogenous constant)	National income, Y (=value of this week's production, i.e., $C+I$)
1	100	20	80	20	100
2	100	20	80	20	100
3	100	20	80	10	90
4	90	18	72	10	82
5	82	16·4	65·6	10	75·6
.	.	.	.	.	.
.	.	.	.	.	.
n	50	10	40	10	50

A quick check of any intermediate values will show that the net contractionary force of an excess of saving over investment exists as long as national income is in excess of 50.[2] Once a national income of 50 has been reached, however, savings of 10 (20 per cent of 50) will just equal investment of 10 and income will remain constant.

1 For example if income is 180 at period x, Y^d will be 180 in the next period, S will be 36, C will be 144, and with an I of 40, income will rise to 184. Also the S of 36 is less than the I of 40.

2 For example if income was 60 last week, Y^d will be 60 this week, saving will be 12, consumption will be 48 and national income will be 58 ($48C + 10I$). Also the saving of 12 is greater than the investment of 10.

In the Frugal economy equilibrium national income occurs where
saving equals investment. When saving exceeds investment, income
falls; when investment exceeds saving, income rises.

Saving and investment are here defined by cols. 3 and 5 of Tables 35.1 and 35.2.

The measurement of saving and investment in the model of the circular flow

We have used definitions of saving and investment that correspond to the actual
flows in a circular flow model. The definitions are illustrated in Figure 35.3. Part (i)
shows the model in equilibrium as shown in weeks 1 and 2 in Tables 35.1 and 35.2.
Part (ii) shows week 3 from Table 35.1. The left-hand flow shows the factor payments actually available to households for spending during the week. The right-hand
flows show money actually laid aside by households for saving, money actually spent
on consumption during the week and actual expenditure on investment goods.[1]
National income is clearly not in equilibrium, and since investment exceeds saving,
income will rise in subsequent weeks – which is what Table 35.1 shows happens.

Part (iii) shows week 3 in Table 35.2. Investment has just fallen from 20 to 10, but
disposable income will not fall until next week. As a result the amount actually

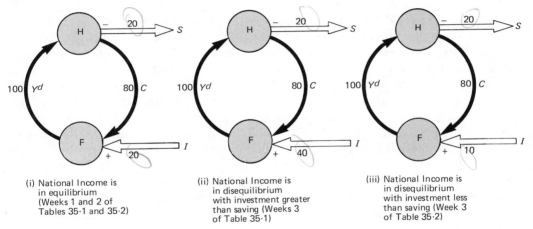

(i) National Income is
    in equilibrium
    (Weeks 1 and 2 of
    Tables 35·1 and 35·2)

(ii) National Income is
    in disequilibrium
    with investment greater
    than saving (Weeks 3
    of Table 35·1)

(iii) National Income is
    in disequilibrium
    with investment less
    than saving (Week 3
    of Table 35·2)

Fig. 35.3 Flows in the Frugal economy in situations of equilibrium and disequilibrium

withdrawn by household saving exceeds the amount actually injected by firms'
investment[2] and we must expect national income to fall in subsequent weeks.

The measurement of saving and investment by the national income statistician[3]

The national income statistician approaches the Frugal economy as follows. He

1 If for example households lend all of their savings to firms by purchasing newly-issued bonds, the amount of
bonds sold by firms to households will be 20 in week 3 (as it is in weeks 1 and 2 as well).

2 For example if firms finance all of their new investment by selling bonds to households there will be 10 units
of bonds sold and households will find themselves with an additional 10 of saving that they are unable to invest
by lending it to firms.

3 This section can be omitted on first reading. It deals with a confusion between saving and investment in the
national income accounts and saving and investment in the circular flow model. If one has not already encountered
the confusion it might be better to omit the discussion until the circular flow model has been mastered.

defines GNP as the value of total output which is made up of consumption and investment goods. Thus

$$\text{GNP} \equiv O \equiv C + I$$

where the three bar signs remind us that we are dealing with relations that hold by definition. The statistician also allocates all the value of output to factor incomes generated in the process of producing the GNP. He then allocates this income between two categories of expenditure: what is spent, C, and what is saved, S. Thus

$$\text{GNP} \equiv Y \equiv C + S.$$

This use of terms makes saving identical with investment:

$$C + I \equiv O \equiv Y \equiv C + S$$
$$I \equiv S.$$

The trick here is that the national income statistician is not making measurements at various points in the circular flow – as we would want to do if we wished to describe its disequilibrium behaviour as in Tables 35.1 and 35.2 and Figure 35.3. He is measuring the circular flow at one point: the point 'F' in Figure 35.3. He is, in fact, measuring the value of total output. When he speaks of factor incomes generated in a particular 'week' (or year) he does not mean the value of incomes actually paid out to households during that 'week' – or year, (not even in the Frugal economy where all income is eventually paid out to households). Instead he means a notional allocation of the value of current output into the income claims that can be put on it – the amount that is owed to land, to labour, to borrowed capital and the amount that is left for the residual claim of profits. Thus in Figure 35.1(ii), the national income statistician would say that national income in week 3 was 120. He would also say that factor incomes were 120. Since only 80 was spent on consumption, savings must have been 40. But households only laid aside 20 out of their disposable income in week 3, so where is the other 20 of what the statistician calls saving? The answer is simple enough: during week 3 firms produced and sold 120 worth of goods; they only paid out 100 in actual payments to factors (because payments are made in arrears), so firms are saving the extra 20 (which will be paid out to factors to become part of their disposable income for next week).

The national income statistician measures the value of output during the week. He also measures the claims on the value of that output on the part of factors (and he measures them in such a way that they add up to exactly the value of the output). Thus in part (ii) of Figure 35.3, the statistician measures the flow of output at point 'F'; he takes this and subtracts C and calls the remainder S. Since output is $C + I$ it follows that S and I are two terms for the same thing. All of these measurements are made at the same point in the circular flow.[1]

The statistician's measurements are extremely useful in telling us the size of the circular flow and whether or not it is changing over time. They are not to be confused, however, with the flows shown at various points in the flow as, for example, in the various parts of Figure 35.3.

---

1 In fact he may take measurements at many points but they are all then adjusted to be consistent with one point, the value of output.

A graphical approach to determining equilibrium national income

Dynamic analysis of the behaviour of the circular flow out of equilibrium rapidly becomes very difficult and requires some relatively advanced mathematics. We can, however, get a long way by confining ourselves to positions of equilibrium and using the method of comparative statics to see how a shift in any of the factors that influence national income changes its equilibrium value.

To do this we need to introduce two new and very useful graphs which show two alternative approaches to determining equilibrium national income.

THE SAVINGS-INVESTMENT APPROACH: Figure 35.4 shows the behavioural assumptions of the example of Tables 1 and 2. National income is plotted on the horizontal axis and expenditure on the vertical one. Investment is exogenous. Since it does not vary with national income, it is shown as a straight line at its assumed value of 20 per week. Savings on the other hand are endogenous. They are always 20 per cent

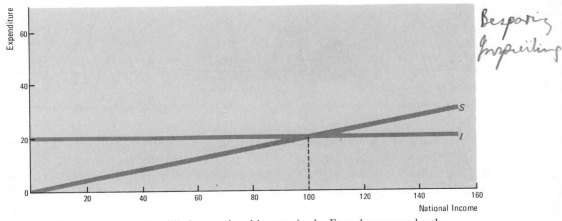

Fig. 35.4 Determination of equilibrium national income in the Frugal economy by the saving-investment approach

of income and the savings function is thus shown as a straight line with a slope of 0·2. The equilibrium level of income is where the savings and investment functions intersect. This is at a value of 100 in the present example. *If* national income were to be held constant at any value less than 100,[1] households would save less than firms wished to invest, and national income would rise under the expansionary pressure of an excess of investment over saving. If national income were to be constant at an amount in excess of 100, households would save more than firms would invest and national income would fall.

> **Graphically the equilibrium level of national income in the Frugal economy occurs where the savings and investment schedules intersect.**

THE INCOME-EXPENDITURE APPROACH: The second method of determining equilibrium national income graphically is shown in Figure 35.5, which is drawn to

1 Holding income constant allows us to ignore the lag between output and disposable factor income. Care must be taken to allow for the lag if the *adjustment process* is to be followed out in the Figure.

conform with the example of weeks 1 and 2 of Tables 35.1 and 35.2. Income and expenditure are again plotted on the two axes. Three lines are shown on the Figure and we must introduce these one at a time.

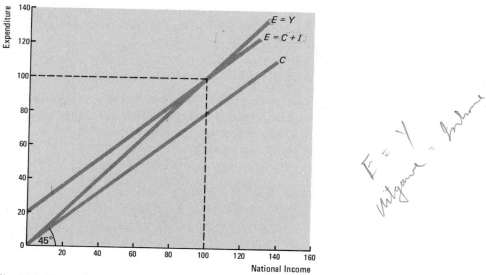

Fig. 35.5 Determination of national income in the Frugal economy by the income-expenditure approach

The 45° line: If we locate all the points showing annual expenditure exactly equal to annual income and join them up, we shall trace out the line labelled $E = Y$ in the figure. This line makes an angle of 45° with the Y-axis and is often referred to as the 45° LINE. Points above or to the left of the 45° line show combinations for which expenditure exceeds income; points below or to the right of the 45° line show combinations for which expenditure is less than income. [1]

Consumption: The line labelled C relates household consumption expenditure to national income. Since consumption expenditure is assumed to be always 80 per cent of income this line slopes upwards with a slope of 0·8. [2] The gap between the C line and the 45° line shows household saving. (Since in the Frugal economy all income must be saved or consumed, consumption plus saving must add to total income so that when Y is plotted against $C + S$ it must yield the 45° line.)

Aggregate expenditure: The third line is labelled E. It is variously called the AGGREGATE EXPENDITURE or the AGGREGATE DEMAND FUNCTION. It relates total demand for all forms of production to national income. Since, in the Frugal economy, there is only consumption and investment, the E line is the sum of C plus I. Since I is assumed constant, the E line is parallel to the C line. [3]

The aggregate expenditure function requires a little care in interpretation. The

---

1 The equation of the 45° line is $E = Y$.
2 The equation of the C line in the present example is $C = 0·8Y$.
3 The equation of the E line in the present example is $E = 20 + 0·8Y$.

E curve relates the two variables (i) the amount of expenditure that all spending units would like to make on currently produced goods and services and (ii) national income. It shows what desired expenditure would be if national income were held constant indefinitely at any particular value. Because of lags in the circular flow, this may not be the amount actually spent at the indicated level of income.[1] For this reason the E line is called a desired expenditure function.

Equilibrium income: In this approach the equilibrium level of national income is determined where the aggregate expenditure function cuts the 45° line. If national income is held at that point, aggregate demand will be just sufficient to buy up the total of all goods produced. If national income is held above that point, aggregate expenditure will be less than the value of output. If, for example, national income were held at 200, aggregate demand would be only 180 ($160C$ plus $20I$). If firms persisted in producing an output of 200 (an assumption *not* made earlier when we assumed that output adjusted instantaneously to demand), inventories of unsold goods would pile up and sooner or later output would have to be cut.

If national income were held week after week at a value below its equilibrium in the Figure, then aggregate desired expenditure would exceed the value of output. If, for example, output were held at 50, total demand would be 60 ($40C + 20I$). If firms did not raise output either inventories would fall as sales exceeded current output or queues of unsatisfied customers would develop. In either case there is a clear signal that firms can increase their sales by increasing their output. Sooner or later output and national income will rise. Only where E cuts the 45° line does aggregate expenditure remain just sufficient, no more and no less, to buy the value of output if that level of output persists week after week.[2]

Graphically, the equilibrium level of national income occurs where the aggregate expenditure function cuts the 45° line.

1 For example, in week 3 in Figure 35.1 actual expenditure and actual output are both 120. But once the 120 is paid out as factor incomes, expenditure rises (week 4) to 136. Because in this particular example there are no lags between *actual* expenditure and *actual* output, these two are always equal. (See the Appendix to this Chapter for an example in which this is not the case.) What spending units *would* spend *if* income were held constant is quite another matter. Table 35.1 shows that if income were held constant at 120 total expenditure would rise to 136 (an I of 40 *plus* a C of 0·8 *times* 120). The expenditure function for this example thus plots $E = 136$ against $Y = 120$. This tells us that if Y were held at 120 over two or more periods, desired E would be 136, (even though when Y passes through 120 in week 3, actual E is only 120 because of the lag between Y and Y^d). In the present example I is constant at 40 and C is $0·8Y^d$. When income is held constant long enough for the lag between Y^d and Y not to matter, we have $E = 40 + 0·8Y$, which is the desired aggregate expenditure function for this example.

2 The equivalence of the savings-investment and the aggregate expenditure approaches can be shown algebraically as follows. Total expenditure, E is $C + I$. Total income is accounted for by C or by S. Thus we have

$$E = C + I$$
$$Y = C + S$$

The equilibrium condition in the income-expenditure approach is

$$E = Y.$$

Substituting in from the above gives

$$C + I = C + S$$
$$I = S$$

which is the equilibrium condition in the savings-investment approach.

A link between savings and investment?

Earlier in this Chapter we stressed that saving and investment decisions were made by different groups, and that there was no necessary reason why households should decide to save the same amount as firms decide to invest. We have just concluded, however, that in the simple Frugal economy, national income is in equilibrium when saving is equal to investment. Does this not mean that we have found a mechanism that ensures that households end up desiring to save an amount equal to what firms desire to invest? The answer is 'yes'. Is there not then a conflict between what we said at first and what we have now concluded? The answer is 'no'.

The explanation of the apparent conflict provides the key to the theory of the determination of national income in the simple Frugal economy. There is no reason why the amount that households wish to save at a randomly selected level of national income should be equal to the amount that firms wish to invest at that same level of income. This is the meaning of the statement made at the outset. But when saving is not equal to investment there are forces at work in the economy that cause national income to change until the two do become equal. This is the meaning of the later statement.

The graphical expression of this is that the saving function does not everywhere coincide with the investment function. Where it does not, saving does not equal investment at the indicated level of income. But the two functions do intersect somewhere, and the equilibrium level of income, in the simple Frugal economy, occurs at the intersection point.

> To recapitulate, there is no reason why saving should equal investment at any randomly-chosen level of income, but, when the level of income is such that they are not equal, national income will change until they are brought into equality.

A GENERALIZATION OF THE THEORY OF EQUILIBRIUM NATIONAL INCOME

Conditions that must be fulfilled if something is to be in equilibrium are called EQUILIBRIUM CONDITIONS. The conditions that must be fulfilled if national income is to be in equilibrium in the model of the Frugal economy can be stated in either of two ways.

(1) Aggregate desired expenditure equals national income. When this happens, desired expenditure is just sufficient to purchase the whole of the nation's output, and there is thus no tendency for output to change.

(2) Saving equals investment. When this happens, the contractionary force of income earned by households but not spent (saving) is just balanced by the expansionary force of income earned by firms that does not arise from household spending (investment). When these two forces are in balance there will be no tendency for total output either to rise or to fall.

These results generalize with surprising ease to all circular flow models. To see this consider the two equilibrium conditions one at a time.

The first condition holds without amendment for any circular flow model.

When aggregate desired expenditure is less than total income, national income will fall; when aggregate desired expenditure exceeds total income, national income will rise; and when aggregate desired expenditure is exactly equal to total national income, an equilibrium pertains so that national income will neither rise nor fall.

All that needs to be done in moving from one circular flow model to another is to identify any new components of aggregate expenditure, and to make assumptions about how each new component is related to national income.

The second equilibrium condition, saving equals investment, requires a slight but important reinterpretation before it can be extended to all circular flow models. We have already noted that saving is an example of what is called a withdrawal from the circular flow of income. Recall that a withdrawal is any income received by households and not passed on through spending to firms, and any income received by firms not passed on as income payments to households. Withdrawals exert a contractionary force on the circular flow. Investment is an example of what is called an injection into the circular flow. Recall that an injection is income received by either a firm or a household that does not arise out of the spending of the other group. Injections exert an expansionary force on the circular flow of income.

In the Frugal economy saving is the only withdrawal and investment is the only injection. Thus it makes no difference if we say that national income is in equilibrium when saving equals investment or when withdrawals equal injections. In more complex models, however, there are many withdrawals and many injections. In such economies national income will be in equilibrium when the aggregate contractionary force of all withdrawals is equal to the aggregate expansionary force of all injections.

The general statement of this equilibrium condition for all circular flow models is thus that withdrawals should equal injections.

All that is required to apply this theory to any particular model is to identify the withdrawals and injections in the model and to make assumptions about how each is related to national income.

These general comments may now be illustrated by extending the theory of the determination of equilibrium national income to cover the cases of the Governed economy and the Open economy.

EQUILIBRIUM NATIONAL INCOME IN THE GOVERNED ECONOMY

The Frugal economy contains only households and firms. The Governed economy allows for the third major spending unit in the economy, the government. We may study the determination of national income in this economy through either of the two equilibrium conditions. When we do this we refer to using the income-expenditure approach and the withdrawals-injections approach.

The withdrawals-injections approach in the Governed economy

THE ELEMENTS OF WITHDRAWALS AND INJECTIONS: In the Frugal economy saving is the only withdrawal from the circular flow. In the Governed economy, taxes levied by the government are a second withdrawal. If the government taxes firms, some of what firms earn is not available to be passed on to households. If the government taxes households, some of what households earn is not available to be passed on to firms. Of course, some of the tax revenue will find its way back into the circular flow if the government subsequently spends it on commodities purchased from firms or factor services purchased from households. If the government does not spend the money, however, but merely lets it accumulate as a reserve against some future expected expenditure, it will remain outside of the flow.

Whatever subsequently happens to the money raised, taxes withdraw expenditure from the circular flow.

In the Frugal economy investment is the only injection. In the Governed economy, however, government expenditure is a second injection. Such expenditure creates income for firms that does not arise from the spending of households, and it creates income for households that does not arise from the spending of firms. If, for example, the government spends money to buy aircraft from private firms, the incomes of these firms will rise, as will the incomes of those households who supply factor services to the firms.

Whatever the source of the funds, government spending injects expenditure into the circular flow.

Letting G stand for government expenditure, T for total taxes, J for injections and W for withdrawals, we can summarize our definitions for the governed economy in symbols as follows:

$$W = S + T \qquad \text{and} \qquad J = G + I.$$

Figure 35.6 shows the model of the circular flow of income in the Governed economy with saving and taxes as withdrawals and investment and government expenditure as injections.

EQUILIBRIUM IN TERMS OF WITHDRAWALS AND INJECTIONS: It is convenient to start by assuming that both injections, I and G, are constant. This allows us to study how national income adjusts to a fixed level of investment and government expenditure. Later we shall study the response of national income to changes in G. We will also see how G is sometimes changed by the government for the express purpose of influencing the level of national income.

Withdrawals, however, cannot be assumed to be constant. We have already seen that the theory of the consumption function predicts that saving will rise as national income rises. The government's tax revenue can also be expected to rise as national income rises: if all tax rates are held constant, tax yields will rise with income. Purchase taxes and taxes on personal and business incomes will all produce more money as the value of total output produced and total incomes earned increases. Thus we expect the withdrawals of both savings and taxes to rise as income rises.

National income will be in equilibrium when total withdrawals, saving plus taxes, is equal to total injections, investment plus government expenditure. The equilibrium condition for national income can thus be written as

$$W = J, \text{ or } S + T = G + I.$$

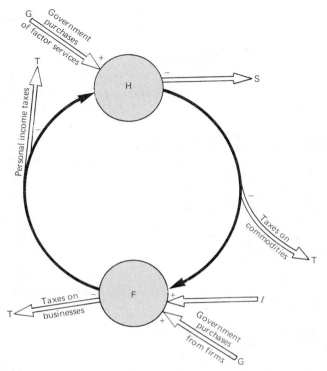

Fig. 35.6 The circular flow of income in the Governed economy

If withdrawals are less than injections there will be a net expansionary force in the economy. Income will rise. Tax receipts and savings will rise along with income and the expansion will come to a halt when total withdrawals have risen to the level of total injections. If withdrawals were to exceed injections there would be a net contractionary force in the economy. Income would fall. Tax receipts and savings would all fall along with income and the contraction would come to a halt when total withdrawals had fallen to the level of injections.

The income-expenditure approach in the Governed economy

In the Governed economy, total expenditure is consumption expenditure, C, and investment expenditure, I, as in the Frugal economy, plus government expenditure, G. Government expenditure is reckoned net of transfer payments, since transfer payments do not of themselves create demand for the nation's output. Of course when households spend their government transfer payments this creates demand – but is shown up as a consumption expenditure; the transfer payment itself does not create demand and thus is not counted as part of aggregate expenditure. Aggregate expenditure, E, may be expressed as

$$E = C + I + G.$$

National income will be in equilibrium when aggregate desired expenditure is equal to national income because in that case desired purchases will exactly equal total production.

EQUILIBRIUM NATIONAL INCOME IN THE OPEN ECONOMY

The Open economy allows for the influence of foreign trade. The effects of such trade need to be introduced into both the withdrawals-injections and the income-expenditure approaches.

The withdrawals-injections approach in the Open economy

THE ELEMENTS OF WITHDRAWALS AND INJECTIONS: As well as the withdrawals of savings and taxes already allowed for, there is now a third withdrawal, imports. When households spend their incomes on imported goods instead of domestic ones, incomes are created for foreign firms and foreign households, instead of for domestic firms and domestic households. If British households decide to buy fewer Cortinas and more Volkswagons, a smaller proportion of the income received by British households will be passed back to the British car producer and a larger proportion will be withdrawn from the circular flow of the British economy. The British motor company will now earn less income and will hire fewer factors of production, so that incomes of British households will fall.

> **Whatever subsequently happens to the money spent, imports withdraw expenditure from the circular flow.**

One country's imports are another country's exports and in the Open economy the list of injections that already includes I and G must be augmented to include exports. In the previous example, there was an increase of imports of Volkswagons into Britain, but there was simultaneously an increase in exports of Volkswagons from Germany. This increase in exports means that the German car company gains an increase in its income and, because more factors of production will be needed to produce more, there will also be an increase in the incomes of German households. This increase in the circular flow in Germany did not arise because of any change in the expenditures of German households (it was the expenditure patterns of British households that changed), and so it constitutes an injection into the German circular flow of income.

> **Whatever the source of the money spent, exports inject expenditure into the circular flow.**

Letting M stand for imports and X for exports we can summarize our definitions of withdrawals and injections as follows:

$$W = S + T + M \qquad \text{and} \qquad J = I + G + X.$$

Figure 35.7 shows the model of the circular flow of income in the Open economy with saving, taxes and imports shown as withdrawals and investment, government expenditure and exports shown as injections. To prevent the Figure from becoming unduly complex all of government taxes are compressed into a single flow and so are government expenditures. Exports are shown as creating income for firms in the first instance. Imports, however, arise both from the spending of households (imported consumers' goods) and from the spending of firms (e.g. imported raw materials).

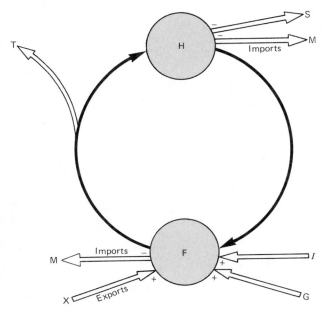

Fig. 35.7 The circular flow of income in the Open economy

EQUILIBRIUM IN TERMS OF WITHDRAWALS AND INJECTIONS: We have already assumed G and I to be fixed. What about the new injection of exports? The amount of our exports depends upon the domestic prices of the goods we sell, on our exchange rate (which determines the foreign prices of these goods), on the prices of competing goods from other countries, and on foreign incomes. As with I and G, it is convenient to see how national income adjusts to a fixed level of exports before seeing how it reacts when exports change. Thus exports are assumed constant for the remainder of this chapter.

The withdrawals already allowed for, S and T, are both assumed to rise with income. Imports are expected to exhibit similar behaviour. They will tend to rise as national income rises, both because domestic households spend a fraction of their consumption expenditure on foreign rather than on domestically-produced commodities, and because almost all domestic output has some import content of raw materials and semi-manufactured goods. Iron ore, oil, paper and lumber are but a few of the many examples. Thus we expect all withdrawals, S, T and M to rise as income rises.

If withdrawals are less than injections there will be a net expansionary force in the economy. Income will rise. Tax receipts, savings and imports will all rise along with income and the expansion will come to a halt when total withdrawals have risen to the level of total injections. If withdrawals were to exceed injections there would be a net contractionary force in the economy. Income would fall. Tax receipts, savings and imports would all fall along with income and the contraction would come to a halt when total withdrawals had fallen to the level of total injections.

National income will be in equilibrium when total desired withdrawals equals total desired injections. Thus the equilibrium condition is, once again, $W = J$, and allowing for all withdrawals and injections this becomes

$$S + T + M = I + G + X.$$

The income-expenditure approach in the Open economy

In the Open economy aggregate expenditure includes expenditure by foreign firms, households and governments on domestically-produced goods and services. Aggregate expenditure thus includes the total of all exports. On the other side of the account, however, some consumption expenditure made by domestic households, some investment expenditure made by domestic firms, and some government expenditure may go to purchase goods and services produced in foreign countries. To arrive at aggregate expenditure on domestically-produced goods, which is domestic national income, we must, as we saw on page 471 of chapter 34, subtract imports to arrive at a total for aggregate expenditure on domestically-produced final goods of

$$E = C + I + G + (X - M).$$

The total is consumption plus investment plus government expenditure plus net exports.

Once again national income will be in equilibrium when aggregate desired expenditure is equal to national income. When this is true, total desired purchases will be just equal to total production.

EQUILIBRIUM NATIONAL INCOME: A GENERAL GRAPHICAL APPROACH

Figure 35.8 shows the equilibrium level of national income in terms of both the income-expenditure and the withdrawals-injections approaches. The analysis is essentially the same whether aggregate expenditure is merely $C + I$, as in the Frugal economy, $C + I + G$, as in the Governed economy, or $C + I + G + (X - M)$, as in the Open economy. Similarly, it is incidental whether there is one injection and one withdrawal, as in the simple Frugal economy, or two of each as in the Governed economy, or three of each, as in the Open economy.

> **Equilibrium income always occurs where desired aggregate expenditure equals national income and where withdrawals equal injections.**

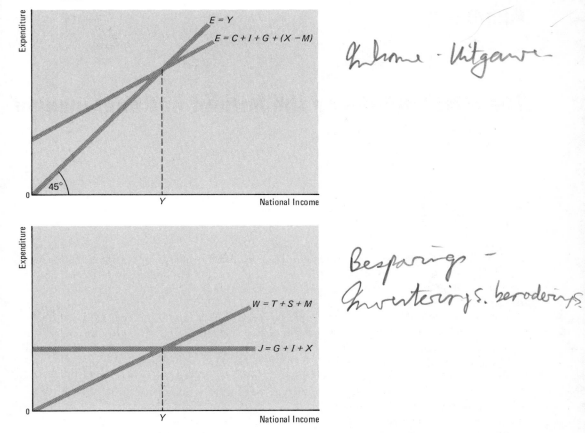

Fig. 35.8 The general graphical expression of equilibrium national income through the income-expenditure and the saving-investment approaches

Appendix

The effect of lags on the path of national income

The path taken by national income when it is not in equilibrium depends critically on the kinds of lags that are assumed to exist in the circular flow. The text used a simple example in which disposable income lagged one 'week' behind actual output, but output adjusted instantaneously to changes in demand. This has the effect of leaving inventories constant. An alternative model, which is often described verbally in elementary texts, has output adjusting to demand with a one period lag, while assuming the existence of sufficient inventories so that any demand can be met out of inventories until production is adjusted.

An example of such a model is given in Table 35.3 in which the lag between output and disposable income is still maintained.

The initial equilibrium, identical to that in Tables 35.1 and 35.2, is shown repeating itself through weeks 1 and 2. Then in week 3 there is an investment boom. Sales of say, machines rise from 20 to 40. Output of machines does not rise and the whole of the additional demand is met by running down inventories. Thus overall investment which is the sum of cols. 5 and 6 remains constant. Current output remains unchanged at 100 and disposable income available in week 4 does not rise.[1] In week 4 sales are 80 of consumption goods and 40 of machines but production is adjusted to meet the expanded

demand for machines. National income thus rises to 120 in week 4 and this amount is available to households for their spending in week 5. Thus in week 5 consumption expenditure rises to 96 (80 per cent of 120) but the rise in demand is unanticipated, so inventories of consumers' goods fall by 16. National income does not rise so neither does disposable income rise in week 6. But in that week production of consumers goods rises to meet the extra demand. The course of national income proceeds in the uneven increases shown in the Table until eventually it reaches its equilibrium level of 200.

In these theories the equilibrium level of national income is independent of the lags that are assumed to exist in the circular flow,

---

1 Since in this case there is a lag between purchases and output, it is possible for expenditure and output, as defined in the flow model, to diverge from each other. In week 3, for example, total expenditure on the purchase of consumption goods and machines rises to 120, while output remains at 100. Thus, using definitions appropriate to measuring the magnitudes of the flows around the circuit, expenditure exceeds output. The national income statistician, in contrast, measures the flow at the output point and measures $E \equiv Y = 100$ in week 3. There is no contradiction because the statistician is measuring the expenditure that *would be needed* to purchase the output of 100 produced in week 3, while in the theoretical model it is the actual expenditure made during week 3 that is referred to.

Table 35.3 The behaviour of the circular flow of income in the Frugal economy with lags between Y^d and Y and between output and expenditure

Col. 1	Col. 2	Col. 3	Col. 4	Col. 5	Col. 6	Col. 7
Week	Disposable income, Y^d (=the value of last week's national income)	Saving, S ($=0.2Y^d$)	Consumption, ($=0.8Y^d$)	Investment, I (=an exogenous constant)	Inventory changes, ΔIv (=last week's Y minus this week's C and I)	National in-come, Y (=value of this week's production, i.e., $C+I+\Delta Iv$)
1	100	20	80	20	0	100
2	100	20	80	20	0	100
3	100	20	80	40	−20	100
4	100	20	80	40	0	120
5	120	24	96	40	−16	120
6	120	24	96	40	0	136
.	.	.	.	.	.	.
.	.	.	.	.	.	.
.	.	.	.	.	.	.
n	200	40	160	40	0	200

but the path of adjustment towards equilibrium is not.

AN ALGEBRAIC TREATMENT

The model of the Frugal economy is easily handled using only simple algebra. The text version runs as follows (see the assumptions on page 484).

$$Y_t = C_t + I_t \qquad (1)$$

$$Y^d_{t+1} = Y_t \qquad (2)$$

$$Y^d_{t+1} \equiv C_{t+1} + S_{t+1}, \qquad (3)$$

where t is time measured in weeks.

Equation (1) states that output adjusts to consumption and investment expenditure without lag. Equation (2) states that household disposable income lags behind output by one week. Equation (3) states that disposable income must be allocated between consumption and saving. Substitution of (3) into (2) yields

$$C_{t+1} + S_{t+1} = Y_t$$

and substitution of this expression into (1) gives

$$C_{t+1} + S_{t+1} = C_t + I_t.$$

Rearranging and writing I for I_t, since I is assumed constant gives

$$C_{t+1} - C_t = I - S_{t+1},$$

or

$$C_t - C_{t-1} = I - S_t.$$

In other words, if consumption is rising, $I > S$; if consumption is falling, $I < S$; and if consumption is constant, $I = S$. Since $C_t = aY^d_t$ (where $0 < a < 1$), and since $Y^d_t = Y_{t-1}$ the same remarks apply substituting Y^d and Y for C.

36

Some predictions of the simple theory of national income

In the last two chapters we have developed the basic model of the circular flow of income, and have determined the conditions for the equilibrium of this flow. In the present chapter we use comparative static analysis to derive some important predictions of the theory. It was noted in the previous chapter that the equilibrium conditions for national income can be stated using either the aggregate expenditure function and the 45° line, or the withdrawals and injections functions. We shall use these approaches interchangeably.

We are interested in predicting what will happen to the level of national income if there is a change in the behaviour of households, firms or the central authorities. We shall consider first the directions of the changes in national income and then raise the question of the magnitudes of the changes.

THE DIRECTIONS OF THE CHANGES IN NATIONAL INCOME

A shift in the injections function

Consider the effect on equilibrium national income of a change in any of the three injections: investment, government expenditure and exports. Fortunately, the same analysis applies to all three changes. In Figure 36.1 an increase in investment, exports or government expenditure is shown by an upward shift in the injections schedule from J_1 to J_2. At the original level of income, Y_1, injections exceed withdrawals so that income must rise. As income rises, the quantity of withdrawals, which is a function of income, also rises, as shown by the upward slope of the withdrawals schedule W. The rise in income continues until withdrawals are again equal to the (now higher level of) injections. This is at income Y_2 in the figure.

It is important to remember that we are dealing with continuous flows measured as so much per period of time. At the original equilibrium level, withdrawals and injections were both steady at E_1 per year, injections then rose autonomously to E_2 per year and, as a result, income rose until withdrawals had risen to the rate E_2 per year as well.

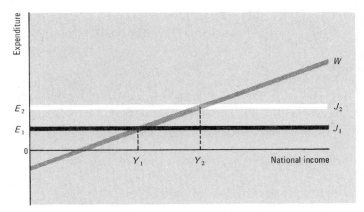

Fig. 36.1 The effect on the equilibrium level of national income of a change in the level of injections

We can analyse a fall in investment, exports, or government spending by assuming that income starts at Y_2, that injections then fall from the level indicated by J_2 (E_2 per year) to that indicated by J_1 (E_1 per year).

We have now derived two sets of predictions from our theory:

> **(1) A rise in autonomous investment expenditure, exports or government expenditure, raises the level of national income.**
>
> **(2) A fall in autonomous investment expenditure, exports or government expenditure, lowers the level of national income.**

A shift in the withdrawals function

A downward shift in the savings, import or tax functions will shift the withdrawals function so that, at each level of income, the flow of withdrawals will be lower than it was previously. Such a shift is shown in Figure 36.2. The original level of income is Y_1, with the annual flows of withdrawals and injections are both equal to E_1. The withdrawals schedule shifts downwards from W_1 to W_2 so that at the original level of

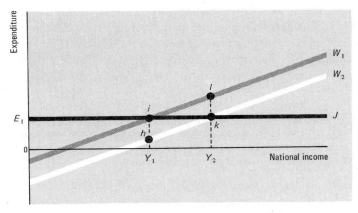

Fig. 36.2 The effect on the equilibrium level of national income of a change in the withdrawals function

income the new annual flow of withdrawals $(Y_1 h)$ is hi less than the annual flow of injections. The fact that less is being withdrawn from the circular flow of income than is being injected into it, causes income to rise until withdrawals are once again equal to injections. This occurs once income has risen to Y_2.

An upward shift in the withdrawals schedule is caused by a rise in the savings, imports or tax schedules. This is shown in Figure 36.2 by starting from the schedule W_2 with income Y_2, and letting the withdrawals schedule rise to W_1, so that at the original level of income, withdrawals exceed injections (by kl per year). Income must fall as a result. As income falls, the volume of actual withdrawals falls as well. This continues until income has fallen to Y_1 and withdrawals are once again equal to injections at the rate E_1 per year.

We have now derived two further important sets of predictions:

(3) A fall in the taxation, savings or imports schedules raises the level of national income.

(4) A rise in the taxation, savings or imports schedules lowers the level of national income.

THE PARADOX OF THRIFT: The above predictions have one interesting and counter-intuitive application. It is normally assumed, by analogy with an individual household, that national thrift is a good thing and prodigality is a bad thing, the former leading to increased wealth and prosperity, and the latter to eventual bankruptcy.

Household saving: What happens if, *ceteris paribus*, all households try to increase the amount they save at each level of income? This increase in thriftiness shifts the withdrawals function upwards as shown in Figure 36.2 by the shift from W_2 to W_1. Indeed, as long as income remains at its original equilibrium level Y_2 the volume of savings is increased by kl. But now income will begin to fall, and it will continue to do so until total withdrawals have been reduced to their original level so that they are again equal to injections.

Now consider an increase in the desire to spend money on purchasing goods and services at each level of income. This means that less will be saved at each level of income so that the withdrawals schedule will be shifted downwards in Figure 36.2, say from W_1 to W_2. But this will mean that income is no longer in equilibrium. Income will rise until withdrawals are once again equal to the unchanged level of injections. In this case the downward shift in the schedule from W_1 to W_2 raises national income from Y_1 to Y_2. We have now derived the predictions of the so-called paradox of thrift.

(5) Other things being equal, the more frugal and thrifty are households, the lower will be the level of national income and total employment. The more prodigal and spendthrift are households, the higher will be the level of national income and employment.

The prediction is not actually a paradox. It is in fact a straightforward, but very important corollary of prediction **4** that in turn follows logically from the theory of the determination of national income. It is called a paradox because it seems paradoxial to those people who expect the advice on how a single household should act if it wishes to raise its wealth and its future income ('save, save and save some more') to be directly applicable to the economy as a whole.

Government taxing and spending: The paradox of thrift applies to governments as well as to households. If governments decide to save more, they must raise taxes or cut expenditure. The first alternative shifts the withdrawals schedule upwards and the second shifts the injections schedule downwards. Either policy causes national income to fall until withdrawals are once again equal to injections. If governments decide to save less (i.e., to become more spendthrift) they lower taxes and/or raise spending. This shifts the withdrawals schedule downwards and/or the injections schedule upwards. Either policy raises national income.

The paradox of thrift leads to the prediction that substantial unemployment is correctly combated by encouraging governments, firms and households to spend as much as possible, and not by encouraging them to save as much as possible. In times of unemployment and depression, frugality and parsimony will only make things worse. This prediction goes directly against our ingrained ideas that we should tighten our belts when times are tough. The idea that it is possible to spend one's way out of a depression touches a very sensitive point in the consciences of people raised in the belief that success is based on hard work and frugality and not on prodigality, and, as a result, the idea very often arouses great emotional hostility.

The paradox of thrift was not generally understood during the Great Depression of the 1930s (indeed it is doubtful if it is well understood today outside the body of professional economists) and we find, at that time, many mistaken policies such as the one suggested in the following passage from King George V's message to the House of Commons on 8 September 1931. The message was delivered on the occasion of the formation of a new national government after the collapse of the Labour administration.[1]

The present condition of the National finances, in the opinion of His Majesty's Ministers, calls for the imposition of additional taxation, and for the effecting of economies in public expenditure.

At the time the unemployment rate stood at 21 per cent of the labour force!

In the US, President Roosevelt, who achieved the reputation of grappling vigorously with the problems of the decade while others shilly-shallied, showed no more appreciation of the real nature of the basic situation than did the British leaders. In his very first inaugural address in 1933 he stated:

Our greatest primary task is to put people to work. . . . [This task] can be helped by insistence that the Federal, State and local governments act forthwith on the demand that their cost be drastically reduced. . . . There must be a strict supervision of all banking and credits and investments.

At the time the American unemployment rate was 23 per cent.

The soul-destroying effects of month after month and year after year looking in vain for work, any work, is hard to imagine for most people below the age of fifty who have neither had the experience themselves nor seen others undergoing it. Yet in the

1 Quoted in David Thomson, *England in the Twentieth Century* (Pelican, 1965), p. 136.

1930s literally millions of respectable citizens were put through this experience. Feelings of frustration, impotence and rage follow from being powerless in a system that just does not provide jobs for those who desperately want to work. Such feelings are not soothed when those lucky enough not to have had their jobs destroyed, and it is largely a matter of luck in a major depression, read lessons on the virtues of hard work, frugality and patience to those who can find no work no matter how hard they try.

You should not read on until you are absolutely sure you know what national income theory predicts to be the outcome of the policies recommended in the 1930s. The suffering and misery of that unhappy decade would have been greatly reduced if those in authority had known even as much economics as is contained in this chapter.

Conditions necessary for the paradox to operate : The striking prediction of the paradox of thrift depends critically on two of the basic assumptions on which the elementary theory of national income is based.
(1) There is a significant amount of unemployment of all resources, so that the level of output depends upon total spending, and anything that reduces spending reduces output and employment.
(2) Injections are assumed to be completely independent of withdrawals; in particular, the volume of investment is independent of the volume of saving. There is no reason, according to the theory, why the amount that firms wish to spend on investment at any level of income should bear any particular relation to the amount that households wish to save.

If the economy is at full employment, then the first assumption will not be correct. In such circumstances a decrease in household saving and an increase in consumption expenditure will not cause an increase in real output and employment since full employment already obtains. In such circumstances the effect of an increase in spending will probably be to cause an inflation. An increase in saving, however, with its accompanying decrease in spending will tend to reduce output and employment.

If the second assumption is not correct the paradox of thrift may not apply. If, for example, the withdrawals and injections functions are linked together because changes in household saving cause changes in investment there would be offsetting shifts in *both* the withdrawals and injections functions whenever the desire to save changed. An increase in the desire to save, for example, would shift upwards the withdrawals function but, by permitting more investment, it would also shift up the injections function and no downward pressure on national income might emerge.

The predictions of the paradox of thrift, and most of the other predictions of the elementary theory of national income depend critically, therefore, on the assumption that savings and investment decisions are taken to a great extent by different groups in society and that there is no mechanism whereby a change in the amount that is desired to be saved at a particular level of income would cause a change in the amount that was desired to be invested at the same level of income.

An alternative method of deriving the basic predictions

We saw in Chapter 35 that the equilibrium level of national income can be determined using either the withdrawals-injections approach or the income-expenditure
approach. You should not be surprised to learn, therefore, that the predictions
derived so far in this Chapter using the withdrawals-injections approach can also be
derived using the income-expenditure approach. Without repeating the whole
analysis in detail the essence of the argument can be illustrated by referring to
Figure 36.5 on page 514.

If the aggregate expenditure schedule is E in the top half of part (i) of the figure,
equilibrium national income is at Y_e, where E cuts the 45° line, indicating total
demand is just sufficient to purchase total output.

Investment expenditure, exports and government expenditure are all components
of aggregate expenditure. An increase in any of these components shifts the aggregate
expenditure function upwards; a decrease shifts it downwards. The effects can be
seen by shifting the expenditure function upwards from that shown in the first panel
to that shown in the second, thus increasing equilibrium income, and by shifting it
downwards from that shown in the second panel to that shown in the first, thus
lowering Y_e. This gives predictions (1) and (2) on page 503.

The aggregate expenditure function is also affected by changes in saving, imports
and taxes. A rise in saving or taxes lowers consumption expenditure and so lowers
aggregate expenditure. A rise in imports has the same effect on aggregate expenditure. (Recall that aggregate expenditure is equal to $C + I + G + (X - M)$.) A fall in
saving, taxes or imports raises aggregate expenditure. Thus a rise in any withdrawal
lowers aggregate expenditure from, say, that shown in the second panel of Figure
36.5 to that shown in the first panel, thus lowering Y_e, while a fall in any withdrawal
raises aggregate expenditure and raises Y_e. This gives predictions (3) and (4) on
page 504.

Compensating shifts in injections and withdrawals

The level of national income is in equilibrium when the total volume of withdrawals
per period of time equals the total volume of injections per period of time. As far as
equilibrium in national income is concerned, there is no need for any particular
withdrawal to equal any particular injection. We may write the condition for
income to be in equilibrium as

$$W = J \tag{1}$$

which was derived on page 493. But specifying withdrawals and injections in more
detail we can rewrite this as:

$$S + T + M = I + G + X. \tag{2}$$

This condition clearly says nothing about pairs of these terms. Specifically it does not
imply that $S = I$, or that $T = G$ or that $M = X$. This means that it is possible to have
compensating changes in various withdrawals and injections. Indeed, if any injection
changes, an equal and opposite change in another injection will leave total injections,

and hence total income, unchanged. Also, an equal change in some withdrawal, but in the same direction as the change in injections, will leave income unchanged.

Consider, for example, an equilibrium situation in which both the budget and international payments are in balance. This means $T = G$, $M = X$, and, since in equilibrium total withdrawals must equal total injections, it follows that $S = I$. Now, assume a decrease in investment by private firms, causing a downward shift in the injections function, say from J_2 to J_1 in Figure 36.1 (page 503). Our theory predicts that, *ceteris paribus*, this will lead to a fall in income and employment. But other things do not have to remain equal. There are two possible offsetting policies.

First, the central authorities can increase governmental spending by exactly the same amount as I has decreased. This restores the injections function to J_2 and leaves equilibrium national income at Y_2. In this new situation $G > T$ and $I < S$, with the fall in investment exactly compensated for by the new government budget deficit. In effect the government will be spending the amount that private firms no longer wish to spend.

The second possible policy is to cut taxes sufficiently to compensate for the fall in investment expenditure. In this case, there is a fall in withdrawals to compensate for the initial fall in injections. In Figure 36.1 it will be necessary to shift the W schedule downwards so that it intersects the new injection schedule J_1 at income Y_2. Again, income will not change but the government will end up with a budget deficit, this time because its tax revenues fall, whereas its expenditures remain unchanged. These compensating changes in injections and withdrawals are extremely important, and they form the basis of the government's fiscal policy intended to stabilize national income in the face of changes in the flow of private spending. We shall consider them in detail in Chapter 40. In the meantime, you should not read on until you have used the equilibrium condition

$$S + M + T = I + X + G \tag{2}$$

to show what the central authorities should do to G or to T in order to offset a rise or a fall in each of the four other withdrawals and injections. In each case, will the government's offsetting action lead to a budget deficit $(G > T)$ or to a budget surplus $(G < T)$?

THE MAGNITUDE OF THE CHANGES IN NATIONAL INCOME: THE MULTIPLIER

In the previous sections we have considered the shifts in the withdrawals and injections schedules on national income, concentrating on the *direction* of movement. We now want to look more precisely at the *magnitude* of the changes. If the annual flow of government expenditures changes by some amount, ΔG, *by how much* will income change? For example, in a severe depression the government might be urged to spend money in order to create employment. The analysis of the previous section suggests that a given increase in government expenditure will in fact increase income and employment, but we will wish to know *by how much*. Likewise, if there is a fall in private investment of some stated amount, we will wish to know by how much this would reduce national income and employment.

The definition of the multiplier

A central prediction of national income theory is that an increase in expenditure, whatever its source, will cause an increase in national income that is greater than the initial increase in expenditure. The MULTIPLIER is defined as the ratio of the change in national income to the change in expenditure that brings it about. The change in expenditure might come, for example, from an increase in private investment, from new government spending or additional household consumption expenditure accompanied by a decline in household saving.

The importance of the multiplier in national income theory makes it worthwhile using more than one approach to develop it and to show why its value exceeds unity.

An intuitive statement

What would you expect to happen to national income if there were a rise in government expenditure on road building of £1 million per year with no corresponding rise in taxes? Would national income rise by only £1 million? Anyone who has mastered the theory developed so far should not have too much trouble in replying 'no, national income will rise by more than £1 million'. This could be argued in either of two ways, remembering that we are dealing with flows and that a rise of £1 million means that much extra spent on roads each year. First, we could say that a permanent increase in government expenditure of £1 million per annum would cause further induced increases in consumption expenditure. The impact of the initial rise will be felt by the construction industry and by all those industries that supply it. Income and the employment of factors will rise by £1 million as a result. But these newly employed factors will spend much of their income buying food, clothing, shelter, holidays, cars, refrigerators and a host of other products. This is the induced rise in consumption expenditure, and when output expands to meet this extra demand, employment will rise in all of the affected industries. When the owners of factors that are newly employed spend their incomes, output and employment will rise further; more income will then be created and more expenditure induced. Indeed, at this stage we might begin to wonder if the increase in income will ever come to an end. This question is more easily answered if we look at the second way in which the process of income expansion might be described.

The initial rise in government expenditure is a rise in injections. This will increase income, but, as income rises, the volume of withdrawals (tax receipts, imports and savings) will rise. Income will continue to rise until additional withdrawals of £1 million have been generated. At this point, withdrawals will have risen by as much as the original (permanent) rise in injections and, assuming we began from a position of equilibrium, we would be back in equilibrium. For example, if 40 per cent of all income is withdrawn through taxes, savings and imports, then the rise in income will come to a halt when income has risen £2·5 million. At this higher level of income an extra £1 million in withdrawals will have been generated, and since the rise in withdrawals equals the initial rise in injections income will no longer be rising.

Thus the increase in income does come to a halt and, in this example, the multiplier is 2·5, since a rise in government expenditure of £1 million causes a rise in national income of £2·5 million.

This is as far as intuitive arguments can take us; and we must look for a more formal demonstration of these propositions.

An algebraic statement

The multiplier is the ratio of the change in income to the permanent change in the flow of expenditure that brought it about. It is symbolized by K and defined by

$$K = \frac{\Delta Y}{\Delta J}. \tag{1}$$

If, for example, $K = 2$ then any permanent rise in the annual flow of injection expenditure will lead to a twofold increase in the annual flow of national income.

We must now see on what the value of K depends. In equilibrium we have

$$W = J, \tag{2}$$

which says that the volume of withdrawals must equal the volume of injections. If J increases by ΔJ, then W must increase by the same amount in order to re-establish equality (2). The symbol Δ means 'a change in', so ΔJ refers to a change in injections. Thus we have

$$\Delta W = \Delta J. \tag{3}$$

This says nothing more than that, if withdrawals equal injections originally, and if injections rise by ΔJ (say by £1 million per year), then withdrawals must rise by the same amount in order to restore the equality of W and J.

Withdrawals depend on income. In the simple theory, withdrawals are a constant fraction, w, of income. We write this $W = wY$. From this it follows that the change in withdrawals must be w *times* the change in income

$$\Delta W = w\Delta Y. \tag{4}$$

If, for example, 20 per cent of extra income is not passed on as new spending, then $w = 0.2$, and the change in withdrawals is 20 per cent of the change in income.

If we substitute (4) into (3), we obtain

$$w\Delta Y = \Delta J,$$

dividing both sides by w,

$$\Delta Y = \frac{1}{w}\Delta J. \tag{5}$$

But we have already written

$$\Delta Y = K\Delta J. \tag{1}$$

Substituting (1) into (5) and cancelling ΔJ yields

$$K = \frac{1}{w}. \tag{6}$$

This demonstrates that the value of the multiplier, K, is equal to the reciprocal of the fraction of income withdrawn from the circular flow. If w is, for example $\frac{1}{5}$, then the multiplier is 5; if it is $\frac{1}{3}$, then the multiplier is 3, and so on.

A graphical statement

The withdrawals and injections functions are depicted in Figure 36.3. When the equilibrium level of income is Y_1, withdrawals and injections are in equilibrium at the amount E_1 ($= Y_1 e$). When the injections function shifts to J_2, income rises to Y_2 where withdrawals and injections are in equilibrium at the amount of E_2 ($= Y_2 g$). In Figure 36.3 the change in income is indicated by the distance bracketed as ΔY,

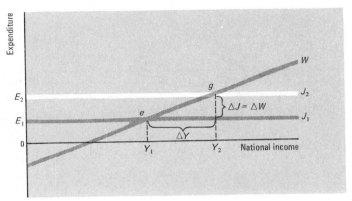

Fig. 36.3 Determining the size of the multiplier

while the changes in withdrawals and injections are indicated by the distances bracketed as $\Delta J = \Delta W$. The slope of the withdrawals line, W, is given by $\Delta W / \Delta Y$. This slope shows the fraction of any new income that is withdrawn from the circular flow, i.e., w. The multiplier, K, is the ratio $\Delta Y / \Delta J$, the change in income divided by the change in injections. This is the reciprocal of $\Delta J / \Delta Y$ and since $\Delta J = \Delta W$ it is also the reciprocal of the slope of the withdrawals function. Thus the value of the multiplier, K, is equal to $1/w$.

To see the influence of the slope of the withdrawals schedule on the multiplier graphically, look at Figure 36.4. The withdrawals line marked W' has a steep slope; the one marked W'' has a very flat slope. In each case, suppose the injection schedule is J_1, and the equilibrium income level is Y_1. Now, *in each case*, suppose injections increase to J_2. The new income level is Y_2' in the case of W' and Y_2'' in the case of W''. The multiplier is much greater for the flatter curve than for the steeper one. The common sense of this is that the flatter the curve, the greater the increase in income necessary to bring forth an addition to withdrawals equal to the increase in injections.

Conclusions

We have now derived two further important predictions:

> **(6) The larger the proportion of income passed on and the smaller the proportion withdrawn (the smaller is w), the greater the change in income for any given shift in aggregate expenditure.**
>
> **(7) The value of the multiplier is equal to the reciprocal of the fraction of income not passed on (w).**

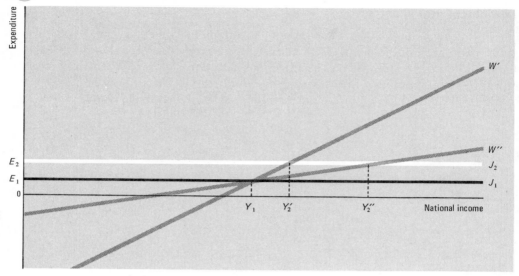

Fig. 36.4 The relation between the value of the multiplier and the slope of the withdrawals schedule

HOW LARGE IS THE MULTIPLIER? Following Keynes' lead, many early national income theories used a model in which saving was the only leakage and investment the only withdrawal. In such a model, the multiplier is the reciprocal of the fraction of extra income saved. In the United States this fraction is around 0·2, and for a long time it was widely believed that the value of the multiplier was around 5. Subsequently, both the experience of post-war fluctuations, and some careful empirical calculations led to the conclusion that the multiplier was substantially smaller than this, and most probably in the range of 1·5 to 2·5. The many leakages of taxes and imports of both raw materials and finished goods cause the fraction of income withdrawn, w, to be much larger than the fraction of income saved.

THE INFLATIONARY AND DEFLATIONARY GAPS

We begin by restating the assumptions of the basic model.

(1) There is a level of national income at which all resources would be fully employed. If aggregate demand is just sufficient to produce that level of income there will be neither unemployment nor inflation.

(2) If aggregate demand is only sufficient to produce an equilibrium level of national income less than the full-employment level, there will be unemployed resources and a constant price level. Fluctuations in aggregate demand in this range will then cause fluctuation in output and employment but will leave prices unchanged.

(3) If aggregate demand is sufficient to produce an equilibrium level of income in excess of the full employment level, there will be full employment of resources and a rising price level. Fluctuations in aggregate demand in this range will leave the level of real output unchanged.

These three situations are illustrated in Figure 36.5. The top half of each panel uses the aggregate expenditure function, E, and the 45° line while the bottom half shows the same situation using the withdrawals and injections functions. In each case the equilibrium level of national income is designated Y_e and the level of income that would produce full employment of resources at the present price level is designated Y_f.

The first panel shows what is called a DEFLATIONARY GAP: the equilibrium level of national income Y_e is less than the full employment level of Y_f. *The deflationary gap may be defined as the amount by which aggregate expenditure would fall short of aggregate income if full employment were achieved.* This is shown by the amount D in the top diagram. The lower diagram illustrates the identical situation. The equilibrium level of income, where withdrawals equal injections, is Y_e and this is less than the full-employment level of Y_f. If Y_f were to be temporarily achieved, injections would fall short of withdrawals by the amount D, and this is the magnitude of the deflationary gap. Of course, in such a situation, income will fall towards its equilibrium level of Y_e.

The third panel differs from the first only by the fact that the injections function, and thus the expenditure function as well, has been raised. This panel illustrates an INFLATIONARY GAP. The equilibrium level of income is Y_e, but there are only sufficient resources available to produce national income of Y_f at the existing price level. *The inflationary gap is the amount by which aggregate expenditure would exceed aggregate output at the full-employment level of national income.* This amount is shown by the bracketed distance F. At full employment there is a situation of excess demand: households, firms and the government are trying to spend an amount greater than the value of total national output. Thus, unless something is done, an inflation will ensue. The figure in the lower half of the panel shows the identical situation. Equilibrium national income exceeds full-employment income, and if income were at Y_f, then injections would exceed withdrawals by the amount F.

Finally, the middle panel shows the intermediate situation where there is neither an inflationary nor a deflationary gap. Here the aggregate expenditure function is high enough to produce full employment, but not high enough to create an inflationary gap. At the full-employment level of income aggregate expenditure is just equal to the value of total output. We shall see in Chapter 51 that such a situation of full employment without inflation may *never* be fully achievable. In the meantime, however, we can proceed a long way in our study of government policy by making this sharp distinction between situations of inflation and situations of unemployment and by assuming that the goal of any government's macro-stabilization policy is to come as close as possible to the situation illustrated in the middle panel of Figure 36.5.

The notion of an inflationary gap received little emphasis in the original formulations of the Keynesian model. Because of the problems of the time, attention was directed mainly to the deflationary gap. But times change and so do economic problems. Theories, if they are effective, have new and perhaps unsuspected applications. As the Second World War succeeded the Great Depression, the world's economies were faced with rising aggregate demand and full employment. A decade of concern with unemployment gave way to concern over rising prices as inflationary pressures became chronic. The concept of the inflationary gap provided a tool for

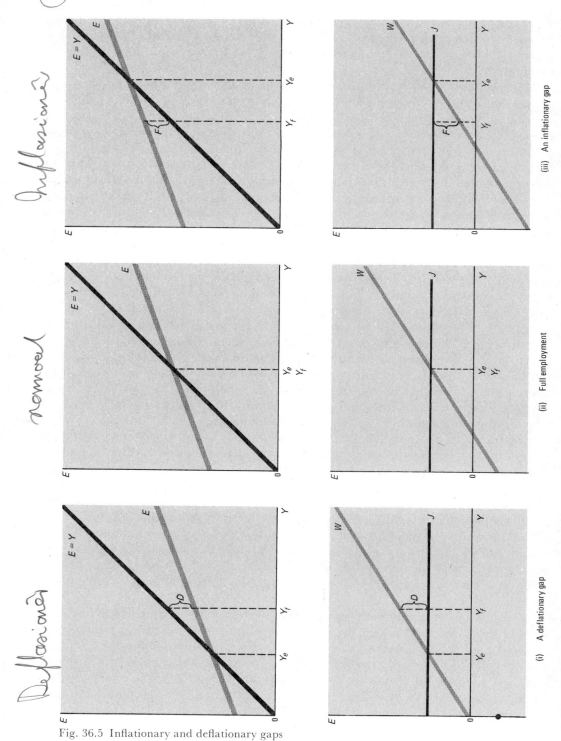

Fig. 36.5 Inflationary and deflationary gaps

(i) A deflationary gap   (ii) Full employment   (iii) An inflationary gap

discussing and measuring the size of these pressures. Thus, the theory of the circular flow can help us to analyse the behaviour of the economy under a wide variety of conditions from the Great Depression of the 1930s, through the highly inflationary period of the 1940s, through the period of alternating mild inflationary and mild deflationary pressures of the 1950s and 1960s, and then on to the more rapid and sustained inflations of the 1970s.

A WORD OF WARNING: The sharp distinction between deflationary and inflationary gaps illustrated in Figure 36.5, is a severe simplification of reality. This simplification can aid us greatly in our study of some problems, and it can be justified on the grounds of wanting to study one thing at a time. Later on we will drop this simplification and study the very important case in which the economy is in between the two situations. In this region there is enough unemployment so that output can be increased, but some resources are so close to being fully employed that there is also some inflationary pressure in the economy. In such circumstances a rise in aggregate expenditure will lead both to a rise in real output and to a rise in prices. Such situations are dealt with in Chapter 51. In the meantime we can make good use of the simplified model in which national income is *either* less than full-employment income and prices are constant, *or* at its full-employment level and prices are constant if there is no inflationary gap, or rising if there is one.

37

The consumption function

The consumption function is one of the most important relations in macro-economics. Consumption is the largest single component of aggregate expenditure and if we are to predict the effects on income and employment of variations in private investment and in government spending, we must know how consumption varies in response to changes in income. Thus it is important to take a closer look at the consumption function.

THE KEYNESIAN THEORY OF THE CONSUMPTION FUNCTION

A basic element in the macro-economic models that grew out of Keynes' *General Theory* was a function that related household expenditure on consumption to national income. In the present section we look at this relation in some detail. In subsequent sections we discuss the empirical tests that revealed certain inadequacies in the simple Keynesian theory and then we go on to some of the more modern theories that have amended the Keynesian hypotheses in the light of the current evidence.

Propensities to consume

We now need to depart from the simple assumption used so far, that a constant fraction of income is always saved. (See page 482.) As a first step we define the twin Keynesian concepts of the marginal and the average propensities to consume.

AVERAGE PROPENSITY TO CONSUME (APC): APC is the proportion of income spent on consumption. To calculate this value, take total consumption expenditure, C, and divide it by Y, total income, $APC = C/Y$. We can obtain an average propensity to consume by using either total income, Y, or disposable income, Y_d, as the divisor. Which of these concepts is being used is almost always obvious from the context.

THE MARGINAL PROPENSITY TO CONSUME (MPC): MPC measures the relation between changes in consumption, ΔC, and changes in income, ΔY. By dividing ΔY

516

into ΔC, we measure how much of the last pound's worth of income is consumed; in symbols, $MPC = \Delta C / \Delta Y$. The MPC may also be stated as a propensity to consume out of either national income or disposable income.

Table 37.1 shows the details of the calculations for the APC and the MPC for two levels of disposable income and consumption. The marginal and average propensities are shown graphically in Figure 37.1. The two points correspond to the data in Table 37.1. At the point labelled a in the figure, consumption is 270 and income is 300. The APC is 270/300, which, geometrically, is the slope of a line joining point a to the origin. Similarly, the APC at point b (320/400) is the slope of the line joining b to the origin. The MPC, when income goes from 300 to 400, is $\Delta C / \Delta Y_d = 50/100$. It is easily seen from the figure that this is the slope of the line joining a and b.

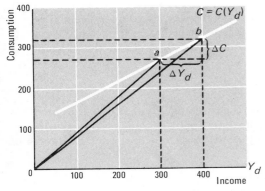

Fig. 37.1 Graphical representation of the average and marginal propensities to consume

Table 37.1 Calculation of the average and marginal propensities to consume

Disposable income, Y_d	Consumption expenditure, C	Average propensity to consume (APC)	Marginal propensity to consume (MPC)
£300	£270	$\dfrac{270}{300} = 0{\cdot}90$	$\dfrac{50}{100} = 0{\cdot}5$
£400	£320	$\dfrac{320}{400} = 0{\cdot}80$	

In the previous Chapter we used the simple assumption that households always consumed a constant proportion of their incomes. In the example it was 80 per cent. This made the APC and the MPC both equal to 0·8.[1] We shall shortly have to introduce a more complex hypothesis to deal with short-term data.

1 Since consumption is always 80 per cent of income then total C divided by total Y must always be $C/Y = 0{\cdot}8$ and the change in consumption induced by a change in income must always be 80 per cent of the change in income.

Consumption and disposable income

Empirical studies suggest that many factors influence consumption. We begin by concentrating on income, assuming that other factors capable of influencing consumption remain constant. Changes in these other factors can then be allowed for by studying how they shift the function relating consumption to income.

Two basic hypotheses provide the core of the Keynesian theory of the consumption function. The first hypothesis is that there is a break-even level of disposable income for which consumption just equals disposable income, and that below the break-even level consumption expenditure will exceed disposable income, while above it consumption expenditure will fall short of disposable income. The second hypothesis was described by Keynes in the *General Theory* in the following words:

The fundamental psychological law, upon which we are entitled to depend with great confidence both *a priori* from our knowledge of human nature and from the detailed facts of experience, is that men are disposed, as a rule and on the average, to increase their consumption as their income increases, but not by as much as the increase in their income.

These two hypotheses can be stated concisely using the concept of average and marginal propensities to consume.

> **(1) There is a break-even level of income at which $APC = 1$. Below this level, APC is greater than unity and above it APC is less than unity.**
> **(2) The MPC is greater than zero but less than unity for all levels of income.**

Figure 37.2 shows two consumption functions that are consistent with these two hypotheses. While the hypotheses greatly restrict the nature of the relationship between consumption and income, it is well to notice that they only predict an MPC between 0 and 1, and are thus consistent with an MPC very near to unity (say, 0·99) or very near to zero (say, 0·01). They are also consistent with an MPC that

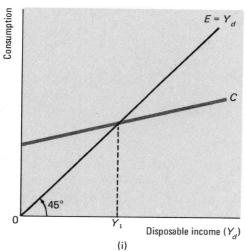
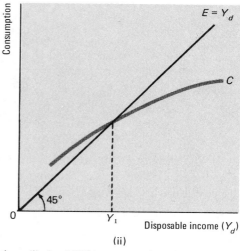

Fig. 37.2 Two possible shapes for a consumption function: (i) the MPC is constant but the APC declines as income rises, (ii) both the APC and the MPC decline as income rises

remains constant as income rises, as shown in the first part of Figure 37.2, or with an *MPC* that declines as income rises, as shown in the second part of the same Figure.

Aggregation problems

An aggregate consumption function shows how the society's total consumption expenditure varies as its total income varies. Conceptually, the society's function is aggregated from all the functions of the individual households that compose it. But aggregation is not without problems. On the one hand, it was noted earlier (see pp. 9–11) that aggregate behaviour would be less capricious than individual behaviour if the odd things done by individual households cancel each other out. On the other hand, a stable aggregate consumption function may not exist even if all households have perfectly stable individual consumption functions. If, for example, households have different *MPC*s then the same total income will lead to different levels of consumption depending on how that income is distributed among households.

What are the conditions under which stable individual consumption functions will give rise to a stable aggregate consumption function? Two conditions, either of which is sufficient, are worth noticing here. The first condition is that all households should have the same *MPC*. In this case, changes in the distribution of income between households will have no effect on the level of total consumption expenditure. If, for example, all households have an *MPC* of 0·8, then redistributing a given national income among households will leave the aggregate level of consumption unchanged, because any household that loses a pound's worth of income cuts its expenditure by 80p while any household that gains an extra pound of income raises expenditure by 80p. Thus, in this situation, the level of total consumption depends only on the level of total income; it is independent of the distribution of this income among households.

If *MPC*s differ among households, a sufficient condition for a stable aggregate consumption function is that the distribution of income among households does not change. Thus, if national income rises or falls by 10 per cent, each household's income will rise or fall by 10 per cent, and total consumption expenditure will be uniquely related to total income. But this is a very strong assumption, and a weaker one is sufficient. It is not necessary to assume that the distribution of income is constant, as long as changes in it are related to changes in national income. If for each level of income there is only one associated distribution of income, then there will be only one associated level of total household consumption.

Thus, the use of a stable aggregate consumption function that relates total disposable income to total consumption expenditures, in a world in which *MPC*s are known to vary among households, requires that most changes that do occur in the distribution of income are themselves associated with changes in the level of income. There is considerable empirical evidence that the distribution of income changes only slowly, so that it is fairly stable from one year to the next, and also that much of the short-period changes that do occur are systematically related to short-period fluctuations in income. This appears to be the explanation of why it has been possible to estimate reasonably stable aggregate consumption functions.

From disposable income to national income

An individual household's consumption is related to its disposable income, and aggregate consumption is thus related to aggregate disposable income. In developing theories of national income, we normally relate aggregate expenditure, of which consumption is an important part, to national income. The transition from a relation between *consumption and disposable income* to one between *consumption and national income*, is easily accomplished if disposable income and national income are themselves related to each other. To illustrate, assume (i) that associated with each level of national income there is a particular level of disposable income, and (ii) that associated with each level of disposable income there is a particular level of consumption. It follows that each level of national income also has a particular level of consumption associated with it.

If, for example, disposable income is always 60 per cent of national income, then, whatever the relation between consumption, C, and disposable income, Y_d, we can always substitute $0.6Y$ for Y_d. Thus, if, to carry the example further, consumption were always 90 per cent of Y_d then C would always be 54 per cent (60 per cent of 90 per cent) of Y. If, to take another example, consumption were $£1{,}000 + \sqrt{Y_d}$ then consumption would be $£1{,}000 + \sqrt{0.6Y}$. From now on we will assume that we can write consumption as a function either of disposable income or of national income.[1]

An important consequence of the relationships just described is that the function relating consumption to national income can shift for two quite distinct reasons:
(1) The relation between consumption and disposable income that describes household spending behaviour may change; and
(2) The relation between national income and disposable income may change.

In the first case, there is a change in the propensity to consume out of disposable income which reflects a change in the basic expenditure decisions of households. In the second case, the relation between national income and disposable income changes while there is no change in the propensity to consume out of disposable income.

Consider an example of each of these changes. Start by recalling that in the previous numerical example the propensity to consume out of disposable income was 0.9 while disposable income was linked to national income by the relation $Y_d = 0.6Y$. This implied a relation between consumption and national income of $C = 0.54Y$. As an example of the first kind of change assume that the propensity to consume out of disposable income falls to $C = 0.75Y_d$ with an unchanged relation between Y_d and Y. This implies a relation between consumption and national income of $C = 0.45Y$. As an example of the second type of change assume that the propensity to consume out of disposable income remains at 0.9, but that disposable income falls from $0.6Y$ to $0.5Y$. This shifts the relation between consumption and national income to $C = 0.45Y$. The changes in both of these examples cause the same shift in the observed relation between consumption and national income (since 0.75 *times* $0.6 = 0.9$ *times* $0.5 = 0.45$).

---

[1] If consumption is any linear function of Y_d and Y_d is a constant fraction of Y we can write $C = a + bY_d$ and $Y_d = eY$. Substitution then gives C as a linear fraction of Y: $C = a + beY$.

Although government policy-makers may find it difficult, if not impossible, to change the propensity to consume out of disposable income (change 1 above), they can very easily change the relation between national income and disposable income (change 2 above) by altering tax rates. An increase in income tax rates will, for example, reduce the amount of disposable income that reaches the hands of households out of any given level of national income. A reduction in tax rates will have the opposite effect. Thus, according to the theory that consumption depends upon disposable income, government policy-makers can shift the aggregate consumption function (and hence shift the aggregate expenditure function) downwards or upwards by increasing or decreasing tax rates, even though they may be unable to affect the propensity to consume out of disposable income.

An increase in tax rates lowers the aggregate expenditure function by lowering the ratio of disposable income to national income. A decrease in tax rates has the opposite effect.

Shifts in the function relating consumption and disposable income

We have seen that government tax policies can shift the aggregate expenditure function by shifting the relation between disposable income and national income. But the aggregate expenditure function can also shift if households change their behaviour in such a way that the relation between consumption and disposable income changes. What factors would cause such a shift?

CHANGES IN INCOME DISTRIBUTION: If households have different *MPC*s, aggregate consumption depends not only on aggregate income but also on the distribution of this income among households. In this case, which was discussed in detail on page 519, a change in the *distribution* of income will cause a change in the aggregate level of consumption expenditure associated with any given *level* of national income.

Since the distribution of income tends to change fairly slowly, such changes do not destroy stable consumption-income relationships. Nevertheless, such changes can occur, and when they do occur they cause the consumption function to shift.

THE TERMS OF CREDIT: Many durable consumer goods are purchased on credit, which may range from a few months to pay for a radio, to two or three years to pay for a car. If credit becomes more difficult or more costly to obtain, many households may postpone their planned, credit-financed purchases. If the typical initial payment required for goods purchased on hire purchase was increased from 10 per cent to 20 per cent, households that had just saved up 10 per cent of the purchase price of the goods they wished to consume would now find this sum inadequate, and would have to postpone their planned purchases until they saved 20 per cent of the purchase price. There would be a temporary reduction in current consumption expenditures until these extra savings had been accumulated.

Monetary authorities can, by controlling the cost and availability of credit, attempt to shift the consumption function in an effort to affect aggregate demand.

EXISTING STOCKS OF DURABLE GOODS: It is now recognized that any period in which durables are difficult or impossible to purchase and in which monetary savings are accumulated is likely to be followed by a sudden outburst of expenditures on durables. Such a flurry of spending will also follow a period of unemployment, in which many families may have refrained from buying durables.

The emphasis here is on durable goods (e.g., cars and refrigerators) because the purchases of non-durable consumer goods (e.g., food and clothing) and of services (e.g., car repairs) cannot be long postponed. While expenditures on non-durables are relatively steady, the purchase of durables is volatile and can lead to sharp shifts in the consumption function.

PRICE EXPECTATIONS: If households expect an inflation to occur, they may be willing to purchase now the durable goods they were otherwise planning to purchase one or two years hence. In such circumstances, purchases made now yield a saving over purchases made in the future. By the same argument, an expected deflation may lead to postponing purchases of durables, in order to purchase them later at a lower price.

Significance of shifts in the consumption function

About 65 per cent of total expenditure in the UK is made up of purchases by UK households of goods and services produced in the UK. If households were to reduce their consumption expenditure by 3 per cent, this would amount to a reduction of 1·95 per cent in total expenditure. Combined with a multiplier of 2, the national income would decline by 3·9 per cent. Perhaps this does not sound like very much. But if employment were to change in proportion to income, this could change a situation of 1·5 per cent unemployment, which is the low achieved in postwar UK experience, to one of 5·4 per cent, which is a very high level judged by the experience of the last 30 years. Clearly, even very small percentage fluctuations can have important effects on the economy. Such shifts have occurred in the past, and to understand aggregate economic behaviour, they must be studied.

From time to time, tastes change and when they do, consumption levels and patterns may change. Households may decide that they do not like this year's motor car models and may save the money they were going to spend on a new motor car this year. If they do, the consumption function will shift downward this year. Incomes earned in Coventry (and many other places) will fall, and unemployment will rise. The unemployed car workers will cut their spending on other products, and a multiplier process will be set up that will magnify the original cut in spending on new cars into a general fall in income and employment.

Some of the factors that cause shifts in the consumption function can be influenced by government policy; others cannot. Whether or not such shifts are controllable and whether or not they can be predicted in advance, their effects, once they do occur, can be offset by public policies. For example, if consumption declines for whatever unforeseen reason, the government can reduce taxes and thus, via an increase in disposable income, attempt to induce additional consumption.

In the last two decades economists' knowledge about the determinants, and thus the control of consumption, has increased greatly and with it the ability to control the economy.

EMPIRICAL TESTING OF THE RELATION BETWEEN CONSUMPTION AND INCOME

We have seen that according to Keynesian theory the larger is the marginal propensity to consume, the larger is the multiplier. This makes an accurate estimation of the marginal propensity to consume important in predicting the effects on the economy of shifts in investment and government expenditure. This important use of the concepts of the marginal propensity to consume and of the multiplier led to a rush to measure their magnitudes soon after the *General Theory* was published in 1936. Early estimates of the *MPC* were based on data gathered from studies of budgets provided by individual households. Studies based on household surveys that had been taken during 1935–6 suggested that the *MPC* out of disposable income was as low as 0·7.

Application of these estimates to a real problem was not long in coming. During the Second World War government expenditure rose to unprecedented heights. True to the predictions of the theory the large rise in *G* removed the deflationary gap that had persisted all through the 1930s. Full employment occurred and an inflationary gap soon opened up.

But what would happen when the war ended and government spending was reduced to its peace-time level? The enormous war-time destruction of capital made predictions for Britain and Europe seem problematical but what of America where no such destruction had occurred? Using the prewar estimates of the *MPC*, many economists predicted that a major American depression would ensue.

The argument ran as follows. When the war came to an end, government war-related expenditures would cease, and thus a major injection would be removed. Although tax cuts would increase disposable income of households, savings were predicted to increase sharply because the *MPC* was well below unity. Thus, there would be a net increase in withdrawals from the circular flow. Unless something changed, this would lead to a decrease in equilibrium income. This gap seemed too large to be filled by the expected amount of private investment expenditure, exports or new government expenditures. Economists forecast, therefore, that aggregate demand would fall short of full-employment output and a major depression with heavy unemployment would develop.

Contrary to this pessimistic view, the immediate postwar period in America turned out to be one of almost uninterrupted prosperity with aggregate demand tending to exceed rather than to fall short of full-employment output. Here was a major setback for those economists who believed that their theories could be usefully applied to predict real-world events.

Postwar studies have shown that there were two major reasons for the failure of the postwar predictions. First, the *MPC* estimated from household-expenditure data turned out to be significantly lower than the *MPC* actually observed when household disposable income rose during the postwar years. Thus, the gap between full-employment income and household consumption expenditure that had to be filled by investment or other injections turned out to be significantly smaller than had been estimated. Second, American households had accumulated large stocks of savings during the war and when peacetime production brought such durables as refrigerators and cars to the market once again, households went on a buying spree to replace prewar equipment. This spree helped create full employment from 1946–8.

Study of the reasons for the failure of this postwar prediction led to a great deal of more sophisticated work on the consumption function and, as a result, we now have much more satisfactory theories and measurements of this function. This modern research into consumption behaviour has distinguished three different types of data all of which throw light on the determinants of consumption: cross-section data, short-period time-series data and long-period time-series data.

Cross-section versus time-series data

Cross-section data on consumption and income show at any instant of time how expenditures of different households are related to their incomes. Such data are made available by budget studies of samples of households. *Time-series* data show how consumption and income have changed over time; such data can be for a single household (i.e., a household's income and consumption expenditure can be observed each year for, say, fifteen years) or for any aggregation of households. Much of the time-series data used is aggregate data showing total consumption and total disposable income for the entire economy.

In effect, these two types of data hold different things constant. Cross-sectional data measure the variation in consumption patterns of different income classes. Because these data are collected at a moment in time, they hold constant the price level, the average standard of living of the population and the distribution of income in the economy, each of which may well affect consumption habits over time. In contrast, a time series showing the consumption behaviour of a fixed panel of households holds constant the identity of the individuals studied, and thus holds constant things such as their ethnic or racial backgrounds, but lets vary all those things that may change over time.

Students of sociology have long known that behaviour of a single household when its income alone rises is not an accurate indication of how it will behave if the whole neighbourhood's income increases. Because it has been shown to be quite a different matter to move up *in* the income distribution (which is what a cross-sectional study examines) than to move up *with* the income distribution (which is one of the things a time-series study can show), it is necessary to distinguish consumption functions based on these two types of data.

CROSS-SECTION STUDIES: Cross-section studies show that household consumption expenditure tends to vary in a consistent fashion as income varies: average household expenditure on consumption rises steadily as income rises, but not as fast as income rises. These findings confirm both of the hypotheses stated on page 518.

Of course, there is a considerable amount of variation among the consumption expenditures of different households that *cannot* be associated with differences in income among households. Of three households with an income of £3,000, the first might have total consumption expenditures of £3,100, the second of £2,800, and the third of £2,300. This suggests that, in making their consumption expenditures, households are not influenced solely by the size of their incomes. The size of the family and the age of its members, their education, occupation and place of residence can all affect the level of consumption.

The data from these studies are valuable in suggesting that income has a significant effect on consumption expenditure. But cross-section data show how consumption expenditure varies as we move up and down the income scale at any moment of time. They do not show how consumption varies as the incomes of all households change over time. For direct evidence of this we must go to time-series data.

TIME-SERIES STUDIES, THE SHORT-TERM CONSUMPTION FUNCTION: Empirical studies of year-to-year changes in income and consumption (i.e., when each observation consists of income and consumption expenditure over the same year) for a period of ten years or so have found a close relation between the two. In general, years with higher-than-average levels of income tend to be years with higher-than-average levels of consumption, and vice versa. The observed *MPC* is less than unity, but larger than that typically found in cross-section studies. The *APC* declines as income rises. Moreover, such studies have tended to find the *MPC* to be constant rather than diminishing as income increases. These observations again support the two hypotheses introduced on page 518 and are consistent with the straight-line consumption function drawn in Figure 37.2(i).

TIME-SERIES STUDIES, THE LONG-TERM CONSUMPTION FUNCTION: Some studies have used ten-year averages of consumption expenditure and income. Thus, the time-series data used consisted of decade-by-decade averages of consumption and income. When plotted on a graph, one point would relate average consumption in, say, 1900–1909 to average income in that period; another point would relate average consumption in 1910–1919 to average income in that period; and so on. The characteristic of such data is that they average out the effects of cyclical fluctuations in national income and allow a concentration on the long-run reaction of consumption to long-run trend changes in national income.

> **When long-run time-series data are studied they show a marginal and average propensity to consume of less than unity but they also show that in the long run the average propensity to consume does not decline as income rises. This implies that the marginal and average propensities must be the same.**[1]

These data support the second hypothesis on page 518 but contradict the first. The consumption function that describes these results is often called a *long-run* consumption function. Figure 37.3 illustrates a consumption function that is consistent with these findings.

Many economists, including Keynes, have thought it reasonable to assume that as households get richer they would tend to save a larger and larger proportion of their income. This would lead to a long-run consumption function of the sort illustrated in Figure 37.2(i). The long-run data lend little support to this assumption and suggest instead the constant long-run *APC* shown in 37.3.

1 If the consumption function has no constant term then we have $C = bY$ and $APC = C/Y = b$ and $MPC = \Delta C/\Delta Y = b$.

SUMMARY: Figure 37.3 summarizes the shapes of the consumption functions that appear from cross-section data, time series of annual observations and time series of decade by decade averages.

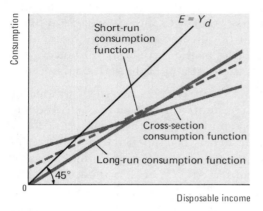

Fig. 37.3 A summary of existing statistical evidence on the shapes of consumption functions

THE PERMANENT-INCOME HYPOTHESIS AND THE LIFE-CYCLE HYPOTHESIS

In everything we have done so far, current consumption expenditure has been related to some concept of current income, either current disposable income or current national income. The concept of a consumption function that related current consumption to current income was basic to national income theory when it was first formulated. Recent attempts to reconcile the apparently conflicting empirical data on short- and long-term consumption behaviour have produced a series of theories that relate consumption to some longer-term concept of income than the income that the household is currently earning.

The two most influential theories of this type are the PERMANENT-INCOME HYPOTHESIS (PIH), developed by Professor Friedman, and the LIFE-CYCLE HYPOTHESIS (LCH), developed by Professors Modigliani and Ando and the late Professor Brumberg. Although there are many significant differences between these theories, their similarities are more important than their differences, and they may be looked at together when studying their major characteristics. In doing this it is important to ask: What variables do these theories seek to explain? What assumptions do the theories make? What are the major implications of these assumptions? How do the theories reconcile the apparently conflicting empirical evidence? And what implications do they have for the overall behaviour of the economy?

Variables

Three important variables need to be considered: consumption, saving and income. Consider consumption first. Keynesian-type theories seek to explain the amounts that households spend on purchasing goods and services for consumption. This concept is called *consumption expenditure*. Permanent-income theories seek to explain the actual flows of consumption of the services that are provided by the commodities that households buy. This concept is called *actual consumption*.[1]

With services and nondurable goods, expenditure and actual consumption occur more or less at the same time, and the distinction between these two concepts is not important. The consumption of a haircut occurs, for example, at the same time as it is purchased, while an orange or a package of corn flakes are consumed very soon after they are purchased. Thus, if we knew purchases of such goods and services at some time, say last year, we would also know last year's consumption of these goods and services. But this is not the case with durable consumer goods. A screwdriver is purchased at one point in time, but it yields up its services over a long time, possibly as long as the purchaser's lifetime. The same is true of a house and a watch and, over a shorter period of time, of a car and a dress. For such products, if we know purchases last year, we do *not* necessarily know last year's consumption of the services that the products yielded.

Thus, one important characteristic of durable goods is that *expenditure* to purchase them is not necessarily synchronized with consumption of the stream of services that the goods provide. If in 1970 Mr Smith buys a car for £1,200, runs it for six years and then discards it as worn out, his expenditure on automobiles is £1,200 in 1970 and zero for the next five years. His consumption of the services of automobiles, however, is spread out at an average annual rate of £200 for six years. If everyone followed Mr Smith's example by buying a new car in 1970 and then replacing it in 1976, the automobile industry would undergo wild booms in 1970 and 1976 with five intervening years of slump, even though the actual consumption of automobile services would be spread more or less evenly over time. Of course, this example is extreme, but it illustrates the possibility of quite different time paths of *consumption expenditure* (which is the subject of Keynesian theories of the consumption function) and of *actual consumption* (which is the subject of permanent-income type theories).

Next consider saving. The change in emphasis from consumption expenditure to actual consumption implies a change in the definition of saving. Saving is no longer disposable income minus consumption expenditure, it is now disposable income minus the value of actual consumption. When Mr Smith spent £1,200 on his car in 1970 but used only £200 worth of its services in that year he was actually consuming £200 and saving £1,000. The purchase of a consumer durable is thus counted as saving, and only the value of its services actually consumed is counted as consumption.

So much for consumption and saving. The third important variable in this type of theory is the income variable. Instead of using current income, the theories use a concept of long-term income. The precise definition varies from one theory to another, but basically it is related to the household's expected income stream over a

---

1 Because Keynes's followers did not always distinguish carefully between the concepts of consumption expenditure and actual consumption, the word 'consumption' is often used in both contexts. We follow this normal practice, but where there is any possible ambiguity in the term we will refer to 'consumption expenditure' and to 'actual consumption'.

fairly long planning period. In the *LCH* it is the income that the household expects to earn over its lifetime. (In the *PIH* theory the household has an infinite time horizon, and the relevant permanent income concept is the amount the household could consume forever without increasing or decreasing its present stock of wealth.)

Every household is assumed to have a view of its expected lifetime earnings. This is not as unreasonable as it might seem. Students training to be doctors, for example, have a very different view of expected lifetime income than those training to become school teachers. Both of these expected income streams, for a doctor and for a school teacher, will be different from that expected by an assembly line worker or an agricultural labourer.

One such possible lifetime income stream is illustrated in Figure 37.4. The Figure shows a hypothetical expected income from work for a household that expects to live 40 years from 1975. The current income rises to a peak, then falls slowly for a while and finally ceases on retirement. The permanent income reflects the amount the household could consume at a steady rate over its lifetime by borrowing against future earnings early on (as do many students and most newly-married couples), then repaying past debts, then saving for retirement when income is at its peak and finally spending past savings during retirement.

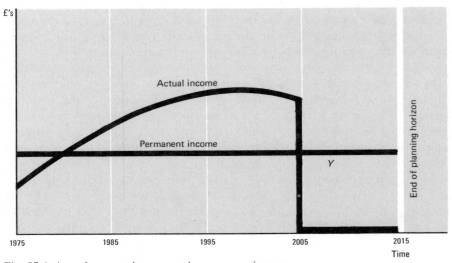

Fig. 37.4 Actual current income and permanent income

The household's expected lifetime income stream is converted into a single figure for ANNUAL PERMANENT INCOME. In the life-cycle hypothesis this permanent income is the maximum amount the household could spend on consumption each year without accumulating debts *that are passed on to future generations*. If a household was to consume a constant amount equal to its permanent income each year, it would add to its debts in years when current income was less than permanent income and reduce its debt or increase its assets in years when its current income exceeded its permanent income; however, over its whole lifetime it would just break even, leaving neither accumulated assets nor debts to its heirs. If the interest rate were zero, permanent income would be merely the sum of all expected incomes divided by the number of expected years of life. With a positive interest rate, permanent income will diverge somewhat from this amount because of the costs of borrowing and the extra income that can be earned by investing savings.

Assumptions

The basic assumption of this type of theory, whether *PIH* or *LCH*, is that the household's actual consumption is related to its permanent rather than to its current income. Two households that have the same permanent income (and are similar in other relevant characteristics) will have the same consumption patterns even though their current incomes behave very differently.

Implications

A major implication of these theories is that changes in a household's current income will affect its actual consumption only so far as it affects its permanent income. Consider, for example, two income changes that could occur to a household with a permanent income of £3,000 per year and an expected lifetime of 30 more years. In the first case, suppose the household receives an unexpected extra income of £600 for this year only. The increase in the household's permanent income is thus very small. If the rate of interest were zero, the household could consume an extra £20 per year for the rest of its expected lifespan, while with a positive rate of interest the extra annual consumption would be more since money not spent this year could be invested and earn interest. In the second case, the household gets a totally unforseen increase of £600 per year for the rest of its life. In this case the household's permanent income has risen by £600 since it can actually consume £600 more every year without accumulating any new debts. Although in both cases the household's *current* income rises by £600, the effect on permanent income is very different in the two cases.

The difference between the two events is illustrated in Figure 37.5. In 1985 current income rises unexpectedly by £600 for both households. The old expected income stream is shown by the heavy black line, while the additional income that was unanticipated before 1985 is shown by the shading on top of the black line. Since the change is only for one year for household (i) its permanent income rises only a small amount from Y to Y'. Since the change is expected to persist for household (ii) its permanent income rises considerably — from Y to Y'' in the Figure.

Keynesian theory assumes that consumption expenditure is related to current income and therefore predicts the same change in the 1985 consumption expenditure of both households. Permanent-income theories relate actual consumption to permanent income and, therefore, predict very different changes in actual consumption in each of these cases. In the first case there would be only a small increase in consumption, while in the second case there would be a large increase.

> **In permanent-income theories, any change in current income that is thought to be temporary will have only a small effect on permanent income, and hence on consumption.**

A RECONCILIATION OF THE DATA: The PIH and the LCH are able to reconcile the observation that the *MPC* appears equal to the *APC* in long-period data while it is less than the *APC* in short-period and cross-section data. They do this by relating changes in observed income to changes in permanent income. Consider long-term data first.

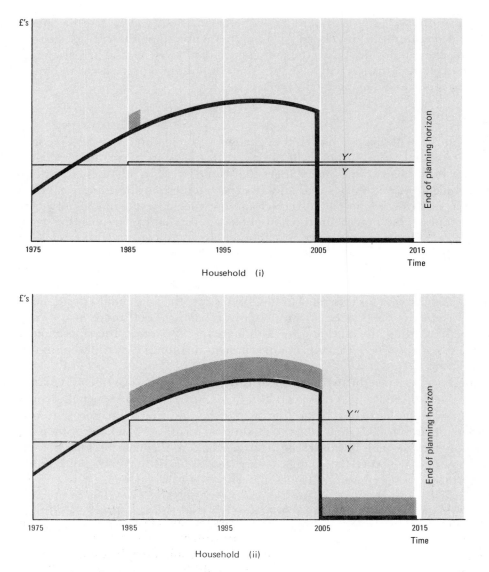

Fig. 37.5 The effect on permanent income of short and long-lived changes in current income

Long-term time-series data using decade-by-decade averages remove the effects of temporary fluctuations in income. The observed changes in income mainly represent permanent increases in real income because of economic growth. Long-term time-series studies will thus tend to measure accurately the propensity to consume out of permanent income.

Now consider short-term data. A study covering 10 or 15 years at the most and using annual observations of C and Y will use an income series dominated by transitory changes caused by cyclical fluctuations: when a household loses employment because of a business recession it does not expect to remain unemployed forever, neither does it expect the extra income that it earns from heavy overtime work during a period of peak demand to persist. It may thus be assumed that households expect these cyclical changes in current income to be temporary so that they will have little effect on permanent income. Since consumption is assumed to depend on permanent income, it follows that the observed relation between consumption and cyclical changes in income will tend to be smaller than the relation shown by the long-term time-series data. What this shows, however, is the lack of relation between changes in consumption and temporary changes in income, not any lack of relation between changes in consumption and changes in permanent income.[1]

IMPLICATIONS FOR THE BEHAVIOUR OF THE ECONOMY: According to the permanent-income and the life-cycle hypotheses, actual consumption is not much affected by temporary changes in income. Does this mean that aggregate expenditure $(C + I + G + X - M)$ is not much affected? Not necessarily. Consider what happens if households get a temporary increase in their incomes. If actual consumption is not greatly affected by this, then households must save most of the temporary increase in their incomes. But from the point of view of these theories, households save when they buy a durable good just as much as when they buy a financial asset such as a stock or a bond. In both cases actual current consumption is not changed.

Thus, spending a temporary increase in income on bonds or on new cars is consistent with both the PIH and the LCH. But it makes a great deal of difference to the short-run behaviour of the economy which one is done. If households buy stocks and bonds, aggregate expenditure on currently produced final goods does not rise when income rises temporarily; if households buy cars or any other durable consumer good, aggregate expenditure on currently produced final goods does rise when income rises temporarily. Thus the PIH and the LCH leave unsettled the question that is critical for the measurement of the size of the multiplier: What is the reaction of *household expenditures* on currently produced goods and services, particularly durables, to short-term, temporary changes in income?

In summary, while permanent-income type theories do succeed in reconciling the various empirical observations of consumption functions referred to above, they leave ambiguous the multiplier effects of temporary increases in income. They are consistent with a constancy in both the MPC and the APC when permanent income

---

1 A similar analysis shows that cross-section studies are strongly influenced by the behaviour of households whose income has temporarily departed from its permanent level. Thus, cross-section studies should be expected to yield a much lower MPC than that yielded by long-term time-series studies.

changes – see the long-run function in Figure 37.3. They also suggest a high degree of stability of the actual flow of consumption in the face of temporary fluctuations in current income, which is consistent with an *APC* out of current income that varies inversely with current income, falling as income rises and rising as income falls – see the short-run function in Figure 37.3.

38

Investment

In 1929, the total investment expenditure of firms and households in the US economy was \$16·2 billion. This was almost double the amount of expenditure needed to replace the capital goods that were used up that year in the process of production. The US economy in 1929 was thus adding rapidly to its stock of new capital equipment. Three years later, in 1932, total investment expenditure was less than \$1 billion. This was less than 15 per cent of the amount needed to keep the stock of capital intact. The US economy in 1932 was thus rapidly reducing its stock of capital equipment. Similar behaviour was observed in the British economy and indeed in most other economies of the Western world. Such enormous fluctuations in investment have not been recorded since that time, but there have been large variations in some countries.

Why do these variations in investment expenditure occur, and what are their effects?

WHAT DETERMINES INVESTMENT?

In previous Chapters we have assumed investment to be constant, in order to examine the equilibrium of the circular flow. We may now relax this assumption and ask what causes investment to vary.

The rate of interest

Much investment is made with borrowed money. As we saw in Chapter 29, it pays a firm to borrow money to finance its investment projects as long as the return on the investment (including an allowance for the riskiness of the project) exceeds the rate of interest. Thus, if a particular investment in a new machine costing £10,000 is expected to yield £1,500 over all costs except interest, then it would clearly pay the firm to borrow £10,000 at, say, 8 per cent (£800 a year) in order to undertake the investment.

Because the lower the rate of interest, the lower the cost of borrowing money for investment purposes, it might seem natural to expect that the lower the rate of interest, the higher the amount of new investment in plant and equipment. And yet this possible relation between investment and the rate of interest has been, and still is, the subject of much controversy and we must take a closer look at it.

THE CAPITAL STOCK AND THE RATE OF INTEREST: Capital equipment is valued because of the stream of income it produces. The amount it is profitable to spend for a capital asset depends on the stream of income that the asset produces each year and the rate of interest. An asset, say a machine that will produce a stream of net income of £100 a year forever, is worth £1,000 at 10 per cent interest because £1,000 invested at 10 per cent per annum will yield £100 interest per year forever. But the same asset is worth £2,000 if the interest rate is 5 per cent per year because it takes £2,000 invested at 5 per cent per annum to yield £100 interest per year. Two important corollaries of this proposition are:

> **(1) If the rate of interest falls, the value of an asset producing a given income stream rises.**
> **(2) If the price of an asset producing a fixed income is forced up, this is equivalent to a decrease in the rate of interest earned by the asset.**

The first of these propositions is of immediate importance in this chapter. The second is a key proposition in understanding the inverse relation between the price of government bonds and the rate of interest on those bonds, which will figure prominently in discussions of economic policy later in this book.

The total stock of capital refers to the total amount of capital in the economy.[1] The desired capital stock refers to the total quantity that everyone in the economy would be willing to hold (and maintain). There is good reason to expect that the desired capital stock will be related to the interest rate. Suppose it costs £1,000 to make a machine that produces £200 worth of net income per year forever. If interest rates are below 20 per cent, it will pay to make such machines because the value of the machine exceeds £1,000. But if the interest rate rises above 20 per cent, the value of the machine will be less than its cost, and it will not pay anyone to make the machine.

This leads to an important prediction:

> **The size of the desired stock of capital rises as the rate of interest falls.**

The relationship between the rate of interest and the desired capital stock is summarized in a schedule first introduced in Chapter 29 and called the MARGINAL EFFICIENCY OF CAPITAL (MEC) SCHEDULE. The MEC relates the stock of capital to the yield an additional unit of capital equipment will produce. This yield, or rate of return on the capital equipment, is related to the rate of interest because it will pay to borrow, say, £100 at 8 per cent, only if the capital purchased with the £100 yields at least £8 to the investor. Thus the *MEC* schedule relates the *desired* quantity

---

1 If we are to talk about the stock of capital we need some common measure which allows us to add up all the diverse physical things that constitute capital. If we use the price of capital to do this and then use the quantity of capital to determine the price of capital we may be involved in a serious circularity. The problems involved are complex and the subject of a prolonged debate among economists. For purposes of this elementary treatment it is convenient to assume that the concept of the stock of capital can be given a clear meaning; but see also the earlier discussions on pages 416–17.

of capital to the interest rate. It is shown as downward sloping in Figure 38.1 because a fall in the rate of interest is hypothesized to increase the capital stock. For example a reduction in the rate of interest from r_1 to r_2 increases the desired capital stock from K_1 to K_2.

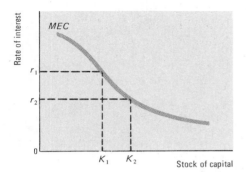

Fig. 38.1 The marginal efficiency of capital schedule

INTEREST RATES AND THE AMOUNT OF INVESTMENT: Investment concerns actual expenditures for investment goods, not the desired level of the stock of capital. A desired increase in capital goods generates investment when the capital goods are actually produced. Suppose for example, that in response to a fall in interest rates there is an increase of £10 billion in the desired capital stock. If the capital stock is raised by £10 billion within a year, net investment will rise for a year and then fall to zero. In this case a fall in the interest rate will lead only to a one-year increase in the amount of investment.

But the timing of investment may be more complicated than this; it may depend on how fast the stock of capital can be built up to its new desired level. The actual volume of investment in plant and equipment that takes place each year is limited by the capacities of the capital-goods and the construction industries. Assume that all the firms in the economy decide that they want a total of 3,000 newly built and equipped factories in operation next year, but that factories can only be built and equipped at the rate of 1,000 a year. And assume also that this situation has just been generated by a fall in the rate of interest. It will take three years before the desired addition to the capital stock is achieved. If, at the end of the first year, a rise in the rate of interest decreases the desired overall addition to the capital stock to 2,000 factories instead of 3,000 factories, this new change will have no effect on investment in 'year two' because the capital-goods industries would still have to work to capacity to create the desired addition. Alternatively, if a fall in interest rates at the end of the first year raised the desired overall addition from 3,000 to 5,000 this, too, would not affect the rate of *current* investment which is already at its maximum. The upper limit to annual investment in plant and equipment is set by the capacity of the capital-goods producing industries. Whenever the desired increase in the capital stock exceeds a year's output of capital, there will be a backlog of orders that cannot be fulfilled 'this year'. Thus substantial variations in the interest rate can have a major effect on the length of the backlog rather than on the level of investment in a particular year. If so, these variations will affect the *duration* of an investment boom generated by changes in desired capital stock, but will have only a minor (or even a zero) effect on the *amount of investment* occurring in one year during that boom.

Of course this picture is over-simplified, since it is always possible to increase the output of capital to some extent by working overtime, or extra shifts. This extra output will usually be produced at higher cost and so will not be profitable unless there is a particularly urgent demand for new capital. The urgency will depend on the expected profitability of new investment which will tend to be higher the lower is the rate of interest. Thus despite the complications mentioned above, most economists believe that *total* private domestic investment (plant and equipment, residential construction and inventory changes combined) does bear an inverse relation to the rate of interest.

The schedule that summarizes the relation between investment and the rate of interest is often called the MARGINAL-EFFICIENCY-OF-INVESTMENT (MEI) SCHEDULE; when graphed it plots the amount of investment per year on the horizontal axis and the rate of interest on the vertical axis. In contrast to the *MEC* schedule, it relates the *flow* of investment per year (rather than the *stock* of capital) to the rate of interest.

Figure 38.2 shows two different *MEI* schedules. The *MEI* curve is relatively flat,

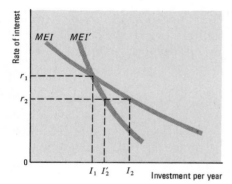

Fig. 38.2 The marginal efficiency of investment schedule

and a decrease in interest rates from r_1 to r_2 leads to a substantial increase in investment, from I_1 to I_2. The steeper curve $M\acute{E}I'$ produces a much smaller increase in investment per year, from I_1 to I_2', in response to the same change in interest rates. A perfectly vertical *MEI* schedule would represent the hypothesis that investment was wholly unresponsive to interest rate changes.

Investment and the level of income

Empirical evidence tends to indicate that investment is more responsive to the level of demand for goods than to interest rates. There are two reasons for this. First, the higher the level of demand and income, the more *willing* businessmen will be to invest in new risky enterprises because they will have favourable expectations about the future. Second, the higher the level of demand, output and hence profits, the more businessmen will *be able* to invest. This aspect of the theory assumes that most businessmen are not able to borrow all the funds they require at the current rate of interest; in fact, so goes the hypothesis, they are severely limited in the quantity of funds they can borrow at any moment of time. As a result of this, the businessman is forced to look within his own firm for funds to finance many of his desired investment projects. These funds can be obtained by not distributing profits to shareholders. If we now add to this the hypothesis that profits will tend to be high when demand and income are high, we obtain the hypothesis that investment will depend on the level of income.[1]

The theory that investment is influenced by the level of profits has been subjected to considerable testing and has occasioned much controversy. The discussion is complex, and much of it concerns the statistical difficulties in determining whether the observations conform to the predictions of the theory. One of the main problems is that the observation that investment is high when profits are high is not necessarily evidence supporting the theory. The causal connection could be in the opposite direction: high investment causes a high level of income (by the multiplier process), which causes high profits. The argument has not yet been settled, and all that we can say at this stage is that there is no really compelling evidence to date that would lead one to reject the theory.

Investment and the rate of change of income: the accelerator theory

According to the 'accelerator' theory, it is not so much the *level* of national income that affects investment, but rather the *rate of change* of national income. The theory is based on the following line of argument: when income is increasing, it will be necessary to invest in order to increase capacity to produce consumption goods; investment may also be high because business *expectations* based on the rising trend of sales are favourable. On the other hand, when income is falling, it may not be necessary even to replace capital equipment as it wears out; furthermore, expectations based on the falling trend of sales may be unfavourable. For both of these reasons investment expenditure need not be great. Thus according to the accelerator theory, investment is a function of changes in income.[2]

The basic idea of the accelerator theory is not a difficult one; it can be elaborated as follows: when income is constant, it will not be necessary to expand existing plant and equipment; investment will be limited to replacing existing machinery as it wears out. If, however, income starts to rise, it will be necessary to invest in new plant and equipment in order to expand the existing capacity to produce (once the expansion of demand is sufficient to employ all of the existing capacity). After this point, every additional rise in income will give rise to additional investment expenditure in order to increase productive capacity. Further, an increase of £1 in income may lead to an increase of more than £1 in investment expenditure; this is because a machine has a long life and may have a value considerably in excess of the value of its output over one year. A machine that has a value of £40,000 may produce an annual output of, say, £10,000. The entrepreneur who wishes to increase his output by using these machines must therefore spend £4 on investment for every £1 that he wishes to add to his annual output. (This is not necessarily a losing proposition, because he only

---

1 In symbols, $I = I(R)$, where R stands for profits; if we add the hypothesis that profits vary with income, $R = R(Y)$, we obtain $I = I(Y)$.
2 In symbols, $I = I(\Delta Y)$.

pays once for the machine, which goes on producing goods over all the years of its life.) In our example, once existing capacity is used to its fullest, every £1 increase in income would entail £4 of additional investment expenditure. In more general terms, new investment is said to be some multiple, α, of the change in income. The multiple α is called the accelerator coefficient.[1] This may be expressed in symbols as follows:

$$I_n = \alpha \Delta Y \qquad (1)$$

when I_n is new investment, ΔY is the change in income, and α is the accelerator coefficient, which depends on the ratio of the value of capital equipment to the annual value of its output.

In summary, there are two aspects of the accelerator theory: (1) that the level of new investment will be a multiple greater than one of the change in income (because the value of a machine is usually well in excess of the value of its annual production), and (2) that the level of new investment varies with the change in income (because *new* capital is needed to expand rather than to maintain output).

In Chapter 39, we shall find that even such a simple theory of investment as the accelerator raises the possibility of dynamic fluctuations in the circular flow of income.

Many attempts have been made to test the accelerator theory of investment. Tests have been made for single industries and for the economy as a whole. Most of the tests of the simple form given in equation (1) above have shown the theory to be a poor explanation of observed fluctuations in investment. On the basis of these tests, many economists have concluded that the actual evidence was unfavourable to the theory.

There is, however, a number of complications that make it unlikely that so simple a relation as equation (1) could accurately describe real data. The theory does not apply to investment that replaces existing equipment, nor does it apply to investment in new techniques (investments that reduce costs of production without necessarily increasing capacity). The theory applies only to some part of net investment – that part that increases the capacity to produce goods. The accelerator will not necessarily apply to increases in demand and output thought to be temporary. (The business-man will build new plant to meet new demand only if he expects the new demand to be maintained long enough for the investment to pay for itself.) The theory may not apply at all when there is excess capacity, because a rise in demand will not lead to a rise in investment when there already exists more capacity than is needed to satisfy the original demand *and* the extra demand. Finally, and most important, all the new capacity will not be established immediately after there is a rise in demand. It takes time to plan an increase in capacity, to let contracts, and to have plant built and machinery installed. Thus, the reaction of investment to a rise in demand will be

1 The basic assumption of the accelerator is that there is an optimal relation between the stock of capital (B) and the level of income, i.e., $B = \alpha Y$. Now assume we start from equilibrium so that at period t the actual stock of capital bears the desired relationship to income, i.e., $B_t = \alpha Y_t$. Now let income rise between period t and $t+1$. If the capital stock is adjusted to its new desired level over the same period, $B_{t+1} = \alpha Y_{t+1}$. Subtracting these two expressions from each other gives $B_{t+1} - B_t = \alpha(Y_{t+1} - Y_t)$. The change in the capital stock *is* new investment, $I \equiv B_{t+1} - B_t$, and $Y_{t+1} - Y_t$ is the change in income. If we denote $Y_{t+1} - Y_t$ as ΔY, this gives us the relation set out in equation (1).

spread out over time. When X (in this case, investment) is a function of Y (in this case, changes in income), but the reaction is spread out over a long period of time, the economist talks of X depending on Y with a *distributed time lag*. The existence of such time lags means that we would not observe a simple relation between investment and income changes of the sort assumed in equation (1). The actual relation would be more complex, and fairly subtle statistical techniques would be needed to observe it if it were present.

More subtle tests have found some evidence of an accelerator-type relation, but one complicated by the factors named above. The simple studies that have failed to find evidence of such a relation are, therefore, not conclusive. The existing evidence does point to a possible accelerator-type relation between new investment and changes in demand, but one complicated by the fact that the relation is subject to a distributed lag of quite long duration.

Investment and expectations

Investment takes time. A businessman who decides this year to expand capacity may not see the fruits of his investment for several years. The decision to invest now is thus to a great extent an act of faith concerning the future. If the businessman guesses wrongly, the penalties can be great. If he decides not to expand capacity and the market for his product expands, he can fall irrevocably behind his more farsighted competitors. If, on the other hand, he decides to expand capacity and his market does not expand, he can be saddled with unused plant and equipment, the fixed costs of which may ruin him. The businessman does his best to predict the extent of his market, but many things can influence it other than the tastes of households. A new government may adopt different taxing and spending policies that affect him profoundly; the apparent success, or failure, of a disarmament conference may cause some lines of production to look more profitable and others less profitable. The rise of a new method of transportation, a revolution in South America, or a relapse in the health of the American President can all influence him in important ways that are hard to predict. Occasionally, mob psychology can become the major determinant of investment decisions, and a feeling of pessimism about the future can snowball into a general cut in investment expenditure, or a feeling of optimism can snowball into an investment boom based on expectations that later turn out to be false.

There is no doubt that the state of business expectations affects investment expenditures, and that a general psychological reaction can cause major shifts in investment. We shall see, in Chapter 39, that such changes in expectations are capable of setting off major expansions or contractions in the level of business activity.

THE EFFECTS OF CHANGES IN INVESTMENT: NATIONAL INCOME AND THE RATE OF INTEREST

If, as in previous chapters, investment is assumed to be autonomous then changes in investment must cause changes in national income. This effect has already been studied and it is summarized in predictions 1 and 2 on page 503.[1]

1 In the long run, changes in investment affect the rate of economic growth. This relation is discussed in Chapter 48. In the present chapter we concentrate on the short run effects of change in investment.

If we allow for the possible dependence of investment on the rate of interest we can no longer take investment as an autonomous constant. We must then consider the possibility that investment may vary causing changes in national income. To see how this possibility arises we first consider how investment is financed.

The financing of investment

Generally, in speaking of the circular flow we speak of withdrawals and injections in pairs: imports and exports, government expenditure and government revenue, and saving and investment. This pairing is no accident and, in the case of saving and investment, it reflects the fact that the savings of firms and households are the major source of finance for investment. When households and firms save funds, the money must go somewhere; when firms spend on investment, the money must come from somewhere. Much of the money spent on current investment projects comes from the current savings of firms and households.

Money required for investment expenditure may be raised in several ways. One is for the firm to save the funds itself (by not distributing all its profits to its share-holders). A second way is by borrowing the savings of others, mainly households. This can be done either directly by selling bonds to households, or indirectly by borrowing the money that households deposit in financial institutions. A third way is by selling equities to households who then become part owners of the firms. If the expenditure on investment is equal to the money saved by households (and by all other units that save out of current income), then the funds spent on investment can be raised completely from funds currently saved with nothing left over.

If the volume of investment expenditure exceeds the volume of funds currently saved, where does the money come from? Basically there are two main sources: the money may come from funds accumulated in the past by firms or households, or it may be money *newly created* by the banking system. In Chapter 42, we shall study in detail how the banking system can create and destroy money within very wide limits. In the meantime, we must note that if banks can create money, they can lend this money to firms for investment expenditure without there being any corresponding saving of funds on the part of households and firms.

There is one more possibility: investment may fall short of savings. In this case all of the money saved cannot be passed back into the circular flow by way of investment expenditure. The excess of savings over investment will pile up in the form of idle funds owned by either households or firms and held by them or by financial institutions on their behalf.

Saving, investment and the rate of interest

How might the rate of interest respond to a situation in which the flow of current savings was not equal to the amount that firms wished to spend on current investment? There could be a shortage of investment funds and competition among would-be borrowers to obtain the available funds might bid up the rate of interest. It is also possible that when desired investment is substantially less than current savings, the rate of interest will fall because some savers will be unable to invest their money at all and so will be prepared to accept lower rates of interest rather than leave their money idle.

Now assume that national income is in equilibrium with savings equal to investment. In Chapter 36, we saw that an autonomous rise in investment would then raise income until new withdrawals sufficient to restore equilibrium had been created. The magnitude of the rise in income depends on the value of the multiplier.

If a rise in investment raises the rate of interest as we have just hypothesized, then this will help to restore equilibrium by choking off some of the extra investment expenditure.

This is shown in Figure 38.3. Suppose the aggregate expenditure function is the one labelled E_1. The equilibrium income is Y_1. Now investment increases by ΔI, thus shifting the aggregate demand function to E_2. If all of the adjustment were thrown onto income changes, income would have to rise to Y_2. But if interest rates rise, and investment falls, the aggregate demand function will shift downward to, say, E_3, and the new equilibrium will be reached at the lower level of income Y_3. If, when investment increases, the rate of interest rises quickly, and this greatly reduces investment, then income need not change much to generate the extra withdrawals to match the (small) increase in investment. On the other hand, if the rate changes only a little or very slowly, and if the change in interest does not affect investment much, then most of the burden of adjustment is placed on changes in income.

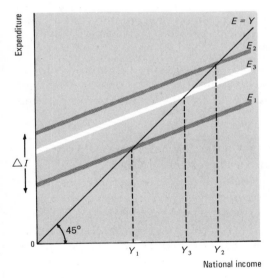

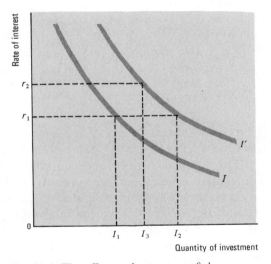

Fig. 38.3 The effect of shifts in investment on the aggregate expenditure function and on the equilibrium level of income

Fig. 38.4 The effect on investment of changes in the rate of interest

We can arrive at this result in another way. In Figure 38.4, the *MEI* schedule is assumed to be I, the current rate of interest is r_1 per cent per year, and the current quantity of investment is I_1 per year.

Now assume that the *MEI* schedule shifts to I'. If the rate of interest remains unchanged at r_1, investment rises by $I_2 - I_1$. This amount is the autonomous ΔI of Figure 38.3. If the interest rate remains unchanged, then the whole of the burden of adjustment is thrown onto national income, and income will rise by the multiplier process until new withdrawals equal to ΔI are generated. If, however, the interest rate rises to r_2, then investment falls to I_3. Investment is now only above its original level by $I_3 - I_1$, and the change in income necessary to restore equilibrium is correspondingly reduced. We now have derived the following predictions:

> **The change in income in response to an autonomous change in investment will be smaller, the greater is the change in interest rates in response to the change in investment, and the more sensitive is the quantity of investment expenditure to changes in the rate of interest.**

Two limiting cases of the relation between investment and the rate of interest

The view about the working of the economy prevailing (at least among English-speaking economists) prior to the publication of Keynes's *General Theory of Employment, Interest and Money* has come to be called 'classical'. Historians are quick to point out that there were many disagreements amongst economists of the time, and that to talk of '*the* Classical Theory' is rather to caricature a complex situation. Nonetheless, there was a more or less common view on many points and, for better or worse, the term the 'Classical Theory' or the 'Classical Model' has come to be used to express one consistent version of the views prevalent amongst economists at the time. The present book is not a treatise on the history of economics and we would not bother to describe this 'classical' theory of investment (and saving) were it not for the fact that some of its predictions have recently gained some substantial support from a group of economists who believe that the economics profession was altogether too uncritical in its total acceptance of the Keynesian theory and accompanying rejection of the classical theory.

THE CLASSICAL THEORY: The basic proposition of the classical theory is that changes in investment and saving cause changes only in the rate of interest.

The classical theory can be summarized as follows: (1) the desired level of investment falls as the rate of interest rises; (2) the desired level of savings rises as the rate of interest rises; (3) the rate of interest changes smoothly and rapidly in such a way as to keep the volume of investment always equal to the volume of saving. As long as the rate of interest always keeps savings and investment equal, there is no reason for changes in either savings or investment to cause changes in income. Consider one case by way of example. Assume that an investment boom causes a greatly increased desire to invest. With the increase in the desire to invest, firms will be trying to increase their borrowings, and they will quickly bid up the rate of interest. This will cause a rightward shift in the *MEI* schedule, say from I to I' in Figure 38.4. As the rate of interest rises, the quantity of money firms wish to borrow and spend on investment falls (since the cost of borrowing rises), and the quantity households are prepared to save and loan to firms increases. The rate of interest continues to rise until the diminished investment is exactly equal to the augmented quantity of saving. The whole process happens quickly enough so that there is no significant rise in income generated during the time in which investment exceeded saving. (You should not read on before you have worked out for yourself the effects of the other three shifts: a fall in the desire to invest, and a rise and a fall in the desire to save.)

The classical theory of saving, investment and interest is built on two important assumptions about the real world: the assumption that the investment schedule is sufficiently interest-elastic, so that suitable variations in the rate of interest can bring about investment sufficient to match any volume of savings that may be forthcoming, and the assumption that the rate of interest is perfectly free to vary, so that saving and investment are quickly brought into equality.

Notice that this theory provides a link between two of the most important withdrawals and injections: the classical theory provides an automatic link between savings and investment. It ensures that, except for temporary fluctuations, the volume of savings will be equal to the volume of investment. Thus as long as the central authorities pursue a balanced budget policy ($G = T$), the volume of withdrawals can only differ from the volume of injections by the difference between imports and exports, which will generally be a trivial amount compared to the whole volume of national income. Thus a major difference between the Keynesian and the classical theory is that in Keynesian theory, income fluctuates in order to bring injections and withdrawals into equality while in classical theory, such fluctuations are not necessary since the job is done by the rate of interest.[1]

Considerable doubt can be cast on the empirical validity of both of these assumptions. First, most empirical studies that have been made seem to suggest that variations in interest rates *over the range actually experienced* do not cause very large variations in the level of investment. Other factors, such as expectations and the level and rate of change of current demand for consumption goods, seem to exert a major influence on investment decisions, with interest-rate variations having only a small effect. In other words, the *MEI* schedule in Figure 38.2 is rather inelastic.[2]

Second, there is some doubt whether the rate of interest is free to vary so as to equate the flow of current savings with the flow of current investment. The central financial authorities exert considerable influence on interest rates, manipulating them in many ways, as we shall see in Chapter 43. Among the most important of these ways is the sale and purchase of bonds on the open market, and such activities can

1 In the classical theory, the equilibrium level of national income was that which, with only temporary aberrations, produced full employment. It was believed that, if there was unemployed labour, wage rates would fall, and the demand for labour increase until full employment prevailed. This labour-market mechanism kept income at the full-employment level; it then did not matter how much people wished to save at this equilibrium level of income, because the interest rate would fluctuate until firms wished to invest exactly what households wished to save.

2 Much of the discussion, both in the classical literature and in the modern, post-Keynesian controversies, is concerned with long-run comparative-static analysis. The question posed in such literature is what would happen to the demand for investment at varying rates of interest if all forces worked themselves out and the economy settled down indefinitely in a completely static position. The possible desire to invest at an interest rate of, say, 1 per cent under such conditions tells us very little about what would happen to the desire to invest if, *under the impact of an excess of saving and a low level of national income and employment*, interest rates were to fall to 1 per cent for a year or two. Yet, if we wish for a theory which is able to handle year-to-year variations in national income, we need a theory that can handle such short-run problems rather than one which tells us what would happen if only the economy would stay put for a longer time than it ever actually does.

prevent the rate of interest from varying to equate current savings with current investment.

THE KEYNESIAN THEORY: The theory that the interest rate will fluctuate so as to equate saving and investment is directly challenged by Keynes's theory of interest rates. By putting forward a plausible alternative theory of the determination of interest rates in a free market, Keynes showed, at the very least, that the classical theory could not be accepted as obviously true. There were now two contradictory theories from which to choose, and the choice between them had to be made on the basis of empirical evidence.

The extreme version of the Keynesian theory was that the interest rate was completely stabilized by the speculative actions of bondholders: bondholders have an idea of the normal rate of interest, and, whenever fluctuations in current savings and investment caused even small changes in the price of bonds, they would buy or sell from their existing stocks of bonds, thus preventing the actual rate from diverging far from what they believe to be the normal rate.

If the interest rate were not free to vary, what would restore equilibrium when there was a large shift in either savings or investment? The equilibrium-restoring mechanism in the Keynesian theory is income fluctuations of the kind we have already analysed. Although the theory that all adjustments take the form of changes in the level of income is now generally regarded as too extreme, it did focus attention on what has come to be understood as an empirically very important mechanism for adjusting savings and investment (even though there may be others): fluctuations in the level of income and employment are *observed to occur* and it is believed that this is often in response to shifts in the schedules of saving and investment.

The balance of empirical evidence seems to many economists to support a modified version of Keynes's theory. According to this theory, fluctuations in savings or investment cause fluctuations *both* in interest rates and in income. Although most economists agree that, as a general rule, more of the burden of equilibriating the system falls on changes in income rather than on changes in interest rates, the relative importance of these two mechanisms varies between times and places according as the interest rate is free to change in response to changes in savings and investment, and as the volume of savings and investment reacts to changes in interest rates. This modified model, in which both national income and the rate of interest change in order to equilibrate the system, is laid out formally in Chapter 43.

39

Fluctuations in the level of economic activity

Output, employment and living standards all tend to rise over time. If you compare any year in the 1970s with any year in the first decade of this century, your overwhelming impression will be one of growth, even if you choose a year of low activity from the 1970s, and compare it with a boom year from the 1900s.

If, however, you take each year of the 1960s and 1970s and compare it with the year following, you will find that economic activity proceeds in an irregular path, with forward spurts followed by pauses and even relapses.

The irregular and often violent movements of the economy over short periods of time have long occupied the attention of economists. These movements were once commonly known as business cycles or trade cycles, the word 'cycle' suggesting a regular oscillation of good times and bad. At some times and places, these movements have been remarkably regular.

Figure 39.1 shows a time series of the percentage of the labour force unemployed in the United Kingdom from 1862 to 1973.[1] The fluctuations are immediately apparent. In the nineteenth century there was a reasonably regular cycle of varying amplitude, with a duration of between eight and ten years. The level of unemployment varied continuously; there were no *prolonged* periods either of full employment or of heavy unemployment. Here then is a regularity in the data that requires explanation. 'Why', the reader should immediately ask, 'did the economy show such fluctuations?'

The period between the two world wars presents a dismal picture of heavy unemployment. The unemployment of the late 1920s was a local British phenomenon associated with the return to the gold standard, and with the long-term decline in some of Britain's staple export industries. This heavy unemployment was not matched elsewhere in the world; in the United States, for example, the middle 1920s was a period of boom. The 1930s, however, saw heavy unemployment throughout the

1 The data for the nineteenth century refer only to trade unions, which probably covered the more volatile parts of the economy. Thus the actual variations for the whole labour force may have been somewhat less than those recorded for the unionized sector.

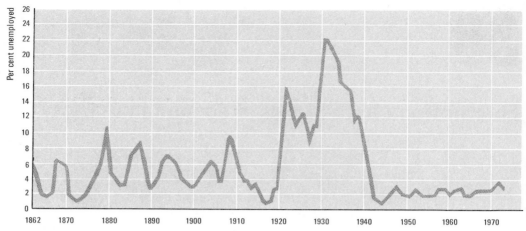

Fig. 39.1 Percentage unemployed in Great Britain 1861–1973 (Figures for 1862–1939 relate to the unionized labour force. The subsequent figures relate to the total registered working population)

world. At the worst point in the depression almost one person in every four was unemployed in the United Kingdom; a similar situation ruled in America and in many other industrialized countries. The data displayed in Figure 39.1 show that the Great Depression of the 1930s was unmatched in severity and duration by any other depression in the last 100 years. It is important to note, however, that unemployment did not remain at a constant level throughout the period; there was considerable variation from one year to the next.

During the Second World War unemployment fell to a very low level indeed, but in spite of the efforts of a total war, it was not until 1942 that all of the unemployed could be put to work. In 1940, one year after the war had begun, 6 per cent of the unionized labour force was still unemployed. Since the war unemployment has fluctuated, but over a very much narrower range than in any other comparable period over the last hundred years. Even when all possible allowances are made for changes in the definitions of the unemployment figures, the postwar experience represents a substantial reduction in the average level of unemployment. Has this been by accident or design?

Unemployment rates since the Second World War have displayed much less regular fluctuations than those of the pre-First World War period. But regular or irregular, the fluctuations have always been present. Figure 39.2 shows the percentage of the labour force unemployed in the United States and the United Kingdom for each year since the Second World War. Fluctuations are present in both economies.

Some students of industrial fluctuations have thought that they were able to discern several types of cycles in economic activity. One such cycle, which is clearly observable in the British nineteenth-century employment series, had a duration of about 9 years from peak to peak. This 9-year cycle was the one usually identified in the past as *the* trade cycle. A second type of cycle, for which there is considerable evidence, is one of much shorter duration, lasting anywhere from 18 to 40 months. This cycle is sometimes associated with variations in business inventories: when

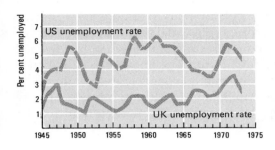

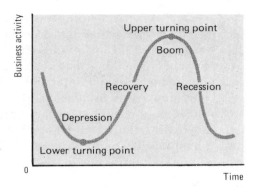

Fig. 39.2 The percentage of the total labour force unemployed in the US and the UK 1945–69

Fig. 39.3 Phases of the trade cycle

inventories are being built up, purchases by firms will exceed their sales; when inventories are being reduced, purchases will be less than sales. We shall see that the building up and running down of inventories can give rise to cyclical oscillations in the economy. Finally, some economists have thought that they could perceive a very long cycle of about 50 years' duration. These cycles were thought to be associated with, among other things, major flourishes of investment activity consequent on some fundamental innovation, each burst being followed by a long pause in investment once all the most obvious new lines have been exploited. Of all the 'cycles', this long-wave one is the most conjectural, and we shall say nothing further about it in this book.[1]

From time to time, many different theories have been put forward to explain these fluctuations in the economy. In the present chapter we can do little more than provide a very general introduction to this interesting and difficult subject.

PHASES OF THE CYCLE

Figure 39.3 shows a stylized cycle and divides it into four periods. We shall first briefly describe the general characteristics of each phase of the cycle, and then describe one possible theory of its causes.

DEPRESSION: A depression is characterized by heavy unemployment and a level of consumers' demand that is low in relation to the capacity of industry to produce goods for consumption. There is, thus, a substantial amount of unused industrial capacity. Some prices may be falling while others will be unchanged, but few if any will be rising. The average level of prices will tend to drift slowly downward. Business profits will be low, and in many individual cases they will be negative. Confidence in the future will be lacking and, as a result, businessmen will be unwilling to take risks in making new investments. Banks and other financial institutions will have surplus cash that no one whom they consider to be a reasonable credit risk wishes to borrow.

1 If there is a long-wave cycle, then the late 1970s should see the downswing into a period of major recession comparable to the 1930s. Perhaps it is the approach of this conjectured period of major depression that accounts for a recent revival of interest in the long-wave cycle.

RECOVERY: When something sets off a recovery, we say, as a matter of terminology, that the *lower turning point* has been reached. Once begun, the pace of recovery is likely to quicken. Old and obsolete machinery will be replaced. Employment, income and consumers' spending all begin to rise. Expectations will become more favourable as a result of increases in production, sales and profits. Investments that once seemed risky may now be undertaken as the climate of business opinion begins to change from one of pessimism to one of optimism. As demand expands, production can be expanded with relative ease merely by re-employing the existing unused capacity and unemployed labour. Prices will stop falling and will generally tend to stay constant or else to rise slowly.

BOOM: As the recovery proceeds, bottlenecks begin to occur in various industries: existing capacity will be fully utilized first in some industries, then in others; labour shortages will begin to occur, particularly in certain skilled categories; and shortages of certain key raw materials will develop. It now becomes difficult to increase output merely by putting unused resources to work, since the supply of unused resources is rapidly disappearing. Output can be raised further only by means of investment, which raises the productivity of already-employed labour. Further rises in demand are now met more by increases in prices than by increases in production. A situation of general excess demand for labour develops. Costs rise and prices rise also, and business remains generally very profitable. Losses are infrequent, since a money profit can be earned merely by holding on to those goods whose prices are rising over time. Investment expenditure is high, investment funds are in short supply, and interest rates will rise in the face of an excess demand for loanable funds. Expectations of the future are favourable, and much investment may be made that is not justified on the basis of current prices and sales, but which requires further rises in prices and sales to render it profitable.

RECESSION: The point at which the boom turns into recession is called the *upper turning point*. Once a recession sets in, it tends to gather its own momentum. Consumption demand falls off. Investments that looked profitable on the expectation of continuously rising sales and prices suddenly become unprofitable. High interest payments, which seemed easily bearable when sales and prices were rising steadily, now become a heavy burden. Business failures, which were very infrequent in the boom period, now become more common. Production and employment fall as a result, and as employment falls, so do income and expenditure; as demand falls, more and more firms get into difficulties. Prices and profits fall, and new investment is reduced to a very low level. It is very often not even worth replacing capital goods as they wear out, since unused capacity is increasing steadily. When the decline is spent, a period of full depression sets in, and we are back where we began.

This discussion is brief and stylized, but it gives some picture of the typical elements found in the various phases of most cycles. No two cycles are exactly the same. In some, the recession phase is short and the resulting depression is not severe; in others, a full-scale period of stagnation sets in. In some cycles, the boom phase develops into a severe inflation; in others, the pressure of excess demand is hardly felt.

A THEORY OF THE CYCLE

We may now ask: Why is it that capitalist societies do not settle down into some position of equilibrium, maintaining more or less full employment at all times? We shall develop a theory of the cyclical behaviour of the economy, a theory which attempts to account for the fact that capitalist economies tend to progress cyclically rather than smoothly. This elementary theory brings together a number of ideas and theories which we have developed throughout Part 7, and it is divided into three steps: first, a theory of cumulative upswings and downswings explaining why, once started, booms and slumps tend to carry on; second, a theory of floors and ceilings, explaining why upward and downward movements are eventually brought to a halt; and third, a theory of instability which explains how, once a process of upward or downward movement is brought to a halt, it tends to reverse itself.

Cumulative movements

Why does a period of expansion or contraction, once begun, tend to go on of its own momentum? First, the multiplier process tends to cause cumulative movements. As soon as a revival begins, some unemployed labourers find work again. These people, with their newly acquired income, can afford to make much needed consumption expenditures. This new demand causes an increase in production and creates new jobs for other unemployed workers. As incomes rise, demand rises; as demand rises, incomes rise. Just the reverse happens in a downswing. Unemployment in one sector causes a fall in demand for the products of other sectors, which leads to a further fall in employment and a further fall in demand.

A second major factor is to be found in the accelerator theory of investment demand, discussed in Chapter 38. New investment is needed to expand existing productive capacity and to introduce new methods of production. When consumer demand is low and there is excess capacity, investment is likely to fall to a very low level; once income starts to rise and entrepreneurs come to expect further rises, investment expenditure may rise very rapidly. Further, when full employment of existing capacity is reached, new investment becomes the only way available for entrepreneurs to increase their output. Since a capital good lasts many years, the value of a machine will generally be greatly in excess of the annual value of consumption goods that it produces. If a machine costing £4,000 produces £1,000 worth of goods every year, then it will be necessary to spend £4 on investment for every desired increase of £1 in the annual production of consumers' goods. For these reasons, investment demand may rise by very much more than consumer demand, and even a moderate fall-off in consumer demand may reduce desired new investment almost to zero. The volatility of investment expenditure is one of the important causes of fluctuations in market economies.

A third major explanation for cumulative movements may be found in the nature and importance of expectations. All production plans take time to fulfil. Current decisions to produce consumers' goods and investment goods are very strongly influenced by the expectations of businessmen. Such expectations can be volatile.

Expectations can, for quite long periods of time, lead to their own realization. If enough people think, for example, that stock-market prices are going to rise, they will all buy stocks in anticipation of a price rise, and these purchases will themselves cause prices to rise; if, on the other hand, enough people think stock-market prices are going to fall, they will sell now at what they regard as a high price and thereby actually cause prices to fall. This is the phenomenon of *self-realizing expectations*. If enough businessmen think the future looks rosy, they may all begin to invest in increasing capacity. This will create new employment and income in the capital-goods industries, and the resulting increase in demand will help to create the rosy conditions, the expectations of which started the whole process. One cannot lay down simple rules about so complicated a psychological phenomenon as the formation of expectations, but it is often, if not always, true that they show a sort of band-wagon effect. Once things begin to improve, people expect further improvements, and their actions based on this expectation help to cause yet further improvements. On the other hand, once things begin to worsen, people often expect further worsenings, and their actions based on this expectation help to make things worse.

There are other reasons too why recoveries and recessions, once started, tend to build up a momentum of their own, but we shall not go into them here. We note in passing that this tendency complicates government anti-cyclical policy. It is not sufficient to know *what* measures will stop a boom; it is necessary to apply these measures at just the right time, and in just the right strength to curb the boom without setting off a downward spiral that will gather momentum of its own accord.

Floors and ceilings

The next question that arises is: Why do these upward and downward processes ever come to an end? Why do we not carry on exploding upwards or downwards once we get started off in one direction or the other? Consider first the revival from a recession. While there is unused capacity, income can continue to rise at a very fast rate. However, once full employment has been achieved, income can rise only as fast as productivity can be increased through new investment. Thus an automatic check is placed on the rapid expansion of real income once full employment is reached. Now consider the recession phase. The worst that can happen to gross investment is that it fall to zero; this would happen if no new investment were occurring, and if existing machinery were not being replaced as it wore out. This is a very extreme situation, but even in this 'worst of all possible worlds' income would not sink to zero. As income falls, fewer and fewer people save, and such saving as does occur is matched by the dissaving of others. Once the society in the aggregate is no longer saving, consumption will equal incomes, and income will no longer decrease. This is the lowest conceivable floor to equilibrium income.[1] Although gross investment may sink to zero in some sectors of the economy, it is unlikely to do so in the whole economy. Between 1930 and 1932, investment fell drastically, but at the depth of the depression it was still well above zero in all Western countries. As long as investment exceeds zero in some sectors, it will exceed zero for the whole economy. In some sectors for example, in the industries providing food, basic clothing and shelter

1 Graphically, it occurs at the point where the consumption function cuts the 45° line.

demands may remain fairly high in spite of quite large reductions in national income. These industries will certainly be carrying out some gross investment to replace equipment as it wears out, and they may even undertake some net investment. The floor to income occurs where withdrawals are equal to the minimum level of injections. Thus, although cumulative movements may continue at very rapid rates in either direction for considerable periods of time, floors and ceilings are eventually encountered. The floor stops the contraction while the ceiling slows down the rate of expansion to that made possible by increases in productivity.

Turning points

Next we introduce a theory that predicts that it is impossible, or at least extremely difficult, to stabilize the level of national income, and that, once income is prevented from either expanding or contracting at a rapid rate, a turning point will occur. We shall develop such a theory in a moment. When we have it, our theory which says (1) that things, once started, tend to go off cumulatively in the same direction; (2) that there are limits, floors and ceilings that slow or stop upward and downward processes; and (3) that, once such a process is stopped or slowed down, it will reverse its direction – will be complete.

Table 39.1 The relation of investment
to changes in income according to
the accelerator hypothesis

Period	Y	ΔY	I
1	100		
2	200	100	300
3	300	100	300
4	375	75	225
5	425	50	150
6	450	25	75
7	460	10	30
8	465	5	15
9	465	0	0

The accelerator theory of investment is probably the best known of the theories accounting for this reversal of direction. This theory was introduced in Chapter 38, and you should now re-read pages 537–9. The accelerator makes the desired level of *new* (not replacement) investment depend upon the rate of change of income. If income is rising at a constant rate, then investment will be at a constant *level*. If the speed at which income is rising slackens,[1] then the level of investment will decline. This is illustrated in Table 39.1 for a hypothetical example where $I = 3\Delta Y$. If income merely levels off to a constant level, then *new* investment may be reduced to a very low amount. This means that a *levelling off* in income at the top of a cycle will lead to a *decline* in the level of investment. The accelerator thus provides a theory of

1 The concept of a declining rate of increase always causes trouble when it is first encountered. The student familiar with the differential calculus will recognize that it refers to a function with a positive first derivative and a negative second derivative with respect to time. Others will recognize the values of Y in Table 39.1 as an example of a series that is increasing at a declining rate.

the upper turning point, although not one for the lower turning point. The decline in investment at the upper turning point will cause a decline in the level of income that will be intensified through the multiplier process. *If* the fall in income continues, the floor will eventually be reached. After a while, investment may rise exogenously. If it does not, then, once existing capacity falls to the level suitable to current output, there will be a revival of replacement investment, and new machines will be bought as old ones wear out. This rise in the level of activity in the capital-goods industries causes, by way of the multiplier, a further rise in income in response to which new investment will take place, leading to yet further rises in income. So a multiplier and an accelerator combined with 'ceilings' and 'floors' may be sufficient to set up an endless cyclical process in the economy.[1]

Such multiplier-accelerator models have been worked out in detail. They provide some real insight into cyclical processes, but it is doubtful if, by themselves, they provide adequate explanations of the cyclical fluctuations in any real economy.

THE INVENTORY CYCLE

Business firms all hold inventories of materials and finished goods and these inventories fluctuate widely. Such sharp fluctuations are a major cause of the short-term variations in the level of activity. The theory of inventory cycles is very similar to the accelerator mechanism, only we now emphasize investment in *inventories* of goods, rather than in plant and equipment.

Start by assuming national income to be in equilibrium, with withdrawals equal to injections at the full-employment level. Now assume, in order to get the process started, that there is an autonomous rise in the propensity to save (a fall in the propensity to consume). The first result of the fall in demand will be a piling up of unsold goods on dealers' shelves. After some time, dealers will reduce their orders so as to prevent inventories from increasing indefinitely: retailers will reduce purchases from wholesalers and, after wholesalers' stocks have risen, they in turn will reduce their purchases from manufacturers. Manufacturers may maintain production for a while, adding the unsold goods to inventories, in the hope that the fall in demand is only temporary. If this proves not to be the case, manufacturers will cut back on production, laying off some workers and reducing the hours worked by the remainder. Thus income and output will begin to fall and, at this stage, inventories will have risen to an abnormally high level. Once production falls to a level equal to the new (lower) level of consumer demand, there will be no further rise in the level of stocks.

Unfortunately, however, matters will not remain at this point. Stocks will now be too high on two counts: first, because sales will be at a lower level than they were originally, and second, because stocks will have increased during the transitional process. In order to work off excess inventories, retailers will buy less from wholesalers than they are selling to consumers, wholesalers will buy less from manufacturers than they are selling to retailers, and manufacturers will produce less than they are selling to wholesalers. Thus the current level of output, and hence of income earned

---

1 The student who wishes to see such a theory handled mathematically should consult William J. Baumol, *Economic Dynamics: An Introduction* (3rd edn., Macmillan, 1970).

by households selling factor services to firms, will fall below the current level of sales. This fall in income will reduce the level of demand still further. As long as production can be held below the level of current sales, then inventories will be falling, even though the level of sales is itself falling.

Once inventories are reduced to the desired level, the retailers and wholesalers will increase their orders, so that their purchases are equal to their current sales. Their inventories will thus be held constant. Manufacturers will also increase the levels of their outputs until output is equal to the (increased) level of sales, thus keeping their own stocks at a constant level. But this means that production, and hence income earned by households, is increased. As this happens, the demand for goods will rise. The initial impact here will be on inventories, which will be run down as sales rise unexpectedly. Now the whole process is set into reverse. For a while, everyone's inventories will be run down, but then orders will increase, first from retailers, then from wholesalers. Finally, the output of manufacturers will increase. This means that income, and with it the level of demand, will rise. Once production is increased to the level of current sales, inventories will no longer be decreasing.

But now the level of inventories is too low for two reasons: first, because the level of sales is higher than it was when inventories were at the correct level, and second, because inventories have been run down during the transitional phase. In order now to build up their inventories, retailers will order more from wholesalers than they sell to consumers, wholesalers will buy more from manufacturers than they sell to retailers, and manufacturers will produce more than they sell to wholesalers. This rise in production will raise incomes and thus raise the level of demand still further. As long as production is kept above the level of sales, however, inventories will be rising in spite of the fact that sales are also rising. Once the inventories are brought up to the desired level, orders will fall off. Retailers and wholesalers will reduce orders to the level of current sales, and manufacturers will reduce output to that level as well. But this fall in output will reduce incomes and with them, demand. For a while, inventories will pile up, but orders and output will be cut back, thus reducing the level of income and demand. Now the whole downward process is set in motion again and, if the reader goes back to the beginning of this section and starts to read there, he will pick up the process again.

Verbal analysis of the sort just given can provide some general ideas of such a cyclical process. But if we should wish to carry our analysis much further, verbal and geometrical reasoning becomes inadequate and mathematical tools become essential. In some branches of economics one can get a long way by means of careful verbal and geometrical analysis. In the field of dynamic fluctuations one can get practically nowhere. We might want to ask such questions as: What are the effects of varying the time lags with which firms react to changes in their sales? What if the reaction does not occur suddenly but is *distributed* through time? Under what circumstances will such a cycle die out rapidly so that income *converges* on its equilibrium level? In what circumstances will the self-exciting process continue indefinitely so that the cycle will itself carry on indefinitely unless stopped by conscious government policy? What will be the effect of government controls built into the system in an attempt to damp down these fluctuations? What difference will it make if the government's control mechanism itself acts with a time lag? To analyse such questions mathematical tools are indispensable; particularly necessary is the sort of mathematics which electrical engineers use to analyse self-exciting (*closed-loop*) control systems. For the student interested in dynamic fluctuations, a knowledge of such techniques has become essential. [1]

[1] One of the best surveys of the formal economic theory of fluctuations and of the mathematics used therein is to be found in the first half of R. G. D. Allen, *Mathematical Economics* (Macmillan, 1956).

40

Government and the circular flow of income

There is no doubt that the government can exert a major influence on the circular flow of income. Prime examples occur during major wars when governments engage in massive military spending and throw fiscal caution to the winds. As more and more money is spent, both Gross National Product (GNP) and employment tend to rise to unprecedented heights. Thus, it is clear that governments can, through their spending and taxing policies, have major impacts on GNP and on employment. The use of these policies *in order to* influence employment and national income is called fiscal policy. This chapter deals with the theory and the actual experience of fiscal policy.

There is little doubt that when appropriately used fiscal policy can be an important tool for influencing the economy. In the heyday of fiscal policy in the 1940s and 1950s, many economists thought that the economy could be adequately regulated solely by varying the size of the government's deficit or surplus. That day is now past, although a few 'pure fiscalists' are still to be found. Today, most economists are aware of the limitations of fiscal policy, and there is much discussion of other tools of stabilization that can complement it.

In Chapter 36 we studied briefly the effects of government taxing and spending policies on the circular flow of income. We now need to consider these policies in much more detail. The subject is vast and we shall organize our introductory discussion around four main headings: (1) A Theory of Fiscal Policy, (2) The Tools of Fiscal Policy, (3) The Use of Fiscal Policy, and (4) The Costs of Government Activity.

THE THEORY OF FISCAL POLICY

Not so many years ago it was generally accepted, and indeed many people still fervently believe, that a prudent government should balance its budget on all occasions. The argument is usually based on an analogy with what seems prudent behaviour for the individual. It is a foolish individual who lets his current expenditure consistently exceed his current revenue, so that he gets steadily further into debt.

It is then argued that what is good for the individual must be good for the nation.

When the government follow a balanced-budget policy, as most governments tried to do even during the Great Depression of the 1930s, it restricts its expenditure during a slump because its tax revenue is falling at that time. On the other hand, during a boom, when its revenue is high and rising, it increases its spending. In other words it rolls with the economy, raising and lowering its expenditures in step with everyone else.

The government, by going along with the crowd, did not seem to some people to be making the most of its potential to control the economy in a beneficial manner. 'Why', they asked, 'should the government not try to stabilize the economy by doing just the opposite of what everyone else is doing – by increasing its demand when private demand is falling and lowering its demand when private demand is rising?' This idea seemed particularly important in view of the fact that government revenues and expenditures were such a large part of the national income of most Western countries. The potential of so large a class of expenditures to influence the economy seemed too obvious to ignore.

In this view, the government's budget is regarded as more than just the revenue-and-expenditure statement of a very large organization. The budget is regarded as a tool for changing the behaviour of the economy.

> **Fiscal policy is defined as the use by the central authorities of government revenues and expenditures in an effort to influence the circular flow of income.**

In this chapter we shall confine ourselves to the major objectives of controlling unemployment and inflation through fiscal policy. Other policy instruments and other objectives will be considered in later chapters.

Budget deficits and surpluses

A household earns income over the year from the sale of the factor services that it controls, and it spends its income on purchasing goods and services. Its deficit or surplus on the year's transactions can be calculated by comparing its total income with its total expenditure. Similarly, governments raise current revenue by levying taxes, and they spend on all the projects that they undertake. If current revenue is exactly equal to current expenditure, the government has a BALANCED BUDGET. If revenues exceed expenditures, there is a BUDGET SURPLUS; while if revenues fall short of expenditures, there is a BUDGET DEFICIT.

If the government raises its spending without raising its taxes, its extra expenditure may be said to be *deficit-financed*. If the extra spending is accompanied by an equal increase in tax revenue, we speak of a *balanced-budget change in spending*.

THE FINANCING OF DEFICITS AND SURPLUSES: If the government spends more than it raises, where does the money come from? If the government raises more than it spends, where does the money go? The difference between expenditure and tax revenue is reflected in changes in the level of the government's debt. If the expenditures exceed revenues, the balance must be borrowed from someone; if revenues exceed expenditures, the balance goes to pay off some of the loans that were made in the past.

A deficit requires an increase in borrowing, for which there are three main sources: the central bank,[1] the commercial banks and the public. The government borrows money from these sources by selling treasury bills or bonds to them. A TREASURY BILL is a promise to repay a stated amount in the near future (usually, 30, 60, or 90 days), and it is sold in return for a smaller amount paid to the government now – the difference between the two sums representing the interest on the loan. A government bond is also a promise to pay a stated sum of money in the future but in the more distant future than a bill — possibly as much as 25 years from now.[2]

A surplus allows the government to reduce its outstanding debt. Treasury bills or bonds in the hands of the central bank, the commercial banks or the public may be redeemed.

THE EFFECT OF DEFICITS AND SURPLUSES ON AGGREGATE EXPENDITURE: Money spent by the government may represent a net addition to aggregate demand, or it may merely represent an expenditure that would have been made in any case, but for other purposes. In the first case, variations in government taxes or expenditure will have a major impact on GNP and total employment. In the second case, such variations will serve to reallocate expenditure between the sectors of the economy but will have little effect on the overall level of aggregate demand, GNP, and total employment.

In this chapter we discuss the important case in which a government deficit represents a net injection of new expenditure into the circular flow and in which a surplus represents a net withdrawal. This may be called the Keynesian case since it was the case mainly assumed in the textbooks written in the wake of Keynes's *General Theory*. Today, it is still recognized as an important extreme case, but not as the only possible case. The opposite extreme case would occur if government expenditure merely replaced an equivalent amount of private expenditure.

The CROWDING-OUT EFFECT refers to a reduction of private expenditure as a direct result of an increase in government expenditure.[3] In the extreme Keynesian case the crowding-out effect is zero, and at the opposite extreme it is 100 per cent (private expenditure falls by £1 for every increase of £1 of government expenditure). Intermediate cases are also possible. If, for example, every extra £1 of government expenditure crowded out 60p worth of private expenditure, the crowding-out effect would be 60 per cent and the net additions to injections would be only 40p. In this case to get a desired net increase of £1 in new injections, the government would have to spend £2·50. Probably the great majority of economists believe that intermediate cases, in which the crowding-out effect exceeds zero but is less than 100 per cent, are more common than either extreme.

1 The central bank controls the money supply and can create as much new money as is needed to finance any amount of government deficit.

2 The date on which the loan will be repaid is called the redemption date or maturity date, and when that date arrives the bond is said to have matured – like a fully matured bottle of wine, there is nothing to be gained by holding it any longer.

3 This term was first used by American monetarist critics of Keynesian fiscal policy, but it has now passed into fairly general use.

The present chapter deals with the Keynesian case, in which the crowding-out effect is zero. The analysis will help in understanding the general consequences of fiscal policy. The results obtained carry over in general terms, even if not in every detail, to all cases in which a deficit-financed increase in government expenditure causes some net increase in injections (the crowding-out effect is less than 100 per cent).[1]

THE EFFECTS OF DEFICITS AND SURPLUSES ON NATIONAL INCOME: We shall study the use of fiscal policy to remove inflationary or deflationary gaps. It would be advisable to review your understanding of these two concepts and of the basic analysis of government in the circular flow by re-reading pages 502–4 and 512–15.

In Figure 40.1 we assume that the aggregate expenditure function is AD_1 and that the full-employment level of income is Y_f. National income is in equilibrium at the level Y_u, and the government's budget is balanced. The deflationary gap is cd. In order to remove it, the government raises its expenditures by ab per year, keeping tax rates constant.[2] Initially, the government will have a deficit of ab per year. This

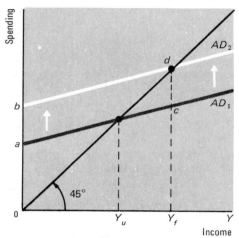

Fig. 40.1 Using a deficit to eliminate a deflationary gap

deficit spending increases injections without increasing withdrawals, and national income is predicted to rise to Y_f, the full-employment level. At this level the extra withdrawals in the form of taxes, savings, and imports will just balance the extra injections in terms of government expenditure. A numerical example of this policy is shown in Table 40.1 on page 560.

1 The crowding-out effect itself will be studied in more detail later after the effects of money and interest rates have been allowed for. In the meantime it may be noted that an important mechanism for the effect is changes in the rate of interest. If an increase in government expenditure of ΔG causes the rate of interest (as well as national income) to increase and investment falls by ΔI as a result, then the net increase in injections is only $\Delta G - \Delta I$ which is less than ΔG because ΔI is negative.

2 The discussion in this Chapter is based on the simplifying assumption that an increase in government expenditure of £1 represents an increase of £1 in demand for domestically-produced commodities. In practice, this is not quite right since there will be some leakages as a result of taxes on the commodities purchased by the government and any import content (in terms of raw materials) that the commodities may have. In detailed statistical studies it is important to know the actual increase in demand for domestically-produced commodities caused by an increase of £1 in G. For purposes of an introductory theoretical discussion the assumption stated in the first sentence of this footnote is very helpful in simplifying the analysis and does not affect any of the conclusions reached.

The government could also raise income from Y_u to Y_f by cutting taxes instead of raising expenditures. A reduction in taxes increases the fraction of national income that remains as disposable income. This shifts upward the line relating consumption to national income. A large enough tax cut can also raise the aggregate demand function from AD_1 to AD_2 and thereby create full employment. This policy alternative is also illustrated in Table 40.1.

Although the theory that we have used up to this point is an extremely simple one it can nonetheless be used to establish a number of predictions that have been very important in the post-war use of macro-economic policy by most Western governments. The first prediction follows from the analysis just concluded.

(1) It is possible for a government to remove a deflationary gap and raise national income to its full-employment level either by raising expenditure with tax rates held constant, or by cutting taxes with expenditure held constant.

To derive the second prediction, compare the effects of cutting tax revenue with those of raising expenditure. If the government raises expenditure by £1 million per year, it injects £1 million worth of new expenditure into the economy. If the multiplier is 2, the final rise in national income will be £2 million. On the other hand, if the government cuts tax rates sufficiently to reduce its revenues by £1 million, the private sector will have an extra £1 million of disposable income. Expenditures, however, will rise by less than £1 million because part of the income will be saved by the private sector and part will be spent on purchasing imports. If 70 per cent of all disposable income is spent on domestically-produced commodities, a cut in tax revenue of £1 million will raise spending on domestic production by only £0·7 million and, combined with a multiplier of 2, will raise national income by £1·4 million. What must the government do if it wishes to generate £2 million of extra national income by a tax cut? It will have to generate (given our assumptions) initial new expenditure of £1 million. This will require a *cut in tax revenue* of £1·43 million. With a propensity to spend on domestically produced commodities of 0·7 this will cause an initial increase in expenditure of £1 million, which is the same as was obtained when the government raised its own expenditure by £1 million. This establishes the second prediction:

(2) A given increase in aggregate demand will require a larger budget deficit if it is accomplished by cutting taxes rather than by raising expenditure.

The third prediction concerns the relative size of the initial budget deficit and the deficit that will exist once the full-employment level of GNP has been established. Consider the case in which the deflationary gap is removed by raising expenditure. In Figure 40.1 we start with an initial rise in government expenditure of *ab* per year; this amount is the initial budget deficit. But, as income rises with tax rates constant, the tax yield will rise and the budget deficit must thus be reduced below *ab*.

Could the deficit ever be erased completely? Not according to our present theory. The extra government expenditure represents new injections into the circular flow.

Table 40.1 Calculation of the final budget deficit for a
numerical example in which the initial deficit is £1 million

1.	The economy is initially in equilibrium with unemployed resources.	
2.	Government expenditure (an injection) rises by	£1 million
3.	The initial budget deficit is	£1 million
4.	Marginal propensities out of GNP are	
	to tax	0·25
	to save	0·18
	to import	0·07
5.	The multiplier is $\dfrac{1}{0\cdot25+0\cdot18+0\cdot07}=2$	
6.	The final rise in GNP is	£2 million
7.	The final rise in tax revenue is (6)×0·25	0·5 million
8.	The final rise in saving is (6)×0·18	0·36 million
9.	The final rise in imports is (6)×0·07	0·14 million
10.	The final rise in all withdrawals is (7)+(8)+(9)	1 million
11.	Equilibrium income is restored since (10) = (2)	
12.	The final budget deficit is (2)−(7)	0·5 million

Income rises until an equivalent extra flow of withdrawals is generated to match the extra injections. Some of these withdrawals will take the form of extra savings, some of extra imports, and only some of extra taxes. The larger taxes are as a proportion of total withdrawals, the more they will increase when income rises, and the smaller will be the final deficit. Unless taxes are the only withdrawal, some deficit is sure to remain. This gives us our third prediction:

(3) There will still be a deficit once full employment has been restored, but it will be less than the initial deficit.

Table 40.1 shows the calculations for a numerical example. The marginal propensities in this example are all out of GNP, and they show that for every £1 increase in GNP, taxes rise by 25p, savings by 18p, and imports by 7p. Thus total withdrawals rise by 50p for every increase in income of £1, and the multiplier has a value of 2. In this case, the induced rise in tax revenue has the effect of halving the initial budget deficit, once the new equilibrium is achieved. Clearly the reduction in the initial deficit depends on the fraction of total withdrawals accounted for by taxes.[1]

So far we have discussed removing a deflationary gap. Exactly the same analysis applies to an inflationary gap. In Figure 40.2, with aggregate demand at AD_1 we assume an inflationary gap of *lm*. The government can remove this gap either by reducing its expenditure by *lm* or by increasing its tax revenue sufficiently to cause the private-expenditure function to shift downward by *lm*. The reader should by now have no trouble in filling in the details of the analysis necessary to derive the following two predictions:

---

1 The final deficit as a fraction of the initial deficit is given by the expression: $\dfrac{\text{Final deficit}}{\text{Initial deficit}} = 1 - \dfrac{t}{w}$, where *t* is the marginal propensity to tax out of GNP and *w* is the total marginal propensity to withdraw from GNP.

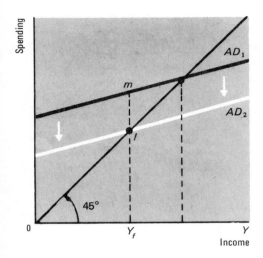

Fig. 40.2 Using a surplus to eliminate an inflationary gap

(4) The government can remove an inflationary gap by an appropriate decrease in its expenditures or increase in its taxes.

(5) The cut in expenditures necessary to remove a given inflationary gap will be less than the rise in tax revenue necessary to accomplish the same job.

THE FULL-EMPLOYMENT DEFICIT OR SURPLUS: It should now be clear that we can talk not only about the *actual* (or 'current') budget deficit or surplus at the current level of national income, but also about the *potential* budget deficit or surplus at any other level of national income, given current rates of taxes and expenditures. The potential deficit or surplus which has been popularized by the Council of Economic Advisers to the President of the United States is the one that would occur if the economy were at full employment. This they call the full-employment deficit, or surplus, and we may refer to it in general as the FULL-EMPLOYMENT BALANCE.

We saw in the example given in Table 40.1 that the current deficit of £1 million produced by an increase in government expenditure of £1 million led to a full-employment deficit of £0·5 million, which was smaller than the current deficit. The concept of the potential balance is elaborated in Figure 40.3. For given tax *rates*, there will be a certain tax yield corresponding to each level of income. This is shown by the line T in the figure. The G line is drawn horizontally, showing that G is assumed not to vary as Y varies. The distance between the two lines shows the potential deficit or surplus corresponding to each level of income. Y_b is the level of national income for which those particular tax and expenditure rates will lead to a balanced budget. If the full-employment income is less than Y_b, say at Y_1, there is a full-employment deficit; if it is to the right of Y_b, say at Y_2, there is a full-employment surplus.

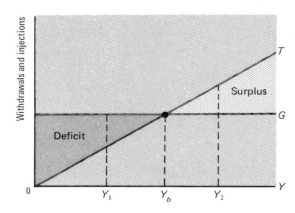

Fig. 40.3 Full-employment balance

Effects of changes in the levels of G and T: the balanced-budget multiplier

So far we have considered the effects of a change in either revenues or expenditures. What would we expect to happen if, during a time of unemployment, the government raises its expenditure but simultaneously raises its taxes, seeking to keep its budget balanced? We have already seen that an increase of £1 million in G will have a different effect on national income from a decrease of £1 million in T. We should not be surprised, therefore, if the effects of an equal increase in G and T did not cancel each other out. Let us see what will happen.

When G rises by £1 million, there is £1 million extra government expenditure, but when T rises by £1 million, consumption expenditure falls by less than £1 million because some of the money would have been withdrawn from the circular flow in any case. Thus, if only £0·7 million of the tax revenue would have been spent on domestically produced goods while the other £0·4 million would have been saved or spent on imported goods, then by reducing disposable incomes by £1 million and spending that amount the government causes a net increase in aggregate demand of £0·3 million. In general, the initial increase in expenditure following on a balanced increase in G and T is equal to that part of T that would otherwise have been withdrawn from the circular flow. Let us call this fraction z so that the total amount by which expenditure rises is zT.

This net addition to expenditure will set up a multiplier process that will lead to a further rise in income. We have already seen that the multiplier is equal to the reciprocal of the marginal propensity to withdraw, $K = 1/w$. Thus the final increase in income will be $\Delta Y = zT/w$ which is, as usual, the initial injection of new expenditure *times* the multiplier.

> **In general, if the marginal propensity to spend tax money is higher for the taxpayers, an increase in the size of the government budget will have an expansionary effect, and a decrease in its size will have a contractionary effect. This effect is called the balanced-budget multiplier.**

The size of the balanced-budget multiplier depends critically on the form the extra taxes take. Two possibilities are discussed below and are included in Table 40.2.

TWO EXAMPLES: (1) Assume that the taxes are levied exclusively on personal incomes. The value of z then is the sum of the marginal propensities to save and to import out of disposable income. Assume for purposes of illustration that this value is 0·30. This means that, of every pound raised in new income taxes, 70p would have been spent in the domestic circular flow in any case, and 30p would have been withdrawn for savings and imports. This means that the impact effect of the increased government expenditure will be to raise aggregate demand by £0·3X. This addition to the circular flow will then be subject to all the withdrawals, including corporate taxes and savings and personal income taxes. If $w = 0·5$, then the balanced budget multiplier, K_B, $= 0·3/0·5 = 0·6$. An increase of £1 million of expenditure financed by £1 million raised from personal income taxes will raise national income by approximately £600,000.

(2) Assume that taxes are increased 'across the board': some on companies, some on persons, some on sales and purchase taxes. In this case, z is difficult to calculate, and we might take w as a good approximation to it. In other words, since we are extracting money from various places in the circular flow, it may be safe to assume that the fraction of it that would not have been spent is the fraction of GNP that is generally withdrawn. If this guess proves correct, z will equal w, and the balanced-budget multiplier will be $K_B = w/w = 1$. The balanced-budget multiplier is unity, if the sum of withdrawal propensities used to calculate the multiplier is the same as the fraction of income that would not have been spent had the tax money remained in private hands.

Pump priming

We have discussed three basic methods of dealing with deflationary and inflationary gaps: changes in G, changes in T and balanced changes in both G and T. A fourth method, pump priming, was popularized by the administration of US President Franklin Roosevelt in the 1930s, and it has supporters even today. The theory of pump priming holds that less than the whole of a deflationary gap needs to be removed by direct government action, because the removal of only a small part of such a gap will create such favourable expectations that private investment expenditure will rise to fill the remainder. Thus, presented with a deflationary gap of cd in Figure 40.1, the government might need, for example, to fill only one tenth of this by new government spending. This would raise the aggregate expenditure schedule only one tenth of the way from AD_1 to AD_2 and raise national income only one tenth of the way from Y_u to Y_f. It is then hoped that this rise in income and demand will generate such favourable expectations among firms that private investment will rise to increase aggregate demand the other nine tenths of the way.

There is nothing self-contradictory about the theory; it describes a world that could exist. Whether or not it can or does work in the real world depends on responses. It depends, first, on how quickly and by how much business expectations respond to a fairly small rise in income occurring during a well-developed slump. During the

Great Depression, this response did not occur as Roosevelt hoped it would. If business expectations do respond as hoped, a second response is then required: private demand must rise sufficiently to justify the favourable business expectations. This latter condition is unlikely to be fulfilled if tax rates are such that much of the new income is siphoned off in taxes. If this happens, private demand may not expand fast enough to persuade firms to continue their expanded investment programme, which is itself the basic cause of the recovery. This problem is now called 'fiscal drag', and we shall discuss it shortly. There is little doubt that it was partly responsible for the very poor results obtained from the very great efforts put into anti-deflationary policies by the American government throughout the 1930s.

An illustration of alternative methods of removing a deflationary gap

Table 40.2 illustrates three of the four methods of removing a deflationary gap of £2 million that we have discussed in this section. If you will follow through the calculations in each case you will obtain a valuable check on your understanding of the general argument that has gone before.

Table 40.2 Alternative devices for achieving an increase of £2 million in GNP during a period of unemployment

Policy method	Assumptions	Policy action	Initial effect on aggregate demand	Final effect on GNP
1. Increase G with no change in tax rates	$w = 0.5$	Increase G by £1 million	Increase by £1 million	Increase by £2 million
2. Decrease T, no change in G	$w = 0.5$; marginal propensity to consume out of disposable income $= 0.7$	Decrease T by £1·43 million	Increase by £1 million	Increase by £2 million
3. Balanced-budget increases in G and T	(a) $w = 0.5$ $z = 0.3$	Increase G and T by £3⅓ million	Increase by £1 million	Increase by £2 million
	(b) $w = 0.5$ $z = 0.5$	Increase G and T by £2 million	Increase by £1 million	Increase by £2 million

Dynamic problems of stabilization policy

Virtually all of the analysis so far has been based on static equilibrium theory. We have taken a *given* inflationary or deflationary gap and have asked how to eliminate it. In fact the economy is continually fluctuating, and some of the reasons for this were analysed in Chapter 39. The problems of stabilization in a continually changing economy can be very much more difficult than those in a static economy with a given inflationary or deflationary gap. Let us briefly consider why.

All of the fiscal policies that stabilize the economy, whether they are automatic or the result of conscious policy decisions, work to create NEGATIVE FEEDBACK. Negative feedback is a technical term that means that, when any system deviates from its target level, forces are set in motion that push the system back *towards* its target level.[1] Thus, when demand is too high so that inflationary conditions prevail, demand is reduced; when demand is too low so that unemployment prevails, demand is increased. It would be grossly misleading to leave the reader with the impression that negative feedback is sufficient to solve all stabilization problems. Negative feedback is a necessary but not a sufficient condition for stability.[2] If any control system operates with delays that are large relative to the period of fluctuations it is seeking to control, it can do the very opposite of stabilizing: the controls can make the system less stable than it would otherwise be; they can actually accentuate rather than check fluctuations.

Controls operate with lags for two main reasons. The first reason is that our knowledge of what is happening is always somewhat out of date. At a minimum, it takes a month or so, and often very much longer, to gather data about current happenings. Our current information thus tells us not what is happening today, but what was happening anywhere from a month to six months ago. The second reason is that it takes time for any policy change to affect the behaviour of firms and households. Such lags may vary from a few weeks to a year, depending on the particular measure.

A simple explanation of this problem can be developed along the following lines.[3] Consider a system that is oscillating around a full-employment level of output as illustrated in Figure 40.4(i). Time is measured along the horizontal axis, and on the vertical axis we measure the difference between full-employment output and current expenditure. The fluctuations are such that a boom in which aggregate expenditure exceeds full-employment output is followed by a slump in which aggregate expenditure falls short of full-employment output. Assume that the government plans to vary its own expenditure so as to offset these fluctuations exactly. The government wants its plan to have the impact pictured by the solid line in Figure 40.4(ii). At first, it plans a surplus that will reduce total expenditure; later, in period 3, it plans a deficit that will raise aggregate expenditure. If the government's plans are fulfilled instantaneously, then the addition of the solid lines in Figure 40.4(i) and Figure 40.4(ii) will produce aggregate expenditure for the private plus the public sectors, which is always equal to full-employment output. The government's deficit or surplus exactly counterbalances the difference between aggregate expenditure and full-employment output in the private sector, so that its stabilization policy is completely successful.

Now, assume that a time lag is involved; further assume, to make the point as clear as possible, that the time lag is equal to half the period of the cycle. Now the planned balanced budget at period zero will not actually occur until period 2; the planned maximum surplus of period 1 will not occur until period 3, when the economy is already in a slump; and the planned maximum deficit of period 3 will not occur until period 5, when the economy is already in a period of boom. Although planned

---

1 The *system* may be anything from an economy to an aeroplane using an automatic pilot; the *target level* may be anything from a set of equilibrium values to a set of values desired and consciously sought after by the central authorities.

2 We illustrated this point in the case of a single competitive market. See page 94, note 1, and the discussion of the cobweb theory in Chapter 12.

3 This particular formulation of the problem is taken from A. W. Phillips, 'Employment, Inflation, and Growth', *Economica*, February 1962.

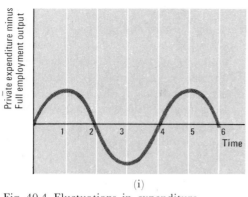 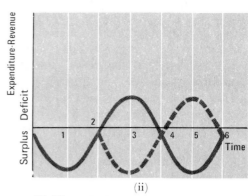 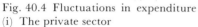

Fig. 40.4 Fluctuations in expenditure (ii) The government sector
(i) The private sector

government expenditure still follows the solid line in Figure 40.4(ii), actual government expenditure now follows the dotted line. Instead of stabilizing the economy as planned, the 'stabilizing' policy actually destabilizes it. The combination of public and private demand will give rise to larger fluctuations than would have occurred if the government had done nothing!

This simple example is sufficient to show that the problem of controlling the economy is not so simple as it sometimes seems. In general, policies designed to stabilize individual markets or the whole economy will have quite widely differing effects, depending on the time lags both in the actual working of the economy and in the functioning of the stabilization scheme.

Professor Frank Paish has compared the problem of stabilizing the economy to that of driving a car with blackened front and side windows and only a rear-view mirror from which to see. The car has brakes and an accelerator, but they take effect only a long time after the driver has used them. Thus the driver often has to have the courage to apply the brake when he estimates that he is going uphill and the accelerator when he estimates that he is going downhill, just as the government, in attempting to influence the economy, often has to make plans to increase its spending during a boom and to decrease it during a slump because of the long time lags that are involved.

THE TOOLS OF FISCAL POLICY
The automatic tools of fiscal policy: built-in stabilizers

The level of aggregate demand is continually fluctuating. A government's full-employment policy thus does not simply require removing an occasional inflationary or deflationary gap. The required size of the deficit or surplus is continually changing.

Fortunately, much of the job of adjusting fiscal policy to an ever-changing economic environment is done automatically by what are called built-in stabilizers. A BUILT-IN STABILIZER is anything that tends to increase government deficits (or decrease surpluses) during slumps, and to increase surpluses (or decrease deficits) during booms, without the central authorities having to make individual policy decisions to bring about each of these changes.

Tax revenues tend to adjust automatically to changes in income in such a way as to stabilize the economy. As incomes rise during a period of prosperity, tax revenues increase and, being a withdrawal, exercise a contractionary effect on national income. As tax revenues fall during a recession, the decrease in withdrawals has an expansionary effect.

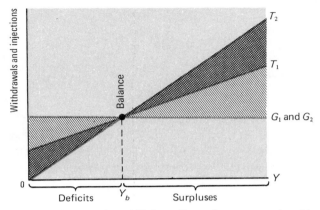

Fig. 40.5 Automatic stabilizing effects of taxes on national income

Figure 40.5 illustrates the stabilizing effect of taxes that rise as national income rises. Suppose the subscripts '1' and '2' refer to different economies. Both economies have the same government expenditure function (G), but each has a different tax function. Economy 2 has a higher degree of built-in stability than economy. 1. As income rises above Y_b, the budget surplus rises faster in 2 than in 1. Also, as income falls below Y_b, the budget deficit increases faster in 2 than in 1.

Government expenditures, which we have so far assumed to be constant, will tend to be automatically stabilizing to the extent that they rise during periods of recession and depression and decline during periods of prosperity and boom. Figure 40.6 shows the potential stabilizing effect of variations in government expenditure. Assume that three economies have the same tax function. Each has a different expenditure function. Economy 1 has the highest degree of built-in stability; economy 3 has the lowest. In economy 1 the level of government expenditure actually falls as Y rises. Thus large surpluses occur rapidly as income rises above Y_b, and large deficits occur when income falls below Y_b. In economy 3 surpluses occur at incomes above Y_b and deficits at incomes below Y_b, but in both cases they are smaller than those in the other two economies because of the tendency for expenditures, as well as revenues, to vary directly with income.

FISCAL DRAG: A large degree of built-in stability is a good thing if the economy is tending to oscillate around a high level of income and employment. The same degree of built-in stability can, however, be very undesirable if the economy is in a serious slump. Fiscal measures that make it difficult to recover from a slump suggest another concept popularized by the American president's Council of Economic Advisers and called by them FISCAL DRAG.

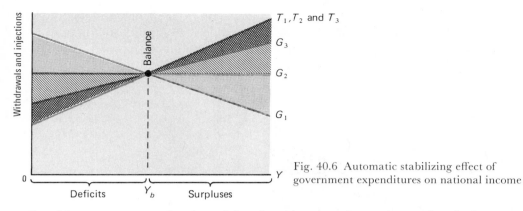

Fig. 40.6 Automatic stabilizing effect of government expenditures on national income

Consider an economy that is reviving from a severe depression under the impetus of new private investment or new government expenditure. The more rapidly tax yields rise as national income rises, the more rapidly withdrawals will rise. Thus the large rise in taxes will tend to bring an expansion quickly to a halt by re-establishing the equality between injections and withdrawals after only a small rise in income.

The concept is illustrated in Figure 40.5. As the lines are drawn in that figure, economy 2 suffers from more fiscal drag than does economy 1. To see this, assume that both economies are in equilibrium at income Y_b with substantial unemployment. Suppose income starts to rise due to an autonomous rise in investment expenditure. The expansion will be less in 2 than in 1 because of the depressing effects of the more rapid rise in tax yields in economy 2 than in economy 1.

TAXES: Most taxes tend to yield more revenue as national income increases. For example, sales and excise tax yields rise as total purchases and sales rise, and this happens as income rises. The same is true of taxes on payrolls such as social security taxes. Thus, with rates constant, the total tax yield and thus the total of withdrawals from the circular flow of income rises and falls as national income rises and falls.

The effect is even more marked with taxes that are progressive rather than proportional. Steeply progressive tax rates ensure that, as income rises, tax receipts rise more than in proportion and, as income falls, tax receipts fall more than in proportion. Whatever else is happening, these extra withdrawals exert a contractionary force on the economy. Conversely, if income falls, tax receipts fall sharply, withdrawals are reduced, and the contractionary pressures on the economy are, to some extent, alleviated.

EXPENDITURES THAT VARY INVERSELY WITH THE LEVEL OF ACTIVITY: The stabilizing effect of government activity can be increased even further if some part of government expenditure can be made to vary inversely with income, rising when incomes fall and falling when incomes rise. An important built-in stabilizer that works in this way is unemployment benefits. When national income falls, expenditure on unemployment benefits rises; when national income rises, the expenditure falls. Unemployment benefits ensure that when workers become unemployed, their consumption expenditure will not fall to zero, since their disposable incomes will not fall to zero. In general, the higher the payment made to the unemployed in relation to the amount they earn when employed, the smaller the fall in their consumption when their employment falls. Most welfare schemes also act as built-in stabilizers.

AGRICULTURAL POLICY: Another stabilizer is provided by agricultural policy. When a slump occurs and the demand for agricultural goods falls off, government price-support policies come into action and prevent farm incomes from falling as drastically as they would without such aid. Since agricultural income is more or less stabilized, the expenditure of the agricultural sector is likewise stabilized. Thus, that part of the multiplier process that would have worked through the agricultural sector is frustrated by policies that automatically support agricultural income. These stabilizers are important in countries such as the United States, in which agricultural sectors are large, but are less important in countries such as the United Kingdom, in which agricultural sectors are small.

UNFORESEEN BENEFITS: Most of these built-in stabilizers are the unforeseen by-products of policies originally adopted for other reasons. The progressive income tax, for example, arose out of a concern to make the distribution of income less unequal. The growth of the government sector has been the result of many factors other than a desire for cyclical stability. But, unforeseen or not, these measures all now constitute potent built-in stabilizers.

THE PARTIAL NATURE OF THE JOB DONE BY BUILT-IN STABILIZERS: Built-in stabilizers can reduce the severity of fluctuations in the economy, but they cannot eliminate them. Stabilizers work by influencing income in such a way as to produce stabilizing reactions to changes in income. But until the income change occurs, the stabilizer is not even brought into play.

The evidence from most Western industrial countries indicates that the magnitude of cyclical fluctuations has been substantially reduced since 1945. Part of this reduction is undoubtedly due to the increased importance of built-in stabilizers. It is also true, however, that the remaining fluctuations have been large enough to cause governments serious concern. Most governments have found it necessary, therefore, to supplement their built-in-stabilizers with what is called DISCRETIONARY FISCAL POLICY: changes in taxes and expenditures consciously designed to remove particular inflationary or deflationary gaps.

Discretionary fiscal policy

If governments are to use fiscal policy to regulate the fluctuations that remain in the economy after the automatic stabilizers have played their part, they need to make conscious decisions to alter their fiscal policy from time to time. Government economists must study current economic trends and predict the probable course of the economy. If the predicted course is unsatisfactory, taxes and/or expenditures must be changed so as to alter that course. In considering discretionary fiscal policy we shall deal with two main questions: Does it matter if the fiscal changes are temporary or relatively long-lived? Does it matter whether it is expenditure or tax revenue that is varied to achieve a desired budget deficit or surplus?

TEMPORARY VERSUS 'PERMANENT' CHANGES: An economist advising on how to stabilize a fluctuating economy through tax policy might advocate temporary tax increases to remove an inflationary gap and temporary tax reductions to remove a deflationary gap. These tax changes would cause changes in household disposable income, and, according to the Keynesian theory of the consumption function, the resulting changes in consumption would tend to stabilize the economy. Consumption expenditure would increase as taxes were cut in times of deflationary gaps and would decrease as taxes were raised in times of inflationary gaps.

This theory of the stabilizing effects of short-term fiscal changes relies on the theory that household consumption depends on current disposable income. Many of the recent theories of the consumption function have emphasized household's expected *lifetime income*, or, *permanent income*, as the major determinant of consumption. According to such theories, households have expectations about their lifetime incomes and they adjust their consumption to these expectations. When temporary fluctuations in income occur, households maintain their long-term consumption plans and use their stocks of wealth as a buffer to absorb income fluctuations. Thus, when there is a purely temporary rise in income, households will save all the extra, and when there is a purely temporary fall in income, households maintain their long-term consumption plans by using up part of their wealth (accumulated through past savings).[1]

To the extent that this kind of influence is at work it has serious consequences for short-run fiscal stabilization policies. A temporary tax reduction raises household disposable income but households, recognizing this as temporary, might not revise their expenditure plans and might save the money instead. Thus the hoped-for increase in aggregate expenditure would not materialize. Seen from the withdrawal-injection approach, the effect is that the decline in one withdrawal, government taxes, is balanced by an equal increase in another withdrawal, household saving. Overall withdrawals are unchanged and so is national income. Similarly, a temporary rise in taxes reduces disposable income, but it may merely cause a fall in saving. Thus, total expenditure and total withdrawals are again unchanged, and a temporary surcharge fails to reduce the inflationary gap.

> **If households' consumption is more closely related to lifetime rather than to current income then the efficacy of fiscal measures that are known to be of short duration is uncertain.**

According to these theories, if a tax reduction is thought to be temporary, households will use most of it to add to their stock of wealth rather than to engage in a temporary burst of present consumption. There remains, however, the important question of what kind of assets households acquire when they add to their wealth. According to these theories, households save and add to their wealth just as much when they buy consumer durables such as washing machines and TV sets (which are consumed slowly over long periods of time) as when they buy financial assets such as municipal bonds or shares in ICI. But the effect on the economy is very different in each of these cases. If households spend their temporary increase in income on

---

1 These theories are discussed in more detail in Chapter 37. See pages 526–32.

financial assets such as stocks and bonds, this will not add directly to aggregate demand for currently produced goods and services.[1] If, however, households spend their temporary increase in income on consumer durables (which add to their present stock of wealth and are consumed slowly over many years), this does add to aggregate demand for current output. Such spending will tend to raise both the GNP and total employment. What matters for the efficacy of short-term tax changes is whether households allow short-term fluctuations in income to affect their expenditures on current output of either durables (including investment goods such as new housing) or nondurables, or whether such fluctuations affect only their expenditures on financial assets such as stocks and bonds, deposits with savings and loan associations, and purchases of life insurance.

Short-term fiscal policies will have the least effect on the economy if both of the following are true: Households feel that the government-induced changes in their disposable income are transitory, and households allow transitory fluctuations in income to affect the rate at which they are accumulating financial assets rather than the rate at which they are spending to purchase currently-produced output.

Short-term fiscal policies will have a strong effect if either, or both, of the following are true: Households regard the government-induced changes in income as permanent, and households allow their temporary fluctuations in income to affect the rate at which they are prepared to spend on currently-produced output.

TAXES VERSUS GOVERNMENT EXPENDITURE: There is often much debate on whether taxes or expenditures or both should be used to achieve those stabilizing changes that are generally agreed to be desirable. What issues are involved in these debates? What factors affect the choice between changes in G and changes in T?

Location of effects: The multiplier effects of an increase in aggregate demand tend to spread over the whole economy, causing a rising demand for virtually every commodity. If a slump is a general one with widespread unemployment, this will be an advantage. If, however, a slump has severely localized characteristics, with a major depression in a particular industry (such as cars) or area (such as the North), then it may be desirable to achieve a disproportionate effect in the seriously depressed industry or area. In this case, raising expenditure has a distinct advantage over cutting taxes. The tax cut will have its initial impact on the entire economy, but by careful choice of projects, much of the initial effect of extra expenditure can be channelled into the depressed industry or area. Thus if specific impact effects are important, G has some advantages over T.

The size of the deficit and the size of the government sector: We saw in Table 40.2 that different fiscal policies can have the same effect on GNP. Because they act in different ways, they have different side effects on the size of government deficits and the size of the government sector. How do these two side effects compare for the three main fiscal policies for eliminating unemployment? A balanced-budget increase in G and T requires no increase in the deficit, but it does require a larger increase in the

1 There may, however, be an indirect effect if the rate of interest is affected by the increased household demand for financial assets.

volume of government spending than either of the other two policies. The policy of increasing only government expenditure produces a smaller increase in the size of G than does the balanced-budget approach, but it does increase the deficit. A tax cut requires the largest deficit of the three policies, but the extra aggregate demand is found in the private rather than in the government sector; thus, the governmental sector need not expand at all.

Clearly, then, someone who wishes to remove some existing unemployment but dislikes both deficits and the rising importance of the government sector faces a conflict if he uses fiscal policy. To minimize the budget deficit, he should encourage a policy that will bring about a balanced increase in G and T, but this policy will maximize the increase in the size of the government sector. To minimize the increase in the government sector, he should call for a tax cut, but this will maximize the increase in the deficit. Some people fear a strong central government and feel that everything should be done to keep the fraction of the GNP that is accounted for by the government as low as possible. They will favour tax cuts as a method of reducing a deflationary gap, because a tax cut will prevent an increase in the importance of the government as a spending agent. Other people feel that we obtain far fewer publicly produced goods and services than we would choose to have if we could purchase what we wanted on the open market.[1] When there is a deflationary gap in the economy, these people will advocate increases in government spending with or without tax increases, in the hope that some of the decreased expenditure will survive the cutback when the next inflationary gap develops.

Time lags: Generally, any discretionary fiscal policy is subject to two major time lags. First, there is a 'decision lag'. Experts must study the problem and agree among themselves on what is required. They must then persuade the Prime Minister or President to call for the action they endorse. The leader of the government must then temper his advice with what he believes to be politically possible or desirable. Then the legislature must enact the necessary legislation. In the American style of government, but not in the British style, the lags involved in this process can be very long.

Second, once the measure is authorized, there is an 'execution lag'. On the one hand, such lags can be very long for expenditure increases. Once the legislature has passed appropriations for a new road-building programme, for example, it will be some time before substantial income payments are made to private firms and households. Routes must be surveyed; land must be acquired, public protests must often be heard; bids must be called for; and contracts must be let. On the other hand, the execution lag can be very short for tax cuts. Only a matter of weeks after a tax cut is passed, wage earners may find themselves with more take-home pay, since their employers are withholding tax payments at a lower rate than previously.

It is often argued that for reducing year-to-year fluctuations in the economy tax changes are superior to expenditure changes because they have a much shorter execution lag. Both, however, suffer from decision lags in American-style political situations. The experience of the 1960s suggests that, until the US Congress is willing

1 There is for example, some significant evidence to suggest that the proportion of resources devoted to health and education increases faster when these services are provided by the private sector than when they are nationalized.

to pass promptly measures that are part of discretionary fiscal policy, the length of the decision lag for tax changes is likely to make differences in execution lags seem minor in comparison. The decision lag for the Kennedy-Johnson tax cut was over two years. In the UK it is typically very short for once the cabinet agrees on a measure the whips will ensure its passage with a minimum of delay.

FISCAL POLICY IN PRACTICE
Fiscal policy in the past

There exists a widespread misconception that massive fiscal policy was tried in the United States during the 1930s and failed and that the American President, Franklin D. Roosevelt, was wedded to deficit financing. Professor E. Cary Brown, after a careful study, concludes: 'Fiscal policy seems to have been an unsuccessful recovery device in the 'thirties – not because it did not work, but because it was not tried.'[1] The *aggregate* government deficit for the entire decade of the 1930s was about $25 billion. This represents less than half of the deficit for the single year 1942 or 1943, and it was clearly a drop in the bucket considering that GNP fell from $103 billion in 1929 to $56 billion in 1933. In 1933, at the depth of the Depression, the federal government was spending $1·6 billion for purchases of *goods and services*, only slightly more than the $1·4 billion spent in 1929. In 1933, state and local governments were spending an additional $6·5 billion, but were collecting $6·3 billion in taxes.

There was a great American outcry at the time against reckless government spending. But the critics of that day did not understand the countercyclical aspects of public expenditure and public deficits. They did not appreciate that projects so financed would *create* income and employment. Professor Brown concludes that the impact on aggregate demand of public expenditures was about what we would expect today, but that it was too small to do much good. *Expenditures were wastefully small, not wastefully large.* This was largely because President Roosevelt and his advisers were committed to the notion of pump priming. They hoped that a small injection of government funds would generate a flow of new private injections that would eliminate the need for further public stimulus. It didn't work, and today it seems hopelessly naïve to have expected that it would. Indeed, at the same time the government was running its small deficits in an effort to prime the pump, it was enacting sharp rises in the tax structure that would nip off any recovery before it got very far. The tax structure was one of a widening full-employment surplus; the 'soak-the-rich' tax changes introduced by Roosevelt in 1932 virtually doubled full-employment tax yields. When the partial recovery of 1936–7 was barely under way, tax yields increased enough to balance the budget, although 14 per cent of the labour force, 7·7 million people, were still unemployed! In modern terminology the economy was labouring under a crushing fiscal drag.

In Britain the same dismal history of enormous unemployment with government activities that either worsened or, at best, did not alleviate the problem was repeated. Only when the Second World War caused governments to spend, without any worry

1 E. Cary Brown, 'Fiscal Policy in the Thirties: A Reappraisal', *American Economic Review*, December 1956, pp. 865–6.

about revenues, in total contradiction to the then orthodox opinion that budgets should be balanced, did the unemployment finally disappear. Whatever else it did, the Second World War showed for once and for all that governments never again had to accept large scale unemployment as unavoidable. After the War the UK government accepted a responsibility to maintain full employment and, although the level of employment has varied, the worst experience of the post-war period has been better than the best experience of any year between the two World Wars.

Fiscal policy in the present

After 1945 the British government embraced fiscal policy as a means of maintaining full employment. The government's fiscal stance has changed almost every year. This is illustrated for the period since 1960 by the following quotation.[1]

> In the early 1960s the [annual] budgets were mildly expansionary, contractionary and more or less neutral respectively. By contrast the 1963 budget was highly expansionary as it planned for a budget deficit – the first for many years – and a substantial borrowing requirement. By comparison the 1964 budget was contractionary as it anticipated a small surplus as did the budget of 1965, whereas the budget of 1966 planned for a considerably larger surplus than in the previous two years and by intention was thus even more contractionary. The 1967 budget reversed this trend and to that extent was expansionary. . . . The 1968 budget was contractionary in that it planned for a large surplus and the 1969 budget for an even larger one. . . . the 1970 budget was essentially neutral in that it anticipated much the same surplus as for the previous year.
>
> The budgets of the last four years can usefully be looked at as a group. Like its two predecessors the 1971 budget planned for a substantial surplus, though somewhat less than that of the 1970 budget, and a *negative* borrowing requirement, thus envisaging a net repayment of debt. During 1971, as for some years previously the growth of output was sluggish and unemployment began to rise. . . .
>
> It was against this background that the budget of 1972 was designed. It was highly expansionary. It planned for a very small surplus and a borrowing requirement of £2,667m – the equivalent of some 17% of the estimated cost of supply services for that year. It was not until 1973 that the economy showed much evidence of a response to this large fiscal stimulus. . . . the 1973 budget carried the expansionary process even further with an anticipated deficit of almost £1,200m, over twice the realized deficit for 1972–73, and a borrowing requirement of some £3,650m.
>
> As had already been seen output grew rapidly during 1973, as did prices, and unemployment fell. . . . Inevitably the 1974 budget had to try and rectify the position. It planned to turn a provisional deficit for 1972–3 of some £1,700m into a surplus of about £980m and a provisional borrowing requirement of £3,100m into one of around £600m. These are dramatic and large changes in relation to overall budgetary figures. . . .

There has been debate about the advisability of some of these changes and the time lags with which they operated. No one, however, has seriously advocated that they have had no effect on the economy. In the United States, where fiscal policy was not seriously used until the mid-1960s, there is a school of extreme monetarists who argue that fiscal policy has no effect on the economy because the crowding-out effect is 100

1 *The UK Economy: A Manual of Applied Economics*, A.R. Prest and D.J. Coppock, editors, (5th edn., Weidenfeld & Nicolson, 1974).

per cent: every change of $1 in government expenditure causes a change in the opposite direction of $1 in private expenditure. In view of the British experience it is difficult to take this monetarist view seriously, although the question of the net gain-or-loss arising from postwar fiscal policy must still be regarded as open.

Fiscal policy in the future

WHAT IF PEACE BROKE OUT: Many people throughout the world ask themselves what would happen to the economies of the United States and Western Europe if US military adventures abroad were suddenly to cease. Karl Marx predicted that the collapse of capitalist economies would be signalled by a series of larger and larger depressions, and the Great Depression of the 1930s seemed to many observers to be a confirmation of Marx's prediction. When the economies of the United States and other Western countries became persistently buoyant after the Second World War, many Marxists argued that it was military expenditure alone that was bolstering them. They argued that, without such expenditures, collapse would be sure and swift. Karl Marx himself had also predicted that, in order to bolster demand and avoid the inevitable collapse, the leaders of capitalist economies would engage in many expensive foreign adventures. What does our theory predict about the effects of large reductions in American military expenditures?

With an American GNP nearly $1,300 billion, it is perfectly clear that, if defence expenditures fell from $74 billion to, say, $10 billion (the level in 1940 in terms of present prices), there would be problems. The magnitude of the problems would depend on what else happened and on how suddenly the change occurred. If the government maintained its tax rates, reduced its expenditures by $64 billion overnight, and allowed the excess tax receipts to be used to reduce the national debt – a course of action that might commend itself to many US Congressmen – our theory predicts that the result would be a major depression. With a multiplier of 2, the reduction in national income would be in the order of 10 per cent, and unemployment might rise as high as 16 or 17 per cent of the labour force.

Suppose, instead, that the government reduced both taxes and expenditures equally by $64 billion. The theory of the balanced-budget multiplier predicts some adverse impact on the economy. The reduction in national income might be in the order of 2 or 3 per cent, and unemployment might rise to 7 or 8 per cent of the labour force.

These two situations, of course, do not exhaust the possibilities. In a country in which households' desires are unlimited but cannot be fully satisfied because of resource limitations, it is perfectly clear that peacetime government expenditures could be substituted for defence expenditures, dollar for dollar if necessary. Such peacetime programmes could absorb funds as rapidly as do major defence programmes. The level of national income *could* thus be maintained at the same time as the standard of living rose in response to more civilian goods per capita produced by the government.

Another strategy would be to let private spending take over from public spending via tax cuts. In the short run, there is a danger in returning too much money to the private sector, because the capacity to produce civilian goods cannot expand over-night. Factories that build rockets do not convert to making civilian aircraft in a hurry. Could America make a gradual phased reduction in both taxes and expenditures, with governmental deficits as transitional devices where necessary? The long-run evidence about consumption functions and investment opportunities suggests it could. The evidence is that, if consumers' disposable income increased by 10 per cent, the long-run effect would be for expenditure to rise by 10 per cent.

The greatest problems would be transitional. First, there would be problems in adjusting the productive capacity and the distribution of resources, geographically and among uses, to a new set of demands. Given what we know about immobility in the economy, we can predict that there would be surpluses in some skills and short-ages in others, and that the adjustments would take time and would cause heavy frictional problems. The second problem would be the lack of wisdom and lack of speed of policy makers, to say nothing of economic advisers. We know much less about the dynamic properties of our economic system than about its equilibrium properties; yet the short-period adjustments are necessarily dynamic. Without both wisdom and substantial authority to act quickly, many problems would persist. We have had little experience with economies faced with sudden changes of great magnitude in peacetime. Such changes in the pattern of demand have, however, occurred during wars, and the evidence seems to suggest that, as long as the level of aggregate demand is held high, substantial reallocations of resources can occur quite rapidly. Although there would be transitional problems, there is no evidence to suggest that they could not be overcome within a few years.

Peace is, of course, unlikely to break out all at once. A gradual reduction in defence expenditure would create less critical transitional problems. The American economy has often had experience with changes of $10 billion to $20 billion per year, and there seems little doubt that increased public nondefence expenditures combined with tax reductions could accommodate a gradual shrinkage in the size of government spending with gain rather than loss in standards of living.

This discussion suggests that the outbreak of peace poses no insurmountable economic problems. Left to themselves economists now know enough to prevent the fulfilment of the Marxist prediction that peace must be accompanied by massive unemployment. Before we become too optimistic, however, we should recall that economists do not have a particularly good record in persuading policy-makers on the correct course of action, even when there is a strong consensus within the profession. If the American administration and the Congress refused to listen to the advice of economists and cut taxes and expenditures too rapidly, they could produce a depression of really serious proportions. Given the record of fiscal conservatism i.e., the desire to reduce the national debt whatever its macro-economic consequences – of so many American legislators, it must at least be taken as a serious possibility that a rapid outbreak of peace would in fact spell massive unemployment for the US economy and, through foreign-trade effects, for the rest of the world, even though the economists know that this outcome is avoidable.

SECULAR STAGNATION: The problem of how to fill the gap left by the decline in government expenditure if peace breaks out is similar to a long-run problem that occupied a great deal of the attention of economists only a few years ago. This problem arose from the belief that the economy might display a continuous long-term tendency for withdrawals to exceed injections at the full-employment level of national income. To see the force of the argument, assume that, with international payments in balance and a balanced budget, there is a continuous tendency for saving to exceed investment at the full-employment level of national income, so that there is a persistent deflationary gap in the economy. There is nothing logically contradictory in such a situation; all that it requires is that the public should desire to save more than businessmen should wish to invest when the economy is at full employment and that the gap between full-employment saving and full-employment investment cannot be removed by driving down the interest rate to a very low level. This situation could arise, for example, if as real incomes rose over the years, households wished to save an ever-increasing fraction of their income, whereas firms did not wish to make investment expenditure an ever-increasing fraction of national income. If such circumstances were to arise, and if the government insisted on following a balanced-budget policy, then there would be a continual tendency for the economy to settle down in an equilibrium at less than full employment. Of course, occasional spurts of investment might sometimes raise the economy to full employment.

If chronic unemployment did become a serious possibility, what could the government do to avoid it? Our national-income theory provides an answer. If the government departs from its balanced-budget policy and adopts a policy of *continuing budget deficits*, national income can be raised to the full-employment level. In this case, resources will not be lying continuously idle; instead, they will be used to create such public goods as schools, roads, opera houses and universities. Clearly, the policy of continued budget deficits creates a higher level of employment and a higher level of real income than does the balanced-budget policy. Yet the national debt will be increasing year after year. Surely, *this* must matter?

To answer this question, let us consider what the government is doing. It is borrowing that amount of full-employment savings that private businesses will not borrow. The total amount of borrowing is the same as it would have been if full employment had come about because the volume of private investment was higher than the level that is actually achieved. All that has happened is that some of the money saved is being channelled into the public sector. The amount that is being so channelled is the amount that the private sector is unwilling to utilize for its own purposes.

There is no reason why such a situation cannot go on forever. There is no reason why the government cannot perpetually borrow and spend those savings that the private sector will not borrow. Indeed, if the private sector will not borrow all the money that the public wishes to save, the alternative to government budget deficits is that income and employment will shrink and the surplus savings will be removed by the reduction of national income to levels sufficiently below full-employment income that actual savings are reduced to the same level as the investment that the private sector is willing to undertake.

Conditions of a chronic excess of desired private saving over desired private investment have been labelled conditions of SECULAR STAGNATION. There has been a long debate in economics about the possibility of such a situation developing. By and large, current opinion is that there is no evidence that such a situation is imminent. The long-run estimates of the consumption function (see pages 525–6) suggest that one of the main postulates of the hypothesis may be factually incorrect. These estimates suggest that, over the long run, the proportion of national income devoted by households to current consumption and the proportion saved tend to remain fairly constant. Furthermore, there is ample evidence that new investment opportunities develop more or less as fast as old ones are utilized. At least, they have so far.

It is important to note, however, that such a situation *could* arise (i.e., there is nothing logically contradictory in the hypothesis of secular stagnation). If it did arise, and if the government had a balanced-budget policy, this policy would lead to a higher level of unemployment and a lower level of real income than would a policy of continued budget deficits.

SECULAR BOOM: The hypothesis of secular stagnation assumes a persistent deflationary gap in the economy. It is possible to imagine a reverse situation in which, with imports equal to exports and the government's budget balanced, there is a chronic tendency for full-employment savings to be less than full-employment investment. In this case the economy would display chronic boom and inflationary conditions. A remedial fiscal policy now would be to run a long-term budgetary surplus, thereby keeping the inflationary gap small or non-existent so that full employment could be maintained without chronic inflation.

THE COSTS OF GOVERNMENT ACTIVITY

We have seen that fiscal policy may well entail government expenditures in excess of tax receipts. This implies increases in the public debt. In recent decades, increases have far outweighed decreases in most Western countries, so that the trend of the debt has been upward. Does an increasing debt matter? Would an ever-increasing debt lead to an ultimate collapse of the free-enterprise economy? Does the debt represent a burden we are passing on to our heirs? It is to these and related questions that we now turn.

The national debt represents money that the government has borrowed via the sale of its bonds – to households, to firms, and to financial institutions. In this sense the national debt is owed by all of us to some of us. All government debt arises because the government has chosen to finance certain of its expenditures not by taxes but by borrowing. In discussing the significance of the debt, it is important to keep distinct the costs of the *actual government expenditure*, and the costs of the *method of financing* the expenditure. Both are important, but only the second is a 'cost of the debt'.

Before discussing the particular consequences of debt financing, let us note certain benefits and costs of government expenditures that exist no matter how the expenditures are financed. This turns out to have a bearing on the questions of financing.

The benefits and costs of government activity

Governments provide a variety of goods and services. Some are clearly current services such as running hospitals, controlling air lanes, providing police and military protection and supporting universities. Others are clearly capital goods, such as dams, roads and university buildings, that will yield a flow of services to some users over many years. Other governmental services are harder to classify, but they are no less important: expenditures on military equipment, and expenditures primarily designed to prevent unemployment may be providing protection from the onset of a depression. Expenditures on satellite programmes or on foreign aid are beneficial in other senses. We often debate whether or not the benefits of some particular governmental activity justify the costs, but, except in rare cases, there are always some benefits.

We saw in Chapter 4 that the cost of doing something can be measured in terms of the things that might have been done instead. *This opportunity cost in terms of foregone alternatives is incurred whether the money to pay for the project is raised by taxes, by borrowing from the public, or by creating new money.*

The opportunity cost of a particular government expenditure depends on what resources the government project will use and from where they are drawn. In times of heavy unemployment, most of the resources used in government activity might otherwise have remained unemployed. In this case there is no opportunity cost in employing them in the government activity because there is no alternative current production sacrificed by so doing. In contrast, if, in a fully employed economy, the government builds dams, roads, schools and nuclear submarines, the opportunity cost of these are the consumer goods, and the capital goods, that would have been produced instead.

In so far as the resources for the government activity were drawn away from the production of consumer goods and services, the opportunity cost is necessarily borne by the present generation in terms of a reduced consumption of goods produced by the private sector of the economy. In so far as the resources are drawn away from the production of capital goods, the opportunity cost will be spread out over the future, because the current generation is giving up, not consumption, but capital goods. This leads to a smaller stock of capital, and to a lower capacity to produce consumption goods in the future than there would have been had the government activity not taken place.

The difference between these capital-good and current-consumption opportunity costs requires further study. In the case in which all the resources for government expenditure are drawn from production of consumption commodities, the sacrifice of consumers could cease the minute the government stopped using these resources, and thus the opportunity cost is all borne by the current generation. However, if the resources used by the government had been drawn entirely from the production of capital goods, once the government activity ceased the production of capital goods could be resumed. In the interim, however, a large supply of capital goods will have gone unproduced, and the consequences of this will be felt in the future. The stock of capital will for a long time be smaller than it would have been had the government activity not occurred. Because it is the stock of capital that provides the means of producing consumption goods, it follows that the output of such goods will be less than it otherwise would have been for as long as the stock of capital (*not* the current output of capital goods) is smaller than it would otherwise have been. Thus, the opportunity cost in terms of a reduced output of goods for current consumption will be spread over a long period of time after the government activity ceases.

The effects of alternative means of financing government activities

There are essentially three different ways in which a government can finance an expenditure: (1) it can raise the money by increasing taxes, thus transferring purchasing power from taxpayers to itself; (2) it can borrow the money from willing lenders, thus transferring current purchasing power from them to itself in return for the promise of future purchasing power; (3) it can (actually or in effect) print enough money to permit itself to bid the resources it needs away from other potential users.

The primary effect of the method of financing concerns who in the community bears the cost of foregone production. In other words, it is concerned with the question of how the cost is distributed among people. This can, as we shall see, have some effect on the division between current production and capital production foregone, and the method of financing can also create some additional costs to society. But the major effect of the method of financing government expenditures is on *who* bears the costs, not on how much they are.

Suppose the economy is at a full-employment level, so that the government must incur real opportunity costs in order to produce its goods. If the cost of a new government programme is met by increases in taxes, then the current taxpayers bear the cost by having their purchasing power reduced. Their purchases of goods and services will be decreased, and resources will be transferred to the production of the government goods.

If the government expenditure is financed by borrowing from households and firms, the reduction in purchasing power for current consumption is suffered by those who lend their money to the government instead of spending it on currently produced goods and services. People who do not buy government bonds do not postpone current consumption and thus do not bear any of the real current cost of the government activity.

The third possibility is that the activity is financed by creating new money. (As we shall see later, the way this is done in the modern world is for the government to sell bonds to the central bank. In return, the central bank credits the government with a deposit on which the government can draw cheques to pay for its purchases.) Because the economy is already in a state of full employment, this method of finance must create an inflationary gap and thus cause a rise in the price level. Aggregate demand, already high enough to purchase all the output the economy is producing, becomes excessive as the government enters the market with its own new demand. The rise in prices will mean that households and firms with fixed budgets will be able to buy less than they would otherwise have bought, and the government will be able to obtain resources for its own activities. Thus fewer resources will be available for private consumption and private capital formation. The result in the aggregate is the same as if the government had reduced private expenditure by taxation.

As far as distributing the opportunity cost is concerned, inflationary finance is similar to financing by taxes, although the identity of the groups forced to cut back on their own purchases is likely to be different in the two cases. By choosing which taxes to increase, the government using tax finance can exert a considerable influence on the distribution of the burden (although we must never forget that taxes may be shifted from the groups on which they are levied to other groups in surprising ways – see pages 122–7). Under inflationary finance, the government bids up prices and leaves it to the market to determine those groups that are to reduce their consumption and thus to pay the current cost. Retired persons and others on fixed incomes will bear much of the cost. Those whose incomes respond only slowly to changes in price levels will bear more of the cost than those whose incomes rise nearly as fast as prices. Some, indeed, will not pay any of the cost. Inflationary finance is usually regarded as a less just method of taxation than income and corporate taxes, because it places much of the burden on the economically weak, the unfortunate, and the uneducated, and taxes least those able to adjust to rising prices, who are often the richest and most powerful groups.

Now consider what happens once the government project is finished. To the extent that it was financed by current taxes (or by inflationary creation of new money) the matter is finished once the government expenditure has been made. Resources can then be transferred back to the production of goods and services, and households' disposable income can be allowed to rise by reducing taxes. But to the extent that the government activity was financed by borrowing from the private sector, the debt remains after the activity has been completed. It is necessary to pay interest each year to the bondholders and eventually to repay the bonds as they reach maturity. To the extent that interest payments and eventual redemption of the bonds are made from tax revenue, taxpayers now suffer a reduction in their consumption below what it would otherwise have been. The transfer is thus reversed. In return for bearing the original reduction in consumption, bondholders (or their heirs) now enjoy a rise in consumption, and taxpayers who are not bondholders suffer a reduction. For a community, the cost in terms of foregone output was borne during the original activity. Once the activity is finished, total production goes back to normal. The opportunity cost could not be postponed, but individuals who did not buy bonds must now pay for their share of the cost of the activity by transferring some claims on current production to other individuals.

Are there real burdens resulting from the method of finance?

We have seen that the current cost of government expenditure is the current production foregone, and that the method of finance can influence the distribution of the cost within the society.

It is easy to see that the method of finance can also affect the extent to which current generations can shift this real cost to future generations. If, for example, new taxes are placed on consumption goods, most of the reduction in private production may be expected to be on consumer goods. If, however, funds for the government activity are raised by a special tax on all business investment, it is likely that the production of capital goods rather than of consumption goods will be reduced.

Is there a systematic difference between tax revenues and sales of bonds in this respect? This is a matter of substantial debate. Some economists believe that the existence of government bonds, by making households feel wealthier than they otherwise would, may make them consume more and save less. This in turn may reduce private capital formation and thus transfer much of the cost of government activity to the future via the reduction in capital stock.

It is possible that the method of finance can impose burdens on the community in addition to the opportunity costs already discussed. These additional burdens are those associated with the existence of a large national debt held within the private sector of the economy. The bonds will continue to exist after the activity is finished, and interest will have to be paid to those households, firms, and financial institutions that hold them. Extra money must be raised in taxes and paid out to bondholders. This is a transfer payment that does not of itself represent a net burden to the society. There is a burden involved, however, because resources, in terms of tax collectors and inspectors and accountants and clerks, will be used to raise taxes and pay bondholders. These resources could otherwise have been employed to make goods and services for current consumption. Such real costs are but a tiny fraction of the interest payments on the national debt. Since these interest payments are themselves only a small fraction of national income, the real collection and disbursement costs are minute.

Is there any economic limit to the size of the debt?

There has been a general trend for national debts to rise in most Western countries and we must wonder if it matters. Are most countries approaching a limit beyond which undesirable or even disastrous consequences will ensue? Let us consider this question in more detail.

To the extent that the money raised by borrowing is spent on items that add to national income, the borrowing creates the extra income out of which extra taxes can be raised to pay the interest. To the extent that the money is spent on items that do not add to our national income, it will be necessary to increase existing taxes in order to provide funds to meet the interest payments. Up to a point, this will not cause any serious problems, since the process of paying interest on the debt involves only a transfer from some citizens (taxpayers) to other citizens (holders of government bonds). That there is a limit beyond which it is not safe to go can be seen by the following example. Suppose the government borrows a sum equal to 5 per cent of the national income each year in order to enhance the beauty of the countryside, and suppose that national income is growing at 2·5 per cent per year. If this policy went on forever, and if no old debt were ever paid off, then eventually the national debt would become so large that current interest payments would exceed current national income. In order to raise enough money to meet its interest bill, the government would have to tax all incomes at a rate exceeding 100 per cent!

Clearly, then, there is a grain of truth in the worry over the size of the interest payments on the national debt. But this worry applies only to those expenditures that do not themselves help to create the extra income out of which interest payments can be met. And the worry becomes significant only if such non-income-creating debt is increasing *very much faster* than the national income. Such a situation existed in most Western countries during the crisis periods of the First and Second World Wars. Both of these periods were, by historical standards, very short. At no other time have we remotely approached a situation in which this class of debt was increasing at a rate anything like the rate at which national income was increasing.

A very good measure of whether the size of the debt is approaching dangerous levels is the willingness of borrowers to take government bonds at various rates of interest. Well before a government reached an absolute debt limit (in terms of its ability to raise the money to pay the interest on its bonds), experienced investors would lose confidence in it. The price of bonds would fall, and interest rates would rise as borrowers demanded a premium for risk. The fact that government bonds in virtually all Western industrial countries are regarded as the least risky sort of investment available provides compelling evidence that the financial community is not concerned about the size of the debt.[1]

1 Lack of confidence in the government's ability to pay interest on the debt and to repay the principal on time should not be confused with an unwillingness to take up new debt at too low a money rate of interest in the face of inflationary expectations. Few investors would be willing, for example, to buy new government bonds yielding an 8 per cent nominal interest rate if they expected a 16 per cent annual rate of inflation.

Part eight

The importance of money in the circular flow

41

The nature and history of money

Up to this point it has been assumed that there is sufficient money to finance any desired level of expenditure. But is there? How are money and credit created, and what effects do they have on the circular flow of income? A considerable portion of both consumption and investment expenditure is made with borrowed money, and the availability and terms of credit may have an influence on both of these expenditure flows.

In this chapter we describe the functions of money and give a brief outline of its history. There is probably more folklore and general nonsense believed about money than about any other aspect of the economy. The purpose of this very stylized bit of history is to remove some of these misconceptions.

WHAT IS MONEY?

We use the term MONEY to refer to any generally accepted medium of exchange – to anything, that is, that will be accepted by virtually everyone in exchange for goods and services. It is customary to distinguish between money's several different functions. The reason for doing this is that different kinds of money vary in the degree of efficiency with which they fulfill each of these functions. The major functions of money are to act as a *medium of exchange,* as a *store of wealth* and as a *unit of account.*

A medium of exchange

An important function of money is to facilitate exchange. Without money, our complicated economic system, which is based on specialization and the division of labour, would be impossible, and we would have to return to a very primitive form of production and exchange. It is not without justification that money has been called one of the great inventions contributing to human freedom.

If there were no money, goods would have to be exchanged by *barter,* one good being swapped directly for another. This system is a cumbersome one in which every transaction requires a *double coincidence of wants.* If I have a donkey to trade, for example,

587

I must search not only for a man who wants a donkey, but also for one who has something that I would like to acquire. Furthermore, there is no way to give change on the transaction. If I find someone who wants my donkey, we must agree on a swap rate. If we decide that a donkey is worth nine chickens, then we are in trouble if my trading partner has only six chickens: I can hardly give him two thirds of my donkey. Thus, goods that are not readily divisible make poor subjects for barter transactions. If we were restricted to barter, we would have to spend a great deal of time searching for satisfactory transactions; we would be unable to specialize in producing some single commodity, for we could not be certain that we could obtain, when we wanted them, all the other goods that we required.

The use of money as a medium of exchange removes these problems, as long as money is readily accepted by everyone. If I wish to trade my donkey, then all I need to do is to find someone who wants a donkey. I then hand over my animal and take money in return; it matters not that the individual who takes my donkey has no goods that I require. I now take my money and search for someone who has chickens that he wishes to trade. When I find him, I hand over my money and take his chickens; it does not matter that my provider of chickens has no use for a donkey. The difficulties of barter force people to become more or less self-sufficient; with money as a medium of exchange, everyone is free to specialize and, with specialization in the direction of one's natural talents and abilities, there comes a great increase in the production of all commodities.

If money is to serve as an efficient medium of exchange, it must have a number of characteristics: it must be readily acceptable; it must have a high value for its weight (otherwise it would be a nuisance to carry around); it must be divisible, for money that comes only in large denominations is useless for transactions having only a small value; and it must not be readily counterfeitable, for if money can be easily duplicated by individuals it will lose its value. [1]

A store of wealth

Money is a handy way to store wealth; with barter, one must take some other good in exchange. With money, you can sell goods today and store the money until you need it. This means that you have a claim on someone else's goods that you can exercise at some future date. The two sides of the barter transaction can be separated in time with the obvious increase in freedom that this confers. To be a satisfactory store of wealth, money must have a stable value. If prices are stable, then one knows exactly how much command over real goods and services has been stored up when a certain sum of money has been accumulated. If prices change rapidly, then one has little idea how many goods one will be able to command when previously accumulated money is spent. Clearly, rapid fluctuations in the general level of prices reduce the usefulness of money as a store of wealth.

Money can serve as a perfectly satisfactory store of accumulated wealth for a single individual, but not for the society as a whole. If a single individual stores up money,

---

1 This last point should be reconsidered after you have studied Chapter 43. In the meantime, you should understand why it does not matter if the money can be counterfeited at very high cost.

he will, when he comes to spend it, be able to command the current output of some other individual. The whole society cannot do this. If all individuals saved their money and all simultaneously retired to live on their savings, there would be no current production to purchase and consume. The society's ability to satisfy wants depends on goods and services being available; if some of this want-satisfying capacity is to be stored up for the *whole society*, then goods that are currently produced must be left unconsumed and carried over to future periods.

A unit of account

Money may also be used purely for accounting purposes without having any real physical existence of its own. For instance, a government store in a truly communist society might say that everyone had so many 'dollars' at his disposal each month. Goods could then be given prices and each consumer's purchases recorded, the consumer being allowed to buy all he wanted until his supply of dollars was exhausted. This money would have no existence other than as entries in the store's books, but it would be serving as a perfectly satisfactory unit of account (although it could serve as a medium of exchange between individuals only if the store agreed to transfer credits from one customer to another at the customers' request).[1]

THE ORIGINS AND GROWTH OF METALLIC MONEY

The origins of money are lost in antiquity; most primitive tribes known today make some use of it. The ability of money to free people from the cumbersome <u>necessity of barter</u> must have led to its early use as soon as some generally accepted commodity appeared. <u>All sorts of commodities</u> have been used as money at one time or another, but precious metals must have asserted their ascendancy early as the most satisfactory ones. They were in heavy and permanent demand for ornament and decoration, and they were in continuous supply (since they do not easily wear out). Thus they tended to have a high and stable price. They were easily recognized and generally known to be commodities which, because of their stable price, would be accepted by most people. They were also divisible into extremely small units (gold, to a single grain).

Precious metals thus came to circulate as money and to be used in many transactions. Before the invention of coins, it was necessary to carry precious metals about in bulk. When a purchase was to be made, the requisite quantity of the metal would have to be weighed out carefully on a scale. A sack of gold and a highly sensitive set of scales were thus the common equipment of the merchant and trader.

Such a system, although better than barter, was still rather cumbersome. Coins eliminated the necessity of weighing the metal at each transaction. The prince or ruler had the metal weighed and made into coins to which an imprint of his own seal was affixed, guaranteeing the weight of precious metal in the coin. Thus a certain coin was stated to contain exactly $\frac{1}{16}$ of an ounce of gold. If a commodity was priced

---

1 A fourth function is sometimes distinguished: that of a standard of deferred payments. Payments that are to be made in the future, on account of debts, etc., are reckoned in money. Money is being used as a unit of account with an added dimension in time, for the account is not settled until the future.

at $\frac{1}{8}$ of an ounce of gold, two coins could be given over without any need of weighing the gold. This is clearly a great convenience, as long as traders know that they can accept the coin at its 'face value'.

The prince's subjects, however, could not let a good thing pass, and someone had the idea of clipping a thin slice off the edge of the coin. If he collected a coin stamped as containing $\frac{1}{2}$ of an ounce of gold, he could clip a slice off the edge and pass the coin off as still weighing $\frac{1}{2}$ of an ounce. ('Doesn't the stamp prove it?', he would argue.) If he were successful, he would have made a profit equal to the market value of the clipped metal. If this practice became common, even the most myopic of traders would notice that things were not quite what they used to be in the coinage world. Mistrust would grow, and it would be necessary to weigh each coin before accepting it at its 'face value'; back would come the scales and most of the usefulness of the coins would be lost. To get around this problem, the princes began to mint their coins with a rough edge. The absence of the rough edge would immediately be apparent and would indicate that the coin had been clipped. This practice still survives today as an interesting anachronism to remind us that there were days when the market value of the metal in the coin (if it were melted down) was equal to the face value of the coin. The coin itself was nothing more than a guarantee that a certain weight of metal, the value of which did not depend on its being stamped into coins, was contained therein. The subjects, when presented with an opportunity of getting something for nothing, were ingenious enough to surmount even the obstacle of the rough edge: they invented the practice of *sweating*. Sweating involved placing a large number of coins in a bag and shaking the bag vigorously. The dust that flaked off the coins was their reward. This practice seems never to have been as disruptive to the money system as that of clipping, possibly because it was difficult to remove very much metal without defacing the coin, but possibly also because the disruptive effects were eclipsed by the upset caused by the princes' periodic debasements of the coinage.

Not to be outdone by the cunning of his subjects, the prince was himself quick to seize the chance of getting something for nothing. Since the prince was empowered to mint the coins, he was in a very good position to work a *really* profitable fraud. When he found himself with bills that he could not pay and that it was inexpedient to repudiate, he used a suitable occasion – a marriage, an anniversary, an alliance – as an excuse to remint the coinage. The subjects would bring their coins to the mint, where they would be melted down and coined afresh with a new stamp. The subject could then go away the proud possessor of one new coin for every one old coin that he had brought in. Between the melting down and the recoining, however, the prince had only to toss some inexpensive base metal into the works to earn himself a handsome profit. If the coinage was debased by adding, say, one part base metal to every four parts of the melted-down metal, then five coins would be made for every four turned in. Thus, for every four coins brought in, the prince could return four and have one left over for himself as profit. With these coins, he could pay his bills.

The result would be an inflation. The subjects would have the same number of coins as before and hence could demand the same number of goods. Once the prince paid his bills, however, the recipients of the extra coins could be expected to spend some or all of them, and this would represent a net increase in demand. The extra demand would bid up prices. Debasing of coinage thus led pretty certainly to a rise in prices. After observing this process in action, early economists propounded the *quantity theory of money*. They argued that there was a relation between the average level of prices and the quantity of money in circulation, such that a change in the quantity of money would lead to a change in the price level in the same direction. We shall have more to say about this theory in Chapter 43.

THE EVOLUTION OF PAPER MONEY

Another important step in the history of money was the evolution of paper currency. Goldsmiths – craftsmen who worked with gold – naturally kept very secure safes in which to store their gold.[1] The practice grew up among the public of storing their gold with the goldsmith for safe-keeping. In return, the goldsmith would give the depositor a receipt promising to hand over the gold on demand. If the depositor wished to make a large purchase, he could go to the goldsmith, reclaim his gold, and hand it over to the seller of the goods. Chances were that the seller would not require the gold, but would carry it back to the goldsmith for safe-keeping. Clearly, if people knew the goldsmith to be reliable, there was no need to go through the cumbersome and risky business of physically transferring the gold. The buyer need only transfer the goldsmith's receipt to the seller, who could accept it secure in the knowledge that the goldsmith would pay over the gold whenever it was needed. If the seller wished to buy a good from a third party who also knew the goldsmith to be reliable, this transaction too could be effected by passing the goldsmith's receipt from the buyer to the seller. The convenience of using these bits of paper instead of gold is obvious. Thus, when paper money first grew up it represented a promise to pay on demand so much gold, the promise being made first by goldsmiths and later by banks; as long as these institutions were known to be reliable, such pieces of paper would be 'as good as gold'. Such paper money was *backed* by precious metal and was *convertible* on demand into this metal.

In the nineteenth century, paper money was commonly issued by banks; in Britain, the commercial banks issued their own notes backed by their own reserves. Also, the Bank of England issued notes backed by the country's gold reserves, for, although it was nominally a private institution until 1947, the Bank always had close links with the government. Since these notes were convertible on demand into gold, the country was said to be on a *gold standard*.

Fractionally backed paper money

For most transactions, individuals were content to use paper currency; it was soon discovered, therefore, that it was not necessary to keep an ounce of gold in the vaults for every claim to an ounce circulating as paper money. It *was* necessary to keep some gold on hand, because, for some transactions, paper would not do. If an individual wished to make a purchase from a distant place where his local bank was

---

1 All the basic ideas about paper money can be displayed by concentrating on the goldsmiths, although there were earlier sources of paper money in various negotiable evidences of debt.

not known, he might have to convert his paper into gold and ship the gold. Further, if he was going to save up money for use in the distant future, he might not have perfect confidence in the bank's ability to honour its pledge to redeem the notes in gold at that time. His alternative was to exchange his notes for gold and store the gold until he needed it. For these and other reasons at any one point in time, some holders of notes would be demanding gold in return for their notes. On the other hand, some of the bank's customers would be receiving gold in various transactions and would be wanting to store this gold in the bank for safe-keeping. They would accept promises to pay (i.e., bank notes) in return. At any one time, therefore, some of the bank's customers would be withdrawing gold, others would be depositing it, and the great majority would be carrying out their transactions using the bank's paper notes without any need or desire to convert them into gold. Thus the bank would be able to issue more money redeemable in gold than it actually had gold in its vaults. This is a profitable thing to do, because the money can be used either to purchase securities that yield a return, or to make interest-earning loans to households and firms.

This discovery was made early on by the goldsmiths; from that time down to the present day, banks have had many more claims to pay cash outstanding against them than they actually had gold available. In such a situation, we say that the currency is *fractionally backed* by gold. A rough rule of thumb is that a 10 per cent backing for these claims is more than sufficient: if a bank holds £10,000 worth of gold and has issued £100,000 in notes, it would be perfectly safe in normal times and would be able to convert into gold all of its notes that were presented for conversion.

The major problem of a fractionally backed currency is that of maintaining its *convertibility* into the precious metal with which it is backed. In the past, the imprudent bank that issued too much paper money found itself unable to redeem its currency in gold when the demand for gold was even slightly higher than usual. This bank would then have to suspend payments, and all holders of its notes would suddenly find them worthless. The prudent bank, which kept a reasonable relation between its note issue and its gold reserve, found that it could meet the normal everyday demand for gold without any trouble. It was always the case with fractionally backed currency, however, that, if all note-holders demanded gold at once, they could not be satisfied. Thus, if ever the public lost confidence and en masse demanded redemption of their currency, the banks would be unable to honour their pledges, and the holders of their notes would lose everything. The history of nineteenth- and early twentieth-century banking on both sides of the Atlantic is replete with examples of banks ruined by momentary runs on their cash and gold reserves. When this happened, the bank's depositors and the holders of its notes would find themselves holding worthless pieces of paper. Future social historians may wonder how it was possible, in the face of such a system, that early economists could have believed that free-market capitalism provided evidence that the hidden hand of perfection was guiding the economic affairs of mankind.

Central banks

The central bank was itself a natural outcome of the whole system. Where were the private banks to keep their cash reserves? Their own vaults, although safer than those of their customers, were not safe against a really determined attempt at robbery. Where were the commercial banks to turn if they had good investments, but were in temporary need of cash? If they provided loans for the public against reasonable security why should not some other institution provide loans to them against the same sort of security? CENTRAL BANKS evolved in response to these and other needs. At first they were private profit-making institutions, providing services to ordinary banks, but their potential to influence the behaviour of commercial banks and through them that of the whole economy led them to develop close ties with central governments. In Europe, these ties eventually became formalized as central banks were taken over by governments. The Bank of England was nationalized in 1947.

The development of fiat currencies

As time went on, note issue by commercial banks became less common, and central banks took over a steadily increasing share of this responsibility. The paper currency was, as it always had been, freely convertible into gold. It was also only fractionally backed by gold. The commercial banks retained the power to create money, but this was no longer done by printing paper money; instead, deposit money was created.

During the period between the two World Wars, virtually all the countries of the world abandoned the gold standard. The reasons for this cannot be gone into in detail here. (They will be mentioned briefly in Chapter 47.) The result of abandoning the gold standard was that currency was no longer convertible into gold.

Some countries (including the United States, until 1965) preserve the fiction that their currency is backed by gold, but none allows it to be converted into gold as a right. The past is recalled by the following statement on the British pound note, 'I promise to pay the bearer on demand the sum of One Pound [signed] Chief Cashier, Bank of England'. (A similar statement appears on the currency of most countries.) If anyone takes this seriously today and demands his 'One Pound', he can hand over his one pound note and receive in return a new one pound note! In the days of the gold standard, paper money was valuable because everyone knew it could be converted into gold on demand.[1] Today, paper money is valuable because it is generally accepted. Because, by habit, everyone accepts it as valuable, it *is* valuable; the fact that it can no longer be converted into anything has no effect on its functioning as a medium of exchange.

This fact, that present-day paper money is not convertible into anything – that it is nothing but bits of paper whose value derives from common acceptance through habit – often disturbs the student. He feels his money should be more substantial than that; after all, what of 'dollar diplomacy' and the 'prestige of the pound'? Well, his money is only bits of paper. There is no point in pretending otherwise.

Once it is accepted that modern money is only bits of paper, the next question that comes to mind is: does it matter? Gold derived its value because it was scarce

1 Originally, the gold had a market value independent of its use as money. Later, however, as large stocks of gold accumulated, gold itself came to have value *because* it was a generally acceptable medium of exchange. There is little doubt that, if at any time in the last few centuries gold had ceased to have value as money (because, say, some superior metal was discovered), the market value of the world's stocks of gold would have fallen very greatly, since the demand for gold for use as a commodity would have been very low in relation to the supply of it.

relative to the heavy demand for it (the demand being derived from its monetary and its nonmonetary uses). Tying a currency to gold meant that the quantity of money in a country was left to such chance occurrences as the discovery of new gold supplies. This was not without advantage, the most important being that it provided a check on the prince's ability to cause inflation. Gold cannot be manufactured at will; paper currency can. There is little doubt that, if the money supply was purely paper, many governments would have succumbed to the temptation to pay their bills by printing new money rather than by raising taxes. Such increases in the money supply would lead to inflation in just the same way as did the debasement of metallic currency. Thus, the gold standard provided some check on inflation by making it difficult for the government to change the money supply. Periods of major gold discoveries, however, brought about inflations of their own. In the sixteenth century, Spanish gold and silver flowed into Europe from the New World, bringing inflation in its wake. On the other hand, it is usually desirable to increase the money supply in a period of rising trade and income. On a gold standard, this cannot be done – unless, by pure chance, gold is discovered at the same time. The gold standard took discretionary powers about the money supply out of the hands of the central authorities. Whether or not one thought that this was a good thing depended on how one thought the central authorities would use this discretion. In general, a gold standard is probably better than having the currency managed by an ignorant or irresponsible government, but worse than having the currency supply adjusted by a well-informed intelligent one. Better and worse in this context are judged by the criterion of having a money supply that varies adequately with the needs of the economy, but that does not vary so as to cause violent inflations or deflations.

DEPOSIT MONEY

In most countries today, the money supply consists of notes and coins issued by the government and the central bank, and DEPOSIT MONEY. Notes and coins (the market value of the metal in the coin is usually a minute fraction of the face value of the coin) are the inconvertible moneys that we have already discussed. Deposit money is *created by the commercial banking system*. We have already explained how bank notes promising to pay gold on demand circulated as money and how, because most people did not require the actual gold, the banks were able to create money by printing and putting into circulation many more notes than they could redeem in gold at any one time. *When the banks lost the right to issue notes of their own, the form of money creation changed but the substance did not.* Today, banks have money in their vaults (or on deposit with the central banks) just as they always did, only the money is no longer gold; it is the legal tender of the times, paper money. Banks' customers sometimes deposit paper money with the banks for safe-keeping just as, in former times, they deposited gold. The bank takes the money and gives the customer a promise to pay it back on demand. Instead of taking the form of a printed bank note, as in the past, this promise to pay is recorded as an entry on the customer's account. If the customer wishes to pay a bill, he may come to the bank and claim his money in pound notes; he may then pay the money over to another person, and this person may redeposit the money in a bank. Just as with the gold transfers, this is a cumbersome procedure, particularly for large payments, and it would be much more convenient if the bank's promise to pay cash could merely be transferred from one person to another. This is done by means of a *cheque*. If individual A deposits £100 in a bank, the entry, a £100 credit in his account, is the bank's promise to pay £100 cash on demand. If A pays B £100 by giving him a cheque that B then deposits in the same bank, the bank merely reduces A's deposit by £100 and increases B's by the same amount. Thus the bank still promises to pay out on demand the £100 originally deposited, but it now promises to pay it to B rather than to A. If B now pays C £100 by cheque and C deposits the cheque, then the promise to pay (i.e., the credit entry in someone's account at the bank) will be transferred from B to C.

The modern deposit is the equivalent of the old bank note: a promise on the bank's behalf to pay out on demand the money of the time. The passing of the bank's note from hand to hand transferred ownership of the claim against the bank; this is now done by means of a cheque, which is merely an order to the bank telling it to transfer from one individual to another its obligation to pay cash. It is true today, just as it was in the past, that most of the bank's customers are content to pay their bills by passing among themselves the bank's promises to pay cash; only a small proportion of the bank's customers want cash at any one time. Thus, just as in the past, the bank can create money by issuing more promises to pay than it actually has cash to pay out. The bank can grant a loan by giving the customer a credit on his account equal to the amount of the loan. If the borrower uses the loan to pay bills by cheque, then the deposit is transferred from person to person. In most circumstances, the bank can have liabilities greatly in excess of the amount of cash that it has in reserve. These deposits can be used to buy goods and services through the medium of cheques. Since they are a generally accepted means of exchange, they are money. The great proportion of transactions (by value) take place by cheque and only a small proportion by notes and coin. Thus, in the modern world, the greater proportion of the money supply is the deposit money that is created by commercial banks. The banks can, if they wish, contract the money supply by not creating deposits, or they can expand it by creating deposits up to the limit of prudence or law (so that there is just enough cash to meet the normal demands of customers who do not wish to pay by cheque). It is, of course, in the bank's interest to expand the supply up to the safety limit because every pound created can be used to grant a loan, to purchase a bond, or to acquire some other asset that pays a return to the bank.

Demand deposits and time deposits

If a customer has a deposit in a bank, he can keep it in one of two forms: in a demand deposit (current account) or a time deposit (deposit account). The distinction between these two types of deposit is commonly made throughout much of the world, although the terms applied to them vary.

The two main characteristics of a DEMAND DEPOSIT are that the owner can withdraw his money on demand, and that the bank agrees to transfer demand deposits from one person to another when ordered to do so by the writing of a cheque. The first characteristic makes the demand deposit as satisfactory a store of value as is currency, since the holder of a demand deposit can withdraw cash from his account without having to give any prior notice. The second characteristic helps to make the demand deposit a medium of exchange. The holder of a demand deposit may make a payment by writing a cheque on his account. The cheque instructs the writer's bank to pay without delay a stated sum to the person in whose favour the cheque is drawn.

Time deposits differ in both of these essential features. The owner of a time deposit must legally give notice (possibly 30 or 60 days) of his intention to withdraw his money. Although banks often do not enforce this law, they could at any time do so if they wished. Furthermore, the holder of a deposit account cannot pay his bills by writing a cheque ordering his bank to pay someone out of his deposit. Banks always pay a higher rate of interest to customers who have deposited money with them on time rather than demand. (Demand deposits frequently, although not invariably, carry a zero interest rate.)

AN OPERATIONAL DEFINITION OF MONEY

Earlier in this chapter we defined money as any generally accepted means of payment. We must now make this definition operational by saying what will be included and what excluded when we reckon the money supply of a country. Clearly, notes and coins are part of the money supply. Current account deposits also fit quite well into our definition. You can pay for most things by cheque, although cheques are not quite so generally acceptable as notes and coins. You may have trouble, for example, buying a packet of cigarettes in a small country store if you offer a cheque in exchange; you will almost certainly have trouble should you try to walk out of a fur store with a £2,000 mink coat if you have offered a cheque in payment and you are not known by the store manager. You will not have much trouble if you offer pound notes in either case. Since demand deposits are a means of exchange and since cheques are widely (if not quite universally) acceptable, we regard demand deposits as part of the money supply. When we ask if we should include anything else as money we immediately encounter the cases of what are called near monies and money substitutes.

Near money and money substitutes

It is generally agreed that over the past two centuries what has been accepted by the public as money has expanded from gold and silver coins to include, first, bank notes and, then, bank deposits subject to transfer by cheque. Until recently, most economists would have agreed that money stopped at that point. No such agreement exists today, and an important debate centres around the definition of money appropriate to the present world.

The two most important functions of money are, first, to act as a medium of exchange and, second, to be a temporary store of value to bridge the gap between receiving and making payments. The problem of deciding what is money stems from the fact that anything that can fulfil the first function can also fulfil the second one, but many things that can fulfil the second do not fulfil the first.

To see what is involved, consider an example. If A has a donkey and wants some chickens, A wants, in effect, to barter the former for the latter. In a monetary society, however, *A* sells his donkey and accepts money, which he may keep until he finds the chickens that he requires. As long as all sales and purchases do not occur at the same moment, everyone needs such a temporary store of value between the act of selling and the act of buying. Whatever serves the function of a medium of exchange can be held and thus can also serve the function of a temporary store of value.

NEAR MONEY: Other assets can also be used for this store-of-value function. If there is another asset in the economy – for instance, time deposits – that is not a medium of exchange, but does have a completely secure capital value, and on which interest can be earned, it may well pay *A* to use this asset as his temporary store of value. Thus *A* accepts pound notes when he sells his donkey for £100, but he does not hold this money. Rather, *A* deposits it in his savings account and earns interest on it, secure in the knowledge that when he finds the chickens he desires he has £100 available. Whether *A* does this or holds the money, depends on the transaction costs (which includes inconvenience) of turning his money into a safe, interest-earning asset and then back into money again, and on the interest that he can earn over the short time that he is holding the purchasing power.

If we concentrate only on the medium-of-exchange function of money, there is little doubt about what is money today. Money consists of notes and coins and demand deposits; no other asset constitutes a generally-accepted medium of exchange. Indeed, even notes and cheques are not universally accepted as you will discover if you try to buy a pack of cigarettes with a very large denomination note, or if you try to walk out of a store on Saturday afternoon with a mink coat having offered your personal cheque in exchange. But these exceptions are unimportant.

Problems arise with the temporary-store-of-value function. Time deposits are perfectly satisfactory for this. If you have a time deposit at a bank you know exactly how much purchasing power you hold (at today's prices) and, given modern banking practices, you can turn your deposit into a medium of exchange – cash or a chequing deposit at a moment's notice. Additionally, your time deposit will earn you some interest during the period that you hold it. Neither currency nor the typical demand deposit will do so. Thus, time deposits fulfil, at least as well as the things traditionally regarded as money, the function of a temporary abode of purchasing power. Time deposits with non-bank financial institutions such as building societies are similar to time deposits with banks except that the requirement that notice be given before a withdrawal is much more likely to be enforced.

Even this is not the end of the story. There is a whole spectrum of assets in the economy that yield an interest return and also serve as reasonably satisfactory temporary stores of value. The difference between these other assets and savings deposits is that their capital values are not quite as certain as are those of savings deposits. If I elect to store my purchasing power in the form of a government bond that matures in 30 days, its price on the market may change between the time I buy it and the time I want to sell it – say 10 days later. If the price changes, I will suffer or enjoy a change in the purchasing power available to me. But because of the short horizon to maturity, the price will not change very much. (After all, the government will pay its face value in a few weeks.) Such a security is, thus, a reasonably satisfactory short-run store of purchasing power. Indeed, any readily saleable capital asset whose value does not fluctuate significantly will satisfactorily fulfil this short-term, store-of-value function. If it also earns an interest rate, it will have an actual advantage over any medium of exchange on which interest cannot be earned, provided that the purchasing power is to be held long enough for the interest to exceed the transaction costs (commissions, etc.) of buying and selling the security, plus an evaluation of the time and trouble involved.

Whether time deposits and short-run government securities are to be regarded as money is still a matter of debate and may depend partly on the problem being studied. Two things are, however, clear: (1) there is a definite distinction between those assets that serve as media of exchange and those that do not; (2) there is a whole range of assets whose capital values vary from being completely insensitive to interest-rate changes to being highly sensitive, and those in the low-sensitivity range constitute acceptable short-term stores of purchasing power between the time of a sale and the time of purchase. These latter assets, which adequately fulfil the temporary-store-of-value function but do not themselves fulfil the medium-of-exchange function, are called NEAR MONEY.

MONEY SUBSTITUTES: A further complication in delineating what is and is not money arises from the existence in the modern economy of short-term MONEY SUBSTITUTES. These serve temporarily as media of exchange but are not themselves money. Credit cards are a prime example. With a credit card many transactions can be made without either cash or a cheque. But the evidence of credit, in terms of the credit slip you sign and hand over to the shop, is not money because it cannot be used to effect further transactions. Furthermore, when your credit card company sends you a bill you have to use money in (delayed) payment for the original transaction. Yet the credit card, like all consumer credit, serves the short-run function of a medium of exchange by allowing you to make purchases even though you have neither cash nor bank deposits currently in your possession. But, of course, this is only temporary, and money remains the final medium of exchange for these transactions once the credit account is settled.

Changing views on what is money

What is an acceptable medium of exchange has changed and will continue to change over time. Furthermore, new monetary assets are continuously being developed to serve some, if not all, of the functions of money, and these are more or less readily convertible into money.

Modern economists now distinguish at least two concepts of money[1]:

> M_1, the narrow definition of money, defines money as currency plus demand deposits. M_3, the broader definition of money, defines money as M_1 plus time deposits with commercial banks.

The first definition concentrates on the medium-of-exchange function. The second definition adds in time deposits with banks, which serve the temporary-store-of-value

---

1 The wider definition of money is called M_2 in America and M_3 in Britain. The magnitude referred to as M_2 in Britain is now seldom used.

function and are in practice instantly convertible into a medium of exchange at a known and completely secure price that does not fluctuate with the rate of interest ($£1$ on deposit in a time account is always convertible into a $£1$ demand deposit or $£1$ in cash).

The supply of money

Economists use the terms the SUPPLY OF MONEY and the MONEY SUPPLY to refer to the total amount of money (defined as either M_1 or M_3), in the economy. It is a relatively easy matter to collect statistics on the total amount of currency in circulation (since the currency is issued by the central bank) and the total of bank deposits (since banks must publish their balance sheets). Thus, we can know with a high degree of accuracy what the money supply is at any moment of time.

The Bank of England has the ultimate legal control over the supply of money in the UK. The supply can also be influenced, as we shall see, by the decisions of the ordinary commercial banks.

DETERMINANTS OF THE MONEY SUPPLY: Two extreme situations are imaginable. In the first situation, the money supply can be determined at exactly the amount decided on by the central bank. In such a case, economists say that the money supply is exogenous and speak of an EXOGENOUS MONEY SUPPLY. This convenient phrase is used to describe a situation in which the money supply is completely determined by the central bank and neither expands nor contracts with the ebb and flow of business activity unless the bank decides to allow it to do so.

In the other extreme situation, the money supply is completely determined by things that are happening in the economy such as the level of business activity and rates of interest and is wholly out of the control of the central bank. In such a case, economists would say that there was an ENDOGENOUS MONEY SUPPLY, which means that the size of the money supply is not imposed from outside by the decisions of the central bank, but is determined by what is happening within the economy (just as is the quantity of steel plates or motor cars).

In practice, the money supply is partly endogenous, because commercial banks are able to change it in response to economic incentives, and partly exogenous, because the central bank is able to set limits beyond which the commercial banks are unable to increase the money supply.

In the next chapter, we shall assume an exogenous money supply, which means that the central bank can make it whatever it wants it to be. This allows us to study the importance of money. Once we have seen how changes in the supply of money can influence the economy, we are ready to study how the supply is determined both by the actions of commercial banks and by the actions of the central bank.

42

The banking system and the supply of money

Our primary concern in this chapter is with the determinants of the supply of money. In order to study these, we must look at the nature of the banking system, at the way in which banks create deposit money, and at the way in which attempts are made to regulate the money supply through public policy. The principles involved are the same in all Western countries although the institutional arrangements through which these operate do differ significantly from one country to another.

The first main element of the banking system is the COMMERCIAL BANK. These banks are privately-owned, profit-seeking firms. They accept demand deposits (often called *current accounts*) and time deposits (often called *savings* or *deposit accounts*), they transfer demand deposits among customers and banks when ordered to do so by cheque, they make loans to customers charging them interest in return, and they invest in interest-earning financial assets.

In the United Kingdom these banks are called DEPOSIT BANKS. There are 18 deposit banks altogether, but the bulk of the deposits are held by the four largest banks. Each bank has many branches throughout the country. (In the United States, by contrast, there are some 14,000 separate commercial banks each with only a small number of branches at most.)

The second main element of the UK banking system is the discount houses. These specialized institutions, which are peculiar to the UK, borrow money at call (i.e., repayable on demand) or at very short notice from banks and other lending institutions. They then use this money to purchase such short-dated financial assets as treasury bills and local authority bills. Since they borrow money that is repayable on demand and lend it out for terms of up to a month or more (as they do when e.g., they buy a treasury bill that has 30 days to run to maturity), they are in the classic exposed position of borrowing short and lending (relatively) long.[1] The advantage

---

1 The discount houses provide a good example of the division of labour. They are specialists in the short term money market. Institutions that specialise in other forms of loans do not find it worth their while to acquire detailed knowledge of the short-term market. They lend those funds that they can only commit for short terms to the discount houses who, guided by their specialist knowledge, can lend them profitably.

to the deposit banks of this arrangement is that they can earn interest on their cash reserves. (Loans to the discount houses are repayable at call and hence are as good as cash – at least as long as the discount houses remain solvent.)

The third main element of the banking system is the central bank. Almost all advanced countries have central banks and their functions are similar in each country: to be banker to the government and the commercial banking system, to manage the public debt, to control the money supply and to regulate the country's monetary and credit system. The central bank is always an instrument of the central authorities whether or not it is owned publicly. The Bank of England, 'The Old Lady of Threadneedle Street', is the oldest and most famous of the central banks. It began to operate as the central bank of England in the seventeenth century, but was not officially nationalized until 1947. It operates in two self-contained sections – the issue department and the banking department – each of which publishes its own balance sheet. In the US the central bank is the Federal Reserve System, which was organized in 1913.

Most banking systems also have a variety of other specialized institutions. Some of these (for example the Building Societies in Great Britain) accept time deposits from the public and lend money out on a longer-term basis. These institutions are often called FINANCIAL INTERMEDIARIES since they stand between those who save money and those who ultimately borrow the money.

THE CREATION AND DESTRUCTION OF DEPOSIT MONEY BY COMMERCIAL BANKS

One part of the money supply, deposit money, is under the control of the privately-owned commercial banks. We have already seen that the ability of banks to create deposit money depends on the fact that bank deposits need to be only fractionally backed by notes and coin. If all deposits had to be backed 100 per cent, banks would be nothing more than safety deposit vaults for their customers' money. If a customer deposited £100 in a bank, that bank would credit the customer's account with £100 and the £100 cash would go into the bank's vault to 'back' the deposit. Nothing further would happen. Because the bank does not need to keep 100 per cent reserves, it can use some of the £100 to purchase income-yielding investments.

A single monopoly bank

Consider first a country with only one bank (with as many physical branches as is necessary) and assume that someone makes a new deposit of £100 in cash. Table 42.1

Table 42.1 A new deposit of £100 is made

Assets	Liabilities
Cash £100	Deposit £100

Table 42.2 £900 is invested in loans and bonds with no cash drain

Assets		Liabilities
Cash	£100	Deposits £1,000
Loan	£500	
Bonds	£400	

shows how this transaction will be recorded on the books of the bank. The balance sheet will show new assets of £100 in the form of cash, and new liabilities of £100 in the form of the customer's deposit. This deposit, and all others like it, is a liability of the bank, since the bank owes this money to the customer and must pay it to him whenever he demands it. Since there is only one bank in the whole country, the bank can immediately create new deposits by some multiple of £100, depending on the reserve requirements. Let us say that all deposits need to be backed by a 10 per cent cash reserve. The monopoly bank could immediately create further deposits of £900. Assume, by way of example, that the bank loans £500 to a customer and buys £400 worth of bonds in the open market. The bank does this by permitting the borrower to write cheques on his account to the amount of £500, and by writing £400 to the credit of the account of the person who sold bonds to the bank. Table 42.2 shows how these transactions will appear on the bank's books once the borrower has written cheques to the allowable amount. The bank's assets include the £100 cash of the original deposit, the loan of £500 (it is an asset of the bank, since the borrower owes this money to the bank and must repay it at some stated date), and the £400 of bonds (these are an asset, since they can be sold again for cash). The bank's liabilities are now £1,000 in deposits, £100 to the account of the original depositor, £500 to the account of the persons who have received payment from the customer who borrowed from the bank, and £400 to the account of the person who sold the bonds to the bank. Note that by a few strokes of the pen the bank has created £900 in deposit money. The customers of the bank are now able to spend £900 more than they could yesterday and no one else is forced to spend any less.

The persons who borrowed the money and sold the bonds can be expected to spend their money. In most cases, they will do so by writing cheques. The bank honours these cheques by reducing the deposit of the person writing the cheque and increasing the deposit of the person in whose favour the cheque is written. Thus, if all the bank's customers are content to hold their money in deposit accounts and to make their payments by cheque, no cash ever leaves the bank, and the bank can effect payments from one person to another merely by debiting and crediting the accounts of individual customers. The total of the bank's deposit liabilities need not change in the process.[1]

Many banks, a single new deposit

The whole system is somewhat more complicated when there are many banks. If a depositor in Bank *A* writes a cheque to someone in Bank *B*, then a mere book transfer will not do, because Bank *A* now owes money to Bank *B*. By writing the cheque, the depositor in Bank *A* is saying, 'I claim the money owed me and ask that it be passed over to the man indicated on the cheque'; when the recipient of the cheque deposits

1 This introductory treatment ignores the fact that people are observed to hold some of their money in cash and some in deposits. If, for example, people hold 10 per cent of their money in the form of cash, then the bank can expect a cash drain when it creates new money. This cash drain would mean that deposits could not safely be expanded by £900. If such an expansion were to occur, £90 would be withdrawn by the public, leaving £810 in new deposits. (This would leave the public satisfied, since 10 per cent of their new money would be held in cash and 90 per cent in deposits, but the bank would have lost £90 in cash and £90 in deposits, leaving it with £10 in cash and £810 in deposits, which gives it a cash-deposit ratio of only 1·23 per cent.) There does exist a smaller deposit expansion that will leave the banks with a 10 per cent cash reserve, in spite of the drain of cash to the public.

it in Bank *B*, he is saying, 'I want my money held for me by Bank *B*'; thus Bank *A* must pay the money over to Bank *B*. It is exactly the same as if one individual withdrew cash from Bank *A* and gave it to the second individual who deposited it in Bank *B*; when the transaction is done by cheque, however, the banks, rather than the individuals, transfer the money.

There are, of course, many such transactions in the course of a day. If the banks are staying the same size in relation to each other, these transactions between banks will tend to cancel each other out. If, for example, Mr Brown who banks with *A* gives a cheque for £100 to Mr Harris who banks with *B*, and if, at the same time, Mr Jones who banks with *B* gives a cheque for £100 to Mr Fitch who banks with *A*, then these two transactions cancel each other out. Bank *A* loses £100 to *B* on account of the first transaction, but gains a like sum from *B* on account of the second. No money need move from bank to bank; all that needs to happen is for *A* to reduce Mr Brown's account by £100 and increase Mr Fitch's by the same amount, and for *B* to reduce Mr Jones's account by £100 and raise Mr Harris's by the same amount.

Multibank systems make use of a CLEARING HOUSE where interbank debts are cancelled out. At the end of the day, all of the cheques drawn by Bank *A*'s customers and deposited in Bank *B* are totalled, and set against the total of all of the cheques drawn by Bank *B*'s customers and deposited in Bank *A*. It is only necessary to settle the difference between these two sums. This is done for every pair of banks. The actual cheques are passed through the clearing house back to the bank on which they are drawn. The bank is then able to adjust each individual's account by a set of book entries; a flow of cash between banks is necessary only if there is a net transfer of deposits from the customers of one bank to those of another.

What would happen if, in a multibank system, one bank received a new deposit of £100 in cash? In this case, the bank could *not* immediately create another £900 in deposits because, when cheques were written on these deposits, the majority would be deposited in other banks. Thus, the bank must expect much of its £100 in cash to be drained away to other banks as soon as it creates new deposits for its own customers.

If, for example, the bank that obtains the new deposit has only 10 per cent of the total deposits held by the community, then 90 per cent of any new deposits it creates will end up in other banks. If other banks are not simultaneously creating new deposits, then this one bank will be severely restricted in its ability to expand deposits. The reason for the restriction is that the bank will suffer a major cash drain as cheques are written in favour of individuals who deal with other banks.

Table 42.3 Bank *A* expands deposits as far as possible while other banks do not

Bank *A*			All other banks in the system	
Assets		Liabilities	Assets	Liabilities
Cash £10·98		Deposits £109·89	New cash £89·02	New deposits £89·02
Loans £54·95				
Bonds £43·96				
£109·89		£109·89		

If the bank illustrated in Table 42.1 were only one bank in a multi-bank system (say with one-tenth of the total deposits in the system), and if the other banks refused to expand deposits, then the final situation would be as illustrated in Table 42.3.

What has happened between Tables 42.1 and 42.3 is that the bank has created £98·91 in new deposits by granting loans and buying bonds. But 90 per cent of these have ended up in other banks, so that the original bank ends up with only £9·89 of the new deposits held by its own customers. The remainder is distributed among the other banks. The total increase in deposits is only 98·91 per cent of the original cash deposit, as opposed to 900 per cent in the monopoly-bank case illustrated in Table 42.2. This leads us to the following conclusion:

> **One bank in a multibank system cannot produce a large multiple expansion of deposits based on an original accretion of cash, unless other banks also expand deposits.**

If all other banks are willing to expand deposits whenever they gain extra cash, the situation shown in Table 42.3 will not represent an equilibrium position. All other banks in the system will have excess cash: the £89·02 in new cash and new deposits will be distributed among them. All these banks will have their new deposits backed 100 per cent by cash. This should lead all banks to expand deposits simultaneously and produce a different situation from the one shown in Table 42.3, since there will no longer be a cash drain from one bank to another. The final outcome will become obvious after the next case has been studied.

Many banks, many new deposits

Assume that, in a system with many banks, each bank obtains new deposits in cash (possibly because of a general increase in the money supply due to a change in government policy).[1] Say, for example, that the community contains ten banks of equal size and that each receives a new deposit of £100 in cash. Now each bank is in the position shown in Table 42.1 and each can begin to expand deposits based on the £100 of reserves (each bank does this by granting loans to customers and by buying bonds and other income-earning assets). On the one hand, since each bank does one-tenth of the total banking business, on average 90 per cent of any newly created deposit will find its way into other banks as customers make payments by cheque to others in the community. This represents a cash drain to these other banks. On the other hand, 10 per cent of the new deposits created by each other bank should find its way into this bank. Thus, if all banks receive new cash and all start creating deposits simultaneously, no bank should suffer a significant cash drain to any other bank. All banks can go on expanding deposits without losing cash to each other; they need only worry about keeping enough cash to satisfy those depositors who occasionally require cash. Thus the expansion can go on, with each bank watching its own ratio of cash reserves to deposits, expanding deposits as long as the ratio exceeds 1:10 and ceasing when it reaches that figure. The process will come to a halt when each bank has created £900 in additional deposits, so that, for each initial

1 The ways in which such changes in the money supply can be effected are discussed later in this chapter.

£100 cash deposit, there is now £1,000 in deposits backed by £100 in cash. Now *each* of the banks will have entries in its books similar to those shown in Table 42.2.

We can think of this process as taking place in steps. During the first day, each bank gets £100 in new deposits and the books of each bank show entries similar to those shown in Table 42.1. During the second day, each bank makes loans, expecting that it will suffer a cash drain on account of these loans. Indeed, 90 per cent of the new loans made by Bank *A* do find their way into other banks when the borrowers pay money to people who are customers of other banks, but 10 per cent of the new loans made by each other bank finds its way into Bank *A* as those borrowing from other banks make payments to people who are customers of Bank *A*. Thus, there is no net movement of cash between banks. Instead of finding itself in a position such as that shown in Table 42.3, each bank's books at the end of the day contain the entries shown in Table 42.4.

Table 42.4 Expansion of credit in expectation of a 90 per cent cash drain to other banks when no cash drain actually occurs

Assets		Liabilities
Cash	£100·00	Deposits £198·91
Loans and		
Bonds	£98·91	
	£198·91	£198·91

Cash is now just over 50 per cent of deposits, instead of being only 10 per cent as is desired. Thus each bank can continue to expand deposits in order to grant loans and to purchase income-earning assets. As long as all banks do this simultaneously, no bank will suffer any significant cash drain to any other bank, and the process can continue until each bank has created £900 worth of new deposits and then finds itself in the position shown in Table 42.2.[1]

> **The fractional reserve requirement is the essential ingredient of deposit creation and thus a multi-bank system creates deposit money just as would a single monopoly bank.**

CENTRAL BANKS

All central banks perform more or less the same functions. The central bank is the agent of MONETARY POLICY which can be defined as the attempt to regulate the economy by regulating the supply of money and the terms and availability of credit.

1 Textbooks often take a case in which one bank creates a deposit on the basis of an accretion of cash, and all of this ends up in a second bank, and the second bank then creates deposits, all of which end up in a third bank, and so on. Two objections can be raised against such a case. First, the situation in which all banks get extra cash is much more common in the real world than the situation in which one bank gets a significant amount of extra cash. Second, even if one bank did get extra cash, the deposits it creates should end up distributed among all other banks. Thus, after round one, we are immediately in the case of many banks and many new deposits, rather than in a case in which a second bank is the sole holder of a new deposit.

Banking institutions and the instruments that central banks use to achieve their goals vary substantially from country to country. These institutional details can have major effects on the workings of central bank policy. In this introductory treatment we concentrate mainly on what can be said about central banks in general.[1]

Banker to the government

Governments need to hold their funds in an account into which they can make deposits and against which they can draw cheques. Such government deposits are usually held by the central bank although in some countries, e.g., the United States, an attempt is made to spread government deposits through the commercial banks while keeping only a bare minimum working balance at the central bank.

Managing the public debt

The central bank helps the government with its debt requirements. They do their best to smooth over the effects that might otherwise ensue from uneven borrowing and lending requirements. The Bank of England generally purchases any part of new issues of public debt that is not taken up by other lenders on the day of issue at what seems like a reasonable interest rate. If the Bank judged the market correctly it will be able to sell the remaining part of the new debt over the next week or so. If it guessed incorrectly it may end up holding some of the new debt indefinitely. We shall see that in this case the money supply will have been increased. The Bank also enters the market if there is a large issue of government debt due for early redemption. The commercial banks buy this issue up over a period of time thus preventing a sudden large accretion of cash to the public on redemption date.

In its capacity as manager of the public debt the central bank is motivated to keep interest rates, and thus the government's interest payments, as low as possible. If the public will not take up all of the government debt being offered at the going rate of interest, either interest rates can rise until all of the debt is taken up, or the bank can buy up whatever the public will not take at the present rate of interest. If banks choose the latter course they are holding down interest rates and, as we shall soon see, this leads to an expansion of the money supply.

Banker to commercial banks

Commercial banks need a place to deposit their funds; they need to be able to transfer their funds among themselves; and they need to be able to borrow money when they are short of cash. The central bank accepts deposits from the commercial banks and will on order transfer these deposits among the commercial banks. In this way the central bank provides the commercial banks with the equivalent of chequing accounts, and with a means of settling debts among themselves.

Lender of last resort

Commercial banks often have sudden needs for cash and one way of getting it is to borrow from the central bank. Historically, the central bank has been the lender of

---

1 It is more important here than almost anywhere else in the book that the text material be supplemented by further reading. For the UK economy the whole of Prest & Coppock (eds.) op. cit., Chapter 2 is relevant.

last resort: if all other sources failed the central bank would lend money to commercial banks with good investments but in temporary need of cash. In many countries the commercial banks borrow directly from the central bank. (They can, of course, only borrow against approved assets.) In the UK the discount houses stand between the deposit banks and the central bank. If the deposit banks find themselves in need of cash they recall some of their demand loans made to the discount houses. But the discount houses will have used their borrowed money to buy short-term financial assets. Thus they are not in a position to repay the deposit banks out of their own cash reserves. If they cannot borrow money from private sources they can always obtain the money by borrowing from the Bank of England. They must put up approved financial assets (mainly short-term government securities) as security. They pay interest on the loan at a rate that used to be called *bank rate* but which is now called the MINIMUM LENDING RATE.

There are two ways in which the central bank can provide assistance when the banking system is short of cash. First, they can lend money to the discount houses as described above. Second they can buy bills and bonds directly. This allows any financial institutions in need of cash to sell those financial assets that the central bank is buying and to gain cash in return.

Regulator of the money supply

The central bank has great power to influence the money supply. The fact that central banks sometimes do not choose to use this power directly does not change the fact that the power is there.

CURRENCY CONTROL: In most countries the central bank has the sole power to issue paper money. In Britain this is done by the Issue Department of the Bank of England. No attempt is made, however, to control the overall money supply by controlling the quantity of bank notes in circulation. Suppose that the public wished to increase the fraction of the total money supply that it holds as notes and coin (as it does, for example, each Christmas season). Faced with a cash drain to the public the commercial banks would withdraw deposits from the Bank of England and the bank would print the necessary bank notes.[1]

RESERVE REQUIREMENTS: The cash held as backing against deposits is called the CASH BASE of the money supply. In most countries the central bank requires that commercial banks hold cash reserves (in their own vaults and on deposit with the central bank) well in excess of what normal prudence would dictate. A rise in the cash reserves required to be held against a given amount of deposits can force a multiple contraction of deposit money on the commercial banks. To see this in its simplest form, return to Table 42.2 and work out for yourself what happens if the single monopoly bank were required to hold 15 per cent cash reserves instead of the 10 per cent required in this example.

1 The accounting would be kept straight by the banking department transferring financial assets to the currency department who would issue currency against these. Thus if the commercial bank withdraws £X cash, the banking department reduces its deposit liabilities to commercial banks by £X and its holdings of interest earning assets by the same amount. The currency department increases its holdings of interest earning assets and increases its note issue (which is a liability) by £X.

In the US the Federal Reserve does change reserve requirements occasionally as a means of influencing the behaviour of the commercial banks. In Britain the Bank of England used to administer an 8 per cent cash reserve requirement. In 1971, however, the Bank introduced a new scheme which required a minimum 12 per cent ratio of deposit liabilities to approved reserve assets. Reserve assets refers to any assets that banks are required to keep as reserves against their deposit liabilities and the RESERVE BASE refers to the quantity of these assets that form the base of the supply of money.[1]

Soon after the scheme was initiated there was an enormous increase in the amount of deposit money. Some economists argued that the new reserve asset scheme gave the Bank of England much less control over the money supply than the old cash reserve scheme. Although it is very difficult if not impossible for commercial banks to increase the cash base without cooperation from the central bank, it may be much easier for them to increase their reserve base. (One reason is that large supplies of reserve assets are in the hands of the non-bank public and the commercial banks can increase their own holdings of reserve assets by buying them on the open market.)

The Special Deposit scheme was introduced in the early 1960s as a method of altering reserve requirements for British banks. From time to time the Bank of England could require that the commercial banks make special deposits with the Bank of England. This had the effect of increasing the required reserve ratio. Whether or not it could be effective in controlling the money supply would depend on whether or not the Bank of England took steps to make it easy for banks to make special deposits when they were required to do so. At the end of 1973 a new variant of the scheme was introduced. The Bank of England announces a target for the expansion of deposit money, and if this target is exceeded, banks must place amounts of money (determined on a sliding scale) in special non-interest-earning deposits with the Bank. This is intended to provide a disincentive against exceeding the target for growth in the money supply.

Open-market operations

The most important tool that the central bank has for influencing the supply of money is the purchase or sale of government bonds on the open market. *If the central bank buys bonds in the open market, this increases the cash reserves of the commercial banks.* If the bank buys a bond from, say, a private citizen, it pays for it with a cheque drawn on the central bank and payable to the seller. The seller will deposit this cheque in his own bank. The commercial bank will present the cheque to the central bank for payment, and the central bank will make a book entry increasing the deposit of the commercial bank at the central bank. At the end of these transactions, the central bank will have acquired a new asset in the form of a bond and a new liability in the form of a deposit by the commercial bank. The individual will have reduced his bond holdings and will have raised his cash holdings. The commercial bank will have a

1 In the UK reserve assets are defined to include normal deposits with the Bank of England, Treasury bills, company tax reserve certificates, money lent at call to the Discount Houses, British government bonds with less than a year to maturity, and certain local authority and commercial bills.

Table 42.5 Changes resulting from the purchase of a £100
bond by the central bank from a private household

Central Bank	
Assets	Liabilities
Bond+£100	Deposits of Commercial Banks+£100

Commercial Banks	
Assets	Liabilities
Deposits with Central Bank+£100	Deposit of Private Household+£100

Private Households	
Assets	Liabilities
Bonds−£100 Deposits with Commercial Banks+£100	No Change

new deposit equal to the amount paid for the bond by the central bank. The commercial bank will find its cash assets and its deposit liabilities increased by the same amount.

The books of the three parties concerned will show the changes indicated in Table 42.5 after £100 worth of open market purchases have been completed.

The commercial banks are now in the position illustrated in Table 42.1. They have received a new deposit of £100 cash and they can engage in a multiple expansion of deposits of the kind already studied in the earlier parts of this chapter. Notice that the whole business has been accomplished by a set of book transactions. The commercial banks have extra cash *to their credit on the books of the central bank*. No new notes or coins have been created. If the subsequent credit expansion causes some cash drain to the public (see note 1, page 602) only then will the commercial banks withdraw some of their deposits from the central bank, and only then will new notes and coins have to be created by the central bank.

If the central bank sells bonds in the open market this reduces the cash reserves of the commercial banks. If the central bank sells a bond to a private citizen, it gives the bond to the individual and receives in return his cheque drawn against his own deposit in his bank and payable to the central bank. The central bank presents the cheque to the commercial bank for payment. The payment is made merely by a book entry reducing the commercial bank's cash held on deposit at the central bank.

Now the central bank has reduced its assets by the value of the bond it sold, and reduced its liabilities in the form of cash owed to commercial banks. The individual has increased his holding of bonds and reduced his cash on deposit with his own bank. The commercial bank has reduced its deposit liability to the individual and reduced its cash assets (on deposit with the central bank) by the same amount. Each of the asset changes is balanced by a liability change. But the commercial bank finds that

Table 42.6 Changes resulting from the sale of a £100 bond by
the central bank to a private household

Central Bank

Assets	Liabilities
Bonds−£100	Deposits of Commercial Banks−£100

Commercial Banks

Assets	Liabilities
Deposits with Central Bank−£100	Deposits of Private Households−£100

Private Households

Assets	Liabilities
Bonds+£100 Deposits with commercial bank−£100	No Change

by suffering an equal change in its cash assets and its deposit liabilities, its ratio of cash to deposit falls. If this ratio was previously at the legal minimum, it will now have fallen below the minimum and the commercial bank will have to take rapid steps to restore its cash ratio. The necessary reduction in deposits can be effected by not making new investments when old ones are redeemed (e.g., by not granting a new loan when old ones are repaid) or by selling existing investments (e.g., by selling bonds to the public and receiving payment in cheques which reduces the deposits held by the public).

The books of the three parties concerned will initially show the changes indicated in Table 42.6 after £100 worth of open market sales have been accomplished. This is not the end of the story for we have already seen that when these initial changes have occurred the commercial banks will have suffered an equal loss of cash and of deposits. Their ratio of cash to deposits will have been upset and they will have to effect a multiple contraction of deposits in order to restore the required ratio of cash reserves to total deposits.

Any open market purchase or sale by the central bank has the effects just analysed. If the Bank buys bills and bonds directly from the government this also increases the cash base and allows a multiple expansion of deposit money. In the first instance it is the government's account with the central bank that gains the new credit balance. But as soon as the government spends the money, writing cheques to households and firms, the money finds its way into the commercial banks who are once again in the position of securing new deposits that simultaneously increase both their cash assets and their deposit liabilities by an equal amount. This permits a multiple expansion of deposit money.

Furthermore it does not matter *why* the central bank engages in open market operations, the effect is the same whatever the purpose of the purchase or sale. The open market operations might have been engaged in for the express purpose of changing the cash base, or for the purpose of assisting the government to float new loans, or to prevent an anticipated rise in short term interest rates. Whatever the reason for a particular open market operation, the effect on the cash base is unavoidable.

Other tools

A central bank can affect the supply of money and credit through a variety of other devices that operate through interest rates and through so-called selective credit controls. Although these devices are much less important than open-market operations or reserve requirements, they are used from time to time.

Open-market operations affect interest rates as well as the quantity of money. Buying large quantities of bonds tends to force up their price. This, as we saw on page 403, is equivalent to forcing down the rate of interest. Selling large quantities of bonds, however, tends to force down the price of bonds and force up the rate of interest. Thus, an open-market policy designed to expand the money supply also tends to lower interest rates, and a policy designed to contract the money supply tends to raise them.

There is a variety of selective credit controls designed not to regulate the over-all volume of money or credit, but rather to limit (or encourage) particular forms of it. Stock-market fluctuations can be controlled to some extent through margin requirements;[1] consumer credit, which can be highly volatile, can be controlled in several ways. Minimum necessary initial payments and maximum terms for hire-purchase contracts can be set. The final tool is direct order or suggestion. If the commercial-banking system is prepared to cooperate, the Central Bank can operate a tight money policy merely by asking banks to be conservative in granting loans; when the restrictive policy is removed, the commercial banks can then be told that it is all right to go ahead granting loans and extending deposits up to the legal maximum.

Supporter of money markets

This is often referred to as the support function and it arose from the operation of the central bank as a lender of last resort to the commercial banks. Today the support function relates to the whole of the financial system. Many financial institutions borrow short and lend long. If their lending rates can only be raised slowly while their borrowing rates rise quickly (because their borrowing contracts are short-term ones while their lending contracts are long-term ones) then a rapid rise in interest rates may put them in danger of insolvency. Rather than let this happen, the central bank may try to slow down the rise in interest rates. To do this it enters the open market and buys bonds thus preventing their prices from falling as much as they otherwise would. In its efforts to control the level and speed of change of interest rates in general support of the financial system the central bank necessarily varies the money supply. The changes in the money supply required if the Bank

---

1 A margin requirement is the proportion of the purchase price of any security that must be put up by the buyer, the remainder being loaned to him.

is to pursue its support function may be very different from the changes in the money supply needed if the Bank seeks to control aggregate demand with a view to removing inflationary and deflationary gaps.

THEORIES OF THE DETERMINATION OF THE MONEY SUPPLY
Exogenous theories

The traditional theory of the determination of the money supply related the total quantity of money to the cash base by means of the so-called MONEY MULTIPLIER. The assumptions of the theory are (1) that the central bank fixes a minimum cash reserve ratio and (2) that the profit incentive of commercial banks leads them to avoid holding excess reserves if at all possible. Idle cash reserves earn nothing for the bank while loans and other investments always yield some interest income. Therefore banks will always try to be fully loaned up (i.e., have no excess reserves).

We can write assumption (1) as

$$\frac{R}{D} \geqslant \alpha$$

where R is cash reserves, D is deposit liabilities, α is the minimum required cash reserve ratio and the sign '$\geqslant$' is read greater than or equal to. Assumption (2) above allows us to replace the '$\geqslant$' sign with an '$=$' sign since banks are assumed never to carry significant amounts of excess reserves. Now re-write the equation as follows:

$$D = \frac{R}{\alpha}.$$

This gives us the quantity of deposit money expressed as a function of the cash base and the required cash reserve ratio.

This is a theory of an exogenous money supply because the cash base is assumed to be under the complete control of the central bank through its open-market operations. Thus the total supply of deposit money can be set by the central bank. Assume, for example, that the central bank wishes to reduce the money supply.

(1) The bank sells bonds on the open market.

(2) The bank receives cheques from the public in payment for the bonds. When it presents these cheques for payment, commercial banks suffer a loss in their cash reserves.

(3) In order to restore their required reserve ratio banks must engage in a multiple contraction of deposit money.

An increase in the quantity of money is generated by open-market purchases that put cash reserves into the hands of commercial banks and engenders an expansion of deposit money.

Endogenous theories

There are many theories of how the money supply may become an endogenous variable. First, the central bank may be concerned to fix the rate of interest rather than the quantity of money. If the bank is to engage in whatever open market operations as are needed to stabilise the price of bonds and other financial assets, then the change in the money supply will be determined by the amount of open-market operations the bank has to conduct. If the price of bonds would be falling on the open market the bank must buy bonds in order to hold their price up. (This as we have seen tends to expand the money supply.) If the price of bonds would be rising on the open market, the bank must sell bonds in order to hold their price down. (This, as we have seen, tends to contract the money supply.)

If the bank behaves in this way the money supply becomes endogenous and it fluctuates with the demand and supply for financial assets since the bank must make up the difference between demand and supply at the fixed price of these assets.

> **If the object of the central bank's open-market policy is to fix interest rates, the cash base becomes endogenous and cannot be fixed by the central bank at any particular predetermined level.**

A second way in which the money supply can become endogenous is if the bank sets a reserve base which the commercial banks themselves can control. Say, for example, that the bank rules that all deposits have to be backed to the extent of 10 per cent of their value by holdings of raw cotton. Banks could then expand deposits by buying up raw cotton. Since cotton production could no doubt be increased greatly, deposits could be increased greatly. Also if cotton remained under private production the central bank would have no power to control the money supply.

A more likely case would occur if the reserve base of the commercial banks were defined to include assets which are held in large quantities by the public. In this case the commercial banks can engage in deposit expansion and maintain their required reserves by buying quantities of the required asset (say short-term bills) currently being held by the public.

> **The central bank loses control of the money supply if it sets a reserve base the size of which it cannot control.**

Some of the most important controversies in economics today – e.g., those concerning the cause and control of the rapid inflation of the 1970s – turn on the question of the degree to which the money supply is exogenous or endogenous. It is hard to mention a more important issue in macro-economics today.

43

The importance of money

So far we have taken a brief look at the historical development of money, and at how its supply is determined by the modern banking system. We now come to the really important question of how money influences the circular flow, and how strongly. Although these questions have interested economists ever since economics began, they are still the subject of controversy. In order to understand some of the current issues of debate, we shall study two extreme theories of the place of money in the circular flow of income, the traditional quantity theory and the modern theory that is accepted by many of today's monetary theorists both Keynesian and monetarist.

The influence of aggregate demand

The main part of our discussion will be carried on under the assumptions first made on page 480. Since they are critically important we shall state them once again: there is a sharp dichotomy between the effect of variations in aggregate demand when the economy is at less than full employment, and the effect when the economy is at full employment; when there is unemployment, variations in aggregate demand cause output and employment to vary but leave the price level unchanged; when there is full employment, variations in aggregate demand cause the rate of inflation to vary but leave the level of output and employment unchanged.

The influence of money

Money is regarded as important because it is thought to influence the level of aggregate demand by affecting spending either directly through the availability of credit or indirectly through the induced changes in the rate of interest. If aggregate demand does vary directly with the supply of money, then the central authorities could seek to operate their stabilization policy by varying the supply of money. A deflationary gap could be removed by increasing the supply of money and so increasing demand until the equilibrium level of income coincided with the full-employment level.

An inflationary gap could be removed by reducing the supply of money until there was no excess demand at full-employment income. To enquire into the possible efficacy of monetary policy as an alternative, or as a supplement to fiscal policy, we first need to study the links between the supply of money and aggregate demand.

The effect of excess demand and supply of money

In the last chapter we studied the determinants of the supply of money. Later in this chapter we shall study the demand for it. Firms and households desire to hold money balances and we may enquire what happens when, in the aggregate, they have either more or less money than they wish to hold. If they hold more than they require, the supply of money exceeds the demand for it, and presumably they will spend the excess. But how will they spend it? Different theories give different answers. When they hold less than they require, the supply of money is less than the demand for it, and, presumably, firms and households will try to add to their money holdings. But where will they get the additional money? Again different theories give different answers. We shall study two extreme hypotheses about what firms and households do when their demand for money is not equal to their supply of it. The first hypothesis, which is associated with the traditional quantity theory, is that all the effects of a difference between the demand for and the supply of money are shown solely in changes in aggregate demand for goods and services: when firms and households have more money than they need, they spend the excess on currently-produced goods and services, while, when they have less money than they wish to hold, they try to build up their balances by reducing their expenditure on goods and services to an amount less than their current incomes, adding the difference to their money holdings. According to this theory disequilibrium between demand for and supply of money causes changes in aggregate demand for currently-produced goods and services.

The second hypothesis is associated with most modern theories of money, and it states that an excess demand for or supply of money is manifested solely in the demand for and the supply of securities. By securities we mean all income-earning assets, such as company shares and bonds, but, for simplicity in developing the basic theory, we shall assume that there is only one such asset, which we shall call a *bond*. According to this theory, when firms and households do not have sufficient money balances they attempt to build them up by selling bonds, and, when they have more money than they need to hold, they attempt to invest the surplus in bonds. Thus, a difference between demand for money and its supply will not have any direct effect on aggregate demand for goods and services. There may, however, be an indirect effect. The attempt on the part of households and firms either to buy or to sell bonds in large quantities will affect the price of bonds. A change in the price of bonds is, as we have already seen, the same thing as a change in the rate of interest. Insofar as investment and consumption decisions are affected by the rate of interest, there may be an effect on aggregate demand. The links between money and aggregate demand are less direct in this theory, and the quantitative effect on aggregate demand of a difference between demand for and supply of money depends on the link between changes in the rate of interest and changes in expenditure.

THE TRADITIONAL QUANTITY THEORY

The traditional quantity theory is based on three main assumptions:
(1) The demand for money is proportional to the value of transactions in the economy.
(2) The supply of money is an exogenously determined constant.
(3) An excess demand for or supply of money is reflected in the aggregate demand for currently-produced goods and services.
Assumption (3) has already been discussed in the previous section. Assumption (2) is common to both the quantity and the Keynesian theories, and it reflects the theory outlined on page 612 of Chapter 42 that the central authorities have control of the money supply, and can determine it at any level that they desire. (We shall have more to say about this later.) The first assumption arises from the theory of the demand for money, and we must now enquire into this in more detail.

Money that is held by a firm or a household has an opportunity cost. If it were not held in idle balances it could be lent out at the going rate of interest, yielding the interest payment as a return. We must wonder, then, why firms and households voluntarily hold any money balances at all. The reason for holding money stressed in the quantity theory is the so-called TRANSACTIONS MOTIVE and money held for this reason is called TRANSACTIONS BALANCES.

The transactions demand for money

Virtually all transactions in our economy use money. Money is passed from households to firms to pay for the goods and services produced by firms; and money is passed from firms to households to pay for the factor services supplied by households to firms. These transactions *force* both firms and households to hold money balances.

Consider, for example, the balances held because of wage payments. The level of balances that must be held depends on the pay period and on the size of the wage bill. Assume, for purposes of illustration, that firms pay wages every Friday, that households spend all their wages on the purchase of goods and services, and that expenditure is spread out evenly over the week. Thus, on Friday morning, firms must hold balances equal to the weekly wage bill, while on Friday afternoon, households will hold these balances. Over the week, households' balances will run down as a result of purchasing goods and services. By the same token, the balances held by firms will build up as a result of selling goods and services until, on the following Friday morning, firms will again have amassed balances equal to the wage bill that must be met on that day. On the average over the week, firms will hold balances equal to half the wage bill and so will households; thus total money balances held will be equal to the total weekly wage bill.

The size of these balances, therefore, depends on the size of the wage bill. If the wage bill doubles, either because twice as many people are employed at the same rate or because the same number is employed at twice the wage rate, the balances held must double. Thus the size of the wage bill tends to vary directly with the level of national income.

In an unreal world where the receipts and disbursements of households and firms were perfectly synchronized it would be unnecessary to hold transactions balances. If every time a household wished to spend £X it received £X as part payment of its income then no transactions balances would be needed.

> **Transactions balances are held because of the non-synchronization of payments and receipts. Transactions balances will be larger (a) the larger are the flows of payments and receipts and (b) the less well synchronized are these two flows.**

To illustrate the importance of point (b) assume that the pay period of one week in the previous example is changed so that wages are now paid monthly. Now payments and receipts are less well synchronised and transactions balances would have to be equal to the month's wage bill. Immediately after pay day households would have money balances equal to a month's wages. As they spent their incomes over the month their balances would run down but firms would be accumulating the money spent as their balances. Just before the next pay day households' transactions balances would have been run down to zero while firms' balances would be equal to the monthly wage bill that they were just about to pay. The average monthly transactions balances held by households would be equal to half a month's wages and the same would be true for firms. Thus total transactions balances would be equal to a month's wages.

The length of the pay period and the other things that determine the degree of non-synchronization of payments and receipts are part of the society's institutional arrangements. In the short-term these may be taken as given, although in the long term they can change significantly.

We have conducted the argument in terms of the wage bill, but a similar analysis holds for payments for all factor services. The critical conclusion for what follows is that, for given institutional arrangements, the demand for money balances depends on the value of transactions in the economy (i.e., all of the payments and receipts of firms and households).

The formal development of the quantity theory

Having stated the assumptions of the theory, we now lay them out and seek to discover their implications. As a first step we take the value of all transactions and split it into two parts; a real part, T, which is the *number* of transactions that occur over some stated time period, say, one year, and a value part, P, which is the average *price* at which these transactions take place.

The value of transactions is larger than the value of national income because, as goods are sold from one firm to another passing through successive stages of production, income is increased only by the value added at each stage, but transactions are increased by the gross value of the sale. As long as the industrial set-up does not change significantly, however, there will be a stable relation between transactions and national income, with a change in one causing a proportionate change in the other.

We can now write assumption (1) on page 616, about the demand for money to hold, in terms of the following equation:

$$M_d = kPT. \tag{1}$$

In this equation, M_d is the demand for money, PT is the annual money value of transactions, and k is the fraction of this value required to be held in transaction balances. It should be noted that we have now related the amount of money people wish to hold as balances, M_d, which is a stock, to the money value of transactions, which is a flow.[1] This job is done by k, which seems so insignificant but which actually is so powerful. The hypothesis that the cash balances one needs to hold are some fraction of the annual value of transactions creates a link between the stock of money and the flow of income.

Next we express assumption (2), that the supply of money is a constant determined by the central authorities, in the following equation:

$$M_s = M, \tag{2}$$

where M_s is the supply of money and M is some constant amount (measured in pounds sterling). Equation (2) merely says that the supply of money does not depend on any other factors in the economy; it is simply what the central authorities want it to be.

Finally we write a condition for equilibrium between the demand for money and the supply of it. This is written as

$$M_d = M_s. \tag{3}$$

When (3) holds, households and firms will have, in the aggregate, just the amount of money balances they require. When (3) does not hold, they will have too much or too little money, and according to assumption (3) on page 616 they will alter their sales or purchases of goods and services in an attempt to bring their money balances to the desired level.

Table 43.1 The equations of the quantity theory

(1)	Demand for money	$M_d = kPT$
(2)	Supply of money	$M_s = M$
(3)	Equilibrium condition	$M_d = M_s$
(4)	Equations (1), (2), and (3) give	$kPT = M$
	or	$P = \dfrac{1}{kT} \cdot M$

If k and T are constant, P varies proportionately with M.

The equations of the quantity theory are summarized in Table 43.1. Substitution of (1) and (2) into the equilibrium condition (3) produces the basic relation between P and M as shown in the fourth equation, which merely states that the demand for money (kPT) should equal its supply (M). If we are dealing with inflationary-gap situations so that transactions are constant at the full-employment level and if k is constant, then the price level must rise in proportion to any increase in the quantity of money.

1 One of the trickiest problems in monetary theory is to distinguish between stocks and flows (see page 32) and to discover relations between stocks of money and assets, on the one hand, and flows of expenditure, on the other.

To see how this result comes about we must consider disequilibrium behaviour. Assume that the economy begins in a situation of full-employment equilibrium with the demand for money equal to its supply. Now assume the central bank increases the supply of money in the hands of households and firms by 10 per cent. According to the behavioural hypothesis of the quantity theory, the firms and households try to convert this extra cash into goods and services but, since the economy is already at full employment, their efforts can only open up an inflationary gap. Indeed, the price level must rise until the demand for money is again equal to its supply. Since the demand for money is kPT, and since k is fixed by assumption, and since T cannot change because the economy remains at the same level of full-employment output, the demand for money will increase by exactly 10 per cent when P increases by 10 per cent. Until that time the demand for money will be less than its supply, and the attempt to convert the excess money into currently-produced goods and services will generate excess demand that will cause further inflation. Thus, equilibrium can be restored only when the price level rises by the same percentage as did the supply of money.

VELOCITY AND BALANCES: Often the quantity theory is presented and discussed using V (VELOCITY OF CIRCULATION) instead of k. V stands for the average number of times a unit of money turns over to effect the volume of transactions. It is defined as the reciprocal of k. Table 43.2 shows the effect of substituting symbols. Of course it makes no difference whether we work with k or V, as long as we are careful about the way we interpret these two variables.

Table 43.2 From k to V

If the demand for money, kPT, equals the supply, M,
we have, from Table 43.1,

(4) $kPT = M$

(5) Rewriting (4) gives $PT = M\dfrac{1}{k}$

(6) Letting V stand for $\dfrac{1}{k}$ gives $\underline{PT = MV}$

$PT = MV$

The stock of money people wish to hold, might, for example, be one-tenth of the annual value of the transactions. If k is 0.1, then V must be 10. This indicates that, if the money supply is to be one-tenth of the value of annual transactions, the average unit of money must change hands ten times in order to bring about an aggregate value of transactions ten times as large as the stock of money.

The quantity theory and unemployment

The quantity theory became a part of the Classical Model in which the *equilibrium level of national income* was always at full employment. Thus, the level of T remained fixed at the full-employment level, and not only did P rise in proportion to a rise in the money supply, but P also *fell* in proportion to a *reduction* in the money supply. Thus T was determined by its full-employment level and P was determined by the quantity of money. Hence the very strong link between the quantity of money and the level of prices in much nineteenth and early twentieth-century economics.

But times change, and with them so do the restrictions that it seems interesting to impose on our theories. Just as the Keynesian theory, which was originally developed to handle situations of deflationary gaps, can be adapted to analyse inflationary gaps (see page 513), so the quantity theory can be adapted to handle situations of unemployment. All that we do is to recall our assumption (see page 480) that in deflationary-gap situations the price level does not fall, but that variations in aggregate demand affect output. This makes P a constant and T a variable but preserves the link provided by the quantity theory between the excess demand for money and changes in aggregate demand.

To see what is implied we take the theory in the form:

$$kPT = M$$

which is equation (4) in Table 43.1 and divide through by kP to obtain:

$$T = \frac{1}{kP}M.$$

This tells us that, if P is constant during periods of unemployment, transactions (and hence output and employment) will vary in proportion to the money supply.

The reason for this is analogous to the reasons given in the discussion of disequilibrium under inflationary conditions. If firms and households have too much money they spend it, and the resulting increase in aggregate demand raises output and employment. If firms and households have too little money they lower their expenditures in an attempt to increase their money balances, and the resulting fall in aggregate demand lowers the equilibrium level of output.

> **If we combine the quantity theory with the set of basic assumptions introduced on page 480, we obtain the predictions that changes in the supply of money will cause proportionate changes in output and employment when unemployment exists in the economy (T can vary but P is constant), and in the price level when full employment already exists (P can vary but T is constant).**

The basic prediction of the quantity theory is that there will be a change in the money value of national income, in proportion to any change in the quantity of money. In some cases the change will be mainly a price change (a change in P) while in other cases it will be a change in output and employment (a change in T). In either case, control over the money supply becomes a potent method of controlling the circular flow of income.

MODERN THEORIES OF MONEY
Assumptions

We state three major assumptions below. The first and third are basic to most modern theories of the demand for money and of the influence of money on the circular flow of income. The second assumption is used because we wish to assume for the moment that the supply of money is determined exogenously by the central authorities. This assumption is not a necessary part of the modern theory of money. (Indeed we shall see in later chapters that much modern controversy over the influence of money turns on the question of the determinants of the money supply.)

(1) The demand for money depends on (a) the money value of national income and (b) the rate of interest.

(2) The supply of money is an exogenously determined constant.

(3) An excess demand for or supply of money is reflected in the demand for and supply of bonds.

The supply assumption (2) used here is the same as the one used in the traditional quantity theory: the supply of money is fully under the control of the central authorities. Part (a) of the demand assumption (1) is the same as that used in the traditional quantity theory,[1] but the second part is critical and depends on motives for holding money other than the transactions motive. The third assumption is basic to the modern theory of money which emphasises the role of money as a store of wealth, in addition to its role as a medium of exchange. We must now examine the theories behind assumptions (1) and (3) in more detail.

Additional factors in the demand for money

THE TRANSACTIONS DEMAND AND INTEREST RATES: Modern versions of the transactions demand for money include interest rates along with income as determining variables. The higher the rate of return on interest-earning assets, the greater is the inducement to invest available funds rather than to hold money to bridge the gaps between receipts and payments. The extent to which an individual will reduce his money holdings to earn interest will be limited by the costs of switching assets.

Assume, for example, that an individual is paid monthly and spends his money regularly over the month. He can hold all of his unspent pay as a transactions balance in his demand deposit at his bank, or as cash in his wallet, in which case he will have an average transaction balance equal to half his monthly salary. But he could keep only a quarter of his salary in cash at pay day and invest the other three-quarters in interest-yielding assets. Then, at the end of the first week, he could cash in a third of his assets and obtain enough cash to finance his second week's expenditure. He would do the same at the start of the third week and at the start of the fourth week when he would cash in the last of his assets. In this way the individual reduces his average transactions holding to one-eighth of a month's income (at the start of each week he has one-fourth of a month's income as a cash balance and by the end of the week he is down to nothing) and correspondingly increases his average holding of interest-earning assets.

It is unlikely that this kind of behaviour would be worthwhile for the typical household. It can, however, be worthwhile for high-income households and, more importantly, for big firms. Big firms hold very large transactions balances, and the interest on these that is foregone each day that they are not invested is quite substantial.

In order to hold a smaller quantity of transactions balances, it is necessary to make more frequent switches between money and other assets and incur higher costs in the

---

1 It requires only that real transactions T bear a constant relation to real national income Y. Thus if $T = aY$ and $M_d = kPT$, substitution yields $M_d^t = akPY$.

form of inconvenience and brokerage fees which are paid when bonds are bought and sold. The modern theory of transactions balances predicts that these costs will be less of an inhibition the higher is the rate of interest, and thus that the amount of money held for transactions purposes will be lower the higher is the rate of interest.

THE PRECAUTIONARY MOTIVE: In addition to the transaction motive, firms and households hold balances because of uncertainty about the exact timing of receipts and payments. Many goods and services are sold on credit, and the seller can never be quite certain when these goods will be paid for, whereas the buyer can never be quite certain of the day of delivery and thus of the day on which payment will fall due; nor can he be certain of the degree to which his suppliers will be pressing for prompt payment at the time at which such payment is due. In order to be able to continue in business during times in which receipts are abnormally low and/or disbursements are abnormally high, firms carry money balances. The larger such balances, the greater is the degree of insurance against being unable to pay bills because of some temporary fluctuation in either receipts or disbursements. If the firm is pressed for cash or has other very profitable uses for its funds, it may run down these balances and take the risk of being caught by some temporary fluctuations in receipts and disbursements. How serious this risk is depends on the penalties of being caught without sufficient reserves by some temporary fluctuation. A firm is unlikely to be pushed into insolvency, but it may have to incur considerable costs if it is forced to borrow money at high interest rates for short periods in order to meet such temporary crises. The cost depends on the lines of short-term credit open to the firm.

The protection provided by PRECAUTIONARY BALANCES depends on the degree to which payments and receipts are subject to haphazard fluctuations and on the volume of payments and receipts. If the volume rises, then a given amount of money held will provide less and less protection. To provide the same degree of protection as the volume of business rises, more money is necessary. Thus, the firm's demand for money is expected to rise as its own sales rise. Aggregating over all firms and households, the total demand for money will rise as national income rises.

Firms can also be expected to hold more funds for precautionary purposes the lower the opportunity cost of holding such funds. If the market rate of interest provides a measure of how expensive it is to hold funds, then the precautionary demand for money can be expected to vary inversely with the rate of interest as well as directly with the level of income.[1]

THE SPECULATIVE MOTIVE: Another major reason for holding money is in order to speculate on the course of future events. The future is never certain, so that any transaction that takes place over time is necessarily somewhat speculative. If one thinks prices are now very low and will soon rise, the tendency is to buy now and to put off selling until prices rise. If one thinks prices are high now and will soon fall, the tendency is to sell now and to postpone buying until prices have fallen. This applies to anything that is bought and sold, including stocks and bonds. For sim-

---

1 Institutional arrangements affect the precautionary demand just as they affect the transactions demand. In the past, for example, a traveller would have to carry a substantial precautionary balance in cash, but today his credit card covers him against almost any unforeseen expense that may arise on his travels.

plicity, attention is confined to bonds and the bond market, but similar statements apply to stocks and the stock market.

If the price of bonds is very high in relation to what people think is the normal price (i.e., the rate of interest is thought to be low), people will tend to sell bonds now and postpone intended purchases until prices have come down. In such a situation, large quantities of money may be held in anticipation of a more favourable chance to purchase bonds in the future. If, however, the price of bonds is very low in relation to what is thought to be the normal price (the rate of interest is high), the tendency will be to buy bonds now and to postpone sales until a more favourable price can be obtained. In this case, the tendency will be to hold as little cash as possible and hold bonds instead.

Whereas the transactions and precautionary motives emphasize money's role as a medium of exchange, the speculative motive emphasizes its role as a store of wealth. A household or firm can hold its wealth in money or in such interest-earning assets as bonds. If there was perfect certainty that the price of bonds would never change there would be no reason to hold any wealth in the form of money since bonds yield an interest payment while money does not. If people believe that the price of bonds may change in the future, there may be a reason to hold bonds rather than money. If, on the one hand, the price of bonds is expected to fall, there will be capital losses for people holding bonds. It will then pay to hold money rather than bonds as long as the expected capital loss from the fall in price exceeds the interest than can be earned by holding the bond. If, on the other hand, the price of bonds is expected to rise, it will pay to hold bonds rather than money since there will be a capital gain when their price rises. People who are certain about the direction in which they expect the price of bonds to move will tend to hold all their wealth in bonds (price of bonds expected to rise) or all their wealth in money (price of bonds expected to fall). It is easy to show, however, that when investors are uncertain about what will happen to bond prices in the future many of them will want to hedge their bets by holding both bonds and money. SPECULATIVE BALANCES are wealth held in the form of money rather than interest-earning assets because of expectations that the prices of those assets may change.

When households and firms decide how much of their monetary assets they will hold as money rather than as bonds (and other interest-earning assets), they are said to be exercising their preference for liquidity. LIQUIDITY PREFERENCE thus refers to the demand to hold assets as money rather than as interest-earning bonds (or stocks). This demand is assumed to vary inversely with the rate of interest.

The total demand for money: recapitulation

The demand for money is defined as the total amount of money balances that every-one in the economy wishes to hold.[1] The previous discussion about the motives for

---

1 Recall that the quantity of money is stock and that the demand for it is a demand for a stock. People wish to hold so many dollars in cash or deposits. This makes the demand for money different from the demand for goods, which is (usually) a flow demand. When we say, for example, that the demand for carrots is 7 million tons, we must say over what time period this is measured. If we specify 'per month', then the demand is to purchase a flow of carrots of 7 millions tons each month.

holding money can be summarized by listing two hypotheses about the demand for money.

The demand for money varies directly with the level of income.

The higher the level of income, the larger the amount of money held for transactions purposes. The higher the level of income, the larger also is the amount needed to provide a given level of security against unforeseen fluctuations in receipts and payments. Both transactions and precautionary motives lead to this hypothesis.

The demand for money varies inversely with the rate of interest.

The market rate of interest reflects the opportunity cost of money holdings (the money could be lent out and earn the market rate). Thus, the higher the rate of interest, the higher the cost of holding money and the less money will be held for precautionary purposes. The rate of interest also influences decisions as to whether to hold money for speculative purposes. Given some expectations about a normal rate of interest, the lower the current rate, the less attractive bonds will seem to be and so the higher the demand will be to hold money instead of bonds. Both precautionary and speculative motives lead to this hypothesis. The schedule relating the demand for money to the rate of interest is often called the LIQUIDITY-PREFERENCE SCHEDULE.

The consequences of the assumptions

We may now follow out the important consequences of the modern theory of money. We shall do this in two stages. In the first stage we compare the traditional quantity theory's predictions with the modern theory's predictions about the effects of a change in the supply of money on the economy. In the second stage we integrate the theory of money fully into the simple macro-theory of the circular flow that we developed in Part 7 of this book.

AN EXCESS DEMAND FOR MONEY: If a single firm or household is short of money balances, it can sell some of its bonds and immediately replenish its stocks of money. On the other hand, if the firm or household has excess stocks of money, it can invest these forthwith by buying bonds on the open market. If everyone tries to do this simultaneously, however, it will not be possible unless there are changes in the stocks of money or of bonds. If the stocks of money and bonds are fixed in size, then general attempts to add to or subtract from bond holdings will only succeed in altering their price. Assume, for example, that the money supply is reduced so that all firms and households are short of money. They try to sell bonds and add to their money holdings. This causes the price of bonds to fall. A fall in the price of bonds is the same thing as a rise in the interest rate. (See page 403.) As the interest rate rises, people will try to economize on cash holdings; they will also tend to reduce speculative balances of cash, since bonds now seem like very good investments. Eventually, the rate will rise high enough so that people will no longer be trying to add to their cash balances by selling bonds. The demand for money will again equal supply. There will no longer be an excess supply of bonds, so the interest rate will stop rising. The net effect of the original excess demand for money will have been an increase in the rate of interest. *Aggregate demand will be affected only in so far as consumption or investment is affected by the change in the interest rate.*

AN EXCESS SUPPLY OF MONEY: Now consider a case in which the money supply increases so that all firms and households have too much money. They try to spend the excess on buying bonds; if everyone tries to do this, however, they will force the price of bonds up (i.e., force the interest rate down). When this happens, people are prepared to hold more money, both because the opportunity cost of doing so is reduced and because bonds now look like a bad buy, so that people will hold large speculative hoards of money in expectation of more favourable bond prices in the future.

Thus, according to the modern theory, a monetary policy that expands the money supply does not lead to any direct increase in aggregate demand, as it does in the traditional quantity theory; it leads only to a fall in the interest rate until everyone is prepared to hold the expanded supply of money. Any effect on aggregate demand occurs in so far as investment or consumption expenditure responds to the change in the interest rate.

Modern debates on the efficacy of monetary policy often turn on the extent to which changes in the quantity of money will affect interest rates and on the extent to which changes in interest rates will affect aggregate expenditure. These debates are considered in detail in Chapter 50.

AN INTEGRATION OF MONEY INTO THE THEORY OF NATIONAL INCOME[1]

In this section we shall show how money can be fitted formally into the national-income model. For simplicity, we shall assume an economy with no foreign trade, and we shall ignore the government sector. (Both the government and foreign trade can be brought in, but none of the basic predictions in which we are interested at this stage is affected.)

The model is shown in Figure 43.1. The first part of the figure shows the consumption function. The second shows that part of the demand for money (mainly the transactions demand) that varies with the level of income. The schedule is labelled T for transactions. The third part of the diagram shows the relation between the rate of interest and that part of the demand for money that depends on the rate of interest. It is called the liquidity preference schedule. The fourth part of the figure shows how investment expenditure varies with the rate of interest. This is the MEI schedule, first introduced in Chapter 29.

The equilibrium of the model

An equilibrium situation is shown in Figure 43.1(i). National income is Y_1 and, according to the consumption function, consumption is c_1 and thus savings are $c_1 s_1$.

---

1 The preceding section has outlined the main differences between the theories. The present section goes on to integrate money into the Keynesian macro-model. This topic is often left for intermediate courses and anyone who wishes to can jump directly to Chapter 44 without missing anything that is critical for an understanding of the material in the rest of this book.

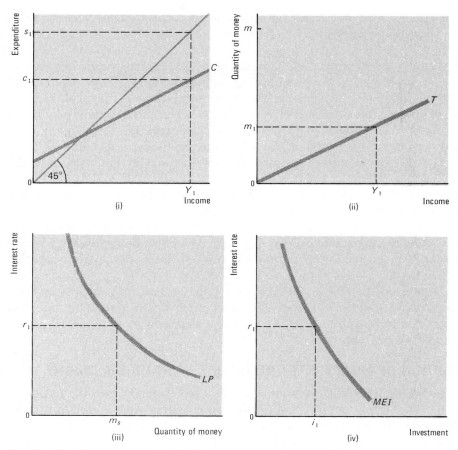

Fig. 43.1 The Keynesian model. (i) The consumption function (ii) The transactions demand for money (T) varies with the level of income (Y) (iii) The speculative and precautionary demand for money (LP) varies with the rate of interest (r) (iv) Investment (MEI) varies with the rate of interest (r)

Since savings are the only withdrawal, consumption plus savings equals income (which is shown by the 45° line). Now we can take this level of income Y_1 and discover in Part (ii) of the figure the level of the transaction demand for money, m_1. We next take the total (fixed) money supply and plot it as m in the figure. Next, by subtracting the quantity needed for transactions purposes, m_1 from the total supply, we obtain the amount available for speculative and precautionary purposes. This is the amount $m - m_1$ in Figure 43.1(ii). We now plot this amount on Figure 43.1(iii) as the point m_s. This shows us that the rate of interest must be r_1 to induce people to hold just the amount of money that is available to be held. If the rate of interest is above r_1 people will be trying to buy bonds in order to run down their cash holdings. If the rate is below r_1 people will be trying to sell bonds in order to increase their cash holdings. In either case the rate of interest will change. Next we go to Figure 43.1(iv) to discover the volume of investment expenditure. We plot on this figure the rate of interest, r_1, that equates the demand and supply of money. The volume of investment expenditure is i_1 at the interest rate r_1. Finally, to check that we really have equilibrium values, we compare the volume of investment i_1 with the volume of savings $c_1 s_1$. Since they are equal as drawn, withdrawals equal injections, and national income will be neither rising nor falling. In short, it is at its equilibrium value. (Note: m_s stands for speculative money balances *not* total money supply.)

The stability of the model

We now show that the model has *negative feedback*, in other words, if income is above the equilibrium, income will tend to fall and, if income is below the equilibrium, it will tend to rise. Consider a level of income above the equilibrium level of Y_1. At this level savings will exceed their equilibrium level of $c_1 s_1$. At this higher income, transactions demand for money will exceed m_1, so that money available for speculative purposes will be less than $m - m_1$ and thus also less than m_s. This means that the rate of interest will be above r_1, and the level of investment will thus be less than i_1. Therefore we see that when income is above the equilibrium level, saving will be higher than, and investment will be lower than, their equilibrium levels. Thus withdrawals exceed injections and income will fall.

Now, consider a level of income less than the equilibrium level. At this level of income saving will be below the equilibrium level. Also the transactions demand for cash will be less than m_1. Thus cash available for speculative purposes exceeds $m - m_1$ and thus also exceeds m_s. The rate of interest will be below r_1, so that investment will exceed i_1. Therefore, at a level of income below the equilibrium level, saving will be less than, and investment will be greater than, their equilibrium level so that withdrawals must be less than injections, and income will rise.

> **The model has negative feedback: income tends to fall when it is above the equilibrium level and to rise when below it.**

Some comparative-static results

We now consider shifts in the functional relations, and by using the method of comparative statics, we see what the theory predicts will happen to the various relevant magnitudes. Most of the analysis is verbal but the reader should follow it through by drawing his own graphs.

AN OUTWARD SHIFT IN THE INVESTMENT FUNCTION: At the existing level of income, saving will fall short of investment so that income will rise. As income rises, more money is needed for transactions purposes, and hence less will be left over for speculative purposes. Thus, the rate of interest will rise as people try to restore their money balances by selling bonds. As the rate of interest rises, investment falls.

At the original level of income, investment exceeds saving because the investment function has shifted upward. Equilibrium is then restored by the rise in savings resulting from the rise of income, and by the fall in investment resulting from the rise in interest rates. The simple multiplier formula of Chapter 36 takes investment as a constant and assumes that the whole of any equilibrating change must come through changes in income. The fall in investment caused by interest-rate increases reduces the value of the multiplier. (This is the process referred to on page 557 as the *crowding out effect*, and also discussed on pages 539–44 under the heading National income and the rate of interest.)

> **The Keynesian model therefore predicts that an upward shift in the investment function will cause a rise in the level of income, a rise in the level of saving, and a rise in the rate of interest.**

A FALL IN THE TRANSACTIONS DEMAND FOR MONEY: In this case, less money is needed for transactions purposes at each level of income than previously. At the original level of income, more money is now available for speculative purposes. This will lower the rate of interest (because people attempt to buy bonds with their surplus cash). The fall in the rate of interest raises the quantity of investment. Thus national income will rise.

The theory thus predicts that a fall in the transactions demand for cash will cause a rise in national income, a fall in interest rates, and a rise in saving and investment.

A DOWNWARD REVISION IN EXPECTATIONS ABOUT THE NORMAL RATE OF INTEREST: If there is a general change so that people come to expect a lower normal rate than they previously expected, the *LP* schedule in Figure 43.1 (iii) will shift to the left. Any given rate of interest will seem higher in relation to the normal rate than it did previously (i.e., any given price of bonds will seem *lower* in relation to the normal price); thus people will be inclined to move from money into bonds and be less inclined to hold money than they were previously.

This leftward shift of the *LP* schedule will create an excess supply of money at the old rate and the rate of interest will fall as people try to swap money for bonds. The fall in the rate of interest will raise investment and this in turn will raise national income. Thus the theory predicts that a downward revision in expectations about the future interest rate will lower the current rate of interest, raise income, and raise saving and investment.

There are, of course, many other shifts that could be studied, and the reader should check his understanding of the theory by working out the consequences of one or two further shifts chosen at random.

The Hicksian representation of the model

If we wish to discover what happens when various components of the model change, we can always shift the functions in Figure 43.1, as we did in the previous section. For some purposes, however, it is convenient to reduce the model to a more compressed form. This form was first developed by John R. Hicks in his famous review of Keynes' *General Theory* entitled 'Mr Keynes and the Classics'.

We plot the level of national income and the rate of interest on the graph in Figure 43.2. We first take the two relations from Figure 43.1 (i) and (iv) *and consider the combinations of income and interest rates that would equate savings (the only withdrawal) and investment (the only injection).* First look at Figure 43.1 (i). It shows us that the higher is the level of income, the higher is the level of savings. This means that, if investment is to remain equal to savings, the volume of investment must rise; Figure 43.1 (iv)

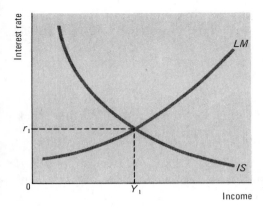

Fig. 43.2 The Hicksian representation of the Keynesian model with money

shows us that this requires a fall in the rate of interest. We have now derived the curve labled *IS* in Figure 43.2. The IS CURVE shows the rate of interest that must rule at each level of income if investment is to be equal to savings at that level of income. One point on the curve, for example, corresponds to the level of income Y_1 and to the rate of interest r_1 in Figure 43.1. The downward slope of the *IS* curve shows that the rate of interest must fall as income rises if additional investment is to be called forth to match the additional savings generated out of the higher level of income.

Next we consider the relations in Figure 43.1(ii) and (iii) *and ask what the rate of interest must be at each level of income if the demand for money is to equal its supply.* Figure 43.1(ii) shows that the higher is the level of national income, the higher will be the quantity of money required for transactions purposes, m_1, and thus the less will there be left over from the fixed supply, m_0. This smaller quantity is all that is available to be held for speculative purposes, and Figure 43.1(iii) shows that, in order to reduce the demand to this smaller available quantity, the rate of interest must rise. We have now derived the curve labelled *LM* in Figure 43.2. The *LM* curve shows all the combinations of income and interest rates that will equate the demand for and the supply of money. Its upward slope indicates that the higher the level of national income (and hence the higher the transactions demand for money), the higher must be the rate of interest if the total demand for money is to remain equal to an unchanged supply of it.[1]

We have now reduced the four curves of Figure 43.1 to the two curves in Figure 43.2. The *IS* curve shows all the combinations of levels of income and rates of interest that equate saving with investment, and the *LM* curve shows all those combinations of the same two variables that equate the demand for money with a given supply of it. The intersection of the two curves shows the level of income and

1 You should not lose sight of the *market mechanism* producing this result. Assume, for example, that with m_s money available for speculative purposes, the market rate was above the equilibrium rate of r_1. At this rate of interest the supply of money would exceed the demand. Having this extra quantity available, the public would attempt to convert it into bonds. This would send up the price of bonds and send down the rate of interest towards r_1. If, on the other hand, the rate were below equilibrium, then the demand for money would exceed the available supply. In an effort to obtain the extra money, bonds would be sold, thus driving down the price of bonds and driving up the rate of interest towards r_1.

the rate of interest at which both sets of equilibrium conditions – investment equals savings and the demand for money equals the supply of money – will be satisfied simultaneously.

Some comparative static results

It is now possible to do comparative static exercises easily by determining the effect on the *IS* and the *LM* curves of any changes in which we are interested. We first check one of the cases studied above and then go on to consider a new case.

AN OUTWARD SHIFT IN THE INVESTMENT FUNCTION: At any combination of *Y* and *r* for which savings equalled investment formerly there is now an excess of investment over saving. To see the effect of this on the *IS* curve, note the following. To restore equilibrium at an unchanged interest rate, income must be increased sufficiently to call forth extra savings equal to the extra investment that was caused by the outward shift in the investment function. In order to restore equilibrium at an unchanged level of income it will be necessary to raise the rate of interest so that the quantity of investment is reduced to its original level (and so is again equal to the unchanged amount of saving). Both of these results show that an outward shift in the investment schedule causes an outward shift in the *IS* curve – any given rate of interest is associated with a higher level of income than previously and any given level of income is associated with a higher rate of interest than previously.

Figure 43.3 shows the effect of an outward shift of the *IS* curve from *IS* to *IS'*. The equilibrium interest rate and national income go from r_1 and Y_1 to r_2 and Y_2 respectively.

An increase in investment increases national income and the rate of interest.

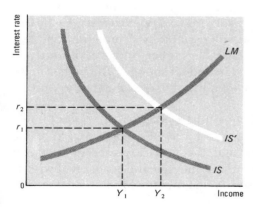

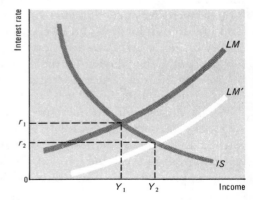

Fig. 43.3 The effect of an outward shift in the *IS* curve

Fig. 43.4 The effect of an outward shift in the *LM* curve

A CHANGE IN THE MONEY SUPPLY: Assume that in exercise of its monetary policy the central bank increases the money supply (which it can do for example by an open market purchase of bonds). At any given levels of national income and the rate of interest, there will now be an excess supply of money. To see the effect of this on the *LM* curve note the following. In order to restore equilibrium at an unchanged level of income, it will be necessary to lower the interest rate thus increasing the demand for money. In order to restore equilibrium at an unchanged rate of interest, it will be necessary to increase income thus increasing the demand for money. Both of these results show that the effect of an increase in the money supply is a shift of the *LM* curve outwards to the right.

Figure 43.4 shows that the effect of an outward shift in the *LM* curve from *LM* to *LM'*. The equilibrium rate of interest and national income go from Y_1 and r_1 to Y_2 and r_2 respectively. This leads to the following key prediction.

An expansionary monetary policy that increases the money supply increases national income and lowers the rate of interest.

The reason for this is that the attempt to turn excess money balances into interest-earning assets bids up the price of bonds which is the same thing as a fall in the rate of interest. The fall in interest rates raises interest-sensitive expenditures and this increases national income.

A contractionary monetary policy that lowers the quantity of money has the opposite effects as can be seen by shifting the *LM* curve from *LM'* to *LM* in Figure 43.4.

We have now accomplished a formal integration of money into the theory of the determination of national income. In subsequent chapters we shall be able to use this expanded model to study some important controversies on current economic policy.

Part nine

The international economy

44

The gains from trade

In Chapter 36 we considered the effects of trade on the circular flow of income. At that time we emphasized the effect of trade on aggregate expenditure, and we were regarding imports as a withdrawal from total domestic expenditure and exports as an injection. We now wish to inquire into the problems of international trade in a more fundamental way. The sequence is as follows: in this chapter we ask if there are gains from international trade and if so, what is the source of the gains; in the Appendix we ask if free international trade will lead to a pattern of imports and exports that will allow the potential gains from trade to be realized. In Chapter 45 we inquire into exchange rates, asking what they are, what they do and why they vary. In Chapter 46 we study reasons that have been advanced for interfering with the free flow of trade that emerges from the operation of the unhindered price system. In Chapter 47 we give a brief account of some of the most important experiences in the world of international trade.

A word of warning

In what follows we shall often speak of nations, e.g., the United Kingdom, and the United States, trading various commodities. This convenient anthropomorphic form of expression should not mislead the student into thinking that all, or even the majority of, decisions about trade are actually taken by governments. In most countries governments do play some, more or less important, role in foreign trade; it must never be forgotten, however, that in market economies most of the decisions determining the size, content and direction of foreign trade are taken by households and firms. Firms may think they see an opportunity of selling goods abroad and may arrange to have these goods exported; other firms may think they see an opportunity of selling foreign goods in the home market and arrange to have these goods imported; and, if households find them attractive and purchase them, the venture will be successful; if they do not, then the goods will remain unsold and will no longer be imported or exported. Governments may, of course, try to influence this process:

they may put subsidies on exports, seeking to encourage foreign sales of domestically-produced goods by making their prices more attractive; they may put tariffs on imports, seeking to discourage domestic sales of foreign-produced goods, by making their prices less attractive. None of this should obscure the basic fact that, in capitalist economies, foreign trade, just like domestic trade, is determined mainly by thousands of independent decisions taken by firms and households and coordinated – more or less effectively – by the price system.

The major difference between foreign trade and domestic trade results from the fact that the domestic trade of different countries makes use of different monies. The money of one country, e.g., the rupee, while generally acceptable within the bounds of that one country, will not be acceptable to the firms and households of another country. If, for example, an importer in India wishes to purchase British goods, he cannot pay for them in rupees, he will have to obtain pounds sterling first. *In general, trade between nations can only occur if it is possible to exchange the currency of one nation for that of another.* For the moment we shall ignore this problem of different currencies and ask the following question: assuming that trade takes place, is there any gain from trade and what is the source of this gain?

Interpersonal, interregional and international trade

Economists have long recognized that the principles governing the gains from trade apply equally well to foreign trade as to domestic trade. Governments tend to regard the two aspects of trade in very different lights, but economists were prominent in the fight to recognize that the causes and consequences of international trade were merely an extension of the principles governing domestic trade. Some of these principles were developed quite early, but it was not until the mid-nineteenth century that the British economist John Stuart Mill advanced a theory that showed satisfactorily how international trade could be explained by exactly the same principles as those explaining domestic trade.

Indeed, economists now recognize that they are asking the same question when they ask what is the advantage of trade between two individuals, between two groups, between two regions, and between two countries. The question of the advantage of trade is usually referred to as that of the *gains from trade*. If we are to search for the advantages of trade, we may consider the differences between a world with trade and one without it. First, consider the individual level. If there were no trade between individuals, each person would have to make himself self-sufficient; he would have to produce for himself all the food, clothing, shelter, medical services, entertainment and luxuries of life that he required. Although this is a wildly unreal situation, it does not take much imagination to realize that living standards would be very low in a world of individual self-sufficiency. Trade between individuals allows each person to specialize in things he can do well, and buy from others the things he cannot easily produce for himself. Thus trade and specialization are intimately connected. Without trade, everyone must be self-sufficient; with trade everyone can specialize.

The same principles apply to regions. Without interregional trade, each region would have to be self-sufficient. With such trade, plains regions can specialize in growing grain, mountain regions in mining and lumbering, and regions with abundant power sources in manufacturing; cool regions can produce wheat and other crops that thrive in such conditions, and tropical regions can produce bananas and coconuts. One would suspect – and soon we shall prove formally – that the living standards of the inhabitants of all regions can be made higher if the inhabitants of each specialize in producing the commodities in the production of which they have some natural or acquired advantage, and obtain other products by trade, than when each region is self-sufficient.

Obviously, identical remarks apply to nations. Whatever the divisions represented by national boundaries, they are usually arbitrary with respect to the advantages of regional specialization and trade. There is no reason to think that a national boundary will define an area that could be fully self-sufficient at no cost to itself. Thus nations, like regions or persons, can gain from specialization and the international trade that would have to accompany it.

THE GAINS FROM RESOURCE RE-ALLOCATION: A SIMPLE EXAMPLE
Absolute and comparative advantage

If there were no trade, everyone would have to produce what he required for himself; with trade, various groups of people specialize in the production of different commodities. Trade therefore results in a different allocation of resources than would occur if there were no trade, and, if we are to search for the source of the gains from trade, we must look to the gains from resource re-allocation that result from it.

Let us first consider a simple example relating to resource allocation within one country. Assume that you are the economic dictator of a country and that you wish to increase the production of commodity X. Assuming that there is full employment, you will have to produce less of something else if you are going to produce more of X. Let us say that you have decided to reduce the production of commodity Y in order to free the resources necessary to produce more of commodity X.

Now assume that there are two distinct groups of labourers producing Y at present, and that the two groups have different capabilities. Your problem is to decide from which of the two groups to take workers in order to raise the production of X by some stated amount, say, 16,000 units per year. Let us imagine two situations. In the first which is shown in Table 44.1, you would probably have no trouble in solving the problem.

Table 44.1 Production of two commodities X and Y, by two groups A and B

	Situation 1	
	Existing annual production of Y per person	Potential annual production of X per person
Group A	1,000	1,600
Group B	500	2,000

Obviously you should move workers from Group B since they can produce more X and less Y than Group-A workers. If you move 8 Group-B workers you will get your 16,000 extra X and the opportunity cost will be the 4,000 Y that these 8 workers could have produced instead. The opportunity cost of 1 X when Group-B workers are moved is $4,000/16,000 = \frac{1}{4}$ unit of Y.

If you had been so silly as to move Group-A workers, you would have had to transfer 10 workers, giving a loss of 10,000 Y to get 16,000 X. When Group-A workers are moved, the opportunity cost of a unit of X is $\frac{5}{8}$ of a unit of Y (10,000/16,000). There is a clear loss of an extra 6,000 Y if Group-A workers rather than Group-B workers are transferred.

Now consider a second situation as shown in Table 44.2.

Table 44.2 Production of two commodities X and Y, by two groups A and B

	Situation II	
	Existing annual production of Y per person	Potential annual production of X per person
Group A	1,000	1,600
Group B	1,500	2,000

Stop and think from which group you would now move workers in order to produce an extra 16,000 X with the least possible loss of Y. Next, ask yourself why it is from that group and not from the other that you would select your workers. The student who answers these questions before reading on will have gone a long way towards discovering for himself the idea of COMPARATIVE ADVANTAGE.

One obvious thing to do might be to transfer workers from Group B, because they are more efficient at producing X than are Group-A workers. But you must also consider the efficiency of each of these groups at producing Y. What matters is not just how efficient is each group at producing X, but how much Y you lose for every extra unit of X you get with each group. You should now calculate the loss in output of Y, per unit of X produced, for each group of workers and then ask yourself again: from which group should I move workers? Clearly, it is Group-A, not Group-B workers who should be moved; with Group-A workers the loss of Y per unit of X gained is less than with Group-B workers. Let us check this calculation. If we transfer Group-A workers we must take 10 workers to get our 16,000 extra X, and the loss is thus 10,000 Y. If we take Group-B workers we only need to transfer 8 workers to get our 16,000 X, but by so doing we lose 12,000 Y. Thus there is a clear extra loss of 2,000 Y in moving Group-B workers rather than Group-A workers. When Group-A workers are transferred, $\frac{5}{8}$ of a unit of Y is lost for every extra unit of X produced; when Group-B workers are transferred, $\frac{6}{8}$ of a unit of Y is lost for every extra unit of X produced.

The moral of this story is that it does not matter that Group-B workers are absolutely more efficient at producing X than are Group-A workers. What matters is the comparative efficiencies of the two groups in both lines, because what we need to compare between the two groups of workers is the amount of the loss of one commodity, per unit gained of the other. In other words we need to know the *opportunity cost* of a unit of X in terms of Y for each group, and we naturally choose to transfer workers from the group with the lower opportunity cost.

The conclusion that Group-A rather than Group-B workers should be transferred depends on the fact that the ratio $\dfrac{\text{annual production of } Y}{\text{annual production of } X}$ is less for members of Group A than Group B. If the annual production of *both* X and Y is changed in the same proportion, there is no change in these ratios. The reader should check for himself that multiplying by the same amount the annual outputs of both X and Y for Group-A workers does nothing to affect the conclusion that it is Group-A workers that should be transferred rather than Group-B workers. (In other words, change the number in the first row of Table 44.2 to read 10,000 and 16,000 and note that the opportunity cost of $1X$ remains unchanged at $\frac{5}{8}Y$.)

Now let us consider whether or not there is any *gain from trade* between our two groups, A and B. Assume that the Group-B workers get together and say: 'This association with these inefficient Group-A characters is only dragging down our standard of living; after all we can produce both X and Y more efficiently than they can. Let us split away and form our own economically independent state with our own dictator; then those poor Group-A workers can wallow in their own poverty without dragging us down with them.'

If the two groups form two independent self-sufficient countries there is no doubt that the people in B will have a higher standard of living than those in A. People in B can produce a higher *per capita* output of both X and Y than can those in A. Now let us suppose that we have our two independent countries, A and B, both producing the X and Y needed to satisfy their own requirements. Is it not possible to do better? A glance at Table 44.2 will show that it is possible. Country B sacrifices $\frac{6}{8}$ unit of Y for every X it produces, while A only sacrifices $\frac{5}{8}$ of a unit. Now do the division the other way, and find the amount of X given up for every unit of Y produced: in country A it is $\frac{8}{5}$ while in B it is only $\frac{4}{3} X$. Thus, B has a lower opportunity cost of producing Y while A has a lower opportunity cost of producing X.[1] Now what would happen if B produced less X and more Y while A produced less Y and more X?

We assume that, in country B, two labourers are moved from the production of X to that of Y, and that in country A, three labourers are moved from the production of Y to that of X. The gains and losses are recorded in Table 44.3. There is, in this case, a clear gain of $800X$ per year. (Remember that we have not changed the total amount of employment in A or B, we have merely re-allocated it between the production of the two commodities.)

The example of Table 44.3 is constructed so that there is only a gain in X, but it is always possible to move resources so that there is an increase in the production of both X and Y. To check on this the reader is left to calculate for himself the gains and losses if 8 labourers in A are moved from producing Y to producing X, while,

1 Question: Is it ever possible for B to have a lower opportunity cost of producing both X and Y than does A?

Table 44.3 Changes in production caused by a re-allocation of resources (derived from Table 44.2)

	Change in annual output	
	Y	X
3 labourers in A are moved from Y to X	−3,000	+4,800
2 labourers in B are moved from X to Y	+3,000	−4,000
Net Gain	0	+ 800

at the same time 6 labourers in B are moved from producing X to producing Y. The changes in output can be calculated from Table 44.2 and should be recorded in a table similar to Table 44.3. This is a most important calculation and no one should proceed without completing it.

We now see that the inhabitants of B were wrong to believe that they could do better by being self-sufficient than by trading with A; if B produces more Y and A produces more X, the total production of both X and Y can be increased, so there is more to go round for everyone. However, since A is producing more X and B more Y than when they were self-sufficient, it will be necessary, so that consumers in each country can have the X and Y they desire, to trade A's X for B's Y. It is necessary, that is, to engage in international trade.

This is the basis of the gains from trade between two countries: different opportunity costs in the two countries. It matters not one bit whether or not one country is absolutely more efficient than the other in all lines (e.g., Table 44.2), or only in some lines (e.g., Table 44.1).

Let us pursue this a step further by expressing the data in Table 44.2 in a slightly different form.

Table 44.4 Opportunity cost ratios (derived from Table 44.2)

	Amount of Y that must be given up to get one unit of X	Amount of X that must be given up to get one unit of Y
Country A	$\frac{5}{8}Y$	$1\frac{3}{5}X$
Country B	$\frac{3}{4}Y$	$1\frac{1}{3}X$

Now it is as simple as this: if B produces *one more unit of Y* the loss is $1\frac{1}{3}X$; if A produces *one less unit of Y*, the gain is $1\frac{3}{5}X$; Y production is unchanged and X production has increased.

We may now state these propositions more formally.

> **DEFINITION: A country has a comparative advantage *vis-à-vis* a second country in the production of the commodity in which it has a lower opportunity cost than the other country.**

PROPOSITION: If two countries are producing some of two commodities, then the total output of both commodities can always be increased if each country transfers resources into the production of the commodity in which it has a comparative advantage.

Comparative advantage must not be confused with ABSOLUTE ADVANTAGE: we say that a country has an absolute advantage in the production of some commodity if, with a given amount of resources, it can produce more of that commodity than can the other country using the same quantity of resources. Thus in Table 44.1, A has an absolute advantage in Y, while B has an absolute advantage in X; in Table 44.2, B has an absolute advantage over A in both X and Y. That comparative advantage is independent of absolute advantage can be seen by multiplying A's figures for X and Y production in Table 44.2 by the same amount. No such multiplication will affect the opportunity costs expressed in Table 44.3. If, for example, A's figures are multiplied by 10, giving $10,000\,Y$ and $16,000\,X$ as the annual outputs of a labourer in these two industries, then A becomes very much more efficient in both X and Y production than B, but the opportunity cost of X in terms of Y or of Y in terms of X is unchanged. The figures in Table 44.4 and the argument immediately below it remain unchanged.[1]

The only time when it is not possible to get more production by re-allocating resources when both countries are producing both commodities, is when the opportunity cost is the same in both countries. Assume, for example, the data in Table 44.5.

Table 44.5 Opportunity cost ratios for which there is no comparative advantage

	Situation III	
	Amount of Y that must be given up to get a unit of X	Amount of X that must be given up to get a unit of Y
Country A	$\frac{1}{2}Y$	$2X$
Country B	$\frac{1}{2}Y$	$2X$

Now if A produces one more Y, then $2X$ is sacrificed, while if B produces one less Y, then $2X$ is gained, making a net gain of zero for both X and Y.

1 Textbooks of economics often quote numerical examples in which the total quantity of resources is stated, and divided in some arbitrary way, between the production of X and that of Y, when A and B are self-sufficient. They then compare this output with the output resulting from a situation in which A produces only one good and B only the other. It is then usually found that, in the latter situation, there is more of one good and less of the other than in the former situation, and it becomes necessary to go through some valuation process to establish that specialization raises the value of production. Such examples tend to obscure the fundamental issue: specialization according to comparative advantage makes it possible to produce more of all goods; if both countries are producing some of both commodities, it is always possible to re-allocate resources so as to get more of both goods.

So far we have only given an example. A simple algebraic proof follows: In country A the opportunity cost of one Y is aX, while in B it is bX. Assume that $a > b$. It follows that the opportunity cost of one X is $1/a$ in A and $1/b$ in B and that $1/a < 1/b$. Thus A has a comparative advantage in producing X and B in Y. Now if B produces one more Y she sacrifices bX, while if A produces one less Y she gains aX. As a result Y production is unchanged and X production changes by $aX - bX = X(a - b)$ which is positive since $a > b$. The increase in X depends on the magnitude of the differences between the two countries in the opportunity cost of producing X.

The importance of comparative rather than absolute costs can again be illustrated by considering the cost data which could have given rise to the opportunity costs in Table 44.5. If in country A a year's labour could produce $200X$ and $100Y$, this would give rise to the costs shown in the table. In country B a year's labour might produce $20X$ and $10Y$, in which case A would have an absolute advantage over B in both commodities, but no comparative advantage. On the other hand, a year's labour in B might produce $2,000X$ and $1,000Y$, in which case B would have an absolute advantage over A in both lines of production, but there is still no comparative advantage. We can multiply the output of a year's labour in X and Y by the same amount without affecting the data in Table 44.5.

The examples in this Chapter have concerned two countries and two commodities, but the argument is readily generalized to many countries and many commodities. The central generalization and basic cornerstone of the theory of the gains from trade can now be stated.

> **Whenever opportunity costs differ among countries, specialization of each country in producing those commodities in which it has comparative advantages will make it possible to increase production of all commodities relative to the quantities available if each country attempted to be self-sufficient.**

It has been shown that regional specialization is efficient in the sense that it makes possible a larger total world production than when regions are self-sufficient. But, as we have already seen, specialization requires trade and so we refer to the increased production brought about by specialization as the gains from trade.

Additional sources of the gains from trade: learning by doing and economies of scale

So far, it has been assumed that costs are constant, and it has been shown that there are gains from specialization and trade as long as there are interregional differences in opportunity costs. If costs are not constant, other sources of gain are possible. The early economists placed great importance on a factor that is now called learning by doing. They felt that as regions specialized in particular tasks, the workers and managers would become more efficient in performing them. As people acquire expertise or 'know-how', costs tend to fall. A substantial body of modern empirical work suggests that this really does happen. If this is the case, then output of X per man may rise in country A as it becomes more specialized in that commodity (see Table 44.2), while the same may happen to output of Y per man in country B. Because there would be a gain from having A and B specialize in cloth and wheat, respectively, even if the output per unit of resources employed were constant (see Table 44.3), it follows that there will be an added gain if output of X per unit of resources rises in country A as A specializes in X, and the same thing happens in country B as B expands her output of Y.

A further reason why costs might fall as regions specialize concerns falling long-run costs. If costs fall as output increases, world output can be greater when there is one large X industry in Country A and one large Y industry in B, rather than two half-size industries one in each country and two half-size Y industries, one in each country.

Terms of trade

So far, it has been shown that world production can be increased if countries A and B specialize in the production of the commodity in which they have a comparative advantage and that specialization requires trade. How will these gains from specialization and trade be shared between the two countries? The division of the gain depends on the terms at which trade takes place. The TERMS OF TRADE are defined as the quantity of domestic goods that must be given up to get a unit of imported goods. Thus, the terms of trade are nothing more than the opportunity cost of obtaining goods through international trade rather than producing them directly.

If the terms of trade are favourable to a country, this means that the country need only export a small amount of domestically-produced goods to obtain a unit of imports. If the terms of trade are unfavourable, the country must export a large quantity of domestically-produced goods to obtain a unit of imports. Since the country always has the opportunity of producing a good itself rather than importing it, there is no need to accept terms of trade less favourable than the domestic opportunity cost of producing the import. (If, for example, a country can produce one unit of Y at home thus sacrificing two units of X, it will only import Y if the terms of trade are less than two units of X per unit of Y.)

Appendix

Does the price system lead to a pattern of trade which accords with the balance of comparative advantage?

In the body of Chapter 44 we showed that potential gains from trade arose wherever there existed comparative advantages between different countries in the production of various commodities. We next need to ask if the price system would lead countries to specialize in the production of goods in which they had comparative advantage and import those in which they had a comparative disadvantage. In other words can we expect the unhampered price system to realize the potential gains from trade?[1]

Exchange rates in a simple two-country, two-commodity world

We can answer this question by considering the simplest possible case with two countries and two commodities. Let us repeat, since we are already familiar with it, the example of Chapter 44, Table 4. The figures in the second column are of course just the reciprocal of the corresponding figures in the first column. (Any student who is not absolutely certain why this is so must go back and reread the previous chapter.)

We have already shown that country A has a comparative advantage in the production of

1 This Appendix is moderately difficult and it can be omitted if you are prepared to accept that the answer to this question is yes.

X and country B has a comparative advantage in the production of Y.

Table 44.6 Opportunity costs of X in terms of Y and of Y in terms of X

	Opportunity cost of X in terms of Y	Opportunity cost of Y in terms of X
Country A	$\frac{5}{8}Y$	$1\frac{3}{5}X$
Country B	$\frac{3}{4}Y$	$1\frac{1}{3}X$

The relation between opportunity costs and prices

In order to see what will happen in a market society, we must discover what will be the prices of the two commodities in each of the two countries. It is convenient to start by assuming that the two countries do not allow trade between each other so that each country must produce those quantities of X and Y that it requires for its own consumption.

The proposition that we shall prove below is as follows: under competitive conditions it will be true for any one country that

Opportunity cost of X in terms of Y

$$= \frac{\text{marginal money cost of production of } X}{\text{marginal money cost of production of } Y}$$

$$= \frac{\text{money price of } X}{\text{money price of } Y}.$$

The opportunity cost of X in terms of Y is the number of units of Y that must be sacrificed in order to produce one more unit of X (by moving resources out of Y production into X production). This is a physical measure. Under competitive conditions this will be equal to the ratio of the (money) costs of producing one more unit of each commodity. Why? Under competitive conditions any factor of production must be paid the same in both the X and the Y industries (otherwise the factor would move from the low-paid industry to the high-paid one). Thus, if it costs twice as much to produce a unit of X as it does to produce a unit of Y, then it must take twice the quantity of factors to produce a unit of X as a unit of Y. In this case, if sufficient factors are transferred from Y in order to produce one more unit of X, two units of Y will be lost. (The reader should pause here and think out carefully for himself the argument of the last two sentences.) Thus, in general, the opportunity cost ratio will conform to the ratio of the marginal costs. Under competitive conditions the ratio of the money prices of the two commodities will be the same as the ratio of the marginal costs. If this is not the case then firms will transfer resources from one line to the other and thereby increase their profits. Assume, for example, that the marginal cost of X is twice that of Y, while the price of X is three times that of Y. By producing two less Y and one more X the firm's outlay will be unchanged but its revenue will be increased because the one unit of X sells for more than the two units of Y which were foregone. Under these conditions profit-maximizing firms will move resources out of Y and into X. The price of X (p_X) will fall as its production increases and the price of Y (p_Y) will rise as its production diminishes. This movement will continue until p_X is only twice p_Y, in which case there will be no gain in producing more X and less Y. The student should now repeat for himself the similar argument for the case in which p_X is less than twice p_Y (say $p_X = p_Y$). It now follows in general that, under competitive conditions, the equilibrium price ratio will conform to the opportunity cost ratio.

Thus, as soon as we know the technical conditions of production, then we also know the relative prices.[1] We do not, however, know the absolute price level so we shall start by assuming it to be anything we wish and later inquire into the consequences of changes in the absolute level of prices. Let us say that the price of X in country A is \$2 while in B it is £1. It now follows that we know the price of Y in A and B. These prices are listed in Table 44.7.

Table 44.7 Money prices of X and Y in countries A and B

	X	Y
Country A	\$2	\$3·20
Country B	£1	£1·33

A comparison of Tables 44.6 and 44.7 will show that in each country the price ratios and the opportunity cost ratios are the same. (We have now given quite a long chain of reasoning. Although each link may be simple enough the whole chain may seem difficult at the first attempt. The student who has any difficulty in understanding the relationship between Tables 44.6 and 44.7 should go back and re-read this section from the beginning.)

The determination of the exchange rate

We now know the prices that will exist in countries A and B when they do not engage in trade. Now let us assume that trade is opened between these two countries and that the cost of transporting X and Y between them is small enough so that it can be ignored. Before we know which way trade will flow we must know the rate of exchange[2] between the

---

1 The reason why price depends only on costs (i.e., supply) and not on both demand and supply as it did earlier, is that costs are assumed to be constant so that supply curves will be perfectly elastic.

2 If you are uncertain what an exchange rate is you should read the first two pages of Chapter 45 at this time.

currencies of the two countries. Let us start by saying that one pound exchanges for one dollar. Now, in these circumstances, B's X which sells for £1 domestically can be sold for $1 in A. Also B's Y can be sold for $1·33 in A. On the other hand A's X must sell in B for £2 and A's Y must sell in B for £3·20. In other words, at the exchange rate $1 = £1, B can undersell A in both X and Y; B will thus export X and Y to A but will buy nothing in return. This means that on the foreign exchange market everyone will be wishing to buy pounds in order to purchase B's goods which are cheaper than A's, but no one will wish to buy dollars in order to purchase A's goods which are more expensive than B's.

This means that everyone will want to trade dollars for pounds but no one will wish to trade pounds for dollars. Clearly this is not a stable situation: the pound is undervalued and the dollar is overvalued. The price of the pound in terms of dollars will rise. Let us say that the price of pounds rises until the exchange rate becomes £1 = $2, the resulting prices are listed in Table 44.8.

Table 44.8 Money prices of goods exported from one country to the other when the rate of exchange is £1 = $2

	X	Y
Sale price in A of the commodity imported from B	$2·00	$2·66
Sale price in B of the commodity imported from A	£1	£1·60

Now it is a matter of indifference whether X is brought from A to B. Clearly this is the cheapest possible rate of exchange for the pound. As long as the pound exchanges for anything less than $2 then both X and Y will be cheaper when bought from B than from A; trade will flow only from B to A; everyone will wish to exchange dollars for pounds but no one will wish to do the opposite, and so the price will change. At the exchange rate of

£1 = $2, B will sell Y to A but A could sell X to B. As soon as the exchange rate rises above £1 = $2 then A's X will definitely be cheaper than B's, while B's Y will still be cheaper than A's. The student should himself work out what the prices will be if the exchange rate is £1 = $2·25.

Now assume that the value of the pound goes as high as £1 = $2·40. Let us see what the prices of imported goods would be at this exchange rate. Country B's X would sell in A for $2·40 while her Y would sell for $3·20 $(= £1\frac{1}{3}$ at $2·40 to the pound). Country A's X would sell for $£\frac{5}{6}$ $(= 2 at $2·40 to the pound) while her Y would sell for $£1\frac{1}{3}$ $(= $3·20$ at $2·40 to the pound). Now, at this exchange rate, A will sell X to B while B could just sell Y to A. At any exchange rate higher than £1 = $2·40, A will be able to undersell B in both X and Y; all trade would flow from A to B; everyone would want dollars and no one would want pounds; and the exchange rate would have to change.

There are a number of things to notice about this example. It was never possible to pick an exchange rate at which A could sell Y to B while at the same time B could sell X to A. At all exchange rates at which trade flowed in both directions, A sold X to B and B sold Y to A. Trade was always in the direction of comparative advantage. We saw in the last chapter that A had a comparative advantage in the production of X and that B had a comparative advantage in the production of Y; *we have now seen that on our assumption the price system ensures that A produces and exports* X *while B produces and exports* Y. We should also note, when constructing other examples, that the limiting exchange rates are easily calculated. Find the rate at which the commodity in which A has a comparative advantage will have the same price as that commodity has when produced in B, then find the exchange rate at which the commodity in which B has a comparative advantage will have the same price as that commodity has when it is produced in A. These two exchange rates will be the limiting rates between which the actual rate must lie. If the rate should be outside these limits one country will be able to undersell the other in both commodities and the exchange rates will have to change. In the present example the exchange rate must lie between the limits $£1 = \$2$ and $£1 = \$2\cdot40$.

45

The theory of exchange rates

In the previous chapter we saw that the sources of the gains from trade are the same for trade between individuals, regions and nations. There is, however, one basic complication that distinguishes international trade from interregional trade: although different regions of the same country use the same money, different nations do not. The currency of one country is generally acceptable within the bounds of that country, but it will not usually be accepted by households and firms in another country. When a British producer sells his products he requires payment in sterling. He must meet his wage bill, pay for his raw materials, and reinvest or distribute his profits. If he sells his goods to British purchasers, there is no problem since they will pay in sterling. If, however, he sells his goods to an Indian importer, either the Indian must exchange his rupees for pounds to pay for the goods, or the UK producer must accept rupees. He will do this only if he knows that he can exchange the rupees for the sterling that he requires. The same holds true for producers in all countries; they must eventually receive payment in terms of the currency of their own country for the goods that they sell. We must now ask what is the mechanism for exchanging currencies and what are the consequences of the need to do so?

FOREIGN EXCHANGE TRANSACTIONS

Suppose that an American dealer wishes to purchase a British sports car to sell in the United States. The British manufacturer requires payment in his own currency. If the car is priced at, say £1,000, the American importer can go to his bank and purchase a cheque for £1,000 and send this to the British seller. The price that he pays for this cheque is called the exchange rate. We shall assume an exchange rate of $2·40 to £1. Given this exchange rate, the US importer would write a cheque on his own account for $2,400 in payment of his £1,000 sterling cheque or 'draft'. The British producer would deposit the cheque in his own bank. When all this was done, the banking system would have exchanged obligations to Americans for obligations to residents of the UK. The deposits of the American purchaser, which are liabilities

Table 45.1 Changes in the balance sheets of two banks

U.K. Bank		U.S. Bank	
Assets	Liabilities	Assets	Liabilities
No change	Deposits of car exporter +£1,000	No change	Deposits of car importer −$2,400
	Deposits of refrigerator importer −£1,000		Deposits of refrigerator exporter +$2,400

of his bank, would be reduced by $2,400, and the deposits of the British seller, which are liabilities of the British bank, would be increased by £1,000. The banking system, as a whole, makes a profit by charging a small commission for effecting these transactions.

Now let us consider a second transaction. Assume that a British wholesaler wishes to purchase ten American refrigerators for sale in Britain. If the refrigerators are priced at $240 each, the American seller will require a total payment of $2,400. To effect this payment, the English importer goes to his bank and writes a cheque on his account for £1,000 and receives a cheque drawn on a US bank for $2,400. This reduces the deposit liabilities of the British bank by £1,000. When the American seller deposits this cheque, his deposits, which are the liabilities of the US banking system, are increased by $2,400. Thus the banking system as a whole has merely switched liabilities, this time from the UK to the US.

These two transactions cancel each other out, and there is no net change in international liabilities. The balance sheets of the British and the American banks will show the changes in Table 45.1. No money need flow between British and American banks to effect these transactions; each bank merely increases the deposits of one domestic customer and lowers those of another, making a profit by charging a commission on its services. Indeed, as long as the flow of payments between the two countries is equal, so that Americans are paying as much to UK residents as UK residents are paying to Americans, all payments can be managed as in the above example and there is no need for a net payment from British banks to American ones. When the flow of payments is not the same in both directions, problems arise, as we shall see very shortly.

The EXCHANGE RATE is the price at which purchases and sales of foreign currency (or claims on it, such as cheques and promises to pay) take place; it is the price of one currency in terms of another. The term FOREIGN EXCHANGE refers to what is traded, actual foreign currency or various claims on it. When the exchange rate between British pounds sterling and American dollars is £1 = $2·40, one pound exchanges for two dollars and forty cents and one dollar exchanges for £0·41⅔. There are similar exchange rates between sterling and every other nation's currency. In 1973 one pound was worth approximately 1,428 Italian lire, 6·5 German Marks, or 132 Spanish pesetas. Once the rates between sterling and any two foreign currencies are determined, there is only one rate between the two foreign currencies that will not

Table 45.2 An example of rates of exchange
giving the possibility of profitable arbitrage
operations

One unit of this currency	Exchanges for the stated number of units of this currency		
	Dollar	Lira	Pound
Dollar	1	600	·41$\frac{2}{3}$
Lira	·00166$\frac{2}{3}$	1	·00083$\frac{1}{3}$
Pound	2·40	1,200	1

allow buyers and sellers to make unlimited profits merely by an endless series of purchases and sales. Such sales and purchases are called ARBITRAGE OPERATIONS. Consider an example in which the US dollar is assumed to be worth £0·41$\frac{2}{3}$ and 600 Italian lire. Given these two rates, the only rate between lire and sterling that rules out profitable arbitrage operations is £0·41$\frac{2}{3}$ = 600 lire, which is the same thing as £1 = 1,440 lire. Table 45.2 gives an example in which the rate between the pound and the lira is out of line with the other two. Anyone could take $2 and buy 1,200 lire. He could then use his 1,200 lire to buy one pound. The pound could then be traded for $2·40, giving the trader a profit of 40¢ on the transaction. Such arbitrage operations ensure that when rates of exchange are set on free markets 'disorderly cross-rates' such as those illustrated in the table will be quickly eliminated. While the disorderly cross-rates shown in Table 45.2 persist, arbitragers will be buying lire with dollars and selling lire against pounds. If rates are free to vary, this will tend to bid the rates toward a consistent level where it is no longer possible to make profits by arbitrage. If rates are fixed by central authorities, such disorderly cross-rates could not long be sustained, and while they were, they would give a free gift to everyone who was informed enough to take advantage of them.

THE BALANCE OF PAYMENTS

The balance of actual payments

In order to know what is happening to the course of international trade, governments keep track of the actual transactions among countries. The record of such transactions is called the *balance of payments*. What we would like to measure in order to study the behaviour of the foreign-exchange market would be the actual payments between nations and the reasons for which they were made. In practice, this cannot be done. What is done instead is to record each transaction, such as the shipment of exports and the arrival of imported goods, and to classify each according to the payments or receipts that would typically arise from it.

> **Any item that typically gives rise to a purchase of foreign currency is recorded as a debit item on the accounts, and any item that typically gives rise to a sale of foreign currency is recorded as a credit item.**

If, for example, a British importer buys a US washing machine to sell in the UK, this appears as a credit in the US balance of payments, because, when the machine is paid for, sterling will be sold and dollars purchased, the US gaining foreign exchange on the deal. On the other hand, if an American shipping firm insures with Lloyd's of London a cargo destined for Egypt, this represents a debit in the US balance of payments because, when the insurance premium is paid, the shipping firm will have to pay Lloyd's in sterling. Since it will purchase sterling in return for dollars, the US stands to lose foreign exchange on the deal. Of course, what is a credit item to one country is a debit item to the other and vice versa. Thus the washing-machine transaction is a debit in the British balance of payments because it used foreign exchange, and the insurance transaction is a credit in the British balance of payments because it earns foreign exchange.

We have seen that in order to study the behaviour of the foreign-exchange market, we would really like to be able to measure purchases and sales of foreign exchange, but that we are able to measure only the movements of goods and services. In order to relate what we can measure to what we want to measure, we have to make a number of assumptions, some of them quite arbitrary. How, for example, should we record gifts of goods to foreigners? If the goods had been sold, they would have given rise to earnings of foreign exchange, but when they are given away, they do not. To take another example, what do we do with an export to a foreign firm that subsequently defaults on the debt it incurred when it bought the good on credit? These, and many related problems, are important both to the statistician who is attempting to measure the balance of payments and to the careful observer who is attempting to account for very detailed movements in the flows of trade and payments. For our more general purposes, however, we can assume that the balance of payments actually measures what we would like it to measure: the actual flow of payments between nations. [1]

The first thing that we need to notice about the record of international transactions is that *the balance of payments always balances*. Although it is quite possible for holders of sterling to want to purchase more dollars in exchange for pounds than holders of dollars want to sell in exchange for pounds, it is not possible for sterling holders actually to buy more dollars than dollar holders sell. Every dollar that is bought must be sold by someone, and every dollar that is sold must be bought by someone. Since the dollars actually bought must be equal to the dollars actually sold, the payments actually made between countries must be in balance, even though desired payments may not be.

In the *balance-of-payments accounts*, an attempt is made to record the reasons for which payments are made. Thus, we hope to be able to tell what volume of payments is (or will be) made by foreigners to UK citizens for such purposes as the purchase of British goods, the use of British services (shipping, insurance, etc.), the lending of money to British households, firms, or governments, or the investment of money in

---

1 The procedure adopted for handling the two problems cited in this paragraph are as follows. The export of a gift is recorded as a credit item just as if the good had been sold, but a compensating debit item is recorded under 'unilateral capital transfers'. Thus we assume that we *give away* the money and that the money is then used to *buy* our goods. The export that is not paid for because the buyer defaults will appear as a normal credit item, and an offsetting debit will probably be recorded under 'residual errors'.

Britain. The accounts also should tell us what volume of payments is (or will be) made by UK residents to foreigners for similar reasons.

Although the total number of pounds bought on the foreign-exchange market must equal the total number sold, this is not true if we look at purchases and sales for a particular purpose. It is quite possible, for example, that more pounds were sold for the purpose of obtaining foreign currency to import foreign cars than were bought for the purpose of buying British cars for export to other countries. In such a case, we would say that the UK had a balance-of-payments deficit on the 'car account', by which we would mean that the value of the UK imports of cars exceeded the value of its exports of cars. For most general purposes, we are not interested in the balance of payments for single commodities but only for larger classes of transactions.

CURRENT ACCOUNT AND CAPITAL ACCOUNT: The most important division in the balance-of-payments accounts is between the *current account* and the *capital account*. The balance of payments on current account includes all payments made because of current purchases of goods and services. There is no automatic reason why current-account payments should balance (any more than the car account should). It is quite possible for more pounds to be sold in order to allow us to purchase our imports, than were bought in order to allow foreigners to purchase our exports. If so, the pounds must have come from somewhere, and the excess of sales over purchases on current account must be exactly matched by an excess of purchases over sales on the capital account.

The capital account records transactions for everything other than what is recorded in the current account. The main items are capital transfers and sales from (or purchases of) stocks of gold and foreign exchange. Consider a British citizen who wishes to invest abroad by lending money to an American industry. We say he is exporting capital from the UK to the US. Suppose he wishes to buy bonds being sold in New York by an expanding American firm. In order to do this, he needs to obtain dollars. He is a demander of foreign exchange and a supplier of sterling. His transaction is, therefore, a debit item in the UK balance-of-payments account.

It sometimes seems confusing to beginners that the export of capital is a debit item and the export of a good is a credit item. The situation is, however, really very simple. In the circular flow, goods and money flows move in opposite directions. The export of a good earns foreign exchange, and the export of capital uses foreign exchange, and therefore they have opposite effects on international payments. Yet another way of looking at it is that the capital transaction involves the purchase, and hence the *import* of a foreign bond; this has the same effect on the balance of payments as the purchase, and hence the import, of a foreign good. Both transactions use foreign exchange and are thus debit items in the UK balance of payments.

Now assume that in a given year, the value of UK imports exceeds the value of UK exports, considering all current-account transactions. The foreign currency necessary to finance the imports that were in excess of exports had to come from somewhere. It must have been lent by someone or else provided out of the government's reserves of gold and foreign exchange. If foreigners are investing funds in the UK, they will be selling foreign currency and buying sterling in order to be able to buy stocks and bonds issued by UK firms. Such foreign lending can provide the foreign exchange necessary to allow the UK to have an excess of imports over exports. The other possibility is that the British central authorities have reduced their holding of gold and foreign exchange by selling some to persons wishing to purchase foreign goods, and accepting sterling in return.

> **A deficit on current account must be matched by a surplus on capital account, which means either borrowing from abroad or reducing the gold and foreign exchange held by the domestic central authorities.**

Now consider a situation in which the value of exports is in excess of the value of imports. This means that foreigners will not have been able to obtain all the sterling they need in order to buy UK goods from the UK sources who wish to supply sterling in return for foreign currency in order to buy foreign goods. The excess of exports over imports could only have been paid for if foreigners obtained sterling from other sources. There are several possibilities. First, sterling may be provided by UK investors wishing to obtain foreign currency so that they can buy foreign stocks and bonds. In this case, the excess of exports over imports is balanced by UK loans and investments abroad. Second, the UK Government, rather than its firms or citizens, may have lent money to foreign governments to finance their purchases of British-produced goods or services. Third, the UK Government may have given money away as aid, particularly to underdeveloped countries. Such gifts allow these countries to purchase more from the UK than they sell to us. The fourth main possibility is that foreign governments may have reduced their holdings of UK pounds or gold by selling these to persons wishing to buy UK goods and accepting their own domestic currency in exchange.

> **A surplus on current account must be matched by a deficit on capital account, which means either loans and gifts to foreigners, or the running down of reserves of gold and foreign exchange held by the foreign central authorities.**

THE MAKE-UP OF THE CURRENT ACCOUNT: The two main divisions within the current account are visibles and invisibles. VISIBLES refer to goods, i.e., to all those things such as cars, pulpwood, aluminium, coffee, and iron ore, that we can see when they cross international borders. INVISIBLES refer to services, to all those things we cannot see, such as insurance and freight haulage and tourist expenditures. When a US firm buys insurance from Lloyd's of London for a shipment of goods consigned to Egypt, the firm consumes a British export just as surely as if it purchased and used a British made car or sent its president on a vacation to Scotland. Payment for the insurance services and for the car and the vacation must be made in pounds, and thus each is a US import and a British export. Another main invisible item on the current account is the receipt of interest and dividends on loans and investments in foreign countries. If for example an American holds shares in a British aircraft company, he will receive dividend payments in pounds sterling. If the American wishes to spend these at home, he will need to exchange the pounds for dollars. Interest and dividends on foreign loans and investments thus provide foreign exchange and are entered as a credit item.

THE MAKE-UP OF THE CAPITAL ACCOUNT: Capital movements can be divided into long-term capital movements, short-term movements, and changes in the exchange reserves. Allowing for risk and other such factors, investors will seek to invest where the return is highest. Just as capital moves in the long run from industry to industry within one country in search of its most productive uses, so would we expect capital to move from country to country in search of the highest rates of return. Such long-term capital movements mean that the households and firms of one country are investing in the firms of another country.

Short-term capital holdings arise in many ways. The mere fact of international trade forces traders to hold money balances. Traders' receipts and expenditures are not perfectly synchronized, and they necessarily hold transactions and precautionary balances because they must be able to pay their bills when these fall due. It usually does not matter where such funds are held. The funds can easily be moved from one currency to another in response to small changes in incentives or because of real or imaginary fears of all sorts. When short-term capital is transferred from one country to another, purchases and sales of foreign exchange must occur.

The final major element in the capital account is changes in gold and foreign-exchange reserves held by central authorities. Central authorities of most countries hold supplies of gold and foreign exchange in order that they may intervene in the foreign-exchange market to stabilize their country's rate of exchange. If a country has a payments deficit on all other accounts (i.e., if it uses more foreign currency than it obtains), this deficit must be made up by an equivalent reduction in its reserves of gold and foreign exchange.[1]

We have already noted that when we add up all the uses to which foreign currency is put, and all the sources from which it came, these two amounts are necessarily equal, and thus the overall accounts of all international payments necessarily balance. What then do we mean when we say that payments are not in balance, that there is a deficit or a surplus on the balance of payments?

When we speak of a balance-of-payments deficit or surplus, we refer to the balance on some part of the accounts. Usually, we are referring to the balance excluding changes in the reserves held by the central authorities. A balance-of-payments deficit thus means that the reserves of the central authorities are being run down while a surplus means that the reserves are rising.

The balance of desired payments

We have seen that *actual* payments must always be in balance, because foreign exchange bought must equal foreign exchange sold, but there is no reason why, at the existing rate of exchange, *desired* payments should be in balance; people may wish to buy more foreign exchange than others wish to sell. If, at the current rate of exchange, the demand for dollars exceeds the supply, it follows that holders of sterling

---

1 A further set of entries has to be made for gifts and other unilateral transfers of capital. If funds are given to foreign sources to allow them to buy British goods and services, the goods appear as an export and thus as a credit, and the money given to purchase them appears as a debit, so that the whole transaction shows neither a net gain nor a net loss of foreign exchange.

are trying to make more payments in dollars than holders of dollars wish to make in sterling. In other words, *desired* payments between the two countries are not in balance. If the total volume of payments that holders of sterling wish to make to America is equal to the total volume of payments that holders of dollars wish to make to Britain, the demand for dollars will equal the supply, and the demand for sterling will equal its supply. Desired payments between the two countries will be equal. Finally, if the amount that holders of dollars wish to pay to Britain exceeds the amount that holders of sterling wish to pay to America, the demand for sterling will exceed the supply and the demand for dollars will be less than the supply. Again, desired payments between the two countries will not be in balance.

We must now develop a theory of how exchange rates are determined on free markets by the balance of desired payments.

A THEORY OF EXCHANGE RATES

The theory we are about to develop applies to all international trade and to all exchange rates, but for the sake of simplicity we shall continue to refer to two countries, Britain and America, and to the rate between their two currencies, pounds and dollars. Since one currency is traded for another on the foreign exchange market, it follows that a demand for dollars implies a supply of pounds while an offer (supply) of dollars implies a need (demand) for pounds. If, at an exchange rate of £1 = $3, a British importer demands $6 he must be offering £2, and if an American importer offers $6 he must be demanding £2. For this reason we can deal either with the demand for and the supply of dollars, or with the demand for and the supply of pounds sterling; we do not need to consider both. We shall conduct the argument in terms of dollars.

The equilibrium exchange rate

THE DEMAND FOR DOLLARS: The demand for dollars arises because holders of sterling wish to make payments in dollars; the demand for dollars thus arises from imports of American goods into Britain and from the movement of investment funds from Britain to the US.

THE SUPPLY OF DOLLARS: Dollars are offered in exchange for sterling because holders of dollars wish to make payments in sterling. The supply of dollars arises therefore on account of British exports to the United States and the movement of investment funds from the United States to Britain.

EXCHANGE RATE CHANGES: When the free-market price of one currency rises in terms of another currency, we say the exchange has APPRECIATED and that the value of the currency has appreciated on the foreign exchange market. When the free-market price of a currency falls in terms of foreign currencies we say the exchange rate has DEPRECIATED.

PRICE CHANGES CAUSED BY EXCHANGE-RATE CHANGES: On the one hand, a British manufacturer is concerned to receive a certain payment for his goods in pounds sterling. It follows that the dollar price at which these goods must be sold in

America depends upon the exchange rate between pounds and dollars. If the manufacturer wishes to obtain one pound each for his goods, then the goods must sell in America (ignoring the cost of transport) for $3 when the exchange rate is £1 = $3, for $2 when the rate is £1 = $2 and for $4 when the rate is £1 = $4. On the other hand, an American manufacturer wishes, when he sells his goods, to be paid a certain number of dollars. It follows that the pound price for which these goods must be sold in Britain depends on the rate of exchange between sterling and dollars. If, for example, the rate of exchange goes from £1 = $2 to £1 = $1, then the dollar price of British exports to America must fall while the sterling price of American exports to Britain must rise. In general a rise in the value of the pound *vis-à-vis* the dollar raises the dollar price of British exports to America, and lowers the sterling price of British imports from America. A fall in the value of the pound has the reverse effect.

THE RELATION BETWEEN THE ELASTICITIES OF DEMAND FOR IMPORTS AND EXPORTS AND THE ELASTICITY OF SUPPLY AND DEMAND FOR DOLLARS: The amount of dollars offered in exchange for sterling depends on the amount of money which American importers need to pay for the purchases they wish to make from Britain. What can we say about how this amount of money will vary if the dollar price of British exports varies? The Americans can be expected to have a downward-sloping demand curve for British goods (as they will have for all goods) and we can therefore say, in general, that the *quantity* of British exports to America will vary inversely with their price, but what happens to the *value* of exports depends on the elasticity of the American demand. If the Americans have an elastic demand for British goods then a fall in the dollar price of British goods will make them spend more dollars on them, while a rise will make them spend less. If, on the other hand, the Americans have an inelastic demand for British goods, then a fall in the dollar price of these goods will cause the Americans to reduce their total expenditure on British goods, while a rise in price will cause them to spend more. We thus reach a most important conclusion:

> **The supply of dollars – i.e., the amount of dollars Americans wish to exchange for pounds in order to purchase British goods, will increase or decrease as the dollar price of British exports falls, according as the American demand for British goods is elastic or inelastic.**

We have already seen that a fall in the exchange value of the pound *vis-à-vis* the dollar will lower the dollar price of British exports. We can therefore restate our previous conclusion in the following manner:

> **A depreciation of the pound will increase or decrease the dollar value of British exports, and hence the supply of dollars, according as the American demand for these exports is elastic or inelastic.**

Now let us consider the demand for dollars. The demand for dollars in exchange for pounds arises on account of the need to obtain dollars to pay for American goods imported into Britain. What can we say about what happens to the volume of this demand for dollars as the pound price of American goods varies? Let us assume that the dollar price of these American goods remains unchanged but that their sterling price changes in consequence of a change in the exchange rate. (For example, an American good with a constant price of \$1 will have a sterling price of $33\frac{1}{3}$p when the exchange rate is \$3 = £1, a price of 50p if the exchange rate falls to \$2 = £1, and a price of 25p if the exchange rate rises to \$4 = £1.) If the sterling price of American goods falls because of a depreciation in the value of the dollar, more goods will be bought and British purchasers will spend more or less sterling on these goods according as their elasticity of demand is greater or less than unity; but, since the quantity of goods bought rises and their dollar price is unchanged, *they will necessarily spend more dollars on them*. On the other hand, if the sterling price of American goods rises as a consequence of a fall in the value of the pound, less goods will be bought and, although the sterling expenditure on them will go up or down depending on the elasticity of demand, the dollar expenditure on these goods necessarily falls since we are assuming that dollar prices are unaffected by the devaluation.[1] We have now reached the following important conclusion:

> **A depreciation of the pound will necessarily decrease the dollar value of British imports and hence decrease the demand for dollars; the more elastic is the British demand for American goods, the more will the demand for dollars fall with any given depreciation.**

The argument leading up to the last three conclusions is not an easy one. The reader should now go back and re-read this section and, when he gets to this point a second time he should put the book down and make sure that he can work out the argument for himself.

We may now introduce a diagram that will be useful for analysing exchange rate problems in terms of the theory just spelled out. In Figure 45.1 we measure the sterling price of a dollar on the vertical axis. (You may be more familiar with the exchange rate expressed the other way round, as the dollar price of one pound sterling and you should, for practice, convert a few of the prices in Figure 45.1 into the more familiar mode of expression. What, for example, is the dollar price of one pound if the sterling price of one dollar is 30p?)

The demand curve for dollars is always downward sloping. This indicates that as the sterling price of dollars falls, a larger quantity of US goods will be sold in Britain and, assuming the dollar price of US goods to be unchanged, a larger quantity of dollars will be needed to purchase these goods. (When considering the demand curve remember that the figures on the vertical axis tell us the number of pence for which an American good costing \$1 must be sold in the UK at each exchange rate.) The elasticity of the supply curve of dollars depends on the elasticity of the US demand for British goods. If the US demand is of unit elasticity then the same number of dollars will be spent on British goods, irrespective of price. In this case the supply of dollars will be the same whatever the exchange rate and the *S* curve in Figure 45.1 will be of zero elasticity. If the US demand for British goods is elastic, the supply

---

1 This is only a very elementary theory and we thus use the simplifying assumption that exports can be increased or decreased without affecting the domestic prices of these products. The theory which allows for variations in domestic prices is much more complex than the present one.

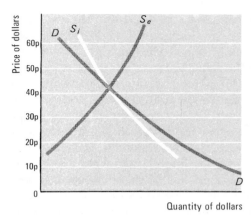

Fig. 45.1 The determination of the equilibrium exchange rate under competitive conditions

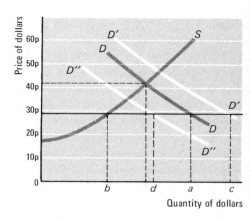

Fig. 45.2 The effects of shifts in the demand for dollars on the equilibrium exchange rate

curve of dollars will slope upwards to the right (e.g., S_e in Figure 45.1), while if the US demand for British goods is inelastic, the supply curve of dollars will slope upwards *to the left* (e.g., S_i in the figure). Before reading on, be sure that you can explain why this is so.

We shall now explicitly assume that the US demand for British goods is elastic. (In the Appendix to this Chapter we consider the effects of dropping this assumption.) In the present Chapter the demand and supply curves will have the slopes shown in Figure 45.2. In the initial situation the demand and supply curves are DD and S respectively.

THE DETERMINATION OF THE EQUILIBRIUM EXCHANGE RATE: Assume that the current price of dollars is too low, say 35p to the dollar. At this exchange rate the demand for dollars exceeds the supply. In other words desired payments are not in balance, for desired payments to the US exceed desired payments from the US to Britain. Dollars will be in scarce supply; some people who require dollars to make payments to America will be unable to obtain them, and the price of dollars will be bid up. The value of the dollar *vis-à-vis* the pound will appreciate or, what is the same thing, the value of the pound *vis-à-vis* the dollar will depreciate. As the price of dollars rises the sterling price of American exports to Britain rises and the quantity for US dollars demanded to buy these goods falls off. On the other hand, as the dollar price of British exports falls a larger quantity will be sold and, on the assumption that the US demand for British goods is elastic, the quantity of US dollars supplied will rise. Thus this rise in the price of the dollar reduces the quantity demanded and increases the quantity supplied. Where the two curves intersect, demand equals supply and the exchange rate is in equilibrium. In Figure 45.2 the equilibrium exchange rate is at $\$1 = 41\frac{2}{3}$p which is $£1 = \$2.40$. Now let us see what happens if the price of dollars is too high. In this case the demand for dollars will fall short of the supply; the dollar will be in excess supply so that some people who wish to convert dollars into pounds will be unable to do so. The price of dollars will fall, fewer dollars will be supplied, more will be demanded and an equilibrium will be re-established.

Some comparative static results

We may now use the theory just developed to generate predictions about certain changes in which we may be interested. Four changes are studied here, but many others could also be examined.

A CHANGE IN TASTES: Consider, for example, the effect of a change whereby the British preference for American goods increases so that there is a rightward shift in the British demand curve for American goods. This means that, at each sterling price, more US goods will be demanded than previously. Thus, at each exchange rate, more US dollars will be demanded (in order to pay for these goods). So the demand curve for dollars will shift to the right, say to D' in Figure 45.2. At the original exchange rate of $41\frac{2}{3}$p per dollar, demand exceeds supply. The price of dollars will rise until a new equilibrium is reached; in Figure 45.2 this new equilibrium is at 47p to the dollar (i.e., £1 = $2·00). We conclude that an increased preference on the part of British consumers for American goods will lead to a rise in the equilibrium value of the dollar (a fall in the value of the pound). The student should work out for himself the effect of an increased preference of American consumers for British goods.

A FALL IN THE DOMESTIC SUPPLY PRICE OF EXPORTS: Assume, for example, that the domestic price of US goods falls. This means that at any given exchange rate the sterling price of US goods will fall. What will this do to the exchange rate? Can you work out the answer before reading on? If the dollar price of US goods falls by X per cent then at each exchange rate the sterling price of these goods will also fall by X per cent. If the British demand for US goods is elastic, the quantity demanded will increase by more than X per cent and, if it is inelastic, the quantity demanded will increase by less than X per cent. Thus the British will demand more or less dollars in order to purchase US goods according as their demand for these goods is elastic or inelastic. Hence a fall in the dollar price of US exports will shift the demand for dollars to the right if the British demand for US goods is elastic, to the left if inelastic, and leave the demand for dollars unchanged if the demand for the goods is of unit elasticity. We conclude therefore that the sterling price of dollars will rise, fall or remain the same according as the UK demand for US goods is elastic, inelastic or of unit elasticity.

A CHANGE IN THE PRICE LEVEL OF ONE COUNTRY: Consider, for example, the case of an inflation in the UK. This means that the sterling price of British goods will rise. British goods will become more expensive in the US and, assuming that US elasticity of demand for British goods exceeds unity, the supply of dollars will diminish. American exports to Britain will have an unchanged sterling price, while the price of British goods sold at home will have increased. Thus US goods will be more attractive compared to British goods (because they have become *relatively* cheaper) and more of them will be bought in Britain, so that at any given exchange rate, the demand for dollars will be increased. The demand curve for dollars shifts to the right while the supply curve shifts to the left so that the equilibrium price of dollars must rise.[1] We conclude that a British inflation leads to a depreciation in the equilibrium value of the pound (an appreciation in the value of the dollar).

AN EQUAL PERCENTAGE CHANGE IN THE PRICE LEVEL IN BOTH COUNTRIES: Let us consider by way of example a 10 per cent inflation in both the US and the UK. In this case, the sterling prices of British goods and the dollar prices of US goods both rise by 10 per cent. At any given exchange rate, the dollar prices of British goods and the sterling price of American goods will also rise by 10 per cent. Thus the relative prices of imports and domestically-produced goods will be unchanged in both countries. There is now no reason to expect any change in either country's demand for imports at the original exchange rate, so that the inflations in the two countries leave the equilibrium exchange rate unchanged. This argument can easily be extended to establish the following important proposition.

> **If the price level of one country is rising faster (falling slower) than is that of another country, then the equilibrium value of its currency will be falling relative to that of the second country.**

FIXED AND FLUCTUATING EXCHANGE RATES

So far we have considered equilibrium exchange rates. If exchange rates are left free to be determined by the market forces of demand and supply, then our theory makes predictions about actual rates of exchange. Such exchange rates are called FREE, or FLEXIBLE, or FLUCTUATING EXCHANGE RATES.

More frequently than not in the last 30 years, governments have not allowed their currencys' exchange rate to fluctuate on the free market. Instead the rates have been fixed within very narrow margins. When this is done, the government states an official price for its currency (usually in terms of US dollars) which is called the currency's PAR VALUE. The government then undertakes to enter the foreign exchange market buying and selling foreign exchange in whatever quantities are necessary to prevent the exchange rate from deviating more than a stated amount in either direction from its par value. (Usually fluctuations were held within 1 per cent of the par value.) Such an exchange rate is called a FIXED or PEGGED EXCHANGE RATE, and when it is changed the country's currency is said to be DEVALUED or REVALUED in the cases, respectively, of a fall or a rise in the currency's par value.

In the case of fixed exchange rates our theory does not predict the actual exchange rate – since this is fixed by government decree. The theory does, however, make predictions about the extent of the deficit or the surplus on the balance of payments at the fixed rate of exchange. Let us consider this further.

Assume, for example, that the exchange rate in Figure 45.2 is fixed by decree at 29p per dollar (i.e., £1 = $3·45). At this rate of exchange demand for dollars is a while the supply is b. There is an excess demand for dollars, a potential 'dollar gap'

---

1 If the US demand for British goods is inelastic then the supply curve of dollars shifts to the right. It can be shown, however, that the supply curve shift in this case must always be less than the demand curve shift so that the conclusion about the equilibrium exchange rate is not upset. The demonstration is too difficult to be included in this introduction to the theory of exchange rates.

of *ba* dollars. If the government does not intervene, some demanders will be able to obtain dollars and others will not; a black market is likely to develop with the available dollars commanding a clandestine price as far in excess of 29p per dollar.

Managing fixed exchange rates

Figure 45.3 shows free market demand and supply curves for dollars. Assume that the British Government fixes the exchange rate between the limits of $40\frac{1}{3}$p and $42\frac{1}{3}$p to the dollar and restricts demand, through an *exchange control* system of rationing and prohibitions, to the curve D'. Certain types of payments will be allowed without limits, others will be subject to quota restrictions setting the maximum amount that can be made, and yet others will be prohibited altogether. By these means, the central authorities keep the demand for dollars lower than it otherwise would be. Even this restricted demand will, however, be subject to seasonal, cyclical and other fluctuations.

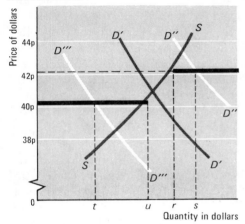

Fig. 45.3 The stabilization of the exchange rate through the intervention of the central authorities

Having restricted demand by the means outlined above, the authorities then control the exchange rate in the following fashion: all transactions go through the normal financial channels with banks and other institutions buying and selling foreign exchange. The government's monetary authority, usually the central bank, stands ready to enter the market to prevent the exchange rate from going outside the permitted band on either side of the par value. When the bank must buy foreign exchange its exchange reserves rise; when it must sell foreign exchange its exchange reserves fall. At the price of $42\frac{1}{3}$p to the dollar, the central bank offers to sell dollars, for permitted purposes, in unlimited amounts; at the price of $40\frac{1}{3}$p per dollar, the bank offers to buy dollars in unlimited amounts.

(1) If the demand curve cuts the supply curve in the range $40\frac{1}{3}$p to $42\frac{1}{3}$p, then the authorities need not touch their exchange reserves. The amount of dollars being supplied for pounds will be equal to the amount of dollars being demanded in exchange for pounds and no intervention into the market is needed.

(2) If the demand curve shifts to D'', then the authorities must sell dollars to the extent of *rs* in order to prevent the price of dollars from rising above $42\frac{1}{3}$p. These dollars must be removed from the exchange reserves.

(3) If the demand curve shifts to D''', the authorities must buy dollars to the extent of tu and add them to the exchange reserves in order to prevent the price of dollars from falling below $40\frac{1}{3}$p.

If the authorities have restricted demand sufficiently so that *on the average* the demand and supply curves intersect in the range $40\frac{1}{3}$p to $42\frac{1}{3}$p, then the exchange reserves will be relatively stable with the authorities buying dollars when the demand is abnormally low and selling them when the demand is abnormally high. In the former case, the reserves will rise, and in the latter case, they will fall; but over a long time their average level may be held fairly stable. [1]

If the central authorities have guessed wrongly or if conditions change (e.g., there is a more rapid inflation in one country than in the other), the exchange reserves will rise or fall more or less continuously. Say that the average level of demand is D'' with fluctuations on either side of this level. Then the average drain on exchange reserves will be rs per period; sometimes it will be more and sometimes less, and occasionally when demand is extremely low, reserves will be added to. *This situation cannot continue indefinitely*. Eventually, if nothing is done, reserves will fall to zero and the controlled price will have to be abandoned. The authorities have two possibilities: they can change the controlled price so that the band of permissible prices straddles the equilibrium price. In other words, they can devalue their currency. Or, they can try to shift the curves so that the intersection is in the band $40\frac{1}{3}$p to $42\frac{1}{3}$p. To accomplish this they must take further steps to restrict demand for dollars: they can impose import quotas and foreign-travel restrictions, or they can seek to increase the supply of dollars by encouraging exports.

The *actual* balance-of-payments surpluses, or deficits, reported in the press are the quantities we have just indicated: the changes in the *reserves* held by the central authorities. This must be sharply distinguished from the potential balance-of-payments surplus or deficit, which is the difference between the demand for and the supply of dollars as they would be if everyone were free to buy and sell dollars without government restriction.

Fixed versus fluctuating exchange rates

We have observed that most governments have maintained fixed exchange rates for their currencies over most of the past 30 years. We must wonder why they have bothered with all this apparatus of control and why they did not allow the rate be set on a free market so that demand and supply could always be brought into equilibrium by suitable and automatic changes in exchange rates?

A long debate has raged among economists and bankers about the relative merits of fixed versus fluctuating exchange rates and no general conclusion has been reached. Contrary to the contentions of some of the protagonists, neither free nor fluctuating rates lead inevitably to disaster, for both policies have been successfully maintained at one time or another by several countries. The debate is considered briefly in Chapter 47.

---

1 Actually, if the fluctuations in demand are normally distributed around their mean value, exchange reserves will remain constant only if the 'average curves' intersect at a price half way between the floor and the ceiling (i.e., $41\frac{1}{3}$p in our example).

Exchange rates and national pride

It is interesting that the value of the exchange rate often becomes an important symbol of national pride. The economist does not seek to explain this phenomenon but he can wonder at it. There can be no doubt that there are circumstances when the rise in the value of a country's currency would be taken as a good sign. There are other circumstances in which such a change would be symptomatic of a domestic situation, about which it would be unusual to be proud. A major domestic depression and deflation could, for example, easily lead to a rise in the external value of a country's currency. On the other hand, major technical innovations which reduced domestic costs and prices will often lead to a fall in the exchange rate. It is not immediately obvious that this should cause a loss of national prestige. A large inflow of foreign capital, leading to a transfer abroad of the control of one's industries, would cause an appreciation of the exchange rate. It is not obvious that such a move is a cause for national congratulation in all circumstances. It would certainly be a peculiar position (frequently held by Canadians) to point with great pride to a high exchange rate and to point with grave concern to the inflow of foreign capital which was the cause of the high rate. In fact exchange rates can appreciate or depreciate for many different reasons and to take the price of one's currency *per se* as a symbol of national pride is to commit oneself in advance to being proud of a great rag bag of varied events.

A similar situation occurs when as a result of fixed exchange rates national pride and national self-confidence become related to fairly trivial changes in the balance of payments, and in the size of foreign exchange reserves held by the central authorities. Throughout the late 1950s and the 1960s the UK was commonly thought of as the sick man of Europe, beset by crises and unable to hold her own in the modern world. To a great extent this view was based on the recurrent crises brought on by an attempt to keep the pound priced at a value well above its equilibrium one. When finally devaluation was forced on an unwilling government in 1967 the balance of payments improved dramatically and the image suddenly changed: Britain was thought to be healthier than any of its continental rivals because it had a stronger balance of payments position than any of them. Yet nothing basic was changed overnight by changing the price of sterling. UK managers remained as good or as bad as they were the year before, the school system and the political decision mechanism were unchanged. Any basic evaluation would show the society to be the same in 1970 as it was in 1967, but the image it presented at home and abroad changed dramatically for what economic theory tells us is a trivial reason. Any country can have a 'favourable' balance of payments if it sets its exchange rate below its equilibrium level, any country will have an unfavourable balance of payments if it sets its rate above the equilibrium level. Economic theory tells us that either situation can be brought about by the stroke of a pen and it thus tells us that the changes in the balance of payments effected by changes in the exchange rate are not necessarily correlated with any more basic characteristics of a society. Thus to judge these basic characteristics by the state of the balance of payments must be misguided, and yet a study of the current or past press will show that this is what is done over and over again.

By 1974 the UK balance of payments was once again in what was judged by many to be a poor state, and sterling was weak on foreign exchange markets. In the press and on the political platform the 'British miracle' of 1970 had given way to the 'British disease' of 1974. Yet the society and the economy were fundamentally no different from what they had been a decade previously.

AN ALTERNATIVE MODEL

The traditional elasticity model presented so far in this Chapter assumes that domestic price levels are independent of exchange rates, and that the effect of a change in exchange rates is to change the relative prices of internationally traded goods. Thus, for example, a depreciation of sterling in the two country examples considered earlier lowers the price of British exports relative to the price of American exports (British imports). This model would seem to make most sense in a world of complete specialization where each country was fully specialized in, and was the only exporter of, a particular commodity or range of commodities.

An alternative model begins with some observations that seem to conflict with the traditional theory. (1) There are many commodities that are produced simultaneously by many different countries. These commodities have a single world price. There is little that one producer, acting on its own, can do to affect that price. (2) Many commodities are highly substitutable for each other and their relative prices cannot change very much as a result. Motor cars are an excellent example. Each country's cars are different from each other country's cars and the relative prices of British and French cars can vary somewhat. Many kinds of cars, however, are closely substitutable for each other, and thus their relative prices cannot change much (e.g., a large rise in the relative price of one type of car would throw most of its market to its close competitors). (3) The domestic price level appears to be quite closely linked to the exchange rate. For example, devaluations of currencies under fixed exchange rates seem usually to be followed by domestic inflations that remove some, but not all, of the competitive advantage conferred on the country's exports by the devaluation.

Assumptions of the model

The extreme version of this alternative model is based on the following assumptions. All commodities can be separated into two categories: internationally-tradeable and non-tradeable commodities. Tradeables are sold on world markets at a single world price; they are, or could be, produced by many countries no one of whom can affect the price significantly by its own actions. Non-tradeables do not enter directly into international trade, either because they cannot be transported – e.g., services such as haircuts, road transport, maid services – or because the cost of transport is prohibitively high – e.g., cement.

The effect of changes in the exchange rate

The main effect of a change in one country's exchange rate under this theory is to change the relative price of tradeables and non-tradeables in the country whose exchange rate is changed. A change in one country's exchange rate does not, however, affect relative prices among different tradeable commodities since these relative prices are all set in world markets.

Consider an example. A small country specializes in the export of a good, X, which has a given international price that can be expressed in US dollars (some X is also consumed at home). It imports a second commodity, Y, which is produced in many countries, and it also consumes a third commodity, Z, which is a non-tradeable commodity. (In a real application there would be three groups of commodities each with its own price index.) The international prices of X and Y are $2 and $4, the price of Z is £1, the current exchange rate is pegged at £1 = $3, and X and Y thus sell domestically for £0·66$\frac{2}{3}$ and £1·33$\frac{1}{3}$.

Now assume that a deficit opens up on the balance of payments due, say, to a growth of real income combined with a high income elasticity of demand for importables and a low income elasticity for non-tradeables. The government eventually decides to devalue the exchange rate to, say £1 = $2. In the traditional theory the price of X falls in the international market. Given the assumptions of the present theory the prices of X and Y remain at $2 and $4 respectively so their domestic prices both rise. The domestic price of X becomes £1 and that of Y becomes £2. Thus the relative price of imported and exported goods does not change in the devaluing country's home market. But both prices rise relative to the price of the non-tradeable, Z, which remains at £1. Domestic demand will now shift away from both the imported and the exported good. This helps to improve the balance of payments by reducing imports and possibly by freeing more goods for export. Demand increases for domestically-produced non-tradeables. If there is excess capacity at home, the extra demand can be met. If there is already full employment, the government must take steps to stop the extra demand from causing a domestic inflation that will raise the price of Z to £1·50. This would restore relative prices to what they were before the devaluation and remove any effect of the devaluation. (In terms of the analysis of Chapter 36 the devaluation shifts up the aggregate expenditure function by reducing imports and raising domestic consumption. If full employment exists already the government must use fiscal and/or monetary measures to shift the expenditure function down again thus preventing the emergence of an inflationary gap.)

CRITICISMS OF DEMAND AND SUPPLY THEORIES OF EXCHANGE RATES

Recently there has been substantial criticism of the market theory of exchange rates, whether it uses the traditional assumptions used earlier in this chapter or the revised assumptions used in the previous section. One line of criticism stems from the so-called monetary theory of the balance of payments. There is no doubt that this new theory emphasises some important monetary factors totally omitted from the demand-supply theories. We will not go into the monetary theory here but will conclude this Chapter with a summary of some points where there seems to be general agreement on the applicability of demand and supply models of exchange rates.

(1) Exchange rates, where they have any flexibility at all, clearly respond to the

conditions of demand and supply.

(2) Insofar as a country's export goods are not perfect substitutes for goods produced in other countries, the exchange rate does influence a country's export performance. Japanese cars, for example, did increasingly well in the US market as their relative prices fell through the 1960s due to an increasing undervaluation of the yen. When the yen was revalued in the early 1970s, the relative prices of Japanese cars rose in the US, and Japanese car exports suffered accordingly.

(3) In spite of point (2) above the most important effects of changes in exchange rates in many cases is to alter the relative prices of tradeable goods against non-tradeable goods, rather than the relative prices of some tradeable goods against other tradeable goods.

(4) Equilibrium exchange rates do change over time, and on a system of fixed rates, occasional rounds of realignments of rates seem necessary if ever-growing balance of payments disequilibria are to be avoided. (This point is taken up again in Chapter 47.)

Appendix

More about exchange rates

In this appendix, we shall deal with two quite different problems: first, the question of the possibility of unstable exchange rates, and, second, some aspects of short- and long-term capital movements.

The possibility of unstable rates of exchange

Although a full treatment is beyond the scope of this book, the problem boils down to the following: if the US demand for British goods and the British demand for US goods are sufficiently inelastic, a devaluation can worsen rather than improve a balance-of-payments deficit. To see that this is a possibility, consider the most extreme case in which the US and the UK both have a perfectly inelastic demand for the goods produced by each other (note that this implies that they have violently dissimilar tastes). Now assume that the UK is in balance-of-payments deficit and the US in surplus. If the UK devalues the pound by 10 per cent to improve its balance-of-payments position, it would, in fact, make things worse, for it has a completely inelastic demand for US imports and will thus buy the same quantity of these goods as before, and will require the same quantity of dollars to effect these purchases. UK export prices will, however, fall by 10 per cent in dollars, but no more will be sold, since the US is assumed to have zero elasticity of demand for UK goods. Thus the UK's dollar earnings will fall by 10 per cent (export prices fall by 10 per cent but quantities sold remain unchanged). In these extreme circumstances, a 10 per cent UK devaluation will *worsen* the UK's balance of payments by approximately 10 per cent.

It is a well-known proposition in the theory of international trade that, if domestic prices are unaffected by variations in foreign demand, the perverse case can occur only if the sum of the elasticities of demand for imported goods in the two countries is less than *one*.[1] In other words, quite highly inelastic demands are required to produce this case. Nonetheless, *if* this situation were commonly encountered, the case for freely fluctuating rates would be dealt a crippling blow, for, far from improving matters, exchange depreciations in the face of balance-of-payments deficits, and exchange appreciation in the face of surpluses would make matters worse.

Shortly after the Second World War, a number of studies of price elasticities in international trade were made and these uniformly produced alarmingly low elastici-

1 Even this is only approximately true if the devaluation occurs when there is already a significant trade deficit. The condition for the perverse case not to occur is only exactly that the elasticities should sum to unity if the initial trade deficit or surplus is *zero*.

ties. Indeed, so low were the estimated elasticities that the efficacy of freely fluctuating rates as an automatic adjustment mechanism was called into serious question. Later, however, both economic and statistical theorists discovered a number of general reasons why the measured figures were likely to have been serious underestimates of the real elasticities. The statistical reasons for a 'downward bias' in the estimated elasticities are beyond the scope of an introductory treatment, but the student who proceeds in economics will want to consult later in his studies the classic treatment of this problem by Guy Orcutt.[1]

Some of the theoretical problems can, however, be mentioned even at this stage. The possibility of very low trade elasticities is made to seem more plausible than it probably is, by the usual assumption of a two-country, two-commodity model. Consider a world of many countries and many commodities. Typically, one commodity will be produced in many countries. Thus if *one* deficit country devalues its exchange rate, it will find a large increase in the demand for its own products, even though the world elasticity of demand for these products is very low. This is because devaluation and the consequent fall in export prices allows the country to increase its share of the world market. This effect is analogous to the proposition in the theory of perfect competition that the elasticity of demand for the product of one perfectly competitive producer can approach infinity, even though the elasticity of the market demand curve is very low. The alternative model presented at the end of the Chapter is an extreme version of this situation. A devaluation does not change the international price of a country's exports at all. The beneficial effects are concentrated on substitutions by domestic consumers between tradeable and non-tradeable goods. The second theoretical consideration concerns the range of commodities in trade. Even though the elasticities of demand for a

1 Guy Orcutt, 'Measurement of Price Elasticities in International Trade', *Review of Economics and Statistics*, May, 1950.

country's existing exports are very low, a sufficiently large devaluation will allow the country to sell new products abroad, and the foreign elasticities of demand for its traditional exports will cease to be the only factors determining the change in the balance of payments when the exchange rate is changed.

For these and many other reasons, most economists today dismiss the perverse case as a theoretical curio of little practical importance – except in the very rare case of a country that accounts for almost the whole of the world's supply of a product that is in highly inelastic demand, and that has few alternative possible lines of production.

Capital movements

What will happen if American investors wish to loan money in Britain, possibly to British firms? The British firm will require pounds, and the Americans will, therefore, have to purchase pounds on the foreign-exchange market. (This is, in effect, what happens. The actual transfer will be accomplished through one of several different institutional channels.) Such a transaction entails a rise in the demand for pounds, which, in a free market, will bid up their price. A transfer of funds from country A to country B will tend to appreciate B's currency and depreciate A's.

MOVEMENTS OF SHORT-TERM CAPITAL: Movements of short-term capital can be induced by the central authorities as part of their policy of keeping a fixed exchange rate in spite of fluctuations in the demand for and supply of foreign exchange. Let us see how a temporary deficit in the balance of payments may be alleviated by attracting short-term capital into the country. Assume that, in Figure 45.3, the demand for dollars is D'' and the supply S, so that the British suffer a balance-of-payments deficit of rs per period. This British deficit is the same thing as an American surplus. Now assume that this high demand is only a temporary one, but that the British central authorities wish neither to put on additional restrictions nor to let reserves run down by rs per period. What else can they do? They can raise the rate of interest they are willing to pay for short-term loans (loans of a few days' to a few months' duration) and attract short-term capital. There is a great deal of money available to traders for short time periods. These traders do not need the money now, but they will require it shortly. If someone is prepared to pay for the use of this money for a short period, then this is better from their point of view than leaving it idle. If the British central authorities raise the rate of interest for short-term loans, people holding dollars will wish to obtain pounds in order to lend them out at the high British rates. Thus the supply of dollars shifts to the right. The horizontal distance between the new curve and the original curve S indicates the amount of dollars supplied on account of the movement of short-term capital out of America and into Britain. If the curve is shifted to cut D'' vertically above s, the inflow of short-term capital is rs per period and this just covers the deficit on current account, and the exchange reserves are not run down. *Provided the government guessed correctly* that the demand was *abnormally* high, the policy will work. If the demand now falls to an abnormally low level, say, D''', the central authorities can stop the capital inflow, letting the supply curve return to S. They can then buy tu dollars per period and add them to their exchange reserves. When the reserves have been built up, they can allow the capital to flow back to America. They do this by lowering short-term rates of interest so that people who have lent money in Britain would now prefer to lend it in, say, New York. There will be a demand on the part of these investors to turn pounds into dollars. The government can now sell tu dollars per period to these investors.

Thus short-term deficits in the balance of payments can be covered by attracting short-term capital into a country, but this policy will be successful only if an equivalent short-term surplus subsequently develops so that the capital can again be transferred out of the country.

MOVEMENTS OF LONG-TERM CAPITAL: Long-term capital is capital lent for long periods of time; anything from a few to twenty or more years is common. Such capital is used by governments and firms for long-range investment projects that normally increase, either directly or indirectly, the productive capacity of the economy. Often people in wealthy countries where savings are high will be prepared to invest funds in less well-developed countries where savings are not high enough to finance a high rate of investment. Money by itself does not build or produce things; only productive resources can do this. When a saver lends his money to an entrepreneur in his own country, the saver is electing not to exercise his claim to the output of the country's resources and is transferring this claim to the entrepreneur. When the latter spends the money on investment, he is directing the productive services of the country towards the manufacture of capital goods and away from the manufacture of the goods they would have made if the saver had spent all his income. Thus, lending means transferring the claim to the productive services of the country from the lender's use to that of the borrower. *International lending has the same effect.* If a person in country A lends money to an entrepreneur in country B, then the claim to the output of country A's resources is transferred to a citizen of country B. *All of the ensuing financial transactions are merely means of making this claim effective.* Assume that an individual in A saves dollars and wishes to buy the bonds sold by a firm in B. Then, in effect, it will be necessary for the saver in A to purchase pounds to purchase the bonds in country B. This means that someone else must have sold pounds and taken dollars in exchange. The simplest case arises when the firm in B wishes to buy machinery from A. The lender in A buys pounds and then uses them to buy bonds in B. The firm in B then uses the pounds to buy dollars and the dollars to buy A's machines. In the foreign-exchange market, there is a rise in the demand for pounds arising from the saver in A and a rise in the demand for dollars (supply of pounds) on the part of the firm in B. Looking at the 'real' flows of production rather than the money flows, we see that the lending from A to B entails a flow of A's production, the machines in this case, from A to B. In general, lending from A to B entails a flow of goods from A to B (either directly, or via third countries, if we consider trade among many countries). The reason is that borrowing represents nothing more than a transfer of claims to the output of productive resources from the lender to the borrower. The income of an individual in A gives him a claim on the output of *his own country*; if he lends to an individual in another country, he is giving the borrower his claim *on output in A*.

It follows that international lending and borrowing affects the demands for, and supplies of, currency in the foreign-exchange market. In terms of the analysis in Chapter 45, lending from A to B entails a rise in the demand for pounds. This will, among other things, raise the price of pounds. We conclude, that a transfer of capital from one country to another tends to appreciate the exchange value of the currency of the borrowing country and to depreciate the exchange value of the currency of the lending country.

46

Tariffs and the gains from trade

In the classical theory specialization according to comparative advantage is the main source of the gains from trade. In this chapter, we first consider this theory of the gains from trade as a positive hypothesis about the real world, and then go on to consider the case for interfering with free trade through tariffs.

We have demonstrated that where opportunity costs differ among countries some degree of specialization with some consequent amount of trade will raise world standards of living. There is abundant evidence to show that such cost differences do occur, so that potential gains from trade do exist. Today, no one seriously advocates complete self-sufficiency, but some people do advocate increasing or diminishing the quantity of trade that we now have. This, as we shall see, is a more difficult issue to settle than the issue of whether we should have any trade at all.

It has sometimes been held that it is impossible for trade between any two parties to be to the mutual advantage of both. According to this view, one trading partner must always reap his gain at the expense of the other. The principle of comparative costs, which shows that it is possible for both parties to gain from trade, even if one of them is more efficient than the other in all lines of production, completely refutes the *exploitation doctrine of trade*. Seen in this light, comparative costs is to be viewed as a *possibility theorem*. It shows that, if opportunity-cost ratios differ in two countries, specialization and the accompanying trade make it possible to produce more of all commodities, and thus make it possible for both parties to get more goods as a result of trade than they could get in its absence. Thus the answer to the question: 'Is it *possible* for trade to be mutually advantageous?' is an emphatic Yes; the answer to the question: 'Is trade *in fact* mutually advantageous?' is quite another matter.

THE CASE FOR FREE TRADE
Free trade versus no trade

The theory of the gains from trade through the exploitation of differences in comparative costs may be looked at not only as a possibility theorem, but as a positive

671

hypothesis about the real world.[1] As such, the theory of comparative costs predicts that, in the real world, there will be gains from trade in the sense of increased world production, and that no country will lose from trade in the sense of having less to consume than it could have if it were self-sufficient. This general theory has not been extensively tested, mainly because it has long been believed to be self-evident. If asked to support it with empirical evidence, most economists would probably point to the widely differing cost conditions in certain countries, the most dramatic being those associated with climate. It would undoubtedly be possible, by using green-houses, to grow oranges, cotton and a whole host of imported raw materials and foodstuffs in Norway or to grow coffee in the United States. But the cost in terms of other commodities foregone would be prodigious, because these artificial means of production require lavish inputs of factors of production. It would likewise be possible for a tropical country currently producing foodstuffs to set up industries to produce all the types of manufactured products that it consumes. The cost, in terms of resources used, for a small country without natural advantages in industrial produc-tion, could be very heavy. It thus appears that there is a large gain to both countries in having specialization and trade. The real output and consumption of both sets of countries would be very much lower if each had to produce domestically all the goods that it consumed.

Thus, almost all economists would agree, the most casual observation reveals such major cost differences among countries that no one could doubt that there are very substantial gains from trade. Careful empirical measurement might put an actual numerical value on it, but it is inconceivable that it could refute the general hypo-thesis that production and consumption in the world, and in each major trading country, is higher with trade than it would be if all countries were forced to be utterly self-sufficient.

Free trade versus the level of tariffs existing today

It is quite a jump from the proposition that 'some trade is better (because it increases production) than no trade' to the proposition that 'A bit more trade than we have at present is better than a bit less trade'. Yet most arguments about commercial policy involve the latter sort of proposition, not the former. Most actual policy disagree-ments concern the relative merits of free trade versus controlled trade with tariffs of the order of, say, 10, 20 or 30 per cent. Such tariffs would not cut out imports of bananas, coffee, sugar, diamonds, iron ore or any of the commodities in whose pro-duction we would be really inefficient. Yet these are just the commodities that defenders of free trade use as examples, when the doctrine of the gains from trade is challenged. If we accept the hypothesis that some trade is better than no trade, we are not necessarily committed to accepting the hypothesis that free trade is better than controlled trade with, say, 20 per cent tariffs.

---

1 The theory is often presented as if it were a general law that cannot be challenged on any grounds. It is unassailable only in the sense that it undoubtedly follows logically from certain postulates. But in this sense, any theory to which the rules of logic have been correctly applied is unassailable. Like any other interesting theory, it is open to testing and to possible refutation. After all, any one of a half-dozen postulates on which it is based might prove to be empirically false.

Let us, then, compare a position of free trade with one of, say, 20 per cent *ad valorem* tariffs on all imports. This is a simplified version of the sort of argument that really does take place over commercial policy, for tariffs are seldom advocated to protect industries that are violently inefficient compared to foreign industries; they are usually advocated to protect industries that can very nearly compete, but not quite.

Let us predict, as comparative cost theory does, that there will be gains when we move from a position of, say, 20 per cent tariffs to one of free trade. If we have any doubt as to the empirical correctness of this prediction, we must look beyond the examples of bananas and sugar, for 20 per cent tariffs will still allow trade in these goods. In fact, there can now be no adequate substitute for a careful empirical test of this hypothesis. But, in the absence of such a test, can we gain any idea of the possibility that the hypothesis might be false? We can get some idea of what is involved by changing some of the assumptions of the theory in ways that seem relevant and seeing what then happens to the prediction about the gains from trade. Let us take a few examples.

The theory is based on an assumption of competition that ensures that relative prices will reflect real opportunity costs. If the degree of competition differs among different industries, relative prices may not reflect comparative costs. Under these circumstances, free trade may force countries to specialize in goods in which they have a comparative disadvantage. In such circumstances, trade will reduce world output. The conclusion that there are gains from trade is thus sensitive to variations in the assumption about the relation between relative prices and relative costs.

The theory is also based on the assumption that the existence of trade does not affect domestic production possibilities. The removal of a 20 per cent tariff might create trade with a neighbouring country, but labour unions might oppose this policy and express their discontent in strikes and slow-downs that would permanently lower output per man-hour. Under such circumstances, trade might reduce the total output of the two countries.[1]

The theory is based on the assumption of full employment. Most people would agree that free trade would not be worth having if its price were massive unemployment. But what if free trade led only to a slightly higher average level of unemployment than a situation of 20 per cent tariffs? If it did, then everything would depend on the *magnitude* of the gains resulting from resource re-allocation under free trade. If, for example, free trade led to a re-allocation of resources that was 0·5 per cent more efficient than one resulting from 20 per cent tariffs, but led simultaneously to an average level of unemployment 1 per cent higher than the one occurring with 20 per cent tariffs, then free trade would bring losses rather than gains. We conclude, therefore, that the assumption that free trade *will* bring gains depends critically upon the assumptions that productivity per man-hour is not lowered and the level of unemployment is not raised by the removal of tariffs. At present, we have very little empirical evidence relating to either of these conditions. It is critical, therefore, that we know

---

1 There is no point in saying this does not upset the theory on the grounds that, if workers could be made to work as hard after trade as they did before, all would be well. We know already that, if all the conditions assumed by the theory are fulfilled, there will be a gain from trade. What we want to know, if we are to give policy advice in the real world, is 'Are the conditions, in fact, fulfilled?'

the order of magnitude of the potential gains from free trade; if these gains are small, they could be wiped out by a small real-world deviation from one of the many assumptions on which the theory is based.

The argument in the previous paragraphs does not refute the hypothesis that there are gains from free trade as compared with, say, 20 per cent tariffs. Such an hypothesis can only be upset by measurement and testing. In the absence of careful tests, such arguments as we have presented can cast doubt on the idea that the hypothesis is self-evident and show that it depends on a large number of circumstances about which we can by no means be certain without careful measurement.

> **We conclude that the proposition, 'Some trade is better than no trade' might be accepted as self-evident on the basis of very casual observation, but that the proposition, 'Free trade is better than some trade (with, say, 20 per cent tariffs)' is by no means self-evident and need not be accepted in the absence of careful empirical tests.**

HOW LARGE ARE THE GAINS FROM ELIMINATING MODEST TARIFFS?: We have seen that most economists would agree that the gains from eliminating prohibitive tariffs were large. Shortly after the Second World War, however, economists found themselves faced with the question of trying to estimate the gains resulting from reducing to zero the tariffs actually found in half a dozen European countries. Six of the present common market countries, France, Germany, Italy, Holland, Belgium and Luxembourg, were to remove all tariffs on trade with each other. As controversy developed about the advantages and disadvantages of such a union, and about the cost to other countries of staying out or the gains from coming in, economists set out to try to measure the gains from such a union. There were three notable empirical measurements: Professor P.J.Verdoorn estimated the gain to the six European Common Market countries to be something in the order of $\frac{1}{20}$ of 1 per cent of their national incomes! Professor Harry Johnson estimated the *maximum cost* to Britain of staying out of the Common Market to be equal to approximately 1 per cent of her national income. Professor W.Welmesfelder estimated the gain to Germany from major tariff reductions in the year 1956–7 to be of the order of less than 1 per cent of German national income.[1]

These measures came as a surprise to those convinced free traders who believed that the losses from existing tariffs were large. Of course there is no satisfactory alternative to careful measurement, but the following rough argument suggests why the correct answer may be in the order of 1 per cent rather than say, 10 or 20 per cent. Typical European tariffs on manufactured goods were in the order of 20 per cent. This means that industries from 1 to 20 per cent less efficient than foreign competitors will be protected by these tariffs. If the costs of different industries were spread out evenly, then some tariff-protected industries would be 20 per cent less efficient than foreign competitors, but others would be only 1 per cent less efficient,

---

1 These studies are not suitable for the elementary student. For the best account of Verdoorn's work, see T. Scitovsky, *Economic Theory and Western European Integration* (Allen & Unwin, 1958). See also H.G.Johnson, 'The Gains from Freer Trade: An Estimate', *Manchester School*, March 1958; and W.Welmesfelder, 'The Short-Run Effects of the Lowering of Import Duties in Germany', *Economic Journal*, March 1960. There are reasons to believe that Welmesfelder's figure is a large overestimate.

and their average inefficiency would be in the order of half the tariff rate, which is 10 per cent less efficient than foreign competitors.[1] A reasonable guess might be that, as a result of tariffs, 10 per cent of a country's resources would be in industries other than they would be in if there were no tariffs. This meant that 10 per cent of a country's resources were producing 10 per cent less efficiently than if there were no tariffs, which made a reduction in national income of something in the order of 1 per cent.

We must conclude that, on the best available evidence, the maximum gains from the extra trade resulting from removing 20 per cent tariffs is in the order of 1 per cent of national income. When one considers the violent feelings and passionate controversies over the differences between a policy of free trade and one of 10, 20 or 30 per cent tariffs, it is understandable that many people were surprised at this figure when it was produced. This figure is itself important, because one would view the use of tariffs for 'non-economic' reasons in quite a different way if the cost of these tariffs were a once-and-for-all reduction of 1 per cent in the national income rather than, say, a 10 per cent reduction.[2] There is, indeed, a world of difference between merely establishing the direction of change and in actually measuring its magnitude.[3]

THE CASE FOR TARIFFS
We shall now consider some of the common arguments used in favour of tariff protection.

Argument 1: 'Mutually advantageous trade is impossible'
Since we have already shown this proposition to be wrong, it is not surprising that the arguments based on it, all contain crude fallacies. Consider, for example, the argument that runs: 'If I buy a foreign good, I have the good and the foreigner has the money, whereas if I buy the same good locally, I have the good and our country has the money too; therefore we are better off.' This argument is based on ignorance of the basic facts of foreign trade because the assumptions are made that domestic money actually goes abroad physically when imports are purchased, and that trade flows in only one direction. When a British importer purchases an Italian-made good, he does not send pounds abroad. He (or some financial agent) buys Italian lire (or claims on them) and uses these to pay the Italian manufacturer. He purchases the lire on the foreign-exchange market by giving up sterling *to someone who wishes to use it for expenditure in the UK*. Even if the Italian accepted a shipload of pound notes so that the money did go abroad physically, he would do so only if he or someone to whom he could sell the pounds wanted them to spend in the only country in which

---

1 If in the absence of foreign competition, the sheltered industries become slack and inefficient, their costs may all come to settle at 20 per cent higher than foreign costs. This implies that foreign competition is more effective for encouraging efficiency than is domestic competition, and it makes the losses from moderate tariffs higher than they appeared in the calculation above.

2 Some economists give the impression that the losses from tariffs would be large when they say that it may be necessary to become partially self-sufficient in certain lines of activity *at great cost* because of fear of future wars. The attempt to imply that the cost will be great is unwarranted in the light of present evidence.

3 This is not to say that the gains from European union are necessarily small; it does say that the gains resulting from a re-allocation of resources according to comparative advantage are probably small.

they are legal tender, the United Kingdom. Pound notes do no one any good except as purchasing power. It would be miraculous indeed if we could export pieces of green paper and receive an unlimited quantity of goods in return. After all, the central bank does have the power to create new money at will. It is only because the green paper can buy British goods that others want it.

Probably the most subtle argument that comes under this heading asserts that it is impossible for a rich, high-wage country to trade profitably with a poor, low-wage country. It is argued that the low-wage country will undersell the high-wage one; that unemployment will ensue; and that the standard of living of the high-wage country will be sacrificed. We considered this argument earlier and saw why it was misleading. You should re-read pages 639–40 for a refutation of this argument.

Argument 2: 'Living standards will be higher with tariffs than with free trade'

Most of the common arguments in this group are concerned with single countries. One argument concerns the effects of trade on employment. The classical argument for the gains from trade assumes full employment. If it were true that a free-trade country had a higher average level of unemployment (perhaps because of wider cyclical movements in unemployment) than a country levying tariffs, then it is possible that the loss in production through unused resources would more than offset the gain through a more efficient allocation of resources. No detailed studies have been made of the effect of trade on employment over any long period of time; in the absence of any evidence one way or the other, no verdict can be rendered on this possibility.

Another argument says that, if a country produces a significant portion of the world output of some commodity, it will be able to exploit its monopoly position by interfering with the free flow of trade. By buying less from abroad and selling less as a result, world prices will be affected and the country concerned can appropriate for itself a larger share of total world production than it would obtain if all prices were set on competitive markets. If other countries follow a fairly passive policy, then one country may be able to reap quite substantial monopoly gains. If, however, several countries all try to do the same thing, then a battle of move and counter-move may ensue until, at the end, everyone may be worse off than they were under free trade.

Probably the most important argument under this heading is the one relating to economies of scale, which is usually referred to as the *infant-industry* case for tariffs. If an industry has large economies of scale, then costs and prices must be high when the industry is small, but they will fall as the industry grows. In such an industry, the country first in the field has a tremendous advantage over latecomers. A newly developing country may find that its industries are unable to compete in the early stages of their development against established foreign rivals. A tariff may protect these industries from foreign competition while they grow up. Once they are large enough, they will be able to produce as cheaply as can foreign rivals and thus be able to stand on their own feet without tariff support.

This has always been recognized as a theoretically sound pro-tariff argument.

Many books, however, wind up the discussion of it with some statement such as the following: 'In practice, these industries never admit to growing up and, even when they are full-grown adults, they cling to their tariff protection; the *infant-industry* argument, although valid theoretically, is thus to be rejected in practice'.

But is it true that such tariffs are seldom removed? This is certainly part of the folklore of tariffs, but it does not seem to have been established by any careful study of the facts. Notable illustrative examples spring to mind, of course, but in order to determine if it is true, we would have to compare the tariff levels existing in the infant industries with the general level of tariffs ruling in the country both when the infants were really infants and again after they had grown up. Only then could we say with any confidence that there was no tendency to remove the tariffs after the infants matured.[1] Second, it is not at all clear, even if this alleged fact is true, that this is a sufficient reason for avoiding such tariffs. If the economies of scale are realized, then the real costs of production are reduced and resources are freed for other uses. *Whether or not the tariff remains*, a cost saving has been effected. The existence of the tariff may protect the grown-up industry from foreign competition and allow it to charge a higher price than it otherwise could. Thus, if the tariff is not removed, all factors in the industry may earn more than they otherwise would. Thus, the continuation of the tariff may redistribute income in favour of factors employed in the protected industry to the cost of the rest of the country. It is quite possible, however, if there are sufficiently large economies of scale, that everyone in the country will have a higher income than if the industry had never been protected in the first place. Other cases are also possible, but the point is that, just because the tariff is not removed, it does not necessarily follow that there is a loss to the country as compared with a situation in which the tariff was not put on at all.

Argument 3: 'Tariffs are required to achieve and encourage goals other than the maximization of output'

Gains from trade, in the classical analysis, stem from increases in production. It is quite possible for someone to accept the classical prediction about output and yet rationally to oppose free trade because of his concern with policy objectives other than production and consumption.

Comparative costs might dictate, for example, that a country should specialize in the production of a few primary products. The central authorities might decide, however, that there were distinct social advantages to having a more diverse economy, one that would give citizens a wider range of occupations in which to develop their talents. The social and psychological gains from having a diverse economy might more than compensate, the authorities decide, for a reduction in living standards to a level, say, 5 per cent below what they could be with free trade.

Another possibility concerns fluctuations in the prices of certain primary goods. Comparative advantage might dictate that a country should specialize in the production of one or two primary commodities that are subject to wide price fluctuations.

1 This kind of comparison is needed because it is not sufficient just to show that the industries keep some tariff protection even after they grow up; instead, we need to show that they keep higher protection than we would have expected them to obtain if they could not have availed themselves of the infant-industry argument.

This would mean that the incomes of the producers would also be subject to such fluctuations. Because the problems caused by this can be serious, even though the average level of income over a long period is high, the central authorities may decide to sacrifice some income in order to reduce such fluctuations. [1] They could encourage the expansion of several stable industries that are protected by tariffs. (They realize also that specialization in one or two products leaves a country highly vulnerable to shifts in demand due to changes in tastes or technological innovations that make some products expendable.)

Many Canadians are passionately concerned with maintaining a separate nation with traditions that differ from those of the United States. Many of these Canadians believe that the tariff helps them to do this, and they are fully prepared to accept even a 5 or 10 per cent cut in living standards in order to maintain this independence. Many Canadian economists have argued that Canadians may be mistaken in believing that the tariff helps them in preserving independence from the United States. The main point, however, is that there is nothing irrational in their being willing to accept substantial costs in order to obtain objects other than the maximizing of living standards. There are many policy goals other than maximizing national income. Although most people would agree that, *ceteris paribus*, they prefer more income to less, the economist cannot pronounce as irrational anyone who chooses to sacrifice some income in order to achieve other goals. The job of the positive economist is to point out what the actual cost in income might be.

Although one can think of many cases, particularly with the older countries of the British Commonwealth, such as Canada, Australia and New Zealand, where a tariff policy was pursued after a rational assessment of the approximate cost, one cannot help feeling that, as often as not, high tariff policies are pursued for rather flimsy objectives of national prestige with very little idea of the actual costs involved. One of the reasons why many economists feel so strongly about free trade is probably that they react against the arguments and motives of politicians advocating high tariffs. Many of the anti-free-trade arguments contain crude fallacies, and many of the motives for advocating tariffs are, to say the least, suspect. The fact that many of the arguments used by tariff advocates are incorrect does not, however, prove the correctness of the free-trade arguments.

Argument 4: 'Since exports raise national income and imports lower it, any policy that encourages exports and discourages imports is desirable'

In the theory of the circular flow we saw that exports were an injection that, *ceteris paribus*, raised national income while imports were a withdrawal that, *ceteris paribus*, lowered national income. Surely then, goes this argument, it is desirable to encourage exports and discourage imports.

When we say exports raise national income we mean that they add to the value of output. But they do not add to the value of domestic consumption. In fact, exports are goods produced at home and consumed abroad, while imports are goods produced abroad and consumed at home. The standard of living in a country depends

---

1 Just as many firms decide to diversify their outputs so as not to have all their eggs in one basket.

on the goods and services available for consumption, not on what is produced. The *average* standard of living of the residents of a country may be thought of in terms of the following equation:

$$\text{average standard of living} = \frac{\text{total of goods and services consumed}}{\text{number of people}}.$$

If exports are really good and imports really bad, then a fully employed economy that obtains an increase in its exports without any corresponding increase in its imports, ought to be made better off thereby. This change will, however, result in a reduction in current standards of living, because, when more goods are sent abroad and no more are brought in from abroad, the total goods available for domestic consumption must fall. The view that exports are good and imports are bad implies that the best of all possible worlds would be the situation in which a country exports all its production and imports nothing. No matter how 'good' or 'bad' this situation may appear to you, you should not fail to notice that all the inhabitants of the country would soon starve to death, since there would be no goods and services of any kind available for domestic consumption.

Now let us ask what happens if a country does achieve a surplus of exports over imports for a considerable period of time? It will be accumulating claims to foreign currency. There are three possible uses for the foreign currency earned by exporting: it may be used to buy foreign goods, to make investments abroad, or to add to foreign-exchange reserves. Let us consider these one at a time.

EXCHANGE RESERVES: We have seen that foreign-exchange reserves are required for the smooth functioning of a system of fixed exchange rates. Such reserves do not help the functioning of the system if they are accumulated beyond the amount necessary to reduce to a very low level the chance of running out of reserves. After that, foreign currencies are useful only if they are spent to purchase goods and services.

THE PURCHASE OF GOODS FOR CURRENT CONSUMPTION: We cannot eat, smoke, drink or wear US dollars or Indian rupees. But we can spend them. US dollars and Indian rupees can be used to buy American and Indian goods that can be eaten, smoked, drunk or worn. When such goods are imported and consumed, they add to UK living standards. Indeed, as we saw in Chapter 44 the main purpose of foreign trade is to take advantage of international specialization; trade allows us to consume more than would be possible if all goods were produced at home. From this point of view, the purpose of exporting is to enable us to import goods that can be produced more cheaply abroad than at home.

FOREIGN INVESTMENT: An excess of exports over imports may be used to acquire foreign exchange needed to purchase foreign assets. But such foreign investments add to living standards only when the interest or profits earned on them is used to buy imports that do not have to be matched by currently-produced exports, i.e., when, in the future, they produce an excess of imports over exports. From this point of view, the purpose of exporting more than one is importing in order to make foreign investments is eventually to be able to import more than one is exporting!

The living standard of a country depends on the goods and services consumed in that country. The importance of exports is that they permit imports to be made. This two-way international exchange is valuable because more goods can be imported than could be obtained if the same goods were produced at home.

AN ECONOMY WITH UNEMPLOYMENT: AN EXCEPTION?: It is sometimes thought that an economy with substantial amounts of unemployment, such as the US economy in the early 1960s or the British economy in the 1930s provides an exception to the principles outlined above. Assume there is a rise in that country's exports without any corresponding rise in its imports, perhaps because the government has put a subsidy on exports and increased the rates of tariffs charged on imports. As we saw in Chapter 36, this rise in exports will increase income and employment. Surely, in a time of unemployment, this is to be regarded as a 'good thing'.

Two points need to be made about such a policy. In the first place, the goods being produced by the newly employed workers in the export sector are not available for domestic consumption and so do not raise domestic standards of living. Would it not be better if, instead of subsidizing exports, the central authorities subsidized the production of goods for the home market, so that the initial rise in employment would also contribute to a rise in domestic living standards? Or if one objects to the government subsidization of private firms, then the government could create new employment by building more roads, schools and research laboratories. Again, income and employment would go up, but, again, there would be something more tangible to show for it than the smoke of ships bearing the subsidized exports to foreign markets disappearing over the horizon.[1]

The second point to be made concerns the foreign effects of such a policy of fostering exports and discouraging imports in a situation of general world unemployment. Although the policy raises domestic employment, it will have the reverse effect abroad – it will create unemployment abroad. Such a policy may therefore be referred to as one of 'exporting one's unemployment'. The foreign countries will suffer a rise in their unemployment, because their exports will fall and their imports rise. This will set up a multiplier process that reduces their levels of income and employment. Even if the governments of these countries are prepared to see their unemployment rise, this policy cannot long continue, because these countries will begin to have balance-of-payments deficits. They will soon be forced to take steps to remove these deficits. If they do this by restricting imports, the original country will lose the stimulus that it originally obtained by encouraging exports. If all countries try such a policy of expanding exports and discouraging imports, the net effect is likely to be a large fall in the volume of international trade without much change in the level of employment in any country.

Our main concern in this chapter has been not to argue a case for or against free trade, but to investigate what can be said about trade and tariffs on the basis of

1 We are here considering the effects of the initial rise in employment in either the export or the investment industries. Of course there will be multiplier effects of an increase in either X or M and these *will* contribute to an increase in domestic living standards.

positive economics. As in all other realms, positive economics investigates the consequences of certain actions: it cannot say which goals one ought to pursue. Whether or not free trade is better than moderate tariffs, depends on the policy goals that one is trying to attain, the magnitude of the gains under a free-trade policy as compared to the gains under a tariff policy, and on the extent to which the policy adopted prohibits the attainment of goals other than maximizing consumption.

47

International economic experience

International economic relations have always been beset by controversy. Should we trade with the foreigners? Won't their cheap labour and unfair practices destroy our basic living standards? Should we have a North Atlantic free-trade area? What about a Latin American one? Although such problems of trading relations have been controversial and may even have been contributing causes of armed skirmishes and minor wars, they have not been the cause of continual world crises; but the international payments systems used in the twentieth century have been the cause of continual crises from the time of the breakdown of the gold standard in the 1920s.

HISTORICAL BACKGROUND

The gold standard

Although the detailed workings of the gold standard are now only of historical interest, a few of its features provide important insights into the present system. The gold standard was not *designed*. Like the price system, it just happened. It arose out of the general acceptance of gold as the commodity to be used as money. In most countries, paper currency was freely convertible into gold at a fixed rate.

Rates of exchange between the standard units of currency of various countries were fixed by their values in terms of the standard unit, gold. In 1914, the US dollar was convertible into 0·053 standard ounce of gold, while the British pound sterling was convertible into 0·257 standard ounce. This meant that the pound was worth 4·86 times as much as the dollar in terms of gold, thus making one pound worth $4·86 US.[1] There was nothing good or bad about this, nor was there any cause for British or American national pride or shame in the fact that the pound sterling was

---

1 In practice, the exchange rate did fluctuate within narrow limits set by the cost of shipping gold. If it cost 2¢ to ship $4·86 worth of gold from New York to London, it would be worth buying pounds in New York as long as their price did not rise above $4·88. At $4·87 to the pound, an American who wished to pay a bill in London would still buy pounds. At $4·89, it would pay him to convert his dollars into gold (at $4·86 per pound) and ship the gold at (2¢ per pound's worth), making the total cost of paying his bill $4·88 per pound rather than $4·89 if he purchased sterling. Thus, no one would buy sterling at a price in excess of $4·88. A similar argument for the British

worth more than the dollar. The British had simply chosen to make their basic unit, the pound, contain a larger amount of gold than was contained in the American basic unit, the dollar.

As long as all countries were on the gold standard, a person in any one country could be sure of being able to make payments to a person in any other country. If he was unable to buy or sell claims to the foreign currencies on the foreign-exchange market, he could always convert the currency he held into gold and then ship the gold.

How the gold standard was supposed to work: Exchange rates were fixed and adjustments were supposed to occur through changes in the relative prices of exports and imports. These changes were supposed to be brought about by changes in the domestic price levels of trading countries. A rise in one country's price level would raise the relative price of its exports in other countries and lower the relative price of imports in its domestic markets.

In a country that bought more foreign goods than it sold, the demand for foreign exchange would exceed its supply, and some people who wished to make foreign payments would be unable to obtain foreign exchange. No matter – they would merely convert their domestic currency into gold and ship the gold. Therefore, some people in a surplus country would secure gold in payment for exports. They would deposit this to their credit and accept claims on gold – in terms of convertible paper money or bank deposits – in return. Thus, deficit countries would be losing gold, while surplus countries would be gaining it.

Under the gold standard, the whole money supply was linked to the supply of gold (see pp. 591–2). The international movements of gold would therefore lead to a fall in the money supply in the deficit country and to a rise in the surplus one.[1] According to the quantity theory of money, changes in the domestic money supply cause changes in domestic price levels. Deficit countries would thus have falling price levels, while surplus countries would have rising price levels. The exports of deficit countries would become relatively cheaper, then, while those of surplus countries would become relatively more expensive. The resulting changes in quantities bought and sold would move the balance of payments toward an equilibrium position.

How the gold standard did work: The half-century before the First World War was the heyday of the gold standard; during this relatively trouble-free period, the automatic mechanism seemed to work well. Subsequent research has suggested, however, that the gold standard succeeded during the period mainly because it was not called on to do much work. Trade flowed between nations in large and rapidly expanding volume, and it is probable that existing price levels were never far from the equilibrium ones. No major trading country found itself with a serious and

---

trader wishing to obtain US funds establishes that the rate cannot fall below $4·84. The values at which it paid to ship gold were known as *gold points*.

1 When the person who received gold deposited it in his bank, this would put the bank in the position shown in Table 42.1, page 601, and a multiple expansion of deposit money would ensue.

persistent balance-of-payments deficit, and so no major country was called upon to restore equilibrium through a large change in its domestic price level.

Inevitably there were short-run fluctuations, but these were ironed out either by movements of short-run capital in response to changes in interest rates or by changes in national income and employment. Interest rates tended to rise in deficit countries, and this tended to attract sufficient short-run capital to cover any balance-of-payments deficit, providing the deficit was shortlived. (The way in which this was accomplished was spelled out in the appendix to Chapter 45.) Also, if a country developed a deficit because of some decline in its exports, its national income would fall through the operation of the multiplier, and the resulting fall in imports would reduce the magnitude of its deficit. If a country developed a surplus, because of either an increase in exports or a switch in domestic expenditure away from imports onto domestically produced goods, national income would rise because of the multiplier effect, and the resulting rise in imports would tend to reduce the surplus.

In the 1920s, the gold standard was called on to do a major job. It failed utterly, and it was abandoned. How did this come about? During the First World War, most belligerent countries had suspended convertibility of currency (i.e., they went off the gold standard). Most countries suffered major inflations, but the degree of inflation differed from country to country. After the war, countries returned to the gold standard (i.e., they restored convertibility of their currencies into gold). For reasons of prestige, some insisted on returning at the prewar rates. This meant that some countries' goods were overpriced and others' underpriced. Furthermore, as a result of major technological changes many countries found much of their industry specialized in products the demand for which was declining. Large deficits and surpluses in the balance of payments inevitably appeared, and the adjustment mechanism required that price levels should change in each of the countries in order to restore equilibrium. Price levels changed very slowly and, by the onset of the Great Depression, equilibrium price levels had not yet been attained. By this time, it was too late to achieve equilibrium and the financial chaos brought on by the Depression destroyed the existing payments system.

The failure of the mechanism of price-level changes to work quickly has often been attributed to the growth of price and wage rigidities in the twentieth century. Recent research has shown, however, that the price and wage levels of the 1920s were no less flexible than in the nineteenth century. The success of the gold standard in the nineteenth century, therefore, is not to be attributed to the fact that the mechanism worked well, but to the fact that it was never presented with a really major job to do.

The 1930s: a period of experimentation

After the abandonment of the gold standard, various experiments were tried with both fixed and fluctuating rates. Often a rate would be allowed to fluctuate on the free market until it had reached what looked like equilibrium, and it would then be fixed at that level. Sometimes, as with the British pound, the rate was left to be determined by a free market throughout the whole period. Sometimes rates would be changed in an attempt to secure domestic full employment without any consideration of the state of the balance of payments.

The period of experimentation coincided with the Great Depression of the 1930s. Trade everywhere was being reduced because of both rising unemployment and the increasing uncertainty and doubt about the future of international markets. Furthermore, this was a period during which many established ideas about the gains from trade were challenged, and many old-fashioned, long-discarded ideas on the desirability of exporting and the undesirability of importing were revived. In the terrible period of mass unemployment of the 1930s, governments began to cast around for any measure, no matter how extreme, that might alleviate domestic unemployment. One superficially plausible way of doing this was to cut back on imports and to produce the goods domestically. If one country managed to reduce its imports, then its unemployment might be reduced because people would be put to work producing goods at home to replace goods formerly imported. Other countries would find their exports falling and unemployment rising as a consequence. When these other countries then retaliated by reducing their own imports and trying to lower their unemployment by producing the goods at home, the first country found its exports falling and unemployment rising as a result. The simultaneous attempts of all countries to cut imports without suffering a comparable cut in exports was bound to be self-defeating. The net effect of such measures was to decrease the volume of trade and thus to sacrifice the gains from trade without raising worldwide employment.

When unemployment is due to insufficient world aggregate demand, it cannot be cured by measures designed to redistribute, among nations, the fixed and inadequate total of demand.

The policy of discouraging imports and encouraging exports was attempted, using the instruments of commercial policy such as import duties, export subsidies, quotas, prohibitions, and, importantly, exchange-rate depreciation. These tools worked to decrease unemployment only as long as other countries remained passive.

Consider now the possibility of devaluing the exchange rate. If a country with a large portion of its labour force unemployed devalues, two effects can be expected: first, exports will rise; second, domestic consumers will buy fewer imports and more domestically-produced goods. Both of these changes will have the effect of lowering the amount of unemployment in the country. If other countries do nothing, the policy succeeds. But again, the volume of unemployment in other countries will have increased because exports to the devaluing country will have been reduced. If other countries try to restore their positions, they may devalue their currencies as well. If all countries devalue their currencies in the same proportion, they will all be right back where they started, with no change in the relative prices of goods from any country and, hence, no change in relative prices from the original situation. A situation in which all countries devalue their currencies in an attempt to gain a competitive advantage over one another is called a situation of competitive devaluations.[1]

1 Under a paper-currency system, a simultaneous devaluation of all currencies would have no effect, beneficial or harmful. In a gold-standard world, however, each country devalues by lowering the gold content of its currency. Thus, a full round of competitive devaluations of X per cent leaves relative exchange rates unchanged, but it raises the price of gold (measured in all currencies) by X per cent. The effect of this is to enrich those producing gold and those holding stocks of it by increasing their claims on the world's output.

The immediate post-Second World War period

The one lesson that everyone thought he had learned from the 1930s was that either a system of freely fluctuating exchange rates or a system of fixed rates with easily accomplished devaluations was the road to disaster in international affairs. In order to achieve a system of orderly exchange rates that would be conducive to the free flow of trade following the Second World War, representatives of most countries that had participated in the alliance against Germany, Italy and Japan met at Bretton Woods, New Hampshire, in 1944 to agree on a system of international payments for the postwar world. The international monetary system that developed out of the agreements reached at Bretton Woods consisted of a large body of rules and understandings for the regulation of international transactions and payments imbalances.

THE INTERNATIONAL MONETARY FUND (IMF): One outcome of the Bretton Woods Conference was the formation of the International Monetary Fund (also referred to as the IMF or the Fund). The Fund was designed to promote international monetary cooperation. To this end, it sought to maintain fixed exchange rates in the face of short-term fluctuations; to guarantee that changes in exchange rates would occur only in the face of long-term, persistent deficits or surpluses in the balance of payments; and to ensure that when such changes did occur they would not spark a series of competitive devaluations.

The rules of the IMF required that members keep a fixed exchange rate between their currencies and the currencies of all other countries. But to avoid the rigidity of a world of completely fixed exchange rates, each member country, after agreeing on its initial par value was allowed to change it by up to five percentage points in either direction. Any larger change was considered a major change. Major changes were to be made only in the face of a serious and persistent disequilibrium in the balance of payments and only after consultation with the IMF. This rule consequently put the world on the ADJUSTABLE PEG system; that is, the exchange rate was pegged, or fixed, by the government but could be adjusted, or changed, from time to time. In practice, the requirement for prior consultation with the IMF proved unworkable, and all major changes in rates since 1950 have been declared unilaterally by the countries concerned.

In order to help governments to maintain fixed rates in the face of temporary fluctuations in imports and exports or speculative movements of short-term capital, the Fund is prepared to lend foreign exchange to members in need of it. A member country that borrows gold or dollars can use it to support its exchange rate by selling these and buying its own currency. Later, it must sell its own currency and buy back the gold or dollars in order to repay the loan. The capital for such loans is subscribed by member countries, partly in terms of gold and partly in terms of their own currencies.

Without doubt, the IMF helped many countries to weather temporary balance-of-payments problems that might otherwise have ended in devaluations. There is no question that the Fund has been a powerful force in favour of maintaining fixed rates of exchange. To those who think fixed exchange rates are the best system, this appears as an advantage; to those who think fixed rates are a poor system, it appears as a disadvantage.

THE INTERNATIONAL BANK FOR RECONSTRUCTION AND DEVELOPMENT: The other major world financial institution emerging from the conference at Bretton Woods was the International Bank for Reconstruction and Development (also referred to as the World Bank or, simply, the Bank). One of the purposes for which the Bank was designed was to facilitate long-term capital movements. This can be done in three ways. The Bank has funds of its own that it can loan to needy countries for development purposes. More important, the Bank can underwrite loans made by others to developing countries. Because the Bank has considerable expertise and inside knowledge, its guarantee that a borrower is reasonably sound may make it possible for a developing country to receive loans when otherwise it could not do so. Finally, the Bank itself can borrow money in member countries to finance its loans.

THE GENERAL AGREEMENT ON TARIFFS AND TRADE (GATT): One of the most notable achievements of the post-Second World War world in moving back from the highwater mark of protectionism achieved in the 1930s was the General Agreement on Tariffs and Trade (GATT). Under this agreement, GATT countries meet periodically to negotiate bilaterally on mutually advantageous cuts in tariffs. They agree in advance that any tariff cuts negotiated in this way will be extended to all member countries. Some significant tariff reductions have been effected by the member countries, but the total results have fallen far short of the hopes of the founders. Although tariffs are not as low as free traders might wish, it is probable that without GATT's imaginative attempt at post-Second World War cooperation, tariffs would be significantly higher than they are now.

The latest in the series of GATT agreements was the so-called Kennedy Round begun in November, 1964, and completed in May, 1967. The reductions finally negotiated averaged about one third of existing world rates. They were phased over five years with the last instalment in 1972. These are the most significant tariff cuts achieved since the Second World War.

To some extent, however, the tariffs were replaced by a series of NONTARIFF BARRIERS to trade. These are defined as anything other than tariffs that impedes the free flow of international trade; they include production and export subsidies, standards purporting to maintain the quality of imports, quotas on imports, complex administrative procedures, variable indirect taxation, and minimum allowed import prices. For this reason, it is hard to assess the overall quantitative effect of the Round, but there can be little doubt that even when all qualifications are allowed, it represented a significant step in the direction of freer international trade.

No new round of tariff reductions was in sight by 1974, and GATT's recent annual reports suggest, if anything, that barriers to trade are beginning to increase throughout much of the world.

THE EUROPEAN ECONOMIC COMMUNITY (EEC): In 1945, Europe seemed on the verge of famine and collapse. Each of the war-devastated countries set out almost immediately to deal with its own crises of insufficient food, shelter and fuel. In 1947, America came forward with the Marshall Plan, which gave US aid and encouragement to the devastated continent. The Marshall Plan gave substantial impetus to the movement for common rather than disjointed action in dealing with the continent-wide crises, a movement that began with an attempt to reject the national rivalries that had caused two world wars within 25 years. A decade after the first tentative steps to cooperative recovery, the nations of Western Europe were no longer in need of economic aid. Indeed, many were achieving rates of economic growth well above that of the United States and were moving toward an economic union that may possibly be the first step in an eventual political union.

In 1957, the Treaty of Rome brought into existence the European Economic Community (EEC). The six original members were France, Germany, Italy, Holland, Belgium and Luxembourg. The EEC is dedicated to bringing about free trade, complete mobility of factors of production and eventual harmonization of fiscal and monetary policies among the member countries. Tariff reductions were made according to a time schedule that eliminated all tariffs on manufactured goods within the Community before 1970. If the development continues, Western Europe will be, before the end of the century, a single economic community with a free movement of goods, labour and capital among the member countries.

In 1972, in the face of strong divisions within each country, Great Britain, the Republic of Ireland and Denmark joined the Community, the first two after close votes in their parliaments and the latter after a plebiscite. At the same time, Norway voted in a plebiscite to remain outside.

With the removal of tariffs on manufactured goods, the EEC transferred its attention to other areas of economic cooperation. Early in 1971, the Community announced that member countries had agreed on the first three-year stage of a plan to achieve full economic and monetary union by the end of the decade. Whether or not a complete monetary integration will be achieved in the future remains to be seen. During 1974 the EEC countries experimented with the initial stage of monetary cooperation in attempting to keep their exchange rates tied to one another. A major purpose of this was to allow their rates to float upward or downward against the US dollar, while not allowing one member country to gain any competitive advantage *vis-à-vis* the other by changes in intracommunity exchange rates.

The Bretton Woods system

Although there are important problems of tariffs, international investment and other trading relations, the most pressing international economic problems today are those monetary problems related to international payments. From 1945 to 1971 the world operated under a payments system known as the BRETTON WOODS SYSTEM, an outgrowth of the Bretton Woods Agreements and the rules subsequently formulated by the IMF. In 1971 that system collapsed because it was unable to cope with persistent US inflation and balance-of-payments deficits. (The IMF itself survived the collapse of the system for whose administration it was originally set up.) Since that time all attempts to obtain agreement on a new system have failed, and the world has been operating on a *de facto* dollar standard with a substantial amount of exchange-rate flexibility.

Whatever system finally emerges, it will, if it is a system of fixed exchange rates, face problems similar to those that beset the Bretton Woods system. Moreover, the design of the new system will inevitably be heavily influenced by the experience of the previous quarter-century. It is important, therefore, to study this experience in some detail.

The basic characteristic of the Bretton Woods system, which was sometimes also called a GOLD-EXCHANGE STANDARD, was that US dollars held by foreign monetary authorities were made directly convertible into gold at a fixed price (of approximately \$35 an ounce) by the US government, while foreign governments fixed the prices at which their currencies were convertible into US dollars. All countries were supposed to make their currencies freely convertible into dollars, but in practice countries with persistent balance-of-payments deficits found it necessary to restrict the conditions under which holders of their currencies could convert them into dollars. The system was thus one of limited convertibility into dollars, the degree of convertibility varying from country to country and from time to time.

In order to maintain convertibility of their currencies at fixed exchange rates, the monetary authorities of each country had to be ready to buy and sell its currency in the foreign-exchange markets. When demand for the currency exceeded the supply, they had no problem, because, as was seen in Chapter 42, they could create unlimited supplies of domestic currency. In this case, they could sell newly created quantities of domestic money and accept foreign currency (or claims on it) in exchange. The reserves of foreign exchange were thereby augmented. When the supply of the domestic currency offered on the foreign-exchange market exceeded the demand for it at the fixed price, the central authorities bought up the excess supply of domestic currency and provided gold or foreign exchange in return. The reserves of foreign exchange were thereby depleted.

In order to be able to support the exchange market by buying domestic currency, the monetary authorities had to have stocks of acceptable foreign exchange to offer in return. In the Bretton Woods system, the authorities held reserves of gold, and claims on key currencies – mainly the American dollar and the British pound sterling. They could also borrow foreign exchange from the IMF to tide them over temporary periods of shortage. When a country's currency was in excess supply, it sold dollars, sterling, or gold. When its currency was in excess demand, it would buy dollars or sterling. If a country wished to increase its gold reserves it used the dollars to purchase gold from the Fed (the commonly used name for the Federal Reserve System, which is the US central bank) (and sterling to purchase dollars if it originally held its reserves in sterling) thus depleting the US gold stock (and the British foreign exchange reserves if it had started with sterling). The problem for the United States was to have enough gold to maintain fixed-price convertibility of the dollar into gold as demanded by foreign monetary authorities. The problem for the UK was to maintain convertibility of sterling into dollars so that other countries would be willing to hold some of their reserves in the form of sterling. The problem for all other countries was to maintain convertibility (on a restricted or unrestricted basis, depending on the country in question) between their currency and either sterling or the US dollar at a fixed rate of exchange.

> **In summary, the Bretton Woods international payments system was an adjustable-peg, gold-exchange standard where the ultimate international money was gold but where countries held much of their exchange reserves in the form of US dollars, which they could convert into gold, and British pounds sterling, which they could convert into dollars.**

MAJOR PROBLEMS WITH AN ADJUSTABLE-PEG SYSTEM

Three major problems of the Bretton Woods system were (1) providing sufficient reserves to iron out short-term fluctuations in international receipts and payments while keeping exchange rates fixed; (2) making adjustments to long-term trends in receipts and payments; and (3) handling speculative crises. Let us look at each of them.

Reserves to accommodate short-term Fluctuations

THE PROBLEM: Reserves are needed to accommodate short-term balance-of-payments fluctuations arising from both the current and the capital account. On current account, normal trade is subject to many short-term variations, some systematic and some random. Exports may be subject to seasonal and cyclical fluctuations, not matched to fluctuations in imports. Strikes, floods, cyclones, revolutions, crop failures, and a host of other natural and man-made factors can disturb exports and imports. This means that even if the value of imports does equal the value of exports, taken on average over several years, there may be considerable imbalances in these over shorter periods of time. Such changes are not fully synchronized across countries, and this causes changes in capital flows so that, even if there is a long-term tendency for capital to flow from country A to country B, this flow may be temporarily reversed by changes in any one of the many factors, such as interest rates, business prospects, and government policy, that affect the attractiveness of investment in a particular country.

On a free market, fluctuations in current- and capital-account payments would cause the exchange rate to fluctuate. To prevent such fluctuations when rates are fixed, the monetary authorities buy and sell foreign exchange as required to keep the exchange rate pegged. These operations require that the authorities hold reserves of foreign exchange.

The demand for reserves: The amount of reserves that the authorities need to hold depends on their estimate of the maximum amount of foreign exchange they might have to sell to stabilize the exchange rate in the face of a particularly unfavourable period of excess demand. If the authorities run out of reserves they cannot maintain the pegged rate, so they will want to hold some safety margin over the maximum they expect to use. It is generally felt that the absolute size of any gap they may have to fill with their own foreign-exchange sales increases as the volume of international payments increases. If, for example, the authorities felt they had to stand ready to meet excess demand of up to 20 per cent of the annual value of foreign payments, then their need for reserves would rise in proportion to the increase in the volume of international payments.

> **Since there is a strong upward trend in the volume of overall international payments, there is also a strong upward trend in the demand for foreign-exchange reserves.**

The supply of reserves: The ultimate reserve in the Bretton Woods gold-exchange standard was gold. The use of gold as a reserve caused two serious problems. First, the world's supply of monetary gold did not grow fast enough to provide adequate total reserves for an expanding volume of trade. During the early 1960s, as a result of a fixed price of gold, rising costs of production and rising commercial uses, the world's stock of monetary gold was rising at about 2 per cent per year while the value of trade was growing at nearly 10 per cent. During the latter half of the decade the stock of monetary gold actually diminished, and by 1970 it was less than it had been in 1960. Gold, which had been 66 per cent of the total monetary reserves in 1959, was only 40 per cent in 1970 and had fallen to 30 per cent by 1972; over this period, reserve holdings of dollars and sterling rose sharply. Clearly, the gold backing needed to maintain convertibility of these currencies was becoming increasingly inadequate. Second, the country whose currency is convertible into gold must maintain sufficient reserves to ensure convertibility. During the 1960s the United States lost substantial gold reserves to other countries that had acquired dollar claims through their balance-of-payments surpluses with the United States. By the late 1960s the loss of US reserves had been sufficiently large to undermine confidence in America's continued ability to maintain dollar convertibility. By 1970 there was an inadequate world supply of gold for monetary uses, and the United States had too small a proportion of the supply that did exist.

POSSIBLE REMEDIES: From the standpoint of 1970, three possible sources of increased reserves seemed to be available: increasing the supply of gold; supplementing gold with an extra reserve asset; and replacing gold by a paper substitute whose supply could be easily increased to meet the needs of trade. All three of these sources could still be used today.

(1) The United States could increase the supply of gold by raising the price that it is prepared to pay for gold above the present free-market price. This would encourage the production of gold and raise the value of the existing gold stock.

US authorities have traditionally been reluctant to adopt this solution for many reasons not the least important of which is that it would represent a free gift to those countries, such as South Africa and Russia, that are able to mine gold at a profit even at a very low price of gold.

(2) A second solution would be to augment the supply of gold with paper substitutes. This was the idea behind the whole key-currency system on which the Bretton Woods gold-exchange standard had always been based. There is not enough gold to satisfy all needs for reserves, so central banks hold claims on sterling, which was convertible into the dollar, and on the dollar, which was convertible into gold. Because the need for reserves expanded much more rapidly than the gold stock in the

period since the Second World War, the system required that nations hold an increasing fraction of their reserves in dollars and sterling and that they maintain confidence in the convertibility of these currencies. This maintenance of confidence was made difficult by a continually declining percentage of gold backing for the dollar.

A major disadvantage of using a national currency as a supplementary reserve is the possible inability to maintain convertibility of that currency into gold. Another major disadvantage occurs if the country whose currency is used for reserves wishes to devalue because of severe balance-of-payments problems. If it does devalue, all countries holding that currency find the value of these reserves slashed. If it tries to avoid devaluation, fear that it may be unable to do so impairs the usefulness of the currency as a reserve because other countries become reluctant to hold it.

The desire to provide a supplementary reserve not tied to the currency of a particular country led to the development in the late 1960s of SPECIAL DRAWING RIGHTS (SDRs) at the IMF. SDRs were designed to provide a supplement to existing reserve assets by setting up a Special Drawing Account kept separate from all other operations of the Fund. Each member country of the Fund is assigned an SDR quota that is guaranteed in terms of a fixed gold value, and that it can use to acquire an equivalent amount of convertible currencies from other participants. SDRs can be used without prior consultation with the Fund, but only to cope with balance-of-payments difficulties.

SDRs might have gone a long way toward alleviating the system's difficulties if the system had not been overwhelmed by much more fundamental problems in the early 1970s.

(3) The United States could permanently demonetize gold. When on 13 August 1971, the Fed stopped selling gold at a fixed price to approved purchasers, this left the price of gold used for all purposes to be determined on the free market.[1] If this nonconvertibility of the US dollar into gold were to be extended indefinitely (i.e., if gold were permanently demonetized), then foreign central banks would have to be satisfied to hold reserves in the form of paper money – dollars or other currencies – or in the form of some new international paper money if an acceptable one could be developed.

The supporters of permanent demonetization argued that the supplies of domestic currencies were no longer tied to gold and that the time had come to do the same for international means of payment. Certainly it would appear to be a waste of resources to mine gold only to rebury it permanently in the vaults of a few dozen central banks. Paper, or better still, book entries, would do just as well. They cost virtually nothing to produce, and their total supply is not limited by any of the factors that limit the total supply of gold.

---

1 Until 1968, a group of countries operated the so-called Gold Pool, which bought and sold gold in free markets in order to stabilize its price at $35 an ounce. This meant that there was a single world price of gold. In 1967–8 the system broke down under pressure of intense speculative demand for gold, which left the Gold Pool countries unable to supply enough gold to hold its price down. In March, 1968, the attempt was abandoned. A two-tier system followed, with official settlement between governments at $35 an ounce and a much higher price for private citizens. This two-tier system exists today although in practice gold is no longer used to settle debts since its official price is well below its free-market price.

Adjusting to long-term disequilibria

THE PROBLEM: With fixed exchange rates, long-term disequilibria (or what the IMF calls *fundamental disequilibria*) can be expected to develop because of secular shifts in the demands for and supplies of foreign exchange. There are two important reasons for these long-term shifts in demands and supplies in the foreign-exchange market. First, there are different rates of inflation in the different trading countries of the world. Chapter 45 discussed how these differing rates of inflation cause changes in the equilibrium rates of exchange and, if the rate is fixed, cause excess supply or excess demand to develop in the foreign-exchange market. Second, changes in the demands for and supplies of imports and exports are associated with long-term economic growth. Because different countries grow at different rates, their demands for imports, and supplies of exports, would be expected to be shifting at different rates.

These long-term shifts in demand and supply imply that, even starting from a current-account equilibrium with imports equal to exports at a given rate of exchange, there is no reason to believe that equilibrium will exist at the same rate of exchange 10 or 20 years later (any more than equilibrium relative prices would be expected to remain unchanged over 20 years within any one country).

> **The rate of exchange that will lead to a balance-of-payments equilibrium will tend to change over time; over a decade the equilibrium rate of exchange can shift substantially.**

POSSIBLE REMEDIES: Governments may react to long-term disequilibria in at least three ways.

(1) The exchange rate can be changed whenever it is clear that a balance-of-payments deficit or surplus is a result of a long-term shift in the demands and supplies in the foreign-exchange market, rather than the result of some transient factor. This was the solution envisaged by the framers of the IMF when they allowed member countries, after consultation with the IMF, to change their exchange rates in the face of a 'fundamental disequilibrium'. During the period of the Bretton Woods system, there were two major rounds of exchange-rate adjustments, each sparked off by a devaluation of the second of the world's two reserve currencies, the British pound sterling. The major changes in each round are summarized in Table 47.1. A further round sparked off by the devaluation of the dollar began in December 1971.

(2) Domestic price levels can be allowed to change in an attempt to establish the equilibrium set of international prices. In Chapter 45 it was shown that a 10 per cent devaluation with the price level constant is the equivalent (as far as the effect on import and export prices is concerned) of a 10 per cent deflation with the exchange rate constant; a 10 per cent revaluation is the equivalent of a 10 per cent inflation. Changes in domestic price levels have all sorts of domestic repercussions (e.g., reductions in aggregate demand intended to lower the price level are more likely to raise unemployment than to lower prices), and one might have expected governments to be more willing to change exchange rates – which can be done by a stroke of a pen – than to try to change the price level. A deflation is difficult to accomplish,

while an inflation is thought to be accompanied by undesirable side effects. None-theless, many governments have sought to vary price levels rather than to rely mainly on changes in exchange rates. Britain, for example, has engaged in several attempts at direct intervention in an effort to control the price level as an alternative to changing the exchange rate.

(3) Restrictions can be imposed on trade and foreign payments. Imports and foreign spending by tourists and governments can be restricted, and exportation of capital can be slowed or even stopped. Surplus countries have often been quick to criticize such restriction on international trade and payments, but it is important to realize that as long as exchange rates are fixed and price levels prove difficult to manipulate, there is little choice for the deficit countries but to restrict the quantity of foreign exchange they demand to the quantity available. Indeed, most of the deficit countries of the world have had to have recourse both to tariffs and other trade and payments restrictions.

Handling speculative crises

THE PROBLEM: When enough people begin to doubt the ability of the central authorities to maintain the current rate, speculative crises develop. Because inter-national monetary reserves are held in the form of gold and foreign exchange – chiefly dollars and sterling – confidence in the system requires confidence in *both* gold and the reserve currencies. In the 1960s, confidence in the reserve currencies weakened as both the dollar and the pound were subject to crises related to persistent American and British balance-of-payments deficits.

The most important reason for such crises is that the equilibrium exchange rates change, and over time they tend to get further and further away from the actual fixed rate. After a while traders become reluctant to hold their working balances in a currency they think may be devalued, but they will be willing to use one that may be revalued. When the disequilibrium becomes obvious to everyone, traders and speculators come to believe that a realignment of rates cannot long be delayed. At such a time, there is a rush to buy currencies expected to be revalued upward and a rush to sell currencies expected to be devalued. Even if the authorities take dramatic steps to remove the payments deficit, there may be doubt as to whether these measures will work before the exchange reserves are exhausted. Speculative flows of funds can reach very large proportions, and it may be impossible to avoid changing the exchange rate under such pressure.

POSSIBLE REMEDIES: Speculative crises were, and will always be, one of the most intractable problems of any adjustable-peg system. The impact of such crises might be reduced if governments had more adequate reserves. If a speculative crisis pre-cedes an exchange-rate adjustment, however, more adequate reserves may just mean that speculators will make larger profits since more of them will be able to sell the currency about to be devalued and to buy the currency about to be revalued before the monetary authorities are forced to act.

In the past, governments have resisted changing their rates until they had no alternative. This tended to make the situation so obvious that speculators could hardly lose, and their actions set off the final crises that forced exchange-rate re-adjustments. It might help to have more frequent, surprise changes made before they had become inevitable. This, however, would remove the day-to-day certainties associated with the system of fixed exchange rates that is its chief advantage. Moreover it might lead to suspicion that a government's surprise devaluation was made to gain a competitive advantage for its exports rather than to remove a fundamental disequilibrium. After all, governments are not supposed to devalue until it is clear that they are faced with a fundamental disequilibrium, and if it is clear to them that they are, there is no reason to think it would not be clear to ordinary traders and speculators too. Basically, then, although the problem of speculative crises might be alleviated somewhat, it will always be present in any adjustable-peg system.

The collapse of the Bretton Woods system

BASIC CAUSES: Despite the difficulties, it still seemed a reasonable bet during the late 1960s that the system would survive with just some patching around the seams. One ray of hope came from the fact the rest of the world had finally begun to be persuaded that the causes of the American balance-of-payments deficits lay outside of American control. Many other countries had previously taken the line that no reform of the system was possible until the United States removed its balance-of-payments deficit. By the mid 1960s the US authorities had come to the view that the American balance-of-payments deficit was caused by the demand of foreign monetary authorities to accumulate US dollars as reserves. If, for example, the French central bank wished to add to its reserves of dollars, it would take steps to encourage a surplus on its country's balance of payments so that it might buy up the excess of foreign exchange that had no private takers. (Indeed, the bank would have to buy up the foreign exchange in order to prevent the franc from appreciating.) Thus, if all central banks were trying to add to their reserves of dollars, each would take steps to generate a balance-of-payments surplus for its country. To the extent that the rest of the world collectively succeeded in doing this, America had to have a balance-of-payments deficit. Indeed the US balance-of-payments deficits of $2 billion to $3 billion per annum throughout the 1960s were consistent with the view that foreign governments wished to add that amount each year to their reserves in order to be able to stabilize their exchange rates in the face of a rising volume of world trade.

It followed from this analysis that America could not remove its deficit by placing restrictions on foreign payments such as were imposed in the latter half of the 1960s. Whenever this was done, foreign governments would respond by increasing their own restrictions in order to maintain their payments surplus so that they could continue adding to their reserves.

Because of this analysis of the cause of its deficit, the American government took the view that a new source of reserves was necessary and that without it the demand that the United States remove its balance-of-payments deficit could not be met – at least so long as foreign governments wished to increase their stocks of reserves.

Ironically, just as the American government managed to persuade its major trading partners of that view, and agreement was reached on the 'brave new experiment' of the SDRs, the whole character of the US deficit changed. The inflationary impact of heavy Vietnam military expenditures began to be felt. America moved into a situation in which her price level rose relative to the price levels of many of her trading partners, and the standard prediction was once again confirmed: countries that inflate relative to the average world price level will tend to generate balance-of-payments deficits. The US payments deficit of $6 billion in 1969 was too large to be explained by desire on the part of foreign monetary authorities to add that amount to their reserves.

The rising US inflation and balance-of-payments deficit revealed an inherent problem in the system that had so far gone virtually unnoted: the American authorities did not, and could not, independently fix their exchange rate against other currencies.[1] Recall that the way the system worked was that each foreign country fixed its exchange rate against the dollar. This system worked reasonably well as long as the American price level was relatively stable. Countries that were inflating a bit too fast could occasionally devalue their exchange rates, and countries that were inflating even more slowly than the United States could occasionally revalue their exchange rates in an upward direction. Occasional upward and downward readjustments relative to the dollar served to keep the system near equilibrium.

But if the United States began to inflate rapidly (or to do anything else that put it in a serious payments deficit with most other countries), it became necessary to devalue the US dollar relative to most (or even conceivably all) other currencies. Any other country in this situation would merely unilaterally devalue its currency relative to the US dollar. But the only way that the required US devaluation could be brought about was for all other countries to agree to revalue their currencies upwards relative to the dollar.

> **Under the Bretton Woods system any country other than the United States could devalue its currency by a unilateral decision; a US devaluation, however, requires the cooperation of all other countries against whose currency the dollar is to be devalued.**

It took a major feat of international bargaining – indeed some countries thought of it as high-handed coercion – to persuade many of the countries of the world to agree to the upward revaluations of their currencies that had the effect of devaluing the dollar. But under a Bretton Woods-type system such cumbersome negotiations would be necessary at frequent intervals as long as the US inflation continues at its present rapid rate. If speculators are able to reap substantial profits by predicting when one currency will be devalued or revalued unilaterally, they will have a field day, reaping enormous profits at the expense of national treasuries by being able to foresee the collective revaluations necessary to devalue the US dollar.

THE PERIOD OF CRISES: The recent history of the international payments crises reveals many of the weaknesses of any adjustable-peg system. In any case, it is a fascinating adventure story of international wheeling and dealing, with fortunes frequently made, and sometimes lost, often in the space of a few days.

1 If, for example, the British authorities pegged the pound sterling at $2·40, then the dollar was pegged at £0·417 and the Fed could not independently decide on another rate. Similar considerations applied to all other currencies.

Devaluation of the pound: 1967. The system worked through the 1950s and 1960s with two reserve currencies, the US dollar and the British pound. The dollar was convertible to gold and the pound convertible to dollars by approved monetary authorities. Since the British economy was more inflationary than the American one, the British balance of payments was in a more unsatisfactory state than the American balance. Foreign monetary authorities, therefore, had less confidence in the British pledge to keep sterling convertible into dollars at a fixed rate than they had in the American pledge to keep dollars convertible into gold. The first crises were thus sterling crises.

Fear of devaluation of the pound caused several speculative crises throughout the 1950s and 1960s. Finally, in 1967, the pound was devalued. Although many other currencies followed (Table 47.1), the dollar did not, in spite of a growing American balance-of-payments deficit. This generated the feeling that the dollar was seriously overvalued.

The gold drain. Believing that the dollar was overvalued, speculators rushed to buy gold before its price was raised by a US devaluation. In early 1968, the gold drain reached crisis proportions. If the US gold stocks were exhausted the price of gold could no longer be kept stable. Speculators everywhere began to believe for the first time since the end of the Second World War that there was a serious chance that the United States could not keep the dollar convertible into gold at the current price. There was a rush to buy gold at that price while it lasted. Of course, *private* speculators could not buy gold from the Fed, but they could buy it on the London and Zurich markets. And buy they did, in massive quantities. The countries of the Gold Pool had to sacrifice official reserves in a vain attempt to hold down the free-market price. The central bankers of the Gold Pool countries met in Washington and decided to abandon official support for the private gold markets of the world. The price in these fluctuated considerably, but it always stayed well above $35 an ounce. (By early 1974 gold was selling for more than $180 an ounce.) Then, at the end of March, 1968, representatives of nine major industrial nations met in Stockholm and signed an agreement to create the Special Drawing Rights that have already been described.

The crisis then receded. The calming was partly due to a temporary improvement in the US balance-of-payments position as a result of government restrictions on direct foreign investments by US firms and requirements for the repatriation of some funds to the United States. Also, tight money with accompanying high interest rates in the United States probably prompted some US firms to borrow abroad, and the resulting inflow of capital improved the balance of payments.

From dollars to marks. But heavy US military expenditures in Vietnam continued to contribute to the US balance-of-payments problems. Additionally, by late 1969 and early 1970, there was once again a substantial outflow of capital from the United States caused partly by US monetary expansion with its accompanying lower interest rates. The outflow contributed heavily to the balance-of-payments deficit. Meanwhile Germany and Japan, among other countries, continued to run large balance-of-payments surpluses. All of these factors contributed to the view that the dollar was overvalued while the mark and the yen were undervalued.

Table 47.1 Adjustments of exchange rates
by IMF countries in the two major rounds
following the devaluations of the pound
on 18 September 1949, and
14 November 1967

Country	Percentage devaluation, 1949–50 round	Percentage devaluation, 1967–8 round
United Kingdom	30·5	14·3
Greece	50·0	—
Australia	30·5	—
Burma	30·5	—
Ceylon	30·5	20·0
Denmark	30·5	7·9
Egypt	30·5	—
Eire	30·5	14·3
Finland	30·5	—
Iceland	30·5	24·6
India	30·5	—
Iraq	30·5	—
Israel	30·5	14·3
Netherlands	30·5	—
New Zealand	30·5	19·4
Norway	30·5	—
South Africa	30·5	—
Southern Rhodesia	30·5	—
Sweden	30·5	—
France	22·8	—
West Germany	20·6	—
Portugal	13·0	—
Belgium	12·0	—
Canada	10·0	—
Brazil	—	18·5
British Honduras	—	14·3
Cyprus	—	14·3
Fiji (net)	—	7·0
Gambia	—	14·3
Guiana	—	14·3
Hong Kong (net)	—	4·3
Jamaica	—	14·3
Macao	—	5·0
Malawi	—	11·9
Malta	—	14·3
Mauritius	—	14·3
Nepal	—	24·8
Sierra Leone	—	14·3
Spain	—	14·3
Trinidad and Tobago	—	14·3

Source: *Keesings Contemporary Archives and IMF
International Financial News Survey.*

From the beginning of 1971, there was a substantial outflow of dollars into marks. If either the dollar were devalued or the mark revalued, speculators holding marks would reap their profit. The full crisis was set off when on 3 May, five German economic institutes published reports recommending that the mark be floated so that it could find its own equilibrium level. On 4 May, $800 million came into Germany within three hours. Then on 5 May, the German foreign-exchange markets were shut down after $1,000 million had been transferred into marks in 40 minutes. During the course of the crisis, $4,000 million dollars came into Germany in two months – $2,000 million in the last two days.

Over the remainder of the week, the Germans debated possible courses of action. Many in Germany wanted to let the mark float, but others in Germany, together with the majority of the other Common Market countries, were opposed. Finally, on 10 May, the mark was allowed to float, and capital controls were instituted, including the elimination of interest payments on all foreign deposits held in German banks. By the end of the week, the mark had appreciated by 3 per cent, and it remained approximately stable at that level.

The hot money left Germany only slowly after the mark was freed. The consensus in the early summer was that speculators wanted to get into the Japanese yen, which was thought to be undervalued by as much as 20 per cent. It proved difficult, however, to move capital into yen because the Japanese had very strict controls on movements of foreign exchange.

The crisis seemed to have died down by early summer, but the general opinion was that exchange rates were seriously out of line, and in particular that the dollar was overvalued. This meant that a new wave of speculation was ready to break out as soon as the inevitable realignment of rates seemed imminent. Such a situation soon arose when US balance-of-payments figures showing a rapidly deteriorating current-account balance were published and when a subcommittee of the influential Joint Economic Committee issued a report admitting that the US dollar was over-valued. A wave of speculation against the dollar began. The German mark was still floating as a result of the May crisis, so the main focus of speculators' attention was the undervalued Japanese yen. Stringent Japanese capital controls prevented an influx of dollars into Japan in the degree to which Germany was flooded in the spring. But the flight from the dollar continued, and a substantial portion of the capital outflow of over $4,000 million ended up in European financial centres.

The dollar crisis of 1971. Prompted by this speculation, by an announced second quarter balance-of-payments deficit of $5,800 million, and by a failure of traditional policies to solve unemployment and inflation at home, President Nixon in August 1971, announced his New Economic Policy. ('New' it was for America but, with the exception of the measure dropping gold convertibility, it was almost exactly the same policy package – including the notorious import surcharge – that successive British governments had used several times in the 1950s and 1960s in a vain attempt to solve the problems that put sterling, the world's second reserve currency, under periodic speculative attacks.)

> **By suspending the gold convertibility of the dollar, the New Economic Policy brought the Bretton Woods gold-exchange standard system officially to an end.**

The policy also sought to achieve a *de facto* devaluation of the dollar by persuading those nations whose balances of payments were in surplus to allow their rates to float upward against the dollar.

The immediate response to this policy was a speculative outflow so severe that for the second time in the year foreign-exchange markets were closed throughout Europe. When the markets were reopened after a week, Britain, Germany, Holland, Italy and the Scandinavian countries allowed their rates to float. The Japanese, however, announced their intention of retaining their existing rate. In spite of their severe controls, $4,000 million of speculative funds managed to find their way into yen in the last two weeks of August, and the Japanese were forced to abandon their fixed-rate policy by allowing the yen to float upward.

Agreement on devaluation. After some very hard bargaining, an agreement between the major trading nations was signed at the Smithsonian Institution in Washington, DC. The main elements of the agreement were as follows: the US import surcharge was to be removed. The United States was to raise the official price of gold from $35 to $38 an ounce, thus causing a *de facto* devaluation of the dollar by approximately 8·5 per cent against all other currencies.

It was agreed, however, that gold would not be used to settle international indebtedness arising from the accumulation of dollars in the hands of foreign monetary authorities, at least until a new basic payments system was worked out. The currencies of some surplus countries were to be revalued upward. In particular, the Dutch guilder, the Belgian franc, the German mark, the Swiss franc and the Japanese yen were increased in value by amounts ranging up to 17 per cent. Canada held out to maintain her policy of a floating exchange rate. The bands of permitted fluctuations of exchange rates were widened.

Thus, the third major realignment of exchange rates since the Second World War was accomplished, and a regime of fixed exchange rates with nominal gold backing of currencies was re-established. The rise in the official price of gold to $38 could not by itself restore gold to its pre-1968 position. In the first place, as long as the free-market price of gold remains substantially above the official price, central banks are unlikely to want to use gold to settle debts. If gold is worth anything over $40 on the free market, it would not be sensible to use it to settle debts at a price of only $38; dollar credits will be used instead.[1] In the second place, the understanding arrived at after 1968 that in effect sealed off monetary from nonmonetary gold, remained in force – foreign central banks were not substantially to convert dollars into gold or to sell existing gold on the free market. Effectively, therefore, by the end of 1971 the world had moved to a dollar standard. American dollars constituted the major source of international reserves.

---

1 This is a splendid example of Gresham's Law, which states that bad money drives good money out of circulation.

Perhaps President Nixon knew he was exaggerating when he called the Smithsonian Agreement 'the greatest monetary agreement in history'. What it did do was (as already stated) bring about the third major realignment of exchange rates since the end of the Second World War. Its uniqueness lay in doing this by multilateral agreement (because the dollar needed to be devalued) rather than by a series of unilateral decisions as in previous rounds (where some of the world's other currencies needed to be devalued *vis-à-vis* the dollar). What it did not do was to set up a new monetary system; it merely bought time during which negotiations for a new system could take place.

THE DE FACTO DOLLAR STANDARD: Since the Smithsonian agreement, the world has effectively been on a *de facto* DOLLAR STANDARD. Foreign monetary authorities hold their reserves in the form of dollars and settle their international debts with dollars. But the dollar is not convertible into gold or anything else. The ultimate value of the dollar is given not by gold but by the American goods and services that dollars can be used to purchase. One major problem with such a dollar system is that the American inflation that upset the Bretton Woods system is no less upsetting to a dollar standard since the real, purchasing-power value of the world's dollar reserves is being continually eroded.

The world's central banks hold dollars because they have little choice unless they want to bring down the whole international payments system. But the private sector has shown its lack of confidence in any paper money including dollars by its desire to hold gold. This desire has been so strong that the price of gold rose from $35 an ounce in 1968 to $180 an ounce in 1974!

THE DRIFT TO A DIRTY FLOAT: We have seen that the Smithsonian agreement brought about the third major realignment of exchange rates since 1945. The two earlier rounds were followed by several years of relatively settled conditions on the world's foreign exchange markets. Not so the Smithsonian round!

The US inflation continued unchecked, and the US balance of payments never returned to the relatively satisfactory position that had been maintained all through the 1960s. Within a year of the agreements, speculation was beginning to build up that a further realignment of rates was necessary. In January of 1973 heavy speculative pressure led the Italian government to adopt a 'two-tier' system in which the lira could be bought and sold for commercial purposes at a stabilized rate but for capital transactions only at a freely floating rate. Shortly afterwards the Swiss national bank stopped stabilizing the price of the Swiss franc.

Then on 12 February 1973 came a bombshell. The US announced that it intended to propose a further 10 per cent devaluation of the dollar which was to be done by raising the dollar value of gold by 10 per cent. This was another first for the Nixon administration: it was the first time in history that a major government had announced in advance its intention to devalue. Needless to say intense speculative activity followed this extraordinary announcement. During the first week of March the major foreign exchange markets were closed down while governments decided how to react. When foreign exchange trading was resumed on 19 March, five of the member countries of the EEC decided to stabilize their currencies against each other but to let them float against the dollar. Norway and Sweden later became associated with this arrangement. The other EEC countries (Ireland, Italy and the UK) as well as Japan announced their intention to allow their currencies to float in value.

Fluctuations in exchange rates were severe. By early July the currencies of the five EEC countries that were involved in the 'joint float' had appreciated about 30 per cent against the dollar but by the end of the year they had returned nearly to their February values.

The dollar devaluation, whose prior announcement has caused such uproar, was formally put into effect on 18 October after congressional approval of the administration's proposal to raise the dollar price of gold by 10 per cent. Most industrialized countries maintained the value of their currencies in terms of gold and SDRs, thus appreciating in terms of the US dollar by 10 per cent.

Throughout 1974, the foreign exchange situation could be summarized as follows: many of the industrial countries – Austria, Canada, Italy, Japan, Switzerland, the UK and the US – were not maintaining rates for exchange transactions within announced margins, while other industrial countries – Belgium, Denmark, France, Germany, Luxembourg, the Netherlands, Norway and Sweden – maintained margins for exchange transactions among their currencies but not against the dollar. A large proportion of the remaining countries maintained stable rates of exchange for their currencies in terms of one of the three major currencies – the US dollar, sterling or the French franc.

Throughout the period following the Smithsonian agreement, central bankers met frequently in an effort to devise a new system that would restore a regime of fixed exchange rates. So far they have been unable to reach agreement on such a system and in the meantime more and more nations have been allowing the values of their currencies to fluctuate on the foreign-exchange market. This system is often described as a DIRTY FLOAT because central banks do try to influence exchange rates by intervening in exchange markets, but they do not try to peg the rate at any publicly announced par value.

THE FUTURE OF THE INTERNATIONAL PAYMENTS SYSTEM

Will any new international payments system that the central bankers may devise over the next few years be subject to the same periodic crises as the old one? The answer is almost certainly yes, if the system involves fixed exchange rates. As long as free-market equilibrium exchange rates change, and as long as governments do not change their fixed rates until the disequilibrium is obvious to everyone, speculative capital movements in anticipation of a new round of exchange-rate adjustments are inevitable.

At the present time, there is debate over how to reform the system to improve its workings and avoid periodic crises. The difficulty of devaluing the dollar as required by persistent US inflation has led the US authorities to look for some way of replacing the dollar as the major means of holding international reserves. The French and some others wish to restore gold to its basic position as the fundamental backing of dollar reserves by re-establishing the gold convertibility of the dollar. This would require that the Fed stand ready to buy gold from all comers at a fixed rate somewhere near the free-market price of gold. Since the free-market price has for several years been in excess of $100 and has several times come close to $200, this would require a major reversal of US policy in now being ready to make very large payments to the USSR and the Union of South Africa in return for the gold that they were able to mine profitably at $35 an ounce!

Other countries feel that nothing can be done until the United States puts its house in order by reducing its inflation rate to the pre-Vietnam level. As of 1974 no agreement on the outlines of a new system has been reached, and none seems to be in the offing. In the meantime, the world continues to drift into a regime of flexible rates as the only way to cope with the situation in which realignment of fixed rates requires multilateral agreement reached after lengthy bargaining and predictably severe speculative crises.

Reform with fixed rates

THE TRIFFIN PLAN: The best known plan for reform with fixed rates is by Professor Robert Triffin, of Yale University. The Triffin plan restores most of the elements of the Bretton Woods system but would replace the US dollar and gold with a genuine international currency as a means of settling official international debts. This would be done by converting the IMF into a world central bank. All countries would hold the bulk of their reserves at this expanded IMF, and these would be denominated in a new international unit of account. The new unit would possibly be called the bancor. This name was suggested by Keynes, whose own plan – rejected in 1944 – bore many similarities to the Triffin plan. International settlements would be made in terms of the bancor. Assume, for example, that Germany has a substantial payments surplus with France and that, in order to prevent the mark from appreciating, the German central bank is buying up francs. It would subsequently accept bancor credits on the books of the IMF in return for the francs, rather than demanding gold or dollars as it now could and usually would. But if the Spanish central bank were entering the market to stop the peseta from depreciating, it could convert its deposits of bancor into any foreign currencies that it required in order to support its own rate of exchange. The IMF could increase the supplies of bancor by the simple expedient of selling securities and so obtaining supplies of a country's currency. Basically, then, the Triffin plan would allow the Bretton Woods system to continue, but it would replace gold with an international paper currency and replace the problem of the adequacy of the gold stock with the monetary-management problem of increasing the supply of bancor quickly enough to meet legitimate demands for increases in liquidity, but slowly enough to prevent runaway world inflation.

THE KRAUSE PLAN: A plan that seeks to correct other shortcomings as well as the inadequacy of international reserves has been developed since the breakdown of the present system by Laurence R. Krause, of the Brookings Institution.[1]

(1) The par values of all currencies should be specified in terms of SDRs rather than

1 Lawrence R. Krause, *Sequel to Bretton Woods* (Brookings Institution, 1971).

gold or US dollars. Under this system the dollar becomes like any other currency and can be devalued or revalued unilaterally merely by changing its SDR par value.

(2) Wider margins for fluctuations on either side of par values should be established. There should also be some narrower range of fluctuations over which central banks agree not to intervene in the foreign-exchange market. This proposal attempts to give more scope to market forces in determining exchange rates while maintaining the assumed advantages of relatively fixed rates.

(3) Gold, dollars and other national currencies should be totally replaced in official reserves by SDRs. (The gold obtained by the IMF in return for SDRs could be sold on the free market and the profit used for such worthy purposes as aid to under-developed countries.)

(4) A market rate of interest would be paid on SDRs. This would make them similar to national currencies that can be invested to earn interest while they are held as reserves.

(5) Countries should be encouraged to make more frequent and smaller adjustments in the par values of their currencies. This feature of the plan seeks to avoid the speculative crises that have preceded each of the major realignments of exchange rates by encouraging changes before, rather than after, disequilibria have reached crisis proportions.

Taken together, these features attempt to maintain the short-run stability provided by fixed exchange rates and to solve the international liquidity problem while providing enough flexibility in rates to prevent the recurrence of serious speculative crises.

Reform with flexible rates

The basic advantages of a fixed-rate system are supposed to be that those planning for trade and capital movements have little uncertainty about the value of different currencies, at least into the near future. This relative lack of uncertainty about the values of exchange rates from one day to the next (except within the very narrow band of permitted fluctuation) is supposed to be very important because it is alleged that speculators will cause wide gyrations of exchange rates when they are left to be determined on free markets.

Many economists do not accept this case. They would point out the fact that the Bretton Woods system led not to certainty about the exchange rates, but rather to a series of periodic crises when large changes in rates were expected. Thus, they argue, the Bretton Woods system was full of serious uncertainties. They would also say that the fact that trade and long-term capital flows have occurred in spite of these uncertainties demonstrates that the supporters of fixed rates have much over-emphasized the effects of exchange-rate uncertainty on trade and capital movements. Each of these points requires careful consideration.

HOW MUCH UNCERTAINTY?: Economists who advocate flexible rates argue that the periodic speculative crises that beset the adjustable-peg system create much more uncertainty than the relatively smooth and gradual changes in rates that normally accompany a flexible system. They argue that the rational behaviour of speculators guarantees periodic crises, with accompanying uncertainty, under fixed rates, and relatively slow and smooth change, with an accompanying reduction in uncertainty, under flexible rates.

These economists hold that under flexible rates the activities of speculators would tend to stabilize the rate of exchange. If there were a temporary rise in imports, demand for foreign exchange would rise and so would the price of foreign exchange. If speculators regarded this change as temporary, they would sell the expensive foreign exchange and buy the cheap domestic currency. Thus, the change in demand on the part of speculators would be in the opposite direction from the change in demand on the part of importers, and the former would partially offset the effects of the latter.

While these economists expect speculation usually to be stabilizing under flexible rates, they hold that it must become very destabilizing under fixed rates. Consider, for example, a holder of sterling who thought a devaluation was likely in late 1967. He speculated by buying dollars at the then current rate of $2·80 to £1. If he had been wrong and the authorities had been able to maintain the existing rate, he would merely have bought sterling again when he needed it and would have lost nothing except the brokers' commission on the deal. If he had been right, as in this case he would have been, he would buy his sterling back at the lower price of $2·40 and would end up with an overall profit of 14 per cent on the deal. Thus, in a fixed-rate system speculators have little to lose if they are wrong when they speculate against a currency, and much to gain if they are right. This asymmetrical position – negligible losses or large profits – encourages speculation. This speculation is destabilizing in the sense that, whenever a currency is in danger of having to be devalued, the speculation will increase the pressure on it and thus increase the chances that it will have to be devalued.

How much does uncertainty matter?: Have the upsetting effects of normal exchange-rate uncertainties been greatly overestimated? Supporters of fluctuating rates answer yes. In support of their argument they point to the ever rising volume of foreign trade and capital movements throughout the whole of the post-Second World War period both in countries with fixed rates and in countries, such as Canada, that adopted flexible rates in defiance of the IMF.

They argue that one of the main reasons why uncertainty about rates causes less upset to trade than one might think is that much of the uncertainty associated with exchange movements in a flexible system can be shifted from those who do not wish to bear it to those who make a business of bearing it. This is done through forward exchange markets in which one buys foreign exchange for delivery in the future at a price agreed to in the present.

To see how risks can be avoided, consider an American exporter who is selling goods to a British importer for a price stated in pounds sterling payable in 90 days. If the American merely holds the British importer's promise to pay, he accepts the risk as to what the US dollar value of pounds will be when he receives his payment in 90 days. But he does not have to do this. He can, for example, cover himself in the forward market by entering into a contract to buy dollars for sterling in 90 days at a price (called the 90-day forward rate) stated now. When the 90 days are up, the exporter takes the pounds he receives in payment for his goods and uses them to fulfil his forward contract, receiving a payment in dollars that was certain the moment he entered into his forward purchase. (If the agreement had been that the British importer had to pay an amount stated in dollars in 90 days, he could have hedged by buying dollars for delivery 90 days hence at a price stated in sterling now.)

The same strategy can be used to protect short-term foreign investments. Assume, for example, that an American wishes to invest $10,000 in London for 90 days to take advantage of very high short-term interest rates in London. If he does not wish to run any exchange risk, he buys $10,000 worth of sterling now and uses it to purchase British securities, and he simultaneously buys $10,000 US on the forward exchange market to be delivered and paid for in pounds sterling in 90 days. Thus, the investor is certain about the price at which he can turn his dollars into sterling now, and about the price at which he can turn his sterling back into dollars in 90 days.

ADVANTAGES OF FLEXIBLE RATES: Many economists argue for a reform that would allow exchange rates to be determined on open markets without substantial government intervention. They ask why in a basically free-market society, in which most people accept that prices and quantities are free to be determined by demand and supply, it is felt that this one price, the foreign-exchange rate, should be rigidly controlled by the central authorities. They believe that the whole set of postwar problems, such as shortages of reserves and restrictions on trade caused by chronic imbalances in payments, are of our own making and would disappear quickly if only the arbitrary government control of this one key market were abandoned. If the free market were allowed to operate, then, when a country's currency turned out to be overvalued, the value would be reduced automatically by the forces of demand and supply. The value would continue to fall until the equilibrium exchange rate was achieved. Central authorities would not need to hold exchange reserves because they would not be trying to restrict movements in exchange rates. There would thus be no problem of international liquidity.

The continuing American inflation and the inability of the world's central bankers to agree on a new payments system has led more and more nations to allow their currencies to float on the exchange market. This drift into a partially flexible exchange-rate system pleases those economists who favour flexible rates. In the words of Professor Harry Johnson:

There is a ... hope that if the central bankers keep on acting as they have been acting, we shall never have a fundamental reform of the international monetary system. This will be all to the good because what is described in the platform oratory as fundamental reform is some sort of restoration of the fixed exchange system. So long as European and American central bankers and their allies remain stalemated ... dirty floating will continue – and the world will eventually become used to floating exchange rates, the system that the majority of academics ... have always recommended.

Who is right?

Historical experiences of experiments with flexible rates do not provide sufficient proof to satisfy everyone of the unequivocal advantages of flexible over fixed rates.

One major concern is with the effects of alternative systems on uncertainty, and through uncertainty on the flows of trade. It is clear that there is some uncertainty under both systems, but how does the uncertainty generated by frequent small changes under a flexible system compare with that caused by the knowledge that infrequent large changes will occur at uncertain dates? It does seem clear, however, that international trade and capital movements can continue in the face of quite substantial uncertainties.

A second major concern in assessing who is right is over the impact of speculative activity. There seems ample evidence that fixed-rate systems are subject to periodic bouts of very heavy speculation. Speculators make enormous profits, at the public expense, when they correctly anticipate change in a pegged exchange rate. When they incorrectly anticipate a change that does not in fact occur, they still cause major upsets to financial markets and often force governments into fiscal and monetary policies that may be undesirable from a domestic point of view.

Under flexible rates the case is less clear. It is possible for speculation to be either stabilizing or destabilizing with fluctuating rates. If the rate falls and speculators take this as a signal that it is going to fall further, they will rush to sell now while the price is high, and their speculative selling will drive the rate down further. However, as was seen above, with a fluctuating rate, speculative behaviour can be stabilizing. Such stabilizing speculation is thought to be impossible with fixed rates, but many economists believe that it is normal with flexible rates.

The evidence from the 1920s and 1930s, which was the first modern period in which flexible rates had ever been applied, is mixed. On the one hand, the British pound sterling floated freely through all of the 1930s without any sign of destabilizing speculative behaviour. On the other hand, the freed French franc showed some wild fluctuations in the 1920s. It is possible to argue that the instability of the French franc was caused by domestic French monetary policy, not by destabilizing speculation *per se*, and that a fixed rate had already proved to be impossible to maintain. Be that as it may, advocates of both views can find some support from the evidence of this period.

The post-Second World War evidence is much clearer. Several countries have experimented with flexible rates, some for decades, and no serious sign of destabilizing speculative behaviour has been observed. Canada, for example, successfully operated flexible rates in the 1950s and dropped them only after the heavy-handed attempts of the central authorities to intervene in the market caused such uncertainty as to destabilize it. Flexible rates were reinstated in 1969 and have existed to the present without sufficient fluctuations to upset the volume of Canadian international trade. Germany had a similar experience when the mark was freed in the spring of 1971. The British pound has been floating since 1971 and the rate has not fluctuated wildly. Furthermore, the British government has been freed for the first time in 25 years from the overriding need to fix domestic fiscal and monetary policy with an eye to the balance of payments.

The value of freeing policy-makers to concentrate on such domestic policy variables as employment, national income and economic growth would not be denied by anyone. Disagreement occurs on whether or not this can be done by leaving the price system, working through free exchange rates, to maintain a sufficiently stable payments equilibrium to encourage a rising volume of trade and capital movements.

The debate on the relative merits of fixed and flexible rates is by no means settled, and it is still possible for economists to take widely divergent stands on it. The majority of the world's central bankers and policy-makers believe that fixed rates are superior to flexible ones, and it is possible that the majority of academic economists believe the opposite. A final verdict on the superiority of one system over the other may have to wait for the research of future generations of economists who can be more detached in studying it than those who are already committed to a specific answer.

The world of international economic relations is in some ways topsy-turvy. It is a world that awaits someone who will do for it what Keynes did for domestic unemployment: remove forever the necessity of accepting crises as inevitable and beyond the power of governments to solve once and for all.

Part ten

Growth and development

48

Economic growth

In Chapter 39 we saw that investment can play a role in causing the economic fluctuations that have been observed for as long as there has been industrial societies and that vary in severity from mild disturbance to major upheaval. In the long run, however, investment has been a major cause of the economic growth that has raised living standards so rapidly over the last two centuries, with eightfold or tenfold increases in material living standards occurring over the space of a single lifetime.

Investment affects growth because it affects the economy's ability to *produce* goods by changing both the quantity and the quality of the capital stock available. In other words:

> **Investment increases the economy's potential, or full-employment, national income.**

The theory of economic growth concentrates on this effect of investment on potential national income. Notice the contrast with the theory of fluctuations, which concentrates on the effects of investment expenditure on aggregate demand and hence on the degree to which actual current national income falls short of, or exceeds, potential national income.

THE NATURE OF ECONOMIC GROWTH

Economic growth has been one of the dominant forces in industrial nations over the last 200 years. It has been the source of some of industrialization's greatest triumphs: the raising of the ordinary person's living standards to levels where leisure, travel and luxury goods are, for the first time, within his reach. It has produced standards of living in industrial nations that are the envy of the peoples of the rest of the world and has led many of them – with varying degrees of success – to strive to copy that performance. Economic growth has also been the source of spectacular failures – perhaps most notably, pollution of the air, water and land by chemicals, heat and noise.

Members of developed societies have come to accept growth. Even when they

711

worry about pollution and other concomitants of growth, they ask 'How can we remove this or that side effect of growth?' Only a few people ask 'How can we stop growth?' and even fewer people take those few seriously.

But growth, which seems inevitable to most of us, has not always been present, nor is it present everywhere today. There have been periods of increases in living standards in human history followed by long periods of no change. One of the latter was documented by Professor Phelps-Brown, of the London School of Economics, who showed that there was no significant trend increase in the real income of English building-trade workers between 1215 and 1798, a period of almost six centuries. Peasants in many underdeveloped countries today enjoy a living standard probably little different from that enjoyed by their ancestors 1,000 or more years ago. (Provided, that is, that they are lucky enough not to have their 'freedom' fought over by some of the more technologically advanced nations.)

Rapid growth, when it occurs, is impressive. Recent data show that *total* world output has doubled in the last 15 years. Despite dramatic population growth, output *per person* for the world as a whole has increased sharply. It was twice as high in 1975 as it had been in 1950.

These figures provide evidence of man's mastery of aspects of his environment, but they are enormously misleading in one respect: Most of this growth in output has occurred in countries that comprise only about one fifth of the world's population, while much of the population growth has occurred in countries that have not experienced economic growth. For many countries, as well as for much of history, the phenomenon of growth is absent. In this chapter, and again in Chapter 49, we ask why.

The definition of economic growth

In a typical Western industrial country where GNP has increased at least tenfold in half a century, and where personal-consumption expenditures per capita have doubled in real terms in less than 30 years, it is easy to recognize the phenomenon of growth. It is harder to measure because of a series of potential confusions. Because each of these is found in some contemporary discussions, it is worth bearing them in mind as you read of country X's spectacular achievements.

CAPACITY VERSUS UTILIZATION: The growth in an economy's national income over three or four years reflects both changes in the productive capacity and changes in the percentage utilization of this capacity. Productive capacity can be measured by the concept of potential national income, Y^F, and percentage utilization by the ratio (expressed in percentage form) of actual income, Y, to potential income $(Y/Y^F) \times 100$.

If there have been large changes in the latter, very high rates of increase in national income will be observed, but such increases will not be sustainable once capacity is 100 per cent utilized. GNP increased by as much as 50 per cent between 1933 and 1936, but this reflected almost entirely increases in utilization of capacity from the depths of the Great Depression, not increases in total productive capacity.

For another example, some undeveloped countries start development with a large backlog of unused resources. Such countries can achieve very rapid rates of increase in income for as long as 10 years and fail to distinguish this change in utilization rates from increases in capacity. In both Yugoslavia and Greece, much of the growth in national income during the 1960s was of this sort.

A great deal of confusion would be avoided if the term 'growth rate' were used to refer only to the growth rate of potential national income and if comparisons of national income figures for one country over several years were divided into two parts: changes due to the growth rate and changes due to variations in the employ-ment of existing productive capacity.

Money versus real output: Part of any increase in the money value of full-employment output may be due to a rise in prices rather than in output. Use of de-flated constant-dollar measures is essential in measuring growth and is now a common practice of all major statistical agencies in reporting growth rates.

Output, output per capita, and output per man-hour: As an example of the relations between these concepts, note that a doubling of real national income com-bined with a doubling of the population would mean no change in per capita income, in spite of a large change in total income. As will be seen in Chapter 49, population growth is a problem plaguing many countries of the world.

To determine a nation's growth in the context of its ability to wage war or to pollute its environment, it is necessary to look at total real output. To measure living standards, per capita income is important. A country's average material living standard depends on real income per person.

Real income per person tends to grow more slowly than the economy's productive capacity per person because, as an economy grows, people choose to spend a shorter portion of their days and lives at work. As standards of living rise, entry into the labour force is delayed by increased schooling, work weeks are shortened to permit greater leisure, and the size of the older nonworking population rises because of both earlier retirement and longer life spans.

In theoretical discussions of growth, a measure of growth in productive capacity per capita is often desired to measure the ability of an economy to convert its re-sources into goods and services. A widely used measure of this is output per man-hour, often called more simply PRODUCTIVITY. It measures the average output per man-hour employed. Obviously, productivity depends not only on labour effort but also on the amount and kind of machinery used, the raw materials available, and so on. The focus of this measure is on the man-hour because special emphasis is put on output per unit of human labour.

The most widely used measure of growth is output per capita, which focuses on the growth of material living standards rather than on the growth of productivity.

The cumulative nature of growth

One of the most important aspects of economic growth is that it is cumulative. If one country grows faster than another, the gap in their living standards will widen pro-gressively. By way of contrast, if one country has a less efficient allocation of resources than another, the gap between their national incomes will not widen progressively on this account. Let us assume that, for one reason or another, country A uses its resources 5 per cent less efficiently than does country B. On this count, therefore, the real national income of A will always be 5 per cent below that of B. If, on the other hand, country A uses its resources so that it grows 5 per cent faster than does B, then the gap in incomes will widen progressively. If the two countries start from the same income, and B grows at 5 per cent per year and A grows at $5\frac{1}{4}$ per cent (i.e., A's growth rate is 5 per cent greater than B's), then in 10 years A's income will be 2·4 per cent

Table 48.1 Effects of different rates of growth on the level of income[a]

| Year | Percentage rate of growth (r) per year | | | | |
	1%	2%	3%	5%	7%
0	100	100	100	100	100
10	111	122	135	165	201
30	135	182	246	448	817
50	165	272	448	1,218	3,312
70	201	406	817	3,312	13,429
100	272	739	2,009	14,841	109,660

[a]National income in year 0 = 100.

higher than B's; in 50 years it will be 12·2 per cent higher, and in 301 years it will be *double* B's. Such are the long-range effects of tiny differences in percentage rates of growth. If we now pick figures closer to currently observed rates of growth, the comparison becomes even more striking. Consider two countries starting with the same level of income, but having different rates of growth. If A grows at 3 per cent while B grows at 2 per cent per year, A's income will be twice B's in 72 years. Table 48.1 shows the effects of alternative rates of growth on levels of income.

Table 48.2 shows the average rates of growth of real national income in a number of countries during the period 1950–70. In many ways, this was an unusual period, dominated as it was by the recovery of so many countries from the devastating effects of the Second World War. In order to illustrate the powerful long-run effects of observed differences in growth rates, we have given, in Column 3, the year in which each of the countries will pass the per capita national income of the United States (which is the country with the highest standard of living in the world at present) *if* the growth rates of the period should continue indefinitely.

In order to illustrate dramatically the powerful long-run effects of observed differences in growth rates, Table 48.2 shows that the United States and Canada would not long remain the world's wealthiest nations if their growth rates were to continue to lag behind those of other countries. Furthermore, if present growth rates continue to the end of the century the UK will look to visitors from France and Germany the way Spain used to look to British visitors: the poor man of Europe.

BENEFITS OF GROWTH
Growth in living standards

A primary reason for desiring growth is to raise the general living standards of the population. A country whose per capita output is growing at 3 per cent per year is

Table 48.2 Effects of differences in growth rates, selected countries

Country	(1) Average annual growth rate of real income per capita,[1] 1950–70	(2) GNP per capita in 1964 US dollars, 1970	(3) Year in which US will be overtaken *if* the growth rates in column (1) persist
United States	2·3	$3,603	—
Canada	2·5	2,255	2198
Japan	8·6	1,218	1986
West Germany	5·0	1,866	1993
France	4·0	2,091	2000
Israel	4·7	1,354	2008
Italy	5·1	1,147	2009
Austria	4·6	1,249	2014
Yugoslavia	5·1	492	2039
United Kingdom	2·2	1,610	—
Venezuela	2·2	842	—

1 Growth rates based on gross domestic product in constant dollars.
Source: World Bank, *World Tables*, 1971.

At the growth rates of the last two decades, many industrial countries were catching up to the American level of per capita national income.
Column (1) shows the average rates of growth of real national income in a number of countries during the period 1950–70. This was an unusual period, dominated by the recovery of many countries from the devastating effects of World War II. Growth rates do change, and thus the projections into the future in column (3) should be taken as illustrative of the force of growth rather than as careful predictions.

doubling its living standards approximately every 24 years. (A helpful approximation device is the 'rule of 72'. Divide any growth rate into 72 and the resulting number approximates the number of years it will take for income to double.)

The extreme importance of economic growth in raising income can be illustrated by comparing the real income of a father with the real income of the son who follows in his father's footsteps. If the son neither rises nor falls in the relative income scale compared with his father, his share of the country's national income will be the same as his father's. If the son is 30 years younger than his father, he can expect to have a real income nearly twice as large as that which his father enjoyed when his father was the same age. These figures assume that the father and son live in a country such as the United Kingdom where the growth rate is about 2 per cent per year. If they live in Japan, where growth has been going on at a rate of about 8 per cent per year, the son's income will be about 10 times as large as his father's.

For those who share in it, growth is a powerful weapon against poverty. A family earning £3,000 today can expect £3,750 within seven years (plus a further increase due to any inflation) if it just shares in a 3 per cent growth rate. The transformation of the life style of the ordinary industrial worker over the present century is a notable example of the escape from poverty that growth makes possible.

Unfortunately, not everyone benefits equally from growth, and many of those who are poorest are not even in the labour force and thus are least likely to share in the higher wages that are a primary means by which the gains from growth are distributed to the working person.

Growth and income redistribution

Economic growth makes many kinds of redistributions easier to achieve. For example, a rapid rate of growth makes it much more feasible politically to alleviate poverty. If existing income is to be redistributed, someone's standard of living will actually have to be lowered. If, however, there is economic growth and if the increment in income is redistributed (through government intervention), then it is possible to reduce income inequalities without actually having to lower anyone's income. It is much easier for a rapidly growing economy to be generous toward its less fortunate citizens – or neighbours – than it is for a static one.

National defence and prestige

If one country is competing with another for power or prestige, then rates of growth are important. If our national income is growing at 2 per cent, for instance, while the other country's is growing at 3 per cent, all the other country has to do is wait for our relative strength to dwindle. Also, a country will find the expenses of an arms race or a space race easier to bear, the faster its productivity is growing.

More subtly, but similarly, growth has become part of the currency of international prestige, and countries that are engaged in persuading other countries of the might or right of their economic and political systems point to their rapid rates of growth as evidence of their achievements.

COSTS OF GROWTH

The benefits discussed above suggest that growth is a great blessing. It is surely true that, *ceteris paribus*, most people would regard a fast rate of growth as preferable to a slow one, but other things are seldom equal.

Social and personal costs of growth

Industrialization, unless very carefully managed, causes deterioration of the environment. Unspoiled landscapes give way to highways and factories and billboards; air and water become polluted; and in some cases unique and priceless relics of earlier ages – from flora and fauna to ancient ruins – disappear. Urbanization tends to move people from the simpler life of farming and small towns into the crowded, slum-ridden life of the urban ghetto. Those remaining behind in the rural areas find that rural life, too, has changed. Larger-scale farming, the decline of population, and the migration of children from the farm to the city all have their costs. The stepped-up tempo of life brings joys to some, but tragedy to others. Accidents, ulcers, crime rates, suicides, divorces, and murder all tend to be higher in periods of rapid change and in more developed societies.

If an economy is growing, it is also changing. Innovation leaves obsolete machines in its wake, and it also leaves partially obsolete people. A rapid rate of growth requires rapid adjustments, and these can cause much upset and misery to the individuals affected. The decline in the number of unskilled jobs makes the lot of the untrained worker much more difficult, and when he loses his job, he may well fail to find another, particularly if he is over 50. No matter how well equipped you are at 25, in another 25 years you are likely to be partially obsolete. This is almost as true if you are a doctor or an engineer as it is if you are a mechanic. The greatest effect is on those whose skills become completely outdated and unneeded.

It is often argued that costs of this kind are a small price to pay for the great benefits that growth can bring. Increasingly, it is being recognized that some of these costs are not so small, and, moreover, that they are very unevenly borne. Indeed, many of those for whom growth is most costly (in terms of jobs) share least in the fruits of growth.[1] An opposite danger is to see only the costs – to yearn for the good old days – while thriving on higher living standards that growth alone has made possible.

The opportunity cost of growth

In a world of scarcity, almost nothing is free. Growth usually requires an investment of resources in capital goods, in education and in health. Such investments do not yield any *immediate* return in terms of goods and services for consumption. Growth, which promises more goods tomorrow, is achieved by consuming fewer goods today. For the economy as a whole, this is a primary cost of growth. A hypothetical example will illustrate the basic choice involved: a more rapid rate of growth may be purchased at the expense of a lower rate of current consumption. Suppose a particular economy has full employment and is experiencing growth at the rate of 2 per cent per year. Its citizens are consuming 85 per cent of the GNP and investing 15 per cent. Suppose that if consumption were reduced to 77 per cent of GNP immediately, the country would produce more capital and that this would shift them at once to a 3 per cent growth rate, which could be maintained as long as saving and investment were held at 23 per cent of the national income. Should this be done?

Table 48.3 and Figure 48.1 represent the choice in terms of time paths of consumption. How expensive is the 'Invest now, consume later' strategy?

Table 48.3 The opportunity cost of growth

	The level of consumption	
	(A)	(A')
In year	2% growth rate of income	3% growth rate of income
0	85·0	77·0
1	86·7	79·3
2	88·5	81·8
3	90·3	84·2
4	92·1	86·8
5	93·9	89·5
6	95·8	92·9
7	97·8	95·0
8	99·7	97·9
9	101·8	100·9
10	103·8	103·9
15	114·7	120·8
20	126·8	140·3
30	154·9	189·4
40	189·2	255·6

1 One aspect of this problem, 'structural unemployment', is discussed in Chapter 51.

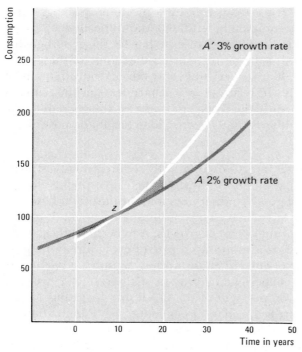

Fig. 48.1 The opportunity costs of growth (a re-allocation of resources occurs at time O)

On the assumed figures, it takes 10 years for the actual level of consumption to catch up to what it would have been had no re-allocation been made (point z in the Figure). But the cumulative losses in consumption must be made up before society can really be said to have broken even. It takes an additional 9 years before total consumption over the whole period is as large as it would have been if the economy had remained on the 2 per cent path. This comparison looks only at actual amounts of consumption. If future income is discounted at a positive rate of interest, so that a quantity of goods now is preferred to the same quantity in the future, it will take longer than 9 years to compensate consumers for the loss of goods during the first 10 years. But at some point after 20 years, the initial sacrifice yields bigger and bigger dividends.

Such a policy of sacrificing present living standards for a gain that one does not begin to reap for a generation is hardly likely to appeal to any but the altruistic or the very young. The question of how much one generation is prepared to sacrifice some of its living standards for its heirs, who are in any case going to be richer, is troublesome. As one sceptic put it: 'Why should we sacrifice for them? What have they ever done for us?'

This example is given only to illustrate some of the costs involved in achieving faster growth through a re-allocation of resources, to suggest approximate orders of magnitude, and to suggest that the case for pursuing a faster rate of growth by this means is possibly not as universally acceptable as it might at first seem.

Many governments have followed this route: the Germans under Hitler, the

Russians under Stalin and the Chinese under Mao Tse-tung adopted four- and five-year plans that shifted resources from consumption to investment. Many countries are using such plans today. They are particularly important when actual growth rates are very small (say less than 1 per cent), for without some current sacrifice there is little or no prospect of real growth in the lifetimes of today's citizens. The very lowest growth rates are frequently encountered in the very poorest countries (as will be seen), and this creates a cruel dilemma, which is discussed in Chapter 49 as the vicious circle of poverty.

GROWTH AS A GOAL OF POLICY: DO THE BENEFITS JUSTIFY THE COSTS?

Suppose that the members of a society want to increase their output of goods by 10 per cent in one year. There are many ways they might try to do it.
(1) They may be able to find idle and unutilized resources and put them to work.
(2) They may be able to schedule extra shifts and overtime labour.
(3) They may, by exhortation or by an appropriate incentive system, induce people to try much harder to increase their output by the required amount.
(4) They may (if they have time) increase the supply of machines and factories and increase output in that way.
(5) They may discover some new techniques that permit them to get more output from the same inputs.

In the short run, the first three of these approaches seem more promising than the last two; in fact, when nations face such crises as wars these devices are used to achieve rapid increases in output. But the gains to be achieved by utilizing unemployed resources, or extending the hours of use of employed ones, or 'working harder' are limited. Eventually, they will be used up. When there are no longer any unutilized resources or under-utilized capacity, further increases in output become more difficult.

For the long-term increases in living standards that have eliminated the 14-hour-day, 6-day-week work load and brought leisure and high material standards of living within the reach of the bulk of people in Western economies (including Australia and New Zealand), there is no substitute for economic growth. Such long-term increases are clearly needed if the ordinary citizen in any underdeveloped country is to escape from abject poverty on the margin of subsistence. But do the already-developed countries need yet more growth? Most people think they do. That poverty is now a solvable problem in the United States is a direct result of its enhanced average living standards. Poverty is still common in particular parts of British society and it might be easier to remove if GNP were higher. Clearly, people in the top quarter of the present income distribution have more opportunities for leisure, travel, culture, good whisky and high living than are open to persons with much lower incomes. Most of those now in the bottom half of the income distribution would like these opportunities too. Only growth can give it to them.

Today, countries that have not yet, or only newly, undergone sustained periods of economic growth in modern times are desperately trying to copy those that have so as to obtain the benefits of growth. There seems little doubt that most nations and most people will pursue the goal of growth for the benefits it brings, despite its costs.

How seriously the costs are taken depends in part on how many of the benefits of growth have already been achieved. With mounting population problems, the poor countries are becoming more and more preoccupied with creating growth, while with mounting awareness of pollution the rich countries are devoting more and more resources to overcoming the problems caused by growth – while at the same time being understandably reluctant to give up further growth.

Indeed, a similar conflict can often be seen in the same country at the same time: one relatively poor community fighting to acquire a new industry for the employment and income it will create; another, relatively affluent community deploring the despoiling of its local environment by an existing industry.

THEORIES OF ECONOMIC GROWTH

Economists have done a great deal of theorising about economic growth over the last twenty years. Although many elegant models have been built and many conceptual issues clarified, it is probably safe to say that such meagre advice as we can give to policy makers in market economies owes little (as yet at least) to these modern theories. In what follows we discuss growth from the strict Classical point of view of the relation between the stock of capital and opportunities for investment in new capital.

Growth in a world without learning

Suppose that there is a known and fixed stock of projects that might be undertaken and that nothing ever happens to increase either the supply of such projects or the knowledge about them. Whenever the opportunity is ripe, some of these investment opportunities are utilized, thus increasing the stock of capital goods and depleting the reservoir of unutilized investment opportunities. Of course, the most productive opportunities will be used first. Such a view of investment opportunities can be represented by a fixed marginal efficiency of capital schedule, of the kind met in Chapter 29. Such a schedule is graphed in Figure 48.2. It relates the stock of capital to the productivity of an additional unit of capital.

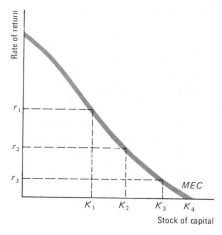

Fig. 48.2 The marginal efficiency of capital schedules

The downward slope of the *MEC* schedule indicates that with knowledge constant increases in the stock of capital are assumed to bring smaller and smaller increases in output per dollar. In other words, the rate of return on successive units of capital declines. This shape is a prediction based on the 'law' of diminishing returns. If, with land, labour and knowledge constant, more and more capital is used, the net amount added by successive increments is predicted to diminish and possibly eventually to reach zero. Given this schedule, as capital is accumulated in a state of constant knowledge the society will move down its *MEC* schedule. Thus when the capital stock increases from K_1 to K_2 to K_3 the marginal return on capital falls from r_1 to r_2 to r_3. Eventually when the capital stock is K_4 the marginal return reaches zero.

In such a 'nonlearning' world, where new investment opportunities do not appear, growth occurs only so long as there are unutilized opportunities to use capital effectively to increase output. Growth is a transitory phenomenon that occurs because the society has a backlog of unutilized investment opportunities.[1]

So far we have discussed the marginal efficiency of capital. The average efficiency of capital refers to the average amount produced in the whole economy per unit of capital employed. It is measured by the ratio of total output to total capital; this is the OUTPUT/CAPITAL RATIO. Its inverse, the amount of capital divided by the amount of output, is the CAPITAL/OUTPUT RATIO.[2]

Suppose, as is commonly believed, that both the average and the marginal efficiencies of capital are declining. In such an economy the output/capital ratio will be falling and the capital/output ratio will be rising as the capital stock grows.

Two important implications of this theory of growth through capital accumulation with constant knowledge are the following:

(1) Successive increases in capital accumulation will be less and less productive, and the capital/output ratio will be increasing.

(2) The marginal efficiency of new capital will be decreasing and will eventually be pushed to zero as the back-log of investment opportunities is used up.

Growth with learning

The steady depletion of the country's growth opportunities in the previous model resulted from the fact that new investment opportunities were never discovered or created. If, however, investment opportunities are created as well as used up by the passage of time, then the *MEC* schedule will shift outward period after period, and the effects of increasing the capital stock may be different. This is illustrated in Figure 48.3. Such outward shifts can be regarded as the consequences of 'learning' either about investment opportunities or about the techniques that create such opportunities. If learning occurs, it is next necessary to know how rapidly it will shift relative to the amount of capital investment being undertaken.

---

1 The argument has been conducted using concepts such as 'the' quality of capital, and the productivity of capital. All that it requires is that there is a finite number of investment opportunities which can be arranged in descending order of the yield that they provide.

2 Of course, the two ratios measure the same thing. If, for example, the average efficiency of capital is declining, the output/capital ratio will be declining, indicating less output on average per unit of capital used; and the capital/output ratio will be rising, indicating more capital used per unit of output produced.

Three possibilities are shown in Figure 48.3. In each case, the economy at period 1 has the MEC curve, a capital stock of K_1, and a rate of return of r_1. In period 2, the curve shifts to MEC_1 and there is investment to increase the stock of capital to K_2. In period 3 the curve shifts to MEC_2 and there is new investment that increases the capital stock from K_2 to K_3. It is the relative size of the shift of the MEC curve and the additions to the capital stock that are important. In part (i), investment occurs more rapidly than increases in investment opportunities and r must fall along the white curve. In (ii), investment occurs at exactly the same rate as investment opportunities and r is constant. In (iii), investment occurs less rapidly than increases in investment opportunities and r will rise.

GRADUAL REDUCTION IN INVESTMENT OPPORTUNITIES, THE CLASSICAL VIEW: If, as in Figure 48.3(i), investment opportunities are created but at a slower rate than they are used up, there will be a tendency for a falling rate of return and an increasing ratio of capital to output. The predictions in this case are the same as those given above for the 'nonlearning state', although the cause is not lack of learning, but too slow a discovery of new investment opportunities.

This figure illustrates one version of the theory of growth held by the Classical economists. They saw the economic problem as one of fixed land, a rising population and a gradual exhaustion of investment opportunities. These things, they said, would ultimately force the economy into a static condition with no growth, very high capital/output ratios and the marginal return on additional units of capital forced down to zero.

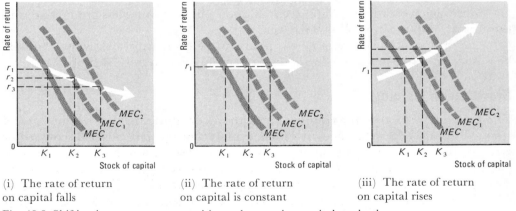

(i) The rate of return on capital falls   (ii) The rate of return on capital is constant   (iii) The rate of return on capital rises

Fig. 48.3 Shifting investment opportunities and a growing capital stock: three cases

CONSTANT OR RISING INVESTMENT OPPORTUNITIES, ONE CONTEMPORARY VIEW: The pessimism of the classical economists was due to their failure to appreciate the possibility of really rapid innovation – of technological progress that could push investment opportunities outward as rapidly or more rapidly than they were used up.

Because the facts (as will be seen in a moment) suggest that the classical economists' predictions are not confirmed, but rather that the economy generates new investment opportunities at least as rapidly as it uses up old ones, a general rethinking of the causes of growth has occurred, with attention devoted more to understanding the *shifts* in the *MEC* schedule over time and less to its *shape*. The record shows that it is the shifts over time that have led to sustained growth.

Factors affecting growth

QUANTITY OF CAPITAL PER MAN: Man has always been a tool user and it is still true today that more and more tools tend to lead to more and more output. As long as a society has unexploited investment opportunities, productive capacity can be increased by increasing the stock of capital. The effect on output per man of 'mere' capital accumulation is so noticeable that it was once regarded as virtually the sole source of growth; but if capital accumulation were the only source of growth, it would lead to movement down the marginal-efficiency schedule, as in Figure 48.2, and to the predictions printed on page 721. The evidence does not support these predictions. In the United States in this century, for example, despite enormous quantities of new capital, the capital/output ratio has remained constant, and there has been no downward trend in the rate of return on capital. This evidence[1] suggests that investment opportunities have expanded as rapidly as investments in capital goods. Thus capital accumulation cannot have been the only source of growth, although such capital accumulation has taken place and has accounted for much observed growth.

INNOVATION: New knowledge and inventions can contribute markedly to the growth of potential national income. In order to see this, assume that the proportion of the society's resources devoted to the production of capital goods is just sufficient to replace capital as it wears out. Thus, if the old capital were merely replaced in the same form, the capital stock would be constant and there would be no increase in the capacity to produce. Now assume, however, that there is a growth of knowledge so that as old equipment wears out, it is replaced by different, more productive equipment. In this situation, national income will be growing because of the growth of knowledge rather than because of the accumulation of more and more capital. This sort of increase in productive capacity is now called EMBODIED TECHNICAL CHANGE because it inheres in the form of capital goods in use.

The historical importance of changes of this kind are clearly visible. The assembly line and now automation are transforming the means of production. The aeroplane has revolutionized transportation, and electronic devices have come to dominate the communications industries. These innovations plus less well-known but no less profound ones – for example, improvements in the strength of metals, the productivity of seeds and the techniques for recovering basic raw materials from the ground – tend to create new investment opportunities.

Less visible but nonetheless important changes occur through DISEMBODIED TECHNICAL CHANGE. These concern innovations in the organization of production that are not embodied in the form of the capital goods or raw materials used. One example is improved techniques of managerial control.

1 This 'evidence' depends on being able to measure the quantity of capital. It is thus open to Cambridge criticisms of the concept of 'the' quantity of capital.

Most innovations involve both embodied and disembodied changes: New processes require new machines, which make yet new processes economical. Computerization promises many such changes in the decade ahead. One of these, which many regard with a mixture of awe and apprehension, is a cashless society, in which banks become parts of vast information networks that receive one's pay, pay one's bills and invest one's savings. But whatever the form of innovation, the nature of the goods and services consumed and the way they are made is continually changing as innovations occur.

THE QUALITY OF HUMAN CAPITAL: 'Labour' is often talked about as if it is a uniform, well-understood input into production. But, clearly, a 'man-hour' of labour is very different for a skilled mechanic, a scientist or a ditchdigger because what each of them produces in an hour is valued differently by the market.

The 'quality' of human capital has several aspects. One of these involves improvements in the health and longevity of the population. These things are, of course, desired as ends in themselves, but they have consequences for production and productivity as well. There is no doubt that they have increased productivity per man-hour by cutting down on illness, accidents and absenteeism. At the same time, the extension of the normal life span with no comparable increase in the working life span has created a larger group of nonworking aged that exercises a claim on total output. Whether health improvements alone have increased output per capita in the United States is not clear.

A second aspect of the quality of human capital concerns technical training, from learning to operate a machine to learning how to be a scientist. Training is clearly required to invent, operate, manage and repair complex machines. More subtly, there are often believed to be general social advantages to an educated population. It has been shown that productivity improves with literacy and that, in general, the longer a person has been educated the more adaptable he is to new challenges, and thus, in the long run, the more productive.

THE QUANTITY OF LABOUR: The size of a country's population and the extent of participation in the labour force are important in and of themselves, not merely because they affect the quantity of a factor of production. For this reason, it is less common to speak of the quantity of people available for work as a source of, or detriment to, growth than it is to speak of the quantity of capital or iron ore in this way. But, clearly, for any given state of knowledge and supplies of other factors of production, the size of the population can affect the level of output per capita. Every child born has both a mouth and a pair of hands, and, on average, it is perfectly possible to speak of overpopulated or underpopulated economies, depending on whether the contribution to production of additional people would raise or lower the level of per capita income.

Figure 48.4 relates population to per capita income and illustrates a case in which there is an optimal population for which living standards are a maximum. The curve is drawn in the shape illustrated because resources and knowledge are assumed constant at any moment of time and alternative populations are assumed to be

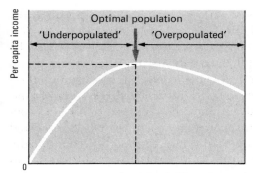

Fig. 48.4 One concept of the optimal population

exploiting them. After a certain size the pressure of more and more population applying given techniques to a given quantity of resources will force diminishing returns into operation. Once output does not grow in proportion to additional population, output per man, must fall.

Many countries have had conscious policies which have attempted to change the size of their population. America in the nineteenth century sought immigrants, as does Australia today. Germany under Hitler paid bonuses for additional children and otherwise offered people incentives to create Germans. Greece today is trying to stem emigration to Western Europe. All of these activities bespeak a belief in insufficient population, although the motives are not in every case purely economic. In contrast, many of the underdeveloped countries of South America and Asia seek means to limit population growth.

SOCIAL AND LEGAL INSTITUTIONS: Social and religious habits can affect economic growth. In a society in which children are expected to stay in their fathers' occupations, it is more difficult for the labour force to change its characteristics and thus to adapt to the requirements of growth than where upward mobility is itself a goal. Max Weber argued that the 'Protestant ethic' encourages the acquisition of wealth and is thus more likely to encourage growth than is an ethic that directs activity away from the economic sphere.

Legal institutions may likewise affect growth. The pattern of ownership of land and natural resources, in affecting the way such resources are used, may affect their productivity. To take one example, if agricultural land is divided into very small parcels, one per family, it may be much more difficult to achieve the advantages of modern agriculture than if the land were available for large-scale farming. Many economists are thus concerned with patterns of land tenure.

Economists are interested in such relationships for positive reasons, not for normative ones. If it is true that social, religious or legal patterns make growth more difficult, this does not mean that they are undesirable; instead, it means that the benefits of these things must now be weighed against the costs, of which the effect on growth is one. If people derive satisfaction from a religion whose beliefs inhibit growth, if they value a society in which every man owns his own land and is more nearly self-sufficient than in another society, they may be quite willing to pay a price in terms of growth opportunities foregone.

Of course, some institutions inhibit growth without having wide appeal to the people. For example, the concentration of land ownership in the hands of a few absentee landowners who are not concerned to maximize their profits can be detrimental to growth. If the landlord's holdings are so vast that he can obtain all the income he desires without using his land effectively, he may have little motivation to introduce advanced techniques. In many societies in which this system of land ownership exists, land reform, which usually implies the confiscation of land, becomes a necessary condition for growth. Not surprisingly, such reforms are resisted by existing governments, which tend to support the interests of the economically powerful. Land reform can often be accomplished only in the wake of a political revolution.

INTERNATIONAL TRADE AND ECONOMIC GROWTH: The most important advantage that the existence of international trade confers on a growing country is that it allows it to escape from its own resource limitations, both natural and human, and concentrate its growth effort in the areas in which it has a genuine advantage. It can be very difficult for a small country to grow in all sectors at once, as would be required if it were a closed economy. With an open economy a small country is free to grow rapidly in sectors in which it enjoys a comparative advantage and meet the rest of its requirements through foreign trade. The policy problem of choosing to foster either *balanced growth* in all sectors of the economy or *unbalanced growth* in some sectors is further discussed in Chapter 49.

POLICIES TO AFFECT GROWTH

Centrally controlled economies, in which growth is the overriding goal of policy, have often shown substantial successes in altering the growth rate. The main policy required is to engineer a massive and fairly abrupt shift of resources from current consumption to investment. There is usually such a backlog of obviously useful investment projects that whether or not they are exploited wastefully, and whatever is the system of free enterprise or central control that is used, the large-scale, new investment pays large dividends in a more rapid growth rate for some considerable time. A long-term, sustained, high growth rate even in an economy in which growth remains the overriding objective may require things other than a high proportion of resources devoted to investment. Research and development of new ideas is important, and at least as important are the entrepreneurial risk-taking activities of innovating. Here there is much debate and little hard knowledge. Economists and historians will no doubt continue to debate the experience of Soviet Russia, India, China and other centrally planned economies for a long time to come. When they do, one of the basic issues will be: Is it possible for the bureaucracy of a centrally planned economy to sustain the risk-taking activities that are one of the basic components of the growth process in the same way that they are sustained by many private profit-seeking entrepreneurs in a free-market system? Past experience with the conservative tendencies of bureaucratic systems must suggest that here is one of the most vulnerable points in the position taken up by the advocates of central planning. (The conservative nature of many bureaucracies is not something that just happens inexplicably; it happens rather for the quite comprehensible reason that the incentive system – punishment for failure is focused on a few individuals while reward for success is diffused throughout the system – works against encouraging individuals to take risks.)

In the mixed economies of Western Europe, North America, and other industrially developed regions, growth is but one of a half a dozen or more of the key objectives of the central authorities. In such economies the problem is much more difficult, than in the 'growth-dominated' economies referred to in the previous paragraph. The policy-makers in these relatively advanced 'mixed economies' want more growth, but only if it does not conflict too much with other goals of policy. Some of the most serious conflicts of economic policy are considered in Chapter 51. In the meantime we may ask what tools are available to the policy-maker who would like to encourage a little more growth without fundamentally changing the present nature of the economy. He may attempt to influence each of the factors listed earlier as affecting growth. The problem, however, is that although we have some qualitative knowledge, we have little quantitative knowledge. If, for example, we spend £10 million more on education each year what will be the quantitative effect on our growth rate and on other goals (there will be £10 million less to spend on other projects)? Nonetheless, central authorities do have growth policies, and they do try to influence the factors thought to affect growth.

The first major policy is to try to increase the overall level of investment. There are two ways in which this can be attempted. First, investment may be encouraged by policies to keep interest rates low and to make borrowing otherwise easy. An easy money policy is thus thought to be a growth policy. Even this is, however, not certain, and Professor Frank Paish has long been an advocate of the view that periods of mild unemployment are more conducive to growth than are periods of very high demand, with consequent inflationary pressures.

The second method of encouraging investment recommends itself to those who are uncertain about the desirability of increasing investment by increasing all of aggregate demand. They wish to encourage investment only by a series of special measures running from direct subsidies on investment expenditures to various types of tax relief. Such measures are largely concerned with the quantity of capital. As noted earlier, recent empirical studies suggest that accumulation of capital is less important and that such factors as innovation and education are more important than had previously been thought. The best guess based on current knowledge is that substantially less than half of the increase in productive capacity in all Western countries is due to capital accumulation, while over half is due to other things.

Invention and innovation clearly play an important role in growth, but it is not so easy to turn them on and off. There is substantial faith that increases in Research and Development (R and D) do pay off in more rapid innovation. The government itself engages in a good deal of R and D, provides research grants to others, and in certain areas participates in joint projects with business firms. We are as yet uncertain about the quantitative importance of R and D in the growth process. Much current research is being devoted to estimating its importance.

Furthermore a great deal of government-fostered R and D goes into industries such as rockets, aeroplanes and other defence or highly technically oriented industries. Currently there is substantial uncertainty about the genuine growth effects of this expenditure. Some feel that the spill over onto the rest of the economy is small and that the government investment merely subsidizes a privileged group of technologists who would otherwise not exist, and who contribute little to the growth of the economy. Others feel that in these activities the government is encouraging research and development that will be generally useful, and thus is contributing significantly to the long-run growth rate. Here there is a very important positive question on which we have too little knowledge now, but about which we will undoubtedly learn much more over the next decade.

Public expenditures on education at all levels, but particularly on higher education and training of scientific personnel, have been high and are growing. It is often thought that these expenditures foster growth, both in the sense of positively promoting it by increasing the likelihood of discovering new and better techniques, and by avoiding barriers to it that arise if there are not enough competent people to operate the new machines that are invented.

Education too requires careful evaluation. Serious empirical studies indicate that, at the present levels of education, further expenditures on education 'pay' in the sense of providing benefits in excess of all costs, including the foregone output during the educational period. Obviously for a society, as for an individual, a point can be reached beyond which further education is not wise, but the present evidence indicates that we have not yet reached that point.

This brief discussion must make it clear that we are not able to control the growth rate with the nice degree of precision with which we can control the level of unemployment or even the balance of payments. Indeed, central authorities in Western countries do not have the ability even to raise or to lower the growth rate at will by changing their policies, let alone to decide that it should be raised or lowered by x per cent. We must conclude therefore that, although we do know something about the growth process, we do not know anything like enough to give policy-makers in mixed economies the ability to exert *measurable* control over the rate of economic growth, at least over small ranges of variation.

CURRENT CONTROVERSIES OVER ECONOMIC GROWTH

Current controversies over economic growth concern first, whether or not further sustained economic growth is desirable and, second, whether or not it is possible. The first question can be reviewed by examining the case that might be made to the ordinary citizen by the advocates and the opponents of further economic growth.

An open letter to the ordinary citizen from a supporter of the 'growth is good' school

DEAR ORDINARY CITIZEN:

You live in the world's first civilization that is devoted principally to satisfying *your* needs rather than those of a privileged minority. Past civilizations have, without exception, been based on leisure and high consumption for a small upper class, a reasonable standard of living for a numerically insignificant middle class and hard work with little more than subsistence consumption for the great mass of people. In the past, the average citizen saw little of the civilized and civilizing products of his economy, except when he was toiling to produce them.

What is unique about the continuing Industrial Revolution is that it is based on the mass production of goods for consumption by the ordinary citizen. It has also ushered in a period of sustained economic growth that has raised the consumption standards of ordinary citizens to levels previously reserved, throughout the entire history of civilization, for a tiny privileged minority. Reflect on a few examples: travel (from motor car to jet), music (in the concert hall or on records), art (from porn to Picasso), good food (a diet of bread, cheese, milk and beer becomes deadly dull when repeated literally day after day with the *possible* exception of feast days), inexpensive books (from pop novels to the classics of ancient and modern literature), universal literacy and a genuine chance to be educated if you want to be. Most important of all there is enough leisure to provide time and energy to enjoy these and a myriad other products of the modern industrial economy.

Could any ordinary citizen seriously doubt the benefits of growth and wish himself back in the world of 150 or 500 years ago – in his same relative social and economic position? Most surely the answer is 'no'. But we cannot say the same for a person with an income in the top 1–2 per cent of the income distribution. Economic growth has destroyed much of his privileged consumption position; he must now vie with the ordinary citizen when he visits the world's beauty spots and be annoyed, as he lounges on the terrace of his palatial mansion, by the sound of jets carrying ordinary people to holidays in far-away places. Many of the rich resent their loss of exclusive rights to luxury consumption. Some complain bitterly, and it is not surprising that they find their intellectual apologists.

Whether they know it or not, the anti-growth men – economists such as John Kenneth Galbraith, Joan Robinson and Ed Mishan – are not the social revolutionaries they assume themselves to be. They are the counter-revolutionaries who would set back the clock of material progress for the ordinary person. They say that growth has produced pollution and wasteful consumption of trivia that contributes nothing to human happiness. But the democratic solution to pollution is not to go back to where so few people consume luxuries that pollution is trivial; it is to accept pollution as a transitional phase connected with the ushering in of mass consumption, to keep the mass consumption and learn to control the pollution that it tends to create.

It is only through further growth that the average citizen can enjoy those consumption standards (of travel, culture, medical and health care etc.) now available to people in the top 25 per cent of the income distribution, which includes the intellectuals who earn large royalties from the books they write denouncing growth. If you think that extra income confers little of real benefit, ask anyone in the top 25 per cent of the income distribution to trade places with the average citizen with his average income.

Ordinary citizens, do not be deceived by disguised elitist doctrines. Remember that the very rich and the elite have much to gain by stopping growth – and more so by rolling it back – but you have very much to gain by letting it go forward.

Yours sincerely
I. Growthman

An open letter to the ordinary citizen from a supporter of the 'growth is bad' school

DEAR ORDINARY CITIZEN:

You live in a world that is being despoiled by a mindless search for ever higher levels of material consumption at the cost of all other values. Once upon a time man knew how to enjoy creative work, and to derive satisfaction from simple activities undertaken in his scarce, and hence highly valued, leisure time. Today the ordinary worker is a mindless cog in an assembly-line process that turns out ever more goods that the advertisers must work overtime to persuade the worker to consume.

Statisticians and politicians count the increasing flow of material output as a triumph of modern civilization. But consider not the flow of output in general, but the individual products that it contains. You arise from your electric-blanketed bed, clean your teeth with an electric toothbrush, go downstairs to open with an electric tin-opener a tin of the sad remnants of a once proud orange, you eat your bread baked from super-refined and chemically refortified flour and you climb into your car to sit in vast traffic jams on exhaust-polluted motorways. And so the day goes on, with endless consumption of high-technology products that give you no more real satisfaction than the simple, cheaply-produced equivalent products consumed by your grandfathers: soft woolly blankets, natural bristle toothbrushes, real oranges, old-fashioned, coarse but healthy bread and public transport that moved on uncongested roads and gave its passengers time to chat with their neighbours, to read or just to daydream.

The slick magazines of today tell you that by consuming more you are happier. But happiness lies not in increasing consumption but in increasing the ratio of *satisfaction of wants to total wants*. Since the more you consume the more the advertisers persuade you that you want to consume, you are almost certainly less happy than the average citizen in a small town in 1900 who we can picture sitting on the village green, sipping a cool beer or a lemonade and enjoying the antics of his children as they play with discarded barrel staves and home-made skipping ropes.

Today the landscape is dotted with countless factories producing the plastic trivia of the modern industrial society and drowning you in a cloud of noise, air and water pollution. The countryside is despoiled by mining tips, petroleum-refining plants and dangerous nuclear power stations that produce the energy that is devoured insatiably by modern factories and motor vehicles. Worse still, our precious heritage of natural resources is fast being used up. Spaceship earth flies, captainless, in its senseless orgy of self-consuming consumption.

Now is the time to stop this madness. We must stabilize production, reduce pollution, conserve our natural resources and seek justice through a more equitable distribution of existing total wealth.

A long time ago Malthus taught us that if we do not limit population voluntarily, nature will do it for us in a cruel and savage manner. Today the same is true of output: if we do not halt its growth voluntarily, the halt will be imposed on us by a disastrous increase in pollution and a rapid exhaustion of natural resources.

Citizen awake! Shake off the shackles of growth worship, learn to enjoy the bounty that is yours already and eschew the endless, self-defeating search for increased happiness through ever-increasing consumption.

Very truly yours

A. Non-growthman

Who is right?

Both of these cases have real merit. Possibly a balanced judgement lies somewhere in between, but both extremes have their sincere supporters. The reader will be interested to ask himself where he stands on these issues.

Are there limits to growth?

DOOMSDAY MODELS: Philosophical anti-growthmen argue that sustained growth for another century is undesirable; some modern no-growthmen argue that it is impossible. Of course all terrestial things have an ultimate limit. Astronomers predict that the solar system itself will die as the sun burns out in another 6,000 million or so years. To be of practical concern a limit must be within our practical planning horizon. Recent models by Jay Forrester (*World Dynamics*) and D.H Meadows *et al* (*The Limits to Growth*) predict the imminence of a growth-induced doomsday. The models predict that living standards will reach a peak about the turn of the century and thereafter, in the words of Professor Norhaus', one of the leading critics of this type of model, 'descend inexorably to the level of Neanderthal man'.

Both of the above works use the same basic model. The model extends into the future trends that have been observed in the recent past. The model's most important variable is the 'quality of life'. This is taken from the year 1900 to date and then projected to the year 2100. The model's two most important influences on the quality of life are population and per capita output. Population growth is determined by per capita consumption, population density, food supply and pollution. Pollution is generated by economic activity and is absorbed only by natural processes. (There is no allowance for human efforts to reduce the creation of pollution or to clean up after it!) Per capita output is determined by capital per worker and the supply of natural resources. (There is no technical progress, no new resources are discovered or rendered usable by the new techniques and there is no substitution of plentiful for scarce resources in production processes!)

The model operates approximately as follows. An increase in capital per worker causes a higher level of output per worker, permitting greater investment, higher capital per worker, and more output and consumption. These initial reinforcing effects are then slowly counteracted by the increase in population due to the higher consumption; as a result output and capital per worker start to fall again. Increasing population and output causes increased pollution and a higher rate of consumption of resources. Fewer natural resources remain for future use, causing extraction costs to rise and lowering the material standard of living.

The model predicts doom from any one of several possible routes: further industrialization with its accompanying resource depletion and pollution is one route, overpopulation resulting in famine is another.

The many possible routes to disaster mean that no single restraint will suffice to prevent it. If both natural resource usage and pollution are controlled, doom results from over-population. Population control may be self-defeating because it leads to an increase in the per capita food supply and in the standard of living which in turn generates forces to trigger a resurgence in population growth. The only way to prevent disaster is to stop economic growth by a comprehensive plan to curtail drastically natural resource use (by 75 per cent) pollution generation (by 50 per cent) investment (by 40 per cent) food production (by 20 per cent) and the birth rate (by 30 per cent). Since the countries of the world are very unlikely, within the next 40 years, to agree on the Draconian measures needed to meet these targets, we can confidently predict, according to the model, a descent down the slippery slope of declining living standards during the lifetimes of readers of this book, and doomsday within the lifetimes of your grandchildren.

CRITICISMS OF DOOMSDAY MODELS: Critics reply that predictions of imminent doomsday are as old as mankind, and about as reliable as predictions of the arrival of universal peace and goodwill among men. They say that the only thing that differentiates the present prophecy from that of its predecessors is that it was spewed forth from a computer. But if enough nonsense is fed in, the computer being an obedient and consistent oracle, will spew out any amount of nonsense. In support of their claim that the computer has been fed mainly nonsense, critics make, among others, the following points:

(1) The assumption of constant technology (the case of growth without learning is analysed on page 720) is nonsense in the light of past human history. Constant technology and a declining marginal efficiency of capital is sufficient by itself to reduce first the marginal and then the average product of capital to zero. The attempt to sustain growth in such a world must eventually produce zero per capita output!

(2) The assumption of a fixed and relatively small supply of resources is nonsense. It defies the law of conservation of mass energy and denies the fact that in the earth's crust beneath the sea and further in towards the core there are vast supplies of mineral resources some located and charted and others known to exist in a general way. As with assumption (1), this assumption is sufficient to produce disaster by itself. A finite supply of limited resources that is destroyed in the course of production must soon be exhausted if output increases exponentially.

(3) The model has no place for the coordinating effects of the price system. As a particular resource becomes scarce its price rises and this has many effects. Four examples: people are induced to try harder to discover new supplies, it becomes profitable to produce from known sources that were previously too costly, producers are induced to substitute other resources within already known technologies and a search for new substitutes and new technologies is encouraged. Such trends are observable in the pattern of use of most resources over the past centuries yet the model makes no allowance for them.

The list has been extended to a score or more of similar points, all of which, say the critics, show the pitfalls ready to trap the person who approaches the economy without using the insights provided by a century of theory and observation of the operation of the price system. Thus say the critics, the model only proves the consistency of logic: from silly assumptions one can only derive silly conclusions.

A FINAL VERDICT?: Whatever the final verdict on world models such as these – and the final verdict is not yet in – there can be no doubt that the debate that has raged around them has helped to give increased awareness of the problems of the pollution and population explosions and the exhaustion of supplies of specific natural resources. For this – even should it turn out to be for nothing else – the authors of the world models deserve the thanks of mankind.

49

Growth and underdeveloped economies

THE UNEVEN PATTERN OF DEVELOPMENT

The problems of economic growth that we considered in Chapter 48 are of particular concern to the poorer countries of the world. In our civilized and comfortable urban life, most of us lose sight of the fact that a very short time ago (very short in terms of the life span of the earth, that is) man lived like any other animal, catching an existence as best he could from what nature threw his way. It is less than 10,000 years since the agricultural revolution when man turned himself from a food gatherer into a food producer, and it is only within the last centuries that any significant proportion of the population of the world could look forward to anything but unremitting work in wresting an existence from a reluctant nature. The idea of leisure as a right to be enjoyed by everyone is very new in human history. There are well over 3,000 million persons alive today. The wealthy parts of the world, where people work no more than forty or fifty hours per week and enjoy substantial amounts of leisure and a level of consumption at or near that attained by the citizens of the US, contain only about 20 per cent of the world's population. Most of the rest struggle for their very subsistence. About 2,000 million people exist at a level at or below that enjoyed by peasants in the more successful civilizations of 5,000 years ago.

If one were studying the effect of variations from year to year in rainfall, one would find that, for rich countries such as Great Britain or Holland, such variations would be reflected in farm output and farm income; for each inch rainfall fell below some critical amount, farm output and income would vary in a regular way. In poor countries, such as China, India and Ethiopia variations in rainfall are reflected in the death rate. Indeed, many live so close to the subsistence level that slight fluctuations in the food supply bring death by starvation.

The fact that fluctuations that are measured in money units in rich countries are often measured in lives in poor ones, makes the problems of economic growth very much more urgent in poor countries than in rich ones. Reformers in poor countries often feel a sense of urgency not felt by their counterparts in rich countries. To get those citizens now alive off a bare subsistence standard in a very poor country requires an immediate change to a very rapid rate of economic growth.

Table 49.1 shows how few countries have made the transition from poverty to relative comfort. It also shows that the rich have been getting *relatively* richer and the poor *relatively* poorer. There are many different ways to look at the inequality of income distribution among the world's population. One way is shown in Columns 5 and 6 of the table and is pictured in Figure 49.1.

Table 49.1 Differences in status among countries

Classification (based on GNP per capita current US dollars)	Number of countries	GNP (billions)	Population (millions)	GNP per capita	Percentage of the worlds		Annual growth rate % (average)
					GNP (%)	Population (%)	1965–71
Less than 100	20	25·990	332·004	78	0·78	9·13	1·28
100–199	30	219·630	1,587·601	138	6·57	43·65	1·14
200–399	45	102·610	335·814	306	3·07	9·23	2·25
400–799	31	177·54	300·603	591	5·31	8·27	4·39
800–1,599	26	525·452	412·892	1,273	15·71	11·35	4·87
1,600–3,199	26	687·920	306·459	2,244	20·57	8·43	4·30
3,200 or more	10	1,605–030	361·547	4,440	67·99	9·94	3·21

Source: World Bank: *Atlas* (published by IBRD 1973).

Figure 49.1 shows the disparity between population and income in terms of a 'Lorenz curve'. If income were distributed proportionally to population, 25 per cent of the population would have 25 per cent of the income, 50 per cent of the population would have 50 per cent of the income, and so on, and the distribution of income would be represented by the 45° line in the figure. The white curve shows the actual distribution. The farther it bends away from the 45° line, the greater the inequality in income distribution. The poorest 55 per cent of the world's countries weighted by population earn less than 9 per cent of its income; the richest 14 per cent earn 58 per cent of its income. Because in addition income distribution is not uniform within countries, the extremes are even greater. The last two columns of the table indicate that in the last fifteen years the poorest countries actually have had lower growth rates than the richer ones. As we shall see, this is both an output problem and a population problem.

Obviously 'underdevelopment' is nothing new in the world. Concern with it as a remediable social condition, however, is recent. It has become a compelling policy concern only within the last half-century. Probably the dominant reason for this new-found concern has been the extraordinary success of planned programmes of 'crash' development of which the Soviet experience is the most remarkable. Leaders in other countries ask, 'If they can do it, why not us?'. It is one thing to remain poor if it is thought to be an unavoidable condition of mankind, and it is quite another thing to remain poor if it is believed that sufficiently determined policies could end

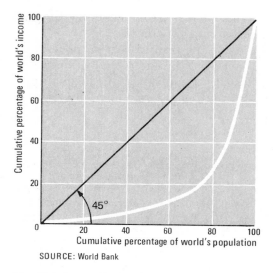

Fig. 49.1 Inequality in distribution of income among nations

poverty. A second push towards development has come from the developed countries, which have fostered policies to aid underdeveloped countries. Some of these
efforts have been ventures of a single developed country; others have been handled
through such international organizations as the World Bank.

In any event, both from the inside and the outside have come pressures for faster
economic development and a search for the causes of underdevelopment and the
techniques of overcoming them.

THE MEANING OF UNDERDEVELOPMENT

We must now see what light economics can shed on the problem of raising living
standards in poor countries. It is often thought that an important step in dealing
with the problem of underdeveloped economies is to find the 'true' definition of
underdevelopment. Books on underdevelopment often start by raising the conceptual problem of how to define *underdevelopment*. The only reason we wish to make clear
the meaning we attach to the term *underdeveloped* is that we wish to delimit our area
of concern – to say, 'We are concerned with these countries and these problems, and
not with those countries and those problems'. Of course, different investigators could
concern themselves with different groups of countries and different problems, and it
would be utterly futile to argue which set of problems should be described by the
term *underdevelopment*, and which set by other terms. One investigator, for example,
defines an underdeveloped country to be one with a per capita national income of
less than $500. Another confines his study to countries with substantial quantities of
underdeveloped resources. Each of these groups of countries can be studied, and it is
completely futile to argue which is the one that is properly defined as underdeveloped.

Underdevelopment has many aspects. We may measure development in dozens of different ways, among them income per head; the percentage of resources un-exploited; capital per head; savings per head; conduciveness to growth of the social system; conduciveness to growth of local religion; amount of 'social capital' (i.e., roads, railroads, schools, etc.); degree of education of the working classes, and so on.

Countries that are 'underdeveloped' in one of these ways may not be under-developed in another. For example, one country may have a lower income per head than others, but have a higher percentage utilization of existing natural resources than others. For this reason we cannot have a unique ranking of the various countries in terms of degree of development. We cannot say one country is more under-developed than another as long as all of these characteristics affect our view of under-development. Furthermore, the problem of raising the income of a country that has low capital per head, much unemployed labour, but few unexploited natural re-sources is likely to be very different from that of raising the income of a country which is underpopulated and has many unexploited natural resources. In either case, the problems will be more difficult if the country has a religious system that places a low value on economic activity and savings. Instead of trying to define *the* problem of underdevelopment, we should look for some common problems in various groups of countries and be prepared to find major differences in both the problems and the solutions in whatever group of countries we study.

BARRIERS TO ECONOMIC DEVELOPMENT

If income per head is taken as a crude index of the level of economic development, a country may develop by any set of devices that causes its aggregate income to grow faster than its population. A growing population, a shortage of natural resources or inefficiency in the way resources are used can each be an important barrier to development.

Population growth

Today, many of the countries of the world have more national income, but they also have more mouths to feed. Thus, their standard of living is no higher than it was a hundred or even a thousand years ago. The average Cambodian and Ethiopian is as hungry as his great-grandfather was. The growth problem faced by these countries is how to get off the treadmill and onto the escalator. Will modest gains in the size of the capital stock eventually add up to enough to produce sustained growth? Not necessarily, because it is the amount of output *per person* that determines whether living standards will rise, and there may be a race between output and population.

Population growth is a central problem of economic development. If population expands as fast as the national income, then per capita income will not increase. If population does expand rapidly, a country may make a great effort to raise the quantity of capital only to find that a corresponding rise in population has occurred, so that the net effect of its 'growth policy' is that a larger population is now main-tained at the original low standard of living. Much of the problem of the poorest countries is due to population growth. They have made appreciable gains in income, but much of it has been eaten up (literally) by the increasing population. This is illustrated in Table 49.2. The differences in growth rates per capita shown in column (3) are more influenced by different rates of population growth (column 2) than by different rates of income growth. For groups I, II and III, almost half of the growth in income was offset by population growth; for groups IV through VII, only 27 per cent was so offset. Thus, the richer countries had a net growth rate (3·6 per cent) half again as large as the poorer countries (2·4 per cent).

Table 49.2 Population and income growth rates, 1950–68 (percentages)

Classification of countries (based on GNP per capita in 1964 US dollars)	(1) Growth rate of income	(2) Average annual Growth rate of population	(3) Growth rate of income per capita	(4) Population growth as a percentage of income growth (2) ÷ (1)
I. Less than $100	3·9	1·8	2·1	46
II. 100–199	4·4	2·6	1·8	59
III. 200–399	5·7	2·9	2·8	51
Average I–III	4·5	2·1	2·4	47
IV. 400–799	5·7	1·7	4·0	30
V. 800–1,599	6·4	1·1	5·3	17
VI. 1,600–3,199	4·7	1·2	3·5	26
VII. 3,200 or more	3·8	1·5	2·3	39
Average IV–VII	4·9	1·3	3·6	27

Source: Computed from World Bank, *World Tables,* 1971.

The population problem has led economists to talk about the 'critical minimum effort' that is required not merely to increase capital, but to increase it fast enough so that the increase in output outraces the increase in population. The problem arises because population size is not independent of the level of income. If population control is left to nature, nature solves it in a cruel way. Population increases until many are forced to live at a subsistence level; further population growth is halted by famine, pestilence and plague. This grim situation was perceived early in the history of economics by Thomas Malthus. In some ways, the population problem is more severe today than it was even a generation ago because advances in medicine and in public health have brought sharp and sudden decreases in death rates. It is ironic that much of the compassion for the poor and underprivileged people of the world has traditionally taken the form of improving their health, thereby doing little to avert their poverty. Men laud the medical missionaries who brought modern medicine to the regions where it was previously unobtainable, but the elimination of malaria has doubled the rate of population growth in Ceylon. Cholera, once a killer, is now largely under control. No one would argue against controlling disease, but other things must also be done if the child who survives the infectious illnesses of infancy is not to die of starvation in early adulthood. In Mexico today the population is growing at more than 3 per cent per year, and thus a rise in production of more than 3 per cent per year is required for Mexico to 'break even'.

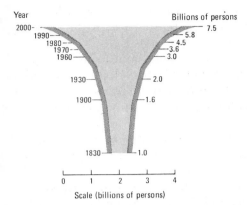

Fig. 49.2 The population bomb

THE POPULATION BOMB: Figure 49.2 illustrates actual and projected population growth in the world today. It took about 40–50 thousand years since the emergence of modern Cro-Magnon Man for the world's population to reach one billion. It took 100 years to add a second billion and 30 years to add the third billion. If present trends continue, the 1970 population of 3·6 billion will be doubled in less than 30 years.

The population problem is not limited to underdeveloped countries (as the concern with pollution in the well-developed countries illustrates), but about two thirds of the expected growth in the world's population is in Africa, Asia and Latin America, areas where underdevelopment is the rule rather than the exception.

Resource limitations

Obviously, a country that has ample fertile land and a large supply of easily developed resources will find growth in income easier to achieve than one that is poorly endowed by nature with such resources. Kuwait has an income per capita second only to the United States, by the accident that it sits on top of the world's greatest known oil field. But natural resource endowments are often the product of man as well as of nature. In fact, a nation's supplies of land and natural resources are often readily expandable in their effective use, if not in their total quantity. Badly fragmented land holdings due to a dowry or inheritance system may effectively limit the productivity of a nation. Lands left idle because of a lack of irrigation or spoiled by excessive irrigation or lack of crop rotation are well-known examples of barriers to development. Ignorance is another. The nations of the Middle East sat through recorded history alongside the Dead Sea not realizing that it was a substantial source of potash. Not until after the First World War were these resources utilized. Now they provide Israel with raw materials for its rapidly growing fertilizer and chemical industries.

FINANCIAL CAPITAL: Investment plays a vital role in economic growth, as was seen in Chapter 48. It may take as much as £10 of capital to increase national income by £1 per year. If this is so, it will take £50,000 million of capital to raise average income per year by £100 in a country of 50 million people such as Mexico. £50,000 million is a lot of money in any country, but it is roughly twice the whole GNP of Mexico. The shortage of investment funds is almost always a bottleneck on the road to development.

One source of financial capital is the savings of households and firms. The particular importance of banks and banking in underdeveloped or developing economies is that if they do not function well and smoothly, the link between private saving and investment may be broken and the problem of finding funds for investment greatly intensified.

Reliance on deposit money and on the good faith of bankers is limited to a small fraction of the world's economies. Many people in undeveloped economies do not trust banks, and they will therefore either not maintain deposits, or they will periodically panic, draw them out and seek security for their money in mattresses, in gold or in real estate. When this happens, increases in savings do not become available for investment in productive capacity. If banks cannot count on their deposits being left in the banking system, they cannot engage in the multiple expansion of credit. Thus, distrust of banks, and of deposit money, may impede economic development, even if private individuals are willing to refrain from current consumption.

SOCIAL-OVERHEAD CAPITAL: The progress of economic development is reflected in the increasing flow of goods and services from a nation's farms and factories to its households. But the ability to sustain and expand these flows depends on many supporting services, particularly transportation and communications, which are sometimes called the 'infra structure' of the economy. Their development is largely left for the government to accomplish.

Roads, bridges, railroads and harbours are needed to transport men, materials and finished goods. The most dramatic confirmation of their importance is in wartime, when belligerents always place very high priority on destroying each other's transportation facilities.

Reasonable phone and postal services, water supply and sanitation are also essential to economic development. The absence, whatever the reason, of a dependable infrastructure can impose severe barriers to economic development.

HUMAN CAPITAL: A well-developed entrepreneurial class of persons motivated and trained to organize resources for efficient production is often lacking in underdeveloped countries. This lack may be a heritage of a colonial system that gave the local population no opportunity to develop; it may result from the fact that managerial positions are awarded on the basis of family status or political patronage; it may reflect the presence of economic or cultural attitudes that do not favour acquisition of wealth by organizing productive activities; or it may simply be due to the nonexistence of the quantity or quality of education or training that is required.

Poor health is likewise a source of inadequate resources. Less time is lost and more effective effort is expended when the labour force is healthy than when it is not. Recently, studies have been undertaken to measure the economic effect of the eradication of certain diseases – malaria, bilharzia and cholera among them – from relatively underdeveloped islands in the West Indies. The economic analysis of medical advances is a very young field, however, and there is a great deal to learn about the quantitative importance of such gains.

Inefficiency in the use of resources

No sharp distinction is possible between resource limitations and inefficient use of resources: Does land rendered unusable by failure to irrigate represent the former or the latter? Despite this problem, it is worth noting certain sources of inefficiency arising out of backwardness rather than mere scarcity that may have contributed to low levels of income and that may impede future development.

ALLOCATIVE INEFFICIENCY AND X-INEFFICIENCY: It is useful to distinguish between two kinds of inefficiency. A man-hour of labour would be used inefficiently, for example, if a labourer was too hungry to concentrate on his task. It would also be used inefficiently even though the labourer was working at top efficiency if he was engaged in making a product that no one wanted. Using society's resources to make the wrong product is an example of ALLOCATIVE INEFFICIENCY. In terms of the production-possibility boundary encountered in Chapter 4, allocation inefficiency represents operation at the wrong place on the boundary. If 2 tons of coal and 50 man-hours of labour are being used to make steel in the most efficient way, this may, nevertheless, be inefficient if this coal and labour could be more productive making electric power to be used to make aluminium. Allocative inefficiency will arise if the signals to which people respond are distorted – both monopoly and tariffs are commonly cited sources of distortions – or if market imperfections prevent resources moving to their best uses.

A second kind of inefficiency has come to be called X-inefficiency, following Professor Harvey Leibenstein. X-INEFFICIENCY arises whenever resources are used in such a way that even if they are making the right product, they are doing so less productively than is possible. If a labourer, for example, is debilitated by disease, unmotivated or inhibited by taboos, a man-hour of his labour may be singularly unproductive, even in its best use. Similarly, land or coal may be poorly used because of ignorance, indifference or poor technology.

While the two kinds of inefficiency can occur simultaneously, X-inefficiency is now believed to be far more important than allocative inefficiency in accounting for both the low levels of income and the difficulties in development of the less developed countries.

SOURCES OF X-INEFFICIENCY: Both inadequate education and poor health, discussed above, may be important sources of X-inefficiency. For example, as modern techniques are introduced, a large rise in the educational standards of the work force is necessary. A man who cannot read or write or do simple calculations will be much less efficient in many jobs than one who can. A manager who is trained in modern methods of bookkeeping, inventory control and personnel management is likely to be much more effective in getting the most output from a given input than one who is ignorant of these techniques.

Traditions, institutions and habitual ways of doing business vary among societies, and not all are equally conducive to productivity. Often personal considerations of family, of past favours or of traditional friendship or enmity are more important than market signals in explaining behaviour. One may find a too small firm struggling to survive against a larger rival and learn that the owner prefers to stay small rather than expand because expansion would require use of nonfamily capital or leadership. To avoid paying too harsh a competitive price for his built-in inefficiency, the firm's owner may then spend half his energies in an attempt to influence the government to prevent larger firms from being formed or to try to secure restrictions on the sale of output, and he may well succeed. Such behaviour is very likely to inhibit economic growth.

Whether a society's customs reflect cherished values or only such things as residual influences of a colonial history or an oligarchical political structure is important to the policy-makers who must decide whether the cost in terms of efficiency should be paid. In any case, cultural attitudes are not easily changed. If people believe that who your father is is more important than what you do, it may take a generation to persuade employers to change their attitudes and another generation to persuade workers that things have changed. Structuring incentives is a widely used form of policy action in market-oriented economies, but this may be harder to do in a personalistic society than in a market economy. If people habitually bribe the tax collector instead of paying taxes, they will not be likely to respond to policies that are supposed to work by changing marginal tax incentives. All that will change is the size of the bribe.

There is a lively current debate on how much to make of the significance of differing cultural attitudes. A widely held hypothesis is that traditional and cultural considerations dominate peasant societies, to the exclusion of economic responses. Recent research suggests that allocative inefficiency may be relatively small. Professor P. A. Yotopoulos studied farming in Epirus, a remote and underdeveloped region of Greece, and found land use adjusting to changes in crop prices, much as would be predicted by micro-economic theory. However, many economists still believe that cultural considerations lead to massive X-inefficiency because managerial personnel are recruited from the wealthy, not the talented, and because there is no basic tradition that one ought to work hard. Max Weber offered the hypothesis that nations adhering to the 'Protestant ethic' of hard work and frugality have an enormous advantage in economic development, but this view, too, is now in dispute.

Advocates of the position that cultural considerations play a major role in problems of developed countries point to what is called the *technology gap* – the fact that the same techniques of production prove less productive in underdeveloped countries than in developed ones. Achieving rapid growth should be easier in one respect for an underdeveloped than for a developed country. More modern techniques of production and distribution can be introduced without spending vast sums on research and development. An underdeveloped country can go a very long way merely by adapting techniques already in use in more developed countries.[1] But this requires imagina-

1 We have used the term 'adapting' rather than 'copying' because an underdeveloped country will often have resource endowments, cultural traditions and institutional arrangements different from those of a developed one and thus must or should use different techniques.

tion, informed personnel, an expansionary view of the future and the motivation on the part of someone to do so. If these are lacking, the result will be to use a less efficient technology than is necessary or to use a given technique less productively than it is used in other countries.

Several empirical studies have shown enormous differences in productivity from country to country in particular industries using the same technologies of production. In some cases, great increases in productivity have been achieved simply by changing incentive systems. These facts suggest a large quantitative importance to X-inefficiency and a large payoff to overcoming it.

FOSTERING ECONOMIC DEVELOPMENT

Economic development policy involves identifying the particular barriers to the level and kind of development desired and then devising policies to overcome them. Planners can seek funds for investment, and they can attempt to identify cultural, legal, social and psychological barriers to growth. They can undertake the programmes of education, legal reform, resource development, negotiation of trade treaties or actual investment that smooth the way to more rapid growth. All of this is more easily said than done. Further, as the dozens of 'development missions' sent out by the World Bank and other international, national and private agencies have discovered, the problems and strategies vary greatly from country to country. Economic development as a field of economic expertise is in its infancy. A few choices seem sufficiently pervasive that it is worth mentioning them here.

Planning or laissez-faire?

How much government control over the economy is necessary and desirable? Practically every shade of opinion from 'The only way to grow is to get the government's dead hand out of everything' to 'The only way to grow is to get a fully planned, centrally controlled economy' has been seriously advocated. Such extreme views are easily refuted by factual evidence. Many economies have grown with very little government assistance. Great Britain and Holland are important examples. Others, such as the Soviet Union and Poland, have sustained growth with a high degree of centralized control. In other countries, there is almost every conceivable mix of government and private initiative in the growth process.

What sense can be made of these apparently conflicting historical precedents? Probably the most satisfactory answer is that the appropriate action depends on the circumstances presently ruling in the country. In some cases, ineffective governments may have been interfering with the economy to the point of discouraging private initiative, in which case growth may well be enhanced by a reduction in government control over the economy. In other cases, where major quantities of social capital are needed or where existing institutional arrangements such as land tenure are harmful to growth, active intervention by the central authorities – 'planning', as it is called – may be essential to encourage growth. There are many possible mixes between state and private initiative that have been used successfully at various times and places. On the question of what is the best mix at a particular time and in a particular place, there is likely to be much disagreement.

THE CASE FOR PLANNING: The active intervention of the central authorities in the management of a country's economy rests upon the real or alleged failure of the market forces to produce satisfactory results. The two major appeals of planning are that it can accelerate the pace of economic development and that it can significantly influence its direction.

Affecting the rate of growth. Any one of the barriers to development may be lowered by actions of the central authorities. Consider, for example, the way that central authorities might seek to mitigate a shortage of investment funds. In a fully employed free-market economy, investment is influenced by the quantity of savings households and firms make, and thus the division of resources between consumption and saving is one determinant of the rate of growth.

When living standards are low, people have urgent uses for their current income. If savings decisions are left to individual determination, savings tend to be low, and this is an impediment to investment and growth. In a variety of ways, central authorities can intervene and force people to save more than they otherwise would have. Such compulsory saving has been one of the main aims of most of the 'plans' of communist governments. The justification offered by the planner for this compulsory sacrifice of the living standards of present generations for the benefit of future ones is that without it growth would be slow or nonexistent, inflicting a low living standard on all future generations.

The goal of the five-year plans of Russia, Poland and now China is to raise savings and thus to lower current consumption below what it would be, given complete freedom of choice. Extra savings may be the subject of planning even in less centrally controlled societies through tax incentives and monetary policies. The object is the same: to increase investment in order to increase growth, and thus to make future generations better off.

Affecting the direction of development. Although the rate of development is important and a desire to increase it might by itself lead to planning, planners are seldom content merely to do everything they can to achieve a particular, more rapid growth rate. This is because they are aware that, as planners, they can choose among *alternative* plans of growth that hold different implications for their country's future. There may be both economic and noneconomic reasons for choosing a different pattern of growth than the free market would provide.

One recent example concerns Greece, which in the period 1958–65 was achieving rapid growth in income per capita largely because of a booming tourist trade and the emigration of many young Greeks to West Germany to work in factories there. The emigrants had been earning incomes in Greece that were substantially below the Greek average, and their remittances home to their families increased both the domestic income and the foreign-exchange reserves. Although it was helpful to the Greek rate of growth to continue to rely on tourism and emigration as bulwarks of the economy, this policy threatened an image of life that visualized 'Greece for the Greeks'. Even at the prospect of some loss in growth, Greek planners recommended the restriction of emigration, the moderation of the size of the tourist role in the economy, and the development of some new industry for the Greek economy.

THE CASE FOR LAISSEZ-FAIRE: Most people would agree that government must play an important part in any development programme. The sectors of the economy that are reserved for public enterprise in most developed economies – education, transportation, communication etc. – are very important to development. But what of the sectors usually left to private enterprise in most advanced capitalist countries?

The advocates of *laissez-faire* in these sectors place great emphasis on human drive, initiative and inventiveness. Once the infrastructure is established, an army of entrepreneurs will do vastly more to develop the economy than will an army of civil servants. People who seem irretrievably lethargic and unenterprising when held down by lack of incentives will show amazing bursts of energy when given sufficient self-interest in economic activity. The market will provide opportunities and direct their efforts and the individual will act energetically within it once he is given a self-interest in doing so.

Furthermore, so goes the argument, individual capitalists are far less wasteful of the country's capital than are civil servants. An individual entrepreneur who risks his own capital will push investment in really productive directions. If he fails to do so, he loses his capital and loses his role in deciding on the allocation of the country's capital. A bureaucrat, however, investing capital that is not his own – possibly raised from the peasants by a state marketing board that buys cheap and sells dear – will behave very differently. His first thought may be to enhance his own prestige by spending too much money on cars, offices and secretaries, and too little on really productive activities. Even if he is genuinely interested in the country's well-being the incentive structure of a bureaucracy does not encourage creative risk-taking. If his ventures fail his own head is likely to roll; if they succeed he will not receive the profits, and his superior may even get the medal. Success and advancement is much more likely for the cautious administrator who takes no risks but cultivates his superiors sycophantically than for a person with genuine entrepreneurial talents.

This is a brief suggestion of the case that is often argued for leaving much of the main thrust of development in the hands of private producers. It is a very emotive subject and readers are likely to have had strong reactions to what they have just read. Those with 'leftish' leanings are likely to have reacted to this case in a hostile fashion, and those with 'rightish' leanings in a favourable fashion. Clearly people have strong, divergent and often doctrinaire views on these matters; equally clearly, these are matters of life and death to millions in underdeveloped countries who will suffer or die if their governments adopt an inappropriate road to development. Human welfare would be well served if these issues could be removed from the realm of emotion into the realm of precise statement and careful testing.

Educational policy

Most studies of underdeveloped countries suggest that undereducation of various kinds is a serious barrier to development and urge increased expenditures on education. This poses a choice of how to spend education funds – whether to spend them on erasing illiteracy and increasing the level of mass education or on training a small cadre of scientifically and technically trained specialists. The problem is serious because education of any kind is very expensive and does not pay off quickly. Basic education requires a large investment in school building, in teacher training and curriculum revision that will result in little visible change in the level of education after 5 or 10 years, and even less payoff to the economy in that time span in terms of greater productivity. Thus, with many urgent demands, the opportunity cost of such expenditures always seems high. Yet it is essential to make them sometime because the gains will be critical to economic development a generation later.

Many, perhaps most, developing countries have put a large fraction of their educational resources into training a small number of highly educated men – often by sending them abroad for periods of advanced study – because the tangible results of a few hundred doctors or engineers or PhDs are relatively more visible than the results from raising the school-leaving age by a year or two, say, from age 10 to age 12. It is not yet clear whether this policy pays off, but it is clear that there are some drawbacks to it. Many of this educated elite are recruited from the privileged classes on the basis of family position, not merit; many regard their education as the passport to a new aristocracy, rather than as a mandate to serve their fellow citizens; and, in addition, an appreciable fraction emigrate to countries where their newly acquired skills bring higher pay than at home. Of those who come home, many seek the security of a government job and become part of the new establishment.

Population control

The race between population and income has been a dominant feature of many underdeveloped countries. There are only two possible ways for a country to win this race. One is to make such a massive push that it achieves a growth rate well in excess of the rate of population growth. The second is to control population growth. The problem *can* be solved by restricting population growth. This is not a matter of serious debate, although the means of restricting it are, for there are considerations of religion, custom and education involved.

Positive economics cannot decide whether population control is morally good or bad, but it can describe the consequences of any choice made. Both Sweden and Venezuela have death rates of about 10 per 1,000 population per year. The birth rate in Sweden is 14; in Venezuela it is 42. While the causes of variations in birth rates are complex, they have inescapable economic consequences. Thus, in Venezuela the net increase of population per year is 32 per 1,000 (3·2 per cent), but it is only 4 per 1,000 (0·4 per cent) in Sweden. If each country achieved an overall rate of growth of production of 3 per cent per year, Sweden would be increasing her living standards by 2·6 per cent per year, while Venezuela would be lowering hers by 0·2 per cent per year. Today, Sweden's income per capita ($4,240) is already four times as high as Venezuela's ($1,060), and Venezuela is the wealthiest country in South and Central America at the present time. (This compares with the US figure of about $5,160 and with the figure for India of about $110.) The gap will widen rapidly, if present population trends continue.

Acquiring capital

A country can get funds for investment in three distinct ways: from the savings (voluntary or forced) of its domestic households and firms, by loans or investment from abroad, or by contributions from foreigners.

CAPITAL FROM DOMESTIC SAVING; THE VICIOUS CIRCLE OF POVERTY: If capital is to be created at home by the country's own efforts, it is necessary to divert resources from the production of goods for current consumption. This requires a cut in present living standards. If living standards are already virtually at the starvation level, such a diversion will be difficult. At best, it will be possible to re-allocate only a small proportion of resources to the production of capital goods. Such a situation is often described as the *vicious circle of poverty*: Because a country has little capital per head, it is poor; because it is poor, it can devote only a few resources to creating new capital rather than producing goods for immediate consumption; because little new capital can be produced, capital per head remains low; because capital per head remains low, the country remains poor. Countries have broken out of the vicious circle of poverty by their own efforts – some slowly over centuries, some rapidly over decades. But the fact that it can be done does not mean that it is easy to do, particularly for a poor country with low savings and a growing population.

IMPORTED CAPITAL: Another way of accumulating the capital needed for growth is to borrow it from abroad. If a poor country, A, borrows from a rich country, B, it can use the borrowed funds to purchase capital goods produced in B. Country A thus accumulates capital and needs to cut its current output of consumption goods only to pay interest on its loans. As the new capital begins to add to current production, it becomes easier to pay the interest on the loan and also to begin to repay the principal out of the increase in output. Thus, income can be raised immediately, and the major sacrifice postponed until later, when part of the increased income that might have been used to raise domestic consumption is used to pay off the loan. This method has the great advantage of allowing a poor country to have an initial increase in capital goods far greater than it could possibly have created by diverting its own resources from consumption industries.

Many countries, developed or undeveloped, are, however, suspicious of foreign capital, for fear that the foreign investor will gain control over their industries or their government. The extent of foreign control depends on the form that foreign capital takes. If the foreigners buy bonds in domestic companies, they do not own or control anything; if they buy common stocks, they own part or all of the company; if they subsidize a government, they may feel justified in exacting political commitments. Whether foreign ownership of one's industries carries political disadvantages is a subject of debate. In Canada, for example, there has been a rising political opposition to having so much of Canadian industry owned by US nationals who are presumably more open to pressure from US central authorities than from Canadian authorities.

Getting foreign capital is easier said than done in the early stages of development. America and Canada were once underdeveloped in the sense of being underpopulated and having many unused resources, but they were latent giants and held promise of rich returns to foreign investors. It is harder to see similar investment opportunities in Pakistan, say, where overpopulation has been a problem for centuries and where the soil is severely damaged by centuries of irrigation without proper drainage. The ability of such a country to borrow from private sources is small. Foreign capital is playing a role, but it is capital provided by foreign governments and international agencies, not by private investors. Investment funds for development are being received today by underdeveloped countries from the governments of the more developed countries acting both unilaterally and through international agencies, such as the World Bank and the Export-Import Bank.

CONTRIBUTED CAPITAL: From the point of view of the receiving country, contributed capital would seem to be ideal. It has the advantage of enabling the country to shift to more rapid growth without either sacrificing consumption now or having to repay later.

Contributed capital in the form of foreign aid expenditures of individual countries and international institutions has played a significant role in post-Second World War economic development. Perhaps surprisingly, there is some significant resistance to accepting aid. The slogan 'Trade Not Aid' reflected political opposition to US economic aid in certain receiving countries. Yugoslavia turned down much aid proffered by the Soviets after 1948. The explanation of this attitude lies in the country's noneconomic goals. It may suspect the motives of the givers and fear that hidden strings may be attached to the offer. Independent countries prize their independence and want to avoid either the fact or the appearance of being satellites. Pride – a desire to be beholden to no one – is also a factor. The economist cannot say that these fears and aspirations are either foolish or unworthy. He can only note that they do have a cost, for there is no doubt that economically it is better to receive than to give.

The motivations behind international giving have themselves become the subject of debate. Do developed nations give aid for humanitarian reasons, because it serves their political objectives, or because it is economically self-serving? Obviously, all three can play a role, but which motive dominates?

Compassion versus political motivation: The distinguished Scandinavian economist Gunnar Myrdal has argued that humanitarian considerations have played a large role. The evidence for the existence of humanitarian motives is, in part, the success of voluntary appeals in developed countries for food, funds and clothes for persons in stricken areas of the world. Although this is not a new concern, as per capita incomes have risen in the Western world, so have contributions, private as well as public. It is the policy of the governments of most of the so-called Western democracies to devote some resources to alleviating poverty throughout the world.

Professor Edward S. Mason, among others, has argued that such American aid as is given can be best understood by looking to political and security motives. He points to the substantial congressional preference for military assistance over economic assistance, the denial of aid to countries such as Ceylon that traded with Communist countries, the fostering of Tito's Yugoslavia because of its anti-Soviet stand – all of which bespeak a strong political motive.

There is little doubt that in the Cold War the struggle for the political allegiance of the uncommitted countries is intense. Because most of the uncommitted countries are underdeveloped and urgently desire to grow, the political system that gives them the best promise of growth is likely to have the strongest appeal.

PATTERNS OF DEVELOPMENT

Because planning can affect the direction of development as well as its rate, a country's economic planners face hard choices. To what extent should a developing country pursue the BALANCED GROWTH POLICY of pushing expansion in all sectors of the economy rather than the UNBALANCED GROWTH POLICY of pushing specialization in certain sectors? How should it decide how much effort to devote to increasing agricultural production, needed to feed its masses, and how much to the industrialization that might change its role in the world economy? If it is to push industrialization, what commodities should it manufacture – those for which there is a large export market, or those that will free it from the need to import?

Comparative advantage: the case for unbalanced growth

The principle of comparative advantage provides the traditional case for the desirability of unbalanced growth. By specializing in those sectors in which it has the greatest comparative advantage, the country can achieve the most rapid growth in the short run. Its potential for growth is certainly not equal in all sectors of the economy. Balanced growth pursued to the extreme of equal growth in all sectors would be virtually sure to result in a lower living standard than would result from some degree of specialization accompanied by increases international trade.

These are cogent reasons in favour of *some* specialization. But specialization involves risks that may be worth avoiding even at the loss of some income. Specialization involves concentrating one's production in one or a few products. This makes the economy highly vulnerable to cyclical fluctuations in world demand and supply. Even more seriously, if technological or taste changes render a product partially or wholly obsolete, the country can face a major calamity for generations. Just as individual firms and regions may become overspecialized, so too may countries.

WHICH COMPARATIVE ADVANTAGES?: Unplanned growth will usually tend to exploit the country's *present* comparative advantages. A planned economy, through the planners, may well choose a pattern of growth that involves changing the country's *future* comparative advantage. One reason for doing so is the belief that the planners can evaluate the future more accurately than the countless individuals whose decisions determine market prices. Thus, the distinguished Latin American economist Raul Prebisch argues that underdeveloped countries are overspecialized in production of agricultural commodities that are sure to enjoy steadily worsening terms of trade relative to manufacturing outputs. Prebisch believes that current market prices fail to anticipate fully this worsening in the terms of trade for agriculture, and thus the planners should intervene and shift the country out of what is sure to be an overreliance on agriculture in the long run.

Whether or not Prebisch is correct in the particular bias he identifies,[1] his concern is an example of a most important general point:

A country need not passively accept its current comparative advantages.

Many skills can be acquired, and the fostering of an apparently uneconomic domestic industry may, by changing the characteristics of the labour force, develop a comparative advantage in that line of production. The Japanese were in a feudal state and showed no visible comparative advantage in any industrial skill when their country was opened to Western influence in 1854, yet they became a major industrial power by the end of the century. Soviet planners in the 1920s and 1930s chose to create an industrial economy out of a predominantly agricultural one and succeeded in vastly changing the mix between agriculture and industry in a single generation. These illustrations should serve as cogent reminders that an excessive reliance on current comparative advantage may lead to an excessive defence of the status quo in the pattern of international specialization.

Agricultural development versus industrialization

Visualize a country (such as Pakistan or India) with a very low level of income, a large and growing population, an historical reliance on agricultural production and a chronic balance-of-payments problem. Suppose that its planners have reduced the myriad choices before them to a choice among three basic development strategies:
(1) The country might choose to devote a major portion of its resources to stimulating agricultural production, say, by mechanizing its farms, irrigating land and utilizing new seeds and fertilizers. If successful in these attempts, it might stave off the spectre of starvation for its current population and even develop an excess over its current needs that would be available for export. This food surplus might earn foreign exchange that could be used to buy needed imports.
(2) The country might attempt to reduce its reliance on foreign trade by using its resources to produce domestic substitutes for the goods it presently imports. If successful, it would find itself with a lesser balance-of-payments deficit and, as its industries developed, a possibility of becoming an exporter of goods it once imported.
(3) The country might seek to develop industrial export industries quickly in order to sell manufactured goods to the rest of the world. Like the previous strategy, this one contemplates industrialization, but with the intent of increasing, not decreasing, its foreign trade.

Any one of these strategies (or any combination of them), if successful, could lead to development. Each has been tried, and each has its advocates. None is without some successes, but none is without difficulties.

AGRICULTURAL DEVELOPMENT AND THE 'GREEN REVOLUTION': India, Pakistan and Taiwan, along with other Asian countries, have begun to achieve dramatic results by the application of new technology – and particularly new seed – to agricultural production. Increases of up to 50 per cent in grain production have been achieved, and it has been estimated that with adequate supplies of water, pesticides,

---

1 A growing world food shortage and rising relative prices of foodstuffs may render some aspects of Prebisch's thesis obsolete as the terms of trade turn in favour of food-producing (and raw material-producing) countries.

fertilizers and modern equipment, production could be doubled or even trebled. This has been labelled the 'green revolution'. When the Nobel Prize Committee gave the 1970 peace prize to Norman Borlaug, it recognized the potential importance of these developments in alleviating, for at least a generation, the shortage of food that the population explosion was expected to bring.

The possibilities of achieving such dramatic gains in agricultural output may seem almost irresistible at first glance, but many economists think they should be resisted and point to a series of problems.[1] One problem is that a vast amount of resources is required to irrigate land and mechanize production, and these resources alternatively could provide industrial development and industrial employment opportunities. Thus, there is a clear opportunity cost. Critics of the agricultural strategy argue that the search for a generation free from starvation will provide at best only a temporary solution because population will surely expand to meet the food supply. Instead, they argue, underdeveloped countries should start at once to reduce their dependence on agriculture. Let someone else grow the food; industrialization should not be delayed.

A second problem with the agricultural strategy is that the great increases in world production of wheat, rice and other agricultural commodities that the 'green revolution' makes possible could depress their prices and not lead to increased earnings from exports. What one agricultural country can do, so can others and there may well be a glut on world markets.

A third problem with the agricultural development strategy has arisen (most sharply in India and Pakistan) where increasing agricultural output has been accompanied by decreasing labour requirements in agricultural production without any compensating increase in employment opportunities elsewhere in the economy. Requirements of labour per acre have dropped by one half. Millions of tenant farmers – and their bullocks – have been evicted from their tenant holdings by owners who are buying tractors to replace them. Many have found no other work and are wandering around the country vainly seeking it. In other areas, unemployment is disguised rather than visible, but it is no less real. If 10 people work full time on a farm because they are all being supported by it and have nothing better to do, even though the same output could be achieved by only 6 people, then the marginal productivity of the last 4 workers is zero. It is as if 6 were gainfully employed and 4 were unemployed. None of the 10, of course, regards himself as an unnecessary worker.

Where there is visible or disguised unemployment, devoting resources to labour-saving innovations makes little sense, unless at the same time there is development of new jobs for the displaced labour. Without such jobs, the potential increases in output that labour-saving techniques make possible will not be achieved.

Import substitution

In the period since the Second World War, industrialization of underdeveloped

---

1 Myrdal and Prebisch are perhaps the most prominent exponents of this view. An excellent account of the issues barely touched in the text is C. R. Wharton, Jr., 'The Green Revolution: Cornucopia or Pandora's Box?' *Foreign Affairs*, April 1969.

countries has largely taken the form of producing domestically goods that were previously imported, largely for sale in the home market. Because these countries characteristically suffered from a significant comparative disadvantage in such production, it proved necessary both to subsidize the home industry and to restrict imports. A recent study of such policies in seven countries – Argentina, Brazil, Mexico, India, Pakistan, the Philippines and Taiwan – concludes that

> although there are arguments for giving special encouragement to industry, this encouragement could be provided in forms which would not, as present policies do, discourage exports, including agricultural exports; which would promote greater efficiency in the use of resources; and which would create a less unequal distribution of income and higher levels of employment in both industry and agriculture.[1]

These conclusions are controversial ones, and critics of them point to the fact that Taiwan, for example, represents one of the great successes of economic development. Its income per capita has averaged a rate of increase of over 6 per cent during the whole of the last two decades.

The use of this import substitution strategy arose out of experience during the Great Depression when the collapse in world agricultural prices caused the value of the exports of agricultural countries to decline drastically, and also during the Second World War when such countries found the manufactured goods they wished to import unavailable.

Implementing an import substitution policy is relatively easy because it can be done by imposing import quotas and by raising tariffs. Such tariffs and other restrictions on imports provide incentives for the development of domestic industry by carving out a ready-made market and by providing a substantial price umbrella that promises high profits to successful local manufacturers and to foreign investors who might enter with both capital and know-how. Subsidies, governmental loans and other forms of encouragement have also been used in many cases.

Little, Scitovsky and Scott concluded that policies of industrialization accomplished by effective rates of protection that varied from 25 per cent for Mexico to over 200 per cent for Pakistan aggravated inequalities in the distribution of income by raising the prices of manufactured goods relative to agricultural goods and by favouring profits over wages. Moreover, they found that productivity increased more than employment opportunities and that unemployment has grown because of the discouraging of such labour-using industries as textiles and the encouraging of the use of capital-intensive labour-saving processes.

In brief, the argument against these industrialization policies is that they have given too much attention to the advantages of self-sufficiency and too little to comparative advantage. Moreover, the opportunities for import substitution are limited: Once the country runs out of imports to substitute for, what then? Industrialization, these critics argue, ought to be encouraged, but along the lines where infant industry arguments are truly valid: where, once the development period is past, the country will have a reliable industry that can compete in world markets.

1 Little, Scitovsky and Scott, *Industry and Trade in Some Developing Countries* (Oxford University Press, 1970), p. 1.

Industrialization

Obviously, if India, Ceylon or South Korea could quickly develop steel, shipbuilding and manufacturing industries that operated as efficiently as those of Japan or West Germany, they, too, might share in the rapid economic growth that has been enjoyed by these industrial countries. Indeed, if a decade or two or even three of protection and subsidization could give infant industries time to mature and to become efficient, the price might be worth paying. After all, both Japan and Russia were underdeveloped countries within the memory of living men.

The greatest problem with such a strategy is that there is no guarantee that it will succeed. Even if the country has the required basic natural resources, it may be backward enough so that it is unlikely to have the labour or managerial talent to achieve success within a reasonable time. India may create a steel industry and have its productivity increase year by year, but it must do more. It must catch up to the steel industries of other countries if it is to compete in world markets.

The catch-up problem is a race against a moving target. Suppose one is committed to having a given industry competitive in 10 years. In such a situation, it is not sufficient to be making gains in productivity; they must be made at a fast enough rate to overcome a present disadvantage against an improving opponent. Suppose you must improve by 50 per cent to achieve the present level of a competitor who is improving at r per cent per year. If you want to catch him in 10 years you must improve at $r + 4$ per cent per year. If r is 6 per cent, you must achieve 10 per cent. To achieve 6 per cent or 7 per cent may be admirable, but you will lose the race just the same.

Thus, while this route to development is available, it depends both on having required resources and on overcoming the things that contribute to X-inefficiency. This often means devoting resources for a long period to education, training, development of an infrastructure, and overcoming the various cultural and social barriers to efficient production.

All of this is hard, although not impossible. Countries sometimes seek a short cut, and pursue certain lines of production on a subsidized basis either for prestige purposes or because of a confusion between cause and effect. Because most wealthy nations have a steel industry, the leaders of many underdeveloped nations regard their countries as primitive until a domestic steel industry has been developed. However, if a country has a serious comparative disadvantage in steel, then having a steel industry will make that country poor. Whether one really gains international prestige by having an uneconomic steel industry or an unprofitable national airline is doubtful. It seems likely that, in the long run, prestige goes to the country that grows rich rather than to the one that stays poor but produces at high cost a few prestigious commodities that are regarded as signs of wealth.

Part eleven

Macro-economic policy

50

Monetarists versus neo-Keynesians

Whoever they are and whatever country they are operating in, macro-economic policy-makers who work in basically free-market societies set themselves some heroic tasks. They would like to bring the economy as close as possible to the full-employment level of national income, while at the same time ensuring both a high growth rate in national income and a low growth rate – zero if possible – in the price level. Furthermore, if the economy is operating with a fixed exchange rate, they must be continually glancing over their shoulders to make sure that the balance of payments does not get into an unsatisfactory state.

In this Chapter we review some of the issues in the debate between the monetarists and the neo-Keynesians.[1] In the following Chapter we widen the perspective to consider the goals and instruments of macro-economic policy in general, paying particular attention to problems that arise when various goals of policy come into conflict with one another.

VIEWS OF MACRO-ECONOMIC POLICY
Two extreme views [2]

There is current controversy over many aspects of macro-economic policy, and in this controversy two extreme views can be discerned. In the first view, the free-market economy has strong self-regulating tendencies: if a satisfactory general climate is maintained, the economy will naturally tend toward full employment and

1 Identifying and attaching names to schools of thought is always a risky business. In the older English universities there are probably as many strands of neo-Keynesian thought as there are Oxbridge colleges. What I have called 'neo-Keynesian' is the line of thought that would, taking all English-speaking economics into account, command the support of a large plurality and probably a simple majority of those economists who build on a Keynesian theory. It is one of the main strands of thought that comes out of the *General Theory*. It was refined by Hicks in his famous article 'Mr Keynes and the Classics' and its *IS, LM* apparatus is the conceptual starting point for a vast amount of theoretical and empirical work which can be lumped into the general category of neo-Keynesian economics.

2 Notice that 'extreme' implies only the descriptive statement that the view lies at one end or the other of a spectrum of views. It does not imply a judgemental statement that the view is wrong or in any way undesirable. The history of ideas is full of examples where extreme views proved correct and moderate views wrong (and vice versa).

a relatively stable price level. At the same time, the exercise of private inventiveness, spurred on by the profit motive, will result in a satisfactory growth rate of real national income. In this view, the government has only to maintain the conditions under which the free-market economy can function effectively. Monetary mismanagement can disturb the economy's natural self-regulation and contribute to severe depressions and inflations, and so one of the government's main problems is to manage the money supply correctly. Indeed, many problems may actually be the result of misguided attempts of government stabilization policies to assist the self-regulatory powers of the free-market economy.

Since, in this view, money does exert an extremely strong influence on the economy, it follows that monetary policy is a potent tool of government policy. Fiscal policy is seen as a relatively ineffective tool except perhaps in the rare situation of a major depression.

According to the second extreme view, the free-enterprise economy has weak self-regulatory powers and may readily settle down into prolonged periods of heavy unemployment. Also, as a result of the restrictive practices of monopolies and a general tendency of the organization man to shun risks and adopt safe policies, the growth rate of income will tend to be sluggish. Furthermore, the enormous power of unions and large firms may cause 'cost-push' inflations that cannot be blamed on monetary mismanagement. In this view, active government intervention is vital. Without such major governmental efforts the economy will tend sometimes to undergo wide cyclical fluctuations and at other times to stagnate in stable positions of heavy unemployment. To prevent these situations from arising, the government must use its instruments of fiscal policy supplemented by monetary policy.

Monetarist and neo-Keynesian views of stabilization policy

The elements of these two extreme views can be combined into many different packages. We can, however, identify two groups of economists who accept two characteristic packages. One group holds that the economy tends to be relatively self-regulating and that monetary policy is much more potent than fiscal policy. Because of the importance they place on monetary factors, these economists are called MONETARISTS. The best known, and probably the most influential, member of this group is Professor Milton Friedman, of the University of Chicago.

The second group holds the view that the economy cannot be relied on to produce full employment if left to itself; they also believe that although fiscal and monetary policy are both useful instruments, fiscal policy is generally the more potent of the two. The economists in this group are called NEO-KEYNESIANS (and sometimes just 'Keynesians') since they accept the macro model of the economy[1] developed by some of the followers of Keynes out of the basic ideas in his *General Theory*.

STABILIZATION POLICY concerns attempts to stabilize the level of national income by ensuring that serious inflationary or deflationary gaps do not persist, so

---

1 This model is what Professor Joan Robinson calls bastard Keynesian. Whether it is a bastard or a legitimate offspring of Keynes, it is a model – sometimes in the simple *IS, LM* form first introduced in Chapter 43, and sometimes in the guise of much more complex econometric and theoretical models – that has been the basis of macro-economic policy since 1945.

that something close to full employment without rapid inflation can be achieved. Many of today's debates concerning stabilization policy involve the issues that divide the monetarists and the neo-Keynesians. We shall study these in terms of disagreements over diagnoses, over the efficiency of alternative policy instruments, and over the cures prescribed.

THE NATURE OF THE PROBLEM (DIAGNOSES)

Why does the economy show the sort of short-run cyclical fluctuations in real income that we studied in Chapter 39? What accounts for inflation, and why does it proceed sometimes at a slow pace and sometimes at a rapid one? Many of the major disagreements between monetarists and neo-Keynesians occur over the first step that any economic doctor must take: diagnosis of the basic problem.

Monetarist views

CYCLICAL FLUCTUATIONS: Monetarists hold that monetary causes are the major source of serious fluctuations in national income.[1] The modern interpretation of business cycles as having mainly monetary causes relies heavily on the evidence advanced by Milton Friedman and Anna Schwartz in their monumental book, *A Monetary History of the United States, 1867–1960*. They establish that there is a strong correlation between changes in the money supply and changes in the level of business activity. Major recessions are found to be associated with absolute declines in the money supply, and minor recessions with the slowing down of the rate of increase in the money supply below its long-term trend. In the worst depression ever experienced, for example, the money supply declined by 35 per cent between 1929 and 1933.[2]

No work of similar detail has been done in modern times for other countries. But a host of smaller studies for particular times and places leaves little doubt that the basic correlation established by Freidman and Schwartz for the US economy applies *mutatis mutandis* throughout advanced industrial countries.

> **The correlation between changes in the money supply and changes in the level of business activity is now accepted by most economists; but there is controversy over how it is to be interpreted: Do changes in the money supply cause changes in the level of business activity, or vice versa?**

Friedman and Schwartz argue that changes in the money supply cause changes in business activity – for example, that the severity of the Great Depression of the 1930s was due to a major contraction in the money supply. Their analysis runs along the following lines: The stock market crash of 1929, and other factors associated with

---

1 The view that fluctuations often have monetary causes is not new. The English economist R.G. Hawtrey, the Austrian economist F.A. von Hayek, and the Swedish economist Knut Wicksell are prominent among those who have given monetary factors an important role in their explanations of the turning points in cycles and/or the tendency for expansions and contractions, once begun, to become cumulative and self-reinforcing. Modern monetarists carry on this tradition.

2 These figures use the definition of the money supply that includes time as well as demand deposits.

a moderate downswing in business activity during the late 1920s, led to a reduction in the public's desire to hold demand deposits and an increase in its desire for cash. The banking system could not meet this increased demand for liquidity without help from the Federal Reserve System.[1] This had been set up to provide just such emergency assistance to banks that were in a basically sound position but unable to meet sudden demands for cash on the part of their depositors.[2] It refused, however, to extend the necessary help, and successive waves of bank failures followed as a direct result. During each wave, literally hundreds of banks failed, ruining many of their depositors and thereby making the already severe depression even worse. During the last half of 1931, for example, almost 2,000 American banks were forced to suspend operations.

A similar monetary contraction, but in the British case without the same wave of bank failures, occurred in Britain and Europe. For the monetarists, the monetary crisis and severe contraction of money and credit that undoubtedly accompanied the Great Depression of the 1930s was a major reason why what might otherwise have been just another short-lived recession turned into a full-blown, long-lived depression.

For the monetarists, fluctuations in the money supply cause fluctuations in national income.

INFLATIONS: Monetarists blame persistent inflationary gaps, with their associated booms and rapid inflations, on excessive increases in the money supply. In doing this, they are the modern spokesmen of a very old tradition in economics. One of the earliest economic 'laws' ever formulated stated that increases in the quantity of money were inevitably followed by inflations (see Chapter 41). Even today, few economists would disagree with the following two propositions: periods of rapid and sustained monetary expansion will cause inflation, and inflation cannot persist indefinitely if the money supply is not expanded.

There is disagreement, however, over two questions. First, are *all* inflations, even the relatively mild ones experienced by Western countries in the 1950s and 1960s, caused by excessive rates of monetary expansion, or are some inflations caused by non-monetary factors? Second, in some inflations is not the causal sequence reversed from that alleged by the monetarists, so that inflations with non-monetary causes induce the increases in the money supply that are observed to accompany them?

Monetarists believe that virtually all inflations are caused by increases in the money supply. The American inflation in the late 1960s, for example, was associated not only with an acceleration of government arms expenditure but also with a rapid expansion of the money supply. The slight slowdown in 1970 and the subsequent renewed outburst of inflation were all due, so the monetarists argue, to variations in the rate at which the central bank was permitting monetary expansion.

In Britain the same association between inflation and changes in the money supply is apparent – when an average lag of 12–18 months between changes in the money

---

1 As we saw in Chapter 42 banks are never able to meet from their own reserves a sudden demand to withdraw currency on the part of a large fraction of their depositors. Their reserves are *always* inadequate for such a task.

2 This is the lender-of-last-resort function of a central bank discussed in Chapter 42.

supply and changes in the price level is allowed for. The recent behaviour of the money supply may be summarized as follows:[1]

For the three years to 1962 inclusive the money supply, M_3, grew at a relatively stable rate of some 2% a year. During 1963 the rate of growth accelerated to over 8% for the year as a whole. The rate of growth, whilst remaining substantially higher than in the early 1960s, declined for the next two years, but for the five years ending December 1968 the compound rate of growth was some 7% a year, though it was far from being regular on a year-to-year basis. In 1969 the rate of growth was only about 3%, whereas over the three years to the end of 1971 the average was about 8·5%. *For 1971 alone the rate was some 13% and for 1972 and 1973 over 27% in each year.*

For the Monetarist the size and variability of the rate of growth of the money supply ... during the greater part of the period since the beginning of the 1960s, would suggest that it was both inflationary and destabilizing. And even those that are sceptical about monetarism are made uneasy by the rapidity of the growth of the money supply in the last few years and the consequences that it may have for inflation, the balance of payments and the operation of the economy generally.

To a monetarist the rapid British inflation of 1972/4 was the inevitable outcome of this unprecedented money expansion, and the incomes policy that caused such disruption to the economy in the winter of 1973/4 ignored the tidal forces of monetary expansion and attempted to order the consequences not to follow with about the same chance as Canute had when he ordered the tide not to rise.

Neo-Keynesian views

CYCLICAL FLUCTUATIONS: Neo-Keynesians emphasize variations in investment as a cause of business cycles and stress non-monetary causes of these variations. Many pre-Keynesian economists had also taken this view.[2] The theories developed by these earlier economists were theories of alternating bouts of prosperity and depression. An economist who accepted such theories might or might not have believed that government policy could significantly shorten a period of depression, but he would almost certainly have believed that in the absence of government intervention, recovery and boom would inevitably follow the period of depression.

Underemployment equilibrium: What was new in Keynes's *General Theory* was the theory of UNDEREMPLOYMENT EQUILIBRIUM: the economy could come to rest with substantial unemployment and without any significant forces operating to push the economy back to full employment. This was more than a theory of cyclical alternations of prosperity and depression; it was a theory of the possibility of permanent (or at least very long-lived) depression.

A great deal of controversy did (and still does) go on about the sense in which we can speak of underemployment *equilibrium*. One of the simplest interpretations, and

1 Prest & Coppock (eds), *op. cit.*, p. 96, italics added.

2 Like the monetarists, the neo-Keynesians are modern advocates of some views that have a long history. The great Austrian (and later American) economist Joseph Schumpeter stressed such explanations early in the present century. The Swedish economist Wicksell and the German Speithoff both stressed this aspect of economic fluctuations before the emergence of the Keynesian school of thought.

one possible view of what Keynes himself meant, is given in the following two paragraphs.

The short-term equilibrium of the economy is at the level of income where withdrawals equal injections (or, as Keynes would have put it, where savings equals investment, since he worked with a one-withdrawal and one-injection model). In the face of any change in withdrawals or injections, the economy will move fairly quickly to a new equilibrium level of national income that may be at, or substantially below, the full-employment level. If withdrawals and injections remain constant, national income will also remain constant, *even if it is well below the full-employment level*. If the economy comes to rest in a state of underemployment equilibrium, there will in fact be forces at work tending to move it back to full employment,[1] but in practice these forces will be so weak and so slow-acting that they can be ignored for all practical purposes.

Since forces tending to move the economy back to full-employment equilibrium probably do exist, it might be more accurate to describe a state of underemployment as a state of *underemployment disequilibrium* that is slowly moving toward a full-employment equilibrium. But since these forces act very slowly, they are of little interest in practical matters and major changes in national income can be understood in terms of the relation between withdrawals and injections.[2]

As Keynes said to those who wanted to wait for these natural forces to produce full employment without government intervention during the 1930s, 'In the long run we are all dead'. A modern Keynesian might add that if the Second World War had not come along to force the adoption of Keynesian remedies in the form of an enormous injection of deficit-financed government expenditure, it might have taken longer than the lifetimes of many of those who lost their jobs in 1929 for the economy's natural forces to produce full employment again.

Keynes did not, of course, hold that the economy would always settle down in a position of underemployment equilibrium, only that it *could* do so. He argued that private investment was usually a volatile element of aggregate demand and that, as a result, there would be fluctuations in national income.

Modern neo-Keynesians use elaborations of the basic model of the circular flow of income developed by Keynes. They also accept the Keynesian views of the importance of such non-monetary factors as new inventions and business confidence in explaining variations in investment. Although the idea of underemployment equilibrium has been muted somewhat, neo-Keynesians mostly accept the view that the economy can come to something like a state of rest at less than full employment and that the forces tending to move the economy back to full employment, if they exist at all, will be weak and slow-acting. Thus, they hold that government action is

1 These forces are supposed to be set in motion by a fall in the real wage rate, that is, money wages were supposed to fall relative to money prices, thus inducing employers to hire more labour. It is a matter of common observation that if such forces do act at all in deflationary situations, they act very slowly since neither the level of money prices nor the average level of money wages has been observed to fall with any rapidity in modern times.

2 Thus, according to the Keynesian view, when withdrawals equal injections and national income is below the full-employment level, it is a matter of practical indifference whether we say that national income is in equilibrium or that it is in a disequilibrium very slowly being corrected by the natural forces that tend to move the economy toward full employment.

necessary when the economy shows signs of settling down to a period of stable but high unemployment.

Money as a cause of fluctuations in national income : There is no single neo-Keynesian view on the importance of money. All neo-Keynesians, however, reject the extreme monetarist view that only money matters in explaining economic fluctuations. Thus they must deny the monetary interpretation of business cycle history given by Friedman and Schwartz. They do accept the statistical correlation between changes in the money supply and changes in the level of economic activity, but they provide explanations that reverse the direction of causality: the neo-Keynesians argue that changes in the level of economic activity tend to cause changes in the money supply, rather than vice versa. A number of reasons can be advanced for this view, although the weight placed on each varies from country to country.

(1) The reserve base may not be under the tight control of the central bank. This would be the case, for example, if the commercial banks' required reserves included assets that were held in substantial quantities by the non-banking public. The banks could then increase their reserves by buying some of these assets on the open market – using newly created deposit money to do so. (This case would not arise if the reserve base were defined in terms of cash in the banks' vaults and on deposit with the central bank, for the cash base is clearly under the control of the central bank.)

(2) The central bank might be unwilling to restrict the reserve base (whether deficit in terms of cash or financial assets). The central bank might provide, through its open market operations, that amount of reserves needed to fulfil legal minimum requirements on whatever amount of deposit money the commercial banks created.

Both (1) and (2) make the money supply endogenously determined rather than being set exogenously by the central bank. The volume of deposit money would be determined by the demand to borrow on the part of customers who were good credit risks. Since this demand (and would-be borrowers' credit-worthiness) will tend to rise on the upswing of a cycle and fall on the downswing, so also will the money supply fluctuate cyclically.

(3) Even if the central bank does control the reserve base the commercial banks may not be fully loaned up at all times. In particular they may hold substantial excess reserves in times of recession because of a dearth of credit-worthy borrowers and because they are unwilling to buy bonds which they expect will soon fall in price. (On the recovery, bond prices will fall as interest rates rise.) As the recovery proceeds, loans will expand, and during the boom demand and interest rates will be high. This will give banks the incentive to lend as much as they can, thus expanding deposits until they are constrained by their legal reserve requirements. During the downswing, excess reserves will pile up, as the demand to borrow shrinks. This behaviour on the part of the commercial banks causes the money supply to fluctuate with the level of economic activity even if the central bank holds the reserve base constant.

(4) The central bank may cause the reserve base, and hence the money supply, to fluctuate cyclically as an incidental result of its pursuit of goals other than control of the money supply. The main alternative goal is the rate of interest. Central banks

sometimes have target levels for the rate of interest. At other times they have targets for the maximum permissible rate of change in the rate of interest. Interest rates tend to rise on upswings as demands to borrow increase, and fall on downswings as demands to borrow decrease. If the central bank wishes to slow down, or prevent altogether these cyclical fluctuations in interest rates, it must engage in a cyclical pattern of open-market operations. The rise in interest rates during the upswing in economic activity means a fall in bond prices. To prevent this happening the bank must buy bonds. The open-market purchase of bonds expands the money supply, and by expanding the monetary base, it permits a multiple expansion of bank credit. The fall in interest rates during the downswing in economic activity means a rise in bond prices. To prevent this from happening the bank must sell bonds on the open market. This contracts the money supply, and by contracting the reserve base it forces a multiple contraction of bank credit. This behaviour causes the money supply to vary directly with the business cycle, even though the money supply, unlike case (1) above, is determined by a reserve base which is controlled by the central bank.

In all of these cases – and others that could be mentioned – the money supply is directly correlated with the level of activity, but it is the level of activity that determines the money supply and not vice versa.

For neo-Keynesians fluctuations in national income cause fluctuations in the money supply.

This much is fairly common ground among neo-Keynesians. Beyond this, however, there are major differences.

A few, such as Professor Nicholas Kaldor, of Cambridge University, hold the extreme view that money does not matter at all. Economists of Professor Kaldor's persuasion hold that the money supply is expanded and contracted by the commercial banking system more or less at will, and that if the central bank tried seriously to control the economy by holding the money supply below what was needed, money substitutes would quickly be invented – as they have been in the past. To these extreme Keynesians (more 'Keynesian' than Keynes himself), money really does not matter at all, and the whole explanation of fluctuations is to be found in non-monetary factors.

Probably the great majority of neo-Keynesians (taking an imaginary census covering all English-speaking economists) would accept the more moderate position which follows from Keynes' own work, that both monetary and non-monetary factors are important in explaining the behaviour of the economy. They would accept that serious monetary mismanagement is one potential source of economic fluctuations, but they would hold that money is not the only, or even the major, source of such fluctuations. In the rest of this chapter we shall confine our attention to this majority, middle-of-the-road, Keynesian view.[1]

INFLATIONS: As we have already noted, most economists agree that sustained very rapid inflations, of the sort commonly experienced in South American countries, and run-away hyperinflation are monetary phenomena: such inflations are almost

---

1 Truth is not of course determined by majority vote or opinion. The *majority*, *moderate* position may be wrong.

invariably caused by excessive monetary expansion used to finance large and sustained government budget deficits.

Disagreement is over mild inflations of the sort experienced in the 1960s and early 1970s in North American and western European countries. Whereas extreme monetarists hold that inflation is *always* a monetary phenomenon, neo-Keynesians hold that non-monetary factors can cause substantial inflations. A prime example would be an investment boom caused by the opening up of some major new set of investment opportunities. Neo-Keynesians agree that such inflations cannot go on indefinitely unless 'validated' by monetary expansions, but they are inclined to stress two further points. First, such inflations may go on for quite a long time even if there is no monetary expansion. Second, the necessary monetary expansion may occur for quite a while *as a response* of the commercial banking system to the heavy investment demand. Some neo-Keynesians also accept the possibility of major cost-push inflation.

INSTRUMENTS OF POLICY (THE POTENCY OF VARIOUS MEDICINES)

Monetarists and neo-Keynesians tend to disagree on the relative potency of fiscal and monetary policy. Monetarists believe that monetary policy has a major influence on the economy and that fiscal policy is relatively powerless except where it is really a disguised way of making changes in the money supply. Neo-Keynesians give a place to both fiscal and monetary policy, although they are usually inclined to place more emphasis on the former rather than on the latter.

Modern monetarists do not use the traditional quantity theory of money outlined in the first half of Chapter 43. They accept, along with neo-Keynesians, the modern view outlined in the second half of that Chapter: the demand for money depends on the rate of interest as well as on income, and excess demand for, or supply of, money is reflected in bond markets rather than in commodity markets. Much of the difference between monetarists and neo-Keynesians is over the empirical magnitudes of relations whose general existence they both accept.

Monetarist views

THE INFLUENCE OF INTEREST RATES: The monetarist view of the power of monetary policy and the relative impotency of fiscal policy follows directly from their assessment of the empirical evidence concerning three critical economic relations, which in all three cases concern the influence of the rate of interest. The first concerns the relation between the rate of interest and the demand for money as summarized in the liquidity-preference schedule. The second concerns the relation between the rate of interest and aggregate expenditure, an important part of which is summarized by the marginal-efficiency-of-investment schedule that relates investment expenditure to the interest rate.[1] The third relation concerns the extent to which the money supply varies with the interest rate.

Monetarists hold that both the demand and supply of money are interest-inelastic (i.e., relatively insensitive to changes in the rate of interest) while the aggregate

---

1 These two relations were discussed in detail in Chapter 43, and the discussion on pages 620–8 is directly relevant.

expenditure function is highly interest-elastic (i.e., relatively sensitive to changes in the rate of interest). They argue as follows.

The most important motive determining the demand for money is the transactions motive, which depends mainly on income and is relatively unaffected by the rate of interest. The speculative motive is the motive most sensitive to the interest rate, but except in times of severe depression it will not, according to the monetarists, be a major motive for holding money. Thus, monetarists see the demand for money in normal times as relatively sensitive to changes in national income but relatively insensitive to changes in the rate of interest.

Monetarists believe that the money supply is also relatively unresponsive to changes in the rate of interest in normal times.

They believe that banks usually tend to lend out as much as they can, keeping a minimum of excess reserves.[1] If this is so, commercial banks will not vary the money supply as the demand for loans and the interest rate varies; they will only expand and contract the money supply when the central bank takes some action, such as changing their excess reserves through open-market operations or varying the legal reserve ratios (either directly, as is done in the US, or by demanding special deposits, as is done in the UK).

While monetarists hold that the money demand and supply is insensitive to interest rates, they take the opposite view with respect to real expenditure, which they believe to be highly sensitive to changes in interest rates. They believe that firms' investment decisions, as summarized in the marginal-efficiency-of-investment schedule, respond significantly to quite small changes in the cost of borrowing money. They also point to certain interest-sensitive household expenditures. Purchases of new housing is defined as investment in the national income accounts, and it is known to be very responsive to changes in mortgage interest rates. Although expenditure on consumers' durables is classified as consumption expenditure in the national income accounts, it is much like investment expenditure. Many consumers' durables are bought on credit at interest rates between 15 and 20 per cent. Such purchases respond to the cost and availability of credit. Taking into account the response of business investment, residential housing and consumers' durables, monetarists hold that aggregate expenditure is highly responsive to changes in interest rates.

The views on these three empirical relations are summarized in Figure 50.1(i).

The monetarists hold that the demand for and supply of money do not respond much to changing the rate of interest, while aggregate expenditure is very sensitive to such changes. Neo-Keynesians hold that the demand for and the supply of money are very sensitive to changes in interest rates, while aggregate expenditure is not.

The significance of these particular shapes become quickly apparent when we study the effects of monetary and fiscal policy.

---

1 They accept that during periods of major crises with accompanying fears of cash drains to the public, banks may hold substantial excess reserves.

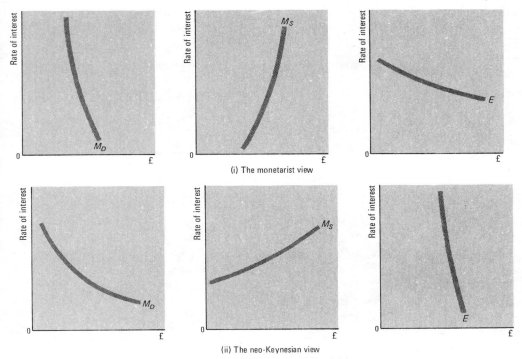

(i) The monetarist view

(ii) The neo-Keynesian view

Fig. 50.1 Monetarist and neo-Keynesian views on interest elasticities

MONETARY POLICY: Given the monetarist view of the interest elasticities outlined in the previous section and summarized in Figure 50.1(i), monetary policy becomes extremely effective. Changes in the money supply engineered by the central bank lead to large changes in interest rates, and these in turn lead to major changes in aggregate expenditure.

The monetarists' scenario for an expansionary monetary policy is illustrated in Figure 50.2(i), and it might run somewhat as follows. The central bank buys bonds on the open market thereby expanding the reserves of the commercial banks. This open-market policy drives up the price of bonds until the public is prepared to hold fewer bonds and more money. Because the demand for money is relatively interest-inelastic, a large fall in interest rates from r_1 to r_2 (i.e., a large rise in the price of bonds) occurs before the public is induced to sell its bonds to the central bank and accept the money in exchange. Aggregate expenditure now responds to this fall in interest rate. Households and firms wish to borrow more for expenditure on such items as plant and equipment, residential housing, and consumer durables, and banks are willing and able to lend more. Thus, a large expansion in expenditure (from E_1 to E_2) and hence in national income is induced.

FISCAL POLICY: The same set of elasticities makes fiscal policy relatively ineffective. Assume that an increase in government expenditure starts off an expansion in the economy shifting the expenditure function from E to E' in Figure 50.3(i). As national incomes increases, more money is needed for transactions purposes, and households

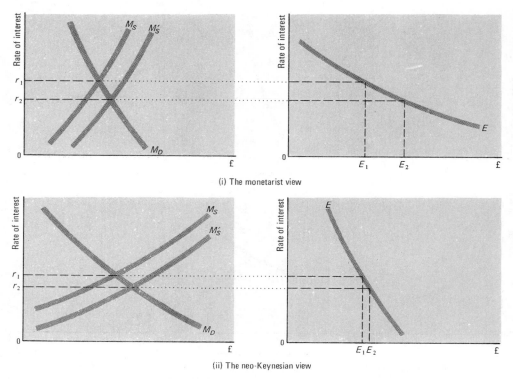

(i) The monetarist view

(ii) The neo-Keynesian view

Fig. 50.2 Monetarist and neo-Keynesian views on monetary policy

and firms try to meet their needs by borrowing money from financial institutions and by selling some of their existing bond holdings. Both of these moves tend to raise interest rates, the first by increasing the demand for loans and the second by forcing down the price of bonds. Because banks have few excess cash reserves, they cannot expand loans significantly in response to both the extra demand and the rise in interest rates. People economize on cash balances until the quantity of money demanded equals the available supply. Because the demand for money is relatively interest-inelastic, a large rise in interest rates is required before this is accomplished (from r_1 to r_3 in Figure 50.3(i)). But the rise in interest rates tends to reduce aggregate expenditure, and the reduction is considerable since this expenditure is highly sensitive to changes in interest rates. The fall in private expenditure (from E_2 to E_3) occasioned by the rise in interest rates largely offsets the initial increase in government expenditure, so that the net effect on aggregate expenditure (from E_1 to E_3) is relatively small. The major effect of the increase in government expenditure is to crowd out private expenditure, and only a minor effect is to make a net increase in aggregate expenditure. (This is the crowding-out effect first studied on page 557.)

Thus, the monetarists' scenario for an expansionary fiscal policy is an increase in government expenditure leading to an initial expansion in income followed by a large rise in interest rates that reduces private expenditure by nearly as much as the increase in government expenditure. The crowding-out effect is close to 100 per cent.

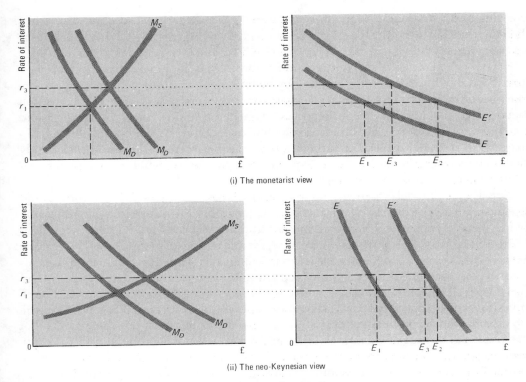

Fig. 50.3 Monetarist and neo-Keynesian views on fiscal policy

CONFUSIONS BETWEEN FISCAL AND MONETARY POLICY: Monetarists also argue that fiscal policy is sometimes given credit that is due to monetary policy because of a confusion between the two policies. They correctly point out that it matters a great deal how any increase in government expenditure is financed. A pure fiscal policy would be a change in government expenditure that left the money supply unaffected. Such a change can be accomplished if the new expenditure is financed either by borrowing money from the public or by taxes. Sometimes, however, government expenditure is financed by the creation of new money by the central bank. In such cases *both* government expenditure *and* the money supply expands. Monetarists agree that in such circumstances a large change in national income can be expected, but they argue that this is due to the expansion in the money supply and not the expansion in government expenditure.

> **Situations in which both the budget balance and the money supply change represent combinations of fiscal and monetary policy and are situations in which both monetarists and neo-Keynesians would expect a significant effect on the level of national income.**

Neo-Keynesian views

THE INFLUENCE OF INTEREST RATES: Neo-Keynesians take a different view from the monetarists on the three critical empirical relations linking the rate of interest to the demand for money, the supply of money, and aggregate expenditure. They believe that both the demand for and the supply of money are highly sensitive to interest rates, while aggregate expenditure is not. Their arguments are as follows.

They believe that the speculative motive for holding money is important because large switches between bonds and money occur when the public expects a change in the interest rate to be temporary. They also stress the very close degree of substitution between money and many short-term assets in the economy that are highly liquid yet yield an interest return. This leads them to argue that relatively small changes in the rate of interest will lead to large substitutions between money and other highly liquid interest-earning assets. As a result the demand for money is itself highly sensitive to changes in the rate of interest.

Neo-Keynesians also believe, for reasons outlined on pages 612–13 above, that the money supply increases as national income and interest rates rise on the upswing of a cycle and decreases as national income and interest rates fall on the downswing.

In contrast to the interest-elastic demand for and supply of money, neo-Keynesians believe that aggregate expenditure is interest-inelastic. The most important interest-sensitive component of aggregate expenditure is private investment by firms, and neo-Keynesians follow the lead given by Keynes himself in believing that such investment is relatively unresponsive to changes in interest rates. They hold, on the one hand, that when business conditions are poor it is not even possible to sell all of the potential output of existing capital, and firms will not then be moved to create more capital just because the interest cost of borrowing money falls a few percentage points. On the other hand, in booms when rates of return are extremely high and the business outlook is rosy, firms will not be deterred from their investment plans by increases of a few percentage points in the cost of borrowing money. Although they grant the interest sensitivity of private residential construction and purchases of some consumer durables, they feel that given the interest inelasticity of the marginal-efficiency-of-investment schedule, the overall aggregate expenditure schedule is relatively interest-inelastic.

The views on these three empirical relations are summarized in Figure 50.1(ii). The particular shapes assumed reverse the relative effectiveness of fiscal and monetary policy from that assumed by the monetarists.

MONETARY POLICY: The Keynesian view of these three critical responses to the interest rate makes monetary policy relatively ineffective. A neo-Keynesian scenario for an expansive monetary policy is illustrated in Figure 50.2(ii) and it might run as follows.

The central bank expands the reserves of the commercial banks by buying bonds in the open market. Because the demand for money is highly interest-elastic, only a small fall in the interest rate is necessary to induce the public to part with bonds and hold more money. This small fall in the interest rate (from r_1 to r_2 in the bottom half of the figure) has only a minute effect on the relatively interest-insensitive aggregate expenditure (increasing it from E_1 to E_2 in the bottom half of the figure). Thus, the expansive monetary policy does not increase national income substantially.

The basic problem, according to the neo-Keynesians, is that the highly interest-sensitive demand for money means that the central bank can induce only small changes in interest rates with its open-market operations. The relatively interest-inelastic aggregate expenditure schedule then guarantees that whatever changes in interest rates the bank is able to engineer will have only a very small effect on aggregate expenditure and hence on the level of economic activity.

FISCAL POLICY: While monetary policy is ineffective given the neo-Keynesian set of interest elasticities, fiscal policy is relatively effective; this is illustrated in Figure 50.3(ii). Assume that the government increases its expenditure in order to raise national income, pushing aggregate expenditure from E to E' in the Figure. As national income increases, more money is needed for transactions purposes, so that the demand for money will now exceed the existing supply. The public will attempt to obtain the extra money that it requires both by borrowing from the banks and by selling bonds on the open market. Both of these actions tend to raise interest rates, but the rise in the demand for loans and in interest rates causes commercial banks to reduce excess reserves, thus increasing the money supply. Also, because of the rise in interest rates (fall in the price of bonds), there is a large fall in the amount of money held for speculative purposes ('Bonds look cheap, so why hold wealth in the form of money?'). Thus, the rate of interest needs to rise by only a small amount (r_1 to r_3 in the lower half of the figure) in order to equate the demand and supply of money once again. This small increase in interest rates has only a negligible effect in reducing the relatively interest-insensitive aggregate expenditure (from E_2 to E_3 in the lower half of the figure).

The crowding-out effect is small: most of the new government expenditure makes a net addition to aggregate expenditure (from E_1 to E_3) and only a small amount is offset by a fall in private expenditure (from E_3 to E_2) due to the rise in interest rates from r_1 to r_3; the expansion will continue until the full multiplier effect of the increase in government expenditure is worked out.

RECOMMENDED POLICIES (PRESCRIPTIONS)

From what has been said so far, one might expect that monetarists would be pushing for an active stabilization policy working through monetary policy and neo-Keynesians for an active stabilization policy with the accent on fiscal policy. Things are not quite so simple as that.

Monetarists

Monetarists do see monetary policy as the major means by which the government can influence national income and the price level. From their view that money matters – indeed, that maybe *only* money matters – they go on to take a possibly surprising position on macro-stabilization policy.

> **Many monetarists argue that money is so important an influence on the short-term behaviour of the economy that monetary policy is too dangerous a tool to be used as an anticyclical device!**

They hold that although the money supply could conceivably be manipulated to control national income, the exercise of monetary policy has, in fact, tended to destabilize the economy and that in practice it is unlikely to do otherwise. One reason for this pessimistic view follows from the monetarists' belief that the money supply exerts its powerful effects on the economy with time lags that are long and that vary for reasons not yet fully understood. Thus, they argue that even the most enlightened attempt to use monetary policy as a short-run stabilizer of the economy may do more harm than good. By the time an anti-inflationary, contractionary policy begins to take hold, for example, the economy may already have turned into a downswing that will only be accentuated by the delayed effects of monetary policy. A second reason for their pessimistic view follows from their belief that the exercise of monetary policy by central banks is often far from enlightened. They believe that central banks tend to overreact to changes in the economy, first indulging in too much monetary restraint and then panicking at the resulting recession and indulging in inordinate monetary expansion that soon causes a severe inflation.

Thus, monetarists feel that our ignorance of the behaviour of the economy, our knowledge of the behaviour of most central-bank decision-makers, and our know-ledge of the potency of the money supply all lead to the conclusion that discretionary control over the money supply should be removed from central banks. The best results, they believe, would be obtained if the money supply were expanded at a constant rate year by year. The actual figure is itself subject to debate, but as a first approximation an expansion equal to the rate of growth of real national income is recommended. This would allow the money supply to expand to suit the needs of business as national income rose, but would eliminate the disturbing effects of large short-term variations in the quantity of money.

The recommended absence of an active stabilization policy does not seriously worry the monetarists. They feel that their rule for monetary expansion will prevent both major declines in the money supply, such as the one that contributed so greatly to the severity of the depression in the 1930s, and too rapid increases in the money supply, such as those that contributed to the accelerating inflationary pressures of the early 1970s. They feel that their rule will put monetary policy in a neutral stance that will allow the economy's own self-regulatory powers to work, producing no more than relatively mild fluctuations around full-employment national income with neither serious inflations nor severe recessions.

Neo-Keynesians

In contrast to the monetarists, neo-Keynesians take the view that an active stabiliza-tion policy is not only possible but is also desirable. They take a more eclectic view of monetary and fiscal policy than do the monetarists. They believe that money does matter somewhat and that monetary policy should be used as an additional anti-cyclical weapon to fiscal policy. The neo-Keynesians believe that monetary policy can influence national income by its effects on interest rates. They tend to deny, therefore, that there is a serious conflict between monetary and fiscal policies; they see the policies rather as complements to each other. Walter Heller, the former chairman of the US President's Council of Economic Advisers, pronounced the official view of the moderate neo-Keynesians when he said, '. . . the "new economics", if you will, assigns an important role to *both* fiscal and monetary policy. Indeed, the appropriate mix of policies has been the cornerstone of the argument. . . . to anyone who fears that the "new economics" is all fiscal policy, the record offers evidence, and the new economics assurance, that money *does* matter.'

Neo-Keynesians do tend, however, to place heavy emphasis on fiscal policy. They do this because they believe that monetary policy may be particularly weak in major depressions when it is particularly important to have some policy intervention. In addition they are disturbed by the uneven incidence of monetary policy. A restrictive monetary policy, for example, tends to hit particularly heavily at home-owners, small businesses, and rapidly expanding firms specializing in the production of new products. It is worth looking at each of these groups briefly.

When monetary restraints are applied, house building tends to be seriously affected because interest costs are such a major part of the total expense of purchasing a house. Thus, monetary policy hits at the home-owner, particularly at those home-owners with modest means who may find it most difficult to raise a mortgage in any case. Small firms tend to find more trouble in acquiring credit than do large firms. Thus, it might be argued, the continual use of monetary policy reinforces the already strong tendencies for large firms to dominate the economy. New products are often produced by a host of small, new, and rapidly expanding firms. Since costs of production must be met before goods are sold, rapidly expanding firms usually find themselves in constant need of more and more credit to meet the gap between paying their costs and receiving money from the sale of their goods. These new firms are the source of much economic growth, but they are just the firms who are hardest hit, and sometimes driven into insolvency, by restrictive monetary policies that make it impossible for them to obtain the credit that they need.

For all these reasons, neo-Keynesians call for an active stabilization policy with fiscal policy playing a major role and monetary policy playing, at most, a supporting role.

THE SIGNIFICANCE OF THE DEBATE OVER PRESCRIPTIONS
More or less intervention

One major debate is over whether we need more or less stabilization policy than we now have. Neo-Keynesians maintain that we could do better in controlling bouts of unemployment and rapid inflation than we now do, and they call for a better informed and more rapidly adjusting set of stabilization policies. Monetarists feel that present stabilization policies are misguided and often accentuate cyclical swings in the economy. They call for a more neutral stance with respect to monetary policy in particular (but for fiscal policy as well) to give the economy's self-regulating powers a chance to work.

Clearly, this debate is important.

> **The neo-Keynesians call for more active monetary and fiscal policies; the monetarists call for more passive policies.**

Which tools?

The debate on appropriate tools is also important. If it is agreed that intervention is required to remove an existing inflationary or deflationary gap, should the main burden fall on fiscal or on monetary policy? Monetarists tend to deride the neo-Keynesian's heavy emphasis on fiscal policy and sometimes argue that appropriate monetary policies are both necessary and sufficient.

Areas of agreement

Although these controversies are important, it is possible to become too impressed with the differences between economists and to forget the amount of agreement that does exist. If, for example, the economy were to be overwhelmed by a recession serious enough to be regarded as a depression – something, say, on the scale of the 1930s – there would be a surprising amount of agreement on what to do.

First, everyone would agree that the central bank should support the banking system by providing loans based on good security. This would allow the public to withdraw from the banks whatever currency that it needed in order to restore confidence that deposits were secure. Once confidence was restored, the currency would soon flow back into the banks, and the loans from the central bank could be repaid.

Second, since almost no one believes that monetary and fiscal policy will cancel each other out, there should be fairly general agreement to use both. Although there would no doubt be argument after the recovery as to which instrument should get most of the credit, at least the debate would take place in a fully employed society rather than in one stagnating in the depths of a prolonged depression.

A plausible scenario for the recovery would be as follows. The central bank expands bank reserves by buying large quantities of government securities on the open market; it also reduces its minimum lending rate. These actions would lower interest rates and thus stimulate the demand to borrow money and at the same time make it easy for the banks to lend to meet this demand. If the monetarists are right, this would be sufficient to set off a recovery phase. If the neo-Keynesians are right, these policies would not by themselves restore confidence in the future, and firms and households would be unwilling to go on a major spending spree financed by borrowed money. The government could then step into the breach and use newly created money to increase its spending. Thus, the deflationary gap is removed by a new government expenditure financed by monetary expansion; but the government increases its expenditure only in so far as private expenditure does not respond to the monetary incentives provided by the central bank. Once the recovery was well under way, confidence would return and as private spending did recover, the government could reduce its own spending to prevent a serious inflationary gap from emerging.

> **As a practical matter, too much should not be made of the distinction between the efficacy of pure fiscal and of pure monetary policies when the job of engineering a recovery from a serious depression could be done by a simple mixture of the two: make money cheap and easily available and have the government spend it to the extent that the private sector refuses to do so.**

The theories of both the monetarists and the neo-Keynesians predict that such a combination of fiscal and monetary policies should be capable of removing any really serious deflationary gap that might emerge in the economy.

Areas of disagreement

Although there would be a significant measure of agreement over how to combat a major depression if one should occur, there is much less agreement on what to do about the major inflations that have beset most Western countries in the 1970s. The debate is complicated by the fact that the neo-Keynesians are themselves seriously divided over the causes of inflation. Some neo-Keynesians believe that all significant inflations are associated with continuing inflationary gaps. These economists agree with the monetarists that the proximate cause of inflation is excess aggregate demand. The only major disagreement between these two groups is over necessary and sufficient reasons for the upward shift in the aggregate demand function that creates the inflationary gap. Other neo-Keynesians accept the cost-push theory that inflation can be caused by the exercise of the powers of unions and monopoly firms whether or not an inflationary gap exists. The inflation controversy thus cuts across the monetarist-neo-Keynesian distinction, and it will be considered further in Chapter 51 where the line will be drawn between cost-push and demand-pull theories of inflation.

Appendix

An IS-LM analysis of the controversy

The debate between the monetarists and the neo-Keynesians can easily be displayed using the *IS* and *LM* curves first introduced in Chapter 43. We will outline the treatment in brief note form, but by relating what is sketched out here to the lengthy discussion of the same problems in the text, the reader can build up a complete treatment for himself.

THE SHAPES OF THE IS AND LM CURVES

The controversy concerning the empirical relations in the economy can be summarized in terms of the shapes of the *IS* and *LM* curves. Monetarists argue that the *IS* curve is flat while the *LM* curve is steep; neo-Keynesians argue the reverse.

Monetarist views

THE *IS* CURVE: According to the monetarists aggregate expenditure is very responsive to changes in the rate of interest. This has the effect of making the *IS* curve very flat. An increase in the national income increases saving, but only a small reduction in the rate of interest is needed to expand investment to restore the equality between saving and investment.

THE *LM* CURVE: According to the monetarists neither the demand for nor the supply of money is very sensitive to the rate of interest. This has the effect of making the *LM* curve very steep. A rise in income raises the transactions demand for money. A large increase in the interest rate is necessary to reduce the speculative demand sufficiently to keep the total demand for money equal to an almost unchanged supply of money.

Neo-Keynesian views

THE *IS* CURVE: The neo-Keynesians argue that investment is not very sensitive to changes in the rate of interest. This makes the *IS* curve relatively steep. A rise in income increases saving and a large fall in the rate of interest is necessary if investment is to increase sufficiently to match the increased volume of saving.

THE *LM* CURVE: The neo-Keynesians argue that both the demand for and the supply of money are highly sensitive to changes in the rate of interest. This has the effect of making the *LM* curve very flat. An increase in the national income increases the transactions demand for money. A small rise in the rate of interest, however, leads banks to expand money supply and leads to a large fall in the speculative demand for money. Thus the total demand for money can be equated with the money supply as income rises, by virtue of only small increases in the rate of interest.

THE REPRESENTATION OF MONETARY AND FISCAL POLICY

Monetary policy

Monetary policy may be shown in this simple model by a shift in the LM curve. If the central bank buys bonds on the open market, it increases the money supply. We have already seen on page 631 that this has the effect of shifting the LM curve to the right. An open market sale contracts the money supply and shifts the LM curve to the left.

Fiscal policy

We have not explicitly incorporated the government sector into this model; to do this note that government expenditure is an injection, as is investment, and that taxes are a withdrawal, as is saving. This suggests that we generalize the IS curve to become a JW curve; the curve shows all the combinations of national income and the rate of interest that will equate injections and withdrawals (as a matter of convention the curve is called an IS curve no matter how many withdrawals and injections are included in the model). Government expenditure is taken as a constant while taxes are a function of national income. The IS curve still slopes downwards as can be seen as follows. G is a constant, I varies with the rate of interest, while S and T vary with national income. As national income rises both withdrawals, S and T, rise and a fall in the rate of interest is necessary to induce sufficient extra investment to maintain equality between $I+G$ on the one hand, and $S+T$ on the other.

Fiscal policy is thus shown by shifts in the IS curve. Suppose the government raises its expenditure, keeping tax rates constant. This shifts the IS curve to the right: any rate of interest is now associated with a higher level of $G+I$ than before, so that a higher level of income is needed to generate the extra savings and taxes necessary if overall withdrawals $(S+T)$ are to remain equal to overall injections $(I+G)$.

An expansionary fiscal policy shifts the IS curve to the right. A contractionary policy shifts it to the left.

THE EFFECTS OF MONETARY AND FISCAL POLICY

Figure 50.4 illustrates the effects of monetary and fiscal policy as seen by two opposing groups. In each of the four parts of the Figure the initial equilibrium is at a national income of Y_1 and an interest rate of r_1. In each case an expansionary policy – fiscal policy in the two left-hand, and monetary policy in the two right-hand, figures – raises the income to Y_2 and moves the rate of interest to r_2. Parts (i) and (ii) show the shape of the curves as assumed by the neo-Keynesians and parts (iii) and (iv) the shapes as assumed by the monetarists.

Inspection of the figures establishes the following results: Given the neo-Keynesian view of the shapes of the IS and the LM curves the effects of fiscal policy are mainly felt in relatively large changes in the national income and relatively small changes in the rate of interest, while the effects of monetary policy are mainly felt in relatively small changes in national income and relatively large changes in the rate of interest.

Given the monetarist view of the shapes of the IS and LM curves, the effects of fiscal policy are mainly felt in relatively small changes in national income and relatively large changes in the rate of interest, while the effects of monetary policy are mainly felt in relatively large changes in the national income and relatively small changes in the rate of interest.[1]

1 An algebraic treatment of the IS–LM curves can be found in Chapters 3 and 16 of G.C. Archibald and R.G. Lipsey, *An Introduction to a Mathematical Treatment of Economics* (2nd edition, Weidenfeld and Nicolson, 1973).

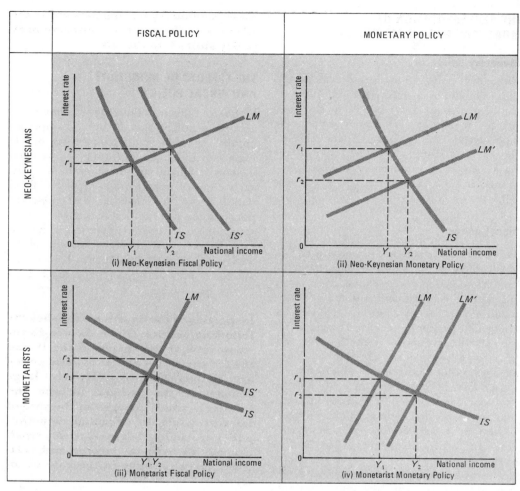

Fig. 50.4 The relative effectiveness of fiscal and monetary policy according to neo-Keynesians and monetarists

51

Goals and instruments of macro-economic policy

Macro-economics is today in a period of crisis. A decade ago there was a majority view that the macro-behaviour of the economy was fairly well understood and instruments were available to help us towards our policy goals. There might be policy conflicts that were imposed by the nature of the economy and that would make it impossible to achieve all of our goals simultaneously. Thus hard choices between alternative goals might be necessary, but, once made, we had sufficient knowledge to enforce through macro-policy any choice that was made. Of course, there were always some dissenters but this majority consensus was a very strong one.

Today the consensus no longer exists. There is great debate over the causes of the severe inflations that have beset western countries in the 1970s. Ten years ago economists spoke confidently about the choice between unemployment and inflation. Today rising unemployment and rising rates of inflation often exist together and have given rise to a new economic disease – STAGFLATION – which refers to the co-existence of high unemployment and rapid inflation.[1]

In the last chapter we discussed the controversy over the efficacy of the two main instruments of macro-policy: fiscal and monetary policy. In the present Chapter we deal more broadly with the goals of macro-policy, with instruments available to achieve these goals, and with problems that arise when various goals conflict with each other.

MACRO-POLICY VARIABLES

The four major goals of macro-policy are (1) to maintain a low and stable level of unemployment; (2) to maintain a relatively stable price level; (3) to maintain a satisfactory balance-of-payments position at a fixed rate of exchange[2]; and (4) to sustain a high rate of growth.

1 The disagreements among economists are serious ones and their outcome will profoundly affect the average citizen. Many of them are over issues that go well beyond introductory economics. Thus although some of the issues can be outlined here, there is no way in which the full nature of what is involved in many of the debates can be appreciated without at least an intermediate, and possibly also an advanced course in macro-economics and monetary theory.

2 As we saw in Chapter 47, this goal has been given much less emphasis in recent years.

In the first part of the Chapter we discuss the four major policy variables separately, asking why each is a cause for concern, why it changes, and how it can be controlled by the central authorities. This discussion helps to bring together much material already introduced, but in widely separated parts of this book. In the rest of the Chapter we consider the new problem of conflicts developing between the desired behaviour of two or more of these policy variables.

At the outset we need to distinguish three kinds of variables. First, we have POLICY VARIABLES which are those variables in which the policy-maker is ultimately interested. In the present context there are (ignoring prestige) four key policy variables: unemployment (U), the price level (P), the balance of payments (B) and the growth rate (G). Second, we have INSTRUMENTAL VARIABLES. These are the variables on which our policies can act directly. They include such things as the rates of taxes and the level of government expenditure, the cash reserves of the commercial banks and laws of all sorts. Between these two we may have a link created by many variables which we call INTERMEDIATE VARIABLES. These are variables that we cannot affect directly, and in whose behaviour we are not directly interested except in so far as they in turn affect the behaviour of our policy variables. The great value of economic theory to the policy-maker is the link that it provides, through intermediate variables, between the instrumental variables the behaviour of which he can change, and the policy variables the behaviour of which he wants to change. In a simple example a change in the instrumental variable, government spending, affects an intermediate variable, aggregate demand, which in turn affects the policy variable of unemployment. Using arrows to indicate these causal links we can summarize the above discussion in Tables 51.1 and 51.2.

Table 51.1　The link between governmental action and the ultimate goals of policy

$$\left\{ \begin{array}{l} \text{Government} \\ \text{policy} \end{array} \right\} \rightarrow \left\{ \begin{array}{l} \text{An instrumental} \\ \text{variable} \end{array} \right\} \rightarrow \left\{ \begin{array}{l} \text{Any number of} \\ \text{intermediate} \\ \text{variables} \end{array} \right\} \rightarrow \left\{ \begin{array}{l} \text{The policy} \\ \text{variable} \end{array} \right\}$$

Table 51.2　The link between governmental action and the level of unemployment

$$\left\{ \begin{array}{l} \text{Government} \\ \text{fiscal policy} \end{array} \right\} \rightarrow \left\{ \begin{array}{l} \text{The level of} \\ \text{government} \\ \text{expenditure} \end{array} \right\} \rightarrow \left\{ \begin{array}{l} \text{The level of} \\ \text{aggregate} \\ \text{expenditure} \end{array} \right\} \rightarrow \left\{ \begin{array}{l} \text{The rate of} \\ \text{employment} \end{array} \right\}$$

We now pass on to a consideration of each of the four main policy variables.

Unemployment

WHAT IS FULL EMPLOYMENT?: We have talked many times in this book about full employment, but every time we have talked about the level of employment we have spoken of such and such a proportion of the labour force as being unemployed. Surely full employment means what it says: no unemployment? The answer to this question is 'No'. Various causes of unemployment can be distinguished, and some of them are regarded as unavoidable aspects of the functioning of a market system. Such unemployment is called FRICTIONAL UNEMPLOYMENT. One source of frictional unemployment is labour turnover. People leave jobs for many different reasons. Some quit, and some are sacked, but almost all of them find new jobs, though it may take time. Since, at every moment of time, there will be a group of individuals moving from one job to another, there will always be some proportion of the labour force out of work. Of course, if the volume of frictional unemployment stays stable over time, it does not mean that the same individuals are out of work. This routine turnover is accentuated by a second source of unemployment, economic growth. As growth proceeds, cost conditions and thus input requirements change; the pattern of demand and thus output requirements change as well. Such changes make it necessary for people to move among occupations, industries and areas, and often necessitates retraining. Thus at any moment of time there will be an amount of unemployment which is associated with resource re-allocation, and which cannot be avoided as long as there is economic growth. A third source of frictional unemployment is the seasonality of some occupations. Finally, about 2 per cent of the labour force every year are new entrants, and it is rare for anyone to walk out of school and into a job without some delay.

For all these reasons some minimum level of unemployment must always occur in an economy. Full employment is usually said to occur when this minimum level is achieved. In Britain, 'full employment' was defined in the White Paper on Employment Policy published by the Government in 1944 as existing when recorded unemployment fell to 3 per cent of the labour force, but this estimate was made to seem too pessimistic by two and a half decades of post-war experience in which unemployment *never* rose as high as 3 per cent.

WHY ARE WE CONCERNED ABOUT UNEMPLOYMENT?: Two main reasons for our concern are, first, that unemployment causes a loss of output and, second, that unemployment is usually unwanted by those who are unemployed.

Factor services are among the least durable of economic commodities. If a fully employed economy has available to it 20 million labour years in 1975, these must either be used in 1975 or wasted. If only 19 million are used in 1975, because 5 per cent of the potential labour force is unemployed, then it is not possible to use 21 million in 1976. The potential output of the one million labour years not employed in 1975 is lost forever. In an economy characterized by scarcity, where there is not nearly enough resources to meet either our individual or our collective needs, this waste of potential output caused by unemployment of resources has seemed to be undesirable, *ceteris paribus*, to almost all observers.

In addition to the lost output, there is the human cost of unemployment. We have already alluded on page 388 to the severe hardship and misery that can be caused by really prolonged periods of unemployment. About these costs there is little argument. But it is wrong to think that a figure of say 2 per cent of the labour force unemployed means 2 per cent of the country's able bodied workers being unemployed indefinitely, and that the cost of a rise of the unemployment rate to 3 per cent is to be measured in terms of the human cost of an extra one worker in each hundred joining the ranks of the permanently unemployed. Modern research has shown that variations in the unemployment rate at or near the full employment level, are to a great extent reflected in changes in the duration of short-term unemployment. For example, assume that 25 per cent of the labour force changes jobs every year. If on average, they take one month between leaving one job and obtaining another, this gives an overall unemployment rate of 2 per cent of the labour force. If jobs should become more difficult to find, so that an average labourer took six weeks between jobs, this would raise the national unemployment figure to 3 per cent. Presumably, most people would value the human costs of every member of the labour force being unemployed for an extra 2 weeks once every four years differently from the human costs of having an extra 1 per cent of the labour force unemployed for a more or less indefinite period.

Before one can make a value judgement about just how high are the costs of a 1 per cent rise in the unemployment rate one would presumably require answers to the positive question of how the extra unemployment was distributed between long- and short-term unemployment. None of this discussion should, however, obscure the general consensus that there are always costs to unnecessary unemployment, but it does suggest that the human costs of an extra 1 per cent unemployment may vary among times and places.

PAST EXPERIENCE: As far back as we have any records, periods of heavy unemployment have been observed. This is illustrated by the data on pages 546 and 547. Up until the 1930s, governments tended to accept periods of unemployment as inevitable. The experience of the rapid end of unemployment as a result of enormous wartime arms expenditures convinced governments otherwise, and after the end of the Second World War they accepted a responsibility to maintain full employment through fiscal policy. Since that time, the British unemployment rate has fluctuated around a rate that would have seemed miraculously low to economists of most earlier generations. By and large taking all Western countries into account the last 30 years has by historical standards been a period of low unemployment.

CAUSES OF UNEMPLOYMENT: Two major causes of serious unemployment are usually distinguished, insufficient aggregate demand and structural changes. We have studied the first cause at length earlier in this book, and we need only recall that macro-theory predicts that the equilibrium national income can be below the full employment level, in which case persistent unemployment will exist.

We may now consider structural changes as a cause of unemployment. As economic growth proceeds, the mix of required inputs (e.g., between skilled and unskilled labourers) changes, as do the proportions in which final goods are demanded. These changes impose considerable demands for readjustment on the economy. When the readjustment does not occur fast enough so that severe pockets of unemployment occur in areas, industries and occupations in which the demand for factors of production is falling faster than is the supply, we speak of STRUCTURAL UNEMPLOYMENT. Strictly speaking structural unemployment is only a severe case of frictional unemployment, but if as growth proceeds, the mix of required inputs (e.g., between skilled and unskilled labour) change fast enough and the movement of labour is slow enough, such unemployment can become very serious.

At any time of heavy unemployment, both structural and deficient-demand causes may be operative. It will not be possible to say that one particular worker is un-employed because of deficient-demand and another for structural reasons, nor will it be possible to say what proportion of the total of unemployment is accounted for by each cause. This should not, however, obscure the fact that both causes can be operative and that both can contribute to the total volume of unemployment.

CONTROL: Deficient aggregate demand can be removed by a satisfactory mixture of the major policies studied in Parts 7 and 8. Structural unemployment is not so easy to cure. Policies for retraining and moving labour can be used as part of a general effort to increase the speed with which the supplies of various types of labour adjust to the changing pattern of demands.

Changes in the price level

By and large, governments do not have policies about the price level *per se*. No one feels that the price level ruling in England in 1275 was intrinsically better or worse than the one ruling in 1975. Standards of living depend on the *purchasing power* of money income, and if, say, we double all money prices and money incomes, standards of living are unchanged. What governments do care about, however, is *changes* in price levels. Whatever is the present level of prices, there will be many economic consequences if it rises or falls by 50 per cent over the next 3 years. It is changes in the level of prices that matter, and that governments seek to control.

WHY ARE WE CONCERNED ABOUT CHANGES IN THE PRICE LEVEL?: A major reason for opposing inflation is that it redistributes income in a haphazard way, from those who cannot protect themselves from the rise in the prices of what they buy by raising the prices of what they sell to those who can. Furthermore, if the country is working in a fixed-exchange-rate world, the policy-maker must worry about the unfavour-able effects on the balance of payments of inflating faster than the average rate of world inflation.

When considering the consequences of inflation, it is important to distinguish anticipated inflation from unanticipated inflation. If an inflation is fully anticipated, it will be allowed for whenever anyone is drawing up a contract agreeing on such things as, for example, money wages to be paid over the next year or interest to be paid on a loan. When this occurs, the real result will be the same whether or not there is an inflation. For example, a 5 per cent increase in money wages with no inflation would merely become a 10 per cent increase if there were a fully anticipated 5 per cent inflation. While some people, such as old-age pensioners, may not be able to avoid the effects of inflation even if they see it coming, most people can.

Unanticipated inflations cause much more upset than do anticipated ones. Contracts freely entered into when the price level was expected to remain constant yield hardships for some and unexpected gains for others once the unanticipated inflation begins. A person who borrowed money at 10 per cent during a year in which the price level rises by more than 10 per cent pays less than nothing (in terms of real purchasing power) for borrowing the money because the purchasing power of the interest that he pays *and* the principle that he returns is less than the purchasing power of the sum that he originally borrowed. The basic harm done by unanticipated inflation is to redistribute income from some groups of the society to others.

Some inflations cause more redistributions than others. Furthermore, an inflation accompanied by an incomes policy that puts legal checks on increases in wages and other incomes usually causes more income redistribution than an inflation that proceeds without any direct government intervention into wage and price setting. Two reasons may be mentioned. The first reason is that even if the government attempts to let all incomes rise at the same rate, it will have more success in controlling some sectors than others. The sectors where the government's control is weakest will gain at the expense of the sectors where government control is strongest. The second reason is that the government may use the tools of an inflation and an incomes policy to bring about an income redistribution that it would find very difficult to accomplish with its fiscal tools of taxes and expenditures operating in the context of a relatively stable price level. The British inflation of 1972–4 seems to have been accompanied by a significant redistribution of income towards skilled workers and away from both many middle-class groups and the poor. The income shifts from the middle-class groups to working-class groups would seem to have been the outcome of direct government policy operated through the setting of differential increases in controlled wages.

Contrary to popular belief, there is no evidence that inflations, whether anticipated or unanticipated, lower total real national income: they do not seem to raise the gap between actual and potential national income, nor do they seem to lower the growth rate of potential income. Thus, the average person's real standard of living is *not* lowered by inflation. Per capita real GNP tends to grow at an average rate of between 2 and 3 per cent per year in the UK whether the rate of inflation is 5 per cent or 15 per cent. Of course, the growth rate of GNP does vary, and a rapid inflation occurring on the upswing of a cycle will be associated with a rapidly rising GNP, while a rapid inflation occurring on the downswing of a cycle will be associated with a constant or even a falling GNP. *There is, however, neither theory nor a solid body of evidence to suggest a systematic association between rates of inflation in the range from 0 to 50 per cent and the rate of growth of real GNP.*

Thus, the *average* housewife is wrong when she says that inflation is pricing everything out of her reach.[1] When the housewife says she would like to see inflation stop, what she really means is that she would like this year's money income to spend at the prices ruling some years ago. But this is impossible since that much output is not available. Few housewives in working households would prefer the prices of, say,

---

1 Some things may go nearly out of her reach if their *relative* prices rise. For example, the rise in the relative price of meat (because of rapidly rising demand as real income rises) certainly has been dramatic, but this is not due, as is often alleged, to inflation, but rather to a change in relative prices. Even if the overall price level were constant meat would be rising in price, and the housewife would find it just as expensive to buy a steak *relative to her overall budget* as she does in today's inflationary world. Similar remarks apply to petroleum products and anything else whose relative price is increasing rapidly.

ten years ago and their money incomes of ten years ago. This is because real income is in fact rising, inflation not withstanding. Of course, some groups are seriously hurt by inflation but the *average* working household is not since its money income rises faster than money prices.

> **Since inflation does not lower overall output, inflation does not reduce average living standards. A main consequence of inflation is to re-distribute income among people, benefiting some and hurting others.**

PAST EXPERIENCE: Practically every form of price-level behaviour has been observed somewhere at some time. Probably the most dramatic occurrences are hyper-inflations, in which prices rise by factors of a thousand-fold in a matter of weeks. One famous example is the hyper-inflation that occurred in Germany in the early 1920s. Most savings were totally destroyed in value by the sky-rocketing prices, and the consequent disruption of the middle classes as a social unit did a great deal to upset the social fabric of Germany and pave the way for the Second World War. It also did a great deal to persuade many people that inflation was one of the worst imaginable social evils, something that was to be avoided at absolutely any cost. Hyper-inflations have invariably been associated with enormous increases in the money supply.

Some indication of the course of price levels in England over a long period of time is given in Figure 51.1, which plots an index of the prices of consumable goods in southern England from 1275 to 1970. The trend line fitted to the whole series shows that on average the price of consumables rose by 0·5 per cent per year over the seven centuries for which data are available. A glance at the figures shows that this general inflationary trend was by no means evenly spread over the centuries. Indeed, most of the permanent rises in the price level occurred in three periods: (1) 1525–

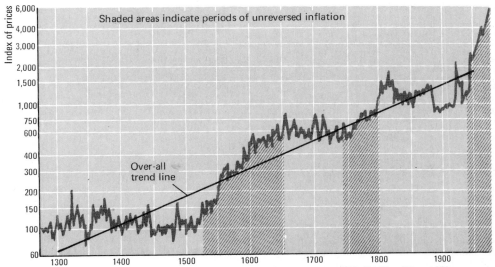

Fig. 51.1 Price index of consumables in southern England 1275–1970 (1451 − 75 = 100)
The cost of living index has been used to extend the series beyond 1959. Source: *Lloyds Bank Review* No. 58, October 1960

1650, when the inflation was associated with local debasements and with the influx of Spanish gold and silver into Europe, (2) 1750–1800, when the inflation was probably due to the large increase in the money supply that followed the rapid spread of banking from London and into the English provincial cities, and (3) 1939–70, when from 1939–50 the inflation was due to the large increases in the money supply that occurred as a result of the deficit financing of the Second World War. (The cause of the inflation during the latter part of this period is a subject of debate among economists although the association between increases in the money supply and increases in the price level was once again in evidence.) There were two other major inflations during the period, one associated with the Napoleonic Wars, 1800–1815, and one associated with the First World War, 1914–20. Both of these inflations were quickly reversed after the wars by almost equivalent deflations.

The period since the Second World War has been one of fairly general inflationary tendencies throughout the world. Table 51.3 shows the average rate of change in the price level of twenty-one countries. Probably the most striking thing about the Table is that it indicates the great range and variability of experience among countries. Evidently, there is no mechanism in the modern world to keep price-level changes even roughly the same across countries.

Although inflation rates differ among countries, the 1970s have witnessed a dramatic and disturbing tendency for inflation rates to accelerate almost everywhere. The annual rate of inflation in Canada and the US reached just into the 'two-figure' category by 1973. In the UK the 'two-figure threshold' (10 per cent)

Table 51.3 Change in the consumer price level of 21
selected countries, 1961–70 (1963=100)

Country	Index of prices			Annual increase, 1961–70 (percentage)
	1961	1970	1972	
Argentina	60	384	812	20·7
Canada	97	125	136	2·6
Chile	54	554	1,277	25·9
China	96	123	131	2·6
Denmark	90	154	169	6·0
Equador	91	140	157	4·8
France	90	131	147	4·1
Germany	95	120	134	2·6
India	91	162	186	6·4
Iran	98	115	126	1·8
Italy	88	128	142	4·2
Japan	90	150	162	5·7
Mexico	98	134	141	3·5
Netherlands	95	141	162	4·4
Norway	95	145	160	4·7
Syria	107	116	127	0·9
United Kingdom	96	139	157	4·1
United States	97	129	157	3·1
Yugoslavia	88	256	337	11·9
Uruguay	62	2,040	5,046	38·8
Vietnam	91	657	875	21·9

was quickly surpassed, and at times the rate approached double that amount. The annual rates of UK inflation as measured by the retail price index through the years 1970 to 1974 were 7·9 per cent, 9·2 per cent, 7·6 per cent, 10·3 per cent and 17·1 per cent.

CAUSES OF CHANGES IN THE PRICE LEVEL: The causes of inflation have been much debated in the last 30 years. Most economists today agree that there are at least two senses in which inflation is a monetary phenomenon. The first is that the very rapid inflations in many countries, particularly those of South America, have been caused by rapid expansions of the money supply. Such expansions have been due to large and persistent government budget deficits, which were often incurred to finance heavy investment expenditure not covered by tax receipts. The second is that inflation, whatever its cause, cannot continue for a sustained period without increases in the money supply. Beyond this much agreement, there is serious controversy over the proximate causes of the inflations that the countries of North America and Western Europe have undergone in the past three decades. Several competing diagnoses – demand-pull, cost-push, price-push, structural rigidity and expectational – have been advanced as explanations.

DEMAND-PULL: The theory of changes in the price level most widely accepted by economists is the one that links price-level changes to inflationary and deflationary gaps. In the last 30 years, inflations have been the concern of policy-makers, so attention has centred on the inflationary-gap, or the demand-pull, theory of inflation.

In essence, the DEMAND-PULL theory says that changes in price levels are to be accounted for by disequilibria in markets caused by changes in aggregate demand. A rise in aggregate demand in a situation of nearly full employment will create excess demand in many individual markets, and prices will be bid upward. The rise in demand for goods and services will cause a rise in demand for factors, and their prices will be bid upward as well. Thus, inflation in the prices both of consumer goods and of factors of production is caused by a rise in aggregate demand.

Virtually all economists agree that excess aggregate demand can be, and often has been, a major cause of inflation. There is room for disagreement, however, on the causes of excess of aggregate demand. Neo-Keynesian economists feel that excess demand can be generated through either an increase in autonomous expenditure or an increase in the money supply, which (by one transitional mechanism or another) will lead to an increase in spending. Some monetarists feel that all inflations have monetary causes. They believe that an increase in the money supply at a faster rate than potential output is increasing is both necessary and sufficient for an inflation.

Although there are real differences between these two groups, the gap between them is not enormous: everyone agrees that a rapid increase in the money supply will cause an inflation, and everyone agrees that without an increase in the money supply inflations cannot exist for very long. Where neo-Keynesians and some monetarists might differ would be on the effect, in a fully employed economy, of a major increase in government expenditure financed either by new taxes or by the sale of bonds to the public but not by the creation of new money. Neo-Keynesians would expect that a tax-financed increase in expenditure would be mildly inflationary via the balanced budget multiplier and the bond-financed increase would be severely inflationary since all of the new expenditure is an injection into the circular flow of income. Some extreme monetarists would expect little inflationary effect from either the tax or bond financial increase in expenditure since the money would not increase in either case.

COST-PUSH: the COST-PUSH theorists believe that rises in costs not themselves associated with excess demand, particularly wage costs, are the initiating cause of inflation. Powerful unions are seen as demanding increases in wages, even when there is no excess demand for labour. Employers, so goes the theory, generally accede to these demands and pass the increased wage costs on to the consumer in terms of higher prices. Thus, the root cause of the inflation is union power, the original upward push to prices being generated from the cost side rather than from the demand side.

The cost-push theory is the one that seems obviously correct to many ordinary people. Surely, they say 'inflation must be caused by these inordinate union wage demands'. There is no doubt that heavy wage demands are found in times of high inflation but as always with a statistical correlation, there is the question of the direction of cause and effect. Monetarists and most neo-Keynesians argue that inflations are caused by excess aggregate demand (possibly caused by excessive monetary expansion) and that the rise in the prices of commodities and factors of production is a consequence of excess demand not a cause of inflation.

Cost-push theorists disagree. They say that union power is a root cause of inflation. They explain away the association between inflation and the money supply by arguing that the money supply is an endogenous variable (see page 613) changes in which are a consequence not a cause of inflation. The main unresolved problem they have to explain arises from the observation that the rate of inflation has varied greatly over the past three decades. Cost-push theorists must explain why, if inflations are caused by union power, the exercise of this power has varied so much over the years. In particular, why did it increase so greatly around 1970? Monetarists say the accelerating inflation of the 1970s was caused by the rapid increases in the money supply (and they point to certain changes in the banking system that in their view helped to cause the monetary expansion). They argue that the power of unions does not vary in such a dramatic way as would be necessary to explain the large variations in the rates of inflation in Western countries since the Second World War.

The most important issues that need to be settled in the debate between cost-push and demand-pull theorists are: (1) can the cost-push theorists develop a measure of the variability of union power that can then be tested as an explanation of the varying rate of inflation;[1] and (2) can the issue of the extent to which the money supply is exogenous or endogenous be settled? Cost-push theorists really require an endogenous money supply that expands passively to permit the inflation caused by the union pressure to continue. The monetarist position would be greatly strengthened by strong evidence that the money supply was exogenous.

[1] A pioneering attempt in this direction was by A. G. Hines, 'Unions and the Change in Money Wages', *Review of Economic Studies*, 1962.

PRICE-PUSH: The PRICE-PUSH, or administered-price theory of inflation, is very close to the cost-push theory. The price-push theory predicts the same sequence of events as does the cost-push theory, but firms rather than unions are the main culprits. The theory says that sellers have monopoly power and would like to raise prices but are restrained from doing so by fear of antitrust action or adverse public opinion. During wage negotiations, sellers grant wage increases and use them as an excuse to raise prices, often by even more than is required to offset the rise in wage costs.

STRUCTURAL RIGIDITY: The STRUCTURAL-RIGIDITY theory assumes that resources do not move quickly from one use to another and that wages and prices can increase but not decrease. Given these conditions, when patterns of demand and costs change, real adjustments occur only very slowly. Shortages appear in potentially expanding sectors, and prices rise because the slow movement of resources prevents the sector from expanding rapidly enough. Contracting sectors keep factors of production on part-time employment or even in full unemployment because mobility is low in the economy. Because their prices are rigid, there is no deflation in these potentially contracting sectors. Thus, the mere process of adjustment in an economy with structural rigidities causes inflation to occur. Prices in expanding sectors rise, and prices in contracting sectors stay the same. On average, therefore, prices rise.

EXPECTATIONAL INFLATION: The EXPECTATIONAL THEORY OF INFLATION depends on a general set of expectations of price and wage increases. Such expectations may have been generated by a continuing demand inflation. Wage contracts may typically include escalator clauses, and price contracts may be made on a cost-plus basis. Such an inflation may persist long after the initial excess-demand causes are removed. Each set of price increases leads, with a lag, to a set of wage increases that leads, with a further lag, to more price increases.

A DOMINANT CAUSE?: Today, few economists would rule out some structural influences, but almost none believe structural rigidity to be the major cause of inflations. Many economists believe that all significant inflations have their initiating causes in excess aggregate demand. Others believe that most of the inflations of the 1950s, 1960s and early 1970s were initiated on the cost side. Most economists agree that demand-pull inflations have occurred in the past and would not rule out cost- or price-push inflations, at least mild ones, as being impossible. Moreover, they believe that inflations once started often generate inflationary expectations that can cause the inflation to persist for some time after the initiating causes had been removed.

   Debate continues on the balance between demand and cost as forces causing inflation in the contemporary inflationary climate. The debate is important because the policy implications of different causes of inflation are different, and different target variables need to be controlled, according to the cause. Until the causes of inflation are fully understood, there will be debate about policies. By the same token, however, the success or failure of particular policies may shed additional light on causes (although we have not always in the past learned the right lessons from our policy futures).

CONTROL OF PRICE-LEVEL CHANGES: Inflations and deflations can be controlled by controlling aggregate demand. A rise in prices can be stopped by a *sufficient* reduction in the level of aggregate demand. Both fiscal and monetary measures can be used to reduce aggregate demand. Although there is some debate about exactly how some of these measures work, there is little doubt that with a sufficiently severe monetary and fiscal contraction any inflation can be brought to a halt. Other undesirable consequences might ensue but there can be little doubt that if control of inflation is desired *to the exclusion of all else*, it could be achieved. What is in doubt as we shall see later is if inflation can be controlled at anything less than a catastrophically high level of unemployment.

Other methods of control are possible only if the orthodox demand-pull theory is not correct. There is still controversy over the competing theories of cost-push and demand-pull and in order to study the control of inflation by means other than the control of aggregate demand, we shall consider some attempts that have actually been made to do so under the inspiration of the cost-push theory. Such theories have been particularly influenced in Britain where several serious attempts at incomes policies have been tried.

Peace-time interventions by the central authorities in an attempt to control the price level are referred to as WAGE-PRICE POLICIES or as INCOMES POLICIES, and they have been tried in most Western countries since the war with varying degrees of seriousness. Believers in the demand-pull and the cost-push theories agree that it is possible, given sufficient controls, to slow down or to stop an inflation at least temporarily. But the kinds of controls necessary and the severity with which they must be applied vary with the theory accepted.

One kind of policy may be called 'exhortation'; it relies on appeals by the central authorities for moderation in setting prices and wages. In America, the President's price and wage guidelines represented such an attempt. The idea that prices can be controlled merely by publishing what the central authorities would like to see happen, represents an extreme view of the economic process. It makes most sense if one is a cost-push and price-push theorist, because, since the inflation is then assumed to be caused by the exercise of arbitrary power on the part of a few industrial or union leaders, it may be possible to persuade them not to exercise their powers. In Britain in 1949, a wage-restraint policy was initiated by the government with the full cooperation of the unions. The rise in wages was very much less than any rise that occurred before or since in the face of the same sort of market conditions. There is little doubt that the policy succeeded temporarily. When cooperation with the unions broke down, higher-than-normal wage increases occurred, so that, by 1951 or 1952, the level of wages was just where one would have expected it to be, given the market conditions that existed over the whole period, but in the absence of a wage-restraint policy.

In the 1950s two attempts were made in Britain to control inflation by controlling wage increases. These experiments reflected the current acceptance by practically everyone, except some professional economists, of the cost-push theory of inflation. In a cost-push situation, control of wages would be sufficient to control inflation, but the problem of how to control wages in a free society has not yet been solved. The unions did not seriously cooperate in the attempt and the policy broke down; its only significant effects were to get wages in the public sector (whose control was possible) seriously out of line with wages in the private sector (whose control was impossible). The belief that a lot of talk and a minimum of effective action by a few officials could seriously change the operation of the economic system pervaded the whole experiment.

In the late 1960s a more determined attempt at wage and price control was made. A Prices and Incomes Board was set up with power to review and prevent proposed wage and price increases. Many proposed increases were reviewed and some were prevented. It would appear to the casual observer that relative prices and wages were significantly affected, but fairly careful empirical research has been unable to locate any significant restraining effect on the overall price level of all of these activities. By and large, attempts to control inflation in the UK between 1950 and 1970 by direct government intervention must be judged to have been a failure.

Undaunted by two decades of failure the British government and the many economists who supported the cost-push theory concluded that incomes policy had failed, not because it was the wrong cure but because it had not been applied with sufficient vigour. In the face of very large inflationary forces, a monetary and fiscal policy aimed at a rapid growth of demand and a rapidly increasing money supply. The Heath government precipitated a major show-down with the unions in an attempt to slow down inflation through incomes policy. After the 1973–4 winter of prolonged industrial strife, a three-day work week, and severe social tensions, the government lost an election. The new Labour government had little alternative but to do what the Conservative government would soon have had to do: give in to the demands of the strikers. The net effect in controlling inflation appeared negligible and the costs in terms of lost output and social stress were significant.

European countries have tried many variants of incomes policies, and these attempts have been studied in a host of detailed research papers and in two important general surveys.

In a study of European experience done when Canada was being urged to adopt an incomes policy, Professor David Smith, of Queen's University, concluded that incomes policies could not, on the available evidence, be judged an effective control of inflation. At best, a really determined policy might decelerate the rate of inflation by 0·5 to 1 per cent per year. Even then, there is evidence that the policy becomes progressively more and more difficult to administer as time passes. Professors Robert Flanagan and Lloyd Ulman, of the University of California, reached similar conclusions in reviewing European experiences a few years after Smith's study.

One of the main problems associated with attempts to control labour costs in Europe can be expressed in terms of the very different behaviour of the *wage rate*, which is the amount workers get per hour, and *wage earnings*, which is the amount they get per week. It was observed that earnings tended to vary with aggregate demand, even though wage rates were held down by an incomes policy. The resulting widening spread between rates and earnings was christened WAGE DRIFT. It resulted from the relative ease with which incomes policy (given union cooperation) could control negotiated wage rates, combined with the extreme difficulty that was encountered in controlling earnings.

Assume for illustration that the officials operating the incomes policy decide that they will allow a rise in wage rates of only 5 per cent in order to keep the increase in purchasing power in line with a 5 per cent increase in output. The average wage is then raised from, say, £1 to £1·05 per hour. If labour is scarce, employers may be bidding against one another both to attract new labour and to hold on to their existing labour. If they are prevented from raising wage rates, they can offer other inducements such as bonuses and guaranteed overtime pay (whether or not the overtime is worked). If, by these devices, they can raise average earnings 10 per cent, from, say, £40 to £44 per week, then the rise in earnings will greatly exceed the rise in output, and inflation will occur in spite of the successful control over wage rates.

Unless wage drift can be controlled, wage-stabilization policy becomes nothing more than a legal fiction, with household incomes responding just as they always did to market conditions, but with increases occurring because of rises in bonuses, overtime pay and other extra earnings rather than because of changes in negotiated wage rates.

America has had one serious attempt at an incomes policy initiated as part of the Nixon Administration's New Economic Policy in 1970 and finally dismantled at the end of 1973. Research by economists such as Professor Robert Gordon of the Brooking Institute have found some effect of the policy on the distribution of income but little or no enduring effect on the rate of inflation.

Summary: Economists still disagree seriously on the need for, and efficacy of, incomes policies. There is always a subjective element in assessing evidence and the reader should be warned that some economists read the evidence differently but to the present author the following conclusions seem hard to avoid on the basis of enormous amounts of evidence of many postwar experiments in incomes policy throughout the Western World.

In essence, the story of wage-price controls commonly runs as follows: (a) successful application of blanket controls on everything, (b) attempt to regulate price changes brought about by innumerable unavoidable circumstances (it would, e.g., be inviting chaos to freeze relative prices permanently), (c) exemption of all sorts of wages and prices for special reasons, (d) the realization that one exception breeds another (since all prices and costs are interrelated) leads to a growing web of exceptions, complex regulations and diminishing effectiveness in controlling overall price rises, (e) the abandonment of the whole system followed by a price explosion taking prices to about where they would have been in the absence of the whole effort at control.

The evidence seems overwhelming that (1) the great majority of incomes policies that have been tried to date have had little or no lasting effects on price levels and (2) that those policies that are pursued with real vigour and determination can be costly in terms of strikes, slow downs, lost output and general social upset. Of course there can be no finality on any social issue, and some observers will continue to draw the lesson that the failure of incomes policies so far means only that they have been pursued with too little vigour and determination. Others, however, will accept the view of the majority of economists *who have made empirical studies of recent incomes policies*: that although they can sometimes have a temporary restraining effect on prices, they are an ineffective method of exerting long-term control over the price level.

The balance of payments

WHY ARE WE CONCERNED ABOUT THE BALANCE OF PAYMENTS?: A necessary condition for concern about the balance of payments is the prior policy decision to support a fixed exchange rate rather than to allow the rate to be determined on the free market. If the latter policy is adopted, fluctuations in the rate would automatically ensure a balance of payments, and this would not need to be a source of concern to the central authorities. (Of course, there might be other problems, and a new policy variable, the variance in the exchange rate, might have to enter our calculations.) The debate about fixed versus flexible exchange rates has been surveyed on pages 702–8. What matters now is that the decision to support a fixed exchange rate forces the central authorities to be concerned about the balance of payments.

Generally, the purpose of international trade is to take advantage of the international division of labour: we export goods in order that we can import those goods that are cheaper to obtain abroad than to produce at home. *Flows of long-term capital aside*, a large import surplus is regarded as undesirable, as is a large export surplus; a situation in which imports equal exports is regarded as desirable. If a country's present reserves of foreign exchange are thought to be inadequate – a position in which many countries find themselves today – it will regard a mild export surplus as its balance-of-payments target, but, once reserves are at an adequate level, it will aim at an equality between imports and exports.

Even the most enlightened government will not regard an export surplus as anywhere nearly as undesirable as an import surplus. An export surplus means that foreign exchange is accumulating, an accumulation that can go on more or less indefinitely, as far as the surplus country is concerned. It does mean that the country is producing without consuming to the extent of its export surplus. Although this depresses living standards below what they could be, it is not a cause of any crisis. Of course, some other country must be suffering an import surplus, and that country may be forced to take steps to remove it. An import surplus can go on only as long as foreign-exchange reserves last. A monthly import surplus equal to, say, 5 per cent of the total exchange reserves can last only for 20 months, and, long before that, it will cause a speculative flight of capital in expectation of a devaluation of the currency. An import surplus is generally the occasion for fairly rapid preventative actions, unless there are reasons to believe that it is the result of genuinely temporary causes so that it will disappear on its own before very long.

PAST EXPERIENCE: We studied past balance-of-payments experience in some detail in Chapter 47. In the past, under the gold standard, governments usually refrained from interfering with the balance of payments. Since the general advent of fixed exchange rates under a paper currency standard (see Chapter 47), however, the central authorities have had no choice but to take a major measure of responsibility for the balance of payments. The drift towards 'dirty floats' in the mid-1970s has taken balance of payments problems from the centre of the stage which they occupied during the 1960s.

CAUSES OF BALANCE OF PAYMENTS PROBLEMS: Causes of balance of payments problems may be divided into changes abroad and changes at home. The central authorities have little or no control over the former, so we shall concentrate on the latter.

Two main causes of balance of payments problems (given a fixed rate of exchange) may be distinguished. The first is domestic inflation. Inflation creates no problems for the balance of payments if all one's competitors are also inflating at the same rate, since it is relative prices that matter in international trade, as in domestic trade. If, however, one country's price level is rising faster than the price levels of competitor countries, imports will rise and exports will fall and balance of payments problems will ensue.

The second cause is in changes in consumption patterns that occur in the course of economic growth. A dramatic example occurred when a technological innovation allowed oil to replace coal as the fuel for ships' boilers. This change greatly reduced Britain's export market for coal, and also increased her import bill since the change over was made by British as well as by foreign ships. Less dramatic shifts occur due to differing income elasticities of demand for imports and exports. Consider two countries with identical rates of economic growth; the first country has a comparative advantage in commodities with low income elasticities while the second has comparative advantages in commodities with high income elasticities. The first country will be in persistent balance of payments problems at a fixed exchange rate. [1]

Capital account problems can be caused both on long-term account if domestic savers wish to invest heavily abroad and on short-term account when short-term capital flows out because of such factors as higher interest rates abroad and fears of devaluation at home.

CONTROL: Broadly speaking, there are two main sets of policies that can be adopted to solve a balance of payments problem. First, national income may be reduced by raising taxes or by lowering government expenditure. The fall in income will reduce the expenditure of households on all goods, including imports. This policy is called an EXPENDITURE-DAMPENING POLICY; it relies on a general reduction in aggregate expenditure to accomplish its goal of a reduction in expenditure on imports. How successful the policy will be depends on the proportion of income that is spent on imports. Where this proportion is small, as it is in the US, a large reduction in income will be needed to accomplish a given change in imports. Where the propor-

---

1 This does not mean that the country will lose if it allows its exchange rate to depreciate steadily. This may well be the policy that maximizes the growth in its standard of living.

tion of income spent on imports is large, as it is in Britain, a smaller change in income will be needed to produce any given change in imports.[1]

The second major policy is an EXPENDITURE-SWITCHING POLICY. The expenditure of domestic households can be switched from foreign to domestic goods to reduce imports, and the expenditures of foreign households can be switched from goods produced abroad to goods produced at home to increase exports. An expenditure-switching policy is accomplished by changing the prices of foreign goods relative to domestic goods. This can be done by taxing imports and subsidizing exports, or by devaluing the exchange rate. Expenditure-switching policies were analysed in detail in Chapter 45.

Expenditure-switching and expenditure-dampening policies can both affect the balance of payments in the desired direction. Both of them, however, have certain side effects.

A policy of expenditure-dampening to reduce imports is somewhat like shooting at a close target with a shotgun. The bull's eye will usually be hit, but so will a lot of other things. Specifically, a reduction in aggregate expenditure will reduce expenditures on all domestically-produced commodities. This means that output and standards of living will fall and that unemployment will rise. These are side effects that are not usually regarded as desirable, especially by those affected.

An expenditure-switching policy will also have an effect on the level of domestic income, output and employment. If a devaluation of the British pound lowers the prices of British goods relative to the prices of foreign ones, both foreign and UK households will buy more UK-produced goods and fewer foreign-produced goods. This will raise incomes in those British industries that produced the newly demanded goods, and, when the extra incomes are spent, a multiplier process will be set up that will raise all incomes in the UK. On the other hand, if the pound is appreciated, then foreign and British households will buy fewer British goods. This will lower the income of those sectors of the UK economy that produced those goods the demand for which has now fallen. Once the incomes of households in these sectors have fallen, their expenditures will be reduced, and incomes throughout the UK will fall. Among the important side effects of such a policy is a redistribution of income among sectors of the UK economy.

Conditions favouring each policy: We have seen that these two policies for removing a balance of payments deficit have opposite effects on income. Expenditure-dampening policies lower demand and income and thus tend to recommend themselves to policy-makers in situations of overfull employment, because, in such situations, it may be considered desirable to reduce demand in order to check inflationary tendencies. The use of expenditure-dampening policies in periods when employment is less than or just equal to the level considered to correspond to full employment, will have the undesirable effect of reducing employment and imposing a sacrifice on the community in terms of foregone domestic output.

1 In general, any change in imports of an amount ΔM can be accomplished by changing income by the amount $\Delta M/m$, where m is the marginal propensity to import. This follows from the relation $\Delta M = m\Delta Y$. Thus if 50 per cent of income goes in imports, a change in M of £1 can be accomplished by changing Y by £2; if only 5 per cent of income goes in imports, then a change in M of £1 requires a change in Y of £20.

Table 51.4 The control of the balance of payments

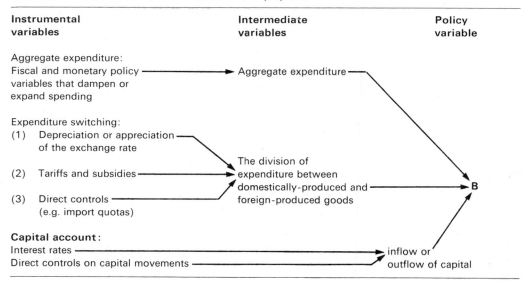

Instrumental variables	Intermediate variables	Policy variable

Aggregate expenditure:
Fiscal and monetary policy variables that dampen or expand spending ——→ Aggregate expenditure ——

Expenditure switching:
(1) Depreciation or appreciation of the exchange rate ——
(2) Tariffs and subsidies ——→ The division of expenditure between domestically-produced and ——→ B foreign-produced goods
(3) Direct controls (e.g. import quotas) ——

Capital account:
Interest rates ——————————→ inflow or
Direct controls on capital movements ——————→ outflow of capital

Expenditure-switching policies tend to raise demand and national income by increasing the volume of domestic expenditure. Such policies will tend to appeal to policy-makers in situations in which income and employment are below the desired level. A successful expenditure-switching policy in these circumstances will simultaneously improve both the balance of payments and the unemployment situation. If an expenditure-switching policy is to be successful in a period of full employment, however, it must be accompanied by a policy of reducing domestic expenditure. There is no point in switching foreign demand onto your products if you are in a situation in which full employment of resources already exists, because it will not be possible to produce more output to meet the extra demand. The appropriate policy in such a situation is to accompany an expenditure-switching policy with an expenditure-dampening one that reduces domestic expenditure by exactly the same amount as the increase in foreign expenditure on domestically-produced goods. This keeps national income and employment unchanged, but directs a larger share of total output to exports, thus improving the balance of payments situation.

On capital account, there are two main tools of control. First, direct controls on movement of capital can be employed as they have been by several countries. Second, the domestic rate of interest can be manipulated. If the central bank raises domestic short-term rates, this will induce an inflow of short-term capital to take advantage of the higher rates. A lowering of domestic interest rates will have the opposite effect as capital moves elsewhere to take advantage of the relatively higher foreign rates.

The policy problem of controlling the balance of payments is illustrated in Table 51.3.

Growth

WHY ARE WE CONCERNED ABOUT GROWTH RATES?: By and large, economic

Capital account:
Interest rates
Direct controls on capital movements
→ inflow or outflow of capital

growth is accepted as desirable. It is the major cause of changes in living standards. With growth, each generation can expect, on the average, to be substantially better off than all preceding generations. The horrors of the early industrial revolution to which we alluded earlier (see page 384) are no longer with us to a great extent because economic growth has removed the necessity of 14-hour days worked in animal-like conditions. Growth, as we have seen is, however, not without its costs. Most people would probably agree that the gains from growth were worth the economic costs incurred by the pockets of persons left behind, *even if they were forced to pay sufficient taxes to fully compensate all those who lost by growth*. Since growth doubles average living standards every 20–30 years it is clearly *possible* by suitable redistributive policies to make *everyone* better off as a result of growth. But growth has other more basic effects on our environment, and, today, people are not so sure that unrestricted growth is worth all of its costs, particularly since the price in terms of change in, deterioration of, or even destruction of the environment is not yet fully known. What does seem clear, however, is that growth is not going to be halted because of environmental problems and that mankind must learn to cope with the problems or face the consequences.

PAST EXPERIENCE: Some discussion of differing growth rates was given on pages 734–6 (see especially Table 49.1). Until recently, concern in Britain over postwar growth rates relative to the countries of Western Europe had suggested that this was a new problem for Britain. The facts are exactly the reverse. By historical standards, the postwar growth rate in Britain has been high. Throughout the nineteenth century the per capita growth rate averaged between $1\frac{1}{2}$ and 2 per cent per annum. Since the Second World War it has averaged just over 2 per cent per annum.

Poor performance by international standards is not a new phenomenon. By 1914 the German growth rate was very much higher than the British one. Were it not for the political idiocies of two world wars, Germany would have gained ascendancy over Britain in the normal course of peacetime events, *provided that the relative growth rate of 1914 had continued to 1960*. This trend was interrupted by 30 years of chaos begun and ended by the two world wars. But it has now reasserted itself and *if* it should continue the standard of living of the average German and French household will be at least double that of the average British household by the end of this century!

CAUSES: Economic growth is the policy variable about which we know least. In spite of a great deal of study, and the accumulation of isolated bits of knowledge, we do not really understand the complex causes of growth sufficiently well to be able to alter the growth rate as easily as we can alter the unemployment rate. No case in which a government has intervened in a free-market society with the purpose of varying the growth rate by 1 or 2 percentage points from year to year is generally agreed to have been a success. Post-war France, which has had a high growth rate combined with an active planning policy, has probably come closest. Many French economists are convinced that their rather loose style of planning has had a significant effect on their growth rate. This is not an easy theory to test and it seems much less obvious when we notice that West Germany has achieved growth rates at least as high as those of

France together with a policy of non-intervention in an almost completely free-market economy. We can only say at this time that the case is 'not proven', one way or the other. Growth, therefore, remains the enigma of macro-policy; we agree that it is one of the most important of all the variables, and we also agree that it is the one we least know how to control.

CONTROL: Since we are not very sure about the causes of growth, we are not very sure about which policy measures will stimulate it. Many economists believe that anything that increases the rate of new investment will be favourable to growth. In addition to preventing reductions in the level of aggregate demand, investment can be encouraged by providing ample funds at low interest rates, by providing tax advantages to investors, and by encouraging research and development. How successful we think we shall be depends on which of the theories of the advancement of knowledge laid out on page 239 we accept.

To encourage growth, we can also seek to change the educational system, health standards and the attitudes towards invention and innovation, as well as to improve business practices.[1] If increasing the rate of economic growth were *the* major objective of economic policy, it is clear that avoiding severe depressions would be important and that stimulating invention, innovation and investment would likewise be desirable. We do not know enough about these processes to be confident of which policies would best achieve the latter objectives.

It is worth noting in this context the utter failure of the policy followed by the British government from 1971 to 1973: a major increase in aggregate demand was engineered in the belief that this would raise the rate of growth of full employment national income. The outcome of the policy was just what conventional theory predicted it would be: first, actual income increased rapidly until it reached full employment income but the growth rate of the latter did not change, and second, a large inflationary gap opened up and was followed by a run-away inflation.

Prestige

An introductory textbook is not the place in which to say much about this goal of policy. It is necessary, however, to mention that a great deal of postwar British economic policy cannot be fully understood unless this goal is recognized. In a full study of British policy the search for international prestige would loom large as an explanation of much otherwise incomprehensible behaviour. The early, and as it now seems premature, venture into atomic power stations; the maintenance of the aircraft industry after it became clear that the British industry was unable to achieve the economies of scale available to the Americans, and in the face of the fact that this unprofitable industry was using the services of a high proportion of Britain's scarce engineering talent; the continuance of the Concorde project in the face of early financial estimates that were obviously unrealistic; the succession of all too predictable failures to develop rockets and other weapons in the face of enormous development costs and the obvious economic superiority of foreign products; the desire to

---

1 The policy followed by the British central authorities in the 1960s of publishing a document saying what they would like the growth rate to be and calling it a 'National Plan' can hardly be regarded as a serious programme.

duplicate the US nuclear deterrent at the cost of a conventional mobile British force that could have supplemented rather than duplicated the American nuclear force; the all too transparent desire to gain entry into the 'nuclear club' so as to be included in the top councils of the world; the desire to maintain the 'prestige of the pound' by not devaluing when it was clearly to the advantage of British industry to do so – all of these and many other decisions in the economic and political sphere are only made comprehensible by the motive of trying to obtain international prestige. It is necessary to note, as we have already done, that much of the behaviour of the central authorities in Britain and in other countries cannot be understood unless the search for prestige is given recognition as one of the major goals governing policy decisions.

POLICY CONFLICTS

We have seen above that economists have sufficient knowledge of the economy to enable policy-makers to achieve any one goal. Growth is the most difficult variable to control but, even here, if we cared about nothing else, massive reallocation policies could increase growth rates.

Inflation seems to many observers to be an intractable problem in today's world, but, here again, if we cared about nothing else it would probably be possible to keep the rate of inflation in the range of, say, 0–3 per cent per annum. The policy package would probably include: a high rate of unemployment for a time – possibly 20 per cent for a year or two until inflationary expectations were removed – and, possibly indefinitely, a flexible exchange rate to insulate the domestic price level from inflation abroad, strict control of the reserve base of commercial banks, restriction on government expenditure and a willingness to accept very high interest rates whenever the free market so dictated.

It may be impossible, however, to fulfil all policy goals simultaneously. It may well be that a policy measure will bring us closer to some of our objectives but take us further away from others. In such cases, policy objectives conflict with one another in the sense that we can get closer to one goal only at the cost of moving further away from another. Thus, it is not sufficient for governments to decide which objectives are worth pursuing, they must also decide on some *rate of substitution* between them; they must decide how much of one it is worth sacrificing in order to get more of the other.

A conflict between unemployment and inflation?

After the Second World War one goal of macro-policy was full employment without inflation. The view that this was a possible goal of policy was commonly held throughout the 1950s. Then, in the 1960s, it came to be believed that there was a policy conflict between full employment and stable prices, so that the best that could be done was to accept some compromise between these two objectives. Now, in the 1970s, with the emergence of stagflation, the idea of a stable trade-off between these two policy variables seems more and more doubtful. At times, Western economies have achieved what would have seemed impossible a decade or so ago: relatively high levels of unemployment combined with rapid rates of inflation. Let us see what is involved.

THE L-SHAPED RELATION: In Part 7 we distinguished between situations of unemployment and constant prices on the one hand and situations of full employment and inflation on the other. The predictions of this theory are illustrated in Figure 51.5. In this figure, the level of resource utilization is plotted on the horizontal axis, and the rate of change of the price level is plotted on the vertical axis. Each point thus indicates the percentage utilization of resources and the accompanying amount of inflation or deflation observed in the economy. According to this theory all observations should be clustered in the shaded band drawn around the axes. When there are unemployed resources, the price level should be observed to be constant. A change in aggregate demand will change the percentage utilization of resources, moving the economy, between, say, points a and b without causing any change in the price level. Prices rise only when full employment exists, so that all observations of inflationary price changes should be clustered in the narrow vertical band at or very near 100 per cent utilization of resources. What is not allowed by the theory is a situation such as that shown by point x in which a significant degree of inflation is combined with a substantial amount of unutilized resources; thus there is no conflict between unemployment and stable prices. The relation shown in Figure 51.5 is often called an

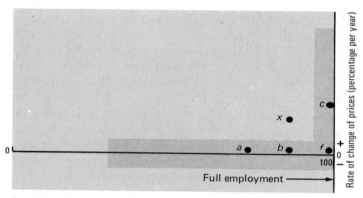

Percentage of resources employed

Fig. 51.5 The L-shaped relation between changes in the price level and the volume of employment

L-shaped curve or an L-shaped reaction function. It is a reaction function because it shows the reactions of the price level to given levels of unemployment (which are in turn related to excess demand). The relation is in fact a reversed L but we shall follow common practice and refer to it as an *L-shaped curve*.

MICRO-ECONOMIC IMPLICATIONS OF THE L-SHAPED CURVE: The L-shaped reaction curve has two basic micro-economic implications. First, prices must be rigid downward in all markets. When the economy is at some point such as a in Figure 51.5, with heavy aggregate unemployment, all markets will have excess supply, and hence there will not be any upward pressure on prices in any market. If prices were flexible downward in any significant number of markets, some prices, and thus the price level, would be falling. Since the price *level* is assumed not to fall, it follows that prices cannot fall in any market. The second micro-implication is more important. It concerns the possibility of the economy really being at a point such as f in Figure 51.5, where full employment is combined with a stable price level. Full employment implies that there is no excess supply in any market; a constant price level implies that there is no excess demand in any market. Thus each and every market in the economy must be in equilibrium when the economy is at the point of full employment without inflation.

Each of these micro-implications contradicts fairly well-established observations about the behaviour of individual markets. Although there are substantial downward rigidities in the prices of manufactured goods and unionized labour, a number of commodities and factors are sold on fairly competitive markets, and their prices do fall during periods of heavy excess supply. Prices of agricultural goods, basic raw materials, and many services decrease in these situations. Thus, when a slump is severe enough so that no individual prices are rising, we would expect the general level of prices to be falling, although the rate of decline may be slow.

Second, we do not expect all of the markets of the economy to be in complete equilibrium relative to each other with none of them displaying either excess demand or excess supply. This is because the economy is continually being subjected to the kinds of changes that necessarily accompany economic growth. As productivity grows, some supplies expand faster than others, and as real incomes grow, some demands expand faster than others. We expect these changes to bring about a re-allocation of resources. Since such changes do not happen instantaneously, we would expect some markets to be exhibiting excess supplies, while other markets exhibited excess demands. Although we expect the price mechanism to direct resources to where demand is greatest, so that there is a continual movement in the direction of equilibrium, we do not expect equilibrium to exist simultaneously in all markets.

This means that, if we start from a period of heavy unemployment and expand aggregate demand, shortages and bottlenecks will develop in some markets while there are still substantial excess supplies in other markets. At this stage prices will begin to rise in the markets where there are shortages. Thus inflation will begin. The level of unemployment can be reduced further, however, by expanding aggregate demand.

As long as excess supply exists in *any* market, the level of resource utilization can be increased (i.e., the level of unemployment lowered) by raising aggregate demand. But the more markets there are in which excess demand already exists, the more any further rise in demand will serve to increase excess demands in these markets (and so speed up the rate of inflation) and the less it will serve to reduce excess supplies in other markets (and so increase the level of resource use). Thus, the higher the level of aggregate demand, the greater the effect on price and the less the effect on employment of yet further increases in demand.

THE PHILLIPS CURVE: If we suppose (as the above suggests we should) (1) that at least some prices fall when there is excess supply, and (2) that all markets do not reach equilibrium simultaneously when aggregate demand is expanded towards its full-employment level, we would predict a relation between price changes and employment in the shape of the curved band illustrated in Figure 51.6. This relation may be called the Phillips curve.[1]

The relation between the level of employment of resources and changes in the price level illustrated in Figure 51.6 shows prices falling slowly for large amounts of unemployment in the economy; for some smaller volume of unused resources, the price level remains steady; and the price level rises when resource utilization is at a high level. The higher the level of resource utilization, the more rapid the rise in prices, but it is always possible to obtain a further increase in resource utilization, and hence in output, at the cost of a more rapid rise in prices. If, for example, excess demand were causing an inflation of de per cent per year, and the percentage of resources unemployed was $(100 - d)$ per cent, then a further rise in excess demand would raise the rate of inflation to, say, kg per cent, but it would simultaneously decrease the level of resource unemployment to $(100 - k)$ per cent.

> **In the Phillips curve, the economy does not abruptly move from a situation of underemployment of resources and constant prices to a situation of full employment with varying prices; instead it moves by degrees from one to another.**

Any increase in expenditure will lower unemployment to some extent, and so raise output, but the lower the level of unemployment already achieved, the less any rise in aggregate demand will affect unemployment and the more it will affect prices.

POLICY IMPLICATIONS OF THE L-SHAPED AND PHILLIPS CURVES: The most important policy implication of the L-shaped curve is that there is no conflict between the two policies of full employment on the one hand and maintaining a stable price level on the other. If there is unemployment in the economy, aggregate demand can be raised until full employment occurs, without any consequent inflationary pressures. Inflation will result only if demand is increased in a situation in which full employment already exists. The economy can be kept in a position such as f in Figure 51.5 with full employment and stable prices. If the economy is at a with unemployment, then aggregate demand need only be expanded to move it to f; if the economy is at c with an inflation under way, then aggregate demand need merely be reduced until the inflation stops and the economy returns to f.

1 The relation is named after Professor A. W. Phillips, formerly of the London School of Economics who first discovered the close relation between the level of unemployment and the rate of change of money wages in the British economy between 1862 and 1958. Phillips worked with a relation between unemployment and the rate of change of wages and derived a curve that sloped downward to the left. Our curve relates the percentage of employment to the rate of change of prices and slopes upwards to the right. We must see how these two curves are related. First write $W = f(U)$ where $\dot{W}$ is the rate of change of money wages and U is percentage unemployment. This is the original Phillips curve. Now define $E = 100 - U$ and write $\dot{W} = g(E)$. This gives us a curve that relates wage changes to employment, and it will slope upwards to the right. Now to replace $\dot{W}$ (the rate of change of wages) by $\dot{P}$ (the rate of change of prices) we specify a simplified theory that is enough to illustrate what is involved. (1) The rate of change of productivity is exogenous. (2) Wages are a major proportion of factor incomes, and other incomes will change in approximately the same proportion as wage incomes. (3) The problem of maintaining a stable price level thus boils down to one of having total wage income (which is the major determinant of aggregate demand) rise at the same speed as productivity (which is the major determinant of aggregate supply). The conflict can then be studied by observing the relation between the level of unemployment and the rate of increase in wages. (More detailed work has used more adequate, and necessarily quite advanced, theories linking these variables together.)

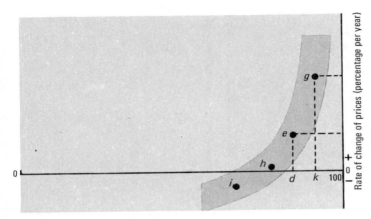

Percentage of resources employed

Fig. 51.6 The Phillips-curve relation between changes in the price level and the volume of employment

With the relationship shown by the Phillips curve, controlling inflation and maintaining the highest possible level of employment become conflicting policy objectives. If the economy is at point e, in Figure 51.6 for example, with $(100-d)$ per cent unemployment and with de per cent inflation per year, then the inflation can be slowed down at the cost of increased unemployment; on the other hand, the level of unemployment can be reduced, but only at the cost of more inflation.

The L-shaped relation lay behind the policy recommendation of full employment without inflation of the 1950s. The Phillips curve lay behind the idea of a policy conflict of the 1960s.

A REVIVAL OF THE L-SHAPED RELATION: Recently Professors Milton Friedman, of the University of Chicago, and Edward Phelps, of Columbia University, have attacked the theoretical underpinnings of the Phillips curve. They hold that it describes a transitory relationship that cannot exist in the 'long run'. They argue that if the economy were to settle down in some position such as e in Figure 51.6 with substantial inflation, people would soon come to realize that the inflation was permanent. Unions would then demand even larger wage increases and others would also change their behaviour to adjust to their expectations of continued inflation. This new behaviour would accelerate the inflation. But once people came to accept the new higher rate as permanent, they would revise their behaviour, and this would accelerate the inflation still further. Their theory is summarized in Figure 51.7, which shows a 'natural rate of unemployment' (indicated by U_N in the figure); if policy-makers try to reduce unemployment below this rate, they bring about an inflation that explodes into ever faster rates of price increases.

According to this theory there is no long-term trade-off between inflation and unemployment. Any government that attempts to hold actual unemployment below the natural rate of unemployment will encounter an accelerating rate of inflation that will sooner or later force the government to accept a rise in unemployment to the natural rate.

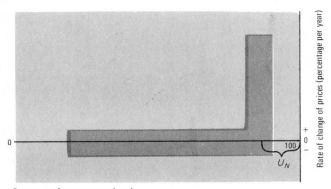

Percentage of resources employed

Fig. 51.7 The new theory of the L-shaped relation with a non-zero natural rate of unemployment (U_N)

The rapid rise in inflation in the 1970s without any fall in unemployment seemed to many to confirm this view: at last inflation was accelerating as a result of a prolonged period when unemployment had been held below its natural rate.

Other economists saw the onset of stagflation as a crisis of conventional economics, a failure of all macro-theory to explain what is happening in the 1970s. The Phelps-Freidman theory is a very conventional market mechanism theory. It holds that the Phillips curve theorists forgot about the expectations of inflation as an influence on prices and wages. They feel that when expectations are added in they can explain the observations of the 1970s with orthodox demand-pull theory, the idea being that aggregate demand can be depressed raising unemployment to very high levels and with inflation persisting but only until expectations of continued inflation are finally revised downwards.

Here is a most important controversy both for current policy and for economic theory. Do we live in a period of a crisis of macro-economics where standard economic theory is unable to explain what is happening in the 1970s? Or is it true that, with the important amendment of expectations, conventional macro-theory can explain what we see?

It may be many years before this debate is settled to the satisfaction of the majority of economists. In the meantime some points that are extremely important for current policy do seem to be agreed upon.

(1) A trade-off between inflation and unemployment does appear to exist in the short term. At least a temporary reduction in unemployment can be obtained by increasing aggregate demand and accepting the resulting higher rate of inflation.

(2) If there is a tendency for the rate of inflation to accelerate when actual unemployment is held below the natural rate (by the persistence of heavy excess demand), the tendency for the rate of inflation to accelerate is slow to operate. After all, the two decades from 1945 to 1965 were characterized by mild inflations that showed no tendency to accelerate and unemployment was no lower than in the decade 1965–75 when the rate of inflation did accelerate.

(3) In the late 1960s there occurred throughout the world an increase in the rate of inflation associated with any given level of unemployment (i.e., an upward shift in

the Phillip's curves). This experience is consistent with the Phelps-Friedman theory of an accelerating inflation, but competing explanations are still in the running.

(4) There is substantial recent empirical evidence suggesting that people have revised their inflationary expectations upwards and that the actual rate of inflation does tend to accelerate as the expected rate accelerates. This evidence is strong enough to suggest a strong note of scepticism to any government that assumes it can reduce unemployment to very low levels and maintain a constant rate of inflation.

(5) If aggregate demand is reduced to remove a persistent inflationary gap, wage and price inflation can be expected to continue as unemployment rises, thus producing a *stagflation*. (Expectations theorists say that it will persist only until inflationary expectations are finally reduced under the impact of falling sales and rising unemployment.)

Unemployment and the balance of payments

With fixed exchange rates, a major policy conflict can occur between unemployment and the balance of payments. If the country's currency is overvalued so that at full employment there is a balance of payments deficit, then an expenditure-dampening policy will reduce imports and thus alleviate the balance of payments problem, but at the cost of raising the level of domestic unemployment. The conflict can be removed, at least temporarily, by raising aggregate demand, while at the same time adopting expenditure-switching policies so that international payments are in balance when full employment is achieved. If, however, the central authorities cannot, or will not, adopt expenditure-switching policies, such as changing the exchange rate, there will be no simple way out of their dilemma, and they will have to choose between INTERNAL and EXTERNAL BALANCE.[1]

In Britain during much of the 1950s and 1960s full employment tended to be associated with payments deficits. As long as expenditure-switching policies could not be adopted, there was pressure to reduce aggregate demand in order to restore external balance. Once external balance had been restored, there was a tendency to worry about the unemployment that was the direct consequence of the expenditure dampening policies. In order to deal with the unemployment, aggregate expenditure would be raised. This would lead to a lowering of the unemployment rate but, no sooner would the unemployment problem appear to be solved, than the rise in demand, with its consequent rise in imports, would cause a new balance-of-payments disequilibrium. Aggregate demand would then have to be depressed again. The history of macro-economic policy in Britain during the period, and, indeed, in other countries similarly situated, was that of a perpetual oscillation between periods of expanding aggregate demand to eliminate unemployment and periods of contracting demand to eliminate balance-of-payments deficits. The policy that led to these alternations was given the name STOP–GO.

The policy conflict between prices and the balance of payments

As far as direct connections are concerned, there is no conflict between prices and the balance of payments. Anything that slows down the rate of domestic inflation

---

1 A situation of full employment is often called a situation of internal balance while a situation in which international payments are in balance is often called one of external balance.

encourages exports and discourages imports and thus helps the balance of payments. An indirect conflict may, however, be set up as a result of a short-term trade-off between inflation and employment that we discussed earlier. If policy-makers decide to go for a very high level of employment and accept some rate of inflation in order to achieve it, they may create a conflict between this combination and a satisfactory balance of payments. Unless the rest of the world is also having a similar inflation, a gradual worsening of the balance of payments will occur. In general, then, the balance of payments problem constrains any choice policy-makers may have between unemployment and inflation if the exchange rate is fixed.

The conflicts between unemployment and growth (structural unemployment)

Conflicts between unemployment and growth could arise in two different ways: if pursuing full employment policies impeded growth, or if rapid growth brought in its wake high and persistent unemployment. We shall discuss the latter possibility because it represents both an ancient fear and the newly revived hypothesis of structural unemployment. Structural unemployment arises because growth brings change, and because labour may be in varying degrees immobile in the face of change. We know that both of these things occur.

Consider first how growth changes the allocation of resources in the economy and thus changes the kind and quantity of labour demanded. Growth brings rising incomes, and rising incomes change the pattern of demand for goods and services. What happens to the demands for various commodities will depend on the income elasticities of demand. The larger this elasticity for a particular commodity, the more rapidly will the demand for it grow as real income grows. Demands for commodities with income elasticities of less than unity will be expanding less rapidly than the average rate of growth in the economy, whereas the demands for commodities with income elasticities greater than unity will be expanding faster than the average rate of growth.

In the United States in recent decades, for example, there has been a significant shift of demand from agricultural to service sectors of the economy, as people spend smaller portions of their income on food and clothing and larger portions on entertainment, recreation and travel. On the supply side, changes also occur. The rates of investment and innovation will differ among industries, and so the rate of growth of productive capacity will also differ among industries.

Together these factors cause dramatic changes in the *output* of an economy over time. But the changes in employment may be even more dramatic. As long as an industry's income elasticity of demand exceeds zero (i.e., as long as the commodity is not an inferior good), output will rise as economic growth proceeds. Employment, however, will not increase unless demand expands *faster than output per manhour*. An industry in which productivity is growing at 3 per cent per year and in which demand is growing at 2 per cent per year will be an expanding industry in terms of output but a declining industry in terms of employment. The displaced worker sees that change (or growth) has destroyed his job, and he is likely to conclude that growth destroys jobs in general and thus creates unemployment in the economy. But this, of course, is not the case if labour let go in one sector of the economy finds employment in another. Few people remain permanently unemployed when they lose a job. Thus the genuine fear should be about the sometimes very heavy short-term costs of moving from one job to another not about the possibility of there being no jobs at all. Of course, movements of labour may be both slow and costly. How much of the economy's gains in output due to growth would be lost if the costs of transitional unemployment were accounted for is an important empirical question.

Moreover, the costs are borne unequally by members of society. The cost to those with heavy investments in education and experience in particular occupations can be enormous. A man of forty-five or fifty whose skills are special to a declining industry may, should he lose his job, find the market value of his services cut drastically. Just as the machine that was built to produce a product no one now wants is worthless, so the human capital invested in skills no longer required is worthless. Further, if the declining industry is a major part of the economy of a particular geographical area, the whole area may be a declining one, and all of its residents may suffer because of the decline in demand for all goods and services in this area. Because of this, the unemployed man who wishes to move to an area where jobs are plentiful may be unable to sell his house for anything near its replacement cost in a growing area. He thus will not be in a position to buy anything like a comparable house in a new area. The costs of growth and change are borne by a small section of the society, and although they may seem small in the aggregate, they are very serious to those who bear them.

THE LONG-RUN EVIDENCE ABOUT TECHNOLOGICAL UNEMPLOYMENT: Every major innovation and every major depression since the Industrial Revolution has rekindled the fear of steadily shrinking employment opportunities. Two pieces of evidence are unmistakable: (1) that in all growing Western economies over the last century, lapses from full employment have been temporary; and (2) that there has been no tendency for average levels of unemployment to rise decade by decade in spite of a prolonged period of sustained growth.

Partly, of course, these things reflect changes in working patterns. We work shorter days and shorter weeks than did our fathers and grandfathers. On the average, we delay longer our entry into the labour force and often enjoy longer periods of retirement. These decreases in the fraction of our lives spent at work have, so far at least, been voluntarily chosen increases in leisure, not a form of disguised unemployment. Thus there is little evidence that over the last century growth has led to any *rising* volume of unemployment. Yet the fear, naturally enough, persists and whenever unemployment rises to undesired levels, the spectre of an ever-rising volume of structural unemployment again arouses many genuine fears. The latest example of this was in the great debate that raged in the early 1960s in the United States over the reasons for the high unemployment of the time.

Between 1958 and 1964 US unemployment remained in excess of 5 per cent per year, despite general prosperity and notable technological developments. Certain economists argued at the time and still maintain that the ancient fear had become a modern reality. This hypothesis is based on two lines of argument. The first argument is that the rate of growth has been accelerating and that there has been a resulting increase in the number of individuals displaced from those industries in which the volume of employment is declining. Since it takes time for such persons to move, retrain, and enter a new job, it is argued that the average level of unemployment will be higher, the greater the rate of growth.

The second argument is that the quality of technological innovation has changed. In the first Industrial Revolution, so goes the argument, technology destroyed the jobs of skilled artisans by inventing machines to do the work and created jobs for unskilled workers who could operate the machines. In other words, formerly skilled jobs were broken up into a series of unskilled ones to be done by men and machines. Although the artisan might suffer a reduction in real income, he was not lacking in employment opportunities, since he was always capable of performing one of the unskilled tasks on the machines. The new Industrial Revolution, automation, so the argument continues, has reversed the technological trend. Now the production process is being reintegrated. The machine in the automated factory now performs all the unskilled tasks, and only a few highly skilled men are necessary to operate the machine and repair it when trouble develops. Thus the unskilled are the immediate sufferers from modern technological advance, and the new jobs are not ones into which they can step without long preparation. The argument concludes that modern technological advance is destroying the jobs of the unskilled and, even if demand and output are expanding everywhere, the jobs for which demand is expanding are not the jobs that the unskilled can perform. At very best, therefore, we would expect to find a rising number of (mainly unskilled) persons unemployed for long periods of time, and, at worst, there may be a rising number of persons who can never acquire the skills necessary to fit into the new industrial processes.

EVALUATION OF THE HYPOTHESIS: The first point to make about these arguments is that they cannot be ruled out on logical grounds alone. They are not self-contradictory, and they describe a state of affairs that *could* exist in the world. This makes the discussion of their relevance to today's world a question of fact: do the arguments actually describe our world, or do they contradict certain observations that we already have?

The first argument rested on an accelerating rate of growth. Despite all the recent advances in technology, the evidence seems to suggest that the US rate of growth now is not higher than it was over the last hundred years, and that it shows no signs of accelerating. In any case, 'structural unemployment' has been alleged to explain unemployment not in Japan or West Germany, where growth rates have indeed jumped, but in the United States, where they have not. It thus appears that the second line of argument must carry the burden of the hypothesis.

There is no question that the demand for unskilled labour has been shrinking. The theory of competitive price determination predicts that this should lead to a substantial fall in the wages earned by the unskilled. We know, however, that there is downward rigidity in wage rates, because unions and such things as minimum-wage laws prevent wages from falling nearly as much as they would in a wholly free market. In the face of this wage rigidity, the theory predicts an excess supply of labour – or, in other words, unemployment.

If the labour supply responds to the probability of getting jobs, as well as to the wage rate earned by those who do get jobs, we would expect a leftward shift in the supply curve of unskilled labour. A sophisticated version of the hypothesis of increasing structural unemployment is, then, that the demand curve for unskilled labour is shifting to the left faster than is the supply curve, so that at more or less constant wages the gap between supply and demand has been increasing. We must now wonder how this hypothesis fits the facts.

The first fact is that, year by year and decade by decade, the education and training of the labour force is increasing. There is no solid evidence of any growing gap between the skills demanded by industry and the training provided by educational institutions and firms. Second, much of the increase in demand for labour is coming in the service sectors that do not require a highly skilled labour force. Thus, although it may be very depressing to contemplate a fully automated manufacturing plant and wonder how to create jobs for the displaced unskilled workers by inducing further increases in demand for the output of the automated plant, it becomes somewhat less depressing if one realizes that a large fraction of any increment in demand will fall on service industries in which there are still many employment opportunities for the unskilled and semiskilled. Third, the evidence on retraining programmes, both within industry and outside, seems to suggest that many of those displaced can be fitted to new employment.

None of these observations is decisive. On the one hand, perhaps the sharpest evidence against the hypotheses is the very substantial decline in the level of unemployment that has occurred since 1964 in response to the increase in aggregate demand. By early 1968, the US unemployment rate had fallen below 3·5 per cent for the first time in 15 years. Clearly, America was not hopelessly locked into a 5 or 6 per cent unemployment rate, as some of the structural unemployment theorists felt in 1964. On the other hand, the rise in unemployment in the 1970s combined with rapid inflation which is usually associated with conditions of excess demand, is consistent with the view that much of the increased unemployment is structural in origin.

The weight of present opinion is that there is no inherent conflict between growth and full employment. Economists now believe that we can have growth at between 2 and 3 per cent per year and, provided we are willing to use appropriate monetary and fiscal policies, have nearly full employment as well.

Because unemployment has decreased sharply since 1964 is not to say that there are no structurally unemployed persons or groups in the United States today. Indeed, there are some severe pockets of unemployment that do not seem to respond significantly to the stimulus of increasing aggregate demand. To remove these depressed pockets special programmes that aim directly at them are without doubt required.

THE COMPOSITION OF MACRO-VARIABLES

We have seen that macro-economic policy is concerned with the behaviour of key averages and aggregates such as the average level of all prices and the overall level of unemployment. In fact, we care about more than just these averages and aggregates. We also care about their composition. Is the overall level of unemployment made up of very unequal rates of unemployment such as those among industries, occupations or areas, or is it made up of rates that are very similar across all of these classifications? We would assess a 4 per cent overall unemployment rate in the UK very differently if it resulted from 4 per cent unemployment in all industries, occupations and geographical areas than if it resulted from 15 per cent unemployment in some areas and only 1 or 2 per cent in others.

Levels of unemployment of 10 or 15 per cent are very serious matters, indeed. They are likely to mean that many people will be out of work for very long periods of time and that there is a level of social and personal upheaval that just does not accompany rates of the order of 4 per cent. The degree of regional and occupational inequality in unemployment rates in both the UK and the US has remained quite large throughout the whole postwar period.[1] Clearly, although we should be satisfied that the overall rate in Britain has been held at a very low level throughout the whole postwar period, we should be very disturbed at the very high rates that persist in some places.

Why do these localized high rates occur – why is it that in the midst of the 'fully employed' society we have these persistent pockets of poverty, pockets that will not respond to the cure of raising aggregate expenditure? Why does the market not adjust to bring about approximate equality in unemployment rates? Shouldn't regions and occupations with excess supplies of labour find their relative wages declining so that there is an incentive to employers to demand more of the relatively cheap labour and for suppliers to move to higher wage markets? Does this market mechanism work at all? How fast does it work? Does the shifting pattern of economic growth continue to disturb markets so that the adjustment mechanism can never catch up? Would things be better if we interfered in the market mechanism? What government policies would reduce these labour-market disequilibria?

A similar set of 'disaggregated observations' could be produced for any macro-variable, and they would provoke a similar set of questions. But to state just one set is enough to show that we have now gone full circle and are back at the *micro*-economics with which we began our study. To tackle these problems, we need to return to market theory, the study of which we began in Part 2 of the book.

There is no sharp distinction between micro- and macro-economics. There are merely higher and lower levels of aggregation and a series of questions appropriate to each level of aggregation, with each series shading one into the other.

THE PROGRESS OF ECONOMICS

The operation of scientific method is not a simple matter in economics. Because of the absence of laboratory experiments we cannot get the holders of opposing views to agree on critical tests and then repeat these tests over and over again until all but those with the heaviest emotional commitments have to agree on the results. The

---

1 But, contrary to popular belief, it has not increased steadily over the period. For the US, see R. A. Gordon, 'Has Structural Unemployment Worsened?', *Industrial Relations*, III, May 1964, pp. 55–77 and for the UK, see the article by F. P. R. Brechling, 'Trends and Cycles in British Regional Unemployment', *Oxford Economic Papers*, vol. 19, NS, No. 1, March 1967.

call that economics try to be a science is the call that it try to relate its theories to observations. If we hold that the truth of economic theories is totally independent of successful empirical applications it is difficult to see how economics can claim to be in any way useful in interpreting the world around us.

The general acceptance of the view that the validity of economic theories should be tested by confronting their predictions with the mass of all available evidence is fairly new in economics. At this point you should re-read the quotation from Lord Beveridge given at the beginning of this book (see pages xi and xii). The controversy that Beveridge was describing was the one that followed the publication in 1936 of Keynes' *General Theory of Employment, Interest and Money*. Keynes' work gave rise to the macro-economics that we have developed in Part 7 and on which we have so often relied in subsequent parts. At many points in the present book, we have raised the question of how various parts of macro-economic theory could be tested; we have also discussed some of the tests that have already been conducted. The student should reflect on how very different this approach to the problem of accepting or rejecting theories is from the approach described by Beveridge.

There is no doubt that since economics first began some, albeit irregular and halting, progress has been made in relating theory to evidence in the world of economic events. This progress has been reflected in the superior ability of governments to achieve their policy objectives. The financial aspects of the Second World War were significantly better handled than those of the First World War. The pathetic efforts of successive British governments to deal with the economic catastrophe that overwhelmed the country after the return to the gold standard and even more so after the great crash of 1929 show measures adopted in all sincerity which in most cases actually served to make things worse. When President Roosevelt tried to reduce American unemployment in the 1930s (with much more vigour than was applied by any British government over the same period) his efforts were greatly hampered by the failure of most economists to realize the critical importance of budget deficits in increasing the level of the circular flow of income. The contrast between the unhappy period of the 1930s and the present is great. When President Kennedy wished to do something about the high levels of unemployment in the 1960s, his main problem was to persuade the American Congress to adopt what most economists agreed was an appropriate cure – a tax cut; and in 1964, when President Johnson finally persuaded Congress to accept the tax cut, the ensuing rise in output and employment was very close to what the economists on the President's Council of Economic Advisers had predicted it would be. Several times during the 1950s and 1960s successive British governments have altered the Budget in pursuit of a 'stop' or a 'go' policy. Many economists are critical of the motives behind these policy oscillations but the fact that each time the economy moved in the direction predicted by economic theory is evidence that we have learned a great deal about the behaviour of the economy in the last 40 years.

Such important policy areas as the running of wars and the curing of major depressions are places in which the general tone of our theories is tested, even if all their specific predictions are not. In some general sense, then, economic theories have always been subjected to empirical tests. When they were wildly at variance with the facts, the ensuing disaster could not but be noticed, and the theories were discarded or amended in the light of what was learned.[1]

The advance of economics in the last 30 years reflect a change in economists' attitudes towards empirical observations. Today, we are much less likely to dismiss theories just because we do not like them and to refuse to abandon theories just because we do like them. Today, we are more likely to try to base our theories as much as possible on empirical observation, and to accept empirical relevance as the ultimate arbiter of the value of our theories. As human beings, the upsetting of a pet theory may cause us much anguish; as scientists we should try to train ourselves to take pleasure in it because of the new knowledge we gain thereby. It has been said that one of the great tragedies of science is the continual slaying of beautiful theories by ugly facts. As economists, we are all too often swayed by aesthetic considerations. In the past, we have too often hung on to our theories because they were beautiful or because we liked their political implications; as scientists, we must always remember that, when theory and fact come into conflict, it is theory, not fact, that must give way.

1 The discussion on page xx of Lord Beveridge's quotation is also relevant here.

Index